Social Research Methods

Qualitative and Quantitative Approaches

SIXTH EDITION

W. Lawrence Neuman
University of Wisconsin at Whitewater

PEARSON

Boston   New York   San Francisco
Mexico City   Montreal   Toronto   London   Madrid   Munich   Paris
Hong Kong   Singapore   Tokyo   Cape Town   Sydney

Senior Series Editor: Jeff Lasser
Series Editorial Assistant: Heather McNally
Senior Marketing Manager: Kelly May
Editoral Production Administrator: Paula Carroll
Editorial Production Service: Omegatype Typography, Inc.
Composition Buyer: Linda Cox
Manufacturing Buyer: JoAnne Sweeney
Electronic Composition: Omegatype Typography, Inc.
Cover Administrator: Linda Knowles

For related titles and support materials, visit our online catalog at www.ablongman.com.

Between the time website information is gathered and then published, it is not unusual for some sites to have closed. Also, the transcription of URLs can result in typographical errors. The publisher would appreciate notification where these errors occur so that they may be corrected in subsequent editions.

Library of Congress Cataloging-in-Publication Data

Neuman, William Lawrence
    Social research methods : qualitative and quantitative approaches / W. Lawrence
Neuman.—6th ed.
        p. cm.
    Includes bibliographical references (p.   ) and index.
    ISBN 0-205-45793-2
        1. Sociology—Research—Methodology.   2. Social sciences—Research—Methodology.   I.
Title.

HM571.N48 2006
301'.072—dc22

                                                                                    2005051336

Printed in the United States of America

10   9   8   7   6   5   4   3   2   1   10   09   08   07   06   05

Contents

Preface   vii

PART THREE
Quantitative Data Collection and Analysis

PART FOUR
Qualitative Data Collection and Analysis

PART FIVE
Communicating With Others

Appendixes

Preface

When I wrote the first edition of this textbook, nearly fifteen years ago, I never imaged that it would become a success and attract a large, loyal following. I continue to strive to make this book a comprehensive, authoritative introduction to social science research that is highly accessible to students who are new to the field.

In addition to generally updating examples and incorporating recent research on specific data collection techniques, I made other changes in the sixth edition. The changes, made in response to teachers who have used previous editions, represent an attempt to improve the clarity of presentation.

First, I moved key term definitions from a separate glossary at the end of the textbook to notes within the text itself. Students told me that they had trouble with some definitions and often turned to the back to read formal definitions after a term was introduced in the text. I thought that moving the definitions to appropriate locations in the text would help students to learn and understand the terms more quickly and in the proper context.

Second, readers of past editions will notice that I rearranged the organization of material in several chapters. This was done to build the sequence of concepts and to make the presentation of material clearer to students. The integration of qualitative and quantitative styles of research remains, but I refined it and clarified how the two styles are different yet complementary. In addition, I now repeat references to a small number of example studies on a few topics, instead of introducing many studies on a disparate range of topics. This should make it easier for students to examine a study in depth and see how multiple studies on one topic can be interrelated to build more general knowledge.

A third change was to reduce some discussions and expand others. For example, information on the web survey was expanded, and in several places didactic charts have been added. Besides rewriting some sections in each chapter, I substantially reorganized and revised the chapters on theory and re-search design. New information on survey research techniques, cross-cultural research, and the negative case study was added. The following supplements are available to assist both students and instructors:

- Instructor's Manual with Test Items
- TestGen EQ Computerized Test Bank for Windows and Macintosh
- Student Workbook with Data CD-ROM
- Student SPSS software (packaged with the text on request at a special price)
- Research Navigator™, an online research database that is searchable by key word and provides access to thousands of full-text articles from scholarly social science journals, popular magazines, and newspapers (free to students when the text is packaged with a Research Navigator™ Guide)
- Allyn & Bacon Social Research Website (www.ablongman.com/socialresearch)

This edition continues a commitment to show students that social research is an exciting, important process that real people conduct. My premise is that social research is not a collection of disembodied, abstract principles or arcane techniques; rather, it is a living, breathing process of discovery and knowledge creation. The process is one that most students can master or at least understand with modest effort and study. Professional researchers need to have a high level of dedication and commitment, but they are only human. They live in the real social, political, and historical world, and it can affect them. The effects include the influence of cultural assumptions, beliefs, and values that can lead to ethnocentric or nationalist views if one is not careful. The text continues to seek an international audience.

I believe social researchers need to be simultaneously detached from and involved in the social-political world around them. A degree of detachment from everyday events and concerns helps maintain a critical scientific perspective. Current fashions, pressing issues, and public concerns can have a negative influence on research. In a quest for relevance, they demand that research provide quick answers, skip steps, and take shortcuts; they rarely allow time for contemplation or examining past accumulated knowledge and alternative points of view. Often economic, political, and practical pressures attempt to turn social research into a nonreflective "quick fix" technology that anyone can apply to resolve a huge range of contemporary problems or issues. When social research is reduced to a simple technology, it leaves behind a vital part of what research really means. The ethos, an attitude, and a perspective of social research is a craftlike process of knowledge creation that extends beyond contemporary society today.

At the same time, excessive detachment can be a danger. If researchers do not apply research in practical applications or ignore the concerns of the day, they may be playing an ivory tower game. Soon, the public and societal leaders will cease to trust, understand, or support research. This requires social researchers to balance a degree of detachment with an awareness of how research is relevant for many practical affairs.

Lastly, this text continues to show students the value of both qualitative and quantitative approaches to research. I believe that maintaining a diversity of perspectives and research techniques will best advance knowledge of the social world, and that a tension between different research styles is healthy.

ACKNOWLEDGMENTS

I would like to thank the reviewers of this edition of *Social Research Methods*: Linda Liska Belgrave, University of Miami; William Gabrenya, Florida Institute of Technology; Kelley Hall, DePauw University; Sandra L. Hofferth, University of Maryland; Bethany L. Letiecq, Montana State University; and Rae S. Shevalier, Metropolitan State College.

Science and Research

> *The sociologist, then, is someone concerned with understanding society in a disciplined way. The nature of this discipline is scientific. This means that what the sociologist finds and says about the social phenomena he studies occurs within a certain rather strictly defined frame of reference.*
> —Peter Berger, *An Invitation to Sociology,* p. 16

Regardless of whether we are aware of it, we are surrounded by social research. Educators, parents, business managers, administrators, government officials, business leaders, human service providers, and health care professionals regularly use social research findings and principles in their jobs. They use social research to raise children, reduce crime, improve public health, sell products, or just understand one's life. Research may seem remote but it has a relevance for daily life. Reports of research appear on broadcast news programs, in magazines, and in newspapers. Recently, I read in my daily newspaper about studies showing that children who watch more TV have lower reading scores and more behavior problems, that the D.A.R.E. antidrug program and "boot camps" for criminal offenders are wholly ineffective, that 10- to 14-year-olds who

watch R-rated films are more likely to start smoking than those who watch only G or PG films, that 31 percent of gay teens were physically threatened or injured while in school, and that medical doctors admitted through Affirmative Action programs are just as successful as those admitted on test scores and grades alone.[1]

Research does not always guide decisions. Political leaders sometimes advance new policies without scientific evidence or that rely on weak or flawed research. For example, shortly after President George W. Bush took office in 2001, he proposed government funding for "faith-based" social programs instead of traditional methods. Critics observed that almost no evidence showed that faith-based programs were effective. Only a single study existed on a faith-based program to reduce drug dependence, but it was unpublished and had many methodological flaws.[2]

This book is about **social research**. In simple terms, research is a way of going about finding answers to questions. Social research is conducted by sociologists, social scientists, and others to seek answers to questions about the social world. You probably already have some notion of what social research entails. First, let me end possible misconceptions. When I ask students what they think research entails, they usually give the following answers:

■ Based on facts alone, without theory or judgment
■ Read or used only by experts or college professors
■ Done only in universities by people with Ph.D. degrees
■ Involves going to the library and finding articles on a topic
■ Hanging around some exotic place and observing people
■ Conducting an experiment in which people are tricked into doing something
■ Drawing a sample of people and giving them questionnaires
■ Looking up lots of tables from government reports or books
■ Using computers, statistics, charts, and graphs

The first three of these answers are wrong, and the others describe only part of what constitutes social research. It is unwise to confuse one part with the whole. Just as you would never mistake wearing shoes for being fully dressed, you should not mistake any one of these items for social research.

Social research involves learning something new about the social world. To do this, a researcher needs to think logically, follow rules, and repeat steps over and over. A researcher combines theories

> **Social research** A collection of methods and methodologies that researchers apply systematically to produce scientifically based knowledge about the social world.

or ideas with facts in a systematic way and uses his or her imagination and creativity. He or she learns to organize and plan carefully and to select the appropriate technique to address a question. A researcher also must treat the people in a study in ethical and moral ways. In addition, a researcher must communicate to others clearly.

Social research is a collection of methods people use systematically to produce knowledge. It is an exciting process of discovery, but it requires persistence, personal integrity, tolerance for ambiguity, interaction with others, and pride in doing quality work. You will learn more about the diversity of social research in Chapter 2.

This book is about research *methodology* and *methods,* two terms often treated as synonyms. Methodology is broader than methods and envelops methods. It is understanding the social-organizational context, philosophical assumptions, ethical principles, and political issues of the enterprise of social researchers who use methods. Methods are sets of specific techniques for selecting cases, measuring and observing aspects of social life, gathering and refining data, analyzing the data, and reporting on results. The two are closely linked and interdependent, but distinct.

ALTERNATIVES TO SOCIAL RESEARCH

You learned most of what you know about the social world by an alternative to social research. A great deal of what you know is based on what your parents and others have told you. You also have knowledge that you have learned from personal experience. The books and magazines you have read and the movies and television you have watched also have given you information. You may also use common sense.

In addition to being a collection of methods, social research is a process for producing knowledge. It is a more structured, organized, and systematic process than the alternatives.[3] Knowledge from the alternatives is often correct, but knowledge based on research is more likely to be true and has fewer errors. It is important to recognize that research does not always produce perfect knowledge. Nonetheless, compared to the alternatives, it is less likely to be flawed. Let us review the alternatives before examining social research.

Authority

You gain knowledge from parents, teachers, and experts as well as from books and television and other media. When you accept something as being true just because someone in a position of authority says it is true or because it is in an authoritative publication, you are using authority as a basis of knowledge. Relying on the wisdom of authorities is a quick, simple, and cheap way to learn something. Authorities often spend time and effort to learn something, and you can benefit from their experience and work.

Relying on authorities also has limitations. It is easy to overestimate the expertise of other people. You may assume that they are right when they are not. Authorities may speak on fields they know little about; they can be plain wrong. An expert in one area may try to use his or her authority in an unrelated area. Have you ever seen television commercials in which an expert in football uses that expertise to try to convince you to buy a car? In addition, there are the questions: Who is or is not an authority? Whom do you believe when different authorities disagree?

Authority is frequently misused. For example, the National Center for Public Policy Research, an advocacy group funded by large corporations, had a list of environmental experts in 27 policy fields. Only 51 of the 141 names on the list had a Ph.D. in any area, and some of the Ph.D.'s were in unrelated areas.[4] All legitimate scientists may not agree 100 percent of the time, but sometimes a person who has training and expertise in one area (e.g., space physics) speaks about an unrelated area (e.g., crime policy). Using the halo effect (discussed later), a person may apply expertise in one area illegitimately to act as an authority in a different area.

A related situation occurs when a person becomes a "senior fellow" or "adjunct scholar" in a private "think tank" that has an impressive name, such as the Center for the Scientific Study of X.

Some think tanks are legitimate research centers, but many are mere fronts created by wealthy special-interest groups to engage in advocacy politics. No regulations control the titles of think tanks, and anyone can become a "scholar" in the group. The purpose is to facilitate the person making authoritative statements to the mass media as if he or she were a neutral third party who had some kind of expertise. In reality, the person may lack expertise and make statements that do not come from serious research.[5]

History is full of past experts whom we now see as being misinformed. For example, some "experts" of the past measured intelligence by counting bumps on the skull; other "experts" used bloodletting to try to cure diseases. Their errors seem obvious now, but can you be certain that today's experts will not become tomorrow's fools? Also, too much reliance on authorities can be dangerous to a democratic society. An overdependence on experts lets them keep others in the dark, and they may promote ideas that strengthen their power and position. When we have no idea of how the experts arrived at their knowledge, we lose some of our ability to make judgments for ourselves.

Tradition

People sometimes rely on tradition for knowledge. Tradition is a special case of authority—the authority of the past. Tradition means you accept something as being true because "it's the way things have always been." For example, my father-in-law said that "drinking a shot of whiskey cures a cold." When I asked about his statement, he said that he had learned it from his father when he was a child, and it had come down from past generations. Tradition was the basis of the knowledge for the cure.

Here is an example from the social world. Many people believe that children who are raised at home by their mothers grow up to be better adjusted and have fewer personal problems than those raised in other settings. People "know" this, but how did they learn it? Most accept it because they believe (rightly or wrongly) that it was true in the past or is the way things have always been done.

Some traditional social knowledge begins as simple prejudice. A belief such as "people from that side of the tracks will never amount to anything" or "you never can trust anyone of that race" comes down from the past. Even if traditional knowledge was once true, it can become distorted as it is passed on, and soon it is no longer true. People may cling to traditional knowledge without real understanding; they assume that because something may have worked or been true in the past, it must always be true.

Common Sense

You know a lot about the social world from your ordinary reasoning or common sense. You rely on what everyone knows and what "just makes sense." For example, it "just makes sense" that murder rates are higher in nations that do not have a death penalty, because people are less likely to kill if they face execution for doing so. This and other widely held commonsense beliefs, such as that poor youth are more likely to commit deviant acts than those from the middle class or that most Catholics do not use birth control, are false.

Common sense is valuable in daily living, but it can allow logical fallacies to slip into your thinking. For example, the "gambler's fallacy" says: "If I have a long string of losses playing a lottery, the next time I play, my chances of winning will be better." In terms of probability and the facts, this is false. Also, common sense contains contradictory ideas that go unnoticed because people use the ideas at different times—for example, "opposites attract" and "birds of a feather flock together." Common sense can originate in tradition. It is useful and sometimes correct, but it also contains errors, misinformation, contradiction, and prejudice.

Media Myths

Television shows, movies, and newspaper and magazine articles are important sources of information about social life. For example, most people who have no contact with criminals learn about crime by watching television shows and movies and by reading newspapers. However, the portrayals of crime and of many other things on television do not accurately reflect social reality. Instead, the writers who invent or "adapt" real life for television shows and movie scripts distort reality either out of ignorance or because they rely on authority, tradition, and common sense. Their primary goal is to entertain. For example, only about 5 of 400 films that portray psychiatric treatment do so accurately (Goode, 2002), and almost all media estimates of the size of the Muslim population in the United States are two to three times greater than scientifically based estimates (Smith, 2002).

The media tend to perpetuate the myths of a culture. For example, the media show that most people who receive welfare are Black (actually, most are White), that most people who are mentally ill are violent and dangerous (only a small percentage actually are), and that most people who are elderly are senile and in nursing homes (a tiny minority are). Also, mass media "hype" can create the idea that a major problem exists when it may not (see Box 1.1). People are misled by visual images more easily than other forms of "lying"; this means that stories or stereotypes that appear on film and television can have a powerful effect on people. For example, television repeatedly shows low-income, inner-city, African American youth using illegal drugs. Eventually, most people "know" that urban Blacks use illegal drugs at a much higher rate than other groups in the United States, even though this notion is false.

The media are also a forum in which competing interests try to win public support. Public relations campaigns often use the media as a vehicle to alter what the public thinks about scientific findings. For example, nearly all scientific research supports the global warming thesis (i.e., that pollutants from industrialization and massive deforestation are raising the earth's temperature and will cause dramatic climate change and bring about environmental disasters). The scientific evidence is growing and getting stronger. In the media, the public sees equal attention to a few dissenters who question global warming. This creates the impression that "no one really knows" or that scientists are undecided about global warming. The media sources rarely say that there are only a few isolated dissenters, that industries with products that are major contributors to global warming pay for most dissenting studies, and that the same industries spend millions of dollars to

BOX **1.1**   Safe Driving and Media Myths

Americans hear a lot about road rage. *Newsweek* magazine, *Time* magazine, and newspapers in most major cities have carried headlines about it. Leading national political officials have held public hearings on it, and the federal government gives millions of dollars in grants to law enforcement and transportation departments to reduce it. A California psychologist now specializes in this disorder and has appeared on several major television programs to discuss it.

The term *road rage* first appeared in 1988, and by 1997, the print media were carrying over 4,000 articles per year on it. Despite media attention about "aggressive driving" and "anger behind the wheel," there is no scientific evidence for road rage. The term is not precisely defined and can refer to anything from gunshots from cars, use of hand gestures, running bicyclists off the road, tailgating, and even anger over auto repair bills! All the data on crashes and accidents show declines during the period when road rage reached an epidemic.

Perhaps media reports fueled perceptions of road rage. After hearing or reading about road rage and having a label for the behavior, people began to notice rude driving behavior and engaged in *selective observation*. We will not know for sure until it is properly studied, but the amount of such behavior may

be unchanged. It may turn out that the national epidemic of road rage is a widely held myth stimulated by reports in the mass media.

Newspapers and television reports are filled with dire warnings about the many traffic accidents that occur on holidays. Thus, the Fourth of July weekend holiday in the United States is presented as very deadly, with an average of 161 people killed each year. Yet, the holiday period may be no more dangerous than other times, and it may even be a bit safer! How can this be? After a careful comparison with other weekends and accounting for the extra amount of driving, the holiday's accident rate is not very different. Safety advocates publicize and distort statistical information in the media to encourage people to drive safer. This is hardly a unique situation; it happens with many social issues. "Problem promoters" often highlight dramatic cases or selectively use statistical information to generate attention and agitate the public about a social problem. The media reports are not so much wrong as they are misleading. They are more effective for public persuasion than is giving a carefully documented presentation of the entire picture.

Sources: Best (2001), Fumento (1998), and Wald (2004).

publicize the dissenting findings to deflect growing criticism and to delay environmental regulations that might harm their business interests.

Personal Experience

If something happens to you, if you personally see it or experience it, you accept it as true. Personal experience, or "seeing is believing," has a strong impact and is a forceful source of knowledge. Unfortunately, personal experience can lead you astray. Something similar to an optical illusion or mirage can occur. What appears true may actually be due to a slight error or distortion in judgment. The power of immediacy and direct personal contact is very strong. Even knowing that, people sometimes make mistakes or fall for illusions. Sometimes people believe what they see or experience rather than what

is revealed by careful research designed to avoid such errors.

The four errors of personal experience reinforce each other and can occur in other areas, as well. They are a basis for misleading people through propaganda, cons or fraud, magic, stereotyping, and some advertising.

1. Overgeneralization occurs when you have some evidence that you believe and then assume that it applies to many other situations, too. Limited generalization may be appropriate; under certain conditions, a small amount of evidence can explain a larger situation. The problem is that people often

Overgeneralization   Statements that go far beyond what can be justified based on the data or empirical observations that one has.

generalize well beyond limited evidence. There are many individuals, areas, and situations about which people know little or nothing, so generalizing from the little they do know might seem reasonable. For example, over the years, I have known five blind people. All of them were very friendly. Can I conclude that all blind people are friendly? Do the five people with whom I had personal experience fully represent all blind people?

Numerous studies cast serious doubt on personal experience and self-knowledge. People often misjudge themselves; eyewitness accounts such as those used in criminal justice tend to be highly inaccurate; most people's estimates of the chance of a mishap are far off from actual probabilities; and people are easily mislead by appearances, such as purchasing an SUV for its safety while it actually is more dangerous.[6]

2. Selective observation occurs when you take special notice of some people or events and generalize from them. People often focus on or observe particular cases or situations, especially when they fit preconceived ideas. We often seek out evidence that confirms what we already know or believe and ignore the range of cases and contradictory information. We are sensitive to features that confirm our ideas—features that might otherwise go unnoticed. For example, I believe overweight people are friendly. This belief may be based on stereotypes, what my mother told me, or whatever. I observe overweight people and, without awareness, pay particular attention to their smiling, laughing, and so on. Without realizing it, I notice and remember people and situations that reinforce my pre-

conceived ideas. Some psychologists have studied people's tendencies to "seek out" and distort their memories to make them more consistent with what they already think. I "overinterpret" gestures or smiles, pay less attention to contradictory evidence, and do not look for unfriendly behavior among overweight people.

3. Premature closure operates with and reinforces the first two errors. Premature closure occurs when you feel you have all the answers and do not need to listen, seek information, or raise questions any longer. Unfortunately, most of us are a little lazy or get a little sloppy. We take a few pieces of evidence or look at events for a short while and then think we have it figured out. We look for evidence to confirm or reject an idea and stop when a small amount of evidence is present. In a word, we jump to conclusions, such as: I know three people who smoked six packs of cigarettes a day and lived to be 80 years old; therefore, people who smoke lots of cigarettes will live to age 80.

4. The **halo effect** states we overgeneralize from what we believe to be highly positive or prestigious. We give things or people we respect a halo, or a strong reputation. We let the prestige "rub off" on other things or people about which we know little. Thus, I pick up a report by a person from a prestigious university, say, Harvard or Cambridge University. I assume that the author is smart and talented and that the report will be excellent. I do not make this assumption about a report by someone from Unknown University. I form an opinion and prejudge the report and may not approach it by considering its own merits alone.

How the various alternatives to social research might address the issue of laundry is shown in Table 1.1.

> **Selective observation**   Making observations in a way that it reinforces preexisting thinking, rather than observing in a neutral and balanced manner.
>
> **Premature closure**   Making a judgment, or reaching a decision and ending an investigation, before one has the amount or depth of evidence required by scientific standards.
>
> **Halo effect**   Allowing the prior reputation of persons, places, or things to color one's evaluations, rather than evaluating all in a neutral, equal manner.

HOW SCIENCE WORKS

Social research involves thinking about questions about the social world and following a set of processes to create new knowledge that is based on science. Let us look at the meaning of *science;* it is a subject that we will examine in more detail in Chapter 4.

TABLE 1.1   Alternatives to Social Research

ALTERNATIVE EXPLANATION TO SOCIAL RESEARCH	EXAMPLE ISSUE: In the division of household tasks by gender, why do women tend to do the laundry?
Authority	Experts say that as children, females are taught to make, select, mend, and clean clothing as part of a female focus on physical appearance and on caring for children or others in a family. Women do the laundry based on their childhood preparation.
Tradition	Women have done the laundry for centuries, so it is a continuation of what has happened for a long time.
Common sense	Men just are not as concerned about clothing as much as women are, so it only makes sense that women do the laundry more often.
Media myth	Television commercials show women often doing laundry and enjoying it, so they do laundry because they think it's fun.
Personal experience	My mother and the mothers of all my friends did the laundry. My female friends did it for their boyfriends, but never the other way around. It just feels natural for the woman to do it.

Science

When most people hear the word *science,* the first image that comes to mind is one of test tubes, computers, rocket ships, and people in white lab coats. These outward trappings are a part of science. The natural sciences—biology, chemistry, physics, and zoology—deal with the physical and material world (e.g., rocks, plants, chemicals, stars, blood, electricity, etc.). The natural sciences are the basis

of new technology and receive a lot of publicity. Most people first think of them when they hear the word *science.*

The social sciences, such as anthropology, psychology, political science, and sociology, involve the study of people—their beliefs, behavior, interaction, institutions, and so forth. Fewer people associate these disciplines with the word *science.* They are sometimes called *soft sciences.* This is not because their work is sloppy or lacks rigor but because their subject matter, human social life, is fluid, formidable to observe, and hard to measure precisely with laboratory instruments. The subject matter of a science (e.g., human attitudes, protoplasm, or galaxies) determines the techniques and instruments (e.g., surveys, microscopes, or telescopes) used by it.

Science is a social institution and a way to produce knowledge. It has not always been around; it is a human invention. What people now call science grew from a major shift in thinking that began with the Age of Reason or Enlightenment period in western European history, which occurred between the

"I'm a social scientist, Michael. That means I can't explain electricity or anything like that, but if you ever want to know about people I'm your man."

Source: © The New Yorker Collection 1986 J. B. Handelsman from cartoonbank.com. All Rights Reserved.

1600s and the early 1800s. The Enlightenment ushered in a wave of new thinking. It included a faith in logical reasoning, an emphasis on experiences in the material world, a belief in human progress, and a questioning of traditional religious authority. It began with the study of the natural world and spread to the study of social life. The importance of science as a basis for seeking knowledge is associated with the societal transformation called the Industrial Revolution. The advancement of science or of fields within science, such as sociology, does not just happen. It is punctuated by the triumphs and struggles of individual researchers. It is also influenced by significant social events, such as war, depression, government policy, or shifts in public support.[7]

Before science became fully entrenched, people used prescientific or nonscientific methods. These included the alternatives discussed previously and other methods that are less widely accepted in modern society (e.g., oracles, mysticism, magic, astrology, or spirits). Such prescientific systems were an unquestioned way to produce knowledge that people took to be true. Such prescientific methods still exist but are secondary to science. Some people use nonscientific methods to study topics beyond the scope of science (e.g., religion, art, or philosophy). Today, few people seriously question science as a legitimate way to produce knowledge about modern society.

> **Social theory** A system of interconnected ideas that condenses and organizes the knowledge about the social world and explains how it works.
>
> **Data** Numerical (quantitative) and nonnumerical (qualitative) information and evidence that have been carefully gathered according to rules or established procedures.
>
> **Empirical** What we can observe and experience directly through human senses (e.g., touch, sight, hearing, smell, taste) or indirectly using techniques that extend the senses.
>
> **Pseudoscience** Ideas or information clothed in the jargon and outward appearance of science to win acceptance but that was not created with the systematic rigor or standards required for the scientific method.

Science refers to both a system for producing knowledge and the knowledge produced from that system. The system evolved over many years and is slowly but constantly changing. It combines assumptions about the nature of the world and knowledge; an orientation toward knowledge; and sets of procedures, techniques, and instruments for gaining knowledge. It is visible in a social institution called the scientific community.

The knowledge of science is organized in terms of theories. For now, **social theory** can be defined as a system of interconnected ideas that condenses and organizes knowledge about the social world. Several types of social theory are discussed in Chapter 3. Social theory is like a map of the social world; it helps people visualize the complexity in the world and explains why things happen.

Scientists gather data using specialized techniques and use the data to support or reject theories. **Data** are the empirical evidence or information that one gathers carefully according to rules or procedures. The data can be *quantitative* (i.e., expressed as numbers) or *qualitative* (i.e., expressed as words, pictures, or objects). **Empirical** evidence refers to observations that people experience through the senses—touch, sight, hearing, smell, and taste. This confuses people, because researchers cannot use their senses to directly observe many aspects of the social world about which they seek answers (e.g., intelligence, attitudes, opinions, feelings, emotions, power, authority, etc.). Researchers have many specialized techniques to observe and indirectly measure such aspects of the social world.

Pseudoscience and Junk Science

We must be cautious about **pseudoscience** posing as real natural or social science. The public faces a constant barrage of pseudoscience through television, magazines, film, newspapers, special seminars or workshops, and the like. Some individuals operating a business, or who strongly embrace a belief system, weave a mix of the outward trappings of science (e.g., technical jargon, fancy-looking machines, complex formulas and statistics, or white lab coats) and a few scientific facts with myths, fantasy, or hopes. They then claim a "miracle cure," "new wonder treatment," "revolutionary learning program," "creationism science," "evidence of alien visitors," or "new age spiritual energy." Pseudoscience may include a few so-called experts who hold mail-order Ph.D. degrees, degrees in unrelated academic fields, or other dubious credentials.

Popular (or "pop") social science books sometimes cross over into pseudoscience. Some are accurate popularization of the knowledge that legitimate social researchers have produced. Others appear to be legitimate social science to a nonspecialist but are a distorted picture or a misuse of social science. They promote particular political or social values in the guise of social science. Such books rarely meet the standards of scientific community. For example, the Hite Report on female sexuality was a seriously flawed study conducted by a nonscientist that grossly distorted actual social relations. That did not prevent it from becoming a best-seller that was widely discussed in the mass media. The *Bell Curve* is an example.[8] There is little quality control on the social science books advertised on television or radio, cited in newspaper articles, or sold at local bookstores. Books that mostly contain personal opinion or political ideology are designed to look like "real" social science texts.

The term **junk science** was invented in the late 1980s by public relations firms hired by major corporations to denigrate the scientific evidence that environmental, public health, and public-interest groups presented against them in the courts. They contrasted it with *sound science* (i.e., studies that supported their position). *Sound* and *junk* are not precise terms, and the quality, methodology, or precision of the research for each does not differ. Instead, people manipulated language to produce the idea that sound science and junk science differ.

> *"Junk science" is the term that corporate defenders apply to any research, no matter how rigorous, that justifies regulations to protect the environment and public health. The opposing term, "sound science," is used in reference to any research, no matter how flawed, that can be used to challenge, defeat, or reverse environmental and public health protection. (Rampton and Stauber, 2001: 223)*

The tobacco industry widely used junk science as a tactic to criticize research on secondhand smoke and spent millions of dollars to deny the harmful health effects of smoking.[9] It tried to confuse the public and create an impression that scientists lacked clear and consistent research evidence.

The Scientific Community

Science is given life through the operation of the scientific community, which sustains the assumptions, attitudes, and techniques of science. The **scientific community** is a collection of people and a set of norms, behaviors, and attitudes that bind them together. It is a professional community because it is a group of interacting people who share ethical principles, beliefs and values, techniques and training, and career paths. It is not a geographic community. For the most part, the scientific community includes both the natural and social sciences.[10]

Many people outside the core scientific community use scientific research techniques. A range of practitioners and technicians apply research techniques that have been developed and refined by the scientific community. For example, many people use a research technique created by the scientific community (e.g., a survey) without possessing a deep knowledge of research, without inventing new methods of research, and without advancing science itself. Yet, those who use the techniques or results of science will be able to do so better if they also understand the principles and processes of the scientific community.

The boundaries of this community and its membership are defined loosely. There is no membership card or master roster. Many people treat a Ph.D. degree in a scientific field as an informal

Junk science A public relations term used to criticize scientific research, even if it is conducted properly, that produces findings that a group opposes.

Scientific community A collection of people who share a system of attitudes, beliefs, and rules that sustains the production and advance of scientific knowledge.

"entry ticket" to membership in the scientific community. The Ph.D., which stands for doctorate of philosophy, is an advanced graduate degree beyond the master's that prepares one to conduct independent research. Some researchers do not have Ph.D.'s and not all those who receive Ph.D.'s enter occupations in which they conduct research. They enter many occupations and may have other responsibilities (e.g., teaching, administration, consulting, clinical practice, advising, etc.). In fact, about one-half of the people who receive scientific Ph.D.'s do not follow careers as active researchers.

At the core of the scientific community are researchers who conduct studies on a full-time or half-time basis, usually with the help of assistants who are students. Working as a research assistant is the way that most scientists gain a real grasp on the details of doing research.

Colleges and universities employ most members of the scientific community's core. Some scientists work for the government or private industry in organizations such as the National Opinion Research Center and the Rand Corporation. Most are found at the approximately 200 research universities and institutes located in half a dozen advanced industrialized countries. Thus, the scientific community may be scattered geographically, but its members tend to work together in small clusters.

How big is the scientific community? This is not an easy question to answer. Using the broadest definition (including all scientists and those in science-related professions, such as engineers), about 15 percent of the labor force in advanced industrialized countries are members of the scientific community. A better way to look at the scientific community is to examine the basic unit of the larger community: the discipline (e.g., sociology, biology, psychology, etc.). Scientists are most familiar with a particular discipline because knowledge is specialized. In the United States, there are about 17,000 professional sociologists, 180,000 architects, 950,000 lawyers, and 1639,000 accountants, and

819,000 medical doctors. Each year, about 600 people receive Ph.D.'s in sociology, 15,000 receive medical degrees, and 38,000 receive law degrees.

A discipline such as sociology may have about 8,000 active researchers. Many of these individuals complete only one or two studies in their careers. A minority conduct dozens of studies. For topic areas or specialties within disciplines (e.g., study of divorce or the death penalty), there are as few as 100 active researchers.[11] The outcomes of the scientific community affect the lives of millions of people, yet most research and new knowledge depend on the efforts of small numbers of people.

The Norms of the Scientific Community

Behavior in any human community is regulated by social norms. The scientific community is governed by a set of professional norms and values that researchers learn and internalize during many years of schooling. The norms are mutually reinforcing and contribute to the unique role of the scientist.[12] The settings in which active researchers work and the operation of the system of science reinforces the norms.[13] Like other social norms, professional norms are ideals of proper conduct. Because researchers are real people, their prejudices, egos, ambitions, personal lives, and the like may affect their professional behavior. The norms of science do not always work perfectly in practice and are occasionally violated.[14] Likewise, it is important to remember that the operation of science does not occur in a vacuum isolated from the real world. Diverse social, political, and economic forces affect its development and influence how it operates.

The five basic **norms of the scientific community** are listed in Box 1.2. They differ from those in other social institutions (e.g., business, government) and set scientists apart. Scientists check on each other to see that the norms are followed. For example, consistent with the norm of *universalism,* scientists will admire a brilliant, creative researcher even if he or she has strange personal habits or a disheveled appearance. Scientists may argue intensely with one another and "tear apart" a research report as part of the norm of *organized skepticism.* They usually listen to new

Norms of the scientific community A set of informal rules, principles, and values that governs how scientists conduct their research.

BOX **1.2** **Norms of the Scientific Community**

1. *Universalism.* Irrespective of who conducts research (e.g., old or young, male or female) and regardless of where it was conducted (e.g., United States or France, Harvard or Unknown University), the research is to be judged only on the basis of scientific merit.
2. *Organized skepticism.* Scientists should not accept new ideas or evidence in a carefree, uncritical manner. They should challenge and question all evidence and subject each study to intense scrutiny. The purpose of their criticism is not to attack the individual, but to ensure that the methods used in research can stand up to close, careful examination.
3. *Disinterestedness.* Scientists must be neutral, impartial, receptive, and open to unexpected observations or new ideas. They should not be rigidly wedded to a particular idea or point of view. They should accept, even look for, evidence that runs against their positions and should honestly accept all findings based on high-quality research.
4. *Communalism.* Scientific knowledge must be shared with others; it belongs to everyone. Creating scientific knowledge is a public act, and the findings are public property, available for all to use. The way in which the research is conducted must be described in detail. New knowledge is not formally accepted until other researchers have reviewed it and it has been made publicly available in a special form and style.
5. *Honesty.* This is a general cultural norm, but it is especially strong in scientific research. Scientists demand honesty in all research; dishonesty or cheating in scientific research is a major taboo.

ideas, no matter how strange. Following *disinterestedness,* scientists are detached and take results, including from their own research, as being tentative. They love to have other scientists read and react to their research, and some have led fights against censorship. This is consistent with the norm of *communalism.* Communalism does not always work, especially when it conflicts with the profit motive. Scientists working in the tobacco, pharmaceutical, and computer chip industries had the publication of research findings suppressed or de-layed by corporate officials for whom the profit motive overrode the scientific norm of communalism.[15] Scientists expect strict *honesty* in the conduct and reporting of research and become morally outraged when anyone cheats at research.

The Scientific Method and Attitude

You have probably heard of the scientific method, and you may be wondering how it fits into all this. The **scientific method** is not one single thing. It refers to the ideas, rules, techniques, and approaches that the scientific community uses. The method arises from a loose consensus within the community of scientists. A discussion of the fundamental methods of social research is found in Chapter 4.

It is better to focus on the **scientific attitude,** or a way of looking at the world. It is an attitude that values craftsmanship, with pride in creativity, high-quality standards, and hard work. As Grinnell (1987:125) stated:

> *Most people learn about the "scientific method" rather than about the scientific attitude. While the "scientific method" is an ideal construct, the scientific attitude is the way people have of looking at the world. Doing science includes many methods; what makes them scientific is their acceptance by the scientific collective.*

Journal Articles in Science

You may be familiar with certain sociology scholarly journals or specialized magazines. When the scientific community creates new knowledge, it appears in academic books or scholarly journal articles. A more detailed discussion of scholarly journals is in Chapter 5. The primary forms in which research findings or new scientific knowledge

Scientific method The ideas, rules, techniques, and approaches that the scientific community uses to create and evaluate knowledge.

Scientific attitude A way of thinking about and looking at the world that reflects a commitment to the norms and values of the scientific community.

appear are **scholarly journal articles.** They are how scientists formally communicate with one another and disseminate the results of scientific research. They are also part of the much discussed explosion of knowledge. Each discipline or field has over 100 journals, each of which publishes many articles every year. For example, a leader among the nearly 200 sociology journals, the *American Sociological Review,* publishes about 65 articles each year. The journal article is a crucial part of the research process and the scientific community, but it is not always well understood.[16]

Consider what happens once a researcher completes a study. First, he or she writes a description of the study and the results as a research report or a paper in a special format. Often, he or she gives an oral presentation of the paper at a meeting of a professional association, such as the American Sociological Association, and sends a copy of it to a few scientists for their comments and suggestions. Next, the researcher sends copies to the editor of a scholarly journal, such as the *Sociological Quarterly* or the *Social Science Quarterly.* Each editor, a respected researcher who has been chosen by other scientists to oversee the journal, removes the title page, which is the only place the author's name appears, and sends the paper to several referees for a **blind review.** The referees are scientists who have conducted research in the same specialty area or topic. The review is "blind" because the referees do not know who conducted the research and the author does not know the referees. This reinforces the norm of universalism, because referees judge the paper on its merits alone. They evaluate the research on the basis of its clarity, originality, standards of good research, and

contribution to knowledge. Journals want to publish research that is well done and that significantly advances knowledge. The referees return their evaluations to the editor, who decides to reject the paper, ask the author for revisions, or accept it for publication.

Almost all academic fields use peer referees for publication, but not all use a blind review process. Sociology, psychology, and political science use blind reviews for almost all scholarly journals, and often three or more scholars review a study. By contrast, fields such as biology, history, and economics use a mix of review processes; sometimes reviewers know the author's identity and only one or two scholars review the study. Blind reviews with many referees slow the process and lower acceptance rates.[17] It is a very cautious method of ensuring quality control that advances the norms of organized skepticism and universalism.

Some scholarly journals are widely read and highly respected. They receive many more papers than they can publish. For example, major social science journals, such as *American Economic Review, American Sociological Review, American Political Science Review,* and *Social Problems* accept only 10 to 15 percent of submitted manuscripts. Even less esteemed journals regularly reject half of the submissions. Thus, publication represents tentative acceptance by the scientific community. Publishing a book involves a somewhat different review process that includes cost and sales considerations, but the acceptance rate is often lower.[18]

Unlike the authors of articles for the popular magazines found at newsstands, who are paid for writing, scientists are not paid for publishing in scholarly journals. In fact, they may have to pay a small fee to help defray costs just to have their papers considered. Researchers are happy to make their research available to their peers (i.e., other scientists and researchers) through scholarly journals. Likewise, the referees are not paid for reviewing papers. They consider it an honor to be asked to conduct the reviews and a responsibility of membership in the scientific community. The scientific community imparts great respect to researchers who publish many articles in the foremost schol-

Scholarly journal article   An article in a specialized publication that has members of the scientific community as its primary audience; it is a means to disseminate new ideas and findings within the scientific community.

Blind review   A process of judging the merits of a research report in which the peer researchers do not know the identity of who conducted a study and the researcher does not know the identity of the evaluators in advance.

arly journals. The articles confirm that these researchers are leaders in advancing the primary goal of the scientific community—to contribute to the accumulation of scientific knowledge.

A researcher gains prestige and honor within the scientific community, respect from peers, and a reputation as an accomplished researcher through such publications. Researchers want to earn the respect of their peers—other highly trained scientists who are knowledgeable about the research issues. In addition, an impressive record of respected publications helps a researcher obtain grants, fellowships, job offers, a following of students, improved working conditions, and increases in salary.[19]

You may never publish an article in a scholarly journal, but you will likely read such articles. They are a vital component of the system of scientific research. Most new scientific knowledge first appears in scholarly journals. Researchers read the journals to learn about the research others conducted, the methods they used, and the results they obtained.

Science as a Transformative Process

You can think of research as the use of scientific methods to transform ideas, hunches, and questions, sometimes called *hypotheses,* into scientific knowledge. In the research process, a researcher starts with guesses or questions and applies specialized methods and techniques to this raw material. At the end of the process, a finished product of value appears: scientific knowledge. A highly productive researcher creates a great deal of new knowledge that greatly improves people's understanding of the world.

You may be starting to feel that the research process is beyond you. After all, it involves complex technical skills and the high-powered scientific community. Yet, the fundamentals of conducting research are accessible to most people. With education and practice, you can learn to do scientific research. In addition to assimilating the scientific attitude or culture, you will need to master how and when to apply research techniques. After reading this book, you should grasp them. Soon you will be able to conduct small-scale research projects yourself.

QUANTITATIVE AND QUALITATIVE SOCIAL RESEARCH

You will learn about both qualitative and quantitative approaches to doing social research in this book. After the first several chapters, the two approaches will be used to help organize most remaining chapters. Each approach uses several specific research techniques (e.g., survey, interview, and historical analysis), yet there is much overlap between the type of data and the approach to research. Most qualitative researchers examine qualitative data, and vice versa.

Unfortunately, there is a lot of ill will between the followers of each research approach. Some find it difficult to understand or appreciate the other approach. Thus, Levine (1993:xii) wrote, "Quantitative social science," which he called "real social science," faced opposition but it "won the battle." Denzin and Lincoln (2003a) argued that qualitative research expanded greatly and is rapidly displacing outdated quantitative research.

Although both share basic principles of science, the two approaches differ in significant ways (see Table 1.2). Each has its strengths and

TABLE 1.2   Quantitative versus Qualitative Approaches

QUANTITATIVE APPROACH	QUALITATIVE APPROACH
Measure objective facts	Construct social reality, cultural meaning
Focus on variables	Focus on interactive processes, events
Reliability is key	Authenticity is key
Value free	Values are present and explicit
Theory and data are separate	Theory and data are fused
Independent of context	Situationally constrained
Many cases, subjects	Few cases, subjects
Statistical analysis	Thematic analysis
Researcher is detached	Researcher is involved

Sources: Creswell (1994), Denzin and Lincoln (2003a), Guba and Lincoln (1994), Marvasti (2004), Mostyn (1985), and Tashakkori and Teddlie (1998).

limitations, topics or issues where it glitters, and classic studies that provide remarkable insights into social life.

No matter what approach they adopt, researchers try to avoid the errors discussed earlier in this chapter, to be systematic in gathering data, and to use the idea of comparison extensively. By understanding both approaches, you will know about a range of research and can use both in complementary ways. Ragin (1994a:92) has explained one way the approaches complement each other:

> *The key features common to all qualitative methods can be seen when they are contrasted with quantitative methods. Most quantitative data techniques are data condensers. They condense data in order to see the big picture. . . . Qualitative methods, by contrast, are best understood as data enhancers. When data are enhanced, it is possible to see key aspects of cases more clearly.*

STEPS IN THE RESEARCH PROCESS

The Steps

Conducting research requires following a sequence of steps. The exact sequence and steps vary somewhat with the type of social research (Chapters 2 and 4 discuss types of research), but there are essentially seven major steps. The steps vary slightly by whether a study involves a quantitative or a qualitative approach and data.

Quantitative Approach.   The process of conducting a quantitative study begins with a researcher selecting a topic. Quantitative researchers typically start with a general area of study or issue of professional or personal interest, such as the effects of divorce, reasons for delinquency, impact of homelessness, or how elites use the media. However, a topic is too broad for conducting a study. This is why the next step is crucial. The researcher must narrow it down to, or focus on, a specific *research question* that can be addressed in the study. Often this requires a careful review of the *research literature* (discussed in Chapter 5) and developing hypotheses (discussed in Chapter 6) that frequently come from *social theory* (discussed in Chapter 3).

For example, a broad topic—reasons for delinquency—becomes the focused research question: Are teenaged East Asian immigrant males who have strong ties to their home culture and who are not assimilated into the new society more likely to engage in delinquent acts than those with weak ties who have assimilated? A rather vague topic, reasons for delinquency, is focused into a specific reason (i.e., degree of assimilation) for a specific group of people (i.e., teenaged immigrant males from East Asia) that is used to pursue the next step, to *design a study* (discussed in Chapters 6–11). Designing the study requires making decisions about the type of case or sample to select, how to measure relevant factors, and what research technique (e.g., questionnaire, experiment) to employ. At this stage as well, theory informs decision making.

After designing the study, a researcher begins to *collect data.* A quantitative researcher will very carefully record and verify information, almost always in the form of numbers, and usually transfers the data into computer-readable format. Once the data are all collected, the researcher begins the fifth step, to *analyze data* (see Chapter 12). This typically involves manipulating the data or numbers using computer software to create many charts, tables, graphs, and statistics. Often the research ends up with a large quantity of computer-generated output that provides the researcher with a condensed picture of the data. The researcher next has to give meaning to or *interpret the data.* By looking at the analyzed data, using background knowledge on the research topic and question, and drawing on theory, a researcher answers the original research question. A researcher also considers alternative interpretations of the data, compares the results of this study with previous studies, and draws out its wider implications. The researcher will be prepared for the final step, to *inform others.* This means writing a report about the study in a specific format (described in Chapter 16) and presenting a description of the study and results to professional audiences and in one or more publications (see Figure 1.1).

Qualitative Approach.   Norman Denzin and Yvonna Lincoln (2003b:31–38) describe a slightly different set of steps for qualitative research. Qualitative researchers begin with a self-assessment

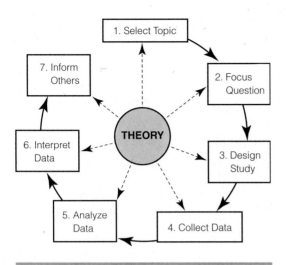

FIGURE 1.1   Steps in the Quantitative Research Process

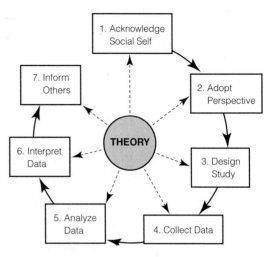

FIGURE 1.2   Steps in the Qualitative Research Process

and reflections about themselves as situated in a sociohistorical context. It is a highly self-aware *acknowledgment of social self,* or of a researcher's position in society. Qualitative researchers do not narrowly focus on a specific question, but ponder the theoretical-philosophical *paradigm* (discussed in Chapter 4) in an inquisitive, open-ended settling-in process as they *adopt a perspective.* Like the quantitative researcher, a qualitative researcher will *design a study* (Chapter 6), *collect data* (Chapters 13–14), *analyze data* (see Chapter 15), and *interpret data.* The qualitative researcher is likely to collect, analyze, and interpret data simultaneously, going back and forth between these steps. He or she also tends to build new theory as well as draw on existing theory during these steps. At the *interpret data* stage, many quantitative researchers test hypotheses they previously developed whereas qualitative researchers tend to create new concepts and emphasize constructing theoretical interpretations. The last step, to *inform others,* is similar for both approaches, but here again, the report styles to present results to other people vary by approach (see Chapter 16). (See Figure 1.2.)

The neat seven-step process shown in Figures 1.1 and 1.2 are oversimplified. In practice, researchers rarely complete step 1, then leave it to move to step 2, and so on. Research is an interactive process in which steps blend into each other. A later step may stimulate reconsideration of a previous one. The process is not strictly linear; it may flow in several directions before reaching an end. Research does not abruptly end at step 7. It is an ongoing process, and the end of one study often stimulates new thinking and fresh research questions.

The seven steps are for one research project. A researcher applies one cycle of the steps in a single research project on a specific topic. Each project builds on prior research and contributes to a larger body of knowledge. The larger process of scientific discovery and accumulating new knowledge requires the involvement of many researchers in numerous research projects all at the same time. A single researcher may be working on multiple research projects at once, or several researchers may collaborate on one project. Likewise, one project may result in one scholarly article or several, and sometimes several smaller projects are reported in a single article.

Quantitative Studies

To illustrate the seven steps in social research, what follows are short summaries of four quantitative and two qualitative studies published in scholarly journals between 2000 and 2004 on the topic of immigration from Mexico to the United States. The authors are from different academic fields and apply various research techniques.

Quantitative Example 1.   R. Michael Alvarez and Tara L. Butterfield (2000) studied why voters supported California's anti-immigrant Proposition 187.

Select a Topic.   California has public referendums on many issues. Proposition 187 in 1994 sought to take away most social services and health care from illegal immigrants. The authors wanted to learn who supported California Proposition 187 and why.

Focus the Question.   In 1994, the California state economy was in the midst of the worst recession since the 1930s Depression. Over a million jobs were lost, creating terrible budget problems for state and local governments. At this time, officials proposed Proposition 187 to end alleged increases in fraud and abuse of public services by illegal immigrants. The authors thought Proposition 187 was diverting public attention away from the real problem—a bad economy and government budget problems—and treating a vulnerable population, immigrants, as scapegoats. They thought nativism could be the real source of voter support for Proposition 187. Nativism periodically has appeared in U.S. history to justify the power and privileges of native-born people over newcomers. It is a competitive response in which settled insiders seek to defend and protect their entrenched interests by blaming their problems on and focusing increased hostility toward politically weak outsiders.

Design the Study.   The authors surveyed a sample of voters to see whether those who fit a nativist profile (i.e., feel competition from, blame various economic problems on, and direct hostility toward immigrants) supported Proposition 187.

Collect the Data.   The authors acquired data from a national survey organization that gave questionnaires to 3,147 registered voters as they left voting booths. Voters were asked about their race, personal finances, beliefs about the state's economy, education level, area of residence, political party,

political ideology, vote for governor, and employment status.

Analyze the Data.   The authors used advanced statistical analysis to measure the impact of opinions and background factors on support for Proposition 187.

Interpret the Data.   The authors found that the strongest predictor of support for Proposition 187 was a voter's beliefs about the state's economy. Voters who blamed California's economic problems on immigrants and who faced the greatest economic and cultural competition from immigrants—non-Latinos with less education who lived close to many recent immigrants—most strongly supported Proposition 187. Political party and ideology had little effect on voting. The authors concluded that nativism was a major source of voter support for Proposition 187.

Inform Others.   The authors presented their findings at the 1996 Southern Political Science Association and later submitted the study to *Social Science Quarterly.*

Quantitative Example 2.   Lisa Magaña and Robert Short (2002) looked at what politicians said about Mexican and Cuban immigrants.

Select a Topic.   The authors examined the statements by political candidates about Mexican and Cuban immigrants.

Focus the Question.   The authors applied social construction theory, which refers to how groups, individuals, and symbols are perceived by the culture at-large. They looked at views expressed by political candidates in the press and how the views might inform political policy or be used to scapegoat certain groups for social problems.

Design the Study.   The authors' content analyzed statements in newspapers over a six-year period (1993–1999), examining federal, state, and local elections during election years and nonelection years, including candidates of both U.S. political parties.

Collect the Data.　Data came from Lexis-Nexus, an electronic database containing full-text newspaper articles. The search was restricted to references of what U.S. politicians said concerning Mexican and Cuban immigration. Their final sample contained 495 articles.

Analyze the Data.　The authors looked at tables with percentages and statistical tests.

Interpret the Data.　The major topic discussed was illegal Mexican immigration during the six years. In the mainstream media press, the topic was treated as very negative because there is little political fallout when candidates appeal to more anti-immigrant constituencies. Republican candidates for federal office made most of the negative statements, primarily about economic and cultural issues. Candidates from neither party discussed Cuban immigrants. The authors suggest that the political rhetoric regarding immigration is a distorted view of immigration issues in the public eye with social policy implications.

Inform Others.　The authors published their results in *Review of Policy Research.*

Quantitative Example 3.　Yeuch-Ting Lee and Victor Ottati (2002) studied attitudes toward U.S. immigration policy and general ingroup/outgroup feelings.

Select a Topic.　The authors examined sources of American attitudes toward immigrants.

Focus the Question.　The authors focused on California Proposition 187 designed to deny public services to illegal immigrants. Past research suggested that some people hold very strong membership feelings about their racial-ethnic group and treat nongroup members unfavorably. They wanted to see whether this general orientation also shaped people's positions about the new law, because it had significant support and in public its supporters claimed they were not motivated by racial-ethnic prejudice. The authors compared three hypotheses about attitudes toward illegal immigrants: (1) an ingroup/outgroup bias (i.e., people favor their own racial-ethnic group), (2) economic concerns (i.e., people

fear a loss of jobs), or (3) obedience to law (i.e., people want everyone to obey the law).

Design the Study.　The authors used a questionnaire with 10 questions about treatment of immigrants. A high score indicated humane treatment for all immigrants. They also asked participants whether an illegal immigrant's children born in the United States (hence U.S. citizens) should have an opportunity for education in the United States and whether they would vote for a law like Proposition 187. The authors conducted three studies in which participants read a story about a Mexican immigrant and answered questions about immigration and other issues. By varying the ethnic background of participants and the story, they sought to test the three hypotheses.

Collect the Data.　Data for study 1 had two sets of 100 college students, one set from Springfield Massachusetts, and one from Mexico City, Mexico. Participants read a story about a hypothetical person who migrated to the United States from Mexico and would suffer many negative consequences if the Proposition 187 became law. In study 2, participants were 286 U.S. citizens of several ethnic groups. They read the same story and were asked about immigration. In study 3, participants were 125 Anglo American college students from California. Some read the same story about a Mexican immigrant, others one where the immigrant was an Anglo-Canadian. In addition to questions on immigration, the child's education, and voting, participants were asked about economic threat due to immigration and about the importance of obeying the law.

Analyze the Data.　For study 1 data, the authors found large differences between U.S. and Mexican college students: 76 percent of the American versus 5 percent of Mexican college students favored Proposition 187. For study 2 data, they found large differences by ethnic group among Americans: Anglo Whites had the lowest favorable treatment scores, next came Asian and African Americans, and highest scores were given by Hispanics. The difference between Asian and African Americans and Hispanics were small, but that between non-Anglos and Anglos was large. For example, 70.0 percent of Anglos, 12.6 percent of Asian and African Americans, and 3.5 percent of Hispanics would vote for Proposition 187. In study 3, the authors statistically compared the impact of the story (Mexican versus Canadian immigrant), belief in economic threat, and law obedience.

Interpret the Data. The first two studies showed that Anglo Whites held a very different position from Mexican nationals and non-Whites. The source of Anglo White opinions was most interesting. Ethnic group membership, fear of economic threat, and law obedience each contributed to an unfavorable view on immigrants and support for Proposition 187. However, only the racial-ethnic factor predicted unfavorably on the question about the immigrant child's education. The authors concluded that although it was not the sole factor, a desire to exclude racial-ethnic outsiders was important for the anti-immigrant views of many Anglo Whites.

Inform Others. The authors submitted their paper to the *Journal of Social Psychology* in July 2000, and it appeared in print in October 2001.

Quantitative Example 4. William Kandel and Douglas Massey (2002) examined Mexican communities with high rates of out-migration coming to the United States.

Select a Topic. The "culture of migration" in which young Mexicans "expect" to live and work in the United States and see migration to the United States as a normal part of the life course.

Focus the Question. The authors examined students in the Mexican state of Zacatecas, a major source of migrants to the United States. The authors developed an equation to express the culture of migration that predicts a desire to migrate and not continue with schooling in Mexico. Predictions are based on a young person's social connections to others who have migrated.

Design the Study. The researchers used a questionnaire and selected schools in the capital city, a medium-sized town, and two dozen smaller agrarian settlements, focusing on students in grades 6

through 12 at upper-level technical schools and senior high schools to get 7,061 students.

Collect the Data. Students completed a 5-page questionnaire in classrooms that asked about social and demographic characteristics of family members (age, education, occupation, job location, marital status, and household membership), the student's educational history, time spent studying and chores or paid labor, whether the student's father had been to the United States, the migratory experience of the student's nuclear and extended families, and the student's own aspirations.

Analyze the Data. Statistical tables and sophisticated statistical tests were used.

Interpret the Data. The odds of wanting to work in the United States rise steadily with families having higher migratory involvement. Students and families reduce their investment in moving up in Mexico and invest in migration, raising the odds that they actually will migrate as they get older. The authors found that aspirations to work in the United States are much lower for females, but rise with age.

Inform Others. Study results were presented at the 1999 annual meeting of the American Sociological Association and later published in the journal *Social Forces*.

Qualitative Studies

Quantitative Example 1. Sofia Villenas (2001) examined the lives of Latina women in a small North Carolina town.

Acknowledge Social Self. The author says she is first-generation Chicana born in Los Angeles of immigrant parents from Ecuador and a detribalized descendant of the Quechua-speaking people of the South American Andes. After getting a degree in Latin American/Chicano/a Studies, she was a bilingual Spanish teacher from Los Angeles. While at the University of North Carolina working on a Ph.D., she was a bilingual instructor for adult English-as-a-second-language (ESL) classes, a bus driver, and an ESL instructor for mothers in parenting classes in a small North Carolina town.

Adopt a Perspective. The author self-consciously applied a race-based feminist perspective to explore connections between racial power and the political economy. She positioned herself as an insider and outsider to both the Latino community and that of English-speaking professionals, to understand both racial ideologies and the daily experience of Latina mothers in rural North Carolina.

Design the Study. The author's community roles also brought her into close relationships with Latino families and with Latina mothers in particular. For two years she participated in social events, community meetings, school meetings, and Catholic mass in Spanish.

Collect and Analyze the Data. The author tape-recorded the oral life histories of 21 Latino community members, including 11 mothers with whom she worked most closely. She engaged in participant observation and analyzed public agency and town documents, including the local daily newspaper.

Interpret the Data. In a kind of benevolent racism, White educators, health care, and social service providers saw "American" (racially coded for "white") women as superior and as models for Latinas to emulate, and saw Latina mothers as "uneducated" and in backward "macho" families. By contrast, the Latina mothers saw themselves as strong and educated, adhering to principles for living that were superior to what they saw in a small American town. They were proud *mujeres de hogar* (women of the home) who imparted distinct moral education that was critical to the Latino community.

Inform Others. The study results were published in *Anthropology and Education Quarterly*. A description of how Villenas's biography and feminist approach affected her research also appeared in the *Harvard Education Review* (1996).

Qualitative Example 2. Tracy J. Andrews, Vickie D. Ybarra, and Teresa Miramontes (2002) explored the experiences of undocumented immigrant women from Mexico.

Acknowledge Social Self. The authors included an anthropologist who had previously conducted research on Native Americans, a clinic worker who was also a public health clinical instructor, and a student who spent six years on ongoing cooperative research and internship projects before going to medical school after working on this study.

Adopt a Perspective. The study was at a health clinic in an area in which there was little prior research on immigrant women. The authors adopted an interdisciplinary, clinical-helping orientation. They assessed propositions of neoclassical economic and social capital theories to explain international migration and compared them to migration decision-making processes of the women in the study.

Design the Study. The study took place at the Yakima Valley Farm Workers Clinic (YVFWC) in Washington State. The clinic addressed the health care and social service needs of migrant and seasonal farmworkers, immigrants, and those without financial resources. It was the largest provider of prenatal care and each year about 1,300 women used the clinic's prenatal services. Approximately 40 percent of these women were undocumented immigrants from Mexico. Researchers used standardized questions and open-ended questions in Spanish to interview 14 women.

Collect the Data. The interviews were tape-recorded in Spanish and addressed three topics: (1) the border crossing experience and its context, (2) reasons for crossing the border, and (3) motivation to cross. The authors also conducted research into the political, historical, economic, and demographic factors of the national and local context for migrants from Mexico. They had access to a unique "First Steps Database" that had detailed health information on pregnant undocumented immigrant women going back to 1989.

Analyze the Data. In addition to describing the historical context and giving a demographic profile, the authors provided information and quotes from the 14 women. Most of the women crossed in remote borderland areas under great danger—including circumstances related to their being women and/or their traveling with children. Their motivations were mixed but joining a husband or family member who had already migrated and finding employment were key factors.

Interpret the Data.   The human social capital and rational economic choice models based on male experiences cannot capture the women's experiences. Age and family history were critical factors, and the decision-making processes combined employment options, being the manager of child care, and a sense of household responsibilities. Many took enormous risks to reunite with husbands and to keep their families intact.

Inform Others.   The findings were published in the *Social Science Journal.*

WHY CONDUCT SOCIAL RESEARCH?

Students, professors, professional researchers, and scientists in universities, research centers, and the government, with an army of assistants and technicians, conduct much social research. This research is not visible to the average person. Although the results may appear only in specialized publications or textbooks, the basic knowledge and research methods of professional researchers are the basis for all social research.

In addition to those in universities, people who work for newspapers, television networks, market research firms, schools, hospitals, social service agencies, political parties, consulting firms, gov-ernment agencies, personnel departments, public interest organizations, insurance companies, and law firms conduct research as part of their jobs. Numerous people make use of social research techniques. The findings from research yield better informed, less biased decisions than the guessing, hunches, intuition, and personal experience that were previously used (see Box 1.3). Unfortunately, those being studied may feel overstudied or overloaded by the research. For example, the many exit poll studies during elections have prompted a backlash of people refusing to vote and debates over legal restrictions on such polling.

Also, some people misuse or abuse social research—use sloppy research techniques, misinterpret findings, rig studies to find previously decided results, and so on. But the hostile reactions to such misuse may be directed at research in general instead of at the people who misuse it.

CONCLUSION

In this chapter, you learned what social research is, how the research process operates, and who conducts research. You also learned about alternatives to research—ways to get fast, easy, and practical knowledge that, nonetheless, often contains error, misinformation, and false reasoning. You saw how the scientific community works, how social research fits into the scientific enterprise, and how the

---

BOX **1.3**   **The Practitioner and Social Science**

Science does not, and cannot, provide people with fixed, absolute Truth. This is because science is a slow, incomplete process of reducing untruth. It is a quest for the best possible answers carried out by a collection of devoted people who labor strenuously in a careful, systematic, and open-minded manner. Many people are uneasy with the painstaking pace, hesitating progress, and incertitude of science. They demand immediate, absolute answers. Many turn to religious fanatics or political demagogues who offer final, conclusive truths in abundance.

What does this mean for diligent practitioners (e.g., human service workers, health care professionals, criminal justice officers, journalists, or policy ana-lysts) who have to make prompt decisions in their daily work? Must they abandon scientific thinking and rely only on common sense, personal conviction, or political doctrine? No. They, too, can use social scientific thinking. Their task is difficult but possible. They must conscientiously try to locate the best knowledge currently available; use careful, independent reasoning; avoid known errors or fallacies; and be wary of any doctrine offering complete, final answers. Practitioners must always be open to new ideas, use multiple information sources, and constantly question the evidence offered to support a course of action.

norms of science and journal articles are crucial to the scientific community. You also learned the steps of research.

Social research is for, about, and conducted by *people*. Despite the attention to the principles, rules, or procedures, remember that social research is a human activity. Researchers are people, not unlike yourself, who became absorbed in a desire to create and discover knowledge. Many find social research to be fun and exciting. They conduct it to discover new knowledge and to gain a richer understanding of the social world. Whether you become a professional social researcher, someone who applies a few research techniques as part of a job, or just someone who uses the results of research, you will benefit from learning about the research process. You will be enriched if you can begin to create a personal link between yourself and the research process.

Mills offered the following valuable advice in his *Sociological Imagination* (1959:196):

> *You must learn to use your life experiences in your intellectual work: continually to examine and interpret it. In this sense craftsmanship is the center of yourself and you are personally involved in every intellectual product upon which you may work.*

KEY TERMS

blind review
data
empirical
halo effect
junk science
norms of the scientific community

overgeneralization
premature closure
pseudoscience
scholarly journal article
scientific attitude
scientific community

scientific method
selective observation
social research
social theory

REVIEW QUESTIONS

1. What sources of knowledge are alternatives to social research?
2. Why is social research usually better than the alternatives?
3. Is social research always right? Can it answer any question? Explain.
4. How did science and oracles serve similar purposes in different eras?
5. What is the scientific community? What is its role?
6. What are the norms of the scientific community? What are their effects?
7. How does a study get published in a scholarly social science journal?
8. What steps are involved in conducting a research project?
9. What does it mean to say that research steps are not rigidly fixed?
10. What types of people do social research? For what reasons?

NOTES

1. See Ethan Bronner, "Study of Doctors Sees Little Effect of Affirmative Action on Careers," *New York Times* (October 8, 1998); Fox Butterfield, "Most Efforts to Stop Crime Fall Far Short, Study Finds," *New York Times* (April 16, 1997); Bob Whitby, "Truth or Dare," *Isthmus* (Madison, WI) (November 8, 1996); "Lies, Damned Lies, and . . . ," *Economist* (July 19, 1997); James Brooke, "Homophobia Often Found in Schools, Data Show," *New York Times* (October 13, 1998); Wysong, Aniskiewicz, and Wright (1994); John O'Neil, "See a Movie, Then Light Up," *New York Times* (July 6, 2004); and Jane Brody, "TV's Toll on Young Minds and Bodies." *New York Times* (August 3, 2004).

2. See Laurice Goodstein, "Church-Based Projects Lack Data on Results," *New York Times* (April 24, 2001).

3. For more on fallacies, see Babbie (1998:20–21), Kaplan (1964), and Wallace (1971).

4. See Rampton and Stauber (2001:256).

5. From Rampton and Stauber (2001:274–277, 305–306).

6. On the limits to self-knowledge, Wilson and Dunn (2004); on inaccurate eyewitness accounts, Wells and Olson (2003); on inaccurate risk evaluation, Gowda and Fox (2002), Paulos (2001); on SUVs, Bradsher (2002).

7. The rise of science is discussed in Camic (1980), Lemert (1979), Merton (1970), Wuthnow (1979), and Ziman (1976). For more on the historical development of the social sciences, see Eastrope (1974), Laslett (1992), Ross (1991), and Turner and Turner (1991).

8. See Herrnstein and Murray (1994) and a critique in Fischer et al. (1996).

9. See Rampton and Stauber (2001:229–252).

10. For more on the scientific community, see Cole (1983), Cole, Cole, and Simon (1981), Collins (1983), Collins and Restivo (1983), Hagstrom (1965), Merton (1973), Stoner (1966), and Ziman (1968).

11. See Cappell and Guterbock (1992) and Ennis (1992) for studies of sociological specialties.

12. For more on the social role of the scientist, see Ben-David (1971), Camic (1980), and Tuma and Grimes (1981).

13. Norms are discussed in Hagstrom (1965), Merton (1973), and Stoner (1966).

14. Violations of norms are discussed in Blume (1974) and Mitroff (1974).

15. See Lawrence K. Altman, "Drug Firm, Relenting, Allows Unflattering Study to Appear," *New York Times* (April 16, 1997); John Markoff, "Dispute over Unauthorized Reviews Leaves Intel Embarassed," *New York Times* (March 12, 1997); and Barry Meier, "Philip Morris Censored Data About Addiction," *New York Times,* (May 7, 1998).

16. The communication and publication system is described in Bakanic and colleagues (1987), Blau (1978), Cole (1983), Crane (1967), Gusfield (1976), Hargens (1988), Mullins (1973), Singer (1989), and Ziman (1968).

17. See Clemens and Powell (1995:446).

18. See Clemens and Powell (1995:444).

19. For more on the system of reward and stratification in science, see Cole and Cole (1973), Cole (1978), Fuchs and Turner (1986), Gaston (1978), Gustin (1973), Long (1978), Meadows (1974), and Reskin (1977).

Dimensions of Research

The objective of academic research, whether by sociologists, political scientists, or anthropologists, is to try to find answers to theoretical questions within their respective fields. In contrast, the objective of applied social research is to use data so that decisions can be made.

—Herbert J. Rubin, *Applied Social Research*, pp. 6–7

Three years after they graduated from college. Tim and Sharon met for lunch. Tim asked Sharon, "So, how is your new job as a researcher for Social Data, Inc.? What are you doing?" Sharon answered. "Right now I'm working on an applied research project on day care in which we're doing a cross-sectional survey to get descriptive data for an evaluation study." Sharon's description of her research project on the topic of day care touches on four dimensions of social research. This chapter discusses those dimensions.

The picture of social research in Chapter 1 was a simplified one. Research comes in multiple shapes and sizes. Before a researcher begins a study, he or she must decide on a specific type of research. Good researchers understand the advantages and disadvantages of each type, although most end up specializing in one.

In this chapter, you will learn four dimensions of research (see Chart 2.1). The first is the distinction between applied and basic research, or the primary audience for and use of research. The next is the purpose of doing research, or the goal of a study. The next two dimensions are more specific. The third dimension is how time is incorporated into the study design, and the last is the specific data collection technique used. The dimensions simplify decision making about research and they overlap in that certain dimensions are often found together (e.g., the goal of a study and a data collection technique). Once you learn the dimensions, you will begin to see how particular research questions you might want to investigate tend to be most compatible with certain ways of designing a study and collecting data.

One way to see the dimensions is as decision points for a researcher when moving from a broad topic to a focused research question to the design of a specific study. An understanding of the dimensions will prepare you to make such decisions. In addition, an awareness of the dimensions of research and how they fit together will make it easier for you to understand the research reports that you hear about or read in scholarly journals.

DIMENSIONS OF RESEARCH

Audience for and Use of Research

For over a century, social research has had two wings. Some researchers adopt a more detached, scientific, and academic orientation; others are more activist, pragmatic, and reform oriented. This is not a rigid separation. Researchers in the two wings cooperate and maintain friendly relations. Some move from one wing to another at different stages in their careers. The difference in orientation revolves around who consumes the findings and who uses them. In simple terms, some use research to advance general knowledge, whereas others use it to solve specific problems. Those who seek an understanding of the fundamental nature of social reality are engaged in **basic research** (also called *academic research* or *pure research*). Applied researchers, by contrast, primarily want to apply and tailor knowledge to address a specific practical issue. They want to answer a policy question or solve a pressing social problem.

Basic Research. Basic research advances fundamental knowledge about the social world. It focuses on refuting or supporting theories that explain how the social world operates, what makes things happen, why social relations are a certain way, and why society changes. Basic research is the source of most new scientific ideas and ways of thinking about the world. Its primary audience is the scientific community.

Many nonscientists criticize basic research and ask, "What good is it?" They consider basic research to be a waste of time and money because it does not have a direct use or help resolve an immediate problem. It is true that knowledge produced by basic research often lacks practical applications in the short term. Yet, basic research provides a foundation for knowledge and understanding that are generalizable to many policy areas, problems, or areas of study. Basic research is the source of most of the tools—methods, theories, and ideas—that applied researchers use. Really big breakthroughs in understanding and significant advances in knowledge usually come from basic research. In contrast to applied researchers, who want quick answers to questions for use within the next month or

year, basic researchers painstakingly seek answers to questions that could have an impact on thinking for over a century.

The questions asked by basic researchers seem impractical. For example, research on an unrelated topic—the causes of cancer in chickens—conducted over a decade before AIDS was discovered now provides the most promising source for advances in research on the AIDS virus. Basic research by the 1975 Nobel Prize–winner Howard Temin laid the foundation for understanding how viruses work and has had major implications for questions that did not even exist when he conducted his path-breaking research years ago. Today's com-

---

CHART 2.1   Dimensions and Major Types of Social Research

AUDIENCE FOR AND USE OF RESEARCH

- Basic
- Applied
  - Evaluation
  - Action
  - Social Impact

PURPOSE OF RESEARCH

- Explore
- Describe
- Explain

TIME DIMENSION IN RESEARCH

- Cross Sectional
- Longitudinal
  - Time series
  - Panel
  - Cohort
- Case study

DATA COLLECTION AND ANALYSIS TECHNIQUES

- Quantitative Data
  - Experiment
  - Survey
  - Nonreactive (content analysis, secondary analysis, existing statistics)
- Qualitative Data
  - Field (ethnography, participant observation)
  - Historical-comparative

Basic research   Research designed to advance fundamental knowledge about how the world works and build/test theoretical explanations. The scientific community is its primary audience.

puters could not exist without the pure research in mathematics conducted over a century ago, for which there was no known practical application at the time.

Police officers, officials trying to prevent delinquency, or counselors of youthful offenders may see little relevance to basic research on the question, "Why does deviant behavior occur?" Basic research rarely helps practitioners directly with their everyday concerns. Nevertheless, it stimulates new ways of thinking about deviance that have the potential to revolutionize and dramatically improve what practitioners do. Although policymakers and service providers often feel that basic research is of little relevance, public policies and social services will be ineffective and misguided without an understanding of actual causes.

Applied research, too, can build new knowledge. Nonetheless, basic research is essential for nourishing the expansion of knowledge. Researchers at the center of the scientific community conduct and consume most of the basic research.

Applied Research. Those doing **applied research** conduct a study to address a specific concern or to offer solutions to a problem of their employer, a club or organization they are affiliated with, their community, or a social movement to which they are committed.[1] Rarely do applied researchers build, test, or connect to a larger theory, develop a long-term general understanding, or carry out a large-scale investigation that might span years. Applied researchers rely on a quick, small-scale study that provides practical results that people can use in the short term. For example, the student government of University X wants to know whether the number of University X students who are arrested for driving while intoxicated or involved in auto accidents will decline if it sponsors alcohol-free parties next year. Applied research would be most applicable for this situation.

People employed in businesses, government offices, health care facilities, social service agencies, political organizations, and educational institutions conduct a great deal of applied research. They use the results of applied research to make decisions. Applied research affects decisions such as starting a new program to reduce the wait time

before a client receives benefits, adopting a new police response to reduce spousal abuse effectively, changing a student discipline procedure to increase fairness, emphasizing a candidate's stand on the environment instead of the economy, and marketing product A to mature adults instead of teenagers.

The primary audience for and consumers of applied research findings are practitioners such as teachers, counselors, and caseworkers, or decision makers such as managers, committees, and officials.

For example, when a court proceeding uses research results, such as survey results, peer researchers are not evaluating them. Instead, nonscientists (judges, jurors, lawyers) will assess research methodology and findings, usually on a nonscientific basis.[2] They can misinterpret the results or use evaluation standards that differ from those of the scientific community. Nonscientists might accept a study that fails to meet basic scientific criteria or reject a study that passes the highest standards of scientific quality and rigor. This means that applied researchers need to be very careful to translate findings from scientific-technical knowledge into a language used by nonspecialist decision makers. They must also provide ample warnings about any limitations of a study's design or the research results. Even if a decision maker is uninterested in details of how a study was conducted and wants only a very short summary of key findings, the applied researcher should also prepare a complete, detailed research report for any others who are interested and who can evaluate the quality of the research.

The results of applied research are less likely to enter the public domain in publications. Results may be available to only a small number of decision makers or practitioners, who decide whether or how to put the research results into practice and who may or may not use the results wisely.

Because applied research has immediate implications, it often generates conflict. This is not

Applied research Research designed to offer practical solutions to a concrete problem or address the immediate and specific needs of clinicians or practitioners.

new. For example, in 1903, Ellwood conducted an applied study of the jails and poorhouses in Missouri and documented serious deficiencies. His research report generated great public indignation, and he was accused of slandering the state that gave him employment.[3]

Whyte (1984) encountered conflict over findings in his applied research on a factory in Oklahoma and on restaurants in Chicago. In the first case, the management was more interested in defeating a union than in learning about employment relations; in the other, restaurant owners sought to make the industry look good rather than have findings about the nitty-gritty of its operations made public.

Indeed, calls for applied research on major policy issues may be a delaying tactic by officials who want to deflect criticism or postpone a decision until after the political heat dies down.

Applied and basic researchers adopt different orientations toward research methodology (see Chart 2.2). Applied researchers make more trade-offs. They may compromise scientific rigor to get quick, usable results. Compromise is no excuse for sloppy research, however. Applied researchers squeeze research into the constraints of an applied setting and balance rigor against practical needs. Such balancing requires an in-depth knowledge of research and an awareness of the consequences of compromising standards.

Three Types of Applied Research. There are many specific types of applied research. Here, you will learn about three major types: evaluation, action, and social impact assessment.

1. *Evaluation research.* The most widely used type of applied research is **evaluation research.**[4] It is widely used in large bureaucratic organizations (e.g., businesses, schools, hospitals, government, large nonprofit agencies) to find out whether a program, a new way of doing something,

| Evaluation research | Applied research in which one tries to determine how well a program or policy is working or reaching its goals and objectives. |

CHART 2.2   Basic and Applied Research Compared

ASPECT	BASIC	APPLIED
Primary audience	Scientific community (other researchers)	Practitioners, participants, or supervisors (nonresearchers)
Evaluators	Researcher peers	Practitioners, supervisors
Autonomy of researcher	High	Low-moderate
Research rigor	Very high	Varies, moderate
Highest priority	Verified truth	Relevance
Purpose	Create new knowledge	Resolve a practical problem
Success indicated by	Publication and impact on knowledge/ scientists	Direct application to address a specific concern/problem

a marketing campaign, a policy, and so forth is effective—in other words, "Does it work?"

Sample evaluation research questions are: Does a Socratic teaching technique improve learning over lecturing? Does a law enforcement program of mandatory arrest reduce spouse abuse? Does a flextime program increase employee productivity? Evaluation research measures the effectiveness of a program, policy, or way of doing something. Evaluation researchers use several research techniques (e.g., survey and field). If it can be used, the experimental technique is usually most effective.

Practitioners involved with a policy or program may conduct evaluation research for their own information or at the request of outside decision makers, who sometimes place limits on researchers by setting boundaries on what can be studied and determining the outcome of interest.

Ethical and political conflicts often arise in evaluation research because people have opposing interests in the findings about a program. Research results can affect getting a job, building political popularity, or promoting an alternative program. People who are personally displeased with the finding often try to attack the researcher or his or her methods as being sloppy, biased, or inadequate. In addition to creating controversy and being attacked, evaluation researchers are sometimes subjected to pressures to rig a study before they begin.

Evaluation research greatly expanded in the 1960s in the United States when many new federal social programs were created. Most researchers adopted a positivist approach (see Chapter 4) and used cost-benefit analysis. By the 1970s, evaluation research was mandated by most federal social programs. Evaluation research has limitations, however. The reports of research rarely go through a peer review process, raw data are rarely publicly available, and the focus is narrowed to select inputs and outputs more than the full process by which a program affects people's lives. In addition, policymakers can selectively use or ignore evaluation reports.

The 1996 welfare reform law in the United States was based on evaluation research. The research focused on amounts of income earned and costs of administering programs, but failed to measure family obligations not fulfilled or harm to children because mothers were forced to work. Policymakers and politicians selectly used the evidence that showed some positive benefits on family income to justify new laws.[5]

Wysong, Aniskiewicz, and Wright (1994) evaluated the effectiveness of the D.A.R.E. (Drug Abuse Resistance Education) program found in 10,000 schools in the United States and 42 other countries. The authors note that the program is widely used, well funded, and very popular with police departments, school officials, parent groups, and others. By having police officers deliver talks in early grades, D.A.R.E. tries to reduce illicit drug use among teens by increasing knowledge of drugs, developing antidrug coping skills, and raising self-esteem. The authors examined two groups of students who were seniors in a high school in Indiana. One group had participated in the D.A.R.E. program in seventh grade and the other group had not. Consistent with past research, the authors found no lasting differences among the groups regarding age of first drug use, frequency of drug use, or self-esteem. The authors suggest that the program's popularity may be due to its political symbolic impact. The program may be effective for latent goals (i.e., helping politicians, school officials, and others feel morally good and involved in antidrug actions) but ineffective for official goals (i.e., reducing illegal drug use by teenagers).

Two types of evaluation research are formative and summative. *Formative evaluation* is built-in monitoring or continuous feedback on a program used for program management. *Summative evaluation* looks at final program outcomes. Both are usually necessary.

Evaluation research is a part of the administration of many organizations (e.g., schools, government agencies, businesses, etc.). One example is the *Planning, Programming, and Budgeting System (PPBS),* first used by the U.S. Department of Defense in the 1960s. The PPBS is based on the idea that researchers can evaluate a program by measuring its accomplishments on the basis of its stated goals and objectives. An evaluator divides a program into components and analyzes each component with regard to its costs (staff, supplies, etc.) and accomplishments in achieving program objectives. For example, a women's health center offers pregnancy education. The program components are outreach, education, counseling, and referrals. The program objectives are to reach out to women who believe they are pregnant, provide education about pregnancy, counsel women about their health risks and concerns, and refer pregnant women to health care providers or family planning agencies. An evaluation researcher will examine the cost of each part of the program and measure how well the program meets its objectives. The researcher may ask how much staff time and how many supplies are used for outreach, how many calls or inquiries have resulted from those efforts, and whether the efforts increased the number of women from targeted groups coming to the center.[6]

2. *Action research.* **Action research** is applied research that treats knowledge as a form of power and abolishes the line between research and social action. There are several types of action research, but most share common characteristics: Those who are being studied participate in the research process; research incorporates ordinary or popular knowledge; research focuses on power with a goal of empowerment; research seeks to raise consciousness or increase awareness; and research is tied directly to political action.

Action researchers try to equalize power relations between themselves and research subjects, and they avoid having more control, status, and authority than those they study. These researchers try to advance a cause or improve conditions by expanding public awareness. They are explicitly political, not value neutral. Because the goal is to improve the conditions and lives of research participants, publishing in formal reports, articles, or books becomes secondary. Action researchers assume that knowledge develops from experience, particularly the experience of sociopolitical action. They also assume that ordinary people can become aware of conditions and learn to take actions that can bring about improvement.

Action research is associated with the critical social science approach discussed in Chapter 4. It attracts researchers who hold specific perspectives (e.g., environmental, radical, African American, feminist, etc.). For example, most feminist research has a dual mission: to create social change by transforming gender relations and to contribute to the advancement of knowledge.[7] A feminist researcher who studies sexual harassment might recommend policy changes both to reduce it as well as to inform potential victims so they can protect themselves and defend their rights. In one situation, action research

involved working to preserve a town that was to be destroyed by a dam project. An action researcher worked together with union officials and management to redesign work to prevent layoffs. In developing nations, action researchers work among illiterate, impoverished peasants to teach literacy, study local conditions, and spread an awareness of conditions, and to attempt to improve them.[8]

Randy Stoecker (1999) argued the ultimate goal of *participatory* action research is to democratize the knowledge-creation process, reveal injustices, highlight the centrality of social conflict, and emphasize the importance of engaging in collection action to alter social structures. This means that the local research participants assume an active role in formulating, designing, and carrying out the research. Professional researchers and local participants cogenerate knowledge in collaborative processes that continuously incorporate the diverse experiences of local groups (Greenwood and Levin, 2003:149). While fully involving participants in problem definition and study implementation, a trained researcher often has to assist and provide expertise that guides participants in the study design, data gathering, and data analysis/interpretation stages. The researcher takes the role of a consultant or collaborator who assists with, but who does not have complete control over, the research process. The researcher has to balance upholding professional standards with adapting to local conditions, involving participants, and addressing their concerns.

Based on his personal experience in several community-based organizations, Stoecker discovered that study success requires research to be community initiated and have substantial community control. This means that the researcher and local participants jointly control and have ownership over research findings (Kemmis and McTaggart, 2003). Stoecker noted that grassroots participants often fear that professional researchers will use findings only to enhance their own careers. He warns (1999:851), "Do not try to publish an article from the research without the community's permission." This can create a dilemma; not only do researchers face career pressures like others, but also scientific norms require a full disclosure of study details and the dissemination of findings.

Action research   Applied research in which the primary goal is to facilitate social change or bring about a value-oriented political-social goal.

BOX 2.1 Areas Assessed in Social Impact Studies

- Community service (e.g., school enrollments, speed of police responses)
- Social conditions (e.g., the races of friends that children are likely to make based on play areas; crime rates; the ability of elderly people to feel that they can care for themselves)
- Economic impact (e.g., changes in income levels, business failure rate)
- Demographic consequences (e.g., changes in the mix of old and young people, population movement into or out of an area)
- Environment (e.g., changes in air quality, noise levels, commuting time)
- Health outcomes (e.g., changes in occurrence of diseases or presence of harmful substances)
- Psychological well-being (e.g., changes in stress, fear, or self-esteem)

Sharing knowledge with professional peers and in publications also helps to ensure quality control over the research and give it legitimacy.

3. *Social impact assessment research.* **Social impact assessment**[9] may be part of a larger environmental impact statement required by government agencies. Its purpose is to estimate the likely consequences of a planned change. Such an assessment can be used for planning and making choices among alternative policies—for example, to estimate the ability of a local hospital to respond to an earthquake; to determine changes in housing if a major new highway is built; or to assess the impact on college admissions and long-term debt if all college students received interest-free loans to be paid back over 20 years, with payments based on the size of their incomes. Researchers conducting social impact assessment examine many outcomes and often work in an interdisciplinary research team. The impact on several areas can be measured or assessed (see Box 2.1).

Various forms of gambling have expanded rapidly in the United States. In 1980, gambling was

legal in only a few states and yielded under $10 billion in profits. Some 20 years later, it was legal in 48 states and profits exceeded $50 billion a year. The reason is simple. Lawmakers sought new sources of revenue without raising taxes and wanted to promote economic development. The gambling industry promised them new jobs, economic revitalization, and a "cut" in the huge flow of money from gambling. This looked ideal to the lawmakers: They could help create jobs, strengthen the local economy, and get revenue without raising taxes.

Today, most promises have gone unrealized and there is widespread disappointment. Job growth has been limited and most has been in the category of low-wage, unskilled jobs. The very high revenue estimates were not reached, because as more areas offered gambling, the supply grew faster than demand. Also, money was diverted from other businesses. As people spent money on gambling, they had less for clothing and other consumer goods. In addition, few public officials anticipated extra costs for law enforcement, social services, street cleaning, and similar areas that accompanied gambling. Gambling hit lower-income people the worst, and the social problem of compulsive gambling has increased. Although only 2 to 4 percent of the population, compulsive gamblers have low work productivity, devastate their families, and often turn to crime.

Were such results predictable? Could anyone have anticipated the outcome? Yes, if the officials had first conducted high-quality *social impact assessment* research and followed results of the research. This rarely occurs. Most officials accept extravagant claims made by industry advocates and cling to the illusion of getting something for next to nothing. Many remain ignorant or distrustful of social science research. The few social impact studies that were conducted made accurate predictions, and the outcome was no surprise.

Social impact assessment Applied research that documents the likely consequences for various areas of social life if a major new change is introduced into a community.

Two Tools in Applied Research. Applied researchers use two tools: needs assessment and cost-benefit analysis.

In a **needs assessment,** a researcher collects data to determine major needs and their severity. It is often a preliminary step before a government agency or charity decides on a strategy to help people. Yet, it often becomes tangled in the complex relations within a community. A researcher may confront dilemmas or difficult issues.

One issue is to decide on the group to target for the assessment. Should the researcher focus on the needs of homeless people sleeping in a park, working people who lose large amounts of money betting at a racetrack, or executives who drink too much at the country club? The most visible need may not be the most serious one. Whom does the researcher ask or observe? Should he or she ask the business owners about the needs of the homeless?

A second issue is that people may not express a need in a way that links it directly to policies or long-term solutions. A researcher may find that homeless people say they need housing. After examining the situation, however, he or she may determine that housing would be available if the homeless had jobs. The housing need is caused by a need for jobs. The need for jobs, in turn, may be caused by a need for skills, a "living wage," and certain types of businesses. Thus, to address the housing need, it may be necessary to attract specific types of businesses, enact a new minimum wage, and provide job training. The apparent need may be linked to a deeper problem or condition. People may not be aware of the causes. For example, a need for health care may be caused by drinking polluted water, poor diet, and a lack of exercise.

Needs assessment An applied research tool in which one gathers descriptive information about a need, issue, or concern, including its magnitude, scope, and severity.

Cost-benefit analysis An applied research tool economists developed in which monetary value is assigned to the inputs and outcomes of a process, and then the researcher examines the balance between them.

Is this a need for more health care or is it a need for better water treatment and a public health education program?

A third issue is that people often have multiple needs. If a researcher finds that people need to reduce pollution, eliminate gangs, and improve transport services, which is most important? A good needs assessment identifies both the expressed and the less visible needs of a target group, as well as the more serious or widespread needs. A researcher must trace links among related needs to identify those of highest priority.

A fourth issue is that a needs assessment may generate political controversy or suggest solutions beyond local control. Powerful groups may not want some needs documented or publicized. The researcher who finds that a city has a lot of unreported crime may tarnish the image of a safe, well-run city promoted by the Chamber of Commerce and the city government. A needs assessment that documents racial discrimination may embarrass civic leaders who prefer to present themselves in public as unprejudiced. The needs of one group, such as people who bet too much at the racetrack, may be linked to the actions of another group that benefits by creating that need, such as the racetrack's owners and employees. Once a researcher documents needs and offers a resolution to them, he or she may be caught between opposing groups.

The second tool is a **cost-benefit analysis.** Economists developed cost-benefit analysis, in which the researcher estimates the future costs and benefits of one or several proposed actions and gives them monetary values. In brief, it works like this: A researcher identifies all the consequences of a proposed action. Next, he or she assigns each consequence a monetary value. The consequences may include intangibles, such as clean air, low crime rates, political freedom, scenic beauty, low stress levels, and even human life itself. Often, the researcher assigns a probability or likelihood to the occurrence of various consequences. Next, policymakers or others identify negative consequences (costs) and positive ones (benefits). Finally, costs are compared to benefits, and policymakers decide whether they balance.

Cost-benefit analysis appears to be a neutral, rational, and technical decision-making strategy, but it can be controversial. People do not necessarily agree on what are positive and negative consequences. For example, I may see widening a nearby road as a benefit because it will let me travel to work much more rapidly. But the homeowner who lives along the road may see the same action as a cost because it will remove some of his or her lot and he or she will then experience more noise, pollution, and congestion.

There are two ways to assign monetary values to costs and benefits. *Contingency evaluation* asks people how much something is worth to them. For example, I may want to estimate the cost of air pollution that has health consequences for the average person. I might ask people: How much is it worth to you not to cough a lot and miss work two days a year due to asthma? If the average value assigned by people is $150 in a town of 20,000, then the contingency evaluation or subjective benefit of health would be $150 × 20,000 per year = $3 million. I might balance this against higher profits for a company or more jobs created by allowing the pollution. A problem with this estimation is that people rarely give accurate estimates and different people may assign very different values. To an impoverished person, coughing and missing work may be worth $500, but for a wealthy person, it may be $10,000. In this example, polluting companies would tend to move to towns with low-income people, worsening their living conditions.

Using the same example, *actual cost evaluation* estimates the actual medical and job loss costs. I would estimate the health impact and then add up medical bills and costs for employers to get replacement workers. For example, if medical treatment averages $100 per person and a replacement worker costs an extra $150, the cost of treating 10,000 people each year and hiring 5,000 replacement workers for two days would be $100 × 10,000 people = $1,000,000 plus $300 × 5,000 workers = $1,500,000, for a total of $2.5 million. This method ignores pain and suffering, inconvenience, and indirect costs (e.g., a parent stays home with a sick child, a child is unable to play sports because of asthma). To balance the costs with benefits by this method, the polluting factory would need to earn an extra $2.5 million in profits.

A significant issue for cost-benefit analysis is the assumption that everything has a price (learning, health, love, happiness, human dignity, chastity, etc.) and that people assign similar valuations. It also raises moral and political concerns. Cost-benefit calculations usually favor upper-income people over low-income or poor people. This occurs because the relative value of a cost or benefit depends on one's wealth and income. Saving 15 minutes in a commute to work is assigned a greater value or benefit for high-income people than for the same 15-minute time savings for low-income people; 15 minutes of a high-income person's time is monetarily worth more. Likewise, cutting a road through an impoverished neighborhood has a lower cost, because of lower property values, than putting the road through an area of high-cost homes.

Cost-benefit analysis tends to conceal the moral-political aspect of questions. For instance, the balance between the human cost of "pulling the plug" on a life-support machine for a very ill person and the benefit of saving large expenses to keep the machine operating has both moral and economic aspects. The moral aspect stands out in decisions that involve a single identifiable person with whom the decision maker has an emotional attachment. Few of us solely look at this issue in terms of economic costs and benefits. The moral aspect can get lost in a decision that involves people who are not easily identified as individuals among a large group and for whom decision makers lack direct, personal contact. A moral aspect remains, even if the focus is on the economic costs and benefits.

Beyond the Basic–Applied Dichotomy. The basic versus applied research dichotomy is simplistic and ignores three related features: (1) the form of knowledge created, (2) various audiences that use research findings, and (3) whether a study is initiated, designed, and controlled by an independent researcher or others who may be nonresearchers. Next, we look at these three factors and an expanded set of research types.

Two Forms of Knowledge. Basic and applied researchers produce two forms of knowledge, instrumental and reflexive. The forms mirror a distinction between neutral, impartial, task-oriented instrumental behavior and principled, value-engaged, reflexive behavior. Most studies published in scholarly journals and conducted by practitioners build and expand instrumental knowledge. Researchers create **instrumental knowledge** as they (1) extend old or invent new research techniques; (2) gather, verify, connect, and accumulate new factual information; and (3) advance, innovate, and elaborate the frontiers of understanding.

The creation of instrumental knowledge often sidesteps or avoids directly engaging moral or value-directed concerns. By contrast, reflexive knowledge is self-aware, value-oriented knowledge. Researchers creating **reflexive knowledge** (1) build on specific moral commitments, (2) consciously reflect on the context and processes of knowledge creation, and (3) emphasize the implications and uses of new knowledge. They ask questions such as, Why and how is this knowledge being created? What is its importance or value? What are its implications for other knowledge, humanity, or moral-value principles?

Audiences for Social Research Findings. Many diverse audiences read and use research findings. One audience is professional researchers or academics in the scientific community who try to expand the foundation of knowledge with new basic research results. There are also four nonresearcher audiences. One is the general public or informed members of a society. They learn about research results in formal schooling or in the mass media outlets. A second type of audience is the political activist, community advocate, or research partici-

Instrumental knowledge Knowledge narrowly focused to answer a basic or applied research question, issue, or concern with an outcome or task-oriented orientation.

Reflexive knowledge Knowledge that broadly examines the assumptions, context, and moral-value positions of basic or applied social research, including the research process itself and the implications of what is learned.

pant in action research. Members of this audience may have personally facilitated, collaborated in, or worked with researchers to carry out a study and have direct, immediate interest in results. A third type of audience is the general practitioner who combines a range of practical, relevant knowledge that may be applicable to an applied issue area or is closely connected to related issues. They may be policy specialists in government or large organizations (e.g., businesses, hospitals, police departments). Last, is the narrowly targeted practitioner audience. This practitioner wants research findings that can help him or her immediately address a specific practical problem or issue that is directly at hand.

Researcher Autonomy and Commissioned Social Research. An idealized and romantic image of a social researcher is someone with total freedom to pursue knowledge without any impediments. The idealized researcher is independent, has sufficient funds for a study, and maintains complete control over what to study and how to study it. A contrast to this image of the autonomous researcher is the reality of commissioned or sponsored research. Researchers often depend on others for employment and research funds or conduct research at the behest of someone else.

Most commissioned studies involve some kind of limitation on researcher autonomy. Someone other than the actively involved researcher provides the funds and directions as to the topic and scope of the research question. Other "strings" with funding may include restrictions to examine certain issues but not others, limits on the time to complete a study, specification of the techniques to be used or people to be contacted in a study, and directions about how to disseminate findings.

Expanded Set of Basic and Applied Research Types. Combining form of knowledge, audience, and whether the study is commissioned gives us an expanded set of basic and applied research and roles of the social researcher (see Chart 2.3). Basic research for the scientific community can be reflexive or instrumental. Burawoy and colleagues (2004) call these critical and professional. Sometimes a large private foundation or government agency commissions researchers to conduct studies; this is basic contract

CHART 2.3   Expanded Set of Basic and Applied Research Types

AUDIENCE	FORM OF KNOWLEDGE		
	REFLEXIVE	INSTRUMENTAL	INSTRUMENTAL
	Autonomous	*Commissioned*	*Autonomous*
Basic Research Type			
Scientific community	Basic critical	Basic contract	Basic professional
Applied Research Types			
General public	Public intellectual	Dedicated policy	Democratic policy
Participants	Public educator	Consultant	Participatory researcher
Generalist practitioner	Democratic deliberation	Democratic contract	Democratic applied
Narrow practitioner	Dedicated deliberation	Dedicated contract	Dedicated applied

research. Sometimes researchers assume a public intellectual role, in which autonomous researchers produce reflexive knowledge to advance public discussion and debate. At other times, the knowledge for the public is instrumental. It may be commissioned and dedicated to a specific policy or autonomous and a democratic contribution to policy discussion. Research shared with and for participants in a study places the researcher in a public educator role when the knowledge is reflexive. When it is instrumental, the researcher may act as a consultant to the participants or a participatory researcher who is more of an equal with the participants. On some occasions, generalist and targeted practitioners create and apply reflexive knowledge in debates and deliberations over issues or decision options. More often practitioners are focused on instrumental knowledge. Hammersley (2000) outlined a distinction between the generalist who creates and uses knowledge as contributions to open, democratic decisions and the narrow practitioner focused on a particular targeted issue with results that have little wider application or distribution. The research may be commissioned by an outside group or employer or created autonomously, giving us contract or applied uses by the two types of practitioners.

Purpose of Research

If you ask someone why he or she is conducting a study, you might get a range of responses: "My boss told me to"; "It was a class assignment"; "I was curious"; "My roommate thought it would be a good idea." There are almost as many reasons to do research as there are researchers. Yet, the purposes of social research may be organized into three groups based on what the researcher is trying to accomplish—explore a new topic, describe a social phenomenon, or explain why something occurs.[10] Studies may have multiple purposes (e.g., both to explore and to describe), but one purpose is usually dominant (see Box 2.2).

Exploration. Perhaps you have explored a new topic or issue in order to learn about it. If the issue was new or no researchers had written about it, you began at the beginning. This is called **exploratory research.** The researcher's goal is to formulate more precise questions that future research can answer. Exploratory research may be the first stage in a sequence of studies. A researcher may need to conduct an exploratory study in order to know enough to design and execute a second, more systematic and extensive study.

Research on AIDS (acquired immune deficiency syndrome) illustrates exploratory research. When AIDS first appeared, around 1980, no one

> **Exploratory research**   Research in which the primary purpose is to examine a little understood issue or phenomenon to develop preliminary ideas and move toward refined research questions by focusing on the "what" question.

BOX **2.2** **Purpose of Research**

EXPLORATORY	DESCRIPTIVE	EXPLANATORY
■ Become familiar with the basic facts, setting, and concerns.	■ Provide a detailed, highly accurate picture.	■ Test a theory's predictions or principle.
■ Create a general mental picture of conditions.	■ Locate new data that contradict past data.	■ Elaborate and enrich a theory's explanation.
■ Formulate and focus questions for future research.	■ Create a set of categories or classify types.	■ Extend a theory to new issues or topics.
■ Generate new ideas, conjectures, or hypotheses.	■ Clarify a sequence of steps or stages.	■ Support or refute an explanation or prediction.
■ Determine the feasibility of conducting research.	■ Document a causal process or mechanism.	■ Link issues or topics with a general principle.
■ Develop techniques for measuring and locating future data.	■ Report on the background or context of a situation.	■ Determine which of several explanations is best.

knew what type of disease it was or even if it was a disease. No one knew what caused it, how it spread, or why it appeared. Officials knew only that people were entering hospitals with symptoms that no one had seen before, that they failed to respond to any treatment, and that they died quickly. It took many exploratory medical and social science studies before researchers knew enough to design precise studies about the disease.

Exploratory studies often go unpublished. Instead, researchers incorporate them into more systematic research that they publish later.

Lavoie, Robitaille, and Martine (2000) conducted an exploratory study that they published in a scholarly journal, *Violence Against Women.* The researchers wanted to learn what teens thought about violence in interpersonal relations. They gathered qualitative data from discussion groups with 24 Canadian teenagers, ages 14 to 19, in Quebec. The researchers found that the teens experienced many forms of violence in their social relations. The teenagers explained the violence and nonconsensual sexual relations by emphasizing individual, couple, and social factors (e.g., the influence of peers or pornography). The teens often blamed the victim and placed the responsibility for violent acts on the victims of violence. The authors suggest that studies of abuse and methods of violence prevention need to be tailored to how teens understand and explain violence.

Exploratory research rarely yields definitive answers. It addresses the "what" question: "What is this social activity really about?" It is difficult to conduct because there are few guidelines to follow. Everything is potentially important, steps are not well defined, and the direction of inquiry changes frequently. This can be frustrating for researchers, who may feel adrift or that they are "spinning their wheels."

Exploratory researchers must be creative, open minded, and flexible; adopt an investigative stance; and explore all sources of information. They ask creative questions and take advantage of *serendipity,* those unexpected or chance factors that have larger implications. For example, researchers expected to find that the younger a child was at immigration to a new nation, the less the negative impact on that child when going on to college. Instead, they unexpectedly discovered that children who immigrated in a specific age group (between ages 6 and 11) were especially vulnerable to the disruption of immigration, more so than either older or younger children.[11]

Exploratory researchers frequently use qualitative techniques for gathering data and they are less wedded to a specific theory or research question. Qualitative research tends to be more open to using a range of evidence and discovering new issues.

Description. You may have a more highly developed idea about a social phenomenon and want to describe it. **Descriptive research** presents a picture of the specific details of a situation, social setting, or relationship. Much of the social research found in scholarly journals or used for making policy decisions is descriptive.

Descriptive and exploratory research have many similarities. They blur together in practice. In descriptive research, the researcher begins with a well-defined subject and conducts research to describe it accurately. The outcome of a descriptive study is a detailed picture of the subject. For example, results may indicate the percentage of people who hold a particular view or engage in specific behaviors—for example, that 10 percent of parents physically or sexually abuse their children.

A descriptive study presents a picture of types of people or of social activities. For example, Donald McCabe (1992) studied cheating among U.S. college students. He was interested in how people rationalize deviance. He thought that they developed justifications that neutralized or turned back moral disapproval, in order to protect their self-images and deflect self-blame. He conducted a survey of over 6,000 students and found that two-thirds admitted to cheating on a major test or assignment at least once. Six major types of cheating appeared to be common. When McCabe asked the students why they cheated, he discovered that they justified their behavior using four major *neutralization strategies.* The most common strategy, cited by over half of the cheaters, was a denial of responsibility. In this strategy, people claim that forces beyond their control, such as a heavy workload or peer behavior, justify the deviance. Other rationalizations given by cheating students included a denial that anyone is hurt, condemnation of the teacher, or an appeal to higher loyalties such as friendship.

Descriptive research focuses on "how" and "who" questions ("How did it happen?" "Who is involved?"). Exploring new issues or explaining why something happens (e.g., why students neutralize cheating or why students hold specific religious beliefs) is less of a concern for descriptive researchers than describing how things are.

A great deal of social research is descriptive. Descriptive researchers use most data-gathering techniques—surveys, field research, content analysis, and historical-comparative research. Only experimental research is infrequent.

Explanation. When you encounter an issue that is already known and have a description of it, you might begin to wonder *why* things are the way they are. The desire to know "why," to explain, is the purpose of **explanatory research.** It builds on exploratory and descriptive research and goes on to identify the reason something occurs. Going beyond focusing on a topic or providing a picture of it, explanatory research looks for causes and reasons. For example, a descriptive researcher may discover that 10 percent of parents abuse their children, whereas the explanatory researcher is more interested in learning *why* parents abuse their children.

Researchers use multiple strategies when doing explanatory research. Some explanatory studies develop a novel explanation and then provide empirical evidence to support it or against it. Other studies outline two or more competing explanations and then present evidence for each, in a type of a "head-to-head" comparison to see which is the strongest. Still others take an existing explanation, often derived from social theory or previous research, and extend it to explain a new issue, setting, or group of people. The goal is to learn how well the explanation holds up and see whether it needs to be modified or is limited to operating in only certain conditions.

For example, Lee, Farrell, and Link (2004) extended the "contact hypothesis" to explain a new area, homeless people in U.S. cities. Social researchers have studied the contact hypothesis since the 1950s, primarily with regard to interracial relations. It explains the degree of prejudice and negative attitudes by saying people tend to hold negative views toward an "outgroup" because of ignorance and negative

Descriptive research Research in which the primary purpose is to "paint a picture" using words or numbers and to present a profile, a classification of types, or an outline of steps to answer questions such as who, when, where, and how.

Explanatory research Research in which the primary purpose is to explain why events occur and to build, elaborate, extend, or test theory.

stereotypes. Once people have contact with and get to know outgroup members, they replace their ignorance and negative stereotypes with more positive views. It answers the question, Why do people hold negative feelings toward outgroups?, with "a lack of contact." Many studies examined the hypothesis, looking at specific conditions of contact and the degree to which an outgroup is perceived as threatening.

Lee, Farrell, and Link (2004) expanded the idea of contact by including 14 measures of exposure to homeless people. These range from having information (e.g., articles, television), personal observation, personal interaction, to having been homeless oneself or having a homeless family member. They also developed comprehensive measures of views on the homeless. These included beliefs about why people become homeless, positive emotions, seeing the homeless as dangerous, feeling empathy, and supporting homeless people's rights. Using telephone survey data from a random sample of 1,388 adults in 200 U.S. metropolitan areas in 1990, they found clear evidence supporting the contact hypothesis. People who had greater contact, and more intimate types of contact, with homeless people held more favorable views and were more likely to support helping the homeless than people who had little or no contact. They also found some variation in views about the homeless based on a person's race, age, education level, and political ideology.

Christian and Lapinski (2003) also conducted explanatory research using the contact hypothesis in a study of high school students' attitudes toward Muslims after the September 11, 2001, New York World Trade Center terrorist attack. The authors surveyed 132 students in two high schools in the Midwest, none themselves Muslim, six months after the terrorist attack. They measured personal contact with Muslims, knowledge of Islam and various religions, and mass media use as well as attitudes toward Muslims and endorsing negative stereotypes of Muslims. Consistent with the contact hypothesis, the authors found that the students who knew the most about Islam and had personal contacts with Muslims or Muslim friends were least likely to hold hostile attitudes or endorse negative stereotypes. Although students with higher media use (especially television) and who discussed issues with their parents had slightly lower negative attitudes, the impact of media and parents was weak. By contrast, direct personal contact had a very strong effect. The contact hypothesis illustrates a powerful explanation extended to many new situations. In yet another study of the contact hypothesis, McLaren (2003) conducted a *secondary analysis* (discussed in Chapter 11) by statistically examining previously collected data in 1997 Eurobarometer surveys. He found that in 17 European nations having contact with immigrants reduced anti-immigrant prejudice. These and many other studies on the contact hypothesis that examined it with different groups, issues, locations, and situations have strengthened its generalizability as an explanation of the sources of (and ways to reduce) hostile attitudes and negative stereotypes about outgroup members.

Time Dimension in Research

Another dimension of social research is the treatment of time. An awareness of the time dimension will help you read or conduct research because different research questions or issues incorporate time in different ways.

Some studies give a snapshot of a single, fixed time point and allow you to analyze it in detail. Other studies provide a moving picture that lets you follow events, people, or social relations over periods of time. Quantitative research is divided into two groups: a single point in time (cross-sectional research) versus multiple time points (longitudinal research). Quantitative research looks at a large group of cases, people, or units and measures a limited number of features. By contrast, a case study involves qualitative methods and focuses on one or a few cases during a limited time period.

Cross-Sectional Research. Most sociological research takes a snapshot approach to the social world. In **cross-sectional research,** researchers ob-

---

Cross-sectional research Any research that examines information on many cases at one point in time.

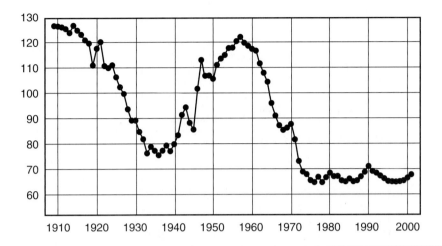

FIGURE 2.1   United States Birth Rate (births per 1,000 women ages 15–44) 1910 to 2000

Source: Calculated by author from U.S. census data.

serve at one point in time. Cross-sectional research is usually the simplest and least costly alternative. Its disadvantage is that it cannot capture social processes or change. Cross-sectional research can be exploratory, descriptive, or explanatory but it is most consistent with a descriptive approach to research. An example of cross-sectional research is the descriptive study by McCabe (1992) on cheating by college students.

Longitudinal Research. Researchers using **longitudinal research** examine features of people or other units at more than one time. It is usually more complex and costly than cross-sectional research, but it is also more powerful, especially when researchers seek answers to questions about social change. Descriptive and explanatory researchers use longitudinal approaches. We will now consider three types of longitudinal research: time series, panel, and cohort.

1. **Time-series research** is a longitudinal study in which the same type of information is collected on a group of people or other units across multiple time periods. Researchers can observe stability or change in the features of the units or can track conditions over time.

Information from time-series data can be very revealing. For example, time-series data on the

U.S. birth rate since 1910 (Figure 2.1) shows how the number of births per woman declined steadily in the 1920s, continued to drop in the 1930s and early 1940s, but sharply reversed direction after World War II ended (1945). It began the dramatic upsurge called the baby boom of the 1950s to 1960s before declining and becoming stable in the 1970s. Time series can reveal changes not easily seen otherwise. For example, since 1967 the Higher Education Research Institute (2004) has gathered annual survey data on large samples of students entering American colleges for use in applied research by colleges. Time-series results on the percentage of students answering which value was very important for them (Figure 2.2) show a clear reversal of priorities between the 1960s and 1970s. The students ceased to value developing a meaningful philosophy of life and instead sought material-financial success.

Longitudinal research   Any research that examines information from many units or cases across more than one point in time.

Time-series research   Longitudinal research in which information can be about different cases or people in each of several time periods.

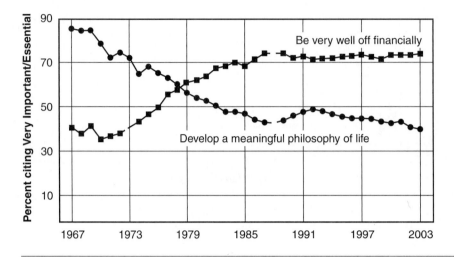

FIGURE 2.2   Value Priorities of U.S. College Freshmen, 1967–2003

Source: From Higher Education Research Institute. (2004). *Recent findings,* Figure 4. Retrieved September 25, 2004, from www.gseis.ucla.edu/heri/findings.html.

Time series is used for many topics. For example, Skog (2003) documented that the level of alcohol consumption in Canada since 1950 has been associated with numbers of fatal accidents such as falls or auto accidents. Davis (1992) used time-series data to show a shift in American political-social attitudes in 1972–1987 on 42 items (e.g., crime, free speech, politics, race, religion, and gender/sexuality), with a general move toward more liberal positions. A time-series study by Pettit and Western (2004) on imprisonment rates among Black and White men in the United States in 1964–1997 found that during a major rise in incarceration rates in the 1980s (up by 300 percent), African American men were six to eight times more likely than White men to go to jail. Young Black men who did not attend college were more likely to be incarcerated, with nearly one in three spending some time behind bars, and these rates doubled for Black men who failed to complete high school.

2. The **panel study** is a powerful type of longitudinal research. It is more difficult to conduct

than time-series research. In a panel study, the researcher observes exactly the same people, group, or organization across time periods. Panel research is formidable to conduct and very costly. Tracking people over time is often difficult because some people die or cannot be located. Nevertheless, the results of a well-designed panel study are very valuable. Even short-term panel studies can clearly show the impact of a particular life event.

Three examples illustrate the value of panel studies. Muriel Egerton (2002) examined the relationship between civic engagement (i.e., volunteering and participating in churches, labor unions, environmental groups, political parties, women's groups, parent–teacher associations, and sports clubs) and higher education among young people in Great Britain. She used the theoretical concept of social capital (i.e., having social connections with other people), which is strengthened by education, such that having more education expands a person's social network and tends to makes him or her more central in it. Data for the study came from nine years of the British Household Panel Study (1991–1999), a survey of a national sample of the same people gathered annually that includes questions on memberships and activity in organizations. Egerton looked at people in the year before they entered

> **Panel study** Longitudinal research in which information is about the identical cases or people in each of several time periods.

higher or tertiary education, at age 17 or 18, and at its completion, about age 22 or 23. She also compared levels of social engagement before and after higher education, and with young people who had not gone into higher education. By tracking information on the same people over six to eight years, she could look at their memberships and activity levels over time. Few people were active in more than one organization, so she focused on being in none or one or more organizations, and for those with an organization, being a member or active participant. She found that young people who entered higher education tended to have been active in an organization before higher education than did those who did not continue with schooling. She also noticed a slight drop-off immediately after completing higher education, because it is a transitional year with new social groups, geographical mobility, and occupational change, but after a year or two it picked up. She found that education has little effect on activity in sports and social clubs, but it increases activity in civic and religious organizations and overall activity. People who were active prior to higher education tended to be from professional families and their activity changed less, whereas those from nonprofessional families showed larger increases. They apparently acquired new values or social networks while in higher education. In general, youth from professional families were more active compared to those from blue-collar families or from the families of business managers. Apparently managers tend to rely on informal social networks within their business, whereas professionals develop wider social networks that include formal civic organizations that are involved in promoting public service or assisting in the community.

M. Kent Jennings and Vicki Zeitner (2003) also looked at civic engagement but focused on how Internet usage among Americans has affected it. They noted that cross-sectional data showed that Internet users have higher levels of civic engagement. Yet, more educated people tend to use the Internet more and to be more engaged in civic organizations. Past studies could not tell us whether over time increasing usage of the Internet affected the level of a person's civic engagement. By using panel data collected from a survey of high school seniors in 1965 who were again studied in 1973, 1982, and 1997 (by which time they were in their fifties), the researchers could measure levels of civic engagement before and after Internet use. The Internet was not available until after 1982 but was in wide use by 1997. Both people previously interviewed and their offspring were surveyed. The measure of civic engagement included a wide range of behaviors and attitudes. In general, the authors found that those who were more engaged prior to the availability of the Internet were more likely to use the Internet, and people who used the Internet also increased their civic engagement once they started using the Internet. Whereas Internet users among people in the panels since 1965, who are now in their fifties, increased all forms of civic engagement as they adopted the Internet, their offspring who use the Internet are less likely to be volunteers or become engaged in their local community. Internet versus non-Internet use increases levels of civic engagement for the older more than the younger generation, especially younger generation Internet users who use the Internet for purposes other than following public affairs.

Susan Mayer (2002) also used a panel design to examine the impact of economic inequality among neighborhoods on schooling. She observed that while economic inequality and residential segregation by income grew in the United States between 1970 and 1990, overall schooling rates remained the same. She wondered whether the schooling might differ in the increasingly separate upper- and lower-income neighborhoods and noted that different theories predicted a rise or fall in schooling as interneighborhood inequality grew. She analyzed U.S. census and other data to track neighborhoods (not individual people) across time and looked at the similarity of levels of family income as well as school attendance rates in each neighborhood. She studied inequality by comparing one neighborhood with other neighborhoods around it at three time points: 1970, 1980, and 1990. Using the neighborhood as the unit, she found that increasing between-neighborhood inequality resulted in schooling improvements for the children in the higher-income neighborhoods, but declines for the children in the lower-income neighborhoods.

Thus, the rise in economic inequality among neighborhoods over time produced opposite effects for the children in higher-income and in lower-income neighborhoods; the children in higher-income neighborhoods were likely to get more schooling, and those in lower-income ones tended to get less schooling.

3. A **cohort study** is similar to the panel study, but rather than observing the exact same people, a category of people who share a similar life experience in a specified time period is studied. Cohort analysis is "explicitly macroanalytic," which means researchers examine the category as a whole for important features (Ryder, 1992:230). The focus is on the cohort, or category, not on specific individuals. Commonly used cohorts include all people born in the same year (called *birth cohorts*), all people hired at the same time, all people who retire in a one- or two-year time frame, and all people who graduate in a given year. Unlike panel studies, researchers do not have to locate the exact same people for cohort studies. They need only identify those who experienced a common life event.

Two examples illustrate the value of cohort studies. Morgan (1998) wanted to find out whether a "glass ceiling" of blocked career advancement or cohort caused an earnings gap between men and women engineers. She examined earnings data for male and female engineers in several college graduation cohorts, from 1971 or earlier to 1988–1992. Women's earnings were lower in past cohorts and women in recent cohorts earn less because they have little seniority. The author found no gender gap in recent cohorts and argued that pay is affected according to when the women started working rather than their career length. A main finding is that an overall gender gap in earnings is caused more by

cohort, or many female engineers in recent years, than a glass ceiling.

Wilhelm (1998) looked at patterns of cohabitation among Americans of different cohorts. She used survey data for 1,187 adult U.S. citizens born between 1943 and 1964 and looked at three birth cohorts: 1943–1950, 1951–1957, and 1958–1964. She found three predictors of cohabitation: political activism, nonreligious beliefs, and being in recent birth cohorts. Certain factors (e.g., nonreligious and politically active) were important predictors in early cohorts, but people in later cohorts were more likely to cohabit independent of the factors. Her main conclusion was that what was once a relatively rare behavior among a few parts of early cohorts has diffused and become a lifestyle option for most sectors of the population in later cohorts.

Case-Study Research. In cross-sectional and longitudinal research, a researcher examines features on many people or units, either at one time period or across time periods. In both, a researcher examines a common set of features on many cases, usually expressed in numbers. In **case-study research,** he or she examines, in depth, many features of a few cases over a duration of time. Cases can be individuals, groups, organizations, movements, events, or geographic units. The data are usually more detailed, varied, and extensive. Most involve qualitative data about a few cases. Qualitative and case-study research are not identical, but "almost all qualitative research seeks to construct representations based on in-depth, detailed knowledge of cases" (Ragin, 1994a:92).[12]

In a case study, a researcher may intensively investigate one or two cases or compare a limited set of cases, focusing on several factors. Case study uses the logic of *analytic* instead of *enumerative* induction. In it, the researcher carefully selects one or a few key cases to illustrate an issue and analytically study it (or them) in detail. He or she considers the specific context of the case and examines how its parts are configured. This contrasts with longitudinal studies in which the researcher collects data on many units or cases, then looks for patterns in the mass of numbers. The researcher looks more for averages or patterns across many units or cases.[13]

Cohort study   Longitudinal research in which information about a category of cases or people that shared a common experience at one time period is traced across subsequent time periods.

Case-study research   Research that is an in-depth examination of an extensive amount of information about very few units or cases for one period or across multiple periods of time.

Case studies help researchers connect the micro level, or the actions of individual people, to the macro level, or large-scale social structures and processes (Vaughan, 1992). "The logic of the case study is to demonstrate a causal argument about how general social forces shape and produce results in particular settings" (Walton, 1992b:122). Case-study research raises questions about the boundaries and defining characteristics of a case. Such questions help in the generation of new thinking and theory. "Case studies are likely to produce the best theory" (Walton, 1992b:129).

Researchers gather case-study data for a period of time. Data may be collected over months, years, or across many decades. Walton's (1992a) *Western Times and Water Wars* is a case study of one community, Owens Valley, California. Walton stated, "I have tried . . . to tell a big story through the lens of a small case" (p. xviii). The community engaged in social protest as it attempted to control its key resource (water) and destiny. The protest took different forms, on and off, for over 100 years. Walton used diverse forms of data, including direct observation, formal and informal interviews, census statistics, maps, old photos and newspapers, various historical documents, and official records.

Most case studies use a qualitative approach, and the example study given in Chapter 1 of Mexican women by Sofia Villenas (2001) on 21 Latino community members in one small town in North Carolina is an example of a case study.

Perhaps you have seen the prize-winning 2002 movie, *The Pianist*, about Wladyslaw Szpilman and the 1943 Jewish uprising in Warsaw, Poland. Einwohner (2003) conducted a historical case study of the 1943 Jewish uprising to examine social movement theory. A major idea in social movement theory is a political opportunity structure (POS), stating that when the POS "opens" the chances of a movement developing or being successful increases and several factors can cause an opening. Yet, this did not happen in the 1943 Jewish uprising.

Social movement theory also recognizes threat, defined as increased costs to a movement for taking certain actions or not taking certain actions. Einwohner also used a third concept from the theory, "motivational frame." A movement "frame" refers to the ways people in a movement think about and perceive something; a "motivational frame" is what people perceive as acceptable reasons or moral justifications for taking action.

In the specific case of the Warsaw Jewish ghetto in 1943, there were no opportunities. By studying diaries and historical reports, Einwohner documented that it was a situation with great threat. The uprising occurred only after the people realized their deaths were inevitable because they faced overwhelming power and a systematic Nazi policy of extermination. They formed a new motivational frame that redefined death in struggle as the only honorable option. In brief, people's thinking shifted to see being killed in a hopeless uprising as the most dignified, honorable action—both for themselves and for the entire Jewish people. Thus, the uprising movement did not arise from an opportunity, but from a total lack of opportunity and great threat. It turned on mass redefinition of the best action to pursue in a totally hopeless situation. See Figure 2.3 for an illustration of how researchers use time.

Data Collection Techniques

This section is a brief overview of the main data collection techniques. In later chapters, you will read about these techniques in detail and learn how to use them. The techniques may be grouped into two categories: *quantitative,* collecting data in the form of numbers, and *qualitative,* collecting data in the form of words or pictures. Some techniques are more effective when addressing specific kinds of questions or topics. It takes skill, practice, and creativity to match a research question to an appropriate data collection technique.

Quantitative Data

Experiments. **Experimental research** uses the logic and principles found in natural science research (see Chapter 9 on experimental research).

> **Experimental research** Research in which the researcher manipulates conditions for some research participants but not others, then compares group responses to see whether it made a difference.

CROSS SECTIONAL: Observe a collection of people at one time.

February 2006

TIME SERIES: Observe different people at multiple times.

| 1950 | 1965 | 1980 | 1995 |

PANEL: Observe the exact same people at two or more times.

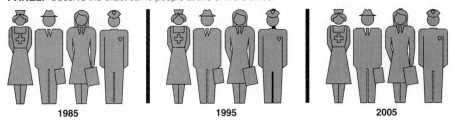

| 1985 | 1995 | 2005 |

COHORT: Observe people who shared an experience at two or more times.

Married in 1962   1982   2002

CASE STUDY: Observe a small set intensely across time.

2002 ➞ 2005

FIGURE 2.3   The Time Dimension in Social Research

Experiments can be conducted in laboratories or in real life. They usually involve a relatively small number of people and address a well-focused question. Experiments are most effective for explanatory research.

In most experiments, the researcher divides the people being studied into two or more groups. He or she then treats both groups identically, except that one group but not the other is given a condition he or she is interested in: the "treatment." The researcher measures the reactions of both groups precisely. By controlling the setting for both groups and giving only one the treatment, the researcher can conclude that any differences in the reactions of the groups are due to the treatment alone.

Patrick and colleagues (2004) described an applied experiment in a field setting. Under a special program that operated for one year, youthful offenders found guilty of status crimes (tobacco or alcohol possession) were randomly assigned to one of the following four options. (1) *Juvenile accountability*—Offender pays restitution, attends a drug and alcohol awareness class, does community service, visits an incarcerated inmate, and writes an essay. A parent accompanies the youth during much of the process. The citation would be removed from the youth's record if followed by a year of good behavior. (2) *Youth court*—A courtlike hearing before a group of other youths. Most offenders were sentenced to 8 hours of counseling, 10 to 20 hours of community service, and had to write an essay with the citation removed from the youth's record if followed by a year of good behavior. (3) *Magistrate court*—A traditional court with most sentences a fine and stern warning by a judge with a permanent record. (4) *Education group*—A brief interview, a voluntary list of services, and viewing of a short film with the citation removed from the youth's record if followed by a year of good behavior.

In a series of experiments Alan Gerber and Donald Green and associates examined factors that increase voting. In one experiment (Gerber and Green, 2000a), shortly before an election they randomly selected 25 streets in the suburban community of Hamden, Connecticut, and placed printed cards at homes urging people to vote. Nothing was done for the "control group" of a matched set of 25

other streets. They then measured whether people voted in the election. They found that people not affiliated with a political party who received the cards were more likely to vote. In another experiment (Gerber and Green, 2000b), they used personal canvassing, telephone calls, and direct mail to urge people to vote in New Haven, Connecticut, in 1998, with some people receiving none of the appeals, some one, and others more than one appeal to vote. The researchers found that face-to-face contact raised voting by over 9 percent, mail by under 1 percent, and telephone contact had no effect over the control group that received no appeal to vote. In a third follow-up experiment (Gerber, Green, and Shachar, 2003), they looked at a 1999 election in New Haven, Connecticut, and asked whether those who had been contacted and voted in 1998 were more likely to vote in 1999. They found that people who had been contacted and voted in 1998 were more likely to return to vote in 1999.

Surveys. Researchers utilize questionnaires or interviews to learn people's beliefs or opinions in many research situations (e.g., experiments, field research). In **survey research,** they use a written questionnaire or formal interview to gather information on the backgrounds, behaviors, beliefs, or attitudes of a large number of people (see Chapter 10 on survey research). Usually, they ask a large number of people dozens of questions in a short time frame. The researcher does not manipulate a situation or condition to see how people react; he or she simply carefully records answers from many people who have been asked the same questions. Often researchers select the people for a survey using a random sampling technique so they can legitimately generalize information from a few people (e.g., one thousand) to many more (e.g., several million) (random sampling is discussed in Chapter 8). Survey data are typically summarized in charts, graphs, or tables and analyzed with statistics. Researchers use surveys in descriptive or explanatory research. The

Survey research   Quantitative research in which the researcher systematically asks a large number of people the same questions and then records their answers.

example study in Chapter 1 by Alvarez and Butterfield (2000) used the survey research technique.

Survey research is widely used. Following is an example of it in the state of Georgia, where a political controversy arose over the Confederate battle emblem on the state flag, which was added to the flag in 1956. Reingold and Wike (1998) wanted to learn whether the symbol was connected with pride in a "New South" identity, as some argued, or was an indirect expression of racism, as others claimed. In fall 1994, the Applied Research Center of Georgia State University surveyed a random sample of 826 Georgia residents by telephone in the "Georgia State Poll." The authors had three questions on New South identity and two questions on racial attitudes. They also asked about other factors (e.g., education, age, sex, race, urban or rural residence, political party, born in the South, etc.). The authors found clear racial divisions; three-fourths of Whites wanted to keep the Confederate symbol, whereas two-thirds of African Americans wanted the flag changed. Their data analysis revealed that New South identity was not related to the flag issue; if anything, it was associated with favoring a change in the flag. Younger people and urban residents also favored changing the flag. Despite public rhetoric, those most strongly in favor of keeping the Confederate symbol on the flag were Whites who had strong anti-Black attitudes.

Nonreactive Research. Most experimental and survey researchers actively engage the people they study by creating experimental conditions or directly asking them questions. These are called *reactive* methods, because a research participant may react in some way due to an awareness that he or she is in a study. Other quantitative research is called **nonreactive research** because the participants or units in the study are not aware that information about them is being used in a study. Three types of nonreactive studies are unobtrusive re-

search, examining statistical information or documents, and secondary data analysis. We can leave unobtrusive research for Chapter 11, which examines all nonreactive methods. *Secondary data analysis* is a new statistical analysis of quantitative data (often originally from a survey) that was previously collected and stored. Here we consider two types of nonreactive research: the study of documents, or content analysis, and existing statistics.

1. *Content analysis.* **Content analysis** is a technique for examining the content, or information and symbols, contained in written documents or other communication medium (e.g., photographs, movies, song lyrics, advertisements). To conduct a content analysis, a researcher identifies a body of material to analyze (e.g., television programs, newspaper articles) and then creates a system for recording specific aspects of its content. The system might include counting how often certain words or themes appear. After the researcher systematically records what was found, he or she analyzes it, often using graphs or charts. It is a nonreactive method because the creators of the content do not know whether anyone will analyze it. Content analysis lets a researcher discover and document specific features in the content of a large amount of material that might otherwise go unnoticed. Content analysis is most often used for descriptive purposes, but can be exploratory or explanatory as well.

The study by Magaña and Short (2002) in Chapter 1 was a content analysis study of newspapers. Ganahl and colleagues (2003) looked at the extensively studied and much debated issue of stereotypes in television commercials. Past studies established that television commercials perpetuate traditional gender stereotypes; the authors asked whether this has ended after the "old days" of the 1960s–1980s. The authors content analyzed a sample of 1,337 prime-time commercials from the three major networks (ABC, CBS, and NBC) in 1998. They recorded the products being advertised and the gender, age, and acting role of the 5,473 characters appearing in the commercials. They compared their results to past studies, census data on the entire population, and information on purchasing behavior. They found little change from the 1980s in how women and men were shown. Purchasing data show that women make most

---

Nonreactive research Research methods in which the people being studied are not aware of it.

Content analysis Research in which the content of a communication medium is systematically recorded and analyzed.

purchases, but except for health and beauty products, they are underrepresented as the primary characters in most commercials. Compared to their size in the population and among buyers of products, women are underrepresented, and those who are shown in commercials tend to be younger. When women and men appear in a commercial, the women tend to be in a supportive role to the man. In short, despite 30 years of public debate and wide acceptance of gender equality, it appears that TV commercials continue to reinforce stereotypical traditional male and female gender roles.

In another example study, Dukes and associates (2003) content-analyzed the 100 most popular songs in the United States (1958–1998) looking at the artist and expressions of love in lyrics. They found that women and Black artists recorded more hits in the 1990s than earlier. Over time, women were less likely to make references to love in lyrics, but references to sex in lyrics increased and peaked during 1976–1984. During that period women used sexual references five times more than men; however, during 1991–1998, there was a shift and men used more sexual references. In the later period, a major theme in most songs, and especially songs performed by White female artists, was that of being self-absorbed, or selfishness. Eschholz and Bufkin (2001) examined the content of movies. They focused on violent criminals and victims in popular, domestic U.S. films in 1996, noting use of sex and gender in depictions of violent crime. They found that masculinity was significantly related to both offending and victimization but not sex. This suggests that the media reinforce the use of violence as a means to project masculinity.

2. *Existing statistics.* In **existing statistics research,** a researcher locates a source of previously collected information, often in the form of government reports or previously conducted surveys (existing statistics research is discussed in Chapter 11). He or she then reorganizes or combines the information in new ways to address a research question. Locating sources can be time consuming, so the researcher needs to consider carefully the meaning of what he or she finds. Frequently, a researcher does not know whether the information of interest is available when he or she begins a study.

Sometimes, the existing quantitative information consists of stored survey or other data that a researcher reexamines using various statistical procedures. This is called *secondary analysis research.* Existing statistics research can be used for exploratory, descriptive, or explanatory purposes but is most frequently used for descriptive research.

Two studies used existing statistics to examine the relationship between industrial restructuring (a massive departure of manufacturing jobs from central cities in the United States during the 1970s and 1980s) and violent death. The manufacturing jobs provided entry-level employment for people with low skills. Shihadeh and Ousey (1998) looked at 100 U.S. cities with over 100,000 people in 1990. They used census data on types of industries located in each city and the prevalence of low-skill jobs by industry. They then combined the census data with data on homicides from the Uniform Crime Reports of the FBI. The authors found that a reduction in entry-level jobs was linked to greater economic deprivation for the local population, and economic deprivation was associated with higher homicide rates for both Blacks and Whites.

On the same general topic, Almgren and associates (1998) looked at homicides, suicides, and accidents in Chicago. They matched census data for 1970 and 1990 with birth and death records for 75 communities and examined the association between unemployment rates and rates of violent death in the communities. They also looked at changes in family composition and racial mix in the community areas. The authors learned that joblessness, more than racial isolation, was associated with both family disruption and violent death rates. Also, they learned that various forms of violent death are interrelated, or appear to have a common cause. The causal relationship between economic dislocation and violent death grew stronger. Thus, economically depressed areas had more violent deaths than nondepressed areas in the 1970s, but the link grew stronger over time.

Existing statistics research Research in which one reexamines and statistically analyzes quantitative data that has been gathered by government agencies or other organizations.

Trovato (1998) used existing statistics to test a theory from Emile Durkheim about social integration. Social integration, or a feeling of belonging, may become stronger during major sports events. Thus, several studies looked at the link between suicide rates and major sports events (e.g., the Superbowl). Trovato looked at the impact of Stanley Cup hockey games on suicide rates in Quebec. He predicted that suicide rates would drop when Montreal was engaged in the playoffs but increase when it was eliminated early. Despite minor changes in suicide rates for single males, he found no evidence of a link between changes in suicide rates and the Stanley Cup tournament.

Qualitative Data

Field Research. Most field researchers conduct case studies on a small group of people for some length of time (field research is discussed in Chapter 13). **Field research** begins with a loosely formulated idea or topic. Next, researchers select a social group or site for study. Once they gain access to the group or site, they adopt a social role in the setting and begin observing. The researchers observe and interact in the field setting for a period from a few months to several years. They get to know personally the people being studied and may conduct informal interviews. They take detailed notes on a daily basis. During the observation, they consider what they observe and refine or focus ideas about its significance. Finally, they leave the field site. They then reread their notes and prepare written reports. Field research is usually used for exploratory and descriptive studies; it is sometimes used for explanatory research.

Mitchell Duneier (1999) conducted a field research of street vendors in Greenwich Village, New York City. He gained entree by being a browser of books at one vendor who he befriended. The vendor introduced him to other vendors, panhandlers,

Field research Qualitative research in which the researcher directly observes and records notes on people in a natural setting for an extended period of time.

Historical-comparative research Qualitative research in which the researcher examines data on events and conditions in the historical past and/or in different societies.

homeless people, and others. Duneier observed on and off over four years, periodically working as a magazine vendor and scavenger. As a White college professor, it took adjustment to learn the daily life and win acceptance among low-income African American men who made a living selling used books and magazines on the sidewalk. In addition to observing and tape-recording life on the sidewalk, Duneier conducted many informal interviews, read related documents, and had a photojournalist take numerous photos of the field site and its people.

Duneier concluded with a critique of the popular "Broken Window" theory of social control and crime reduction. Where others saw only a disorderly street environment causing deviant behavior and crime, he found a rich informal social life with honor, dignity, and entrepreneurial vigor among poor people who were struggling to survive. He noted that the upper-middle-class government officials and corporate leaders often advocate laws and regulations that threaten to destroy the fluid, healthy informal social structure he discovered because they do not know the people or understand life on the sidewalk. They see only social disorganization because the vibrant daily lives of those who make a living among the flow of people on the sidewalk do not mesh with the upper-middle-class world that is centered in large complex organizations with formal regulations, official procedures, fixed hierarchies, and standardized occupations.

Historical-Comparative Research. **Historical-comparative research** examines aspects of social life in a past historical era or across different cultures (historical-comparative research is discussed in Chapter 14). Researchers who use this technique may focus on one historical period or several, compare one or more cultures, or mix historical periods and cultures. This kind of research combines theory with data collection. As with field research, a researcher begins with a loosely formulated question, refining and elaborating on it during the research process. Researchers often use a mix of evidence, including existing statistics, documents (e.g., books, newspapers, diaries, photographs, and maps), observations, and interviews. Historical-comparative research can be exploratory, descriptive, or explanatory and can blend types, but it is usually descriptive.

Anthony Marx (1998) conducted an historical-comparative study of race in the United States, South Africa, and Brazil. His initial goal was to understand racial mobilization in South Africa, which led him to examine African American protests. He soon asked why legal institutions of racial domination, Jim Crow segregation in the United States, and apartheid in South Africa did not develop in Brazil, which also had a large subordinate African population. Marx spent six years examining the histories of the three nations, traveling to numerous research centers, archives, and libraries in each country, and he interviewed hundreds of people in English and Portuguese in the three countries. He concluded that the pattern of nation formation was critical. The government-supported racial division and legal forms of domination arose in countries that had violent conflict among Whites (the U.S. Civil War and Boer War). Racially dominating Blacks was a way to unify all Whites around national goals and override regional, political, and class differences among them. This form of racial oppression shaped how Blacks politically mobilized to gain inclusion as full citizens.

James Mahoney (2003) presented a puzzle about the countries of Spanish America, specifically 15 countries that had been mainland territories of the Spanish colonial empire. He observed that their relative ranking, from most to least developed in 1900, remained unchanged in 2000; that is, the least developed country in 1900 (Bolivia) remained the least developed. This picture of great stability contrasts with dramatic changes and improvements in the region during the twentieth century. Going back to the height of the Spanish empire in the seventeenth century, Mahoney noted that the richest, most central colonies in that period were later the poorest countries, while marginal, backwater, poor colonies were the developed, richest countries by the late nineteenth century.

To solve this puzzle, Mahoney used two qualitative data analysis tools, path dependency and qualitative comparative analysis (QCA) (both are discussed later in Chapter 15). His data included maps, national economic and population statistics, and several hundred historical studies on the specific countries. He concluded that the most central, prosperous Spanish colonies were located

where natural resources were abundant (for extraction and shipment to Europe) and large indigenous populations existed (to work as coerced labor). In these colonies, local elites arose and created rigid racial-ethnic stratification systems that concentrated economic-political power and excluded broad parts of society. The systems continued into the nineteenth century when new political events, trade patterns, and economic conditions appeared. In the 1700–1850 era, liberal-minded elites who were open to new ideas did not succeed in them. In contrast, colonies that had been on the fringe of the Spanish empire in South America were less encumbered by rigid systems. New elites arose who were better able to innovate and adapt, so there was a "great reversal" of positions. After this historical "turning point" some countries got a substantial head start toward social-economic development in the late 1800s. These countries built political-economic systems and institutions that propelled them forward; that is, they "locked into" a particular direction or path that brought increasing returns.

Mahoney (2003:53) argued, "explanations of differences in units that draw on the current attributes of those units will often be inadequate." In other words, a cross-sectional approach that tries to explain differences among the countries by using data at only one time point cannot capture significant long-term dynamic processes. An explanation that includes the impact of distant historical events and takes a long-term view is superior.

CONCLUSION

This chapter gave you an overview of the dimensions of social research. You saw that research can be classified in a number of different ways (e.g., by its purpose, by its research technique, etc.) and that the dimensions of research loosely overlap with each other (see Chart 2.1). The dimensions of research provide a "road map" through the terrain that is social research.

In the next chapter, we turn to social theory. You read about theory in Chapter 1 and it was mentioned again in this chapter. In Chapter 3, you will learn how theory and research methods work together and about several types of theory.

KEY TERMS

action research
applied research
basic research
case-study research
cohort study
content analysis
cost-benefit analysis
cross-sectional research
descriptive research

evaluation research
existing statistics research
experimental research
explanatory research
exploratory research
field research
historical-comparative research
instrumental knowledge
longitudinal research

needs assessment
nonreactive research
panel study
reflexive knowledge
social impact assessment
survey research
time-series research

REVIEW QUESTIONS

1. When is exploratory research used, and what can it accomplish?
2. What types of results are produced by a descriptive research study?
3. What is explanatory research? What is its primary purpose?
4. What are the major differences between basic and applied research?
5. Who is likely to conduct basic research, and where are results likely to appear?
6. Explain the differences among the three types of applied research.
7. How do time-series, panel, and cohort studies differ?
8. What are some potential problems with cost-benefit analysis?
9. What is a needs assessment? What complications can occur when conducting one?
10. Explain the differences between qualitative and quantitative research.

NOTES

1. Finsterbusch and Motz (1980), Freeman (1983), Lazarsfeld and Reitz (1975), Olsen and Micklin (1981), and Rubin (1983) discuss applied research. Also see Whyte's (1986) critique of social research that is not applied and instances in which social research affects public issues. McGrath and colleagues (1982) discuss judgment calls that are relevant in applied research.
2. See Crespi (1987) for a discussion of survey research in court proceedings.
3. See Turner and Turner (1991:181).
4. For a brief introduction to evaluation research, see Adams and Schvaneveldt (1985:315–328), Finsterbusch and Motz (1980:119–158), and Smith and Glass (1987). A more complete discussion can be found in Burnstein and associates (1985), Freeman (1992), Rossi (1982), Rossi and Freeman (1985), Saxe and Fine (1981), and Weiss (1972).
5. See Oliker (1994).
6. PPBS and related evaluation research are discussed in Smith and Glass (1987:41–49).

7. See Reinharz (1992:252).
8. See Cancian and Armstead (1992), Reason (1994), and Whyte (1989).
9. Social impact research is discussed in Chadwick and associates (1984:313–342), Finsterbusch and Motz (1980:75–118), and Finsterbusch and Wolf (1981). Also see Rossi and colleagues (1982) and Wright and Rossi (1981) on "natural hazards" and social science.
10. Explanatory, exploratory, and descriptive research are also discussed in Babbie (1998), Bailey (1987:38–39), and Churchill (1983:56–77).
11. See Guy and colleagues (1987:54–55) for discussion.
12. For discussions of case-study research, see Miller (1992), Mitchell (1984), Ragin (1992a, 1992b), Stake (1994), Vaughan (1992), Walton (1992b), and Yin (1988).
13. See Mitchell (1984) and Stake (1994).

Theory and Research

> *One of the major functions of theory is to order experience with the help of concepts.*
> *It also selects relevant aspects and data among the enormous multitude of "facts"*
> *that confront the investigator of social phenomena.*
> —Lewis Coser, "The Uses of Classical Sociological Theory," p. 170

Suppose you want to make sense of the hostility between people of different races. Trying to understand it, you ask a teacher, who responds:

> *Most racially prejudiced people learn negative stereotypes about another racial group from their families, friends, and others in their immediate surroundings. If they lack sufficient intimate social contact with members of the group or intense information that contradicts those stereotypes, they remain prejudiced.*

This makes sense to you because it is consistent with what you know about how the social world works. This is an example of a small-scale social theory, a type that researchers use when conducting a study.

What do you think of when you hear the word *theory*? Theory is one of the least well understood terms for students learning social science. My stu-

dents' eyelids droop if I begin a class by saying, "Today we are going to examine the theory of . . . ." The mental picture many students have of theory is something that floats high among the clouds. My students have called it "a tangled maze of jargon" and "abstractions that are irrelevant to the real world." The beginning of one textbook on social theory (Craib, 1984:3) echoes this perspective:

> *The very word "theory" sometimes seems to scare people, and not without good reason. Much modern social theory is either unintelligible, or banal, or pointless. . . . Few people feel at home with theory or use it in a productive way.*

Contrary to these views, theory has an important role in research and is an essential ally for the researcher. Researchers use theory differently in various types of research, but some type of theory is present in most social research. It is less evident in applied or descriptive than in basic or explanatory research. In simple terms, researchers interweave a story about the operation of the social world (the theory) with what they observe when they examine it systematically (the data).

WHAT IS THEORY?

In Chapter 1, *social theory* was defined as a system of interconnected ideas that condenses and organizes knowledge about the social world. People are always creating new theories to talk about how the world works.

Many people confuse the history of social thought, or what great thinkers said, with social theory. The classical social theorists (e.g., Durkheim, Weber, Marx, and Tonnies) played an important role in generating innovative ideas. They developed original theories that laid the foundation for subsequent generations of social thinkers. People study the classical theorists because they provided many creative and interrelated ideas at once. They radically changed the way people understood and saw the social world. We still study them because geniuses who generate many original, insightful ideas and fundamentally shift how people look at the social world are very rare.

People often use theories without making them explicit or labeling them as such. For example, newspaper articles or television reports on social issues usually have unstated social theories embedded within them. A news report on the difficulty of implementing a school desegregation plan will contain an implicit theory about race relations. Likewise, political leaders frequently express social theories when they discuss public issues. Politicians who claim that inadequate education causes poverty or that a decline in traditional moral values causes higher crime rates are expressing theories. Compared to the theories of social scientists, such laypersons' theories are less systematic, less well formulated, and harder to test with empirical evidence.

Parsimony   The idea that simple is better. Everything else being equal, a social theory that explains more with less complexity is better.

Social science theory seems complicated compared to laypersons' theories. Fortunately, a principle of good theory called **parsimony** helps. Parsimony means simpler is better. A parsimonious theory has minimal complexity, with no redundant or excess elements. Parsimony says a more powerful theory does more with less, and the less complex of two equally convincing theories is better.

Almost all research involves some theory, so the question is less *whether* you should use theory than *how* you should use it. Being explicit about the theory makes it easier to read someone else's research or to conduct your own. An awareness of how theory fits into the research process produces better designed, easier to understand, and better conducted studies. Most researchers disparage atheoretical or "crude empiricist" research.

Theories come in many shapes and sizes. In this chapter, I provide an elementary introduction to social theory. You will encounter theory in later chapters, as well.

SOCIAL THEORY VERSUS IDEOLOGY

Many people confuse a social scientific theory and a sociopolitical ideology. Most people encounter diverse ideologies in the mass media or from the champions of particular points of view. Controversy occurs because the scientific community recognizes theory as essential for clarifying and building scientific knowledge, while it condemns ideology as illegitimate obfuscation that is antithetical to science. Confusion arises because both explain similar events in the world, and they can overlap in places.

There are similarities between theory and ideology (see Box 3.1). Both explain many events in the world: why crime occurs, why some people are poor, why divorce rates are high in some places, and so on. Social scientific theory and an ideology both contain assumptions about the nature of the social world. They both focus on what is or is not important in it, contain a system of ideas or concepts, and specify relations among the concepts. Both explain why things are the way they are and what needs to be changed to alter conditions.

BOX **3.1**   Social Theory and Ideology

SIMILARITIES

▪ Contains a set of assumptions or a starting point
▪ Explains what the social world is like, how/why it changes
▪ Offers a system of concepts/ideas
▪ Specifies relationships among concepts, tells what causes what
▪ Provides an interconnected system of ideas

DIFFERENCES

Ideology	Social Theory
▪ Offers absolute certainty	▪ Conditional, negotiated understandings
▪ Has all the answers	▪ Incomplete, recognizes uncertainty
▪ Fixed, closed, finished	▪ Growing, open, unfolding, expanding
▪ Avoids tests, discrepant findings	▪ Welcomes tests, positive and negative evidence
▪ Blind to opposing evidence	▪ Changes based on evidence
▪ Locked into specific moral beliefs	▪ Detached, disconnected, moral stand
▪ Highly partial	▪ Neutral considers all sides
▪ Has contradictions, inconsistencies	▪ Strongly seeks logical consistency, congruity
▪ Rooted in specific position	▪ Transcends/crosses social positions

An **ideology** is a quasi-theory that lacks critical features required of a true scientific theory. Many ideologies look like legitimate scientific theories. Ideologies have fixed, strong, and unquestioned assumptions. They are full of unquestioned absolutes and normative categories (what is right/wrong, moral/immoral, good/bad, etc.). The assumptions may be founded on faith or rooted in particular social circumstances. Many ideologies advance or protect the interests of a particular group or sector of society.

Ideologies are belief systems closed to contradictory evidence that use circular reasoning. Ideologies are logically "slippery" and prevent falsification. This makes them immune to change. Their capacity to develop is extremely limited, because they already have all the answers. In ideology, lines between assertions about what *is* the case and beliefs about what *should be* the case blur together. (See Box 3.2.)

Ideologies selectively present and interpret empirical evidence. They often use personal experience or conviction (e.g., overgeneralization, selective observation, and premature closure) that fall short of a scientific approach. It is difficult to test ideological

principles or confront them with opposing evidence. In a way, ideology cannot acknowledge contradictory evidence. Even if overwhelming evidence is amassed, the ideology will not bend or change. A true, hard-core believer in an ideology will reject or refuse to recognize evidence. He or she will rigidly adhere to core value premises and principles. It is a "Don't confuse me with facts, I know I'm right" attitude. Supporters often react with fear and hostility to anyone who disagrees or presents carefully gathered contradictory information.

The distinction between ideology and theory has implications for how a person conducts research. A researcher can never show an ideology to its followers. By contrast, a researcher can test a scientific theory or parts of it and show them to be false. Social scientific theories are empirically testable, and they are constantly evolving.

Ideology   A nonscientific quasi-theory, often based on political values or faith, with assumptions, concepts, relationships among concepts, and explanations. It is a closed system that resists change, cannot be directly falsified with empirical data, and makes normative claims.

BOX **3.2**   **How Ideology and Social Theory Might Explain Divorce**

EXAMPLE OF IDEOLOGY

American society has experienced a moral-social breakdown over the past several decades. Families used to be strong, mothers did not work but spent lots more time with children, and divorce was rare. Moral decay, a loss of respect, and bad media messages have weakened the family and caused divorce to rise.

An Evaluation: This explanation uses the concepts of *moral-social breakdown, strength of family, divorce, time mothers spend with children, moral decay, loss of respect, and media messages.* It does not precisely specify the meaning and measurement of each concept or its timing. Besides divorce and time with children, the concepts are vague and highly evaluative (e.g., *decay, breakdown, bad*). The long time frame suggests considering the impact of alternative factors that were occurring in the same period.

EXAMPLE OF SOCIAL THEORY

Families are strongest (i.e., less likely to divorce, spend more time together, devote more time nurturing children, have positive interaction patterns) when they have abundant resources and little stress. Resources can be material (income, education, good housing), social (friends and extended family, involvement in community organizations), and psychological (members with positive self-images, maturity, and respect for others). Those with more resources and fewer sources of stress (e.g., family members irregularly employed, with poor or declining health, who are crime victims, or emotionally unstable) are the strongest.

An Evaluation: This explanation uses three concepts: *resources* (with three types), *stress,* and *family strength.* Measures of each concept are suggested and have been developed. The relationship among concepts is straightforward and can be empirically tested.

Researchers try to directly confront a theory with evidence. They look at all relevant evidence, both that supporting and that opposing a theory, in a disinterested way. They do not know for sure whether the evidence will support a theory when they begin. If the evidence repeatedly fails to support a theory, it is changed or replaced.

Theories are logically consistent. If a contradiction occurs, researchers try to resolve it. Theories are also open ended, always growing or developing to higher levels. Theories that fail to develop get replaced. Rarely do theories claim to have all the answers. Instead, they contain areas of uncertainty or incomplete knowledge and offer only partial or tentative answers. Researchers constantly test theories and are skeptical toward them. The theory itself is disinterested or detached from the position of any specific social group or sector of society.

Assumption   An untested starting point or belief in a theory that is necessary to build a theoretical explanation.

THE PARTS OF SOCIAL THEORY

Assumptions

Theories contain built-in **assumptions,** statements about the nature of things that are not observable or testable. We accept them as a necessary starting point, such as assumptions about the nature of human beings, social reality, or a particular phenomenon. Assumptions often remain hidden or unstated. One way for a researcher to deepen his or her understanding is to identify the assumptions on which a theory is based.

For example, theory about a *book* assumes a system of writing, people who can read, and the existence of paper. Without such assumptions, the idea of a *book* makes little sense. Theories about social science issues, such as *racial prejudice,* rest on several assumptions. These include people who make distinctions among individuals based on their racial heritage, attach specific motivations and characteristics to membership in a racial group, and make judgments about the goodness of specific motivations and characteristics. If race became irrelevant, people would cease to distinguish among individuals on the basis of race, to attach specific characteristics to a racial group, and to make judgments about characteristics. If that occurred, the concept of *racial prejudice* would cease to be useful for research.

Concepts

Concepts are the building blocks of theory.[1] A **theoretical concept** is an idea expressed as a symbol or in words. Natural science concepts are often expressed in symbolic forms, such as Greek letters (e.g., π) or formulas (e.g., $s = d/t$; s = speed, d = distance, t = time). Most social science concepts are expressed as words. The exotic symbols of natural science theory make many people nervous, but the use of everyday words in specialized ways can create confusion.

I do not want to exaggerate the distinction between concepts expressed as words and concepts expressed as symbols. Words, after all, are symbols, too; they are symbols we learn with language. Height is a concept with which you are already familiar. For example, I can say the word *height* or write it down; the spoken sounds and written words are part of the English language. The combination of letters in the sound symbolizes, or stands for, the idea of a *height*. Chinese or Arabic characters, the French word *hauteur*, the German word *höhe*, the Spanish word *altura*—all symbolize the same idea. In a sense, a language is an agreement to represent ideas by sounds or written characters that people learned at some point in their lives. Learning concepts and theory is like learning a language.[2]

Concepts are everywhere, and you use them all the time. Height is a simple concept from everyday experience. What does it mean? It is easy to use the concept of *height,* but describing the concept itself is difficult. It represents an abstract idea about physical relations. How would you describe it to a very young child or a creature from a distant planet who was totally unfamiliar with it? A new concept from a social theory may seem just as alien when you encounter it for the first time. Height is a characteristic of a physical object, the distance from top to bottom. All people, buildings, trees, mountains, books, and so forth have a height. We can measure height or compare it. A height of zero is possible, and height can increase or decrease over time. As with many words, we use the word in several ways. Height is used in the expressions *the height of the battle, the height of the summer,* and *the height of fashion.*

The word *height* refers to an abstract idea. We associate its sound and its written form with that idea. There is nothing inherent in the sounds that make up the word and the idea it represents. The connection is arbitrary, but it is still useful. People can express the abstract idea to one another using the symbol alone.

Concepts have two parts: a *symbol* (word or term) and a *definition*. We learn definitions in many ways. I learned the word *height* and its definition from my parents. I learned it as I learned to speak and was socialized to the culture. My parents never gave me a dictionary definition. I learned it through a diffuse, nonverbal, informal process. My parents showed me many examples; I observed and listened to others use the word; I used the word incorrectly and was corrected; and I used it correctly and was understood. Eventually, I mastered the concept.

This example shows how people learn concepts in everyday language and how we share concepts. Suppose my parents had isolated me from television and other people, then taught me that the word for the idea *height* was *zdged*. I would have had difficulty communicating with others. People must share the terms for concepts and their definitions if they are to be of value.

Everyday life is filled with concepts, but many of them have vague and unclear definitions. Likewise, the values and experiences of people in a culture may limit everyday concepts. Everyday concepts are often rooted in misconceptions or myth. Social scientists refine these concepts and add new ones. Many concepts social scientists first developed have diffused into the larger culture and become less precise. Concepts such as sexism, lifestyle, peer group, urban sprawl, and social class began as precise, technical concepts in social theory.

Theoretical concept   An idea that is thought through, carefully defined, and made explicit in a theory.

We create concepts from personal experience, creative thought, or observation. The classical theorists originated many concepts.

Social science concepts form a specialized language, or *jargon.* Specialists use jargon as a shorthand way to communicate with one another. Most fields have their own jargon. Physicians, lawyers, engineers, accountants, plumbers, and auto mechanics all have specialized languages. They use their jargon to refer to the ideas and objects with which they work. I read a book with the terms used by publishers and printers in order to understand their jargon—terms such as *idiot tape, fonts, cropping, halftone, galley proof, kiss impression, hickeys, widows,* and *kerning.* For people on the inside, jargon is a speedy, effective, and efficient way to communicate. But jargon also has negative connotations. Some people misuse it to confuse, exclude, or denigrate others. Using jargon among nonspecialists fails to communicate; it is like speaking English to people who know only Korean.

Level of Abstraction. Concepts vary by their **level of abstraction.** They range from very concrete ones easily evident in the familiar empirical world to highly abstract mental creations far removed from direct, daily empirical life. Abstract concepts refer to aspects of the world we do not directly or easily experience but nonetheless help organize thought and expand understanding. Elementary, concrete concepts, such as *books* or *height,* are defined by simple nonverbal processes. Complex, abstract concepts that are more frequently used in the social sciences often require formal, dictionarylike definitions and are defined by other concepts. We often define higher-level, more abstract concepts with lower-level ones. *Top, bottom,* and *distance* are less abstract than *height* and are used in its definition. Similarly, the concept of *aggression* is more

abstract than *hit, slap, shout, push, yell, punch, physically injure,* or *threaten serious harm.*

Researchers define theoretical concepts more precisely than those we use in daily discourse. Social theory requires well-defined concepts. The definition helps to link theory with research. A valuable goal of exploratory research, and of most good research, is to clarify and refine concepts. Weak, contradictory, or unclear definitions of concepts restrict the advance of knowledge. After noting that there are many definitions of a *gang* with little consensus, Ball and Curry (1995:239) argued that lack of a clear, consistent definition seriously hampered our understanding of gangs.

Single versus Concept Clusters. Concepts are rarely used in isolation. Rather, they form interconnected groups, or **concept clusters.** This is true for concepts in everyday language as well as for those in social theory. Theories contain collections of associated concepts that are consistent and mutually reinforcing. Together, they form a web of meaning. For example, if I want to discuss a concept such as *urban decay,* I will need a set of associated concepts (e.g., *urban expansion, economic growth, urbanization, suburbs, center city, revitalization, mass transit,* and *racial minorities*).

Some concepts take on a range of values, quantities, or amounts. Examples of this kind of concept are *amount of income, temperature, density of population, years of schooling,* and *degree of violence.* These are called *variables,* and you will read about them in Chapter 6. Other concepts express types of nonvariable phenomena (e.g., *bureaucracy, family, revolution, homeless,* and *cold*). Theories use both kinds of concepts.

Simple versus Complex Concepts. Some concepts are simple; they have only one dimension and vary along a single continuum. Others are complex; they have multiple dimensions or many subparts. You can break complex concepts into a set of simple, or single-dimension, concepts. For example, Rueschemeyer and associates (1992:43–44) stated that democracy has three dimensions. *Democracy* means (1) regular, free elections with universal suffrage; (2) an elected legislative body

---

Level of abstraction   A characteristic of a concept that ranges from empirical and concrete, often easily observable in daily experience, to very abstract, unseen mental creations.

Concept cluster   A collection of interrelated concepts that share common assumptions, refer to one another, and operate together in a social theory.

that controls government; and (3) freedom of expression and association. The authors recognized that each dimension varies by degree. They combined the dimensions to create a set of types of regimes. Regimes very low on all three dimensions are totalitarian, those high on all three are democracies, and ones with other mixes are either authoritarian or liberal oligarchies.

Concept classifications are partway between a single, simple concept and a theory.[3] They help to organize abstract, complex concepts. To create a new classification, a researcher logically specifies and combines the characteristics of simpler concepts. You can best grasp this idea by looking at some examples.

The **ideal type** is a well-known classification. Ideal types are pure, abstract models that define the essence of the phenomenon in question. They are mental pictures that define the central aspects of a concept. Ideal types are not explanations because they do not tell why or how something occurs. They are smaller than theories, and researchers use them to build a theory. They are broader, more abstract concepts that bring together several narrower, more concrete concepts. Qualitative researchers often use ideal types to see how well observable phenomena match up to the ideal model. For example, Max Weber developed an ideal type of the concept *bureaucracy*. Many people use Weber's ideal type (see Box 3.3). It distinguishes a bureaucracy from other organizational forms (e.g., social movements, kingdoms, etc.). It also clarifies critical features of a kind of organization that people once found nebulous and hard to think about. No real-life organization perfectly matches the ideal type, but the model helps us think about and study bureaucracy.

Another type of classification is the **typology,** or taxonomy,[4] in which a researcher combines two or more unidimensional, simple concepts, such that the intersection of simple concepts forms new concepts. The new concepts or types express the complex interrelation between the simple concepts.

One of the chief merits of a typology is parsimony. . . . A well constructed typology can work miracles in bringing order out of chaos. It can transform the overwhelming complexity of an apparent eclectic congeries of numerous apparently

---

- ■ It is a continuous organization governed by a system of rules.
- ■ Conduct is governed by detached, impersonal rules.
- ■ There is division of labor, in which different offices are assigned different spheres of competence.
- ■ Hierarchical authority relations prevail; that is, lower offices are under control of higher ones.
- ■ Administrative actions, rules, and so on are in writing and maintained in files.
- ■ Individuals do not own and cannot buy or sell their offices.
- ■ Officials receive salaries rather than receiving direct payment from clients in order to ensure loyalty to the organization.
- ■ Property of the organization is separate from personal property of officeholders.

Source: Adapted from Chafetz (1978:72).

---

diverse cases into a well-ordered set of a few rather homogenous types. (Bailey, 1992:2193)

Robert Merton's anomie theory of deviance argues that people can understand nondeviance, or conformity, and deviance by considering two key concepts: the goals a culture defines as worth pursuing and the means to achieve those goals that a society defines as legitimate. Merton's typology rests on two concepts: (1) whether people accept or reject the goals and (2) whether the means people use to reach the goals are legitimate. His typology identifies types of deviance and conformity based on the two concepts (see Table 3.1).

Concept classification A complex, multidimensional concept that has subtypes that are in between a single concept and a complete theoretical explanation.

Ideal type A type of concept classification that presents a pure, abstract model of an event, process, or idea. It is used in building social theory and in the analysis of data.

Typology A theoretical classification or quasi-theory that is created by cross-classifying or combining two or more simple concepts to form a set of interrelated subtypes.

TABLE 3.1   Robert Merton's Modes of Individual Adaptation

MODE OF ADAPTATION	SOCIETAL GOALS	INSTITUTIONAL MEANS
I Conformity	Accept	Accept
II Innovation	Accept	Reject
III Ritualism	Reject	Accept
IV Retreatism	Reject	Reject
V Revolution	Substitute new	Substitute new

TABLE 3.2   Erik Wright's System of Social Classes

SOCIAL CLASS	CONTROL OVER SOCIETAL RESOURCE		
	Investments	Production	Labor
Capitalists	+	+	+
Managers	–	+	+
Supervisors	–	–	+
Workers	–	–	–
Petite bourgeoisie	+	+	–

+ means has control, – means no or little control

Conformity, or nondeviance, occurs when people accept cultural goals (e.g., obtaining a high income) and use a socially legitimate means to reach them (e.g., getting a good job and working hard). Deviance occurs when this is not the case (e.g., when someone robs a bank instead of working hard). Merton's classification of how individuals adapt to cultural goals and means to reach them summarizes his complex concept and labels each subpart. For example, *retreatism* describes a person who rejects both cultural goals and the socially legitimate means to achieve them—such as a chronic alcohol user or a religious hermit. This type of deviant rejects the cultural goal of appearing respectable and acquiring material possessions (e.g., house, car, etc.). He or she also rejects the legitimate means of reaching the goal (e.g., being honest, working at a job, etc.).

Erik O. Wright updated Karl Marx's theory of social classes in capitalism. He noted that, for Marx, inequality and exploitation are based on control over three types of resources: investments (i.e., profit-making property or capital), the organization of production, and labor power (i.e., the work of other people). Wright said that the organization of a society defines social classes. The organization of a class society creates positions that confer control over the three types of resources to those occupying the positions (see Table 3.2). People in positions that control all three resources constitute the most powerful or dominant class. In market economies, this is the capitalist class. Its members include the major investors, owners, and presidents of banks or corporations. Capitalists make investment decisions

(e.g., whether and where to build a new factory), determine how to organize production (e.g., use robots or low-wage workers), and give orders to others. The class near the bottom consists of workers. They occupy positions in which they have no say over investments or how to organize production. They lack authority over others and must follow orders to keep their jobs. Managers and supervisors, who assist the capitalists, are between the two major classes. They are a quasi-class that had not yet fully appeared in the 1800s when Marx developed his theory. They control some but not all of the major resources of society.

Wright's classification also points out the position of another class about which Marx wrote, the petite (small) bourgeoisie, consisting of small-scale self-employed proprietors or farmers. Members of this class own and operate their own businesses but employ no one except family members. Marx thought this class would shrink and disappear, but it is still with us today. Like Merton's classification, Wright's scheme shows how to combine simpler concepts (i.e., types of resources owned or not owned) into a more powerful idea (i.e., the structure of social classes in capitalist society).

A last example of a concept classification can be found in Walder (2003), who examined the transition from a communist regime with a command economy to a market economy. He found four transition patterns that were based on two factors: (1) limits on seizing assets and (2) how much political change took place. By cross-classifying these

TABLE 3.3 Four Transition Paths from a Communist to a Postcommunist Economy

		HOW EXTENSIVE WAS POLITICAL CHANGE?	
		High	*Low*
Limits on taking assets	*High*	1	2
	Low	3	4

Path 1: Communist hierarchies collapse, the ruling party shrinks and loses power, privatization is smooth, and elite turnover is high. Only a few old elites with more education/skills succeed in the new society. (example nations: Hungary, Poland, and Estonia)

Path 2: Past political hierarchies survive, the Communist Party stays in control and holds onto assets, and privatization is very slow. There are low elite turnover rates and many old elites and their families get rich in the new society. (example nations: China and Vietnam)

Path 3: Past communist hierarchies collapse, the ruling party shrinks and loses power, privatization is chaotic, and elite turnover is high. Some old elites manage to succeed in the new system. (example nations: Ukraine and Russia)

Path 4: Past communist hierarchies survive, the Communist Party stays in control and holds on to assets, and it directs privatization. There is little elite turnover so the new elite is formed out of the old one. (example nations: Kazakhstan and Uzbekistan)

two factors, he created a conceptual typology that explained the smoothness of the transition and which social-political groups gained power in the various postcommunist societies (see Table 3.3).

Scope. Concepts vary by scope. Some are very narrow; they apply only to specific social settings or activities, are narrowly limited in time or place, and cannot be easily applied beyond a particular setting. Other concepts are very broad and apply to many diverse settings or activities across expanses of time and space. Narrow concepts tend to be less abstract. An example concept with a narrow scope is "football hooliganism," which refers to acts of violence by British and, to a degree, other European soccer fans that has accelerated since the late 1960s. The concept is restricted in time and location, although observers or fans of other mass spectator events have

engaged in rioting or acts of violence and property destruction. Another example is the Japanese phenomena of *karoshi,* or death by overwork. People have died from excessive labor throughout history and across cultures, but this concept narrowly refers to men working for companies in white-collar jobs who are under intense social pressure to put in extremely long working hours without rest for an extended period of time. The concept is associated with a specific Japanese company work culture during a period of economic boom. By contrast, concepts that have a broader scope, such as physical aggression or labor, widely apply across historical time, diverse cultural settings, and numerous activities.

Concepts with a narrow scope have an advantage of being close to concrete daily life, so they are easily recognized and incorporate specific contextual features and the texture of a social setting. Yet, they are difficult to generalize and cannot be used easily to build a broad theoretical understanding of social life. Concepts with a very broad scope have the opposite advantages and disadvantages; they can easily bridge diverse settings to facilitate general understanding but often overlook and disregard significant contextual details in a social setting or activity.

Relationships

In addition to making assumptions and providing concepts, social theories specify relationships among concepts. Theories tell us whether the concepts are related to one another and, if they are related, the kind of relationship. By outlining an entire complex of assumptions, concepts, and interconnections, a theory often states why a specific relationship does or does not exist.

Kinds of Relationships. Beyond stating that concepts are or are not related, theories often specify other characteristics of the relationship. If two concepts are interrelated, the theory can specify whether they are related strongly or weakly, directly or indirectly, such that they accelerate/accentuate one another or depress/reduce each another, or are related immediately or only after a time delay. One concept might relate to another alone, or only when it is in combination with other conditions and concepts (these are called an *interaction effect* and a *contingent relationship* and are discussed later in the book). A theory may identify a concept as a necessary (i.e., essential and required) precondition for another concept or state that is it sufficient (i.e., it may be involved but does not have to be present). Beyond these kinds of relationships, different forms of theoretical explanations (see later in this chapter) also specify the particular form of a relationship (e.g., causal, structural, and so forth).

Propositions and Hypotheses. Many theories contain propositions, or statements, about the connection among concepts. A **proposition** is a theoretical statement that specifies the relationship between two or more concepts and says something about the kind of relationship it is. A researcher will try to learn the truthfulness of a proposition by evaluating whether it conforms to empirical evidence or data. To do this he or she converts the proposition into a hypothesis. A **hypothesis** is an empirically testable version of a proposition. It is a tentative statement about a relationship; that is, researchers are uncertain as to its truthfulness, or whether it actually operates in the empirical world. After repeated empirical evaluations of a hypothesis in many situations, their certainty in the truthfulness of a theoretical proposition increases if it is found to hold. Thus, propositions in a theory are converted into hypotheses for empirical testing, and after the hypothesis has been evaluated, the empirical results inform us whether the proposition is likely to be truthful, or if it needs to be modified or rejected. Sometimes researchers develop propositions after they examine empirical evidence, and in some types of research they proceed without using hypotheses.

> **Proposition** A theoretical statement about the relationship between two or more concepts.
>
> **Hypothesis** An empirically testable version of a theoretical proposition that has not yet been tested or verified with empirical evidence. It is most used in deductive theorizing and can be restated as a prediction.
>
> **Units of analysis** The unit, case, or part of social life that is under consideration. They are key in concept development, empirically measuring or observing concepts, and in data analysis.

Units of Analysis

We can think of the social world as being comprised of many units, such as individual people, groups, organizations, movements, institutions, countries, and so forth. Researchers tailor theoretical concepts to apply to one or more of these **units of analysis.** For example, the concept *aggression* can be applied to several units, the individual, group, organization, or country. This is illustrated by the statements "Joseph is an aggressive child," "The basketball team was very aggressive last night," "The XYZ Corporation has aggressively moved into a new market," and "The United Nations condemned country X for acts of *aggression* toward its neighbor." Aggression by a child (slapping another 4-year-old and kicking his teacher) looks different than aggression by a sports team (physical contact and blocking), a company (lowering prices and launching a massive advertising campaign that targets a competing product), or a nation (moving troops and tanks across an international border). Researchers fit a concept to the specific type of unit they wish to analyze, like a glove fitting over a hand. They use the concepts with analysis units to design a study and measure concepts (discussed in Chapters 6 and 7). When an abstract concept, such as aggression, is applicable across multiple units of analysis, a researcher must decide explicitly the unit he or she wants to focus on and tailor the concept to that unit before proceeding with a study. The abstract concepts facilitate establishing theoretical connections that could operate across the units of analysis.

ASPECTS OF THEORY

Now that you know the parts of social theory, we can look at its various forms. Social theory can be baffling because it has many aspects, but these can be divided into five major ones: (1) the direction of theorizing, either deductive or inductive; (2) the level of analysis, either micro, macro, or meso; (3) the focus as a substantive or formal theory; (4) the form of explanation, either causal, structural, or interpretative; and (5) the range at which it operates, as an empirical generalization, a middle-range theory, or

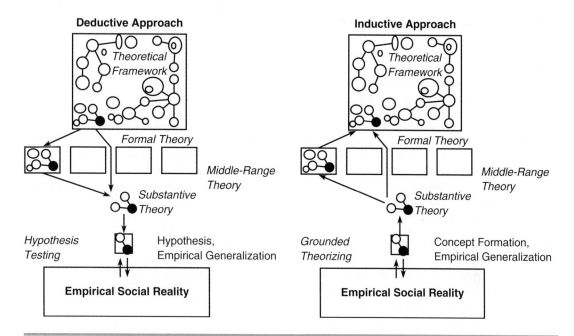

FIGURE 3.1   Deductive and Inductive Theorizing

a framework. Although these aspects may appear intimidating at first, fortunately only a few major combinations of them are in frequent use.

Direction of Theorizing

Researchers approach the building and testing of theory from two directions. Some begin with abstract thinking. They logically connect the ideas in theory to concrete evidence, then test the ideas against the evidence. Others begin with specific observations of empirical evidence. On the basis of the evidence, they generalize and build toward increasingly abstract ideas. In practice, most researchers are flexible and use both approaches at various points in a study (see Figure 3.1).

Deductive.   To theorize in a **deductive direction,** you begin with abstract concepts or a theoretical proposition that outlines the logical connection among concepts and then move toward concrete, empirical evidence. Thus, you start with ideas, or a mental picture of the social world, and then test

your thinking against observable empirical evidence. The studies of the contact hypothesis that you read about in Chapter 2 used deductive theorizing. They began with a theoretical proposition: The absence of interpersonal contact between people and others in a social "outgroup" causes the negative views toward an outgroup to arise due to ignorance and negative stereotypes. The researchers turned the abstract proposition into an empirical hypothesis; that is, increased social contact with, knowledge of, and familiarity among individuals and an outgroup will lessen their negative beliefs, attitudes, and statements. The theorizing proceeded deductively from the abstract level logically to a more concrete, empirical level that included specific outgroups, forms of social contact, and beliefs or attitudes.

> **Deductive direction**   An approach to developing or confirming a theory that begins with abstract concepts and theoretical relationships and works toward more concrete empirical evidence.

BOX **3.4 What Is Grounded Theory?**

Grounded theory is a widely used approach in qualitative research. It is not the only approach and it is not used by all qualitative researchers. *Grounded theory* is "a qualitative research method that uses a systematic set of procedures to develop an inductively derived theory about a phenomenon" (Strauss and Corbin, 1990:24). The purpose of grounded theory is to build a theory that is faithful to the evidence. It is a method for discovering new theory. In it, the researcher compares unlike phenomena with a view toward learning similarities. He or she sees micro-level events as the foundation for a more macro-level explanation. Grounded theory shares several goals with more positivist-oriented theory. It seeks theory that is comparable with the evidence that is precise and rigorous, capable of replication, and generalizable. A grounded theory approach pursues generalizations by making comparisons across social situations.

Qualitative researchers use alternatives to grounded theory. Some qualitative researchers offer an in-depth depiction that is true to an informant's worldview. They excavate a single social situation to elucidate the micro processes that sustain stable social interaction. The goal of other researchers is to provide a very exacting depiction of events or a setting. They analyze specific events or settings in order to gain insight into the larger dynamics of a society. Still other researchers apply an existing theory to analyze specific settings that they have placed in a macro-level historical context. They show connections among micro-level events and between micro-level situations and larger social forces for the purpose of reconstructing the theory and informing social action (see Burawoy, 1991:271–287; Charmaz, 2003; and Hammersley, 1992, for a summary of several alternatives).

Inductive. To theorize in an **inductive direction,** you begin with observing the empirical world and then reflect on what is taking place, thinking in increasingly more abstract ways, moving toward theoretical concepts and propositions. Whereas deductive theorizing requires you to begin with a clearly thought-out theoretical picture, with inductive theorizing you can begin with a general topic and some vague ideas that you then refine and elaborate into more exact theoretical concepts. In inductive theorizing you build from observations on the ground toward more abstract thinking, whereas in deductive theorizing you move from ideas toward grounded empirical observations. In his study of street vendors in New York City that you read about in Chapter 2, Duneier used inductive theorizing. He developed a

theoretical understanding only during and after he had collected data. He stated (1999:341), "I began to get ideas from the things I was seeing and hearing on the street." Duneier (1999:342) described the process like a medical professional who sees many diverse symptoms and then comes up with a diagnosis or coherent story that can explain the underlying reason for the many symptoms on the surface.

Many researchers use a specific kind of inductive theorizing called **grounded theory** (see Box 3.4). You will learn more about grounded theory in Chapters 6 and 14. It involves formulating new theoretical ideas from the ground up instead of testing existing theoretical ideas. A researcher builds theoretical generalizations out of the process of trying to explain, interpret, and render meaning from observed data.

Inductive direction An approach to developing or confirming a theory that begins with concrete empirical evidence and works toward more abstract concepts and theoretical relationships.

Grounded theory A type of inductive social theory often used in qualitative research that builds toward abstract theory, often by making comparisons of empirical observations.

Level of Analysis

Social reality exists on many levels, from the micro to macro level. At the micro level it includes short-term face-to-face interactions of a few individuals in a small-scale setting (e.g., a female and two male students exchange comments for a few minutes as they are leaving a classroom). Micro-level reality typically involves few people in direct contact over a short time period in a close setting. Social scientists develop **micro-level theory** and concepts tailored to analyze this level of social reality, or that operate best at this level of analysis. For example, Dellinger and Williams (2002) conducted field research among the editorial staff at two magazine offices, *Gentleman's Sophisticate* (heterosexual male pornography) and *Womyn* (feminist works) to examine on-the-job sexual harassment. They observed face-to-face interactions, listened to comments, and conducted interviews to inductively develop a micro-level theory of the distinctive workplace culture that operated in each editorial office. McFarland (2004) developed a micro-level theory of disruptive behaviors in high school classrooms. Based on detailed observations of interactions inside classrooms among students and teachers, he noted how protagonists and antagonists acted in patterned ways and had different outcomes.

At the opposite extreme is the macro level; it includes large-scale events (e.g., the patterns of encounters between western European imperialist powers and Chinese civilization during the eighteenth century). **Macro-level theorizing** is designed for this level of analysis—to explain events, processes, patterns, and structures that operate among large social units with direct and indirect contacts over long time periods and often covering large expanses of space. The study of Black–White race relations in the United States, South Africa, and Brazil, and the study of the colonial experience and later development of South American nations, described in Chapter 2, both illustrate macro-level theorizing.

The study by Anthony Marx (1998) explained the conditions that led Black people to engage in protest to gain full citizenship rights and he examined patterns of national racial politics in three counties across two centuries. His theory states that protest resulted in an interaction between (1) race-based political mobilization and (2) national government policies of racial domination (i.e., apartheid in South Africa, Jim Crow laws in southern United States, and no legalized race-based domination in Brazil). Policies of racial domination developed from practices of slavery, exploitation,

and discrimination that justified White superiority. The policies reinforced specific racial ideologies that shaped national development during the twentieth century. A critical causal factor was how national political elites used the legalized domination of Blacks to reduce divisions among Whites. In nations that had large regional or class divisions among Whites, national elites tried to increase White backing for the national government by creating legalized forms of racial domination. Over time, such legalized domination froze racial divisions, which promoted a sense of racial identity and consciousness among Blacks. The strong sense of racial identity became a key resource when Blacks mobilized politically to demand full citizenship rights. Legalized racial domination also intensified the Blacks' protest and directed it against the national government as the societal institution that reinforced their experience of racial inequality.

Between the micro level and macro level is an intermediate level, the meso level. **Meso-level theory** focuses on the level of analysis of organizations, social movements, or communities. Thus, as social scientists examine different levels of the social world, they develop theories and concepts that operate at a corresponding level of analysis. The study by Mayer (2002) on the impact of economic inequality in neighborhoods on schooling described in Chapter 2 was at the meso level of analysis.

Krysan (2002) used quantitative and qualitative data to examine the responses of Blacks and Whites in four U.S. cities about what makes a

---

Micro-level theory Social theory focusing on the micro level of social life that occurs over short durations (e.g., face-to-face interactions and encounters among individuals or small groups).

Macro-level theory Social theory focusing on the macro level of social life (e.g., social institutions, major sectors of society, entire societies, or world regions) and processes that occur over long durations (many years, multiple decades, or a century or longer).

Meso-level theory Social theory focusing on the relations, processes, and structures at a midlevel of social life (e.g., organizations, movements, and communities) and events operating over moderate durations (many months, several years, or a decade).

desirable neighborhood for them. She examined how people of different races evaluated various factors, including racial composition, crime rates, social class, and racial climate, in hypothetical neighborhoods. Her meso-level theory explained neighborhood preferences based on a mixture of people's racial stereotypes, past experiences with racial discrimination, public policies, and formation of neighborhood-level reputations or climates of hostility. McVeigh, Welch, and Bjarnason (2003) used meso-level theorizing to explain hate crime reporting in the United States. They found that social movement resources and local context affected whether local civil rights organizations urged the reporting of hate crimes. Kelly (2003) explained the development of employee benefits among U.S. employers with a meso-level theory. She found that organizations added employee benefits in response to changes in their legal-political environment, including tax laws and policies shared among firms, as well as factors internal to the organizations such as activities by specific departments of an organization and form of the organization.

Focus of Theory

Researchers construct, elaborate, and test or verify substantive and formal theories. **Substantive theory** focuses on a particular content or topic area in social reality. For example, it might be about family relations, delinquent behavior, or racial-ethnic relations. **Formal theory** focuses on general processes or structures that operate across multiple topic areas. For example, a formal theory might be about forming a social identity, engaging in conflict, or exercising power. The two focuses can intersect. Social identity, conflict, and power can operate in

> **Substantive theory** A type of theory that is specifically tailored to a particular topic area.
>
> **Formal theory** A type of theory that is general and applies across many specific topic areas.
>
> **Theoretical explanation** A logical argument or "story" that tells why something takes a specific form or occurs, and does so by referring to more general ideas and abstract principles.

families, among delinquents, and across racial-ethnic groups. Substantive theory on one topic will often draw on and combine formal theories; a formal theory often has applications in several substantive areas. As Layder (1993:44) remarked, "the cumulative process of theory is enhanced by the encouragement of multiple substantive and formal theories."

Each theoretical focus has its strengths. Substantive theory offers powerful explanations for a topic area because it is tailored to it and incorporates rich details from specific settings, processes, or events. Nonetheless, substantive theory is often difficult to generalize to different topic areas. Compared to formal theory, substantive theory employs concepts at lower levels of abstraction and narrower scope, which makes it harder to connect across diverse topics and build general knowledge. Formal theory's strength is its ability to operate and build bridges across multiple topics, which advances more general knowledge. Its weakness is that it is less attached to specific social settings and may require adjustment to be applied a particular issue or topic. Formal theories help researchers recognize and explain similar features that operate across several divergent topics. Because they are more abstract, researchers find them easier to elaborate into more complex forms, compare and connect ideas from several theories, and express the theory in a very logical or purely analytic form.

Forms of Explanation

Prediction and Explanation. A theory's primary purpose is to explain. Many people confuse prediction with explanation. There are two meanings or uses of the term *explanation.* Researchers focus on **theoretical explanation,** a logical argument that tells why something takes a specific form or occurs. It refers to a general rule or principle. These are a researcher's theoretical argument or connections among concepts. The second type of explanation, *ordinary explanation,* makes something clear or describes something in a way that illustrates it and makes it intelligible. For example, a good teacher "explains" in the ordinary sense. The two types of explanation can blend together. This occurs when a researcher explains (i.e., makes intelligible) his or her explanation (i.e., a logical argument involving theory).

Prediction is a statement that something will occur. It is easier to predict than to explain, and an explanation has more logical power than prediction because good explanations also predict. An explanation rarely predicts more than one outcome, but the same outcome may be predicted by opposing explanations. Although it is less powerful than explanation, many people are entranced by the dramatic visibility of a prediction.

A gambling example illustrates the difference between explanation and prediction. If I enter a casino and consistently and accurately predict the next card to appear or the next number on a roulette wheel, it will be sensational. I may win a lot of money, at least until the casino officials realize I am always winning and expel me. Yet, my method of making the predictions is more interesting than the fact that I can do so. Telling you what I do to predict the next card is more fascinating than being able to predict.

Here is another example. You know that the sun "rises" each morning. You can predict that at some time, every morning, whether or not clouds obscure it, the sun will rise. But why is this so? One explanation is that the Great Turtle carries the sun across the sky on its back. Another explanation is that a god sets his arrow ablaze, which appears to us as the sun, and shoots it across the sky. Few people today believe these ancient explanations. The explanation you probably accept involves a theory about the rotation of the earth and the position of the sun, the star of our solar system. In this explanation, the sun only appears to rise. The sun does not move; its apparent movement depends on the earth's rotation. We are on a planet that both spins on its axis and orbits around a star millions of miles away in space. All three explanations make the same prediction: The sun rises each morning. As you can see, a weak explanation can produce an accurate prediction. A good explanation depends on a well-developed theory and is confirmed by empirical observations.

Nobel Prize–winning physicist Steven Weinberg (2001:47) has given a "hard science" view of explanation:

Scientists who do pure rather than applied research commonly tell the public and funding agencies that their mission is the explanation of something or other. . . .Within the limited context of physics, I think one can . . . [distinguish] explanation from mere description, which captures what physicists mean when they say that they have explained some regularity. . . .We explain a physical principle when we show that it can be deduced from a more fundamental physical principle. (emphasis added)

Thus, *explanation* implies logically connecting what occurs in a specific situation to a more abstract or basic principle about "how things work." A researcher explains or answers the question Why? by showing that one particular situation is a case of, or a particular instance of, the more general principle.

We next examine three major forms of theoretical explanation that social researchers use: causal, structural, and interpretative. Each explains, or answers, the question of why things occur, by making connections to general principles, but they do so in different ways. We begin with the best known and most widely used form, causal explanation.

Causal Explanation. **Causal explanation** is used when the relationship is one of cause and effect. We use it all the time in everyday language, which tends to be sloppy and ambiguous. What do we mean when we say *cause*? For example, you may say that poverty causes crime or that looseness in morals causes an increase in divorce. This does not tell how or why the causal process works. Researchers try to be more precise and exact when discussing causal relations.

Philosophers have long debated the idea of cause. It has been a controversial idea since the writings of the eighteenth-century Scottish philosopher David Hume (1711–1776). Some people argue that causality occurs in the empirical world, but it cannot be proved. Causality is "out there" in objective reality, and researchers can only try to find evidence

Causal explanation A type of theoretical explanation about why events occur and how things work expressed in terms of causes and effects, or as one factor producing certain results.

BOX **3.5** **Three Elements of Causality**

I read that several politicians visited a Catholic school in Chicago that had a record of being much more successful than public schools in educating children. The next day, the politicians called a news conference and advocated new laws and the redirection of tax money to Catholic schools. As a person who wants children to get a good education, I was interested in the story, but as a social scientist, I critically evaluated it. The politicians' theory said Catholic schools cause more learning than public schools. They had two elements of causality: temporal order (first the children attended a Catholic school, then learning improved) and association (those attending Catholic schools performed better than those attending public school). Social researchers know this is not enough information. They first try to eliminate alternative explanations and then try to understand the causal mechanism (i.e., what happens in Catholic schools that helps students learn more). For example, the

politicians failed to eliminate the alternative explanation that children in the two types of schools had different family circumstances that affect learning and that this caused learning differences. If the family circumstances (e.g., parents' education and income, family religious belief and intensity of belief, two-parent versus single-parent households, degree of parental interest in a child's education, etc.) are the same for children who attend both types of schools, then the politicians are on the right track. The focus, then, is on what Catholic schools are doing that improves learning. If the family circumstances are very different, then the politicians are making a big mistake. Unfortunately, politicians are rarely trained in social research and most make quick, high-publicity decisions without the careful reasoning or the patience for precise empirical investigation. Fortunately, sociologist James S. Coleman and others have studied this issue (see Coleman and Hoffer, 1987).

for it. Others argue that causality is only an idea that exists in the human mind, a mental construction, not something "real" in the world. This second position holds that causality is only a convenient way of thinking about the world. Without entering into the philosophical debate, many researchers pursue causal relationships.

You need three things to establish causality: temporal order, association, and the elimination of plausible alternatives (see Box 3.5). An implicit fourth condition is an assumption that a causal relationship makes sense or fits with broader assumptions or a theoretical framework. Let us examine the three basic conditions.

The *temporal order* condition means that a cause must come before an effect. This common-sense assumption establishes the direction of causality: from the cause toward the effect. You may ask: How can the cause come after what it is to affect? It cannot, but temporal order is only one of the conditions needed for causality. Temporal order is necessary but not sufficient to infer causality. Sometimes people make the mistake of talking about "cause" on the basis of temporal order alone. For example, a professional baseball player pitches no-

hit games when he kisses his wife just before a game. The kissing occurred before the no-hit games. Does that mean the kissing is the cause of the pitching performance? It is very unlikely. As another example, race riots occurred in four separate cities in 1968, one day after an intense wave of sunspots. The temporal ordering does not establish a causal link between sunspots and race riots. After all, all prior human history occurred before some specific event. The temporal order condition simply eliminates from consideration potential causes that occurred later in time.

It is not always easy to establish temporal order. With cross-sectional research, temporal order is tricky. For example, a researcher finds that people who have a lot of education are also less prejudiced than others. Does more education cause a reduction in prejudice? Or do highly prejudiced people avoid education or lack the motivation, self-discipline, and intelligence needed to succeed in school? Here is another example. The students who get high grades in my class say I am an excellent teacher. Does getting high grades make them happy, so they return the favor by saying that I am an excellent teacher (i.e., high grades cause a positive evalua-

Lower Income   Upper Income

FIGURE 3.2   Association of Income and Race

tion)? Or am I doing a great job, so students study hard and learn a lot, which the grades reflect (i.e., their learning causes them to get high grades)? It is a chicken-and-egg problem. To resolve it, a researcher needs to bring in other information or design research to test for the temporal order.

Simple causal relations are unidirectional, operating in a single direction from the cause to the effect. Most studies examine unidirectional relations. More complex theories specify reciprocal-effect causal relations—that is, a mutual causal relationship or simultaneous causality. For example, studying a lot can cause a student to get good grades, but getting good grades also motivates the student to continue to study. Theories often have reciprocal or feedback relationships, but these are difficult to test. Some researchers call unidirectional relations nonrecursive and reciprocal-effect relations recursive.

A researcher also needs an **association** for causality. Two phenomena are associated if they occur together in a patterned way or appear to act together. People sometimes confuse correlation with association. Correlation has a specific technical meaning, whereas association is a more general idea. A correlation coefficient is a statistical measure that indicates the amount of association, but there are many ways to measure association. Some-

times, researchers call association *concomitant variation* because two variables vary together. Figure 3.2 shows 38 people from a lower-income neighborhood and 35 people from an upper-income neighborhood. Can you see an association between race and income level?

More people mistake association for causality than confuse it with temporal order. For example, when I was in college, I got high grades on the exams I took on Fridays but low grades on those I took on Mondays. There was an association between the day of the week and the exam grade, but it did not mean that the day of the week caused the exam grade. Instead, the reason was that I worked 20 hours each weekend and was very tired on Mondays. As another example, the number of children born in India increased until the late 1960s, then slowed in the 1970s. The number of U.S.-made cars driven in the United States increased until the late 1960s, then slowed in the 1970s. The number of Indian children born and the number of U.S. cars driven are associated: They vary together or increase

Association   The co-occurrence of two events, characteristics, or factors such that when one happens/is present, the other one is likely to happen/be present as well.

BOX **3.6** Learning to See Causal Relations

As I was driving home from the university one day, I heard a radio news report about gender and racial bias in standardized tests. A person who claimed that bias was a major problem said that the tests should be changed. Because I work in the field of education and disdain racial or gender bias, the report caught my attention. Yet, as a social scientist, I critically evaluated the news story. The evidence for a bias charge was the consistent pattern of higher scores in mathematics for male high school seniors versus female high school seniors, and for European-background students versus African American students. Was the cause of the pattern of different test scores a bias built into the tests?

When questioned by someone who had designed the tests, the person charging bias lacked a crucial piece of evidence to support a claim of test bias: the

educational experience of students. It turns out that girls and boys take different numbers and types of mathematics courses in high school. Girls tend to take fewer math courses. Among the girls who complete the same mathematics curriculum as boys, the gender difference dissolves. Likewise, a large percentage of African Americans attend racially segregated, poor-quality schools in inner cities or in impoverished rural areas. For African Americans who attend high-quality suburban schools and complete the same courses, racial differences in test scores disappear. This evidence suggests that inequality in education causes test score differences. Although the tests may have problems, identifying the real cause implies that changing the tests without first improving or equalizing education could be a mistake.

---

and decrease at the same time. Yet there is no causal connection. By coincidence, the Indian government instituted a birth control program that slowed the number of births at the same time that Americans were buying more imported cars.

If a researcher cannot find an association, a causal relationship is unlikely. This is why researchers attempt to find correlations and other measures of association. Yet, a researcher can often find an association without causality. The association eliminates potential causes that are not associated, but it cannot definitely identify a cause. It is a necessary but not a sufficient condition. In other words, you need it for causality, but it is not enough alone.

An association does not have to be perfect (i.e., every time one variable is present, the other also is) to show causality. In the example involving exam grades and days of the week, there is an association if on 10 Fridays I got 7 As, 2 Bs, and 1 C, whereas my exam grades on 10 Mondays were 6 Ds, 2 Cs, and 2 Bs. An association exists, but the days of the week and the exam grades are not perfectly associated. The race and income-level association shown in Figure 3.2 is also an imperfect association.

Eliminating alternatives means that a researcher interested in causality needs to show that

the effect is due to the causal variable and not to something else. It is also called *no spuriousness* because an apparent causal relationship that is actually due to an alternative but unrecognized cause is called a spurious relationship, which is discussed in Chapter 6 (see Box 3.6).

Researchers can observe temporal order and associations. They cannot observe the elimination of alternatives. They can only demonstrate it indirectly. Eliminating alternatives is an ideal because eliminating all possible alternatives is impossible. A researcher tries to eliminate major alternative explanations in two ways: through built-in design controls and by measuring potential hidden causes. Experimental researchers build controls into the study design itself to eliminate alternative causes. They isolate an experimental situation from the influence of all variables except the main causal variable.

Researchers also try to eliminate alternatives by measuring possible alternative causes. This is common in survey research and is called *controlling for* another variable. Researchers use statistical techniques to learn whether the causal variable or something else operates on the effect variable.

Causal explanations are usually in a linear form or state cause and effect in a straight line: *A* causes

B, B causes *C, C* causes *D*. For example, *A* (the main earner of a family loses his or her job and the income supporting the family stops) causes *B* (rapid and significant economic hardship within a family), *B* causes *C* (increased interpersonal stress and arguments and inflames pre-existing tensions or issues that have been controlled), *C* causes *D* (marital distress and maybe even the breakup of a marriage). This explanation is in a linear form, in that each variable or part is causally connected to each subsequent part or variable in a straight line. We can restate it as a causal proposition: Job loss and ending the income flow from a family's main earner creates major economic difficulties for a family, which greatly intensifies interpersonal tension and stress, which in turn, can seriously destabilize and disrupt a marital relationship. Good causal explanations identify a causal relationship and specify a causal mechanism. A simple causal explanation is: *X* causes *Y, Y* occurs because of *X*, where *X* and *Y* are concepts (e.g., early marriage and divorce). Some researchers state causality in a predictive form: If *X* occurs, then *Y* follows. Causality can be stated in many ways: *X* leads to *Y, X* produces *Y, X* influences *Y, X* is related to *Y*, the greater *X* the higher *Y*.

Here is a simple causal theory: A rise in unemployment causes an increase in child abuse. The subject to be explained is an increase in the occurrence of child abuse. What explains it is a rise in unemployment. We "explain" the increase in child abuse by identifying its cause. A complete explanation also requires elaborating the causal mechanism. My theory says that when people lose their jobs, they feel a loss of self-worth. Once they lose self-worth, they become easily frustrated, upset, and angry. Frustrated people often express their anger by directing violence toward those with whom they have close personal contact (e.g., friends, spouse, children, etc.). This is especially true if they do not understand the source of the anger or cannot direct it toward its true cause (e.g., an employer, government policy, or "economic forces").

The unemployment and child abuse example illustrates a chain of causes and a causal mechanism. Researchers can test different parts of the chain. They might test whether unemployment rates and child abuse occur together, or whether frus-

trated people become violent toward the people close to them. A typical research strategy is to divide a larger theory into parts and test various relationships against the data.

Diagrams of Causal Relations among Variables. At minimum, you need a cause and an effect for a causal relationship. Researchers express theories in words, pictures, or both. They often draw diagrams of the causal relations to present a simplified picture of a relationship and see it at a glance. Such symbolic representations supplement verbal descriptions of causal relations and convey complex information. They are a shorthand way to show theoretical relations.

The simplest diagram is a two-variable model, as in Figure 3.3(a). Researchers represent variables using letters, circles, or boxes. The convention is to represent a cause by an *X* and the effect by a *Y*. The arrow shows the direction of causality (e.g., from independent to dependent variable). Sometimes, researchers use subscripts when there is more than one cause (e.g., X_1, X_2). Relationships among variables are symbolized by lines with arrows. Causal relations are represented by straight lines. Associations that do not imply a causal relationship are represented by curved lines with arrows on each end. A single arrow on a line represents a unidirectional relationship. Arrows on both ends of a straight line represent reciprocal relationships.

Relationships between variables can be positive or negative. Researchers imply a positive relationship if they say nothing. A **positive relationship** means that a higher value on the causal variable goes with a higher value on the effect variable. For example, the more education a person has, the longer his or her life expectancy is. A **negative relationship** means that a higher value on the causal

---

Positive relationship An association between two concepts or measures, such that as one increases, the other also increases, or when one is present the other is also present.

Negative relationship An association between two concepts or measures, such that as one increases, the other decreases, or when one is present the other is absent.

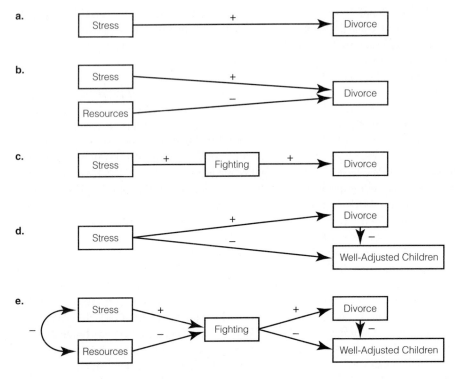

Explanation of relationship in each diagram

a. Level of stress (financial, social, emotional, etc.) is positively associated with the likelihood that a couple will get a divorce.

b. Level of stress is positively associated with the likelihood that a couple gets a divorce, but the amount of resources (financial, social, emotional, etc.) they possess is negatively associated with it.

c. Level of stress is positively associated with the frequency of fighting by a couple, which is associated with the likelihood that the couple gets a divorce.

d. Level of stress is positively associated with the likelihood that a couple gets a divorce and negatively associated with the likelihood that the couple will have emotionally well-adjusted children. In addition, the divorce process itself has a negative effect on the emotional adjustment of children.

e. Level of stress and amount of resources are negatively associated with each other (i.e., people who tend to have a lot of resources are less likely to experience or better able to deal with stress). Level of stress is positively associated with frequency of fighting by a couple, but the amount of resources is negatively associated with it. Amount of fighting is positively associated with the likelihood that a couple gets a divorce. Both fighting and the divorce itself are negatively associated with the likelihood that the couple will have emotionally well-adjusted children.

FIGURE 3.3 Causal Diagrams

variable goes with a lower value on the effect variable. For example, the more frequently a couple attends religious services, the lower the chances of their divorcing each other. In diagrams, a plus sign (+) signifies a positive relationship and a negative sign (–) signifies a negative relationship.

Figure 3.3 presents some samples of relationships that can be diagrammed. Researchers would not use a diagram for a very simple two-variable relationship like the one in Figure 3.3(a). As researchers add variables and increase the complexity of relationships, they find diagrams more helpful.

Studies you read about in Chapter 2 that tested the contact hypothesis used a causal explanation. They found that contact caused a decrease in negative attitudes. Behrens, Uggen, and Manza (2003) used a causal explanation to study felon disenfranchisement in the United States. The authors begin by noting that the United States has the most restrictive voting laws in the advanced world for people convicted of committing a crime. The state-level voting laws vary widely—some states have no restrictions, others bar incarcerated felons from voting, and others bar felons who served their sentences from voting for life. The authors extended the racial threat hypothesis originally used to explain interracial economic competition. They looked at the year a restrictive voting law was passed, the types of restrictions, and the percentage of Blacks in the state population and in prisons. They found that restrictive voting laws for felons were passed after more direct forms of denying voting rights to Blacks were no longer legal, and that restrictive voting laws were associated with a state having a large Black population and more Blacks in its prisons. The temporal order and association between racial composition and restrictive laws fit the explanation that White fears of Blacks weakening White political power caused the passage of voting laws whose primary result was to prevent many Blacks from voting.

McVeigh (2004) used a causal explanation to explain why racist organizations succeed in certain locations of the United States. Using quantitative data on counties in the United States, he noted that racist organizations are most successful where local conditions matched the racist claims; that is, Whites are declining economically relative to non-Whites. Because they appeal to Whites experiencing downward social mobility, the racist messages succeed in areas of racial diversity, changing economic conditions, and rising income inequality. The racist messages were less successful when White education levels were very mixed in an area. This was because the more educated Whites spread information that offered alternatives to the diagnosis of conditions offered by racists. Thus, the cause of racist organizational success was a combination of certain conditions (Whites economically falling behind visible non-Whites) plus the absence of an alternative

diagnosis (e.g., changes in the economy and technology, Whites without needed education and job skills) to racist or xenophobic messages (i.e., domestic or immigrant non-Whites are displacing and advancing over Whites unfairly).

Structural Explanation. In a causal explanation one or more factors cause factors to respond, like one ball that rolls and hits others causing them to begin rolling. By contrast, the logic of a **structural explanation** locates a social process, event, or factor within a larger structure. The structure is like a spider web, a wheel with spokes, or a machine with interconnected parts. Aspects of social life are explained by noting where they fit within the larger structure. Three major theories that use a structural explanation are sequential theories, network theories, and functional theories (see Figure 3.4).

Sequential theory emphasizes the order or sequence by which events occur; it identifies the necessary earlier steps and possible subsequent steps in an unfolding pattern of development across time. A sequential theory maps out an ordered set of stages that all or almost all people, organizations, or events follow. There may be a single path or a narrow range of paths for a specific process—moral development of a child, intimate relationship maturing, family formation, urban expansion, organizational growth or death, conflict intensification or resolution, or societal development. In addition to identifying the steps or stages of a process, sequential theories explain the speed of movement along the steps, stagnation at a stage, and key points that may turn a process in a different direction or start the pursuit of a different set of steps. A sequential theory may identify essential versus optional prior steps, or ways that a specific prior step restricts

Structural explanation A type of theoretical explanation about why events occur and how things work expressed by outlining an overall structure and emphasizing locations, interdependences, distances, or relations among positions in that structure.

Sequential theory A type of theory that uses a structural explanation, outlines a sequential pattern, and specifies the ordered sequence, stages, steps, or phases by which events occur.

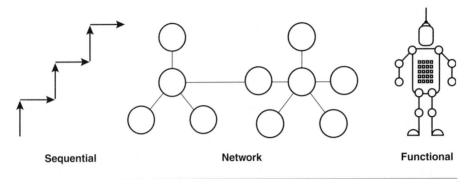

Sequential   **Network**   **Functional**

FIGURE 3.4   Forms of Structural Explanation

possible next steps. It is not a causal theory—being in an earlier step does not *cause* movement along the sequence; instead, the structure of a staged sequence constrains how events or processes can occur. Thus a sequential theory may state that unless step A was taken, it is impossible to move onto step B, and the only way to move from step A to step C is to pass through step B.

A sequential theory was used in the example of historical-comparative research you read in Chapter 2 by Mahoney (2003) on Spanish American countries. He found that events at an early stage in a Spanish American country's development, during colonialism, affected the direction of its path in later stages. Oesterle, Johnson, and Mortimer (2004) used sequential theory in their panel study on voluntarism. The authors adopted a "life course" perspective in which "the meaning of roles and activities differs across life stage" (2004:1124). Thus, the impact of something happening at a specific phase of a person's life may differ from its happening in other phases, and it shapes the events in later phases. The authors sought to explain levels of volunteering among young adults. They noted the transition to adulthood is a critical stage when a person learns new social roles and adult expectations. They examined panel data of ninth-grade students (15–16 years old) begun in 1988 that continued across nine

years, when the research subjects were 18–19 and 26–27. The authors found that what happened at last stage was strongly influenced by activities at a prior stage. People who devoted full time to working or parenting at an earlier stage (18–19 years old) were less likely to volunteer at a later state (26–27 years old) than those whose major activity was attending school. Also, volunteering at an earlier stage had a strong effect on whether one volunteered at a later stage.

Network theory also discusses structure, but it is positional structure.[5] The position in a structured network of positions, size and shape of a network, type and existence of connections among positions, overlap or density of connections, centrality in a network, and direction of flows among positions or nodes in a network are all key ideas for network theory. The positions might be points or nodes in a network of relations among people, organizations, cities, or nations. Positions and the structure of a network help to explain ease of communication, power relationships, hierarchical relations, and speed of flows in the network.

A network theorist explains something by referring to a broader pattern, a set of syntax rules, or structures. His or her explanation shows how a specific event is just one part of a larger pattern, is one building block in a bigger structure, or is a one link within a much larger system of linkages. It is a form of reasoning like that used to explain why people use language in specific ways; that is, there are syntax rules that state that X goes with Y or that sentences need a noun and a verb. The researcher

> **Network theory**   A type of theory that uses a structural explanation in which the emphasis is on locations and connections within an interconnected web or network and on the shape or overall pattern of the network.

explains an event by identifying the syntax rule that covers the event.

Gould's (1991) theory of the social mobilization in the Paris Commune of 1871 used network theory. The Paris Commune was a famous rebellion and takeover of the city of Paris—and very nearly of the government of France—by masses of poor and working people who were led by socialists, Marxists, and radicals. It was a two-month experiment in democratic socialism with free education, worker cooperatives, and radical social reforms. The Commune ended with a brutal battle in which 25,000 Parisians died, most of them shot after surrendering to the national army.

Gould said that people came from different social networks, which shaped their involvement in collective action. Thus, prior to their recruitment into the Paris Commune rebellion, people had social ties to one another. By knowing these ties, Gould predicted who was likely to join. His theory said that isolated people are unlikely to join. People join when those with whom they have intimate social relations join. In addition, a person's location within a web of social ties is important. People at the center of a dense web of ties (i.e., those who have multiple strong ties) are pulled more strongly than those on the periphery (i.e., those with only one or a few weak ties). Gould found that people from the same Paris neighborhood were recruited into a single battalion in the revolutionary defense guard. The new organization, the guard, was built on previous informal ties from the neighborhood—ties of family, neighbor, co-worker, or friend. This created intense intrabattalion loyalty. At the same time, a few people from the neighborhood, some whom were central in it, went to other battalions. This created loyalty across guard battalions. Gould predicted the pattern of battalion behavior from the positions people held in the overlapping social networks of the neighborhood and the guard battalion. He explained the actions of battalions and their responses to events by referring to a broader pattern of social ties among people.

Sanders, Nee, and Sernau (2002) used network theory to explain Asian immigrant job seeking. Using interview data with immigrants from the Philippines, Korea, Taiwan, and China in Los An-

geles, they found that networks matched and sorted immigrants with jobs. New immigrants with limited language and job skills sought employment either with a co-ethnic employer or through informal social ties; that is, they consulted experienced friends, relatives, and acquaintances and asked them to be intermediaries. Network users expanded job opportunities beyond employers in their own ethnic group. Thus, ethnic network ties were "bridge ties"; that is, they helped immigrants get jobs beyond their ethnic community by using co-ethnics who had made the transition to mainstream employment. Over time as language and job skills improved, these immigrants moved on to better mainstream jobs. Immigrants without social ties, in limited networks, or who worked for co-ethnics found getting mainstream jobs difficult. Thus, network location, access to a large and diverse network, and using network ties facilitated getting mainstream jobs and upward social mobility in mainstream society.

Alderson and Beckfield (2004) used network theory to study city power and prestige. According to the "world city thesis" globalization has broken down the old hierarchies of cities and replaced them with a new pattern of centrality (or marginality). Certain cities have risen in the world economy. They are nodes in international networks of information, investment, and financial flows around the world; that is, they are command posts in running the world economy. The authors looked at information and resource flows among 500 largest companies and their branches that linked 3,692 cities across the globe, and they ranked 50 cities in terms of several types of power and prestige. The authors mapped connections among major companies and between company headquarters and less important branches. They found that corporate headquarters were located in a few major world cities, and minor branches were in lesser cities as predicted by the world city thesis.

Functional theory uses the idea of a system with a set of mutually interdependent relations.[6]

Functional theory A type of theory that uses a structural explanation in which the emphasis is on how interdependent parts fit into and operate to sustain an overall system, with specific parts serving complementary and specialized supporting roles for the whole.

Various parts of a system depend on other parts, and in combination, all the parts work together as a whole. Success or failure of one part has ramifications for other parts and for the entire system. The system might refer to a family, a social group, a formal organization, or an entire society. Functional theories often assume long-term system survival or continuity over time, with a need for balance or equilibrium for a system to continue smooth operation. A failure of a critical part means the inability to fulfill a vital system function, and unless the part is "repaired" or a replacement found for a vital function, a system is in danger of failing. Parts of a system tend to be specialized or more efficient/effective in fulfilling different system needs or functions, and fit a patterned division of labor. The parts fill functions and parts are explained by how they fit into the structure of all functions in a system. Like the part of a human body or part of a robot, each part (e.g., head, hand, foot) performs specialized functions.

A functional theory of social change says that, over time, a social system, or society, moves through developmental stages, becoming increasingly differentiated and more complex. It evolves a specialized division of labor and develops greater individualism. These developments create greater efficiency for the system as a whole. Specialization and individualism create temporary disruptions. The traditional ways of doing things weaken, but new social relations emerge. The system generates new ways to fulfill functions or satisfy its needs.

Kalmijn (1991) used a functional explanation to explain a shift in how Americans select marriage partners. He relied on secularization theory, which holds that ongoing historical processes of industrialization and urbanization shape the development of society. During these modernization processes, people rely less on traditional ways of doing things. Religious beliefs and local community ties weaken, as does the family's control over young adults. People no longer live their entire lives in small, homogeneous communities. Young adults become more

independent from their parents and from the religious organizations that formerly played a critical role in selecting marriage partners.

Society has a basic need to organize the way people select marriage partners and find partners with whom they share fundamental values. In modern society, people spend time away from small local settings in school settings. In these school settings, especially in college, they meet other unmarried people. Education is a major socialization agent in modern society. Increasingly, it affects a person's future earnings, moral beliefs and values, and ways of spending leisure time. This explains why there has been a trend in the United States for people to marry less within the same religion and increasingly to marry persons with a similar level of education. In traditional societies, the family and religious organization served the function of socializing people to moral values and linking them to potential marriage partners who held similar values. In modern society, educational institutions largely fulfill this function for the social system.

Interpretive Explanation. The purpose of **interpretive explanation** is to foster understanding. The interpretive theorist attempts to discover the meaning of an event or practice by placing it within a specific social context. He or she tries to comprehend or mentally grasp the operation of the social world, as well as get a feel for something or to see the world as another person does. Because each person's subjective worldview shapes how he or she acts, the researcher attempts to discern others' reasoning and view of things. The process is similar to decoding a text or work of literature. Meaning comes from the context of a cultural symbol system.

A study by Williams, Alvarez, and Hauck (2002) on recently immigrated Latina high school students in the midwestern United States used an interpretative explanation. The authors studied students in an English-as-a-second-language (ESL) class in a large high school. They asked, What is the students' assimilation/acculturate experience? They found that the students used a mix of adaptation strategies that involved their ethnicity, gender identity, and immigration status. In particular, they noted that ethnicity is gendered; this was shown by how

Interpretative explanation A type of theoretical explanation about why events occur and how things work expressed in terms of the socially constructed meanings and subjective worldviews.

girls learned English and felt parental controls over them in ways that sharply differed from boys. While the Latina girls felt pressure to "fit in," they also felt strong pressures to resist peers based on family obligations and norms. In school the girls were frustrated with poor-quality teaching and racial stereotypes that treated them as "illiterate peasants," when in fact most of them migrated from large Mexican cities where they had been pursuing serious academic studies. Unlike the boys who had opportunities for outside work experience and faced less restrictive family controls, the girls saw education as their main avenue to success, but they had to balance education with fulfilling their family obligations. The girls created a bicultural self in which they learned to assimilate and present one side of themselves to the English-speaking world and the teachers; another side was for their family and Latino friends.

Futrell and Siml (2004) used interpretative explanation to study the U.S. White power movement. The authors focused on movement collective identity, or a shared sense of "we." They examined members of a racist movement that is fragmented into many organizations (e.g., Ku Klux Klan, Christian identity groups, Aryan Nation, neo-Nazi groups) and whose members are marginalized from larger society. The authors asked, How do members communicate their beliefs and engage in activism when their radical beliefs can get them fired and destroy most personal relations? After interviewing and collecting data on 56 activists from 1996 and 2003, the authors discovered the members participated in small domestic gatherings (e.g., study groups, ritual parties) at which they reaffirmed their commitments and discouraged conformity to the mainstream outside of others. The gatherings were small, inclusive, and rooted in ongoing personal relations. In them members felt that they could safely and openly express racial ideologies. Family members and close friends supported these "cultural havens." Thus, members created and sought out "free spaces" in which they could affirm their radical beliefs among like-minded people. By embedding opportunities for political expressions in what looked on the surface to be "normal" activities (homeschooling, study groups, camping trips, parties), they reduced the distance between themselves and the outside world. They built a protective social environment so they could maintain and celebrate a radical ideology and identity, but it was camouflaged to appear mainstream.

Range of Theorizing

Theoretical statements also vary by range. At one extreme is the **empirical generalization.** It is a narrow statement that mostly relies on concrete concepts and fits into a substantive theory; it is a low-level descriptive statement about a relationship believed to operate empirically. It generalizes beyond a specific case or set of observations but not by very much. For example, people who marry when they are very young (under age 21) are more likely than those who marry when they are older (over age 31) to divorce. A researcher might wish to qualify the generalization by specifying historical, cultural, or other conditions that make it more or less likely. If empirical generalization includes an explanation it is simple and concrete, and not a full social theory. For example, people who marry when they are younger are more likely to divorce because they are less mature.

Middle-range theorizing has a broader theoretical range and uses more abstract concepts in a substantive or formal theory. It is the range most frequently used to guide research studies. A **middle-range theory** about divorce would include a number of empirical generalizations interlocked with more abstract concepts. Divorce might become part of the large idea of marital instability, and age of marriage might be linked to stage in the life cycle and the social roles a person learns. Maintaining a marital relationship may be placed in a context of other social forces (e.g., gender ideologies, societal

Empirical generalization A narrow, quasi-theoretical statement that expresses empirical patterns or describes empirical regularities using concepts that are not very abstract.

Middle-range theory Social theory between general frameworks and empirical generalization, that has limited abstraction/range and is in the form of empirically verifiable statements capable of being connected to observable phenomena.

BOX **3.7**   Kalmijn's Levels of Theory in "Shifting Boundaries"

Theoretical Framework: Structural functionalism holds that the processes of industrialization and urbanization change human society from a traditional to a modern form. In this process of modernization, social institutions and practices evolve. This evolution includes those that fill the social system's basic needs, socialize people to cultural values, and regulate social behavior. Institutions that filled needs and maintained the social system in a traditional society are superseded by modern ones.

Formal Theory: Secularization theory says that during modernization, people shift away from a reliance on traditional religious beliefs and local community ties. In traditional society, institutions that conferred ascribed social status (family, church, and community) also controlled socialization and regulated social life. In modern society, they are superseded by secular institutions (e.g., education, government, and media) that confer achievement-oriented status.

Middle-Range Substantive Theory: A theory of intermarriage patterns notes that young adults in modern society spend less time in small, local settings, where family, religion, and community all have a strong influence. Instead, young adults spend increasing amounts of time in school settings. In these settings, especially in college, they have opportunities to meet other unmarried people. In modern society, education has become a major socialization agent. It affects future earnings, moral beliefs and values, and leisure interests. Thus, young adults select marriage partners less on the basis of shared religious or local ties and more on the basis of common educational levels.

Empirical Generalization: Americans once married others with similar religious beliefs and affiliation. This practice is being replaced by marriage to others with similar levels of education.

disapproval or acceptance, laws affecting divorce, friendship or kinship groups, religious pressures). A study may elaborate and test specific parts of the middle-range theory, and accumulating empirical support for many parts of the theory over time helps the theory to advance as an explanation.

Theoretical frameworks (also called theoretical systems or paradigms) are at the widest range and the opposite extreme from empirical generalizations. It is more than a formal or substantive theory, and includes many specific formal and substantive theories that may share basic assumptions and general concepts in common. Sociology has several major frameworks.[7] They are orientations or sweeping ways to see and think about the social world. They provide assumptions, concepts, and forms of explanation. For example, each framework

may have its own theory of the family, theory of crime, theory of social change. Some frameworks (e.g., symbolic interactionism) are more oriented toward the micro level of analysis whereas others (e.g., conflict) are stronger at the macro level. Specific studies rarely test or contrast entire frameworks. More often a study will seek evidence for one part of a theory within one framework (e.g., one proposition from a conflict theory of crime). Box 3.7 illustrates the ranges of theory with Kalmijn's study of changing marriage partner selection.

As you will see in Chapter 4, each framework is associated with an overall approach to doing research. Box 3.8 briefly describes the key concepts of assumption of the four major theoretical frameworks of sociology.

Combining the Aspects of Theory

Now that you have learned the aspects of social theory, we can put them together (see Table 3.4). Let us look at an example study in which the re-

Theoretical framework   A very general theoretical system with assumptions, concepts, and specific social theories.

BOX **3.8** Major Theoretical Frameworks in Sociology

STRUCTURAL FUNCTIONALISM

Major Concepts: system, equilibrium, dysfunction, division of labor

Key Assumptions: Society is a system of interdependent parts that is in equilibrium or balance. Over time, society has evolved from a simple to a complex type, which has highly specialized parts. The parts of society fulfill different needs or functions of the social system. A basic consensus on values or a value system holds society together.

EXCHANGE THEORY (ALSO RATIONAL CHOICE)

Major Concepts: opportunities, rewards, approval, balance, credit

Key Assumptions: Human interactions are similar to economic transactions. People give and receive resources (symbolic, social approval, or material) and try to maximize their rewards while avoiding pain, expense, and embarrassment. Exchange relations tend to be balanced. If they are unbalanced, persons with credit can dominate others.

SYMBOLIC INTERACTIONISM

Major Concepts: self, reference group, role-playing, perception

Key Assumptions: People transmit and receive symbolic communication when they socially interact. People create perceptions of each other and social settings. People largely act on their perceptions. How people think about themselves and others is based on their interactions.

CONFLICT THEORY

Major Concepts: power, exploitation, struggle, inequality, alienation

Key Assumptions: Society is made up of groups that have opposing interests. Coercion and attempts to gain power are ever-present aspects of human relations. Those in power attempt to hold onto their power by spreading myths or by using violence if necessary.

searchers deductively theorized a middle-range, substantive causal theory at the meso level of analysis. You should recognize the theory's direction (deductive), the level of analysis (meso), the form of explanation (causal), and the range (middle). Because it has a substantive focus, the theory is about

a specific topic. In this example, it is about the outcomes of social movements. In the example study, researchers (McVeigh et al., 2003) defined the local reports of hate crime (a 1990 federal law that collected data on crimes motivated by prejudice based on race, religion, sexual orientation, or ethnicity)

TABLE 3.4 The Parts and Aspects of Social Theory

FOUR PARTS OF SOCIAL THEORY	FIVE ASPECTS OF SOCIAL THEORY
1. Assumptions	1. Direction of theorizing—deductive (abstract to concrete) or inductive (concrete to abstract)
2. Concepts—vary by level of abstraction (concrete versus abstract), single versus concept clusters, simple versus complex (e.g., classifications, typologies), and scope (narrow versus broad)	2. Level of analysis—micro level, meso level, macro level
	3. Focus of theory—substantive theory or formal theory
3. Relationships—forms of relationships, propositions, and hypotheses	4. Forms of explanation—causal, structural (sequential, network, functional), or interpretative
4. Units of analysis	5. Range of theorizing—empirical generalization, middle-range theory, or theoretical framework

as a movement outcome. They deduced from two movement theories (political mediation theory and discursive rivalry) to elaborate and test a middle-range theory that would explain variation in hate crime reporting across counties of the United States. From political mediation theory, they deduced that more reporting would occur in counties with active, strong civil rights organizations and where local political contexts gave the organizations influence in electing local officials. From discursive rivalry theory, they deduced that more reporting would occur in counties where movement organizations had been able to define the meaning of hate crimes as important crimes that had to be treated seriously. Thus, they answered the question, Why are hate crime reported more in certain counties?, with three causal factors that worked together—the presence of strong civil rights organizations, vulnerable elected officials, and hate crimes defined as serious ones. In other counties that lacked these factors, their theory predicted that the law would be nearly ignored and few hate crimes that occurred would go unreported.

THE DYNAMIC DUO

You have seen that theory and research are interrelated. Only the naive, new researcher mistakenly believes that theory is irrelevant to research or that a researcher just collects the data. Researchers who attempt to proceed without theory may waste time collecting useless data. They easily fall into the trap of hazy and vague thinking, faulty logic, and imprecise concepts. They find it difficult to converge onto a crisp research issue or to generate a lucid account of their study's purpose. They find themselves adrift as they attempt to design or conduct empirical research.

The reason is simple. Theory frames how we look at and think about a topic. It gives us concepts, provides basic assumptions, directs us to the important questions, and suggests ways for us to make sense of data. Theory enables us to connect a single study to the immense base of knowledge to which other researchers contribute. To use an analogy, theory helps a researcher see the forest instead of just

a single tree. Theory increases a researcher's awareness of interconnections and of the broader significance of data.

Theory has a place in virtually all research, but its prominence varies. It is generally less central in applied-descriptive research than in basic-explanatory research. Its role in applied and descriptive research may be indirect. The concepts are often more concrete, and the goal is not to create general knowledge. Nevertheless, researchers use theory in descriptive research to refine concepts, evaluate assumptions of a theory, and indirectly test hypotheses.

Theory does not remain fixed over time; it is provisional and open to revision. Theories grow into more accurate and comprehensive explanations about the makeup and operation of the social world in two ways. They advance as theorists toil to think clearly and logically, but this effort has limits. The way a theory makes significant progress is by interacting with research findings.

The scientific community expands and alters theories based on empirical results. Researchers who adopt a more deductive approach use theory to guide the design of a study and the interpretation of results. They refute, extend, or modify the theory on the basis of results. As researchers continue to conduct empirical research testing a theory, they develop confidence that some parts of it are true. Researchers may modify some propositions of a theory or reject them if several well-conducted studies have negative findings. A theory's core propositions and central tenets are more difficult to test and are refuted less often. In a slow process, researchers may decide to abandon or change a theory as the evidence against it mounts over time and cannot be logically reconciled.

Researchers adopting an inductive approach follow a slightly different process. Inductive theorizing begins with a few assumptions and broad orienting concepts. Theory develops from the ground up as the researchers gather and analyze the data. Theory emerges slowly, concept by concept and proposition by proposition in a specific area. The process is similar to a long pregnancy. Over time, the concepts and empirical generalizations emerge and mature. Soon, relationships become visible, and researchers weave together knowledge from different studies into more abstract theory.

CONCLUSION

In this chapter, you learned about social theory—its parts, purposes, and types. The dichotomy between theory and research is an artificial one. The value of theory and its necessity for conducting good research should be clear. Researchers who proceed without theory rarely conduct top-quality research and frequently find themselves in a quandary. Likewise, theorists who proceed without linking theory to research or anchoring it to empirical reality are in jeopardy of floating off into incomprehensible speculation and conjecture. You are now familiar with the scientific community, the dimensions of research, and social theory. In the next chapter, you will examine the competing approaches researchers adopt when they do social science.

KEY TERMS

association
assumption
causal explanation
concept classification
concept cluster
deductive direction
empirical generalization
formal theory
functional theory
grounded theory
hypothesis

ideal type
ideology
inductive direction
interpretative explanation
level of abstraction
macro-level theory
meso-level theory
micro-level theory
middle-range theory
negative relationship
network theory

parsimony
positive relationship
proposition
sequential theory
structural explanation
substantive theory
theoretical concept
theoretical explanation
theoretical framework
typology
units of analysis

REVIEW QUESTIONS

1. How do concrete and abstract concepts differ? Give examples.
2. How do researchers use ideal types and classifications to elaborate concepts?
3. How do concepts contain built-in assumptions? Give examples.
4. What is the difference between inductive and deductive approaches to theorizing?
5. Describe how the micro, meso, and macro levels of social reality differ.
6. Discuss the differences between prediction and theoretical explanation.
7. What are the three conditions for causality? Which one is never completely demonstrated? Why?
8. Why do researchers use diagrams to show causal relationships?
9. How do structural and interpretive explanations differ from one another?
10. What is the role of the major theoretical frameworks in research?

NOTES

1. For more detailed discussions of concepts, see Chafetz (1978:45–61), Hage (1972:9–85), Kaplan (1964:34–80), Mullins (1971:7–18), Reynolds (1971), and Stinchcombe (1973).

2. Turner (1980) has provided an interesting discussion of how sociological explanation and theorizing can be conceptualized as translation.

3. Classifications are discussed in Chafetz (1978: 63–73) and Hage (1972).

4. For more on typologies and taxonomies, see Blalock (1969:30–35), Chafetz (1978:63–73), Reynolds (1971: 4–5), and Stinchcombe (1968:41–47).

5. Network theory is discussed in Collins (1988: 412–428) and Galaskiewicz and Wasserman (1993).

6. An introduction to functional explanation can be found in Chafetz (1978:22–25).

7. Introductions to alternative theoretical frameworks and social theories are provided in Craib (1984), Phillips (1985:44–59), and Skidmore (1979). An elementary introduction is given in Chapter 1 of Bart and Frankel (1986).

The Meanings of Methodology

> *The confusion in the social sciences—it should now be obvious—is wrapped up with the long-continuing controversy about the nature of Science.*
> —C. Wright Mills, *The Sociological Imagination,* p. 119

Many people, including professionals outside the social sciences, ask, Are the social sciences *real* science? They think only of the natural sciences (e.g., physics, chemistry, and biology). In this chapter, we examine the meaning of *science* in the social sciences. We build on the ideas about the scientific community and the varieties of social research and theory discussed in the previous three chapters. This chapter is concerned more with the method of inquiry—how we know—than with specific techniques for gathering and examining data. It looks at the question: What are researchers trying to do when they conduct research?

The question, Where is science in social science? is relevant to anyone wishing to learn social research methods, because research methodology is what makes social science scientific. The question is an important one, with a long history of debate. It has been asked repeatedly since the social sciences originated. Classical social theorists such as Auguste Comte, Émile Durkheim, Karl Marx, John Stuart Mill, and Max Weber pondered this question. Despite two centuries of debate, the ques-

tion remains with us today. Obviously, it does not have a simple answer.

A question for which there are multiple answers does not mean that anything goes; it means that social researchers choose from *alternative approaches* to science. Each approach has its own set of philosophical assumptions and principles and its own stance on how to do research. The approaches are rarely declared explicitly in research reports, and many researchers have only a vague awareness of them. Yet, the approaches play an important role and are found across the social sciences and their related applied fields.[1]

Collins (1989:134) argued that the debate comes from an overly rigid definition of *science*. He remarked, "Modern philosophy of science does not destroy sociological science; it does not say that science is impossible, but gives us a more flexible picture of what science is." The approaches in this chapter link abstract issues in philosophy to concrete research techniques. They proscribe what good social research involves, justify why one should do research, relate values to research, and guide ethical behavior. They are broad frameworks within which researchers conduct studies. Couch (1987:106) summarized it as follows:

> *The ontological and epistemological positions of these . . . research traditions provide the foundation of one of the more bitter quarrels in contemporary sociology. . . . Each side claims that the frame of thought they promote provides a means for acquiring knowledge about social phenomena, and each regards the efforts of the other as at best misguided. . . . They differ on what phenomena should be attended to, how one is to approach phenomena, and how the phenomena are to be analyzed.*

By the end of this chapter, you should have three answers to the question, What is scientific about social scientific research? One answer will be for each of the three approaches to be discussed. You may find the pluralism of approaches confusing at first, but once you learn them, you will find that other aspects of research and theory become clearer. Specific research techniques are based on the general approaches discussed in this chapter. The techniques (e.g., experiments and participant observation) will make more sense to you if you are aware of the logic and assumptions on which they are based. In addition, the approaches presented here will help you understand the diverse perspectives you may encounter as you read social research studies. Equally important, the three approaches give you an opportunity to make an informed choice among alternatives for the type of research you may want to pursue. You might feel more comfortable with one approach or another.

THE THREE APPROACHES

We need to begin with the meaning of science. It was not written in stone or handed down as a sacred text; it has been an evolving human creation. Until the early 1800s, only philosophers and religious scholars who engaged in armchair speculation studied or wrote about human behavior. The classical theorists made a major contribution to modern civilization when they argued that the social world could be studied using science. They contended that rigorous, systematic observation of the social world, combined with careful, logical thinking, could pro-

vide a new and valuable type of knowledge about human relations. In modern times, science has become the accepted way to gain knowledge.

Once the idea of a science of the social world gained acceptance, the issue became: What does such a science look like, and how is it conducted? Some people went to the already accepted natural sciences (e.g., physics, biology, and chemistry) and copied their methods. Their argument was simple: The legitimacy of the natural sciences rests on the scientific method, so social scientists should adopt the same approach.

Many researchers accepted this answer, but it poses certain difficulties. First, there is a debate over what *science* means, even in the natural sciences. The scientific method is a loose set of abstract, vague principles that provide little guidance. Scholars who specialize in the history and philosophy of science have found that scientists use several methods. Second, some scholars say that human beings are qualitatively different from the objects of study in the natural sciences (stars, rocks, plants, chemical compounds, etc.). Humans think and learn, have an awareness of themselves and their past, and possess motives and reasons. These unique human characteristics mean that a special science is needed to study the social life of people.

Social researchers did not stop while the philosophers debated. Practicing researchers developed ways to do research based on their informal notions of science. This added to the confusion. Leading researchers used techniques to conduct social research that sometimes deviated from the philosopher's ideal model of good science.

The three approaches in this chapter are based on a major reevaluation of social science that began in the 1960s[2] and are the core ideas distilled from many specific arguments. They are ideal types or idealized, simplified models of more complex arguments. In practice, few social researchers agree with all parts of an approach. Often, they mix elements from each. Yet, these approaches represent fundamental differences in outlook and alternative assumptions about social science research.[3] The approaches are different ways of looking at the world—ways to observe, measure, and understand social reality.

1. What is the ultimate purpose of conducting social scientific research?

2. What is the fundamental nature of social reality?

3. What is the basic nature of human beings?

4. What is the view on human agency (free will, volition, and rationality)?

5. What is the relationship between science and common sense?

6. What constitutes an explanation or theory of social reality?

7. How does one determine whether an explanation is true or false?

8. What does good evidence or factual information look like?

9. What is the relevance or use of social scientific knowledge?

10. Where do sociopolitical values enter into science?

To simplify the discussion, I have organized the assumptions and ideas of the approaches into answers to ten questions (see Chart 4.1).

The three approaches are *positivist social science, interpretive social science,* and *critical social science.* Most ongoing social research is based on the first two. Positivism is the oldest and the most widely used approach. The interpretive approach has held a strong minority position in debates for over a century. Critical social science is less commonly seen in scholarly journals. It is included to show the full range of debate and because it criticizes the other approaches and tries to move beyond them.

Each approach is associated with different traditions in social theory and diverse research techniques. The linkage among the broad approaches to science, social theories, and research techniques is not strict. The approaches are similar to a research program, research tradition, or scientific paradigm. A **paradigm**, an idea made famous by Thomas Kuhn (1970), means a basic orientation to theory and research. There are many definitions of *paradigm.* In general, a scientific paradigm is a whole

system of thinking. It includes basic assumptions, the important questions to be answered or puzzles to be solved, the research techniques to be used, and examples of what good scientific research looks like. Sociology is called a multiparadigm science because no single paradigm is all-powerful; instead, several compete with each other.[4]

POSITIVIST SOCIAL SCIENCE

Positivist social science (PSS) is used widely, and *positivism,* broadly defined, is the approach of the natural sciences. In fact, most people assume that the positivist approach *is* science. There are many versions of positivism, and it has a long history within the philosophy of science and among researchers.[5] Yet, for many researchers, it has come to be a pejorative label to be avoided. Turner (1992:1511) observed, "*Positivism* no longer has a clear referent, but it is evident that, for many, being a positivist is not a good thing." Varieties of PSS go by names such as logical empiricism, the accepted or conventional view, postpositivism, naturalism, the covering law model, and behaviorism.

Positivism arose from a nineteenth-century school of thought by the Frenchman who founded sociology—Auguste Comte (1798–1857). Comte's major work in six volumes, *Cours de Philosophie Positivistic (The Course of Positive Philosophy)* (1830–1842), outlined many principles of positivism still used today. British philosopher John Stuart Mill (1806–1873) elaborated and modified the principles in his *A System of Logic* (1843). Classical French sociologist Émile Durkheim (1858–1917) outlined a version of positivism in his *Rules of the Sociological Method* (1895), which became a key textbook for positivist social researchers.

Paradigm   A general organizing framework for theory and research that includes basic assumptions, key issues, models of quality research, and methods for seeking answers.

Positivist social science   One of three major approaches to social research that emphasizes discovering causal laws, careful empirical observations, and value-free research.

Positivism is associated with many specific social theories. Best known is its linkage to the structural-functional, rational choice, and exchange-theory frameworks. PSS researchers prefer precise quantitative data and often use experiments, surveys, and statistics. They seek rigorous, exact measures and "objective" research, and they test hypotheses by carefully analyzing numbers from the measures. Many applied researchers (administrators, criminologists, market researchers, policy analysts, program evaluators, and planners) embrace positivism. Critics charge that PSS reduces people to numbers and that its concerns with abstract formulas are not relevant to the actual lives of real people.

PSS dominated the articles of major sociology journals in Britain, Canada, Scandinavia, and the United States during the 1960s and 1970s. By the 1980 and 1990s, it had declined sharply in European journals but the approach remained in position of dominance in North American journals.[6]

According to positivism, "there is only *one* logic of science, to which any intellectual activity aspiring to the title of 'science' must conform" (Keat and Urry, 1975:25, emphasis in original). Thus, the social sciences and the natural sciences use the same method. In this view, differences between the social and natural sciences are due to the immaturity or youth of the social sciences and their subject matter. Eventually, all science, including the social sciences, will eventually become like the most advanced science, physics. Differences among the sciences may exist as to their subject matter (e.g., geology requires techniques different from astrophysics or microbiology because of the objects being studied), but all sciences share a common set of principles and logic.

Positivist social science is an *organized method for combining deductive logic with precise empirical observations of individual behavior in order to* discover and confirm a set of probabilistic causal laws that can be used to predict general patterns of human activity.

The Questions

1. *What is the ultimate purpose of social scientific research?*

The ultimate purpose of research is scientific explanation—to discover and document universal **causal laws** of human behavior. Turner (1985:39), a defender of the positivist approach, stated that the "social universe is amenable to the development of abstract laws that can be tested through the careful collection of data" and that researchers need to "develop abstract principles and models about invariant and timeless properties of the social universe."

Positivists say that scientists are engaged in a never-ending quest for knowledge. As more is learned, new complexities are discovered and there is still more to learn. Early versions of PSS maintained that humans can never know everything because only God possesses such knowledge; however, as creatures placed on this planet with great capacity for knowledge, humans have a duty to discover as much as they can.

2. *What is the fundamental nature of social reality?*

Modern positivists adopt an **essentialist orientation** to reality: Reality is real; it exists "out there" and is waiting to be discovered. Human perception and intellect may be flawed, and reality may be difficult to pin down, but it does exist. Moreover, social reality is not random; it is patterned and has order. Without this assumption (i.e., if the world were chaotic and without regularity), logic and prediction would be impossible. Science lets humans discover this order and the laws of nature. "The basic, observational laws of science are considered to be true, primary and certain, because they are built into the fabric of the natural world. Discovering a law is like discovering America, in the sense that both are already waiting to be revealed" (Mulkay, 1979:21).

Essentialist (also called *objectivist*) assumptions are built into commonsense thinking prevalent in Anglo-European societies. An essentialist position states that what people see and touch (i.e., em-

---

Causal laws General cause–effect rules that are used in causal explanations of social theory and whose discovery is a primary objective of positivist social science.

Essentialist orientation An orientation toward social reality that assumes people experience empirical conditions directly and the experiences reflect the essence of reality.

pirical reality) is not overly complex. It reflects the deeper essence of things, people, and relations in the world. It is a "what you see is what you get" or "show me" type of stance. Things are the way they are by nature, or created out of a natural order of the world. Thus, race, gender, and measurements of space and time just "are." This has many implications. For example, men commit more crime than women because of something to do with their "maleness." An essentialist assumption about time is that it is linear or flows in a straight line. This means that what happened in the past will not be directly repeated, because time moves in only one direction—forward to the future.

Two other PSS assumptions are that basic patterns of social reality are stable and knowledge of them is additive. The regularity in social reality does not change over time, and laws discovered today will hold in the future. We can study many parts of reality one at a time, then add the fragments together to get a picture of the whole. Some early versions of this assumption said that the order in nature was created by and is evidence of the existence of God or a supreme being.

3. *What is the basic nature of human beings?*

Humans are assumed to be self-interested, pleasure-seeking, rational mammals. A cause will have the same effect on everyone. We can learn about people by observing their behavior, what we see in external reality. This is more important than what happens in internal, subjective reality. Sometimes, this is called a **mechanical model of man** or a behaviorist approach. It means people respond to external forces that are as real as physical forces on objects. Durkheim (1938:27) stated, "Social phenomena are things and ought to be studied as things." This emphasis on observable, external reality suggests that researchers may not have to examine unseen, internal motivations.

4. *What is the view on human agency (free will, volition, and rationality)?*

PSS emphasizes **deterministic** relationships and looks for determining causes or mechanisms that produce effects. PSS looks at how external forces, pressures, and structures that operate on individuals, groups, organizations, or societies produce out-

comes (e.g., behaviors, attitudes, and so forth). PSS downplays an individual's subjective or internal reasons and any sense of free choice or volition. Mental processes are less central than the structural forces or conditions beyond individual control that exert influence over choices and behavior. While individual people may feel that they can act freely and can make any decisions, positivists emphasize the powerful social pressures and situations that operate on people to shape most if not all of their actions. Even positivists who use rational choice explanations focus less on how individuals reason and make choices, than on identifying sets of conditions that allow them to predict what people will choose. They assume that once they know external factors, individual reasoning will largely follows a machinelike rational logic of decision making.

Few positivists believe in absolute determinism, wherein people are mere robots or puppets who must always respond exactly the same. Rather, the causal laws are probabilistic. Laws hold for large groups of people or occur in many situations. Researchers can estimate the odds of a predicted behavior. In other words, the laws enable us to make accurate predictions of how often a social behavior will occur within a large group. The causal laws cannot predict the specific behavior of a specific person in each situation. However, they can say that under conditions *X, Y,* and *Z,* there is a 95 percent probability that one-half of the people will engage in a specified behavior. For example, researchers cannot predict how John Smith will vote in the next election. However, after learning dozens of facts about John Smith and using laws of political behavior, researchers can accurately state that there is an 85 percent chance that he (and people like him) will vote for candidate C. This does not mean that

Mechanical model of man A model of human nature used in positivist social science stating that observing people's external behaviors and documenting outside forces acting on them are sufficient to provide adequate explanations of human thought and action.

Determinism An approach to human agency and causality that assumes human actions are largely caused by forces external to individuals that can be identified.

Mr. Smith cannot vote for whomever he wants. Rather, his voting behavior is patterned and shaped by outside social forces.

5. *What is the relationship between science and common sense?*

PSS sees a clear separation between science and nonscience. Of the many ways to seek truth, science is special—the "best" way. Scientific knowledge is better than and will eventually replace the inferior ways of gaining knowledge (e.g., magic, religion, astrology, personal experience, and tradition). Science borrows some ideas from common sense, but it replaces the parts of common sense that are sloppy, logically inconsistent, unsystematic, and full of bias. The scientific community—with its special norms, scientific attitudes, and techniques—can regularly produce "Truth," whereas common sense does so only rarely and inconsistently.

Many positivist researchers create a whole new vocabulary that is more logically consistent and carefully thought out and refined than terms for ideas found in everyday common sense. The positivist researcher "should formulate new concepts at the outset and not rely on lay notions. . . . There is a preference for the precision which is believed possible in a discipline-based language rather than the vague and imprecise language of everyday life" (Blaikie, 1993:206). In his *Rules of the Sociological Method,* Durkheim warned the researcher to "resolutely deny himself the use of those concepts formed outside of science" and to "free himself from those fallacious notions which hold sway over the mind of the ordinary person" (quoted in Gilbert, 1992:4).

6. *What constitutes an explanation or theory of social reality?*

PSS explanation is **nomothetic** (*nomos* means law in Greek); it is based on a system of general laws. Science explains why social life is the way it is by discovering causal laws. Explanation takes the form; *Y* is caused by *X* because *Y* and *X* are specific instances of a causal law. In other words, a PSS explanation states the general causal law that applies to or covers specific observations about social life. This is why PSS is said to use a **covering law model** of explanation.

PSS assumes that the laws operate according to strict, logical reasoning. Researchers connect causal laws and the specific facts observed about social life with deductive logic. Positivists believe that eventually laws and theories of social science will be expressed in formal symbolic systems, with axioms, corollaries, postulates, and theorems. Someday, social science theories will look similar to those in mathematics and the natural sciences.

The laws of human behavior should be universally valid, holding in all historical eras and in all cultures. As noted before, the laws are stated in a probabilistic form for aggregates of people. For example, a PSS explanation of a rise in the crime rate in Toronto in 2005 refers to factors (e.g., rising divorce rate, declining commitment to traditional moral values, etc.) that could be found anywhere at any time: in Buenos Aires in the 1890s, Chicago in the 1940s, or Singapore in the 2010s. The factors logically obey a general law (e.g., the breakdown of a traditional moral order causes an increase in the rate of criminal behavior).

7. *How does one determine whether an explanation is true or false?*

Positivism developed during the Enlightenment (post–Middle Ages) period of Western thinking.[7] It includes an important Enlightenment idea: People can recognize truth and distinguish it from falsehood by applying reason, and, in the long run, the human condition can improve through the use of reason and the pursuit of truth. As knowledge grows and ignorance declines, conditions will improve. This optimistic belief that knowledge accumulates over time plays a role in how positivists sort out true from false explanations.

PSS explanations must meet two conditions: They must (1) have no logical contradictions and (2) be consistent with observed facts. Yet, this is not

> **Nomothetic**   A type of explanation used in positivist social science in which the explanation relies heavily on causal laws and lawlike statements and interrelations.
>
> **Covering law model**   A positivist social science principle that a few higher-level, very abstract theories cover and allow deducing to many lower-level, more concrete situations.

sufficient. Replication is also needed.[8] Any researcher can replicate or reproduce the results of others. This puts a check on the whole system for creating knowledge. It ensures honesty because it repeatedly tests explanations against hard, objective facts. An open competition exists among opposing explanations, impartial rules are used, neutral facts are accurately observed, and logic is rigorously followed. Over time, scientific knowledge accumulates as different researchers conduct independent tests of a theory and add up the findings. For example, a researcher finds that rising unemployment is associated with increased child abuse in San Diego, California. A causal relationship between unemployment and child abuse is not demonstrated with just one study, however. Confirming a causal law depends on finding the same relationship in other cities with other researchers conducting independent tests using careful measures of unemployment and child abuse.

8. *What does good evidence or factual information look like?*

PSS is dualist; it assumes that the cold, observable facts are fundamentally distinct from ideas, values, or theories. Empirical facts exist apart from personal ideas or thoughts. We can observe them by using our sense organs (eyesight, smell, hearing, and touch) or special instruments that extend the senses (e.g., telescopes, microscopes, and Geiger counters). Some researchers express this idea as a language of empirical fact and a language of abstract theory. If people disagree over facts, it must be due to the improper use of measurement instruments or to sloppy or inadequate observation. "Scientific explanation involves the accurate and precise measurement of phenomena" (Derksen and Gartell, 1992:1714). Knowledge of observable reality obtained using our senses is superior to other knowledge (e.g., intuition, emotional feelings, etc.); it allows us to separate true from false ideas about social life.

Positivists assign a privileged status to empirical observation and assume that subjective understanding of the empirical world is shared. This means that factual knowledge is not based on just one person's observations and reasoning. It must be capable of being communicated and shared by others. Rational people who independently observe facts will agree on them. This is called **intersubjectivity**, or the shared subjective acknowledgment of the facts.

Many positivists also endorse the falsification doctrine outlined by the Anglo-Austrian philosopher Sir Karl Popper (1902–1991) in *The Logic of Scientific Discovery* (1934). Popper argued that claims to knowledge "can never be proven or fully justified, they can only be refused" (Phillips, 1987:3). Evidence for a causal law requires more than piling up supporting facts; it involves looking for evidence that contradicts the causal law. In a classic example, if I want to test the claim that all swans are white, and I find 1,000 white swans, I have not totally confirmed a causal law or pattern. All it takes is locating one black swan to refute my claim—one piece of negative evidence. This means that researchers search for disconfirming evidence, and even then, the best they can say is, "Thus far, I have not been able to locate any, so the claim is probably right."

9. *What is the relevance or use of social scientific knowledge?*

Positivists try to learn about how the social world works to enable people to exercise control over it and make accurate predictions about it. In short, as we discover the laws of human behavior, we can used that knowledge to alter and improve social conditions. This instrumental form of knowledge (discussed in Chapter 2) sees research results as a tool or instrument people use to satisfy their desires and control the social environment. Thus, PSS uses an **instrumental orientation**, in which the relevance of knowledge is its ability to enable people to master or control events in the world around them.

Intersubjectivity   A principle for evaluating empirical evidence in positivist social science that states different people can agree on what is in the empirical world by careful observations based on using the senses.

Instrumental orientation   A means–end orientation toward social knowledge in which knowledge is like an instrument or tool that people can use to control their environment or achieve some goal. The value of knowledge is in its use to achieve goals.

PSS has a **technocratic perspective** toward applying knowledge. The word *technocratic* combines *technology* with *bureaucracy*. PSS says after many years of professional training, researchers develop in-depth technical expertise. As an expert, the researcher tries to satisfy the information needs of large-scale bureaucratic organizations (e.g., hospitals, business corporations, government agencies). The questions such organization ask tend to be oriented to improving the efficiency of operations and effectiveness of reaching organizational goals or objectives. A technical expert role has the researcher provide answers to questions asked by others and *not* to ask different questions, redirect an inquiry into new areas, challenge the basic premises of questions, or defy the objectives set by leaders in control of the bureaucratic organizations.

10. *Where do sociopolitical values enter into science?*

PSS argues for objectives of **value-free science.** There are two meanings of the term *objective:* that observers agree on what they see and that scientific knowledge is not based on values, opinions, attitudes, or beliefs.[9] Positivists see science as a special, distinctive part of society that is free of personal, political, or religious values. It is able to operate independently of the social and cultural forces affecting other human activity because it involves applying strict rational thinking and systematic observation in a manner that transcends personal prejudices, biases, and values. Thus the norms and operation of the scientific community keep science objective. Researchers accept and internalize the norms as part of their membership in the scientific community. The scientific community

has an elaborate system of checks and balances to guard against value bias. A researcher's proper role is to be a "disinterested scientist."[10] PSS has had an immense impact on how people see ethical issues and knowledge:

> To the degree that a positivist theory of scientific knowledge has become the criterion for all knowledge, moral insights and political commitments have been delegitimized as irrational or reduced to mere subjective inclination. Ethical judgments are now thought of as personal opinion. (Brown, 1989:37)

Summary

Positivist social science is widely taught as being the same as science. Few people are aware of the origins of PSS assumptions. Scholars who developed it in western Europe during the eighteenth and nineteenth centuries had religious training and lived in a cultural-historical setting that assumed specific religious beliefs. Many PSS assumptions will reappear when you read about quantitative research techniques and measurement in later chapters. A positivist approach implies that a researcher begins with a cause–effect relationship that he or she logically derives from a possible causal law in general theory. He or she logically links the abstract ideas to precise measurements of the social world. The researcher remains detached, neutral, and objective as he or she measures aspects of social life, examines evidence, and replicates the research of others. These processes lead to an empirical test of and confirmation for the laws of social life as outlined in a theory. Chart 4.2 provides a summary of PSS.

When and why did PSS become dominant? The story is long and complicated. Many present it as a natural advance or the inevitable progress of pure knowledge. PSS expanded largely due to changes in the larger political-social context. Positivism gained dominance in the United States and became the model for social research in many nations after World War II, once the United States became the leading world power. A thrust toward objectivism—a strong version of positivism—developed in U.S. sociology during the 1920s. Objectivism grew as researchers shifted away from social reform-oriented studies with less formal or

Technocratic perspective An applied orientation in which the researcher unquestioningly accepts any research problems and limits on the scope of study requested by government, corporate, or bureaucratic officials, uncritically conducts applied research for them, and obediently supplies the officials with information needed for their decision making.

Value-free science A positivist social science principle that social research should be conducted in an objective manner based on empirical evidence alone and without inference from moral-political values.

CHART 4.2   Summary of Positivist Social Science

1. The purpose of social science is to discover laws.

2. An *essentialist* view is that reality is empirically evident.

3. Humans are rational thinking, individualistic mammals.

4. A *deterministic* stance is taken regarding human agency.

5. Scientific knowledge is different from and superior to all other knowledge.

6. Explanations are *nomothetic* and advance via deductive reasoning.

7. Explanations are verified using *replication* by other researchers.

8. Social science evidence requires *intersubjectivity*.

9. An *instrumental orientation* is taken toward knowledge that is used from a *technocratic perspective*.

10. Social science should be *value free* and objective.

precise techniques toward rigorous techniques in a "value-free" manner modeled on the natural sciences. They created careful measures of the external behavior of individuals to produce quantitative data that could be subjected to statistical analysis. Objectivism displaced locally based studies that were action oriented and largely qualitative. It grew because competition among researchers for prestige and status combined with other pressures, including funds from private foundations (e.g., Ford Foundation, Rockefeller Foundation, etc.), university administrators who wanted to avoid unconventional politics, a desire by researchers for a public image of serious professionalism, and the information needs of expanding government and corporate bureaucracies. These pressures combined to redefine social research. The less technical, applied local studies conducted by social reformers (often women) were often overshadowed by apolitical, precise quantitative research by male professors in university departments.[11] Decisions made during a large-scale expansion of federal government fund-

ing for research after World War II also pushed the social sciences in a positivist direction.

INTERPRETIVE SOCIAL SCIENCE

Interpretive social science (ISS) can be traced to German sociologist Max Weber (1864–1920) and German philosopher Wilhem Dilthey (1833–1911). In his major work, *Einleitung in die Geisteswissenshaften (Introduction to the Human Sciences)* (1883), Dilthey argued that there were two fundamentally different types of science: *Naturwissenschaft* and *Geisteswissenschaft*. The former is based on *Erklärung,* or abstract explanation. The latter is rooted in an empathetic understanding, or *Verstehen*, of the everyday lived experience of people in specific historical settings. Weber argued that social science needed to study social action with a purpose. He embraced *Verstehen* and felt that we must learn the personal reasons or motives that shape a person's internal feelings and guide decisions to act in particular ways.

> We shall speak of "social action" wherever human action is subjectively related in meaning to the behavior of others. An unintended collision of two cyclists, for example, shall not be called social action. But we will define as such their possible prior attempts to dodge one another. . . . Social action is not the only kind of action significant for sociological causal explanation, but it is the primary object of an "interpretive sociology." (Weber, 1981:159)

Interpretive social science is related to **hermeneutics,** a theory of meaning that originated in the nineteenth century. The term comes from a

Interpretative social science (ISS) One of three major approaches to social research that emphasizes meaningful social action, socially constructed meaning, and value relativism.

Verstehen A word from German that means empathetic understanding that interpretative social science takes as a primary goal for social research.

Hermeneutics A method associated with interpretative social science that originates in religious and literary studies of textual material, in which in-depth inquiry into text and relating its parts to the whole can reveal deeper meanings.

god in Greek mythology, Hermes, who had the job of communicating the desires of the gods to mortals. It "literally means making the obscure plain" (Blaikie, 1993:28). Hermeneutics is largely found in the humanities (philosophy, art history, religious studies, linguistics, and literary criticism). It emphasizes a detailed reading or examination of *text,* which could refer to a conversation, written words, or pictures. A researcher conducts "a reading" to discover meaning embedded within text. Each reader brings his or her subjective experience to a text. When studying the text, the researcher/reader tries to absorb or get inside the viewpoint it presents as a whole, and then develop a deep understanding of how its parts relate to the whole. In other words, true meaning is rarely obvious on the surface; one reaches it only through a detailed study of the text, contemplating its many messages, and seeking the connections among its parts.[12]

There are several varieties of interpretive social science (ISS): hermeneutics, constructionism, ethnomethodology, cognitive, idealist, phenomenological, subjectivist, and qualitative sociology.[12] An interpretive approach is associated with the symbolic interactionist, or the 1920s–1930s Chicago, school in sociology. It is often called a qualitative method of research.

Interpretive researchers often use participant observation and field research. These techniques require that researchers spend many hours in direct personal contact with those being studied. Other ISS researchers analyze transcripts of conversations or study videotapes of behavior in extraordinary detail, looking for subtle nonverbal communication, to understand details of interactions in their context. A positivist researcher will precisely measure selected quantitative details about thousands of people and use statistics, whereas an interpretive researcher may live a year with a dozen people to gather large quantities of detailed qualitative data to acquire an in-depth understanding of how they create meaning in everyday life.

Meaningful social action Social action in social settings to which people subjectively attach significance, and that interpretative social science treats as being the most important aspect of social reality.

Interpretive social science is concerned with how people interact and get along with each other. In general, the interpretive approach is *the systematic analysis of socially meaningful action through the direct detailed observation of people in natural settings in order to arrive at understandings and interpretations of how people create and maintain their social worlds.*

The Questions

1. *What is the ultimate purpose of conducting social scientific research?*

For interpretive researchers, the goal of social research is to develop an understanding of social life and discover how people construct meaning in natural settings. An interpretive researcher wants to learn what is meaningful or relevant to the people being studied, or how individuals experience daily life. The researcher does this by getting to know a particular social setting and seeing it from the point of view of those in it. The researcher shares the feelings and interpretations of the people he or she studies and sees things through their eyes. Summarizing the goal of his 10-year study of Willie, a repair shop owner in a rural area, interpretive researcher Harper (1987:12) said, "The goal of the research was to share Willie's perspective."

Interpretive researchers study **meaningful social action,** not just the external or observable behavior of people. Social action is the action to which people attach subjective meaning; it is activity with a purpose or intent. Nonhuman species lack culture and the reasoning to plan out things and attach purpose to their behavior; therefore, social scientists should study what is unique to human social behavior. The researcher must take into account the social actor's reasons and the social context of action. For example, a physical reflex such as eye blinking is human behavior that is rarely an intentional social action (i.e., done for a reason or with human motivation), but in some situations, it can be such a social action (i.e., a wink). More than simply having a purpose, the actions must also be social and "for action to be regarded as social and to be of interest to the social scientist, the actor must attach subjective meaning to it and it must be directed towards the activities of other people" (Blaikie, 1993:37).

Human action has little inherent meaning, but it acquires meaning among people who share a meaning system that permits them to interpret the action as a socially relevant sign or action. For example, raising one finger in a situation with other people can express social meaning; the specific meaning it expresses (e.g., a direction, an expression of friendship, a vulgar sign) depends on the cultural meaning system that the social actors share.

2. *What is the fundamental nature of social reality?*

The interpretive approach sees human social life as an accomplishment. It is intentionally created out of the purposeful actions of interacting social beings. In contrast to the positivist view that social life is "out there" waiting to be discovered, ISS states the social world is largely what people perceive it to be. Social life exists as people experience it and give it meaning. It is fluid and fragile. People construct it by interacting with others in ongoing processes of communication and negotiation. They operate on the basis of untested assumptions and taken-for-granted knowledge about people and events around them.

The interpretive approach holds that social life is based on social interactions and socially constructed meaning. People possess an internally experienced sense of reality. This subjective sense of reality is crucial to grasp human social life. In ISS, "access to other human beings is possible, however, only by indirect means: what we experience initially are gestures, sound, and actions and only in the process of understanding do we take the step from external signs to the underlying inner life" (Bleicher, 1980:9).

In contrast to an essentialist orientation view, those with a **constructionist orientation** assume that the interactions and beliefs of people create reality. There is no inner essence that causes the reality people see; it is a product of social processes. For example, when you see a chair, there is no "chairness" in it; rather, what you see as a chair arises from what a people of particular society define, accept, and understand to be a chair. What you

see as solid empirical reality is actually a fluid process of appearances that you have come to define as real. In general, what people see and experience is socially constructed. Do not think that because what people see and experience is social constructed makes it illusionary, immaterial, or unimportant. Once people accept social creations as being facts, or as real, very real consequences follow. For example, if socially constructed reality tells me that the person moving into an apartment next to mine is someone who has committed violent crimes and carries a gun, I will behave accordingly, whether or not my constructed belief fits actual physical reality.

For the constructionists, people live in, believe, and accept the constructed reality that is linked to but distinct from physical reality. Essentialists say people live in the actual physical reality.

A constructionist notes that people take most things around them "for granted" and act as if they were as natural, objective, and part of fixed reality. For example, people accept that a week has 7 days. Very few people realize that a week could be very different. Cultures have had 3-day, 5-day, and even 10-day weeks. The 7-day week that we now accept is a social construction. It was created in particular places and under specific historical circumstances.

A constructionist and essentialist differ on the relation between language and reality. An essentialist believes language can connect to reality and tries to make language pure, logical, and precise so that it accurately reflects the essential physical reality. A constructionist sees language as filled with built-in social constructions, so that as people learn language, they learn to think and see the world in certain ways. Language cannot connect to essential reality but contains a worldview that colors how people see and experience the world.

Constructionist and essentialist assumptions affect social concepts, such as gender and race. For example, Anglo-European society divides gender into two categories and race into six categories,

Constructionist orientation An orientation toward social reality that assumes the beliefs and meaning people create and use fundamentally shape what reality is for them.

primarily based on shades of skin color. An essentialist says the genders and races are real (i.e., males and females or races are essential distinctions in reality). A constructionist says language and habitual ways of thinking dictate that people see a world with two genders and six races. People in some cultures see more than two genders or a different number of races or they base racial groupings on something other than skin color. Constructionists say the essentialist view tends to blind people to the processes of social construction and that people treat constructions as if they were real "things." Essentialists say constructionists take the simple facts of reality and turn them into vague processes. Essentialists argue that hard, cold facts are needed to study the world objectively.[13]

PSS assumes that everyone experiences the world in the same way. The interpretive approach questions whether people experience social or physical reality in the same way. Key questions for an interpretive researcher are: How do people experience the world? Do they create and share meaning? Interpretive social science points to numerous examples in which several people have seen, heard, or even touched the same physical object, yet come away with different meanings or interpretations of it. The interpretive researcher argues that positivists impose one way of experiencing the world on others. By contrast, ISS assumes that multiple interpretations of human experience, or realities, are possible. In sum, the ISS approach sees social reality as consisting of people who construct meaning and create interpretations through their daily social interaction.

3. *What is the basic nature of human beings?*

Ordinary people are engaged in an ongoing process of creating systems of meaning through social interaction. They then use such meanings to interpret their social world and make sense of their lives. Human behavior may be patterned and regular, but this is not due to preexisting laws waiting to be discovered. The patterns result from evolving meaning systems or social conventions that people

Voluntarism An approach to human agency and causality that assumes human actions are based on the subjective choices and reasons of individuals.

generate as they socially interact. Important questions for the interpretive researcher are: What do people believe to be true? What do they hold to be relevant? How do they define what they are doing?

Interpretive researchers want to discover what actions mean to the people who engage in them. It makes little sense to try to deduce social life from abstract, logical theories that may not relate to the feelings and experiences of ordinary people. People have their own reasons for their actions, and researchers need to learn the reasons people use. Individual motives are crucial to consider even if they are irrational, carry deep emotions, and contain false facts and prejudices.

Some interpretive researchers say that the laws sought by positivists may be found only after the scientific community understands how people create and use meaning systems, how common sense develops, and how people apply their common sense to situations. Others say there are no such laws of human social life, so the search is futile. For example, an interpretive researcher sees the desire to discover laws of human behavior in which unemployment causes child abuse as premature at best and dangerous at worst. Instead, he or she wants to understand how people subjectively experience unemployment and what the loss of a job means in their everyday lives. Likewise, the interpretive researcher wants to learn how child abusers account for their actions, what reasons they give for abuse, and how they feel about abusing a child. He or she explores the meaning of being unemployed and the reasons for abusing a child in order to understand what is happening to the people who are directly involved.

4. *What is the view on human agency (free will, volition, and rationality)?*

Whereas PSS emphasizes deterministic relations and external forces, ISS emphasizes voluntary individual free choice, sometimes called human agency. ISS adopts **voluntarism** and sees people as having volition and being able to make conscious choices. Social settings and subjective points of views help to shape the choices a person makes, but people create and change those settings and have the ability to develop or form a point of view. ISS researchers emphasize the importance of taking into account individual decision-making processes, subjective feelings, and ways to understanding events. To ISS this inner world and a person's way of seeing and thinking are equally if not more significant for a person's actions than the external, objective conditions and structural forces that are emphasized by positivists.

5. *What is the relationship between science and common sense?*

Positivists see common sense as inferior to science. By contrast, interpretive researchers argue that ordinary people use common sense to guide them in daily living; people use common sense all the time. It is a stockpile of everyday theories people use to organize and explain events in the world. It is critical for researchers to understand common sense because it contains the meanings that people use when they engage in routine social interactions.

An interpretive approach says that common sense and the positivist's laws are alternative ways to interpret the world; that is, they are distinct meaning systems. Neither common sense nor scientific law has all the answers. Instead, interpretive researchers see each as important in its own domain; each is created in a different way for a different purpose.

Ordinary people could not function in daily life if they based their actions on science alone. For example, in order to boil an egg, people use unsystematic experiences, habits, and guesswork. A strict application of natural science would require one to know the laws of physics that determine heating the water and the chemical laws that govern the changes in the egg's internal composition. Even natural scientists use common sense when they are not "doing science" in their area of expertise.

ISS states that common sense is a vital source of information for understanding people. A person's common sense and sense of reality emerge from a pragmatic orientation and set of assumptions about the world. People do not know that common sense is true, but they must assume that it is true in order to get anything accomplished. The interpretive philosopher, Alfred Schutz (1899–1959), called this the natural attitude. It is the assumption that the

world existed before you arrived and it will continue to exist after you depart. People develop ways to maintain or reproduce a sense of reality based on systems of meaning that they create in the course of social interactions with others.

6. *What constitutes an explanation or theory of social reality?*

PSS theory tries to mimic natural science theory with deductive axioms, theorems, and interconnected causal laws. Instead of a maze of interconnected laws and propositions, theory for ISS tells a story. Interpretive social science theory describes and interprets how people conduct their daily lives. It contains concepts and limited generalizations, but it does not dramatically depart from the experience and inner reality of the people being studied.

The interpretive approach is idiographic and inductive. **Idiographic** means the approach provides a symbolic representation or "thick" description of something else. An interpretive research report may read like a novel or a biography. It is rich in detailed description and limited in abstraction. Like the interpretation of a literary work, it has internal coherence and is rooted in the text, which here refers to the meaningful everyday experiences of the people being studied.

ISS theory gives the reader a feel for another's social reality by revealing the meanings, values, interpretive schemes, and rules of living used by people in their daily lives. For example, it may describe major typifications people use in a setting to recognize and interpret their experiences. A typification is an informal model, scheme, or set of beliefs that people use to categorize and organize the flow of the daily events they experience.

Thus, ISS theory resembles a map. It outlines a social world and describes local customs and informal norms. For example, an interpretive report on professional gamblers tells the reader about the careers and daily concerns of such people. It

---

Idiographic   A type of explanation used in interpretative social science in which the explanation is an in-depth description or picture with specific details but limited abstraction about a social situation or setting.

describes the specific individuals studied, the locations and activities observed, and the strategies used to gamble. The reader learns how professional gamblers speak, how they view others, and what their fears or ambitions are. The researcher provides some generalizations and organizing concepts, but the bulk of the report is a detailed description of the gambling world. The theory and evidence are interwoven to create a unified whole; the concepts and generalizations are wedded to their context.

7. How does one determine whether an explanation is true or false?

PSS logically deduces from theory, collects data, and analyzes facts in ways that allow replication. For ISS, a theory is true if it makes sense to those being studied and if it allows others to enter the reality of those being studied. The theory or description is accurate if the researcher conveys a deep understanding of the way others reason, feel, and see things. Prediction may be possible, but it is a type of prediction that occurs when two people are very close, as when they have been married for a long time. An interpretive explanation documents the actor's point of view and translates it into a form that is intelligible to readers. Smart (1976:100) calls this the **postulate of adequacy**:

> The postulate of adequacy asserts that if a scientific account of human action were to be presented to an individual actor as a script it must be understandable to that actor, translatable into action by the actor and furthermore comprehensible to his fellow actors in terms of a common sense interpretation of everyday life.

Like a traveler telling about a foreign land, the researcher is not a native. Such an outside view never equals the insider account given by those being studied, but the closer it is to the native's account, the better. For example, one way to test the truthfulness of an ISS study of professional gambling is to have professional gamblers read it and verify its accuracy. A good report tells a reader

Postulate of adequacy An interpretative social science principle that explanations should be understandable in commonsense terms by the people being studied.

enough about the world of professional gambling so that if the reader absorbed it and then met a professional gambler, the understanding of gambling jargon, outlook, and lifestyle might lead the gambler to ask whether the reader was also a professional gambler.

8. What does good evidence or factual information look like?

Good evidence in positivism is observable, precise, and independent of theory and values. By contrast, ISS sees the features of specific contexts and meanings as essential to understand social meaning. Evidence about social action cannot be isolated from the context in which it occurs or the meanings assigned to it by the social actors involved. As Weber (1978:5) said, "Empathic or appreciative accuracy is attained when, through sympathetic participation, we can adequately grasp the emotional context in which the action took place."

For ISS, facts are fluid and embedded within a meaning system; they are not impartial, objective, and neutral. Facts are contingent and context specific; they depend on combinations of specific events with particular people in a social setting. What the positivist assumes—that neutral outsiders observe behavior and see unambiguous, objective facts—an ISS researcher takes as a question to be addressed: How do people observe ambiguities in social life and assign meaning? Interpretive researchers say that social situations are filled with ambiguity. Most behaviors or statements can have several meanings and can be interpreted in multiple ways. In the flow of social life, people are constantly "making sense" by reassessing clues in the situation and assigning meanings until they "know what's going on." For example, I see a woman holding her hand out, palm forward. Even this simple act carries multiple potential meanings; I do not know its meaning without knowing the social situation. It could mean that she is warding off a potential mugger, drying her nail polish, hailing a taxi, admiring a new ring, telling oncoming traffic to stop for her, or requesting five bagels at a deli counter.[14] People are able to assign appropriate meaning to an act or statement only if they take the social context in which it occurs into account.

ISS researchers rarely ask survey questions, aggregate the answers of many people, and claim to have something meaningful to them. To them each person's interpretation of the survey question must be placed in a context (e.g., the individual's previous experiences or the survey interview situation), and the true meaning of a person's answer will vary according to the interview or questioning context. Moreover, because each person assigns a somewhat different meaning to the question and answer, combining answers produces only nonsense.

When studying a setting or data, interpretive researchers of the ethnomethodological school often use bracketing. Bracketing is a mental exercise in which the researcher identifies then sets aside taken-for-granted assumptions used in a social scene. The researcher questions and reexamines ordinary events that have an "obvious" meaning to those involved. For example, at an office work setting, one male co-worker in his late twenties says to the male researcher, "We're getting together for softball after work tonight. Do you want to join us?" What is *not said* is that the researcher should know the rules of softball, own a softball glove, and change from a business suit into other clothing before the game. Bracketing reveals what "everyone knows"—what people assume but rarely say. It makes visible key features of the social scene that make other events possible and is the underlying scaffolding of understandings on which actions are based.

9. *What is the relevance or use of social scientific knowledge?*

Interpretative social scientists want to learn about how the world works so they can acquire an in-depth understanding of other people, appreciate the wide diversity of lived human experience, and better acknowledge shared humanity. Instead of viewing knowledge as a kind of tool or instrument, ISS researchers try to capture the inner lives and subjective experience of ordinary people. This humanistic approach focuses on how people manage their practical affairs in everyday life and treats social knowledge as a pragmatic accomplishment.

In the ISS **practical orientation**, the relevance of social science knowledge comes from its ability

to reflect in an authentic and comprehensive way how ordinary people get things done in commonplace situations. ISS also emphasizes incorporating the social context of knowledge creation and creates a reflexive form of knowledge (discussed in Chapter 2).

ISS researchers tend to apply a **transcendent perspective** toward the use and application of new knowledge. To *transcend* means to go beyond ordinary material experiences and perceptions. In social research, it means do not stop at the surface or observable level, but go on to an inner and subjective level of human experience. Rather than treating people as external objects that a researcher studies, the perspectives urges researchers to examine people's complex inner lives. Also rather than study social conditions as they now appear, researchers should examine processes by which people actively construct and can transform the existing conditions. ISS researchers try to engage and participate with the people being studied as a way to gain an intimate familiarity with them. A transcendent perspective emphasizes researchers and people being studied working together to create mutual understandings and affect conditions.

10. *Where do sociopolitical values enter into science?*

The PSS researcher calls for eliminating values and operating within an apolitical environment. The ISS researcher, by contrast, argues that researchers should reflect on, reexamine, and analyze personal points of view and feelings as a part of the process of studying others. The ISS researcher needs, at least temporarily, to empathize with and share in the social and political commitments or values of those he

Practical orientation   A pragmatic orientation toward social knowledge in which people apply knowledge in their daily lives. The value of knowledge is ability to be integrated with a person's practical everyday understandings and choices.

Transcendent perspective   The researcher develops research together with the people being studied, examines people's inner lives to gain an intimate familiarity with them, and works closely with people being studied to create mutual understandings.

or she studies. This is why ISS adopts the position of **relativism** with regard to values.

ISS questions the possibility of being value free because interpretive research sees values and meaning infused everywhere in everything. What PSS calls value freedom is just another meaning system and value—the value of positivist science. The interpretive researcher adopts relativism and does not assume that any one set of values is better or worse. Values should be recognized and made explicit.

Summary

The interpretive approach existed for many years as the loyal opposition to positivism. Although some positivist social researchers accept the interpretive approach as useful in exploratory research (see Chapter 2), few positivists consider it to be fully scientific. You will read again about the interpretive outlook when you examine field research and, to a lesser degree, historical-comparative research in later chapters. The interpretive approach is the foundation of social research techniques that are sensitive to context, that get inside the ways others see the world, and that are more concerned with achieving an empathic understanding than with testing lawlike theories of human behavior. Chart 4.3 provides a summary of the interpretive approach.

CRITICAL SOCIAL SCIENCE

Versions of **critical social science (CSS)** are called dialectical materialism, class analysis, and structuralism.[15] CSS mixes nomothetic and ideographic approaches. It agrees with many of the criticisms the interpretive approach directs at PSS, but it adds some of its own and disagrees with ISS on some points. This approach is traced to Karl Marx (1818–1883)

CHART 4.3 Summary of Interpretative Social Science

1. The purpose of social science is to understand social meaning in context.

2. A *constructionist* view that reality is socially created.

3. Humans are interacting social beings who create and reinforce shared meaning.

4. A *voluntaristic* stance is taken regarding human agency.

5. Scientific knowledge is different from but no better than other forms.

6. Explanations are *idiographic* and advance via *inductive* reasoning.

7. Explanations are verified using the *postulate of adequacy* with people being studied.

8. Social scientific evidence is contingent, context specific, and often requires *bracketing*.

9. A *practical orientation* is taken toward knowledge that is used from a *transcendent perspective*.

10. Social science should be *relativistic* regarding value positions.

---

and Sigmund Freud (1856–1939), and was elaborated on by Theodor Adorno (1903–1969), Erich Fromm (1900–1980), and Herbert Marcuse (1898–1979). Often, CSS is associated with conflict theory, feminist analysis, and radical psychotherapy. It is also tied to critical theory, first developed by the Frankfurt School in Germany in the 1930s.[16] Critical social science criticized positivist science as being narrow, antidemocratic, and nonhumanist in its use of reason. This was outlined in Adorno's essays, "Sociology and Empirical Research" (1976a) and "The Logic of the Social Sciences" (1976b). The well-known living representative of the school, Jurgen Habermas (1929–), advanced critical social science in his *Knowledge and Human Interests* (1971). In the field of education, Freire's *Pedagogy of the Oppressed* (1970) also falls within the CSS approach.

Another example is the French sociologist Pierre Bourdieu (1930–2002).[17] Bourdieu rejected

---

Relativism A principle used in interpretative social science that no single point of view or value position is better than others, and all are equally valid for those who hold them.

Critical social science (CSS) One of three major approaches to social research that emphasizes combating surface-level distortions, multiple levels of reality, and value-based activism for human empowerment.

both the objective, lawlike quantitative empirical approach of positivists and the subjective, voluntarist approach of ISS. Bourdieu argued that social research must be reflexive (i.e., study and criticize itself as well as its subject matter) and it is necessarily political. He also held that a goal of research is to uncover and demystify ordinary events.

ISS criticizes PSS for failing to deal with the meanings of real people and their capacity to feel and think, ignoring social context, and being antihumanist. CSS agrees with these criticisms of PSS. It also believes that PSS defends the status quo because it assumes an unchanging social order instead of seeing current society as a particular stage in an ongoing process.

CSS researchers criticize ISS for being too subjective and relativist. CSS states the interpretive approach treats people's ideas as more important than actual conditions and focuses on localized, microlevel, short-term settings while ignoring the broader and long-term context. To CSS researchers, ISS is amoral and passive. It fails to take a strong value position or actively help people to see false illusions around them so that they can improve their lives. In general, CSS defines social science as a *critical process of inquiry that goes beyond surface illusions to uncover the real structures in the material world in order to help people change conditions and build a better world for themselves.*

The Questions

1. *What is the ultimate purpose of conducting social scientific research?*

The purpose of critical social research is not simply to study the social world but to change it. CSS researchers conduct research to critique and transform social relations by revealing the underlying sources of social relations and empowering people, especially less powerful people. More specifically, they uncover myths, reveal hidden truths, and help people to change the world for themselves. In CSS, the purpose is "to explain a social order in such a way that it becomes itself the catalyst which leads to the transformation of this social order" (Fay, 1987:27).

The CSS researcher asks embarrassing questions, exposes hypocrisy, and investigates conditions in order to encourage grassroots action. "The point of all science, indeed all learning, is to change and develop out of our understandings and reduce illusion. . . . Learning is the reducing of illusion and ignorance; it can help free us from domination by hitherto unacknowledged constraints, dogmas and falsehoods" (Sayer, 1992:252).

For example, a CSS researcher conducts a study showing that there is racial discrimination in rental housing. White landlords refuse to rent to minority tenants. A critical researcher does not just publish a report and then wait for the fair housing office of the city government to act. The researcher gives the report to newspapers and meets with grassroots organizations to discuss the results of the study. He or she works with activists to mobilize political action in the name of social justice. When grassroots people picket the landlords' offices, flood the landlords with racial minority applicants for apartments, or organize a march on city hall demanding action, the critical researcher predicts that the landlords will be forced to rent to minorities. The goal of research is to empower. Kincheloe and McLaren (1994:140) stated:

> Critical research can be best understood in the context of the empowerment of individuals. Inquiry that aspires to the name critical must be connected to an attempt to confront the injustice of a particular society or sphere within the society. Research thus becomes a transformative endeavor unembarrassed by the label "political" and unafraid to consummate a relationship with an emancipatory consciousness.

2. *What is the fundamental nature of social reality?*

CSS shares aspects of PSS's premise that there is an empirical reality independent of our perceptions, and ISS's focus that we construct what we take to be reality from our subjective experiences, cultural beliefs, and social interactions. CSS uses a **realist orientation** that states reality has three

---

Realist orientation An orientation toward social reality that assumes reality has several levels and that what is observed on surface level does not easily reveal significant structures or causal mechanisms at deeper levels.

layers: the empirical, the real, and the actual.[18] We can observe the empirical reality with our senses. Yet, the surface empirical layer is generated by structures and causal mechanisms that operate at the deeper, unobservable layers. Theories and systematic research over time help us to understand structures operating at the real level and causal mechanisms at the actual level that generate and modify structures.

Structures at the real level are not directly observable and not fixed, but can evolve or be modified. For example, gender structures at the real level shape the specific actions of people at the surface level that we can observe. With theoretical insight and careful investigation, researchers can slowly uncover these deep structures, but the task is complicated because the structures can change. Structures at deeper levels do not produce a direct and immediate surface appearance at the empirical level. They can lie inactive or dormant and then became activated and emerge on the surface. Also, various structures are not insulated from one another. Counteracting structures may suppress or complicate the surface appearances of another structure.

Causal mechanisms at the actual level can have internal contradictions and operate in a paradoxical manner creating structural conflicts. They may contain forces or processes that appear to be opposites, or to be in conflict, but are actually parts of a single larger process. A biological analogy helps illustrate this idea. We see birth and life as the opposites of death. Yet, death begins the day we are born and each day of living moves us toward death as our body ages and decays. There is a contradiction between life and death; to live we move toward its opposite, death. Living and dying appear to be opposites, but actually they are two parts of a single process. Discovering and understanding such paradoxical processes, called the **dialectic,** is a central task in CSS.

CSS says that our observations and experiences with empirical reality are not pure, neutral, and un-

mediated; rather, ideas, beliefs, and interpretations color or influence what and how we observe. Our knowledge of empirical reality can capture the way things really are, yet in an incomplete manner, because our experiences of it depend on ideas and beliefs. CSS states our experiences of empirical reality are always theory or concept dependent. Our theories and concepts, both commonsense and scientific, sensitize us to particular aspects of empirical reality, inform what we recognize as being relevant in it, and influence how we categorize and divide its features. Over time, new theoretical insights and concepts enable us to recognize more aspects in the surface, empirical reality and improve our understandings of the deeper levels of reality.

In sum, PSS emphasizes how external reality operates on people, whereas ISS emphasizes the inner subjective construction of reality. CSS states there is a deeper reality that is prestructured, not invented by us. It has existed before we experience or think about it and has real effects on people. At the same time, we construct ways of seeing and thinking that shape our experience of empirical reality. Our thinking can lead to us to take actions that will change the structures in deeper levels of reality. CSS views our ability to understand reality as an interactive process in which thoughts, experiences, and actions interact with one another over time.

CSS notes that social change and conflict are not always apparent or easily observable. The social world is full of illusion, myth, and distortion. Initial observations of the world are only partial and often misleading because the human senses are limited. The appearances in surface reality do not have to be based on conscious deception. The immediately perceived characteristics of objects, events, or social relations rarely reveal everything. These illusions allow some groups in society to hold power and exploit others. Karl Marx, German sociologist and political thinker, stated this forcefully (Marx and Engels, 1947:39):

> *The ideas of the ruling class are in every epoch the ruling ideas; . . . The class which has the means of material production at its disposal, has control at the same time over the means of mental production, so that . . . the ideas of those who lack the means of mental production are subject to it.*

Dialectic   A change process emphasized in critical social science in which social relationships contain irresolvable inner contradictions; over time they will trigger a dramatic upset and a total restructuring of the relationship.

CSS states that although subjective meaning is important, there are real, objective relations that shape social relations. The critical researcher probes social situations and places them in a larger historical context.

For example, an ISS researcher studies the interactions of a male boss and his female secretary and provides a rich account of their rules of behavior, interpretive mechanisms, and systems of meaning. By contrast, the CSS researcher begins with a point of view (e.g., feminist) and notes issues ignored in an interpretive description: Why are bosses male and secretaries female? Why do the roles of boss and secretary have unequal power? Why are such roles created in large organizations throughout society? How did the unequal power come about historically, and were secretaries always female? Why can the boss make off-color jokes that humiliate the secretary? How are the roles of boss and secretary in conflict based on the everyday conditions faced by the boss (large salary, country club membership, new car, large home, retirement plan, stock investments, etc.) and those of the secretary (low hourly pay, children to care for, concerns about how to pay bills, television as her only recreation, etc.)? Can the secretary join with others to challenge the power of her boss and similar bosses?

3. *What is the basic nature of human beings?*

PSS sees humans as mammals and focuses on their behavior as rationally acting individuals. ISS sees humans as fundamentally social beings defined by their capacity to create and sustain social meanings. CSS recognizes that people are rational decision makers who are shaped by social structures and creative beings that construct meaning and social structures. Society exists prior to and apart from people, yet it can exist only with their active involvement. People create society and society creates people, who in turn create society, in a continuous process.[19] Thus, human beings exist within an ongoing relational process.

CSS notes that humans can be misled and have unrealized potential. One important way this happens is through reification. **Reification** occurs when we become detached from and lose sight of our connection or relationship to something that we created our-

selves. By severing connections to our own creations, we no longer recognize ourselves in our creations and we treat them as being alien, external forces that have control over us. By "forgetting" and not seeing connections, we lose control over our creations. Humans are filled with tremendous potential, yet this often goes unrealized because we find it difficult to break free from beliefs, conditions, and situations largely of their own making. To fully realize their potential, people must look beyond immediate surface appearance and break through what they reified to see how they possess the capacity to change situations.

4. *What is the view on human agency (free will, volition, and rationality)?*

CSS blends determinism and voluntarism to emphasize **bounded autonomy,** or how agency and structure cooperate. Bounded autonomy suggests that free will, choices, and decision making are not unlimited or open ended; rather, they either must stay within restricted boundaries of options or are confined within limits, which can be cultural or material limits or boundaries. A CSS researcher identifies a range of options, or at least what people see as being realistic alternatives, and allows for some volition among those options. People make choices, but the choices are confined to what they feel is possible. Material factors (e.g., natural resources, physical abilities) and cultural-subjective schemes (e.g., beliefs, core values, deeply felt norms) set what people feel to be possible or impossible, and people act based on what they believe is possible.

Sewell (1992) observed that social structures are simultaneously cultural and material. Thus, what a person does in the material world is shaped by how he or she sees, thinks, and feels (i.e., culture). Material objects, conditions, and resources depend on the cultural schemas. If a person's

Reification An idea used in critical social science referring to when people become detached from and lose sight of their connection to their own creations and treat them as being alien, external forces.

Bounded autonomy An approach to human agency and causality used in critical social science that assumes human action is based on subjective choices and reasons but only within identifiable limits.

worldview defines some action as impossible, a material resource as being unavailable, or a choice as blocked, his or her "free will" choices are limited. If for reasons of culture, a person does not see an insect a source of food nor as having three wives simultaneously as morally possible, then the cultural beliefs restrict the use of material resources and taking some actions. Material and subjective-cultural factors interact. Cultural-subjective beliefs that define material resources as available restrict volition, and material conditions can shape people's cultural-subjective experiences and beliefs. Under certain conditions collective human actions can alter deep structures of the material conditions and cultural beliefs, and this can expand the range of volition.

5. *What is the relationship between science and common sense?*

The CSS position on common sense is based on the idea of **false consciousness**—that people are often mistaken and act against their own true best interests as defined in objective reality. Objective reality lies behind myth and illusion. False consciousness is meaningless for ISS because it implies that a social actor uses a meaning system that is false or out of touch with objective reality. ISS states that people create and use such systems and that researchers can only describe such systems, not judge their value. CSS states that social researchers should study subjective ideas and common sense because these shape human behavior. Yet, they contain myth and illusion that can mask an objective world in which there is unequal control over resources and power.

The structures that critical researchers talk about are not easy to see. Researchers must first

demystify them and pull back the veil of surface appearances. Careful observation is not enough. It does not tell what to observe, and observing an illusion does not dispel it. A researcher must use theory to dig beneath surface relations, to observe periods of crisis and intense conflict, to probe interconnections, to look at the past, and to consider future possibilities. Uncovering the deeper level of reality is difficult, but it is essential because surface reality is full of ideology, myth, distortion, and false appearances. "Common sense tends to naturalize social phenomena and to assume that what is, must be. A social science which builds uncritically on common sense . . . reproduces these errors" (Sayer, 1992:43).

6. *What constitutes an explanation or theory of social reality?*

Beyond deduction and induction, CSS uses abduction to create explanatory critiques. American philosopher Charles S. Peirce (1839–1914) developed **abduction** by extending the other forms of reasoning. Instead of beginning with many observations, or starting with a theoretical premise, abduction "tries on" a potential rule and asks, What might follow from this rule? Both ideas and observations are placed into alternative frames and then examined, and the "what if" question is asked. A researcher using abduction applies and evaluates the efficacy of multiple frameworks sequentially, and creatively recontexualizes or redescribes both data and ideas in the process.

Abduction rarely produces a single, definitive truth; instead it eliminates some alternatives as it advances a deeper understanding. In certain ways, it is an aspect of all human perception. Abduction is similar to how an insightful, creative detective may solve a crime—by taking the data (clues) and putting them into alternative possible scenarios (what might have caused the crime). Considering alternative scenarios gives the same observations new meanings. Thus, abduction means repeated reevaluations of ideas and data based on applying alternative rules or schemes and learning from each.

Explanatory critique begins with the premise that studying social life means studying both the thing "itself" and how people think about or under-

---

False consciousness An idea used by critical social science that people often have false or misleading ideas about empirical conditions and their true interests.

Abduction An approach to theorizing in which several alternative frameworks are applied to data and theory that are redescribed in each and evaluated.

Explanatory critique A type of explanation used in critical social science in which the explanation simultaneously explains (or tells why events occur) and critiques (or points out discrepancies, reveals myths, or identifies contradictions).

stand the "thing" being studied. Actual conditions and people's beliefs about conditions are both relevant and have effects, and the two may not match. An explanatory critique has practical, moral, and political implications in itself, because it can differ from the prevailing beliefs. The explanation simultaneously explains (or tells why events occur) and critiques (or points out discrepancies, reveals myths, or identifies contradictions).

The rendering of social conditions in an explanatory critique often will enlighten and help to emancipate people. As the explanation reveals aspects of reality beyond the surface level, people are awakened to the underlying structures of society. As it reveals deep causal mechanisms, people learn how to change those structures. In this way, the explanations are critiques that show a pathway for taking action and achieving change.

7. *How does one determine whether an explanation is true or false?*

PSS deduces hypotheses, tests hypotheses with replicated observations, and then combines results to confirm causal laws. ISS asks whether the meaning system and rules of behavior make sense to those being studied. CSS tests theory by accurately describing conditions generated by underlying structures and then by applying that knowledge to change social relations. A CSS theory teaches people about their own experiences, helps them understand their historical role, and can be used to improve conditions.

CSS theory informs practical action and is modified on the basis of its use. A CSS theory grows and interacts with the world it seeks to explain. Because CSS tries to explain and change the world by penetrating hidden structures that are in flux, the test of an explanation is not static. Testing theory is a dynamic, ongoing process of applying theory and modifying it. Knowledge grows by an ongoing process of eroding ignorance and enlarging insights through action.

CSS separates good from bad theory by putting the theory into practice and uses the outcome of these applications to reformulate theory. **Praxis** means that explanations are valued when they help people understand the world and to take action that changes it. As Sayer (1992:13) argued, "Knowledge

is primarily gained through activity both in attempting to change our environment (through labor or work) and through interaction with other people."

Critical praxis eliminates the division between the researcher and those being researched, the distinction between science and everyday life. For example, a critical researcher develops an explanation for housing discrimination. He or she tests the explanation by using it to try to change conditions. If the explanation says that underlying economic relations cause discrimination and that landlords refuse to rent to minorities because it is profitable to rent only to nonminorities, then political actions that make it profitable to rent to minorities should change the landlords' behavior. By contrast, if the explanation says that an underlying racial hatred causes landlords to discriminate, then actions based on profit will be unsuccessful. The critical researcher would then examine race hatred as the basis of landlord behavior through new studies combined with new political action.

8. *What does good evidence or factual information look like?*

PSS assumes that there are incontestable neutral facts on which all rational people agree. Its dualist doctrine says that social facts are like objects. They exist separate from values or theories. ISS sees the social world as made up of created meaning, with people creating and negotiating meanings. It rejects positivism's dualism, but it substitutes an emphasis on the subjective. Evidence is whatever resides in the subjective understandings of those involved. The critical approach bridges the object–subject gap. It says that the facts of material conditions exist independent of subjective perceptions, but that facts are not theory neutral. Instead, facts require an interpretation from within a framework of values, theory, and meaning.

For example, it is a "fact" that the United States spends a much greater percentage of its gross national product (GNP) on health care than any other

> **Praxis** A way to evaluate explanations in critical social science in which theoretical explanations are put into real-life practice and the outcome is used to refine explanation.

advanced industrial nation, and yet it ranks as the 29th lowest infant death rate (7 deaths per 1,000 live births). A CSS interprets the fact by noting that the United States has many people without health care and no system to cover everyone. The fact includes the way the health care is delivered to some through a complex system of for-profit insurance companies, pharmaceutical firms, hospitals, and others who benefit greatly from the current arrangement. Some powerful groups are getting rich while weaker or poor sectors of society are getting low quality or no health care. CSS researchers look at the facts and ask who benefits and who loses?

Theory helps a critical researcher find new facts and separate the important from the trivial ones. The theory is a type of map telling researchers where to look for facts and how to interpret them once they are uncovered. The critical approach says that theory does this in the natural sciences, as well. For example, a biologist looks into a microscope and sees red blood cells—a "fact" based on a theory about blood and cells and a biologist's education about microscopic phenomena. Without this theory and education, a biologist sees only meaningless spots. Clearly, then, facts and theories are interrelated.

All theories are not equally useful for finding and understanding key facts. Theories are based on beliefs and assumptions about what the world is like and on a set of moral-political values. CSS states that some values are better than others.[20] Thus, in order to interpret facts, one must understand history, adopt a set of values, and know where to look for underlying structures. Different versions of critical science offer different value positions (e.g., Marxism versus feminism).

Reflexive-dialectic orientation An orientation toward social knowledge used in critical social science in which subjective and objective sides are blended together to provide insights in combination unavailable from either side alone. The value of knowledge is as a process that integrates making observations, reflecting on them, and taking action.

Transformative perspective The researcher probes beyond the surface level of reality in ways that can shift subjective understandings and provide insights into how engaging in social-political action may dramatically improve the conditions of people's lives.

---

9. *What is the relevance or use of social scientific knowledge?*

As CSS researchers learn how the world works, they link subjective understandings with ways to analyze objective conditions to reveal unseen forces and unrecognized injustices. This spurs people to take action. For CSS, knowledge is not an instrument for people to manipulate, nor is it a capturing and rendering of people's inner, subjective experiences; instead, knowledge means active involvement in the world. Knowledge can free people from the shackles of past thinking and help them take control of events around them. It is not a thing to be possessed, but a process that combines greater awareness with taking action.

CSS researchers blend aspects of the instrumental and practical orientations and bridge duality of the positivist's external, empirical reality and the inner, subjective reality emphasized in ISS. CSS uses reflexive knowledge (see Chapter 2) to offer a "third way," **reflexive-dialectic orientation.** This third way is "not a conflation of, or compromise between these perspectives; it represents a standpoint in its own right" (Danermark et al., 2002:202). Instead of treating external and internal reality as being opposites, a reflexive-dialectic orientation see them as two sides of a single dynamic whole that is in a process of becoming. An external or internal orientation alone is incomplete. The two sides work together as one and are interwoven to affect each other.

CSS adopts a **transformative perspective** toward applying knowledge. To transform means to change fundamentally, to reorganize basic structures, and to breach current limits. The perspective goes beyond a surface level of reality to realign subjective understandings with the external reality, and then uses renewed consciousness as a basis for engaging in actions that have the potential to modify external conditions and future consciousness. The relevance of knowledge is its ability to connect consciousness with people engaging in concrete actions, reflecting on the consequences of those actions, then advancing consciousness to a new level in an ongoing cycle.

10. *When do sociopolitical values enter into science?*

CSS has an activist orientation. Social research is a moral-political activity that requires the researcher to commit to a value position. CSS rejects PSS value freedom as a myth. It also attacks ISS for

BOX **4.1**   **The Extended Case Method and CSS**

Michael Burawoy's (1998) extended case method is an example of critical social science. He says it applies *reflexive science* to ethnography or field research. Reflexive science is a type of CSS that states social research should be a dialogue between the researcher and the people being studied. Thus, intersubjectivity is not only among scientists, as in positivism; rather, it occurs between the researcher and people under study. Burawoy identifies four features of reflexive science:

1. The researcher interacts with subject-participants. Disruptions or disturbances that develop out of their mutual interaction help to expose and better illuminate social life.
2. The researcher adopts the subject-participant's view of the world in specific situations, but does not stop there. The researcher adds together many views from individual subjects and specific situations, aggregating them into broader social processes.
3. The researcher sees the social world simultaneously from inside outward (i.e., from the subjective view-

point of the people being studied) and from the outside inward (i.e., from the viewpoint of external forces that act on people).
4. The researcher constantly builds and rebuilds theory. This takes place in a dialogue with the people studied and in a dialogue with other researchers in the scientific community.

Burawoy used the extended case method to study mine workers in Zambia. He argued that positivist social science best fits situations in which people are "powerless to resist wider systems of economy and polity" (p. 30)—in other words, situations in which people are dominated and have little control over their lives. The CSS approach strives in contexts in which people try to resist or reduce power distinctions and domination. It highlights conditions of emancipation in which people come to question or challenge the external forces of power and control under which they live.

---

its relativism. In ISS, the reality of the genius and the reality of the idiot are equally valid and important. There is little, if any, basis for judging between alternative realities or conflicting viewpoints. For example, the interpretive researcher does not call a racist viewpoint wrong, because any viewpoint is true for those who believe in it. CSS states that there is only one, or a very few, correct point of view. Other viewpoints are plain wrong or misleading. All social research *necessarily* begins with a value or a moral point of view. For CSS, being objective is not being value free. Objectivity means a nondistorted, true picture of reality; "it challenges the belief that science must be protected from politics. It argues that some politics—the politics for emancipatory social change—can increase the objectivity of science" (Harding, 1986:162).

CSS holds that to deny that a researcher has a point of view is itself a point of view. It is a technician's point of view: Conduct research and ignore the moral questions; satisfy a sponsor and follow orders. Such a view says that science is a tool or instrument anyone can use. This view was strongly

criticized when Nazi scientists committed inhumane experiments and then claimed that they were blameless because they "just followed orders" and were "just scientists." PSS adopts such an approach and produces technocratic knowledge—a form of knowledge best suited for use by the people in power to dominate or control other people.[21]

CSS rejects PSS and ISS as being detached and concerned with studying the world instead of acting on it. CSS holds that knowledge is power. Social science knowledge can be used to control people, it can be hidden in ivory towers for intellectuals to play games with, or it can be given to people to help them take charge of and improve their lives. What a researcher studies, how he or she studies it, and what happens to the results involve values and morality, because knowledge has tangible effects on people's lives. The researcher who studies trivial behavior, who fails to probe beneath the surface, or who buries the results in a university library is making a moral choice. The choice is to take information from the people being studied without involving them or liberating them (see Box 4.1).

CHART 4.4 Summary of Critical Social Science

1. The purpose of social science is to reveal what is hidden to liberate and empower people.

2. Social reality has multiple layers.

3. People have unrealized potential and are misled by reification; social life is relational.

4. A *bounded autonomy* stance is taken toward human agency.

5. Scientific knowledge is imperfect but can fight *false consciousness*.

6. *Abduction* is used to create *explanatory critiques*.

7. Explanations are verified through *praxis*.

8. All evidence is theory dependent and some theories reveal deeper kinds of evidence.

9. A *reflexive-dialectic orientation* is adopted toward knowledge that is used from a *transformative perspective*.

10. Social reality and the study of it necessarily contain a moral-political dimension, and moral-political positions are unequal in advancing human freedom and empowerment.

CSS questions the morality of such a choice, even if it is not a conscious one.

Summary

Although few full-time researchers adopt the critical science approach, it is often adopted by community action groups, political organizations, and social movements. It only rarely appears in scholarly journals. CSS researchers may use any research technique, but they tend to favor the historical-comparative method. This is because of its emphasis on change and because it helps researchers uncover underlying structures. CSS researchers differ from the others less in the research techniques they use than in how they approach a research problem, the kinds of questions they ask, and their purposes for doing research. Chart 4.4 provides a summary of CSS.

FEMINIST AND POSTMODERN RESEARCH

Two additional approaches that are less well known than the three major ones are feminist and postmodern social research. Both criticize positivism and offer alternatives that build on interpretive and critical social science. They gained visibility only since the 1980s.

Feminist Research

Feminist research is conducted by people, most of them women, who hold a feminist self-identity and consciously use a feminist perspective. They use multiple research techniques, attempt to give a voice to women, and work to correct the predominant male-oriented perspective. Works such as *Women's Ways of Knowing* (Belenky et al., 1986) argue that women learn and express themselves differently than men.

Feminist research assumes that the subjective experience of women differs from that of men.[22] Many feminist researchers see positivism as being a male point of view; it is objective, logical, task oriented, and instrumental. It reflects a male emphasis on individual competition, on dominating and controlling the environment, and on the hard facts and forces that act on the world. In contrast, women emphasize accommodation and gradually developing human bonds. They see the social world as a web of interconnected human relations, full of people linked together by feelings of trust and mutual obligation. Women emphasize the subjective, empathetic, process-oriented, and inclusive sides of social life. Feminist research is also action oriented and seeks to advance feminist values (see Box 4.2).

Feminist researchers argue that much nonfeminist research is sexist, largely as a result of broader cultural beliefs and a preponderance of male researchers. The research overgeneralizes from the experience of men to all people, ignores gender as a fundamental social division, focuses on men's problems, uses males as points of reference, and assumes traditional gender roles. For example, a traditional researcher would say that a family has a problem of unemployment when the adult male in it cannot find stable work. When a woman in the same family cannot find stable work outside the

Characteristics of Feminist Social Research

- Advocacy of a feminist value position and perspective
- Rejection of sexism in assumptions, concepts, and research questions
- Creation of empathic connections between the researcher and those he or she studies
- Sensitivity to how relations of gender and power permeate all spheres of social life
- Incorporation of the researcher's personal feelings and experiences into the research process
- Flexibility in choosing research techniques and crossing boundaries between academic fields
- Recognition of the emotional and mutual-dependence dimensions in human experience
- Action-oriented research that seeks to facilitate personal and societal change

home, it is not considered an equal family problem. Likewise, the concept *unwed mother* is widely used by traditional researchers, but is not a parallel of *unwed father.*

The feminist approach sees researchers as fundamentally gendered beings. Researchers necessarily have a gender that shapes how they experience reality, and therefore it affects their research. In addition to gender's impact on individual researchers, basic theoretical assumptions and the scientific community appear as gendered cultural contexts. Gender has a pervasive influence in culture and shapes basic beliefs and values that cannot be isolated and insulated in the social processes of scientific inquiry.[23]

Feminist researchers are not objective or detached; they interact and collaborate with the people they study. They fuse their personal and professional lives. For example, feminist researchers will attempt to comprehend an interviewee's experiences while sharing their own feelings and experiences. This process may give birth to a personal relationship between researcher and interviewee that might mature over time. Reinharz (1992:263) argued, "This blurring of the disconnection between formal and personal relations, just

as the removal of the distinction . . . between the research project and the researcher's life, is a characteristic of much, if not all, feminist research."

The impact of a woman's perspective and her desire to gain an intimate relationship with what she studies occurs even in the biological sciences. Feminist researchers tend to avoid quantitative analysis and experiments. They use multiple methods, often qualitative research and case studies. Gorelick (1991) criticized the affinity of many feminist researchers for interpretive social science. ISS is limited to the consciousness of those being studied and fails to reveal hidden structures. Gorelick wants feminist researchers to adopt a critical approach and to advocate social change more assertively.

Feminist researchers reject the value-neutral claim of positivists. For example, Risman (2001), among others, sharply criticized a study that tried to explain gender differences almost entirely with biological factors. She argued (2001:606) that "the positivist model of science not only failed in this particular instance to recognize and exclude the expression of particular political values, but that value-free science as such is not only an impossible goal but it is an inappropriate one that distorts the research and publication." She (p. 609) noted that "value-neutrality can be a cloak that hides (perhaps even from scientists themselves) values that are so embedded in the folk wisdom of our culture so as to be invisible. Researchers who believe they are working within an apolitical, value-neutral version of science are, often without any conscious decision at all, simply ignoring the ways in which dominant presumptions frame their questions."

Postmodern Research

Postmodern research is part of the larger postmodern movement that includes art, music, literature, and cultural criticism. It began in the humanities and has roots in the philosophies of existentialism, nihilism, and anarchism and in the ideas of Heidegger, Nietzsche, Sartre, and Wittgenstein. Postmodernism is a rejection of modernism. *Modernism* refers to basic assumptions, beliefs, and values that arose in the Enlightenment era. Modernism relies on logical reasoning; it is optimistic about the future and believes in progress, it has confidence in technology and science, and it embraces humanist values (i.e., judging ideas based on their effect on human welfare). Modernism holds that there are standards of beauty, truth, and morality about which most people can agree.[24]

Postmodern researchers see no separation between the arts or humanities and social sciences. They share the critical social science goal of demystifying the social world, want to deconstruct or tear apart surface appearances and reveal the hidden structure. Like extreme forms of ISS, postmodernism distrusts abstract explanation and holds that research can never do more than describe, with all descriptions equally valid. A researcher's description is neither superior nor inferior to anyone else's and describes only the researcher's personal experiences. Going beyond interpretive and critical social science, it attempts to dismantle social science. Extreme postmodernists reject the possibility of a science of the social world, distrust all systematic empirical observation, and doubt that knowledge is generalizable or accumulates over time. They see knowledge as taking numerous forms and as unique to particular people or specific locales. Rosenau (1992:77) argued, "Almost all postmodernists reject truth as even a goal or ideal because it is the very epitome of modernity. . . . Truth makes reference to order, rules, and values; depends on logic, rationality and reason, all of which the postmodernists question."

Postmodernists object to presenting research results in a detached and neutral way. The researcher or author of a report should never be hidden when someone reads it; his or her presence needs to be unambiguously evident in the report. Thus, a postmodern research report is similar to a work of art. Its purpose is to stimulate others, to give pleasure, to evoke a response, or to arouse curiosity. Postmodern reports often have a theatrical, expressive, or dramatic style of presentation. They may be in the form of a work of fiction, a movie, or a play. The postmodernist argues that the knowledge about social life created by a researcher may be better communicated through a skit or musical piece than by a scholarly journal article. Its value lies in telling a

---

BOX 4.3 Characteristics of Postmodern Social Research

- Rejection of all ideologies and organized belief systems, including all formal social theory
- Strong reliance on intuition, imagination, personal experience, and emotion
- Sense of meaninglessness and pessimism; belief that the world will never improve
- Extreme subjectivity in which there is no distinction between the mental and the external world
- Ardent relativism in which there are infinite interpretations, none superior to another
- Espousal of diversity, chaos, and complexity that is constantly changing
- Rejection of studying the past or different places because only the here and now is relevant
- Belief that causality cannot be studied because life is too complex and rapidly changing
- Assertion that research can never truly represent what occurs in the social world

---

story that may stimulate experiences within the people who read or encounter it. Postmodernism is antielitist and rejects the use of science to predict and to make policy decisions. Postmodernists oppose those who use positivist science to reinforce power relations and bureaucratic forms of control over people (see Box 4.3).

CONCLUSION

You have learned two important things in this chapter. First, there are competing approaches to social research based on philosophical assumptions about the purpose of science and the nature of social reality. Second, the ideal-type approaches answer basic questions about research differently (see Table 4.1). Most researchers operate primarily within one approach, but many also combine elements from the others.

Remember that you can study the same topic from any of these approaches, but each approach implies going about it differently. This can be illustrated

TABLE 4.1   A Summary of Differences among the Three Approaches to Social Research

	POSITIVISM	INTERPRETIVE SOCIAL SCIENCE	CRITICAL SOCIAL SCIENCE	FEMINIST	POSTMODERN
1. Reason for research	To discover natural laws so people can predict and control events	To understand and describe meaningful social action	To smash myths and empower people to change society	To empower people to advance values of nurturing others and equality	To express the subjective self, to be playful, and to entertain and stimulate
2. Nature of social reality	Stable preexisting patterns or order that can be discovered	Fluid definitions of a situation created by human interaction	Multiple layers and governed by hidden, underlying structures	Gender-structured power relations that keep people oppressed	Chaotic and fluid without real patterns or master plan
3. Human nature	Self-interested and rational individuals who are shaped by external forces	Social beings who create meaning and who constantly make sense of their worlds	Creative, adaptive people with unrealized potential, trapped by illusion.	Gendered beings with unrealized potential often trapped by unseen forces	Creative, dynamic beings with unrealized potential
4. Human agency	Powerful external social pressures shape people's actions; free will is largely illusion	People have significant volition; they develop meanings and have freedom to make choices	Bounded autonomy and free choice structurally limited, but the limits can be moved	Structural limits based on gender confines choices, but new thinking and action can breach the limits	People have great volition, and all structures are illusionary
5. Role of common sense	Clearly distinct from and less valid than science	Powerful everyday theories used by ordinary people	False beliefs that hide power and objective conditions	False beliefs that hide power and objective conditions	The essence of social reality that is superior to scientific or bureaucratic forms of reasoning
6. Theory looks like	A logical, deductive system of interconnected definitions, axioms, and laws	A description of how a group's meaning system is generated and sustained	A critique that reveals true conditions and helps people take action	A critique that reveals true conditions and helps people see the way to a better world	A performance or work of artistic expression that can amuse, shock, or stimulate others
7. An explanation that is true	Is logically connected to laws and based on facts	Resonates or feels right to those who are being studied	Supplies people with tools needed to change the world	Supplies ideas/tools to help liberate people from oppressive relations	No one explanation is more true; all are true for those who accept them
8. Good evidence	Is based on precise observations that others can repeat	Is embedded in the context of fluid social interactions	Is informed by a theory that penetrates the surface level	Is informed by theory that reveals gender structures	Has aesthetic properties and resonates with people's inner feelings
9. Relevance of knowledge	An instrumental orientation is used; knowledge enables people to master and control events	A practical orientation is used; knowledge helps us embrace/share empathetically others' life worlds and experiences	A dialectiical orientation is used; knowledge lets people see and alter deeper structures	Knowledge raises awareness and empowers people to make change	Former knowledge has no special value; it can amuse or bring personal enjoyment.
10. Place for values	Science is value free, and values have no place except when choosing a topic	Values are an integral part of social life: no group's values are wrong, only different	All science must begin with a value position; some positions are right, some are wrong	Values are essential to research, and feminist ones are clearly preferred	Values are integral to research, but all value positions are equal

with the topic of discrimination and job competition between minority and majority groups in four countries: aborigines in the Australian outback, Chinese in western Canada, African Americans in the midwestern United States, and Pakistanis in London.

PSS researchers first deduce hypotheses from a general theory about majority–minority relations. The theory is probably in the form of causal statements or predictions. The researchers next gather data from existing government statistics or conduct a survey to precisely measure the factors that the theory identifies, such as the form of initial contact, the ratio of numbers in majority versus minority groups, or the visibility of racial differences. Finally, PSS researchers use statistics to formally test the theory's predictions about the degree of discrimination and the intensity of job competition.

An ISS researcher personally talks with and observes specific people from both the minority groups and the majority groups in each of the four countries. His or her conversations and observations are used to learn what each group feels to be its major problem and whether group members feel that discrimination or job competition are everyday concerns. The researcher puts what people say into the context of their daily affairs (e.g., paying rent, getting involved in family disputes, having run-ins with the law, getting sick, etc.). After he or she sees what the minority or majority people thinks about discrimination, how they get jobs, how people in the other group get jobs, and what they actually do to get or keep jobs, he or she describes findings in terms that others can understand.

A CSS researcher begins by looking at the larger social and historical context. This includes factors such as the invasion of Australia by British colonists and the nation's history as a prison colony, the economic conditions in China that caused people to migrate to Canada, the legacy of slavery and civil rights struggles in the United States, and the rise and fall of Britain's colonial empire and the migration of people from its ex-colonies. He or she inquires from a moral-critical standpoint: Does the majority group discriminate against and economically exploit the minority? The researcher looks at many sources to document the underlying pattern

of exploitation and to measure the amount of discrimination in each nation. He or she may examine statistical information on income differences between groups, personally examine living situations and go with people to job interviews, or conduct surveys to find out what people now think. Once the researcher finds out how discrimination keeps a minority group from getting jobs, he or she gives results to minority group organizations, gives public lectures on the findings, and publishes results in newspapers read by minority group members in order to expose the true conditions and to encourage political-social action.

What does all this about three approaches mean to you in a course on social research? First, it means that there is no single, correct approach to social science research. This does not mean that anything goes, nor that there is no ground for agreement (see Box 4.4). Rather, it means that the basis for doing social research is not settled. In other words, more than one approach is currently "in the running." Perhaps this will always be the case. An awareness of the approaches will help you to read research reports. Often, researchers will rely on one approach, but rarely will they tell you which one they are using.

Second, it means that what you try to accomplish when you do research (i.e., discover laws, identify underlying structures, describe meaning systems) will vary with the approach you choose. The fit between the three approaches and types of research discussed in Chapter 2 is loose. For example, PSS is likely to conduct cost-benefit analysis, ISS researchers tend to do exploratory research, and CSS researchers favor action-oriented research. By being aware of the approaches when you do social research, you can make an informed decision about the type of study to conduct.

Third, the various techniques used in social research (sampling, interviewing, participant observation, etc.) are ultimately based on assumptions and ideas from the approaches. Often, you will see a research technique presented without the background reasoning on which it was originally based. By knowing about the approaches, you can better understand the principles on which the specific research techniques are based. For example,

BOX **4.4** **Common Features of the Three Major Approaches to Social Science**

1. *All are empirical.* Each is rooted in the observable reality of the sights, sounds, behaviors, situations, discussions, and actions of people. Research is never based on fabrication and imagination alone.
2. *All are systematic.* Each emphasizes meticulous and careful work. All reject haphazard, shoddy, or sloppy thinking and observation.
3. *All are theoretical.* The nature of theory varies, but all emphasize using ideas and seeing patterns. None holds that social life is chaos and disorder; all hold that explanation or understanding is possible.
4. *All are public.* All say a researcher's work must be candidly expressed to other researchers; it should be made explicit and shared. All oppose keeping the research processes hidden, private, or secret.
5. *All are self-reflective.* Each approach says researchers need to think about what they do and be self-

conscious. Research is never done in a blind or unthinking manner. It involves serious contemplation and requires self-awareness.
6. *All are open-end processes.* All see research as constantly moving, evolving, changing, asking new questions, and pursuing leads. None see it as static, fixed, or closed. Current knowledge or research procedures are not "set in stone" and settled. They involve continuous change and an openness to new ways of thinking and doing things.

Thus, despite their differences, all the approaches say that the social sciences strive to create systematically gathered, empirically based theoretical knowledge through public processes that are self-reflective and open ended.

the precise measures and logic of experimental research flow directly from positivism, whereas field research is based on an interpretive approach.

So far, we have looked at the overall operation of the research process, different types of studies

and theory, and the three fundamental approaches to social research. By now, you should have a grasp of the basic contours of social research. In the next chapter, you will see how to locate reports of specific research projects.

KEY TERMS

abduction	idiographic	praxis
bounded autonomy	instrumental orientation	realist orientation
causal laws	interpretative social science	reflexive-dialectic orientation
constructionist orientation	(ISS)	reification
covering law model	intersubjectivity	relativism
critical social science (CSS)	meaningful social action	technocratic perspective
determinism	mechanical model of man	transcendent perspective
dialectic	nomothetic	transformative perspective
essentialist orientation	paradigm	value-free science
explanatory critique	positivist social science (PSS)	*verstehen*
false consciousness	postulate of adequacy	voluntarism
hermeneutics	practical orientation	

REVIEW QUESTIONS

1. What is the purpose of social research according to each approach?
2. How does each approach define social reality?
3. What is the nature of human beings according to each approach?
4. How are science and common sense different in each approach?
5. What is social theory according to each approach?
6. How does each approach test a social theory?
7. What does each approach say about facts and how to collect them?
8. How is value-free science possible in each approach? Explain.
9. How are the criticisms of positivism by the interpretive and critical science approaches similar?
10. How does the model of science and the scientific community presented in Chapter 1 relate to each of the three approaches?

NOTES

1. For educational research, see Bredo and Feinberg (1982) and Guba and Lincoln (1994); for psychology, see Harré and Secord (1979) and Rosnow (1981); for political science, see Sabia and Wallulis (1983); and for economics, see Hollis (1977) and Ward (1972). A general discussion of alternatives can be found in Nowotny and Rose (1979).

2. See especially Friedrichs (1970), Giddens (1976), Gouldner (1970), and Phillips (1971). General introductions are provided by Harré (1972), Suppe (1977), and Toulmin (1953).

3. Divisions of the philosophies of social science similar to the approaches discussed in this chapter can be found in Benton (1977), Blaikie (1993), Bredo and Feinberg (1982), Fay (1975), Fletcher (1974), Guba and Lincoln (1994), Keat and Urry (1975), Lloyd (1986), Miller (1987), Mulkay (1979), Sabia and Wallulis (1983), Smart (1976), and Wilson (1970).

4. For discussions of paradigms, see Eckberg and Hill (1979), Kuhn (1970, 1979), Masterman (1970), Ritzer (1975), and Rosnow (1981).

5. In addition to the works listed in note 3, Halfpenny (1982) and Turner (1984) have provided overviews of positivism in sociology. Also see Giddens (1978). Lenzer (1975) is an excellent introduction to Auguste Comte.

6. See Gartell and Gartell (1996, 2002).

7. From Bernard (1988:12–21).

8. See Hegtvedt (1992).

9. For a discussion, see Derksen and Gartell (1992: 1715).

10. See Couch (1987). Also see Longino (1990:62–82) for an excellent analysis of objectivity in positivism and more broadly.

11. For a discussion, see Bannister (1987), Blumer (1991a, 1991b, 1992), Deegan (1988), Geiger (1986), Gillespie (1991), Lagemann (1989), Ross (1991), Schwendinger and Schwendinger (1974), Silva and Slaughter (1980), and Smith (1996).

12. In addition to the works in note 3, interpretive science approaches are discussed in Berger and Luckman (1967), Bleicher (1980), Cicourel (1973), Garfinkel (1967, 1974b), Geertz (1979), Glaser and Strauss (1967), Holstein and Gubrium (1994), Leiter (1980), Mehan and Wood (1975), Silverman (1972), and Weber (1974, 1981).

13. See Roy (2001:7–13) on the essentialist versus constructionist orientation.

14. See Brown (1989:34) for more examples and explanation.

15. In addition to the works in note 3, critical science approaches are discussed in Burawoy (1990), Dickson (1984), Fay (1987), Glucksmann (1974), Harding (1986), Harvey (1990), Keat (1981), Lane (1970), Lemert (1981), Mayhew (1980, 1981), Sohn-Rethel (1978), Veltmeyer (1978), Wardell (1979), Warner (1971), and Wilson (1982).

16. For a discussion of the Frankfurt School, see Botto-more (1984), Held (1980), Martin (1973), and Slater (1977). For more on the works of Habermas, see Holub (1991), McCarthy (1978), Pusey (1987), and Roderick (1986).

17. See Swartz (1997) on Bourdieu.

18. For discussions of realism, see Bhaskar (1975), Miller (1987), and Sayer (1992).

19. For discussion of critical realism, see Bhaskar (2003), Danermark et al. (2002), and Groff (2004), Archer et al. (1998).

20. See Sprague and Zimmerman (1989) on feminists' privileged perspectives of women and see Rule (1978a, 1978b) on constituencies that researchers favor.

21. See Habermas (1971, 1973, 1979) for a critical sci-ence critique of positivism as being technocratic and used for domination. He has suggested an emancipatory al-ternative.

22. See Olsen (1994).

23. See Evelyn Fox Keller's (1983) biography of Bar-bara McClintock and her other essays on gender and sci-ence (1985, 1990). Also see Longino (1990), Chapters 6 and 7.

24. From Brannigan (1992).

The Literature Review and Ethical Concerns

But since we do not as yet live in a period free from mundane troubles and beyond history, our problem is not how to deal with a kind of knowledge which shall be "truth in itself," but rather how man deals with his problems of knowing, bound as he is in his knowledge by his position in time and society.
—Karl Mannheim, *Ideology and Utopia*, p. 188

Jorge is getting ready to design a study on race relations. As he focuses his topic into a specific research question (e.g., Do children attending elementary school for three or more years in classes in which at least one-third of the students are of other races see race differently from those in single-race classes?), he confronts two issues. First, he must find out what others have said, or review the scholarly literature on race relations. In practice, the process of focusing a topic into a research question overlaps nicely with reviewing the literature. Second, Jorge needs to think about how to treat the respondents of his study in an ethical manner. Specific ethical concerns become salient depending on the research question he examines and the data collection technique he employs. Human subject issues are more salient in survey research, experiments, and field research than in existing documents, secondary data analysis, content analysis, or historical-comparative research. They are more significant for controversial topics or areas that might violate a person's privacy (e.g., illegal behavior, sexuality) than for "safe topics" that raise few privacy concerns. The topic of race can evoke intense emotions and be controversial depending on the research question asked.

In previous chapters, we looked at the norms of the scientific community, steps in the research process, various types of studies, the place of theory, and basic approaches to social science. In this chapter, we move to more concrete and practical concerns that a person will encounter early as he or she designs a study. We will examine literature reviews and human subject protection. The researcher needs to conduct a literature review and think about human-subject considerations as he or she starts to design a study.

THE LITERATURE REVIEW

Reviewing the accumulated knowledge about a question is an essential early step in the research process, no matter which approach to social science you adopt. As in other areas of life, it is best to find out what is already known about a question before trying to answer it yourself. The cliché about wasting time reinventing the wheel is a reminder to do your homework before beginning an endeavor that requires an investment of time and effort. This is true for the consumer of research and for the professional researcher beginning a study.

We begin by looking at the various purposes the review can serve. We will also discuss what the *literature* is, where to find it, and what it contains. Next, we will explore techniques for systematically conducting a review. Finally, we will look at how to write a review and its place in a research report.

A literature review is based on the assumption that knowledge accumulates and that people learn from and build on what others have done. Scientific research is a collective effort of many researchers who share their results with one another as a community. Although some studies may be especially important and individual researchers may become famous, a specific research project is just a tiny part of the overall process of creating knowledge. Today's studies build on those of yesterday. Researchers read studies to compare, replicate, or criticize them for weaknesses.

Reviews vary in scope and depth. Different kinds of reviews are stronger at fulfilling one or another of four goals (see Box 5.1). It may take a researcher over a year to complete an extensive professional summary review of all the literature on a broad question. The same researcher might complete a highly focused review in a very specialized area in a week. When beginning a review, a researcher decides on a topic, how much depth to go into, and the kind of review to conduct. The six kinds listed in Box 5.2 are ideal types. A specific review often combines features of several kinds.

A **meta-analysis** is a special technique to create an integrative review, or more often, a methodological review.[1] The researcher gathers the details about a large number of research projects (e.g., sample size, when published, size of the effects of variables) and then statistically analyzes this information.

Cox and Davidson (1995) used meta-analysis to examine findings on whether alternative educa-

BOX **5.1**   **Goals of a Literature Review**

1. *To demonstrate a familiarity with a body of knowledge and establish credibility.* A review tells a reader that the researcher knows the research in an area and knows the major issues. A good review increases a reader's confidence in the researcher's professional competence, ability, and background.
2. *To show the path of prior research and how a current project is linked to it.* A review outlines the direction of research on a question and shows the development of knowledge. A good review places a research project in a context and demonstrates its relevance by making connections to a body of knowledge.
3. *To integrate and summarize what is known in an area.* A review pulls together and synthesizes different results. A good review points out areas where prior studies agree, where they disagree, and where major questions remain. It collects what is known up to a point in time and indicates the direction for future research.
4. *To learn from others and stimulate new ideas.* A review tells what others have found so that a researcher can benefit from the efforts of others. A good review identifies blind alleys and suggests hypotheses for replication. It divulges procedures, techniques, and research designs worth copying so that a researcher can better focus hypotheses and gain new insights.

tion programs help juvenile delinquents. These nontraditional programs are designed specifically for troubled youth, using low student/teacher ratios, an unstructured environment, and individualized learning. They looked for all articles that mentioned alternative education programs for youth and found 241. They next read each to see whether the article met three criteria: (1) mentioned a separate curriculum, (2) was held in a separate location or building, (3) included quantitative measures of program outcomes. Of the 241 studies, only 87 met all three criteria. The researchers then checked whether the

Meta-analysis A special type of literature review in which a writer organizes the results from many studies and uses statistical techniques to identify common findings in them.

BOX **5.2** Six Types of Literature Reviews

1. *Context review.* A common type of review in which the author links a specific study to a larger body of knowledge. It often appears at the beginning of a research report and introduces the study by situating it within a broader framework and showing how it continues or builds on a developing line of thought or study.
2. *Historical review.* A specialized review in which the author traces an issue over time. It can be merged with a theoretical or methodological review to show how concept, theory, or research method developed over time.
3. *Integrative review.* A common type of review in which the author presents and summarizes the current state of knowledge on a topic, highlighting agreements and disagreements within it. It is often combined with a context review or may be published as an independent article as a service to other researchers.
4. *Methodological review.* A specialized type of integrative review in which the author compares and evaluates the relative methodological strength of various studies and shows how different methodologies (e.g., research designs, measures, samples) account for different results.
5. *Self-study review.* A review in which an author demonstrates his or her familiarity with a subject area. It is often part of an educational program or course requirement.
6. *Theoretical review.* A specialized review in which the author presents several theories or concepts focused on the same topic and compares them on the basis of assumptions, logical consistency, and scope of explanation.

---

three criteria for inclusion: (1) It used direct ethnographic observation over a period of at least six months, (2) it focused on a single organizational setting, and (3) it focused on at least one clearly identified group of workers (an assembly line, a typing pool, a task group, etc.). He located 83 publications, but because some were books with multiple case studies, the 83 publications generated 108 cases.

Over a period of six months, a team of four researchers read and coded eight case studies. After coding each, they met to decide whether to keep or remove items and how to develop response categories. In this process, they created a coding instrument with a list of concepts. Next, members of a graduate research practicum read the entire collection of 108 case studies. All coders were trained on a common case study and met twice weekly to discuss questions. After a coder finished a book, he or she was debriefed by a member of the research staff to check the accuracy of the codings and review codings in detail. Three of the coders independently read and coded each book to ensure consistency. Coders recorded passages and looked for behavioral indicators or specific descriptions for each category. They did not rely on the ethnographers' summary statements or evaluations They coded items such as how well an organization was run, whether work was based on a traditional craft, the degree of job autonomy, and the prevalence of injuries. The researchers next turned the codes into quantitative data and subjected them to statistical analysis.

Where to Find Research Literature

Researchers report their research projects in several forms: books, scholarly journal articles, dissertations, government documents, or policy reports. They also present them as papers at the meetings of professional societies. This section briefly discusses each type and gives you a simple road map on how to access them.

Periodicals. You can find the results of social research in newspapers, in popular magazines, on television or radio broadcasts, and in Internet news summaries, but these are not the full, complete reports of research required to prepare a literature re-

studies used specific statistical measures or tests; they found that 57 studies had the statistics. After statistically analyzing the results of the 57 studies, the authors learned that such programs slightly improve school performance and self-esteem but do not directly reduce delinquent behavior.

Although most meta-analyses summarize quantitative research, Hodson (1998) conducted a meta-analysis of qualitative field research case studies on workplace settings. He initially examined hundreds of case studies in books and articles using

CHART 5.1   Types of Publications

TYPE OF PUBLICATION	EXAMPLES	AUTHORS	PURPOSE	STRENGTHS	WEAKNESSES
Peer-reviewed scholarly journal	*Social Science Quarterly, Social Forces, Journal of Contemporary Ethnography*	Professional researchers	Report on empirical research studies to professionals and build knowledge	Highest quality, most accurate, and most objective with complete details	Technical, difficult to read, requires background knowledge, not always current issues
Semischolarly professional publication	*American Prospect, Society, American Demographics*	Professors, professional policy-makers, or politicians	Share and discuss new findings and implications with the educated public	Generally accurate, somewhat easy to read	Lacks full detail and explanation, often includes opinion mixed in with discussion
Newsmagazines and newspapers	*Wall Street Journal, Christian Science Monitor, Newsweek, Time*	Respected journalists	Report on current events in an easy-to-read, accessible way for the lay public	Easy to read, accessible, very current	Semi-accurate, incomplete, distorted or one-sided views may be presented
Serious opinion magazines	*Nation, Human Events, Public Interest, Commentary*	Professors, professional policy-makers, politicians	Offer value-based ideas and opinions to the educated public	Carefully written and reasoned	One-sided view and highly value based
Popular magazines for the public	*Esquire, Ebony, Redbook, Forbes, Fortune*	Journalists, other writers	Entertain; present and discuss current events for lay public	Easy to read, easy to locate	Often shallow, inaccurate, and incomplete

view. They are selected, condensed summaries prepared by journalists for a general audience, and they lack many essential details needed for a serious evaluation of the study. Textbooks and encyclopedias also present condensed summaries as introductions to readers who are new to a topic, but, again, these are inadequate for preparing a literature review because many essential details about the study are absent.

Navigating published articles often confuses beginning research students. This is not surprising. When asked to do a "literature review," many students first go to familiar nonprofessional, nonscholarly magazine or newspaper articles they may have used for a high school term paper or freshman-level report. Social science students need to learn to distinguish between scholarly publications that report on research studies and popular or layperson entertainment or news articles for the general public (see Chart 5.1). They should move away from lay public sources and instead begin to rely on scholarly publications written for a professional audience.

Professional researchers present the results of empirical studies in one of several forms: academic research books (often called monographs), articles in scholarly journals, chapters in edited academic books, and papers presented at professional meetings. One can also read about these studies, in a summarized, simplified, abbreviated, and "predigested" form, in textbooks written for students who are first learning about a topic and in magazines or newspapers articles written for the general public. The simplified summaries, especially in publications for the general public, often give an incomplete or distorted picture of the full original study. Whenever possible, go to the original scholarly journal article to see what the author said and the data show.

Upper-level students writing a term paper or a serious research paper should rely on the academic literature, that is, original articles in academic scholarly journals. A downside is that students will find some of the scholarly articles too difficult or technical to follow. The upside is that the articles are original reports—and not another person's (mis)reading of the original. Also, they have been carefully screened for professional use and are of high quality—and are not the sloppy, inaccurate, or incomplete low-quality reports on research that often appear in publications for the general public.

Another type of nonresearch publication is the opinion magazine. Professionals of various types and others write in these magazines for the educated public or professionals. They do not contain original empirical research or actual scientific studies. Instead, they have essays expressing individuals' opinions, beliefs, value-based ideas, and speculation. A student can use them for term papers—but with caution—because they present an individual's opinions and judgments not empirical research. When writing a research paper that uses empirical research (e.g., an experiment, survey data, field research), it is best to rely on empirical studies or official statistical documents (e.g., Census Bureau). If one uses an opinion essay article, it should be treated as such and never confused with an empirically based study or data.

Specialized computer-based search tools help one locate articles in the scholarly literature, and there are specialized formats or styles for referring to sources. It is important to learn how to use the search tools and how to refer correctly to sources through citation styles and bibliographic reference formats. Professional social scientists use the search tools to tap into and build on a growing body of research studies and scientifically based knowledge. Knowing how to locate the studies, recognize and read an empirical research study, and properly cite scholarly articles as sources are important skills for students to learn.

Scholarly Journals. The primary type of periodical to use for a literature review is the scholarly journal filled with peer-reviewed reports of research. (See the back inside cover of this book for a list.) One rarely finds them outside of college and university libraries. Recall from Chapter 1 that scholarly journals are where most researchers disseminate findings of new studies, and they are the heart of the scientific community's communication system.

Some scholarly journals are specialized. Instead of reports of research studies, they have only book reviews that provide commentary and evaluations on a book (e.g., *Contemporary Sociology*), or they contain only literature review essays (e.g., *Annual Review of Sociology, Annual Review of Psychology,* and *Annual Review of Anthropology*) in which researchers give a "state of the field" essay for others. Publications that specialize in literature reviews can be helpful if an article was recently published on a topic of interest. Many scholarly journals have a mix of literature reviews, book reviews, reports on research studies, and theoretical essays.

No simple solution or "seal of approval" distinguishes scholarly journals from other periodicals, or instantly distinguishes the report on a research study from other types of articles. One needs to develop judgment or ask experienced researchers or professional librarians. Nonetheless, distinguishing among types of publications is essential to build on a body of research. One of the best ways to distinguish among types of publications is to read many articles in scholarly journals.

The number of journals varies by field. Psychology has over 400 journals, whereas sociology has about 250 scholarly journals, political science and communication have slightly fewer than sociology, anthropology-archaeology and social work have about 100, urban studies and women's studies have about 50, and there are about a dozen journals in criminology. Each publishes from a few dozen to over 100 articles a year.

You may wonder if anyone ever reads all the articles. One study found that in a sample of 379 sociology articles, 43 percent were cited in another study in the first year after publication and 83 percent within six years.[2] As mentioned in Chapter 1, scholarly journals vary by prestige and acceptance rates, with some prestigious journals rejecting as much as 90 percent of the reports submitted to them. Overall rejection rates are higher in the social science than in other academic fields and have been rising.[3] This does not mean that researchers are doing lower-quality studies. Rather, the review process is becoming more rigorous, standards are rising, and more researchers are conducting studies, thus increasing the competition to publish in a well-respected journal.

Many, but not all, scholarly journals may be viewed via the Internet. Usually, this is limited to selected years and to libraries that paid special subscription fees. A few Internet services provide full, exact copies of scholarly journal articles over the Internet. For example, JSTOR provides exact copies, but only for a small number of scholarly journals and only for past years. Other Internet services, such as Proquest or EBSCO HOST, offer a full-text version of recent articles for a limited number of scholarly journals, but they are not always in the same format as a print version of an article. This can make it impossible to find a specific page number or see an exact copy of a chart. It is best to visit the library and see what a full-print version of the scholarly article looks like. An added benefit is that makes it easy for you to browse the table of contents of the journals. Browsing can be very useful for generating new ideas for research topics, seeing an established topic in creative ways, or expanding an idea into new areas. Only a tiny handful of new Internet-only scholarly journals, called *e-journals,* present peer-reviewed research studies (e.g., *Sociological Research Online, Current Research in Social Psychology,* and *Journal of World Systems Research).* Eventually, the Internet format may re-

place print versions. But for now, 99 percent of scholarly journals are available in print form and less than one-half of these are also available in a full-text version over the Internet, only for some years, and only then if a library pays for a special on-line subscription service.

Once you locate a scholarly journal with research studies, you need to make sure that a particular article presents the results of a study, because the journal may have other types of articles. It is easier to identify quantitative studies because they usually have a methods or data section and charts, statistical formulas, and tables of numbers. Qualitative research articles are more difficult to identify, and many students confuse them with theoretical essays, literature review articles, idea-discussion essays, policy recommendations, book reviews, and legal case analyses. To distinguish among these types requires a grasp of the varieties of research as well as experience in reading many articles.

Your college library has a section for scholarly journals and magazines, or, in some cases, they may be mixed with books. Look at a map of library facilities or ask a librarian to find this section. The most recent issues, which look like magazines, are often physically separate in a "current periodicals" section. This is done to store them temporarily and make them available until the library receives all the issues of a volume. Most often, libraries bind all issues of a volume together as a book before adding it to their permanent collection.

Scholarly journals from many different fields are placed together with popular magazines. All are periodicals, or serials in the jargon of librarians. Thus, you will find popular magazines (e.g., *Time, Road and Track, Cosmopolitan,* and *Atlantic Monthly*) next to journals for astronomy, chemistry, mathematics, literature, and philosophy as well as sociology, psychology, social work, and education. Some fields have more scholarly journals than others. The "pure" academic fields usually have more than the "applied" or practical fields such as marketing or social work. The journals are listed by title in a card catalog or a computerized catalog system. Libraries can provide you with a list of the periodicals to which they subscribe.

Scholarly journals are published as rarely as once a year or as frequently as weekly. Most appear four to six times a year. For example, *Sociological Quarterly* appears four times a year. To assist in locating articles, scholars have a system for tracking scholarly journals and the articles in them. Each issue is assigned a date, volume number, and issue number. This information makes it easier to locate an article. Such information—along with details such as author, title, and page number—is called an article's *citation* and is used in bibliographies. When a journal is first published, it begins with volume 1, number 1, and continues increasing the numbers thereafter. Although most journals follow a similar system, there are enough exceptions that you have to pay close attention to citation information. For most journals, each volume is one year. If you see a journal issue with volume 52, for example, it probably means that the journal has been in existence for 52 years. Most, but not all, journals begin their publishing cycle in January.

Most journals number pages by volume, not by issue. The first issue of a volume usually begins with page 1, and page numbering continues throughout the entire volume. For example, the first page of volume 52, issue 4, may be page 547. Most journals have an index for each volume and a table of contents for each issue that lists the title, the author's or authors' names, and the page on which the article begins. Issues contain as few as 1 or 2 articles or as many as 50. Most have 8 to 18 articles, which each may be 5 to 50 pages long. The articles often have **abstracts**, short summaries on the first page of the article or grouped together at the beginning of the issue.

Many libraries do not retain physical paper copies of older journals. To save space and costs, they retain only microfilm versions. There are hundreds of scholarly journals in most academic fields, with each costing $75 to $2,500 per year. Only the large

research libraries subscribe to all of them. You may have to borrow a journal or photocopy of an article from a distant library through an *interlibrary loan service,* a system by which libraries lend books or materials to other libraries. Few libraries allow people to check out recent issues of scholarly journals. You should plan to use these in the library. Some, not all, scholarly journals are available via the Internet.

Once you find the periodicals section, wander down the aisles and skim what is on the shelves. You will see volumes containing many research reports. Each title of a scholarly journal has a call number like that of a regular library book. Libraries often arrange them alphabetically by title. Because journals change titles, it may create confusion if the journal is shelved under its original title.

Scholarly journals differ by field and by type. Most contain articles on research in an academic field. Thus, most mathematics journals contain reports on new mathematical studies or proofs, literature journals contain commentary and literary criticism on works of literature, and sociology journals contain reports of sociological research. Some journals cover a broad field (e.g., sociology, psychology, education, political science) and contain reports from the entire field. Others specialize in a subfield (e.g., the family, criminology, early childhood education, comparative politics).

Citation Formats. An article's **citation** is the key to locating it. Suppose you want to read the study on student cheating discussed in Chapter 2. This book's bibliography says the following:

> McCabe, Donald L. (1992). The influence of situational ethics on cheating among college students. *Sociological Inquiry,* 62:365–374.

It tells you to go to an issue of the scholarly journal *Sociological Inquiry* published in 1992. The citation does not provide the issue or months, but it gives the volume number (62) and the page numbers (365–374).

There are many ways to cite the literature. Formats for citing literature in the text itself vary, with the internal citation format of using an author's last name and date of publication in parentheses being very popular. The full citation appears in a separate bibliography or reference section. There are many

Citation Details of a scholarly publication's location that helps people to find it quickly.

Abstract A term with two meanings: a short summary of a scholarly journal article that usually appears at its beginning, and a reference tool for locating journal articles.

FIGURE 5.1   Different Reference Citations for a Journal Article

---

The oldest journal of sociology in the United States, *American Journal of Sociology,* reports on a study of virginity pledges by Peter Bearman and Hannah Bückner. It appeared on pages 859 to 912 of the January 2001 issue (number 4) of the journal, which begins counting issues in March. It was in volume 106, or the journal's 106th year. Here are ways to cite the article. Two very popular styles are those of *American Sociological Review (ASR)* and *American Psychological Association (APA).*

ASR STYLE

Bearman, Peter and Hannah Bückner. 2001. "Promising the Future: Virginity Pledges and First Intercourse." *American Journal of Sociology* 106:859–912.

APA STYLE

Bearman, P., and Bückner, H. (2001). Promising the future: Virginity pledges and first intercourse. *American Journal of Sociology 106,* 859–912.

OTHER STYLES

Bearman, P., and H. Bückner. "Promising the Future: Virginity Pledges and First Intercourse," *American Journal of Sociology* 106 (2001), 859–912.

Bearman, Peter and Hannah Bückner, 2001.
    "Promising the future: Virginity pledges and first intercourse." *Am. J. of Sociol.* 106:859–912.

Bearman, P. and Bückner, H. (2001). "Promising the Future: Virginity Pledges and First Intercourse." *American Journal of Sociology* 106 (January): 859–912.

Bearman, Peter and Hannah Bückner. 2001.
    "Promising the future: Virginity pledges and first intercourse." *American Journal of Sociology* 106 (4):859–912.

Bearman, P. and H. Bückner. (2001). "Promising the future: Virginity pledges and first intercourse." *American Journal of Sociology* 106, 859–912.

Peter Bearman and Hannah Bückner, "Promising the Future: Virginity Pledges and First Intercourse," *American Journal of Sociology* 106, no. 4 (2001): 859–912.

---

styles for full citations of journal articles, with books and other types of works each having a separate style. When citing articles, it is best to check with an instructor, journal, or other outlet for the desired format. Almost all include the names of authors, article title, journal name, and volume and page numbers. Beyond these basic elements, there is great variety. Some include the authors' first names, others use initials only. Some include all authors; others give only the first one. Some include information on the issue or month of publication; others do not (see Figure 5.1).

Citation formats can get complex. Two major reference tools on the topic in social science are *Chicago Manual of Style,* which has nearly 80 pages on bibliographies and reference formats, and *American Psychological Association Publication Manual,* which devotes about 60 pages to the topic. In sociology, the *American Sociological Review* style, with 2 pages of style instructions, is widely followed.

Books. Books communicate many types of information, provoke thought, and entertain. There are many types of books: picture books, textbooks, short story books, novels, popular fiction or nonfiction, religious books, children's books, and others. Our concern here is with those books containing reports of original research or collections of research articles. Libraries shelve these books and assign call numbers to them, as they do with other types of books. You can find citation information on them (e.g., title, author, publisher) in the library's catalog system.

It is not easy to distinguish a book that reports on research from other books. You are more likely to find such books in a college or university library. Some publishers, such as university presses, specialize in publishing them. Nevertheless, there is no guaranteed method for identifying one without reading it.

Some types of social research are more likely to appear in book form than others. For example, studies by anthropologists and historians are more likely to appear in book-length reports than are those of economists or psychologists. Yet, some anthropological and historical studies are reported in articles, and some economic and psychological studies appear as books. In education, social work, sociology, and political science, the results of long, complex studies may appear both in two or three articles and in book form. Studies that involve detailed clinical or ethnographic descriptions and complex theoretical or philosophical discussions usually appear as books. Finally, an author who wants to communicate to scholarly peers and to the educated public may write a book that bridges the scholarly, academic style and a popular nonfiction style.

Locating original research articles in books can be difficult because there is no single source listing them. Three types of books contain collections of articles or research reports. The first is designed for teaching purposes. Such books, called *readers,* may include original research reports. Usually, articles on a topic from scholarly journals are gathered and edited to be easier for students to read and understand.

The second type of collection is designed for scholars and may gather journal articles or may contain original research or theoretical essays on a specific topic. Some collections contain articles from journals that are difficult to locate. They may include original research reports organized around a specialized topic. The table of contents lists the titles and authors. Libraries shelve these collections with other books, and some library catalog systems include article or chapter titles.

Finally, there are annual research books that contain reports on studies that are not found elsewhere. These are hybrids between scholarly journals and collections of articles: They appear year after year, with volume numbers for each year. These volumes, such as the *Review of Research in Political Sociology* and *Comparative Social Research,* are shelved with books. Some annual books specialize in literature reviews (e.g., *Annual Review of Sociology* and *Annual Review of Anthropology*). There is no comprehensive list of these books as there is for scholarly journals. The only way someone new to an area can find out about them is by spending a lot of time in the library or asking a researcher who is already familiar with a topic area.

Citations or references to books are shorter than article citations. They include the author's name, book title, year and place of publication, and publisher's name.

Dissertations. All graduate students who receive the Ph.D. degree are required to complete a work of original research, which they write up as a dissertation thesis. The dissertation is bound and shelved in the library of the university that granted the Ph.D. About half of all dissertations are eventually published as books or articles. Because dissertations report on original research, they can be valuable sources of information. Some students who receive the master's degree conduct original research and write a master's thesis, but fewer master's theses involve serious research, and they are much more difficult to locate than unpublished dissertations.

Specialized indexes list dissertations completed by students at accredited universities. For example, *Dissertation Abstracts International* lists dissertations with their authors, titles, and universities. This index is organized by topic and contains an abstract of each dissertation. You can borrow most dissertations via interlibrary loan from the degree-granting university if the university permits this. An alternative is to purchase a copy from a national dissertation microfilm/photocopy center such as the one at the University of Michigan, Ann Arbor, for U.S. universities. Some large research libraries contain copies of dissertations from other libraries if others have previously requested them.

Government Documents.

The federal government of the United States, the governments of other nations, state or provincial-level governments, the United Nations, and other international agencies such as the World Bank, all sponsor studies and publish reports of the research. Many college and university libraries have these documents in their holdings, usually in a special "government documents" section. These reports are rarely found in the catalog system. You must use specialized lists of publications and indexes, usually with the help of a librarian, to locate these reports. Most college and university libraries hold only the most frequently requested documents and reports.

Policy Reports and Presented Papers.

A researcher conducting a thorough review of the literature will examine these two sources, which are difficult for all but the trained specialist to obtain. Research institutes and policy centers (e.g., Brookings Institute, Institute for Research on Poverty, Rand Corporation, etc.) publish papers and reports. Some major research libraries purchase these and shelve them with books. The only way to be sure of what has been published is to write directly to the institute or center and request a list of reports.

Each year, the professional associations in academic fields (e.g., sociology, political science, psychology) hold annual meetings. Thousands of researchers assemble to give, listen to, or discuss oral reports of recent research. Most of these oral reports are available as written papers to those attending the meeting. People who do not attend the meetings but who are members of the association receive a program of the meeting, listing each paper to be presented with its title, author, and author's place of employment. They can write directly to the author and request a copy of the paper. Many, but not all, of the papers are later published as articles. The papers may be listed in indexes or abstract services (to be discussed).

How to Conduct a Systematic Literature Review

Define and Refine a Topic.

Just as a researcher must plan and clearly define a topic and research question when beginning a research project, you need to begin a literature review with a clearly defined, well-focused research question and a plan. A good review topic should be as focused as a research question. For example, "divorce" or "crime" is much too broad. A more appropriate review topic might be "the stability of families with stepchildren" or "economic inequality and crime rates across nations." If you conduct a context review for a research project, it should be slightly broader than the specific research question being examined. Often, a researcher will not finalize a specific research question for a study until he or she has reviewed the literature. The review usually helps bring greater focus to the research question.

Design a Search.

After choosing a focused research question for the review, the next step is to plan a search strategy. You must decide on the type of review, its extensiveness, and the types of materials to include. The key is to be careful, systematic, and organized. Set parameters on your search: how much time you will devote to it, how far back in time you will look, the minimum number of research reports you will examine, how many libraries you will visit, and so forth.

Also, decide how to record the bibliographic citation for each reference you find and how to take notes (e.g., in a notebook, on 3 × 5 cards, in a computer file). Develop a schedule, because several visits are usually necessary. You should begin a file folder or computer file in which you can place possible sources and ideas for new sources. As the review proceeds, it should become more focused.

Locate Research Reports.

Locating research reports depends on the type of report or "outlet" of research being searched. As a general rule, you should use multiple search strategies to counteract the limitations of a single search method.

Articles in Scholarly Journals.

As discussed earlier, most social research is published in scholarly journals. There are dozens of journals, each containing many articles. The task of searching for articles can be formidable. Luckily, specialized publications and source tools make the task easier.

You may have used an index for general publications, such as *Reader's Guide to Periodical Literature.* Many academic fields have "abstracts" or "indexes" for the scholarly literature (e.g., *Psychological Abstracts, Social Sciences Index, Sociological Abstracts,* and *Gerontological Abstracts*). For education-related topics, the Educational Resources Information Center (ERIC) system is especially valuable. There are over 100 such source tools. You can usually find them in the reference section of a library or available via computer access.

Source tools are updated on a regular basis (monthly, six times a year, etc.) and allow a reader to look up articles by author name or subject. The journals covered by the source tool are listed in it. An index, such as the *Social Sciences Index,* lists only the citation, whereas an abstract, such as *Sociological Abstracts,* lists the citation and has a copy of the article's abstract. Abstracts do not give you all the findings and details of a research project. Researchers use abstracts to screen articles for relevance, then locate the more relevant articles. Abstracts may also include papers presented at professional meetings.

It may sound as though all you have to do is to go find the source tool and look up a topic. Unfortunately, things are more complicated than that. The subjects or topics listed in the abstracts or indexes are broad. The specific research question that interests you may fit into several subject areas. You should check each one. For example, for the topic of illegal drugs in high schools, you might look up these subjects: drug addiction, drug abuse, substance abuse, drug laws, illegal drugs, high schools, and secondary schools. Many of the articles under a subject area will not be relevant for your literature review. Also, there is a 3- to 12-month time lag between the publication of an article and its appearance in the abstracts or indexes. Unless you are at a major research library, the most useful article may not be available in your library. You can obtain it only by using an interlibrary loan service, or it may be in a foreign language that you do not read.

Most research-oriented libraries subscribe to the *Social Science Citation Index (SSCI)* of the Institute for Scientific Information. This is a valuable resource with information on over 1,400 journals. It is similar to other indexes and abstracts, but it takes time to learn how to use it. The SSCI comes in four books. One is a source index, which provides complete citation information on journal articles. The other three books refer to articles in the source book. They are organized by subject, by university or research center for which the researcher works, or by authors who are cited in the reference sections of other articles.

You can begin a SSCI search in one of three ways: (1) with a subject (e.g., alcohol use among children); (2) with a known research center (e.g., the Center for Alcohol Studies at Rutgers, the State University of New Jersey); or (3) with an earlier article (e.g., Kandel's "Drug and Drinking Behavior among Youth" in the 1980 *Annual Review of Sociology*). The first search directs you to the authors of current research reports. The second search identifies all authors from the same research center who published articles. The third search directs you to all citations included in earlier article's reference section. This last type of search is important when a researcher wants to trace research that influenced other research. For example, you find a 1980 article relevant. The SSCI tells you all articles published since 1980 that listed it in their reference sections. Even if your library does not have the *Social Science Citation Index,* a good search principle is to examine the bibliography of articles to find additional articles or books on a topic.

Researchers organize computerized searches in several ways—by author, by article title, by subject, or by keyword. A keyword is an important term for a topic that is likely to be found in a title. You will want to use six to eight keywords in most computer-based searches and consider several synonyms. The computer's searching method can vary and most look for a keyword only in a title or abstract. If you choose too few words or very narrow terms, you will miss a lot of relevant articles. If you choose too many words or very broad terms, you will get a huge number of irrelevant articles. The best way to learn the appropriate breadth and number of keywords is by trial and error.

In a study I conducted on how college students define *sexual harassment* (Neuman, 1992), I used the following keywords: *sexual harassment, sexual assault, harassment, gender equity, gender fairness,* and *sex discrimination.* I later discovered a few important studies that lacked any of these keywords in their titles. I also tried the keywords *college student* and *rape,* but got huge numbers of unrelated articles that I could not even skim.

There are numerous computer-assisted search databases or systems. A person with a computer and an Internet hookup can search some article index collections, the catalogs of libraries, and other information sources around the globe if they are available on the Internet.

All computerized searching methods share a similar logic, but each has its own method of operation to learn. In my study, I looked for sources in the previous seven years and used five computerized databases of scholarly literature: *Social Science Index, CARL (Colorado Area Research Library), Sociofile, Social Science Citation Index,* and *PsychLit.*

Often, the same articles will appear in multiple scholarly literature databases, but each database may identify a few new articles not found in the others. This points to a critical lesson: "Do not rely exclusively on computerized literature searches, on abstracting services, [or] on the literature in a single discipline, or on an arbitrarily defined time period" (Bausell, 1994:24). For example, I discovered several excellent sources not listed in any of the computerized databases that had been published in earlier years by studying the bibliographies of the relevant articles.

The process in my study was fairly typical. Based on my keyword search, I quickly skimmed or scanned the titles or abstracts of over 200 sources. From these, I selected about 80 articles, reports, and books to read. I found about 49 of the 80 sources valuable, and they appear in the bibliography of the published article.

Scholarly Books. Finding scholarly books on a subject can be difficult. The subject topics of library catalog systems are usually incomplete and too broad to be useful. Moreover, they list only books

that are in a particular library system, although you may be able to search other libraries for interlibrary loan books. Libraries organize books by call numbers based on subject matter. Again, the subject matter classifications may not reflect the subjects of interest to you or all the subjects discussed in a book. Librarians can help you locate books from other libraries. For example, the *Library of Congress National Union Catalog* lists all books in the U.S. Library of Congress. Librarians have access to sources that list books at other libraries, or you can use the Internet. There is no surefire way to locate relevant books. Use multiple search methods, including a look at journals that have book reviews and the bibliographies of articles.

Dissertations. A publication called *Dissertation Abstracts International* lists most dissertations. Like the indexes and abstracts for journal articles, it organizes dissertations by broad subject category, author, and date. Researchers look up all titles in the subject areas that include a topic. Unfortunately, after you have located the dissertation title and abstract, you may find that obtaining a copy of it takes time and involves added costs.

Government Documents. The "government documents" sections of libraries contain specialized lists of government documents. A useful index for documents issued by the U.S. federal government is the *Monthly Catalog of Government Documents,* which is often available on computer. It has been issued since 1885, but other supplemental sources should be used for research into documents more than a decade old. The catalog has an annual index, and monthly issues have subject, title, and author indexes. *Indexes to Congressional Hearings,* another useful source, lists committees and subjects going back to the late 1930s. The *Congressional Record* contains debate of the U.S. Congress with synopses of bills, voting records, and changes in bills. *United States Statutes* lists each individual U.S. federal law by year and subject. The *Federal Register,* a daily publication of the U.S. government, contains all rules, regulations, and announcements of federal agencies. It has both monthly and annual indexes. There are other indexes that cover treaties, technical announcements, and so forth. Other governments have similar lists. For example, the British government's *Government Publications Index* lists government publications issued during a year. *Parliamentary Papers* lists official social and economic studies going back 200 years. It is usually best to rely on the expertise of librarians for assistance in using these specialized indexes. The topics used by index makers may not be the best ones for your specific research question.

Policy Reports and Presented Papers. The most difficult sources to locate are policy reports and presented papers. They are listed in some bibliographies of published studies; some are listed in the abstracts or indexes. To locate these studies, try several methods: Write to research centers and ask for lists of publications, obtain lists of papers presented at professional meetings, and so forth. Once you locate a research report, try writing to the relevant author or institute.

Evaluating Research Articles

After you locate published studies, you need to read and evaluate them. At first, this is not easy, but it gets easier over time. Here are general guidelines to help you read and evaluate reports you find and locate models for writing your own research reports. First, look at the title carefully. A good title is specific, indicates the nature of the research without describing the results, and avoids asking a yes or no question. It describes the topic, may mention one or two major variables, and tells about the setting or people being studied. An example of a good title is "Parental involvement in schooling and reduced discipline problems among junior high school students in the Singapore." A good title informs readers about a study whereas a bad title either is vague or overemphasizes technical details or jargon. The same study could have been titled "A three-step correlation analysis of factors that affect segmented behavioral anxiety reduction."

Next read the abstract. A good abstract summarizes critical information about a study. It gives the study's purpose, tells methods used, and highlights major findings. It will avoid vague references to future implications. After an initial screening by title, a reader should be able to decide a report's relevance from a well-prepared abstract. In addition to screening for relevance, a title and abstract prepare the interested reader for examining a report in detail.

I recommend a two-stage screening process. Use the title and abstract to determine initial relevance. If it appears relevant, quickly scan the introduction and conclusion sections to decide whether it is a real "keeper" and worth investing in a slow, careful reading of the entire article or picking out a few details. Most likely, you will discover a few articles are very central to your purpose and many others with tangential relevance that are only worth skimming to locate one or two specific relevant details. Exercise caution not to pull specific details out of context.

Three factors will influence the amount of time and effort and overall payoff from reading a scholarly article. The time and effort are lower and results greater when (1) the article is of high quality with a well-defined purpose, clear writing, and smooth, logical organization; (2) the reader is sharply focused on a particular research issue or question; and (3) the reader has a solid background on the theoretical issues, knows a great deal about the substantive topic, and is familiar with multiple research methodologies. A great deal depends on reader preparation. A reader who can quickly "size up" an article by recognizing the dimensions of a study (see Chapter 2), its use of theory (Chapter 3), and the author's approach to doing research (Chapter 4) will find it less burdensome to read, evaluate, and extract information from a scholarly article. Also, be aware that authors write with different audiences in mind. They may target a narrow, highly specialized sector of the scientific community; write for a broad cross section of interested students and scholars in one or more academic disciplines; or address policymakers, issue advocates, and applied professionals.

When you read a highly relevant article, begin with the introduction section. The introduction section has three purposes: (1) introduce a broad topic and show a transition to a specific research question that is the primary focus of the study, (2) establish the significance of the problem (in terms of expanding knowledge, linking to past studies, or addressing an applied concern), and (3) outline the theoretical framework and define major concepts being used. Sometimes an article blends the introduction with a context literature review; at other times the literature review is a separate section.

A good literature review is selective, comprehensive, critical, and current. By being selective, it does not list everything ever written on a topic, but picks the most relevant past studies. By being comprehensive, it includes past studies that are highly relevant and does not omit any important ones. More than merely recounting past studies, the review should be critical-evaluative. This means it comments on the details of some specific studies and evaluates them as they relate to current study. Because the writer does not know everything about a study until it is done, a literature review prepared before conducting a study must be fine-tuned and rewritten after the study is completed.

Literature reviews should include recent studies, those published in the past year. Depending on its size and complexity, a review may distinguish among theory, methods, findings, and evaluation. For example, one section may review theoretical issues and disputes, another cover the methods used in prior studies used, and another summarize findings, highlighting any gaps or inconsistencies. An evaluation often serves to justify the importance of conducting the current study.

Depending on the type of research study, a hypothesis or methods section may follow the literature review. They outline what will be examined in detail, inform readers of specific data sources or methods of data collection, describe how variables were measured and whether sampling was used, and if so, details about it. These sections are usually tightly written and packed with technical details. They are often longer in quantitative than qualitative studies.

After a methods section come the results or findings. The results section is a descriptive essay. If it is quantitative research, it needs to do more than present a collection of statistical tables or coefficients and percentages. If it is qualitative research, it should be more than a list of quotations or straight description.

Each paragraph flows sequentially, describing results in a logical order determined by the author.

The organization of data presentation usually begins simply, painting a broad scope, and then goes into complexities and specific findings. Data presentation includes a straightforward discussion of the central findings and notes their significance. In quantitative research, it is not necessary to discuss every detail in a table or chart, but to note major findings and any unexpected or unusual findings. The author guides the reader through the data, pointing out what is in the study, but lets the reader see details for him or herself. In qualitative research, the organization of data often "tells a story" or presents a line of reasoning. Readers follow the author's story but are free to make inquiries of it.

Some researchers combine a discussion section with a results section; others keep them separate. A discussion section goes beyond straight description to elaborating on the implications of results for past findings, theory, or applied issues. Implications and interpretation take two forms: (1) implications for the building of knowledge as outlined in the literature review, and (2) implications for the specific research question of this study, as well as what was unexpected.

Researchers usually include methodological limitations in the discussion. An author may state how the specific measures, sampling, cases, location, or other factors restrict the generalizability of findings or open up alternative explanations. Full candor and openness are expected. An author should show readers that he or she was self-critical and has thought through the results and is aware of what is in them. This is not the place to include new references, but terms, theories, or ideas from the introduction and literature review will be used.

Last, read through the conclusion or summary at the end. A good conclusion/summary reviews the research problem, major findings, and significant unexpected results. It also outlines future implications and directions. It is sometimes useful to read the introduction and skim the conclusion before reading through the entire report step by step. Also look for an appendix that may include additional study details. You might also want to review the reference or bibliography section. An article's bibliography may give you some leads to related studies or theoretical statements.

Reading and critically evaluating scholarly articles improves with practice. Despite the peer-review process and manuscript rejection rates, articles vary in quality and may contain errors, sloppy logic, or gaps. Beware that a title and introduction may not mesh with specific details in the results section. Authors do not always describe all the findings, and a reader with a clearly focused purpose may notice new details in the findings by carefully poring over an article. For example, an author may not mention important results evident in a statistical table or chart or may place too much attention on minor or marginal results. A careful reader will evaluate how the study was done, how logically tight the parts of an article fit together, and whether the major conclusions really flow from all the findings.

Taking Notes

As you gather the relevant research literature, it is easy to feel overwhelmed by the quantity of information, so you need a system for taking notes. The old-fashioned approach was to write notes onto index cards. You then shifted and sorted the note cards, placed them in piles, and so forth as you looked for connections among them or developed an outline for a report or paper. This method still works. Today, however, most people use word-processing software and gather photocopies or printed versions of many articles.

As you discover sources, it is a good idea to create two kinds of files for your note cards or computer documents: a *Source File* and a *Content File.* Record *all* the bibliographic information for each source in the Source File, even though you may not use some and later erase them. Do not forget anything in a complete bibliographic citation, such as a page number or the name of the second author; you will regret it later. It is far easier to erase a source you do not use than to try to locate bibliographic information later for a source you discover that you need or from which you forgot one detail.

I recommend creating two kinds of Source Files, or divide a master file into two parts: *Have File* and *Potential File.* The Have File is for sources that you have found and for which you have already taken content notes. The Potential File is for leads and possible new sources that you have yet to track down or read. You can add to the Potential File anytime you come across a new source or in the bibliography of something you read. Toward the end of writing a report, the Potential File will disappear while the Have File will become your bibliography.

Your note cards or computer documents go into the Content File. This file contains substantive information of interest from a source, usually its major findings, details of methodology, definitions of concepts, or interesting quotes. If you directly quote from a source or want to take some specific information from a source, you need to record the specific page number(s) on which the quote appears. Link the files by putting key source information, such as author and date, on each content file.

What to Record. Researchers have to decide what to record about an article, book, or other source. It is better to err in the direction of recording too much rather than too little. In general, record the hypotheses tested, how major concepts were measured, the main findings, the basic design of the research, the group or sample used, and ideas for future study (see Figure 5.2). It is wise to examine the report's bibliography and note sources that you can add to your search.

Photocopying all relevant articles or reports will save you time recording notes and will ensure that you will have an entire report. Also, you can make notes on the photocopy. There are several warnings about this practice. First, photocopying can be expensive for a large literature search. Second, be aware of and obey copyright laws. U.S. copyright laws permit photocopying for personal research use. Third, remember to record or photocopy the entire article, including all citation information. Fourth, organizing entire articles can be cumbersome, especially if several different parts of a single article are being used. Finally, unless you highlight carefully or take good notes, you may have to reread the entire article later.

Organize Notes. After gathering a large number of references and notes, you need an organizing scheme. One approach is to group studies or specific findings by skimming notes and creating a

FIGURE 5.2   Example of Notes on an Article

FULL CITATION ON BIBLIOGRAPHY (SOURCE FILE)

Bearman, Peter, and Hannah Bückner. 2001. "Promising the Future: Virginity Pledges and First Intercourse." *American Journal of Sociology* 106:859–912. (January, issue no. 4).

NOTE CARD (CONTENT FILE)

Bearman and Bückner 2001

Topics: Teen pregnancy & sexuality, pledges/promises, virginity, first sexual intercourse, S. Baptists, identity movement

Since 1993, the Southern Baptist Church sponsored a movement among teens whereby the teens make a public pledge to remain virgins until marriage. Over 2.5 million teens have made the pledge. This study examines whether the pledge affected the timing of sexual intercourse and whether pledging teens differ from nonpledging teens. Critics of the movement are uncomfortable with it because pledge supporters often reject sex education, hold an overly romanticized view of marriage, and adhere to traditional gender roles.

Hypothesis
Adolescents will engage in behavior that adults enjoy but that is forbidden to them based on the amount of social controls that constrain opportunities to engage in forbidden behavior. Teens in nontraditional families with greater freedom and less supervision are more likely to engage in forbidden behavior (sex). Teens in traditional families and who are closer to their parents will delay sexual activity. Teens closely tied to "identity movements" outside the family will modify behavior based on norms the movements teach.

Method
Data are from a national health survey of U.S. teens in grades 7–12 who were in public or private schools in 1994–1995. A total of 90,000 students in 141 schools completed questionnaires. A second questionnaire was completed by 20,000 of the 90,000 students. The questionnaire asked about a pledge, importance of religion, and sexual activity.

Findings
The study found a substantial delay in the timing of first intercourse among pledgers. Yet, the effect of pledging varies by the age of the teen. In addition, pledging only works in some social contexts (i.e., where it is at least partially a social norm). Pledgers tend to be more religious, less developed physically, and from more traditional social and family backgrounds.

mental map of how they fit together. Try several organizing schemes before settling on a final one. Organizing is a skill that improves with practice. For example, place notes into piles representing common themes, or draw charts comparing what different reports state about the same question, noting agreements and disagreements.

In the process of organizing notes, you will find that some references and notes do not fit and should be discarded as irrelevant. Also, you may discover gaps or areas and topics that are relevant but that you did not examine. This necessitates return visits to the library.

There are many organizing schemes. The best one depends on the purpose of the review. A context review implies organizing recent reports around a specific research question. A historical review implies organizing studies by major theme and by the date of publication. An integrative review implies organizing studies around core common findings of a field and the main hypotheses tested. A methodological review implies organizing studies by the topic and, within topic, by the design or method used. A theoretical review implies organizing studies by the theories and major thinkers being examined.

What Does a Good Review Look Like?

A literature review requires planning and clear writing, which requires a lot of rewriting. This step is often merged with organizing notes. All the rules of good writing (e.g., clear organizational structure, an introduction and conclusion, transitions between sections, etc.) apply to writing a literature review. Keep your purposes in mind when you write, and communicate clearly and effectively.

An author should communicate a review's purpose to the reader by its organization. The *wrong* way to write a review is to list a series of research reports with a summary of the findings of each. This fails to communicate a sense of purpose. It reads as a set of notes strung together. Perhaps the reviewer got sloppy and skipped over the important organizing step in writing the review. The *right* way to write a review is to organize common findings or arguments together. A well-accepted approach is to address the most important ideas first, to logically link statements or findings, and to note discrepancies or weaknesses in the research (see Box 5.3 for an example).

Using the Internet for Social Research

The Internet has revolutionized how social researchers work. Only a decade ago, it was rarely used; today, most social researchers use the Internet regularly to help them review the literature, to communicate with other researchers, and to search for other information sources. The Internet continues to expand and change at an explosive rate.

The Internet has been a mixed blessing for social research, but it has not proved to be the panacea that some people first thought it might be. It provides new and important ways to find information, but it remains one tool among others. It can quickly make some specific pieces of information accessible. The Internet is best thought of as a supplement rather than as a replacement for traditional library research. There are "up" and "down" sides to using the Internet for social research.

The Upside

1. The Internet is easy, fast, and cheap. It is widely accessible and can be used from many locations. This near-free resource allows people to find source material from almost anywhere—local public libraries, homes, labs or classrooms, or anywhere a computer is connected to the Internet system. Also, the Internet does not close; it operates 24 hours a day, 7 days a week. With minimal training, most people can quickly perform searches and get information on their computer screens that would have required them to take a major trip to large research libraries a few years ago. Searching a vast quantity of information electronically is easier and faster than a manual search, and the Internet greatly expands the amount and variety of source material. More and more information (e.g., *Statistical Abstract of the United States*) is available on the Internet. In addition, once the information is located, a researcher can often store it electronically or print it at a local site.

2. The Internet has "links" that provide additional ways to find and connect to many other sources of information. Many websites, home pages, and other

BOX **5.3**   **Examples of Bad and Good Reviews**

EXAMPLE OF BAD REVIEW

Sexual harassment has many consequences. Adams, Kottke, and Padgitt (1983) found that some women students said they avoided taking a class or working with certain professors because of the risk of harassment. They also found that men and women students reacted differently. Their research was a survey of 1,000 men and women graduate and undergraduate students. Benson and Thomson's study in *Social Problems* (1982) lists many problems created by sexual harassment. In their excellent book, *The Lecherous Professor,* Dziech and Weiner (1990) give a long list of difficulties that victims have suffered.

Researchers study the topic in different ways. Hunter and McClelland (1991) conducted a study of undergraduates at a small liberal arts college. They had a sample of 300 students and students were given multiple vignettes that varied by the reaction of the victim and the situation. Jaschik and Fretz (1991) showed 90 women students at a mideastern university a videotape with a classic example of sexual harassment by a teaching assistant. Before it was labeled as *sexual harassment,* few women called it that. When asked whether it was sexual harassment, 98 percent agreed. Weber-Burdin and Rossi (1982) replicated a previous study on sexual harassment, only they used students at the University of Massachusetts. They had 59 students rate 40 hypothetical situations. Reilley, Carpenter, Dull, and Bartlett (1982) conducted a study of 250 female and 150 male undergraduates at the University of California at Santa Barbara. They also had a sample of 52 faculty. Both samples completed a questionnaire in which respondents were presented vignettes of sexual-harassing situations that they were to rate. Popovich et al. (1986) created a nine-item scale of sexual harassment. They studied 209 undergradu-

ates at a medium-sized university in groups of 15 to 25. They found disagreement and confusion among students.

EXAMPLE OF BETTER REVIEW

The victims of sexual harassment suffer a range of consequences, from lowered self-esteem and loss of self-confidence to withdrawal from social interaction, changed career goals, and depression (Adams, Kottke, and Padgitt, 1983; Benson and Thomson, 1982; Dziech and Weiner, 1990). For example, Adams, Kottke, and Padgitt (1983) noted that 13 percent of women students said they avoided taking a class or working with certain professors because of the risk of harassment.

Research into campus sexual harassment has taken several approaches. In addition to survey research, many have experimented with vignettes or presented hypothetical scenarios (Hunter and McClelland, 1991; Jaschik and Fretz, 1991; Popovich et al., 1986; Reilley, Carpenter, Dull, and Bartlett, 1982; Rossi and Anderson, 1982; Valentine-French and Radtke, 1989; Weber-Burdin and Rossi, 1982). Victim verbal responses and situational factors appear to affect whether observers label a behavior as harassment. There is confusion over the application of a sexual harassment label for inappropriate behavior. For example, Jaschik and Fretz (1991) found that only 3 percent of the women students shown a videotape with a classic example of sexual harassment by a teaching assistant initially labeled it as *sexual harassment.* Instead, they called it "sexist," "rude," "unprofessional," or "demeaning." When asked whether it was sexual harassment, 98 percent agreed. Roscoe et al. (1987) reported similar labeling difficulties.

Internet resource pages have "hot links" that can call up information from related sites or sources simply by clicking on the link indicator (usually a button or a highlighted word or phrase). This connects people to more information and provides "instant" access to cross-referenced material. Links make embedding one source within a network of related sources easy.

3. The Internet speeds the flow of information around the globe and has a "democratizing" effect. It provides rapid transmission of information (e.g., text, news, data, and photos) across long distances and international borders. Instead of waiting a week for a report or having to send off for a foreign publication and wait for a month, the information is often available in seconds at no cost. There are

BOX **5.4**   **Websites: Surfer Beware**

The rapid diffusion of Internet access and increased reliance on the Internet for information has provided many benefits. The Internet is unregulated, so almost anyone can create a website saying almost anything. In 2000, over 60 million U.S. residents went on-line in search of health information. Among those who use the Internet, more than 70 percent report the health information they find will influence a decision about treatment. A study (Berland et al., 2001) on health information available on the Internet found that health information is often incomplete or inaccurate. The researchers used 10 English and 4 Spanish search engines looking for 4 search terms: breast cancer, childhood asthma, depression, and obesity.

They found that less than one-fourth of the linked background information on health web pages provided valid, relevant information.

Thirty-four physicians evaluated the quality of 25 health websites. They concluded that less than one-half more than minimally covered a topic and were completely accurate. The researchers found that, more than half the time, information in one part of a site contradicted information elsewhere on the same site and same topic. They also found wide variation in whether the site provided full source documentation. On average, only 65 percent of the site provided accurate documentation of the author and date of its sources.

virtually no restrictions on who can put material on the Internet or what appears on it, so many people who had difficulty publishing or disseminating materials can now do so with ease. Because of its openness, the Internet reinforces the norm of universalism.

4. The Internet is the provider of a very wide range of information sources, some in formats that are more dynamic and interesting. It can send and be a resource for more than straight black-and-white text, as in traditional academic journals and sources. It transmits information in the form of bright colors, graphics, "action" images, audio (e.g., music, voices, sounds), photos, and even video clips. Authors and other creators of information can be creative in their presentations.

The Downside.

1. There is no quality control over what gets on the Internet. Unlike standard academic publications, there is no peer-review process or any review. Anyone can put almost anything on a website. It may be poor quality, undocumented, highly biased, totally made up, or plain fraudulent. There is a lot of real "trash" out there! Once a person finds material, the real work is to distinguish the "trash" from valid information. One needs to treat a web page with the same caution that one applies to a paper flyer someone hands out on the street; it could contain the dri-

vel of a "nut" or be really valuable information. A less serious problem is that the "glitz" of bright colors, music, or moving images found in sites can distract unsophisticated users. The "glitz" may attract them more than serious content, and they may confuse glitz for high-caliber information. The Internet is better designed for a quick look and short attention spans rather than the slow, deliberative, careful reading and study of content (see Box 5.4).

2. Many excellent sources and some of the most important resource materials (research studies and data) for social research are *not* available on the Internet (e.g., *Sociofile,* GSS datafiles, and recent journal articles). Much information is available only through special subscription services that can be expensive. Contrary to popular belief, the Internet has *not* made all information free and accessible to everyone. Often, what is free is limited, and fuller information is available only to those who pay. In fact, because some libraries redirected funds to buy computers for the Internet and cut the purchases for books and paper copies of documents, the Internet's overall impact may have actually reduced what is available for some users.

3. Finding sources on the Internet can be very difficult and time consuming. It is not easy to locate specific source materials. Also, different "search engines" can produce very different results. It is wise to use multiple search engines because they work

differently. Most search engines simply look for specific words in a short description of the web page. This description may not reveal the full content of the source, just as a title does not fully tell what a book or article is about. In addition, search engines often come up with tens of thousands of sources, far too many for anyone to examine. The ones at the "top" may be there because they were recently added to the Internet or because their short description had several versions of the search word. The "best" or most relevant source might be buried as the 150th item found in a search. Also, one must often wade through a lot of commercials and advertisements to locate "real" information.

4. Internet sources can be "unstable" and difficult to document. After one conducts a search on the Internet and locates web pages with information, it is important to note the specific "address" (usually it starts http://) where it resides. This address refers to an electronic file sitting in a computer somewhere. If the computer file is moved, it may not be at the same address two weeks later. Unlike a journal article that will be stored on a shelf or on microfiche in hundreds of libraries for many decades to come and available for anyone to read, web pages can quickly vanish. This means it may not be possible to check someone's web references easily, verify a quote in a document, or go back to original materials and read them for ideas or to build on them. Also, it is easy to copy, modify, or distort, then reproduce copies of a source. For example, a person could alter a text passage or a photo image and then create a new web page to disseminate the false information. This raises issues about copyright protection and the authenticity of source material.

Understanding the Internet, its jargon and how to identify a worthwhile site takes time and practice. There are few rules for locating the best sites on the Internet—ones that have useful and truthful information. Sources that originate at universities, research institutes, or government agencies usually are more trustworthy for research purposes than ones that are individual home pages of unspecified origin or location, or that a commercial organization or a political/social issue advocacy group sponsors. In addition to moving or disappearing, many web pages or sources fail to provide complete information to make citation easy. Better sources provide fuller or more complete information about the author, date, location, and so on.

ETHICS IN SOCIAL RESEARCH

We now turn from reviewing the literature to a second major concern one needs to address before designing a study. Research has an ethical-moral dimension, although as you saw in Chapter 4, different approaches to science address each concern somewhat differently. All approaches recognize an ethical dimension to research. It is difficult to appreciate the ethical dilemmas that researchers face until one is doing research, but waiting until the middle of doing a study is too late. Researchers need to prepare themselves and consider ethical concerns as they design a study so that sound ethical practice is built in to the study design.

Codes of ethics and other researchers provide guidance, but ethical conduct ultimately depends on the individual researcher. The researcher has a moral and professional obligation to be ethical, even when research subjects are unaware of or unconcerned about ethics. Indeed, many subjects are less concerned about protecting their privacy and other rights than are researchers.[4]

The ethical issues are the concerns, dilemmas, and conflicts that arise over the proper way to conduct research. Ethics define what is or is not legitimate to do, or what "moral" research procedure involves. There are few ethical absolutes. Although there are few fixed rules, there are agreed-on principles. These principles may conflict in practice. Many ethical issues involve a balance between two values: the pursuit of scientific knowledge and the rights of those being studied or of others in society. Potential benefits—such as advancing the understanding of social life, improving decision making, or helping research participants—must be weighed against potential costs—such as a loss of dignity, self-esteem, privacy, or democratic freedoms.

The standards for ethical research are stricter than those in many other areas (e.g., collection agencies, police departments, advertisers, etc.). Professional social research requires both knowledge of proper research techniques (e.g., sampling) and sensitivity to ethical concerns in research. This is not easy.

The Individual Researcher

Ethics begin and end with you, the researcher. A researcher's personal moral code is the best defense against unethical behavior. Before, during, and after conducting a study, a researcher has opportunities to, and *should,* reflect on research actions and consult his or her conscience. Ethical research depends on the integrity of the individual researcher and his or her values. "If values are to be taken seriously, they cannot be expressed and laid aside but must instead be guides to actions for the sociologist. They determine who will be investigated, for what purpose and in whose service" (Sagarin, 1973:63).

Why Be Ethical?

Given that most people who conduct social research are genuinely concerned about others, why would a researcher act in an ethically irresponsible manner? Outside of the rare disturbed individual, most unethical behavior results from a lack of awareness and pressures on researchers to take ethical shortcuts. Researchers face pressures to build a career, publish, advance knowledge, gain prestige, impress family and friends, hold on to a job, and so forth. Ethical research takes longer to complete, costs more money, is more complicated, and is more likely to be terminated before completion. Moreover, written ethical standards are in the form of vague principles. There are many places where it is possible to act unethically, and the odds of getting caught are small.

There are few rewards available for ethical research. The unethical researcher, if caught, faces

---

Scientific misconduct When someone engages in research fraud, plagiarism, or other unethical conduct that significantly deviates from the accepted practices for conducting and reporting research established by the scientific community.

Research fraud A type of unethical behavior in which a researcher fakes or creates false data, or falsely reports on the research procedure.

---

public humiliation, a ruined career, and possible legal action, but the ethical researcher wins no praise. Ethical behavior arises from a sensitivity to ethical concerns that researchers internalize during their professional training, from a professional role, and from personal contact with other researchers. Moreover, the norms of the scientific community reinforce ethical behavior with an emphasis on honesty and openness. Researchers who are oriented toward their professional role, who are committed to the scientific ethos, and who interact regularly with other researchers are likely to act ethically.

Scientific Misconduct. The research community and agencies that fund research oppose unethical behavior called scientific misconduct, which includes research fraud and plagiarism. **Scientific misconduct** occurs when a researcher falsifies or distorts the data or the methods of data collection, or plagiarizes the work of others. It also includes significant departures from the generally accepted practices of the scientific community for doing or reporting on research. Research institutes and universities have policies and procedures to detect misconduct, report it to the scientific community and funding agencies, and penalize researchers who engage in it (e.g., through a pay cut or loss of job).[5]

Research fraud occurs when a researcher fakes or invents data that were not really collected, or falsely reports how research was conducted. Though rare, it is treated very seriously. The most famous case of fraud was that of Sir Cyril Burt, the father of British educational psychology. Burt died in 1971 as an esteemed researcher who was famous for his studies with twins that showed a genetic basis of intelligence. In 1976, it was discovered that he had falsified data and the names of coauthors. Unfortunately, the scientific community had been misled for nearly 30 years.

Plagiarism is fraud that occurs when a researcher steals the ideas or writings of another or uses them without citing the source. A special type of plagiarism is stealing the work of another researcher, an assistant, or a student, and misrepresenting it as one's own. These are serious breaches of ethical standards.[6] Plagiarism is discussed further in Chapter 16.

Unethical but Legal. Behavior may be unethical but not break the law. The distinction between legal and ethical behavior is illustrated in a plagiarism case. The American Sociological Association documented that a 1988 book without footnotes by a dean from Eastern New Mexico University contained large sections of a 1978 dissertation written by a sociology professor at Tufts University. The copying was not *illegal;* it did not violate copyright law because the sociologist's dissertation did not have a copyright filed with the U.S. government. Nevertheless, it was clearly *unethical* according to standards of professional behavior.[7] (See Figure 5.3 for relations between legal and moral actions.)

	ETHICAL	
LEGAL	*Yes*	*No*
Yes	Moral and Legal	Legal but Immoral
No	Illegal but Moral	Immoral and Illegal

FIGURE 5.3   Typology of Legal and Moral Actions in Social Research

Power

The relationship between the researcher and subjects or employee-assistants involves power and trust. The experimenter, survey director, or research investigator has power relative to subjects or assistants. The power is legitimated by credentials, expertise, training, and the role of science in modern society. Some ethical issues involve an abuse of power and trust.

The researcher's authority to conduct research, granted by professional communities and the larger society, is accompanied by a responsibility to guide, protect, and oversee the interests of the people being studied. For example, a physician was discovered to have conducted experimental gynecological surgery on 33 women without their permission. The women had trusted the doctor, but he had abused the trust that the women, the professional community, and society placed in him.[8]

The researcher seeking ethical guidance is not alone. He or she can turn to a number of resources: professional colleagues, ethical advisory committees, institutional review boards or human subjects committees at a college or institution, codes of ethics from professional associations, and writings on ethics in research.

Ethical Issues Involving Research Participants

Have you ever been a participant in a research study? If so, how were you treated? More attention is fo-cused on the possible negative effects of research on those being studied than any other ethical issue, beginning with concerns about biomedical research. Ethical research requires balancing the value of advancing knowledge against the value of noninterference in the lives of others. Giving research subjects absolute rights of noninterference could make empirical research impossible, but giving researchers absolute rights of inquiry could nullify participants' basic human rights. The moral question becomes: When, if ever, are researchers justified in risking physical harm or injury to those being studied, causing them great embarrassment, or frightening them?

The law and codes of ethics recognize some clear prohibitions: Never cause unnecessary or irreversible harm to subjects; secure prior voluntary consent when possible; and never unnecessarily humiliate, degrade, or release harmful information about specific individuals that was collected for research purposes. These are minimal standards and are subject to interpretation (e.g., what does *unnecessary* mean in a specific situation?).

Origins of Research Participant Protection.
Concern over the treatment of research participants arose after the revelation of gross violations of basic human rights in the name of science. The most notorious violations were "medical experiments" conducted on Jews and others in Nazi Germany. In these experiments, terrible tortures were committed. For example, people were placed in freezing water to see how long it took them to die, people were purposely starved to death, and limbs were severed from children and transplanted onto others.[9]

Such human rights violations do not occur only in Germany, nor did they happen only long ago. A symbol of unethical research is the Tuskegee Syphilis Study, also known as *Bad Blood.* Until the 1970s, when a newspaper report caused a scandal to erupt, the U.S. Public Health Service sponsored a study in which poor, uneducated African American men in Alabama suffered and died of untreated syphilis, while researchers studied the severe physical disabilities that appear in advanced stages of the disease. The study began in 1929, before penicillin was available to treat the disease, but it continued long after treatment was available. Despite their unethical treatment of the subjects, the researchers were able to publish their results for 40 years. The study ended in 1972, but the president of the United States did not admit wrongdoing and formally apologize to the participant-victims until 1997.[10]

Unfortunately, the Bad Blood scandal is not unique. During the Cold War era, the U.S. government periodically compromised ethical research principles for military and political goals. In 1995, reports revealed that the government authorized injecting unknowing people with radioactive material in the late 1940s. In the 1950s, the government warned Eastman Kodak and other film manufacturers about nuclear fallout from atomic tests to prevent fogged film, but it did not warn nearby citizens of health hazards. In the 1960s, the U.S. army gave unsuspecting soldiers LSD (a hallucinogenic drug), causing serious trauma. Today, these are widely recognized to be violations of two fundamental ethical principles: avoid physical harm and get informed consent.[11]

Physical Harm, Psychological Abuse, and Legal Jeopardy.

Social research can harm a research participant in several ways: physical harm, psychological harm, legal harm, and harm to a person's career or income. Physical harm is rare, even in biomedical research, in which the intervention is much greater; 3 to 5 percent of studies involved any person who suffered any harm. Different types of harm are more likely in different types of research (e.g., in experiments versus field research). Researchers need to be aware of all types of harm and minimize them at all times.[12]

Physical Harm.

A straightforward ethical principle is that researchers should not cause physical harm. An ethical researcher anticipates risks before beginning research, including basic safety concerns (safe buildings, furniture, and equipment). He or she screens out high-risk subjects (those with heart conditions, mental breakdown, or seizures) if stress is involved and anticipates the danger of injury or physical attacks on research participants or assistants. The researcher accepts moral and legal responsibility for injury due to participation in research and terminates a project immediately if he or she can no longer guarantee the physical safety of the people involved (see the Zimbardo study in Box 5.5).

Psychological Abuse, Stress, or Loss of Self-Esteem.

The risk of physical harm is rare, but researchers may place people in stressful, embarrassing, anxiety-producing, or unpleasant situations. Researchers learn about how people respond in real-life, highly anxiety-producing situations by placing subjects in realistic situations of psychological discomfort or stress. Is it unethical to cause discomfort? The ethics of the famous Milgram obedience study are still debated (see Box 5.5). Some say that the precautions taken and the knowledge gained outweighed the stress and potential psychological harm that subjects experienced. Others believe that the extreme stress and the risk of permanent harm were too great.

Social researchers have created high levels of anxiety or discomfort: exposing participants to gruesome photos; falsely telling male students that they have strongly feminine personality traits; falsely telling students that they have failed; creating a situation of high fear (e.g., smoke entering a room in which the door is locked); asking participants to harm others; placing people in a situation in which they face social pressure to deny their convictions; and having participants lie, cheat, or steal.[13] Researchers who study helping behavior often place participants in emergency situations to see whether they will lend assistance. For example, Piliavin and associates (1969) studied helping behavior in subways by faking someone's collapse onto the floor. In the field experiment, the riders in the subway car were unaware of the experiment and did not volunteer to participate in it.

A sensitive researcher is also aware of harm to a person's self-esteem. For example, Walster (1965)

BOX **5.5**   **Three Cases of Ethical Controversy**

Stanley Milgram's *obedience study* (Milgram, 1963, 1965, 1974) attempted to discover how the horrors of the Holocaust under the Nazis could have occurred by examining the strength of social pressure to obey authority. After signing "informed consent forms," subjects were assigned, in rigged random selection, to be a "teacher" while a confederate was the "pupil." The teacher was to test the pupil's memory of word lists and increase the electric shock level if the pupil made mistakes. The pupil was located in a nearby room, so the teacher could hear but not see the pupil. The shock apparatus was clearly labeled with increasing voltage. As the pupil made mistakes and the teacher turned switches, she or he also made noises as if in severe pain. The researcher was present and made comments such as "You must go on" to the teacher. Milgram reported, "Subjects were observed to sweat, tremble, stutter, bite their lips, groan and dig their fingernails into their flesh. These were characteristic rather than exceptional responses to the experiment" (Milgram, 1963:375). The percentage of subjects who would shock to dangerous levels was dramatically higher than expected. Ethical concerns arose over the use of deception and the extreme emotional stress experienced by subjects.

In Laud Humphreys's (Humphreys, 1975) *tearoom trade study* (a study of male homosexual encounters in public restrooms), about 100 men were observed engaging in sexual acts as Humphreys pretended to be a "watchqueen" (a voyeur and lookout). Subjects were followed to their cars, and their license numbers were secretly recorded. Names and addresses were obtained from police registers when Humphreys posed as a market researcher. One year later, in disguise, Humphreys used a deceptive story about a health survey to interview the subjects in their homes. Humphreys was careful to keep names in safety deposit boxes, and identifiers with subject names were burned. He significantly advanced knowledge of homosexuals who frequent "tearooms" and overturned previous false beliefs about them. There has been controversy over the study: The subjects never consented; deception was used; and the names could have been used to blackmail subjects, to end marriages, or to initiate criminal prosecution.

In the *Zimbardo prison experiment* (Zimbardo, 1972, 1973; Zimbardo et al., 1973, 1974), male students were divided into two role-playing groups: guards and prisoners. Before the experiment, volunteer students were given personality tests, and only those in the "normal" range were chosen. Volunteers signed up for two weeks, and prisoners were told that they would be under surveillance and would have some civil rights suspended, but that no physical abuse was allowed. In a simulated prison in the basement of a Stanford University building, prisoners were deindividualized (dressed in standard uniforms and called only by their numbers) and guards were militarized (with uniforms, nightsticks, and reflective sunglasses). Guards were told to maintain a reasonable degree of order and served 8-hour shifts, while prisoners were locked up 24 hours per day. Unexpectedly, the volunteers became too caught up in their roles. Prisoners became passive and disorganized, while guards became aggressive, arbitrary, and dehumanizing. By the sixth day, Zimbardo called off the experiment for ethical reasons. The risk of permanent psychological harm, and even physical harm, was too great.

---

wanted to see whether changes in feelings of female self-worth affect romantic liking. In her experiment, undergraduate women were given personality tests followed by phony feedback. Some were told that they lacked imagination and creativity. Next, a handsome male graduate student who pretended to be another research participant struck up a conversation with the women. The student acted very interested in one woman and asked her out for a dinner date. The researcher wanted to measure the woman's romantic attraction to the male. After the experiment, the woman was told of the hoax; there was no date and the man was not interested in her. Although the participants were debriefed, they suffered a loss of self-esteem and possible psychological harm.[14]

Only experienced researchers who take precautions before inducing anxiety or discomfort should consider conducting experiments that induce significant stress or anxiety. They should consult with others who have conducted similar studies and mental health professionals when planning the study, screen out high-risk populations (e.g., those with emotional problems or a weak heart), and arrange for emergency interventions or termination of the research if dangerous situations arise. Researchers should always get informed consent (to be discussed) before the research and debrief subjects immediately afterward.

Researchers should never create *unnecessary* stress, beyond the minimal amount needed to create the desired effect, or stress that has no direct, legitimate research purpose. Knowing the minimal amount comes with experience. It is better to begin with too little stress, risking finding no effect, than to create too much. If the level of stress could have long-term effects, the researcher should follow up and offer free psychological counseling.

Research that creates stress and anxiety also carries the danger that experimenters will develop a callous or manipulative attitude toward others. Researchers report guilt and regrets after conducting experiments that caused psychological harm to subjects. Experiments that place subjects in anxiety-producing situations may produce discomfort for the ethical researcher.

Legal Harm. A researcher is responsible for protecting research participants from increased risk of arrest. If participation in research increases the risk of arrest, individuals will distrust researchers and be unwilling to participate in future research. Researchers may be able to secure clearance from law enforcement authorities before conducting certain types of research. For example, the U.S. Department of Justice provides written waivers for researchers studying criminal behavior.

Potential legal harm is one criticism of the 1975 "tearoom trade" study by Humphreys (see Box 5.5). In the New Jersey Negative Income Tax Experiment, those participating in the experiment received income supplements, but no explicit provision was made for monitoring whether they also received welfare checks. A local prosecuting attorney requested data on participants to identify "welfare cheats." In other words, subjects were at legal risk

because they had participated in the experiment. Eventually, the conflict was resolved, but it illustrates that researchers should be aware of potential legal problems.

A related ethical issue arises when a researcher learns of illegal activity when collecting data. A researcher must weigh the value of protecting the researcher–subject relationship and the benefits to future researchers against potential harm to innocent people. A researcher bears the cost of his or her judgment. For example, in his field research on police, Van Maanen (1982:114–115) reported seeing police beat people and witnessing illegal acts and irregular procedures, but said, "On and following these troublesome incidents . . . I followed police custom: I kept my mouth shut."

Field researchers often face difficult ethical decisions. For example, when studying a mental institution, Taylor (1987) discovered the mistreatment and abuse of inmates by the staff. He had two choices: Abandon the study and call for an investigation, or keep quiet and continue with the study for several months, publicize the findings afterward, and then advocate an end to abuse. After weighing the situation, he followed the latter course and is now an activist for the rights of mental institution inmates.

A similar ethical dilemma is illustrated by the case of a New York restaurant fire that was complicated by the issue of confidentiality. A sociology graduate student was conducting a participant observation study of waiters. During the research project, the field site, a restaurant, burned down, and arson was suspected. Local legal authorities requested the field notes and wanted to interrogate the researcher about activity in the restaurant. The researcher faced a dilemma: He could cooperate with the investigation and violate the trust, confidentiality, and integrity of ethical research, or he could uphold confidentiality and protect his subjects but face contempt of court and obstruction of justice penalties, including fines and jail. He wanted to behave ethically but he also wanted to stay out of jail. After years of legal battles, the situation was resolved with limited cooperation by the researcher and a judicial ruling upholding the confidentiality of field notes.

Nevertheless, the issue took years to resolve, and the researcher bore substantial financial and personal costs.[15]

Observing illegal behavior may be central to a research project. A researcher who covertly observes and records illegal behavior and then supplies information to law enforcement authorities, violates ethical standards regarding research participants and undermines future research. Yet, a researcher who fails to report illegal behavior indirectly permits criminal behavior and could be charged as an accessory to a crime. Is the researcher a professional seeking knowledge or a freelance undercover informant?

Other Harm to Participants. Research participants may face other types of harm. For example, a survey interview may create anxiety and discomfort among people who are asked to recall unpleasant events. The ethical researcher is sensitive to any harm to participants, considers possible precautions, and weighs potential harm against potential benefits. Another risk of harm to subjects is that of a negative effect on their careers or incomes. For example, a researcher conducts a survey of employees and concludes that the supervisor's performance is poor. As a consequence, the supervisor loses her job. Or a researcher studies welfare recipients. As a consequence, the recipients lose their health insurance and their quality of life declines. What is the researcher's responsibility? The ethical researcher considers the consequences of research for those being studied. But there is no fixed answer to such questions. A researcher must evaluate each case, weigh potential harm against potential benefits, and bear the responsibility for the decision.

Deception. Has anyone ever told you a half-truth or lie to get you to do something? How did you feel about it? Social researchers follow the ethical **principle of voluntary consent:** Never force anyone to participate in research, and do not lie unless it is required for legitimate research reasons. The people who participate in social research should explicitly agree to participate. The right of a person not to participate becomes a critical issue whenever the researcher uses deception, disguises the research, or uses covert research methods.[16]

Social researchers sometimes deceive or lie to participants in field and experimental research. A researcher might misrepresent his or her actions or true intentions for legitimate methodological reasons: If participants knew the true purpose, they would modify their behavior, making it impossible to learn of their real behavior, or access to a research site might be impossible if he or she told the truth. Deception is never preferable if the researcher could accomplish the same thing without deception. Experimental researchers often deceive subjects to prevent them from learning the true hypothesis and to reduce reactive effects.

Deception is acceptable only if there is a specific methodological purpose for it, and even then, it should be used only to the minimal degree necessary. A researcher who uses deception should obtain informed consent, never misrepresent risks, and always debrief the participants afterward. He or she can describe the basic procedures involved and conceal only specific information about hypotheses being tested.

Informed Consent. A fundamental ethical principle of social research is: Never coerce anyone into participating; participation *must* be voluntary. It is not enough to get permission from people; they need to know what they are being asked to participate in so that they can make an informed decision. Participants can become aware of their rights and what they are getting involved in when they read and sign a statement giving **informed consent,** a written agreement to participate given by people after they learn something about the research procedure.

Principle of voluntary consent   An ethical principle that people should never participate in research unless they explicitly and freely agree to participate.

Informed consent   A statement, usually written, that explains aspects of a study to participants and asks for their voluntary agreement to participate before the study begins.

BOX **5.6** **Informed Consent**

Informed consent statements contain the following:

1. A brief description of the purpose and procedure of the research, including the expected duration of the study
2. A statement of any risks or discomfort associated with participation
3. A guarantee of anonymity and the confidentiality of records
4. The identification of the researcher and of where to receive information about subjects' rights or questions about the study
5. A statement that participation is completely voluntary and can be terminated at any time without penalty
6. A statement of alternative procedures that may be used
7. A statement of any benefits or compensation provided to subjects and the number of subjects involved
8. An offer to provide a summary of findings

The U.S. federal government does not require informed consent in all research involving human subjects. Nevertheless, researchers should get written consent unless there are good reasons for not obtaining it (e.g., covert field research, use of secondary data, etc.) as judged by an institutional review board (IRB) (see the later discussion of IRBs).

Informed consent statements provide specific information (see Box 5.6).[17] A general statement about the kinds of procedures or questions involved and the uses of the data are sufficient for informed consent. In a study by Singer (1978), one random group of survey respondents received a detailed informed consent statement and another did not. No significant differences were discovered. If anything, people who refused to sign such a statement were more likely to guess or answer "no response" to questions.

In their analysis of the literature, Singer and colleagues (1995) found that assuring confidentiality modestly improved responses when researchers asked about highly sensitive topics. In other situa-

tions, extensive assurances of confidentiality failed to affect how or whether subjects responded.

Signed informed consent statements are optional for most survey, field, and secondary data research, but are often mandated for experimental research. They are impossible to obtain in documentary research and in most telephone interview studies. The general rule is: The greater the risk of potential harm to subjects, the greater the need for a written consent statement. In sum, there are many reasons to get informed consent and few reasons not to get it.

Covert Observation. Obtaining informed consent may be easy in survey and experimental research, but some field researchers feel it is inappropriate when observing real-life field settings, and say they could not gain entry or conduct a study unless it were covert. In the past, field researchers used covert observation, such as feigning alcoholism to present a false cover story to join a group seeking treatment so it could be studied. Field researchers have three choices blurring the line between informed consent and a not fully informed acquiescence. Borrowing from the language of espionage, Fine (1980) distinguished deep cover (the researcher tells nothing of the research role but acts as a full participant), shallow cover (the researcher reveals that research is taking place but is vague about details), and explicit cover (the researcher fully reveals his or her purpose and asks permission).

Two arguments are made in favor of covert observation and exempting field research from informed consent (Herrera, 1999). The first is that informed consent is impractical and disruptive in field research, and may even create some harm by disturbing the participants or the setting by upsetting the ongoing flow of activities. The problem with this reasoning is the moral principle that ensuring participant dignity outweighs practical expediency for researchers. This reasoning is self-serving; it puts a higher value on doing research than on upholding honesty or privacy, and it assumes that researchers are better at judging the risk of being in study than are the participants. The moral-ethical standard is that researchers need to respect the freedom/autonomy of all the people they study and let them make their own decisions. Participants may not remain naïve and may be offended once they learn of an unauthorized invasion of their "privacy" for research purposes.

A second argument favoring covert observations is that human communication and daily affairs are already filled with covert activity. Ordinary activities involve some amount of covert activity with many "people watchers" or harmless eavesdroppers. Covert and deceptive behaviors are pervasive in daily life by many retail sales outlets, law enforcement, or security personnel and people almost expect it. It is expected and harmless, so why must social researchers act differently? Opposing this reason for exemption is that "everyone else is doing it" and "it would happen anyway" are not valid justifications on which to base a morally sound professional research role. The issue here is setting moral-ethical standards for the professional researcher. Perhaps voyeurism, surveillance, and the use of undercover informants are increasing in some societies. Are they models for building greater respect and trust for the higher goals of social research? More likely they lead to public cynicism, distrust, and noncooperation in research. An absence of informed consent is an ethical gray area, and many feel that the moral-ethical risk of not getting informed consent is likely to cause greater harm.

Covert research remains controversial, and many researchers feel that all covert research is unethical.[18] The code of ethics of the American Anthropological Association condemns it as "impractical and undesirable." Even those who accept covert research as ethical in some situations argue that it should be used only when overt observation is impossible. In addition, the researcher should inform participants afterward and give them an opportunity to express concerns.

Deception and covert research may increase mistrust and cynicism, and diminish public respect for social research. Misrepresentation in field research is analogous to being an undercover agent or informer in nondemocratic societies. Deception can increase distrust by people who are frequently studied. In one case, the frequent use of deception reduced helping behavior. When a student was shot at the University of Washington in Seattle in 1973,

students crossing the campus made no attempt to assist. Later, it was discovered that many of the bystanders did not help because they thought that the shooting was staged as part of an experiment.[19]

Special Populations and New Inequalities
Special Populations and Coercion. Some populations or groups of research participants are not capable of giving true voluntary informed consent. **Special populations** may lack the necessary competency or may be indirectly coerced. Students, prison inmates, employees, military personnel, the homeless, welfare recipients, children, or the mentally disabled may agree to participate in research. Yet, they may not be fully capable of making a decision, or may agree to participate only because some desired good—such as higher grades, early parole, promotions, or additional services—requires an agreement to participate.

It is unethical to involve "incompetent" people (e.g., children, mentally disabled, etc.) in research unless two conditions are met: A legal guardian grants written permission, and the researcher follows all ethical principles against harm to participants. For example, a researcher wants to conduct a survey of smoking and drug/alcohol use among high school students. If it is conducted on school property, school officials must give permission, and written parental permission is needed for any subject who is a legal minor. It is best to ask permission from each student, as well.

It is unethical to coerce people to participate, including offering them special benefits that they cannot otherwise attain. For example, it is unethical for a commanding officer to order a soldier to participate in a study, for a professor to require a student to be a research subject in order to pass a course, or for an employer to expect an employee to complete a survey as a condition of continued employment. It is unethical even if someone other than

> **Special population**   Research participants who, because of age, incarceration, potential coercion, or less than full physical, mental, emotional, or other capabilities, may lack complete freedom or awareness to grant voluntary consent to participate in a study.

the researcher (e.g., an employer) coerced people (e.g., employees) to participate in research.

Whether coercion to participate is involved can be a complex issue, and a researcher must evaluate each case. For example, a convicted criminal is given the alternative of imprisonment or participation in an experimental rehabilitation program. The convicted criminal may not believe in the benefits of the program, but the researcher may believe that it will help the criminal. This is a case of coercion, but the researcher must judge whether the benefits to the subject and to society outweigh the ethical prohibition on coercion.

Teachers sometimes require students in social science courses to participate as subjects in research projects. This is a special case of coercion. Three arguments have been made in favor of requiring participation: (1) It would be difficult and prohibitively expensive to get participants otherwise; (2) the knowledge created from research with students serving as subjects will benefit future students and society; (3) students will learn more about research by experiencing it directly in a realistic research setting. Of the three arguments, only the third justifies limited coercion. Limited coercion is acceptable only as long as it has a clear educational objective, the students are given a choice of research experience, and all other ethical principles are upheld.[20]

Creating New Inequalities. Another type of harm occurs when one group of people is denied a service or benefit as a result of participation in a research project. For example, a researcher might have a new treatment for subjects with a terrible disease, such as acquired immune deficiency syndrome (AIDS). In order to determine the effects of the new treatment, some individuals receive it while others are given a placebo. The design will show whether the drug is effective, but subjects in the control group who receive the placebo may die. Of course, those receiving the drug may also die, until more is known about whether it is effective. Is it eth-

ical to deny people who have been randomly assigned to the control group the potentially lifesaving treatment? What if a clear, definitive test of whether the drug is effective requires a control group that receives a placebo?

A researcher can reduce new inequality among research participants in three ways. First, subjects who do not receive the "new, improved" treatment continue to receive the best previously acceptable treatment. In other words, the control group is not denied all assistance, but they receive the best treatment available prior to the new one being tested. This ensures that people in the control group will not suffer in absolute terms, even if they temporarily fall behind in relative terms. Second, researchers can use **crossover designs,** whereby the control group for the first phase of the experiment becomes the experimental group in the second phase, and vice versa. Finally, the researcher carefully and continuously monitors results. If it appears early in the experiment that the new treatment is highly effective, the new treatment should be offered to those in the control group. Also, in high-risk experiments with medical treatments or possible physical harm, researchers may use animal or other surrogates for humans.

Privacy, Anonymity, and Confidentiality.
How would you feel if private details about your personal life were shared with the public without your knowledge? Because social researchers transgress the privacy of subjects in order to study social behavior, they must take precautions to protect subjects' privacy.

Privacy. Survey researchers invade a person's privacy when they probe into beliefs, backgrounds, and behaviors in a way that reveals intimate private details. Experimental researchers sometimes use two-way mirrors or hidden microphones to "spy" on subjects. Even if people are told they are being studied, they are unaware of what the experimenter is looking for. Field researchers may observe very private aspects of another's behavior or eavesdrop on conversations. In field experimentation and ethnographic field research, privacy may be violated without advance warning. When Humphreys (1975)

Crossover design A type of experimental design in which all groups receive the treatment so that discomfort or benefits are shared and inequality is not created.

served as a "watchqueen" in a public restroom where homosexual contacts took place, he observed very private behavior without informing subjects. When Piliavin and colleagues (1969) had people collapse on subways to study helping behavior, those in the subway car had the privacy of their ride violated. People have been studied in public places (e.g., in waiting rooms, walking down the street, in classrooms, etc.), but some "public" places are more private than others (consider, for example, the use of periscopes to observe people who thought they were alone in a public toilet stall).[21]

The ethical researcher violates privacy only to the minimum degree necessary and only for legitimate research purposes. In addition, he or she protects the information on research participants from public disclosure.

In a few situations, privacy is protected by law. One case of the invasion of privacy led to the passage of a federal law. In the *Wichita Jury Study* of 1954, University of Chicago Law School researchers recorded jury discussions to examine group processes in jury deliberations. Although the findings were significant and great precautions were taken, a congressional investigation followed and a law was passed in 1956 to prohibit the "bugging" of any grand or petit jury for any purpose, even with the jurors' consent.[22]

Anonymity. Researchers protect privacy by not disclosing a participant's identity after information is gathered. This takes two forms: anonymity and confidentiality.

Anonymity means that people remain anonymous, or nameless. For example, a field researcher provides a social picture of a particular individual, but gives a fictitious name and location, and alters some characteristics. The subject's identity is protected, and the individual is unknown or anonymous. Survey and experimental researchers discard the names or addresses of subjects as soon as possible and refer to participants by a code number only, to protect anonymity. If a researcher using a mail survey includes a code on the questionnaire to determine which respondents failed to respond, the respondent's anonymity is not being fully protected. In panel studies, where the same individuals are

traced over time, anonymity is not possible. Likewise, historical researchers use specific names in historical or documentary research. They may do so if the original information was from public sources; if the sources were not publicly available, a researcher must obtain written permission from the owner of the documents to use specific names.

It is difficult to protect research participant anonymity. In one study about a fictitious town, "Springdale," in *Small Town in Mass Society* (Vidich and Bensman, 1968), it was easy to identify the town and specific individuals in it. Town residents became upset about how the researchers portrayed them and staged a parade mocking the researchers. As in the famous Middletown study of Muncie, Indiana, people often recognize the towns studied in community research. Yet, if a researcher protects the identities of individuals with fictitious information, the gap between what was studied and what is reported to others raises questions about what was found and what was made up.

Confidentiality. Even if anonymity is not possible, researchers should protect confidentiality. Anonymity protects the identity of specific individuals from being known. **Confidentiality** means that information may have names attached to it, but the researcher holds it in confidence or keeps it secret from the public. The information is not released in a way that permits linking specific individuals to responses and is publicly presented only in an aggregate form (e.g., percentages, means, etc.).

A researcher may provide anonymity without confidentiality, or vice versa, although they usually go together. Anonymity without confidentiality means that all the details about a specific individual

---

Anonymity The ethical protection that participants remain nameless; their identity is protected from disclosure and remains unknown.

Confidentiality The ethical protection for those who are studied by holding research data in confidence or keeping them secret from the public; not releasing information in a way that permits linking specific individuals to specific responses. Researchers do this by presenting data only in an aggregate form (e.g., percentages, means, etc.).

are made public, but the individual's name is withheld. Confidentiality without anonymity means that information is not made public, but a researcher privately links individual names to specific responses.

Attempts to protect the identity of subjects from public disclosure has resulted in elaborate procedures: eliciting anonymous responses, using a third-party list custodian who holds the key to coded lists, or using the random-response technique (discussed in Chapter 10). Past abuses suggest that such measures may be necessary. For example, Diener and Crandall (1978:70) reported that during the 1950s, the U.S. State Department and the FBI requested research records on individuals who had been involved in the famous Kinsey sex study. The Kinsey Sex Institute refused to comply with the government. The institute threatened to destroy all records rather than release any. Eventually, the government agencies backed down. The moral duty and ethical code of the researchers obligated them to destroy the records to protect confidentiality.

Confidentiality may protect participants from physical harm. For example, I met a researcher who studied the inner workings of the secret police in a nondemocratic society. Had he released the names of informants, they would have faced certain death or imprisonment. To protect the subjects, he wrote all notes in code and kept all records secretly locked away. Although he resided in the United States, he was physically threatened by the foreign government and discovered attempts to burglarize his office. In other situations, other principles may take precedence over protecting confidentiality. For example, when studying patients in a mental hospital, a researcher discovers that a patient is preparing to kill an attendant. The researcher must weigh the benefit of confidentiality against the potential harm to the attendant.

Social researchers can pay high personal costs for being ethical. Although he was never accused or convicted of breaking any law and he closely followed the ethical principles outlined by the American Sociological Association, Rik Scarce, a doctoral sociology student at Washington State University, spent 16 weeks in a Spokane jail for contempt of court. He was jailed because he refused to testify before a grand jury and break the confidentiality of

social research data. Scarce had been studying radical animal liberation groups and already published one book on the subject. He had interviewed a research participant who was suspected of leading a group that broke into animal facilities and caused $150,000 damage. Two judges refused to acknowledge the confidentiality of social research data.[23]

Participants' Information as Private Property. If you freely give information about yourself for research purposes, do you lose all rights to it? Can it be used against you? People who participate in research have knowledge about them taken away and analyzed by others. The information can then be used for a number of purposes, including actions against the subjects' interests.

Information about people is collected, bought, sold, analyzed, and exchanged by large organizations. Information about buying habits, personal taste, spending patterns, credit ratings, voting patterns, and the like is used by many private and public organizations. Information is a form of private property. Like other "intellectual" property (copyrights, software, patents, etc.) and unlike most physical property, information continues to have value after it is exchanged.

Most people give a researcher their time and information for little or no compensation. Yet, concerns about privacy and the collection of information make it reasonable to see personal information as private property. If it is private property, a person's right to keep, sell, or give it away becomes clear. The ethical issue is strongest where the information could be used against subjects or used in ways they would disapprove of if they were fully informed.

For example, a group of committed nonsmokers is studied to learn about their habits and psychological profiles. A market research firm obtains the information and is hired by a tobacco company to design a campaign to promote smoking among nonsmokers. Had the nonsmokers been informed about the use of their responses, they might have chosen not to participate. A researcher can increase fairness by giving subjects a copy of the findings and describing the sponsor and the uses to which the information will be put in an informed consent statement.

The issue of who controls data on research participants is relevant to the approaches to social science outlined in Chapter 4. Positivism implies the collection and use of information by experts separate from research participants and the ordinary citizen. The two alternatives to positivism, each in its own way, argue for the involvement and participation of those who are studied in the research process and in the use of research data and findings.[24]

Mandated Protections of Research Participants. The U.S. federal government and governments of other nations have regulations and laws to protect research participants and their rights. In the United States the legal restraint is found in rules and regulations issued by the U.S. Department of Health and Human Services Office for the Protection from Research Risks. Although this is only one federal agency, most researchers and other government agencies look to it for guidance. Current U.S. government regulations evolved from Public Health Service policies adopted in 1966 and expanded in 1971. The National Research Act (1974) established the National Commission for the Protection of Human Subjects in Biomedical and Behavioral Research, which significantly expanded regulations, and required informed consent in most social research. The responsibility for safeguarding ethical standards was assigned to research institutes and universities. The Department of Health and Human Services issued regulations in 1981, which are still in force. Regulations on scientific misconduct and protection of data confidentiality were expanded in 1989.

Federal regulations follow a biomedical model and protect subjects from physical harm. Other rules require **institutional review boards (IRBs)** at all research institutes, colleges, and universities to review all use of human subjects. The IRB is staffed by researchers and community members. Similar committees oversee the use of animals in research. The board also oversees, monitors, and reviews the impact of all research procedures on human participants and applies ethical guidelines. The board also reviews research procedures at the preliminary stage when first proposed. Educational tests, "normal educational practice," most surveys, most observation of public behavior, and studies of existing data in which individuals cannot be identified are exempt from the IRB.[25]

Ethics and the Scientific Community

Physicians, attorneys, counselors, and other professionals have a **code of ethics** and peer review boards or licensing regulations. The codes formalize professional standards and provide guidance when questions arise in practice.[26] Social researchers do not provide a service for a fee, receive limited ethical training, and are rarely licensed. They incorporate ethical concerns into research because it is morally and socially responsible, and to protect social research from charges of insensitivity or abusing people.

Professional social science associations around the world have codes of ethics. The codes state proper and improper behavior and represent a consensus of professionals on ethics. All researchers may not agree on all ethical issues, and ethical rules are subject to interpretation, but researchers are expected to uphold ethical standards as part of their membership in a professional community.

Codes of research ethics can be traced to the **Nuremberg code,** which was adopted during the Nuremberg Military Tribunal on Nazi war crimes held by the Allied Powers immediately after World War II. The code, developed as a response to the cruelty of concentration camp experiments, outlines ethical principles and rights of human subjects.

Institutional review board (IRB)   A committee at U.S. colleges, hospitals, and research institutes required by federal law to ensure that research involving humans is conducted in a responsible, ethical manner. It examines study details before the research begins.

Code of ethics   Principles and guidelines developed by professional organizations to guide research practice and clarify the line between ethical and unethical behavior.

Nuremberg code   An international code of moral, ethical behavior that was the beginning of codes of ethics for human research. It was adopted after the war crime trials of World War II in response to inhumane Nazi medical experiments.

BOX **5.7** **Basic Principles of Ethical Social Research**

▣ Ethical responsibility rests with the individual researcher.
▣ Do not exploit subjects or students for personal gain.
▣ Some form of informed consent is highly recommended or required.
▣ Honor all guarantees of privacy, confidentiality, and anonymity.
▣ Do not coerce or humiliate subjects.
▣ Use deception only if needed, and always accompany it with debriefing.
▣ Use a research method that is appropriate to the topic.
▣ Detect and remove undesirable consequences to research subjects.
▣ Anticipate repercussions of the research or publication of results.
▣ Identify the sponsor who funded the research.
▣ Cooperate with host nations when doing comparative research.
▣ Release the details of the study design with the results.
▣ Make interpretations of results consistent with the data.
▣ Use high methodological standards and strive for accuracy.
▣ Do not conduct secret research.

The principles in the Nuremberg code dealt with the treatment of human subjects and focused on medical experimentation, but they became the basis for the ethical codes in social research. Similar codes of human rights, such as the 1948 Universal Declaration of Human Rights by the United Nations and the 1964 Declaration of Helsinki, also have implications for social researchers.[27] Box 5.7 lists some of the basic principles of ethical social research.

Whistle-blower A person who recognizes unethical or illegal practices in an organization and voices opposition to them. He or she attempts to stop the practices through organizational channels but is not successful and may be punished for the attempt. He or she continues to voice opposition to the unethical or illegal practices beyond the organization.

Professional social science associations (e.g., the American Psychological Association, American Anthropological Association, American Political Science Association, and American Sociological Association) adopted codes of ethics beginning in the 1960s or 1970s. A copy of the code of ethics for the American Sociological Association is provided in Appendix A.

Professional social science associations have committees that review codes of ethics and hear about possible violations, but there is no strict enforcement of the codes. The penalty for a minor violation rarely goes beyond a letter. If laws have not been violated, the main penalty is the negative publicity surrounding a well-documented and serious ethical violation. The publicity may result in the loss of employment, a refusal to publish research findings in scholarly journals, and a prohibition from receiving funding for research—in other words, banishment from the community of professional researchers.

Codes of ethics do more than codify thinking and provide guidance; they also help universities and other institutions defend ethical research against abuses. For example, after interviewing 24 staff members and conducting observations, a researcher in 1994 documented that the staff at the Milwaukee Public Defenders Office were seriously overworked and could not effectively provide legal defense for poor people. Learning of the findings, top officials at the office contacted the university and demanded to know who on their staff had talked to the researcher, with implications that there might be reprisals. The university administration defended the researcher and refused to release the information, citing widely accepted codes that protect human research subjects.[28]

Among the codes of ethics, Greenwald (1992: 585–586) remarked, "Sociology stands out among the learned professions as critical of the authority of established institutions such as government or large business firms" and in its provision to "explicitly state the shortcoming of methodologies and the openness of findings to varying interpretations."

Ethics and the Sponsors of Research

Whistle-blowing. You might find a job in which you do research for a sponsor—an employer, a government agency, or a private firm that contracts with a researcher to conduct research. Special ethical problems arise when a sponsor pays for research, especially applied research. Researchers may be asked to compromise ethical or professional research standards as a condition for receiving a contract or for continued employment. Researchers need to set ethical boundaries beyond which they will refuse sponsor demands. When confronted with an illegitimate demand, a researcher has three basic choices: loyalty to an organization or larger group, exiting from the situation, or voicing opposition.[29] These present themselves as caving in to the sponsor, quitting, or becoming a whistle-blower. The researcher must choose his or her own course of action, but it is best to consider ethical issues early in a relationship with a sponsor and to express concerns up front.

Whistle-blowing can be strenuous and risky. Three parties are involved: the researcher who sees ethical wrongdoing, an external agency or the media, and supervisors in an employing organization. The researcher must be convinced that the breach of ethics is serious and approved of in the organization. After exhausting internal avenues to resolve the issue, he or she turns to outsiders. The outsiders may or may not be interested in the problem or able to help. Outsiders often have their own priorities (making an organization look bad, sensationalizing the problem, etc.)—ones that differ from the researcher's main concern (ending unethical behavior). Supervisors or managers may try to discredit or punish anyone who exposes problems and acts disloyal (see Box 5.8). As Frechette-Schrader (1994:78) noted, "An act of whistle blowing is a special kind of organizational disobedience or, rather, obedience to a higher principle than loyalty to an employer." Under the best of conditions, the issue may take a long time to resolve and create great emotional strain. By acting moral, a whistle-blower needs to be prepared to make sacrifices— losing a job or promotions, lowered pay or undesirable transfer, being abandoned by friends at work, or incurring legal costs. There is no guarantee that doing the right thing will change the unethical behavior or protect the researcher from retaliation.

BOX **5.8** **The Story of a Whistle-Blower**

A Ph.D. microbiologist, David Franklin, was hired by Warner-Lambert to be a medical liaison. His job was to gain the trust of physicians and provide them with scientific information to sell pharmaceuticals. During his training, he was asked to make false claims about a drug and told how to circumvent legal-ethical rules to increase sales. He was also told to exaggerate the results of studies that did show a few benefits of the drug and hide reports of side effects. When he raised concerns and showed published reports of dangerous side effects to his superiors, his complaints were dismissed. He observed that the company paid tens of thousands of dollars to physicians to give testimonials as to the drug's benefits or to be the authors of articles that were actually written by the firm's marketing department. He felt that the company was acting illegally and endangering people. He resigned after just four months on the job, but was threatened not to reveal anything about the company. It took seven years to settle his whistle-blower legal case against the firm.

Source: Melody Petersen, "Doctor Explains Why He Blew the Whistle," *New York Times* (March 12, 2003).

Applied social researchers in sponsored research settings need to think seriously about their professional roles and maintain some independence from an employer. Many find a defense against sponsor pressures by participating in professional organizations (e.g., the Evaluation Research Society), maintaining regular contacts with researchers outside the sponsoring organization, and staying current with the best research practices. The researcher least likely to uphold ethical standards in a sponsored setting is someone who is isolated and professionally insecure. Whatever the situation, unethical behavior is never justified by the argument, "If I didn't do it, someone else would have."

Arriving at Particular Findings. What should you do if a sponsor tells you, directly or indirectly, what results you should come up with? An ethical researcher refuses to participate if he or she must arrive at specific results as a precondition for doing research. All research should be conducted without restrictions on the findings that the research yields. For example, a survey organization obtained a contract to conduct research for a shopping mall association. The association was engaged in a court battle with a political group that wanted to demonstrate at a mall. An interviewer in the survey organization objected to many survey questions that he believed were invalid and slanted to favor the shopping mall association. After he contacted a newspaper and exposed the biased questions, the interviewer was fired. Several years later, however, in a "whistle-blower lawsuit," the interviewer was awarded more than $60,000 for back pay, mental anguish, and punitive damages against the survey organization.[30]

Another example of pressure to arrive at particular findings is in the area of educational testing. Standardized tests to measure achievement by U.S. school children have come under criticism. For example, children in about 90 percent of school districts in the United States score "above average" on such tests. This was called the *Lake Wobegon effect* after the mythical town of Lake Wobegon, where, according to radio show host Garrison Keillor, "all the children are above average." The main reason for this finding was that the researchers compared current students to standards based on tests taken by students many years ago. The researchers faced pressure from teachers, school principals, superintendents, and school boards for results that would allow them to report to parents and voters that their school district was "above average."[31]

Limits on How to Conduct Studies. Can a sponsor limit research by defining what can be studied or by limiting the techniques used, either directly or indirectly (by limiting funding)? Sponsors can legitimately set conditions on research techniques used (e.g., survey versus experiment) and limit costs for research. However, the researcher must follow generally accepted research methods.

> **Contract research**   A type of applied research that is sponsored, that is, paid for by a government agency, foundation, company, and so on. The researcher agrees to conduct a study on the sponsor's research question and finish the study by a set deadline for a fixed price.

Researchers should give a realistic appraisal of what can be accomplished for a given level of funding.

The issue of limits is common in **contract research,** when a firm or government agency asks for work on a particular research project. A trade-off may develop between quality and cost in contract research. Abt (1979), the president of a major private social research firm, Abt Associates, argued that it is difficult to get a contract by bidding what the research actually costs. Once the research begins, a researcher may need to redesign the project, or costs may be higher. The contract procedure makes midstream changes difficult. A researcher may find that he or she is forced by the contract to use research procedures or methods that are less than ideal. The researcher then confronts a dilemma: Complete the contract and do low-quality research, or fail to fulfill the contract and lose money and future jobs.

A researcher should refuse to continue if he or she cannot uphold generally accepted standards of research. If a sponsor wants biased samples or leading questions, the ethical researcher refuses to cooperate. If legitimate research shows the sponsor's pet idea or project to be a bad course of action, a researcher may anticipate the end of employment or pressure to violate professional research standards. In the long run, the sponsor, the researcher, the scientific community, and the larger society are harmed by the violation of sound research practice. The researcher has to decide whether he or she is a "hired hand" who gives the sponsors whatever they want, even if it is ethically wrong, or a professional who is obligated to teach, guide, or even oppose sponsors in the service of higher moral principles.

A researcher should ask: Why would sponsors want the social research conducted if they are not interested in using the findings or in the truth? The answer is that such sponsors see social research only as a cover they can use to legitimate a decision or practice that they could not otherwise carry out. They are abusing the researcher's status as a professional, being deceitful, and trying to "cash in" on the reputation of social research for honesty and integrity. When it occurs, an ethical researcher has a moral responsibility to expose and stop the abuse.

Suppressing Findings. What happens if you conduct research and the findings make the sponsor look bad or the sponsor does not want to release the results? This is not an uncommon situation. For example, a sociologist conducted a study for the Wisconsin Lottery Commission on the effects of state government-sponsored gambling. After she completed the report, but before the report was released to the public, the commission asked her to remove sections that outlined many negative social effects of gambling and to eliminate her recommendations to create social services to help compulsive gamblers. The researcher was in a difficult position. Which ethical value took precedence: covering up for the sponsor that had paid for the research, or revealing the truth for all to see but then suffering the consequences?[32] A Roman Catholic priest who surveyed American bishops on their dissatisfaction with official church policy was ordered by his superiors to suppress findings and destroy the questionnaires. Instead, he resigned after 24 years in the priesthood and made his results public.[33] Researchers pay high personal and economic costs for being ethical.

Government agencies may suppress scientific information that contradicts official policy or embarrasses high officials. Retaliation against social researchers employed by government agencies who make the information public also occurs. For example, a social researcher employed by the U.S. Census Bureau who studied deaths caused by the 1991 Gulf War against Iraq reported that government officials suppressed findings for political reasons. The researcher, whom the agency attempted to fire, reported that findings of high death rates were delayed and underestimated by the U.S. government's agency for statistics. Before information could be released, it had to go through an office headed by a political appointee. She charged that the political appointee was most interested in protecting the administration's foreign policy. In another example, the U.S. Defense Department ordered studies destroyed that showed 10 percent of the U.S. military to be gay or lesbian and that showed no support for the banning of gays from the military.[34]

In sponsored research, a researcher can negotiate conditions for releasing findings *prior to beginning* the study and sign a contract to that effect.

It may be unwise to conduct the study without such a guarantee, although competing researchers who have fewer ethical scruples may do so. Alternatively, a researcher can accept the sponsor's criticism and hostility and release the findings over the sponsor's objections. Most researchers prefer the first choice, because the second one may scare away future sponsors.

Social researchers sometimes restrict or delay the release of findings to protect the identity of informants, to maintain access to a research site, to hold on to their jobs, or to protect the personal safety of themselves or of family members.[35] This is a less disturbing type of censorship because it is not imposed by an outside power. It is done by someone who is close to the research and who is knowledgeable about possible consequences. Researchers shoulder the ultimate responsibility for their research. Often, they can draw on many different resources but they face many competing pressures, as well (see Box 5.9).

BOX **5.9** **Common Types of Misuse in Evaluation Research**

■ Asking "wrong" research questions (e.g., asking summative yes/no questions when formulative questions are most appropriate or asking questions that exclude major stakeholders)

■ Requesting an evaluation study after a decision on a program has been made, using the study only as a way to delay or justify the decision already made

■ Demanding the use of a research design/data collection technique that is inappropriate for the program evaluation task

■ Interfering with the research design or data collection process to ensure that it produces desired results

■ Continuing a program when the evaluation results unambiguously show it to be ineffective or ending a program when the results unambiguously show it to be highly effective

■ Suppressing/deleting positive results to eliminate/reduce a program, or suppressing/deleting negative results to continue/expand a program

Source: Adapted from Stevens and Dial (1994), who also provide examples of misuse.

Concealing the True Sponsor. Is it ethical to keep the identity of a sponsor secret? For example, an abortion clinic funds a study on the attitudes of religious groups opposed to abortion. The researcher must balance the ethical value of making the sponsor's identity public to subjects and releasing results against the sponsor's desire for confidentiality and the likelihood of reduced cooperation from subjects. If the results are published, there is a clear overriding ethical mandate to reveal the true sponsor. There is less agreement on the ethical issue of revealing the true sponsor to subjects. Presser and colleagues (1992) found that the answers given by respondents may depend on the sponsor of a survey. If a respondent believes a survey is conducted by a newspaper that has taken a strong position on an issue, the respondent is less likely to contradict the newspaper's public stand on the issue. This is less of a problem if the respondent believes the survey sponsor is a neutral academic organization. It is ethical to inform the subjects of the sponsor unless one has a good methodological reason for not doing so.

Feminist Communitarian Research Ethics

Some researchers who adopt the interpretative or critical social science approaches (see Chapter 4) view most ethical debates, codes of ethics, and review boards as inadequate and rooted in positivist assumptions about individual rationality. They propose a feminist communitarian model of research ethics as an alternative to research ethics based on formal procedures and a rational utilitarian balancing of costs versus benefits and abstract principles of moral good. They hold that "the moral task cannot be reduced to professional ethics" (Christians 2003:232). Aligned with participatory action research (see Chapter 2), they argue that research participants should have a say in how research is conducted and be actively involved in conducting it. Ethics should reflect the ultimate purpose of research—to empower research participants in terms of their own everyday experiences and advance the goal of human freedom.

The feminist communitarian model is based on three moral principles. First, ethical research is multivocal, that is, it recognizes a diversity of human experiences and incorporates that diversity. It begins with the premise that all human life is situated in the socially constructed contexts of gender, race, class, and religion. People live in multiple communities and each has something important to say. Second, ethical research requires engaging in a dialogue over moral concerns that is phased in terms of the participants' everyday life experiences. Researchers have to engage and participate in the ongoing moral debates and discussions occurring within the communities of the people they wish to study, and they should not superimpose their own abstract legalistic rights or principles. Third, research processes that involve researchers and participants on open, equal terms will unmask power relations and generate social criticism that can facilitate greater reflection and mutual awareness. In the end, a collaborative relationship between researcher and participant will emerge in which "invasion of privacy, informed consent, and deception are non-issues" (Christians 2003:234).

The feminist communitarian model of research ethics is in a preliminary stage of development and has yet to be implemented. Nonetheless, it critiques the dominant approach to research ethics for being overly formal-legalistic, procedure based, and abstract. It also highlights how an approach to social sciences, as outlined in Chapter 4, is connected with moral issues in research ethics.

CONCLUSION

This chapter is a transition between the general foundation of social research and the specifics of study design. As such, it has discussed two issues that are part of the preparation for designing a study: the literature review and ethical concerns. Both involve placing one's study in the context of the larger community of researchers and attaching a specific study to larger concerns.

In Chapter 1, we discussed the distinctive contribution of science to society and how social research is a source of knowledge about the social world. The perspectives and techniques of social research can be powerful tools for understanding the world. Nevertheless, with that power comes responsibility—a responsibility to yourself, a responsibility to your sponsors, a responsibility to the community of researchers, and a responsibility to the larger society. These responsibilities can and do come into conflict with each other at times.

Ultimately, you personally must decide to conduct research in an ethical manner, to uphold and defend the principles of the social science approach you adopt, and to demand ethical conduct by others.

The truthfulness of knowledge produced by social research and its use or misuse depends on individual researchers like you, reflecting on their actions and on how social research fits into society.

In the next chapter, we examine basic design approaches and issues that appear in both qualitative and quantitative research.

KEY TERMS

abstract	crossover design	principle of voluntary consent
anonymity	informed consent	research fraud
citation	institutional review board	scientific misconduct
code of ethics	(IRB)	special population
confidentiality	meta-analysis	whistle-blower
contract research	Nuremberg code	

REVIEW QUESTIONS

1. What are the four major goals of a literature review?

2. Which outlets of research are easiest to locate and which are the most difficult?

3. How would you go about locating a Ph.D. dissertation?

4. What distinguishes a strong from a weak literature review?

5. What are the major strengths and weaknesses of using the Internet for social research?

6. What is the primary defense against unethical conduct in research?

7. How do deception and coercion to participate in research conflict with the principle of voluntary consent?

8. Explain the ethical issues in the Milgram, Humphreys, and Zimbardo examples.

9. What is *informed consent,* and how does it protect research subjects?

10. What is the difference between *anonymity* and *confidentiality?*

NOTES

1. See Hunt (1997) and Hunter and associates (1982).
2. From Hargens (1988).
3. Based on Hargens (1991).
4. See Reynolds (1979:56–57) and Sieber (1993).
5. Research fraud is discussed by Broad and Wade (1982), Diener and Crandall (1978:154–158), and Weinstein (1979). Also see Hearnshaw (1979) and Wade (1976) on Cyril Burt. Kusserow (1989) and the Septem-

ber 1, 1989, issue of the National Institutes of Health weekly *Guide* summarize some recent scientific misconduct issues.
6. See "Noted Harvard Psychiatrist Resigns Post after Faculty Group Finds He Plagiarized," *Chronicle of Higher Education* (December 7, 1988).
7. See Blum (1989) and D'Antonio (1989) on this case of plagiarism.

8. See "Doctor Is Accused of 'Immoral' Tests,'" *New York Times* (December 9, 1988). For a more general discussion of power and trust, see Reynolds (1979:32).

9. Lifton (1986) provided an account of Nazi medical experimentation.

10. See Jones (1981) and Mitchell (1997) on the Bad Blood case.

11. Diener and Crandall (1978:128) discuss these examples.

12. See Warwick (1982) on types of harm to research participants. See Reynolds (1979:62–68) on rates of harm in biomedical research. Kelman (1982) discusses different types of harms from different types of research.

13. College counselors report that anxiety and low self-esteem over dating are major problems among college women (Diener and Crandall, 1978:21–22). Also see Kidder and Judd (1986:481–484).

14. See Dooley (1984:330) and Kidder and Judd (1986:477–484).

15. See Hallowell (1985), and "Threat to Confidentiality of Fieldnotes," *ASA Footnotes,* Volume 12 (October 1984), p. 6.

16. For more on the general issue of the right not to be researched, see Barnes (1979), Boruch (1982), Moore (1973), and Sagarin (1973).

17. Informed consent requirements and regulations are discussed in detail in Maloney (1984). Also see Capron (1982) and Diener and Crandall (1978:64–66).

18. The debate over covert research is discussed in Denzin and Erikson (1982), Homan (1980), and Sieber (1982). Also see Miller and Tewksbury (2000), especially Sections 1 and 4.3.

19. See Diener and Crandall (1978:87) and Warwick (1982:112).

20. See Diener and Crandall (1978:173–177) and Kidder and Judd (1986:469).

21. See Boruch (1982), Caplan (1982), Katz (1972), and Vaughan (1967) on privacy.

22. For more on the Wichita Jury Study, see Dooley (1984:338–339), Gray (1982), Robertson (1982), Tropp (1982:391), and Vaughan (1967).

23. See Monaghan (1993a, 1993b, 1993c).

24. See Gustavsen (1986).

25. IRBs are discussed in Maloney (1984) and Chadwick and associates (1984:20). See Taylor (1994) for an international survey of ethical standards.

26. See Abbott (1988), Brint (1994), and Freidson (1986, 1994) on professionals.

27. See Beecher (1970:227–228) and Reynolds (1979:28–31, 428–441).

28. See "UW Protects Dissertation Sources," *Capital Times* (December 19, 1994), p. 4.

29. See Hirschman (1970) on loyalty, exit, or voice. Also see Rubin (1983:24–40) on ethical issues in applied research.

30. Additional discussion can be found in Schmeling and Miller (1988).

31. See Fiske (1989), Koretz (1988), and Weiss and Gruber (1987) on educational statistics.

32. See "State Sought, Got Author's Changes in Lottery Report," *Capital Times* (July 28, 1989), p. 21.

33. See Chambers (1986).

34. See Dale W. Nelson, "Analyst: War Death Counts Falsified," *Wisconsin State Journal* (April 14, 1992), p. 3A, and "Ex-Official Says Pentagon Dumped Findings on Gays," *Capital Times* (April 1, 1993).

35. See Adler and Adler (1993).

CHAPTER 6

Qualitative and Quantitative Research Designs

> *Substantive problems must thus be translated into the vocabulary of social inquiry. . . . Working out a way of thinking through the choices and some appropriate sequence of tasks will allow you to answer a research question.*
> —Robert Alford, *The Craft of Inquiry*, p. 25

This chapter begins Part Two, in which we look at strategies for designing a study, creating measures, and sampling. Differences between quantitative and qualitative styles of doing research will be more evident. Quantitative researchers are more concerned about issues of design, measurement, and sampling because their deductive approach emphasizes detailed planning prior to data collection and analysis. Qualitative researchers are more concerned about issues of the richness, texture, and feeling of raw data because their inductive approach emphasizes developing insights and generalizations out of the data collected.

TRIANGULATION

Surveyors and sailors measure distances between objects by making observations from multiple po-

sitions. By observing something from different angles or viewpoints, they get a fix on its true location (see Figure 6.1). This process, called **triangulation,** is used also by quantitative and qualitative social researchers. Applied to social research, it means it is better to look at something from several angles than to look at it in only one way.

There are several types of triangulation (see Box 6.1). The most common type is *triangulation of measures.* Researchers take multiple measures of the same phenomena. By measuring something in more than one way, researchers are more likely to see all aspects of it. For example, a teacher has students write answers to essay questions, complete a series

Triangulation The idea that looking at something from multiple points of view improves accuracy.

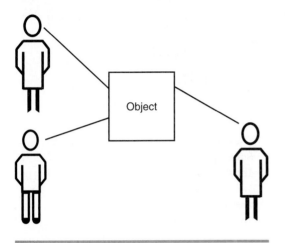

FIGURE 6.1 Triangulation: Observing from Different Viewpoints

of multiple-choice questions, give an oral presentation, and complete a term paper or applied project. The teacher's confidence in getting an accurate measure of the student's learning is greater if the student scores similarly on all four testing methods than on just one or two. Any differences in results for the measures become interesting, informative data, as well.

Another type is *triangulation of observers*. In many studies, one researcher conducts interviews or is the sole observer of people's behavior. A single person means the limitations of the one observer are the limitations of the study. Multiple observers add alternative perspectives, backgrounds, and social characteristics and will reduce the limitations. For example, observed patient behavior in a hospital by one person—a White 55-year-old male who has substantial medical training—may differ if the observer was female, was 30 years old, was of a different race, or lacked medical training. Combining data from a variety of observers is more likely to yield a more complete picture of the setting.

Triangulation of theory occurs when a researcher uses multiple theoretical perspectives in the planning stages of research, or when interpreting the data. For example, the researcher plans the study using the concepts and assumptions of both conflict theory and exchange theory, or looks at the data coming from each theoretical perspective.

Last, *triangulation of method* means mixing qualitative and quantitative styles of research and data. Most researchers develop an expertise in one style, but the styles have complementary strengths. Because there is only partial overlap, a study using both is fuller or more comprehensive. Mixing the styles can occur several ways.[1] One way is to use the methods sequentially, first one and then the other. Another way is to use the two methods in parallel, or both simultaneously. For example, Dressler (1991) used sequential methods. He wanted to study

---

BOX **6.1** Example of Four Types of Triangulation

TOPIC

The amount of violence in popular American films

Measures: Create three quantitative measures of violence: the frequency (e.g., number of killings, punches, etc.), intensity (e.g., volume and length time screaming, amount of pain shown in face or body movement), and level of explicit, graphic display (e.g., showing a corpse, blood flowing, amputated body parts, close-ups of injury) in films.

Observers: Have five different people independently watch, evaluate, and record the forms and degrees of violence in a set of 10 highly popular American films.

Theory: Compare how a feminist, a functional, and a symbolic interaction theory each explains the forms, causes, and societal results of violence that is in popular films.

Method: Conduct a content analysis of a set of 10 popular films, an experiment to measure the responses of experimental subjects to violence in each film, a survey of attitudes toward film violence among the movie-attending public, and field observations on audience behavior during and immediately after a showing of the films.

how various household factors, lifestyle, and family resources affected whether African Americans in a community in the U.S. South developed depression. He began using the qualitative style, with open-ended ethnographic interviews, then followed with a quantitative survey questionnaire from which he gathered data for statistical analysis.

QUALITATIVE AND QUANTITATIVE ORIENTATIONS TOWARD RESEARCH

Qualitative and quantitative research differ in many ways, but they complement each other, as well. All social researchers systematically collect and analyze empirical data and carefully examine the patterns in them to understand and explain social life. One of the differences between the two styles comes from the nature of the data. *Soft data,* in the form of impressions, words, sentences, photos, symbols, and so forth, dictate different research strategies and data collection techniques than *hard data,* in the form of numbers. Other differences are different assumptions about social life and different objectives. These differences can make tools used by the other style inappropriate or irrelevant. People who judge qualitative research by standards of quantitative research are often disappointed, and vice versa. It is best to appreciate the strengths each style offers on its own terms.

Qualitative researchers often rely on interpretive or critical social science. They apply "logic in practice" and follow a nonlinear research path. Qualitative researchers speak a language of "cases and contexts." They emphasize conducting detailed examinations of cases that arise in the natural flow of social life. They try to present authentic interpretations that are sensitive to specific social-historical contexts. Interestingly, more female than male social researchers adopt the qualitative approach.[2]

Most quantitative researchers rely on a positivist approach to social science. They apply "reconstructed logic," and follow a linear research path. They speak a language of "variables and hypotheses." Quantitative researchers emphasize precisely measuring variables and testing hypotheses that are linked to general causal explanations.

Researchers who use one style alone do not always communicate well with those using the other, but the languages and orientations of the styles are mutually intelligible. It takes time and effort to understand both styles and to see how they can be complementary.

Reconstructed Logic and Logic in Practice

The way social researchers learn and discuss research usually follows one of two logics: reconstructed logic or logic in practice.[3] Most researchers will mix the two logics, but the proportion of each varies. Quantitative researchers apply more of the reconstructed logic, whereas qualitative researchers tend to apply logic in practice. The two logics represent the degree that discussions of social research are explicit, codified, and standardized.

Reconstructed logic means that the logic of how to do research is highly organized and restated in an idealized, formal, and systematic form. It is reconstructed into logically consistent rules and terms. It is a cleansed model of good research. This logic appears in textbooks and in published research reports. For example, the rules for conducting a simple random sample are very straightforward and follow a step-by-step procedure.

Logic in practice is the logic of how research is actually carried out. It is relatively messy, with ambiguity, and is tied to specific cases and oriented toward the practical completion of a task. It has fewer set rules and is based on judgment calls or norms shared among experienced researchers. It depends on an informal folk wisdom passed among researchers when they get together over lunch or coffee and discuss doing research.

Reconstructed logic A logic of research based on reorganizing, standardizing, and codifying research knowledge and practices into explicit rules, formal procedures, and techniques; it is characteristic of quantitative research.

Logic in practice A logic of research based on an apprenticeship model and the sharing of implicit knowledge about practical concerns and specific experiences; it is characteristic of qualitative research.

Reconstructed logic is easier to define and learn from books or formal instruction. Quantitative researchers describe the technical research procedures they use (e.g., a systematic random sample of 300 drawn from a telephone directory; Likert scaling).

Qualitative research relies more on the informal wisdom that has developed from the experiences of researchers. Qualitative research reports may not discuss method (common for historical-comparative research) or may have a personal autobiographical account tailored to a particular study (common for field research). Few procedures or terms are standardized and there is a debate among qualitative researchers about whether they ever should be. Many qualitative researchers learned how to do research by reading many reports, by trial and error, and by working in an apprentice role with an experienced researcher. This does not mean that qualitative research is less valid, but it may be more difficult for someone learning about it for the first time to grasp.

Linear and Nonlinear Paths

Researchers follow a path when conducting research. The path is a metaphor for the sequence of things to do: what is finished first or where a researcher has been, and what comes next or where he or she is going. The path may be well worn and marked with signposts where many other researchers have trod. Alternatively, it may be a new path into unknown territory where few others have gone, and without signs marking the direction forward.

In general, quantitative researchers follow a more linear path than do qualitative researchers. A **linear research path** follows a fixed sequence of steps. It is like a staircase leading in one clear direction. It is a way of thinking and a way of looking at issues—the direct, narrow, straight path that is

---

Linear research path Research that proceeds in a clear, logical, step-by-step straight line and is often used in quantitative research.

Nonlinear research path Research that proceeds in a cyclical, iterative, or back-and-forth pattern and is often used in qualitative research.

---

most common in western European and North American culture.

Qualitative research is more nonlinear and cyclical. Rather than moving in a straight line, a **nonlinear research path** makes successive passes through steps, sometimes moving backward and sideways before moving on. It is more of a spiral, moving slowly upward but not directly. With each cycle or repetition, a researcher collects new data and gains new insights.

People who are used to the direct, linear approach may be impatient with a less direct cyclical path. From a strict linear perspective, a cyclical path looks inefficient and sloppy. But the diffuse cyclical approach is not merely disorganized, undefined chaos. It can be highly effective for creating a feeling for the whole, for grasping subtle shades of meaning, for pulling together divergent information, and for switching perspectives. It is not an excuse for doing poor-quality research, and it has its own discipline and rigor. It borrows devices from the humanities (e.g., metaphor, analogy, theme, motif, and irony) and is oriented toward constructing meaning. A cyclical path is suited for tasks such as translating languages, in which delicate shades of meaning, subtle connotations, or contextual distinctions can be important. "Circularity is one of the strengths of the approach, because it forces the researcher to permanently reflect on the whole research process and on particular steps in light of the other steps" (Flick, 1998:43).

Objectivity and Integrity

Opportunities for being biased, dishonest, or unethical exist in all research. All social researchers want to be fair, honest, truthful, and unbiased in their research activity. Nevertheless, the qualitative and quantitative styles emphasize different ways to ensure honest, truthful research.

Qualitative researchers emphasize intimate firsthand knowledge of the research setting; they avoid distancing themselves from the people or events they study. This does not mean arbitrarily interjecting personal opinion, being sloppy about data collection, or using evidence selectively to support personal prejudices. It means taking advantage of personal insight, feelings, and human perspectives to understand social life more fully. The researcher makes his or her presence explicit and is sensitive to prior assumptions. In place of "objective" techniques, the qualitative researcher is forthright and open about his or her personal involvement.

Researcher integrity is central to qualitative research. Quantitative researchers stress objectivity and more "mechanical" techniques. They use the principle of replication, adhere to standardized methodological procedures, measure with numbers, and then analyze the data with statistics, an area of applied mathematics.[4] Quantitative research tries to control or eliminate the human factor. As Porter (1995:7, 74) has argued,

> *Ideally, expertise should be mechanized and objectified . . . grounded in specific techniques. . . . This ideal of objectivity is a political as well as scientific one. Objectivity means rule of law, not of men. It implies the subordination of personal interests and prejudices to public standards.*

Quantitative research addresses the issue of integrity by relying on an objective technology—such as precise statements, standard techniques, numerical measures, statistics, and replication. This is the same as in the natural sciences.

Qualitative researchers emphasize trustworthiness as a parallel idea to objective standards in quantitative research design. This ensures that their research is dependable and credible.[5] Qualitative researchers have checks on their evidence.[6] For example, the field researcher listens to and records a student who says, "Professor Smith threw an eraser at Professor Jones." The field researcher treats this evidence carefully. To strengthen the claim, the researcher considers what other people say, looks for confirming evidence, and checks for internal consistency. The researcher asks whether the student has firsthand knowledge of the event and whether the student's feelings or self-interest would lead him to lie (e.g., the student might dislike Professor Smith for other reasons). Even if the student made a false statement, it is evidence about the student's perspective. Similarly, the researcher examining historical evidence uses techniques for verifying the authenticity of sources.

Another check is the great volume of detailed written notes that qualitative researchers record. Besides a detailed verbatim description of the evidence, notes include references to the sources, commentaries by the researcher, and key terms to help organize the notes, as well as quotes, photographs, maps, diagrams, paraphrasing, and counts.

Although qualitative researchers usually work alone, others know about the evidence. For example, a field researcher studies people who are alive and in a specific setting. The subjects being observed can read the details of a study. Likewise, historical documents are cited and other researchers can check references and sources.

The most important way that a qualitative researcher creates trust is how he or she presents evidence. A qualitative researcher does not present all of his or her detailed notes in a report; rather, he or she spins a web of interlocking details, providing sufficient texture and detail so that the readers feel that they are there. A qualitative researcher's firsthand knowledge of events, people, and situations cuts two ways. It raises questions of bias, but it also provides a sense of immediacy, direct contact, and intimate knowledge.

Preplanned and Emergent Research Questions

Your first step when beginning a research project is to select a topic.[7] There is no formula for this task. Whether you are an experienced researcher or just beginning, the best guide is to conduct research on something that interests you. There are many sources of topics; Box 6.2 suggests ways to make your selection.

All research begins with a topic but a topic is only a starting point that researchers must narrow into a focused research question. Qualitative researchers often begin with vague or unclear research questions. The topic emerges slowly during the study. The researchers often combine focusing on a specific question with the process of deciding the details of study design that occurs while they are gathering data. By contrast, quantitative researchers narrow a topic into a focused question as a discrete

BOX **6.2**   **Ways to Select Topics**

1. *Personal experience.* You can choose a topic based on something that happens to you or those you know. For example, while you work a summer job at a factory, the local union calls a strike. You do not have strong feelings either way, but you are forced to choose sides. You notice that tensions rise. Both management and labor become hostile toward each other. This experience suggests unions or organized labor as a topic.

2. *Curiosity based on something in the media.* Sometimes you read a newspaper or magazine article or see a television program and leave with questions. What you read raises questions or suggests replicating what others' research found. For example, you read a *Newsweek* article on the homeless, but you do not really know much about who they are, why they are homeless, whether this has always been a problem, and so forth. This suggests the homeless as a topic.

3. *The state of knowledge in a field.* Basic research is driven by new research findings and theories that push at the frontiers of knowledge. As theoretical explanations are elaborated and expanded, certain issues or questions need to be answered for the field to move forward. As such issues are identified and studied, knowledge advances. For example, you read about attitudes toward capital punishment and realize that most research points to an underlying belief in the innate wickedness of criminals among capital punishment supporters. You notice that no one has yet examined whether people who belong to certain religious groups that teach such a belief in wicked-

ness support capital punishment, nor has anyone mapped the geographic location of these religious groups. Your knowledge of the field suggests a topic for a research project, beliefs about capital punishment, and religion in different regions.

4. *Solving a problem.* Applied research topics often begin with a problem that needs a solution. For example, as part of your job as a dorm counselor, you want to help college freshmen establish friendships with each other. Your problem suggests friendship formation among new college students as a topic.

5. *Social premiums.* This is a term suggested by Singleton and colleagues (1988:68). It means that some topics are "hot" or offer an opportunity. For example, you read that there is a lot of money available to conduct research on nursing homes, but few people are interested in doing so. Your need of a job suggests nursing homes as a topic.

6. *Personal values.* Some people are highly committed to a set of religious, political, or social values. For example, you are strongly committed to racial equality and become morally outraged whenever you hear about racial discrimination. Your strong personal belief suggests racial discrimination as a topic.

7. *Everyday life.* Potential topics can be found throughout everyday life in old sayings, novels, songs, statistics, and what others say (especially those who disagree with you). For example, you hear that the home court advantage is very important in basketball. This statement suggests "home court advantage" as a topic for research.

---

planning step before they finalize study design. They use it as a step in the process of developing a testable hypothesis (to be discussed later) and to guide the study design before they collect any data.[8]

The qualitative research style is flexible and encourages slowly focusing the topic throughout a study. Only a small amount of topic narrowing occurs in an early research planning stage, and much of the narrowing occurs after a researcher has begun to collect data.

Focusing and refining continues after he or she has gathered some of the data and started preliminary analysis. Qualitative researchers use early data

collection to adjust and sharpen the research question(s) because they rarely know the most important issues or questions until after they become immersed in the data. Developing a focused research question is a part of the data collection process, during which the researcher actively reflects on and develops preliminary interpretations. The qualitative researcher is open to unanticipated data and constantly reevaluates the focus early in a study. He or she is prepared to change the direction of research and follow new lines of evidence.

Typical research questions for qualitative researchers include: How did a certain condition or social situation originate? How is the condition/ situation maintained over time? What are the processes by which a condition/situation changes, develops, or operates? A different type of question tries to confirm existing beliefs or assumptions. A last type of question tries to discover new ideas.[9]

Research projects are designed around research problems or questions. Before designing a project, quantitative researchers focus on a specific research problem within a broad topic. For example, the personal experience example in Box 6.2 suggests labor unions as a topic. "Labor unions" is a topic, not a research question or a problem. In any large library, you will find hundreds of books and thousands of articles written by sociologists, historians, economists, lawyers, management officials, political scientists, and others on unions. The books and articles focus on different aspects of the topic and adopt many perspectives on it. Before proceeding to design a research project, you must narrow and focus the topic. An example research question is, "How much did U.S. labor unions contribute to racial inequality by creating barriers to skilled jobs for African Americans in the post–World War II period?"

When starting research on a topic, ask yourself: What is it about the topic that is of greatest interest? For a topic about which you know little, first get background knowledge by reading about it. Research questions refer to the relationships among a small number of variables.

Box 6.3 lists some ways to focus a topic into a research question. For example, the question, "What causes divorce?", is not a good research question. A better research question is, "Is age at marriage associated with divorce?" The second question suggests two variables: age of marriage and divorce (also see Box 6.4).

Another technique for focusing a research question is to specify the **universe** to which the answer to the question can be generalized. All research questions and studies apply to some group or category of people, organizations, or other units. The universe is the set of all units that the research covers, or to which it can be generalized. For example, your research question is about the effects of a new attendance policy on learning by high school students. The universe is all high school students.

BOX **6.3** **Techniques for Narrowing a Topic into a Research Question**

1. *Examine the literature.* Published articles are an excellent source of ideas for research questions. They are usually at an appropriate level of specificity and suggest research questions that focus on the following:
   a. Replicate a previous research project exactly or with slight variations.
   b. Explore unexpected findings discovered in previous research.
   c. Follow suggestions an author gives for future research at the end of an article.
   d. Extend an existing explanation or theory to a new topic or setting.
   e. Challenge findings or attempt to refute a relationship.
   f. Specify the intervening process and consider linking relations.
2. *Talk over ideas with others.*
   a. Ask people who are knowledgeable about the topic for questions about it that they have thought of.
   b. Seek out those who hold opinions that differ from yours on the topic and discuss possible research questions with them.
3. *Apply to a specific context.*
   a. Focus the topic onto a specific historical period or time period.
   b. Narrow the topic to a specific society or geographic unit.
   c. Consider which subgroups or categories of people/units are involved and whether there are differences among them.
4. *Define the aim or desired outcome of the study.*
   a. Will the research question be for an exploratory, explanatory, or descriptive study?
   b. Will the study involve applied or basic research?

When refining a topic into a research question and designing a research project, you also need to consider practical limitations. Designing a perfect research project is an interesting academic exercise,

---

Universe The entire category or class of units that is covered or explained by a relationship or hypothesis.

BOX **6.4**   **Examples of Bad and Good Research Questions**

BAD RESEARCH QUESTIONS

Not Empirically Testable, Nonscientific Questions
- Should abortion be legal?
- Is it right to have capital punishment?

General Topics, Not Research Questions
- Treatment of alcohol and drug abuse
- Sexuality and aging

Set of Variables, Not Questions
- Capital punishment and racial discrimination
- Urban decay and gangs

Too Vague, Ambiguous
- Do police affect delinquency?
- What can be done to prevent child abuse?

Need to Be Still More Specific
- Has the incidence of child abuse risen?
- How does poverty affect children?
- What problems do children who grow up in poverty experience that others do not?

GOOD QUESTIONS

Exploratory Questions
- Has the incidence of new forms of child abuse appeared in Wisconsin in the past 10 years?

Descriptive Questions
- Is child abuse, violent or sexual, more common in families that have experienced a divorce than in intact, never-divorced families?
- Are the children raised in poverty households more likely to have medical, learning, and social-emotional adjustment difficulties than nonpoverty children?

Explanatory Questions
- Does the emotional instability created by experiencing a divorce increase the chances that divorced parents will physically abuse their children?
- Is a lack of sufficent funds for preventive treatment a major cause of more serious medical problems among children raised in families in poverty?

but if you expect to carry out a research project, practical limitations will have an impact on its design.

Major limitations include time, costs, access to resources, approval by authorities, ethical concerns, and expertise. If you have ten hours a week for five weeks to conduct a research project, but the answer to a research question will take five years, reformulate the research question more narrowly. Estimating the amount of time required to answer a research question is difficult. The research question specified, the research technique used, and the type of data collected all play significant roles. Experienced researchers are the best source of good estimates.

Cost is another limitation. As with time, there are inventive ways to answer a question within limitations, but it may be impossible to answer some questions because of the expense involved. For example, a research question about the attitudes of all sports fans toward their team mascot can be answered only with a great investment of time and money. Narrowing the research question to how students at two different colleges feel about their mascots might make it more manageable.

Access to resources is a common limitation. Resources can include the expertise of others, special equipment, or information. For example, a research question about burglary rates and family income in many different nations is almost impossible to answer because information on burglary and income is not collected or available for most countries. Some questions require the approval of authorities (e.g., to see medical records) or involve violating basic ethical principles (e.g., causing serious physical harm to a person to see the person's reaction). The expertise or background of the researcher is also a limitation. Answering some research questions involves the use of data collection techniques, statistical methods, knowledge of a foreign language, or skills that the researcher may not have. Unless the researcher can acquire the necessary training or can pay for another person's services, the research question may not be practical.

In summary, qualitative and quantitative researchers have much in common, but they differ on design issues, such as using a design logic of study design, taking a linear or nonlinear research path, using a mode of verification, and developing a re-

TABLE 6.1   Quantitative Research versus Qualitative Research

QUANTITATIVE RESEARCH	QUALITATIVE RESEARCH
Test hypothesis that the researcher begins with.	Capture and discover meaning once the researcher becomes immersed in the data.
Concepts are in the form of distinct variables.	Concepts are in the form of themes, motifs, generalizations, and taxonomies.
Measures are systematically created before data collection and are standardized.	Measures are created in an ad hoc manner and are often specific to the individual setting or researcher.
Data are in the form of numbers from precise measurement.	Data are in the form of words and images from documents, observations, and transcripts.
Theory is largely causal and is deductive.	Theory can be causal or noncausal and is often inductive.
Procedures are standard, and replication is frequent.	Research procedures are particular, and replication is very rare.
Analysis proceeds by using statistics, tables, or charts and discussing how what they show relates to hypotheses.	Analysis proceeds by extracting themes or generalizations from evidence and organizing data to present a coherent, consistent picture.

search question (see Table 6.1). In addition, researchers tend to adopt a different language and approach to study design, which we will consider next.

QUALITATIVE DESIGN ISSUES

The Language of Cases and Contexts

Qualitative researchers use a language of cases and contexts, employ bricolage, examine social processes and cases in their social context, and look at interpretations or the creation of meaning in specific settings. They look at social life from multiple points of view and explain how people construct identities. Only rarely do they use variables or test hypotheses, or convert social life into numbers.

Qualitative researchers see most areas of social life as intrinsically qualitative. To them, qualitative data are not imprecise or deficient; they are highly meaningful. Instead of trying to convert social life into variables or numbers, qualitative researchers borrow ideas from the people they study and place them within the context of a natural setting. They examine motifs, themes, distinctions, and ideas instead of variables, and they adopt the inductive approach of *grounded theory* (discussed in Chapter 3).

Some people believe that qualitative data are "soft," intangible, and immaterial. Such data are so fuzzy and elusive that researchers cannot really capture them. This is not necessarily the case. Qualitative data involve documenting real events, recording what people say (with words, gestures, and tone), observing specific behaviors, studying written documents, or examining visual images. These are all concrete aspects of the world. For example, some qualitative researchers closely scrutinize photos or videotapes of people or social events.[10] This evidence is just as "hard" and physical as that used by quantitative researchers to measure attitudes, social pressure, intelligence, and the like.

Grounded Theory

A qualitative researcher develops theory during the data collection process. This more inductive method means that theory is built from data or grounded in the data. Many researchers use grounded theory. It makes qualitative research flexible and lets data and theory interact. Qualitative researchers remain open to the unexpected, are willing to change the direction or focus of a research project, and may abandon their original research question in the middle of a project.[11]

A qualitative researcher builds theory by making comparisons. For example, when a researcher observes an event (e.g., a police officer confronting a speeding motorist), he or she immediately ponders questions and looks for similarities and differences. When watching a police officer stop a speeder, a qualitative researcher asks: Does the police officer always radio in the car's license number before proceeding? After radioing the car's location, does the officer ask the motorist to get out of the car sometimes, but in others casually walk up to the car and talk to the seated driver? When data collection and theorizing are interspersed, theoretical questions arise that suggest future observations, so new data are tailored to answer theoretical questions that came from thinking about previous data.

The Context Is Critical

Qualitative researchers emphasize the social context for understanding the social world. They hold that the meaning of a social action or statement depends on the context in which it appears. When a researcher removes an event, social action, answer to a question, or conversation from the social context in which it appears, social meaning and significance are distorted.

Attention to social context means that a qualitative researcher notes what came before or what surrounds the focus of study. It also implies that the same events or behaviors can have different meanings in different cultures or historical eras. For example, instead of ignoring the context and counting votes across time or cultures, a qualitative researcher asks: What does voting mean in the context? He or she may treat the same behavior (e.g., voting for a presidential candidate) differently depending on the social context in which it occurs (see Box 6.5). Qualitative researchers place parts of social life into a larger whole. Otherwise, the meaning of the part may be lost. For example, it is hard to understand what a baseball glove is without knowing something about the game of baseball. The whole of the game—innings, bats, curve balls, hits—gives meaning to each part, and each part without the whole has little meaning.

Bricolage

Qualitative researchers are *bricoleurs;* they learn to be adept at doing many things, drawing on a variety of sources, and making do with whatever is at hand.[12] The qualitative style emphasizes developing an ability to draw on a variety of skills, materials, and approaches as they may be needed, usually without being able to plan for them in advance. A **bricolage** technique means working with one's hands and being pragmatic at using an assortment of odds and ends in an inventive manner to accomplish a specific task. It requires having a deep knowledge of one's materials, a collection of esoteric skills, and the capacity to combine them flexibly. The mixture of using diverse materials, applying disparate approaches, and assembling bits and pieces gives qualitative researchers the aura of being similar to a skilled craftperson who seems to be able to make or repair almost anything.

The Case and Process

Qualitative researchers tend to use a "case-oriented approach [that] places cases, not variables, center stage" (Ragin, 1992a:5). They examine a wide variety of aspects of one or a few cases. Their analyses emphasize contingencies in "messy" natural settings (i.e., the co-occurrence of many specific factors and events in one place and time). Explanations or interpretations are complex and may be in the form of an unfolding plot or a narrative story about particular people or specific events. Rich detail and astute insight into the cases replace the sophisticated statistical analysis of precise measures across a huge number of units or cases found in quantitative research.

Bricolage Improvising by drawing on diverse materials that are lying about and using them in creative ways to accomplish a pragmatic task.

BOX **6.5**   **Example of the Importance of Context for Meaning**

"Voting in a national election" has different meanings in different contexts:

1. A one-party dictatorship with unopposed candidates, wherein people are required by law to vote. The names of nonvoters are recorded by the police. Nonvoters are suspected of being antigovernment subversives. They face fines and possible job loss for not voting.
2. A country in the midst of violent conflict between rebels and those in power. Voting is dangerous because the armed soldiers on either side may shoot voters they suspect of opposing their side. The outcome of the vote will give power to one or the other group and dramatically restructure the society. Anyone over the age of 16 can vote.
3. A context in which people choose between a dozen political parties of roughly equal power that represent very different values and policies. Each party has a sizable organization, with its own newspapers, social clubs, and neighborhood organizers. Election days are national holidays, when no one has to work. A person votes by showing up with an identification card at any of many local voting locations. Voting itself is by secret ballot, and everyone over age 18 can vote.
4. A context in which voting is conducted in public by white males over age 21 who have regular jobs. Family, friends, and neighbors see how one another vote. Political parties do not offer distinct policies; instead,

they are tied to ethnic or religious groups and are part of a person's ethnic-religious identity. Ethnic and religious group identities are very strong. They affect where one lives, where one works, whom one marries, and the like. Voting follows massive parades and week-long community events organized by ethnic and religious groups.
5. A context in which one political party is very powerful and is challenged by one or two very small, weak alternatives. The one party has held power for the past 60 years through corruption, bribery, and intimidation. It has the support of leaders throughout society (in religious organizations, educational institutions, business, unions, and the mass media). The jobs of anyone working in any government job (e.g., every police officer, post office clerk, schoolteacher, garbage collector, etc.) depend on the political party staying in power.
6. A context in which the choice is between two parties and there is little difference between them. People select candidates primarily on the basis of television advertising. Candidates pay for advertising with donations by wealthy people or powerful organizations. Voting is a vague civic obligation that few people take seriously. Elections are held on a workday. In order to vote, a person must meet many requirements and register to vote several weeks in advance. Recent immigrants and anyone arrested for a crime cannot vote.

The passage of time is integral to qualitative research. Qualitative researchers look at the sequence of events and pay attention to what happens first, second, third, and so on. Because qualitative researchers examine the same case or set of cases over time, they can see an issue evolve, a conflict emerge, or a social relationship develop. The researcher can detect process and causal relations.

In historical research, the passage of time may involve years or decades. In field research, the passage of time is shorter. Nevertheless, in both, a researcher notes what is occurring at different points in time and recognizes that *when* something occurs is often important.

Interpretation

Interpretation means to assign significance or coherent meaning. Quantitative research expresses meaning by using numbers (e.g., percentages or statistical coefficients), and a researcher tells how they relate to hypotheses.

Qualitative research reports rarely include tables with numbers. The only visual presentations of data may be maps, photographs, or diagrams showing how ideas are related. A researcher weaves the data into discussions of their significance. The data are in the form of words, including quotes or descriptions of particular events. Any numerical information is supplementary to the textual evidence.

A qualitative researcher gives data meaning, translates them, or makes them understandable. He or she begins with the point of view of the people being studied, and then finds out how the people being studied see the world, how they define the situation, or what it means for them.

The first step in qualitative interpretation is to learn about its meaning for the people being studied.[13] The people who created the social behavior have personal reasons or motives for their actions. This is **first-order interpretation.** A researcher's discovery and reconstruction of this first-order interpretation is a **second-order interpretation,** because the researcher comes in from the outside to discover what has occurred. In a second-order interpretation, the researcher elicits an underlying coherence or sense of meaning in the data. Because meaning develops within a set of other meanings, not in a vacuum, a second-order interpretation places the human action being studied in the "stream of behavior" or events to which it is related—its context.

A researcher who adopts a strict interpretive approach may stop at a second-order interpretation—that is, once he or she understands the significance of the action for the people being studied. Many qualitative researchers go further to generalize or link the second-order interpretation to general theory. They move to a broader level of interpretation, or **third-order interpretation,** whereby a researcher assigns general theoretical significance.

First-order interpretation   Interpretations from the point of view of the people being studied.

Second-order interpretation   Qualitative interpretations from the point of view of the researcher who conducted a study.

Third-order interpretation   Qualitative interpretations made by the readers of a research report.

Variable   A concept or its empirical measure that can take on multiple values.

Attributes   The categories or levels of a variable.

QUANTITATIVE DESIGN ISSUES

The Language of Variables and Hypotheses

Variation and Variables.   The **variable,** simply defined, is a concept that varies. Quantitative research uses a language of variables and relationships among variables.

In Chapter 3, you learned about two types of concepts: those that refer to a fixed phenomenon (e.g., the ideal type of bureaucracy) and those that vary in quantity, intensity, or amount (e.g., amount of education). The second type of concept and measures of the concepts are variables. Variables take on two or more values. Once you begin to look for them, you will see variables everywhere. For example, gender is a variable; it can take on one of two values: male or female. Marital status is a variable; it can take on the value of never married single, married, divorced, or widowed. Type of crime committed is a variable; it can take on values of robbery, burglary, theft, murder, and so forth. Family income is a variable; it can take on values from zero to billions of dollars. A person's attitude toward abortion is a variable; it can range from strongly favoring legal abortion to strongly believing in the sanctity of life.

The values or the categories of a variable are its **attributes.** It is easy to confuse variables with attributes. The confusion arises because the attribute of one variable can itself become a separate variable with a slight change in definition. The distinction is between concepts themselves that vary and conditions within concepts that vary. For example, "male" is not a variable; it describes a category of gender and is an attribute of the variable "gender." Yet, a related idea, "degree of masculinity," is a variable. It describes the intensity or strength of attachment to attitudes, beliefs, and behaviors associated with the concept of *masculine* within a culture. "Married" is not a variable; it is an attribute of the variable "marital status." Related ideas such as "number of years married" or "depth of commitment to a marriage" are variables. Likewise, "robbery" is not a variable; it is an attribute of the variable "type of crime." "Number of robberies," "robbery rate," "amount taken during a robbery," and "type of robbery" are all variables because they vary or take on a range of values.

Quantitative researchers redefine concepts into the language of variables. As the examples of variables and attributes illustrate, slight changes in definition change a nonvariable into a variable concept. As you saw in Chapter 3, concepts are the building blocks of theory; they organize thinking about the social world. Clear concepts with careful definitions are essential in theory.

Types of Variables. Researchers who focus on causal relations usually begin with an effect, then search for its causes. Variables are classified depending on their location in a causal relationship. The cause variable, or the one that identifies forces or conditions that act on something else, is the **independent variable.** The variable that is the effect or is the result or outcome of another variable is the **dependent variable.** The independent variable is "independent of" prior causes that act on it, whereas the dependent variable "depends on" the cause.

It is not always easy to determine whether a variable is independent or dependent. Two questions help you identify the independent variable. First, does it come before other variables in time? Independent variables come before any other type. Second, if the variables occur at the same time, does the author suggest that one variable has an impact on another variable? Independent variables affect or have an impact on other variables. Research topics are often phrased in terms of the dependent variables because dependent variables are the phenomenon to be explained. For example, suppose a researcher examines the reasons for an increase in the crime rate in Dallas, Texas; the dependent variable is the crime rate.

A basic causal relationship requires only an independent and a dependent variable. A third type of variable, the **intervening variable,** appears in more complex causal relations. It comes between the independent and dependent variables and shows the link or mechanism between them. Advances in knowledge depend not only on documenting cause-and-effect relationships but also on specifying the mechanisms that account for the causal relation. In a sense, the intervening variable acts as a dependent variable with respect to the independent variable

and acts as an independent variable toward the dependent variable.

For example, French sociologist Émile Durkheim developed a theory of suicide that specified a causal relationship between marital status and suicide rates. Durkheim found evidence that married people are less likely to commit suicide than single people. He believed that married people have greater social integration (i.e., feelings of belonging to a group or family). He thought that a major cause of one type of suicide was that people lacked a sense of belonging to a group. Thus, his theory can be restated as a three-variable relationship: marital status (independent variable) causes the degree of social integration (intervening variable), which affects suicide (dependent variable). Specifying the chain of causality makes the linkages in a theory clearer and helps a researcher test complex explanations.[14]

Simple theories have one dependent and one independent variable, whereas complex theories can contain dozens of variables with multiple independent, intervening, and dependent variables. For example, a theory of criminal behavior (dependent variable) identifies four independent variables: an individual's economic hardship, opportunities to commit crime easily, membership in a deviant subgroup of society that does not disapprove of crime, and lack of punishment for criminal acts. A multicause explanation usually specifies the independent variable that has the greatest causal effect.

A complex theoretical explanation contains a string of multiple intervening variables. For example, family disruption causes lower self-esteem among children, which causes depression, which

Independent variable   A cause variable that produces an effect or results on a dependent variable in a causal hypothesis.

Dependent variable   The effect or result variable that is caused by an independent variable in a causal hypothesis.

Intervening variable   A variable is logically or temporally after the independent variable and before the dependent variable, and through which their causal relation operates.

causes poor grades in school, which causes reduced prospects for a good job, which causes a lower adult income. The chain of variables is family disruption (independent), childhood self-esteem (intervening), depression (intervening), grades in school (intervening), job prospects (intervening), adult income (dependent).

Two theories on the same topic may have different independent variables. In addition, theories may agree about the independent and dependent variables but differ on the intervening variable or causal mechanism. For example, two theories say that family disruption causes lower adult income, but for different reasons. One theory holds that disruption encourages children to join deviant peer groups that are not socialized to norms of work and thrift. Another emphasizes the impact of the disruption on childhood depression and poor academic performance, which directly affect job performance.

A single research project usually tests only part of a causal chain. For example, a research project examining six variables may take the six from a large, complex theory with two dozen variables. Explicit links to a larger theory strengthen and clarify a research project.

Causal Theory and Hypotheses

The Hypothesis and Causality.

A **causal hypothesis** is a proposition to be tested or a tentative statement of a relationship between two variables. Hypotheses are guesses about how the social world works; they are stated in a value-neutral form. Kerlinger (1979:35) noted that

> hypotheses are much more important in scientific research than they would appear to be just by knowing what they are and how they are constructed. They have a deep and highly significant purpose of taking man out of himself. . . . Hypotheses are powerful tools for the advancement of knowledge, be-

---

Causal hypothesis   A statement of a causal explanation or proposition that has at least one independent and one dependent variable, and has yet to be empirically tested.

BOX 6.6   Five Characteristics of Causal Hypotheses

1. It has at least two variables.
2. It expresses a causal or cause-effect relationship between the variables.
3. It can be expressed as a prediction or an expected future outcome.
4. It is logically linked to a research question and a theory.
5. It is falsifiable; that is, it is capable of being tested against empirical evidence and shown to be true or false.

> cause, although formulated by man, they can be tested and shown to be correct or incorrect apart from man's values and beliefs.

A causal hypothesis has five characteristics (see Box 6.6). For example, the hypothesis that attending religious services reduces the probability of divorce can be restated as a prediction: Couples who attend religious services frequently have a lower divorce rate than do couples who rarely attend religious services. The prediction can be tested against empirical evidence. The hypothesis should be logically tied to a research question and to a theory. Researchers test hypotheses to answer the research question or to find empirical support for a theory. Statements that are necessarily true as a result of logic or questions that are impossible to answer through empirical observation (e.g., What is the "good life"? Is there a God?) cannot be scientific hypotheses.

Causal hypotheses can be stated in several ways. Sometimes the word *cause* is used, but this is not necessary. For example, a causal hypothesis between religious attendance and a reduced likelihood of divorce can be stated in 10 different ways (see Box 6.7).

Researchers avoid using the term *proved* when testing hypotheses. You might hear the word *proof* used in journalism, courts of law, or advertisements, but you will rarely hear research scientists use it. A jury says that the evidence "proves" someone guilty, or a television commercial states, "Studies prove that our aspirin cures headaches the fastest." This is

BOX **6.7** **Ways to State Causal Relations**

■ Religious attendance *causes* reduced divorce.
■ Religious attendance *leads* to reduced divorce.
■ Religious attendance *is related* to reduced divorce.
■ Religious attendance *influences* the reduction of divorce.
■ Religious attendance *is associated with* reduced divorce.
■ Religious attendance *produces* reduced divorce.
■ Religious attendance *results* in reduced divorce.
■ If people attend religious services, *then* the likelihood of divorce will be reduced.
■ *The higher* religious attendance, *the lower* the likelihood of divorce.
■ Religious attendance *reduces* the likelihood of divorce.

---

not the language of scientific research. In science, knowledge is tentative, and creating knowledge is an ongoing process that avoids premature closure.

Proof implies finality, absolute certainty, or something that does not need further investigation. *Proof* is too strong a term for the cautious world of science. Evidence supports or confirms, but does not prove, the hypothesis. Even after hundreds of studies show the same results, as with the link between cigarette smoking and lung cancer, scientists do not say that they have absolute proof. They can say that overwhelming evidence, or all studies to date, support or are consistent with the hypothesis. Scientists do not want to close off the possibility of discovering new evidence that might contradict past findings. They do not want to cut off future inquiry or stop exploring intervening mechanisms. History contains many examples of relationships that were once thought to be proved but were later found to be in error. *Proof* is used when referring to logical or mathematical relations, as in a mathematical proof, but not in discussing empirical research.

Testing and Refining a Hypothesis. Knowledge rarely advances on the basis of one test of a single hypothesis. In fact, it is easy to get a distorted

picture of the research process by focusing on a single research project that tests one hypothesis. Knowledge develops over time as researchers throughout the scientific community test many hypotheses. It grows from shifting and winnowing through many hypotheses. Each hypothesis represents an explanation of a dependent variable. If the evidence fails to support some hypotheses, they are gradually eliminated from consideration. Those that receive support remain in contention. Theorists and researchers constantly create new hypotheses to challenge those that have received support. Figure 6.2 represents an example of the process of shifting through hypotheses over time.

Scientists are a skeptical group. Support for a hypothesis in one research project is not sufficient for them to accept it. The principle of replication says that a hypothesis needs several tests with consistent and repeated support to gain broad acceptance. Another way to strengthen confidence in a hypothesis is to test related causal linkages in the theory from which it comes.

The strongest contender with the greatest empirical support is accepted as the best explanation at the time. The logic suggests that the more alternatives we test a hypothesis against, the greater our confidence in it. Some tests of hypotheses are called **crucial experiments** or crucial studies. This is a type of study whereby

> two or more alternative explanations for some phenomenon are available, each being compatible with the empirically given data; the crucial experiment is designed to yield results that can be accounted for by only one of the alternatives, which is thereby shown to be "the correct explanation." (Kaplan, 1964:151–152)

Thus, the infrequent crucial experiment is an important test of theory. Hypotheses from two different theories confront each other in crucial experiments, and one is knocked out of the competition. It is rare, but significant, when it occurs.

Crucial experiment A direct comparison and evaluation of competing explanations of the same phenomenon designed to show that one is superior to the other.

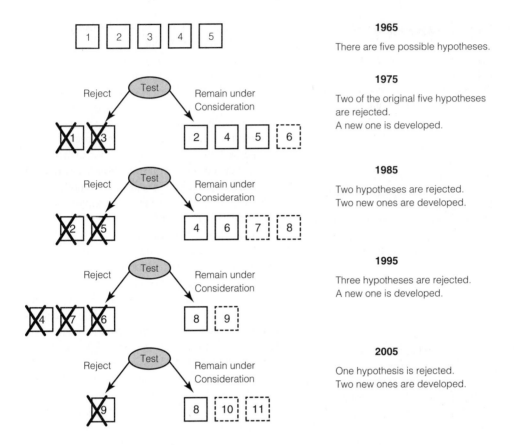

1965

There are five possible hypotheses.

1975

Two of the original five hypotheses are rejected.
A new one is developed.

1985

Two hypotheses are rejected.
Two new ones are developed.

1995

Three hypotheses are rejected.
A new one is developed.

2005

One hypothesis is rejected.
Two new ones are developed.

In 2005, 3 hypotheses are in contention, but from 1965 to 2005, 11 hypotheses were considered, and over time, 8 of them were rejected in one or more tests.

FIGURE 6.2   How the Process of Hypotheses Testing Operates over Time

Types of Hypotheses. Hypotheses are links in a theoretical causal chain and are used to test the direction and strength of a relationship between variables. When a hypothesis defeats its competitors, it supports the researcher's explanation. A curious aspect of hypothesis testing is that researchers treat evidence that supports a hypothesis differently from

evidence that opposes it. They give negative evidence more importance. The idea that negative evidence is critical when evaluating a hypothesis comes from the **logic of disconfirming hypotheses.**[15] It is associated with Karl Popper's idea of falsification (see Chapter 4 in the section on positivism) and with the use of *null hypotheses* (see later in this section).

Recall the preceding discussion of proof. A hypothesis is never proved, but it can be disproved. A researcher with supporting evidence can say only that the hypothesis remains a possibility or that it is still in the running. Negative evidence is more significant because the hypothesis becomes "tarnished"

Logic of disconfirming hypothesis The logic for the null hypothesis. It is based on the idea that confirming empirical evidence makes a weak case for the existence of a relationship. Instead of gathering supporting evidence, test that no relationship exists that provides more cautious, indirect support for its possible existence.

or "soiled" if the evidence fails to support it. This is because a hypothesis makes predictions. Negative and disconfirming evidence shows that the predictions are wrong. Positive or confirming evidence for a hypothesis is less critical because alternative hypotheses may make the same prediction. A researcher who finds confirming evidence for a prediction may not elevate one explanation over its alternatives.

For example, a man stands on a street corner with an umbrella and claims that his umbrella protects him from falling elephants. His hypothesis that the umbrella provides protection has supporting evidence. He has not had a single elephant fall on him in all the time he has had his umbrella open. Yet, such supportive evidence is weak; it also is consistent with an alternative hypothesis—that elephants do not fall from the sky. Both predict that the man will be safe from falling elephants. Negative evidence for the hypothesis—the one elephant that falls on him and his umbrella, crushing both—would destroy the hypothesis for good.

Researchers test hypotheses in a straightforward way and a null hypothesis way. Many quantitative researchers, especially experimenters, frame hypotheses in terms of a **null hypothesis** based on the logic of the disconfirming hypotheses. They look for evidence that will allow them to accept or reject the null hypothesis. Most people talk about a hypothesis as a way to predict a relationship. The null hypothesis does the opposite. It predicts no relationship. For example, Sarah believes that students who live on campus in dormitories get higher grades than students who live off campus and commute to college. Her null hypothesis is that there is no relationship between residence and grades. Researchers use the null hypothesis with a corresponding **alternative hypothesis** or experimental hypothesis. The alternative hypothesis says that a relationship exists. Sarah's alternative hypothesis is that students' on-campus residence has a positive effect on grades.

For most people, the null hypothesis approach seems like a backward way of hypothesis testing. Null hypothesis thinking rests on the assumption that researchers try to discover a relationship, so hypothesis testing should be designed to make finding a relationship more demanding. A researcher who uses the null hypothesis approach only directly tests the null hypothesis. If evidence supports or leads the researcher to accept the null hypothesis, he or she concludes that the tested relationship does not exist. This implies that the alternative hypothesis is false. On the other hand, if the researcher can find evidence to reject the null hypothesis, then the alternative hypotheses remain a possibility. The researcher cannot prove the alternative; rather, by testing the null hypotheses, he or she keeps the alternative hypotheses in contention. When null hypothesis testing is added to confirming evidence, the argument for an alterative hypothesis can grow stronger over time.

The scientific community is extremely cautious. It prefers to consider a causal relationship to be false until mountains of evidence show it to be true. This is similar to the Anglo-American legal idea of innocent until proved guilty. A researcher assumes, or acts as though, the null hypothesis is correct until *reasonable doubt* suggests otherwise. Researchers who use null hypotheses generally use them with specific statistical tests (e.g., *t*-test or *F*-test). Thus, a researcher says there is reasonable doubt in a null hypothesis if a statistical test suggests that the odds of it being false are 99 in 100. This is what a researcher means when he or she says that statistical tests allow him or her to "reject the null hypothesis at the .01 level of significance."

Another type of hypothesis is the **double-barreled hypothesis.**[16] Researchers should avoid using it; it shows unclear thinking and creates confusion. A double-barreled hypothesis puts two relationships in one hypothesis. For example, a researcher states, Poverty and a high concentration of

---

Null hypothesis   A hypothesis that states there is no significant effect of an independent variable on a dependent variable.

Alternative hypothesis   A hypothesis paired with the null hypothesis that says an independent variable has a significant effect on a dependent variable.

Double-barreled hypothesis   A confusing and poorly designed hypothesis with two independent variables in which it is unclear whether one or the other variable, or both in combination, produces an effect.

teenagers in an area cause property crime to increase. This is double barreled. It could mean either of two things: that poverty *or* a high concentration of teenagers causes property crime, or that *only* the combination of poverty with a high concentration of teenagers causes property crime. If "either one" is intended, and only one independent variable has an effect, the results of hypothesis testing are unclear. For example, if evidence shows that poverty causes crime but a concentration of teenagers does not, is the hypothesis supported? If the combination hypothesis is intended, then a researcher really means that the joint occurrence of poverty with a high concentration of teenagers only, and neither alone, causes property crime. If a researcher intends the combination meaning, it is not double barreled. Researchers should be clear and state the combination hypothesis explicitly. This is called an *interaction effect* (interaction effects are discussed later; see Figure 6.3).

Potential Errors in Causal Explanation

Developing a good explanation for any kind of theory (i.e., causal, interpretive, or network) requires avoiding common logical errors. These errors can enter at the stage of beginning research, or while interpreting and analyzing quantitative data, or while collecting and analyzing qualitative data. It is easiest to think of them as fallacies or false explanations that may appear to be legitimate on the surface.

Tautology. A **tautology** is a form of circular reasoning in which someone appears to say something new but is really talking in circles and making a statement that is *true by definition.* Tautologies can-

---

Tautology An error in explanation in which the causal factor (independent variable) and the result (dependent variable) are actually the same or restatements of one another. This is making an apparent causal relationship true by definition.

Teleology An error in explanation in which the causal relationship is empirically untestable because the causal factor does not come earlier in time than the result, or because the causal factor is a vague, general force that cannot be empirically measured.

---

not be tested with empirical data. For example, I heard a news report about a representative in the U.S. Congress who argued for a new crime law that would send many more 14- and 15-year-olds to adult courts. When asked why he was interested only in harsh punishment and not prevention, the representative said that offenders would learn that crime does not pay and that would prevent crime. He believed that the only prevention that worked was harsh punishment. This sounded a bit odd when I heard it. So, I reexamined the argument and realized it was tautological (i.e., it contained a logic error). The representative essentially said punishment resulted in prevention, because he had redefined *prevention* as being the same as *punishment.* Logically, he said punishment caused prevention because harsh punishment was prevention. Politicians may confuse the public with circular reasoning, but social researchers need to learn how to see through and avoid such garble.

Example. A conservative is a person with certain attitudes, beliefs, and values (desires less government regulation, no taxes on upper-income people, a strong military, religion in public schools, an end to antidiscrimination laws, etc.). It is a tautology to say that wanting less regulation, a strong military, and so on *causes* conservatism. In sloppy everyday usage, we can say, "Sally is conservative *because* she believes that there should be less regulation." This looks like a causal statement, but it is not a causal explanation. The set of attitudes is a *reason* to label Sally as a conservative, but those attitudes cannot be the *cause* of Sally's conservatism. Her attitudes *are* conservatism, so the statement is true by definition. It would be impossible ever to come up with evidence showing that those attitudes were not associated with conservatism.

Teleology. A **teleology** is something directed by an ultimate purpose or goal, and it takes two forms. First, it may be associated with events that occur because it is in "God's plan." In other words, an event occurs because God, or a deity, predetermined that it must occur. It appears when saying something occurs because it is part of the "natural unfolding" of an all-powerful inner spirit or *Geist* (German for

HYPOTHESIS: Poverty and a high concentration of teenagers in an area cause property crime to increase.

DOUBLE-BARRELED HYPOTHESIS: This can mean one of three things—

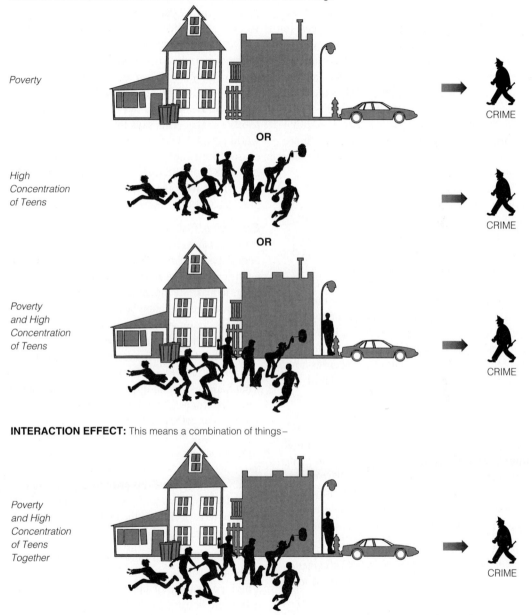

Poverty

OR

*High
Concentration
of Teens*

OR

*Poverty
and High
Concentration
of Teens*

CRIME

INTERACTION EFFECT: This means a combination of things—

*Poverty
and High
Concentration
of Teens
Together*

CRIME

FIGURE 6.3   Double-Barreled Hypothesis versus Interaction Effect

spirit). Thus, society develops in a certain direction because of the "spirit of the nation" or a "manifest destiny." This is similar to arguments that use human nature as a cause, as in, "Crime occurs because it is just human nature." Teleology appears in theories of history in which an "ideal society" or a utopia toward which the theory says society is moving explains events occurring now. It occurs in functional arguments. Thus, the family takes a certain form (e.g., nuclear) because the family fulfills social system "needs" for continuation (i.e., functional needs of the social system's survival into the future cause the family form now). These cannot be empirically measured.

Second, teleologies violate the temporal order requirement of causality. They lack a true independent variable because the "causal factor" is so extremely vague. Many people confuse goal motivation (i.e., a desire for something yet to occur) with teleology. I might say a goal causes an action; for example, my goal to get an A in a class caused me to get a good grade. A person's conscious goal or desire can be a legitimate cause, and not be teleological. First, a person's mental condition (e.g., goals, desires, or aspirations) can be empirically measured. Second, the mental condition exists now. This clarifies the temporal order issue. Third, the mental condition can be compared to future events that may or may not occur and is not itself a direct cause. The mental condition can cause current behaviors, and the behaviors increase the chances that a future event will occur. Conscious human goals differ from the will of God, a society's *Geist,* or system needs—which we can never empirically measure, have no fixed existence in time, and always match what occurs.

Example.   The statement *The nuclear family is the dominant family form in Western industrial societies* because *it is functional for the survival of the soci-*

Ecological fallacy   An error in explanation in which empirical data about associations found among large-scale units of analysis are greatly overgeneralized and treated as evidence for statements about relationships among much smaller units.

---

ety is an untestable teleological statement from structural functional theory. It is saying "society's survival" *causes* "development of family form." Yet, the only way we can observe whether a society survives is after the fact, or as a consequence of its having had a form of the family. Here is another example of a teleological statement: *Because it was the destiny of the United States to become a major world power, we find thousands of immigrants entering the Western frontier during the early nineteenth century.* This says that "becoming a major world power," which occurred from 1920 to 1945, caused "westward migration," which took place between 1850 and 1890. It uses the obscure term *destiny,* which, like other similar terms (e.g., "in God's plan"), cannot be observed in causal relationships.

Ecological Fallacy.   The **ecological fallacy** arises from a mismatch of units of analysis. It refers to a poor fit between the units for which a researcher has empirical evidence and the units for which he or she wants to make statements. It is due to imprecise reasoning and generalizing beyond what the evidence warrants. Ecological fallacy occurs when a researcher gathers data at a *higher* or an *aggregated* unit of analysis but wants to make a statement about a *lower* or *disaggregated* unit. It is a fallacy because what happens in one unit of analysis does not always hold for a different unit of analysis.[17] Thus, if a researcher gathers data for large aggregates (e.g., organizations, entire countries, etc.) and then draws conclusions about the behavior of individuals from those data, he or she is committing the ecological fallacy. You can avoid this error by ensuring that the unit of analysis you use in an explanation is the same as or very close to the unit on which you collect data (see Box 6.8).

Example.   Tomsville and Joansville each have about 45,000 people living in them. Tomsville has a high percentage of upper-income people. Over half of the households in the town have family incomes of over $160,000. The town also has more motorcycles registered in it than any other town of its size. The town of Joansville has many poor people. Half its households live below the poverty line. It also has fewer motorcycles registered in it than

BOX **6.8** **The Ecological Fallacy**

Researchers have criticized the famous study *Suicide* ([1897] 1957) by Émile Durkheim for the ecological fallacy of treating group data as though they were individual-level data. In the study, Durkheim compared the suicide rates of Protestant and Catholic districts in nineteenth-century western Europe and explained observed differences as due to differences between people's beliefs and practices in the two religions. He said that Protestants had a higher suicide rate than Catholics because they were more individualistic and had lower social integration. Durkheim and early researchers had data only by district. Because people tended to reside with others of the same religion, Durkheim used group-level data (i.e., region) for individuals.

Later researchers (van Poppel and Day, 1996) re-examined nineteenth-century suicide rates with only individual-level data that they discovered for some areas. They compared the death records and looked at the official reason of death and religion, but their results differed from Durkheim's. Apparently, local officials at that time recorded deaths differently for people of different religions. They recorded "unspecified" as a reason for death far more often for Catholics because of a strong moral prohibition against suicide among Catholics. Durkheim's larger theory may be correct, yet the evidence he had to test it was weak because he used data aggregated at the group level while trying to explain the actions of individuals.

any other town its size. But it is a *fallacy* to say, on the basis of this information alone, that rich people are more likely to own motorcycles or that the evidence shows a relationship between family income and motorcycle ownership. The reason is that we do not know which families in Tomsville or Joansville own motorcycles. We know about only the two variables—average income and number of motorcycles—for the towns as a whole. The unit of analysis for observing variables is the town as a whole. Perhaps all of the low- and middle-income families in Tomsville belong to a motorcycle club, and not a single upper-income family belongs. Or perhaps one rich family and five poor ones in Joansville each own motorcycles. In order to make a statement about the relationship between family ownership of motorcycles and family income, we have to collect information on families, not on towns as a whole.

Reductionism. Another problem involving mismatched units of analysis and imprecise reasoning about evidence is **reductionism,** also called the *fallacy of nonequivalence* (see Box 6.9). This error occurs when a researcher explains macro-level events using evidence about specific individuals. It occurs when a researcher observes a *lower* or *disaggregated* unit of analysis but makes statements about

the operations of *higher* or *aggregated* units. It is a mirror image of the mismatch error in the ecological fallacy. A researcher who has data on how individuals behave but makes statements about the dynamics of macro-level units is committing the error of reductionism. It occurs because it is often easier to get data on concrete individuals. Also, the operation of macro-level units is more abstract and nebulous. Lieberson has argued that this error, which he says is common in social research, leads to inconsistencies, contradictions, and confusion. He (1985:108, 113–114) forcefully stated:

> *Associations on the lower level are irrelevant for determining the validity of a proposition about processes operating on the higher level. As a matter of fact, no useful understanding of the higher-level structure can be obtained from lower-level analysis. . . . If we are interested in the higher-level processes and events, it is because we operate with the understanding that they have distinct qualities that are not simply derived by summing up the subunits.*

Reductionism   An error in explanation in which empirical data about associations found among small-scale units of analysis are greatly overgeneralized and treated as evidence for statements about relationships among much larger units.

BOX **6.9** Error of Reductionism

Suppose you pick up a book and read the following:

American race relations changed dramatically during the Civil Rights Era of the 1960s. Attitudes among the majority, white population shifted to greater tolerance as laws and court rulings changed across the nation. Opportunities that had been legally and officially closed to all but the white population—in the areas of housing, jobs, schooling, voting rights, and so on—were opened to people of all races. From the Brown vs. *Board of Education decision in 1955, to the Civil Rights Act of 1964, to the War on Poverty from 1966 to 1968, a new, dramatic outlook swept the country. This was the result of the vision, dedication, and actions of America's foremost civil rights leader, Dr. Martin Luther King, Jr.*

This says: *dependent variable* = major change in U.S. race relations over a 10- to 13-year period; *independent variable* = King's vision and actions.

If you know much about the civil rights era, you see a problem. The entire civil rights movement and its successes are attributed to a single individual. Yes, one individual does make a difference and helps build and guide a movement, but the *movement* is missing. The idea of a social-political movement as a causal force is reduced to its major leader. The distinct social phenomenon—a movement—is obscured. Lost are the actions of hundreds of thousands of people (marches, court cases, speeches, prayer meetings, sit-ins, rioting, petitions, beatings, etc.) involved in advancing a shared goal and the responses to them. The movement's ideology, popular mobilization, politics, organization, and strategy are absent. Related macro-level historical events and trends that may have influenced the movement (e.g., Vietnam War protest, mood shift with the killing of John F. Kennedy, African American separatist politics, African American migration to urban North) are also ignored.

This error is not unique to historical explanations. Many people think in terms of only individual actions and have an individualist bias, sometimes called *methodological individualism*. This is especially true in the extremely individualistic U.S. culture. The error is that it disregards units of analysis or forces beyond the individual. The *error of reductionism* shifts explanation to a much lower unit of analysis. One could continue to reduce from an individual's behavior to biological processes in a person, to micro-level neurochemical activities, to the subatomic level.

Most people live in "social worlds" focused on local, immediate settings and their interactions with a small set of others, so their everyday sense of reality encourages seeing social trends or events as individual actions or psychological processes. Often, they become blind to more abstract, macro-level entities—social forces, processes, organizations, institutions, movements, or structures. The idea that all social actions cannot be reduced to individuals alone is the core of sociology. In his classic work *Suicide,* Émile Durkheim fought methodological individualism and demonstrated that larger, unrecognized social forces explain even highly individual, private actions.

As with the ecological fallacy, you can avoid this error by ensuring that the unit of analysis in your explanation is very close to the one for which you have evidence.

Researchers who fail to think precisely about the units of analysis and those who do not couple data with the theory are likely to commit the ecological fallacy or reductionism. They make a mistake about the data appropriate for a research question, or they may seriously overgeneralize from the data.

You can make assumptions about units of analysis other than the ones you study empirically. Thus, research on individuals rests on assumptions that individuals act within a set of social institutions. Research on social institutions is based on assumptions about individual behavior. We know that many micro-level units form macro-level units. The danger is that it is easy to slide into using the behavior of micro units, such as individuals, to explain the actions of macro units, such as social institutions. What happens among units at one level does not necessarily hold for different units of analysis. Sociology rests on the belief that a distinct level of social reality exists beyond the individual. Explanations of this level require data and theory that go beyond the individual alone. The causes, forces, structures, or processes that exist among macro units cannot be reduced to individual behavior.

Example. Why did World War I occur? You may have heard that it was because a Serbian shot an archduke in the AustroHungarian Empire in 1914. This is reductionism. Yes, the assassination was a factor, but the macro-political event between nations—war—cannot be reduced to a specific act of one individual. If it could, we could also say that the war occurred because the assassin's alarm clock worked and woke him up that morning. If it had not worked, there would have been no assassination, so the alarm clock caused the war! The event, World War I, was much more complex and was due to many social, political, and economic forces that came together at a point in history. The actions of specific individuals had a role, but only a minor one compared to these macro forces. Individuals affect events, which eventually, in combination with larger-scale social forces and organizations, affect others and move nations, but individual actions alone are not the cause. Thus, it is likely that a war would have broken out at about that time even if the assassination had not occurred.

Spuriousness. To call a relationship between variables *spurious* means that it is false, a mirage. Researchers get excited if they think they have found a spurious relationship because they can show the world to be more complex than it appears on the surface. Because any association between two variables might be spurious, researchers are cautious when they discover that two variables are associated; upon further investigation, it may not be the basis for a causal relationship. It may be an illusion, just like the mirage that resembles a pool of water on a road during a hot day.

Spuriousness occurs when two variables are associated but are not causally related because there is actually an unseen third factor that is the real cause (see Boxes 6.10 and 6.11). The third variable causes both the apparent independent and the dependent variable. It accounts for the observed association. In terms of conditions for causality, the unseen third factor represents a more powerful alternative explanation.

BOX **6.10** **Spuriousness**

In their study of the news media, Neuman and colleagues (1992) found a correlation between type of news source and knowledge. People who prefer to get their news from television are less knowledgeable than those who get it from print sources. This correlation is often interpreted as the "dumbing down" of information. In other words, television news causes people to know little.

The authors found that the relationship was spurious, however. "We were able to show that the entire relationship between television news preference and lower knowledge scores is spurious" (p. 113). They found that a third variable, initially unseen, explained both to a preference for television news and a level of knowledge about current events. They said, "We find that what is really causing the television-is-the-problem effect is the preference for people with lower cognitive skill to get their news from television" (p. 98). The missing or hidden variable was "cognitive skill." The authors defined cognitive skill as a person's ability to use reason and manipulate abstract ideas. In other words, people who find it difficult to process abstract, complex information turn to television news. Others may also use the high-impact, entertaining television news sources, but they use it less and heavily supplement it with other more demanding, information-rich print sources. People who have weak information skills also tend to be less knowledgeable about current events and about other topics that require abstract thought or deal with complex information.

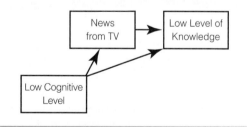

Spuriousness An apparent causal relationship that is illusionary due to the effect of an unseen or initially hidden causal factor. If the unseen factor has a causal impact on both an independent and dependent variable, it produces the false impression that there is a relationship between them.

BOX **6.11** Night-Lights and Spuriousness

For many years, researchers observed a strong positive association between the use of a night-light and children who were nearsighted. Many thought that the night-light was somehow causing the children to develop vision problems (illustrated as **a** below). Other researchers could think of no reason for a causal link between night-light use and developing nearsightedness. A 1999 study provided the answer. It found that nearsighted parents are more likely to use night-lights; they also genetically pass on their vision deficiency to their children. The study found no link between night-light use and nearsightedness once parental vision was added to the explanation (see **b** below). Thus the initial causal link was misleading or spurious (from *New York Times,* May 22, 2001).

a. Initial relationship

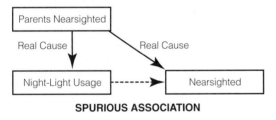

POSITIVE ASSOCIATION

b. Addition of the missing true causal factor

SPURIOUS ASSOCIATION

How can you tell whether a relationship is spurious, and how do you find out what the mysterious third factor is? You will need to use statistical techniques (discussed later in this book) to test whether an association is spurious. To use them, you need a theory or at least a guess about possible third factors. Actually, spuriousness is based on some common-sense logic that you already use. For example, you already know that there is an association between the use of air conditioners and ice cream cone consumption. If you measured the number of air conditioners in use and the number of ice cream cones sold for each day, you would find a strong correlation, with more cones sold on the days when more air conditioners are in use. But you know that eating ice cream cones does not cause people to turn on air conditioners. Instead, both variables are caused by a third factor: hot days. You could verify the same thing through statistics by measuring the daily temperature as well as ice cream consumption and air conditioner use. In social research, opposing theories help people figure out which third factors are relevant for many topics (e.g., the causes of crime or the reasons for war or child abuse).

Example. Some people argue that taking illegal drugs causes suicide, school dropouts, and violent acts. Advocates of "drugs are the problem" position point to the positive correlations between taking drugs and being suicidal, dropping out of school, and engaging in violence. They argue that ending drug use will greatly reduce suicide, dropouts, and violence. Others argue that many people turn to drugs because of their emotional problems or high levels of disorder of their communities (e.g., high unemployment, unstable families, high crime, few community services, lack of civility). The people with emotional problems or who live in disordered communities are also more likely to commit suicide, drop out, and engage in violence. This means that reducing emotional problems and community disorder will cause illegal drug use, dropping out, suicide, and violence all to decline greatly. Reducing drug taking alone will have only a limited effect because it ignores the root cause, and drugs are not the root cause. The "drugs are the problem" argument is spurious because the initial relationship between taking illegal drugs and the problems is misleading. The emotional problems and community disorder are the true and often unseen causal variables.

We can now turn from the errors in causal explanation to avoid and more to other issues involving hypotheses. Table 6.2 provides a review of the major errors, and Figure 6.4 illustrates them.

From the Research Question to Hypotheses

It is difficult to move from a broad topic to hypotheses, but the leap from a well-formulated re-

TABLE 6.2   Summary of Errors in Explanation

TYPE OF ERROR	SHORT DEFINITION	EXAMPLE
Tautology	The relationship is true by definition and involves circular reasoning.	Poverty is caused by having very little money.
Teleology	The cause is an intention that is inappropriate, or it has misplaced temporal order.	People get married in religious ceremonies because society wants them to.
Ecological fallacy	The empirical observations are at too high a level for the causal relationship that is stated.	New York has a high crime rate. Joan lives in New York. Therefore, she probably stole my watch.
Reductionism	The empirical observations are at too low a level for the causal relationship that is stated.	Because Steven lost his job and did not buy a new car, the country entered a long economic recession.
Spuriousness	An unseen third variable is the actual cause of both the independent and dependent variable.	Hair length is associated with TV programs. People with short hair prefer watching football; people with long hair prefer romance stories. (*Unseen:* Gender)

search question to hypotheses is a short one. Hints about hypotheses are embedded within a good research question. In addition, hypotheses are tentative answers to research questions.

Consider an example research question: "Is age at marriage associated with divorce?" The question contains two variables: "age at marriage" and "divorce." To develop a hypothesis, a researcher asks, "Which is the independent variable?" The independent variable is "age at marriage" because marriage must logically precede divorce. The researcher also asks, "What is the direction of the relationship?" The hypothesis could be: "The lower the age at time of marriage, the greater the chances that the marriage will end in divorce." This hypothesis answers the research question and makes a prediction. Notice that the research question can be reformulated and better focused now: "Are couples who marry younger more likely to divorce?"

Several hypotheses can be developed for one research question. Another hypothesis from the same research question is: "The smaller the difference between the ages of the marriage partners at the time of marriage, the less likely that the mar-

riage will end in divorce." In this case, the variable "age at marriage" is specified differently.

Hypotheses can specify that a relationship holds under some conditions but not others. As Lieberson (1985:198) remarked, "In order to evaluate the utility of a given causal proposition, it is important that there be a clear-cut statement of the conditions under which it will operate." For example, a hypothesis states: "The lower the age of the partners at time of marriage, the greater the chances that the marriage will end in divorce, unless it is a marriage between members of a tight-knit traditional religious community in which early marriage is the norm."

Formulating a research question and a hypothesis does not have to proceed in fixed stages. A researcher can formulate a tentative research question and then develop possible hypotheses; the hypotheses then helps the researcher state the research question more precisely. The process is interactive and involves creativity.

You may be wondering: Where does theory fit into the process of moving from a topic to a hypothesis I can test? Recall from Chapter 3 that theory

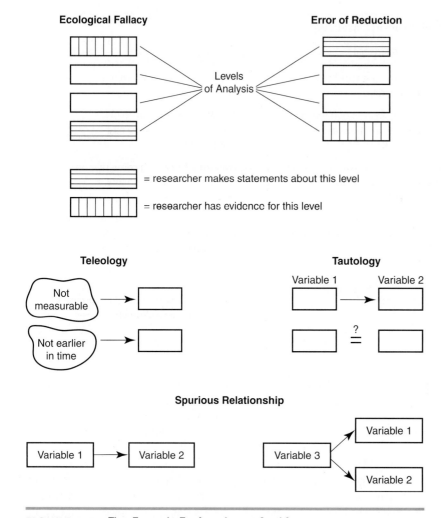

FIGURE 6.4   Five Errors in Explanation to Avoid

takes many forms. Researchers use general theoretical issues as a source of topics. Theories provide concepts that researchers turn into variables as well as the reasoning or mechanism that helps researchers connect variables into a research question. A hypothesis can both answer a research question and be an untested proposition from a theory. Researchers can express a hypothesis at an abstract, conceptual level or restate it in a more concrete, measurable form.

Examples of specific studies may help to illustrate the parts of the research process. For examples of three quantitative studies, see Chart 6.1; for two qualitative studies, see Chart 6.2.

CONCLUSION

In this chapter, you encountered the groundwork needed to begin a study. You saw how differences in the qualitative and quantitative styles direct a researcher to prepare for a study differently. All social researchers narrow their topic into a more specific, focused research question. The styles of research suggest a different form and sequence of

CHART 6.1   Examples of Quantitative Studies

Study Citation and Title	Ridgeway and Erickson (2000), "Creating and Spreading Status Beliefs"	Musick, Wilson, and Bynum (2000), "Race and Formal Volunteering: The Differential Effects of Class and Religion"	Barlow, Barlow, and Chiricos (1995), "Economic Conditions and Ideologies of Crime in the Media"
Methodological Technique Used	Experiment	Survey	Content analysis
Topic	Processes by which people develop beliefs about the social status of others	Rates of volunteering by White and Black adults	U.S. mass media portrayals of law-breakers
Research Question	As individuals interact, do external, structural factors that affect the interaction mold the beliefs they come to hold about entire categories of people in the future?	What different kinds of resources are available to Blacks and Whites that explain why Blacks are less likely to volunteer?	Do economic conditions affect how the media portray offenders?
Main Hypothesis Tested	People can be "taught" to make status distinctions among categories of people, who are actually equal, based on limited interaction in which one category exerts more skill.	Social class and religion affect whether a person volunteers differently for Whites and Blacks.	The media distortion of crime shows offenders in a more negative way (blames them) when economic conditions are bad.
Main Independent Variable(s)	Whether a person's interaction with someone in a category that shows members of the category to have superior or inferior skill at tasks	Social class, religious attendance, race	Unemployment rate in several years, 1953–1982
Main Dependent Variable	Whether individuals develop and apply a belief of inequality to an entire category of people	Whether a person said he or she volunteered for any of five organizations (religious, education, political or labor, senior citizen, or local)	Whether distortion occurred, measured as a mismatch between media attention (articles in *Time* magazine) and crime statistics for several years
Unit of Analysis	Individual undergraduate student	Individual adults	The media report
Universe	All individuals	All adult Whites and Blacks in the U.S.	All American mass media reports

CHART 6.2   Examples of Qualitative Studies

Study Citation and Title	Lu and Fine (1995), "The Presentation of Ethnic Authenticity: Chinese Food as a Social Accomplishment"	Molotch, Freudenburg, and Paulsen (2000), "History Repeats Itself, but How? City Character, Urban Tradition, and the Accomplishment of Place"
Methodological Technique Used	Field research	Historical-comparative research
Topic	The ways ethnic cultures are displayed within the boundaries of being acceptable in the U.S. and how they deploy cultural resources	The ways cities develop a distinct urban "character"
Research Question	How do Chinese restaurants present food to balance authenticity and to satisfy non-Chinese U.S. customers?	Why did the California cities of Santa Barbara and Ventura, which appear very similar on the surface, develop very different characters?
Grounded Theory	Ethnic restaurants Americanize their food to fit local tastes but also construct an impression of authenticity. It is a negotiated process of meeting the customer's expectations/taste conventions and the desire for an exotic and authentic eating experience.	The authors use two concepts, "lash up" (interaction of many factors) and structure (past events create constraints on subsequent ones), to elaborate on character and tradition. Economic, political, cultural, and social factors combine to create distinct cultural-economic places. Similar forces can have opposite results depending on context.
Bricolage	The authors observed and interviewed at four Chinese restaurants, but relied on evidence from past studies.	The authors used historical records, maps, photos, official statistical information, and interviews. In addition to economic, social conditions, they examined voluntary associations and physical materials.
Process	Restaurants make modifications to fit available ingredients, their market niche, and the cultural and food tastes of local customers.	Conditions in the two cities contributed to two different economic development responses to oil and highways. Ventura formed an industrial-employment base around oil and allowed new highways. Santa Barbara limited both and instead focused on creating a tourism industry.
Context	Chinese restaurants, especially four in Athens, Georgia	The middle part of California's coast over the past 100 years

decisions, and different answers to when and how to focus the research. The style that a researcher uses will depend on the topic he or she selects, the researcher's purpose and intended use of study results, the orientation toward social science that he or she adopts, and the individual researcher's own assumptions and beliefs.

Quantitative researchers take a linear path and emphasize objectivity. They are more likely to use explicit, standardized procedures and a causal explanation. Their language of variables and hypotheses is found across many areas of science that are based on a positivist tradition. The process is often deductive with a sequence of discrete steps that precede data collection: Narrow the topic to a more focused question, transform nebulous theoretical concepts into more exact variables, and develop one or more hypotheses to test. In actual practice, researchers move back and forth, but the general process flows in a single, linear direction. In addition, quantitative researchers take special care to avoid logical errors in hypothesis development and causal explanation.

Qualitative researchers follow a nonlinear path and emphasize becoming intimate with the details of a natural setting or a particular cultural-historical context. They use fewer standardized procedures or explicit steps, and often devise on-the-spot techniques for one situation or study. Their language of cases and contexts directs them to conduct detailed investigations of particular cases or processes in their search for authenticity. They rarely separate planning and design decisions into a distinct pre–data collection stage, but continue to develop the study design throughout early data collection.

In fact, the more inductive qualitative style encourages a slow, flexible evolution toward a specific focus based on what the researcher is learning from the data. Grounded theory emerges from the researcher's continuous reflections on the data and the context.

The qualitative and quantitative distinction is often overdrawn and presented as a rigid dichotomy. Too often, adherents of one style of social research judge the other style on the basis of the assumptions and standards of their own style. The quantitative researcher demands to know the variables used and the hypothesis tested. The qualitative researcher balks at turning humanity into cold numbers. The well-versed, prudent social researcher understands and appreciates each style on its own terms and recognizes the strengths and limitations of each. The ultimate goal of developing a better understanding and explanation of the social world comes from an appreciation of what each has to offer.

KEY TERMS

alternative hypothesis	independent variable	reductionism
attributes	intervening variable	second-order interpretation
bricolage	linear research path	spuriousness
causal hypothesis	logic in practice	tautology
crucial experiment	logic of disconfirming	teleology
dependent variable	hypothesis	third-order interpretation
double-barreled hypothesis	nonlinear research path	triangulation
ecological fallacy	null hypothesis	universe
first-order interpretation	reconstructed logic	variable

REVIEW QUESTIONS

1. What are the implications of saying that qualitative research uses more of a logic in practice than a reconstructed logic?

2. What does it mean to say that qualitative research follows a nonlinear path? In what ways is a nonlinear path valuable?

3. Describe the differences between independent, dependent, and intervening variables.

4. Why don't we *prove* results in social research?

5. Take a topic of interest and develop two research questions for it. For each research question specify the units of analysis and universe.

6. What two hypotheses are used if a researcher uses the logic of disconfirming hypotheses? Why is negative evidence stronger?

7. Restate the following in terms of a hypothesis with independent and dependent variables: "The number of miles a person drives in a year affects the number of visits a person makes to filling stations, and there is a positive unidirectional relationship between the variables."

8. Compare the ways quantitative and qualitative researchers deal with personal bias and the issue of trusting the researcher.

9. How do qualitative and quantitative researchers use theory?

10. Explain how qualitative researchers approach the issue of interpreting data. Refer to first-, second-, and third-order interpretations.

NOTES

1. See Tashakkori and Teddlie (1998).
2. Ward and Grant (1985) and Grant and colleagues (1987) analyzed research in sociology journals and suggested that journals with a higher proportion of qualitative research articles address gender topics, but that studies of gender are not themselves more likely to be qualitative.
3. See Kaplan (1964:3–11) for a discussion.
4. On the issue of using quantitative, statistical techniques as a substitute for trust, see Collins (1984), Porter (1995), Smith and Heshusius (2004).
5. For discussion, see Schwandt (1997), Swanborn (1996), and Tashakkori and Teddlie (1998:90–93).
6. For examples of checking, see Agar (1980) and Becker (1970c).
7. Problem choice and topic selection are discussed in Campbell and associates (1982) and in Zuckerman (1978).
8. Exceptions are secondary data analysis and existing statistics research. In these situations, a quantitative researcher often focuses the research question and develops a specific hypothesis to test after he or she examines the available data.

9. See Flick (1998:51).
10. See Ball and Smith (1992) and Harper (1994).
11. For place of theory in qualitative research, see Hammersley (1995).
12. See Harper (1987:9, 74–75) and Schwandt (1997: 10–11).
13. See Blee and Billings (1986), Ricoeur (1970), and Schneider (1987) on the interpretation of text in qualitative research.
14. See Lieberson (1985:185–187) for a discussion of basic and superficial variables in a set of causal linkages. Davis (1985) and Stinchcombe (1968) provide good general introductions to making linkages among variables in social theory.
15. The logic of disconfirming hypothesis is discussed in Singleton and associates (1988:56–60).
16. See Bailey (1987:43) for a discussion of this term.
17. The general problem of aggregating observation and making causal inferences is discussed in somewhat technical terms in Blalock (1982:237–264) and in Hannan (1985). O'Brien (1992) argues that the ecological fallacy is one of a whole group of logical fallacies in which levels and units of analysis are confused and overgeneralized.

Qualitative and Quantitative Measurement

> *Measurement, in short, is not an end in itself. Its scientific worth can be appreciated only in an instrumentalist perspective, in which we ask what ends measurement is intended to serve, what role it is called upon to play in the scientific situation, what functions it performs in inquiry.*
>
> —Abraham Kaplan, *The Conduct of Inquiry*, p. 171

You may have heard of the Stanford Binet IQ test to measure intelligence, the Index of Dissimilarity to measure racial segregation, the Poverty Line to measure whether one is poor, or Uniform Crime Reports to measure the amount of crime. When social researchers test a hypothesis, evaluate an explanation, provide empirical support for a theory, or study an applied issue, they measure concepts and variables. How social researchers measure the numerous aspects of the social world—such as intelligence, segregation, poverty, crime, self-esteem, political power, alienation, or racial prejudice—is the focus of this chapter.

Quantitative researchers are far more concerned about measurement issues than are qualitative researchers. Quantitative researchers treat measurement as a distinct step in the research process that occurs prior to data collection, and they developed special terminology and techniques for it. They adopt a deductive approach, and begin with a concept, then create empirical measures that precisely capture it in a form that can be expressed in numbers.

Qualitative researchers approach measurement very differently. They develop ways to capture and express concepts using various alternatives to numbers. They often take an inductive approach, creating new concepts as part of measuring.

How people think about variables affects social issues beyond concerns of research methodology. For example, psychologists debate the meaning and measurement of intelligence. Most intelligence tests that people use in schools, on job applications, and in making statements about racial or other inherited superiority measure only analytic reasoning (i.e., one's capacity to think abstractly and to infer logically). Yet, many argue that there are types of intelligence in addition to analytic, such as practical and creative intelligence. Others suggest more types, such as social-interpersonal, emotional, body-kinesthetic, musical, or spatial. If there are many forms of intelligence but people narrowly limit measurement to one type, it seriously restricts how schools identify and nurture learning; how larger society evaluates, promotes, and recognizes the contributions of people; and how a society values diverse human abilities.

Likewise, different policymakers and researchers measure poverty differently. How people measure poverty will determine whether people get assistance from numerous social programs (e.g., subsidized housing, food aid, health care, child care, etc.). For example, some say that people are poor only if they cannot afford the food required to prevent malnutrition. Others say that people are poor if they have an annual income that is less than one-half of the average (median) income. Still others say that people are poor if they earn below a "living wage" based on a judgment about the income needed to meet minimal community standards of health, safety, and decency in hygiene, housing, clothing, diet, transportation, and so forth. Decisions about a variable—poverty—can greatly influence the daily living conditions of millions of people.

Brady (2003) noted that many academics and policymakers criticized the official U.S. poverty measure. He concluded, "the U.S. measure clearly provides inaccurate results about trends" (p. 743). For example, the official poverty rate in 1997 was 13.3 percent, while other methodologically superior measures stated that 17.6 to 30.1 percent were poor.

WHY MEASURE?

We use many measures in our daily lives. For example, this morning I woke up and hopped onto a bathroom scale to see how well my diet is working. I glanced at a thermometer to find out whether to wear a coat. Next, I got into my car and checked the gas gauge to be sure I could make it to campus. As I drove, I watched the speedometer so I would not get a speeding ticket. By 8:00 A.M., I had measured weight, temperature, gasoline volume, and speed—all measures about the physical world. Such precise, well-developed measures, which we use in daily life, arc fundamental in the natural sciences.

We also measure the nonphysical world in everyday life, but in less exact terms. We are measuring when we say that a restaurant is excellent, that Pablo is really smart, that Karen has a negative attitude toward life, that Johnson is really prejudiced, or that the movie last night had a lot of violence in it. However, such everyday judgments as "really prejudiced" or "a lot of violence" are imprecise, vague, or intuitive measures.

Measurement also extends our senses. The astronomer or biologist uses the telescope or the microscope to extend natural vision. In contrast to our senses, scientific measurement is more sensitive, varies less with the specific observer, and yields more exact information. You recognize that a thermometer gives more specific, precise information about temperature than touch can. Likewise, a good bathroom scale gives you more specific, constant, and precise information about the weight of a 5-year-old girl than you get by lifting her and calling her "heavy" or "light." Social measures provide information about social reality.

In addition, measurement helps people observe what is otherwise invisible. Measurement extends human senses. It lets us observe things that were once unseen and unknown but were predicted by theory.

Before you can measure, you need a clear idea about what you are interested in. For example, you cannot see or feel magnetism with your natural senses. Magnetism comes from a theory about the physical world. You observe its effects indirectly; for instance, metal flecks move near a magnet. The magnet allows you to "see" or measure the magnetic fields. Natural scientists have invented thousands of measures to "see" very tiny things (molecules or insect organs) or very large things (huge geological land masses or planets) that are not observable through ordinary senses. In addition, researchers are constantly creating new measures.[1]

Some of the things a social researcher is interested in measuring are easy to see (e.g., age, sex, skin color, etc.), but most cannot be directly observed (e.g., attitudes, ideology, divorce rates, deviance, social roles, etc.). Like the natural scientist who invents indirect measures of the "invisible" objects and forces of the physical world, the social researcher devises measures for difficult-to-observe aspects of the social world. For example, suppose you heard a principal complain about teacher morale in a school. You can create a measure for the morale of teachers.

QUANTITATIVE AND QUALITATIVE MEASUREMENT

Both qualitative and quantitative researchers use careful, systematic methods to gather high-quality data. In both styles, data are empirical representations of concepts, and measurement links data to concepts. Yet, differences in the styles of research and the types of data mean they approach the measurement process differently. Designing measures of variables is a vital step in planning a study for quantitative researchers. Qualitative researchers measure with a wider variety of techniques. The two approaches to measurement have three distinctions.

One difference between the two styles involves timing. Quantitative researchers think about variables and convert them into specific actions during a planning stage that occurs before and separate from gathering or analyzing data. Qualitative researchers measure during the data collection process.

A second difference involves the data itself. Quantitative researchers develop techniques that produce data in the form of numbers. The researcher moves deductively from abstract ideas, to specific data collection techniques, to precise numerical information produced by the techniques. The numer-

ical information is an empirical representation of the abstract ideas.

Data for qualitative researchers sometimes is in the form of numbers; more often, it includes written or spoken words, actions, sounds, symbols, physical objects, or visual images (e.g., maps, photographs, videos, etc.). The qualitative researcher does not convert all observation into a single, common medium such as numbers. Instead, he or she develops many flexible, ongoing processes that leave the data in various shapes, sizes, and forms.

A third difference is how the two styles make construct-to-data linkages. Quantitative researchers contemplate and reflect on concepts before they gather any data. They construct measurement techniques that bridge concepts and data. Qualitative researchers also reflect on ideas before data collection, but they develop many, if not most, of their concepts during data collection. The qualitative researcher reexamines and reflects on the data and concepts simultaneously and interactively. Researchers start gathering data and measuring based on what they encounter. As they gather data, they reflect on the process and develop new ideas that give them direction and suggest new ways to measure. In turn, the new ways to measure determine how the researchers will continue to collect data. They bridge ideas and data in a continuing, interactive process.

PARTS OF THE MEASUREMENT PROCESS

When a researcher measures, he or she takes a concept, idea, or construct[2] and develops a measure (i.e., a technique, a process, a procedure, etc.) by which he or she can observe the idea empirically. Quantitative researchers begin with an abstract idea, follow with a measurement procedure, and end with empirical data that represent the ideas. Qualitative researchers primarily begin with empirical data, follow with abstract ideas, relate ideas and data, and end with a mixture of ideas and data. Actually, the process is more interactive in both styles of research. As a quantitative researcher develops measures, the constructs become refined and clearer, and as the researcher applies the measures to gather data, he or she often adjusts the measurement technique. As a qualitative researcher gathers data, he or she uses some preexisting ideas to assist in data collection, and will then mix old with new ideas that are developed from the data.

All researchers use two processes: conceptualization and operationalization in measurement. **Conceptualization** is the process of taking a construct and refining it by giving it a conceptual or theoretical definition. A **conceptual definition** is a definition in abstract, theoretical terms. It refers to other ideas or constructs. There is no magical way to turn a construct into a precise conceptual definition. It involves thinking carefully, observing directly, consulting with others, reading what others have said, and trying possible definitions.

A good definition has one clear, explicit, and specific meaning. There is no ambiguity or vagueness. Some scholarly articles have been devoted to conceptualizing key concepts. Melbin (1978) conceptualized *night* as a frontier, Gibbs (1989) analyzed the meaning of the concept of *terrorism,* and Ball and Curry (1995) discussed ways to conceptualize what a *street gang* means. Researchers need clear, unambiguous definitions of concepts to develop sound explanations.

A single construct can have several definitions, and people may disagree over definitions. Conceptual definitions are linked to theoretical frameworks. For example, a conflict theorist may define *social class* as the power and property a group of people in society has or lacks. A structural functionalist defines it in terms of individuals who share a social status, lifestyle, or subjective identification. Although people disagree over definitions, the researcher should always state explicitly which definition he or she is using.

Some constructs (e.g., alienation) are highly abstract and complex. They contain lower-level concepts within them (e.g., powerlessness), which

can be made even more specific (e.g., a feeling of little power over where one can live). Other constructs are concrete and simple (e.g., age). A researcher needs to be aware of how complex and abstract a construct is. For example, a concrete construct such as *age* is easier to define (e.g., number of years that have passed since birth) than is a complex, abstract concept such as *morale.*

Before you can measure, you need to distinguish what you are interested in from other things. How can you observe or measure something unless you know what you are looking for? For example, a biologist cannot observe a cell unless he or she first knows what a cell is, has a microscope, and has learned to distinguish it from noncell "stuff" or "junk" under the microscope. The process of measurement involves more than just having a measurement instrument (e.g., a microscope). The researcher needs three things to measure: a construct, a measure, and an ability to recognize what one is looking for.[3]

For example, I want to measure teacher morale. I first define *teacher morale.* What does the construct of *morale* mean? As a variable construct, it takes on different values—high versus low or good versus bad morale. Next, I create a measure of my construct. This could take the form of survey questions, an examination of school records, or observations of teachers. Finally, I distinguish morale from other things in the answers to survey questions, school records, or observations.

A social researcher's job is more difficult than that of the natural scientist because social measurement involves talking with people or observing their behavior. Unlike the planets, cells, or chemicals, the answers people give and their actions can be ambiguous. People can react to the very fact that they are being asked questions or observed. Thus, the social researcher has a double burden. First, he or she must have a clear construct, a good measure, and an ability to recognize what is being looked for. Second, he or she tries to measure fluid and confusing social life that may change just because of an awareness that a researcher is trying to measure.

How can I develop a conceptual definition of *teacher morale,* or at least a tentative working def-

---

Conceptualization The process developing clear, rigorous, systematic conceptual definitions for abstract ideas/concepts.

Conceptual definition A careful, systematic definition of a construct that is explicitly written down.

inition to get started? I begin with my everyday understanding of morale—something vague such as "how people feel about things." I ask some of my friends how they define it. I also look at an unabridged dictionary and a thesaurus. They give definitions such as "confidence, spirit, zeal, cheerfulness, esprit de corps, mental condition toward something." I go to the library and search the research literature on morale or teacher morale to see how others have defined it. If someone else has already given an excellent definition, I might borrow it (citing the source, of course). If I do not find a definition that fits my purposes, I turn to theories of group behavior, individual mental states, and the like for ideas. As I collect various definitions, parts of definitions, and related ideas, I begin to see the boundaries of the core idea.

By now, I have a lot of definitions and need to sort them out. Most say that morale is a spirit, feeling, or mental condition toward something, or a group feeling. I separate the two extremes of my construct. This helps me turn the concept into a variable. High morale involves confidence, optimism, cheerfulness, feelings of togetherness, and willingness to endure hardship for the common good. Low morale is the opposite; it is a lack of confidence, pessimism, depression, isolation, selfishness, and an unwillingness to put forth effort for others.

I am interested in *teacher* morale, I learn about teachers to specify the construct to them. One strategy is to make a list of examples of high or low teacher morale. High teacher morale includes saying positive things about the school, not complaining about extra work, or enjoying being with students. Low morale includes complaining a lot, not attending school events unless required to, or looking for other jobs.

Morale involves a feeling toward something else; a person has morale with regard to something. I list the various "somethings" toward which teachers have feelings (e.g., students, parents, pay, the school administration, other teachers, the profession of teaching). This raises an issue that frequently occurs when developing a definition. Are there several kinds of teacher morale or are all these "somethings" aspects of one construct? There is no perfect answer. I have to decide whether morale means a

single, general feeling with different parts or dimensions, or several distinct feelings.

What unit of analysis does my construct apply to: a group or an individual? Is morale a characteristic of an individual, of a group (e.g., a school), or of both? I decide that for my purposes morale applies to groups of people only. This tells me that the unit of analysis in my research project will be a group: all teachers in a school.

A researcher must distinguish the construct of interest from related ones. How is my construct of teacher morale similar to or different from related concepts? For example, does *morale* differ from *mood?* I decide that mood is more individual and temporary than morale. Likewise, morale differs from optimism and pessimism, which are outlooks about the future held by individuals. Morale is a group feeling that includes positive or negative feelings about the future as well as other beliefs and feelings.

Conceptualization is a process of thinking through the meanings of a construct. By now, I know that teacher morale is a mental state or feeling that ranges from high (optimistic, cheerful) to low (pessimistic, depressed); it has several dimensions (morale regarding students, morale regarding other teachers); it is a characteristic of a group; and it persists for a period of months. I have a much more specific mental picture of what I want to measure than when I began. If I had not conceptualized, I would have tried to measure what I started with—"how people feel about things."

Even with all the conceptualization about teacher morale, some ambiguity remains. To complete the conceptualization process, I need to think about exactly what I intend to include within it. For example, what is a teacher? Does a teacher include guidance counselors, principals, athletic coaches, and librarians? What about student teachers or part-time, temporary, or substitute teachers? Does it include everyone who teaches for a living, even if someone is not employed by schools (e.g., a corporate trainer, an on-the-job supervisor who instructs an apprentice, a hospital physician who trains residents, etc.)? Even if I restrict my definition to people in schools, what is a school? A school could include a nursery school, a training hospital, a university's Ph.D. program, a for-profit business that prepares people to take standardized tests, a dog obedience school, a summer camp that teaches students to play basketball, and a vocational school that teaches how to drive semitrailer trucks.

Some people assume "a teacher" means a full-time, professionally trained employee of a school, grades 1 through 12, who spends most of the day in a classroom with students. Others think of the legal or official government definition, which could include people who are certified to teach, even if they are not in classrooms, and exclude people who are uncertified even if they are in classrooms with students. The main point is that conceptualization means I need to be very clear in my own thinking of what I mean by *teachers* as well as by *morale* before I develop measures. I need to state what I mean very clearly and explicitly for other people to see.

Operationalization links a conceptual definition to a specific set of measurement techniques or procedures, the construct's **operational definition** (i.e., a definition in terms of the specific operations or actions a researcher carries out). An operational definition could be a survey questionnaire, a method of observing events in a field setting, a way to measure symbolic content in the mass media, or any process carried out by the researcher that reflects, documents, or represents the abstract construct as it is expressed in the conceptual definition.

There are usually multiple ways to measure a construct. Some are better or worse and more or less practical than others. The key is to fit your measure to your specific conceptual definition, to the practical constraints within which you must operate (e.g., time, money, available subjects, etc.), and to the research techniques you know or can learn. You can develop a new measure from scratch, or it can be a measure that is already being used by other researchers (see Box 7.1).

Operationalization The process of moving from a construct's conceptual definition to specific activities or measures that allow a researcher to observe it empirically.

Operational definition The definition of a variable in terms of the specific actions to measure or indicate it in the empirical world.

BOX **7.1**   **Five Suggestions for Coming Up with a Measure**

1. *Remember the conceptual definition.* The underlying principle for any measure is to match it to the specific conceptual definition of the construct that will be used in the study.
2. *Keep an open mind.* Do not get locked into a single measure or type of measure. Be creative and constantly look for better measures. Avoid what Kaplan (1964:28) called the "law of the instrument," which means being locked into using one measurement instrument for all problems.
3. *Borrow from others.* Do not be afraid to borrow from other researchers, as long as credit is given. Good ideas for measures can be found in other studies or modified from other measures.
4. *Anticipate difficulties.* Logical and practical problems often arise when trying to measure variables of interest. Sometimes a problem can be anticipated and avoided with careful forethought and planning.
5. *Do not forget your units of analysis.* Your measure should fit with the units of analysis of the study and permit you to generalize to the universe of interest.

Operationalization links the language of theory with the language of empirical measures. Theory is full of abstract concepts, assumptions, relationships, definitions, and causality. Empirical measures describe how people concretely measure specific variables. They refer to specific operations or things people use to indicate the presence of a construct that exists in observable reality.

Quantitative Conceptualization and Operationalization

The measurement process for quantitative research follows a straightforward sequence: first conceptualization, followed by operationalization, followed by applying the operational definition or measuring to collect the data. Quantitative researchers developed several ways to rigorously link abstract ideas to measurement procedures that will produce precise quantitative information about empirical reality.

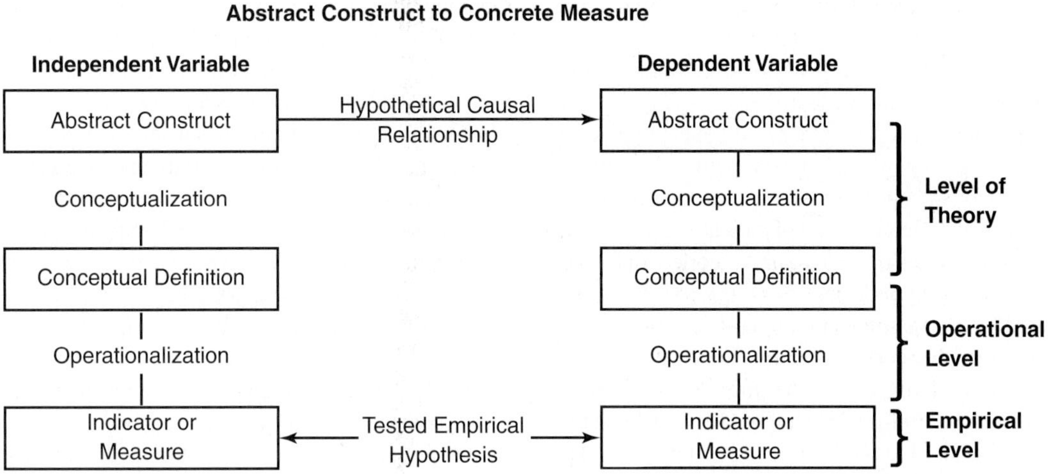

Abstract Construct to Concrete Measure

FIGURE 7.1   Conceptualization and Operationalization

Rules of correspondence or auxiliary theory link the conceptual definitions of constructs to concrete measures or operations for measuring constructs.[4] **Rules of correspondence** are logical statements of how an indicator corresponds to an abstract construct. For example, a rule of correspondence states that a person's verbal agreement with a set of 10 specific statements is evidence that the person holds strongly antifeminist beliefs and values. They are an auxiliary theory that explains how and why indicators and constructs connect. Carmines and Zeller (1979:11) noted, "The auxiliary theory specifying the relationship between concepts and indicators is equally important to social research as the substantive theory linking concepts to one another." For example, a researcher wants to measure alienation. The construct has four parts, each in a different sphere of life: family relations, work relations, relations with community, and relations with friends. The auxiliary theory specifies that certain behaviors or feelings in each sphere of life express alienation. For instance, in the sphere of work, an indicator of alienation is that a person feels a total lack of control over when, where, and with whom he or she works, what he or she does when working, or how fast he or she must work.

Figure 7.1 illustrates the measurement process for two variables that are linked together in a theory and a hypothesis. There are three levels to consider: conceptual, operational, and empirical.[5] At the most abstract level, the researcher is interested in the causal relationship between two constructs, or a **conceptual hypothesis.** At the level of operational definitions, the researcher is interested in testing an **empirical hypothesis** to determine the degree of association between indicators. This is the level at which correlations, statistics, questionnaires, and the like are used. The third level is the concrete empirical world. If the operational indicators of variables (e.g., questionnaires) are logically linked to a construct (e.g., racial discrimination), they will

Rules of correspondence   Rules that researchers use to connect abstract constructs with measurement operations in empirical social reality.

Conceptual hypothesis   A type of hypothesis that expresses variables and the relationships among them in abstract, conceptual terms.

Empirical hypothesis   A type of hypothesis in which the researcher expresses variables in specific empirical terms and expresses the association among the measured indicators in observable, empirical terms.

capture what happens in the empirical social world and relate it to the conceptual level.

The measurement process links together the three levels, moving deductively from the abstract to the concrete. A researcher first conceptualizes a variable, giving it a clear conceptual definition. Next, he or she operationalizes it by developing an operational definition or set of indicators for it. Last, he or she applies the indicators to collect data and test empirical hypotheses. Those tests are logically linked back to a conceptual hypothesis and causal relations in the world of theory.

How do I give my teacher morale construct an operational definition? First, I read the research reports of others and see whether a good indicator already exists. If there are no existing indicators, I must invent one from scratch. Morale is a mental state or feeling, so I measure it indirectly through people's words and actions. I might develop a questionnaire for the teachers and ask them about their feelings toward the dimensions of morale in my definition. I might go to the school and observe the teachers in the teachers' lounge, interacting with students, and at school activities. I might use school personnel records on teacher behaviors for statements that indicate morale (e.g., absences, requests for letters of recommendation for other jobs, performance reports, etc.). I might survey students, school administrators, and others to find out what they think about teacher morale. Whichever indicator I choose, I further refine my conceptual definition as I develop it (e.g., write specific questionnaire questions).

The processes of conceptualization and operationalization are necessary for each variable. In the preceding example, morale is not a hypothesis. It is one variable. It could be a dependent variable caused by something else, or it could be an independent variable causing something else. It depends on my theoretical explanation.

Qualitative Conceptualization and Operationalization

Conceptualization. The conceptualization process in qualitative research differs from quantitative research. Instead of refining abstract ideas into theoretical definitions early in the research process, qualitative researchers refine rudimentary "working ideas" during the data collection and analysis process. Conceptualization is a process of forming coherent theoretical definitions as one struggles to "make sense" or organize the data and one's preliminary ideas about it.

As the researcher gathers and analyzes qualitative data, he or she develops new concepts, formulates definitions for major constructs, and considers relationships among them. Eventually, he or she links concepts and constructs to create theoretical relationships. Qualitative researchers form and refine constructs as they examine their data (i.e., field notes, photos and maps, historical documents, etc.) and ask theoretical questions about the data (e.g., Is this a case of class conflict? What is the sequence of events and could it be different? Why did this happen here and not somewhere else?).

A qualitative researcher conceptualizes by developing clear, explicit definitions linked to other ideas and closely tied to specific data. They are expressed in the words and concrete actions of the people being studied. In qualitative research, conceptualization flows largely from the data.

Operationalization. The operationalization process for qualitative research often precedes conceptualization. (Figure 7.2 gives an example of the measurement process for quantitative research and Figure 7.3 gives an example of the measurement process for qualitative research.) A researcher forms conceptual definitions out of rudimentary "working ideas" while making observations or gathering data. Instead of turning refined conceptual definitions into measurement operations, a qualitative researcher operationalizes by describing how specific observations and thoughts about the data contributed to working ideas that are the basis of conceptual definitions and constructs.

Operationalization is a description of how a researcher developed working ideas while making observations and collecting data. It is a description of how specific observations or data, preliminary ideas about the data, and struggles to understand the data become constructs. It is an after-the-fact description more than a preplanned technique.

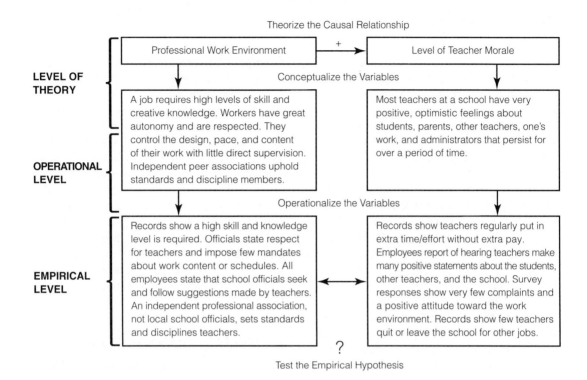

FIGURE 7.2   Example of the Deductive Measurement Process for the Hypothesis: A Professional Work Environment Increases the Level of Teacher Morale

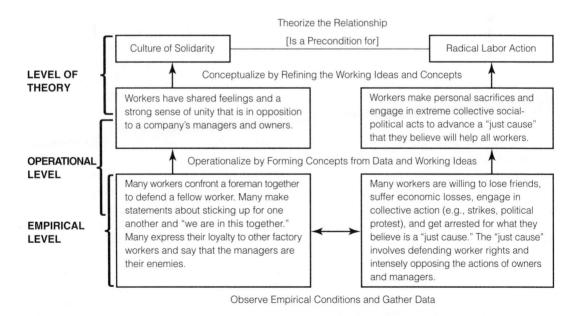

FIGURE 7.3   Example of the Inductive Measurement Process for the Proposition: Radical Labor Action Is Likely to Occur Where a Culture of Solidarity Has Been Created

Just as quantitative operationalization deviates from a rigid deductive process, qualitative researchers may draw on ideas from beyond the data of a specific research setting. Qualitative operationalization includes the researcher's use of pre-existing techniques and concepts that were blended with those that emerged during the data collection process.

An example of qualitative operationalization is found in Fantasia's (1988) field research on contested labor actions using the *cultures of solidarity* as the construct. A culture of solidarity is related to ideas of conflictual workplace relations and growing class consciousness among nonmanagerial workers. His conceptual definition is that it is a kind of cultural expression by workers that evolves in particular places over time. It is a process in which workers develop shared feelings and a sense of unity that is in opposition to management and business owners. It is an interactive process during which workers come to common ideas, understandings, and actions. It is "less a matter of disembodied mental attitude than a broader set of practices and repertoires available for empirical investigation" (Fantasia, 1988:14).

Fantasia operationalized the construct by describing how he gathered data, by presenting data that portrays the construct, and by explaining his thinking about the data. He describes what he specifically did to collect the data (e.g., he worked in a particular factory, attended a press conference, and interviewed people) and he presents the data in detail (e.g., he describes specific events that document the construct, such as several maps showing where people stood during a confrontation with a foreman, retelling sequence of events in a factory, recounting actions by management officials, and repeating statements individual workers made). He also provides a look into his own thinking as he reflected and tried to understand his experiences, including developing new ideas and drawing on the ideas of other scholars.

Casing The development of cases in qualitative research.

Casing. In qualitative research, ideas and evidence are mutually interdependent. This applies particularly to case study analysis. Cases are not given preestablished empirical units or theoretical categories apart from data; they are defined by data and theory. By analyzing a situation, the researcher organizes data and applies ideas simultaneously to create or specify a case. Making or creating a case, called **casing,** brings the data and theory together. Determining what to treat as a case resolves a tension or strain between what the researcher observes and his or her ideas about it. "Casing viewed as a methodological step, can occur at any phase of the research process, but occurs especially at the beginning of the project and at the end" (Ragin, 1992b:218).

RELIABILITY AND VALIDITY

Reliability and validity are central issues in all measurement. Both concern connecting measures to constructs. Reliability and validity are salient because constructs are often ambiguous, diffuse, and not directly observable. Perfect reliability and validity are virtually impossible to achieve. Rather, they are ideals researchers strive for.

All social researchers want their measures to be reliable and valid. Both ideas help to establish the truthfulness, credibility, or believability of findings. Both terms also have multiple meanings. Here, they refer to related, desirable aspects of measurement.

Reliability means dependability or consistency. It suggests that the same thing is repeated or recurs under the identical or very similar conditions. The opposite of reliability is a measurement process that yields erratic, unstable, or inconsistent results.

Validity suggests truthfulness. It refers to how well an idea "fits" with actual reality. The absence of validity occurs if there is poor fit between the constructs a researcher uses to describe, theorize, or analyze the social world and what actually occurs in the social world. In simple terms, validity addresses the question of how well the social reality being measured through research matches with the constructs researchers use to understand it.

Qualitative and quantitative researchers want reliable and valid measurement, but beyond an agreement on the basic ideas at a general level, each style sees reliability and validity in the research process differently.

Reliability and Validity in Quantitative Research

Reliability. **Measurement reliability** means that the numerical results produced by an indicator do not vary because of characteristics of the measurement process or measurement instrument itself. For example, I get on my bathroom scale and read my weight. I get off and get on again and again. I have a reliable scale if it gives me the same weight each time—assuming, of course, that I am not eating, drinking, changing clothing, and so forth. An unreliable scale will register different weights each time, even though my "true" weight does not change. Another example is my car speedometer. If I am driving at a constant slow speed on a level surface, but the speedometer needle jumps from one end to the other, my speedometer is not a reliable indicator of how fast I am traveling. Actually, there are three types of reliability.[6]

Three Types of Reliability.
Stability Reliability. **Stability reliability** is reliability across time. It addresses the question: Does the measure deliver the same answer when applied in different time periods? The weight-scale example just given is of this type of reliability.

You can verify an indicator's degree of stability reliability by using the *test-retest method.* This has you retest or readminister the indicator to the same group of people. If what you are measuring is stable and the indicator has stability reliability, then you will get the same results each time. A variation of the test-retest method is to give an alternative form of the test, but the alternative form has to be very similar. For example, I have a hypothesis about gender and seating patterns in a college cafeteria. I measure my dependent variable (seating patterns) by observing and recording the number of male and female students at tables, and noting who sits down

first, second, third, and so on for a three-hour period. If, as I am observing, I get tired or distracted, or I forget to record and miss more people toward the end of the three hours, then my indicator does not have a high degree of stability reliability.

Representative Reliability. **Representative reliability** is reliability across subpopulations or groups of people. It addresses the question: Does the indicator deliver the same answer when applied to different groups? An indicator has high representative reliability if it yields the same result for a construct when applied to different subpopulations (e.g., different classes, races, sexes, age groups, etc.). For example, I ask a question about a person's age. If people in their twenties answered my question by overstating their true age, whereas people in their fifties understated their true age, then the indicator has a low degree of representative reliability. To have representative reliability, the measure needs to give accurate information for every age group.

A *subpopulation analysis* verifies whether an indicator has this type of reliability. The analysis compares the indicator across different subpopulations or subgroups and uses independent knowledge about subpopulations. For example, I want to test the representative reliability of a questionnaire item that asks about a person's education. I conduct a subpopulation analysis to see whether the question works equally well for men and women. I ask men and women the question and then obtain independent information (e.g., check school records) and check to see whether the errors in answering the question are equal for men and women. The item has representative reliability if men and women have the same error rate.

Measurement reliability The dependability or consistency of the measure of a variable.

Stability reliability Measurement reliability across time; a measure that yields consistent results at different time points assuming what is being measured does not itself change.

Representative reliability Measurement reliability across groups; a measure that yields consistent results for various social groups.

Equivalence Reliability. **Equivalence reliability** applies when researchers use *multiple indicators*—that is, when a construct is measured with multiple specific measures (e.g., several items in a questionnaire all measure the same construct). It addresses the question: Does the measure yield consistent results across different indicators? If several different indicators measure the same construct, then a reliable measure gives the same result with all indicators.

Researchers verify equivalence reliability with the *split-half method.* This involves dividing the indicators of the same construct into two groups, usually by a random process, and determining whether both halves give the same results. For example, I have 14 items on a questionnaire. All measure political conservatism among college students. If my indicators (i.e., questionnaire items) have equivalence reliability, then I can randomly divide them into two groups of 7 and get the same results. For example, I use the first 7 questions and find that a class of 50 business majors is twice as conservative as a class of 50 education majors. I get the same results using the second 7 questions. There are also special statistical measures (e.g., Cronbach's alpha) to determine this type of reliability.

A special type of equivalence reliability, intercoder reliability, arises when there are several observers, raters, or coders of information (explained in Chapter 11). In a sense, each observer is an indicator. A measure is reliable if the observers, raters, or coders agree with each other. It is a common type of reliability reported in content analysis studies. For example, I hire six students to observe student seating patterns in a cafeteria. If all six are equally skilled at observing and recording, I can combine the information from all six into a single reliable measure. But if one or two students are lazy, inattentive, or sloppy, then my measure will have lower reliability. Intercoder reliability is tested by having several coders measure the exact same thing, then comparing the measures. For instance, I have three coders independently code the seating patterns during the same hour on three different days. I compare the recorded observations. If they agree, I can be confident of my measure's intercoder reliability. Special statistical techniques measure the degree of intercoder reliability.

How to Improve Reliability. It is rare to have perfect reliability. Four ways to increase the reliability of measures are (1) clearly conceptualize constructs, (2) use a precise level of measurement, (3) use multiple indicators, and (4) use pilot tests.

Clearly Conceptualize All Constructs. Reliability increases when each measure indicates one and only one concept. This means developing unambiguous, clear theoretical definitions. Constructs should be specified to eliminate "noise" (i.e., distracting or interfering information) from other constructs. For example, the indicator of a pure chemical compound is more reliable than one in which the chemical is mixed with other material or dirt. In the latter case, it is difficult to separate the "noise" of other material from the pure chemical.

Let us return to teacher morale. I should separate morale from related ideas (e.g., mood, personality, spirit, job attitude). If I did not do this, I could not be sure what I was really measuring. I might develop an indicator for morale that also indicates personality; that is, the construct of personality contaminates that of morale and produces a less reliable indicator. Bad measurement occurs when one indicator is used to operationalize different constructs (e.g., using the same questionnaire item to indicate morale and personality).

Increase the Level of Measurement. Levels of measurement are discussed later in this chapter. Indicators at higher or more precise levels of measurement are more likely to be reliable than less precise measures because the latter pick up less detailed information. If more specific information is measured, then it is less likely that anything other than the construct will be captured. The general principle is: Try to measure at the most precise level possible. However, it is more difficult to measure at higher levels of measurement. For example, if I have a choice of measuring morale as either high or low,

Equivalence reliability Measurement reliability across indicators; a measure that yields consistent results using different specific indicators, assuming that all measure the same construct.

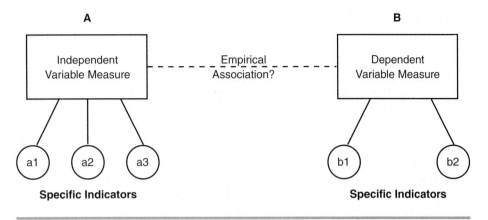

FIGURE 7.4 Measurement Using Multiple Indicators

or in 10 categories from extremely low to extremely high, it would be better to measure it in 10 refined categories.

Use Multiple Indicators of a Variable. A third way to increase reliability is to use **multiple indicators,** because two (or more) indicators of the same construct are better than one.[7] Figure 7.4 illustrates the use of multiple indicators in hypothesis testing. Three indicators of the one independent variable construct are combined into an overall measure, *A,* and two indicators of a dependent variable are combined into a single measure, *B.* For example, I have three specific measures of *A,* which is teacher morale: answers to a survey question on attitudes about school, number of absences for reasons other than illness and requests for transfers, and number of complaints others heard a teacher voice. I also have two measures of my dependent variable *B,* giving students extra attention: number of hours teacher spent staying after school hours to meet individually with students and whether the teacher inquires frequently about a student's progress in other classes.

Multiple indicators let a researcher take measurements from a wider range of the content of a conceptual definition. Some writers call this sampling from the conceptual domain. Different aspects of the construct can be measured, each with its own indicator. Also, one indicator (e.g., one question on

a questionnaire) may be imperfect, but several measures are less likely to have the same (systematic) error. Multiple indicator measures tend to be more stable than measures with one item.

Use Pretests, Pilot Studies, and Replication. Reliability can be improved by using a pretest or pilot version of a measure first. Develop one or more draft or preliminary versions of a measure and try them before applying the final version in a hypothesis-testing situation. This takes more time and effort. For example, in my survey of teacher morale, I go through many drafts of a question before the final version. I test early versions by asking people the question and checking to see whether it is clear.

The principle of using pilot tests extends to replicating the measures other researchers have used. For example, I search the literature and find measures of morale from past research. I may want to build on and use a previous measure if it is a good one, citing the source, of course. In addition, I may want to add new indicators and compare them to the previous measure (see Box 7.2). In this way, the quality of the measure can improve over time, as long as the same definition is used. See Table 7.1 for a summary of reliability types.

Multiple indicators Using multiple procedures or seven specific measures to provide empirical evidence of the levels of a variable.

BOX **7.2**   Improving the Measure of U.S. Religion Affiliation

Quantitative researchers measure individual religious beliefs (e.g., Do you believe in God? in a devil? in life after death? What is God like to you?), religious practices (e.g., How often do you pray? How frequently do you attend services?), and religious affiliation (e.g., If you belong to a church or religious group, which one?). They have categorized the hundreds of U.S. religious denominations into either a three-part grouping (Protestant, Catholic, Jewish) or a three-part classification of fundamentalist, moderate, or liberal that was introduced in 1990.

Steensland and colleagues (2000) reconceptualized affiliation, and, after examining trends in reli-

gious theology and social practices, argued for classifying all American denominations into six major categories: Mainline Protestant, Evangelical Protestant, Black Protestant, Roman Catholic, Jewish, and Other (including Mormon, Jehovah's Witnesses, Muslim, Hindu, and Unitarian). The authors evaluated their new six-category classification by examining people's religious views and practices as well as their views about contemporary social issues. Among national samples of Americans, they found that the new classification better distinguished among religious denominations than previous measures.

Validity.   Validity is an overused term. Sometimes, it is used to mean "true" or "correct." There are several general types of validity. Here, we are concerned with **measurement validity.** There are also several types of measurement validity. Nonmeasurement types of validity are discussed later.

When a researcher says that an indicator is valid, it is valid for a particular purpose and definition. The same indicator may be less valid or invalid for other purposes. For example, the measure of morale discussed here (e.g., questions about feelings toward school) might be valid for measuring morale among teachers but invalid for measuring morale of police officers.[8]

At its core, measurement validity refers to how well the conceptual and operational definitions mesh with each other. The better the fit, the greater the measurement validity. Validity is more difficult to achieve than reliability. We cannot have absolute confidence about validity, but some measures are *more valid* than others. The reason is that constructs are abstract ideas, whereas indicators refer to con-

crete observation. This is the gap between our mental pictures about the world and the specific things we do at particular times and places. Validity is part of a dynamic process that grows by accumulating evidence over time, and without it, all measurement becomes meaningless.

Some researchers use rules of correspondence (discussed earlier) to reduce the gap between abstract ideas and specific indicators. For example, a rule of correspondence is: If a teacher agrees with statements that "things have gotten worse at this school in the past five years" and that "there is little hope for improvement," this indicates low morale on the part of the teacher. Some researchers talk about the *epistemic correlation,* a hypothetical correlation between an indicator and the construct that the indicator measures. We cannot empirically measure such correlations, but they can be estimated.[9]

Four Types of Measurement Validity

Face Validity.   The easiest to achieve and the most basic kind of validity is **face validity.** It is a judgment by the scientific community that the indicator really measures the construct. It addresses the question: On the face of it, do people believe that the definition and method of measurement fit? For example, few people would accept a measure of college student math ability using a question that asked students: $2 + 2 = ?$ This is not a valid measure of college-level math ability on the face of it. Recall that

---

Measurement validity   How well an empirical indicator and the conceptual definition of the construct that the indicator is supposed to measure "fit" together.

Face validity   A type of measurement validity in which an indicator "makes sense" as a measure of a construct in the judgment of others, especially in the scientific community.

TABLE 7.1   Summary of Measurement Reliability and Validity Types

RELIABILITY (Dependable Measure)	VALIDITY (True Measure)
Stability—over time (verify using test-retest method)	Face—in the judgment of others
Representative—across subgroups (verify using split-half method)	Content—captures the entire meaning
Equivalence—across indicators (verify using subpopulation analysis)	Criterion—agrees with an external source ■ Concurrent—agrees with a preexisting measure ■ Predictive—agrees with future behavior
	Construct—multiple indicators are consistent ■ Convergent—alike ones are similar ■ Discriminant—different ones differ

the principle of organized skepticism in the scientific community means that aspects of research are scrutinized by others.[10] See Table 7.1 for a summary of types of measurement validity.

Content Validity. **Content validity** addresses the question: Is the full content of a definition represented in a measure? A conceptual definition holds ideas; it is a "space" containing ideas and concepts. Measures should sample or represent all ideas or areas in the conceptual space. Content validity involves three steps. First, specify the content in a construct's definition. Next, sample from all areas of the definition. Finally, develop one or more indicators that tap all of the parts of the definition.

An example of content validity is my definition of *feminism* as a person's commitment to a set of beliefs creating full equality between men and women in areas of the arts, intellectual pursuits, family, work, politics, and authority relations. I create a measure of feminism in which I ask two survey questions: (1) Should men and women get equal pay for equal work and (2) Should men and women share household tasks? My measure has low content validity because the two questions ask only about pay and household tasks. They ignore the other areas (intellectual pursuits, politics, authority relations, and other aspects of work and family). For a content-valid measure, I must either expand the measure or narrow the definition.[11]

Criterion Validity. **Criterion validity** uses some standard or criterion to indicate a construct accurately. The validity of an indicator is verified by comparing it with another measure of the same construct in which a researcher has confidence. There are two subtypes of this kind of validity.[12]

Concurrent Validity. To have **concurrent validity,** an indicator must be associated with a preexisting indicator that is already judged to be valid (i.e., it has face validity). For example, you create a new test to measure intelligence. For it to be concurrently valid, it should be highly associated with existing IQ tests (assuming the same definition of intelligence is used). This means that most people who score high on the old measure should also score high on the new one, and vice versa. The two measures may not be perfectly associated, but if they measure the same or a similar construct, it is logical for them to yield similar results.

> **Content validity**   Measurement validity that requires that a measure represent all the aspects of the conceptual definition of a construct.
>
> **Criterion validity**   Measurement validity that relies on some independent, outside verification.
>
> **Concurrent validity**   Measurement validity that relies on a preexisting and already accepted measure to verify the indicator of a construct.

Predictive Validity. Criterion validity whereby an indicator predicts future events that are logically related to a construct is called **predictive validity.** It cannot be used for all measures. The measure and the action predicted must be distinct from but indicate the same construct. Predictive measurement validity should not be confused with prediction in hypothesis testing, where one variable predicts a different variable in the future. For example, the Scholastic Assessment Test (SAT) that many U.S. high school students take measures scholastic aptitude—the ability of a student to perform in college. If the SAT has high predictive validity, then students who get high SAT scores will subsequently do well in college. If students with high scores perform the same as students with average or low scores, then the SAT has low predictive validity.

Another way to test predictive validity is to select a group of people who have specific characteristics and predict how they will score (very high or very low) vis-à-vis the construct. For example, I have a measure of political conservatism. I predict that members of conservative groups (e.g., John Birch Society, Conservative Caucus, Daughters of the American Revolution, Moral Majority) will score high on it, whereas members of liberal groups (e.g., Democratic Socialists, People for the American Way, Americans for Democratic Action) will score low. I "validate" it by pilot-testing it on members of the groups. It can then be used as a measure of political conservatism for the general public.

Predictive validity   Measurement validity that relies on the occurrence of a future event or behavior that is logically consistent to verify the indicator of a construct.

Construct validity   A type of measurement validity that uses multiple indicators and has two subtypes: how well indicators of one construct converge or how well indicators of different constructs diverge.

Convergent validity   A type of measurement validity for multiple indicators based on the idea that indicators of one construct will act alike or converge.

Discriminant validity   A type of measurement validity for multiple indicators based on the idea that indicators of different constructs diverge.

Construct Validity. **Construct validity** is for measures with multiple indicators. It addresses the question: If the measure is valid, do the various indicators operate in a consistent manner? It requires a definition with clearly specified conceptual boundaries.

Convergent Validity. This kind of validity applies when multiple indicators converge or are associated with one another. **Convergent validity** means that multiple measures of the same construct hang together or operate in similar ways. For example, I measure the construct "education" by asking people how much education they have completed, looking up school records, and asking the people to complete a test of school knowledge. If the measures do not converge (i.e., people who claim to have a college degree have no records of attending college, or those with college degrees perform no better than high school dropouts on my tests), then my measure has weak convergent validity and I should not combine all three indicators into one measure.

Discriminant Validity. **Discriminant validity** is the opposite of convergent validity and means that the indicators of one construct hang together or converge, but also are negatively associated with opposing constructs. It says that if two constructs *A* and *B* are very different, then measures of *A* and *B* should not be associated. For example, I have 10 items that measure political conservatism. People answer all 10 in similar ways. But I also put 5 questions on the same questionnaire that measure political liberalism. My measure of conservatism has discriminant validity if the 10 conservatism items both hang together and are negatively associated with the 5 liberalism ones. (See Figure 7.5 for a review of measurement validity.)

Reliability and Validity in Qualitative Research

Most qualitative researchers accept the basic principles of reliability and validity, but rarely use the terms because of their association with quantitative measurement. In addition, qualitative researchers apply the principles differently.

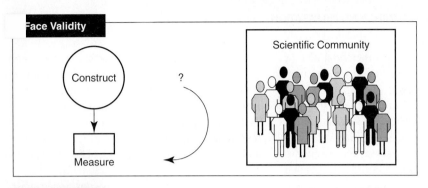

Face Validity

Construct

?

Measure

Scientific Community

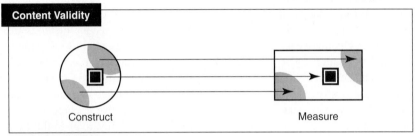

Content Validity

Construct

Measure

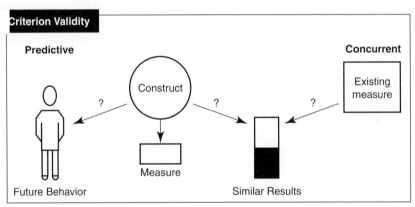

Criterion Validity

Predictive

Concurrent

Construct

?

?

?

Existing measure

Measure

Future Behavior

Similar Results

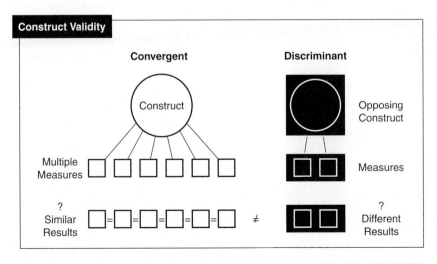

Construct Validity

Convergent

Discriminant

Construct

Opposing Construct

Multiple Measures

Measures

?
Similar Results

□=□=□=□=□=□ ≠

?
Different Results

FIGURE 7.5   Types of Validity

195

Reliability. Reliability means dependability or consistency. Qualitative researchers use a variety of techniques (e.g., interviews, participation, photographs, document studies, etc.) to record their observations consistently. Qualitative researchers want to be consistent (i.e., not vacillating and erratic) in how, over time, they make observations, similar to the idea of stability reliability. One difficulty is that they often study processes that are not stable over time. Moreover, they emphasize the value of a changing or developing interaction between the researcher and what he or she studies. Qualitative researchers believe that the subject matter and a researcher's relationship to it should be an evolving process. The metaphor for the relationship between a researcher and the data is one of an evolving relationship or living organism (e.g., a plant) that naturally matures. Most qualitative researchers see the quantitative approach to reliability as a cold, fixed mechanical instrument that one repeatedly applies to some static, lifeless material.

Qualitative researchers consider a range of data sources and employ multiple measurement methods. They question the quantitative-positivist ideas of replication, equivalence, and subpopulation reliability. They accept that different researchers or researchers using alternative measures will get distinctive results. This is because data collection is an interactive process in which particular researchers operate in an evolving setting and the setting's context dictates using a unique mix of measures that cannot be repeated. The diverse measures and interactions with different researchers are beneficial because they can illuminate different facets or dimensions of a subject matter. Many qualitative researchers question the quantitative researcher's quest for standard, fixed measures. They fear such measures ignore benefits of having a variety of researchers with many approaches and may neglect key aspects of diversity that exist in the social world.

Validity. Validity means truthful. Qualitative researchers are more interested in authenticity than in the idea of a single version of truth. *Authenticity* means giving a fair, honest, and balanced account of social life from the viewpoint of someone who lives it every day. Qualitative researchers are less concerned with matching an abstract construct to empirical data and more concerned with giving a candid portrayal of social life that is true to the experiences of people being studied. Most qualitative researchers concentrate on capturing an inside view and providing a detailed account of how those being studied understand events (see Box 7.3).

Qualitative researchers have developed substitutes for the quantitative approach to validity: ecological validity or natural history methods (see Chapter 13). These emphasize conveying the insider's view to others. Historical researchers use internal and external criticisms (see Chapter 14) to determine whether the evidence they have is real or they believe it to be. Qualitative researchers adhere to the core principle of validity, to be truthful (i.e., avoid false or distorted accounts). They try to create a tight fit between their understanding, ideas, and statements about the social world and what is actually occurring in it.

Relationship between Reliability and Validity

Reliability is necessary for validity and is easier to achieve than validity. Although reliability is necessary in order to have a valid measure of a concept, it does not guarantee that a measure will be valid. It is not a sufficient condition for validity. A measure can produce the same result over and over (i.e., it has reliability), but what it measures may not match the definition of the construct (i.e., validity).

A measure can be reliable but invalid. For example, I get on a scale and get weighed. The weight registered by the scale is the same each time I get on and off. But then I go to another scale—an "official" one that measures true weight—and it says that my weight is twice as great. The first scale yielded reliable (i.e., dependable and consistent) results, but it did not give a valid measure of my weight.

A diagram might help you see the relationship between reliability and validity. Figure 7.6 illustrates the relationship between the concepts by using the analogy of a target. The bull's-eye represents a fit between a measure and the definition of the construct.

BOX **7.3**   Meanings of Validity in Qualitative Research

Measurement validity in qualitative research does not require demonstrating a fixed correspondence between a carefully defined abstract concept and a precisely calibrated measure of its empirical appearance. Other features of the research measurement process are important for establishing validity.

First, to be considered valid, a researcher's truth claims need to be plausible and, as Fine (1999) argued, intersubjectively "good enough" (i.e., understandable by many other people). *Plausible* means that the data and statements about it are not exclusive; they are not the only possible claims nor are they exact accounts of the one truth in the world. This does not make them mere inventions or arbitrary. Instead, they are powerful, persuasive descriptions that reveal a researcher's genuine experiences with the empirical data.

Second, a researcher's empirical claims gain validity when supported by numerous pieces of diverse empirical data. Any one specific empirical detail alone may be mundane, ordinary, or "trivial." Validity arises out of the cumulative impact of hundreds of small, diverse details that only together create a heavy weight of evidence.

Third, validity increases as researchers search continuously in diverse data and consider the connections among them. Raw data in the natural social world are not in neatly prepackaged systematic scientific concepts; rather, they are numerous disparate elements that "form a dynamic and coherent ensemble" (Molotch et al., 2000:816). Validity grows as a researcher recognizes a dense connectivity in disparate details. It grows with the creation of a web of dynamic connections across diverse realms and not only with the number of specifics that are connected.

Validity and *reliability* are usually complementary concepts, but in some special situations they conflict with each other. Sometimes, as validity increases, reliability is more difficult to attain, and vice versa. This occurs when the construct has a highly abstract and not easily observable definition. Reliability is easiest to achieve when the measure is precise and observable. Thus, there is a strain between the true essence of the highly abstract construct and measuring it in a concrete manner. For example, "alienation" is a very abstract, highly subjective construct, often defined as a deep inner sense of loss of one's humanity that diffuses across many aspects of one's life (e.g., social relations, sense of self, orientation toward nature). Highly precise questions in a questionnaire give reliable measures, but there is a danger of losing the subjective essence of the construct.

A Bull's-Eye = A Perfect Measure

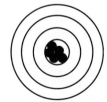

Low Reliability
and Low Validity

High Reliability
but Low Validity

High Reliability
and High Validity

FIGURE 7.6   Illustration of Relationship between Reliability and Validity

Source: Adapted from Babbie (1998:128).

Other Uses of the Terms *Reliable* and *Valid*

Many words have multiple definitions, including reliability and validity, creating confusion unless we distinguish among uses of the same word.

Reliability. Reliability is a word in everyday language. A reliable person is one who is dependable, stable, and responsible; a reliable car is dependable and trustworthy. This means the person responds in similar, predictable ways in different times and conditions; the same can be said for the car. In addition to measurement reliability, researchers sometimes say a study or its results are reliable, meaning that other researchers can reproduce the method of conducting a study or the results from it.

Internal Validity. Internal validity means there are no errors internal to the design of the research project.[13] It is used primarily in experimental research to talk about possible errors or alternative explanations of results that arise despite attempts to institute controls (see Chapter 9 for discussion).

External Validity. External validity is used primarily in experimental research. It is the ability to generalize findings from a specific setting and small group to a range of settings and people. It addresses the question: If something happens in a laboratory or among a particular group of subjects (e.g., college students), can the findings be generalized to the "real" (nonlaboratory) world or to the general public (nonstudents)? (discussed in Chapter 9).

Statistical Validity. Statistical validity means that the correct statistical procedure is chosen and its assumptions are fully met. Different statistical tests or procedures are appropriate for different conditions, which are discussed in textbooks that describe the statistical procedures.

All statistics are based on assumptions about the mathematical properties of the numbers being

used. A statistic will be invalid and its results nonsense if the major assumptions are violated. For example, to compute an average (actually the mean, which is discussed in a later chapter), one cannot use information at the nominal level of measurement (to be discussed). For example, suppose I measure the race of a class of students. I give each race a number: White = 1, African American = 2, Asian = 3, others = 4. It makes no sense to say that the "mean" race of a class of students is 1.9 (almost African American?). This is a misuse of the statistical procedure, and the results are invalid even if the computation is correct. The degree to which statistical assumptions can be violated or bent (the technical term is *robustness*) is a topic in which professional statisticians take great interest.

A GUIDE TO QUANTITATIVE MEASUREMENT

Thus far, you have learned about the principles of measurement. Quantitative researchers have developed ideas and specialized measures to help them in the process of creating operational definitions that will be reliable and valid measures and yield numerical data for their variable constructs. This section of the chapter is a brief guide to these ideas and a few of the measures.

Levels of Measurement

Levels of measurement is an abstract but important and widely used idea. It states that some measures are at a higher or more refined level, and others are crude or less precisely specified. The level of measurement depends on how a construct is conceptualized—that is, assumptions about whether it has particular characteristics. The level of measurement affects the kinds of indicators chosen and is tied to basic assumptions in a construct's definition. The way in which a researcher conceptualizes a variable limits the levels of measurement that he or she can use and has implications for how measurement and statistical analysis can proceed.

Continuous and Discrete Variables. Variables are continuous or discrete. **Continuous variables** have an infinite number of values or attributes

Levels of measurement   A system for organizing information in the measurement of variables into four levels, from nominal level to ratio level.

Continuous variables   Variables measured on a continuum in which an infinite number of finer gradations between variable attributes are possible.

that flow along a continuum. The values can be divided into many smaller increments; in mathematical theory, there is an infinite number of increments. Examples of continuous variables include temperature, age, income, crime rate, and amount of schooling. **Discrete variables** have a relatively fixed set of separate values or variable attributes. Instead of a smooth continuum of values, discrete variables contain distinct categories. Examples of discrete variables include gender (male or female), religion (Protestant, Catholic, Jew, Muslim, atheist), and marital status (never married single, married, divorced or separated, widowed). Whether a variable is continuous or discrete affects its level of measurement.

Four Levels of Measurement

Precision and Levels. The idea of levels of measurement expands on the difference between continuous and discrete variables. The four levels of measurement categorize the precision of measurement.[14]

Deciding on the appropriate level of measurement for a construct often creates confusion. The appropriate level of measurement for a variable depends on (1) how a construct is conceptualized and (2) the type of indicator or measurement that a researcher uses.

The construct itself limits the level of precision. The way a researcher conceptualizes a construct can limit how precisely it can be measured. For example, some of the variables listed earlier as continuous can be reconceptualized as discrete. Temperature can be a continuous variable (e.g., degrees, fractions of degrees) or it can be crudely measured with discrete categories (e.g., hot or cold). Likewise, age can be continuous (how old a person is in years, months, days, hours, and minutes) or treated as discrete categories (infancy, childhood, adolescence, young adulthood, middle age, old age). Yet, most discrete variables cannot be conceptualized as continuous variables. For example, sex, religion, and marital status cannot be conceptualized as continuous; however, related constructs *can* be conceptualized as continuous (e.g., femininity, degree of religiousness, commitment to a marital relationship, etc.).

The level of measurement limits the statistical measures that can be used. A wide range of powerful statistical procedures are available for the higher levels of measurement, but the types of statistics that can be used with the lowest levels are very limited.

There is a practical reason to conceptualize and measure variables at higher levels of measurement. You can collapse higher levels of measurement to lower levels, but the reverse is not true.

Distinguishing among the Four Levels. The four levels from lowest to greatest or highest precision are nominal, ordinal, interval, and ratio. Each level gives a different type of information (see Table 7.2). **Nominal-level measurement** indicates only that there is a difference among categories (e.g., religion: Protestant, Catholic, Jew, Muslim; racial heritage: African, Asian, Caucasian, Hispanic, other). **Ordinal-level measurement** indicates a difference, *plus* the categories can be ordered or ranked (e.g., letter grades: A, B, C, D, F; opinion measures: Strongly Agree, Agree, Disagree, Strongly Disagree). **Interval-level measurement** does everything the first two do, *plus* it can specify the amount of distance between categories (e.g., Fahrenheit or Celsius temperature: 5°, 45°, 90°; IQ scores: 95, 110, 125). Arbitrary zeros may be used in interval measures; they are just there to help keep score. **Ratio-level measurement** does everything all the other levels do, *plus* there is a true zero, which

Discrete variables   Variables in which the attributes can be measured with only a limited number of distinct, separate categories.

Nominal-level measurement   The lowest, least precise level of measurement for which there is a difference in type only among the categories of a variable.

Ordinal-level measurement   A level of measurement that identifies a difference among categories of a variable and allows the categories to be rank ordered as well.

Interval-level measurement   A level of measurement that identifies differences among variable attributes, ranks categories, and measures distance between categories, but there is no true zero.

Ratio-level measurement   The highest, most precise level of measurement; variable attributes can be rank ordered, the distance between them precisely measured, and there is an absolute zero.

TABLE 7.2 Characteristics of the Four Levels of Measurement

LEVEL	DIFFERENT CATEGORIES	RANKED	DISTANCE BETWEEN CATEGORIES MEASURED	TRUE ZERO
Nominal	Yes			
Ordinal	Yes	Yes		
Interval	Yes	Yes	Yes	
Ratio	Yes	Yes	Yes	Yes

makes it possible to state relations in terms of proportion or ratios (e.g., money income: $10, $100, $500; years of formal schooling: 1 year, 10 years, 13 years). In most practical situations, the distinction between interval and ratio levels makes little difference. The arbitrary zeros of some interval measures can be confusing. For example, a rise in temperature from 30 to 60 degrees is not really a doubling of the temperature, although the numbers double, because zero degrees is not the absence of all heat.

Discrete variables are nominal and ordinal, whereas continuous variables can be measured at the interval or ratio level. A ratio-level measure can be turned into an interval, ordinal, or nominal level. The interval level can always be turned into an ordinal or nominal level, but the process does not work in the opposite way!

In general, if it is necessary to use ordinal measurement, use at least five ordinal categories and obtain many observations. This is because the distortion created by collapsing a continuous construct into a smaller number of ordered categories is minimized as the number of categories and the number of observations increase.[15]

For most purposes, the ratio level is indistinguishable from interval measurement. The only difference is that ratio measurement has a "true zero." This can be confusing because some measures, such as temperature, have zeros that are not true zeros.

Temperature scales use numbers, but this does not make them ratio measures because the zero may be arbitrary. For example, water freezes at 32° on a Fahrenheit temperature scale. It freezes at 0° on a Celsius or Centigrade scale and 273° on a Kelvin scale. Water boils at 212°, 100°, or 373.15°, respectively. Although two temperature numbers may be double, say 25 to 50° Fahrenheit. It is not "twice

as warm" because an actual ratio relation does not exist without a true zero. For example, the ratio of boiling to freezing water temperatures varies; it is 6.625 times greater in Fahrenheit, 100 times in Celsius, and 1.366 times in Kelvin. The Kelvin scale has an absolute zero (the absence of all heat) and its ratio corresponds to physical conditions.

Another common example of arbitrary—not true—zeros occurs when measuring attitudes in numbers are assigned to statements (e.g., -1 = disagree, 0 = no opinion, $+1$ = agree). True zeros exist for variables such as income, age, or years of education. Examples of the four levels of measurement are shown in Table 7.3.

Specialized Measures: Scales and Indexes

In this last section we will look at a number of specialized measures, including scales and indexes. Researchers have created thousands of different scales and indexes to measure social variables.[16] For example, scales and indexes measure the degree of formalization in bureaucratic organizations, the prestige of occupations, the adjustment of people to a marriage, the intensity of group interaction, the level of social activity in a community, the degree to which a state's sexual assault laws reflect feminist values, and the level of socioeconomic development of a nation. We will focus on principles of scale and index construction and explore some major types.

Keep two things in mind. First, virtually every social phenomenon can be measured. Some constructs can be measured directly and produce precise numerical values (e.g., family income). Other constructs require the use of surrogates or proxies that indirectly measure a variable and may not be as

TABLE 7.3 Example of Levels of Measurement

VARIABLE (LEVEL OF MEASUREMENT)	HOW VARIABLE IS MEASURED
Religion (nominal)	Different religious denominations (Jewish, Catholic, Lutheran, (nominal) Baptist) are not ranked, just different (unless one belief is conceptualized as closer to heaven).
Attendance (ordinal)	"How often do you attend religious services? (0) Never, (1) less than once a year, (3) several times a year, (4) about once a month, (5) two or three times a week, or (8) several times a week?" This might have been measured at a ratio level if the exact number of times a person attended was asked instead.
IQ score (interval)	Most intelligence tests are organized with 100 as average, middle, or normal. Scores higher or lower indicate distance from the average. Someone with a score of 115 has somewhat above average measured intelligence for people who took the test, whereas 90 is slightly below. Scores of below 65 or above 140 are rare.
Age (ratio)	Age is measured by years of age. There is a true zero (birth). Note that a 40-year-old has lived twice as long as a 20-year-old.

precise (e.g., predisposition to commit a crime). Second, a lot can be learned from measures used by other researchers. You are fortunate to have the work of thousands of researchers to draw on. It is not always necessary to start from scratch. You can use a past scale or index, or you can modify it for your own purposes. The process of creating measures is an ongoing process with constant change; new concepts are developed, theoretical definitions are refined, and scales or indexes that measure old or new constructs are improved.

Indexes and Scales. You might find the terms *index* and *scale* confusing because they are often used interchangeably. One researcher's scale is another's index. Both produce ordinal- or interval-level measures of a variable. To add to the confusion, scale and index techniques can be combined in one measure. Scales and indexes give a researcher more information about variables and make it possible to assess the quality of measurement. Scales and indexes increase reliability and validity, and they aid in data reduction; that is, they condense and simplify the information that is collected (see Box 7.4).

Mutually Exclusive and Exhaustive Attributes. Before discussing scales and indexes, it is important to review features of good measurement.

The attributes of all measures should be mutually exclusive and exhaustive.

Mutually exclusive attributes means that an individual or case fits into one and only one attribute of a variable. For example, a variable measuring type of religion—with the attributes Christian, non-Christian, and Jewish—is not mutually exclusive. Judaism is both a non-Christian religion and a Jewish religion, so a Jewish person fits into both the non-Christian and the Jewish category. Likewise, a variable measuring type of city, with the attributes river port city, state capital, and international airport, lacks mutually exclusive attributes. One city could be all three (a river port state capital with an international airport), any one of the three, or none of the three.

Exhaustive attributes means that all cases fit into one of the attributes of a variable. When measuring religion, a measure with the attributes Catholic, Protestant, and Jewish is not exclusive. The individual who is a Buddhist, a Muslim, or an

Mutually exclusive attributes The principle that variable attributes or categories in a measure are organized so that responses fit into only one category and there is no overlap.

Exhaustive attributes The principle that attributes or categories in a measure should provide a category for all possible responses.

BOX **7.4**   **Scales and Indexes: Are They Different?**

For most purposes, you can treat scales and indexes as interchangeable. Social researchers do not use a consistent nomenclature to distinguish between them.

A *scale* is a measure in which a researcher captures the intensity, direction, level, or potency of a variable construct. It arranges responses or observations on a continuum. A scale can use a single indicator or multiple indicators. Most are at the ordinal level of measurement.

An *index* is a measure in which a researcher adds or combines several distinct indicators of a construct into a single score. This composite score is often a simple sum of the multiple indicators. It is used for content and convergent validity. Indexes are often measured at the interval or ratio level.

Researchers sometimes combine the features of scales and indexes in a single measure. This is common when a researcher has several indicators that are scales (i.e., that measure intensity or direction). He or she then adds these indicators together to yield a single score, thereby creating an index.

---

agnostic does not fit anywhere. The attributes should be developed so that every possible situation is covered. For example, Catholic, Protestant, Jewish, or other is an exclusive and mutually exclusive set of attributes.

Unidimensionality. In addition to being mutually exclusive and exhaustive, scales and indexes should also be unidimensional or one dimensional. **Unidimensionality** means that all the items in a scale or index fit together, or measure a single construct. Unidimensionality was hinted at in the previous discussions of construct and content validity. Unidimensionality states: If you combine several specific pieces of information into a single score or measure, have all the pieces measure the same thing. One of the more advanced techniques—factor

analysis (see Appendix D)—is often used to test for the unidimensionality of data.

There is an apparent contradiction between using a scale or index to combine parts or subparts of a construct into one measure and the criteria of unidimensionality. It is only an apparent contradiction, however, because constructs are theoretically defined at different levels of abstraction. Higher-level or more abstract constructs can be defined as containing several subparts. Each subdimension is a part of the construct's overall content.

For example, "feminist ideology" is a highly abstract and general construct. It includes specific beliefs and attitudes toward social, economic, political, family, and sexual relations. The ideology's five belief areas are parts of the single general construct. The parts are mutually reinforcing and together form a system of beliefs about the dignity, strength, and power of women.

If feminist ideology is unidimensional, then there is a unified belief system that varies from very antifeminist to very profeminist. We can test the convergence validity of the measure that includes multiple indicators that tap the construct's subparts. If one belief area (e.g., sexual relations) is consistently distinct from the other areas in empirical tests, then we question its unidimensionality.

It is easy to become confused: A specific measure can be an indicator of a unidimensional construct in one situation and indicate a part of a different construct in another situation. This is possible because constructs can be used at different levels of abstraction.

For example, a person's attitude toward gender equality with regard to pay is more specific and less abstract than feminist ideology (i.e., beliefs about gender relations throughout society). An attitude toward equal pay can be both a unidimensional construct in its own right and a subpart of the more general and abstract unidimensional construct, *ideology toward gender relations.*

INDEX CONSTRUCTION

The Purpose

You hear about indexes all the time. For example, U.S. newspapers report the Federal Bureau of Inves-

---

Unidimensionality   The principle that when using multiple indicators to measure a construct, all the indicators should consistently fit together and indicate a single construct.

tigation (FBI) crime index and the consumer price index (CPI). The FBI index is the sum of police reports on seven so-called index crimes (criminal homicide, aggravated assault, forcible rape, robbery, burglary, larceny of $50 or more, and auto theft). It began with the Uniform Crime Report in 1930 (see Rosen, 1995). The CPI, which is a measure of inflation, is created by totaling the cost of buying a list of goods and services (e.g., food, rent, and utilities) and comparing the total to the cost of buying the same list in the previous year. The consumer price index has been used by the U.S. Bureau of Labor Statistics since 1919; wage increases, union contracts, and social security payments are based on it. An **index** is a combination of items into a single numerical score. Various components or subparts of a construct are each measured, then combined into one measure.

There are many types of indexes. For example, if you take an exam with 25 questions, the total number of questions correct is a kind of index. It is a composite measure in which each question measures a small piece of knowledge, and all the questions scored correct or incorrect are totaled to produce a single measure.

Indexes measure the most desirable place to live (based on unemployment, commuting time, crime rate, recreation opportunities, weather, and so on), the degree of crime (based on combining the occurrence of different specific crimes), the mental health of a person (based on the person's adjustment in various areas of life), and the like.

Creating indexes is so easy that it is important to be careful that every item in the index has face validity. Items without face validity should be excluded. Each part of the construct should be measured with at least one indicator. Of course, it is better to measure the parts of a construct with multiple indicators.

An example of an index is a college quality index (see Box 7.5). My theoretical definition says that a high-quality college has six distinguishing characteristics: (1) fewer students per faculty member, (2) a highly educated faculty, (3) more books in the library, (4) fewer students dropping out of college, (5) more students who go on to advanced degrees, and (6) faculty members who publish books or scholarly articles. I score 100 colleges on each item, then add the scores for each to create an index

score of college quality that can be used to compare colleges.

Indexes can be combined with one another. For example, in order to strengthen my college quality index, I add a subindex on teaching quality. The index contains eight items: (1) average size of classes, (2) percentage of class time devoted to discussion, (3) number of different classes each faculty member teaches, (4) availability of faculty to students outside the classroom, (5) currency and amount of reading assigned, (6) degree to which assignments promote learning, (7) degree to which faculty get to know each student, and (8) student ratings of instruction. Similar subindex measures can be created for other parts of the college quality index. They can be combined into a more global measure of college quality. This further elaborates the definition of the construct "quality of college."

Weighting

An important issue in index construction is whether to weight items. Unless it is otherwise stated, assume that an index is unweighted. Likewise, unless you have a good theoretical reason for assigning different weights, use equal weights. An *unweighted index* gives each item equal weight. It involves adding up the items without modification, as if each were multiplied by 1 (or –1 for items that are negative).

In a weighted index, a researcher values or weights some items more than others. The size of weights can come from theoretical assumptions, the theoretical definition, or a statistical technique such as factor analysis (see Appendix D). Weighting changes the theoretical definition of the construct.

For example, I elaborate the theoretical definition of the college quality index. I decide that the student/faculty ratio and number of faculty with Ph.D's are twice as important as the number of books in the library per student or the percentage of students pursuing advanced degrees. Also, the percentage of freshmen who drop out and the number of publications per faculty member are three times

Index The summing or combining of many separate measures of a construct or variable to create a single score.

BOX **7.5**   **Example of Index**

In symbolic form, where:

Q = overall college quality

A quality-of-college index is based on the following six items:

R = number of students per faculty member
F = percentage of faculty with Ph.D.s
B = number of books in library per student
D = percentage of freshmen who drop out or do not finish
A = percentage of graduates who go for an advanced degree
P = number of publications per faculty member

Unweighted formula: $(-1)R + (1)F + (1)B + (-1)D + (1)A + (1)P = Q$
Weighted formula: $(-2)R + (2)F + (1)B + (-3)D + (1)A + (3)P = Q$

Old Ivy College

Unweighted: $(-1)13 + (1)80 + (1)334 + (-1)14 + (1)28 + (1)4 = 419$
Weighted: $(-2)13 + (2)80 + (1)334 + (-3)14 + (1)28 + (3)4 = 466$

Local College

Unweighted: $(-1)20 + (1)82 + (1)365 + (-1)25 + (1)15 + (1)2 = 419$
Weighted: $(-2)20 + (2)82 + (1)365 + (-3)25 + (1)15 + (3)2 = 435$

Big University

Unweighted: $(-1)38 + (1)95 + (1)380 + (-1)48 + (1)24 + (1)6 = 419$
Weighted: $(-2)38 + (2)95 + (1)380 + (-3)48 + (1)24 + (3)6 = 392$

more important than books in the library or percentage pursuing an advanced degree. This is easier to see when it is expressed as a formula.

The number of students per faculty member and the percentage who drop out have negative signs because, as they get larger, the quality of the college gets lower. The weighted and unweighted indexes can produce different results. Consider Old Ivy College, Local College, and Big University. All have identical unweighted index scores, but the colleges have different quality scores after weighting.

Weighting produces different index scores in this example, but in most cases, weighted and unweighted indexes yield similar results. Researchers are concerned with the relationship between variables, and weighted and unweighted indexes usually give similar results for the relationships between variables.[17]

Missing Data

Missing data can be a serious problem when constructing an index. Validity and reliability are threat-ened whenever data for some cases are missing. There are four ways to attempt to resolve the problem (see Box 7.6), but none fully solves it.

For example, I construct an index of the degree of societal development in 1975 for 50 nations. The index contains four items: life expectancy, percentage of homes with indoor plumbing, percentage of population that is literate, and number of telephones per 100 people. I locate a source of United Nations statistics for my information. The values for Belgium are 68 + 87 + 97 + 28; for Turkey, the scores are 55 + 36 + 49 + 3; for Finland, however, I discover that literacy data are unavailable. I check other sources of information, but none has the data because they were not collected.

Rates and Standardization

You have heard of crime rates, rates of population growth, or the unemployment rate. Some indexes and single-indicator measures are expressed as

BOX **7.6** **Ways to Deal with Missing Data**

1. *Eliminate all cases for which any information is missing.* If Finland is removed from the study, the index will be reliable for the nations on which information is available. This is a problem if other nations have missing information. A study of 50 nations may become a study of 20 nations. Also, the cases with missing information may be similar in some respect (e.g., all are in eastern Europe or in the Third World), which limits the generalizability of findings.
2. *Substitute the average score for cases in which data are present.* The average literacy score from the other nations is substituted. This "solution" keeps Finland in the study but gives it an incorrect value. For an index with few items or for a case that is not "average," this creates serious validity problems.
3. *Insert data based on nonquantitative information about the case.* Other information about Finland (e.g., percentage of 13- to 18-year-olds in high school) is used to make an informed guess about the literacy rate. This "solution" is marginally acceptable in this situation. It is not as good as measuring Finland's literacy, and it relies on an untested assumption—that one can predict the literacy rate from other countries' high school attendance rate.
4. *Insert a random value.* This is unwise for the development index example. It might be acceptable if the index had a very large number of items and the number of cases was very large. If that were the situation, however, then eliminating the case is probably a better "solution" that produces a more reliable measure.

Source: Also see Allison (2001).

then the murder rate per 100,000 is 10 for City A and 5 for City B.

Standardization makes it possible to compare different units on a common base. The process of standardization, also called *norming,* removes the effect of relevant but different characteristics in order to make the important differences visible. For example, there are two classes of students. An art class has 12 smokers and a biology class has 22 smokers. A researcher can compare the rate or incidence of smokers by standardizing the number of smokers by the size of the classes. The art class has 32 students and the biology class has 143 students. One method of standardization that you already know is the use of percentages, whereby measures are standardized to a common base of 100. In terms of percentages, it is easy to see that the art class has more than twice the rate of smokers (37.5 percent) than the biology class (15.4 percent).

A critical question in standardization is deciding what base to use. In the examples given, how did I know to use city size or class size as the base? The choice is not always obvious; it depends on the theoretical definition of a construct.

Different bases can produce different rates. For example, the unemployment rate can be defined as the number of people in the workforce who are out of work. The overall unemployment rate is

$$\text{Unemployment rate} = \frac{\text{Number of unemployed people}}{\text{Total number of people working}}$$

We can divide the total population into subgroups to get rates for subgroups in the population such as White males, African American females, African American males between the ages of 18 and 28, or people with college degrees. Rates for these subgroups may be more relevant to the theoretical definition or research problem. For example, a researcher believes that unemployment is an experience that affects an entire

rates. Rates involve standardizing the value of an item to make comparisons possible. The items in an index frequently need to be standardized before they can be combined.

Standardization involves selecting a base and dividing a raw measure by the base. For example, City A had 10 murders and City B had 30 murders in the same year. In order to compare murders in the two cities, the raw number of murders needs to be standardized by the city population. If the cities are the same size, City B is more dangerous. But City B may be safer if it is much larger. For example, if City A has 100,000 people and City B has 600,000,

Standardization Procedures to adjust measures statistically to permit making an honest comparison by giving a common basis to measures of different units.

BOX **7.7**   **Standardization and the Real Winners at the Olympics**

Sports fans in the United States were jubilant about "winning" at the 2000 Olympics by carrying off the most gold medals. However, because they failed to *standardize,* the "win" is an illusion. Of course, the world's richest nation with the third largest population does well in one-on-one competition among all nations. To see what really happened, one must standardize on a base of the population or wealth. Standardization yields a more accurate picture by adjusting the results as if the nations had equal pop-

ulations and wealth. The results show that the Bahamas, with less than 300,000 citizens (smaller than a medium-sized U.S. city), proportionately won the most gold. Adjusted for its population size or wealth, the United States is not even near the top; it appears to be the leader only because of its great size and wealth. Sports fans in the United States can perpetuate the illusion of being at the top only if they ignore the comparative advantage of the United States.

TOP TEN GOLD MEDAL WINNING COUNTRIES AT THE 2000 OLYMPICS IN SYDNEY

Unstandardized Rank			*Standardized Rank**			
RANK	COUNTRY	TOTAL	COUNTRY	TOTAL	POPULATION	GDP
1	USA	39	Bahamas	1	33.3	20.0
2	Russia	32	Slovenia	2	10	10.0
3	China	28	Cuba	11	9.9	50.0
4	Australia	16	Norway	4	9.1	2.6
5	Germany	14	Australia	16	8.6	4.1
6	France	13	Hungry	8	7.9	16.7
7	Italy	13	Netherlands	12	7.6	3.0
8	Netherlands	12	Estonia	1	7.1	20.0
9	Cuba	11	Bulgaria	5	6.0	41.7
10	Britain	11	Lithuania	2	5.4	18.2
	EU15**	80	EU 15	80	2.1	0.9
			USA	39	1.4	0.4

Note: *Population is gold medals per 10 million people and GDP is gold medals per $10 billion.

**EU15 is the 15 nations of the European Union treated as a single unit.

Source: Adapted from *The Economist,* October 7, 2000, p. 52.

household or family and that the base should be households, not individuals. The rate will look like this:

$$\text{New unemployment rate} = \frac{\text{Number of households with at least one unemployed person}}{\text{Total number of households}}$$

Different conceptualizations suggest different bases and different ways to standardize. When com-

bining several items into an index, it is best to standardize items on a common base (see Box 7.7).

SCALES

The Purpose

Scales are common in situations in which a researcher wants to measure how an individual feels or thinks about something. Some call this the hardness or potency of feelings. Scales also help in the conceptualization and operationalization processes.

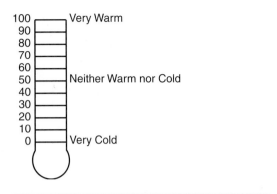

FIGURE 7.7   "Feeling Thermometer" Graphic Rating Scale

For example, a researcher believes that there is a single ideological dimension that underlies people's judgments about specific policies (e.g., housing, education, foreign affairs, etc.). Scaling can help determine whether a single construct—for instance, "conservative/liberal ideology"—underlies the positions people take on specific policies.

Scaling produces quantitative measures used to test hypotheses.

Logic of Scaling

Scaling measures the intensity, direction, level, or potency of a variable. Graphic rating **scales** are an elementary form of scaling. People indicate a rating by checking a point on a line that runs from one extreme to another. This type of scale is easy to construct and use. It conveys the idea of a continuum, and assigning numbers helps people think about quantities. Scales assume that people with the same subjective feeling mark the graphic scale at the same place.

Figure 7.7 is an example of a "feeling thermometer" scale that is used to find out how people feel about various groups in society (e.g., the National Organization of Women, the Ku Klux Klan, labor unions, physicians, etc.). This type of measure has been used by political scientists in the National Election Study since 1964 to measure attitudes toward candidates, social groups, and issues.[18]

Commonly Used Scales

Likert Scale. You have probably used **Likert scales;** they are widely used in survey research. They were developed in the 1930s by Rensis Likert to provide an ordinal-level measure of a person's attitude.[19] Likert scales are called *summated-rating* or *additive scales* because a person's score on the scale is computed by summing the number of responses the person gives. Likert scales usually ask people to indicate whether they agree or disagree with a statement. Other modifications are possible; people might be asked whether they approve or disapprove, or whether they believe something is "almost always true." Box 7.8 presents several examples of Likert scales.

Likert scales need a minimum of two categories, such as "agree" and "disagree." Using only two choices creates a crude measure and forces distinctions into only two categories. It is usually better to use four to eight categories. A researcher can combine or collapse categories after the data are collected, but data collected with crude categories cannot be made more precise later.

You can increase the number of categories at the end of a scale by adding "strongly agree," "somewhat agree," "very strongly agree," and so forth. Keep the number of choices to eight or nine at most. More distinctions than that are not meaningful, and people will become confused. The choices should be evenly balanced (e.g., "strongly agree," "agree" with "strongly disagree," "disagree"). Nunnally (1978:521) stated:

> As the number of scale steps is increased from 2 up through 20, the increase in reliability is very rapid at first. It tends to level off at about 7, and after about 11 steps, there is little gain in reliability from increasing the number of steps.

Scale   A class of quantitative data measures often used in survey research that captures the intensity, direction, level, or potency of a variable construct along a continuum. Most are at the ordinal level of measurement.

Likert scale   A scale often used in survey research in which people express attitudes or other responses in terms of ordinal-level categories (e.g., agree, disagree) that are ranked along a continuum.

BOX **7.8** **Examples of Types of Likert Scales**

THE ROSENBERG SELF-ESTEEM SCALE
All in all, I am inclined to feel that I am a failure:

(1) Almost always true   (4) Seldom true
(2) Often true   (5) Never true
(3) Sometimes true

A STUDENT EVALUATION OF INSTRUCTION SCALE
Overall, I rate the quality of instruction in this course as:

Excellent   Good   Average   Fair   Poor

A MARKET RESEARCH MOUTHWASH RATING SCALE

Brand	Dislike Completely	Dislike Somewhat	Dislike a Little	Like a Little	Like Somewhat	Like Completely
X	_____	_____	_____	_____	_____	_____
Y	_____	_____	_____	_____	_____	_____

WORK GROUP SUPERVISOR SCALE
My supervisor:

	Never	Seldom	Sometimes	Often	Always
Lets members know what is expected of them	1	2	3	4	5
Is friendly and approachable	1	2	3	4	5
Treats all unit members as equals	1	2	3	4	5

Researchers have debated about whether to offer a neutral category (e.g., "don't know," "undecided," "no opinion") in addition to the directional categories (e.g., "disagree," "agree"). A neutral category implies an odd number of categories.

A researcher can combine several Likert scale questions into a composite index if they all measure a single construct. Consider the Index of Equal Opportunity for Women and the Self-Esteem Index that Sniderman and Hagen (1985) created for their study (see Box 7.9). In the middle of larger surveys, respondents were asked three questions about the position of women. The researchers later scored answers and combined items into an index that ranged from 3 to 15. Respondents also answered questions about self-esteem. Notice that when scoring these items, one item (question 2) is scored in reverse. The reason for switching directions in this way is to avoid the problem of the **response set.** The response set, also called *response style* and *response bias,* is the tendency of some people to answer a large number of items in the same way (usually agreeing) out of laziness or a psychological predisposition. For example, if items are worded so that saying "strongly agree" always indicates self-esteem, we would not know whether a person who always strongly agreed had high self-esteem or simply had a tendency to agree with questions. The person might be answering "strongly agree" out of habit or a tendency to agree. Researchers word statements in alternative directions, so that anyone who agrees all the time appears to answer inconsistently or to have a contradictory opinion.

Response set   A tendency to agree with every question in a series rather than carefully thinking through one's answer to each.

BOX **7.9**   **Examples of Using the Likert Scale to Create Indexes**

Sniderman and Hagen (1985) created indexes to measure beliefs about equal opportunity for women and self-esteem. For both indexes, scores were added to create an unweighted index.

INDEX OF EQUAL OPPORTUNITY FOR WOMEN

Questions

1. Women have less opportunity than men to get the education for top jobs.

Strongly Agree	Somewhat Agree	Somewhat Disagree	Disagree a Great Deal	Don't Know

2. Many qualified women cannot get good jobs; men with the same skills have less trouble.

Strongly Agree	Somewhat Agree	Somewhat Disagree	Disagree a Great Deal	Don't Know

3. Our society discriminates against women.

Strongly Agree	Somewhat Agree	Somewhat Disagree	Disagree a Great Deal	Don't Know

Scoring: For all items, Strongly Agree = 1, Somewhat Agree = 2, Somewhat Disagree = 4, Disagree a Great Deal = 5, Don't Know = 3.

Highest Possible Index Score = 15, respondent feels opportunities for women are equal
Lowest Possible Index Score = 3, respondent feels opportunities are not equal

SELF-ESTEEM INDEX

Questions

1. On the whole, I am satisfied with myself.   Agree   Disagree   Don't Know

2. At times, I think I am no good at all.   Agree   Disagree   Don't Know

3. I sometimes feel that (other) men do not
   take my opinion seriously.   Agree   Disagree   Don't Know

Scoring: Items 1 and 3: 1 = Disagree, 2 = Don't Know, 3 = Agree, Item 2: 1 = Disagree, 2 = Don't Know, 1 = Agree.

Highest Possible Index Score = 9, high self-esteem
Lowest Possible Index Score = 3, low self-esteem

Researchers often combine many Likert-scaled attitude indicators into an index. The scale and indexes have properties that are associated with improving reliability and validity. An index uses multiple indicators, which improves reliability. The use of multiple indicators that measure several aspects of a construct or opinion improves content validity. Finally, the index scores give a more precise quantitative measure of a person's opinion. For example, each person's opinion can be measured with a number from 10 to 40, instead of in four categories: "strongly agree," "agree," "disagree," "strongly disagree."

Instead of scoring Likert items, as in the previous example, the scores –2, –1, +1, +2 could be used. This scoring has an advantage in that a zero implies neutrality or complete ambiguity, whereas a high negative number means an attitude that opposes the opinion represented by a high positive number.

The numbers assigned to the response categories are arbitrary. Remember that the use of a zero does not give the scale or index a ratio level of measurement. Likert scale measures are at the ordinal level of measurement because responses indicate a ranking only. Instead of 1 to 4 or –2 to +2, the numbers 100, 70, 50, and 5 would have worked. Also, do not be fooled into thinking that the distances between the ordinal categories are intervals just because numbers are assigned. The numbers are used for convenience only. The fundamental measurement is only ordinal.[20]

The simplicity and ease of use of the Likert scale is its real strength. When several items are combined, more comprehensive multiple indicator measurement is possible. The scale has two limitations: Different combinations of several scale items can result in the same overall score or result, and the response set is a potential danger.

Thurstone Scaling. Researchers sometimes want a measure with one numerical continuum, but the attitude variable in which they are interested has several characteristics or aspects. For example, a dry-cleaning business, Quick and Clean, wants to find out its image in Greentown compared to that of its major competitor, Friendly Cleaners. The researcher working for Quick and Clean conceptualizes a person's attitude toward the business as having four subparts or aspects: attitude toward location, hours, service, and cost. Quick and Clean is seen as having more convenient hours and locations, but higher costs and discourteous service, whereas Friendly Cleaners is seen as having low cost and friendly service, but inconvenient hours and locations. Unless the researcher knows how the four aspects relate to the core attitude—image of the dry cleaner—he or she cannot say which business is generally viewed more favorably. During the late 1920s, Louis Thurstone developed scaling methods for assigning numerical values in such situations. These are now called **Thurstone scaling** or the *method of equal-appearing intervals.*[21]

Thurstone scaling uses the law of comparative judgment. The law addresses the issue of comparing attitudes when each person makes a unique judgment. It anchors or fixes the position of one person's attitude relative to that of others as each makes an individual judgment.

The law of comparative judgment states that it is possible to identify the "most common response" for each object or concept being judged. Although different people arrive at different judgments, the individual judgments cluster around a single most common response. The dispersion of individual judgments around the common response follows a statistical pattern called the normal distribution. From the law, it follows that, if many people agree that two objects differ, the most common responses for the two objects will be distant from each other. By contrast, if many people are confused or disagree, the common responses of the two objects will be closer to each other.

In Thurstone scaling, a researcher develops many statements (e.g., more than 100) regarding the object of interest, then uses judges to reduce the number to a smaller set (e.g., 20) by eliminating ambiguous statements. Each judge rates the statements on an underlying continuum (e.g., favorable to unfavorable). The researcher examines the ratings and keeps statements based on two factors: (1) agreement among the judges and (2) the statement's location on a range of possible values. The final set of statements is a measurement scale that spans a range of values.

Thurstone scaling begins with a large number of statements that should cover all shades of opinion. Each should be clear and precise. Good statements refer to the present and are not capable of being interpreted as facts. They are unlikely to be endorsed by everyone, are stated as simple sentences, and avoid words such as *always* and *never.* Researchers get ideas for writing the statements from reviewing the literature, from the mass media, from personal experience, and from asking others. For example, statements about the dry-cleaning

Thurstone scaling   A scale in which the researcher gives a group of judges many items and asks them to sort the items into categories along a continuum, and then looks at sorting results to select items on which the judges are in agreement.

business might include the four aspects listed before, plus the following:

- I think X Cleaners dry cleans clothing in a prompt and timely manner.
- In my opinion, X Cleaners keeps its stores looking neat and attractive.
- I do not think that X Cleaners does a good job removing stains.
- I believe that X Cleaners charges reasonable prices for cleaning coats.
- I believe that X Cleaners returns clothing clean and neatly pressed.
- I think that X Cleaners has poor delivery service.

A researcher next locates 50 to 300 judges. The judges should be familiar with the object or concept in the statements. Each judge receives a set of statement cards and instructions. Each card has one statement on it, and the judges place each card in one of several piles. The number of piles is usually 7, 9, 11, or 13. The piles represent a range of values (e.g., favorable to neutral to unfavorable) with regard to the object or concept being evaluated. Each judge places cards in rating piles independently of the other judges.

After the judges place all cards in piles, the researcher creates a chart cross-classifying the piles and the statements. For example, 100 statements and 11 piles results in an 11 × 100 chart, or a chart with 11 × 100 = 1,100 boxes. The number of judges who assigned a rating to a given statement is written into each box. Statistical measures (beyond the present discussion) are used to compute the average rating of each statement and the degree to which the judges agree or disagree.

The researcher keeps the statements with the greatest between-judge agreement, or interrater reliability, as well as statements that represent the entire range of values. (See Box 7.10 for an example.)

With Thurstone scaling, a researcher can construct an attitude scale or select statements from a larger collection of attitude statements. The method is seldom used because of its limitations:

1. It measures only agreement or disagreement with statements, not the intensity of agreement or disagreement.

2. It assumes that judges and others agree on where statements appear in a rating system.
3. It is time consuming and costly.
4. It is possible to get the same overall score in several ways because agreement or disagreement with different combinations of statements can produce the same average.

Bogardus Social Distance Scale. The **Bogardus social distance scale** measures the social distance separating ethnic or other groups from each other. It is used with one group to determine how much distance it feels toward a target or "outgroup." It was developed in the 1920s by Emory Bogardus to measure the willingness of members of different ethnic groups to associate with each other. It can be used to see how close or distant people feel toward some other group (e.g., a religious minority or a deviant group).[22]

The scale has a simple logic. People respond to a series of ordered statements; those that are most threatening or most socially distant are at one end, and those that might be least threatening or socially intimate are at the other end. The logic of the scale assumes that a person who refuses contact or is uncomfortable with the socially distant items will refuse the socially closer items.

Researchers use the scale in several ways. For example, people are given a series of statements: People from Group X are entering your country, are in your town, work at your place of employment, live in your neighborhood, become your personal friends, and marry your brother or sister. People are asked whether they feel comfortable with the statement or if the contact is acceptable. It is also possible to ask whether they feel uncomfortable with the relationship. People may be asked to respond to all statements, or they may keep reading statements until they are not comfortable with a relationship. There is no set number of statements required; the number usually ranges from five to nine.

Bogardus social distance scale A scale measuring the social distance between two or more social groups by having members of one group indicate the limit of their comfort with various types of social interaction or closeness with members of the other group(s).

BOX **7.10** Example of Thurstone Scaling

Variable Measured: Opinion with regard to the death penalty.

Step 1:   Develop 120 statements about the death penalty using personal experience, the popular and professional literature, and listening to others.

Example Statements
1. I think that the death penalty is cruel and unnecessary punishment.
2. Without the death penalty, there would be many more violent crimes.
3. I believe that the death penalty should be used only for a few extremely violent crimes.
4. I do not think that anyone was ever prevented from committing a murder because of fear of the death penalty.
5. I do not think that people should be exempt from the death penalty if they committed a murder even if they are insane.
6. I believe that the Bible justifies the use of the death penalty.
7. The death penalty itself is not the problem for me, but I believe that electrocuting people is a cruel way to put them to death.

Step 2:   Place each statement on a separate card or sheet of paper and make 100 sets of the 120 statements.

Step 3:   Locate 100 persons who agree to serve as judges. Give each judge a set of the statement and instructions to place them in one of 11 piles, from 1 = highly unfavorable statement through 11 = highly favorable statement.

Step 4:   The judges place each statement into one of the 11 piles (e.g., Judge #1 puts statement 1 into pile #2; Judge #2 puts the same statement into pile #1; Judge #3 also puts it into pile #2, Judge #4 puts it in pile #3, and so on).

Step 5:   Collect piles from judges and create a chart summarizing their responses. See the example chart that follows.

CHART OF NUMBER OF JUDGES RATING EACH STATEMENT RATING PILE

Statement	Unfavorable				Neutral				Favorable			Total
	1	2	3	4	5	6	7	8	9	10	11	
1	23	60	12	5	0	0	0	0	0	0	0	100
2	0	0	0	0	2	12	18	41	19	8	0	100
3	2	8	7	13	31	19	12	6	2	0	0	100
4	9	11	62	10	4	4	0	0	0	0	0	100

Step 6:   Compute the average rating and degree of agreement by judges. For example, the average for question 1 is about 2, so there is high agreement; the average for question 3 is closer to 5, and there is much less agreement.

Step 7:   Choose the final 20 statements to include in the death penalty opinion scale. Choose statements if the judges showed agreement (most placed an item in the same or a nearby pile) and ones that reflect the entire range of opinion, from favorable to neutral to unfavorable.

Step 8:   Prepare a 20-statement questionnaire, and ask people in a study whether they agree or disagree with the statements.

BOX **7.11** Example of Bogardus Social Distance Scale

A researcher wants to find out how socially distant freshmen college students feel from exchange students from two different countries: Nigeria and Germany. She wants to see whether students feel more distant from students coming from Africa or from Europe. She uses the following series of questions in an interview:

> Please give me your first reaction, yes or no, whether you personally would feel comfortable having an exchange student from (name of country):

> _____ As a visitor to your college for a week

> _____ As a full-time student enrolled at your college

> _____ Taking several of the same classes you are taking

> _____ Sitting next to you in class and studying with you for exams

> _____ Living a few doors down the hall on the same floor in your dormitory

> _____ As a same-sex roommate sharing your dorm room

> _____ As someone of the opposite sex who has asked you to go out on a date

Hypothetical Results

	Percentage of Freshmen Who Report Feeling Comfortable	
	Nigeria	*Germany*
Visitor	100%	100%
Enrolled	98%	100%
Same class	95%	98%
Study together	82%	88%
Same dorm	71%	83%
Roommate	50%	76%
Go on date	42%	64%

The results suggest that freshmen feel more distant from Nigerian students than from German students. Almost all feel comfortable having the international students as visitors, enrolled in the college, and taking classes. Feelings of distance increase as interpersonal contact increases, especially if the contact involves personal living settings or activities not directly related to the classroom.

A researcher can use the Bogardus scale to see how distant people feel from one outgroup versus another (see Box 7.11). The measure of social distance can be used as either an independent or a dependent variable. For example, a researcher believes that social distance from a group is greatest for people who have some other characteristic. A hypothesis might be that feelings of social distance by whites from Vietnamese is negatively associated with education; that is, the least educated feel the most distant. Social distance is the dependent variable, and amount of education is the independent variable.

The social distance scale has two potential limitations. First, a researcher needs to tailor the categories to a specific outgroup and social setting. Second, it is not easy for a researcher to compare how a respondent feels toward several different groups unless the respondent completes a similar social distance scale for all outgroups at the same time. Of course, how a respondent completes the scale and the respondent's actual behavior in specific social situations may differ.

Semantic Differential. **Semantic Differential** was developed in the 1950s to provide an indirect measure of how a person feels about a concept, object, or other person. It measures subjective feelings toward something by using adjectives, because people communicate evaluations through adjectives in spoken and written language. Most adjectives have polar opposites (e.g., *light/dark, hard/soft, slow/fast*). The Semantic Differential captures the connotations associated with whatever is being evaluated and provides an indirect measure of it.

To use the Semantic Differential, a researcher presents subjects with a list of paired opposite adjectives with a continuum of 7 to 11 points between them. The subjects mark the spot on the continuum between the adjectives that expresses their feelings. The adjectives can be very diverse and should be well mixed (e.g., positive items should not be located mostly on either the right or the left side). Studies of a wide variety of adjectives in English found that they fall into three major classes of meaning: evaluation *(good–bad)*, potency *(strong–weak)*, and activity *(active–passive)*. Of the three classes, evaluation is usually the most significant. The analysis of results is difficult, and a researcher needs to use statistical procedures to analyze a subject's feelings toward the concept.

Results from a Semantic Differential tell a researcher how one person perceives different concepts or how different people view the same concept. For example, political analysts might discover that young voters perceive their candidate as traditional, weak, and slow, and as halfway between good and bad. Elderly voters perceive the candidate as leaning toward strong, fast, and good, and as halfway between traditional and modern. In the example in Box 7.12, a person rated two concepts. The pattern of responses for each concept illustrates how this individual feels about the concepts. This person views the two concepts differently and appears to feel rather negatively about the idea of divorce.

There are techniques for creating three-dimensional diagrams of results.[23] The three aspects are diagrammed in three-dimensional "semantic space." In the diagram, "good" is up and "bad" is down, "active" is left and "passive" is right, "strong" is away from the viewer and "weak" is close.

Guttman Scaling. **Guttman scaling index,** or cumulative scaling, differs from the previous scales or indexes in that researchers use it to evaluate data after they are collected. This means that researchers must design a study with the Guttman scaling technique in mind. Louis Guttman developed the scale in the 1940s to determine whether a relationship existed among a set of indicators or measurement items. He used multiple indicators to document an underlying single dimension or cumulative intensity of a construct.[24]

Guttman scaling begins with measuring a set of indicators or items. These can be questionnaire items, votes, or observed characteristics. The indicators are usually measured in a simple yes/no or present/absent fashion. From 3 to 20 indicators can be used. The researcher selects items on the belief that there is a logical relationship among them. He or she then places the results into a Guttman scale and determines whether the items form a pattern that corresponds to the relationship.

Once a set of items is measured, the researcher considers all possible combinations of responses for the items. For example, three items are measured: whether a child knows her age, her telephone number, and three local elected political officials. The little girl may know her age but no other answer, or all three, or only her age and telephone number. In fact, for three items there are eight possible combinations of answers or patterns of responses, from

Semantic Differential   A scale that indirectly measures feelings or thoughts. People are presented with a topic or object and a list of polar opposite adjectives or adverbs, and then indicate feelings by marking one of several spaces between the two adjectives or adverbs.

Guttman scaling index   A scale that researchers use after data are collected to reveal whether a hierarchical pattern exists among responses, such that people who give responses at a "higher level" also tend to give "lower-level" ones.

BOX **7.12** **Example of Semantic Differential**

Please read each pair of adjectives below, then place a mark on the blank space that comes closest to your first impression feeling. There are no right or wrong answers.

How do you feel about the idea of divorce?

	1	2	3	4	5	6	7	8	9	
Bad		x								Good
Deep								x		Shallow
Weak			x							Strong
Fair								x		Unfair
Quiet									x	Loud
Modern	x									Traditional
Simple						x				Complex
Fast		x								Slow
Dirty		x								Clean

How do you feel about the idea of marriage?

	1	2	3	4	5	6	7	8	9	
Bad								x		Good
Deep		x								Shallow
Weak								x		Strong
Fair		x								Unfair
Quiet			x							Loud
Modern								x		Traditional
Simple						x				Complex
Fast								x		Slow
Dirty							x			Clean

not knowing any through knowing all three. There is a mathematical way to compute the number of combinations (e.g., 2^3), but you can write down all the combinations of yes or no for three questions and see the eight possibilities.

The logical relationship among items in Guttman scaling is hierarchical. Most people or cases have or agree to lower-order items. The smaller number of cases that have the higher-order items also have the lower-order ones, but not vice versa. In other words, the higher-order items build on the lower ones. The lower-order items are necessary for the appearance of the higher-order items.

An application of Guttman scaling, known as *scalogram analysis,* lets a researcher test whether a hierarchical relationship exists among the items. For example, it is easier for a child to know her age than her telephone number, and to know her telephone number than the names of political leaders. The items are called scalable, or capable of forming a Guttman scale, if a hierarchical pattern exists.

The patterns of responses can be divided into two groups: scaled and errors (or nonscalable). The scaled patterns for the child's knowledge example would be as follows: not knowing any item, knowing only age, knowing only age plus phone number, knowing all three. Other combinations of answers (e.g., knowing the political leaders but not her age) are possible but are nonscalable. If a hierarchical relationship exists among the items, then most answers fit into the scalable patterns.

The strength or degree to which items can be scaled is measured with statistics that measure whether the responses can be reproduced based on a hierarchical pattern. Most range from zero to 100 percent. A score of zero indicates a random pattern, or no hierarchical pattern. A score of 100 percent indicates that all responses to the answer fit the hierarchical or scaled pattern. Alternative statistics to

BOX **7.13** Guttman Scale Example

Crozat (1998) examined public responses to various forms of political protest. He looked at survey data on the public's acceptance of forms of protest in Great Britain, Germany, Italy, Netherlands, and the United States in 1974 and 1990. He found that the pattern of the public's acceptance formed a Guttman scale. Those who accepted more intense forms of protest (e.g., strikes and sit-ins) almost always accepted more modest forms (e.g., petitions or demonstrations), but not all who accepted modest forms accepted the more intense forms. In addition to showing the usefulness of the Guttman scale, Crozat also found that people in different nations saw protest similarily and the degree of Guttman scalability increased over time. Thus, the pattern of acceptance of protest activities was Guttman "scalable" in both time periods, but it more closely followed the Guttman pattern in 1990 than in 1974.

	FORM OF PROTEST				
	Petitions	*Demonstrations*	*Boycotts*	*Strike*	*Sit-In*
Guttman Patterns					
	N	N	N	N	N
	Y	N	N	N	N
	Y	Y	N	N	N
	Y	Y	Y	N	N
	Y	Y	Y	Y	N
	Y	Y	Y	Y	Y
Other Patterns (examples only)					
	N	Y	N	Y	N
	Y	N	Y	Y	N
	Y	N	Y	N	N
	N	Y	Y	N	N
	Y	N	N	Y	Y

measure scalability have also been suggested.[25] (See Box 7.13 for an example of a study using Guttman scaling.)

Clogg and Sawyer (1981) studied U.S. attitudes toward abortion using Guttman scaling by looking at different conditions under which people thought abortion was acceptable (e.g., mother's health in danger, pregnancy resulting from rape). They discovered that 84.2 percent of responses fit into a scaled response pattern.

CONCLUSION

In this chapter, you learned about the principles and processes of measurement in quantitative and qual-

itative research. All researchers conceptualize—or refine and clarify their ideas into conceptual definitions. All researchers operationalize—or develop a set of techniques or processes that will link their conceptual definitions to empirical reality. Qualitative and quantitative researchers differ in how they approach these processes, however. The quantitative researcher takes a more deductive path, whereas the qualitative researcher takes a more inductive path. The goal remains the same: to establish unambiguous links between a reseacher's abstract ideas and empirical data.

You also learned about the principles of reliability and validity that are shared by all researchers. Reliability refers to the dependability of a measure;

validity refers to its truthfulness, or how well a construct and data for it fit together. Quantitative and qualitative researchers diverge in how they understand these principles but try to measure in a consistent way and seek a tight fit between the abstract ideas and the empirical social world. In addition, you saw how quantitative researchers apply the principles of measurement when they create indexes and scales, and you read about some major scales they use.

Beyond the core ideas of reliability and validity, you now know principles of good measurement: Create clear definitions for concepts, use multiple indicators, and, as appropriate, weigh and standardize the data. These principles hold across all fields of study (e.g., family, criminology, inequality, race relations, etc.) and across the many research techniques (e.g., experiments, surveys, etc.).

As you are probably beginning to realize, a sound research project involves doing a good job in each phase of research. Serious mistakes or sloppiness in any one phase can do irreparable damage to the results, even if the other phases of the research project were conducted in a flawless manner.

KEY TERMS

Bogardus social distance scale
casing
conceptual definition
conceptual hypothesis
conceptualization
concurrent validity
construct validity
content validity
continuous variables
convergent validity
criterion validity
discrete variables
discriminant validity
empirical hypothesis

equivalence reliability
exhaustive attributes
face validity
Guttman scaling index
index
interval-level measurement
levels of measurement
Likert scale
measurement reliability
measurement validity
multiple indicators
mutually exclusive attributes
nominal-level measurement
operational definition

operationalization
ordinal-level measurement
predictive validity
ratio-level measurement
representative reliability
response set
rules of correspondence
scale
Semantic Differential
stability reliability
standardization
Thurstone scaling
unidimensionality

REVIEW QUESTIONS

1. What are the three basic parts of measurement, and how do they fit together?
2. What is the difference between reliability and validity, and how do they complement each other?
3. What are ways to improve the reliability of a measure?
4. How do the levels of measurement differ from each other?
5. What are the differences between convergent, content, and concurrent validity? Can you have all three at once? Explain your answer.
6. Why are multiple indicators usually better than one indicator?
7. What is the difference between the logic of a scale and that of an index?
8. Why is unidimensionality an important characteristic of a scale?
9. What are advantages and disadvantages of weighting indexes?
10. How does standardization make comparisons easier?

NOTES

1. Duncan (1984:220–239) presented cautions from a positivist approach on the issue of measuring anything.
2. The terms *concept, construct,* and *idea* are used more or less interchangeably, but there are differences in meaning between them. An *idea* is any mental image, belief plan, or impression. It refers to any vague impression, opinion, or thought. A *concept* is a thought, a general notion, or a generalized idea about a class of objects. A *construct* is a thought that is systematically put together, an orderly arrangement of ideas, facts, and impressions. The term *construct* is used here because its emphasis is on taking vague concepts and turning them into systematically organized ideas.
3. See Grinnell (1987:5–18) for further discussion.
4. See Blalock (1982:25–27) and Costner (1985) on rules of correspondence or the auxiliary theories that connect abstract concept with empirical indicators. Also see Zeller and Carmines (1980:5) for a diagram that illustrates the place of the rules in the process of measurement. In his presidential address to the American Sociological Association in 1979, Hubert Blalock (1979a:882) said, "I believe that the most serious and important problems that require our immediate and concerted attention are those of conceptualization and measurement."
5. See Bailey (1984, 1986) for a discussion of the three levels.
6. See Bohrnstedt (1992a, b) and Carmines and Zeller (1979) for discussions of reliability and various types of reliability.
7. See Sullivan and Feldman (1979) on multiple indicators. A more technical discussion can be found in Herting (1985), Herting and Costner (1985), and Scott (1968).
8. See Carmines and Zeller (1979:17). For a discussion of the many types of validity, see Brinberg and McGrath (1982).
9. The epistemic correlation is discussed in Costner (1985) and in Zeller and Carmines (1980:50–51, 137–139).
10. Kidder (1982) discussed the issue of disagreements over face validity, such as acceptance of a measure's meaning by the scientific community, but not the subjects being studied.
11. This was adapted from Carmines and Zeller (1979: 20–21).
12. For a discussion of types of criterion validity, see Carmines and Zeller (1979:17–19) and Fiske (1982) for construct validity.
13. See Cook and Campbell (1979) for elaboration.

14. See Borgatta and Bohrnstedt (1980) and Duncan (1984:119–155) for a discussion and critique of the topic of levels of measurement.
15. Johnson and Creech (1983) examined the measurement errors that occur when variables that are conceptualized as continuous are operationalized in a series of ordinal categories. They argued that errors are not serious if more than four categories and large samples are used.
16. For compilations of indexes and scales used in social research, see Brodsky and Smitherman (1983), Miller (1991), Robinson and colleagues (1972), Robinson and Shaver (1969), and Schuessler (1982).
17. For a discussion of weighted and unweighted index scores, see Nunnally (1978:534).
18. Feeling thermometers are discussed in Wilcox and associates (1989).
19. For more information on Likert scales, see Anderson and associates (1983:252–255), Converse (1987: 72–75), McIver and Carmines (1981:22–38), and Spector (1992).
20. Some researchers treat Likert scales as interval-level measures, but there is disagreement on this issue. Statistically, it makes little difference whether the Likert scale has at least five response categories and an approximately even proportion of people answer in each category.
21. McIver and Carmines (1981:16–21) have an excellent discussion of Thurstone scaling. Also see discussions in Anderson and colleagues (1983:248–252), Converse (1987:66–77), and Edwards (1957). The example used here is partially borrowed from Churchill (1983:249–254), who described the formula for scoring Thurstone scaling.
22. The social distance scale is described in Converse (1987:62–69). The most complete discussion can be found in Bogardus (1959).
23. The Semantic Differential is discussed in Nunnally (1978:535–543). Also see Heise (1965, 1970) on the analysis of scaled data.
24. See Guttman (1950).
25. See Bailey (1987:349–351) for a discussion of an improved method for determining scalability called Minimal Marginal Reproducibility. Guttman scaling can involve more than yes/no choices and a large number of items, but the complexity increases quickly. A more elaborate discussion of Guttman scaling can be found in Anderson and associates (1983:256–260), Converse (1987:189–195), McIver and Carmines (1981:40–71), and Nunnally (1978:63–66). Clogg and Sawyer (1981) presented alternatives to Guttman scaling.

Qualitative and Quantitative Sampling

Sampling is a major problem for any type of research. We can't study every case of whatever we're interested in, nor should we want to. Every scientific enterprise tries to find out something that will apply to everything *of a certain kind by studying a few examples, the results of the study being, as we say, "generalizable."*
—Howard Becker, *Tricks of the Trade,* p. 67

Qualitative and quantitative researchers approach sampling differently. Most discussions of sampling come from researchers who use the quantitative style. Their primary goal is to get a representative **sample,** or a small collection of units from a much larger collection or population, such that the researcher can study the smaller group and produce accurate generalizations about the larger group. Researchers focus on the specific techniques that will yield highly representative samples (i.e., samples that are very much like the population). The sampling is based on theories of probability from mathematics (called *probability sampling*).

Researchers have two motivations for using probability or random sampling. The first motivation is *time and cost.* If properly conducted, results from a sample may yield results at 1/1000 the cost and time. For example, instead of gathering data from 20 million people, a researcher may draw a sample of 2,000; for accurate generalizations the

data from those 2,000 are equal to the data from all 20 million. The second motivation is *accuracy.* The results of a well-designed, carefully executed probability sample will produce results that are equally if not more accurate than trying to reach every single person in the whole population. A census is usually an attempt to count everyone.

Qualitative researchers focus less on a sample's representativeness than on how the sample or small collection of cases, units, or activities illuminates social life. The primary purpose of sampling is to collect specific cases, events, or actions that can clarify and deepen understanding. Qualitative researchers' concern is to find cases that will enhance what the researchers learn about the processes of social life in a specific context.

Sample A smaller set of cases a researcher selects from a larger pool and generalizes to the population.

NONPROBABILITY SAMPLING

Qualitative researchers rarely draw a representative sample from a huge number of cases to intensely study the sampled cases. For qualitative researchers, "it is their relevance to the research topic rather than their representativeness which determines the way in which the people to be studied are selected" (Flick, 1998: 41). Qualitative researchers tend to use nonprobability or **nonrandom samples.** This means they rarely determine the sample size in advance and have limited knowledge about the larger group or population from which the sample is taken. Unlike the quantitative researcher who uses a preplanned approach based on mathematical theory, the qualitative researcher selects cases gradually, with the specific content of a case determining whether it is chosen. Table 8.1 shows a variety of nonprobability sampling techniques.

Haphazard, Accidental, or Convenience Sampling

Haphazard sampling can produce ineffective, highly unrepresentative samples and is not recommended. When a researcher haphazardly selects cases that are convenient, he or she can easily get a sample that seriously misrepresents the population. Such samples are cheap and quick; however, the systematic errors that easily occur make them worse than no sample at all.[1] The person-on-the-street interview conducted by television programs is an example of a haphazard sample. Television interviewers go out on the street with camera and microphone to talk to a few people who are convenient to interview. The people walking past a television studio in the middle of the day do not represent everyone. Likewise, television interviewers often select people who look "normal" to them

TABLE 8.1   Types of Nonprobability Samples

TYPE OF SAMPLE	PRINCIPLE
Haphazard	Get any cases in any manner that is convenient.
Quota	Get a preset number of cases in each of several predetermined categories that will reflect the diversity of the population, using haphazard methods.
Purposive	Get all possible cases that fit particular criteria, using various methods.
Snowball	Get cases using referrals from one or a few cases, and then referrals from those cases, and so forth.
Deviant case	Get cases that substantially differ from the dominant pattern (a special type of purposive sample).
Sequential	Get cases until there is no additional information or new characteristics (often used with other sampling methods).
Theoretical	Get cases that will help reveal features that are theoretically important about a particular setting/topic.

Nonrandom sample A sample in which the sampling elements are selected using something other than a mathematically random process.

Haphazard sampling A nonrandom sample in which the researcher selects anyone he or she happens to come across.

---

and avoid people who are unattractive, poor, very old, or inarticulate.

Another example of a haphazard sample is that of a newspaper that asks readers to clip a questionnaire from the paper and mail it in. Not everyone reads the newspaper, has an interest in the topic, or will take the time to cut out the questionnaire and mail it. Some people will, and the number who do so may seem large (e.g., 5,000), but the sample cannot be used to generalize accurately to the population. Such haphazard samples may have entertainment value, but they can give a distorted view and seriously misrepresent the population.

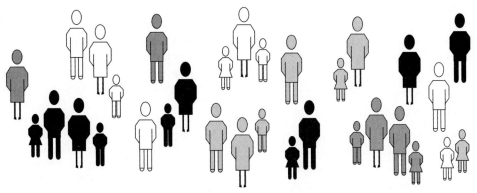

Of 32 adults and children in the street scene, select 10 for the sample:

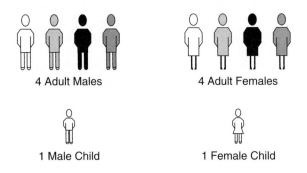

4 Adult Males   4 Adult Females

1 Male Child   1 Female Child

FIGURE 8.1   Quota Sampling

Quota Sampling

Quota sampling is an improvement over haphazard sampling.[2] In quota sampling, a researcher first identifies relevant categories of people (e.g., male and female; or under age 30, ages 30 to 60, over age 60, etc.), then decides how many to get in each category. Thus, the number of people in various categories of the sample is fixed. For example, a researcher decides to select 5 males and 5 females under age 30, 10 males and 10 females aged 30 to 60, and 5 males and 5 females over age 60 for a 40-person sample. It is difficult to represent all population characteristics accurately (see Figure 8.1).

Quota sampling ensures that some differences are in the sample. In haphazard sampling, all those interviewed might be of the same age, sex, or background. But once the quota sampler fixes the categories and number of cases in each category, he

or she uses haphazard sampling. For example, the researcher interviews the first 5 males under age 30 he or she encounters, even if all 5 just walked out of the campaign headquarters of a political candidate. Nothing prevents the researcher from selecting people who "act friendly" or who want to be interviewed.

A case from the history of sampling illustrates the limitations of quota sampling. George Gallup's American Institute of Public Opinion, using quota sampling, successfully predicted the outcomes of the 1936, 1940, and 1944 U.S. presidential elections. But in 1948, Gallup predicted the wrong candidate. The incorrect prediction had several causes

Quota sampling   A nonrandom sample in which the researcher first identifies general categories into which cases or people will be selected, and then he or she selects cases to reach a predetermined number of cases in each category.

(e.g., many voters were undecided, interviewing stopped early), but a major reason was that the quota categories did not accurately represent all geographical areas and all people who actually cast a vote.

Purposive or Judgmental Sampling

Purposive sampling is a valuable kind of sampling for special situations. It is used in exploratory research or in field research.[3] It uses the judgment of an expert in selecting cases or it selects cases with a specific purpose in mind. It is inappropriate if it is used to pick the "average housewife" or the "typical school." With purposive sampling, the researcher never knows whether the cases selected represent the population.

Purposive sampling is appropriate to select unique cases that are especially informative. For example, a researcher wants to use content analysis to study magazines to find cultural themes. He or she selects a specific popular women's magazine to study because it is trend setting.

A researcher may use purposive sampling to select members of a difficult-to-reach, specialized population. For example, the researcher wants to study prostitutes. It is impossible to list all prostitutes and sample randomly from the list. Instead, he or she uses subjective information (e.g., locations where prostitutes solicit, social groups with whom prostitutes associate, etc.) and experts (e.g., police who work on vice units, other prostitutes, etc.) to identify a "sample" of prostitutes for inclusion in the research project. The researcher uses many different methods to identify the cases, because his or her goal is to locate as many cases as possible. For example, McCall (1980) identified 31 female artists in St. Louis by asking a friend about other artists and by joining a local arts organization.

Another situation for purposive sampling occurs when a researcher wants to identify particular

---

> **Purposive sampling**   A nonrandom sample in which the researcher uses a wide range of methods to locate all possible cases of a highly specific and difficult-to-reach population.

---

types of cases for in-depth investigation. The purpose is to gain a deeper understanding of types. For example, Hochschild intensively interviewed 28 people about their beliefs. She selected some because they had low incomes and some because they had high incomes. Some were male and some were female.

> *Obviously, one cannot safely generalize from a sample of this kind to a national population: it would be worthless, for example, for me to point out what percentage of my sample sought more or fewer government services. . . . Intensive interviews are a device for generating insights, anomalies, and paradoxes, which later may be formalized into hypotheses that can be tested by quantitative social science methods. (1981:23–24)*

Gamson (1992) used purposive sampling in a focus group study of what working-class people think about politics. (Chapter 10 discusses focus groups.) Gamson wanted a total of 188 working-class people to participate in one of 37 focus groups. He sought respondents who had not completed college but who were diverse in terms of age, ethnicity, religion, interest in politics, and type of occupation. He recruited subjects from 35 neighborhoods in the Boston area by going to festivals, picnics, fairs, and flea markets and posting notices on many public bulletin boards. In addition to explaining the study, respondents were well paid so as to attract people who would not traditionally participate in a study.

Snowball Sampling

Social researchers are often interested in an interconnected network of people or organizations.[4] The network could be scientists around the world investigating the same problem, the elites of a medium-sized city, the members of an organized crime family, persons who sit on the boards of directors of major banks and corporations, or people on a college campus who have had sexual relations with each other. The crucial feature is that each person or unit is connected with another through a direct or indirect linkage. This does not mean that each person directly knows, interacts with, or is influenced

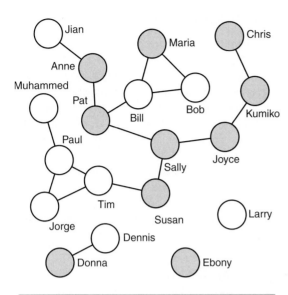

FIGURE 8.2   Sociogram of Friendship Relations

by every other person in the network. Rather, taken as a whole, with direct and indirect links, most are within an interconnected web of linkages.

For example, Sally and Tim do not know each other directly, but each has a good friend, Susan, so they have an indirect connection. All three are part of the same friendship network. Researchers represent such a network by drawing a *sociogram*—a diagram of circles connected with lines. The circles represent each person or case, and the lines represent friendship or other linkages (see Figure 8.2).

Snowball sampling (also called *network, chain referral,* or *reputational sampling*) is a method for sampling (or selecting) the cases in a network. It is based on an analogy to a snowball, which begins small but becomes larger as it is rolled on wet snow and picks up additional snow. Snowball sampling is a multistage technique. It begins with one or a few people or cases and spreads out on the basis of links to the initial cases.

For example, a researcher examines friendship networks among the teenagers in a community. He or she begins with three teenagers who do not know each other. Each teen names four close friends. The researcher then goes to the four friends and asks each

to name four close friends, then goes to those four and does the same thing again, and so forth. Before long, a large number of people are involved. Each person in the sample is directly or indirectly tied to the original teenagers, and several people may have named the same person. The researcher eventually stops, either because no new names are given, indicating a closed network, or because the network is so large that it is at the limit of what he or she can study. The sample includes those named by at least one other person in the network as being a close friend.

Deviant Case Sampling

A researcher uses **deviant case sampling** (also called *extreme case sampling*) when he or she seeks cases that differ from the dominant pattern or that differ from the predominant characteristics of other cases. Similar to purposive sampling, a researcher uses a variety of techniques to locate cases with specific characteristics. The goal is to locate a collection of unusual, different, or peculiar cases that are not representative of the whole. The cases are selected because they are unusual, and a researcher hopes to learn more about the social life by considering cases that fall outside the general pattern or including what is beyond the main flow of events.

For example, a researcher is interested in studying high school dropouts. Let us say that previous research suggested that a majority of dropouts come from families that have low income, are single parent or unstable, have been geographically mobile, and are racial minorities. The family environment is one in which parents and/or siblings have low education or are themselves dropouts. In addition, dropouts are often engaged in illegal behavior and

Snowball sampling   A nonrandom sample in which the researcher begins with one case, and then based on information about interrelationships from that case, identifies other cases, and repeats the process again and again.

Deviant case sampling   A nonrandom sample, especially used by qualitative researchers, in which a researcher selects unusual or nonconforming cases purposely as a way to provide greater insight into social processes or a setting.

have a criminal record prior to dropping out. A researcher using deviant case sampling would seek majority-group dropouts who have no record of illegal activities and who are from stable two-parent, upper-middle-income families who are geographically stable and well educated.

Sequential Sampling

Sequential sampling is similar to purposive sampling with one difference. In purposive sampling, the researcher tries to find as many relevant cases as possible. The principle is to get every possible case. In sequential sampling, a researcher continues to gather cases until the amount of new information or diversity of cases is filled. The principle is to gather cases until a saturation point is reached. In economic terms, information is gathered until the marginal utility, or incremental benefit for additional cases, levels off or drops significantly. It requires that a researcher continuously evaluate all the collected cases. For example, a researcher locates and plans in-depth interviews with 60 widows over 70 years old who have been living without a spouse for 10 or more years. Depending on the researcher's purposes, getting an additional 20 widows whose life experiences, social backgrounds, and worldviews differ little from the first 60 may be unnecessary.

Sequential sampling   A nonrandom sample in which a researcher tries to find as many relevant cases as possible, until time, financial resources, or his or her energy is exhausted, or until there is no new information or diversity from the cases.

Theoretical sampling   A nonrandom sample in which the researcher selects specific times, locations, or events to observe in order to develop a social theory or evaluate theoretical ideas.

Sampling element   The name for a case or single unit to be sampled.

Population   The abstract idea of a large group of many cases from which a researcher draws a sample and to which results from a sample are generalized.

Target population   The concretely specified large group of many cases from which a researcher draws a sample and to which results from a sample are generalized.

Theoretical Sampling

In **theoretical sampling,** what is sampled (e.g., people, situations, events, time periods, etc.) comes from grounded theory. A growing theoretical interest guides the selection of sample cases. The researcher selects cases based on new insights they may provide. For example, a field researcher may be observing a site and group of people during weekdays. Theoretically, the researcher may question whether the people act the same at other times or other aspects of the site change. He or she could then sample other time periods (e.g., nights and weekends) to get a more full picture and learn whether important conditions are the same.

PROBABILITY SAMPLING

A specialized vocabulary is used in probability sampling. Before examining probability sampling, it is important to review its language.

Populations, Elements, and Sampling Frames

A researcher draws a sample from a larger pool of cases, or *elements*. A **sampling element** is the unit of analysis or case in a population. It can be a person, a group, an organization, a written document or symbolic message, or even a social action (e.g., an arrest, a divorce, or a kiss) that is being measured. The large pool is the **population,** which has an important role in sampling. Sometimes, the term *universe* (defined in Chapter 6) is used interchangeably with *population.* To define the population, a researcher specifies the unit being sampled, the geographical location, and the temporal boundaries of populations. Consider the examples of populations in Box 8.1. All the examples include the elements to be sampled (e.g., people, businesses, hospital admissions, commercials, etc.) and geographical and time boundaries.

A researcher begins with an idea of the population (e.g., all people in a city) but defines it more precisely. A **target population** is the specific pool of cases that he or she wants to study. The ratio of the size of the sample to the size of the target pop-

BOX **8.1** Examples of Populations

1. All persons ages 16 or older living in Australia on December 2, 1989, who were not incarcerated in prison, asylums, and similar institutions
2. All business establishments employing more than 100 persons in Ontario Province, Canada, that operated in the month of July 2005
3. All admissions to public or private hospitals in the state of New Jersey between August 1, 1988, and July 31, 1993
4. All television commercials aired between 7:00 A.M. and 11:00 P.M. Eastern Standard Time on three major U.S. networks between November 1 and November 25, 2004
5. All currently practicing physicians in the United States who received medical degrees between January 1, 1960, and the present
6. All African American male heroin addicts in the Vancouver, British Columbia, or Seattle, Washington, metropolitan areas during 2004

ulation is the **sampling ratio.** For example, the population has 50,000 people, and a researcher draws a sample of 150 from it. Thus, the sampling ratio is 150/50,000 = 0.003, or 0.3 percent. If the population is 500 and the researcher samples 100, then the sampling ratio is 100/500 = 0.20, or 20 percent.

A population is an abstract concept. You may ask, how can population be an abstract concept, when there are a given number of people at a certain time? Except for specific small populations, one can never truly freeze a population to measure it. For example, in a city at any given moment, some people are dying, some are boarding or getting off airplanes, and some are in cars driving across city boundaries. The researcher must decide exactly who to count. Should he or she count a city resident who happens to be on vacation when the time is fixed? What about the tourist staying at a hotel in the city when the time is fixed? Should he or she count adults, children, people in jails, those in hospitals? A population, even the population of all people over the age of 18 in the city limits of Milwaukee, Wisconsin, at 12:01 A.M. on March 1,

2005, is an abstract concept. It exists in the mind but is impossible to pinpoint concretely.

Because a population is an abstract concept, except for small specialized populations (e.g., all the students in a classroom), a researcher needs to estimate the population. As an abstract concept, the population needs an operational definition, similar to that used in the measurement process (see Chapter 7).

A researcher operationalizes by developing a specific list that closely approximates all the elements in the population. This list is a **sampling frame.** He or she can choose from many types of sampling frames: telephone directories, tax records, driver's license records, and so on. Listing the elements in a population sounds simple. It is often difficult because there may be no good list of elements in a population.

A good sampling frame is crucial to good sampling. A mismatch between the sampling frame and the conceptually defined population can be a major source of error. Just as a mismatch between the theoretical and operational definitions of a variable creates invalid measurement, so a mismatch between the sampling frame and the population causes invalid sampling. Researchers try to minimize mismatches. For example, you would like to sample all people in a region of the United States, so you decide to get a list of everyone with a driver's license. But some people do not have driver's licenses, and the lists of those with licenses, even if updated regularly, quickly go out of date. Next, you try income tax records. But not everyone pays taxes; some people cheat and do not pay, others have no income and do not have to file, others have died or have not begun to pay taxes, and still others have entered or left the area since the last time taxes were due. Telephone directories are not much better; some people are not listed in a telephone

Sampling ratio The number of cases in the sample divided by the number of cases in the population or the sampling frame, or the proportion of the population in a sample.

Sampling frame A list of cases in a population, or the best approximation of it.

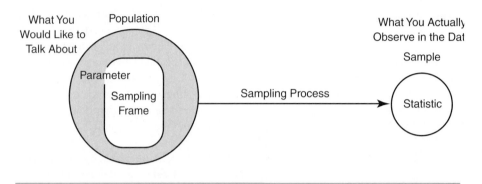

FIGURE 8.3   A Model of the Logic of Sampling

directory, some people have unlisted numbers, and others have recently moved. With a few exceptions (e.g., a list of all students enrolled at a university), sampling frames are almost always inaccurate. A sampling frame can include some of those outside the target population (e.g., a telephone directory that lists people who have moved away) or might omit some of those inside it (e.g., those without telephones).

Any characteristic of a population (e.g., the percentage of city residents who smoke cigarettes, the average height of all women over the age of 21, the percent of people who believe in UFOs) is a population **parameter.** It is the true characteristic of the population. The parameter is never known with absolute accuracy for large populations (e.g., an entire nation), so researchers must estimate it on the basis of samples. They use information from the sample, called a **statistic,** to estimate population parameters (see Figure 8.3).

A famous case in the history of sampling illustrates the limitations of the technique. The *Literary Digest,* a major U.S. magazine, sent postcards to people before the 1920, 1924, 1928, and 1932 U.S. presidential elections. The magazine

took the names for the sample from automobile registrations and telephone directories—the sampling frame. People returned the postcards indicating whom they would vote for. The magazine correctly predicted all four election outcomes. The magazine's success with predictions was well known, and in 1936, it increased the sample to 10 million. The magazine predicted a huge victory for Alf Landon over Franklin D. Roosevelt. But the *Literary Digest* was wrong; Franklin D. Roosevelt won by a landslide.

The prediction was wrong for several reasons, but the most important were mistakes in sampling. Although the magazine sampled a large number of people, its sampling frame did not accurately represent the target population (i.e., all voters). It excluded people without telephones or automobiles, a sizable percentage of the population in 1936. The frame excluded as much as 65 percent of the population and a segment of the voting population (lower income) that tended to favor Roosevelt.[5] The magazine had been accurate in earlier elections because people with higher and lower incomes did not differ in how they voted. Also, during earlier elections, before the Great Depression, more lower-income people could afford to have telephones and automobiles.

You can learn two important lessons from the *Literary Digest* mistake. First, the sampling frame is crucial. Second, the size of a sample is less important than whether it accurately represents the population. A representative sample of 2,500 can

Parameter   A characteristic of the entire population that is estimated from a sample.

Statistic   A word with several meanings, including a numerical estimate of a population parameter computed from a sample.

Source: © 1996 Thaves. Newspaper dist. by NEA, Inc.

give more accurate predications about the U.S. population than a nonrepresentative sample of 10 million or 50 million.

Why Random?

The probability theory in applied mathematics relies on random processes. The word *random* in mathematics refers to a process that generates a mathematically random result. If the selection process operates in a truly random method (i.e., no pattern), a researcher can calculate the probability of outcomes. In a true random process, each element has an equal probability of being selected.

Random or probability samples that rely on random processes require more work than nonrandom ones. A researcher must identify specific sampling elements (e.g., person) to include in the sample. For example, if conducting a telephone survey, the researcher needs to try to reach the specific sampled person, by calling back four or five times, to get an accurate random sample.[6]

Random samples are most likely to yield a sample that truly represents the population and lets a researcher statistically calculate the relationship between the sample and the population—that is, the size of the **sampling error.** The sampling error is the deviation between sample results and a population parameter due to random processes.

This chapter does not cover the technical and statistical details of random sampling. Instead, it focuses on the fundamentals of how sampling works, the difference between good and bad samples, how

to draw a sample, and basic principles of sampling in social research. If you plan to pursue a career using quantitative research, you should get more statistical background than space permits here.

Types of Probability Samples

Simple Random. The **simple random sample** is the one on which other types are modeled. In simple random sampling, a researcher develops an accurate sampling frame, selects elements from the sampling frame according to a mathematically random procedure, then locates the exact element that was selected for inclusion in the sample.

After numbering all elements in a sampling frame, a researcher uses a list of random numbers to decide which elements to select. He or she needs as many random numbers as there are elements to be sampled; for example, for a sample of 100, 100 random numbers are needed. The researcher can get

Random sample   A sample in which the researcher uses a random number table or similar mathematical random process so that each sampling element in the population will have an equal probability of being selected.

Sampling error   How much a sample deviates from being representative of the population.

Simple random sample   A random sample in which a researcher creates a sampling frame and uses a pure random process to select cases so that each sampling element in the population will have an equal probability of being selected.

random numbers from a **random-number table.** Random-number tables are available in most statistics and research methods books, including this one (see Appendix B). The numbers are generated by a pure random process so that any number has an equal probability of appearing in any position. Computer programs can also produce lists of random numbers.

You may ask, Once I select an element from the sampling frame, do I then return it to the sampling frame or do I keep it separate? Unrestricted random sampling is random sampling with replacement—that is, replacing an element after sampling it so it can be selected again. In simple random sampling without replacement, the researcher ignores elements already selected into the sample.

The logic of simple random sampling can be illustrated with an elementary example—sampling marbles from a jar. I have a large jar full of 5,000 marbles, some red and some white. The 5,000 marbles are my population, and the parameter I want to estimate is the percentage of red marbles in it. I randomly select 100 marbles (I close my eyes, shake the jar, pick one marble, and repeat the procedure 100 times). I now have a random sample of marbles. I count the number of red marbles in my sample to estimate the percentage of red versus white marbles in the population. This is a lot easier than counting all 5,000 marbles. My sample has 52 white and 48 red marbles.

Does this mean that the population parameter is 48 percent red marbles? Maybe not. Because of random chance, my specific sample might be off. I can check my results by dumping the 100 marbles back in the jar, mixing the marbles, and drawing a second random sample of 100 marbles. On the second try, my sample has 49 white marbles and 51 red ones. Now I have a problem. Which is correct? How good is this random sampling business if different samples from the same population can yield different results? I repeat the procedure over and over until I have drawn 130 different samples of 100 marbles each (see Chart 8.1 for results). Most people might empty the jar and count all 5,000, but I want to see what is going on. The results of my 130 different samples reveal a clear pattern. The most common mix of red and white marbles is 50/50. Samples that are close to that split are more frequent than those with more uneven splits. The population parameter appears to be 50 percent white and 50 percent red marbles.

Mathematical proofs and empirical tests demonstrate that the pattern found in Chart 8.1 always appears. The set of many different samples is my **sampling distribution.** It is a distribution of different samples that shows the frequency of different sample outcomes from many separate random samples. The pattern will appear if the sample size is 1,000 instead of 100; if there are 10 colors of marbles instead of 2; if the population has 100 marbles or 10 million marbles instead of 5,000; and if the population is people, automobiles, or colleges instead of marbles. In fact, the pattern will become clearer as more and more independent random samples are drawn from the population.

The pattern in the sampling distribution suggests that over many separate samples, the true population parameter (i.e., the 50/50 split in the preceding example) is more common than any other result. Some samples deviate from the population parameter, but they are less common. When many different random samples are plotted as in the graph in Chart 8.1, the sampling distribution looks like a normal or bell-shaped curve. Such a curve is theoretically important and is used throughout statistics.

The **central limit theorem** from mathematics tells us that as the number of different random samples in a sampling distribution increases toward infinity, the pattern of samples and the population parameter become more predictable. With a huge number of random samples, the sampling distribution forms a normal curve, and the midpoint of the

Random-number table   A list of numbers that has no pattern and that researchers use to create a random process for selecting cases and other randomization purposes.

Sampling distribution   A distribution created by drawing many random samples from the same population.

Central limit theorem   A mathematical relationship that states: Whenever many random samples are drawn from a population, a normal distribution is formed, and the center of the distribution for a variable equals the population parameter.

CHART 8.1 Example of Sampling Distribution

RED	WHITE	NUMBER OF SAMPLES
42	58	1
43	57	1
45	55	2
46	54	4
47	53	8
48	52	12
49	51	21
50	50	31
51	49	20
52	48	13
53	47	9
54	46	5
55	45	2
57	43	1
	Total	130

Number of red and white marbles that were randomly drawn from a jar of 5,000 marbles with 100 drawn each time, repeated 130 times for 130 independent random samples.

NUMBER OF SAMPLES

#	42	43	44	45	46	47	48	49	50	51	52	53	54	55	56	57
31									*							
30									*							
29									*							
28									*							
27									*							
26									*							
25									*							
24									*							
23									*							
22									*							
21								*	*							
20								*	*	*						
19								*	*	*						
18								*	*	*						
17								*	*	*						
16								*	*	*						
15								*	*	*						
14								*	*	*						
13								*	*	*	*					
12							*	*	*	*	*					
11							*	*	*	*	*					
10							*	*	*	*	*					
9							*	*	*	*	*	*				
8						*	*	*	*	*	*	*				
7						*	*	*	*	*	*	*				
6						*	*	*	*	*	*	*				
5						*	*	*	*	*	*	*	*			
4					*	*	*	*	*	*	*	*	*			
3					*	*	*	*	*	*	*	*	*			
2				*	*	*	*	*	*	*	*	*	*	*		
1	*	*		*	*	*	*	*	*	*	*	*	*	*		*

| | 42 | 43 | 44 | 45 | 46 | 47 | 48 | 49 | 50 | 51 | 52 | 53 | 54 | 55 | 56 | 57 |

NUMBER OF RED MARBLES IN A SAMPLE

curve approaches the population parameter as the number of samples increases.

Perhaps you want only one sample because you do not have the time or energy to draw many different samples. You are not alone. A researcher rarely draws many samples. He or she usually draws only one random sample, but the central limit theorem lets him or her generalize from one sample to the population. The theorem is about many samples, but lets the researcher calculate the probability of a particular sample being off from the population parameter.

Random sampling does not guarantee that every random sample perfectly represents the population. Instead, it means that most random samples will be close to the population most of the time. Plus, you can calculate the probability of a particular sample being inaccurate. A researcher estimates the chance that a particular sample is off or unrepresentative (i.e., the size of the sampling error) by using information from the sample to estimate the sampling distribution. He or she combines this information with knowledge of the central limit theorem to construct **confidence intervals.**

The confidence interval is a relatively simple but powerful idea. When television or newspaper polls are reported, you may hear about something called the margin of error being plus or minus 2 percentage points. This is a version of confidence intervals. A confidence interval is a range around a specific point used to estimate a population parameter. A range is used because the statistics of random processes do not let a researcher predict an exact point, but they let the researcher say with a high level of confidence (e.g., 95 percent) that the true population parameter lies within a certain range.

The calculations for sampling errors or confidence intervals are beyond the level of this discussion. The sampling distribution is the key idea that lets a researcher calculate the sampling error and confidence interval. Thus, he or she cannot say, "This sample gives a perfect measure of the population parameter," but can say, "I am 95 percent certain that the true population parameter is no more than 2 percent different from what I have found in my sample."

For example, I cannot say, "There are precisely 2,500 red marbles in the jar based on a random sample." I can say, "I am 95 percent certain that the population parameter lies between 2,450 and 2,550." I can combine characteristics of the sample (e.g., its size, the variation in it) with the central limit theorem to predict specific ranges around the parameter with a great deal of confidence.

Systematic Sampling. **Systematic sampling** is simple random sampling with a shortcut for random selection. Again, the first step is to number each element in the sampling frame. Instead of using a list of random numbers, a researcher calculates a **sampling interval,** and the interval becomes his or her quasi-random selection method. The sampling interval (i.e., 1 in k, where k is some number) tells the researcher how to select elements from a sampling frame by skipping elements in the frame before selecting one for the sample.

For instance, I want to sample 300 names from 900. After a random starting point, I select every third name of the 900 to get a sample of 300. My sampling interval is 3. Sampling intervals are easy to compute. I need the sample size and the population size (or sampling frame size as a best estimate). You can think of the sampling interval as the inverse of the sampling ratio. The sampling ratio for 300 names out of 900 is $300/900 = .333 = 33.3$ percent. The sampling interval is $900/300 = 3$.

In most cases, a simple random sample and a systematic sample yield equivalent results. One important situation in which systematic sampling cannot be substituted for simple random sampling occurs when the elements in a sample are organized in some kind of cycle or pattern. For example, a researcher's sampling frame is organized by married couples with the male first and the female second

Confidence intervals   A range of values, usually a little higher and lower than a specific value found in a sample, within which a researcher has a specified and high degree of confidence that the population parameter lies.

Systematic sampling   A random sample in which a researcher selects every kth (e.g., 12th) case in the sampling frame using a sampling interval.

Sampling interval   The inverse of the sampling ratio that is used when selecting cases in systematic sampling.

TABLE 8.2   Problems with Systematic Sampling of Cyclical Data

CASE	
1	Husband
2[a]	Wife
3	Husband
4	Wife
5	Husband
6[a]	Wife
7	Husband
8	Wife
9	Husband
10[a]	Wife
11	Husband
12	Wife

Random start = 2; Sampling interval = 4.
[a]Selected into sample.

(see Table 8.2). Such a pattern gives the researcher an unrepresentative sample if systematic sampling is used. His or her systematic sample can be nonrepresentative and include only wives because of how the cases are organized. When his or her sample frame is organized as couples, even-numbered sampling intervals result in samples with all husbands or all wives.

Figure 8.4 illustrates simple random sampling and systematic sampling. Notice that different names were drawn in each sample. For example, H. Adams appears in both samples, but C. Droullard is in only the simple random sample. This is because it is rare for any two random samples to be identical.

The sampling frame contains 20 males and 20 females (gender is in parentheses after each name). The simple random sample yielded 3 males and 7 females, and the systematic sample yielded 5 males and 5 females. Does this mean that systematic sampling is more accurate? No. To check this, draw a new sample using different random numbers; try taking the first two digits and beginning at the end (e.g., 11 from 11921, then 43 from 43232). Also draw a new systematic sample with a different random start. The last time the random start was 18. Try a random start of 11. What did you find? How many of each sex?[7]

Stratified Sampling. In **stratified sampling,** a researcher first divides the population into subpopulations (strata) on the basis of supplementary information.[8] After dividing the population into strata, the researcher draws a random sample from each subpopulation. In stratified sampling, the researcher controls the relative size of each stratum, rather than letting random processes control it. This guarantees representativeness or fixes the proportion of different strata within a sample. Of course, the necessary information about strata is not always available.

In general, stratified sampling produces samples that are more representative of the population than simple random sampling if the stratum information is accurate. A simple example illustrates why this is so. Imagine a population that is 51 percent female and 49 percent male; the population parameter is a sex ratio of 51 to 49. With stratified sampling, a researcher draws random samples among females and among males so that the sample contains a 51 to 49 percent sex ratio. If the researcher had used simple random sampling, it would be possible for a random sample to be off from the true sex ratio in the population. Thus, he or she makes fewer errors representing the population and has a smaller sampling error with stratified sampling.

Researchers use stratified sampling when a stratum of interest is a small percentage of a population and random processes could miss the stratum by chance. For example, a researcher draws a sample of 200 from 20,000 college students. He or she gets information from the college registrar indicating that 2 percent of the 20,000 students, or 400, are divorced women with children under the age of 5. This group is important to include in the sample. There would be 4 such students (2 percent of 200) in a representative sample, but the researcher could miss them by chance in one simple random sample. With stratified sampling, he or she obtains a list of the 400 such students from the registrar and

Stratified sampling   A random sample in which the researcher first identifies a set of mutually exclusive and exhaustive categories, divides the sampling frame by the categories, and then uses random selection to select cases from each category.

FIGURE 8.4 How to Draw Simple Random and Systematic Samples

1. Number each case in the sampling frame in sequence. The list of 40 names is in alphabetical order, numbered from 1 to 40.
2. Decide on a sample size. We will draw two 25 percent (10-name) samples.
3. For a *simple random sample,* locate a random-number table (see excerpt; a fuller table appears in Appendix B). Before using random-number table, count the largest number of digits needed for the sample (e.g., with 40 names, two digits are needed; for 100 to 999, three digits; for 1,000 to 9,999, four digits). Begin anywhere on the random-number table (we will begin in the upper left) and take a set of digits (we will take the last two). Mark the number on the sampling frame that corresponds to the chosen random number to indicate that the case is in the sample. If the number is too large (over 40), ignore it. If the number appears more than once (10

and 21 occurred twice in the example), ignore the second occurrence. Continue until the number of cases in the sample (10 in our example) is reached.

4. For a *systematic sample,* begin with a random start. The easiest way to do this is to point blindly at the random-number table, then take the closest number that appears on the sampling frame. In the example, 18 was chosen. Start with the random number, then count the sampling interval, or 4 in our example, to come to the first number. Mark it, and then count the sampling interval for the next number. Continue to the end of the list. Continue counting the sampling interval as if the beginning of the list were attached to the end of the list (like a circle). Keep counting until ending close to the start, or on the start if the sampling interval divides evenly into the total of the sampling frame.

No.	Name (Gender)	Simple Random	Systematic	No.	Name (Gender)	Simple Random	Systematic
01	Abrams, J. (M)			21	Hjelmhaug, N. (M)	Yes*	
02	Adams, H. (F)	Yes	Yes (6)	22	Huang, J. (F)	Yes	Yes (1)
03	Anderson, H. (M)			23	Ivono, V. (F)		
04	Arminond, L. (M)			24	Jaquees, J. (M)		
05	Boorstein, A. (M)			25	Johnson, A. (F)		
06	Breitsprecher, P. (M)	Yes	Yes (7)	26	Kennedy, M. (F)		Yes (2)
07	Brown, D. (F)			27	Koschoreck, L. (F)		
08	Cattelino, J. (F)			28	Koykkar, J. (M)		
09	Cidoni, S. (M)			29	Kozlowski, C. (F)	Yes	
10	Davis, L. (F)	Yes*	Yes (8)	30	Laurent, J. (M)		Yes (3)
11	Droullard, C. (M)	Yes		31	Lee, R. (F)		
12	Durette, R. (F)			32	Ling, C. (M)		
13	Elsnau, K. (F)	Yes		33	McKinnon, K. (F)		
14	Falconer, T. (M)		Yes (9)	34	Min, H. (F)	Yes	Yes (4)
15	Fuerstenberg, J. (M)			35	Moini, A. (F)		
16	Fulton, P. (F)			36	Navarre, H. (M)		
17	Gnewuch, S. (F)			37	O'Sullivan, C. (M)		
18	Green, C. (M)		START, Yes (10)	38	Oh, J. (M)		Yes (5)
19	Goodwanda, T. (F)	Yes		39	Olson, J. (F)		
20	Harris, B. (M)			40	Ortiz y Garcia, L. (F)		

Excerpt from a Random-Number Table (for Simple Random Sample)

150<u>10</u>	18590	001<u>02</u>	422<u>10</u>	94174	22099
901<u>22</u>	382<u>21</u>	215<u>29</u>	000<u>13</u>	047<u>34</u>	60457
67256	13887	941<u>19</u>	11077	01061	27779
13761	23390	12947	21280	445<u>06</u>	36457
81994	666<u>11</u>	16597	44457	076<u>21</u>	51949
79180	25992	46178	23992	62108	43232
07984	47169	88094	82752	15318	11921

*Numbers that appeared twice in random numbers selected.

BOX **8.2** **Illustration of Stratified Sampling**

Sample of 100 Staff of General Hospital, Stratified by Position

POSITION	POPULATION		SIMPLE RANDOM SAMPLE	STRATIFIED SAMPLE	ERRORS COMPARED TO THE POPULATION
	N	Percent	n	n	
Administrators	15	2.88	1	3	−2
Staff physicians	25	4.81	2	5	−3
Intern physicians	25	4.81	6	5	+1
Registered nurses	100	19.23	22	19	+3
Nurse assistants	100	19.23	21	19	+2
Medical technicians	75	14.42	9	14	+5
Orderlies	50	9.62	8	10	−2
Clerks	75	14.42	5	14	+1
Maintenance staff	30	5.77	3	6	−3
Cleaning staff	25	4.81	3	5	−2
Total	520	100.00	100	100	

Randomly select 3 of 15 administrators, 5 of 25 staff physicians, and so on.

Note: Traditionally, N symbolizes the number in the population and n represents the number in the sample.
The simple random sample overrepresents nurses, nursing assistants, and medical technicians, but underrepresents administrators, staff physicians, maintenance staff, and cleaning staff. The stratified sample gives an accurate representation of each position.

randomly selects 4 from it. This guarantees that the sample represents the population with regard to the important strata (see Box 8.2).

In special situations, a researcher may want the proportion of a stratum in a sample to differ from its true proportion in the population. For example, the population contains 0.5 percent Aleuts, but the researcher wants to examine Aleuts in particular. He or she oversamples so that Aleuts make up 10 percent of the sample. With this type of disproportionate stratified sample, the researcher cannot generalize directly from the sample to the population without special adjustments.

In some situations, a researcher wants the proportion of a stratum or subgroup to differ from its true proportion in the population. For example, Davis and Smith (1992) reported that the 1987 General Social Survey (explained in Chapter 11) oversampled African Americans. A random sample of the U.S. population yielded 191 Blacks. Davis and Smith conducted a separate sample of African Americans to increase it to 544. The 191 Black respondents are about 13 percent of the random sam-

ple, roughly equal to the percentage of Blacks in the U.S. population. The 544 Blacks are 30 percent of the disproportionate sample. The researcher who wants to use the entire sample must adjust it to reduce the number of sampled African Americans before generalizing to the U.S. population. Disproportionate sampling helps the researcher who wants to focus on issues most relevant to a subpopulation. In this case, he or she can more accurately generalize to African Americans using the 544 respondents than using a sample of only 191. The larger sample is more likely to reflect the full diversity of the African American subpopulation.

Cluster Sampling. **Cluster sampling** addresses two problems: Researchers lack a good sampling frame for a dispersed population and the cost to

Cluster sampling A type of random sample that uses multiple stages and is often used to cover wide geographic areas in which aggregated units are randomly selected and then samples are drawn from the sampled aggregated units, or clusters.

reach a sampled element is very high.[9] For example, there is no single list of all automobile mechanics in North America. Even if I got an accurate sampling frame, it would cost too much to reach the sampled mechanics who are geographically spread out. Instead of using a single sampling frame, researchers use a sampling design that involves multiple stages and clusters.

A *cluster* is a unit that contains final sampling elements but can be treated temporarily as a sampling element itself. First sample clusters, and then draw a second sample from within the clusters selected in the first stage of sampling. You randomly sample clusters, then randomly sample elements from within the selected clusters. This has a big practical advantage when you can create a good sampling frame of clusters, even if it is impossible to create one for sampling elements. Once you get a sample of clusters, creating a sampling frame for elements within each cluster becomes manageable. A second advantage for geographically dispersed populations is that elements within each cluster are physically closer to one another. This may produce a savings in locating or reaching each element.

You draw several samples in stages in cluster sampling. In a three-stage sample, stage 1 is random sampling of big clusters; stage 2 is random sampling of small clusters within each selected big cluster; and the last stage is sampling of elements from within the sampled small clusters. For example, you want a sample of individuals from Mapleville. First, you randomly sample city blocks, then households within blocks, then individuals within households (see Chart 8.2). Although there is no accurate list of all residents of Mapleville, there is an accurate list of blocks in the city. After selecting a random sample of blocks, you count all households on the selected blocks to create a sample frame for each block. You then use the list of households to draw a random sample at the stage of sampling households. Finally, you choose a specific individual within each sampled household.

Cluster sampling is usually less expensive than simple random sampling, but it is less accurate. Each stage in cluster sampling introduces sampling errors, so a multistage cluster sample has more sampling errors than a one-stage random sample.[10]

A researcher who uses cluster sampling must decide the number of clusters and the number of elements within clusters. For example, in a two-stage cluster sample of 240 people from Mapleville, you could randomly select 120 clusters and select 2 elements from each, or randomly select 2 clusters and select 120 elements in each. Which is best? A design with more clusters is better because elements within clusters (e.g., people living on the same block) tend to be similar to each other (e.g., people on the same block tend to be more alike than those on different blocks). If few clusters are chosen, many similar elements could be selected, which would be less representative of the total population. For example, you could select two blocks with relatively wealthy people and draw 120 people from each. This would be less representative than a sample with 120 different city blocks and 2 individuals chosen from each.

When a researcher samples from a large geographical area and must travel to each element, cluster sampling significantly reduces travel costs. As usual, there is a trade-off between accuracy and cost.

For example, Alan, Ricardo, and Barbara each personally interview a sample of 1,500 students who represent the population of all college students in North America. Alan obtains an accurate sampling frame of all students and uses simple random sampling. He travels to 1,000 different locations to interview one or two students at each. Ricardo draws a random sample of three colleges from a list of all 3,000 colleges, then visits the three and selects 500 students from each. Barbara draws a random sample of 300 colleges. She visits the 300 and selects 5 students at each. If travel costs average $250 per location, Alan's travel bill is $250,000, Ricardo's is $750, Barbara's is $75,000. Alan's sample is highly accurate, but Barbara's is only slightly less accurate for one-third the cost. Ricardo's sample is the cheapest, but it is not representative at all.

Within-Household Sampling. Once a researcher samples a household or similar unit (e.g., family or dwelling unit) in cluster sampling, the question arises: Whom should the researcher choose? A potential source of bias is introduced if the first person who answers the telephone, the door, or the mail is used in the sample. The first person who answers

---

CHART 8.2   Illustration of Cluster Sampling

Goal: Draw a random sample of 240 people in Mapleville.

Step 1:   Mapleville has 55 districts. Randomly select 6 districts.

1 2 3* 4 5 6 7 8 9 10 11 12 13 14 15* 16 17 18 19 20 21 22 23 24 25 26
27* 28 29 30 31* 32 33 34 35 36 37 38 39 40* 41 42 43 44 45 46 47 48
49 50 51 52 53 54* 55
* = Randomly selected.

Step 2:   Divide the selected districts into blocks. Each district contains 20 blocks. Randomly select 4 blocks from the district.

Example of District 3 (selected in step 1):

1 2 3 4* 5 6 7 8 9 10* 11 12 13* 14 15 16 17* 18 19 20
* = Randomly selected.

Step 3:   Divide blocks into households. Randomly select households.

Example of Block 4 of District 3 (selected in step 2):

Block 4 contains a mix of single-family homes, duplexes, and four-unit apartment buildings. It is bounded by Oak Street, River Road, South Avenue, and Greenview Drive. There are 45 households on the block. Randomly select 10 households from the 45.

1	#1 Oak Street	16	"	31*	"	
2	#3 Oak Street	17*	#154 River Road	32*	"	
3*	#5 Oak Street	18	#156 River Road	33	"	
4	"	19*	#158 River Road	34	#156 Greenview Drive	
5	"	20*	"	35*	"	
6	"	21	#13 South Avenue	36	"	
7	#7 Oak Street	22	"	37	"	
8	"	23	#11 South Avenue	38	"	
9*	#150 River Road	24	#9 South Avenue	39	#158 Greenview Drive	
10*	"	25	#7 South Avenue	40	"	
11	"	26	#5 South Avenue	41	"	
12	"	27	#3 South Avenue	42	"	
13	#152 River Road	28	#1 South Avenue	43	#160 Greenview Drive	
14	"	29*	"	44	"	
15	"	30	#152 Greenview Drive	45	"	

* = Randomly selected.

Step 4:   Select a respondent within each household.

Summary of cluster sampling:
1 person randomly selected per household
10 households randomly selected per block
4 blocks randomly selected per district
6 districts randomly selected in the city
1 x 10 x 4 x 6 = 240 people in sample

TABLE 8.3   Within-Household Sampling

Selecting individuals within sampled households. Number selected is the household chosen in Chart 8.2.

Number	Last Name	Adults (over Age 18)	Selected Respondent
3	Able	1 male, 1 female	Female
9	Bharadwaj	2 females	Youngest female
10	DiPiazza	1 male, 2 females	Oldest female
17	Wucivic	2 males, 1 female	Youngest male
19	Cseri	2 females	Youngest female
20	Taylor	1 male, 3 females	Second oldest female
29	Velu	2 males, 2 females	Oldest male
31	Wong	1 male, 1 female	Female
32	Gray	1 male	Male
35	Mall-Krinke	1 male, 2 females	Oldest female

EXAMPLE SELECTION TABLE (ONLY ADULTS COUNTED)

Males	Females	Whom to Select	Males	Females	Whom to Select
1	0	Male	2	2	Oldest male
2	0	Oldest male	2	3	Youngest female
3	0	Youngest male	3	2	Second oldest male
4+	0	Second oldest male	3	3	Second oldest female
0	1	Female	3	4	Third oldest female
0	2	Youngest female	4	3	Second oldest male
0	3	Second oldest female	4	4	Third oldest male
0	4+	Oldest female	4	5+	Youngest female
1	1	Female	5+	4	Second oldest male
1	2	Oldest female	5+	5+	Fourth oldest female
1	3	Second oldest female			
2	1	Youngest male			
3	1	Second oldest male			

+ = or more

should be selected only if his or her answering is the result of a truly random process. This is rarely the case. Certain people are unlikely to be at home, and in some households one person (e.g., a husband) is more likely than another to answer the telephone or door. Researchers use within-household sampling to ensure that after a random household is chosen, the individual within the household is also selected randomly.

Researchers can randomly select a person within a household in several ways.[11] The most common method is to use a selection table specifying who is to be chosen (e.g., oldest male, youngest female, etc.) after the size and composition of the household are known (see Table 8.3). This removes any bias that might arise from choosing the first person to answer the door or telephone, or from the interviewer's selecting the person who appears to be friendliest.

Probability Proportionate to Size (PPS). There are two ways to cluster sample. The method just described is proportionate or unweighted cluster sampling. It is proportionate because the size of each cluster (or number of elements at each stage) is the same. The more common situation is for the cluster groups to be of different sizes. When this is the case, the researcher must adjust the probability for each stage in sampling.

The foregoing cluster sampling example with Alan, Barbara, and Ricardo illustrates the problem with unweighted cluster sampling. Barbara drew a simple random sample of 300 colleges from a list of all 3,000 colleges, but she made a mistake—unless every college has an identical number of students. Her method gave each college an equal chance of being selected—a 300/3,000 or 10 percent chance. But colleges have different numbers of students, so each student does not have an equal chance to end up in her sample.

Barbara listed every college and sampled from the list. A large university with 40,000 students and a small college with 400 students had an equal chance of being selected. But if she chose the large university, the chance of a given student at that college being selected was 5 in 40,000 (5/40,000 = 0.0125 percent), whereas a student at the small college had a 5 in 400 (5/400 = 1.25 percent) chance of being selected. The small-college student was 100 times more likely to be in her sample. The total probability of being selected for a student from the large university was 0.125 percent (10 × 0.0125), while it was 12.5 percent (10 × 1.25) for the small-college student. Barbara violated a principle of random sampling—that each element has an equal chance to be selected into the sample.

If Barbara uses **probability proportionate to size (PPS)** and samples correctly, then each final sampling element or student will have an equal probability of being selected. She does this by adjusting the chances of selecting a college in the first stage of sampling. She must give large colleges with more students a greater chance of being selected and small colleges a smaller chance. She adjusts the probability of selecting a college on the basis of the proportion of all students in the population who attend it. Thus, a college with 40,000 students will be 100 times more likely to be selected than one with 400 students. (See Box 8.3 for another example.)

Random-Digit Dialing.

Random-digit dialing (RDD) is a sampling technique used in research projects in which the general public is interviewed by telephone.[12] It does not use the published telephone directory as the sampling frame.

Three kinds of people are missed when the sampling frame is a telephone directory: people without telephones, people who have recently moved, and people with unlisted numbers. Those without phones (e.g., the poor, the uneducated, and transients) are missed in any telephone interview study, but 95 percent of people have a telephone in advanced industrialized nations. Several kinds of people have unlisted numbers: people who want to avoid collection agencies; the very wealthy; and those who want privacy and want to avoid obscene calls, salespeople, and prank calls. In some urban areas in the United States, the percentage of unlisted numbers 50 percent. In addition, people change their residences, so directories that are published annually or less often have numbers for people who have left and do not list those who have recently moved into an area. A researcher using RDD randomly selects telephone numbers, thereby avoiding the problems of telephone directories. The population is telephone numbers, not people with telephones. RDD is not difficult, but it takes time and can frustrate the person doing the calling.

Here is how RDD works in the United States. Telephone numbers have three parts: a three-digit area code, a three-digit exchange number or central office code, and a four-digit number. For example, the area code for Madison, Wisconsin, is 608, and there are many exchanges within the area code (e.g., 221, 993, 767, 455); but not all of the 999 possible three-digit exchanges (from 001 to 999) are active. Likewise, not all of the 9,999 possible four-digit numbers in an exchange (from 0000 to 9999) are being used. Some numbers are reserved for future expansion, are disconnected, or are temporarily withdrawn after someone moves. Thus, a possible U.S. telephone number consists of an active area

Probability proportionate to size (PPS) An adjustment made in cluster sampling when the each cluster does not have the same number of sampling elements.

Random-digit dialing (RDD) A method of randomly selecting cases for telephone interviews that uses all possible telephone numbers as a sampling frame.

BOX **8.3** **Example of Probability Proportionate to Size (PPS) Sampling**

Henry wants to conduct one-hour, in-person interviews with people living in the city of Riverdale. Riverdale is spread out over a large area; Henry wants to reduce his travel time and expenses, so he uses a *cluster sampling design*. The last census reported that the city had about 490,000 people. Henry can interview only about 220 people, or about 0.05 percent of the city population. He first gathers maps from the city tax office and fire department, and retrieves census information on city blocks. He learns that there are 2,182 city blocks. At first, he thinks he can randomly select 10 percent of the blocks (i.e., 218), go to a block and count housing units, then locate one person to interview in each housing unit (house, apartment, etc.), but the blocks are of unequal geographic and population size. He studies the population density of the blocks and estimated number of people in each, then develops a five-part classification based on the average size of a block:

Density	Number of Blocks	Average Number of People
Very high density	20	2,000
High density	200	800
Medium density	800	300
Low density	1,000	50
Semirural	162	10

Henry realizes that randomly selecting city blocks without adjustment will not give each person an equal chance of being selected. For example, 1 very high-density block has the same number people as 40 low-density blocks. Henry adjusts proportionate to the block size. The easiest way to do this is to convert all city blocks to equal-sized units based on the smallest cluster, or the semirural city blocks. For example, there are 2,000/10 or 200 times more people in a high-density block than a semirural block, so Henry increases the odds of selecting such a block to make its probability 200 times greater than a semirural block. Essentially, Henry creates adjusted-cluster units of 10 persons each (because that is how

many there are in the semirural blocks) and substitutes them for city blocks in the first stage of sampling. The 162 semirural blocks are unchanged, but after adjustment, he has $20 \times 200 = 4,000$ units for the very high-density blocks, $200 \times 80 = 16,000$ units for the high-density blocks, and so forth, for a total of 49,162 such units. Henry now numbers each block, using the adjusted cluster units, with many blocks getting multiple numbers. For example, he assigns numbers 1 to 200 to the first very high-density block, and so forth, as follows:

1	Very high-density block #1
2	Very high-density block #1
3	Very high-density block #1

. . . and so forth

3,999	Very high-density block #20
4,000	Very high-density block #20
4,001	High-density block #1
4,002	High-density block #2

. . . and so forth

49,160	Semirural block #160
49,161	Semirural block #161
49,162	Semirural block #162

Henry still wants to interview about 220 people and wants to select one person from each adjusted cluster unit. He uses simple random sample methods to select 220 of the 49,162 adjusted cluster units. He can then convert the cluster units back to city blocks. For example, if Henry randomly selected numbers 25 and 184, both are in very high density block #1, telling him to select two people from that block. If the number 49,161 was randomly selected, he selects one person in semirural block #161. Henry now goes to each selected block, identifies all housing units in that block, and randomly selects housing units. Of course, Henry may use within-household sampling after he selects a housing unit.

BOX **8.4** Example Sample

Sampling has many terms for the different parts of samples or types of samples. A complex sample illustrates how researchers use them. Look at the 1980 sample for the best-known national U.S. survey in sociology, the General Social Survey (discussed in Chapter 11).

The *population* is defined as all resident adults (18 years or older) in the United States for the *universe* of all Americans. The *target population* consists of all English-speaking adults who live in households, excluding those living in institutional settings such as college dormitories, nursing homes, or military quarters. The researchers estimated that 97.3 percent of all resident adults lived in households and that 97 percent of the household population spoke sufficient English to be interviewed.

The researchers used a complex multistage probability sample that is both a *cluster sample* and a *stratified sample*. First, they created a national *sampling frame* of all U.S. counties, independent cities, and Standard Metropolitan Statistical Areas (SMSAs), a Census Bureau designation for larger cities and surrounding areas. Each *sampling element* at this first level had about 4,000 households. They divided these elements into strata. The strata were the four major geographic regions as defined by the Census Bureau, divided into metropolitan and nonmetropolitan areas. They then sampled from each strata using *probability proportionate to size (PPS)* ran-

dom selection, based on the number of housing units in each county or SMSA. This gave them a sample of 84 counties or SMSAs.

For the second stage, the researchers identified city blocks, census tracts, or the rural equivalent in each county or SMSA. Each *sampling element* (e.g., city block) had a minimum of 50 housing units. In order to get an accurate count of the number of housing units for some counties, a researcher counted addresses in the field. The researchers selected 6 or more blocks within each county or SMSA using PPS to yield 562 blocks.

In the third stage, the researchers used the household as a *sampling element.* They randomly selected households from the addresses in the block. After selecting an address, an interviewer contacted the household and chose an eligible respondent from it. The interviewer looked at a selection table for possible respondents and interviewed a type of respondent (e.g., second oldest) based on the table. In total, 1,934 people were contacted for interviews and 75.9 percent of interviews were completed. This gave a final sample size of 1,468. We can calculate the *sampling ratio* by dividing 1,468 by the total number of adults living in households, which was about 150 million in 1980, which is 0.01 percent. To check the representativeness of their sample, the researchers also compared characteristics of the sample to census results (see Davis and Smith, 1992:31–44).

code, an active exchange number, and a four-digit number in an exchange.

In RDD, a researcher identifies active area codes and exchanges, then randomly selects four-digit numbers. A problem is that the researcher can select any number in an exchange. This means that some selected numbers are out of service, disconnected, pay phones, or numbers for businesses; only some numbers are what the researcher wants—working residential phone numbers. Until the researcher calls, it is not possible to know whether the number is a working residential number. This means spending a lot of time getting numbers that are disconnected, for businesses, and so forth. Research organizations often use computers

to select random digits and dial the phone automatically. This speeds the process, but a human must still listen and find out whether the number is a working residential one.

The sampling element in RDD is the phone number, not the person or the household. Several families or individuals can share the same phone number, and in other situations each person may have a separate phone number. This means that after a working residential phone is reached, a second stage of sampling is necessary, within household sampling, to select the person to be interviewed.

Box 8.4 presents an example of how the many sampling terms and ideas can be used together in a specific real-life situation.

Hidden Populations

In contrast to sampling the general population or visible and accessible people, sampling **hidden populations** (i.e., people who engage in clandestine or concealed activities) is a recurrent issue in the studies of deviant or stigmatized behavior. It illustrates the creative application of sampling principles, mixing qualitative and quantitative styles of research and combining probability with nonprobability techniques. Three studies in which AIDS researchers drew samples of "hidden populations" are instructive.

Watters and Biernacki (1989) studied HIV-positive intravenous drug users in San Francisco and sought to evaluate a new AIDS prevention program. They combined chain referral (a kind of snowball sampling), stratified sampling, and quota sampling. They also used purposive sampling in carefully selected geographic districts with high concentrations of drug users. They remarked, "While they are not random samples, it is particularly important to emphasize that targeted samples are not convenience samples" (1989:420).

Martin and Dean (1993) sampled gay men from New York City. The men had to live in the city, be over age 18, not be diagnosed as having AIDS, and engage in sex with other men. The authors began with a purposive sample using five diverse sources to recruit 291 respondents. They first contacted 150 New York City organizations with predominately homosexual or bisexual members. They next screened these to 90 organizations that had eligible men for the study. From the 90, they drew a stratified random sample of 52 organizations by membership size. They randomly selected 5 members from each of the organizations. Reports of Martin and Dean's study appeared in local news sources. This brought calls from which they got 41 unsolicited volunteers. Another source of 32 men were referrals from respondents who had participated in a small pilot study. In addition, 72 men were identified at an annual New York City Gay Pride Parade.

Hidden population   A population of people who engage in clandestine, socially disapproved, or concealed activities and who are difficult to locate and study.

And 15 eligible men were contacted at a New York City clinic and asked to participate.

They next used snowball sampling by asking each of the 291 respondents to give a recruitment packet to three gay male friends. Each friend who agreed to participate was also asked to give packets to three friends. This continued until it had gone five levels out from the initial 291 men. Eventually, 746 men were recruited into the study. Martin and Dean checked their sample against two random samples of gay men in San Francisco, a random-digit dialing sample of 500, and a cluster sample of 823 using San Francisco census tracts. Their sample paralleled those from San Francisco on race, age, and the percent being "out of the closet."

Heckathorn (1997, 2002) studied active drug injectors in two small Connecticut cities and the surrounding area. As of July 1996, 390 AIDS cases had been diagnosed in the towns; about half the cases involved drug-injection. The sampling was purposive in that each sampled element had to meet certain criteria. Heckathorn also used a modified snowball sampling with a "dual reward system." He gave each person who completed an interview a monetary reward and a second monetary reward for recruiting a new respondent. The first person was asked not to identify the new person to the researcher, at times referred to as *masking* (i.e., protecting friends). This gets around the "snitching" issue and "war on drugs" stigma, especially strong in the U.S. context. This modified snowball sampling is like sequential sampling in that after a period of time, fewer and fewer new recruits are found, until the researcher comes to saturation or an equilibrium.

You are now familiar with several major types of probability samples (see Box 8.5) and supplementary techniques used with them (e.g., PPS, within household, and RDD) that may be appropriate. In addition, you have seen how researchers combine nonprobability and probability sampling for special situations, such as hidden populations. Next, we turn to determining a sample size for probability samples.

How Large Should a Sample Be?

Students often ask, "How large does my sample have to be?" The best answer is, "It depends." It de-

BOX **8.5**   Types of Probability Samples

TYPE OF SAMPLE	TECHNIQUE
Simple random	Create a sampling frame for all cases, then select cases using a purely random process (e.g., random-number table or computer program).
Systematic	Create a sampling frame, calculate the sampling interval 1/k, choose a random starting place, then take every 1/k case.
Stratified	Create a sampling frame for each of several categories of cases, draw a random sample from each category, then combine the several samples.
Cluster	Create a sampling frame for larger cluster units, draw a random sample of the cluster units, create a sampling frame for cases within each selected cluster unit, then draw a random sample of cases, and so forth.

pends on the kind of data analysis the researcher plans, on how accurate the sample has to be for the researcher's purposes, and on population characteristics. As you have seen, a large sample size alone does not guarantee a representative sample. A large sample without random sampling or with a poor sampling frame is less representative than a smaller one with random sampling and an excellent sampling frame.

The question of sample size can be addressed in two ways. One is to make assumptions about the population and use statistical equations about random sampling processes. The calculation of sample size by this method requires a statistical discussion that goes beyond the level of this text.[13] The researcher must make assumptions about the degree of confidence (or number of errors) that is acceptable and the degree of variation in the population.

A second method is a rule of thumb—a conventional or commonly accepted amount. Researchers use it because they rarely have the information required by the statistical method and because it gives sample sizes close to those of the statistical method. Rules of thumb are not arbitrary but are based on past experience with samples that have met the requirements of the statistical method.

One principle of sample sizes is, the smaller the population, the bigger the sampling ratio has to be for an accurate sample (i.e., one with a high probability of yielding the same results as the entire population). Larger populations permit smaller sampling ratios for equally good samples. This is because as the population size grows, the returns in accuracy for sample size shrink.

For small populations (under 1,000), a researcher needs a large sampling ratio (about 30 percent). For example, a sample size of about 300 is required for a high degree of accuracy. For moderately large populations (10,000), a smaller sampling ratio (about 10 percent) is needed to be equally accurate, or a sample size of around 1,000. For large populations (over 150,000), smaller sampling ratios (1 percent) are possible, and samples of about 1,500 can be very accurate. To sample from very large populations (over 10 million), one can achieve accuracy using tiny sampling ratios (0.025 percent) or samples of about 2,500. The size of the population ceases to be relevant once the sampling ratio is very small, and samples of about 2,500 are as accurate for populations of 200 million as for 10 million. These are approximate sizes, and practical limitations (e.g., cost) also play a role in a researcher's decision.

A related principle is that for small samples, small increases in sample size produce big gains in accuracy. Equal increases in sample size produce more of an increase in accuracy for small than for large samples. For example, an increase in sample size from 50 to 100 reduces errors from 7.1 percent to 2.1 percent, but an increase from 1,000 to 2,000 only decreases errors from 1.6 percent to 1.1 percent.[14] (See Table 8.4.)

A researcher's decision about the best sample size depends on three things: (1) the degree of

TABLE 8.4   Sample Size of a Random Sample for Different Populations with a 99 Percent Confidence Level

POPULATION SIZE	SAMPLE SIZE	% POPULATION IN SAMPLE
200	171	85.5%
500	352	70.4%
1,000	543	54.3%
2,000	745	37.2%
5,000	960	19.2%
10,000	1,061	10.6%
20,000	1,121	5.6%
50,000	1,160	2.3%
100,000	1,173	1.2%

accuracy required, (2) the degree of variability or diversity in the population, and (3) the number of different variables examined simultaneously in data analysis. Everything else being equal, larger samples are needed if one wants high accuracy, if the population has a great deal of variability or heterogeneity, or if one wants to examine many variables in the data analysis simultaneously. Smaller samples are sufficient when less accuracy is acceptable, when the population is homogeneous, or when only a few variables are examined at a time.

The analysis of data on subgroups also affects sample size. If you want to analyze subgroups in the population, you need a larger sample. For example, you want to analyze four variables for males between the ages of 30 and 40 years old. If this sample is of the general public, then only a small proportion (e.g., 10 percent) of sample cases will be males in that age group. A rule of thumb is to have about 50 cases for each subgroup to be analyzed. Thus, if you want to analyze a group that is only 10 percent of the population, then you should have 10 × 50 or 500 cases in the sample to get enough for the subgroup analysis.

Drawing Inferences

A researcher samples so he or she can draw inferences from the sample to the population. In fact, a subfield of statistical data analysis is called *inferential statistics* (see Chapter 12). The researcher directly observes variables using units in the sample. Researchers are not interested in samples in themselves; they want to infer to the population. Thus, a gap exists between what the researcher concretely has (a sample) and what is of real interest (a population) (see Figure 8.5).

In the last chapter, you saw how the logic of measurement could be stated in terms of a gap between abstract constructs and concrete indicators. Measures of concrete, observable data are approximations for abstract constructs. Researchers use the approximations to estimate what is of real interest (i.e., constructs and causal laws). Conceptualization and operationalization bridge the gap in measurement just as the use of sampling frames, the sampling process, and inference bridge the gap in sampling.

Researchers put the logic of sampling and the logic of measurement together by directly observing measures of constructs and empirical relationships in samples (see Figure 8.5). They infer or generalize from what they can observe empirically in samples to the abstract causal laws and constructs in the population.

Validity and sampling error have similar functions. This is illustrated by an analogy between the logic of sampling and the logic of measurement—that is, between what is observed and what is discussed. In measurement, you want valid indicators of constructs—that is, concrete indicators that accurately represent abstract constructs. In sampling, you want samples that have little sampling error—concrete collections of cases that accurately represent unseen and abstract populations. A valid measure deviates little from the construct it represents. A sample with little sampling error permits estimates that deviate little from population parameters.

Researchers try to reduce sampling errors. The sampling error is based on two factors: the sample size and the amount of diversity in the sample. Everything else being equal, the larger the sample size, the smaller the sampling error. Likewise, the greater the homogeneity (or the less the diversity) in a sample, the smaller its sampling error.

A Model of the Logic of Sampling

What You
Would Like to
Talk About

Population

Sampling
Frame

Sampling Process

What You Actually
Observe in the Data

Sample

A Model of the Logic of Measurement

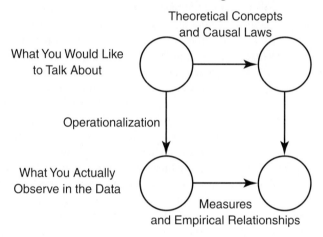

Theoretical Concepts
and Causal Laws

What You Would Like
to Talk About

Operationalization

What You Actually
Observe in the Data

Measures
and Empirical Relationships

A Model Combining Logics of Sampling and Measurement

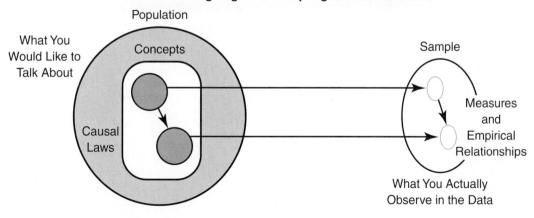

Population

What You
Would Like to
Talk About

Concepts

Causal
Laws

Sample

Measures
and
Empirical
Relationships

What You Actually
Observe in the Data

FIGURE 8.5   Model of the Logic of Sampling and of Measurement

Sampling error is also related to confidence intervals. If two samples are identical except that one is larger, the one with more cases will have a smaller sampling error and narrower confidence intervals. Likewise, if two samples are identical except that the cases in one are more similar to each other, the one with greater homogeneity will have a smaller sampling error and narrower confidence intervals. A narrow confidence interval means more precise estimates of the population parameter for a given level of confidence. For example, you want to estimate average annual family income. You have two samples. Sample 1 gives a confidence interval of $30,000 to $36,000 around the estimated population parameter of $33,000 for an 80 percent level of confidence. For a 95 percent level of confidence, the range is $25,000 to $45,000. A sample with a smaller sampling error (because it is larger or is more homogeneous) might give a $30,000 to $36,000 range for a 95 percent confidence level.

CONCLUSION

In this chapter, you learned about sampling. You learned about types of sampling that are not based on random processes. Only some are acceptable, and even then their use depends on special circumstances.[15] In general, probability sampling is preferred by quantitative researchers because it produces a sample that represents the population and enables the researcher to use powerful statistical techniques. In addition to simple random sampling, you learned about systematic, stratified, and cluster sampling. Although this book does not cover the statistical theory used in random sampling, from the discussion of sampling error, the central limit theorem, and sample size, it should be clear that random sampling produces more accurate and precise sampling.

Before moving on to the next chapter, it may be useful to restate a fundamental principle of social research: Do not compartmentalize the steps of the research process; rather, learn to see the interconnections between the steps. Research design, measurement, sampling, and specific research techniques are interdependent. Unfortunately, the constraints of presenting information in a textbook necessitate presenting the parts separately, in sequence. In practice, researchers think about data collection when they design research and develop measures for variables. Likewise, sampling issues influence research design, measurement of variables, and data collection strategies. As you will see in future chapters, good social research depends on simultaneously controlling quality at several different steps—research design, conceptualization, measurement, sampling, and data collection and handling. The researcher who makes major errors at any one stage may make an entire research project worthless.[16]

KEY TERMS

central limit theorem
cluster sampling
confidence intervals
deviant case sampling
haphazard sampling
hidden populations
nonrandom sample
parameter
population
probability proportionate to
    size (PPS)

purposive sampling
quota sampling
random-digit dialing (RDD)
random-number table
random sample
sample
sampling distribution
sampling element
sampling error
sampling frame
sampling interval

sampling ratio
sequential sampling
simple random sample
snowball sampling
statistic
stratified sampling
systematic sampling
target population
theoretical sampling

REVIEW QUESTIONS

1. When is purposive sampling used?
2. When is the snowball sampling technique appropriate?
3. What is a sampling frame and why is it important?
4. Which sampling method is best when the population has several groups and a researcher wants to ensure that each group is in the sample?
5. How can you get a sampling interval from a sampling ratio?
6. When should a researcher consider using probability proportionate to size?
7. What is the population in random-digit dialing? Are sampling frame problems avoided? Explain.
8. How do researchers decide how large a sample to use?
9. How are the logic of sampling and the logic of measurement related?
10. When is random-digit dialing used, and what are its advantages and disadvantages?

NOTES

1. See Stern (1979:77–81) on biased samples. He also discusses ways to identify problems with samples in published reports.

2. Quota sampling is discussed in Babbie (1998:196), Kalton (1983:91–93), and Sudman (1976a:191–200).

3. For further discussion on purposive sampling, see Babbie (1998:195), Grosof and Sardy (1985:172–173), and Singleton and associates (1988:153–154, 306). Bailey (1987:94–95) describes "dimensional" sampling, which is a variation of purposive sampling.

4. For additional discussion of snowball sampling, see Babbie (1998:194–196), Bailey (1987:97), and Sudman (1976a:210–211). Also see Bailey (1987:366–367), Dooley (1984:86–87), Kidder and Judd (1986:240–241), Lindzey and Byrne (1968:452–525), and Singleton and associates (1988:372–373) for discussions of sociometry and sociograms. Network sampling issues are discussed in Galaskiewicz (1985), Granovetter (1976), and Hoffmann-Lange (1987).

5. For a discussion of the *Literary Digest* sampling mistake, see Babbie (1998:192–194), Dillman (1978:9–10), Frey (1983:18–19), and Singleton and colleagues (1988:132–133).

6. See Traugott (1987) on the importance of persistence in reaching sampled respondents for a representative sample. Also see Kalton (1983:63–69) on the importance of nonresponse.

7. Only one name appears in both. The stratified sample has 6 males and 4 females; the simple random sample has 5 males and 5 females. (Complete the lower block of numbers, then begin at the far right of the top block.)

8. Stratified sampling techniques are discussed in more detail in Frankel (1983:37–46), Kalton (1983:19–28), Mendenhall and associates (1971:53–88), Sudman (1976a:107–130), and Williams (1978:162–175).

9. Cluster sampling is discussed in Frankel (1983:47–57), Kalton (1983:28–38), Kish (1965), Mendenhall and associates (1971:121–141, 171–183), Sudman (1976a: 69–84), and Williams (1978:144–161).

10. For a discussion, see Frankel (1983:57–62), Kalton (1983:38–47), Sudman (1976a:131–170), and Williams (1978:239–241).

11. Within-household sampling is discussed in Czaja and associates (1982) and in Groves and Kahn (1979:32–36).

12. For more on random-digit dialing issues, see Dillman (1978:238–242), Frey (1983:69–77), Glasser and Metzger (1972), Groves and Kahn (1979:20–21, 45–63), Kalton (1983:86–90), and Waksberg (1978). Kviz (1984) reported that telephone directories can produce relatively accurate sampling frames in rural areas, at least for mail questionnaire surveys. Also see Keeter (1995).

13. See Kraemer and Thiemann (1987) for a technical discussion of selecting a sample size.

14. See Sudman (1976a:99).

15. Berk (1983) argued that sampling that is nonrandom or a sampling process that excludes a nonrandom subset of cases can create seriously inaccurate estimates of causal relations.

16. For a further discussion of sample size calculation, see Grosof and Sardy (1985:181–185), Kalton (1983: 82–90), Sudman (1976a:85–105), and Williams (1978: 211–227).

Experimental Research

Experimentation, the principal scientific method to be emphasized here, involves at a simple level the comparison of groups or individuals who have been differentially exposed to changes in their environment.
—Leonard Saxe and Michelle Fine, *Social Experiments,* p. 45

This chapter begins a new section of the book. In the previous three chapters, you learned about the foundations of research design. This chapter and the three that follow it focus on quantitative research techniques. We begin with experimental research. It is the easiest to grasp, it is used across many fields of science, and it is most "pure" in terms of the standards of the positivist, quantitative style.

Experimental research builds on the principles of a positivist approach more directly than do the other research techniques.[1] Researchers in the natural sciences (e.g., chemistry and physics) and related applied fields (e.g., agriculture, engineering, and medicine) conduct experiments. The logic that guides an experiment on plant growth in biology or testing a metal in engineering is applied in experi-ments on human social behavior. Although it is most widely used in psychology, the experiment is found in education, criminal justice, journalism, market-ing, nursing, political science, social work, and so-ciology. This chapter focuses first on the experiment conducted in a laboratory under controlled condi-tions and then looks at experiments conducted in the field.

Commonsense experiments are less careful or systematic than scientifically based experiments. In commonsense language, an *experiment* means modifying something in a situation, then compar-ing an outcome to what existed without the modifi-cation. For example, I try to start my car. To my surprise, it does not start. I "experiment" by clean-ing off the battery connections, then try to start it again. I modified something (cleaned the connections) and compared the outcome (whether the car started) to the previous situation (it did not start). I began with an implicit "hypothesis"—a buildup of crud on the connections is the reason the car is not starting, and once the crud is cleaned off, the car will start. This illustrates three things researchers do in experiments: (1) begin with a hypothesis, (2) modify something in a situation, and (3) compare outcomes with and without the modification.

Compared to the other social research techniques, experimental research is the strongest for testing causal relationships because the three conditions for causality (temporal order, association, and no alternative explanations) are clearly met in experimental designs.

RESEARCH QUESTIONS APPROPRIATE FOR AN EXPERIMENT

The Issue of an Appropriate Technique

New researchers often ask which research technique best fits which problem. This is difficult to answer because there is no fixed match between problem and technique. The answer is: Make an informed judgment. You can develop judgment from reading research reports, understanding the strengths and weaknesses of different techniques, assisting more experienced researchers with their research, and gaining practical experience.

Research Questions for Experimental Research

The experiment is a powerful way to focus sharply on causal relations, it closely fits the canons of positivist science, and it has practical advantages over other techniques, but it also has limitations. The research questions most appropriate for an experiment fit its strengths and limitations. These include its basic logic and practical restraints, its narrow scope, its ability to isolate causes, and the convention of researchers.

The questions appropriate for using an experimental logic confront ethical and practical limitations of intervening in human affairs for research purposes. It is immoral or impossible to manipulate many areas of human life for research purposes. The pure logic of an experiment has an experimenter induce a change in some focused part of social life, then examine the consequences that result from the change or intervention. This means that the experiment is limited to research questions in which a researcher is able to manipulate conditions. Experimental research cannot answer questions such as, Do people who complete a college education increase their annual income more than people who do not? Do children raised with younger siblings develop better leadership skills than only children? Do people who belong to more organizations vote more often in elections? This is because an experimenter cannot randomly assign thousands to attend college and prevent others from attending to discover who later earns more income. He or she cannot induce couples to have either many children or a single child so he or she can examine how leadership skills develop in children. He or she cannot compel people to join or quit organizations and then see whether they vote. Experimenters are highly creative in simulating such interventions or conditions, but they cannot manipulate many variables of interest to fit the pure experimental logic.

The experiment is usually best for issues that have a narrow scope or scale. This strength allows experimenters to assemble and "run" many experiments with limited resources in a short period. Some carefully designed experiments require assembling only 50 or 60 volunteers and can be completed in one or two months. In general, the experiment is better suited for micro-level (e.g., individual or small-group phenomena) than for macro-level theoretical concerns or questions. This is one reason why psychologists, social psychologists in sociology, and political psychologists in political science all tend to use experiments. Experiments rarely address questions that require looking at conditions across an entire society or across decades.

Experiments encourage researchers to isolate and target the impact that arises from one or a few causal variables. This strength in demonstrating causal effects is a limitation in situations in which a researcher tries to examine numerous variables simultaneously. The experiment is rarely appropriate for research questions or issues that require a researcher to examine the impact of dozens of diverse variables all together. Rarely do experiments permit assessing conditions across a wide range of complex settings or numerous social groups all at the same time. Accumulated knowledge from many individual experiments, each focused on one or two variables, may advance understanding, yet the experiment differs from research on a complex situation that examines how dozens of variables operate simultaneously.

A last factor that influences the research questions that fit the experimental method is convention. For some topics or research questions, numerous researchers depended on the experimental method to create a large body of literature with hundreds of studies. This facilitates quick, smooth communication. More importantly, it allows researchers to advance knowledge rapidly by replicating previous experiments with only minor adjustments in study design and to isolate precisely the effects of specific conditions or variables. It is a limitation because those who specialize in a topic tend to evaluate new research by the criteria of a good experiment. They may be slower to accept and assimilate new knowledge from a nonexperimental study.

Often, it is possible to conduct research on closely related topics using either an experimental or a nonexperimental method. For example, a researcher may wish to study attitudes toward people in wheelchairs. A survey researcher might ask people their opinions about people in wheelchairs. The field researcher might observe people's reactions to someone in a wheelchair, or the experimenter himself or herself might be in a wheelchair and carefully note the reactions of others.

A SHORT HISTORY OF THE EXPERIMENT IN SOCIAL RESEARCH

The experimental method was borrowed from the natural sciences and began in psychology. It was not widely accepted in psychology until after 1900.[2]

Wilhelm M. Wundt (1832–1920), a German psychologist and physiologist, introduced the experimental method into psychology. During the late 1800s, Germany was the center of graduate education, and leading social scientists from around the world went to Germany to study. Wundt established a laboratory for experimentation in psychology that became a model for many other social researchers. By 1900, researchers at many U.S. and other universities established psychology laboratories to conduct experimental social research. The experiment replaced a more philosophical, introspective, integrative approach that was closer to interpretive social science. For example, William James (1842–1910), the foremost U.S. philosopher and psychologist of the 1890s, did not use or embrace the experimental method.

From the turn of the century to the time of World War II, the experimental method was elaborated and became entrenched in social research. The method's appeal was that it offered an objective, unbiased, scientific way to study human mental and social life at a time when the scientific study of social life was just gaining acceptance.

Four trends speeded the expansion of the experimental method in this period: the rise of behaviorism, the spread of quantification, changes in research subjects, and practical applications.

1. *Behaviorism* is a school of psychology founded in the 1920s by the American John B. Watson (1878–1958) and extended by B. F. Skinner (1904–1990). It emphasized measuring observable behavior or outcomes of mental life and advocated the experimental method for conducting rigorous empirical tests of hypotheses.

2. *Quantification,* or measuring social phenomena with numbers, also grew between 1900 and 1940. Researchers reconceptualized social constructs so that they could be quantified, and other constructs (e.g., spirit, consciousness, will) were jettisoned from empirical research. An example is measuring mental ability by the IQ test. Originally developed by Alfred Binet (1857–1911), a Frenchman, the intelligence test was translated into English and revised by 1916. It was widely used, and the ability to express something as subjective as mental ability in a single score had public appeal as an objective way to rank and sort people. In fact, between the years of 1921 and 1936, over 5,000 articles were published on intelligence tests.[3] Many scaling and index techniques were developed in this period, and social researchers began to use applied statistics.

3. Early reports of empirical social research included the names of the people who participated in research, and most early subjects were professional researchers. Later reports treated subjects anonymously and reported only the results of their actions. Subjects were increasingly college students or schoolchildren. These changes reflected an increasingly objective and distant relationship between the researcher and the people studied.

4. People increasingly used experimental methods for applied purposes. For example, intelligence testing was adopted by the U.S. Army during World War I to sort thousands of men into different positions. The leader of the "scientific management" movement, Frederick W. Taylor (1856–1915), advocated the use of the experimental method in factories and worked with management to modify factory conditions to increase worker productivity.

Through the 1950s and 1960s, researchers continued to use the experimental method. They became concerned with sources of alternative explanations that could slip into experimental design. They created ways to reduce these possible sources of systematic error in experiments with new research designs and statistical procedures. Experiments became more logically rigorous, and by the 1970s, methodological criteria were increasingly used to evaluate research. A related trend that began in the 1960s was the increased use of deception and a concern with ethical issues. For example, a now common practice of debriefing did not come into use until the mid-1960s.[4] The experiment is still widely used because of its logical rigor and simplicity, consistency with positivist assumptions, and relatively low cost.

RANDOM ASSIGNMENT

Social researchers frequently make comparisons. For example, a researcher has two groups of 15 students and wants to compare the groups on the basis of a key difference between them (e.g., a course that one group completed). Or a researcher has five groups of customers and wants to compare the groups on the basis of one characteristic (e.g., geo-

graphic location). The cliché, "Compare apples to apples, don't compare apples to oranges," is not about fruit; it is about comparisons. It means that a valid comparison depends on comparing things that are fundamentally alike. Random assignment facilitates comparison in experiments by creating similar groups.

When making comparisons, experimenters want to compare cases that do not differ with regard to variables that offer alternative explanations. For example, when comparing two groups of students to determine the impact of completing a course, the two groups must be similar in most respects except for taking the course. If the group that completed the course is also older than the group that did not, for example, the researcher cannot determine whether completing the course or being older accounts for differences between the groups.

Why Randomly Assign?

Random assignment is a method for assigning cases (e.g., individuals, organizations, etc.) to groups for the purpose of making comparisons. It is a way to divide a collection of cases into two or more groups in order to increase one's confidence that the groups do not differ in a systematic way. It is a mechanical method; the assignment is automatic, and the researcher cannot make assignments on the basis of personal preference or the features of specific cases.

Random assignment is random in a statistical or mathematical sense, not in an everyday sense. In everyday speech, *random* means unplanned, haphazard, or accidental. In probability theory, *random* describes a process in which each case has an equal chance of being selected. Random selection lets a researcher calculate the odds that a specific case will be sorted into one group over another. For example, a random process is one in which all cases have an exactly equal chance of ending up in one or the other group.

> **Random assignment** Dividing subjects into groups at the beginning of experimental research using a random process, so the experimenter can treat the groups as equivalent.

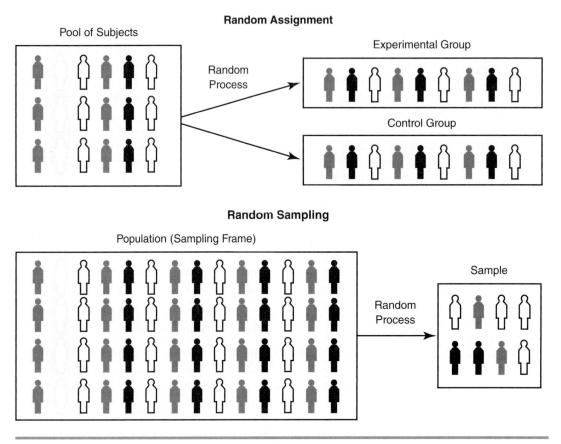

FIGURE 9.1   Random Assignment and Random Sampling

The wonderful thing about a random process is that over many separate random occurrences, predictable things happen. Although the process is entirely due to chance and it is impossible to predict a specific outcome at a specific time, very accurate predictions are possible over many situations.

Random assignment or randomization is unbiased because a researcher's desire to confirm a hypothesis or a research subject's personal interests do not enter into the selection process. *Unbiased* does not mean that groups with identical characteristics are selected in each specific situation of random assignment. Instead, it says something close to that: The probability of selecting a case can be math-ematically determined, and, in the long run, the groups will be identical.

Sampling and random assignment are processes of systematically selecting cases for inclusion in a study. When a researcher randomly assigns, he or she sorts a collection of cases into two or more groups using a random process. By contrast, in random sampling, he or she selects a smaller subset of cases from a larger pool of cases (see Figure 9.1). A researcher can both sample and randomly assign. He or she can first sample to obtain a smaller set of cases (e.g., 150 people out of 20,000) and then use random assignment to divide the smaller set into groups (e.g., divide the 150 people into three groups of 50).

Step 1: Begin with a collection of subjects.

Step 2: Devise a method to randomize that is purely mechanical (e.g., flip a coin).

Step 3: Assign subjects with "Heads" to one group   and "Tails" to the other group.

           Control Group   **Experimental Group**

FIGURE 9.2   How to Randomly Assign

How to Randomly Assign

Random assignment is very simple in practice. A researcher begins with a collection of cases (individuals, organizations, or whatever the unit of analysis is), and then divides it into two or more groups by a random process, such as asking people to count off, tossing a coin, or throwing dice. For example, a researcher wants to divide 32 people into two groups of 16. A random method is writing each person's name on a slip of paper, putting the slips in a hat, mixing the slips with eyes closed, then drawing the first 16 names for group 1 and the second 16 for group 2.

A specific situation can be unusual and the groups can differ. For example, it is possible, though extremely unlikely, that all cases with one characteristic will end up in one group (see the example in Figure 9.2).

Matching versus Random Assignment

You may ask, If the purpose of random assignment is to get two (or more) equivalent groups, would it not be simpler to match the characteristics of cases in each group? Some researchers match cases in

groups on certain characteristics, such as age and sex. Matching is an alternative to random assignment, but it is an infrequently used one.

Matching presents a problem: What are the relevant characteristics to match on, and can one locate exact matches? Individual cases differ in thousands of ways, and the researcher cannot know which might be relevant. For example, a researcher compares two groups of 15 students. There are 8 males in one group, which means there should be 8 males in the other group. Two males in the first group are only children; one is from a divorced family, one from an intact family. One is tall, slender, and Jewish; the other is short, heavy, and Catholic. In order to match groups, does the researcher have to find a tall Jewish male only child from a divorced home and a short Catholic male only child from an intact home? The tall, slender, Jewish male only child is 22 years old and is studying to become a physician. The short, heavy Catholic male is 20 years old and wants to be an accountant. Does the researcher also need to match the age and career aspirations of the two males? True matching soon becomes an impossible task.

EXPERIMENTAL DESIGN LOGIC

The Language of Experiments

In experimental research, the cases or people used in research projects and on whom variables are measured are called the **subjects.**

Parts of the Experiment. The experiment has seven parts. Not all experiments have all these parts, and some have all seven parts plus others.

1. Treatment or independent variable
2. Dependent variable
3. Pretest
4. Posttest
5. Experimental group
6. Control group
7. Random assignment

In most experiments, a researcher creates a situation or enters into an ongoing situation, and then modifies it. The **treatment** (or the stimulus or manipulation) is what the researcher modifies. The term comes from medicine, in which a physician administers a treatment to patients; the physician intervenes in a physical or psychological condition to change it. It is the independent variable or a combination of independent variables. In earlier examples of measurement, a researcher developed a measurement instrument or indicator (e.g., a survey question), then applied it to a person or case. In experiments, researchers "measure" independent variables by creating a condition or situation. For example, the independent variable is "degree of fear or anxiety"; the levels are high fear and low fear. Instead of asking subjects whether they are fearful, experimenters put subjects into either a high-fear or a low-fear situation. They measure the independent variable by manipulating conditions

so that some subjects feel a lot of fear and others feel little.

Researchers go to great lengths to create treatments. Some are as minor as giving different groups of subjects different instructions. Others can be as complex as putting subjects into situations with elaborate equipment, staged physical settings, or contrived social situations to manipulate what the subjects see or feel. Researchers want the treatment to have an impact and produce specific reactions, feelings, or behaviors.

For example, a mock jury decision is one type of treatment. Johnson (1985) asked subjects to watch a videotape of a child-abuse trial about a man who brought his 2-year-old son to an emergency room with a skull fracture. The videotapes were the same, except that in one, the man's attorney argued that the father was a highly religious person who followed the word of God in the Bible in all family affairs. In the other videotape, no such statement was made. The dependent variable was a decision of guilty or innocent and a recommended sentence for guilty decisions. Contrary to common sense, Johnson found that subjects were more likely to find the religious defendant guilty and to recommend longer sentences.

Dependent variables or outcomes in experimental research are the physical conditions, social behaviors, attitudes, feelings, or beliefs of subjects that change in response to a treatment. Dependent variables can be measured by paper-and-pencil indicators, observation, interviews, or physiological responses (e.g., heartbeat or sweating palms). An example is a study by Stephens and colleagues (1985) on helping people who have disabilities. In the experiment, subjects were 40 males and 40 females walking across a university campus, who encountered either a woman with severe physical disabilities in a wheelchair or a woman with no disabilities. The woman asked for help in finding a lost earring in a hallway. The dependent variable was the number of minutes the subject spent helping find the earring, as measured by an observer a short distance away who appeared to be reading a book.

Frequently, a researcher measures the dependent variable more than once during an experiment. The **pretest** is the measurement of the dependent

Subjects The name for the participants in experimental research.

Treatment What the independent variable in experimental research is often called.

Pretest Measurement of the dependent variable of an experiment prior to the treatment.

BOX **9.1** **Steps in Conducting an Experiment**

1. Begin with a straightforward hypothesis that is appropriate for experimental research.
2. Decide on an experimental design that will test the hypothesis within practical limitations.
3. Decide how to introduce the treatment or create a situation that induces the independent variable.
4. Develop a valid and reliable measure of the dependent variable.
5. Set up an experimental setting and conduct a pilot test of the treatment and dependent variable measures.
6. Locate appropriate subjects or cases.
7. Randomly assign subjects to groups (if random assignment is used in the chosen research design) and give careful instructions.
8. Gather data for the pretest measure of the dependent variable for all groups (if a pretest is used in the chosen design).
9. Introduce the treatment to the experimental group only (or to relevant groups if there are multiple experimental groups) and monitor all groups.
10. Gather data for posttest measure of the dependent variable.
11. *Debrief* the subjects by informing them of the true purpose and reasons for the experiment. Ask subjects what they thought was occurring. Debriefing is crucial when subjects have been deceived about some aspect of the experiment.
12. Examine data collected and make comparisons between different groups. Where appropriate, use statistics and graphs to determine whether the hypothesis is supported.

not receive the treatment is called the **control group.** When the independent variable takes on many different values, more than one experimental group is used.

Steps in Conducting an Experiment. Following the basic steps of the research process, experimenters decide on a topic, narrow it into a testable research problem or question, and then develop a hypothesis with variables.

A crucial early step is to plan a specific experimental design (to be discussed). The researcher decides the number of groups to use, how and when to create treatment conditions, the number of times to measure the dependent variable, and what the groups of subjects will experience from beginning to end. He or she also develops measures of the dependent variable and pilot tests the experiment (see Box 9.1).

The experiment itself begins after a researcher locates subjects and randomly assigns them to groups. Subjects are given precise, preplanned instructions. Next, the researcher measures the dependent variable in a pretest before the treatment. One group is then exposed to the treatment. Finally, the researcher measures the dependent variable in a posttest. He or she also interviews subjects about the experiment before they leave. The researcher records measures of the dependent variable and examines the results for each group to see whether the hypothesis receives support.

Control in Experiments. Control is crucial in experimental research.[5] A researcher wants to control all aspects of the experimental situation to isolate the effects of the treatment and eliminate alternative explanations. Aspects of an experimental situation that are not controlled by the researcher are alternatives to the treatment for change in the

variable prior to introduction of the treatment. The **posttest** is the measurement of the dependent variable after the treatment has been introduced into the experimental situation.

Experimental researchers often divide subjects into two or more groups for purposes of comparison. A simple experiment has two groups, only one of which receives the treatment. The **experimental group** is the group that receives the treatment or in which the treatment is present. The group that does

Posttest   Measurement of the dependent variable of an experiment after the treatment.

Experimental group   The group that receives the treatment in experimental research.

Control group   The group that does not get the treatment in experimental research.

dependent variable and potentially undermine attempts to establish causality.

Experimental researchers sometimes use deception to control the experimental setting. **Deception** is when the researcher intentionally misleads subjects through written or verbal instructions, the actions of others, or aspects of the setting. It may involve the use of confederates or stooges—people who pretend to be other subjects or bystanders but who actually work for the researcher and deliberately mislead subjects. Through deception, the researcher tries to control what the subjects see and hear and what they believe is occurring. For example, a researcher's instructions falsely lead subjects to believe that they are participating in a study about group cooperation. In fact, the experiment is about male–female verbal interaction, and what subjects say is being secretly tape recorded. Deception lets the researcher control the subjects' definition of the situation. It prevents them from altering their cross-sex verbal behavior because they are unaware of the true research topic. By focusing their attention on a false topic, the researcher induces the unaware subjects to act "naturally." For realistic deception, researchers may invent false treatments and dependent variable measures to keep subjects unaware of the true ones. The use of deception in experiments raises ethical issues.

Types of Design

Researchers combine parts of an experiment (e.g., pretests, control groups, etc.) together into an **experimental design.** For example, some designs lack pretests, some do not have control groups, and oth-

---

Deception When an experimenter lies to subjects about the true nature of an experiment or creates a false impression through his or her actions or the setting.

Experimental design Planning and arranging the parts of an experiment.

Classical experimental design An experimental design that has random assignment, a control group, an experimental group, and a pretest and posttest for each group.

---

ers have many experimental groups. Certain widely used standard designs have names.

You should learn the standard designs for two reasons. First, in research reports, researchers give the name of a standard design instead of describing it. When reading reports, you will be able to understand the design of the experiment if you know the standard designs. Second, the standard designs illustrate common ways to combine design parts. You can use them for experiments you conduct or create your own variations.

The designs are illustrated with a simple example. A researcher wants to learn whether wait staff (waiters and waitresses) receive more in tips if they first introduce themselves by first name and return to ask, "Is everything fine?" 8 to 10 minutes after delivering the food. The dependent variable is the size of the tip received. The study occurs in two identical restaurants on different sides of a town that have had the same types of customers and average the same amount in tips.

Classical Experimental Design. All designs are variations of the **classical experimental design,** the type of design discussed so far, which has random assignment, a pretest and a posttest, an experimental group, and a control group.

Example. The experimenter gives 40 newly hired wait staff an identical two-hour training session and instructs them to follow a script in which they are not to introduce themselves by first name and not to return during the meal to check on the customers. They are next randomly divided into two equal groups of 20 and sent to the two restaurants to begin employment. The experimenter records the amount in tips for all subjects for one month (pretest score). Next, the experimenter "retrains" the 20 subjects at restaurant 1 (experimental group). The experimenter instructs them henceforth to introduce themselves to customers by first name and to check on the customers, asking, "Is everything fine?" 8 to 10 minutes after delivering the food (treatment). The group at restaurant 2 (control group) is "retained" to continue without an introduction or checking during the meal. Over the second month, the amount of tips for both groups is recorded (posttest score).

Preexperimental Designs. Some designs lack random assignment and are compromises or shortcuts. These **preexperimental designs** are used in situations in which it is difficult to use the classical design. They have weaknesses that make inferring a causal relationship more difficult.

One-Shot Case-Study Design. Also called the one-group posttest-only design, the **one-shot case-study design** has only one group, a treatment, and a posttest. Because there is only one group, there is no random assignment.

Example. The experimenter takes a group of 40 newly hired wait staff and gives all a two-hour training session in which they are instructed to introduce themselves to customers by first name and to check on the customers, asking, "Is everything fine?" 8 to 10 minutes after delivering the food (treatment). All subjects begin employment, and the experimenter records the amount in tips for all subjects for one month (posttest score).

One-Group Pretest-Posttest Design. This design has one group, a pretest, a treatment, and a posttest. It lacks a control group and random assignment.

Example. The experimenter takes a group of 40 newly hired wait staff and gives all a two-hour training session. They are instructed to follow a script in which they are not to introduce themselves by first name and not to return during the meal to check on the customers. All begin employment, and the experimenter records the amount in tips for all subjects for one month (pretest score). Next, the experimenter "retrains" all 40 subjects (experimental group). The experimenter instructs the subjects henceforth to introduce themselves to customers by first name and to check on the customers, asking, "Is everything fine?" 8 to 10 minutes after delivering the food (treatment). Over the second month, the amount of tips for both groups is recorded (posttest score).

This is an improvement over the one-shot case study because the researcher measures the dependent variable both before and after the treatment. But it lacks a control group. The researcher cannot know whether something other than the treatment occurred between the pretest and the posttest to cause the outcome.

Static Group Comparison. Also called the posttest-only nonequivalent group design, **static group comparison design** has two groups, a posttest, and treatment. It lacks random assignment and a pretest. A weakness is that any posttest outcome difference between the groups could be due to group differences prior to the experiment instead of to the treatment.

Example. The experimenter gives 40 newly hired wait staff an identical two-hour training session and instructs them to follow a script in which they are not to introduce themselves by first name and not to return during the meal to check on the customers. They can choose one of the two restaurants to work at, as long as each restaurant ends up with 20 people. All begin employment. After one month, the experimenter "retrains" the 20 subjects at restaurant 1 (experimental group). The experimenter instructs them henceforth to introduce themselves to customers by first name and to check on the customers, asking, "Is everything fine?" 8 to 10 minutes after delivering the food (treatment). The group at restaurant 2 (control group) is "retained" to continue without an introduction or checking during the meal. Over the second month, the amount of tips for both groups is recorded (posttest score).

Quasi-Experimental and Special Designs. These designs, like the classical design, make identifying a causal relationship more certain than do

Preexperimental designs Experimental designs that lack random assignment or use shortcuts and are much weaker than the classical experimental design. They are be substituted in situations in which an experimenter cannot use all the features of a classical experimental design, but have weaker internal validity.

One-shot case-study design An experimental design with only an experimental group and a posttest, no pretest.

Static group comparison design An experimental design with two groups, no random assignment, and only a posttest.

TABLE 9.1   A Comparison of the Classical Experimental Design with Other Major Designs

DESIGN	RANDOM ASSIGNMENT	PRETEST	POSTTEST	CONTROL GROUP	EXPERIMENTAL GROUP
Classical	Yes	Yes	Yes	Yes	Yes
One-Shot Case Study	No	No	Yes	No	Yes
One-Group Pretest Postest	No	Yes	Yes	No	Yes
Static Group Comparison	No	No	Yes	Yes	Yes
Two-Group Posttest Only	Yes	No	Yes	Yes	Yes
Time-Series Designs	No	Yes	Yes	No	Yes

preexperimental designs. **Quasi-experimental designs** help researchers test for causal relationships in a variety of situations in which the classical design is difficult or inappropriate. They are called *quasi* because they are variations of the classical experimental design. Some have randomization but lack a pretest, some use more than two groups, and others substitute many observations of one group over time for a control group. In general, the researcher has less control over the independent variable than in the classical design (see Table 9.1).

Two-Group Posttest-Only Design. This is identical to the static group comparison, with one exception: The groups are randomly assigned. It has all the parts of the classical design except a pretest. The random assignment reduces the chance that the groups differed before the treatment, but without a

> **Quasi-experimental designs** Experimental designs that are stronger than preexperimental designs. They are variations on the classical experimental design and are used in special situations or when an experimenter has limited control over the independent variable.
>
> **Interrupted time-series design** An experimental design in which the dependent variable is measured periodically across many time points, and the treatment occurs in the midst of such measures, often only once.
>
> **Equivalent time-series design** An experimental design in which there are several repeated pretests, posttests, and treatments for one group often over a period of time.

pretest, a researcher cannot be as certain that the groups began the same on the dependent variable.

In a study using a two-group posttest-only design with random assignment, Rind and Strohmetz (1999) examined restaurant tips. The treatment was messages about a upcoming special written on the back of customers' checks. The subjects were 81 dining parties eating at an upscale restaurant in New Jersey. The treatment was whether a female server wrote a message about an upcoming restaurant special on the back of a check and the dependent variable was the size of tips. The server with two years' experience was given a randomly shuffled stack of cards, half of which said No Message and half of which said Message. Just before she gave a customer his or her check, she randomly pulled a card from her pocket. If it said Message, she wrote about an upcoming special on the back of the customer's check. If it said No Message, she wrote nothing. The experimenters recorded the amount of the tip and the number of people at the table. They instructed the server to act the same toward all customers. The results showed that higher tips came from customers who received the message about upcoming specials.

Interrupted Time Series. In an **interrupted time-series design,** a researcher uses one group and makes multiple pretest measures before and after the treatment.

Equivalent Time Series. An **equivalent time-series design** is another one-group design that extends over a time period. Instead of one treatment, it has a pretest, then a treatment and posttest, then treatment and posttest, then treatment and posttest, and so on. For example, people who drive motorcycles were not required to wear helmets before 1975, when a law was passed requiring helmets. In 1981, the law was repealed because of pressure from motorcycle clubs. The helmet law was reinstated in 1998. The researcher's hypothesis is that wearing protective helmets results in a lower number of head injury deaths in accidents. The researcher plots head injury death rates in motorcycle accidents over time. He or she finds the rate was very high prior to 1975, dropped sharply between 1975 and 1981, then rose to pre-1975 levels between 1981 and 1998, then dropped again from 1998 to the present.

Latin Square Designs. Researchers interested in how several treatments given in different sequences or time orders affect a dependent variable can use a **Latin square design.** For example, a geography instructor has three units to teach students: map reading, using a compass, and the longitude/latitude (LL) system. The units can be taught in any order, but the teacher wants to know which order most helps students learn. In one class, students first learn to read maps, then how to use a compass, then the LL system. In another class, using a compass comes first, then map reading, then the LL system. In a third class, the instructor first teaches the LL system, then compass usage, and ends with map reading. The teacher gives tests after each unit, and students take a comprehensive exam at the end of the term. The students were randomly assigned to classes, so the instructor can see whether presenting units in one sequence or another resulted in improved learning.

Solomon Four-Group Design. A researcher may believe that the pretest measure has an influence on the treatment or dependent variable. A pretest can sometimes sensitize subjects to the treatment or improve their performance on the posttest (see the discussion of testing effect to come). Richard L. Solomon developed the **Solomon four-group design** to address the issue of pretest effects. It combines the classical experimental design with the two-group posttest-only design and randomly assigns subjects to one of four groups. For example,

a mental health worker wants to determine whether a new training method improves clients' coping skills. The worker measures coping skills with a 20-minute test of reactions to stressful events. Because the clients might learn coping skills from taking the test itself, a Solomon four-group design is used. The mental health worker randomly divides clients into four groups. Two groups receive the pretest; one of them gets the new training method and the other gets the old method. Another two groups receive no pretest; one of them gets the new method and the other the old method. All four groups are given the same posttest and the posttest results are compared. If the two treatment (new method) groups have similar results, and the two control (old method) groups have similar results, then the mental health worker knows pretest learning is not a problem. If the two groups with a pretest (one treatment, one control) differ from the two groups without a pretest, then the worker concludes that the pretest itself may have an effect on the dependent variable.

Factorial Designs. Sometimes, a research question suggests looking at the simultaneous effects of more than one independent variable. A **factorial design** uses two or more independent variables in combination. Every combination of the categories in variables (sometimes called *factors*) is examined. When each variable contains several categories, the number of combinations grows very quickly. The treatment or manipulation is not each independent variable; rather, it is each combination of the categories.

The treatments in a factorial design can have two kinds of effects on the dependent variable: main

---

Latin square design An experimental design used to examine whether the order or sequence in which subjects receive multiple versions of the treatment has an effect.

Solomon four-group design An experimental design in which subjects are randomly assigned to two control groups and two experimental groups. Only one experimental group and one control group receive a pretest. All four groups receive a posttest.

Factorial design A type of experimental design that considers the impact of several independent variables simultaneously.

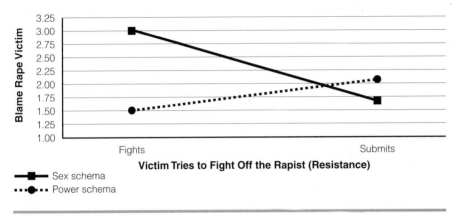

FIGURE 9.3   Blame, Resistance, and Schema

effects and interaction effects. Only *main effects* are present in one-factor or single-treatment designs. In a factorial design, specific combinations of independent variable categories can also have an effect. They are called **interaction effects** because the categories in a combination interact to produce an effect beyond that of each variable alone. For example, Bardack and McAndrew (1985) wanted to determine the effects of physical attractiveness and appropriate dress on the decision to hire someone. They had six photographs of females with either high, average, or low attractiveness and appropriate or inappropriate clothing. Subjects saw one of the six photographs with identical resumés and were asked to decide whether to hire the person for an entry-level managerial position in a major corporation. Both variables affected the decision to hire; that is, subjects were more likely to hire attractive and appropriately dressed people. In addition to these main effects, the experimenters found interaction effects; attractive and well-dressed women were much more likely to be hired than would be expected as a result of either dress or appearance alone. Combined, the two factors gave an extra

boost to the hiring decision, with physical attractiveness having a stronger effect.

Interaction effects are illustrated in Figure 9.3, which uses data from a study by Ong and Ward (1999). As part of a study of 128 female undergraduates at the National University of Singapore, Ong and Ward measured which of two major ways subjects understood the crime of rape. Some of the women primarily understood it as sex and due to the male sex drive (sex schema); others understood it as primarily an act of male power and domination of a woman (power schema). The researchers asked the subjects to read a realistic scenario about the rape of a college student at their university. One randomly selected group of subjects read a scenario in which the victim tried to fight off the rapist. In the other set, she passively submitted. The researchers next asked the subjects to evaluate the degree to which the rape victim was at blame or responsible for the rape.

Results showed that the women who held the sex schema (and who also tended to embrace traditionalist gender role beliefs) more strongly blamed the victim when she resisted. Blame decreased if she submitted. The women who held a power schema (and who also tended to be nontraditionalists) were less likely to blame the victim if she fought. They blamed her more if she passively submitted. Thus, the subjects' responses to the victim's act of resisting the attack varied by, or interacted with, their understanding of the crime of rape (i.e., the rape

Interaction effect   An effect of two independent variables operating simultaneously and in combination on a dependent variable. It is a larger effect than occurs from the sum of each independent variable working separately.

schema held by each subject). The researchers found that the two rape schemas caused subjects to interpret victim resistance in opposite ways for the purpose of assigning responsibility for the crime.

Researchers discuss factorial design in a shorthand way. A "two by three factorial design" is written 2×3. It means that there are two treatments, with two categories in one and three categories in the other. A $2 \times 3 \times 3$ design means that there are three independent variables, one with two categories and two with three categories each.

Valentine-French and Radtke (1989) used a $2 \times 2 \times 3$ factorial design to study the effect of victim reaction to sexual harassment blame. The subjects were 120 male and 120 female undergraduate volunteers from the University of Calgary. The researchers operationalized the independent variable as an audiotaped vignette in which a professor guaranteed a good grade to a student if she or he were willing to cooperate, permitted caressing of the student's shoulder, and let the professor kiss her or him on the cheek. The experimenters varied the situation by having the student victim be male or female and by using one of three endings: The victim blamed his or her own behavior for the incident, blamed the professor, or gave no reaction. Thus, there were six combinations of victim gender and endings.

The subjects did not know the purpose of the study and listened to the vignette alone. The experimenters measured various background characteristics of the subjects with a questionnaire, as well as the main dependent variable—attribution of blame, or who was at fault. They operationalized the variable as an eight-item index measured with a 7-point Likert scale. The authors found that women were more likely to label the incident as sexual harassment and blame the professor. Male subjects, more than females, blamed the victim when the victim made a statement of self-blame. This was a $2 \times 2 \times 3$ factorial design because three independent variables were examined: the subject's gender, the victim's gender, and the victim's reactions. (Also see Box 9.2.)

Design Notation

Experiments can be designed in many ways. **Design notation** is a shorthand system for symbolizing the parts of experimental design.[6] It expresses a complex, paragraph-long description of the parts of an experiment in five or six symbols arranged in two lines. Once you learn design notation, you will find it easier to think about and compare designs. It uses the following symbols: O = observation of dependent variable; X = treatment, independent variable; R = random assignment. The Os are numbered with subscripts from left to right based on time order. Pretests are O_1, posttests O_2. When the independent variable has more than two levels, the Xs are numbered with subscripts to distinguish among them. Symbols are in time order from left to right. The R is first, followed by the pretest, the treatment, and then the posttest. Symbols are arranged in rows, with each row representing a group of subjects. For example, an experiment with three groups has an R (if random assignment is used), followed by three rows of Os and Xs. The rows are on top of each other because the pretests, treatment, and posttest occur in each group at about the same time. Table 9.2 gives the notation for many standard experimental designs.

INTERNAL AND EXTERNAL VALIDITY

The Logic of Internal Validity

Internal validity is when the hypothesized independent variable alone affects the dependent variable. Variables, other than the treatment, that affect the dependent variable are threats to internal validity. They threaten the researcher's ability to say that the treatment was the true causal factor producing change in the dependent variable. Thus, researchers try to rule out variables other than the treatment by controlling experimental conditions and through

---

Design notation   The name of a symbol system used to show parts of an experiment and to make diagrams of them.

Internal validity   The ability of experimenters to strengthen the logical rigor of a causal explanation by eliminating potential alternative explanations for an association between the treatment and dependent variable through an experimental design.

BOX **9.2**   **What Did the "Willie Horton" Television Advertisement Do?**

Willie Horton became well known in a political advertisement aired during the 1988 U.S. presidential campaign. He was a convicted murderer who, on a weekend leave from a Massachusetts state prison, committed rape and torture. Candidate George Bush ran the advertisement against his opponent Michael Dukakis, the governor of Massachusetts when Horton was released. Despite misleading information in it, observers felt the advertisement played on public fears of crime. Critics claimed it also contained a racial message because viewers were shown that Horton was an African American.

Mendelberg (1997) designed an experiment to test whether White viewers responded to the crime or the racist message. Experimental subjects were 77 White non-Hispanic students from the University of Michigan with a median age of 18 years. Subjects completed a modern racism index with seven items using a 5-point Likert scale and were classified as prejudiced or not based on scores. The students were randomly assigned to two groups and viewed a 50-minute news program. They were told the study was on "horse race" versus "substantive issue" coverage in political campaigns. The experimental group saw a news segment on Willie Horton in the middle of the program, while the control group viewed a segment about pollution that also criticized candidate Dukakis.

In the posttest, the students completed questionnaires on a range of public issues, including crime control and government programs to reduce racial inequality. After completing the posttest, they were debriefed. The experiment used a two-group posttest only 2×2 factorial design (racial prejudice or not by Willie Horton advertisement or not). The results suggest that the advertisement was more about race than crime. Viewers of the Horton advertisement did not become greater proponents of anticrime, but prejudiced viewers of it became more opposed to racial equality. The author concluded, "When it is activated by a racially implicit symbol like the Horton story, prejudice will lead to perceptions that African Americans' position has improved and to a sense that whites are losing their jobs to African Americans.... People who are prejudiced become even more resistant to racial equality with exposure to Horton."

In a related experiment, Valentino (1999) compared the rating of candidates in the 1996 U.S. presidential election. Research participants saw news programs with one of three conditions inserted. Some saw a program with no crime story, others saw a non-White suspect in a story about gang-related crime, and still others saw a White suspect. Subjects who saw no crime report rated Bill Clinton most favorable, those who saw a White suspect rated Clinton lower, and those who saw a non-White suspect rated him the lowest. The author concluded that news reports can "prime" racial attitudes in a way that affects voting preferences.

---

experimental designs. Next, we examine major threats to internal validity.

Threats to Internal Validity

The following are 10 common threats to internal validity.[7]

Selection Bias. Selection bias is the threat that research participants will not form equivalent

> **Selection bias** A threat to internal validity when groups in an experiment are not equivalent at the beginning of the experiment with regard to the dependent variable.

groups. It is a problem in designs without random assignment. It occurs when more subjects in one group have a characteristic that affects the dependent variable. For example, in an experiment on physical aggressiveness, the treatment group unintentionally contains subjects who are football, rugby, and hockey players, whereas the control group is made up of musicians, chess players, and painters. Another example is an experiment on the ability of people to dodge heavy traffic. All subjects assigned to one group come from rural areas, and all subjects in the other grew up in large cities. An examination of pretest scores helps a researcher detect this threat, because no group differences are expected.

TABLE 9.2   Summary of Experimental Designs with Notation

NAME OF DESIGN	DESIGN NOTATION
Classical experimental design	R O X O O O
Preexperimental Designs One-shot case study	X O
One-group pretest/posttest	O X O
Static group comparison	X O O
Quasi-Experimental Designs Two-group posttest only	R X O O
Interrupted time series	O O O O X O O O
Equivalent time series	O X O X O X O X O

Latin square designs	R O X_a O X_b O X_c O
	     O X_b O X_a O X_c O
	     O X_c O X_b O X_a O
	     O X_a O X_c O X_b O
	     O X_b O X_c O X_a O
	     O X_c O X_a O X_b O

Solomon four-group design	O X O
	 O O
	 R
	     X O
	        O

Factorial designs	X_1 Z_1 O X_1 Z_2 O R X_2 Z_1 O X_2 Z_2 O

History. This is the threat that an event unrelated to the treatment will occur during the experiment and influence the dependent variable. **History effects** are more likely in experiments that continue over a long time period. For example, halfway through a two-week experiment to evaluate subjects' attitudes toward space travel, a spacecraft explodes on the launchpad, killing the astronauts.

Maturation. This is the threat that some biological, psychological, or emotional process within the subjects and separate from the treatment will change over time. A **maturation effect** is more common in experiments over long time periods. For example,

during an experiment on reasoning ability, subjects become bored and sleepy and, as a result, score lower. Another example is an experiment on the styles of children's play between grades 1 and 6. Play styles are affected by physical, emotional, and

History effects A threat to internal validity due to something that occurs and affects the dependent variable during an experiment, but which is unplanned and outside the control of the experimenter.

Maturation effect A threat to internal validity in experiments due to natural processes of growth, boredom, and so on that occur during the experiment and affect the dependent variable.

maturation changes that occur as the children grow older, instead of or in addition to the effects of a treatment. Designs with a pretest and control group help researchers determine whether maturation or history effects are present, because both experimental and control groups will show similar changes over time.

Testing. Sometimes, the pretest measure itself affects an experiment. This **testing effect** threatens internal validity because more than the treatment alone affects the dependent variable. The Solomon four-group design helps a researcher detect testing effects. For example, a researcher gives students an examination on the first day of class. The course is the treatment. He or she tests learning by giving the same exam on the last day of class. If subjects remember the pretest questions and this affects what they learned (i.e., paid attention to) or how they answered questions on the posttest, a testing effect is present. If testing effects occur, a researcher cannot say that the treatment alone has affected the dependent variable.

Instrumentation. This threat is related to stability reliability. It occurs when the *instrument* or dependent variable measure changes during the experiment. For example, in a weight-loss experiment, the springs on the scale weaken during the experiment, giving lower readings in the posttest. Another example might have occurred in an experiment by Bond and Anderson (1987) on the reluctance to transmit bad news. The experimenters asked subjects to tell another person the results of an intelligence test and varied the test results to be either well above or well below average. The dependent variable was the length of time it took to tell the test taker the results. Some subjects were told that the session was being videotaped. During the experiment, the video equipment failed to work for one subject. If it had failed to work for more than one subject or had worked for only part of the session, the experiment would have had instrumentation problems. (By the way, subjects took longer to deliver bad news only if they thought they were doing so publicly—that is, being videotaped.)

Experimental mortality. Experimental mortality, or attrition, arises when some subjects do not continue throughout the experiment. Although the word *mortality* means death, it does not necessarily mean that subjects have died. If many subjects leave partway through an experiment, a researcher cannot know whether the results would have been different had the subjects stayed. For example, a researcher begins a weight-loss program with 50 subjects. At the end of the program, 30 remain, each of whom lost 5 pounds with no side effects. The 20 who left could have differed from the 30 who stayed, changing the results. Maybe the program was effective for those who left, and they withdrew after losing 25 pounds. Or perhaps the program made subjects sick and forced them to quit. Researchers should notice and report the number of subjects in each group during pretests and posttests to detect this threat to internal validity.

Statistical Regression. *Statistical regression* is not easy to grasp intuitively. It is a problem of extreme values or a tendency for random errors to move group results toward the average. It can occur in two ways.

One situation is when subjects are unusual with regard to the dependent variable. Because they begin as unusual, subjects are unlikely to respond further in one direction. For example, a researcher wants to see whether violent films make people act violently. He or she chooses a group of violent criminals from a high-security prison, gives them a pretest, shows violent films, then administers a posttest. To the researcher's shock, the criminals are slightly less violent after the film, whereas a control group of nonprisoners who did not see the film are more violent than before. Because the violent criminals were unusual and began at an extreme, a treatment could make them more violent; by random chance alone, they appear less extreme when measured a second time.[8]

Testing effect   A threat to internal validity that occurs when the very process of measuring in the pretest can have an impact on the dependent variable.

Experimental mortality   Threats to internal validity due to subjects failing to participate through the entire experiment, especially if it is many participants or more from one group than another.

A second situation involves a problem with the measurement instrument. If many research participants score very high (at the ceiling) or very low (at the floor) on a variable, random chance alone will produce a change between the pretest and the posttest. For example, a researcher gives 80 subjects a test, and 75 get perfect scores. He or she then gives a treatment to raise scores. Because so many subjects already had perfect scores, random errors will reduce the group average because those who got perfect scores can randomly move in only one direction—to get some answers wrong. An examination of scores on pretests will help researchers detect this threat to internal validity.

Diffusion of Treatment or Contamination.

Diffusion of treatment is the threat that research participants in different groups will communicate with each other and learn about the other's treatment. Researchers avoid it by isolating groups or having subjects promise not to reveal anything to others who will become subjects. For example, subjects participate in a daylong experiment on a new way to memorize words. During a break, treatment group subjects tell those in the control group about the new way to memorize, which control group subjects then use. A researcher needs outside information such as postexperiment interviews with subjects to detect this threat.

Compensatory Behavior.

Some experiments provide something of value to one group of subjects but not to another, and the difference becomes known. The inequality may produce pressure to reduce differences, competitive rivalry between groups, or resentful demoralization. These types of **compensatory behavior** can affect the dependent variable in addition to the treatment. For example, one school system receives a treatment (longer lunch breaks) to produce gains in learning. Once the inequality is known, participants in the control group demand equal treatment and work extra hard to learn and overcome the inequality. Another group becomes demoralized by the unequal treatment and withdraws from learning. It is difficult to detect this threat unless outside information is available (see the discussion of diffusion of treatment).

Experimenter Expectancy.

Although it is not always considered a traditional internal validity problem, the experimenter's behavior, too, can threaten causal logic.[9] A researcher may threaten internal validity by indirectly communicating **experimenter expectancy** to subjects. Researchers may be highly committed to the hypothesis and indirectly communicate desired findings to subjects. For example, a researcher studying reactions toward those with disabilities deeply believes that females are more sensitive toward those with disabilities than males are. Through eye contact, tone of voice, pauses, and other nonverbal communication, the researcher unconsciously encourages female research participants to report positive feelings toward those with disabilities; the researcher's nonverbal behavior is the opposite for male subjects.

Here is a way to detect experimenter expectancy. A researcher hires assistants and teaches them experimental techniques. The assistants train subjects and test their learning ability. The researcher gives the assistants fake transcripts and records showing that subjects in one group are honor students and the others are failing, although in fact the subjects are identical. Experimenter expectancy is present if the fake honor students, as a group, do much better than the fake failing students.

The **double-blind experiment** is designed to control researcher expectancy. In it, people who have direct contact with subjects do not know the

---

Diffusion of treatment   A threat to internal validity that occurs when the treatment "spills over" from the experimental group and control group subjects modify their behavior because they learn of the treatment.

Compensatory behavior   A threat to internal validity that occurs when subjects in the control group modify their behavior to make up for not getting the treatment.

Experimenter expectancy   A type of reactivity and threat to internal validity due to the experimenter indirectly making subjects aware of the hypothesis or desired results.

Double-blind experiment   A type of experimental research in which neither the subjects nor the person who directly deals with the subjects for the experimenter knows the specifics of the experiment.

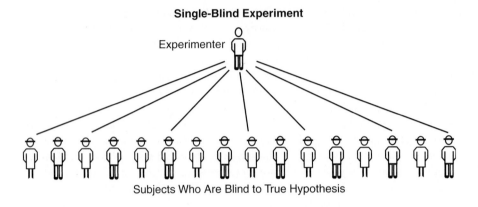

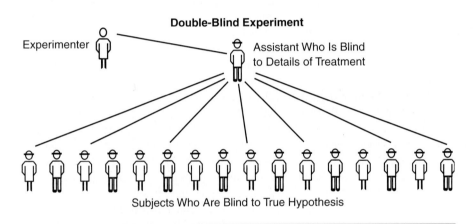

FIGURE 9.4   Double-Blind Experiments: An Illustration of Single-Blind, or Ordinary, and Double-Blind Experiments

details of the hypothesis or the treatment. It is *double* blind because both the subjects and those in contact with them are blind to details of the experiment (see Figure 9.4). For example, a researcher wants to see if a new drug is effective. Using pills of three colors—green, yellow, and pink—the researcher puts the new drug in the yellow pill, puts an old drug in the pink one, and makes the green pill a *placebo*—a false treatment that appears to be real (e.g., a sugar pill without any physical effects). Assistants who give the pills and record the effects do not know which color contains the new drug. Only

another person who does not deal with subjects directly knows which colored pill contains the drug and examines the results. The double-blind design is nearly mandatory in medical research because experimenter expectancy effects are well recognized.

External Validity and Field Experiments

Even if an experimenter eliminates all concerns about internal validity, external validity remains a potential problem. **External validity** is the ability to generalize experimental findings to events and settings outside the experiment itself. If a study lacks external validity, its findings hold true only in experiments, making them useless to both basic and applied science.

External validity   The ability to generalize findings beyond a specific study.

Realism.   Are experiments realistic? There are two types of realism to consider.[10] **Experimental realism** is the impact of an experimental treatment or setting on subjects; it occurs when experimental subjects are caught up in the experiment and are truly influenced by it. It is weak if subjects remain unaffected by the treatment, which is why researchers go to great lengths to create realistic conditions. Aronson and Carlsmith (1968:25) noted:

> *All experimental procedures are "contrived" in the sense that they are invented. Indeed, it can be said that the art of experimentation rests primarily on the skill of the investigator to judge the procedure which is the more accurate realization of his conceptual variable and has the greatest impact and the more credibility for the subject.*

Mundane realism asks: Is the experiment like the real world? For example, a researcher studying learning has subjects memorize four-letter nonsense syllables. Mundane realism would be stronger if he or she had subjects learn factual information used in real life instead of something invented for an experiment alone.

Mundane realism most directly affects external validity—the ability to generalize from experiments to the real world.[11] Two aspects of experiments can be generalized. One is from the subjects to other people. If the subjects are college students, can the researcher generalize results to the entire population, most of whom are not college students? Another aspect is generalizing from an artificial treatment to everyday life. For example, can one generalize from undergraduate subjects watching a two-hour horror movie in a classroom to the impact of the general public watching violent television programs over many years?

Reactivity.   Research participants might react differently in an experiment than they would in real life because they know they are in a study; this is called **reactivity**. The **Hawthorne effect** is a specific kind of reactivity.[12] The name comes from a series of experiments by Elton Mayo at the Hawthorne, Illinois, plant of Westinghouse Electric during the 1920s and 1930s. Researchers modified many aspects of working conditions (e.g., lighting,

time for breaks, etc.) and measured productivity. They discovered that productivity rose after each modification, no matter what it was. This curious result occurred because the workers did not respond to the treatment but to the additional attention they received from being part of the experiment and knowing that they were being watched. Later research questioned whether this had occurred, but the name is used for an effect from the attention of researchers. A related effect is the effect of something new, which may wear off over time.

Demand characteristics are another type of reactivity. Subjects may pick up clues about the hypothesis or goal of an experiment, and they may change their behavior to what they think is demanded of them (i.e., support the hypothesis) in order to please the researcher. For example, Chebat and Picard (1988) wanted to see whether people are more persuaded by one-sided (showing only positive features) versus two-sided (showing both positive features and limitations) advertisements. They created professional advertisements for a new soap and a car, with a one-sided and a two-sided advertisement for each. They presented the advertisements to 434 undergraduates at the University of Québec at Montréal who were asked to complete questionnaires with eight Likert-type questions on the acceptance of the advertising message. They stated (1988:356), "To avoid any potential bias or

---

Experimental realism   External validity in which the experiment is made to feel realistic, so that experimental events have a real impact on subjects.

Mundane realism   A type of external validity in which the experimental conditions appear to be real and very similar to settings or situations outside a lab setting.

Reactivity   A general threat to external validity that arises because subjects are aware that they are in an experiment and being studied.

Hawthorne effect   A reactivity effect named after a famous case in which subjects responded to the fact that they were in an experiment more than to the treatment.

Demand characteristics   A type of reactivity in which the subjects in experimental research pick up clues about the hypothesis and alter their behavior accordingly.

TABLE 9.3   Major Internal and External Validity Concerns

INTERNAL VALIDITY	EXTERNAL VALIDITY AND REACTIVITY
Selection bias	Experimental realism
History effect	Mundane realism
Maturation effect	Hawthorne effect
Testing effect	Demand characteristics
Instrumentation	Placebo effect
Experimental mortality	
Statistical regression	
Diffusion of treatment	
Compensatory behavior	
Experimenter expectancy	

experimental 'demand' that the presence of the researchers might introduce . . . , the questionnaires were administered by graduate research assistants."

A last type of reactivity is the **placebo effect,** observed when subjects are given the placebo but respond as if they have received the real treatment. For example, in an experiment on stopping smoking, subjects are given either a drug to reduce their dependence on nicotine or a placebo. If subjects who received the placebo also stop smoking, then participating in an experiment and taking something that subjects believed would help them quit smoking had an effect. The subjects' belief in the placebo alone affected the dependent variable. See Table 9.3 for a review of internal and external validity.

Field Experiments. This chapter has focused on experiments conducted under the controlled conditions of a laboratory. Experiments are also conducted in real-life or field settings in which a

---

Placebo effect When subjects do not receive the real treatment and instead receive a placebo or imitation treatment but respond as though they have received the real treatment.

Laboratory experiment Experimental research in an artificial setting over which the experimenter has great control.

Field experiment Experimental research that takes place in a natural setting.

---

researcher has less control over the experimental conditions. The amount of control varies on a continuum. At one end is the highly controlled **laboratory experiment,** which takes place in a specialized setting or laboratory; at the opposite end is the **field experiment,** which takes place in the "field"—in natural settings such as a subway car, a liquor store, or a public sidewalk. Subjects in field experiments are usually unaware that they are involved in an experiment and react in a natural way. For example, researchers have had a confederate fake a heart attack on a subway car to see how the bystanders react.[13]

A dramatic example is a field experiment by Harari and colleagues (1985) on whether a male passerby will attempt to stop an attempted rape. In this experiment, conducted at San Diego State University, an attempted rape was staged on a somewhat isolated campus path in the evening. The staged attack was clearly visible to unsuspecting male subjects who approached alone or in groups of two or three. In the attack, a female student was grabbed by a large man hiding in the bushes. As the man pulled her away and tried to cover her mouth, the woman dropped her books. She struggled and screamed, "No, no! Help, help, please help me!" and "Rape!" Hidden observers told the actors when to begin to stage the attack and noted the actions of subjects. Assistance was measured as movement toward the attack site or movement toward a police officer visible across a nearby parking lot. The study found that 85 percent of men in groups and 65 percent of men walking alone made a detectable move to assist the woman.

The amount of experimenter control is related to internal and external validity. Laboratory experiments tend to have greater internal validity but lower external validity. They are logically tighter and better controlled, but less generalizable. Field experiments tend to have greater external validity but lower internal validity. They are more generalizable but less controlled. Quasi-experimental designs are more common. For example, in the experiment involving the staged attempted rape, the experimenters re-created a very realistic situation with high external validity. It had more external validity than putting people in a laboratory setting and asking them what they would do hypothetically. Yet, subjects were not randomly assigned. Any man who happened to walk by became a subject. The experimenters could not precisely control what the subject heard or saw. The measurement of subject response was based on hidden observers who may have missed some subject responses. Moreover, subjects did not give informed consent.

PRACTICAL CONSIDERATIONS

Every research technique has "tricks of the trade" that are pragmatic strategies learned from experience. They account for the difference between the successful research projects of an experienced researcher and the difficulties a novice researcher faces. Three are discussed here.

Planning and Pilot Tests

All social research requires planning. During the planning phase, a researcher anticipates alternative explanations or threats to internal validity and how to avoid them, develops a well-organized system for recording data, and pilot-tests any apparatus (e.g., computers, video cameras, tape recorders, etc.) that will be used in the study. After the pilot tests, the researcher should interview the pilot subjects to uncover aspects of the experiment that need refinement.

Instructions to Subjects

Most experiments involve giving instructions to subjects to set the stage. A researcher should word instructions carefully and follow a prepared script so that all subjects hear the same thing. This ensures reliability. The instructions are also important in creating a realistic cover story when deception is used. Aronson and Carlsmith (1968:46) noted, "One of the most common mistakes the novice experimenter makes is to present his instructions too briefly."

Postexperiment Interview

At the end of an experiment, the researcher should interview subjects, for three reasons. First, if deception was used, the researcher needs to **debrief**

the research participants, telling them the true purpose of the experiment and answering questions. Second, he or she can learn what the subjects thought and how their definitions of the situation affected their behavior. Finally, he or she can explain the importance of not revealing the true nature of the experiment to other potential participants.

RESULTS OF EXPERIMENTAL RESEARCH: MAKING COMPARISONS

Comparison is the key to all research. By carefully examining the results of experimental research, a researcher can learn a great deal about threats to internal validity, and whether the treatment has an impact on the dependent variable. For example, in the Bond and Anderson (1987) experiment on delivering bad news, discussed earlier, it took an average of 89.6 and 73.1 seconds to deliver favorable versus 72.5 or 147.2 seconds to deliver unfavorable test scores in private or public settings, respectively. A comparison shows that delivering bad news in public takes the longest, whereas good news takes a bit longer in private.

A more complex illustration of such comparisons is shown in Figure 9.5 on the results of a series of five weight-loss experiments using the classical experimental design. In the example, the 30 research participants in the experimental group at Enrique's Slim Clinic lost an average of 50 pounds, whereas the 30 in the control group did not lose a single pound. Only one person dropped out during the experiment. Susan's Scientific Diet Plan had equally dramatic results, but 11 people in her experimental group dropped out. This suggests a problem with experimental mortality. People in the experimental group at Carl's Calorie Counters lost 11 pounds, compared to 2 pounds for the control group, but the control group and the experimental group began with an average of 31 pounds difference in weight. This suggests a problem with

Debrief Talking with subjects after an experiment to give a true explanation of the experiment if deception has been used or to learn their perceptions.

FIGURE 9.5 **Comparisons of Results, Classical Experimental Design, Weight-Loss Experiments**

**ENRIQUE'S
SLIM CLINIC**

	Pretest	Posttest
Experimental	190 (30)	140 (29)
Control group	189 (30)	189 (30)

**NATALIE'S
NUTRITION CENTER**

	Pretest	Posttest
Experimental	190 (30)	188 (29)
Control group	192 (29)	189 (28)

**SUSAN'S SCIENTIFIC
DIET PLAN**

	Pretest	Posttest
Experimental	190 (30)	141 (19)
Control group	189 (30)	189 (28)

**PAULINE'S
POUNDS OFF**

	Pretest	Posttest
Experimental	190 (30)	158 (30)
Control group	191 (29)	159 (28)

**CARL'S CALORIE
COUNTERS**

	Pretest	Posttest
Experimental	160 (30)	152 (29)
Control group	191 (29)	189 (29)

**SYMBOLS FOR
COMPARISON
PURPOSES**

	Pretest	Posttest
Experimental	A (A)	C (C)
Control group	B (B)	D (D)

COMPARISONS

	A–B	C–D	A–C	B–D	(A)–(C)	(B)–(D)
Enrique's	1	49	−50	0	−1	0
Susan's	1	48	−49	0	−11	0
Carl's	31	37	−8	−2	−1	0
Natalie's	2	1	−2	−3	−1	−1
Pauline's	1	1	−32	−32	0	−1

A–B   Do the two groups begin the same? If not, selection bias may be possibly occurring.

C–D   Do the two groups end the same? If not, the treatment may be ineffective, or there may be strong history, maturation, or diffusion or treatment effects.

A–C   Did the experimental group change? If not, treatment may be ineffective.

(A)–(C) and (B)–(D)   Did the number of subjects in the experimental group or control group change? If a large drop occurs, experimental mortality may be a threat to internal validity.

INTERPRETATION

Enrique's: No internal validity threats evident, treatment effects

Susan's: Experimental mortality threat likely problem

Carl's: Selection bias likely problem

Natalie's: No internal validity threat evident, no treatment effects

Pauline's: History, maturation, diffusion of treatment threats are a likely problem

Note: Numbers are average number of pounds. Numbers in parentheses ( ) are number of subjects per group. Random assignment is made to the experimental or control group.

BOX **9.3**   **Use of Experiments for Evaluation Research**

In a study that you read about earlier in Chapter 2, Wysong and colleagues (1994) used an experiment to evaluate the effectiveness of the D.A.R.E. (Drug Abuse Resistance Education) program. Now that you better understand experiments, let us review its design.

The authors examined two groups of students that were not randomly divided but were separated into groups without a pattern. The experimental group participated in the D.A.R.E. program in grade 7; the control group did not. The treatment was participation in D.A.R.E., a program of presentations and discussions led by trained police officers in schools.

The program claims to help students resist peer pressure to use alcohol and illegal drugs and to raise student self-esteem. The dependent variables included age of first drug use, frequency of drug use, and student's self-esteem. The authors measured the variables four years after the treatment to determine whether it had any lasting impact on student behavior in the high school years. When the authors compared measures of the dependent variables for the two groups, they found no difference between them. They failed to reject the null hypothesis that the program had no effect.

---

selection bias. Natalie's Nutrition Center had no experimental mortality or selection bias problems, but those in the experimental group lost no more weight than those in the control group. It appears that the treatment was not effective. Pauline's Pounds Off also avoided selection bias and experimental mortality problems. People in her experimental group lost 32 pounds, but so did those in the control group. This suggests that the maturation, history, or diffusion of treatment effects may have occurred. Thus, the treatment at Enrique's Slim Clinic appears to be the most effective one.

A WORD ON ETHICS

Ethical considerations are a significant issue in experimental research because experimental research is intrusive (i.e., it interferes). Treatments may involve placing people in contrived social settings and manipulating their feelings or behaviors. Dependent variables may be what subjects say or do. The amount and type of intrusion is limited by ethical standards. Researchers must be very careful if they place research participants in physical danger or in embarrassing or anxiety-inducing situations. They must painstakingly monitor events and control what occurs.

Deception is common in social experiments. Researchers may mislead or lie to subjects for research purposes. Such dishonesty is acceptable only as the means to achieve a goal that cannot be

achieved otherwise. Even for a worthy goal, deception can be used only with restrictions. The amount and type of deception should not go beyond what is minimally necessary, and research participants should be debriefed.

CONCLUSION

In this chapter, you learned about random assignment and the methods of experimental research. Random assignment is an effective way to create two (or more) groups that can be treated as equivalent and hence compared. Experimental research provides precise and relatively unambiguous evidence for a causal relationship. It follows the positivist approach, produces quantitative results that can be analyzed with statistics, and is often used in evaluation research (see Box 9.3).

This chapter also examined how the parts of an experiment can be combined to produce different experimental designs. In addition to the classical experimental design, you learned about preexperimental and quasi-experimental designs and design notation.

You learned about threats to internal validity that are possible alternative explanations to the treatment. You also learned about external validity and how field experiments maximize external validity.

The real strength of experimental research is its control and logical rigor in establishing evidence for causality. In general, experiments tend to be easier to replicate, less expensive, and less time consuming than the other techniques. Experimental research also has limitations. First, some questions cannot be addressed using experimental methods because control and experimental manipulation are impossible. Another limitation is that experiments usually test one or a few hypotheses at a time. This fragments knowledge and makes it necessary to synthesize results across many research reports. External validity is a potential problem because many experiments rely on small nonrandom samples of college students.[14]

You learned how a careful examination and comparison of results can alert you to potential problems in research design. Finally, you saw some practical and ethical considerations in experiments.

In the next chapters, you will examine other research techniques. The logic of the nonexperimental methods differs from that of the experiment. Experimenters focus narrowly on a few hypotheses. They usually have one or two independent variables, a single dependent variable, small groups of subjects, and an independent variable that the researcher induces. By contrast, in other techniques researchers test many hypotheses at once, measure a large number of independent and dependent variables, and use a larger number of randomly sampled research participants.

KEY TERMS

classical experimental design
compensatory behavior
control group
debrief
deception
demand characteristics
design notation
diffusion of treatment
double-blind experiment
equivalent time-series design
experimental design
experimental group
experimental mortality
experimental realism

experimenter expectancy
external validity
factorial design
field experiment
Hawthorne effect
history effects
interaction effect
internal validity
interrupted time-series design
laboratory experiment
Latin square design
maturation effect
mundane realism
one-shot case-study design

placebo effect
posttest
preexperimental designs
pretest
quasi-experimental designs
random assignment
reactivity
selection bias
Solomon four-group design
static group comparison design
subjects
testing effect
treatment

REVIEW QUESTIONS

1. What are the seven elements or parts of an experiment?
2. What distinguishes preexperimental designs from the classical design?
3. Which design permits the testing of different sequences of several treatments?
4. A researcher says, "It was a three by two design, with the independent variables level of fear (low, medium, high) and ease of escape (easy/difficult) and the dependent variable anxiety." What does this mean? What is the design notation, assuming that random assignment with posttest only was used?
5. How do the interrupted and the equivalent time-series designs differ?
6. What is the logic of internal validity and how does the use of a control group fit into that logic?
7. How does the Solomon four-group design show the testing effect?

8. What is the double-blind experiment and why is it used?

9. Do field or laboratory experiments have greater internal validity? External validity? Explain.

10. What is the difference between experimental and mundane realism?

NOTES

1. Cook and Campbell (1979:9–36, 91–94) argued for a modification of a more rigid positivist approach to causality for experimental research. They suggested a "critical-realist" approach, which shares some features of the critical approach outlined in Chapter 4.

2. For discussions of the history of the experiment, see Danziger (1988), Gillespie (1988), Hornstein (1988), O'Donnell (1985), and Scheibe (1988).

3. See Hornstein (1988:11).

4. For events after World War II, see Harris (1988) and Suls and Rosnow (1988). For a discussion of the increased use of deception, see Reynolds (1979:60).

5. For a discussion of control in experiments, see Cook and Campbell (1979:7–9) and Spector (1981:15–16).

6. The notation for research design is discussed in Cook and Campbell (1979:95–96), Dooley (1984:132–137), and Spector (1981:27–28).

7. For additional discussions of threats to internal validity, see Cook and Campbell (1979:51–68), Kercher (1992), Spector (1981:24–27), Smith and Glass (1987), and Suls and Rosnow (1988).

8. This example is borrowed from Mitchell and Jolley (1988:97).

9. Experimenter expectancy is discussed in Aronson and Carlsmith (1968:66–70), Dooley (1984:151–153), and Mitchell and Jolley (1988:327–329).

10. Also see Aronson and Carlsmith (1968:22–25).

11. For a discussion of external validity, see Cook and Campbell (1979:70–80).

12. The Hawthorne effect is described in Roethlisberger and Dickenson (1939), Franke and Kaul (1978), and Lang (1992). Also see the discussion in Cook and Campbell (1979:123–125) and Dooley (1984:155–156). Gillespie (1988, 1991) discussed the political context of the experiments and how it shaped them.

13. See Piliavin and associates (1969).

14. See Graham (1992).

Survey Research

> *Every method of data collection, including the survey, is only an approximation to knowledge. Each provides a different glimpse of reality, and all have limitations when used alone. Before undertaking a survey the researcher would do well to ask if this is the most appropriate and fruitful method for the problem at hand. The survey is highly valuable for studying some problems, such as public opinion, and worthless for others.*
>
> —Donald P. Warwick and Charles A. Lininger, *The Sample Survey*, pp. 5–6

Someone hands you a sheet of paper full of questions. The first reads: "I would like to learn your opinion of the Neuman research methods textbook. Would you say it is (a) well organized, (b) adequately organized, or (c) poorly organized?" You probably would not be shocked by this. It is a kind of survey, and most of us are accustomed to surveys by the time we reach adulthood.

The survey is the most widely used data-gathering technique in the social sciences and in related applied fields. In fact, people sometimes say, "Do a survey," to get information when they should be asking, "What is the most appropriate research design?" Despite the popularity of surveys, it is easy to conduct a survey that yields misleading or worthless results. Good surveys require thought and effort. "Surveys, like other scientific and technical tools, can be well made or poorly made and can be used in appropriate or inappropriate ways" (Bradburn and Sudman, 1988:37).

All surveys are based on the professional social research survey. In this chapter, you will learn the main ingredients of good survey research, as well as its limitations.

RESEARCH QUESTIONS APPROPRIATE FOR A SURVEY

Survey research developed within the positivist approach to social science.[1] As Robert Groves remarked, "Surveys produce information that is inherently statistical in nature. Surveys are quantitative beasts" (1996:389). The survey asks many people (called *respondents*) about their beliefs, opinions, characteristics, and past or present behavior.

Surveys are appropriate for research questions about self-reported beliefs or behaviors. Researchers usually ask about many things at one time in surveys, measure many variables (often with multiple indicators), and test several hypotheses in a single survey (see Box 10.1).

Scholars warn against using surveys to ask "why" questions (e.g., Why do you think crime occurs?).[2] "Why" questions are appropriate, however, if a researcher wants to discover a respondent's subjective understanding or informal theory (i.e., the respondent's own view of "why" he or she acts a certain way). Because few respondents are fully aware of the causal factors that shape their beliefs or behavior, such questions are not a substitute for the researcher developing a consistent causal theory of his or her own that builds on the existing scientific literature.

A HISTORY OF SURVEY RESEARCH

The modern survey can be traced back to ancient forms of the census.[3] A *census* includes information on characteristics of the entire population in a territory. It is based on what people tell officials or what officials observe. For example, the *Domesday Book* was a famous census of England conducted in 1085 to 1086 by William the Conqueror. Early censuses assessed the property available for taxation or the young men available for military service. With the development of representative democracy, offi-

---

BOX **10.1** **What Is Asked in a Survey**

Although the categories overlap, the following can be asked in a survey:

1. *Behavior.* How frequently do you brush your teeth? Did you vote in the last city election? When did you last visit a close relative?
2. *Attitudes/beliefs/opinions.* What kind of job do you think the mayor is doing? Do you think other people say many negative things about you when you are not there? What is the biggest problem facing the nation these days?
3. *Characteristics.* Are you married, never married, single, divorced, separated, or widowed? Do you belong to a union? What is your age?
4. *Expectations.* Do you plan to buy a new car in the next 12 months? How much schooling do you think your child will get? Do you think the population in this town will grow, shrink, or stay the same?
5. *Self-classification.* Do you consider yourself to be liberal, moderate, or conservative? Into which social class would you put your family? Would you say you are highly religious or not religious?
6. *Knowledge.* Who was elected mayor in the last election? About what percentage of the people in this city are nonwhite? Is it legal to own a personal copy of Karl Marx's *Communist Manifesto* in this country?

---

cials used the census to assign the number of elected representatives based on the population in a district.

The survey has a long and varied history. Its use for social research in the United States and Great Britain began with social reform movements and social service professions documenting the conditions of urban poverty. At first, surveys were overviews of an area based on questionnaires and other data. Scientific sampling and statistics were absent. For example, between 1851 and 1864, Henry Mayhew published the 4-volume *London Labour and the London Poor,* based on conversations with street people and observations of daily life. Charles Booth's 17-volume (1889–1902) *Labour and Life of the People of London* and B. Seebohm Rowntree's *Poverty: A Study of Town Life* (1906) also examined the extent of urban poverty.

Similar work appeared in the United States in *Hull House Maps and Papers of 1895* and in W. E. B. DuBois's *Philadelphia Negro* (1899).

The *social survey* grew into both the modern quantitative survey research and qualitative field research in a community. From the 1890s to the 1930s, it was the major method of social research practiced by the Social Survey Movement in Canada, Great Britain, and the United States. The Social Survey Movement used systematic empirical inquiry to support sociopolitical reform goals. Today, the social survey would be called an action-oriented community survey. By the mid-1940s, the modern quantitative survey had largely displaced it.

Early social surveys were detailed empirical studies of specific local areas based on many sources of quantitative and qualitative data. Most were exploratory and descriptive. Researchers wanted to inform the public of the problems of industrialism and provide information for democratic decision making. Some leaders of the early social survey—Florence Kelly and Jane Addams of the Hull House and settlement movement, and African American W. E. B. DuBois—were unable to secure regular work in universities because of race and gender discrimination. Social surveys provide impressive pictures of daily community life. For example, the six-volume *Pittsburgh Survey* published in 1914 was based on face-to-face interviews; existing statistical data on health, crime, and industrial injury; and direct observations.

Four forces reshaped the social survey into modern quantitative survey research. First, researchers applied statistically based sampling techniques and precise measurement to the survey, especially after the *Literary Digest* debacle (discussed in Chapter 8). Second, researchers created scales and indexes to gather systematic quantitative data on attitudes, opinions, and subjective aspects of social life. Third, many others adapted the survey to applied areas. Market research emerged as a distinct field and adapted surveys to study consumer behavior. Journalists used surveys to measure public opinion and the impact of the radio. Religious organizations and charities used surveys to identify areas of need. Government agencies used surveys to improve services for agricultural and social programs. Also, more social scientists used the survey for basic research.

Fourth, empirical social research was reoriented away from nonacademics using a mixture of methods to focus on local social problems, and toward respectable, "scientific" methods modeled after the natural sciences. Social research became more professional, objective, and nonpolitical. This reorientation was stimulated by (1) a competition among researchers and universities for status, prestige, and funds; (2) researchers turning away from social reform ideals after the end of the Progressive Era (1895–1915) in U.S. politics; and (3) a program of major private foundations (Carnegie, Rockefeller, and Sage) to fund the expansion of quantitative, positivist social research.[4]

Survey research expanded during World War II, especially in the United States. Academic social researchers and practitioners from industry converged in Washington, DC, to work in the war effort. Survey researchers studied morale, consumer demand, production capacity, enemy propaganda, and the effectiveness of bombing. The wartime cooperation helped academic researchers and applied practitioners learn from each other and gain experience in conducting many large-scale surveys. Academic researchers helped practitioners appreciate precise measurement, sampling, and statistical analysis, while practitioners helped academics learn the practical side of organizing and conducting large-scale surveys.

After World War II, officials dismantled the extensive government survey research establishment. This was, in part, a cost-cutting move. Also, some members of the U.S. Congress feared that others might use survey results to advance social policies that they opposed, such as helping the unemployed or promoting equal rights for African Americans who lived in racially segregated southern states.

Many researchers returned to universities and created new social research organizations. At first, the universities were hesitant to embrace survey research. Survey research was expensive and involved many people. In addition, traditional social researchers were wary of quantitative research and skeptical of a technique used in private industry. The culture of applied researchers and business-oriented poll takers clashed with that of traditional basic researchers who lacked statistical training. Yet, surveys grew in use. This growth was not limited to the United States. Within three years of the end of World War II, national survey research institutes had been established in France, Norway, Germany, Italy, the Netherlands, Czechoslovakia, and Britain.[5]

Despite initial uncertainty, survey research grew through the 1970s. For example, about 18 percent of articles published in sociology journals used the survey method in 1939–1940; this rose to 55 percent by 1964–1965. A dramatic expansion of higher education and of the social science during the 1960s also spurred the growth of survey research. More people learned about survey research, and the method gained in popularity. Five factors contributed to the postwar growth of survey research[6] (see Box 10.2).

Today, quantitative survey research is a major industry. The professional survey industry probably employs over 60,000 people in the United States alone. Most of these are part-time workers, assistants, or semiprofessionals. About 6,000 full-time professional survey researchers design and analyze surveys.[9]

Researchers in many fields (communication, education, economics, political science, social psychology, and sociology) conduct and analyze surveys. Many U.S. universities have centers for survey research. Major centers include the Survey Research Center at the University of California at Berkeley, the National Opinion Research Center (NORC) at the University of Chicago, and the Institute for Social Research (ISR) at the University of Michigan.

Several applied areas rely heavily on the survey: government, marketing, private policy research, and mass media. Governments around the world at the national and local levels regularly conduct surveys to inform policy decisions. Private-sector survey research can be divided into three types of organizations: opinion polling organizations (e.g., Gallup, Harris, Roper, Yankelovich and Associates, etc.), marketing firms (e.g., Nielsen, Market Facts, Market Research Corporation, etc.), and nonprofit research organizations (e.g., Mathematica Policy Research, Rand Corporation, etc.).[10]

BOX **10.2** **Factors Contributing to Post-1950 Growth in Survey Research**

1. *Computers.* Computer technology that became available to social scientists by the 1960s made the sophisticated statistical analysis of large-scale survey data sets feasible for the first time. Today, the computer is an indispensable tool for analyzing data from most surveys.

2. *Organizations.* New social research centers with an expertise and interest in quantitative research were established at universities. About 50 such centers were created in the years after 1960.

3. *Data storage.* By the 1970s, data archives were created to store and permit the sharing of the large-scale survey data for secondary analysis (discussed in Chapter 11). The collection, storage, and sharing of information on hundreds of variables for thousands of respondents expanded the use of surveys.

4. *Funding.* For about a decade (late 1960s to late 1970s), the U.S. federal government expanded funds for social science research. Total federal spending for research and development in the social sciences increased nearly tenfold from 1960 to the mid-1970s before it declined in the 1980s.

5. *Methodology.* By the 1970s, substantial research was being conducted on ways to improve the validity of surveys. The survey technique advanced as errors were identified and corrected.[7] In addition, researchers created improved statistics for analyzing quantitative data and taught them to a new generation of researchers. Since the 1980s, new cognitive psychology theories have been applied to survey research.[8]

Major television and newspaper organizations regularly conduct surveys. In addition, there are many ad hoc or in-house surveys. Businesses, schools, and other organizations conduct small-scale surveys of employees, clients, students, and the like to address specific applied questions.

Survey researchers have formed professional organizations. The American Association for Public Opinion Research, founded in 1947, sponsors a scholarly journal devoted to survey research called *Public Opinion Quarterly.* The Council of American Survey Research Organization is an organization for commercial polling firms. There is also an international survey research organization—the World Association of Public Opinion Research.[11]

Modern survey research techniques have been used for 75 years and there are many "how to" sources on survey research, but during the past decade researchers have developed theories and conducted studies on the survey process itself. They have become sophisticated about modeling the communication-interaction process of survey interviews, pinpointing the effectiveness of visual and other clues in questionnaire design, recognizing the impact of question wording or ordering, adjusting to social desirability or threatening question issues (discussed later), incorporating computer-related technologies, and theorizing the reasons for respondent cooperation or refusals (see Schaeffer and Presser, 2003; Tourangeau, 2004a for overviews).

THE LOGIC OF SURVEY RESEARCH

What Is a Survey?

In experiments, researchers place people in small groups, test one or two hypotheses with a few variables, control the timing of the treatment, note associations between the treatment and the dependent variable, and control for alternative explanations. By contrast, survey researchers sample many respondents who answer the same questions, measure many variables, test multiple hypotheses, and infer temporal order from questions about past behavior, experiences, or characteristics. For example, years of schooling or a respondent's race are prior to current attitudes. An association among variables is measured with statistical techniques. They think of alternative explanations when planning a survey, measure variables that represent alternative explanations (i.e., control variables), then statistically examine their effects to rule out alternative explanations.

Survey research is often called *correlational*. Survey researchers use control variables to approximate the rigorous test for causality that experimenters achieve with their physical control over temporal order and alternative explanations.

Steps in Conducting a Survey

The survey researcher begins with a theoretical or applied research problem and ends with empirical measurement and data analysis. The basic steps in a survey research project can be divided into the steps outlined in Figure 10.1.

In the first phase, the researcher develops an instrument—a survey questionnaire or interview schedule. Respondents read the questions themselves and mark answers on a *questionnaire*. An *interview schedule* is a set of questions read to the respondent by an interviewer, who also records responses. To simplify the discussion, I will use only the term *questionnaires*.

A survey researcher conceptualizes and operationalizes variables as questions. He or she writes and rewrites questions for clarity and completeness, and organizes questions on the questionnaire based on the research question, the respondents, and the type of survey. (The types of surveys are discussed later.)

When preparing a questionnaire, the researcher thinks ahead to how he or she will record and organize data for analysis. He or she pilot tests the questionnaire with a small set of respondents similar to those in the final survey. If interviewers are used, the researcher trains them with the questionnaire. He or she asks respondents in the pilot test whether the questions were clear and explores their interpretations to see whether his or her intended meaning was clear.[12] The researcher also draws the sample during this phase.

After the planning phase, the researcher is ready to collect data. This phase is usually shorter than the planning phase. He or she locates sampled respondents in person, by telephone, or by mail. Respondents are given information and instructions on completing the questionnaire or interview. The questions follow, and there is a simple stimulus/response or question/answer pattern. The researcher accurately records answers or responses immediately after they are given. After all respondents complete the questionnaire and are thanked, he or she organizes the data and prepares them for statistical analysis.

Survey research can be complex and expensive and it can involve coordinating many people and steps. The administration of survey research re-

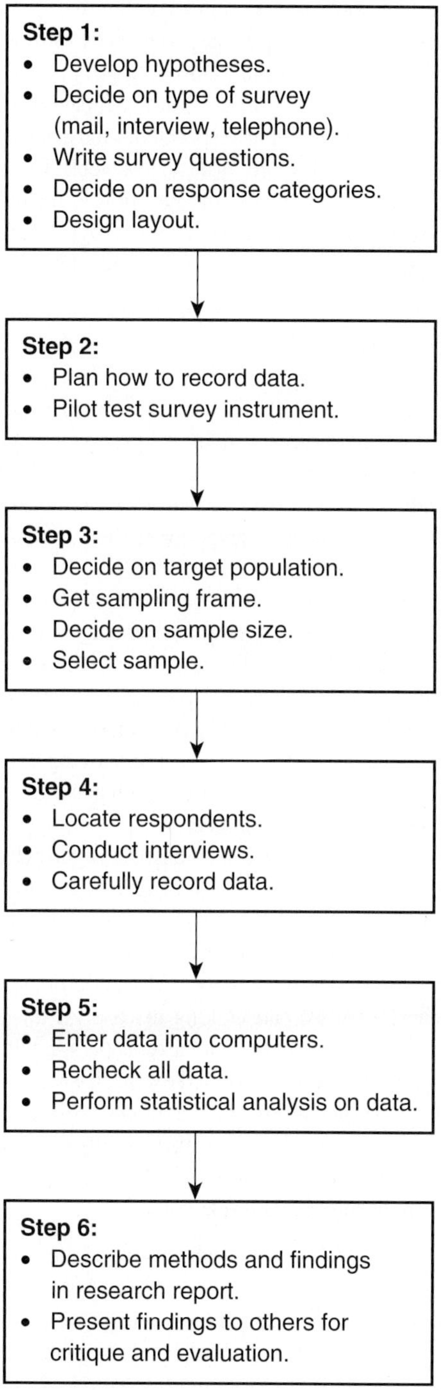

Step 1:
- Develop hypotheses.
- Decide on type of survey (mail, interview, telephone).
- Write survey questions.
- Decide on response categories.
- Design layout.

↓

Step 2:
- Plan how to record data.
- Pilot test survey instrument.

↓

Step 3:
- Decide on target population.
- Get sampling frame.
- Decide on sample size.
- Select sample.

↓

Step 4:
- Locate respondents.
- Conduct interviews.
- Carefully record data.

↓

Step 5:
- Enter data into computers.
- Recheck all data.
- Perform statistical analysis on data.

↓

Step 6:
- Describe methods and findings in research report.
- Present findings to others for critique and evaluation.

FIGURE 10.1   Steps in the Process of Survey Research

quires organization and accurate record keeping.[13] The researcher keeps track of each respondent, questionnaire, and interviewer. For example, each sampled respondent receives an identification number, which also appears on the questionnaire. Next, the researcher reviews responses on individual questionnaires, stores original questionnaires, and transfers information from questionnaires to a format for statistical analysis. Meticulous bookkeeping and labeling are essential. Otherwise, the researcher may find that valuable data and effort are lost through sloppiness.

CONSTRUCTING THE QUESTIONNAIRE

Principles of Good Question Writing

A good questionnaire forms an integrated whole. The researcher weaves questions together so they flow smoothly. He or she includes introductory remarks and instructions for clarification and measures each variable with one or more survey questions.

Two key principles for good survey questions are: Avoid confusion and keep the respondent's perspective in mind. Good survey questions both give the researcher valid and reliable measures, and help respondents feel that they understand the question and that their answers are meaningful. Questions that do not mesh with a respondent's viewpoint or that respondents find confusing are not good measures. A survey researcher exercises extra care if the respondents are heterogeneous or come from different life situations than his or her own.

Researchers want each respondent to hear exactly the same question, but will the questions be equally clear, relevant, and meaningful to all respondents? If respondents have diverse backgrounds and frames of reference, the same wording may not have the same meaning. Yet, tailoring question wording to each respondent makes comparisons almost impossible. A researcher would not know whether the wording of the question or differences in respondents accounted for different answers.

Question writing is more of an art than a science. It takes skill, practice, patience, and creativity. The principles of question writing are illustrated in the 10 things to avoid when writing survey questions. The list does not include every possible error, only the more frequent problems.[14]

1. *Avoid jargon, slang, and abbreviations.* Jargon and technical terms come in many forms. Plumbers talk about *snakes,* lawyers about a contract of *uberrima fides,* psychologists about the *Oedipus complex.* Slang is a kind of jargon within a subculture. For example, the homeless talk about a *snowbird* and skiers about a *hotdog.* Also avoid abbreviations. *NATO* usually means North Atlantic Treaty Organization, but for a respondent, it might mean something else (National Auto Tourist Organization, Native Alaskan Trade Orbit, or North African Tea Office). Avoid slang and jargon unless a specialized population is being surveyed. Target the vocabulary and grammar to the respondents sampled. For the general public, this is the language used on television or in the newspaper (about an eighth-grade reading vocabulary). Survey researchers learned that respondents may not understand some basic terminology. For example, one-fourth of respondents who had less than a high school degree (about 20 percent of the U.S. population) have difficulty understanding the meaning of sexual terms such as *vaginal intercourse* (Binson and Catania, 1998).

2. *Avoid ambiguity, confusion, and vagueness.* Ambiguity and vagueness plague most question writers. A researcher might make implicit assumptions without thinking of the respondents. For example, the question, "What is your income?" could mean weekly, monthly, or annual; family or personal; before taxes or after taxes; for this year or last year; from salary or from all sources. The confusion causes inconsistencies in how different respondents assign meaning to and answer the question. The researcher who wants before-tax annual family income for last year explicitly asks for it.[15]

Another source of ambiguity is the use of indefinite words or response categories. For example, an answer to the question, "Do you jog regularly? Yes _____ No _____ ," hinges on the meaning of the word *regularly.* Some respondents may define *regularly* as every day, others as once a week. To reduce respondent confusion and get more information, be specific—ask whether a person jogs "about once a day," "a few times a week," "once a week," and so on. (See Box 10.3 on improving questions.)

3. *Avoid emotional language and prestige bias.* Words have implicit connotative as well as explicit denotative meanings. Likewise, titles or positions in society (e.g., president, expert, etc.) carry prestige or status. Words with strong emotional connotations and stands on issues linked to people with high social status can color how respondents hear and answer survey questions.

Use neutral language. Avoid words with emotional "baggage" because respondents may react to the emotionally laden words rather than to the issue. For example, the question, "What do you think about a policy to pay murderous terrorists who threaten to steal the freedoms of peace-loving people?" is full of emotional words—such as *murderous, freedoms, steal,* and *peace.*

Also avoid **prestige bias**—associating a statement with a prestigious person or group. Respondents may answer on the basis of their feelings toward the person or group rather than addressing the issue. For example, saying, "Most doctors say that cigarette smoke causes lung disease for those near a smoker. Do you agree?" affects people who want to agree with doctors. Likewise, a question such as, "Do you support the president's policy regarding Uzbekistan?" will be answered by respondents who have never heard of Uzbekistan on the basis of their view of the president.

4. *Avoid double-barreled questions.* Make each question about one and only one topic. A **double-barreled question** consists of two or more questions joined together. It makes a respondent's answer ambiguous. For example, if asked, "Does this company have pension and health insurance benefits?" a respondent at a company with health insurance benefits only might answer either yes or

BOX **10.3** Improving Unclear Questions

Here are three survey questions written by experienced professional researchers. They revised the original wording after a pilot test revealed that 15 percent of respondents asked for clarification or gave inadequate answers (e.g., don't know). As you can see, question wording is an art that may improve with practice, patience, and pilot testing.

ORIGINAL QUESTION	PROBLEM	REVISED QUESTION
Do you exercise or play sports regularly?	What counts as exercise?	Do you do any sports or hobbies, physical activities, or exercise, including walking, on a regular basis?
What is the average number of days each week you have butter?	Does margarine count as butter?	The next question is just about butter—not including margarine. How many days a week do you have butter?
[Following question on eggs] What is the number of servings in a typical day?	How many eggs is a serving? What is a typical day?	On days when you eat eggs, how many eggs do you usually have?

	RESPONSES TO QUESTION		PERCENTAGE ASKING FOR CLARIFICATION	
	Original	*Revision*	*Original*	*Revision*
Exercise question (% saying "yes")	48%	60%	5%	0%
Butter question (% saying "none")	33%	55%	18%	13%
Egg question (% saying "one")	80%	33%	33%	0%

Source: Adapted from Fowler (1992).

no. The response has an ambiguous meaning, and the researcher cannot be certain of the respondent's intention. A researcher who wants to ask about the joint occurrence of two things—for example, a company with both health insurance and pension benefits—should ask two separate questions.

5. *Avoid leading questions.* Make respondents feel that all responses are legitimate. Do not let them become aware of an answer that the researcher wants. A *leading* (or *loaded*) *question* is one that leads the respondent to choose one response over another by its wording. There are many kinds of leading questions. For example, the question, "You don't smoke, do you?" leads respondents to state that they do not smoke.

Loaded questions can be stated to get either positive or negative answers. For example, "Should the mayor spend even more tax money trying to keep the streets in top shape?" leads respondents to disagree, whereas "Should the mayor fix the potholed and dangerous streets in our city?" is loaded for agreement.

6. *Avoid asking questions that are beyond respondents' capabilities.* Asking something that few respondents know frustrates respondents and produces poor-quality responses. Respondents cannot always recall past details and may not know specific factual information. For example, asking an adult, "How did you feel about your brother when you were 6 years old?" is probably worthless. Asking respondents to make a choice about something they know nothing about (e.g., a technical issue in foreign affairs or an internal policy of an organization) may result in an answer, but one that is unreliable and meaningless.

"Next question: I believe that life is a constant striving for balance, requiring frequent tradeoffs between morality and necessity, within a cyclic pattern of joy and sadness, forging a trail of bittersweet memories until one slips, inevitably, into the jaws of death. Agree or disagree?"

When many respondents are unlikely to know about an issue, use a full-filter question form (to be discussed).

Phrase questions in the terms in which respondents think. For example, few respondents will be able to answer, "How many gallons of gasoline did you buy last year for your car?" Yet, respondents may be able to answer a question about gasoline purchases for a typical week, which the researcher can multiply by 52 to estimate annual purchases.[16]

Being very clear in asking questions reduces respondent errors. Clear questions have built-in clues and make contrasts explicit. For example, instead of asking, "Do you pay money to the children of your past marriage?" It would be better to ask, "Do you pay child support?" For those answering yes, follow-up questions could be, "Did you pay alimony in addition to child support?" and "Did you have any other financial obligations, such as paying health insurance, tuition, or contributing to the mortgage or rent payments?" (Dykema and Schaeffer, 2000).

7. *Avoid false premises.* Do not begin a question with a premise with which respondents may not agree, then ask about choices regarding it. Respondents who disagree with the premise will be frustrated and not know how to answer. For example, the question, "The post office is open too many hours. Do you want it to open four hours later or close four hours earlier each day?" leaves those who either oppose the premise or oppose both alternatives without a meaningful choice.

A better question explicitly asks the respondent to assume a premise is true, then asks for a preference. For example, "Assuming the post office has to cut back its operating hours, which would you find more convenient, opening four hours later or closing four hours earlier each day?" Answers to a hypothetical situation are not very reliable, but being explicit will reduce frustration.

8. *Avoid asking about distant future intentions.* Avoid asking people about what they might do under hypothetical circumstances. Questions such as "Suppose a new grocery store opened down the road. Would you shop at it?" are usually a waste of time. It is better to ask about current or recent attitudes and behavior. In general, respondents answer specific, concrete questions that relate to their experiences more reliably than they do those about abstractions that are beyond their immediate experiences.

9. *Avoid double negatives.* Double negatives in ordinary language are grammatically incorrect and confusing. For example, "I ain't got no job" logically means that the respondent does have a job, but the second negative is used in this way for emphasis. Such blatant errors are rare, but more subtle forms of the double negative are also confusing. They arise when respondents are asked to agree or disagree with a statement. For example, respondents who *dis*agree with the statement, "Students should not be required to take a comprehensive exam to graduate" are logically stating a double negative because they *disagree* with *not* doing something.

10. *Avoid overlapping or unbalanced response categories.* Make response categories or choices mutually exclusive, exhaustive, and balanced (mutually exclusive and exhaustive attributes were discussed in Chapter 7). *Mutually exclusive* means that response categories do not overlap. Overlapping categories that are numerical ranges (e.g., 5–10, 10–20, 20–30) can be easily corrected (e.g., 5–9, 10–19, 20–29). The ambiguous verbal choice is another type of overlapping response category—for example, "Are you satisfied with your job or are there things you don't like about it?" *Exhaustive* means that every respondent has a choice—a place to go. For example, asking respondents, "Are you working or unemployed?" leaves out respondents who are not working but do not consider themselves unemployed (e.g., full-time homemakers, people on vacation, students, people with disabilities, retired people, etc.). A researcher first thinks about what he or she wants to measure and then considers the circumstances of respondents. For example, when asking about a respondent's employment, does the researcher want information on the primary job or on all jobs? On full-time work only or both full- and part-time work? On jobs for pay only or on unpaid or volunteer jobs as well?

Keep response categories *balanced.* A case of unbalanced choices is the question, "What kind of job is the mayor doing: outstanding, excellent, very good, or satisfactory?" Another type of unbalanced question omits information—for example, "Which of the five candidates running for mayor do you favor: Eugene Oswego or one of the others?"

Researchers can balance responses by offering bipolar opposites. It is easy to see that the terms *honesty* and *dishonesty* have different meanings and connotations. Asking respondents to rate whether a mayor is highly, somewhat, or not very *honest* is not the same as asking them to rate the mayor's level of *dishonesty*. Unless there is a specific purpose for doing otherwise, it is better to offer respondents equal polar opposites at each end of a continuum.[17] For example, "Do you think the mayor is: very honest, somewhat honest, neither honest nor dishonest, somewhat dishonest, or very dishonest?" (see Table 10.1).

Aiding Respondent Recall

Survey researchers have studied the ability of respondents to recall past behavior and events accurately when answering survey questions.[18] Recalling events accurately takes more time and effort than the seconds that respondents have to answer survey questions. Also, one's ability to recall accurately declines over time. Studies in hospitalization and crime victimization show that although most respondents can recall significant events that occurred in the past several weeks, half are inaccurate a year later.

Survey researchers recognize that memory is less trustworthy than once assumed. It is affected by many factors—the topic (threatening or socially desirable), events occurring simultaneously and subsequently, the significance of an event for a person, situational conditions (question wording and interview style), and the respondent's need to have internal consistency.

The complexity of respondent recall does not mean that survey researchers cannot ask about past events; rather, they need to customize questions and interpret results cautiously. Researchers should provide respondents with special instructions and extra thinking time. They should also provide aids to respondent recall, such as a fixed time frame or location references. Rather than ask, "How often did you attend a sporting event last winter?" they should say, "I want to know how many sporting events you attended last winter. Let's go month by month. Think back to December. Did you attend any sporting events for which you paid admission in December? Now, think back to January. Did you attend any sporting events in January?"

Mooney and Gramling (1991) asked students two types of questions about drinking behavior and found that standard questions, such as "On the average, how many days a month have you had something to drink (wine, beer, liquor)?" and "On the average, how many drinks do you have each of these times?" yielded much lower results than asking the same question about 12 locations (e.g., bar, relative's home, fraternity/sorority house, etc.) and summing the total. Such aided recall reduces omissions

TABLE 10.1   Summary of Survey Question Writing Pitfalls

THINGS TO AVOID	NOT GOOD	A POSSIBLE IMPROVEMENT
Jargon, slang, abbreviations	Did you drown in brew until you were totally blasted last night?	Last night, about how much beer did you drink?
Vagueness	Do you eat out often?	In a typical week, about how many meals do you eat away from home, at a restaurant, cafeteria, or other eating establishment?
Emotional language and prestige bias	"The respected Grace Commission documents that a staggering $350 BILLION of our tax dollars are being completely wasted through poor procurement practices, bad management, slopping bookkeeping, 'defective' contract management, personnel abuses and other wasteful practices. Is cutting pork barrel spending and eliminating government waste a top priority for you?"*	How important is it to you that Congress adopt measures to reduce government waste? Very Important Somewhat Important Neither Important or Unimportant Somewhat Unimportant Not Important at All
Double-barreled questions	Do you support or oppose raising social security benefits and increased spending for the military?	Do you support or oppose raising social security benefits? Do you support or oppose increasing spending on the military?
Leading questions	Did you do your patriotic duty and vote in the last election for mayor?	Did you vote in last month's mayoral election?
Issues beyond respondent capabilities	Two years ago, how many hours did you watch TV every month?	In the past two weeks, about how many hours do you think you watched TV on a typical day?
False premises	When did you stop beating your girl-/boyfriend?	Have you ever slapped, punched, or hit your girl/boyfriend?
Distant future intentions	After you graduate from college, get a job, and are settled, will you invest a lot of money in the stock market?	Do you have definite plans to put some money into the stock market within the coming two months?
Double negatives	Do you disagree with those who do not want to build a new city swimming pool?	There is a proposal to build a new city swimming pool. Do you agree or disagree with the proposal?
Unbalanced responses	Did you find the service at our hotel to be: Outstanding, Excellent, Superior, or Good?	Please rate the service at our hotel: Outstanding, Very Good, Adequate, or Poor.

*Actual question taken from a mail questionnaire that was sent to me in May 1998 by the National Republican Congressional Committee. It is also a double-barreled question.

and enhances accuracy, but it does not produce over-estimating.

Respondents often compress time when asked about past events, or use **telescoping.** They recall an event but earlier (backward telescope) or later (forward telescope) than it actually occurred. Three techniques reduce telescoping: (1) *Situational framing*—Ask the respondent to recall a specific situation and ask details about it ("Tell me what happened on the day you were married"); (2) *Decomposition*—Ask the respondent about specific events and then to add them up ("Last week did you buy anything from a vending machine? Now, for the week before that, did you buy any items?"); and (3) *Landmark anchoring*—Ask the respondent whether something occurred before or after a major event ("Did that occur before or after the major earthquake that happened here in June 2003?").

Getting Honest Answers

Questions on Sensitive Topics. Survey researchers sometimes ask about sensitive issues or issues that respondents may feel threaten their presentation of self, such as questions about sexual behavior, drug or alcohol use, mental health problems, or deviant behavior. Respondents may be reluctant to answer the questions or to answer completely and truthfully. Survey researchers who wish to ask such questions must do so with great care and must be extra cautious about the results[19] (see Table 10.2).

Threatening questions are part of a larger issue, ego protection. Respondents try to present a positive image of themselves to others. They may be ashamed, embarrassed, or afraid to give truthful answers, or find it emotionally painful to confront their own actions honestly, let alone admit them to other people. They underreport behavior or attitudes they wish to hide or believe to be in violation of social norms. Alternatively, they may overreport positive behaviors or generally accepted beliefs (social desirability bias is discussed later).

People are likely to underreport having an illness or disability (e.g., cancer, mental illness, venereal disease), engaging in illegal or deviant behavior (e.g., evading taxes, taking drugs, consuming alcohol, engaging in uncommon sexual practices), or revealing their financial status (e.g., income, savings, debts) (see Table 10.3).

Survey researchers use many techniques to increase honest answering to questions about sensitive topics. One technique is to establish a comfortable setting before asking the questions. They state guarantees of anonymity and confidentiality explicitly and emphasize the need for honest answers. They ask sensitive questions following a "warm-up period" of other nonthreatening questions and after creating an atmosphere of trust and comfort. A second technique is to use an "enhanced" phasing of questions. For example, rather than asking, "Have you shoplifted?"—which has an accusatory tone and uses the word *shoplift,* which implies committing an illegal act—instead get at the same behavior by asking, "Have you even taken anything from a store without paying for it?"

TABLE 10.2   Threatening Questions and Sensitive Issues

TOPIC	PERCENTAGE VERY UNEASY
Masturbation	56
Sexual intercourse	42
Use of marijuana or hashish	42
Use of stimulants and depressants	31
Getting drunk	29
Petting and kissing	20
Income	12
Gambling with friends	10
Drinking beer, wine, or liquor	10
Happiness and well-being	4
Education	3
Occupation	3
Social activities	2
General leisure	2
Sports activity	1

Source: Adapted from Bradburn and Sudman (1980:68).

Telescoping   When survey research respondents compress time when answering about past events, overreporting recent events, and underreporting distant past ones.

TABLE 10.3   Over- and Underreporting Behavior on Surveys

	PERCENTAGE DISTORTED OR ERRONEOUS ANSWERS		
	Face to Face	Phone	Self-Administered
Low Threat/Normative			
Registered to vote	+15	+17	+12
Voted in primary	+39	+31	+36
Have own library card	+19	+21	+18
High Threat			
Bankruptcy	− 32	− 29	− 32
Drunk driving	− 47	− 46	− 54

Source: Adapted from Bradburn and Sudman (1980:8).

Researchers also try to reduce threat and make it easier for respondents to answer honestly about sensitive topics by providing contextual background information. In one study, researchers asked heterosexual males the following enhanced question, "In past surveys, many men have reported that at some point in their lives they have had some type of sexual experience with another male. This could have happened before adolescence, during adolescence, or as an adult. Have you ever had a sexual experience with another male at some point in your life?" While 3.5 percent of men had answered "yes" to a standard form of this question, 8.2 percent answered "yes" when asked in an enhanced form. The authors also found that enhanced questions lowered the age that young women reported their first sexual relationship, but raised it for men (see Catania et al., 1996). Another technique to improve honest answers is to create a context by first asking about more serious actions. For example, a respondent may hesitate to answer a question about shoplifting, but it appears to be less threatening if it comes after a series of questions about more serious crimes (e.g., armed robbery, burglary).

The questioning format affects how respondents answer questions. Studies show that survey formats

> **Randomized response technique (RRT)**   A specialized technique in survey research that is used for very sensitive topics. With it a respondent randomly receives a question without the interviewer being aware of the question the respondent is answering.

that permit greater respondent anonymity, such as a self-administered questionnaire or web-based survey, increase the likelihood of honest responses over formats that involve interacting with another person, such as in a face-to-face or telephone interview.[20]

Technological innovations such as computer-assisted self-administered interviews (CASAI) and computer-assisted personal interviewing (CAPI) also increase respondent comfort and honesty in answering questions on sensitive topics. In CASAI, respondents are "interviewed" with questions asked on a computer screen or over earphones. They answer by moving a computer mouse or typing on a keyboard. Even when an interviewer or others are present, the respondent is semi-insulated from human contact and interacts with an automated system. In CAPI, an interviewer sets up a laptop computer and is available for questions, but respondents hear questions over earphones and read them on a screen and enter their own answers. Respondents do not appear to feel their privacy is reduced if others are present while they complete computer-based interviews.[21]

A complicated invention for asking threatening questions in face-to-face interview situations is the **randomized response technique (RRT)**. The technique uses statistics beyond the level of this book, but the basic idea is to use known probabilities to estimate unknown proportions. Here is how RRT works. An interviewer gives the respondent two questions: One is threatening (e.g., "Do you use heroin?"), the other not threatening (e.g., "Were you born in September?"). A random method (e.g., toss of coin) is used to select the question to answer. The interviewer does not see which question was chosen but records the respondent's answer. The researcher uses knowledge about the probability of the random outcome and the frequency of the nonthreatening behavior to estimate the frequency of the sensitive behavior.

Social Desirability Bias. In addition to getting honest answers to questions on sensitive topics and not having respondents understate an attitude or behavior, survey resarchers also want to reduce the chances that respondents overstate an attitude or behavior, called **social desirability bias.**

Social desirability bias occurs when respondents distort answers to make their reports conform to social norms. As Wentworth (1993:180) noted, "False claim exaggerations of socially desirable behavior occur more frequently than untruthful denials, false classes or minimizations, or exaggerations of socially undesirable behavior." People tend to overreport being cultured (i.e., reading, attending high-culture events), giving money to charity, having a good marriage, loving their children, and so forth. For example, one study found that 34 percent of people who reported in a survey that they gave money to a local charity, really did not.[22] Because a norm says that one should vote in elections, many report voting when they did not. In the United States, those under the greatest pressure to vote (i.e., highly educated, politically partisan, highly religious people who had been contacted by an organization that urged them to vote) are the people most likely to overreport voting. This patterned misrepresentation of voting "substantially distorts" studies of voting that rely on self-reported survey data (Bernstein et al., 2001:41).

Questionnaire writers try to reduce social desirability bias by phrasing questions in ways that make norm violation appear less objectionable or give respondents "face-saving" alternatives. For example, Belli and colleagues (1999) reduced overreports of voting and permitted respondents to "save face." Their question on voting included statements such as "A lot of people were not able to vote because they were not registered, were sick, or just didn't have time." They offered four response choices: "I did not vote in the November 5 election,

I thought about voting but did not vote, I usually vote but did not vote this time, I am sure I voted on November 5." Only the last response choice is a clear, unambiguous indication that the person voted.

Knowledge Questions. Studies suggest that a large majority of the public cannot correctly answer elementary geography questions or identify important political documents (e.g., the Declaration of Independence). Researchers sometimes want to find out whether respondents know about an issue or topics, but knowledge questions can be threatening because respondents do not want to appear ignorant.[23]

Surveys may measure opinions better if they first ask about factual information, because many people have inaccurate factual knowledge. For example, Nadeau and colleagues (1993) found that most Americans seriously overestimate the percent of racial minorities in the population. Only 15 percent of U.S. adults accurately report (plus or minus 6 percent) that 12.1 percent of the U.S. population is African American. Over half believe it is above 30 percent. Similarly, Jews make up about 3 percent of the U.S. population, but a majority (60 percent) of Americans believe the proportion to be 10 percent. A follow-up study by Sigelman and Niemi (2001:93) found that "African Americans themselves overestimate the black population by at least as much." Nearly twice as many African Americans as Whites, about 30 percent of Blacks, thought that African Americans were one-half of the U.S. population.

Simple knowledge questions, such as the number of people living in a household, are not always answered accurately. In some households, a marginal person—the boyfriend who left for a week, the adult daughter who left after an argument about her pregnancy, or the uncle who walked out after a dispute over money—may be reported as not living in a household, but he or she may not have another permanent residence and consider himself or herself to live there.[24]

For example, many Americans oppose foreign aid spending based on high overestimates of the

Social desirabilty bias   A bias in survey research in which respondents give a "normative" response or a socially acceptable answer rather than a honest answer.

amount spent on the programs. When asked openly what they would prefer to spend on foreign aid, most report an amount much higher than the government now spends.

In another example, 65 percent of Americans said that covering college costs for their children is a major concern, but most estimated the tuition at public universities to be double its true amount.[25] They also overestimated tuition for private colleges and vastly underestimated the availability of financial aid. Survey questions about the public's knowledge can reveal serious distortions, but researchers have to phrase them carefully.

First, a researcher pilot tests questions so that questions are at an appropriate level of difficulty. Little is gained if 99 percent of respondents cannot answer the question. Word questions so that respondents feel comfortable saying they do not know the answer—for example, "How much, if anything, have you heard about . . . ."

One way to check whether respondents are overstating their knowledge is to use a **sleeper question**—a question or response choice about which a respondent could not possibly know. For example, in a study to determine which U.S. civil rights leaders respondents recognized, the name of a fictitious person was added. The person was "recognized" by 15 percent of the respondents. This implies that actual leaders who were recognized by only 15 percent were probably actually unknown. Another method is to ask respondents to "tell me about the person" after they say they recognize a name in a list.

Contingency Questions. Some questions apply only to specific respondents and researchers avoid asking questions that are irrelevant for a re-

---

Sleeper question Survey research questions about nonexistent people or events to check whether respondents are being truthful.

Contingency question A two-part survey question in which a respondent's answer to a first question directs him or her either to the next questionnaire item or to a more specific and related second question.

Open-ended question A type of survey research question in which respondents are free to offer any answer they wish to the question.

BOX **10.4** **Example of a Contingency Question**

QUESTION VERSION 1 (NOT CONTINGENCY QUESTION)
In the past year, how often have you used a seat belt when you have ridden in the backseat of a car?

QUESTION VERSION 2 (CONTINGENCY QUESTION)
In the past, have you ridden in the backseat of a car?

  No [Skip to next question]

  Yes → When you rode in the backseat, how often do you use a seat belt?

Results:	Always use	Never use
Version 1:	30%	24%
Version 2:	42%	4%

During pilot testing, researchers learned that many respondents who answered "never" to Version 1 did not ride in the backseat of a car. Version 1 created ambiguity, because respondents who never rode in the backseat plus those who rode there but did not use a seat belt both answered, "never." Version 2 using a contingency question format clarified the question.

Source: Adapted from Fowler, 2004:184–185.

---

spondent. A **contingency question** is a two- (or more) part question.[25] The answer to the first part of the question determines which of two different questions a respondent next receives. Contingency questions select respondents for whom a second question is relevant. Sometimes they are called *screen* or *skip questions*. On the basis of the answer to a first question, the respondent or an interviewer is instructed to go to another or to skip certain questions (see Box 10.4).

Open versus Closed Questions

There has been a long debate about open versus closed questions in survey research.[27] An **open-ended** (unstructured, free response) **question** asks a question (e.g., "What is your favorite television program?") to which respondents can give any an-

BOX **10.5** Closed versus Open Questions

ADVANTAGES OF CLOSED

- It is easier and quicker for respondents to answer.
- The answers of different respondents are easier to compare.
- Answers are easier to code and statistically analyze.
- The response choices can clarify question meaning for respondents.
- Respondents are more likely to answer about sensitive topics.
- There are fewer irrelevant or confused answers to questions.
- Less articulate or less literate respondents are not at a disadvantage.
- Replication is easier.

DISADVANTAGES OF CLOSED

- They can suggest ideas that the respondent would not otherwise have.
- Respondents with no opinion or no knowledge can answer anyway.
- Respondents can be frustrated because their desired answer is not a choice.
- It is confusing if many (e.g., 20) response choices are offered.
- Misinterpretation of a question can go unnoticed.
- Distinctions between respondent answers may be blurred.
- Clerical mistakes or marking the wrong response is possible.
- They force respondents to give simplistic responses to complex issues.
- They force people to make choices they would not make in the real world.

ADVANTAGES OF OPEN

- They permit an unlimited number of possible answers.
- Respondents can answer in detail and can qualify and clarify responses.
- Unanticipated findings can be discovered.
- They permit adequate answers to complex issues.
- They permit creativity, self-expression, and richness of detail.
- They reveal a respondent's logic, thinking process, and frame of reference.

DISADVANTAGES OF OPEN

- Different respondents give different degrees of detail in answers.
- Responses may be irrelevant or buried in useless detail.
- Comparisons and statistical analysis become very difficult.
- Coding responses is difficult.
- Articulate and highly literate respondents have an advantage.
- Questions may be too general for respondents who lose direction.
- Responses are written verbatim, which is difficult for interviewers.
- A greater amount of respondent time, thought, and effort is necessary.
- Respondents can be intimidated by questions.
- Answers take up a lot of space in the questionnaire.

swer. A **closed-ended** (structured, fixed response) **question** both asks a question and gives the respondent fixed responses from which to choose (e.g., "Is the president doing a very good, good, fair, or poor job, in your opinion?").

Each form has advantages and disadvantages (see Box 10.5). The crucial issue is not which form is best. Rather, it is under what conditions a form is most appropriate. A researcher's choice to use an open- or closed-ended question depends on the purpose and the practical limitations of a research

Closed-ended question   A type of survey research question in which respondents must choose from a fixed set of answers.

project. The demands of using open-ended questions, with interviewers writing verbatim answers followed by time-consuming coding, may make them impractical for a specific project.

Large-scale surveys have closed-ended questions because they are quicker and easier for both respondents and researchers. Yet something important may be lost when an individual's beliefs and feelings are forced into a few fixed categories that a researcher created. To learn how a respondent thinks, to discover what is really important to him or her, or to get an answer to a question with many possible answers (e.g., age), open questions may be best. In addition, sensitive topics (e.g., sexual behavior, liquor consumption) may be more accurately measured with closed questions.

The disadvantages of a question form can be reduced by mixing open-ended and closed-ended questions in a questionnaire. Mixing them also offers a change of pace and helps interviewers establish rapport. Periodic probes (i.e., follow-up questions by interviewers) with closed-ended questions can reveal a respondent's reasoning.

Having interviewers periodically use probes to ask about a respondent's thinking is a way to check whether respondents are understanding the questions as a researcher intended (probes are discussed later). However, probes are not substitutes for writing clear questions or creating a framework of understanding for the respondent. Unless carefully stated, probes might shape the respondent's answers or force answers when a respondent does not have an opinion or information. Yet, flexible or conversational interviewing in which interviewers can improve accuracy on questions about complex issues on which respondents do not clearly understand basic terms or about which they have difficulty expressing their thoughts. For example, to the question, "Did you do any work for money last week?" a respondent might hesitate then reply, "Yes." An interviewer probes, "Could you tell me exactly what

work you did?" The respondent may reply, "On Tuesday and Wednesday, I spent a couple of hours helping my buddy John move into his new apartment. For that he gave me $40, but I didn't have any other job or get paid for doing anything else." If the researcher's intention was only to get reports of regular employment, the probe revealed a misunderstanding. Researchers also use **partially open questions** (i.e., a set of fixed choices with a final open choice of "other"), which allows respondents to offer an answer that the researcher did not include.

A total reliance on closed questions can distort results. For example, a study compared open and closed versions of the question, "What is the major problem facing the nation?" Respondents ranked different problems as most important depending on the form of the question. As Schuman and Presser (1979:86) reported, "Almost all respondents work within the substantive framework of the priorities provided by the investigators, *whether or not it fits their own priorities*" (emphasis added). In another study, respondents were asked open and closed questions about what was important in a job. Half of the respondents who answered the open-ended version gave answers that were outside closed-question responses.

Open-ended questions are especially valuable in early or exploratory stages of research. For large-scale surveys, researchers use open questions in pilot tests, then develop closed-question responses from the answers given to the open questions.

Researchers writing closed questions have to make many decisions. How many response choices should be given? Should they offer a middle or neutral choice? What should be the order of responses? What types of response choices? How will the direction of a response be measured?

Answers to these questions are not easy. For example, two response choices are too few, but more than five response choices are rarely a benefit. Researchers want to measure meaningful distinctions and not collapse them. More specific responses yield more information, but too many specifics create confusion. For example, rephrasing the question, "Are you satisfied with your dentist?" (which has a yes/no answer) to "How satisfied are you with your dentist: very satisfied, somewhat sat-

Partially open question   A type of survey research question in which respondents are given a fixed set of answers to choose from, but in addition an "other" category is offered so that they can specify a different answer.

isfied, somewhat dissatisfied, or not satisfied at all?" gives the researcher more information and a respondent more choices.

Neutral Positions, Wild Guesses, and Selective Refusals.

The failure to get valid responses from each respondent can weaken a survey and can take three forms. The first type, mentioned earlier, occurs when a respondent gives inaccurate information (i.e., overstates as with the social desirability bias or understates or withholds information about sensitive topics). The second type is "false positive" error when a respondent selects an attitude position but has no knowledge about an issue and no opinion on it. A third type is "false negative" error in which a respondent refuses to answer some questions or withholds an answer when he or she has information or an opinion. The three types overlap: The first involves an inaccurate direction of a response toward a normative position; the second involves lacking information but substituting wild guesses for a serious response; and the last type is the partial and selective nonresponse to the survey.[28]

Neutral Positions.

Survey researchers debate whether they should offer respondents who lack knowledge or have no position a neutral position and a "no opinion" choice.[29]

One group of researchers argue against offering a neutral or middle position and the no opinion option, and instead favor putting pressure on respondents to give a response.[30] This perspective holds that respondents "satisfice"; that is, they pick no opinion or a neutral response to avoid the cognitive effort of answering. These researchers maintain that the least educated respondents are lazy and pick a no opinion option when they actually have one and that pressuring respondents for an answer does not lower data quality.

Others argue that it is usually best to offer a nonattitude choice, because people will express opinions on fictitious issues, objects, and events. By offering a nonattitude (middle or no opinion) choice, researchers identify those holding middle positions or those without opinions.

The issue of nonattitudes can be approached by distinguishing among three kinds of attitude questions: standard-format, quasi-filter, and full-filter questions (see Box 10.6). The **standard-format question** does not offer a "don't know" choice; a respondent must volunteer it. A **quasi-filter question** offers respondents a "don't know" alternative. A **full-filter question** is a special type of contingency question. It first asks whether respondents have an opinion, and then asks for the opinion of those who state that they do have an opinion.

Many respondents will answer a question if a "no opinion" choice is missing, but they will choose "don't know" when it is offered, or say that they do not have an opinion if asked. Such respondents are called **floaters** because they "float" from giving a response to not knowing. Their responses are affected by minor wording changes, so researchers screen them out using quasi-filter or full-filter questions. Filtered questions do not eliminate all answers to nonexistent issues, but they reduce the problem.

Middle alternative floaters choose a middle position when it is offered, or another alternative if it is not. They have less intense feelings about an issue. There is also a slight **recency effect;** that is, respondents are more likely to choose the last alternative offered. The recency effect suggests

---

Standard-format question   A type of survey research question in which the answer categories do not include a "no opinion" or "don't know" option.

Quasi-filter question   A survey research question that includes the answer choice "no opinion," "unsure," or "don't know."

Full-filter question   A survey research question in which respondents are first asked whether they have an opinion or know about a topic; then only those with an opinion or knowledge are asked a specific question about the topic.

Floaters   Survey research respondents without the knowledge or an opinion to answer a survey question but who answer it anyway, often giving inconsistent answers.

Recency effect   An effect in survey research that occurs when respondents choose the last answer response offered rather than seriously considering all answer choices.

BOX **10.6** Standard-Format, Quasi-Filter, and Full-Filter Questions

STANDARD FORMAT

Here is a question about another country. Do you agree or disagree with this statement? "The Russian leaders are basically trying to get along with America."

QUASI-FILTER

Here is a statement about another country: "The Russian leaders are basically trying to get along with America." Do you agree, disagree, or have no opinion on that?

FULL FILTER

Here is a statement about another country. Not everyone has an opinion on this. If you do not have an opinion, just say so. Here's the statement: "The Russian leaders are basically trying to get along with America." Do you have an opinion on that? No (go to next question), Yes (continue). Do you agree or disagree?

Example of Results from Different Question Forms

	Standard Form (%)	Quasi-Filter (%)	Full Filter (%)
Agree	48.2	27.7	22.9
Disagree	38.2	29.5	20.9
No opinion	13.6*	42.8	56.3

*Volunteered

Source: Adapted from Schuman and Presser (1981:116–125). Standard format is from Fall 1978; quasi- and full-filter are from February 1977.

that it is best to present responses on a continuum, with the middle or neutral position stated in the middle.

Researchers have two choices: offering a middle position for those who are truly ambiguous or moderate, or omitting the middle choice and forcing respondents to choose a position but following it immediately with a question asking how strongly they feel about the choice. This latter choice is preferred because attitudes have two aspects: direction (for or against) and intensity (strongly held or weakly held). For example, two respondents both oppose abortion, but one holds the opinion fiercely, with a strong commitment, whereas the other holds it weakly.

Selective Refusals. In addition to the issue of satisficing, by which respondents pick no response to avoid expending the effort of answering, some respondents may refuse to answer questions about a sensitive issue rather than indicate a socially inappropriate answer. For example, in 1992 over one-third of Americans refused to answer a sensitive question about racial integration. When many respondents fail to answer a question, it can create misleading findings if most of the nonresponding people hold the same opinion. For example, if the respondents who oppose racial integration instead answer don't know, the results will appear more favorable toward integration than if everyone had answered the question. After adjusting for this type of error, Berinsky (1999) found that the percentage of Americans who favored racial integration declined from 49.4 to 34.9 percent. He warned (p. 1225), "the opinions respondents express in the survey interview are not necessarily identical to the opinions they construct when coming to grips with a survey question."

Agree/Disagree, Rankings or Ratings? Survey researchers who measure values and attitudes have debated two issues about the responses offered.[31] Should a questionnaire item make a statement and ask respondents whether they agree or disagree with it, or should it offer respondents specific alternatives? Should the questionnaire include a set of items and ask respondents to rate them (e.g., approve, disapprove), or should it give them a list of items and force them to rank-order items (e.g., from most favored to least favored)?

It is best to offer respondents explicit alternatives. For example, instead of asking, "Do you agree or disagree with the statement, 'Men are better suited to . . . ,' " instead ask, "Do you think men are better suited, women are better suited, or both are equally suited?" Less well-educated respondents are more likely to agree with a statement, whereas forced-choice alternatives encourage thought and avoid the *response set* bias—a tendency of some respondents to agree and not really decide (discussed in Chapter 7).

Survey respondents asked about values tend to show little differentiation and to pile up responses along extremes. One solution is a "rank-then-rate" procedure. Researchers first ask respondents to rank values, most to least important. Next, respondents assign a rating to each. For example, respondents rank values (e.g., world peace, personal wealth, family security) in importance, and then they assign a value, 1 to 10, from extremely important to not important at all. A respondent may rank the value of world peace ahead of personal wealth, but when asked to rate the importance of world peace or its personal significance, a respondent may give it a 4 and personal wealth a rating of 8.[32]

Researchers must present the alternatives fairly and not create bias by giving respondents a reason for choosing one alternative. For example, respondents were asked whether they supported or opposed a law on energy conservation. The results changed when respondents heard, "Do you support the law or do you oppose it because the law would be difficult to enforce?" instead of simply, "Do you support or oppose the law?"

It is better to ask respondents to choose among alternatives by ranking instead of rating items along an imaginary continuum. Respondents can rate several items equally high, but will place them in a hierarchy if asked to rank them.[33]

Attaching numbers to a response scale can assist respondents and give them clues for understanding. Positive and negative numbers at the extremes (e.g., +5 to –5) are best when a researcher conceptualizes the variable as bipolar opposites, and a series of positive numbers (e.g., 0 to 10) is best if he or she conceptualizes the variable as a single continuum.

Visual presentations, including the use of colors, symbols, and pictures, can make large differences in how respondents react to questionnaires, sometimes having a larger impact than changes in wording. Respondents tend to interpret the middle of a set of responses as a typical or middle option, treat closeness in space on the questionnaire as indicating similarity in meaning, view the top items in a vertical list as being most desirable, and see differences in space between answers or the use of different colors as indicating bigger differences in meaning. Also, they find vertical response categories less confusing than horizontal ones.[34]

Details in question and questionnaire design can matter. For example, one study asked college students how many hours they studied per day. Some students saw five answer choices ranging from a half hour to more than 2.5 hours; others saw five answer choices ranging from less than 2.5 hours to more than 4.5 hours. Of students who saw the first set, 77 percent said they studied under 2.5 hours versus 31 percent of those receiving the second set. When mail questionnaires and telephone interviews were compared, 58 percent of students hearing the first set said under 2.5 hours whereas there was no change in those hearing the second set. This involves more than differences in response categories, because when students were asked about hours of television watching per day with similar changes in response categories, the response categories made no difference. What can we learn from this? When respondents lack clear answers, they tend to rely on the response categories of a question for guidance, and more anonymous formats generally yield more honest responses (see Dillman, 2000:32–39).

Wording Issues

Survey researchers face two wording issues. The first, discussed earlier, is to use simple vocabulary and grammar to minimize confusion. The second issue involves effects of specific words or phrases. It is trickier because it is not possible to know in advance whether a word or phrase affects responses.[35]

The well-documented difference between *forbid* and *not allow* illustrates the problem of wording differences. Both terms have the same meaning, but many more people are willing to "not allow" something than to "forbid" it. In general, less well educated respondents are most influenced by minor wording differences.

Certain words seem to trigger an emotional reaction, and researchers are just beginning to learn of them. For example, Smith (1987) found large differences (e.g., twice as much support) in U.S. survey responses depending on whether a question asked about spending "to help the poor" or "for welfare." He suggested that the word *welfare* has such strong negative connotations for Americans (lazy people, wasteful and expensive programs, etc.) that it is best to avoid it.

Possible **wording effects** are illustrated by what appears to be a noncontroversial question. Peterson (1984) examined four ways to ask about age: "How old are you?" "What is your age?" "In what year were you born?" and "Are you . . . 18–24, 25–34, . . . ?" He checked responses against birth certificate records and found that from 98.7 to 95.1 percent of respondents gave correct responses depending on the form of question used. He also found that the form of the question that had the fewest errors had the highest percentage of refusals to answer, and the form with the most errors had the lowest refusal rate. This example suggests that errors in a noncontroversial factual question vary with minor wording changes and that increasing the respondent's willingness to answer may increase errors in responses.

Many respondents are confused by words or their connotations. For example, respondents were

> **Wording effects**   An effect in survey research when a specific term or word used strongly influences how some respondents answer a survey question.

asked whether they thought television news was impartial. Researchers later learned that large numbers of respondents had ignored the word *impartial*—a term the middle-class, educated researchers assumed everyone would know. Less than half the respondents had interpreted the word as intended with its proper meaning. Over one-fourth had no idea of its meaning; others gave it unusual meanings, and one-tenth thought it was directly opposite to its true meaning. Researchers need to be cautious, because wording effects (e.g., the difference between *forbid* and *not allow*) may remain the same for decades, while other effects may appear.[36]

Questionnaire Design Issues

Length of Survey or Questionnaire. How long should a questionnaire be or an interview last?[37] Researchers prefer long questionnaires or interviews because they are more cost effective. The cost for extra questions—once a respondent has been sampled, has been contacted, and has completed other questions—is small. There is no absolute proper length. The length depends on the survey format (to be discussed) and on the respondent's characteristics. A 10-minute telephone interview is rarely a problem. Mail questionnaires are more variable. A short (3- or 4-page) questionnaire is appropriate for the general population. Some researchers have had success with questionnaires as long as 10 pages (about 100 items) with the general public, but responses drop significantly for longer questionnaires. For highly educated respondents and a salient topic, using questionnaires of 15 pages may be possible. Face-to-face interviews lasting an hour are not uncommon. In special situations, face-to-face interviews as long as three to five hours have been conducted.

Question Order or Sequence. A survey researcher faces three question sequence issues: organization of the overall questionnaire, question order effects, and context effects.

Organization of Questionnaire. In general, you should sequence questions to minimize the discomfort and confusion of respondents. A question-

BOX **10.7** Question Order Effects

QUESTION 1

"Do you think that the United States should let Communist newspaper reporters from other countries come in here and send back to their papers the news as they see it?"

QUESTION 2

"Do you think a Communist country like Russia should let American newspaper reporters come in and send back to America the news as they see it?"

PERCENTAGE SAYING YES

Heard First	Yes to #1 (Communist Reporter)	Yes to #2 (American Reporter)
#1	54%	75%
#2	64%	82%

The context created by answering the first question affects the answer to the second question.

Source: Adapted from Schuman and Presser (1981:29).

naire has opening, middle, and ending questions. After an introduction explaining the survey, it is best to make opening questions pleasant, interesting, and easy to answer so that they help a respondent to feel comfortable about the questionnaire. Avoid asking many boring background questions or threatening questions first. Organize questions in the middle into common topics. Mixing questions on different topics causes confusion. Orient respondents by placing questions on the same topic together and introduce the section with a short introductory statement (e.g., "Now I would like to ask you questions about housing"). Make question topics flow smoothly and logically, and organize them to assist respondents' memory or comfort levels. Do not end with highly threatening questions, and always end with a "thank you."

Order Effects. Researchers are concerned that the order in which they present questions may influence respondent answers.[38] Such **order effects** appear to be strongest for people who lack strong views, for less educated respondents, and for older respondents or those with memory loss.[39] For example, support for a single woman having an abortion regularly rises if the question precedes a question about

abortion being acceptable when a fetus has serious defects, but not when the question is by itself or before a question about fetus defects. A classic example of order effects is presented in Box 10.7.

Respondents may not perceive each issue as isolated and separate, but respond to survey questions based on the set of issues and their order of presentation. Previous questions can influence later ones in two ways: through their content (i.e., the issue) and through the respondent's response. For example, a student respondent is asked, "Do you support or favor an educational contribution for students?" Answers vary depending on the topic of the preceding question. If it comes after "How much tuition does the average U.S. student pay?" respondents interpret "contribution" to mean support for what students will pay. If it comes after "How much does the Swedish government pay to students?" respondents interpret it to mean a contribution that the government will pay. Previous answers can also influence responses, because having

Order effects   An effect in survey research in which a topic or some questions asked before others influence respondents' answers to later questions.

already answered one part will assume no overlap. For example, a respondent is asked, "How is your wife?" The next question is, "How is your family?" Most respondents will assume that the second question means family members other than the wife because they already gave an answer about the wife.[40]

Context Effects. Survey researchers noted how powerfully context affects surveys.[41] "Context includes more than just the influence of one question on another. It includes the effects of the interviewer, the interview setting, and indeed the historical setting. . . . At present, we do not have a good grasp of how questionnaire context effects relate to response effects on surveys" (Schuman, 1992:18). The context is more evident in mail than phone surveys, because a respondent can see all the questions.[42] No simple solution exists to control context effects.

As a practical matter, two things can be done regarding context effects. Use a **funnel sequence** of questions—that is, ask more general questions before specific ones (e.g., ask about health in general before asking about specific diseases). Or, divide the number of respondents in half and give one-half questions in one order and the other half in the alternative order, and then examine the results to see whether question order mattered. If question order effects are found, which order tells you what the respondents really think? The answer is that you cannot know for sure.

For example, a few years ago, my students conducted a telephone survey on two topics: concern about crime and attitudes toward a new anti-drunk-driving law. A random half of the respondents heard questions about the drunk-driving law first; the other half heard about crime first. I examined the results to see whether there was any **context effect**—a difference by topic order. I found that respondents who were asked about the drunk-driving

law first expressed less fear about crime than did those who were asked about crime first. Likewise, they were more supportive of the drunk-driving law than were those who first heard about crime. The first topic created a context within which respondents answered questions on the second topic. After they were asked about crime in general and thought about violent crime, drunk driving may have appeared to be a less important issue. By contrast, after they were asked about drunk driving and thought about drunk driving as a crime, they may have expressed less concern about crime in general.

Respondents answer all questions based on a context of preceding questions and the interview setting. A researcher needs to remember that the more ambiguous a question's meaning, the stronger the context effects, because respondents will draw on the context to interpret and understand the question. Previous questions on the same topic and heard just before a question can have a large context effect. For example, Sudman and associates (1996:90–91) contrasted three ways of asking how much a respondent followed politics. When they asked the question alone, about 21 percent of respondents said they followed politics "now and then" or "hardly at all." When they asked the question after asking what the respondent's elected representative recently did, the percentage who said they did not follow nearly doubled, going to 39 percent. The knowledge question about the representative made many respondents feel that they did not really know much. When a question about the amount of "public relations work" the elected representative provided to the area came between the two questions, 29 percent of respondents said they did not follow politics. This question gave respondents an excuse for not knowing the first question—they could blame their representative for their ignorance. The context of a question can make a difference and researchers need to be aware of it at all times: "Question comprehension is not merely a function of the wording of a question. Respondents use information provided by the context of the question to determine its intended meaning" (Sudman et al., 1996:69).

Format and Layout. There are two format or layout issues: the overall physical layout of the

---

Funnel sequence Organizing survey research questions in a questionnaire from general to specific questions.

Context effect An effect in survey research when an overall tone, setting, or set topics heard by respondents affect how they interpret the meaning of subsequent questions.

questionnaire and the format of questions and responses.

Questionnaire Layout. Layout is important, whether a questionnaire is for an interviewer or for the respondent.[43] Questionnaires should be clear, neat, and easy to follow. Give each question a number and put identifying information (e.g., name of organization) on questionnaires. Never cramp questions together or create a confusing appearance. A few cents saved in postage or printing will ultimately cost more in terms of lower validity due to a lower response rate or of confusion of interviewers and respondents. Make a cover sheet or face sheet for each interview, for administrative use. Put the time and date of interview, the interviewer, the respondent identification number, and the interviewer's comments and observations on it. A professional appearance with high-quality graphics, space between questions, and good layout improves accuracy and completeness and helps the questionnaire flow.

Give interviewers or respondents instructions on the questionnaire. Print instructions in a different style from the questions (e.g., in a different color or font or in all capitals) to distinguish them. This is so that an interviewer can distinguish between questions for respondents and instructions intended for the interviewer alone.

Layout is crucial for mail and web questionnaires because there is no friendly interviewer to interact with the respondent. Instead, the questionnaire's appearance persuades the respondent. In mail surveys, include a polite, professional cover letter on letterhead stationery, identifying the researcher and offering a telephone number for questions. Details matter. Respondents will be turned off if they receive a bulky brown envelope with bulk postage addressed to Occupant or if the questionnaire does not fit into the return envelope. Always end with "Thank you for your participation." Interviewers and questionnaires should leave respondents with a positive feeling about the survey and a sense that their participation is appreciated.

Question Format. Survey researchers decide on a format for questions and responses. Should respondents circle responses, check boxes, fill in dots, or put an × in a blank? The principle is to make responses unambiguous. Boxes or brackets to be checked and numbers to be circled are usually clearest. Also, listing responses down a page rather than across makes them easier to see (see Box 10.8). As mentioned before, use arrows and instructions for contingency questions. Visual aids are also helpful. For example, hand out thermometer-like drawings to respondents when asking about how warm or cool they feel toward someone. A **matrix question** (or grid question) is a compact way to present a series of questions using the same response categories. It saves space and makes it easier for the respondent or interviewer to note answers for the same response categories.

Sanchez (1992) examined two questionnaire layouts on questions about religion and found that a clearer layout reduced "not ascertained" responses from 8.8 to 2.04 percent. In addition, when she changed the format for a contingency question to make it clearer, the percentage of interviewers who probed for specific religious denomination increased from about 91 percent to over 99 percent.

Nonresponse. The failure to get a valid response from every sampled respondent weakens a survey. In addition to research surveys, people are asked to respond to many requests from charities, marketing firms, candidate polls, and so forth. Charities and marketing firms get low response rates, whereas government organizations get much higher cooperation rates. Nonresponse can be a major problem for survey research because if a high proportion of the sampled respondents do not respond, researchers may not be able to generalize results, especially if those who do not respond differ from those who respond.

Most U.S. citizens will be interviewed at some time during their lives, and the reporting of survey or poll results in major newspapers grew rapidly after the 1960s. By the 1970s, there was about one newspaper story per day that cited survey or poll results, compared to about ten per year in the 1940s.

> **Matrix question** A survey research question in which a set of questions are listed in a compact form together and all the questions share the same answer categories.

BOX **10.8** **Question Format Examples**

EXAMPLE OF HORIZONTAL VERSUS VERTICAL RESPONSE CHOICES

Do you think it is too easy or too difficult to get a divorce, or is it about right?
○ Too Easy   ○ Too Difficult   ○ About Right

Do you think it is too easy or too difficult to get a divorce, or is it about right?
○ Too Easy
○ Too Difficult
○ About Right

EXAMPLE OF A MATRIX QUESTION FORMAT

	Strongly Agree	Agree	Disagree	Strongly Disagree	Don't Know
The teacher talks too fast.	○	○	○	○	○
I learned a lot in this class.	○	○	○	○	○
The tests are very easy.	○	○	○	○	○
The teacher tells many jokes.	○	○	○	○	○
The teacher is organized.	○	○	○	○	○

EXAMPLES OF SOME RESPONSE CATEGORY CHOICES

Excellent, Good, Fair, Poor
Approve/Disapprove
Favor/Oppose
Strongly Agree, Agree, Somewhat Agree, Somewhat Disagree, Disagree, Strongly Disagree
Too Much, Too Little, About Right
Better, Worse, About the Same
Regularly, Often, Seldom, Never
Always, Most of Time, Some of Time, Rarely, Never
More Likely, Less Likely, No Difference
Very Interested, Interested, Not Interested

Nonresponse rates in surveys vary greatly; for most academic organizations they range from 25 to 33 percent. In commercial polls (Roper, Gallop, CBS, etc.) and campaign polls the nonresponse rates tend to be higher, reaching as high as 50 percent. Nonresponse rates have been climbing over time. In the United States, nonresponse rates for major academic surveys climbed from under 10 percent in the 1950s to 25 percent in the 1980s. Public cooperation in survey research has declined across most countries, with the Netherlands having the highest refusal rate. Refusal rates are as high as 30 percent in the United States.[44]

There is both a growing group of "hard core" refusing people and a general decline in participation because many people feel there are too many surveys. Other reasons for refusal include a fear of crime and strangers, a more hectic lifestyle, a loss of privacy, and a rising distrust of authority or government. The misuse of the survey to sell products or persuade people, poorly designed questionnaires, and inadequate explanations of surveys to respondents also increase refusals for legitimate surveys.

The people most likely to participate in surveys and polls are the most interested, informed, and active in society. This means that nonresponse both harms survey validity and omits a specific segment of the population from being counted or having a voice. In the United States, nonrespondents tend to be male, younger, non-White, and less educated. After reviewing studies of the types of people least likely to participate, Brehm (1993) found that they tend to have a lower self-image, be more suspicious of strangers, and distrust people of a different race. They tend to be less informed about public events and less involved in social-political organizations or activities.

Researchers have identified five types of nonresponse (see Box 10.9):[45]

1. Nonlocation (could not find a sampled respondent)
2. Noncontact (respondent was not at home or not reached after many attempts)
3. Ineligible (respondent was reached but was not the proper age, race, sex, citizenship, etc., for the survey purposes)
4. Refusal to participate (respondent was not willing to be interviewed)
5. Incomplete participation (respondent stopped answering before the end or began answering every question with "do not know" or "no opinion")

Improving the overall survey response rate requires reducing each type of nonresponse. Improving location means better sampling frames and maps or phone directories. Improving contact necessitates making many repeat calls, varying the time of day the calls are made, and lengthening the period to try contacts. Several factors are associated with noncontact in the United States—high population density, urban central city, non-owner-occupied housing (i.e., rental), high crime rate, high percentage of minority race population, presence of physical barriers (i.e., fence, bars on window, beware of dog or no trespassing signs), and a single adult living alone or households without young children. Although they may be easier to locate and contact, people who have higher income and more education may be less likely to cooperate once contacted. As Groves and Couper

---

BOX **10.9** Confusion about Response Rates

There is some confusion about response rates because the total response rate depends on success at several prior steps, each of which has its own rate:

Location Rate: Percentage of respondents in the sampling frame who are located.

Contact Rate: Percentage of located respondents who are contacted.

Eligibility Rate: Percentage of contacted respondents who are eligible.

Cooperation Rate: Percentage of contacted, eligible respondents who agree to participate.

Completion Rate: Percentage of cooperating respondents who complete the survey.

Total Response Rate: Percentage of all respondents in the initial sampling frame who were located, contacted, eligible, agreed to participate, and completed the entire questionnaire.

For example, researchers begin with 1,000 respondents in a sampling frame, locate 950 by telephone or an address, can contact 800 (by an interviewer or successful mailing), and determine that 780 are eligible (i.e., meet basic criteria, speak the language, are mentally competent). They find that 700 people cooperate with questionnaire or interview and 690 complete the entire questionnaire or interview. This yields the following rates: *location rate:* 95 percent, *contact rate:* 84.2 percent, *eligibility rate:* 97.5 percent, *cooperation rate:* 89.8 percent, *completion rate:* 98.6 percent, *total response rate:* 69 percent. The *total response rate* is the product of all the other rates: $.95 \times .842 \times .975 \times .898 \times .986 = .690$.

(1998:130) observed, "We find support in our data for the notion that those in high SES households cooperate less with surveys than those in low SES groups." Studies suggest that few respondents use caller ID and telephone machine screening technologies to block survey research in a significant way.[46]

Survey researchers can improve eligibility rates by careful respondent screening, better sample-frame definition, and multilingual interviewers.

They can decrease refusals by sending letters in advance of an interview, offering to reschedule interviews, using small incentives (i.e., small gifts), adjusting interviewer behavior and statements (i.e., making eye contact, expressing sincerity, explaining the sampling or survey, emphasizing importance of the interview, clarifying promises of confidentiality, etc.). Survey researchers can also use alternative interviewers (i.e., different demographic characteristics, age, race, gender, or ethnicity), use alternative interview methods (i.e., phone versus face to face), or accept alternative respondents in a household.

A critical area of nonresponse or refusal to participate occurs with the initial contact between an interviewer and a respondent. Cooperation increases by showing a respondent that the survey topic or results will be highly salient to him or her (i.e., are of great interest or will produce direct benefits), tailoring introductions to respondents (tailoring is discussed later in this chapter), or offering a small incentive.

For example, researchers increased cooperation among inner-city, low-income racial-ethnic minorities by using a journalistic-style letter and a personal phone call, compared to the standard academic letter. Respondents who were pessimistic about government and social service agencies and who felt misunderstood were more likely to respond once someone explained the survey to them in their terms.[47]

Research on the use of incentives found that prepaid incentives increase respondent cooperation in all types of surveys. They do not appear to have negative effects on survey composition or future participation. For example, Brehm (1994) found that without advance contact, 71 percent of respondents cooperated, but the rate rose to 78 percent with advance contact (a letter) and an incentive (one dollar), plus the respondents were more talkative. Moreover, respondents do not feel that differential payments for participation are unfair.[48]

There is a large body of literature on ways to increase response rates for mail questionnaires (see Box 10.10).[49] Heberlein and Baumgartner (1978) reported 71 factors affecting mail questionnaire response rates.

A meta-analysis (meta-analysis is explained in Chapter 5) of 115 articles on mail survey responses taken from 25 journals published between 1940 and

BOX **10.10** **Ten Ways to Increase Mail Questionnaire Response**

1. Address the questionnaire to specific person, not "Occupant," and send it first class.
2. Include a carefully written, dated cover letter on letterhead stationery. In it, request respondent cooperation, guarantee confidentiality, explain the purpose of the survey, and give the researcher's name and phone number.
3. *Always* include a postage-paid, addressed return envelope.
4. The questionnaire should have a neat, attractive layout and reasonable page length.
5. The questionnaire should be professionally printed and easy to read, with clear instructions.
6. Send two follow-up reminder letters to those not responding. The first should arrive about one week after sending the questionnaire, the second a week later. Gently ask for cooperation again and offer to send another questionnaire.
7. Do not send questionnaires during major holiday periods.
8. Do not put questions on the back page. Instead, leave a blank space and ask the respondent for general comments.
9. Sponsors that are local and are seen as legitimate (e.g., government agencies, universities, large firms, etc.) get a better response.
10. Include a small monetary inducement ($1) if possible.

1988 revealed that cover letters, questionnaires of four pages or less, a return envelope with postage, and a small monetary reward all increase returns (Yammarino et al., 1991). Many of the techniques suggested follow the total design method (to be discussed next) and help to make the task easy and interesting for respondents.

Dillman (2000:252) reports much higher self-administered questionnaire completion rates when a respondent was personally handed the questionnaire, as opposed to receiving it on the doorstep or via mail. Response rates of 77 percent were obtained for the combination of personally handing a questionnaire to a respondent, sending two follow-up reminders, and including a monetary incentive for completion (compared to 53 to 71 percent rates when one or more technique was not included).

Researchers rely on two theories to explain survey response behavior. Social exchange theory, also called the total design method (Dillman, 1978, 2000), holds that the formal survey is a special type of social interaction in which respondent behavior is based on what respondents expect to receive in return for cooperation. To increase response rates and accuracy, researchers need to minimize the burdens of cooperating by designing guides to make participation very easy and to maximize rewards by providing benefits (i.e., feelings of esteem, material incentives, and emotional rewards) for cooperation.

The more recent **leverage saliency theory** holds that the salience or interest/motivation varies by respondent. Different people value, either positively or negatively, specific aspects of the survey process differently (e.g., length of time, topic of survey, sponsor, etc.). To maximize cooperation, a survey researcher needs to identify and present positively valued aspects early in the survey process. Two practical implications are sponsorship and tailoring. Sponsorship refers to the organization carrying out or paying for the survey.

Respondent cooperation increases with **tailoring** (i.e., when interviewers adjust what they say in an introduction to specific respondents). As Groves and Couper (1998:216) have argued, "While standardization during the interview process has value for scientific replicability of measurement, we see little in the scientific method to argue for standardization during the recruitment of sample persons. Rather, the evidence points to each person taking her or his own route to the participation decision." They suggest training survey interviewers to be sensitive to a range of household types and concerns, so the interviews can "read" the setting and the various verbal and nonverbal cues. Interviewers should be able to shift quickly to alternative scripts for persuading a respondent and tailor the persuasion to a specific respondent.[50]

TYPES OF SURVEYS: ADVANTAGES AND DISADVANTAGES

Mail and Self-Administered Questionnaires

Advantages. Researchers can give questionnaires directly to respondents or mail them to respondents who read instructions and questions, then record their answers. This type of survey is by far the cheapest, and it can be conducted by a single researcher. A researcher can send questionnaires to a wide geographical area. The respondent can complete the questionnaire when it is convenient and can check personal records if necessary. Mail questionnaires offer anonymity and avoid interviewer bias. They are very effective, and response rates may be high for a target population that is well educated or has a strong interest in the topic or the survey organization.

Disadvantages. Because people do not always complete and return questionnaires, the biggest problem with mail questionnaires is a low response rate. Most questionnaires are returned within two weeks, but others trickle in up to two months later. Researchers can raise response rates by sending nonrespondents reminder letters, but this adds to the time and cost of data collection.

A researcher cannot control the conditions under which a mail questionnaire is completed. A questionnaire completed during a drinking party by a dozen laughing people may be returned along with one filled out by an earnest respondent. Also, no one is present to clarify questions or to probe for more information when respondents give incomplete answers. Someone other than the sampled respondent (e.g., spouse, new resident, etc.) may open the mail and complete the questionnaire without the researcher's knowledge. Different respondents can complete the questionnaire weeks apart or answer questions in a different order than that intended by researchers. Incomplete questionnaires can also be a serious problem.

Researchers cannot visually observe the respondent's reactions to questions, physical characteristics, or the setting. For example, an impoverished 70-year-old White woman living alone on a farm

Leverage salience theory A theory of survey research cooperation that states that different respondents find different aspects of a survey interview to be salient and will decide whether to cooperate based on different specific aspects of it.

Tailoring A technique to encourage respondent cooperation in survey research interviews in which interviewers highlight specific aspects of the interview that a respondent finds salient and positively values.

TABLE 10.4   Types of Surveys and Their Features

FEATURES	TYPE OF SURVEY			
	Mail Questionnaire	*Telephone Interview*	*Face-to-Face Interview*	*Web Survey*
Administrative Issues				
Cost	Cheap	Moderate	Expensive	Cheapest
Speed	Slowest	Fast	Slow to moderate	Fastest
Length (number of questions)	Moderate	Short	Longest	Moderate
Response rate	Lowest	Moderate	Highest	Moderate
Research Control				
Probes possible	No	Yes	Yes	No
Specific respondent	No	Yes	Yes	No
Question sequence	No	Yes	Yes	Yes
Only one respondent	No	Yes	Yes	No
Visual observation	No	No	Yes	Yes
Success with Different Questions				
Visual aids	Limited	None	Yes	Yes
Open-ended questions	Limited	Limited	Yes	Yes
Contingency questions	Limited	Yes	Yes	Yes
Complex questions	Limited	Limited	Yes	Yes
Sensitive questions	Some	Limited	Limited	Yes
Sources of Bias				
Social desirability	No	Some	Worse	No
Interviewer bias	No	Some	Worse	No
Respondent's reading skill	Yes	No	No	Some

could falsely state that she is a prosperous 40-year-old Asian male doctor living in a town with three children. Such extreme lies are rare, but serious errors can go undetected.

The mail questionnaire format limits the kinds of questions that a researcher can use. Questions requiring visual aids (e.g., look at this picture and tell me what you see), open-ended questions, many contingency questions, and complex questions do poorly in mail questionnaires. Likewise, mail questionnaires are ill suited for the illiterate or near-illiterate in English. Questionnaires mailed to illiterate respondents are not likely to be returned; if they are completed and returned, the questions were probably misunderstood, so the answers are meaningless (see Table 10.4).

Telephone Interviews

Advantages. The telephone interview is a popular survey method because about 95 percent of the population can be reached by telephone. An interviewer calls a respondent (usually at home), asks questions, and records answers. Researchers sample respondents from lists, telephone directories, or use RDD, and can quickly reach many people across long distances. A staff of interviewers can interview 1,500 respondents across a nation within a few days and, with several callbacks, response rates can reach 90 percent. Although this method is more expensive than a mail questionnaire, special reduced long distance phone rates help. In general, the telephone interview is a flexible method with most of the strengths of face-to-face interviews but for about half the cost. Interviewers control the sequence of questions and can use some probes. A specific respondent is chosen and is likely to answer all the questions alone. The researcher knows when the questions were answered and can use contingency questions effectively.

Several kinds of computer-assisted technologies have been developed for use in telephone interviews: CATI and Interactive Voice Response interviews. Advances and lower costs for computer technology in the late 1970s to 1980s enabled professional survey research organizations to install **computer-assisted telephone interviewing (CATI)** systems.[51] With CATI, the interviewer sits in front of a computer and makes calls. Wearing a headset and microphone, the interviewer reads the questions from a computer screen for the specific respondent who is called, then enters the answer via the keyboard. Once he or she enters an answer, the computer shows the next question on the screen.

Computer-assisted telephone interviewing speeds interviewing and reduces interviewer errors. It also eliminates the separate step of entering information into a computer and speeds data collection.

Interactive Voice Response (IVR) includes several computer-automated systems through phone technology and is widely used in marketing (Tourangeau, 2004a:791–792). With IVR, a respondent listens to questions and response options over the telephone, and responses are recorded by touch-tone entry or voice recognition software. Studies suggest that IVR has some advantages over live interviewers, such as rapid and automated data collection, few errors, and high anonymity. Some IVR interviewers involve a live interviewer to recruit and set up the respondent; others have direct automated systems. IVR is relatively successful for very short and simple surveys, but has sharp drop-off rates (as many as 40 percent do not complete the survey) for longer questionnaires (Tourangeau and colleagues, 2002).

Disadvantages. Relatively high cost and limited interview length are disadvantages of telephone interviews. In addition, respondents without telephones are impossible to reach, and the call may come at an inconvenient time. The use of an interviewer reduces anonymity and introduces potential interviewer bias. Open-ended questions are difficult to use, and questions requiring visual aids are impossible. Interviewers can note only serious disruptions (e.g., background noise) and respondent tone of voice (e.g., anger or flippancy) or hesitancy.

Face-to-Face Interviews

Advantages. Face-to-face interviews have the highest response rates and permit the longest questionnaires. They have the advantages of the telephone interview, and interviewers also can observe the surroundings and can use nonverbal communication and visual aids. Well-trained interviewers can ask all types of questions, can ask complex questions, and can use extensive probes.

Disadvantages. High cost is the biggest disadvantage of face-to-face interviews. The training, travel, supervision, and personnel costs for interviews can be high. Interviewer bias is also greatest in face-to-face interviews. The appearance, tone of voice, question wording, and so forth of the interviewer may affect the respondent. In addition, interviewer supervision is less than for telephone interviews, which supervisors monitor by listening in.[52]

Web Surveys

Access to the Internet and e-mail did not become widespread until the late 1990s across the advanced world. For example, in 1994 only 3 percent of the U.S. population had e-mail, but by February 2004 an estimated 75 percent of homes were connected to the Internet.[53]

Computer-assisted telephone interviewing (CATI) Survey research telephone interviewing in which the interviewer sits before a computer screen and keyboard, reads from the screen questions, and enters answers directly into the computer.

Interactive Voice Response (IVR) A technique in telephone interviewing in which respondents hear computer-automated questions and indicate their responses by touch-tone phone entry or voice-activated software.

Advantages. Web-based surveys over the Internet or by e-mail are very fast and inexpensive, they allow flexible design and can use visual images, or even audio or video in some Internet versions. The great flexibility in design can be a disadvantage as well, but principles for paper questionnaires generally apply. Commenting on the efficiency of e-mail or web-based survey technologies compared to past methods, Dillman (2000:352) observed, "These efficiencies include the nearly complete elimination of paper, postage, mailout, and data entry costs . . . [they] also provide a potential for overcoming international boundaries as significant barriers . . . [and] the time required for survey implementation can be reduced from weeks to days, or even hours."

Disadvantages. Web surveys have three disadvantages or areas of concern: coverage, privacy and verification, and design issues. The first concern involves sampling, and unequal access and use of the Internet. Older, less educated, lower-income, and rural people are less likely to have access, and a majority without access now say they do not plan to acquire it in the future. In addition, many people have multiple e-mail addresses. As Tourangeau (2004a:792) remarked, "the sampling problems with Web surveys are formidable."

A second concern involves protecting respondent privacy. This may be addressed technologically with secure websites and high confidentiality protection. Respondent verification to ensure that the sampled respondents alone participate and do so only once may also be resolved with a technical fix, such as giving each respondent a unique PIN number limiting who can complete the questionnaire.

A third concern involves the complexity of design. Researchers need to check and verify the compatibility of various web software and hardware combinations for respondents using different types of computers. Researchers are just beginning to learn what is effective on this relatively new way to administer questionnaires. For example, it appears best to provide screen-by-screen questions and make each entire question visible on the screen at one time in a consistent format with drop-down boxes for answer choices. It is best to include a progress indicator (as motivation) such as clock or waving hand. Visual appearance, such as the range of colors and fonts, should be limited for easy readability and consistency. Be sure to provide very clear instructions for any computer actions (e.g., use of drop-down screens) where they are needed and include "click here" instruction. Also, it is best to make it easy for respondents to move back and forth across questions (see Dillman, 2000:376–400 for summary). It is also important to avoid technical glitches and "bugs" at the implementation stage with dedicated servers and sufficient broadband to handle demand. As Tarnai and Moore (2004:320) remarked, "The increased complexity of CAI [computer-assisted interview] instruments means significant increases in the amount of testing that must be done to ensure an accurately fielded survey."

Special Situations

There are many kinds of special surveys. One is a survey of organizations (e.g., businesses, schools, etc.). Mail questionnaires are usually used, but other methods are possible. A researcher writes questions to ask about the organization. He or she learns who in the organization has the necessary information, because it is essential to contact someone capable of responding. He or she then makes the significance of the survey clear because officials receive many requests for information and do not answer all of them.

Surveying white-collar elites requires special techniques.[54] Powerful leaders in business, government, and so on are difficult to reach. Assistants may intercept mail questionnaires, and restricted access can present a formidable obstacle to face-to-face or telephone interviewing. Access is facilitated when a prestigious source calls or sends a letter of introduction. Once the researcher makes an appointment, the researcher, not a hired interviewer, conducts the interviews. Personal interviews with a high percentage of open-ended questions are usually more successful than all closed-ended questions. Confidentiality is a crucial issue and should be guaranteed, because elites often have information that few others do.

Time budget surveys are a special type of survey used to study how people allocate their time. Studies of urban planning, the sexual division of labor, quality of life, mass media usage, and leisure use time budget surveys.[55] In the survey, a respondent agrees to record his or her activities in detail over several days, usually in a diary, noting activities for each 10- or 15-minute period. For example, about 10 years ago, several professors who work at my university were asked to be part of a time budget survey. The survey was by government officials who wanted to learn how much time professors devoted to academic work activities. The professors filled in a detailed diary, recording what they did each 15-minute period at home and work over two weeks.

Some government officials periodically request such surveys because they believe that professors at public universities work only 25 to 30 hours a week. Dozens of such time budget surveys have consistently shown the same results: When all the meetings, community service activities, research work, course preparation and planning, writing and grading exams, paper evaluation, student advising, and direct teaching time are totaled, most professors work about 55 hours a week. By the way, undergraduate students tend to believe professors put in about 40 hours a week.[56]

Time budget surveys can reveal more interesting findings than the total hours worked. For example, Bittman and Wajcman (2000) analyzed cross-national data on time usage in 10 countries and used data from time diaries to investigate the "double burden" of working women who must perform household tasks in addition to paid work outside the home. Women report they have very little leisure time, but the data show that men and women have nearly equal amounts of total leisure time. The authors discovered that although the total quantity of time is similar, women's leisure time is more likely to be interrupted than that of men and less likely to be adult leisure (i.e., women's leisure may involve playing with or going on an outing with children). Thus, detailed data on time usage showed that gender inequality appears more in the different character of the time than the total amount of leisure time.

You may have heard of *focus groups* in regard to applied studies in political campaign or marketing research. Focus groups are a special kind of nonquantitative data collection technique that we will explore in Chapter 13.

Costs

Professional-quality survey research can be expensive if all costs are considered. The cost varies according to the type of survey used. A simple formula is that for every $1 in cost for a mail survey, a telephone interview survey costs about $5 and a face-to-face interview about $20.

Costs vary greatly.[57] Beyond modest supply costs, the biggest expenses are labor costs for professional staff who develop and pilot test a questionnaire, costs to train interviewers, and labor costs for clerical staff and interviewers. Beginning researchers and students tend to seriously underestimate the expenses and the amount of time required. In 1998, a two-page mail questionnaire sent to 300 respondents cost me $1,500, or about $5 each. This did not include pay for the 24 hours I spent writing and checking the questionnaire nor any costs to prepare the data for the computer or to analyze the data. With a 70 percent response rate, the real cost was closer to $7.50 per respondent.

Professional survey organizations often charge $60 and up per completed 15-minute telephone interview. The costs for a face-to-face interview study are higher. Professionally completed face-to-face interviews can cost over $200 per completed interview, depending on the interview length and travel expenses. At one extreme, a face-to-face survey of 1,000 geographically dispersed respondents from the general public may cost over $250,000 and take over a year to complete. At the other extreme, a simple one-page, self-administered questionnaire that a teacher photocopies and distributes to 100 students in one school can cost very little, except for the teacher's time and effort. The teacher might be able to prepare

Time budget survey   A specialized type of survey in which respondents record details about the timing and duration of their activities over a period of time.

BOX **10.11** Types of Nonresearch Interviews

1. *Job interview.* An employer asks open-ended questions to gather information about a candidate for a job and to observe how the candidate presents himself or herself. The candidate (respondent) initiates the contact and attempts to present a positive self-image. The employer (interviewer) tries to discover the candidate's true talents and flaws. A serious, judgmental tone exists, with the employer having the power to accept or reject the candidate. This often creates tension and limited trust. The parties may have conflicting goals and each may use some deception. The results are not confidential.

2. *Assistance interview.* A helping professional (counselor, lawyer, social worker, medical doctor, etc.) seeks information on a client's problem, including background and current conditions. The helping professional (interviewer) uses the information to understand and translate the client's (respondent's) problem into professional terms for problem resolution. The tone is serious and concerned. There is usually low tension and high mutual trust. The parties share the goal of resolving the client's problem, and deception is rare. The interview results are usually confidential.

3. *Journalistic interview.* A journalist gathers information from a celebrity, newsmaker, witness, or background person for later use in constructing a newsworthy story. The journalist (interviewer) uses various skills in attempting to get novel information, some that may not be easily revealed, and "quotable quotes" from the news source (respondent). The journalist uses the interview information selectively in combination with other information, usually beyond the respondent's control. The tone and degree of trust and tension vary greatly. The goals of the parties may diverge and each may use deception. The

interview results are not confidential and they may get a lot of publicity.

4. *Interrogation or investigative interview.* A criminal justice official, auditor, or other person in authority seriously asks questions to obtain information from an accused person or others with information about wrongdoing. The official (interviewer) will use the information as evidence to construct a case against someone (possibly the respondent). The tension is often extreme with mutual distrust. The goals of the parties diverge sharply and each often uses deception. Interview results are rarely confidential and may become part of an official, public record.

5. *Entertainment interview.* An emcee or show host offers comments and asks open-ended questions to a celebrity or other person who may digress in answers or begin a monologue. The primary goal is to stimulate interest, enjoyment, or gaiety among an audience. Often, the style displayed by each is more central than any information revealed. The host (interviewer) seeks an immediate response or reaction in the audience, while the celebrity (respondent) tries to increase his or her fame or reputation. The tone is light, tension is low, and trust is moderately high. The limited goals of each often converge. They may deceive each other or join in deceiving the audience. The situation is the opposite to one in which confidentially can occur.

People can mix the types of interviews, and people often use several types. For example, the social worker in a social control role instead of a helping role may conduct an investigative interview. Or a police officer helping a crime victim may use an assistance interview instead of an interrogation.

---

and distribute the questionnaire, collect responses, and tabulate results in as little as one week.

INTERVIEWING

The Role of the Interviewer

Interviews to gather information occur in many settings. Employers interview prospective employees,

medical personnel interview patients, mental health professionals interview clients, social service workers interview the needy, reporters interview politicians and others, police officers interview witnesses and crime victims, and talk-show hosts interview celebrities (see Box 10.11). Survey research interviewing is a specialized kind of interviewing. As with most interviewing, its goal is to obtain accurate information from another person.[58]

TABLE 10.5   Differences between Ordinary Conversation and a Structured Survey Interview

ORDINARY CONVERSATION	THE SURVEY INTERVIEW
1. Questions and answers from each participant are relatively equally balanced.	1. Interviewer asks and respondent answers most of the time.
2. There is an open exchange of feelings and opinions.	2. Only the respondent reveals feelings and opinions.
3. Judgments are stated and attempts made to persuade the other of particular points of view.	3. Interviewer is nonjudgmental and does not try to change respondent's opinions or beliefs.
4. A person can reveal deep inner feelings to gain sympathy or as a therapeutic release.	4. Interviewer tries to obtain direct answers to specific questions.
5. Ritual responses are common (e.g., "Uh huh," shaking head, "How are you?" "Fine").	5. Interviewer avoids making ritual responses that influence a respondent and also seeks genuine answers, not ritual responses.
6. The participants exchange information and correct the factual errors that they are aware of.	6. Respondent provides almost all information. Interviewer does not correct a respondent's factual errors.
7. Topics rise and fall and either person can introduce new topics. The focus can shift directions or digress to less relevant issues.	7. Interviewer controls the topic, direction, and pace. He or she keeps the respondent "on task," and irrelevant diversions are contained.
8. The emotional tone can shift from humor, to joy, to affection, to sadness, to anger, and so on.	8. Interviewer attempts to maintain a consistently warm but serious and objective tone throughout.
9. People can evade or ignore questions and give flippant or noncommittal answers.	9. Respondent should not evade questions and should give truthful, thoughtful answers.

Source: Adapted from Gorden (1980:19–25) and Sudman and Bradburn (1983:5–10).

The interview is a short-term, secondary social interaction between two strangers with the explicit purpose of one person's obtaining specific information from the other. The social roles are those of the interviewer and the interviewee or respondent. Information is obtained in a structured conversation in which the interviewer asks prearranged questions and records answers, and the respondent answers. It differs in several ways from ordinary conversation (see Table 10.5).

An important problem for interviewers is that many respondents are unfamiliar with the survey respondents' role and "respondents often do not have a clear conception of what is expected of them" (Turner and Martin, 1984:282). As a result, they substitute another role that may affect their responses. Some believe the interview is an intimate conversation or therapy session, some see it as a bu-

reaucratic exercise in completing forms, some view it as a citizen referendum on policy choices, some view it as a testing situation, and some see it as a form of deceit in which interviewers are trying to trick or entrap respondents. Even in a well-designed, professional survey, follow-up research found that only about half the respondents understand questions exactly as intended by researchers. Respondents reinterpreted questions to make them applicable to their idiosyncratic, personal situations or to make them easy to answer.[59]

The role of interviewers is difficult. They obtain cooperation and build rapport, yet remain neutral and objective. They encroach on the respondents' time and privacy for information that may not directly benefit the respondents. They try to reduce embarrassment, fear, and suspicion so that respondents feel comfortable revealing information.

They may explain the nature of survey research or give hints about social roles in an interview. Good interviewers monitor the pace and direction of the social interaction as well as the content of answers and the behavior of respondents.

Survey interviewers are nonjudgmental and do not reveal their opinions, verbally or nonverbally (e.g., by a look of shock). If a respondent asks for an interviewer's opinion, he or she politely redirects the respondent and indicates that such questions are inappropriate. For example, if a respondent asks, "What do you think?" the interviewer may answer, "Here, we are interested in what *you* think; what I think doesn't matter." Likewise, if the respondent gives a shocking answer (e.g., "I was arrested three times for beating my infant daughter and burning her with cigarettes"), the interviewer does not show shock, surprise, or disdain but treats the answer in a matter-of-fact manner. He or she helps respondents feel that they can give any truthful answer.

You might ask, "If the survey interviewer must be neutral and objective, why not use a robot or machine?" Machine interviewing has not been successful because it lacks the human warmth, sense of trust, and rapport that an interviewer creates. An interviewer helps define the situation and ensures that respondents have the information sought, understand what is expected, give relevant answers, are motivated to cooperate, and give serious answers.

Interviewers do more than interview respondents. Face-to-face interviewers spend only about 35 percent of their time interviewing. About 40 percent is spent in locating the correct respondent, 15 percent in traveling, and 10 percent in studying survey materials and dealing with administrative and recording details.[60]

Stages of an Interview

The interview proceeds through stages, beginning with an introduction and entry. The interviewer gets

in the door, shows authorization, and reassures and secures cooperation from the respondent. He or she is prepared for reactions such as "How did you pick me?" "What good will this do?" "I don't know about this." "What's this about, anyway?" The interviewer can explain why the specific respondent is interviewed and not a substitute.

The main part of the interview consists of asking questions and recording answers. The interviewer uses the exact wording on the questionnaire—no added or omitted words and no rephrasing. He or she asks all applicable questions in order, without returning to or skipping questions unless the directions specify this. He or she goes at a comfortable pace and gives nondirective feedback to maintain interest.

In addition to asking questions, the interviewer accurately records answers. This is easy for closed-ended questions, for which interviewers just mark the correct box. For open-ended questions, the interviewer's job is more difficult. He or she listens carefully, must have legible writing, and must record what is said verbatim without correcting grammar or slang. More important, the interviewer never summarizes or paraphrases. This causes a loss of information or distorts answers. For example, the respondent says, "I'm really concerned about my daughter's heart problem. She's only 10 years old and already she has trouble climbing stairs. I don't know what she'll do when she gets older. Heart surgery is too risky for her and it costs so much. She'll have to learn to live with it." If the interviewer writes, "concerned about daughter's health," much is lost.

The interviewer knows how and when to use probes. A **probe** is a neutral request to clarify an ambiguous answer, to complete an incomplete answer, or to obtain a relevant response. Interviewers recognize an irrelevant or inaccurate answer and use probes as needed.[61] There are many types of probes. A three- to five-second pause is often effective. Nonverbal communication (e.g., tilt of head, raised eyebrows, or eye contact) also works well. The interviewer can repeat the question or repeat the reply and then pause. She or he can ask a neutral question, such as, "Any other reasons?" "Can you tell me more about that?" "How do you mean?" "Could you explain more for me?" (see Box 10.12).

Probe   A follow-up question in survey research interviewing that asks a respondent to clarify or elaborate on an incomplete or inappropriate answer.

BOX **10.12** **Example of Probes and Recording Full Responses to Closed Questions**

Interviewer Question: What is your occupation?

Respondent Answer: I work at General Motors.
    Probe: What is your job at General Motors? What type of work do you do there?

Interviewer Question: How long have you been unemployed?

Respondent Answer: A long time.
    Probe: Could you tell me more specifically when your current period of unemployment began?

Interviewer Question: Considering the country as a whole, do you think we will have good times during the next year, or bad times, or what?

Respondent Answer: Maybe good, maybe bad, it depends, who knows?
    Probe: What do you expect to happen?

Record Response to a Closed Question
Interviewer Question: On a scale of 1 to 7, how do you feel about capital punishment or the death penalty, where 1 is strongly in favor of the death penalty, and 7 is strongly opposed to it? (Favor) 1 _ 2 _ 3 _ 4 _ 5 _ 6 _ 7 _ (Oppose)

Respondent's Answer: About a 4. I think that all murderers, rapists, and violent criminals should get death, but I don't favor it for minor crimes like stealing a car.

Human responses in interviews are more complex than outlined by the **naïve assumption model.** For example, "Inaccurate reporting is not a response tendency or a predisposition to be untruthful. Individuals who are truthful on one occasion or in response to particular questions may not be truthful at other times or to other questions" (Wentworth, 1993:130).

Respondents often interpret straightforward questions differently than intended by the survey designer. Techniques to reduce misunderstanding, such as conversational interviewing (in which interviewers reword questions and explain the meaning of questions to respondents) deviate from the simple, standardized interview model. In conversational interviewing, the interviewer guides the respondent to the interpretation intended by the survey designer. Beyond concerns about introducing bias, such interviewing requires more time and more intense interviewer training. Yet, as Conrad and Schober (2000:20) have observed, respondent "comprehension

can be made more consistent—and responses more comparable—when certain interviewer behaviors (discussions about the meaning of questions) are *less* consistent." Paradoxically, nonstandardized interviewing can increase the reliability of survey research by improving the consistency in how respondents interpret the meaning of survey questions and responses.

Given this complexity and possible distortion, what should the diligent survey researcher do? Survey researcher should at least supplement closed-ended questionnaires with open-ended questions and probes. This takes more time, requires better-trained interviewers, and produces responses that may be less standardized and more difficult to quantify. Fixed-answer questionnaires based on the naive assumption model imply a more simple and

Naïve assumption model A model of standardized survey research in which there are no communication problems and respondents' responses perfectly match their thoughts.

mechanical way of responding than occurs in many situations. The inquiry into interviewer bias, cultural meanings, and the interview as a social situation provides a lesson in how qualitative and quantitative styles of social research complement one another. As quantitative survey researchers strived to eliminate sources of interviewer bias and respondent confusion, they discovered that qualitative researchers offered valuable insights into how people construct meaning in various social settings.

The last stage is the exit, when the interviewer thanks the respondent and leaves. He or she then goes to a quiet, private place to edit the questionnaire and record other details such as the date, time, and place of the interview; a thumbnail sketch of the respondent and interview situation; the respondent's attitude (e.g., serious, angry, or laughing); and any unusual circumstances (e.g., "Telephone rang at question 27 and respondent talked for four minutes before the interview started again"). He or she notes anything disruptive that happened during the interview (e.g., "Teenage son entered room, sat at opposite end, turned on television with the volume loud, and watched a baseball game"). The interviewer also records personal feelings and anything that was suspected (e.g., "Respondent became nervous and fidgeted when questioned about his marriage").

Training Interviewers

A large-scale survey requires hiring several interviewers.[62] A professional-quality interview requires the careful selection of interviewers and good training. As with any employment situation, adequate pay and good supervision are important for consistent high-quality performance.

Unfortunately, professional interviewing has not always paid well or provided regular employment. In the past, interviewers were largely drawn from a pool of middle-aged women willing to accept irregular part-time work. Good interviewers are pleasant, honest, accurate, mature, responsible, moderately intelligent, stable, and motivated. They have a nonthreatening appearance, have experience with many types of people, and possess poise and tact. If the survey involves interviewing in high-crime areas, interviewers need extra protection. Researchers may consider interviewers' physical

appearance, age, race, sex, languages spoken, and even the voice. For example, in a study using trained female telephone interviewers from homogeneous social backgrounds, Oksenberg and colleagues (1986) found fewer refusals for interviewers whose voices had higher pitch and greater pitch variation, and who spoke louder, faster, with clear pronunciation and sounded more pleasant and cheerful.

Researchers train professional interviewers in a one- to two-week training course, which usually includes lectures and reading, observation of expert interviewers, mock interviews in the office and in the field that are recorded and critiqued, many practice interviews, and role playing. The interviewers learn what survey research is about and the role of the interviewer. They become familiar with the questionnaire and the purpose of questions, although not with the answers expected.

Although interviewers largely work alone, researchers use an interviewer supervisor in large-scale surveys with several interviewers. Supervisors are familiar with the area, assist with problems, oversee the interviewers, and ensure that work is completed on time. For telephone interviewing, this includes helping with calls, checking when interviewers arrive and leave, and monitoring interview calls. In face-to-face interviews, supervisors check to find out whether the interview actually took place. This means calling back or sending a confirmation postcard to a sample of respondents. They can also check the response rate and incomplete questionnaires to see whether interviewers are obtaining cooperation, and they may reinterview a small subsample, analyze answers, or observe interviews to see whether interviewers are accurately asking questions and recording answers.

Interviewer Bias

Survey researchers proscribe interviewer behavior to reduce bias. Ideally, the actions of a particular interviewer will not affect how a respondent answers, and responses will not vary from what they would be if asked by any other interviewer. This goes beyond reading each question exactly as worded (see Box 10.13).

Survey researchers are still learning about the factors that influence survey interviews. They know

10.13 Interview Bias Falls into Six Categories

1. Errors by the respondent—forgetting, embarrassment, misunderstanding, or lying because of the presence of others
2. Unintentional errors or interviewer sloppiness—contacting the wrong respondent, misreading a question, omitting questions, reading questions in the wrong order, recording the wrong answer to a question, or misunderstanding the respondent
3. Intentional subversion by the interviewer—purposeful alteration of answers, omission or rewording of questions, or choice of an alternative respondent
4. Influence due to the interviewer's expectations about a respondent's answers based on the respondent's appearance, living situation, or other answers
5. Failure of an interviewer to probe or to probe properly
6. Influence on the answers due to the interviewer's appearance, tone, attitude, reactions to answers, or comments made outside of the interview schedule

that interviewer expectations can create significant bias. Interviewers who expect difficult interviews have them, and those who expect certain answers are more likely to get them (see Box 10.14). Proper interviewer behavior and exact question reading may be difficult, but the issue is larger.

In addition, interviewer bias can arise from expectations based on a respondent's age and race. In a major national U.S. survey, researchers learned that interviewers regularly coded Black respondents as being less intelligent and coded younger respondents as both less intelligent and less informed. Better interviewer training is needed to reduce such bias in survey results.[63]

The social setting in which the interview occurs can affect answers, including the presence of other people. For example, students answer differently depending on whether they are asked questions at home or at school. In general, survey researchers do not want others present because they may affect respondent answers. It may not always make a difference, however, especially if the others are small children.[64] For example, Zipp and Toth (2002) found greater agreement on numerous

10.14 Interviewer Characteristics Can Affect Responses

EXAMPLE OF INTERVIEWER EXPECTATION EFFECTS

Asked by Female Interviewer Whose Own	Female Respondent Reports That Husband Buys Most Furniture
Husband buys most furniture	89%
Husband does not buy most furniture	15%

EXAMPLE OF RACE OR ETHNIC APPEARANCE EFFECTS

	PERCENTAGE ANSWERING YES TO:	
Interviewer	"Do you think there are too many Jews in government jobs?"	"Do you think that Jews have too much power?"
Looked Jewish with Jewish-sounding name	11.7	5.8
Looked Jewish only	15.4	15.6
Non-Jewish appearance	21.2	24.3
Non-Jewish appearance and non-Jewish-sounding name	19.5	21.4

Source: Adapted from Hyman (1975:115,163).

Note: Racial stereotypes held by respondents can affect how they respond in interviews.

attitude items when the other spouse was present at an interview, with wives modifying their answers to conform to their husbands', while husbands changed little. Aquilino (1993) found that both spouses are more likely to say that a divorce will make them worse when the other spouse is present, and the wives report husbands do more housework when the husbands are present.

An interviewer's visible characteristics, including race and gender, often affect interviews and respondent answers, especially for questions about issues related to race or gender. For example, African American and Hispanic American respondents express different policy positions on race- or ethnic-related issues depending on the apparent race or ethnicity of the interviewer. This occurs even with telephone interviews when a respondent has clues about the interviewer's race or ethnicity. In general, interviewers of the same racial-ethnic group get more accurate answers.[65] Gender also affects interviews both in terms of obvious issues, such as sexual behavior, as well as support for gender-related collective action or gender equality.[66] Survey researchers need to note the race and gender of both interviewers and respondents.

Interview characteristics can influence answers in many ways. For example, when the interviewer was a person with disabilities, respondents lowered their self-reported level of "happiness," compared to when they answered a self-administered questionnaire. Apparently, they did not want to sound too well off compared to the interviewer. However, when respondents completed a self-administered questionnaire while a person with disabilities was in the same room, they reported higher levels of happiness. Apparently, respondents felt comparatively better off due to the physical presence of the person with the disability compared to when there was no immediate reminder of the life situations of others.[67] When a respondent answers identical questions differently depending on the race, gender, or physical conditions of the person who asks it, it threatens representative reliability.

Cultural Meanings and Survey Interviews

Research into survey errors and interview bias has advanced thinking about larger issues of how people

---

BOX **10.15** Naïve Assumption Model of Survey Interviews

1. Researchers have clearly conceptualized all variables being measured.
2. Questionnaires have no wording, question order, or related effects.
3. Respondents are motivated and willing to answer all the questions asked.
4. Respondents possess complete information and can accurately recall events.
5. Respondents understand each question exactly as the reseacher intends it.
6. Respondents give more truthful answers if they do not know the hypotheses.
7. Respondents give more truthful answers if they receive no hints or suggestions.
8. The interview situation and specific interviewers have no effects on answers.
9. The process of the interview has no impact on the respondents' beliefs or attitudes.
10. Respondents' behaviors match perfectly their verbal responses in an interview.

---

create social meaning and achieve cultural understanding.[68] Survey researchers are troubled when the same words have different meanings and implications depending on the social situation, who speaks them, how they are spoken, and the social distance between the speaker and listener. Also, respondents do not always understand the social situation of the survey interview, may misinterpret the nature of survey research, and may seek clues for how to answer in the wording of questions or subtle actions of the interviewer. Moreover, "it is important not to lose sight of the fact that the interview setting is itself distinct from other settings in which attitudes are expressed, and hence we should not expect to find complete congruence between attitudes expressed in interviews and in other social contexts."[69]

Initially, survey research was based on a naïve assumption model (Foddy, 1993:13). Researchers try to improve survey research by reducing the gap between actual experience in conducting surveys and the ideal survey expressed as the model's assumptions (see Box 10.15).

Some researchers question the assumptions of this model. For example, as an interviewer strives

BOX **10.16** Interviewing: Positivist and Feminist Approaches

In this chapter, you have learned the positivist approach to survey research interviewing. In the ideal survey interview, the interviewer withholds her or his own feelings and beliefs. The interviewer should be so objective and neutral that it should be possible to substitute another interviewer and obtain the same responses.

Feminist researchers approach interviewing very differently. Feminist interviewing is similar to qualitative interviewing (to be discussed in Chapter 14). Oakley (1981) criticized positivist survey interviewing as being part of a masculine paradigm. It is a social situation in which the interviewer exercises control and dominance while suppressing the expression of personal feelings. It is manipulative and instrumental. The interviewer and the respondent become merely the vehicles for obtaining the objective data.

The goals of feminist research vary, but two common goals are to give greater visibility to the subjective experience of women and to increase the involvement of the respondent in the research process. Features of feminist interviewing include the following:

- A preference for an unstructured and open-ended format
- A preference for interviewing a person more than once
- Creation of social connections and building a trusting social relationship
- Disclosure of personal experiences by the interviewer
- Drawing on female skills of being open, receptive, and understanding
- Avoiding control and fostering equality by downplaying professional status
- Careful listening, interviewers become emotionally engaged with respondents
- Respondent-oriented direction, not researcher oriented or questionnaire oriented
- Encouragement of respondents to express themselves in ways they are most comfortable—for example, by telling stories or following digressions
- Creation of a sense of empowerment and an esprit de corps among women

to act in a more neutral and uniform way, he or she reduces the type of bias that causes unreliability because of individual interviewer behavior. Yet, such attempts cause other problems according to interpretive or critical social science researchers (see Box 10.16).[70] They argue that meaning is created in social context; therefore, standard wording will not produce the same meaning for all respondents. For example, some respondents express their values and feelings by telling stories instead of answering straightforward questions with fixed answers.

These researchers note that few survey interviews ever meet the pure standardized form of the naive assumption model and substitute the model of an interview as a collaborative encounter between an interviewer and respondent in which they work together to exchange information. A collaborative encounter model views all human encounters as highly dynamic, complex mutual interactions in which even minor, unintended forms of feedback (e.g., saying hmmm, laughter, smiles, nods) have an influence. The collaborative encounter model also allows interviewers to incorporate information offered by respondents in response to fixed-choice questions but that the standardized interview prohibits or treats as an error because it does not correspond to a preset, standardized format.

In complex human interaction, people often add interpretative meaning to simple questions. For example, my neighbor asks me the simple question, "How often do you mow your lawn?" I could interpret his question in the following ways:

- How often do I personally mow the lawn (versus having someone else mow it for me)?
- How often do I mow it to cut grass (versus run my lawnmower over it to chop up leaves)?
- How often do I mow the entire lawn (versus cutting the quick-growing parts only)?
- How often do I mow it during an entire season, a month, a week?
- How often do I mow it most seasons (versus last year when my lawnmower was broken several times and it was very dry and the grass grew less tall, so I did not mow it as frequently)?

Within seconds, I make an interpretation and give an answer, but the open-ended, ongoing interaction between myself and the neighbor permits me to ask for clarification and for several follow-up questions that help us arrive at mutual understanding.

A dilemma arises because a survey interview interaction differs from ordinary conversation. A survey research interview is a standardized, artificial interaction that treats diverse respondents alike to control the communication situation and yield a uniform measure. Ordinary interaction contains built-in features to detect and correct misinterpretation; it relies on nuance and give and take. People achieve social meaning in ordinary conversation by relying on clues in the context, adjusting the interaction flow to specific people involved, and building on a cultural frame (often based on race, class, gender, region, or religion). The fluid interaction of ordinary conversation is self-adjusting because different people do not always assign the same meaning to the same words, phases, and questions. For example, men and women report health differently. A man saying he is in excellent health means something different from a woman answering the same question with the same response. By standardizing human interaction, the survey interview strips away features in ordinary conversation that provide self-correction, promote the construction of a shared meaning among different people, and increase human mutual understanding.[71]

Pilot Testing

It is best to pilot-test survey interviews and questionnaires prior to implementation. In recent years, researchers have begun the systematic study of pilot tests in the survey process. Many use a model of cognitive processing that divides the tasks of answering survey questions into four steps: (1) interpret and comprehend the question, (2) retrieve

Cognitive interviewing A technique used in pilot testing surveys in which researchers try to learn about a questionnaire and improve it by interviewing respondents about their thought processes or have respondents "think out loud" as they answer survey questions.

BOX **10.17** Methods of Improving Questionnaire with Pilot Tests

1. *Think aloud interviews.* A respondent explains his or her thinking out loud during the process of answering each question.
2. *Retrospective interviews and targeted probes.* After completing a questionnaire, the respondent explains to researchers the process used to select each response or answer.
3. *Expert evaluation.* An independent panel of experienced survey researchers reviews and critiques the questionnaire
4. *Behavior coding.* Researchers closely monitor interviews, often using audio or videotapes, for misstatements, hesitations, missed instructions, nonresponse, refusals, puzzled looks, answers that do not fit any of the response categories, and so forth.
5. *Field experiments.* Researchers administer alternative forms of the questionnaire items in field settings and compare results.
6. *Vignettes and debriefing.* Interviewers and respondents are presented with short, invented "lifelike" situations and asked which questionnaire response category they would use.

Sources: Dillman and Redine (2004), Fowler (2004), Martin (2004, Tourangeau (2004a, 2004b), Willis (2004), and van der Zouwen and Smit (2004).

relevant information, (3) integrate and evaluate the information, and (4) select a response category (see Willis, 2004, and van der Zouwen and Smit, 2004). Another development has been **cognitive interviewing,** in which researchers examine how respondents answer questions during pilot tests. They use this information to refine the questionnaire or interviewing process. Cognitive interviewing is used with a collection of pilot test evaluation techniques (see Box 10.17). In his discussion of memory processing and interview behavior, Willis (2004:31) noted that "verbal reports may be limited to cases when the investigator and research participants fail to share an identical mental representation of the task."

Another related development draws on ethnomethodology (see Chapter 13) and conversation analysis to study the interview process as a special type of social interaction and speech event. Some researchers have observed that even standardized interviews vary a lot and suggested viewing interviews as more of a collaborative encounter between interviewer and respondent. This suggests treating nonstandardized interview behaviors, such as respondent queries or minor forms of interviewer feedback (saying humm, laughter, smiling), as opportunities to learn more about the interview.[72]

THE ETHICAL SURVEY

Like all social research, people can conduct surveys in ethical or unethical ways. A major ethical issue in survey research is the invasion of privacy.[73] Survey researchers can intrude into a respondent's privacy by asking about intimate actions and personal beliefs. People have a right to privacy. Respondents decide when and to whom to reveal personal information. They are likely to provide such information honestly when it is asked for in a comfortable context with mutual trust, when they believe serious answers are needed for legitimate research purposes, and when they believe answers will remain confidential. Researchers should treat all respondents with dignity and reduce discomfort. They are also responsible for protecting the confidentiality of data.

A second issue involves voluntary participation by respondents. Respondents agree to answer questions and can refuse to participate at any time. They give "informed consent" to participate in research. Researchers depend on respondents' voluntary cooperation, so researchers need to ask well-developed questions in a sensitive way, treat respondents with respect, and be very sensitive to confidentiality.

A third ethical issue is the exploitation of surveys and pseudosurveys. Because of its popularity, some people use surveys to mislead others. A **pseudosurvey** is when someone uses the survey format in an attempt to persuade someone to do something and has little or no real interest in learning information from a respondent. Charlatans use the guise of conducting a survey to invade privacy, gain entry into homes, or "suggle" (sell in the guise of a survey). An example of a pseudosurvey occurred in the 1994 U.S. election campaign as "suppression polls." In this situation, an unknown survey organi-

zation telephoned a potential voter and asked whether the voter supported a given candidate. If the voter supported the candidate, the interviewer asked whether the respondent would still support the candidate if he or she knew that the candidate had an unfavorable characteristic (e.g., had been arrested for drunk driving, used illegal drugs, raised the wages of convicted criminals in prison, etc.). The goal of the interview was not to measure candidate support; rather, it was to identify a candidate's supporters and then attempt to suppress voting. I received such calls, as did an unsuccessful candidate for governor who was the object of the suppression poll. No one has been prosecuted for using this campaign tactic.

Another ethical issue is when people misuse survey results or use poorly designed or purposely rigged surveys. People may demand answers from surveys that surveys cannot provide or may not understand a survey's limitations. Those who design and prepare surveys may lack sufficient training to conduct a legitimate survey. Policy decisions made based on careless or poorly designed surveys may result in waste and human hardship. Such misuse makes it important that legitimate researchers conduct methodologically rigorous survey research.

Mass media reporting of survey results and the quality of surveys being reported permits abuse.[74] Few people reading survey results may appreciate it, but researchers should include details about the survey (see Box 10.18) to reduce the misuse of survey research and increase questions about surveys that lack such information. Survey researchers urge the media to include such information, but it is rarely included. Over 88 percent of reports on surveys in the mass media fail to reveal the researcher who conducted the survey, and only 18 percent provide details on how the survey was conducted.[75] This occurs while the media report more surveys than other types of social research.

Currently, there are no quality-control standards to regulate the opinion polls or surveys reported in the U.S. media (see Box 10.19).

> **Pseudosurvey**   A false and deceptive survey-like action in which someone uses the format of a survey interview but the true purpose is to persuade a respondent.

10.18 Ten Items to Include When Reporting Survey Research

1. The sampling frame used (e.g., telephone directories)
2. The dates on which the survey was conducted
3. The population that the sample represents (e.g., U.S. adults, Australian college students)
4. The size of the sample for which information was collected
5. The sampling method (e.g., random)
6. The exact wording of the questions asked
7. The method of the survey (e.g., face to face, telephone)
8. The organizations that sponsored the survey (who paid for it and conducted it)
9. The response rate or percentage of those contacted who actually completed the questionnaire
10. Any missing information or "don't know" responses when results on specific questions are reported

Researchers have made unsuccessful attempts since World War II to require adequate samples, interviewer training and supervision, satisfactory questionnaire design, public availability of results, and controls on the integrity of survey organizations.[76]

As a result, the mass media report both biased and misleading survey results and rigorous, professional survey results without distinction. The media report "the commonly cited margins of error . . . [that] promote overconfidence in survey estimates. These figures commonly account only for sampling variations and do not take into account other sources of variation in survey estimates" (Turner and Martin, 1984:107). It is not surprising that public confusion and a distrust of all surveys occurs.

CONCLUSION

In this chapter, you learned about survey research. Survey research is the most widely used social research technique. You also learned some principles of writing good survey questions. There are many things to avoid and to include when writing questions. You learned about the advantages and disadvantages of four types of survey research: mail, telephone interviews, face-to-face interviews, and web surveys. You saw that interviewing, especially face-to-face interviewing, can be difficult.

Although this chapter focused on survey research, researchers use questionnaires to measure variables in other types of quantitative research

10.19 Problems with *Money* Magazine's "Best Places to Live" Poll

Each year since the late 1980s, *Money* magazine has published a list of the "Best Places to Live in America" that ranks 300 U.S. metropolitan areas. The results get widespread publicity. Because the city in which I reside has often ranked at or near the top, I was interested in a study by Gutterbock (1997) stating that the magazine "does an unfortunate misservice to the credibility of survey research" (p. 355). The *Money* data are based on an annual telephone interview survey of 250 subscribers to *Money* magazine, with a substantial oversampling of new subscribers. Respondents are asked to rate 40 characteristics (e.g., crime rate, sunny weather, property taxes, etc.) on a scale from 1 to 10. Little information on details of the methods is published, and Gutterbock could learn only a little more from the magazine officials. In the telephone surveys, there are

few "callbacks" and within-household sampling is not used. The sampling frame is unclear, but it is apparently a list of subscribers who provide phone numbers. The estimated response rate is a low 36 percent. The magazine does not provide question wording but changes questions slightly over the years. A ranking index is created by combining responses, but the weights for the index are not made public. Of the 40 items included, a large number (10) involve the economy. Far fewer cover other issues (e.g., 3 on education, 4 on housing). Gutterbock argues that the "Best Places to Live" poll is based on inadequate survey methods, reporting on methodology that is far below professional standards, and a presentation of findings in a manner that "substantially misrepresents the public's views" (p. 535).

(e.g., experiments). The survey, often called the sample survey because random sampling is usually used with it, is a distinct technique. It is a process of asking many people the same questions and examining their answers.

Survey researchers try to minimize errors, but survey data often contain them. Errors in surveys can compound each other. For example, errors can arise in sampling frames, from nonresponse, from question wording or order, and from interviewer bias. Do not let the existence of errors discourage you from using the survey, however. Instead, learn to be very careful when designing survey research and cautious about generalizing from the results of surveys.

KEY TERMS

closed-ended question
cognitive interviewing
computer-assisted telephone
   interviewing (CATI)
context effects
contingency question
double-barreled question
floaters
full-filter question
funnel sequence
Interactive Voice Response
   (IVR)

leverage salience theory
matrix question
naïve assumption model
open-ended question
order effects
partially open question
prestige bias
probe
pseudosurvey
quasi-filter question
randomized response technique
   (RRT)

recency effect
sleeper question
social desirability bias
standard-format question
tailoring
telescoping
time budget survey
wording effects

REVIEW QUESTIONS

1. What are the six types of things surveys often ask about? Give an example of each that is different from the examples in the book.

2. Why are surveys called *correlational,* and how do they differ from experiments?

3. What five changes occurred in the 1960s and 1970s that dramatically affected survey research?

4. Identify 5 of the 10 things to avoid in question writing.

5. What topics are threatening to respondents, and how can a researcher ask about them?

6. What are advantages and disadvantages of open-ended versus closed-ended questions?

7. What are filtered, quasi-filtered, and standard-format questions? How do they relate to floaters?

8. How does ordinary conversation differ from a survey interview?

9. Under what conditions are mail questionnaires, telephone interviews, web surveys, or face-to-face interviews best?

10. What are CATI and IVR, and when might they be useful?

NOTES

1. For such criticism of a strict positivist approach, see Carr-Hill (1984b), Denzin (1989), Mishler (1986), and Phillips (1971).

2. "Why" questions require special techniques. See Barton (1995) and Wilson and colleagues (1996).

3. The history of survey research is discussed in Converse (1987), Hyman (1991), Marsh (1982:9–47), Miller (1983:19–125), Moser and Kalton (1972:6–15), Rossi and colleagues (1983), Sudman (1976b), and Sudman and Bradburn (1987).

4. See Bannister (1987), Blumer (1991a, 1991b), Blumer and associates (1991), Camic and Xie (1994), Cohen (1991), Deegan (1988), Ross (1991), Sklar (1991), Turner (1991), and Yeo (1991). Also see R. Smith (1996) on how political ideological conflicts and how private foundations in the United States in the 1950s and 1960s affected how survey research developed.

5. See Scheuch (1990) for an introduction to national surveys conducted in various countries.

6. See Converse (1987:383–385), *Statistical Abstract of the United States,* and Rossi and colleagues (1983:8).

7. As Hyman (1975:4) remarked, "All scientific inquiry is subject to error, and it is far better to be aware of what it is, to study the sources in an attempt to reduce it, and to estimate the magnitudes of errors in our findings, than to be ignorant of errors concealed in the data." Examples include Bishop and colleagues (1983, 1984, 1985), Bradburn (1983), Bradburn and Sudman (1980), Cannell and colleagues (1981), Converse and Presser (1986), Groves and Kahn (1979), Hyman (1991), Schuman and Presser (1981), Sudman and Bradburn (1983), and Tanur (1992).

8. For more on studies of behavior in survey situations, see Groves and colleagues (2000), Groves and Couper (1998), Lacy (2001), Lyberg et al. (1997), Schacter (2001), Schwarz and Sudman (1992, 1994), Sniderman and Grob (1996), and Sudman and colleagues (1996).

9. See Rossi and associates (1983:10).

10. See Bayless (1981) on the Research Triangle Institute.

11. For a list of survey organizations, see Bradburn and Sudman (1988).

12. For a discussion of pilot-testing techniques, see Bishop (1992), Bolton and Bronkhorst (1996), Fowler and Cannell (1996), and Sudman and colleagues (1996).

13. The administration of survey research is discussed in Backstrom and Hursh-Cesar (1981:38–45), Dillman (1978:200–281; 1983), Frey (1983:129–169), Groves and Kahn (1979:40–78, 186–212), Prewitt (1983), Tanur (1983), and Warwick and Lininger (1975:20–45, 220–264).

14. Similar lists of prohibitions can be found in Babbie (1990:127–132), Backstrom and Hursh-Cesar (1981: 140–153), Bailey (1987:110–115), Bradburn and Sudman (1988:145–153), Converse and Presser (1986:13–31), de-Vaus (1986:71–74), Dillman (1978:95–117), Fowler (1984:75–86), Frey (1983:116–127), Moser and Kalton (1972:318–341), Sheatsley (1983:216–217), Sudman and Bradburn (1983:132–136), and Warwick and Lininger (1975:140–148).

15. Sudman and Bradburn (1983:39) suggest that even simple questions (e.g., "What brand of soft drink do you usually buy?") can cause problems. Respondents who are highly loyal to one brand of traditional carbonated sodas can answer the question easily. Other respondents must implicitly address several questions to answer the question as it was asked.

16. See Schaeffer (2000) and Sudman and colleagues (1996:197–226).

17. See Ostrom and Gannon (1996).

18. See Abelson and associates (1992), Auriat (1993), Bernard and associates (1984), Croyle and Loftus (1992), Gaskell and colleagues (2000), Krosnick and Abelson (1992), Loftus and colleagues (1990), Loftus and colleagues (1992), Pearson and Dawes (1992), and Sudman and colleagues (1996).

19. See Bradburn (1983), Bradburn and Sudman (1980), and Sudman and Bradburn (1983) on threatening or sensitive questions. Backstrom and Hursh-Cesar (1981:219) and Warwick and Lininger (1975:150–151) provide useful suggestions as well. Fox and Tracy (1986) discuss the randomized response technique. Also see DeLamater and MacCorquodale (1975) on measuring sexual behavior and Herzberger (1993) for design issues when examining sensitive topics.

20. For studies on survey format and answer honesty, see Holbrook and associates (2004), Johnson et al. (1989), Schaeffer and Presser (2003:75), and Tourangeau and colleagues (2002).

21. See Couper and associates (2003), DeMaio (1984), and Sudman and Bradburn (1983:59).

22. For more on surveys with threatening or sensitive topics and computer-assisted techniques, see Aquilino and Losciuto (1990), Couper and Rowe (1996), Johnson and associates (1989), Tourangeau and Smith (1996), and Wright and associates (1998).

23. For a discussion of knowledge questions, see Backstrom and Hursh-Cesar (1981:124–126), Converse and Presser (1986:24–31), Sudman and Bradburn (1983:88–118), and Warwick and Lininger (1975:158–160).

24. On how "Who knows who lives here?" can be complicated, see Martin (1999) and Tourangeau et al. (1997).

25. See Archibald (1998).

26. Contingency questions are discussed in Babbie (1990:136–138), Bailey (1987:135–137), deVaus (1986:78–80), Dillman (1978:144–146), and Sudman and Bradburn (1983:250–251).

27. For a further discussion of open and closed questions, see Bailey (1987:117–122), Converse (1984), Converse and Presser (1986:33–34), deVaus (1986:74–75), Geer (1988), Moser and Kalton (1972:341–345), Schuman and Presser (1979; 1981:79–111), Sudman and Bradburn (1983:149–155), and Warwick and Lininger (1975:132–140).

28. See Gilljam and Grandberg (1993).

29. For a discussion of the "don't know," "no opinion," and middle positions in response categories, see Backstrom and Hursh-Cesar (1981:148–149), Bishop (1987), Bradburn and Sudman (1988:154), Brody (1986), Converse and Presser (1986:35–37), Duncan and Stenbeck (1988), Poe and associates (1988), Sudman and Bradburn (1983:140–141), and Schuman and Presser (1981:113–178). For more on filtered questions, see Bishop and colleagues (1983, 1984) and Bishop and colleagues (1986).

30. See Krosnick et al. (2002), Schaefer and Presser (2003:79–80), and Tourganeau (2004:786).

31. The disagree/agree versus specific alternatives debate is discussed in Bradburn and Sudman (1988:149–151), Converse and Presser (1986:38–39), Schuman and Presser (1981:179–223), and Sudman and Bradburn (1983: 119–140). Backstrom and Hursh-Cesar (1981:136–140) discuss asking Likert, agree/disagree questions.

32. See McCarty and Shrum (2000) and Narayan and Krosnick (1996).

33. The ranking versus ratings issue is discussed in Alwin and Krosnick (1985), Krosnick and Alwin (1988), and Presser (1984). Also see Backstrom and Hursh-Cesar (1981:132–134) and Sudman and Bradburn (1983: 156–165) for formats of asking rating and ranking questions.

34. For more on specific design issues, see Christian and Dillman (2004), Dillman and Redline (2004), Kaplowitz and associates (2004), Ostrom and Gannon (1996), Schwarz and associates (1991), and Tourangeau and colleagues (2004).

35. For a discussion of wording effects in questionnaires, see Bradburn and Miles (1979), Peterson (1984), Schuman and Presser (1981:275–296), Sheatsley (1983), and Smith (1987). Hippler and Schwarz (1986) found the same difference between *forbid* and *not allow* in the Federal Republic of Germany.

36. See Foddy (1993) and Presser (1990).

37. The length of questionnaires is discussed in Dillman (1978:51–57; 1983), Frey (1983:48–49), Herzog and Bachman (1981), and Sudman and Bradburn (1983: 226–227).

38. For a discussion of the sequence of questions or question order effects, see Backstrom and Hursh-Cesar (1981:154–176), Bishop and colleagues (1985), Bradburn (1983:302–304), Bradburn and Sudman (1988: 153–154), Converse and Presser (1986:39–40), Dillman (1978:218–220), McFarland (1981), McKee and O'Brien (1988), Moser and Kalton (1972:346–347), Schuman and Ludwig (1983), Schuman and Presser (1981:23–74), Schwartz and Hippler (1995), and Sudman and Bradburn (1983:207–226). Also see Knäuper (1999), Krosnick (1992), Lacy (2001), and T. Smith (1992) on the issue of question-order effects.

39. A study by Krosnick (1992) and a meta-analysis (Narayan and Krosnick, 1996) show that education reduces response-order (primacy or recency) effects, but Knäuper (1999) found that age is strongly associated with response-order effects.

40. This example comes from Strack (1992).

41. For additional discussions of context effects, see Schuman (1992), Smith (1992), Todorov (2000a, 2000b), and Tourangeau (1992).

42. Tarnai and Dillman (1992) discuss how the method of survey affects context effects.

43. For a discussion of format and layout, see Babbie (1990), Backstrom and Hursh-Cesar (1981:187–236), Dillman (1978, 1983), Mayer and Piper (1982), Sudman and Bradburn (1983:229–260), Survey Research Center (1976), and Warwick and Lininger (1975:151–157).

44. For a discussion, see Couper, Singer et al. (1998), de Heer (1999), Keeter et al. (2000), Sudman and Bradburn (1983:11), and "Surveys Proliferate, but Answers Dwindle," *New York Times* (October 5, 1990), p. 1. Smith (1995) and Sudman (1976b:114–116) also discuss refusal rates.

45. For additional discussion of nonresponse and refusal rates, see Backstrom and Hursh-Cesar (1981:140–141, 274–275), DeMaio (1980), Frey (1983:38–41), Groves and Couper (1998), Groves and Kahn (1979:218–223), Martin (1985:701–706), Nederhof (1986), Oksenberg and associates (1986), Schuman and Presser (1981:

331–336), Sigelman (1982), Stech (1981), Sudman and Bradburn (1983), and Yu and Cooper (1983). For a discussion of methods for calculating response rates, see Bailey (1987:169), Dillman (1978:49–51), Fowler (1984:46–52), and Frey (1983:38).

46. Link and Oldendick (1999) examined telephone screening.

47. See Pottick and Lerman (1991) for a discussion of the study.

48. Introductions and incentives are discussed in Brehm (1994), Couper (1997), Goldstein and Jennings (2002), Singer (1999), Singer and associates (1998), Singer and associates (1999), Singer and associates (2000), and Trussell and Lavrakas (2004). Dillman and colleagues (1996) discuss mandatory appeals.

49. More extensive discussions of how to increase mail questionnaire return rates can be found in Bailey (1987:153–168), Church (1993), Dillman (1978, 1983), Fox and colleagues (1988), Goyder (1982), Heberlein and Baumgartner (1978, 1981), Hubbard and Little (1988), Jones (1979), and Willimack and colleagues (1995).

50. The importance of tailoring and related entry techniques is discussed in Brehm (1994), Groves and Couper (1996, 1998, 2004), and Groves, Presser, and Dipko (2004).

51. CATI is discussed in Bailey (1987:201–202), Bradburn and Sudman (1988:100–101), Freeman and Shanks (1983), Frey (1983:24–25, 143–149), Groves and Kahn (1979:226), Groves and Mathiowetz (1984), and Karweit and Meyers (1983).

52. For comparison of surveys, see Backstrom and Hursh-Cesar (1981:16–23), Bradburn and Sudman (1988:94–110), Dillman (1978:39–78), Fowler (1984:61–73), and Frey (1983:27–55).

53. For Internet usage, see Robyn Greenspan "Three-Quarters of Americans Have Access from Home," *ClickZ News* (March 18, 2004), www.clickz.com/news/article.php/3328091; Amanda Lenhart, "Who's Not Online," Pew Internet and American Life Project, Washington, DC (September 21, 2000), www.pewinternet.org/report_display.asp?r=21. For discussions of web and e-mail surveys see Birnhaum (2004), Couper (2000), Couper et al. (2001), Fox and associates (2003), Koch and Emrey (2001), and Tourangeau (2004a:792–794).

54. Elite interviewing is discussed in Dexter (1970). Also see Galaskiewicz (1987), Useem (1984), Verba and Orren (1985), and Zuckerman (1972).

55. See Andorka (1987).

56. See ERIC (1976), Hornsby-Smith (1974), Jordan and Layzell (1992), Meyer (1998), Milem and colleagues (2000), and Wiedmer (1993) for faculty hours.

57. Dillman (1983) and Groves and Kahn (1979: 188–212) discuss costs.

58. For more on interviewing, see Brenner and colleagues (1985), Cannell and Kahn (1968), Converse and Schuman (1974), Dijkstra and van der Zouwen (1982), Foddy (1993), Gorden (1980), Hyman (1975), Moser and Kalton (1972:270–302), and Survey Research Center (1976). For a discussion of telephone interviewing, see Frey (1983), Groves and Mathiowetz (1984), Jordan and colleagues (1980), and Tucker (1983).

59. See Turner and Martin (1984:262–269, 282).

60. From Moser and Kalton (1972:273).

61. The use of probes is discussed in Backstrom and Hursh-Cesar (1981:266–273), Foddy (1995), Schober and Conrad (1997), and Smith (1989). Gorden (1980:368–390), Hyman (1975:236–241), Scholer and Conrad (1997), and Smith (1989).

62. For a discussion of interviewer training, see Backstrom and Hursh-Cesar (1981:237–307), Billiet and Loosveldt (1988), Bradburn and Sudman (1980), Oksenberg and associates (1986), Singer and Kohnke-Aguirre (1979), and Tucker (1983).

63. See Leal and Hess (1999).

64. See Bradburn and Sudman (1980), Pollner and Adams (1997), and Zane and Matsoukas (1979).

65. The race or ethnicity of interviewers is discussed in Anderson and colleagues (1988), Bradburn (1983), Cotter and colleagues (1982), Finkel and colleagues (1991), Gorden (1980:168–172), Reese and colleagues (1986), Schaeffer (1980), Schuman and Converse (1971), and Weeks and Moore (1981). Davis (1997) found that when African Americans are interviewed by Whites, they put "self-imposed limits on free expression" and are less likely to say that Whites keep Blacks down or that Blacks do not have the power to affect change.

66. See Catania and associates (1996) and Kane and MacAulay (1993).

67. See Sudman and associates (1996:74–76).

68. See Bateson (1984), Clark and Schober (1992), Foddy (1993), Lessler (1984), and Turner (1984).

69. From Turner and Martin (1984:276).

70. See Briggs (1986), Cicourel (1982), and Mishler (1986) for critiques of survey research interviewing.

71. For additional discussion of ordinary conversation and survey interviews, see Beatty (1995), Conrad and Schober (2000), Groves and colleagues (1992), Moore

(2004), Schaeffer (2004), Schober and Conrad (2004), Smith (1984), and Suchman and Jordan (1992).

72. Maynard and Schaeffer (2004), Moore (2004), Schaeffer (2004), and Schober and Conrad (2004) discuss pilot testing methods such as the cognitive interview and related techniques.

73. For a discussion of ethical concerns specific to survey research, see Backstrom and Hursh-Cesar (1981:46–50), Fowler (1984:135–144), Frey (1983:177–185), Kelman (1982:79–81), and Reynolds (1982:48–57). Marsh (1982:125–146) and Miller (1983:47–96) provided useful discussions for and against the use of survey research. The use of informed consent is discussed in Singer and Frankel (1982) and in Sobal (1984).

74. On reporting survey results in the media, see Channels (1993) and MacKeun (1984).

75. See Singer (1988).

76. From Turner and Martin (1984:62).

Nonreactive Research and Secondary Analysis

There are a number of research conditions in which the sole use of the interview or questionnaire leaves unanswerable rival explanations. The purpose of those less popular measurement classes emphasized here is to bolster these weak spots and provide intelligence to evaluate threats to validity. The payout for using these measures is high, but the approach is more demanding of the investigator.
—Eugene Webb et al., *Nonreactive Measures in the Social Sciences*, pp. 315–316

Experiments and survey research are both *reactive*; that is, the people being studied are aware of that fact. In this chapter you will learn about four research techniques that are *nonreactive;* that is, those being studied are not aware that they are part of a research project. Nonreactive techniques are largely based on positivist principles but are also used by interpretive and critical researchers.

The first technique you will learn about is a loose collection of inventive **nonreactive measures.** It is followed by content analysis, which builds on the fundamentals of quantitative research design and is a well-developed research technique in the social sciences. Existing statistics and secondary analysis, the last two techniques, refer to the collection of existing information from government

documents or previous surveys. Researchers examine the data in new ways to address new questions. Although the data may have been reactive when first collected, a researcher can address new questions without reactive effects.

NONREACTIVE MEASUREMENT

The Logic of Nonreactive Research

Nonreactive measurement begins when a researcher notices something that indicates a variable of inter-

> **Nonreactive measures** A class of measures in which people being studied are unaware that they are part of a study.

est. In nonreactive or **unobtrusive measures** (i.e., measures that are not obtrusive or intrusive), the people being studied are not aware of it but leave evidence of their social behavior or actions "naturally." The observant researcher infers from the evidence to behavior or attitudes without disrupting those being studied. Unnoticed observation is also a type of nonreactive measure. For example, McKelvie and Schamer (1988) unobtrusively observed whether drivers stopped at stop signs. They made observations during both daytime and nighttime. Observers noted whether the driver was male or female; whether the driver was alone or with passengers; whether other traffic was present; and whether the car came to a complete stop, a slow stop, or no stop. Later, we will contrast this type of observation to a slightly different type used in field research.

Varieties of Nonreactive or Unobtrusive Observation

Nonreactive measures are varied, and researchers have been creative in inventing indirect ways to measure social behavior (see Box 11.1). Because the measures have little in common except being nonreactive, they are best learned through examples. Some are **erosion measures,** whereby selective wear is used as a measure, and some are **accretion measures,** whereby the measures are deposits of something left behind.[1]

Researchers have examined family portraits in different historical eras to see how gender relations within the family are reflected in seating patterns. Urban anthropologists have examined the contents of garbage dumps to learn about lifestyles from what is thrown away (e.g., liquor bottles indicate level of alcohol consumption). Based on garbage, people underreport their liquor consumption by 40 to 60 percent (Rathje and Murphy, 1992:71). Researchers have studied the listening habits of drivers by checking what stations their radios are tuned to when cars are repaired. They have measured interest in different exhibits by noting worn tiles on the floor in different parts of a museum. They have studied differences in graffiti in male versus female high school restrooms to show gender differences in themes. Some have examined high school yearbooks

BOX **11.1** Finding Data on Tombstones

Foster and colleagues (1998) examined the tombstones in 10 cemeteries in an area of Illinois for the period from 1830 to 1989. They retrieved data on birth and death dates and gender from over 2,000 of the 2,028 burials. The researchers learned the area differed from some national trends. They found that conceptions had two peaks (spring and winter), females ages 10 to 64 had a higher death rate than males, and younger people died in late summer but older people in late winter.

to compare the high school activities of those who had psychological problems in latter life versus those who did not. Researchers have noted bumper stickers in support of different political candidates to see if one candidate's supporters are more likely than another's to obey traffic laws. Some have even measured television-watching habits by noting changes in water pressure due to the use of toilets during television commercials.[2] (Also see Box 11.2.)

Recording and Documentation

Creating nonreactive measures follows the logic of quantitative measurement, although qualitive researchers also use nonreactive observation. A researcher first conceptualizes a construct, then links the construct to nonreactive empirical evidence, which is its measure. The operational definition of the variable includes how the researcher systematically notes and records observations.

Because nonreactive measures indicate a construct indirectly, the researcher needs to rule out

Unobtrusive measures Another name for nonreactive measures that emphasizes how the people being studied are not aware of it because the measures do not intrude.

Erosion measures Nonreactive measures of the wear or deterioration on surfaces due to the activity of people.

Accretion measures Nonreactive measures of the residue of the activity of people or what they leave behind.

BOX **11.2** **Examples of Nonreactive Measures**

PHYSICAL TRACES

Erosion: Wear suggests greater use.
Example: A researcher examines children's toys at a day care that were purchased at the same time. Worn-out toys suggest greater interest by the children.

Accretion: Accumulation of physical evidence suggests behavior.
Example: A researcher examines the brands of aluminum beverage cans in trash or recycling bins in male and female dormitories. This indicates the brands and types of beverages favored by each sex.

ARCHIVES

Running Records: Regularly produced public records may reveal much.
Example: A researcher examines marriage records for the bride and groom's ages. Regional differences suggest that the preference for males marrying younger females is greater in certain areas of the country.

Other Records: Irregular or private records can reveal a lot.
Example: A researcher finds the number of reams of paper purchased by a college dean's office for 10

years when student enrollment was stable. A sizable increase suggests that bureaucratic paperwork has increased.

OBSERVATION

External Appearance: How people appear may indicate social factors.
Example: A researcher watches students to see whether they are more likely to wear their school's colors and symbols after the school team has won or lost.

Count Behaviors: Counting how many people do something can be informative.
Example: A researcher counts the number of men and women who come to a full stop and those who come to a rolling stop at a stop sign. This suggests gender difference in driving behavior.

Time Duration: How long people take to do things may indicate their attention.
Example: A researcher measures how long men and women pause in front of the painting of a nude man and in front of a painting of a nude woman. Time may indicate embarrassment or interest in same or cross-sex nudity by each sex.

---

reasons for the observation other than the construct of interest. For example, a researcher wants to measure customer walking traffic in a store. The researcher's measure is dirt and wear on floor tiles. He or she first clarifies what the customer traffic means (e.g., Is the floor a path to another department? Does it indicate a good location for a visual display?). Next, he or she systematically measures dirt or wear on the tiles, compares it to that in other locations, and records results on a regular basis (e.g., every month). Finally, the researcher rules out other reasons for the observations (e.g., the floor tile is of lower quality and wears faster, or the location is near an outside entrance).

> **Text** A general name for a communication medium from which symbolic meaning is measured in content analysis.

CONTENT ANALYSIS

What Is Content Analysis?

Content analysis is a technique for gathering and analyzing the content of text. The *content* refers to words, meanings, pictures, symbols, ideas, themes, or any message that can be communicated. The **text** is anything written, visual, or spoken that serves as a medium for communication. It includes books, newspaper or magazine articles, advertisements, speeches, official documents, films or videotapes, musical lyrics, photographs, articles of clothing, or works of art. For example, Cerulo (1989) studied national anthems.

Content analysis goes back nearly a century and is used in many fields—literature, history, journalism, political science, education, psychology, and so on. At the first meeting of the German

BOX **11.3** How Qualitative Researchers Study Documents or Statistical Reports

Qualitative researchers who use the interpretative or critical approaches also study documents and reports with statistical information, but they tend to do so differently. They consider documents and statistical reports to be cultural objects, or media that communicate social meaning. They see the documents as belonging to a range of other cultural objects (e.g., monuments, diaries, musical scores, shopping lists, films, photographs, paintings, engineering drawings, web pages) that carry meaning. For example, an architectural floor plan is a document that expresses spatial arrangements that convey social meanings. Some offices are located in desirable locations with large windows designed for holders of certain job positions.

Instead of treating a document or statistical report as a neutral container of content, qualitative researchers examine the larger context of its creation, distribution, and reception. Consistent with a constructionist perspective (discussed in Chapter 4), qualitative researchers emphasize the entire process, from a document's creation (including the intentions of creators) through its consumption or reception by various receivers/consumers, and they situate the document in a social context. In short, they treat the document or report itself as a cultural object that carries social meaning in its own right. Although they may examine the content inside a document or report, they do not limit themselves to content.

Qualitative researchers emphasize that people think and interact on the basis of meaning as well as with words or numbers. For example, the content in one document may convey medical information to health care workers, grant a person access to a social service, sell products to a consumer, inform officials of geographic areas where problems exist, or allow/prevent a person's entry into a country. Different people may put the same document or report to different uses at different times, and processes of "reading" or interpreting documents often depend on training and following rules. For example, people learn what to look for in a medical record, statistical report, or passport. People looking at the same document may see different things, follow different rules, and use it for different purposes (e.g., grant insurance reimbursement or prescribe a medical treatment, test a hypothesis or allocate funds for a new public building, allow someone into a country, or cash a check). They look at multiple facets of a document and its content. For example, a magazine article can carry content that entertains readers, is a vehicle that allows an author to build a reputation, triggers a public controversy, and is a way to boost magazine sales (see Griswold, 1987, 1994, and Prior, 2003, on the study of cultural objects and documents).

Sociological Society, in 1910, Max Weber suggested using it to study newspapers.[3]

In quantitative content analysis, a researcher uses objective and systematic counting and recording procedures to produce a numerical description of the symbolic content in a text.[4] There are qualitative or interpretive versions of content analysis (see Box 11.3). The emphasis here is on quantitative data about a text's content.

Content analysis is nonreactive because the process of placing words, messages, or symbols in a text to communicate to a reader or receiver occurs without influence from the researcher who analyzes its content. For example, I, as author of this book, wrote words or drew diagrams to communicate research methods content to you, the student. The way the book was written and the way you read it are without any knowledge or intention of its ever being content analyzed.

Content analysis lets a researcher reveal the content (i.e., messages, meanings, etc.) in a source of communication (i.e., a book, article, movie, etc.). It lets him or her probe into and discover content in a different way from the ordinary way of reading a book or watching a television program.

With content analysis, a researcher can compare content across many texts and analyze it with quantitative techniques (e.g., charts and tables). In addition, he or she can reveal aspects of the text's content that are difficult to see. For example, you might watch television commercials and feel that non-Whites rarely appear in commercials for expensive consumer goods (e.g., luxury cars, furs, jewelry, perfume, etc.). Content analysis can document—in objective, quantitative terms—whether your vague feelings based on unsystematic observation are true. It yields repeatable, precise results about the text. As a content analysis researcher gathers the data, he or she analyzes them with statistics in the same way that an experimenter or survey researcher would.

Topics Appropriate for Content Analysis

Researchers have used content analysis for many purposes: to study themes in popular songs and religious symbols in hymns, trends in the topics that newspapers cover and the ideological tone of newspaper editorials, sex-role stereotypes in textbooks or feature films, how often people of different races appear in television commercials and programs, answers to open-ended survey questions, enemy propaganda during wartime, the covers of popular magazines, personality characteristics from suicide notes, themes in advertising messages, gender differences in conversations, and so on.

Generalizations that researchers make on the basis of content analysis are limited to the cultural communication itself. Content analysis cannot determine the truthfulness of an assertion or evaluate the aesthetic qualities of literature. It reveals the content in text but cannot interpret the content's significance. Researchers should examine the text directly. Holsti (1968a:602) warned, "Content analysis may be considered as a supplement to, not as a substitute for, subjective examination of documents."

Content analysis is useful for three types of research problems. First, it is helpful for problems involving a large volume of text. A researcher can measure large amounts of text (e.g., years of newspaper articles) with sampling and multiple coders. Second, it is helpful when a topic must be studied "at a distance." For example, content analysis can be

used to study historical documents, the writings of someone who has died, or broadcasts in a hostile foreign country. Finally, content analysis can reveal messages in a text that are difficult to see with casual observation. The creator of the text or those who read it may not be aware of all its themes, biases, or characteristics. For example, authors of preschool picture books may not consciously intend to portray children in traditional stereotyped sex roles, but a high degree of sex stereotyping has been revealed through content analysis.[5] Another example is that of conversations in all-male versus all-female groups. Although people may be unaware of it, in same-sex groups, women talk more about interpersonal matters and social relationships, whereas men talk more about achievement and aggressive themes.[6]

Measurement and Coding

General Issues. Careful measurement is crucial because a researcher takes diffuse and murky symbolic communication and turns it into precise, objective, quantitative data. He or she carefully designs and documents procedures for coding to make replication possible. For example, a researcher wants to determine how frequently television dramas portray elderly characters in terms of negative stereotypes. He or she develops a measure of the construct "negative stereotypes of the elderly." The conceptualization may result in a list of stereotypes or negative generalizations about older people (e.g., senile, forgetful, cranky, frail, hard of hearing, slow, ill, in nursing homes, inactive, conservative, etc.) that do not accurately reflect the elderly. For example, if 5 percent of people over age 65 are in nursing homes, yet 50 percent of those over age 65 on television are portrayed as being in nursing homes, it is evidence of negative stereotyping.[7]

Constructs in content analysis are operationalized with a **coding system,** a set of instructions or rules on how to systematically observe and record content from text. A researcher tailors it to the type of text or communication medium being studied (e.g., television drama, novels, photos in magazine advertisements, etc.). It also depends on the researcher's unit of analysis.

Coding system   A set of instructions or rules used in content analysis to explain how a researcher systematically converted the symbolic content from text into quantitative data.

Units. The unit of analysis can vary a great deal in content analysis. It can be a word, a phrase, a theme, a plot, a newspaper article, a character, and so forth. In addition to units of analysis, researchers use other units in content analysis that may or may not be the same as units of analysis: recording units, context units, and enumeration units. There are few differences among them, and they are easily confused, but each has a distinct role. In simple projects, all three are the same.

What Is Measured? Measurement in content analysis uses **structured observation:** systematic, careful observation based on written rules. The rules explain how to categorize and classify observations. As with other measurement, categories should be mutually exclusive and exhaustive. Written rules make replication possible and improve reliability. Although researchers begin with preliminary coding rules, they often conduct a pilot study and refine coding on the basis of it.

Coding systems identify four characteristics of text content: frequency, direction, intensity, and space. A researcher measures from one to all four characteristics in a content analysis research project.

Frequency. *Frequency* simply means counting whether or not something occurs and, if it occurs, how often. For example, how many elderly people appear on a television program within a given week? What percentage of all characters are they, or in what percentage of programs do they appear?

Direction. *Direction* is noting the direction of messages in the content along some continuum (e.g., positive or negative, supporting or opposed). For example, a researcher devises a list of ways an elderly television character can act. Some are positive (e.g., friendly, wise, considerate) and some are negative (e.g., nasty, dull, selfish).

Intensity. *Intensity* is the strength or power of a message in a direction. For example, the characteristic of forgetfulness can be minor (e.g., not remembering to take your keys when leaving home, taking time to recall the name of someone who you have not seen in years) or major (e.g., not remembering your name, not recognizing your children).

Space. A researcher can record the size of a text message or the amount of space or volume allocated to it. *Space* in written text is measured by counting words, sentences, paragraphs, or space on a page (e.g., square inches). For video or audio text, space can be measured by the amount of time allocated. For example, a TV character may be present for a few seconds or continuously in every scene of a two-hour program.

Coding, Validity, and Reliability

Manifest Coding. Coding the visible, surface content in a text is called **manifest coding.** For example, a researcher counts the number of times a phrase or word (e.g., *red*) appears in written text, or whether a specific action (e.g., a kiss) appears in a photograph or video scene. The coding system lists terms or actions that are then located in text. A researcher can use a computer program to search for words or phrases in text and have a computer do the counting work. To do this, he or she learns about the computer program, develops a comprehensive list of relevant words or phrases, and puts the text into a form that computers can read.[8]

Manifest coding is highly reliable because the phrase or word either is or is not present. Unfortunately, manifest coding does not take the connotations of words or phrases into account. The same word can take on different meanings depending on the context. The possibility that there are multiple meanings of a word limits the measurement validity of manifest coding.

For example, I read a book with a *red* cover that is a real *red* herring. Unfortunately, its publisher drowned in *red* ink because the editor could not deal with the *red* tape that occurs when a book is *red* hot. The book has a story about a *red* fire truck that stops

---

Structured observation A method of watching what is happening in a social setting that is highly organized and follows systematic rules for observation and documentation.

Manifest coding A type of content analysis coding in which a researcher first develops a list of words, phrases, or symbols and then locates them in a communication medium.

at *red* lights only after the leaves turn *red.* There is also a group of *Reds* who carry *red* flags to the little *red* schoolhouse. They are opposed by *red*-blooded *red*necks who eat *red* meat and honor the *red,* white, and blue. The main character is a *red*-nosed matador who fights *red* foxes, not bulls, with his *red* cape. *Red*-lipped little *Red* Riding Hood is also in the book. She develops *red* eyes and becomes *red*-faced after eating a lot of *red* peppers in the *red* light district. She is given a *red* backside by her angry mother, a *red*head.

Latent Coding.

A researcher using **latent coding** (also called *semantic analysis*) looks for the underlying, implicit meaning in the content of a text. For example, a researcher reads an entire paragraph and decides whether it contains erotic themes or a romantic mood. His or her coding system has general rules to guide his or her interpretation of the text and for determining whether particular themes or moods are present.

Latent coding tends to be less reliable than manifest coding. It depends on a coder's knowledge of language and social meaning.[9] Training, practice, and written rules improve reliability, but still it is difficult to consistently identify themes, moods, and the like. Yet, the validity of latent coding can exceed that of manifest coding because people communicate meaning in many implicit ways that depend on context, not just in specific words.

A researcher can use both manifest and latent coding. If the two approaches agree, the final result is strengthened; if they disagree, the researcher may want to reexamine the operational and theoretical definitions.

Intercoder Reliability.

Content analysis often involves coding information from a very large number of units. A research project might involve observing the content in dozens of books, hundreds of hours of television programming, or thousands of newspaper articles. In addition to coding the information personally, a researcher may hire assistants to help with the coding. He or she teaches coders the coding system and trains them to fill out a recording sheet. Coders should understand the variables, follow the coding system, and ask about ambiguities. A researcher records all decisions he or she makes about how to treat a new specific coding situation after coding begins so that he or she can be consistent.

A researcher who uses several coders must *always* check for consistency across coders. He or she does this by asking coders to code the same text independently and then checking for consistency across coders. The researcher measures **intercoder reliability,** a type of equivalence reliability, with a statistical coefficient that tells the degree of consistency among coders.[10] The coefficient is *always* reported with the results of content analysis research.

When the coding process stretches over a considerable time period (e.g., more than three months), the researcher also checks stability reliability by having each coder independently code samples of text that were previously coded. He or she then checks to see whether the coding is stable or changing. For example, six hours of television episodes are coded in April and coded again in July without the coders looking at their original coding decisions. Large deviations in coding necessitate retraining and coding the text a second time.

Content Analysis with Visual Material.

Researchers have used content analysis to study visual "text," such as photographs, paintings, statues, buildings, clothing, and videos and film. Visual "text" is difficult to analyze because it communicates messages or emotional content indirectly through images, symbols, and metaphors. Moreover, visual images often contain mixed messages at multiple levels of meaning.

To conduct content analysis on visual text, the researcher must "read" the meaning(s) within visual text. He or she must interpret signs and discover the meanings attached to symbolic images. Such "reading" is not mechanical (i.e., image *X* al-

---

Latent coding   A type of content analysis coding in which a researcher identifies subjective meaning such as themes or motifs and then systematically locates them in a communication medium.

Intercoder reliability   Equivalence reliability in content analysis with multiple content coders that require a high degree of consistency across coders.

ways means *G*); it depends heavily on the cultural context because the meaning of an image is culture bound. For example, a red light does not inevitably mean "stop"; it means "stop" only in cultures in which people have given it that meaning. People construct cultural meanings that they attach to symbolic images, and the meanings can change over time. Some meanings are clearer and more firmly attached to symbols and images than others.

Most people share a common meaning for key symbols of the dominant culture, but various people may read a symbol differently. For example, one group of people "reads" a national flag to mean patriotism, duty to nation, and honor of tradition. For others, the flag evokes fear, because they read it to mean government domination, abuse of power, and military aggression. A researcher pursuing the content analysis of images needs to be aware of potentially divergent readings of symbols.

Sociopolitical groups may invent or construct new symbols with attached meanings (e.g., a pink triangle came to mean gay pride). They may wrestle for control of the meaning of major existing symbols. For example, some people want to assign a religious meaning to the Christmas tree; others want it to represent a celebration of tradition and family values without religious content; and still others want it to mean a festive holiday season for commercial reasons. Because images have symbolic content with complex, multilayer meaning, researchers often combine qualitative judgments about the images with quantitative data in content analysis.

For example, Chavez (2001) conducted a content analysis of the covers of major American magazines that dealt with the issue of immigration into the United States. Looking at the covers of 10 magazines from the mid-1970s to the mid-1990s, he classified the covers as having one of three major messages: affirmative, alarmist, or neutral or balanced. Beyond his classification and identifying trends in messages, he noted how the mix of people (i.e., race, gender, age, and dress) in the photographs and the recurrent use of major symbols, such as the Statute of Liberty or the U.S. flag, communicated messages.

Chavez argued that magazine covers are a site, or location, where cultural meaning is created. Visual images on magazine covers have multiple levels of meaning, and viewers construct specific meanings as they read the image and use their cultural knowledge. Collectively, the covers convey a worldview and express messages about a nation and its people. For example, a magazine cover that displayed the icon of the Statute of Liberty as strong and full of compassion (message: welcome immigrants) was altered to have strong Asian facial features (message: Asian immigrants distorted the national culture and altered the nation's racial makeup), or holding a large stop sign (message: go away immigrants). Chavez (2001: 44) observed that "images on magazines both refer to and, in the process, help to structure and construct contemporary 'American' identity." (See Box 11.4 for another example.)

How to Conduct Content Analysis Research

Question Formulation. As in most research, content analysis researchers begin with a research question. When the question involves variables that are messages or symbols, content analysis may be appropriate. For example. I want to study how newspapers cover a political campaign. My construct "coverage" includes the amount of coverage, the prominence of the coverage, and whether the coverage favors one candidate over another. I could survey people about what they think of the newspaper coverage, but a better strategy is to examine the newspapers directly using content analysis.

Units of Analysis. A researcher decides on the units of analysis. It is the amount of text that is assigned a code. For example, for a political campaign, each issue (or day) of a newspaper could be the unit of analysis, or each newspaper article, or each paragraph of an article.

Sampling. Researchers often use random sampling in content analysis. First, they define the population and the sampling element. For example, the population might be all words, all sentences, all paragraphs, or all articles in certain types of documents over a specified time period. Likewise, it could include each conversation, situation, scene,

BOX **11.4** A Study of the Social Content in American Films

Eschholz and associates (2001) examined the 50 most popular U.S.-made films in 1996. They compared gender and racial-ethnic representations in the films with the percentages in the U.S. population and looked at whether major actors and actresses reproduced traditional gender and racial-ethnic stereotypes. The authors noted that media images, especially repeated images, form a basis for people's background knowledge and understandings about the world and people and can reinforce or weaken preexisting stereotypes. Past research on U.S. film and television documented a mismatch between the proportion of women and racial-ethnic minority film characters and their proportion in the population and found they tended to be cast in stereotypical roles. In addition, the age distribution shown was for women much younger and males slightly older than the population. Films tend to show young women peaking in their late teens to early twenties, then declining, while males are shown to maintain their intelligence and sexuality, aging gracefully. The authors noted that most all writers (85 percent), directors (93 percent), and producers (84 percent) in the Hollywood film industry are White males, and that the industry has become more concentrated with fewer companies making more films.

After two weeks of intensive training, three individuals coded each of the 50 films. The coders were well educated and varied by gender and race-ethnicity, and a fourth coder checked on their accuracy. Six of the top 50 films were dropped because they were animations without live human characters. Leading characters, up to four per film, were coded to provide 147 characters. Females were found to be underrepresented. Non-Whites were equally represented, if not slightly overrepresented. Of the non-White male characters, more were in comedies or action-adventure than in dramas, while non-White leading females were in action-adventure films. Virtually all the non-Whites in 1996 were African American. Leading characters were more likely to be employed full time and have higher prestige occupations than occurs in the entire population. In addition, most male characters had traditional male occupations, while under one-half females (46 percent) were shown in traditional female occupations.

Last, the age distribution of film characters did not reflect that of the U.S. population. Female characters tended to be much younger than males. In addition, almost all African American females were shown in one of two stereotypes, either a "mammy" or a "Jezebel" role (wild and highly erotic).

Reflecting on research of American-made films over the last 50 years, the authors concluded that the most popular films continued to disseminate images that misrepresented major aspects of social life and reinforced traditional cultural stereotypes.

---

or episode of certain types of television programs over a specified time period. For example, I want to know how women and minorities are portrayed in U.S. weekly newsmagazines. My unit of analysis is the article. My population includes all articles published in *Time, Newsweek,* and *U.S. News and World Report* between 1985 and 2005. I first verify that the three magazines were published in those years and define precisely what is meant by an article. For example, do film reviews count as articles? Is there a minimum size (two sentences) for an article? Is a multipart article counted as one or two articles?

Because I am interested in positive leadership roles, my measure indicates whether the role was positive or negative. I can do this with either latent or manifest coding. With manifest coding, I create a list of adjectives and phrases. If someone in a sampled article is referred to with one of the adjectives, then the direction is decided. For example, the terms *brilliant* and *top performer* are positive, whereas *drug kingpin* and *uninspired* are negative. For latent coding, I create rules to guide judgments. For example, I classify stories about a diplomat resolving a difficult world crisis, a business executive unable to make a firm profitable, or a lawyer winning a case into positive or negative terms. (Relevant questions for coding each article are in Box 11.5.)

In addition to written rules for coding decisions, a content analysis researcher creates a recording sheet (also called a coding form or tally sheet) on which to record information (see Box 11.6). Each unit should have a separate recording sheet. The sheets do not have to be pieces of paper; I develop a sampling frame worksheet to keep track of

BOX **11.5** **Example of Latent Coding Questions, Magazine Article Leadership Role Study**

1. *Characteristics of the article.* What is the magazine? What is the date of the article? How large is the article? What was its topic area? Where did it appear in the issue? Were photographs used?
2. *People in the article.* How many people are named in the article? Of these, how many are significant in the article? What is the race and sex of each person named?
3. *Leadership roles.* For each significant person in the article, which ones have leadership roles? What is the field of leadership or profession of the person?
4. *Positive or negative roles.* For each leadership or professional role, rate how positively or negatively it is shown. For example, 5 = highly positive, 4 = positive, 3 = neutral, 2 = negative, 1 = highly negative, 0 = ambiguous.

BOX **11.6** **Example of Recording Sheet**

BLANK EXAMPLE

Professor Neuman, Sociology Department   Coder:_____

Minority/Majority Group Representation in Newsmagazines Project

ARTICLE #_____   MAGAZINE:_____   DATE:_____   SIZE:_____ col. in.

Total number of people named_____   Number of Photos_____
No. people with significant roles:_____   Article Topic:_____

Person____:	Race:_____	Gender:_____	Leader?:_____	Field?_____	Rating:_____
Person____:	Race:_____	Gender:_____	Leader?:_____	Field?_____	Rating:_____
Person____:	Race:_____	Gender:_____	Leader?:_____	Field?_____	Rating:_____
Person____:	Race:_____	Gender:_____	Leader?:_____	Field?_____	Rating:_____
Person____:	Race:_____	Gender:_____	Leader?:_____	Field?_____	Rating:_____
Person____:	Race:_____	Gender:_____	Leader?:_____	Field?_____	Rating:_____
Person____:	Race:_____	Gender:_____	Leader?:_____	Field?_____	Rating:_____
Person____:	Race:_____	Gender:_____	Leader?:_____	Field?_____	Rating:_____

EXAMPLE OF COMPLETED RECORDING SHEET FOR ONE ARTICLE

Professor Neuman, Sociology Department   Coder: Susan J.

Minority/Majority Group Representation in Newsmagazines Project

ARTICLE # 0454   MAGAZINE: Time   DATE: March 1–7, 2005   SIZE: 14 col. in.

Total number of people named 5   Number of Photos 0
No. people with significant roles: 4   Article Topic: Foreign Affairs

Person 1 :	Race: White	Gender: M	Leader?: Y	Field? Banking	Rating: 5
Person 2 :	Race: White	Gender: M	Leader?: N	Field? Government	Rating: NA
Person 3 :	Race: Black	Gender: F	Leader?: Y	Field? Civil Rights	Rating: 2
Person 4 :	Race: White	Gender: F	Leader?: Y	Field? Government	Rating: 0
Person ____:	Race: _____	Gender: ____	Leader?: ____	Field? _____	Rating: ____
Person ____:	Race: _____	Gender: ____	Leader?: ____	Field? _____	Rating: ____
Person ____:	Race: _____	Gender: ____	Leader?: ____	Field? _____	Rating: ____
Person ____:	Race: _____	Gender: ____	Leader?: ____	Field? _____	Rating: ____

TABLE 11.1   Excerpt from Sampling Frame Worksheet

MAGAZINE	ISSUE	ARTICLE	NUMBER	ARTICLE IN SAMPLE?[a]	SAMPLED ARTICLE ID
Time	January 1–7, 1985	pp. 2–3	000001	No	
Time	"	p. 4, bottom	000002	No	
Time	"	p. 4, top	000003	Yes—1	0001
.					
.					
Time	March 1–7, 2005	pp. 2–5	002101	Yes—10	0454
Time	"	p. 6, right column	002102	No	
Time	"	p. 6, left column	002103	No	
Time	"	p. 7	002104	No	
.					
.					
Time	December 24–31, 2005	pp. 4–5	002201	Yes—22	0467
Time	"	p. 5, bottom	002202	No	
Time	"	p. 5, top	002203	Yes—23	0468
Newsweek	January 1–7, 1985	pp. 1–2	010030	No	
Newsweek	"	p. 3	010031	Yes—1	0469
.					
.					
U.S. News	December 25–31, 2005	p. 62	140401	Yes—23	1389

[a]"Yes" means the number was chosen from a random number table. The number after the dash is a count of the number of articles selected for a year.

my sampling procedure. See Table 11.1 for a sampling frame worksheet in which 1,398 sample articles are randomly selected from 140,401 articles.

Variables and Constructing Coding Categories. In my example, I am interested in the construct of an African American or Hispanic American woman portrayed in a significant leadership role. I must define "significant leadership role" in operational terms and express it as written rules for classifying people named in an article. For example, if an article discusses the achievements of someone who is now dead, does the dead person have a significant role? What is a significant role—a local Girl Scout leader or a corporate president?

I must also determine the race and sex of people named in the articles. What if the race and sex are not evident in the text or accompanying photographs? How do I decide on the person's race and sex?

I next examine the three magazines and find that the average issue of each contains 45 articles and that

the magazines are published 52 weeks per year. With a 20-year time frame, my population contains over 140,000 articles ($3 \times 45 \times 52 \times 20 = 140,400$). My sampling frame is a list of all the articles. Next, I decide on the sample size and design. After looking at my budget and time, I decide to limit the sample size to 1,400 articles. Thus, the sampling ratio is 1 percent. I also choose a sampling design. I avoid systematic sampling because magazine issues are published cyclically according to the calendar (e.g., an interval of every 52nd issue results in the same week each year). Because issues from each magazine are important, I use stratified sampling. I stratify by magazine, sampling $1,400/3 = 467$ articles from each. I want to ensure that articles represent each of the 20 years, so I also stratify by year. This results in about 23 articles per magazine per year.

Finally, I draw the random sample using a random-number table to select 23 numbers for the 23 sample articles for each magazine for each year. They can be 3" × 5" or 4" × 6" file cards, or lines in a computer record or file. When a lot of information is recorded for each recording unit, more than one sheet of paper can be used. When planning a project, researchers calculate the work required. For example, during my pilot test, I find that it takes an average of 15 minutes to read and code an article. This does not include sampling or locating magazine articles. With approximately 1,400 articles, that is 350 hours of coding, not counting time to verify the accuracy of coding. Because 350 hours is about nine weeks of nonstop work at 40 hours a week, I should consider hiring assistants as coders.

Each recording sheet has a place to record the identification number of the unit and spaces for information about each variable. I also put identifying information about the research project on the sheet in case I misplace it or it looks similar to other sheets I have. Finally, if I use multiple coders, the sheet notes the coder to check intercoder reliability and, if necessary, makes it possible to recode information for inaccurate coders. After completing all recording sheets and checking for accuracy, I can begin data analysis.

Inferences

The inferences a researcher can or cannot make on the basis of results is critical in content analysis. Content analysis describes what is in the text. It cannot reveal the intentions of those who created the text or the effects that messages in the text have on those who receive them. For example, content analysis shows that children's books contain sex stereotypes. That does not necessarily mean that children's beliefs or behaviors are influenced by the stereotypes; such an inference requires a separate research project on children's perceptions.

EXISTING STATISTICS/DOCUMENTS AND SECONDARY ANALYSIS

Appropriate Topics

Many types of information about the social world are available in statistical documents (books, reports, etc.). Other information is in the form of published compilations available in a library or on computerized records. In either case, the researcher can search through collections of information with a research question and variables in mind, and then reassemble the information in new ways to address the research question.

It is difficult to specify topics that are appropriate for existing statistics research because they are so varied. Any topic on which information has been collected and is publicly available can be studied. In fact, existing statistics projects may not fit neatly into a deductive model of research design. Rather, researchers creatively reorganize the existing information into the variables for a research question after first finding what data are available.

Experiments are best for topics where the researcher controls a situation and manipulates an independent variable. Survey research is best for topics where the researcher asks questions and learns about reported attitudes or behavior. Content analysis is for topics that involve the content of messages in cultural communication.

Existing statistics research is best for topics that involve information collected by large bureaucratic organizations. Public or private organizations systematically gather many types of information. Such information is gathered for policy decisions or as a public service. It is rarely collected for purposes directly related to a specific research question. Thus, existing statistics research is appropriate when a researcher wants to test hypotheses involving variables that are also in official reports of social, economic, and political conditions. These include descriptions of organizations or the people in them. Often, such information is collected over long time periods. For example, existing statistics can be used by a researcher who wants to see whether unemployment and crime rates are associated in 150 cities across a 20-year period.

Existing statistics are valuable over time or across nations. Firebaugh and Chen (1995) studied the legacy of the Nineteenth Amendment to the U.S. Constitution, which gave women the right to vote. They wanted to see whether there was a cohort effect (discussed in Chapter 2) of an enduring gender gap in voting. Looking at time-series existing statistics on voting turnout by gender, they found that between 1952 and 1988, the women who grew up in an era before the amendment voted less often. In other words, cohorts from the pre–Nineteenth

Amendment era never voted as much as women who grew up later.

Social Indicators

During the 1960s, some social scientists, dissatisfied with the information available to decision makers, spawned the "social indicators' movement" to develop indicators of social well-being. Many hoped that information about social well-being could be combined with widely used indicators of economic performance (e.g., gross national product) to better inform government and other policy-making officials. Thus, researchers wanted to measure the quality of social life so that such information could influence public policy.[11]

Today, there are many books, articles, and reports on social indicators, and even a scholarly journal, *Social Indicators Research,* devoted to the creation and evaluation of social indicators. The U.S. Census Bureau produced a report, *Social Indicators,* and the United Nations has many measures of social well-being in different nations.

A **social indicator** is any measure of social well-being used in policy. There are many specific indicators that are operationalizations of well-being. For example, social indicators have been developed for the following areas: population, family, housing, social security and welfare, health and nutrition, public safety, education and training, work, income, culture and leisure, social mobility, and participation.

A more specific example of a social indicator is the FBI's uniform crime index. It indicates the amount of crime in U.S. society. Social indicators can measure negative aspects of social life, such as the infant mortality rate (the death rate of infants during the first year of life) or alcoholism, or they can indicate positive aspects, such as job satisfaction or the percentage of housing units with indoor plumbing. Social indicators often involve implicit value judgments (e.g., which crimes are serious or what constitutes a good quality of life).

Social indicator A quantitative indicator of social well-being.

Researchers at the Institute for Innovation in Social Policy at Fordham University in New York created a social indicator called the "Index of Social Well-Being" for the United States. The index combines measures of 16 social problem areas (e.g., child abuse rates, teenage suicide rates, high school dropout rates, alcohol-related traffic accidents, percent of population without health insurance, etc.) from various existing U.S. government statistics. The level in a year is compared to the best level recorded for an item since 1970, when the index began. It is placed on a scale of 0 to 100, with 100 being the best score. The United States reached its highest level of social well-being in 1973, when the index score was 77.5. It has since declined to about 38. This suggests that the current social well-being of Americans is sharply lower than in the recent past[12] (see Miringoff and Miringoff, 1999).

Locating Data

Locating Documents and Existing Statistics.

The main sources of existing statistics are government or international agencies and private sources. If you plan to conduct existing statistics research, it is wise to discuss your interests with an information professional—in this case, a reference librarian, who can point you in the direction of possible sources.

Many existing documents are "free"—that is, publicly available at libraries—but the time and effort it takes to search for specific information can be substantial. Researchers who conduct existing statistics research spend many hours in libraries or on the Internet. After the information is located, it is recorded on cards, graphs, or recording sheets for later analysis. Often, it is already available in a format for computers to read. For example, instead of recording voting data from books, a researcher could use a social science data archive at the University of Michigan (to be discussed). Also see Box 11.7 on newspapers as data sources.

There are so many sources that only a sample of what is available is discussed here. The single-most valuable source of statistical information about the United States is the *Statistical Abstract of the United States,* which has been published annually

BOX **11.7 Newspaper Reports as a Data Source**

Many social researchers use reports in newspapers as a data source, not only to analyze the content of articles but also as a way to identify and count key events, such as social protests. Newspapers can be an invaluable source of public information, even if newspapers do not cover all events (i.e., selection bias) or do not report all information on the events covered (i.e., description bias). In addition, these types of bias may vary by geographic area or historical period. Although major newspapers have subject indexes, these are not always organized to be useful for social research purposes. Especially in countries with a free press, newspapers can be a way to measure social events across time. In particular, "for many historical and comparative research designs, newspapers remain the only source of data on protest events" (Earl et al., 2004:76).

(with a few exceptions) since 1878. The *Statistical Abstract* is available in all public libraries and on the Internet and can be purchased from the U.S. Superintendent of Documents. It is a selected compilation of the many official reports and statistical tables produced by U.S. government agencies. It contains statistical information from hundreds of more detailed government reports. You may want to examine more specific government documents. (The detail of what is available in government documents is mind boggling. For example, you can learn that there were two African American females over the age of 75 in Tucumcari City, New Mexico, in 1980.)

The *Statistical Abstract* has 1,400 charts, tables, and statistical lists from over 200 government and private agencies. It is hard to grasp all that it contains until you skim through the tables. A two-volume set summarizes similar information across many years; it is called *Historical Statistics of the U.S.: Colonial Times to 1970.*

Most governments publish similar statistical yearbooks. Australia's Bureau of Statistics produces *Yearbook Australia,* Statistics Canada produces *Canada Yearbook,* New Zealand's Department of Statistics publishes *New Zealand Official Yearbook,*

and in the United Kingdom, the Central Statistics Office publishes *Annual Abstract of Statistics.*[13] Many nations publish books with historical statistics, as well.

Locating government statistical documents is an art in itself. Some publications exist solely to assist the researcher. For example, the *American Statistics Index: A Comprehensive Guide* and *Index to the Statistical Publications of the U.S. Government and Statistics Sources: A Subject Guide to Data on Industrial, Business, Social Education, Financial and Other Topics for the U.S. and Internationally* are two helpful guides for the United States.[14] The United Nations and international agencies such as the World Bank have their own publications with statistical information for various countries (e.g., literacy rates, percentage of the labor force working in agriculture, birth rates)—for example, the *Demographic Yearbook, UNESCO Statistical Yearbook,* and *United Nations Statistical Yearbook.*

Other publications offer sources of data on specialized topics. For example, there are publications that contain social background, career, and other biographical information on famous individuals identified as important by some criteria. They depend on voluntary information provided by those deemed important. Another source of information covers businesses or their executives.[15] Last, there are publications that specialize on information about politics, voting, and politicians (see Box 11.8 for source publications covering the United States).

Secondary Survey Data. Secondary analysis is a special case of existing statistics; it is the reanalysis of previously collected survey or other data that were originally gathered by others. As opposed to primary research (e.g., experiments, surveys, and content analysis), the focus is on analyzing rather than collecting data. Secondary analysis is increasingly used by researchers. It is relatively inexpensive; it permits comparisons across groups, nations, or time; it facilitates replication; and it permits asking about issues not thought of by the original researchers.

Large-scale data collection is expensive and difficult. The cost and time required for a major national survey that uses rigorous techniques are prohibitive for most researchers. Fortunately, the

---

11.8   Specialized Publications That Provide Social Data

PUBLISHED INFORMATION SOURCES ON FAMOUS INDIVIDUALS

Who's Who in America is a popular biographic source that has been published since 1908. It lists the name, birth date, occupation, honors, publications, memberships, education, positions held, spouse, and children's names for those included. Specialized editions are devoted to regions of the United States (e.g., *Who's Who in the East*), to specific occupations (e.g., *Who's Who in Finance and Industry*), and to specific subgroups (e.g., women, Jews, African Americans).

Dictionary of American Biography is a more detailed listing on fewer people than *Who's Who*. It began in 1928 and has supplements to update information. For example, Supplement 7 lists 572 people and devotes about a page to each. It has details about careers, travels, the titles of publications, and relations with other famous people.

Biographical Dictionaries Master Index is an index listing names in the various *Who's Who* publications and many other biographic sources (e.g., *Who's Who in Hockey*). If a researcher knows a name, the index tells where biographic information can be found for the person.

SOURCES ON BUSINESSES AND COMPANIES

Dun and Bradstreet Principal Industrial Businesses is a guide to approximately 51,000 businesses in 135 countries with information on sales, number of employees, officers, and products.

Who Owns Whom comes in volumes for nations or regions (e.g., North America, the United Kingdom, Ireland, and Australia). It lists parent companies, subsidiaries, and associated companies.

Standard and Poor's Register of Corporations, Directors and Executives lists about 37,000 U.S. and Canadian companies. It has information on corporations, products, officers, industries, and sales figures.

SOURCES ON POLITICAL ISSUES (UNITED STATES)

Almanac of American Politics is a biannual publication that includes photographs and a short biography of U.S. government officials. Committee appointments, voting records, and similar information are provided for members of Congress and leaders in the executive branch.

America Votes: A Handbook of Contemporary American Election Statistics contains detailed voting information by county for most statewide and national offices. Primary election results are included down to the county level.

Vital Statistics on American Politics provides dozens of tables on political behavior, such as the campaign spending of every candidate for Congress, their primary and final votes, ideological ratings by various political organizations, and a summary of voter registration regulations by state.

---

organization, preservation, and dissemination of major survey data sets have improved. Today, there are archives of past surveys that are open to researchers (see Appendix C).

The Inter-University Consortium for Political and Social Research (ICPSR) at the University of Michigan is the world's major archive of social science data. Over 17,000 survey research and related sets of information are stored and made available to researchers at modest costs. Other centers hold survey data in the United States and other nations.[16]

A widely used source of survey data for the United States is the *General Social Survey (GSS)*,

which has been conducted annually in most years by the National Opinion Research Center at the University of Chicago. In recent years, it has covered other nations as well. The data are made publicly available for secondary analysis at a low cost[17] (see Box 11.9).

Limitations

Despite the growth and popularity of secondary data analysis and existing statistics research, there are limitations in their use. The use of such techniques is not trouble free just because a government agency or research organization gathered the data. One dan-

BOX **11.9** The General Social Survey

The General Social Survey (GSS) is the best-known set of survey data used by social researchers for secondary analysis. The mission of the GSS is "to make timely, high quality, scientifically relevant data available to the social science research community" (Davis and Smith, 1992:1). It is available in many computer-readable formats and is widely accessible for a low cost. Neither datasets nor codebooks are copyrighted. Users may copy or disseminate them without obtaining permission. You can find results using the GSS in over 2,000 research articles and books.

The National Opinion Research Center (NORC) has conducted the GSS almost every year since 1972. A typical year's survey contains a random sample of about 1,500 adult U.S. residents. A team of researchers selects some questions for inclusion, and individual researchers can recommend questions. They repeat some questions and topics each year, include some on a four- to six-year cycle, and add other topics in specific years. For example, in 1988, the special topic was religion, and in 1990, it was intergroup relations.

Interviewers collect the data through face-to-face interviews. The NORC staff carefully selects interviewers and trains them in social science methodology and survey interviewing. About 120 to 140 interviewers work on the GSS each year. About 95 percent are women, and most are middle aged. The NORC recruits bilingual and minority interviewers. Interviewers with respondents are race-matched with respondents. Interviews are typically 90 minutes long and contain approximately 500 questions. The response rate has been 71 to 79 percent. The major reason for nonresponse is a refusal to participate.

The International Social Survey Program conducts similar surveys in other nations. Beginning with the German ALLBUS and British Social Attitudes Survey, participation has grown to include Australia, Austria, Italy, Hungary, Ireland, Israel, the Netherlands, Switzerland, and Poland. The goal is to conduct on a regular basis large-scale national general surveys in which some common questions are asked across cooperating nations.

ger is that a researcher may use secondary data or existing statistics that are inappropriate for his or her research question. Before proceeding, a researcher needs to consider units in the data (e.g., types of people, organizations), the time and place of data collection, the sampling methods used, and the specific issues or topics covered in the data (see Box 11.10). For example, a researcher wanting to examine racial-ethnic tensions between Latinos and Anglos in the United States uses secondary data that includes only the Pacific Northwest and New England states should reconsider the question or the use of data.

A second danger is that the researcher does not understand the substantive topic. Because the data are easily accessible, researchers who know very little about a topic and use the data could make erroneous assumptions or false interpretations about results. Before using any data, a researcher needs to be well informed about the topic. For example, if a researcher uses data on high school graduation rates in Germany without understanding the German sec-

ondary education system with its distinct academic and vocational tracks, he or she may make serious errors in interpreting results.

A third danger is that a researcher may quote statistics in great detail to give an impression of scientific rigor. This can lead to the **fallacy of misplaced concreteness,** which occurs when someone gives a false impression of precision by quoting statistics in greater detail than warranted and "overloading" the details. For example, existing statistics report that the population of Australia is 19,169,083, but it is better to say that it is a little over 19 million. One might calculate the percentage of divorced people as 15.65495 in a secondary data analysis of the 2000 General Social Survey, but it is better to report that about 15.7 percent of people are divorced.[18]

Fallacy of misplaced concreteness Using too many digits in a quantitative measure in an attempt to create the (mis)impression that data are accurate.

11.10 The Census

Almost every country conducts a census, or a regular count of its population. For example, Australia has done so since 1881, Canada since 1871, and the United States since 1790. Most nations conduct a census every 5 or 10 years. In addition to the number of people, census officials collect information on topics such as housing conditions, ethnicity, religious affiliation, education, and so forth.

The census is a major source of high-quality existing statistical data, but it can be controversial. In Canada, an attempt to count the number of same-sex couples living together evoked public debate about whether the government should document the changes in society. In Great Britain, the Muslim minority welcomed questions about religion in the 2001 census because they felt that they had been officially ignored. In the United States, the measurement of race and ethnicity was hotly debated, so in the 2000 census, people could place themselves in multiple racial-ethnic categories.

The U.S. 2000 census also generated a serious public controversy because it missed thousands of people, most from low-income areas with concentrations of recent immigrants and racial minorities. Some double counting also occurred of people in high-income areas where many owned second homes. A contentious debate arose among politicians to end miscounts by using scientific sampling and adjusting the census. The politicians proved to be less concerned about improving the scientific accuracy of the census than retaining traditional census methods that would benefit their own political fortunes or help their constituencies, because the government uses census data to draw voting districts and allocate public funds to areas.

Units of Analysis and Variable Attributes.

A common problem in existing statistics is finding the appropriate units of analysis. Many statistics are published for aggregates, not the individual. For example, a table in a government document has information (e.g., unemployment rate, crime rate, etc.) for a state, but the unit of analysis for the research question is the individual (e.g., "Are unemployed people more likely to commit property crimes?"). The potential for committing the eco-logical fallacy is very real in this situation. It is less of a problem for secondary survey analysis because researchers can obtain raw information on each respondent from archives.

A related problem involves the categories of variable attributes used in existing documents or survey questions. This is not a problem if the initial data were gathered in many highly refined categories. The problem arises when the original data were collected in broad categories or ones that do not match the needs of a researcher. For example, a researcher is interested in people of Asian heritage. If the racial and ethnic heritage categories in a document are "White," "Black," and "Other," the researcher has a problem. The "Other" category includes people of Asian and other heritages. Sometimes information was collected in refined categories but is published only in broad categories. It takes special effort to discover whether more refined information was collected or is publicly available.

Validity. Validity problems can occur when the researcher's theoretical definition does not match that of the government agency or organization that collected the information. Official policies and procedures specify definitions for official statistics. For example, a researcher defines a *work injury* as including minor cuts, bruises, and sprains that occur on the job, but the official definition in government reports includes only injuries that require a visit to a physician or hospital. Many work injuries, as defined by the researcher, would not be in official statistics. Another example occurs when a researcher defines people as *unemployed* if they would work if a good job were available, if they have to work part time when they want full-time work, and if they have given up looking for work. The official definition, however, includes only those who are now actively seeking work (full or part time) as unemployed. The official statistics exclude those who stopped looking, who work part time out of necessity, or who do not look because they believe no work is available. In both cases, the researcher's definition differs from that in official statistics (see Box 11.11).

Another validity problem arises when official statistics are a proxy for a construct in which a re-

BOX **11.11**   Official Unemployment Rates versus the Nonemployed

In most countries, the official unemployment rate measures only the unemployed (see below) as a percent of all working people. It would be 50 percent higher if two other categories of nonemployed people were added: involuntary part-time workers and discouraged workers (see below). In some countries (e.g., Sweden and United States), it would be nearly double if it included these people. This does not consider other nonworking people, transitional self-employed, or the underemployed (see below). What a country measures is a theoretical and conceptual definition issue: What construct should an unemployment rate measure and why measure it?

An economic policy or labor market perspective says the rate should measure those ready to enter the labor market immediately. It defines nonworking people as a supply of high-quality labor, an input for use in the economy available to employers. By contrast, a social policy or human resource perspective says the rate should measure those who are not currently working to their fullest potential. The rate should represent people who are not or cannot fully utilize their talents, skills, or time to the fullest. It defines nonworking people as a social problem of individuals unable to realize their capacity to be productive, contributing members of society.

CATEGORIES OF NONEMPLOYED/FULLY UTILIZED

Unemployed people	People who meet three conditions: lack a paying job outside the home, are taking active measures to find work, can begin work immediately if it is offered.
Involuntary part-time workers	People with a job, but work irregularly or fewer hours than they are able and willing.
Discouraged workers	People able to work and who actively sought it for some time, but being unable to find it, have given up looking.
Other nonworking	Those not working because they are retired, on vacation, temporarily laid off, semidisabled, homemakers, full-time students, or in the process of moving.
Transitional self-employed	Self-employed who are not working full time because they are just starting a business or are going through bankruptcy.
Underemployed	Persons with a temporary full-time job for which they are seriously overqualified. They seek a permanent job in which they can fully apply their skills and experience.

Source: Adapted from *The Economist,* July 22, 1995, p. 74.

searcher is really interested. This is necessary because the researcher cannot collect original data. For example, the researcher wants to know how many people have been robbed, so he or she uses police statistics on robbery arrests as a proxy. But the measure is not entirely valid because many robberies are not reported to the police, and reported robberies do not always result in an arrest.

A researcher who wants to measure marriages "forced" by a premarital pregnancy serves as another example. The researcher can use the date of marriage and the date of the birth of a child in offi-

cial records to estimate whether a marriage was "forced" by a pregnancy. This does not tell him or her that pregnancy was the motivation for the marriage, however. A couple may have planned to marry and the pregnancy was irrelevant, or the pregnancy may have been unknown at the date of marriage. Likewise, some marriages without a recorded birth could be forced by a false belief in pregnancy or a pregnancy that ended in a miscarriage or abortion instead of a birth. In addition, a child might be conceived after the date of marriage, but be born very prematurely. If a researcher measures forced marriages as those in which a child was born less than nine months after a marriage date, some will be mislabeled, thereby lowering validity.

A third validity problem arises because the researcher lacks control over how information is collected. All information, even that in official government reports, is originally gathered by people in bureaucracies as part of their jobs. A researcher depends on them for collecting, organizing, reporting, and publishing data accurately. Systematic errors in collecting the initial information (e.g., census people who avoid poor neighborhoods and make up information, or people who put a false age on a driver's license); errors in organizing and reporting information (e.g., a police department that is sloppy about filing crime reports and loses some); and errors in publishing information (e.g., a typographical error in a table) all reduce measurement validity.

This kind of problem happened in U.S. statistics on the number of people permanently laid off from their jobs. A university researcher reexamined the methods used to gather data by the U.S. Bureau of Labor Statistics and found an error. Data on permanent job losses come from a survey of 50,000 people, but the government agency failed to adjust for a much higher survey nonresponse rate. The corrected figures showed that instead of a 7 percent decline in the number of people laid off between 1993 and 1996, as had been first reported, there was no change.[19]

Reliability. Problems with reliability can plague existing statistics research. Stability reliability problems develop when official definitions or the method of collecting information changes over time. Official definitions of work injury, disability, unemployment, and the like change periodically. Even if a researcher learns of such changes, consistent measurement over time is impossible. For example, during the early 1980s, the method for calculating the U.S. unemployment rate changed. Previously, the unemployment rate was calculated as the number of unemployed persons divided by the number in the civilian workforce. The new method divided the number of unemployed by the civilian workforce plus the number of people in the

military. Likewise, when police departments computerize their records, there is an apparent increase in crimes reported, not because crime increases but due to improved record keeping.

Equivalence reliability can also be a problem. For example, a measure of crime across a nation depends on each police department's providing accurate information. If departments in one region of a country have sloppy bookkeeping, the measure loses equivalence reliability. Likewise, studies of police departments suggest that political pressures to increase arrests are closely related to the number of arrests. For example, political pressure in one city may increase arrests (e.g., a crackdown on crime), whereas pressures in another city may decrease arrests (e.g., to show a drop in crime shortly before an election in order to make officials look better).

Representative reliability can be a problem in official government statistics. For example, the U.S. Bureau of Labor Statistics found a 0.6 percent increase in the female unemployment rate after it used gender-neutral measurement procedures. Until the mid-1990s, interviewers asked women only whether they had been "keeping house or something else?" The women who answered "keeping house" were categorized as housewives, and not unemployed. Because the women were not asked, this occurred even if the women had been seeking work. Once women were asked the same question as men, "Were you working or something else?" more women said they were not working but doing "something else" such as looking for work. This shows the importance of methodological details in how government statistics get created.

Researchers often use official statistics for international comparisons but national governments collect data differently and the quality of data collection varies. For example, in 1994, the official unemployment rate reported for the United States was 7 percent, Japan's was 2.9 percent, and France's was 12 percent. If the nations defined and gathered data the same way, including discouraged workers and involuntary part-time workers rates, the rates would have been 9.3 percent for the United States, 9.6 percent for Japan, and 13.7 percent for France. To evaluate the quality of official government statistics, *The Economist* magazine asked a team of 20 leading statisticians to evaluate the statistics of 13 nations based on freedom from political interference, reliability, statistical methodology, and coverage of topics. The top five nations in order were Canada, Australia, Holland, France, and Sweden. The United States was tied for sixth with Britain and Germany. The quality of U.S. statistics suffered from being highly decentralized, having fewer statisticians employed than any nation, and politically motivated cutbacks on the range of data collected. (See Box 11.12 for a creative use of existing statistics.)

Data collected internationally can be controversial. The International Labor Organization of the United Nations reported in 1998 that the official statistics of total economic activity for several nations are inaccurate because they exclude the sex industry. In some countries (especially Thailand and the Philippines), millions of workers (primarily young women) are employed and billions of dollars in revenue are generated from prostitution and the sex industry. This has a large impact on the economy, but it does not appear in any official reports or statistics.[20]

Missing Data. One problem that plagues researchers who use existing statistics and documents is that of missing data (missing data were discussed in Chapter 7). Sometimes, the data were collected but have been lost. More frequently, the data were never collected. The decision to collect official information is made within government agencies. The decision to ask questions on a survey whose data are later made publicly available is made by a group of researchers. In both cases, those who decide what to collect may not collect what another researcher needs in order to address a research question. Government agencies start or stop collecting information for political, budgetary, or other reasons. For example, during the early 1980s, cost-cutting measures by the U.S. federal government stopped the collection of information that social researchers found valuable. Missing information is especially a problem when researchers cover long time periods. For instance, a researcher interested in the number of work stoppages and strikes in the United States can obtain data from the 1890s to the present, except for a five-year period after 1911 when the federal government did not collect the data.

BOX **11.12** **Existing Statistics, Androgynous First Names, and Collective Behavior**

An androgynous first name is one that can be for either a girl or boy without clearly marking the child's gender. Some argue that the feminist movement decreased gender marking in a child's name as part of its broader societal influence to reduce gender distinctions and inequality. Others observe that gender remains the singlemost predominant feature of naming in most societies. Even when racial groups or social classes invent distinctive new first names, the gender distinctions are retained.

Lieberson and colleagues (2000) examined existing statistical data in the form of computerized records from the birth certificates of 11 million births of White children in the state of Illinois from 1916 to 1989. They found that androgynous first names are rare (about 3 percent) and that there has been a very slight historical trend toward androgyny, but only in very recent years. In addition, parents give androgynous names to girls more than to boys, and gender segregation in naming is unstable (i.e., a name tends to lose its androgynous meaning over time). The authors noted that the way parents name children mimics a pattern of collective behavior found to operate in another research area: the racial segregation of neighborhoods. Change in residence is unequal among races with less movement by the dominant group; the less powerful group moves to occupy areas that the dominant group has abandoned; and integration is unstable, with new segregation reappearing after some time.

ISSUES OF INFERENCE AND THEORY TESTING

Inferences from Nonreactive Data

A researcher's ability to infer causality or test a theory on the basis of nonreactive data is limited. It is difficult to use unobtrusive measures to establish temporal order and eliminate alternative explanations. In content analysis, a researcher cannot generalize from the content to its effects on those who read the text, but can only use the correlation logic of survey research to show an association among variables. Unlike the ease of survey research, a researcher does not ask respondents direct questions to measure variables, but relies on the information available in the text.

Ethical Concerns

Ethical concerns are not at the forefront of most nonreactive research because the people being studied are not directly involved. The primary ethical concern is the privacy and confidentiality of using information gathered by someone else. Another ethical issue is that official statistics are social and political products. Implicit theories and value assumptions guide which information is collected and the categories used when gathering it. Measures or statistics that are defined as official and collected on a regular basis are objects of political conflict and guide the direction of policy. By defining one measure as official, public policy is shaped to lead to outcomes that would be different if an alternative, but equally valid, measure had been used. For example, the collection of information on many social conditions (e.g., the number of patients who died while in public mental hospitals) was stimulated by political activity during the Great Depression of the 1930s. Previously, the conditions were not defined as sufficiently important to warrant public attention. Likewise, information on the percentage of non-White students enrolled in U.S. schools at various ages is available only since 1953, and for various non-White races only since the 1970s. Earlier, such information was not salient for public policy.

The collection of official statistics stimulates new attention to a problem, and public concern about a problem stimulates the collection of new official statistics. For example, drunk driving became an issue once statistics were collected on the number of automobile accidents and on whether alcohol was a factor in an accident.

Political and social values influence decisions about which existing statistics to collect. Most official statistics are designed for top-down bureaucratic or administrative planning purposes. They may not conform to a researcher's purposes or the purposes of those opposed to bureaucratic decision makers. For example, a government agency measures the number of tons of steel produced, miles of highway paved, and average number of people in a household. Information on other conditions such as drinking-water quality, time needed to commute to work, stress related to a job, or number of children needing child care may not be collected because officials say it is unimportant. In many countries, the gross national product (GNP) is treated as a critical measure of societal progress. But GNP ignores noneconomic aspects of social life (e.g., time spent playing with one's children) and types of work (e.g., housework) that are not paid. The information available reflects the outcome of political debate and the values of officials who decide which statistics to collect.[21]

CONCLUSION

In this chapter, you have learned about several types of nonreactive research techniques. They are ways to measure or observe aspects of social life without affecting those who are being studied. They result in objective, numerical information that can be analyzed to address research questions. The techniques can be used in conjunction with other types of quantitative or qualitative social research to address a large number of questions.

As with any form of quantitative data, researchers need to be concerned with measurement issues. It is easy to take available information from a survey or government document, but this does not mean that it measures the construct of interest to the researcher.

You should be aware of two potential problems in nonreactive research. First, the availability of existing information restricts the questions that a researcher can address. Second, the nonreactive variables often have weaker validity because they do not measure the construct of interest. Although existing statistics and secondary data analysis are low-cost research techniques, the researcher lacks control over, and substantial knowledge of, the data collection process. This potential source of errors means that researchers need to be especially vigilant and cautious.

In the next chapter, we move from designing research projects and collecting data to analyzing data. The analysis techniques apply to the quantitative data you learned about in the previous chapters. So far, you have seen how to move from a topic, to a research design and measures, to collecting data. Next, you will learn how to look at data and see what they can tell you about a hypothesis or research question.

KEY TERMS

accretion measures
coding system
erosion measures
fallacy of misplaced
    concreteness

intercoder reliability
latent coding
manifest coding
nonreactive measures
social indicator

structured observation
text
unobtrusive measures

REVIEW QUESTIONS

1. For what types of research questions is content analysis appropriate?

2. What are the four characteristics of content that are observed and recorded in coding systems?

3. Of what reliability problems should the researcher using existing statistical data be aware?

4. What are the advantages and disadvantages of secondary data analysis?

5. Why do content analysis researchers use multiple coders, and what is the possible problem with doing this?

6. How are inferences limited in content analysis?

7. What units of analysis are used in content analysis?

8. What is the aggregation problem in existing statistics?

9. What are the three validity problems in content analysis?

10. Of what limitations of using existing statistics should researchers be aware?

NOTES

1. See Webb and colleagues (1981:7–11).
2. For an inventory of nonreactive measures, see Bouchard (1976) and Webb and associates (1981).
3. See Krippendorff (1980:13).
4. For definitions of content analysis, see Holsti (1968a: 597), Krippendorff (1980:21–24), Markoff and associates (1974:5–6), Stone and Weber (1992), and Weber (1985:81, note 1).
5. Weitzman and colleagues (1972) is a classic in this type of research.
6. See Ariés (1977) for an example.
7. Examples of content analysis studies can be found in Berelson (1952), Carney (1972), McDiarmid (1971), Myers and Margavio (1983), Namenwirth (1970), Sepstrup (1981), Stempel (1971), Stewart (1984), and Stone

and colleagues (1966). Also see Weber (1983) for a discussion of measurement issues in content analysis.
8. Stone and Weber (1992) and Weber (1984, 1985) review computerized content analysis techniques.
9. See Andren (1981:58–66) on reliability and latent or semantic analysis, and Holsti (1969:94–126).
10. See Krippendorff (1980) for various measures of intercoder reliability. Also see Fiske (1982) for the related issue of convergent validity.
11. A discussion of social indicators can be found in Carley (1981). Also see Bauer (1966), Duncan (1984:233–235), Juster and Land (1981), Land (1992), Rossi and Gilmartin (1980), and Taylor (1980). Also see Ferriss (1988) on the using of social indicators for planning and social forecasting.

12. See Herbert (2003) and Ravo (1996).

13. Many non-English yearbooks are also produced; for example, *Statistiches Jahrbuch* for the Federal Republic of Germany, *Annuaire Statistique de la France* for France, *Year Book Australia* for Australia, and Denmark's *Statiskisk Ti Arsoversigt.* Japan produces an English version of its yearbook called the *Statistical Handbook of Japan.*

14. Guides exist for the publications of various governments—for example, the *Guide to British Government Publications, Australian Official Publications,* and *Irish Official Publications.* Similar publications exist for most nations. For example, *DOD's Parliamentary Companion for the United Kingdom* and the *Parliamentary Handbook of the Commonwealth of Australia* are both similar to the *Almanac of American Politics.*

15. See Churchill (1983:140–167) and Stewart (1984) for lists of business information sources.

16. Other major U.S. archives of survey data include the National Opinion Research Center, University of Chicago; the Survey Research Center, University of California–Berkeley; the Behavioral Sciences Laboratory, University of Cincinnati; Data and Program Library Service, University of Wisconsin–Madison; the Roper Center, University of Connecticut–Storrs; and the Institute for Research in Social Science, University of North Carolina–Chapel Hill. Also see Kiecolt and Nathan (1985) and Parcel (1992).

17. See Alwin (1988) and Davis and Smith (1992).

18. For a discussion of these issues, see Dale and colleagues (1988:27–31), Horn (1993:138), Maier (1991), and Parcel (1992).

19. See Stevenson (1996).

20. See *The Economist,* "The Good Statistics Guide" (September 11, 1993), "The Overlooked Housekeeper" (February 5, 1994), and "Fewer Damned Lies?" (March 30, 1996). Also see "U.N. Urges Fiscal Accounting to Include Sex Trade," *New York Times* (August 20, 1998).

21. See Block and Burns (1986), Carr-Hill (1984a), Hindess (1973), Horn (1993), Maier (1991), and Van den Berg and Van der Veer (1985). Discussions by Norris (1981) and Starr (1987) are also very helpful.

Analysis of Quantitative Data

> *Statistics may also be regarded as a method of dealing with data. This definition stresses the view that statistics is a tool concerned with the collection, organization, and analysis of numerical facts or observations. . . . The major concern of descriptive statistics is to present information in a convenient, usable, and understandable form.*
> —Richard Runyon and Audry Haber, *Fundamentals of Behavioral Statistics,* p. 6.

If you read a research report or article based on quantitative data, you will probably find it has charts, graphs, and tables full of numbers. Do not be intimidated by them. A researcher provides the charts, graphs, and tables to give you, the reader, a condensed picture of the data. The charts and tables allow you to see the evidence collected by the researcher and learn for yourself what is in it. When you collect your own quantitative data, you will have to use similar techniques to help you to see what is inside the data. You will need to organize and manipulate the quantitative data to get them to reveal things of interest about the social world. In this chapter, you will learn the fundamentals of organizing and analyzing quantitative data. The analy-

sis of quantitative data is a complex field of knowledge. This chapter cannot substitute for a course in social statistics. It covers only the basic statistical concepts and data-handling techniques necessary to understand social research.

Data collected using the techniques in the past chapters are in the form of numbers. The numbers represent values of variables, which measure characteristics of subjects, respondents, or other cases. The numbers are in a raw form, on questionnaires, note pads, recording sheets, or paper.

Researchers do several things to the raw data in order to see what they can say about the hypotheses: Reorganize them into a form suitable for computers, present them in charts or graphs to summarize their features, and interpret or give theoretical meaning to the results.

DEALING WITH DATA

Coding Data

Before a researcher examines quantitative data to test hypotheses, he or she needs to put them in a different form. You encountered the idea of coding data in the last chapter. Here, data *coding* means systematically reorganizing raw data into a format that is machine readable (i.e., easy to analyze using computers). As with coding in content analysis, researchers create and consistently apply rules for transferring information from one form to another.[1]

Coding can be a simple clerical task when the data are recorded as numbers on well-organized recording sheets, but it is very difficult when, for example, a researcher wants to code answers to open-ended survey questions into numbers in a process similar to latent content analysis.

Researchers use a coding procedure and a codebook. The **coding procedure** is a set of rules stating that certain numbers are assigned to variable attributes. For example, a researcher codes males as 1 and females as 2. Each category of a variable and missing information needs a code. A **codebook** is a document (i.e., one or more pages) describing the coding procedure and the location of data for variables in a format that computers can use.

When you code data, it is very important to create a well-organized, detailed codebook and make

multiple copies of it. If you do not write down the details of the coding procedure, or if you misplace the codebook, you have lost the key to the data and may have to recode the data again.

Researchers begin thinking about a coding procedure and codebook before they collect data. For example, a survey researcher precodes a questionnaire before collecting data. *Precoding* means placing the code categories (e.g., 1 for male, 2 for female) on the questionnaire.[2] Sometimes, to reduce dependence on a codebook, researchers also place the location in the computer format on the questionnaire.

If a researcher does not precode, his or her first step after collecting data is to create a codebook. He or she also gives each case an identification number to keep track of the cases. Next, the researcher transfers the information from each questionnaire into a format that computers can read.

Entering Data

Most computer programs designed for data analysis need the data in a grid format. In the grid, each row represents a respondent, subject, or case. In computer terminology, these are called **data records.** Each is the record of data for a single case. A column or a set of columns represents specific variables. It is possible to go from a column and row location (e.g., row 7, column 5) back to the original source of data (e.g., a questionnaire item on marital status for respondent 8). A column or a set of columns assigned to a variable is called a **data field** or just a *field.*

For example, a researcher codes survey data for three respondents in a format for computers like that presented in Figure 12.1. People cannot easily read it, and without the codebook, it is worthless. It condenses answers to 50 survey questions for three respondents into three lines or rows. The raw data for many research projects look like this, except that there may be over 1,000 rows, and the lines may be over 100 columns long. For example, a 15-minute telephone survey of 250 students produces a grid of data that is 250 rows by 240 columns.

The codebook in Figure 12.1 states that the first two numbers are identification numbers. Thus, the

---

Coding procedure A set of rules created by a quantitative researcher for assigning numbers to specific variable attributes, usually in preparation for statistical analysis and carefully recorded in a codebook.

Codebook A document that describes the procedure for coding variables and their location in a format that computers can use.

Data records The units or records in computer-based data that contain information on the variables for a case.

Data field One or more columns in data already organized for a computer representing the location of information on a specific variable.

FIGURE 12.1   Coded Data for Three Cases and Codebook

EXCERPT FROM SURVEY QUESTIONNAIRE

Respondent ID _____   Interviewer Name _____

Note the Respondent's Sex: _____ Male _____ Female

1. The first question is about the president of the United States. Do you Strongly Agree, Agree, Disagree, Strongly Disagree, or Have No Opinion About the following statement:

   The president of the United States is doing a great job.

   _____ Strongly Agree _____ Agree _____ Disagree _____ Strongly Disagree _____ No Opinion

2. How old are you? _____

EXCERPT OF CODED DATA

Column

```
00000000011111111112222222222333333333444 ... etc. (tens)
123456789012345678901234567890123456789012 ... etc. (ones)
01 212736302 182738274 10239 18.82 3947461 ... etc.
02 213334821 124988154 21242 18.21 3984123 ... etc.
03 420123982 113727263 12345 17.36 1487645 ... etc.
etc.
```

Raw data for first three cases, columns 1 through 42.

EXCERPT FROM CODEBOOK

Column	Variable Name	Description
1–2	ID	Respondent identification number
3	BLANK	
4	Interviewer	Interviewer who collected the data:
		1 = Susan
		2 = Carlos
		3 = Juan
		4 = Sophia
		5 = Clarence
5	Sex	Interviewer report of respondent's sex
		1 = Male, 2 = Female
6	PresJob	The president of the United States is doing a great job.
		1 = Strongly Agree
		2 = Agree
		3 = No Opinion
		4 = Disagree
		5 = Strongly Disagree
		Blank = missing information

---

example data are for the first (01), second (02), and third (03) respondents. Notice that researchers use zeros as place holders to reduce confusion between 1 and 01. The 1s are always in column 2; the 10s are in column 1. The codebook states that column 5 contains the variable "sex": Cases 1 and 2 are male and Case 3 is female. Column 4 tells us that Carlos interviewed Cases 1 and 2, and Sophia Case 3.

There are four ways to get raw quantitative data into a computer:

1. *Code sheet.* Gather the information, then transfer it from the original source onto a grid format (code sheet). Next, type what is on the code sheet into a computer line by line.
2. *Direct-entry method, including CATI.* As information is being collected, sit at a computer keyboard (or similar recording device) while listening to or observing the information and enter the information, or have a respondent/subject enter the information him or herself. To use the **direct-entry method,** the computer must be preprogrammed to accept the information.
3. *Optical scan.* Gather the information, then enter it onto optical scan sheets (or have a respondent/subject enter the information) by filling in the correct "dots." Next, use an optical scanner or reader to transfer the information into a computer.
4. *Bar code.* Gather the information and convert it into different widths of bars that are associated with specific numerical values; then use a bar-code reader to transfer the information into a computer.

Cleaning Data

Accuracy is extremely important when coding data. (See Box 12.1 for an example.) Errors made when coding or entering data into a computer threaten the validity of measures and cause misleading results. A researcher who has a perfect sample, perfect measures, and no errors in gathering data, but who makes errors in the coding process or in entering data into a computer, can ruin a whole research project.

After very careful coding, the researcher checks the accuracy of coding, or "cleans" the data. He or she may code a 10 to 15 percent random sample of the data a second time. If no coding errors appear, the researcher proceeds; if he or she finds errors, the researcher rechecks all coding.

Researchers verify coding after the data are in a computer in two ways. **Possible code cleaning** (or *wild code checking*) involves checking the categories of all variables for impossible codes. For example, respondent sex is coded 1 = Male, 2 = Female. Finding a 4 for a case in the field for the sex variable indicates a coding error. A second method, **contingency cleaning** (or *consistency checking*), involves cross-classifying two variables and looking for logically impossible combinations. For example, education is cross-classified by occupation. If a respondent is recorded as never having passed the eighth grade and also is recorded as being a legitimate medical doctor, the researcher checks for a coding error.

A researcher can modify data after they are in a computer. He or she may not use more refined categories than were used when collecting the original data, but may combine or group information. For example, the researcher may group ratio-level income data into five ordinal categories. Also, he or she can combine information from several indicators to create a new variable or add the responses to several questionnaire items into an index score.

Direct-entry method   Entering data directly into a computer by typing data without bar codes or optical scan sheets.

Possible code cleaning   Cleaning data using a computer in which the researcher looks for responses or answer categories that cannot have cases.

Contingency cleaning   Cleaning data using a computer in which the researcher looks at the combination of categories for two variables for logically impossible cases.

RESULTS WITH ONE VARIABLE

Frequency Distributions

The word *statistics* has several meanings. It can mean a set of collected numbers (e.g., numbers telling how many people live in a city) as well as a branch of applied mathematics used to manipulate and summarize the features of numbers. Social researchers use both types of statistics. Here, we focus on the second type—ways to manipulate and summarize numbers that represent data from a research project.

BOX **12.1**   **Example of Dealing with Data**

There is no good substitute for getting your hands dirty with the data. Here is an example of data preparation from a study I conducted with my students. My university surveyed about one-third of the students to learn their thinking and experience with sexual harassment on campus. A research team drew a random sample, then developed and distributed a self-administered questionnaire. Respondents put answers on optical scan sheets that were similar to the answer sheets used for multiple-choice exams. The story begins with the delivery of over 3,000 optical scan sheets.

After the sheets arrived, we visually scanned each one for obvious errors. Despite instructions to use pencil and fill in each circle neatly and darkly, we found that about 200 respondents used a pen, and another 200 were very sloppy or used very light pencil marks. We cleaned up the sheets and redid them in pencil. We also found about 25 unusable sheets that were defaced or damaged, or were too incomplete (e.g., only the first 2 of 70 questions answered).

Next, we read the usable optical scan sheets into a computer. We had the computer produce the number of occurrences, or frequency, of the attributes for each variable. Looking at them, we discovered several kinds of errors. Some respondents had filled in two responses for a question to which only one answer was requested or possible. Some had filled in impossible response codes (e.g., the numeral 4 for sex, when the only legitimate codes were 1 for male and 2 for female), and some had filled in every answer in the same way, suggesting that they did not take the survey seriously. For each case with an error, we returned to the optical scan sheet to see whether we could recover any information. If we could not recover information, we reclassified the case as a nonresponse or recoded a response as missing information.

The questionnaire had two contingency questions. For each, a respondent who answered "no" to one question was to skip the next five questions. We created a table for each question. We looked to see whether all respondents who answered "no" to the first question skipped or left blank the next five. We found about 35 cases in which the respondent answered "no" but then went on to answer the next five questions. We returned to each sheet and tried to figure out which the respondent really intended. In most cases, it appeared that the respondent meant the "no" but failed to read the instructions to skip questions.

Finally, we examined the frequency of attributes for each variable to see whether they made sense. We were very surprised to learn that about 600 respondents had marked "Native American" for the racial heritage question. In addition, over half of those who had done so were freshmen. A check of official records revealed that the university enrolled a total of about 20 Native Americans or American Indians, and that over 90 percent of the students were White, non-Hispanic Caucasians. The percentage of respondents marking Black, African American, or Hispanic-Chicano matched the official records. We concluded that some White Caucasian respondents had been unfamiliar with the term "Native American" for "American Indian." Apparently, they had mistakenly marked it instead of "White, Caucasian." Because we expected about 7 Native Americans in the sample, we recoded the "Native American" responses as "White, Caucasian." This meant that we reclassified Native Americans in the sample as Caucasian. At this point, we were ready to analyze the data.

Descriptive statistics describe numerical data. They can be categorized by the number of variables involved: univariate, bivariate, or multivariate (for one, two, and three or more variables). **Univariate statistics** describe one variable (*uni-* refers to one; *-variate* refers to variable). The easiest way to describe the numerical data of one variable is with a **frequency distribution.** It can be used with nominal-, ordinal-, interval-, or ratio-level data and takes many forms. For example, I have data for 400 re-

Descriptive statistics   A general type of simple statistics used by researchers to describe basic patterns in the data.

Univariate statistics   Statistical measures that deal with one variable only.

Frequency distribution   A table that shows the distribution of cases into the categories of one variable, that is, the number or percent of cases in each category.

FIGURE 12.2 **Examples of Univariate Statistics**

RAW COUNT FREQUENCY DISTRIBUTION		PERCENTAGE FREQUENCY DISTRIBUTION	
Gender	*Frequency*	*Gender*	*Percentage*
Male	100	Male	25%
Female	300	Female	75%
Total	400	Total	100%

BAR CHART OF SAME INFORMATION

Males

Females

EXAMPLE OF GROUPED DATA FREQUENCY DISTRIBUTION

First Job Annual Income	*N*
Under $5,000	25
$5,000 to $9,999	50
$10,000 to $15,999	100
$16,000 to $19,999	150
$20,000 to $29,999	50
$30,000 and over	25
Total	400

EXAMPLE OF FREQUENCY POLYGON

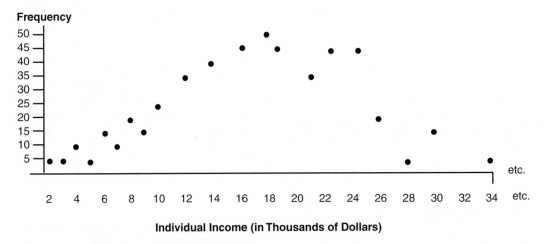

spondents. I can summarize the information on the gender of respondents at a glance with a raw count or a percentage frequency distribution (see Figure 12.2). I can present the same information in graphic form. Some common types of graphic representations are the **histogram,** *bar chart,* and *pie chart.* Bar charts or graphs are used for discrete variables. They can have a vertical or horizontal orientation

histogram A graphic display of univariate frequencies or percentages, usually with vertical lines indicating the amount or proportion.

with a small space between the bars. The terminology is not exact, but histograms are usually upright bar graphs for interval or ratio data.[3]

For interval- or ratio-level data, a researcher often groups the information into categories. The grouped categories should be mutually exclusive. Interval- or ratio-level data are often plotted in a **frequency polygon.** In it the number of cases or frequency is along the vertical axis, and the values of the variable or scores are along the horizontal axis. A polygon appears when the dots are connected.

Measures of Central Tendency

Researchers often want to summarize the information about one variable into a single number. They use three **measures of central tendency,** or measures of the center of the frequency distribution: mean, median, and mode, which are often called *averages* (a less precise and less clear way of saying the same thing).

The **mode** is the easiest to use and can be used with nominal, ordinal, interval, or ratio data. It is simply the most common or frequently occurring number. For example, the mode of the following list is 5: 6 5 7 10 9 5 3 5. A distribution can have more than one mode. For example, the mode of this list is both 5 and 7: 5 6 1 2 5 7 4 7. If the list gets long, it is easy to spot the mode in a frequency distribution—just look for the most frequent score. There will always be at least one case with a score that is equal to the mode.

The **median** is the middle point. It is also the 50th percentile, or the point at which half the cases are above it and half below it. It can be used with ordinal-, interval- or ratio-level data (but not nominal level). You can "eyeball" the mode, but computing a median requires a little more work. The easiest way is first to organize the scores from highest to lowest, then count to the middle. If there is an odd number of scores, it is simple. Seven people are waiting for a bus; their ages are 12 17 20 27 30 55 80. The median age is 27. Note that the median does not change easily. If the 55-year-old and the 80-year-old both got on one bus, and the remaining people were joined by two 31-year-olds, the median remains unchanged. If there is an even number of scores, things

are a bit more complicated. For example, six people at a bus stop have the following ages: 17 20 26 30 50 70. The median is halfway between 26 and 30. Compute the median by adding the two middle scores together and dividing by 2, or $26 + 30 = 56/2 = 28$. The median age is 28, even though no person is 28 years old. Note that there is no mode in the list of six ages because each person has a different age.

The **mean,** also called the arithmetic average, is the most widely used measure of central tendency. It can be used *only* with interval- or ratio-level data.[4] Compute the mean by adding up all scores, then divide by the number of scores. For example, the mean age in the previous example is $17 + 20 + 26 + 30 + 50 + 70 = 213$; $213/6 = 35.5$. No one in the list is 35.5 years old, and the mean does not equal the median.

The mean is strongly affected by changes in extreme values (very large or very small). For example, the 50- and 70-year-old left and were replaced with two 31-year-olds. The distribution now looks like this: 17 20 26 30 31 31. The median is unchanged 28. The mean is $17 + 20 + 26 + 30 + 31 + 31 = 155$; $155/6 = 25.8$. Thus, the mean dropped a great deal when a few extreme values were removed.

If the frequency distribution forms a, **normal distribution** or bell-shaped curve, the three measures of central tendency equal each other. If the

Frequency polygon   A graph of connected points showing the distribution of how many cases fall into each category of a variable.

Measures of central tendency   A class of statistical measures that summarizes information about the distribution of data for one variable into a single number.

Mode   A measure of central tendency for one variable that indicates the most frequent or common score.

Median   A measure of central tendency for one variable that indicates the point or score at which half the cases are higher and half are lower.

Mean   A measure of central tendency for one variable that indicates the arithmetic average, that is, the sum of all scores divided by the total number of scores

Normal distribution   A bell-shaped frequency polygon for a distribution of cases, with a peak in the center and identical curving slopes on either side of the center. It is the distribution of many naturally occurring phenomena and is a basis of much statistical theory.

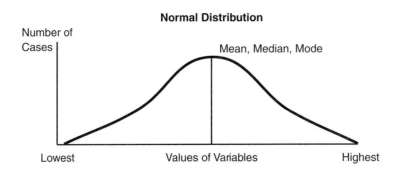

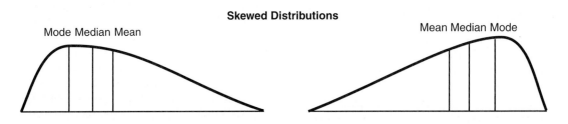

FIGURE 12.3   Measures of Central Tendency

distribution is a **skewed distribution** (i.e., more cases are in the upper or lower scores), then the three will not be equal. If most cases have lower scores with a few extreme high scores, the mean will be the highest, the median in the middle, and the mode the lowest. If most cases have higher scores with a few extreme low scores, the mean will be the lowest, the median in the middle, and the mode the highest. In general, the median is best for skewed distributions, although the mean is used in most other statistics (see Figure 12.3).

Measures of Variation

Measures of central tendency are a one-number summary of a distribution; however, they give only its *center*. Another characteristic of a distribution is

its spread, dispersion, or variability around the center. Two distributions can have identical measures of central tendency but differ in their spread about the center. For example, seven people are at a bus stop in front of a bar. Their ages are 25 26 27 30 33 34 35. Both the median and the mean are 30. At a bus stop in front of an ice cream store, seven people have the identical median and mean, but their ages are 5 10 20 30 40 50 55. The ages of the group in front of the ice cream store are spread more from the center, or the distribution has more variability.

Variability has important social implications. For example, in city X, the median and mean family income is $25,600 per year, and it has zero variation. *Zero variation* means that every family has an income of exactly $25,600. City Y has the same median and mean family income, but 95 percent of its families have incomes of $12,000 per year and 5 percent have incomes of $300,000 per year. City X has perfect income equality, whereas there is great inequality in city Y. A researcher who does not know the variability of income in the two cities misses very important information.

Researchers measure variation in three ways: range, percentile, and standard deviation. **Range** is

Skewed distribution   A distribution of cases among the categories of a variable that is not normal, that is, not a bell shape. Instead of an equal number of cases on both ends, more are at one of the extremes.

Range   A measure of dispersion for one variable indicating the highest and lowest scores.

the simplest. It consists of the largest and smallest scores. For example, the range for the bus stop in front of the bar is from 25 to 35, or 35 – 25 = 10 years. If the 35-year-old got onto a bus and was replaced by a 60-year-old, the range would change to 60 – 25 = 45 years. Range has limitations. For example, here are two groups of six with a range of 35 years: 30 30 30 30 30 65 and 20 45 46 48 50 55.

Percentiles tell the score at a specific place within the distribution. One percentile you already learned is the median, the 50th percentile. Sometimes the 25th and 75th percentiles or the 10th and 90th percentiles are used to describe a distribution. For example, the 25th percentile is the score at which 25 percent of the distribution have either that score or a lower one. The computation of a percentile follows the same logic as the median. If I have 100 people and want to find the 25th percentile. I rank the scores and count up from the bottom until I reach number 25. If the total is not 100, I simply adjust the distribution to a percentage basis.

Standard deviation is the most difficult to compute measure of dispersion; it is also the most comprehensive and widely used. The range and percentile are for ordinal-, interval-, and ratio-level data, but the standard deviation requires an interval or ratio level of measurement. It is based on the mean and gives an "average distance" between all scores and the mean. People rarely compute the standard deviation by hand for more than a handful of cases because computers and calculators can do it in seconds.

Look at the calculation of the standard deviation in Figure 12.4. If you add up the absolute difference between each score and the mean (i.e., subtract each score from the mean), you get zero. This is because the mean is equally distant from all scores. Also notice that the scores that differ the most from the mean have the largest effect on the sum of squares and on the standard deviation.

The standard deviation is of limited usefulness by itself. It is used for comparison purposes. For example, the standard deviation for the schooling of parents of children in class A is 3.317 years; for class B, it is 0.812; and for class C, it is 6.239. The standard deviation tells a researcher that the parents of children in class B are very similar, whereas those for class C are very different. In fact, in class B, the schooling of an "average" parent is less than a year

above or below than the mean for all parents, so the parents are very homogeneous. In class C, however, the "average" parent is more than six years above or below the mean, so the parents are very heterogeneous.

The standard deviation and the mean are used to create z-scores. **Z-scores** let a researcher compare two or more distributions or groups. The z-score, also called a *standardized score,* expresses points or scores on a frequency distribution in terms of a number of standard deviations from the mean. Scores are in terms of their relative position within a distribution, not as absolute values.

For example, Katy, a sales manager in firm A, earns $50,000 per year, whereas Mike in firm B earns $38,000 per year. Despite the absolute income differences between them, the managers are paid equally relative to others in the same firm. Katy is paid more than two-thirds of other employees in her firm, and Mike is also paid more than two-thirds of the employees in his firm.

Here is another example of how to use z-scores. Hans and Heidi are twin brother and sister, but Hans is shorter than Heidi. Compared to other girls her age, Heidi is at the mean height; she has a z-score of zero. Likewise, Hans is at the mean height among boys his age. Thus, within each comparison group, the twins are at the same z-score, so they have the same relative height.

Z-scores are easy to calculate from the mean and standard deviation (see Box 12.2). For example, an employer interviews students from Kings College and Queens College. She learns that the colleges are similar and that both grade on a 4.0 scale. Yet, the mean grade-point average at Kings College is 2.62 with a standard deviation of .50, whereas the mean grade-point average at Queens College is 3.24

Percentile   A measure of dispersion for one variable that indicates the percentage of cases at or below a score or point.

Standard deviation   A measure of dispersion for one variable that indicates an average distance between the scores and the mean.

Z-score   A standardized location of a score in a distribution of scores based on the number of standard deviations it is above or below the mean.

FIGURE 12.4   The Standard Deviation

STEPS IN COMPUTING THE STANDARD DEVIATION

1. Compute the mean.
2. Subtract the mean from each score.
3. Square the resulting difference for each score.
4. Total up the squared differences to get the sum of squares.
5. Divide the sum of squares by the number of cases to get the variance.
6. Take the square root of the variance, which is the standard deviation.

EXAMPLE OF COMPUTING THE STANDARD DEVIATION

[8 respondents, variable = years of schooling]

Score	Score – Mean	Squared (Score – Mean)
15	15 – 12.5 = 2.5	6.25
12	12 – 12.5 = –0.5	.25
12	12 – 12.5 = –0.5	.25
10	10 – 12.5 = –2.5	6.25
16	16 – 12.5 = 3.5	12.25
18	18 – 12.5 = 5.5	30.25
8	8 – 12.5 = 4.5	20.25
9	9 – 12.5 = –3.5	12.25

Mean = 15 + 12 + 12 + 10 + 16 + 18 + 8 + 9 = 100, 100/8 = 12.5
Sum of squares = 6.25 + .25 + .25 + 6.25 + 12.25 + 30.25 + 20.25 + 12.25 = 88
Variance = Sum of squares/Number of cases = 88/8 = 11
Standard deviation = Square root of variance = $\sqrt{11}$ = 3.317 years.
Here is the standard deviation in the form of a formula with symbols.

Symbols:
X = SCORE of case Σ = Sigma (Greek letter) for sum, add together
$\bar{X}$ = MEAN N = Number of cases

Formula:[a]

$$\text{Standard deviation} = \sqrt{\frac{\Sigma(X - \bar{X})^2}{N-1}}$$

---

[a] There is a slight difference in the formula depending on whether one is using data for the population or a sample to estimate the population parameter.

---

with a standard deviation of .40. The employer suspects that grades at Queens College are inflated. Suzette from Kings College has a grade-point average of 3.62, while Jorge from Queens College has a grade-point average of 3.64. Both students took the same courses. The employer wants to adjust the grades for the grading practices of the two colleges (i.e., create standardized scores). She calculates z-scores by subtracting each student's score from the mean, then dividing by the standard devi-

ation. For example, Suzette's z-score is 3.62 – 2.62 = 1.00/.50 = 2, whereas Jorge's z-score is 3.64 – 3.24. = .40/.40 = 1. Thus, the employer learns that Suzette is two standard deviations above the mean in her college, whereas Jorge is only one standard deviation above the mean for his college. Although Suzette's absolute grade-point average is lower than Jorge's, relative to the students in each of their colleges, Suzette's grades are much higher than Jorge's.

BOX **12.2** Calculating Z-Scores

Personally, I do not like the formula for z-scores, which is:

Z-score = (Score − Mean)/Standard Deviation, or in symbols:

$$z = \frac{X - \bar{X}}{\delta}$$

where: X = score, $\bar{X}$ = mean, δ = standard deviation

I usually rely on a simple conceptual diagram that does the same thing and that shows what z-scores really do. Consider data on the ages of schoolchildren with a mean of 7 years and a standard deviation of 2 years. How do I compute the z-score of 5-year-old Miguel, or what if I know that Yashohda's z-score is a +2 and I need to know her age in years? First, I draw a little chart from −3 to +3 with zero in the middle. I will put the mean value at zero, because a z-score of zero is the mean and z-scores measure distance above or below it. I stop at 3 because virtually all cases fall within 3 standard deviations of the mean in most situations. The chart looks like this:

```
|____|____|____|____|____|____|
 −3   −2   −1    0   +1   +2   +3
```

Now, I label the values of the mean and add or subtract standard deviations from it. One standard deviation above the mean (+1) when the mean is 7 and standard deviation is 2 years is just 7 + 2, or 9 years. For a −2 z-score, I put 3 years. This is because it is 2 standard deviations, of 2 years each (or 4 years), lower than the mean of 7. My diagram now looks like this:

```
 1    3  5  7    9   11   13   age in years
|____|__|__|____|____|____|
 −3  −2 −1  0   +1   +2   +3
```

It is easy to see that Miguel, who is 5 years old, has a z-score of −1, whereas Yashohda's z-score of +2 corresponds to 11 years old. I can read from z-score to age, or age to z-score. For fractions, such as a z-score of −1.5, I just apply the same fraction to age to get 4 years. Likewise, an age of 12 is a z-score of +2.5.

RESULTS WITH TWO VARIABLES

A Bivariate Relationship

Univariate statistics describe a single variable in isolation. **Bivariate statistics** are much more valuable. They let a researcher consider two variables together and describe the relationship between variables. Even simple hypotheses require two variables.

Bivariate statistical analysis shows a **statistical relationship** between variables—that is, things that appear together. For example, a relationship exists between water pollution in a stream and the fact that people who drink the water get sick. It is a statistical relationship between two variables: pollution in the water and the health of the people who drink it.

Statistical relationships are based on two ideas: covariation and statistical independence. **Covariation** means that things go together or are associated. To covary means to vary together; cases with certain values on one variable are likely to have certain values on the other one. For example, people with higher values on the income variable are likely to have higher values on the life expectancy variable. Likewise, those with lower incomes have lower life expectancy. This is usually stated in a shorthand way by saying that income and life expectancy are related to each other, or covary. We could also say that knowing one's income tells us one's probable life expectancy, or that life expectancy depends on income.

Statistical independence is the opposite of covariation. It means there is no association or no

Bivariate statistics Statistical measures that involve two variables only.

Statistical relationship Expressing whether two or more variables affect one another based on the use of elementary applied mathematics, that is, whether there is an association between them or independence.

Covariation The idea that two variables vary together, such that knowing the values on one variable provides information about values found on another.

Statistical independence The absence of a statistical relationship between two variables, that is, when knowing the values on one variable provides no information about the values one will find on another variable. There is no association between them.

relationship between variables. If two variables are independent, cases with certain values on one variable do not have any particular value on the other variable. For example, Rita wants to know whether number of siblings is related to life expectancy. If the variables are independent, then people with many brothers and sisters have the same life expectancy as those who are only children. In other words, knowing how many brothers or sisters someone has tells Rita nothing about the person's life expectancy.

Most researchers state hypotheses in terms of a causal relationship or expected covariation; if they use the null hypothesis, the hypothesis is that there is independence. It is used in formal hypothesis testing and is frequently found in inferential statistics (to be discussed).

Three techniques help researchers decide whether a relationship exists between two variables: (1) a scattergram, or a graph or plot of the relationship; (2) cross-tabulation, or a percentaged table; and (3) measures of association, or statistical measures that express the amount of covariation by a single number (e.g., correlation coefficient). Also see Box 12.3 on graphing data.

Seeing the Relationship: The Scattergram

What Is a Scattergram? A **scattergram** is a graph on which a researcher plots each case or observation, where each axis represents the value of one variable. It is used for variables measured at the interval or ratio level, rarely for ordinal variables, and never if either variable is nominal. There is no

fixed rule for which variable (independent or dependent) to place on the horizontal or vertical axis, but usually the independent variable (symbolized by the letter X) goes on the horizontal axis and the dependent variable (symbolized by Y) on the vertical axis. The lowest value for each should be the lower left corner and the highest value should be at the top or to the right.

How to Construct a Scattergram. Begin with the range of the two variables. Draw an axis with the values of each variable marked and write numbers on each axis (graph paper is helpful). Next, label each axis with the variable name and put a title at the top.

You are now ready for the data. For each case, find the value of each variable and mark the graph at a place corresponding to the two values. For example, a researcher makes a scattergram or scatterplot of years of schooling by number of children. He or she looks at the first case to see years of schooling (e.g., 12) and at the number of children (e.g., 3). Then he or she goes to the place on the graph where 12 for the "schooling" variable and 3 for the "number of children" variable intersect and puts a dot for the case.

The scattergram in Figure 12.5 is a plot of data for 33 women. It shows a negative relationship between the years of education the woman completed and the number of children she gave birth to.

What Can You Learn from the Scattergram? A researcher can see three aspects of a bivariate relationship in a scattergram: form, direction, and precision.

Form. Relationships can take three forms: independence, linear, and curvilinear. *Independence* or no relationship is the easiest to see. It looks like a random scatter with no pattern, or a straight line that is exactly parallel to the horizontal or vertical axis. A **linear relationship** means that a straight line can be visualized in the middle of a maze of cases running from one corner to another. A **curvilinear relationship** means that the center of a maze of cases would form a U curve, right side up or upside down, or an S curve.

Scattergram   A diagram to display the statistical relationship between two variables based on plotting each case's values for both of the variables.

Linear relationship   An association between two variables that is positive or negative across the levels of variables. When plotted in a scattergram, the pattern of the association forms a straight line, without a curve.

Curvilinear relationship   A relationship between two variables such that as the values of one variable increase, the values of the second show a changing pattern, for example, first decrease then increase then decrease. It is not a linear relationship.

BOX **12.3** Graphing Accurately

The pattern in graph A shows drastic change. A steep drop in 1980 is followed by rapid recovery and instability. The pattern in graph B is much more constant. The decline from 1979 to 1980 is smooth, and the other years are almost level. Both graphs are for identical data, the U.S. business failure rate from 1975 to 1992. The X axis (bottom) for years is the same.

The scale of the Y axis is 60 to 160 in graph A and 0 to 400 in graph B. The pattern in graph A only looks more dramatic because of the Y axis scale. When reading graphs, be careful to check the scale. Some people purposely choose a scale to minimize or dramatize a pattern in the data.

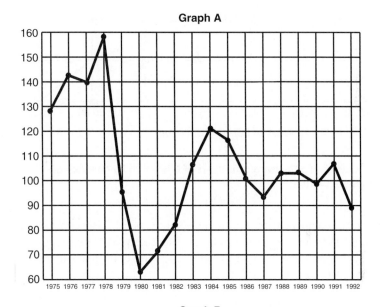

Graph A

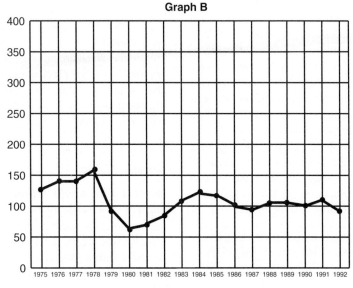

Graph B

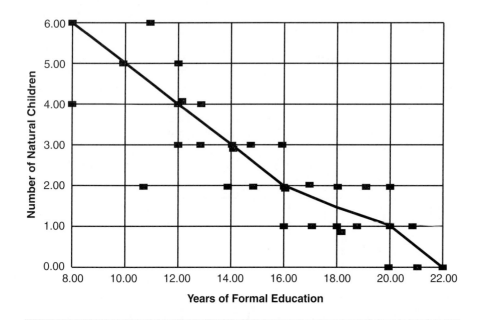

FIGURE 12.5   Example of a Scattergram: Years of Education by Number of Natural Children for 33 Women

Direction. Linear relationships can have a positive or negative direction. The plot of a *positive* relationship looks like a diagonal line from the lower left to the upper right. Higher values on *X* tend to go with higher values on *Y,* and vice versa. The income and life expectancy example described a positive linear relationship.

A *negative* relationship looks like a line from the upper left to the lower right. It means that higher values on one variable go with lower values on the other. For example, people with more education are less likely to have been arrested. If we look at a scattergram of data on a group of males where in years of schooling (*X* axis) are plotted by number of arrests (*Y* axis), we see that most cases (or men) with many arrests are in the lower right, because most of them completed few years of school. Most cases with few arrests are in the upper left because most have had more schooling. The imaginary line for

the relationship can have a shallow or a steep slope. More advanced statistics provide precise numerical measures of the line's slope.

Precision. Bivariate relationships differ in their degree of precision. *Precision* is the amount of spread in the points on the graph. A high level of precision occurs when the points hug the line that summarizes the relationship. A low level occurs when the points are widely spread around the line. Researchers can "eyeball" a highly precise relationship. They can also use advanced statistics to measure the precision of a relationship in a way that is analogous to the standard deviation for univariate statistics.

Bivariate Tables

What Is a Bivariate Table? The bivariate contingency table is widely used. It presents the same information as a scattergram in a more condensed form. The data can be measured at any level of measurement, although interval and ratio data must be grouped if there are many different values. The table is based on **cross-tabulation;** that is, the cases are

Cross-tabulation   The process of placing data for two variables in a contingency table to show the percentage or number of cases at the intersection of variable categories.

organized in the table on the basis of two variables at the same time.

A **contingency table** is formed by cross-tabulating two or more variables. It is contingent because the cases in each category of a variable get distributed into each category of a second (or additional) variable. The table distributes cases into the categories of multiple variables at the same time and shows how the cases, by category of one variable, are "contingent upon" the categories of other variables.

Constructing Percentaged Tables.
It is easy to construct a percentaged table, but there are ways to make it look professional. We will first review the steps for constructing a table by hand. The same principles apply if a computer makes the table. We begin with the raw data, which can be organized into a format for computers. They might look like data from an imaginary survey in Box 12.4.

If creating a table by hand, the next step is to create a *compound frequency distribution (CFD)*. This is similar to the frequency distribution, except that it is for each combination of the values of two variables. For example, a researcher wants to see the relationship between age and attitude. Age is a ratio measure, so it is grouped to treat the ratio-level variable as if it were ordinal. Ratio- or interval-level data are converted to the ordinal level for percentaged tables. Otherwise, there could be 50 categories for a variable and a table that was impossible to read.

The CFD is an intermediate step that makes table construction easier. Computer programs give you the completed table right away.

The CFD has every combination of categories. Age has four categories and Attitude three, so there are $3 \times 4 = 12$ rows. The steps to create a CFD are as follows:

1. Figure all possible combinations of variable categories.
2. Make a mark next to the combination category into which each case falls.
3. Add up the marks for the number of cases in a combination category.

If there is no missing information problem, add up the numbers of categories (e.g., all the "Agree"s, or all the "61 and Older"s). In the example, missing data are an issue. The four "Agree" categories in the CFD add up to 37 (20 + 10 + 4 + 3), not 38, as in the univariate frequency distribution, because one of the 38 cases has missing information for age.

The next step is to set up the parts of a table (see Figure 12.6) by labeling the rows and columns. The independent variable usually is placed in the columns, but this convention is not always followed. Next, each number from the CFD is placed in a cell in the table that corresponds to the combination of variable categories. For example, the CFD shows that 20 of the under-30-year-olds agree (top number), and so does Figure 12.6 (upper left cell).

Figure 12.6 is a raw count or frequency table. Its cells contain a count of the cases. It is easy to make, but interpreting a raw count table is difficult because the rows or columns can have different totals, and what is of real interest is the relative size of cells compared to others.

Researchers convert raw count tables into percentaged tables to see bivariate relationships. There are three ways to percentage a table: by row, by column, and for the total. The first two are often used and show relationships.

Is it best to percentage by row or column? Either can be appropriate. Let us first review the mechanics of percentaging a table. When calculating column percentages, compute the percentage each cell is of the column total. This includes the total column or marginal for the column variable. For example, the first column total is 26 (there are 26 people under age 30), and the first cell of that column is 20 (there are 20 people under age 30 who agree). The percentage is 20/26 = 0.769 or 76.9 percent. Or, for the first number in the marginal,

---

Contingency table   A table of the cross-tabulation of two or more variables showing bivariate quantitative data for variables in the form of percentages across rows or down columns for the categories of one variable.

BOX **12.4** Raw Data and Frequency Distributions

EXAMPLE OF RAW DATA

Case	Age	Gender	Schooling	Attitude	Political Party, etc. . . .
01	21	F	14	1	Democrat
02	36	M	8	1	Republican
03	77	F	12	2	Republican
04	41	F	20	2	Independent
05	29	M	22	3	Democratic Socialist
06	45	F	12	3	Democrat
07	19	M	13	2	Missing Information
08	64	M	12	3	Democrat
09	53	F	10	3	Democrat
10	44	M	21	1	Conservative
etc.					

(Attitude scoring, 1 = Agree, 2 = No Opinion, 3 = Disagree)

TWO FREQUENCY DISTRIBUTIONS:
AGE AND ATTITUDE TOWARD CHANGING THE DRINKING AGE

Age Group	Number of Cases	Attitude	Number of Cases
Under 30	26		
30–45	30	Agree	38
46–60	35	No Opinion	26
61 and older	15	Disagree	40
Missing	3	Missing	5
Total	109	Total	109

COMPOUND FREQUENCY DISTRIBUTION:
AGE GROUP AND ATTITUDE TOWARD CHANGING THE DRINKING AGE

Age	Attitude	Number of Cases
Under 30	Agree	20
Under 30	No Opinion	3
Under 30	Disagree	3
30–45	Agree	10
30–45	No Opinion	10
30–45	Disagree	5
46–60	Agree	4
46–60	No Opinion	10
46–60	Disagree	21
61 and older	Agree	3
61 and older	No Opinion	2
61 and older	Disagree	10
	Subtotal	101
Missing on either variable		8
Total		109

FIGURE 12.6   Age Group by Attitude about Changing the Drinking Age, Raw Count Table

---

RAW COUNT TABLE (a)

ATTITUDE (b)	AGE GROUP (b)				TOTAL (c)
	Under 30	*30–45*	*46–60*	*61 and Older*	
Agree	20	10	4	3	37
No opinion	3 (d)	10	10	2	25
Disagree	3	5	21	10	39
Total (c)	26	25	35	15	101

Missing cases (f) = 8.   (e)

THE PARTS OF A TABLE
(a) Give each table a *title,* which names variables and provides background information.
(b) Label the row and column variable and give a name to each of the variable categories.
(c) Include the totals of the columns and rows. These are called the **marginals.** They equal the univariate frequency distribution for the variable.
(d) Each number or place that corresponds to the intersection of a category for each variable is a **cell of a table.**
(e) The numbers with the labeled variable categories and the totals are called the **body of a table.**
(f) If there is missing information (cases in which a respondent refused to answer, ended interview, said, "don't know," etc.), report the number of missing cases near the table to account for all original cases.

37/101 = 0.366 = 36.6 percent (see table 12.1) except for rounding, the total should equal 100 percent.

Computing row percentages is similar. Compute the percentage of each cell as a percentage of the row total. For example, using the same cell with 20 in it, we now want to know what percentage it is of the row total of 37, or 20/37 = 0.541 = 54.1 percent. Percentaging by row or column gives different percentages for a cell unless the marginals are the same.

The row and column percentages let a researcher address different questions. The row-percentaged table answers the question: Among those who hold an attitude, what percentage come from each age group? It says of respondents who agree, 54.1 percent are in the under-30 age group. The column-percentaged table addresses the question: Among those in each age group, what percentage hold different attitudes? It says that among those who are under 30, 76.9 percent agree. From the row percentages, a researcher learns that a little over half of those who agree are under 30 years old,

whereas from column percentages, the researcher learns that among the under-30 people, over three-quarters agree. One way of percentaging tells about people who have specific attitudes; the other tells about people in specific age groups.

A researcher's hypothesis may imply looking at row percentages or the column percentages. When beginning, calculate percentages each way and practice interpreting, or figuring out, what each says. For example, my hypothesis is that age affects attitude, so column percentages are most helpful. However, if my interest is in describing

---

Marginals   The row and column totals in a contingency table, outside the body of a table.

Cell of a table   A part of the body of a contingency table that shows the distribution of cases into categories of variables as a number or percentage.

Body of a table   The center part of a contingency table. It contains all the cells, but not the totals or labels.

TABLE 12.1   Age Group by Attitude about Changing the Drinking Age, Percentaged Tables

COLUMN-PERCENTAGED TABLE

	AGE GROUP				
ATTITUDE	*Under 30*	*30–45*	*46–60*	*61 and Older*	**TOTAL**
Agree	76.9%	40%	11.4%	20%	36.6%
No opinion	11.5	40	28.6	13.3	24.8
Disagree	11.5	20	60	66.7	38.6
Total	99.9	100	100	100	100
(N)	(26)*	(25)*	(35)*	(15)*	(101)*
Missing cases = 8					

ROW-PERCENTAGED TABLE

	AGE GROUP					
ATTITUDE	*Under 30*	*30–45*	*46–60*	*61 and Older*	**TOTAL**	*(N)*
Agree	54.1%	27%	10.8%	8.1%	100%	(37)*
No opinion	12	40	40	8	100	(25)*
Disagree	7.7	12.8	53.8	25.6	99.9	(39)*
Total	25.7	24.8	34.7	14.9	100.1	(101)*
Missing cases = 8						

*For percentaged tables, provide the number of cases or *N* on which percentages are computed in parentheses near the total of 100%. This makes it possible to go back and forth from a percentaged table to a raw count table and vice versa.

the age makeup of groups of people with different attitudes, then row percentages are appropriate. As Zeisel (1985:34) noted, whenever one factor in a cross-tabulation can be considered the cause of the other, percentage will be most illuminating if they are computed in the direction of the causal factor.

Unfortunately, there is no "industry standard" for putting the independent and dependent variable in a percentage table as row or column, or for percentage by row and column. A majority of researchers place the independent variable on the column and percentage by column, but a large minority put the independent variable as row and percentage by row.

Reading a Percentaged Table. Once you understand how a table is made, reading it and figuring out what it says are much easier. To read a table,

first look at the title, the variable labels, and any background information. Next, look at the direction in which percentages have been computed—in rows or columns. Notice that the percentaged tables in Table 12.1 have the same title. This is because the same variables are used. It would have helped to note how the data were percentaged in the title, but this is rarely done. Sometimes, researchers present abbreviated tables and omit the 100 percent total or the marginals, which adds to the confusion. It is best to include all the parts of a table and clear labels.

Researchers read percentaged tables to make comparisons. Comparisons are made in the opposite direction from that in which percentages are computed. A rule of thumb is to compare across rows if the table is percentaged down (i.e., by column) and to compare up and down in columns if the table is percentaged across (i.e., by row).

For example, in row-percentaged Table 12.1, compare columns or age groups. Most of those who agree are in the youngest group, with the proportion declining as age increases. Most no-opinion people are in the middle-age groups, whereas those who disagree are older, especially in the 46-to-60 group. When reading column-percentaged Table 12.1, compare across rows. For example, a majority of the youngest group agree, and they are the only group in which most people agree. Only 11.5 percent disagree, compared to a majority in the two oldest groups.

It takes practice to see a relationship in a percentaged table. If there is no relationship in a table, the cell percentages look approximately equal across rows or columns. A linear relationship looks like larger percentages in the diagonal cells. If there is a curvilinear relationship, the largest percentages form a pattern across cells. For example, the largest cells might be the upper right, the bottom middle, and the upper left. It is easiest to see a relationship in a moderate-sized table (9 to 16 cells) in which most cells have some cases (at least five cases are recommended) and the relationship is strong and precise.

Principles of reading a scattergram can help you see a relationship in a percentaged table. Imagine a scattergram that has been divided into 12 equal-sized sections. The cases in each section correspond to the number of cases in the cells of a table that is superimposed onto the scattergram. The table is a condensed form of the scattergram. The bivariate relationship line in a scattergram corresponds to the diagonal cells in a percentaged table. Thus, a simple way to see strong relationships is to circle the largest percentage in each row (for row-percentaged tables) or column (for column-percentaged tables) and see whether a line appears.

The circle-the-largest-cell rule works—with one important caveat. The categories in the percentages table *must* be ordinal or interval and in the same order as in a scattergram. In scattergrams the lowest variable categories begin at the bottom left. If the categories in a table are not ordered the same way, the rule does not work.

For example, Table 12.2a looks like a positive relationship and Table 12.2b like a negative relationship. Both use the same data and are percentaged by row. The actual relationship is negative.

TABLE 12.2A   Age by Schooling

| | YEARS OF SCHOOLING | | | | |
AGE	0–11	12	13–14	16+	TOTAL
Under 30	5%	25	30	40	100
30–45	15	25	40	20	100
46–60	35	45	12	8	100
61 +	45	35	15	5	100

TABLE 12.2B   Age by Schooling

| | YEARS OF SCHOOLING | | | | |
AGE	0–11	12	13–14	16+	TOTAL
61 +	45%	35	15	5	100
46–60	35	45	12	8	100
30–45	15	25	40	20	100
Under 30	5	25	30	40	100

Look closely—Table 12.2b has age categories ordered as in a scattergram. When in doubt, return to the basic difference between positive and negative relationships. A positive relationship means that as one variable increases, so does the other. A negative relationship means that as one variable increases, the other decreases.

Bivariate Tables without Percentages. Researchers condense information in another kind of bivariate table with a measure of central tendency (usually the mean) instead of percentages. It is used when one variable is nominal or ordinal and another is measured at the interval or ratio level. The mean (or a similar measure) of the interval or ratio variable is presented for each category of the nominal or ordinal variable. Such tables are not constructed from the CFD. Instead, all cases are divided into the ordinal or nominal variable categories; then the mean is calculated for the cases in each variable category from the raw data.

Table 12.3 shows the mean age of people in each of the attitude categories. The results suggest that the mean age of those who disagree is much higher than for those who agree or have no opinion.

TABLE 12.3   Attitude about Changing the Drinking Age by Mean Age of Respondent

DRINKING AGE ATTITUDE	MEAN AGE	(N)
Agree	26.2	(37)
No opinion	44.5	(25)
Disagree	61.9	(39)

Missing cases = 8

Measures of Association

A measure of association is a single number that expresses the strength, and often the direction, of a relationship. It condenses information about a bivariate relationship into a single number.

There are many measures of association. The correct one depends on the level of measurement. Many measures are called by letters of the Greek alphabet. Lambda, gamma, tau, chi (squared), and rho are commonly used measures. The emphasis here is on interpreting the measures, not on their calculation. In order to understand each measure, you will need to complete a beginning statistics course. See Box 12.5 on the correlation.

Most of the elementary measures discussed here follow a *proportionate reduction in error (PRE)* logic. The logic asks: How much does knowledge of one variable reduce the errors that are made when guessing the values of the other variable? Independence means that knowledge of one variable does not reduce the chance of errors on the other variable. Measures of association equal zero if the variables are independent.

If there is a strong association or relationship, then few errors are made predicting a second variable on the basis of knowledge of the first, or the proportion of errors reduced is large. A large number of correct guesses suggests that the measure of association is a nonzero number if an association exists between the variables. Table 12.4 describes

> **Control variable** A "third" variable that shows whether a bivariate relationship holds up to alternative explanations; it can occur before or between other variables.

five commonly used bivariate measures of association. Notice that most range from −1 to +1, with negative numbers indicating a negative relationship and positive numbers a positive relationship. A measure of 1.0 means a 100 percent reduction in errors, or perfect prediction.

MORE THAN TWO VARIABLES

Statistical Control

Showing an association or relationship between two variables is not sufficient to say that an independent variable *causes* a dependent variable. In addition to temporal order and association, a researcher must eliminate alternative explanations—explanations that can make the hypothesized relationship spurious. Experimental researchers do this by choosing a research design that physically controls potential alternative explanations for results (i.e., that threaten internal validity).

In nonexperimental research, a researcher controls for alternative explanations with statistics. He or she measures possible alternative explanations with **control variables,** then examines the control variables with multivariate tables and statistics that help him or her decide whether a bivariate relationship is spurious. They also show the relative size of the effect of multiple independent variables on a dependent variable.

A researcher controls for alternative explanations in multivariate (more than two variables) analysis by introducing a third (or sometimes a fourth or fifth) variable. For example, a bivariate table shows that taller teenagers like baseball more than shorter ones do. But the bivariate relationship between height and attitude toward baseball may be spurious because teenage males are taller than females, and males tend to like baseball more than females do. To test whether the relationship is actually due to sex, a researcher must *control* for gender; in other words, effects of sex are statistically *removed*. Once this is done, a researcher can see whether the bivariate relationship between height and attitude toward baseball remains.

A researcher controls for a third variable by seeing whether the bivariate relationship persists within

BOX **12.5** Correlation

The formula for a correlation coefficient (rho) looks awesome to most people. Calculating it by hand, especially if the data have multiple digits, can be a very long and arduous task. Nowadays, computers do the calculation. However, the problem with relying on computers to do the work is that a researcher may not understand what the coefficient means. Here is a short, simplified example to show how it is done.

The purpose of a correlation coefficient is to show how much two variables "go together" or covary. Ideally, the variables have a ratio level of measurement (some use variables at the interval level). To calculate the coefficient, we first convert each score on a variable into its z-score. This "standardizes" the variable based on its mean and standard deviation. Next, we multiply the z-scores for each case together. This tells us how much the variables for a case vary together—cases with high z-scores on both variables get much bigger, while those low on both are much smaller. Finally, we divide the sum of the multiplied z-scores

by the number of cases. It yields a type of "average" covariation that has been standardized. In short, a correlation coefficient is the product of z-scores added together, then divided by the number of cases. It is always between +1.0 and −1.0 and summarizes scattergram information about a relationship into a single number.

Let us look at the correlation between the age and price for five small bottles of red wine. First, anyone who is brave or lacks math-symbol phobia can look at one of the frequently used formulas for a correlation coefficient:

$$(\Sigma \; [\text{z-score}_1][\text{z-score}_2])/N$$

where: Σ = sum, z-score_1 = z-score for 1st variable (see Box 12.2), z-score_2 = z-score for 2nd variable, N = number of cases

Here is how to calculate a correlation coefficient without directly using the formula:

WINE	AGE	PRICE	(DIFFERENCE) Age	Price	SQUARED DIFF. Age	Price	Z-SCORES Age	Price	Z-SCORE Product
A	2	$10	−2	−5	4	25	−1.43	−0.70	1.0
B	3	$ 5	−1	−10	1	100	−0.71	−1.41	1.0
C	5	$20	+1	+5	1	25	0.71	+0.70	0.50
D	6	$25	+2	+10	4	100	+1.43	+1.41	2.0
E	4	$15	0	0	0	0	0	0	0
Total	20	$75			10	250			4.50

Mean: Age = 4; Price = $15
Variance: Age = 10/5 = 2; Price = 250/5 = 50.
Stnd. Dev.:   Age = square root of 2 = 1.4; Price = square root of 50 = 7.1
Correlation: 4.50/5 = .90

Step 1: Calculate the mean and standard deviation for each variable. (For the standard deviation, first subtract each score from its mean, next square the difference, now sum squared differences, then divide the sum by the number of cases for the variance. Then take the square root of the variance.)

Step 2: Convert each score for the variables into their z-scores. (Just subtract each score from its mean and divide by its standard deviation.)

Step 3: Multiply the z-scores together for each case.

Step 4: Sum the products of z-scores, then divide by the number of cases.

TABLE 12.4 Five Measures of Association

Lambda is used for nominal-level data. It is based on a reduction in errors based on the mode and ranges between 0 (independence) and 1.0 (perfect prediction or the strongest possible relationship).

Gamma is used for ordinal-level data. It is based on comparing pairs of variable categories and seeing whether a case has the same rank on each. Gamma ranges from −1.0 to +1.0, with 0 meaning no association.

Tau is also used for ordinal-level data. It is based on a different approach than gamma and takes care of a few problems that can occur with gamma. Actually, there are several statistics named tau (it is a popular Greek letter), and the one here is Kendall's tau. Kendall's tau ranges from −1.0 to +1.0, with 0 meaning no association.

Rho is also called Pearson's product moment correlation coefficient (named after the famous statistician Karl Pearson and based on a product moment statistical procedure). It is the most commonly used measure of correlation, the correlation statistic people mean if they use the term *correlation* without identifying it further. It can be used only for data measured at the interval or ratio level. Rho is used for the mean and standard deviation of the variables and tells how far cases are from a relationship (or regression) line in a scatterplot. Rho ranges from −1.0 to +1.0, with 0 meaning no association. If the value of rho is squared, sometimes called *R*-squared, it has a unique proportion reduction in error meaning. *R*-squared tells how the percentage in one variable (e.g., the dependent) is accounted for, or explained by, the other variable (e.g., the independent). Rho measures linear relationships only. It cannot measure nonlinear or curvilinear relationships. For example, a rho of zero can indicate either no relationship or a curvilinear relationship (see Box 12.5).

Chi-squared has two different uses. It can be used as a measure of association in descriptive statistics like the others listed here, or in inferential statistics. Inferential statistics are briefly described next. As a measure of association, chi-squared can be used for nominal and ordinal data. It has an upper limit of infinity and a lower limit of zero, meaning no association (see Box 12.8).

SUMMARY OF MEASURES OF ASSOCIATION

Measure	Greek Symbol	Type of Data	High Association	Independence
Lambda	λ	Nominal	1.0	0
Gamma	γ	Ordinal	+1.0, −1.0	0
Tau (Kendall's)	τ	Ordinal	+1.0, −1.0	0
Rho	ρ	Interval, ratio	+1.0, −1.0	0
Chi-square	χ^2	Nominal, ordinal	Infinity	0

categories of the control variable. For example, a researcher controls for sex, and the relationship between height and baseball attitude persists. This means that tall males and tall females both like baseball more than short males and short females do. In other words, the control variable has no effect. When this is so, the bivariate relationship is not spurious.

If the bivariate relationship weakens or disappears after the control variable is considered, it means that tall males are no more likely than short males to like baseball, and tall females are no more likely to like baseball than short females. It indicates that the initial bivariate relationship is spurious and suggests that the third variable, sex, and not height, is the true cause of differences in attitudes toward baseball.

Statistical control is a key idea in advanced statistical techniques. A measure of association such as the correlation coefficient only suggests a relationship. Until a researcher considers control variables, the bivariate relationship could be spurious. Researchers are cautious in interpreting bivariate relationships until they have considered control variables.

After they introduce control variables, researchers talk about the **net effect** of an independent variable—the effect of the independent variable "net of," or in spite of, the control variable. There are two ways to introduce control variables: trivariate percentaged tables and multiple regression analysis. Each will be briefly discussed next.

The Elaboration Model of Percentaged Tables

Constructing Trivariate Tables. In order to meet all the conditions needed for causality, researchers want to "control for" or see whether an alternative explanation explains away a causal relationship. If an alternative explanation explains a relationship, then the bivariate relationship is spurious. Alternative explanations are operationalized as third variables, which are called *control variables* because they control for alternative explanation.

One way to take such third variables into consideration and see whether they influence the bivariate relationship is to statistically introduce control variables using trivariate or three-variable tables. Trivariate tables differ slightly from bivariate tables; they consist of multiple bivariate tables.

A trivariate table has a bivariate table of the independent and dependent variable for each category of the control variable. These new tables are called **partials.** The number of partials depends on the number of categories in the control variable. Partial tables look like bivariate tables, but they use a subset of the cases. Only cases with a specific value on the control variable are in the partial. Thus, it is possible to break apart a bivariate table to form partials, or combine the partials to restore the initial bivariate table.

Trivariate tables have three limitations. First, they are difficult to interpret if a control variable has more than four categories. Second, control variables can be at any level of measurement, but interval or ratio control variables must be grouped (i.e., converted to an ordinal level), and how cases are grouped can affect the interpretation of effects. Finally, the total number of cases is a limiting factor because the cases are divided among cells in partials. The number of cells in the partials equals the number of cells in the bivariate relationship multiplied by the number of categories in the control variable. For example, a control variable has three categories, and a bivariate table has 12 cells, so the partials have $3 \times 12 = 36$ cells. An average of five cases per cell is recommended, so the researcher will need $5 \times 36 = 180$ cases at minimum.

Like bivariate table construction, a trivariate table begins with a compound frequency distribution (CFD), but it is a three-way instead of a two-way CFD. An example of a trivariate table with "gender" as a control variable for the bivariate table in Figure 12.4 is shown in Table 12.5.

As with the bivariate tables, each combination in the CFD represents a cell in the final (here the partial) table. Each partial table has the variables in an initial bivariate table.

For three variables, three bivariate tables are logically possible. In the example, the combinations are: (1) gender by attitude, (2) age group by attitude, and (3) gender by age group. The partials are set up on the basis of the initial bivariate relationship. The independent variable in each is "age group" and the dependent variable is "attitude." "Gender" is the control variable. Thus, the trivariate table consists of a pair of partials, each showing the age/attitude relationship for a given gender.

A researcher's theory suggests the hypothesis in the initial bivariate relationship; it also tells him

Net effect The effect of one variable (usually independent) on another (usually dependent) after the impact of control variables that affects both has been statistically removed.

Partials In contingency tables for three variables, tables between the independent and dependent variables for each category of a control variable.

TABLE 12.5 CFD and Tables for a Trivariate Analysis

COMPOUND FREQUENCY DISTRIBUTION FOR TRIVARIATE TABLE

	MALES			FEMALES	
Age	*Attitude*	*Number of Cases*	*Age*	*Attitude*	*Number of Cases*
Under 30	Agree	10	Under 30	Agree	10
Under 30	No Opinion	1	Under 30	No Opinion	2
Under 30	Disagree	2	Under 30	Disagree	1
30–45	Agree	5	30–45	Agree	5
30–45	No Opinion	5	30–45	No Opinion	5
30–45	Disagree	2	30–45	Disagree	3
46–60	Agree	2	46–60	Agree	2
46–60	No Opinion	5	46–60	No Opinion	5
46–60	Disagree	11	46–60	Disagree	10
61 and older	Agree	3	61 and older	Agree	0
61 and older	No Opinion	0	61 and older	No Opinion	2
61 and older	Disagree	5	61 and older	Disagree	5
	Subtotal	51		Subtotal	50
Missing on either variable		4	Missing on either variable		4
Number of males		55	Number of females		54

PARTIAL TABLE FOR MALES

	AGE GROUP				
ATTITUDE	*Under 30*	*30–45*	*46–60*	*61 and Older*	**TOTAL**
Agree	10	5	2	3	20
No Opinion	1	5	5	0	11
Disagree	2	2	11	5	20
Total	13	12	18	8	51

Missing cases = 4

PARTIAL TABLE FOR FEMALES

	AGE GROUP				
ATTITUDE	*Under 30*	*30–45*	*46–60*	*61 and Older*	**TOTAL**
Agree	10	5	2	0	17
No Opinion	2	5	5	2	14
Disagree	1	3	10	5	19
Total	13	13	17	7	50

Missing cases = 4

or her which variables provide alternative explanations (i.e., the control variables). Thus, the choice of the control variable is based on theory.

As with bivariate tables, the CFD provides the raw count for cells (partials here). A researcher converts them into percentages in the same way as for a bivariate table (i.e., divide cells by the row or column total). For example, in the partial table for females, the upper left cell has a 10. The row percentage for that cell is 10/17 = 58 percent.

The **elaboration paradigm** is a system for reading percentaged trivariate tables.[5] It describes the pattern that emerges when a control variable is introduced. Five terms describe how the partial tables compare to the initial bivariate table, or how the original bivariate relationship changes after the control variable is considered (see Box 12.6). The examples of patterns presented here show strong cases. More advanced statistics are needed when the differences are not as obvious.

The **replication pattern** is the easiest to understand. It is when the partials replicate or reproduce the same relationship that existed in the bivariate table before considering the control variable. It means that the control variable has no effect.

The **specification pattern** is the next easiest pattern. It occurs when one partial replicates the initial bivariate relationship but other partials do not. For example, you find a strong (negative) bivariate relationship between automobile accidents and college grades. You control for gender and discover that the relationship holds only for males (i.e., the strong negative relationship was in the partial for males, but not for females). This is specification because a researcher can specify the category of the control variable in which the initial relationship persists.

The control variable has a large impact in both the interpretation and explanation patterns. In both, the bivariate table shows a relationship that disappears in the partials. In other words, the relationship appears to be independence in the partials. The two patterns cannot be distinguished by looking at the tables alone. The difference between them depends on the location of the control variable in the causal order of variables. Theoretically, a control variable

can be in one of two places, either between the original independent and dependent variables (i.e., the control variable is intervening), or before the original independent variable.

The **interpretation pattern** describes the situation in which the control variable intervenes between the original independent and dependent variables. For example, you examine a relationship between religious upbringing and abortion attitude. Political ideology is a control variable. You reason that religious upbringing affects current political ideology and abortion attitude. You theorize that political ideology is logically prior to an attitude about a specific issue, such as abortion. Thus, religious upbringing causes political ideology, which in turn has an impact on abortion attitude. The control variable is an intervening variable, which helps you interpret the meaning of the complete relationship.

The **explanation pattern** looks the same as interpretation. The difference is the temporal order of the control variable. In this pattern, a control variable comes before the independent variable in the initial bivariate relationship. For example, the

---

Elaboration paradigm   A system for describing patterns evident among tables when the bivariate contingency table is compared with partials after the control variable has been added.

Replication pattern   A pattern in the elaboration paradigm in which the partials show the same relationship as in a bivariate contingency table of the independent and dependent variable alone.

Specification pattern   A pattern in the elaboration paradigm in which the bivariate contingency table shows a relationship. One of the partial tables shows the relationship, but other tables do not.

Interpretation pattern   A pattern in the elaboration paradigm in which the bivariate contingency table shows a relationship, but the partials show no relationship and the control variable is intervening in the causal explanation.

Explanation pattern   A pattern in the elaboration paradigm in which the bivariate contingency table shows a relationship, but the partials show no relationship and the control variable occurs prior to the independent variable.

BOX **12.6** **Summary of the Elaboration Paradigm**

Pattern Name	Pattern Seen When Comparing Partials to the Original Bivariate Table
Replication	Same relationship in both partials as in bivariate table.
Specification	Bivariate relationship is seen only in one of the partial tables.
Interpretation	Bivariate relationship weakens greatly or disappears in the partial tables (control variable is intervening).
Explanation	Bivariate relationship weakens greatly or disappears in the partial tables (control variable is before independent variable).
Suppressor variable	No bivariate relationship; relationship appears in partial tables only.

EXAMPLES OF ELABORATION PATTERNS

Replication

	BIVARIATE TABLE			PARTIALS			
				Control = Low		Control = High	
	Low	*High*		*Low*	*High*	*Low*	*High*
Low	85%	15%	Low	84%	16%	86%	14%
High	15%	85%	High	16%	84%	14%	86%

Interpretation or Explanation

	BIVARIATE TABLE			PARTIALS			
				Control = Low		Control = High	
	Low	*High*		*Low*	*High*	*Low*	*High*
Low	85%	15%	Low	45%	55%	55%	45%
High	15%	85%	High	55%	45%	45%	55%

Specification

	BIVARIATE TABLE			PARTIALS			
				Control = Low		Control = High	
	Low	*High*		*Low*	*High*	*Low*	*High*
Low	85%	85%	Low	95%	5%	50%	50%
High	15%	15%	High	5%	95%	50%	50%

Suppressor Variable

	BIVARIATE TABLE			PARTIALS			
				Control = Low		Control = High	
	Low	*High*		*Low*	*High*	*Low*	*High*
Low	54%	46%	Low	84%	16%	14%	86%
High	46%	54%	High	16%	84%	86%	14%

original relationship is between religious upbringing and abortion attitude, but now gender is the control variable. Gender comes before religious upbringing because one's sex is fixed at birth. The explanation pattern changes how a researcher explains the results. It implies that the initial bivariate relationship is spurious (see the discussion of spuriousness in Chapter 6).

The **suppressor variable pattern** occurs when the bivariate tables suggest independence but a relationship appears in one or both of the partials. For example, religious upbringing and abortion attitude are independent in a bivariate table. Once the control variable "region of the country" is introduced, religious upbringing is associated with abortion attitude in the partial tables. The control variable is a suppressor variable because it suppressed the true relationship. The true relationship appears in the partials.

Multiple Regression Analysis

Multiple regression is a statistical technique whose calculation is beyond the level in this book. Although it is quickly computed by the appropriate statistics software, a background in statistics is needed to prevent making errors in its calculation and interpretation. It requires interval- or ratio-level data. It is discussed here for two reasons. First, it controls for many alternative explanations and variables simultaneously (it is rarely possible to use more than one control variable at a time using percentaged tables). Second, it is widely used in sociology, and you are likely to encounter it when reading research reports or articles.

Multiple regression results tell the reader two things. First, the results have a measure called *R*-squared (R^2), which tells how well a set of variables explains a dependent variable. *Explain* means reduced errors when predicting the dependent variable scores on the basis of information about the independent variables. A good model with several independent variables might account for, or explain, a large percentage of variation in a dependent variable. For example, an R^2 of .50 means that knowing the independent and control variables improves the accuracy of predicting the dependent variable by 50 percent, or half as many errors are made as would be made without knowing about the variables.

Second, the regression results measure the direction and size of the effect of each variable on a dependent variable. The effect is measured precisely and given a numerical value. For example, a researcher can see how five independent or control variables simultaneously affect a dependent variable, with all variables controlling for the effects of one another. This is especially valuable for testing

BOX 12.7 Example of Multiple Regression Results

DEPENDENT VARIABLE IS POLITICAL IDEOLOGY INDEX (HIGH SCORE MEANS VERY LIBERAL)

Independent Variable	Standardized Regression Coefficients
Region = South	−.19
Age	.01
Income	−.44
Years of education	.23
Religious attendance	−.39
$R^2 = .38$	

theories that state that multiple independent variables cause one dependent variable. (See Chapter 3 for examples of causal diagrams.)

The effect on the dependent variable is measured by a standardized regression coefficient or the Greek letter beta (ß). It is similar to a correlation coefficient. In fact, the beta coefficient for two variables equals the *r* correlation coefficient.

Researchers use the beta regression coefficient to determine whether control variables have an effect. For example, the bivariate correlation between *X* and *Y* is .75. Next, the researcher statistically considers four control variables. If the beta remains at .75, then the four control variables have no effect. However, if the beta for *X* and *Y* gets smaller (e.g., drops to .20), it indicates that the control variables have an effect.

Consider an example of regression analysis with age, income, education, and region as independent variables. The dependent variable is a score on a political ideology index. The multiple regression results show that income and religious attendance have large effects, education and region minor effects, and age no effect. All the independent variables together have a 38 percent accuracy in predicting a person's political ideology (see Box 12.7).[6]

> **Suppressor variable pattern** A pattern in the elaboration paradigm in which no relationship appears in a bivariate contingency table, but the partials show a relationship between the variables.

CHART 12.1 Summary of Major Types of Descriptive Statistics

TYPE OF TECHNIQUE	STATISTICAL TECHNIQUE	PURPOSE
Univariate	Frequency distribution, measures of central tendency, standard deviation, z-score	Describe one variable.
Bivariate	Correlation, percentage table, chi-square	Describe a relationship or the association between two variables.
Multivariate	Elaboration paradigm, multiple regression	Describe relationships among several variables, or see how several independent variables have an effect on a dependent variable.

The example suggests that high income, frequent religious attendance, and a southern residence are positively associated with conservative opinions, whereas having more education is associated with liberal opinions. The impact of income is more than twice the size of the impact of living in a southern region.

Chart 12.1 summarizes the types and techniques of descriptive statistics. Next we turn our attention to inferential statistics.

INFERENTIAL STATISTICS

The Purpose of Inferential Statistics

The statistics discussed so far in this chapter are descriptive statistics. But researchers often want to do more than describe; they want to test hypotheses, know whether sample results hold true in a population, and decide whether differences in results (e.g., between the mean scores of two groups) are big enough to indicate that a relationship really exists. Inferential statistics use probability theory to test hypotheses formally, permit inferences from a sample to a population, and test whether descriptive results are likely to be due to random factors or to a real relationship.

This section explains the basic ideas of inferential statistics but does not deal with inferential statistics in any detail. This area is more complex than descriptive statistics and requires a background in statistics.

Inferential statistics rely on principles from probability sampling, whereby a researcher uses a random process (e.g., a random-number table) to select cases from the entire population. Inferential statistics are a precise way to talk about how confident a researcher can be when inferring from the results in a sample to the population.

You have already encountered inferential statistics if you have read or heard about "statistical significance" or results "significant at the .05 level." Researchers use them to conduct various statistical tests (e.g., a t-test or an F-test). Statistical significance is also used in formal hypothesis testing, which is a precise way to decide whether to accept or to reject a null hypothesis.[7]

Statistical Significance

Statistical significance means that results are not likely to be due to chance factors. It indicates the probability of finding a relationship in the sample when there is none in the population. Because probability samples involve a random process, it is always possible that sample results will differ from a

Inferential statistics A branch of applied mathematics based on random sampling that allows researchers to make precise statements about the level of confidence they can have that measures in a sample are the same as a population parameter.

Statistical significance A way to discuss the likelihood that a finding or statistical relationship in a sample's results is due to the random factors rather than due to the existence of an actual relationship in the entire population.

population parameter. A researcher wants to estimate the odds that sample results are due to a true population parameter or to chance factors of random sampling. Statistical significance uses probability theory and specific statistical tests to tell a researcher whether the results (e.g., an association, a difference between two means, a regression coefficient) are produced by random error in random sampling.

Statistical significance tells only what is likely. It cannot prove anything with absolute certainty. It states that particular outcomes are more or less probable. Statistical significance is *not* the same as practical, substantive, or theoretical significance. Results can be statistically significant but theoretically meaningless or trivial. For example, two variables can have a statistically significant association due to coincidence, with no logical connection between them (e.g., length of fingernails and ability to speak French).

Levels of Significance

Researchers usually express statistical significance in terms of levels (e.g., a test is statistically significant at a specific level) rather than giving the specific probability. The **level of statistical significance** (usually .05, .01, or .001) is a way of talking about the likelihood that results are due to chance factors—that is, that a relationship appears in the sample when there is none in the population. If a researcher says that results are significant at the .05 level, this means the following:

- Results like these are due to chance factors only 5 in 100 times.
- There is a 95 percent chance that the sample results are not due to chance factors alone, but reflect the population accurately.
- The odds of such results based on chance alone are .05, or 5 percent.
- One can be 95 percent confident that the results are due to a real relationship in the population, not chance factors.

These all say the same thing in different ways. This may sound like the discussion of sampling distributions and the central limit theorem in the chapter on sampling. It is not an accident. Both are based on probability theory, which researchers use to link sample data to a population. Probability theory lets us predict what happens in the long run over many events when a random process is used. In other words, it allows precise prediction over many situations in the long run, but not for a specific situation. Because we have one sample and we want to infer to the population, probability theory helps us estimate the odds that our particular sample represents the population. We cannot know for certain unless we have the whole population, but probability theory lets us state our confidence—how likely it is that the sample shows one thing while something else is true in the population. For example, a sample shows that college men and women differ in how many hours they study. Is the result due to an unusual sample, and there is really no difference in the population, or does it reflect a true difference between the sexes in the population? (See Box 12.8 on chi-square.)

Type I and Type II Errors

If the logic of statistical significance is based on stating whether chance factors produce results, why use the .05 level? It means a 5 percent chance that randomness could cause the results. Why not use a more certain standard—for example, a 1 in 1,000 probability of random chance? This gives a smaller chance that randomness versus a true relationship caused the results.

There are two answers to this way of thinking. The simple answer is that the scientific community has informally agreed to use .05 as a rule of thumb for most purposes. Being 95 percent confident of results is the accepted standard for explaining the social world.

A second, more complex answer involves a trade-off between making Type I and Type II errors. A researcher can make two kinds of logical errors.

> **Level of statistical significance**   A set of numbers researchers use as a simple way to measure the degree to which a statistical relationship results from random factors rather than the existence of a true relationship among variables.

BOX **12.8** Chi-Square

The chi-square (χ^2) is used in two ways. This creates confusion. As a *descriptive statistic*, it tells us the strength of the association between two variables; as an *inferential statistic*, it tells us the probability that any association we find is likely to be due to chance factors. The chi-square is a widely used and powerful way to look at variables measured at the nominal or ordinal level. It is a more precise way to tell whether there is an association in a bivariate percentaged table than by just "eyeballing" it.

Logically, we first figure out "expected values" in a table. We do this based on information from the marginals alone. Recall that marginals are frequency distributions of each variable alone. An expected value can be thought of as our "best guess" without looking at the body of the table. Next, we look at the data to see how much differs from the "expected value." If it differs by a lot, then there may be an association between the variables. If the data in a table are identical or very close to the expected values, then the variables are not associated; they are independent. In other words, *independence* means "what is going on" in a table is what we would expect based on the marginals alone. Chi-square is zero if there is independence that gets bigger as the association gets stronger. If the data in the table greatly differ from the expected values, then we know something is "going on" beyond what we would expect from the marginals alone (i.e., an association between the variables). See the example of an association between height and grade.

Raw or Observed Data Table

STUDENT HEIGHT	GRADE IN RESEARCH METHODS			TOTAL
	C	B	A	
Tall	30	10	10	50
Medium	10	30	10	50
Short	30	20	50	100
Total	70	60	70	200

Expected Values Table

Expected value = (Column total × Row total)/Grand total). EXAMPLE (70 × 50)/200 = 17.5

STUDENT HEIGHT	GRADE IN RESEARCH METHODS			TOTAL
	C	B	A	
Tall	17.5	15	17.5	50
Medium	17.5	15	17.5	50
Short	35	30	35	100
Total	70	60	70	200

Difference Table

Difference = (Observed − Expected). EXAMPLE (30 − 17.5) = 12.5

STUDENT HEIGHT	GRADE IN RESEARCH METHODS			TOTAL
	C	B	A	
Tall	12.5	−5	−7.5	0
Medium	−7.5	15	−7.5	0
Short	−5	−10	15	0
Total	0	0	0	0

(continued)

BOX **12.8** **(continued)**

Chi-square = Sum of each difference squared, then divided by the expected value of the cell. Example: 12.5 squared = 156.25, divided by 17.5 = 8.93.

Chi-square = 1st row (8.93 + 1.67 + 3.21) +
     2nd row (3.21 + 15 + 3.21) +
     3rd row (.71 + 3.33 + 6.43) = 45.7

Because chi-squared is not zero, the data are not independent; there is an association. The chi-square coefficient cannot tell us the direction (e.g., negative) of the association. For inferential statistics, we need to use a chi-square table or computer program to evaluate the association (i.e., to see how likely such a large chi-square is to occur by chance alone). Without going into all the details about the chi-square table, this association is rare; it occurs by chance less than 1 in 1,000 times. For a table with nine cells, a chi-square of 45.7 is significant at the .001 level.

A **Type I error** occurs when the researcher says that a relationship exists when in fact none exists. It means falsely rejecting a null hypothesis. A **Type II error** occurs when a researcher says that a relationship does not exist, when in fact it does. It means falsely accepting a null hypothesis (see Table 12.6). Of course, researchers want to avoid both errors. They want to say that there is a relationship in the data only when it does exist and that there is no relationship only when there really is none, but they face a dilemma: As the odds of making one type of error decline, the odds of making the opposite error increase.

The idea of Type I and Type II errors may seem difficult at first, but the same logical dilemma appears outside research settings. For example, a jury can err by deciding that an accused person is guilty when in fact he or she is innocent. Or the jury can err by deciding that a person is innocent when in fact he or she is guilty. The jury does not want to make either error. It does not want to jail the innocent or to free the guilty, but the jury must make a judgment using limited information. Likewise, a pharmaceutical company has to decide whether to sell a new drug. The company can err by stating that the drug has no side effects when, in fact, it has the side effect of causing blindness. Or it can err by holding back a drug because of fear of serious side effects when in fact there are none. The company does not want to make either error. If it makes the first error, the company will face lawsuits and injure people. The second error will prevent the company from selling a drug that may cure illness and produce profits.

Let us put the ideas of statistical significance and the two types of error together. An overly cautious researcher sets a high level of significance and is likely to make one kind of error. For example, the researcher might use the .0001 level. He or she attributes the results to chance unless they are so rare that they would occur by chance only 1 in 10,000 times. Such a high standard means that the researcher is most likely to err by saying results are due to chance when in fact they are not. He or she may falsely accept the null hypothesis when there is a causal relationship (a Type II error). By contrast, a risk-taking researcher sets a low level of significance, such as .10. His or her results indicate a relationship would occur by chance 1 in 10 times. He or she is likely to err by saying that a causal relationship exists, when in fact random factors (e.g., random sampling error) actually cause the results.

Type I error   The logical error of falsely rejecting the null hypothesis.

Type II error   The logical error of falsely accepting the null hypothesis.

TABLE 12.6   Type I and Type II Errors

WHAT THE RESEARCHER SAYS	TRUE SITUATION IN THE WORLD	
	No Relationship	*Causal Relationship*
No relationship	No error	Type II error
Causal relationship	Type I error	No error

The researcher is likely to falsely reject the null hypothesis (Type I error). In sum, the .05 level is a compromise between Type I and Type II errors.

This section outlines the basics of inferential statistics. The statistical techniques are precise and rely on the relationship between sampling error, sample size, and central limit theorem. The power of inferential statistics is their ability to let a researcher state, with specific degrees of certainty, that specific sample results are likely to be true in a population. For example, a researcher conducts statistical tests and finds that a relationship is statistically significant at the .05 level. He or she can state that the sample results are probably not due to chance factors. Indeed, there is a 95 percent chance that a true relationship exists in the social world.

Tests for inferential statistics are useful but limited. The data must come from a random sample, and tests only take into account sampling errors. Nonsampling errors (e.g., a poor sampling frame or a poorly designed measure) are not considered. Do not be fooled into thinking that such tests offer easy, final answers.

Before concluding this chapter, we discuss statistical programs for the computer, as presented in Box 12.9.

CONCLUSION

You learned about organizing quantitative data to prepare them for analysis, and analyzing them (organizing data into charts or tables, or summarizing them with statistical measures). Researchers use statistical analysis to test hypotheses and answer research questions. You saw how data must first be coded and then analyzed using univariate or bivariate statistics. Bivariate relationships might be spurious, so control variables and multivariate analysis are often necessary. You also learned some basics about inferential statistics.

Beginning researchers sometimes feel they have done something wrong if their results do not support a hypothesis. *There is nothing wrong with rejecting a hypothesis.* The goal of scientific research is to produce knowledge that truly reflects the social world, not to defend pet ideas or hypotheses. Hypotheses are theoretical guesses based on limited knowledge; they need to be tested. Excellent-quality research can find that a hypothesis is wrong, and poor-quality research can support a hypothesis. Good research depends on high-quality methodology, not on supporting a specific hypothesis.

Good research means guarding against possible errors or obstacles to true inferences from data to the social world. Errors can enter into the research process and affect results at many places: research design, measurement, data collection, coding, calculating statistics and constructing tables, or interpreting results. Even if a researcher can design, measure, collect, code, and calculate without error, another step in the research process remains. It is to interpret the tables, charts, and statistics, and to answer the question: What does it all mean? The only way to assign meaning to facts, charts, tables, or statistics is to use theory.

Data, tables, or computer output cannot answer research questions. The facts do not speak for themselves. As a researcher, you must return to your theory (i.e., concepts, relationships among concepts, assumptions, theoretical definitions) and give the results meaning. Do not lock yourself into the ideas with which you began. There is room for creativity, and new ideas are generated by trying to figure out what results really say. It is important to be careful

12.9 Statistical Programs on Computers

Almost every social researcher who needs to calculate many statistics does so with a computer program. One can do some statistics using a basic spreadsheet program, such as Excel. Unfortunately, spreadsheets are designed for accounting and bookkeeping functions. They include statistics, but are clumsy and limited for that purpose. There are many computer programs designed for calculating general statistics. The marketplace can be confusing to a beginner, for products rapidly evolve with changing computer technology. One or two decades ago, one had to know a computer language or do simple programming to have a computer calculate statistics.

In recent years, the software has become less demanding for a user. The most popular programs in the social sciences are Minitab, Microcase, and SPSS (Statistical Package for the Social Sciences). Others include SAS (Statistical Analysis System), BMPD (bought out by SPSS, Inc.), STATISTICA by StratSoft, and Strata. Many began as simple, low-cost programs for research purposes. Today, private corporations own many of these and are interested in selling a sophisticated set of software products to many diverse corporate and government users.

The most widely used program for statistics in the social sciences is SPSS. Its advantages are that social researchers have used it extensively for over three decades, it includes many ways to manipulate quantitative data, and it contains most statistical measures. Its disadvantage is that it can take a long time to learn because of its many options and complex statistics. Also, it is expensive to purchase unless one gets an inexpensive, "stripped down" student version included with a textbook or workbook.

As computer technology makes using a statistics program easier, the danger increases that some people will use the programs but not understand statistics or what the programs are doing. They can easily violate basic assumptions required by a statistical procedure, use the statistics improperly, and produce results that are pure nonsense yet look very technically sophisticated.

in designing and conducting research so that you can look at the results as a reflection of something in the social world and not worry about whether they are due to an error or an artifact of the research process itself.

Before we leave quantitative research, there is one last issue. Journalists, politicians, and others increasingly use statistical results to make a point or bolster an argument. This has not produced greater accuracy and information in public debate. More often, it has increased confusion and made it more important to know what statistics can and cannot do. The cliché that you can prove anything with statis-

tics is false; however, people can and do *misuse* statistics. Through ignorance or conscious deceit, some people use statistics to manipulate others. The way to protect yourself from being misled by statistics is not to ignore them or hide from the numbers. Rather, it is to understand the research process and statistics, think about what you hear, and ask questions.

We turn next to qualitative research. The logic and purpose of qualitative research differ from those of the quantitative, positivist approach of the past chapters. It is less concerned with numbers, hypotheses, and causality and more concerned with words, norms and values, and meaning.

KEY TERMS

bivariate statistics	contingency cleaning	curvilinear relationship
body of a table	contigency table	data field
cell of a table	control variable	data records
codebook	covariation	descriptive statistics
coding procedure	cross-tabulation	direct-entry method

elaboration paradigm	measures of central tendency	skewed distribution
explanation pattern	median	specification pattern
frequency distribution	mode	standard deviation
frequency polygon	net effect	statistical independence
histogram	normal distribution	statistical relationship
inferential statistics	partials	statistical significance
interpretation pattern	percentile	suppressor variable pattern
level of statistical significance	possible code cleaning	Type I error
linear relationship	range	Type II error
marginals	replication pattern	univariate statistics
mean	scattergram	z-score

REVIEW QUESTIONS

1. What is a codebook and how is it used in research?
2. How do researchers clean data and check their coding?
3. Describe how researchers use the optical scan sheets.
4. In what ways can a researcher display frequency distribution information?
5. Describe the differences between mean, median, and mode.
6. What three features of a relationship can be seen from a scattergram?
7. What is a covariation and how is it used?
8. When can a researcher generalize from a scattergram to a percentaged table to find a relationship among variables?
9. Discuss the concept of control as it is used in trivariate analysis.
10. What does it mean to say "statistically significant at the .001 level," and what type of error is more likely: Type I or Type II?

NOTES

1. Some of the best practical advice on coding and handling quantitative data come from survey research. See discussions in Babbie (1998:366–372), Backstrom and Hursh-Cesar (1981:309–400), Fowler (1984:127–133), Sonquist and Dunkelberg (1977:210–215), and Warwick and Lininger (1975:234–291).

2. Note that coding sex as 1 = Male, 2 = Female, or as 0 = Male, 1 = Female, or reversing the sex for numbers is arbitrary. The only reason one uses numbers instead of letters (e.g., M and F) is because many computer programs work best with all numbers. Sometimes coding data as a zero can create confusion, so the number 1 is usually the lowest value.

3. For discussions of many different ways to display quantitative data, see Fox (1992), Henry (1995), Tufte (1983, 1991), and Zeisel (1985:14–33).

4. There are other statistics to measure a special kind of mean for ordinal data and for other special situations, which are beyond the level of discussion in this book.

5. For a discussion of the elaboration paradigm and its history, see Babbie (1998:400–409) and Rosenberg (1968).

6. Beginning students and people outside the social sciences are sometimes surprised at the low (10 to 50 percent) predictive accuracy in multiple regression results. There are three responses to this. First, a 10 to 50 per-

cent reduction in errors is really not bad compared to purely random guessing. Second, positivist social science is still developing. Although the levels of accuracy may not be as high as those of the physical sciences, they are much higher than for any explanation of the social world possible 10 or 20 years ago. Finally, the theoretically important issue in most multiple regression models is less the accuracy of overall prediction than the effects of specific variables. Most hypotheses involve the effects of specific independent variables on dependent variables.

7. In formal hypothesis testing, researchers test the *null hypothesis*. They usually want to reject the null because rejection of the null indirectly supports the alternative hypothesis to the null, the one they deduced from theory as a tentative explanation. The null hypotheis was discussed in Chapter 6.

Field Research

*Field research is the study of people acting in the natural courses of their daily lives.
The fieldworker ventures into the worlds of others in order to learn firsthand about
how they live, how they talk and behave, and what captivates and distresses them. . . .
It is also seen as a method of study whose practitioners try to understand the
meanings that activities observed have for those engaging in them.*
—Robert Emerson, *Contemporary Field Research,* p. 1

This chapter and the two that follow shift away from the quantitative style of the past several chapters to the qualitative research style. This chapter describes field research, also called *ethnography* or *participant-observation research*. It is a qualitative style in which a researcher directly observes and participates in small-scale social settings in the present time and usually in the researcher's home culture.

Chapter 14 will examine historical-comparative research, which can have a macro- or micro-level focus. In it, the researcher examines a different time period and/or a different culture. Chapter 15 will discuss the analysis of qualitative data.

Many students are excited by field research because it involves hanging out with some exotic group of people. There are no cold mathematics or complicated statistics, no abstract deductive hypotheses. Instead, there is direct, face-to-face social interaction with "real people" in a natural setting.

Field research appeals to those who like people watching. In addition, field research reports can be fascinating accounts of unfamiliar social worlds: nude beaches, the homeless, professional gamblers, street gangs, police squads, emergency rooms, artists' colonies, and so on.

In field research, the individual researcher directly talks with and observes the people being studied. Through interaction over months or years, the researcher learns about them, their life histories, their hobbies and interests, and their habits, hopes, fears, and dreams. Meeting new people, developing friendships, and discovering new social worlds can be fun. It is also time consuming, emotionally draining, and sometimes physically dangerous.

RESEARCH QUESTIONS APPROPRIATE FOR FIELD RESEARCH

When should you use field research? Field research is appropriate when the research question involves learning about, understanding, or describing a group of interacting people. It is usually best when the question is: How do people do Y in the social world? or What is the social world of X like? It can be used when other methods (e.g., survey, experiments) are not practical, as in studying street gangs.

Field researchers study people in a location or setting. It has been used to study entire communities. Beginning field researchers should start with a relatively small group (30 or fewer) who interact with each other on a regular basis in a relatively fixed setting (e.g., a street corner, church, barroom, beauty parlor, baseball field, etc.). Field research is also used to study amorphous social experiences that are not fixed in place, but where intensive interviewing and observation are the only way to gain access to the experience—for example, the feelings of a person who has been mugged, or who is the widow of someone who committed suicide.[1]

In order to use consistent terminology, we can call the people who are studied in a field setting *members*. They are insiders or natives in the field and belong to a group, subculture, or social setting that the "outsider" field researcher wants to learn about.

Field researchers have explored a wide variety of social settings, subcultures, and aspects of social life[2] (see Figure 13.1). Places my students have conducted successful short-term, small-scale field research studies include a beauty parlor, day-care center, bakery, bingo parlor, bowling alley, church, coffee shop, laundromat, police dispatch office, nursing home, tattoo parlor, and weight room.

A SHORT HISTORY OF FIELD RESEARCH

Early Beginnings

Field research can be traced back to the reports of travelers to distant lands.[3] Since the 1200s, European explorers and missionaries have written descriptions of the strange cultures and peoples they have encountered. Others read these descriptions to learn about foreign cultures. Later, in the nineteenth century, when European trade and empires rapidly expanded and there were more literate, educated travelers, the number of reports grew.

Academic field research began in the late nineteenth century with anthropology. The first anthropologists only read the reports of explorers, government officials, or missionaries but lacked direct contact with the people they studied. The reports focused on the exotic and were highly racist and ethnocentric. Travelers rarely spoke the local language and had to rely on interpreters. Not until the 1890s did European anthropologists begin to travel to faraway lands to learn about other cultures.

British social anthropologist Bronislaw Malinoski (1844–1942) was the first researcher to live with a group of people for a long period of time and write about collecting data. In the 1920s, he presented intensive field work as a new method and argued for separating direct observation and native statements from the observer's inferences. He said that social researchers should directly interact with and live among the native peoples and learn their customs, beliefs, and social processes.

Researchers also used field research to study their own society. The observations of the London poor by Charles Booth and Beatrice Webb in the

FIGURE 13.1   Examples of Field Research Sites/Topics

SMALL-SCALE SETTINGS

Passengers in an airplane
Bars or taverns
Battered women's shelters
Camera clubs
Laundromats
Social movement organizations
Social welfare offices
Television stations
Waiting rooms

COMMUNITY SETTINGS

Retirement communities
Small towns
Urban ethnic communities
Working-class neighborhoods

CHILDREN'S ACTIVITIES

Children's playgrounds
Little League baseball
Youth in schools
Junior high girl groups
Summer camps

OCCUPATIONS

Airline attendants
Artists
Cocktail waitresses

Dog catchers
Door-to-door salespersons
Factory workers
Gamblers
Medical students
Female strippers
Police officers
Restaurant chefs
Social workers
Taxi drivers

DEVIANCE AND CRIMINAL ACTIVITY

Body/genital piercing and branding
Cults
Drug dealers and addicts
Hippies
Nude beaches
Occult groups
Prostitutes
Street gangs, motorcycle gangs
Street people, homeless shelters

MEDICAL SETTINGS AND MEDICAL EVENTS

Death
Emergency rooms
Intensive care units
Pregnancy and abortion
Support groups for Alzheimer's caregivers

1890s began both survey research and field research outside of anthropology. Booth and Webb directly observed people in natural settings and used an inductive data-gathering approach. Participant observation may have originated in Germany in 1890. Paul Gohre worked and lived as a factory apprentice for three months and took detailed notes each night at home in order to study factory life. His published work influenced scholars in the universities, including the sociologist Max Weber.

Chicago School of Sociology

Sociological field research in the United States began at the University of Chicago Department of Sociol-

ogy in what is known as the Chicago school of sociology. The Chicago school's influence on field research had two phases. In the first phase, from the 1910s to 1930s, the school used a variety of methods based on the case study or life history approach, including direct observation, informal interviews, and reading documents or official records. Important influences came from Booker T. Washington, William James, and John Dewey. In 1916, Robert E. Park (1864–1944) drew up a research program for the social investigation of the city of Chicago. Influenced by his background as a newspaper reporter, he said that social researchers should leave the libraries and "get their hands dirty" by direct observations and conversations on street corners, in barrooms, and in luxury hotel lobbies. Early studies such as *The Hobo* (Anderson, 1923), *The Jack Roller* (Shaw, 1930), and *The Gang* (Thrasher, 1927) established early Chicago school sociology as the descriptive study of street life with little analysis.

Journalistic and anthropological models of research were combined in the first phase. The journalistic model has a researcher get behind fronts, use informants, look for conflict, and expose what is "really happening." In the anthropological model, a researcher attaches himself or herself to a small group for an extended period of time and reports on the members' views of the world.

In the second phase, from the 1940s to the 1960s, the Chicago school developed participant observation as a distinct technique. It expanded an anthropological model to groups and settings in the researcher's society. Three principles emerged:

1. Study people in their natural settings, or in situ.
2. Study people by directly interacting with them.
3. Gain an understanding of the social world and make theoretical statements based on the members' perspective.

Over time, the method moved from strict description to theoretical analyses based on involvement by the researcher in the field.

After World War II, field research faced increased competition from survey and quantitative research and declined as a proportion of all social research. In the 1970s and 1980s, however, several changes rejuvenated field research. First, field researchers borrowed ideas and techniques from cognitive psychology, cultural anthropology, folklore, and linguistics. Second, researchers reexamined the epistemological roots and philosophical assumptions of social science (see Chapter 4) that justified their method. Finally, field researchers became more self-conscious about their techniques and methods. They wrote about methodology and became more systematic about it as a research technique.

Today, field researchers directly observe and interact with members in natural settings to get inside their perspective. They embrace an activist or social constructionist perspective on social life. They do not see people as a neutral medium through which social forces operate, nor do they see social meanings as something "out there" to observe. Instead, they hold that people create and define the social world through their interactions. Human experiences are filtered through a subjective sense of reality, which affects how people see and act on events. Thus, they focus on the everyday, face-to-face social processes of negotiation, discussion, and bargaining to construct social meaning.

Field researchers see research as simultaneously a description of the social world and a part of it. As part of a socially created setting, a researcher's presence in the field cannot be just neutral data gathering.

Ethnography and Ethnomethodology

Two extensions of field research, ethnography and ethnomethodology, build on the social constructionist perspective.

Ethnography comes from cultural anthropology.[4] *Ethno* means people or folk, and *graphy* refers to describing something. Thus *ethnography* means describing a culture and understanding another way of life from the native point of view. As Franke (1983:61) stated, "Culture, the object of our description, resides within the thinking of natives." Ethnography assumes that people make inferences—that is, go beyond what is explicitly seen or said to what is meant or implied. People display their culture (what people think, ponder, or believe) through behavior (e.g., speech and actions) in specific social contexts. Displays of behavior do not give meaning; rather, meaning is inferred, or someone figures out meaning. Moving from what is heard or observed to what is meant is at the center of ethnography. For example, when a student is invited to a "kegger," the student infers that it is an informal party with other student-aged people at which beer will be served, based on his or her cultural knowledge. Cultural knowledge includes symbols, songs, sayings, facts, ways of behaving, and objects (e.g., telephones, newspapers, etc.). We

> **Ethnography** Field research that emphasizes providing a very detailed description of a different culture from the viewpoint of an insider in the culture to facilitate understanding of it.

learn the culture by watching television, listening to parents, observing others, and the like.

Cultural knowledge includes both explicit knowledge, what we know and talk about, and tacit knowledge, what we rarely acknowledge. For example, *explicit knowledge* includes the social event (e.g., a "kegger"). Most people can easily describe what happens at one. *Tacit knowledge* includes the unspoken cultural norm for the proper distance to stand from others. People are generally unaware that they use this norm. They feel unease or discomfort when the norm is violated, but it is difficult to pinpoint the source of discomfort. Ethnographers describe the explicit and tacit cultural knowledge that members use. Their detailed descriptions and careful analysis take what is described apart and put it back together.

Anthropologist Clifford Geertz stated that a critical part of ethnography is **thick description**,[5] a rich, detailed description of specifics (as opposed to summary, standardization, generalization, or variables). A thick description of a three-minute event may go on for pages. It captures what occurred and the drama of events, thereby permitting multiple interpretations. It places events in a context so that the reader of an ethnographic report can infer cultural meaning.

Ethnomethodology is a distinct approach developed in the 1960s, with its own unique terminology.[6] It combines theory, philosophy, and method. Some do not consider it a part of sociology. Mehan and Wood (1975:3, 5) argued that

Thick description Qualitative data in which a researcher attempts to capture all the details of a social setting in an extremely detailed description and convey an intimate feel for the setting and the inner lives of people in it.

Ethnomethodology An approach to social science that combines philosophy, social theory, and method to study commonsense knowledge. It looks at ordinary social interaction in small-scale settings to reveal the rules that people use to construct and maintain their everyday social reality.

Breaching experiment When a field researcher intentionally breaks social rules and patterns of behavior to reveal aspects about social meanings and relationships.

ethnomethodology is not a body of findings, nor a method, nor a theory, nor a world view. I view ethnomethodology as a form of life. . . . Ethnomethodology is an attempt to display the reality of a level which exists beyond the sociological level. . . . It differs from sociology much as sociology differs from psychology.

Ethnomethodology is the study of common-sense knowledge. Ethnomethodologists study common sense by observing its creation and use in ongoing social interaction in natural settings. Ethnomethodology is a radical or extreme form of field research, based on phenomenological philosophy and a social constructionist approach. It involves the specialized, highly detailed analysis of microsituations (e.g., transcripts of short conversations or videotapes of social interactions). Compared to Chicago school field research, it is more concerned about method and argues that research findings result as much from the method used as from the social life studied.

Ethnomethodology assumes that social meaning is fragile and fluid, not fixed, stable, or solid. Meaning is constantly being created and re-created in an ongoing process. For this reason, ethnomethodologists analyze language, including pauses and the context of speech. They assume that people "accomplish" commonsense understanding by using tacit social-cultural rules, and social interaction is a process of reality construction. People interpret everyday events by using cultural knowledge and clues from the social context. Ethnomethodologists examine how ordinary people in everyday settings apply tacit rules to make sense of social life (e.g., to know whether or not someone is joking).

Ethnomethodologists examine ordinary social interaction in great detail to identify the rules for constructing social reality and common sense, how these rules are applied, and how new rules are created. For example, they argue that standardized tests or survey interviews measure a person's ability to pick up implicit clues and apply common sense more than measuring objective facts.

Ethnomethodologists sometimes use **breaching experiments** to demonstrate the simple tacit rules that people rely on to create a sense of reality in everyday life (also see the discussion of breakdown later on). The researchers purposefully violate a tacit social norm. The breach usually creates a powerful social response, which verifies the rule's existence, shows the fragility of social reality, and demonstrates that such tacit rules are essential for the flow of ordinary life. For example, ethnomethodology's founder, Harold Garfinkel, sent students to stores where they were told to "mistake" customers for salesclerks. At first, the customers were confused and stammered explanations. But as the students persisted in the misinterpretation, the bewildered customers either reluctantly accepted the new definition of the situation and awkwardly filled the salesclerk role, or "blew up" and "lost their cool." The breach illustrated how the operation of social reality depended on tacit knowledge (e.g., distinguishing sales clerks from customers). Filmmakers use similar situations for comic effect when people from a different culture who do not share the same tacit rules or who are unaware of the unspoken rules of proper behavior are seen as humorous.[7] Mental health practitioners use the ability to apply tacit cultural knowledge as an indicator of mental competence.

THE LOGIC OF FIELD RESEARCH

What Is Field Research?

Field research is more of an orientation toward research than a fixed set of techniques to apply.[8] A field researcher uses various methods to obtain information. As Schatzman and Strauss (1973:14) said, "Field method is more like an umbrella of activity beneath which any technique may be used for gaining the desired knowledge, and for processes of thinking about this information." A *field researcher* is a "methodological pragmatist" (Schatzman and Strauss, 1973:7), a resourceful, talented individual who has ingenuity, and an ability to think on her feet while in the field.

Field research is based on naturalism, which is also used to study other phenomena (e.g., oceans, animals, plants, etc.). **Naturalism** involves observing ordinary events in natural settings, not in contrived, invented, or researcher-created settings. Research occurs in the field and outside the safe settings of an office, laboratory, or classroom.

BOX **13.1** **What Do Field Researchers Do?**

A field researcher does the following:

1. Observes ordinary events and everyday activities as they happen in natural settings, in addition to any unusual occurrences
2. Becomes directly involved with the people being studied and personally experiences the process of daily social life in the field setting
3. Acquires an insider's point of view while maintaining the analytic perspective or distance of an outsider
4. Uses a variety of techniques and social skills in a flexible manner as the situation demands
5. Produces data in the form of extensive written notes, as well as diagrams, maps, or pictures to provide very detailed descriptions
6. Sees events holistically (e.g., as a whole unit, not in pieces) and individually in their social context
7. Understands and develops empathy for members in a field setting, and does not only record "cold" objective facts
8. Notices both explicit (recognized, conscious, spoken) and tacit (less recognized, implicit, unspoken) aspects of culture
9. Observes ongoing social processes without imposing an outside point of view
10. Copes with high levels of personal stress, uncertainty, ethical dilemmas, and ambiguity

A field researcher examines social meanings and grasps multiple perspectives in natural social settings. He or she gets inside the meaning system of members and then goes back to an outside or research viewpoint. As Van Maanen (1982:139) noted, "Fieldwork means involvement and detachment, both loyalty and betrayal, both openness and secrecy, and most likely, love and hate." The researcher switches perspectives and sees the setting from multiple points of view simultaneously.

Let us look at what practicing field researchers do (see Box 13.1). Research is usually conducted by a single individual, although small teams have

Naturalism The principle that researchers should examine events as they occur in natural, everyday ongoing social settings.

been effective. A researcher is directly engaged in the social world studied, so his or her personal characteristics are relevant in research. Wax (1979:509) noted:

> *Informal and quantitative methods, the peculiarities of the individual tend to go unnoticed. Electronic data processing pays no heed to the age, gender, or ethnicity of the research director or programmer. But, in fieldwork, these basic aspects of personal identity become salient; they drastically affect the process of field research.*

The researcher's direct involvement in the field often has an emotional impact. Field research can be fun and exciting, but it can also disrupt one's personal life, physical security, or mental well-being. More than other types of social research, it reshapes friendships, family life, self-identity, or personal values:

> *The price of doing fieldwork is very high, not in dollars (fieldwork is less expensive than most other kinds of research) but in physical and mental effort. It is very hard work. It is exhausting to live two lives simultaneously. (Bogdan and Taylor, 1975:vi)*

Field research requires time, as Fine (1996: 244) remarked in his study of four restaurant kitchens:

> *I attempted to be present six days each week . . . and I attempted to stagger my observation times. . . . I spent a month observing in the kitchen in each restaurant then interviewed all the full-time cooks for a total of thirty in-depth interviews. Each interview lasted from one to three hours.*

Steps in a Field Research Project

Field research is more flexible or less structured than quantitative research. This makes it essential to be well organized and prepared for the field. The steps of a project only serve as only an approximate guide or road map (see Box 13.2).

Flexibility. Field researchers rarely follow fixed steps. Flexibility is a key advantage of field research, which lets a researcher shift direction and follow leads. Good field researchers recognize and seize opportunities, "play it by ear," and rapidly adjust to fluid social situations.

BOX **13.2** **Steps in Field Research**

1. Prepare oneself, read the literature, and defocus.
2. Select a field site and gain access to it.
3. Enter the field and establish social relations with members.
4. Adopt a social role, learn the ropes, and get along with members.
5. Watch, listen, and collect quality data.
6. Begin to analyze data and to generate and evaluate working hypotheses.
7. Focus on specific aspects of the setting and use theoretical sampling.
8. Conduct field interviews with member informants.
9. Disengage and physically leave the setting.
10. Complete the analyses and write the research report.

Note: There is no fixed percentage of time needed for each step. For a rough approximation, Junker (1960:12) suggested that, once in the field, the researcher should expect to spend approximately one-sixth of his or her time observing, one-third recording data, one-third of the time analyzing data, and one-sixth reporting results. Also see Denzin (1989:176) for eight steps of field research.

A field researcher does not begin with a set of methods to apply or explicit hypotheses to test. Rather, he or she chooses techniques on the basis of their value for providing information. In the beginning, the researcher expects little control over data and little focus. Once socialized to the setting, however, he or she focuses the inquiry.

Getting Organized in the Beginning. Human and personal factors can play a role in any research project, but they are crucial in field research. Field projects often begin with chance occurrences or a personal interest. Field researchers can begin with their own experiences, such as working at a job, having a hobby, or being a patient or an activist.[9]

Field researchers use the skills of careful looking and listening, short-term memory, and regular writing. Before entering the field, you should practice observing the ordinary details of situations and later writing them down. Attention to details and short-term memory can improve with practice. Likewise, keeping a daily diary or personal journal is good practice for writing field notes.

As with all social research, reading the scholarly literature helps you learn concepts, potential pitfalls, data collection methods, and techniques for resolving conflicts. In addition, you may find diaries, novels, journalistic accounts, and autobiographies useful for gaining familiarity and preparing emotionally for the field.

You should not get locked into any initial misconceptions, but be open to discovering new ideas. Finding the right questions to ask about the field takes time.

You first need to empty your mind of preconceptions and defocus. There are two types of **defocusing.**[10] The first is casting a wide net in order to witness a broad range of situations, people, and settings—getting a feel for the overall setting before deciding what to include or exclude. The second type of defocusing means not focusing exclusively on the role of researcher. As Douglas (1976:122) noted, it is important to extend one's experience beyond a strictly professional role. You should move outside your comfortable social niche to experience as much as possible in the field without betraying a primary commitment to being a researcher.

Another preparation for field research is self-knowledge. A field researcher needs to know himself or herself and reflect on personal experiences. You should expect anxiety, self-doubt, frustration, and uncertainty in the field. Especially in the beginning, you may feel that you are collecting the wrong data and may suffer emotional turmoil, isolation, and confusion. You may feel doubly marginal: an outsider in the field setting and also distant from friends, family, and other researchers.[11] The relevance of your emotional makeup, personal biography, and cultural experiences makes it important to be aware of your personal commitments and inner conflicts (see the later section on stress; see also Box 13.3).

Fieldwork can have a strong impact on a researcher's identity and outlook. Researchers have been personally transformed by the field experience. Some adopt new values, interests, and moral commitments, or change their religion or political ideology.[12] Hayano (1982:148) remarked from his study on gambling:

> *By this time I felt more comfortable sitting at a poker table than I did at faculty meetings and in my classes. Most of my social life focused on poker playing, and often, especially after a big win, I felt the desire to give up my job as a university professor in order to spend more time in the cardroom.*

CHOOSING A SITE AND GAINING ACCESS

Although a field research project does not proceed by fixed steps, some common concerns arise in the early stages. These include selecting a site, gaining access to the site, entering the field, and developing rapport with members in the field.

Selecting a Site

Where to Observe. Field researchers talk about doing research on a setting, or **field site,** but this term is misleading. A site is the context in which events or activities occur, a socially defined territory with shifting boundaries. A social group may interact across several physical sites. For example, a college football team may interact on the playing field, in the locker room, in a dormitory, at a training camp, or at a local hangout. The team's field site includes all five locations.

The field site and research question are bound up together, but choosing a site is not the same as focusing on a *case* for study. A case is a social relationship or activity; it can extend beyond the boundaries of the site and have links to other social settings. A researcher selects a site, then identifies cases to examine within it—for example, how football team members relate to authority figures.

Defocusing   A technique early in field research when the researcher removes his or her past assumptions and preconceptions to become more open to events in a field site.

Field site   The one or more natural locations where a researcher conducts field research.

BOX **13.3** Field Research at a Country and Western Bar

Eliasoph (1998) conducted field research on several groups in a California community to understand how Americans avoid political expression. One was a social club. Eliasoph describes herself as an "urban, bicoastal, bespectacled, Jewish, Ph.D. candidate from a long line of communists, atheists, liberals, bookreaders, ideologues, and arguers" (p. 270). The social club's world was very foreign to her. The social club, the Buffalos, centered on country and western music at a bar, the Silverado Club. She describes it:

The Silverado huddled on a vast, rutted parking lot on what was once wetlands and now was a truck stop, a mile and a half from Amargo's [town name] nuclear battleship station. Occasional gulleys of salt water cattails poked through the wide flat miles of paved malls and gas stations. Giant four-wheeled-drive vehicles filled the parking lot, making my miniature Honda look like a toy. . . . Inside the windowless Silverado, initial blinding darkness gave way to a huge Confederate flag pinned up behind the bandstand, the standard collection of neon beer signs and beer

mirrors, men in cowboys hats, cowboys shirts and jeans, women in curly perms and tiered flounces of lace or denim skirts, or jeans, and belts with their names embroidered in glitter on the back. (1998:92)

Eliasoph introduced herself as a student. During her two years of research, she endured smoke-filled rooms as well as expensive beer and bottled-water prices; attended a wedding and many dance lessons; and participated in countless conversations and heard many abusive sexist/racist jokes. She listened, asked questions, observed, and took notes in the bathroom. When she returned home after spending hours with club members, it was to a university crowd who had little understanding of the world she was studying. For them, witty conversation was central and being bored was to be avoided. By contrast, club members used more nonverbal than verbal communication and being bored, or sitting and doing nothing, was just fine. The research forced Eliasoph to reexamine her own views and tastes, which she had taken for granted.

Selecting a field site is an important decision, and you should take notes on the site selection processes. Three factors are relevant when choosing a field research site: richness of data, unfamiliarity, and suitability.[13] Some sites are more likely than others to provide rich data. Sites that present a web of social relations, a variety of activities, and diverse events over time provide richer, more interesting data. Beginning field researchers should choose an unfamiliar setting because it is easier to see cultural events and social relations in a new site. Bogdan and Taylor (1975:28) noted, *"We would recommend that researchers choose settings in which the subjects are strangers and in which they have no particular professional knowledge or expertise"* (emphasis in original). When "casing" possible field sites, you must consider such practical issues as your time and skills, serious conflicts among people in the site, personal characteristics and feelings, and access to parts of a site.

Your ascriptive characteristics can limit access. For example, an African American researcher cannot hope to study the Ku Klux Klan or neo-Nazis,

although some researchers have successfully crossed ascriptive lines.[14] Sometimes "insider" and "outsider" teams can work together. For example, the outsider Douglas teamed up with a member insider, Flanagan, for a study of nude beaches, and a White collaborated with a Black to study a Black housing project.[15]

Physical access to a site can be an issue. Sites are on a continuum, with open and public areas (e.g., public restaurants, airport waiting areas, etc.) at one end and closed and private settings (e.g., private firms, clubs, activities in a person's home, etc.) at the other. You may find that you are not welcome or not allowed on the site, or there are legal and political barriers to access. Laws and regulations in institutions (e.g., public schools, hospitals, prisons, etc.) restrict access. In addition, institutional review boards may limit field research on ethical grounds (discussed in Chapter 5).

Level of Involvement. Field roles can be arranged on a continuum by the degree of detachment or involvement a researcher has with members. At one extreme is a detached outsider; at the other extreme is an intimately involved insider. The range of field roles is described in three systems developed by Junker, Gans, and the Adlers.

Junker (1960, but also see Denzin, 1989, Gold, 1969, and Roy, 1970) describes four roles. The range is from *complete observer* (e.g., researcher is behind a one-way mirror or taking on an "invisible role" such as an eavesdropping janitor), to *observer as participant* (e.g., researcher is known from the beginning but has limited contact), to *participant as observer* (e.g., researcher is overt and is an intimate friend of participants), and finally to *complete participant* (e.g., researcher acts as member and shares secret information of insiders). This range is similar to that of Gans (1982), who collapses the two middle categories into *researcher participant.* He emphasizes the degree of attachment/emotional involvement or detachment at each level.

Adler and Adler (1987) suggest three roles. *Peripheral membership* means maintaining distance between self and those studied, or setting limits by the researcher's beliefs or discomfort with the members' activities. *Active membership* is when the researcher assumes a membership role and goes through a similar induction into membership and participates like a member. The researcher maintains high levels of trust and can withdraw from the field periodically. *Complete membership* is when the researcher converts and **goes native.** As a fully committed member, the researcher experiences the same emotions as others and finds it very difficult or impossible to leave the field and return to being a researcher.

Your level of involvement depends on negotiations with members, specifics of the field setting, your personal comfort, and the particular role adopted in the field. You may move from outsider to insider levels with more time in the field. Each level has its advantages and disadvantages. Different field researchers advocate different levels of involvement. For example, the Adlers' complete member role is criticized by some for overinvolvement and loss of a researcher's perspective. Others argue that it is the only way to really understand a member's social world.

Roles at the outsider end of the continuum reduce the time needed for acceptance, make overrap-

port less an issue, and can sometimes help members open up. They facilitate detachment and protect the researcher's self-identity. This was the role assumed by Rueben May over the 18 months he studied Trena's bar, visiting it three to four times a week. He said (2001:174), "My goal as an ethnographyer was to document the daily lifestyle of Trena's regulars, while being as unobtrusive as possible . . . I spent most of my time listening to the patrons' exchanges and documenting those topics patrons thought important." Although there is less risk of *going native,* he or she is also less likely to know an insider's experience and misinterpretation is more likely.

To really understand social meaning for those being studied, you must participate in the setting, as others do. Holy (1984:29–30) observed:

> *The researcher does not participate in the lives of subjects in order to observe them, but rather observes while participating fully in their lives . . . through living with the people being studied. . . . She comes to share the same meanings with them in the process of active participation in their social life. . . . Research means, in this sense, socialization to the culture being studied.*

Roles at the insider end of the continuum facilitate empathy and sharing of a member's experience. The goal of fully experiencing the intimate social world of a member is achieved. Nevertheless, a lack of distance from, too much sympathy for, or overinvolvement with members is likely. Your reports may be questioned, data gathering is difficult, there can be a dramatic impact on the self, and the distance needed for analysis may be hard to attain.[16]

Gatekeepers. A **gatekeeper** is someone with the formal or informal authority to control access to a site.[17] It can be the thug on the corner, an administrator of a hospital, or the owner of a business. Informal public areas (e.g., sidewalks, public waiting rooms, etc.) rarely have gatekeepers; formal

---

Go native   When a researcher in field research gets overly involved and loses all distance or objectivity and becomes joined with the people being studied.

Gatekeeper   A person in an official or unofficial role who controls access to a setting.

organizations have authorities from whom permission must be obtained.

You should expect to negotiate with gatekeepers and bargain for access. The gatekeepers may not appreciate the need for conceptual distance or ethical balance. You need to set nonnegotiable limits to protect research integrity. If there are many restrictions initially, you can often reopen negotiations later, and gatekeepers may forget their initial demands as trust develops. It is ethically and politically astute to call on gatekeepers. Many gatekeepers do not care about the findings, except insofar as these findings might provide evidence for someone to criticize them.

Dealing with gatekeepers is a recurrent issue as you enter new levels or areas of a field site. In addition, a gatekeeper can shape the direction of research:

> *Even the most friendly and co-operative gatekeepers or sponsors will shape the conduct and development of research. To one degree or another, the ethnographer will be channeled in line with existing networks of friendship and enmity, territory, and equivalent boundaries. (Hammersley and Atkinson, 1983:73)*

In some sites, gatekeeper approval creates a stigma that inhibits the cooperation of members. For example, prisoners may not be cooperative if they know that the prison warden gave approval to the researcher.

Strategy for Entering

Planning. Entering and gaining access to a field site depend on commonsense judgment and social skills. Field sites usually have different levels or areas, and entry is an issue for each. Entry is more analogous to peeling the layers of an onion than to opening a door. Moreover, bargains and promises of entry may not remain stable over time. You need fallback plans or may have to return later for rene-

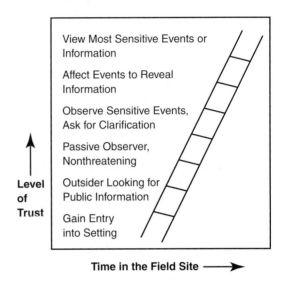

FIGURE 13.2   The Access Ladder

gotiation. Because the specific focus of research may not emerge until later in the research process or may change, it is best to avoid being locked into specifics by gatekeepers.

Entry and access can be visualized as an **access ladder** (see Figure 13.2). You begin at the bottom rung, where access is easy and where you are an outsider looking for public information. The next rung requires increased access. Once close on-site observation begins, you become a passive observer, not questioning what members say. With time in the field, you observe specific activities that are potentially sensitive or seek clarification of what you see or hear. Reaching this access rung is more difficult. Finally, you may try to shape interaction so that it reveals specific information, or you may want to see highly sensitive material. This highest rung of the access ladder is rarely attained and requires deep trust.[18]

Negotiation. Social relations are negotiated and formed throughout the process of fieldwork.[19] Negotiation occurs with each new member until a stable relationship develops to gain access, develop trust, obtain information, and reduce hostile reactions. You should expect to negotiate and explain

> **Access ladder**   Field researchers may be able to see and learn about only public, non controversial events in the beginning, but with time and effort they can gain entry to more hidden, intimate, and controversial information.

what you are doing over and over in the field (see the discussion of normalizing social research, to follow).

Deviant groups and elites often require special negotiations for gaining access. To gain access to deviant subcultures, field researchers have used contacts from the researcher's private life, gone to social welfare or law enforcement agencies where the deviants are processed, advertised for volunteers, offered a service (e.g., counseling) in exchange for access, or gone to a location where deviants hang out and joined a group. For example, Harper (1982) gained access by living in a skid-row mission without any money and befriending homeless men who knew street life. Bart (1987) argued that her background as a feminist activist and nonprofessional demeanor were essential for gaining access to an illegal feminist abortion clinic.[20]

Field researchers use connections with other people, or networking, and use one informant to suggest another. Often, the social relations developed are maintained over years. Access to elites and professionals often depends on luck or personal ties.[21] Hoffmann (1980) gained access to wealthy individuals on the boards of directors by using her family ties and including personal references in letters requesting interviews. Danziger (1979) gained access to physicians' activities because her father was a doctor. Johnson's (1975) access to a social work agency was aided by mentioning that someone in the agency was a friend of his wife.

Disclosure. You must decide how much to reveal about yourself and the research project. Disclosing your personal life, hobbies, interests, and background can build trust and close relationships, but you also lose privacy and need to ensure that the focus remains on events in the field.

Disclosure ranges on a continuum from fully covert research, in which no one in the field is aware that research is taking place, to the opposite end, where everyone knows the specifics of the research project (see Chapter 5 on covert research). The degree and timing of disclosure depends on a researcher's judgment and particulars in the setting. Disclosure may unfold over time as you feel more secure.

Disclose the project to gatekeepers and others unless there is a good reason for not doing so, such as the presence of gatekeepers who would seriously limit or inhibit research for illegitimate reasons (e.g., to hide graft or corruption). Even in these cases, you may disclose your identity as a researcher, but may pose as one who seems submissive, harmless, and interested in nonthreatening issues (see Acceptable Incompetent, later).

Entering the Field

After a field site is selected and access obtained, you must learn the ropes, develop rapport with members, adopt a role in the setting, and maintain social relations. Before confronting such issues, you should ask: How will I present myself? What does it mean for me to be a "measurement instrument"? How can I assume an "attitude of strangeness"?

Presentation of Self. People explicitly and implicitly present themselves to others. We display who we are—the type of person we are or would like to be—through our physical appearance, what we say, and how we act. The presentation of self sends a symbolic message. It may be, "I'm a serious, hard-working student," "I'm a warm and caring person," "I'm a cool jock," or "I'm a rebel and party animal." Many selves are possible, and presentations of selves can differ depending on the occasion.

A good field researcher is very conscious of the presentation of self in the field. For example, how should you dress in the field? The best guide is to respect both yourself and those being studied. Do not overdress so as to offend or stand out, but copying the dress of those being studied is not always necessary. A professor who studies street people does not have to dress or act like one; dressing and acting informally is sufficient. Likewise, more formal dress and professional demeanor are usually required when studying corporate executives or top officials.[22]

A researcher must be aware that self-presentation will influence field relations to some degree. It is difficult to present a highly deceptive front or to present oneself in a way that deviates sharply from the person one is ordinarily.

Being herself and revealing her personal background as a Jewish woman helped Myerhoff (1989) gain access and develop rapport in a field site of elderly residents in a Jewish senior citizen home. At the same time, her understanding and awareness of her identity changed as a result of her field interactions. Stack (1989) began as an outsider—a White woman studying a low-income Black industrial community. Eventually, she was accepted into a kin-like relationship with the women she studied. Assigned nickname "White Caroline" was a signal of acceptance and endearment. She performed many small favors, such as driving people to the hospital or welfare office, shopping, and visiting sick children. She achieved this by how she interacted with others—her openness and willingness to share personal feelings. Although he was a Black man in a Black bar, Anderson (1989) found social class to be a barrier. The setting was a corner bar and liquor store on the south side of Chicago in a poor African American neighborhood. Anderson developed a social relationship of trust and was "sponsored." This occurred when he befriended "Herman," a witty, easygoing person who was street smart and socially well connected in the setting. Anderson succeeded by "the low-key, nonassertive role I assumed . . . not to disrupt the consensual definition of the social order in this type of setting" (Anderson, 1989:19).

Researcher as Instrument.   The researcher is the instrument for measuring field data. This has two implications. First, it puts pressure on the researcher to be alert and sensitive to what happens in the field and to be disciplined about recording data. Second, it has personal consequences. Fieldwork involves social relationships and personal feelings. Field researchers are flexible about what to include as data and admit their own subjective insights and feelings, or "experiential data."[23] Personal, subjective experiences are part of field data. They are valuable both in themselves and for interpreting events in the field. Instead of trying to be

objective and eliminate personal reactions, field researchers treat their feelings toward field events as data. For example, Karp's (1973, 1980) personal feelings of tension in his study of pornographic bookstores were a critical part of the data. His personal discomfort in the field revealed some dynamics of the setting. "If we avoid writing about our reactions, we cannot examine them. We cannot achieve immersion without bringing our subjectivity into play" (Kleinman and Copp, 1993:19).

Field research can heighten a researcher's awareness of personal feelings. For example, a researcher may not be fully aware of personal feelings about nudity until he or she is in a nudist colony, or about personal possessions until he or she is in a setting where others "borrow" many items. The researcher's own surprise, indignation, or questioning then may become an opportunity for reflection and insight.[24]

An Attitude of Strangeness.   It is hard to recognize what we are very close to. The everyday world we inhabit is filled with thousands of details. If we paid attention to everything all the time, we would suffer from severe information overload. We manage by ignoring much of what is around us and by engaging in habitual thinking. Unfortunately, we fail to see the familiar as distinctive, and assume that others experience reality just as we do. We tend to treat our own way of living as natural or normal.

Field research in familiar surroundings is difficult because it is easy to be blinded by the familiar. In fact, "intimate acquaintance with one's own culture can create as much blindness as insight" (McCracken, 1988:12). By studying other cultures, researchers encounter dramatically different assumptions about what is important and how things are done. This confrontation of cultures, or culture shock, has two benefits: It makes it easier to see cultural elements and it facilitates self-discovery. Researchers adopt the attitude of strangeness to gain these benefits. The **attitude of strangeness** means you question and notice ordinary details or look at the ordinary through the eyes of a stranger. Strangeness helps you overcome the boredom of observing ordinary details. It helps you see in a way, that re-

---

Attitude of strangeness   A field research technique in which researchers mentally adjust to "see" events in the field as if for the first time or as an outsider.

veals aspects of the setting of which members are not consciously aware.

People rarely recognize customs they take for granted. For example, when someone gives us a gift, we say thank you and praise the gift. By contrast, gift-giving customs in many cultures include complaining that the gift is inadequate. The attitude of strangeness helps make the tacit culture visible—for example, that gift givers expect to hear "thank you" and "the gift is nice," and become upset otherwise. A field researcher adopts both a stranger's and an insider's point of view. The stranger sees events as specific social processes, whereas to an insider, they seem natural. Davis (1973) called this the Martian and the convert: The Martian sees everything as strange and questions assumptions, whereas the convert accepts everything and wants to become a believer. Researchers need both views, as well as the ability to switch back and forth.[25]

Strangeness also encourages you to reconsider your own social world. Immersion in a different setting breaks old habits of thought and action. You will find reflection and introspection easier and more intense when encountering the unfamiliar, whether it is a different culture or a familiar culture seen through a stranger's eyes.

Building Rapport

A field researcher builds rapport by getting along with members in the field. He or she forges a friendly relationship, shares the same language, and laughs and cries with members. This is a step toward obtaining an understanding of members and moving beyond understanding to empathy—that is, seeing and feeling events from another's perspective.

It is not always easy to build rapport. The social world is not all in harmony, with warm, friendly people. A setting may contain fear, tension, and conflict. Members may be unpleasant, untrustworthy, or untruthful; they may do things that disturb or disgust a researcher. An experienced researcher is prepared for a range of events and relationships. He or she may find, however, that it is impossible to penetrate a setting or get really close to members. Settings where cooperation, sympathy, and collaboration are impossible require different tech-

niques.[26] Also, the researcher accepts what he or she hears or sees at face value, but without being gullible. As Schatzman and Strauss (1973:69) remarked, "The researcher believes 'everything' and 'nothing' simultaneously."

Charm and Trust. You need social skills and personal charm to build rapport. Trust, friendly feelings, and being well liked facilitate communication and help you understand the inner feelings of others. There is no magical way to do this. Showing a genuine concern for and interest in others, being honest, and sharing feelings are good strategies, but they are not foolproof. It depends on the specific setting and members.

Many factors affect trust and rapport—how you present yourself; the role you choose for the field; and the events that encourage, limit, or make it impossible to achieve trust. Trust is not gained once and for all. It is a developmental process built up over time through many social nuances (e.g., sharing of personal experiences, storytelling, gestures, hints, facial expressions). It is constantly recreated and seems easier to lose once it has been built up than to gain in the first place.

Establishing trust is important, but it does not ensure that all information will be revealed. It may be limited to specific areas. For example, trust can be built up regarding financial matters but not to disclose intimate dating behavior. Trust may have to be created anew in each area of inquiry; it requires constant reaffirmation.

Freeze Outs. Some members may not be open and cooperative. **Freeze outs** are members who express an uncooperative attitude or an overt unwillingness to participate. Field researchers may never gain the cooperation of everyone, or a lukewarm relationship may develop only after prolonged persistence.

Understanding. Rapport helps you understand members, but understanding is a precondition for

Freeze outs When one or more people studied in field research refuse to cooperate with the researcher or to become involved in the study.

greater depth, not an end in itself. It slowly develops in the field as you overcome an initial bewilderment with a new or unusual language and system of social meaning. Once you attain an understanding of the member's point of view, the next step is to learn how to think and act within a member's perspective. This is *empathy,* or adopting another's perspective. Empathy does not necessarily mean sympathy, agreement, or approval; it means feeling things as another does.[27]

Rapport helps create understanding and ultimately empathy, and the development of empathy facilitates greater rapport. The novel *To Kill a Mockingbird* notes the link between rapport and empathic understanding in the following passage:

> *"First of all," he said, "if you can learn a simple trick, Scout, you'll get along a lot better with all kinds of folks. You never really understand a person until you consider things from his point of view."*
>
> *"Sir?"*
>
> *"—until you climb into his skin and walk around in it." (Lee, 1960:34)*

RELATIONS IN THE FIELD

You play many social roles in daily life—daughter/son, student, customer, sports fan—and maintain social relations with others. You choose some roles and others are structured for you. Few have a choice but to play the role of son or daughter. Some roles are formal (e.g., bank teller, police chief, etc.); others are informal (flirt, elder statesperson, buddy, etc.). You can switch roles, play multiple roles, and play a role in a particular way. Field researchers play roles in the field. In addition, they learn the ropes and maintain relations with members.

Roles in the Field

Social psychological theories and studies on social roles, self identity, and self-presentation inform access in field research. Harrington (2003) noted that a field researcher's success depends on how skillfully he or she negotiates symbolic interaction processes, such as presentation of self and performing social roles. She observed (p. 609):

> *researchers entering a field site encounter not only participants but participants' preexisting categories for understanding the world—categories which will be applied to researchers as a way of getting a definitional "handle" on their presence, and figuring out how to interact with them . . . researchers must be defined in terms that either enhance or do not threaten participants' group identity.*

Field researchers negotiate which preexisting role the field site members assign early field site interactions. The assigned role and how a researcher performs in that role influence not only the ease and degree of access but also the success in developing social trust and securing cooperation in the field.

Some existing roles provide access to all areas of the site, the ability to observe and interact with all members, the freedom to move around, and a way to balance the requirements of researcher and member. At other times, a researcher creates a new role or modifies an existing one. For example, Fine (1987) created a role of the "adult friend" and performed it with little adult authority when studying preadolescent boys. He was able to observe parts of their culture and behavior that were otherwise inaccessible to adults. A researcher may adopt several different field roles over time in the field.

Limits on the Role Chosen. The field roles open to you are affected by ascriptive factors and physical appearance. You can change some aspects of appearance, such as dress or hairstyle, but not ascriptive features such as age, race, gender, and attractiveness. Nevertheless, such factors can be important in gaining access and can restrict the available roles. For example, Gurney (1985) reported that being a female in a male-dominated setting required extra negotiations and "hassles." Nevertheless, her gender provided insights and created situations that would have been absent with a male researcher.

Because many roles are sex-typed, gender is an important consideration. Female researchers often have more difficulty when the setting is perceived as dangerous or seamy and where males are in control (e.g., police work, fire fighting, etc.). They may be shunned or pushed into limiting gender stereotypes (e.g., "sweet kid," "mascot," "loud mouth," etc.). Male researchers have more problems in routine and administrative sites where males are in control (e.g., courts, large offices, etc.). They may not be accepted in female-dominated territory. In sites where both males and females are involved, both sexes may be able to enter and gain acceptance.[28]

Other Considerations. Almost any role limits access to some parts of a field site. For example, the role of a bartender in a bar limits knowledge of intimate customer behavior or presence at customer gatherings in other locations. A field researcher takes care when choosing roles but recognizes that all roles involve trade-offs.

Most social settings contain cliques, informal groups, hierarchies, and rivalries. A role can help you gain acceptance into or be excluded from a clique, be treated as a person in authority or as an underling, and be a friend or an enemy of some members. You need to be aware that by adopting a role, you may be forming allies and enemies who can assist or limit research.

Danger and high risk are aspects of some settings (e.g., police work, violent criminal gangs). A field researcher should be aware of risks to his or her safety, assess the risks, and then decide what he or she is willing to do. Some observers argue that a field researcher needs to share in the risks and danger of a setting to truly understand it and the experiences of participants. For example, Westmarland (2000) argued that only by putting on a safety vest while rushing to the scene of violent crime and then dodging bullets along with police officers can a researcher acquire an insider's view. Taking risks means that some researchers have had "near misses" or been injured.

In addition to physical injury, researchers can face legal or financial risks, and damage to their professional or personal reputation based on actions in a field setting. Research into some settings (e.g., the severely mentally ill, trauma centers, war zones) may create extreme emotional-psychological discomfort and cause permanent damage to a researcher's sense of inner well-being. Field researchers who have studied high-risk settings, such as inner-city drug dealers, offer suggestions for staying safe (see Box 13.4).

BOX **13.4** **Staying Safe in Unsafe Settings**

1. First impressions matter; adopt a personal style and demeanor appropriate to the setting.
2. Learn "street life" and fit in; do not dress or act too much like an outsider.
3. Explain yourself, who you are, and why you are there.
4. Scan the physical environment for obvious signs of danger (e.g., floors likely to collapse, a ceiling likely to fall).
5. Stay alert and be prepared to respond quickly to potentially dangerous circumstances (paranoia, sexual approaches, robbery, theft, shootings, police raids, and arrests).
6. Find a "protector" (i.e., a powerful person in the setting with whom strong trust is created and who will provide verbal/physical protection).
7. Develop an assertive, confident mind-set and do not act like a victim; overly fearful behavior can invite aggression.
8. Acquire a "sixth sense" and use prudence or common sense for changing conditions. Keep some money hidden for an emergency.
9. Develop a "safety zone" of people whom you trust and feel comfortable with, and who accept you.
10. If feeling discomfort, it is best to leave the setting and return another time. The threat of sexual assault or rape is often a real concern for female researchers and should be taken seriously.

Sources: Adapted from Bourgeois (1996), Lee-Treweek and Linkogle (2000), and Williams and Dunlap (1992).

Learning the Ropes

As you learn the ropes on the field site, you learn how to cope with personal stress, how to normalize the social research, and how to act like an "acceptable incompetent" (discussed later).

Stress. Fieldwork can be highly rewarding, exciting, and fulfilling, but it also can be difficult:

> *Fieldwork must certainly rank with the more disagreeable activities that humanity has fashioned for itself. It is usually inconvenient, to say the least, sometimes physically uncomfortable, frequently embarrassing, and, to a degree, always tense. (Shaffir et al., 1980:3)*

New researchers face embarrassment, experience discomfort, and are overwhelmed by the details in the field. For example, in her study of U.S. relocation camps for Japanese Americans during World War II, respected field researcher Rosalie Wax (1971) reported that she endured the discomfort of 120-degree Fahrenheit temperatures, filthy and dilapidated living conditions, dysentery, and mosquitoes. She felt isolated, she cried a lot, and she gained 30 pounds from compulsive eating. After months in the field, she thought she was a total failure; she was distrusted by members and got into fights with the camp administration.

Maintaining a "marginal" status is stressful; it is difficult to be an outsider who is not fully involved, especially when studying settings full of intense feelings (e.g., political campaigns, religious conversions, etc.). The loneliness and isolation of fieldwork may combine with the desire to develop rapport and empathy to cause overinvolvement. A researcher may *go native* and abandon the professional researcher's role to become a full member of the group being studied. Or the researcher may feel guilt about learning intimate details as members drop their guard and may overidentify with members.[29]

Some emotional stress is inevitable in field research. Instead of suppressing emotional responses, you need to be sensitive to emotional reactions. You can cope in the field by keeping a personal diary, emotional journal, or written record of inner feelings, or by having sympathetic people outside the field site to confide in.[30]

Normalizing Social Research. A field researcher not only observes and investigates members in the field but is observed and investigated by members as well: "While the fieldworker is undertaking a study of others, others are undertaking a study of the fieldworker" (Van Maanen, 1982:110). Fieldwork is not performed by an isolated individ-

ual but is created by everyone in the field setting (Wax 1979:363).

In overt field research, members are usually initially uncomfortable with the presence of a researcher. Most are unfamiliar with field research and fail to distinguish between sociologists, psychologists, counselors, and social workers. They may see the researcher as an outside critic or spy, or as a savior or all-knowing expert.

An overt field researcher must **normalize social research**—that is, help members redefine social research from something unknown and threatening to something normal and predictable. You can help members manage research by presenting your own biography, explaining field research a little at a time, appearing nonthreatening, or accepting minor deviance in the setting (e.g., minor violations of official rules).[31] For example, in a study of social workers, Johnson (1975:99–104) was accepted after the social workers realized that he accepted their minor deviance (e.g., leaving work early to go swimming) and said that he thought others did it also.

Another way to normalize research is to explain it in terms members understand. Sometimes, members' excitement about being written up in a book is useful, as Fine and Glassner (1979) and LeMasters (1975) found. In his study of a neighborhood tavern in Wisconsin, LeMasters became a regular over a five-year period, going to the bar several nights a week. He (1975:7) stated how he explained what he was doing to members:

> *I initially assumed the role of patron—just another person who liked to drink beer and shoot some pool. This finally became difficult because the amount of time I spent in the tavern began to raise questions. Some of the regular customers, I learned later, had decided I must be an undercover agent from the state liquor commission. . . . I adopted the following stance when queried about being in the tavern: that sociologists have to have some knowledge of various aspects of American society to be effective teachers, that I found The Oasis men and women to be helpful in understanding how blue-collar people feel about American society, and, further, that I became bored by constant association with white-collar people and that the tavern contacts were refreshing. All of the above statements were true.*

Normalize social research   Techniques in field research to make the people being studied feel more comfortable with the research process and to help them accept the researcher's presence.

Acceptable Incompetent. As a researcher, you are in the field to learn, not to be an expert. Depending on the setting, you should be a friendly but naive outsider, an acceptable incompetent who is interested in learning about the social life of the field. An **acceptable incompetent** is someone who is only partially competent (skilled or knowledgeable) in the setting but who is accepted as a non-threatening person who needs to be taught.[32]

You may know little about the setting or subculture at first. You may be seen as a fool who is hoodwinked or shortchanged, and may be the butt of jokes for your lack of adeptness in the setting. Even when you are knowledgeable, you can display less than full information to draw out a member's knowledge. Of course, you might overdo this and appear so ignorant that you are not taken seriously.

Maintaining Relations

Social Relations. With time, a field researcher develops and modifies social relationships. Members who are cool at first may warm up later. Or they may put on a front of initial friendliness, and their fears and suspicions surface only later. You are in a delicate position. Early in a project, when not yet fully aware of everything about a field site, you should not rush to form close relationships because circumstances may change. Yet, if you develop close friends, they can become allies who will defend your presence and help you gain access.

You need to monitor how your actions or appearance affects members. For example, a physically attractive researcher who interacts with members of the opposite sex may encounter crushes, flirting, and jealousy. He or she develops an awareness of these field relations and learns to manage them.[33]

In addition to developing social relationships, you must be able to break or withdraw from relationships as well. Ties with one member may have to be broken in order to forge ties with others or to explore other aspects of the setting. As with the end of any friendly relationship, the emotional pain of social withdrawal can affect both the researcher and the member. You must balance social sensitivity and the research goals.

Small Favors. *Exchange relationships* develop in the field, in which small tokens or favors, including deference and respect, are exchanged.[34] You may gain acceptance by helping out in small ways. Exchange helps when access to sensitive issues is limited. You may offer small favors but not burden members by asking for return favors. As you and members share experiences and see each other again, members recall the favors and reciprocate by allowing access. For example, Fine (1987:242) learned a lot when he was providing small favors (e.g., driving the boys to the movies) as part of his "adult friend" role. Fine (1996:x) also reported that he washed potatoes, cleaned beans, and performed many small chores during his study of restaurant kitchens.

Conflicts in the Field. Fights, conflict, and disagreements can erupt in the field, or you may study groups with opposing positions. In such situations, you will feel pressure to take sides and will be tested to see whether you can be trusted. In such occasions, you usually want to stay on the neutral sidelines and walk a tightrope between opposing sides. This is because once you become aligned with one side, you will be cut off from access to the other side.[35] In addition, you will see the situation from only one point of view. Nevertheless, some (e.g., Van Maanen, 1982:115) argue that true neutrality is illusory. As a researcher becomes involved with members and embroiled in webs of relationships and commitments, neutrality becomes almost impossible.

Appearing Interested. Field researchers maintain an **appearance of interest** in the field. An experienced researcher appears to be interested in and involved with field events by statements and behaviors (e.g., facial expression, going for coffee,

---

Acceptable incompetent When a field researcher pretends to be less skilled or knowledgeable in order to learn more about a field site.

Appearance of interest A technique field researchers use to maintain relations in a field site in which they pretend to be interested in and excited by the activities of those studied even though they are actually uninterested.

organizing a party, etc.) even if he or she is not truly interested. This is because field relations may be disrupted if you appear to be bored or distracted. Putting up such a temporary front of involvement is a common small deception in daily life and is part of being polite.[36]

Of course, selective inattention (i.e., not staring or appearing not to notice) is also part of acting polite. If a person makes a social mistake (e.g., accidentally uses an incorrect word, passes gas, etc.), the polite thing to do is to ignore it. Selective inattention is used in fieldwork, as well. It gives an alert researcher an opportunity to learn by casually eavesdropping on conversations or observing events not meant to be public.

Social Breakdowns. A social breakdown occurs when two cultural traditions or social assumptions fail to mesh. **Social breakdowns** highlight social meaning because hidden routine expectations and assumptions become explicit in a breakdown. They appear as misunderstandings or confusion over which of several implicit social rules to apply. For example, I go to a restaurant and sit down and wait for a server to appear. Twenty minutes later, having gotten no service, I become angry. I look around and notice that I have not seen any servers. I see customers enter from a doorway carrying their own food and realize my misunderstanding. My implicit expectation was that the restaurant had table service; in fact, it is one where patrons go to a counter, order, and pick up their own food. Once I recognize which rules to apply in the context, I can resolve the breakdown.

Social breakdowns produce embarrassment because the mismatch of cultural meanings often causes a person to look foolish, ignorant, or uninformed. For example, you are invited to a party that begins at 8:00. You show up in your usual attire, old jeans and a wrinkled sweater, and arrive at your usual time for an 8:00 party—8:30. The door opens and you enter. Shocked, you see that everyone else

is formally dressed and sitting at a formal dinner, which was served about 30 minutes ago. People stare at you, and you feel out of place. Your cultural expectation (this is an informal student party with loud music, dancing, beer, and informal dress) does not match the setting (this is a formal dinner party, where people expect to eat, engage in polite conversation, and act professionally). The breakdown makes explicit the unspoken social rules that "everyone knows" or assumes.

Social breakdowns can be unexpected or can be purposefully created to test working hypotheses. As with an ethnomethodologist's breaching experiments, a researcher may violate social rules to illustrate the existence of tacit rules and their importance. Researchers observe unplanned breakdowns, or they create breakdowns and watch reactions in order to pinpoint implicit social expectations.

OBSERVING AND COLLECTING DATA

This section looks at how to get good qualitative field data. Field data are what you experience, remember, and record in field notes.

Watching and Listening

Observing. A great deal of what researchers do in the field is to pay close attention, watch, and listen carefully. They use all the senses, noticing what is seen, heard, smelled, tasted, or touched. The researcher becomes an instrument that absorbs all sources of information.

A field researcher carefully scrutinizes the physical setting to capture its atmosphere. He or she asks: What is the color of the floor, walls, ceiling? How large is a room? Where are the windows and doors? How is the furniture arranged, and what is its condition (e.g., new or old and worn, dirty or clean)? What type of lighting is there? Are there signs, paintings, plants? What are the sounds or smells?

Why bother with such details? You may have noticed that stores and restaurants often plan lighting, colors, and piped-in music to create a certain atmosphere. Maybe you know that used-car sales people spray a new-car scent into cars or that shops

Social breakdown When social rules and patterns of behavior in a field site do not operate as expected and reveal a great deal about social meanings and relationships.

in shopping malls intentionally send out the odor of freshly made cookies. These subtle, unconscious signals influence human behavior.

Observing in field research is often detailed, tedious work. Silverman (1993:30) noted, "If you go to the cinema to see action [car chases, hold-ups, etc.], then it is unlikely that you will find it easy to be a good observer." Instead of the quick flash, motivation arises out of a deep curiosity about the details. Good field researchers are intrigued about details that reveal "what's going on here" through careful listening and watching. Field researchers believe that the core of social life is communicated through the mundane, trival, everyday minutia. This is what people often overlook, but field researchers need to learn how to notice.

In addition to physical surroundings, you want to observe people and their actions, noting each person's observable physical characteristics: age, sex, race, and stature. People socially interact differently depending on whether another person is 18, 40, or 70 years old; male or female; White or non-White; short and frail or tall, heavyset, and muscular. When noting such characteristics, include yourself. For example, an attitude of strangeness heightens sensitivity to a group's racial composition. A researcher who ignores the racial composition of a group of Whites in a multiracial society because he or she too is White is being racially insensitive. Likewise, "Gender insensitivity occurs when the sex of participants in the research process is neglected" (Eichler, 1988:51).

You record such details because something of significance *might* be revealed. It is better to err by including everything than to ignore potentially significant details. For example, "the tall, White muscular 19-year-old male in a torn tee shirt and dirty jeans sprinted into the brightly lit room just as the short, overweight light-skinned black woman in her sixties who was professionally dressed eased into a battered chair" says much more than "one person entered, another sat down."

You should note aspects of physical appearance such as neatness, dress, and hairstyle because they express messages that can affect social interactions. People spend a great deal of time and money selecting clothes, styling and combing hair, grooming with makeup, shaving, ironing clothes, and using deodorant or perfumes. These are part of their presentation of self. Even people who do not groom, shave, or wear deodorant present themselves and send a symbolic message by their appearance. No one dresses or looks "normal." Such a statement suggests that you are insensitive to social signals.

What people do is also significant. A field researcher notices where people sit or stand, the pace at which they walk, and their nonverbal communication. People express social information, feelings, and attitudes through nonverbal communication, including gestures, facial expressions, and how one stands or sits (standing stiffly, sitting in a slouched position, etc.). People express relationships by how they position themselves in a group and through eye contact. A researcher may read social communication by noting that people are standing close together, looking relaxed, and making eye contact.

You can also notice the context in which events occur: Who was present? Who just arrived or left the scene? Was the room hot and stuffy? Such details may help you assign meaning and understand why an event occurred. If they are not noticed, the details are lost, as is a full understanding of the event.

Serendipity is important in field research. Many times, a field researcher does not know the relevance of what he or she is observing until later. This has two implications. First is the importance of keen observation and excellent notes at all times, even when "nothing seems to be happening." Second is the importance of looking back over time and learning to appreciate wait time. Most field researchers say that they spend a lot of time "waiting." Novice field researchers get frustrated with the amount of time they seem to "waste," either waiting for other people or waiting for events to occur. What novices need to learn is that wait time is a necessary part of fieldwork, and it can be valuable.

You need to learn the rhythms of the setting, to operate on other people's schedules, and to observe how events occur within their own flow of time. Also, wait time is not always wasted time. Wait time is time for reflection, for observing details, for developing social relations, for building rapport, and for becoming a familiar sight to people in the field setting. Wait time also displays that you are committed and serious; perseverance is a significant trait to cultivate. You may be impatient to get in, get the research over, and get on with your "real life" but for the people in the field site, this *is* real life. You should subordinate your personal wants to the demands of the field site.

Listening. A good field researcher listens carefully to phrases, accents, and incorrect grammar, listening both to *what* is said and *how* it is said or what was implied. For example, people often use phrases such as "you know" or "of course" or "et cetera." A field researcher knows the meaning behind such phrases. You can try to hear everything, but listening is difficult when many conversations occur at once or when eavesdropping. Luckily, significant events and themes usually recur.

Argot. People who interact with each other over a time period develop shared symbols and terminology. They create new words or assign new meanings to ordinary words. New words develop out of specific events, assumptions, or relations. Knowing and using the language can signal membership in a distinct subculture. A field researcher learns the specialized language, or **argot**.[37]

> *Researchers must start with the premise that words and symbols used in their world may have different meaning in the world of their subjects. They must also be attuned to new words and words used in contexts other than those with which they are familiar. (Bogdan and Taylor, 1975:53)*

A field researcher discovers how the argot fits into social relations or meanings. The argot gives a researcher clues to what is important to members and how they see the world. For example, Douglas (1976:125) discovered the term *vultching* in a study of nude beaches. It was a member's label for the practice of some males who sat around an attractive nude woman on the beach.

Argot The special language or terminology used by the members of a subculture or group that interacts regularly.

In their study of sales practices of a vacation condominium ownership firm, Katovich and Diamond (1986) conducted observations and informal interviews over six months when one researcher was employed and the other was a trainee. They analyzed the salesroom as a stage in which a series of events are presented to prospective buyers and discussed the argot used. For example, "drops" occurred when the finance manager enters and "drops" information during a discussion between the salesperson and potential buyers. The purpose of such staged events is to stimulate sales. Common revelations were: A major corporation that bought 20 units just decided it needed only 15, so 5 are suddenly available at a special price; a previous client was denied financing, so a property can be offered at a reduced price; or only a few charter members can qualify for a special deal.

A field researcher translates back and forth between the field argot and the outside world. Spradley (1970:80) provided an example of argot when quoting an "urban nomad" he studied as saying, "If a man hasn't made the bucket, he isn't a tramp." This translates: A man is not considered a true member of the subculture (i.e., a tramp) until he has been arrested for public drunkenness and spent the night in the city or county jail (i.e., "made the bucket"). After you have been in the field for some time, you may feel comfortable using the argot, but it is unwise to use the argot too soon and risk looking foolish.

Taking Notes

Most field research data are in the form of field notes. Full field notes can contain maps, diagrams, photographs, interviews, tape recordings, videotapes, memos, objects from the field, notes jotted in the field, and detailed notes written away from the field. You can expect to fill many notebooks or the equivalent in computer memory. You may spend more time writing notes than being in the field. Some researchers produce 40 single-spaced pages of notes for three hours of observation. With practice, you should produce several pages of notes for each hour in the field.

Writing notes is often boring, tedious work that requires self-discipline. The notes contain extensive descriptive detail drawn from memory.

Direct Observation	Inference	Analytic	Personal Journal
Sunday, October 4. Kay's Kafe 3:00 pm. Large White male in mid-40s, overweight, enters. He wears worn brown suit. He is alone; sits at booth #2. Kay comes by, asks, "What'll it be?" Man says, "Coffee, black for now." She leaves and he lights cigarette and reads menu. 3:15 pm. Kay turns on radio.	Kay seems friendly today, humming. She becomes solemn and watchful. I think she puts on the radio when nervous.	Women are afraid of men who come in alone since the robbery.	It is raining. I am feeling comfortable with Kay but am bored today.

FIGURE 13.3   Types of Field Notes

Emerson and colleagues (1995) argued that good field notes are as much a mind-set as an activity and (p. 40) remarked, "Perhaps more crucial than how long the ethnographer spends in the field is the timing of writing up field notes. . . . Writing field notes *immediately* after leaving the setting provides fresher, more detailed recollections . . ." (emphasis in original). If possible, write notes before the day's thoughts and excitement begin to fade, without retelling events to others. Pouring fresh memories into the notes with an intense immediacy often triggers an emotional release and stimulates insightful reflection. At times, especially after a long, tiring day, writing may feel more like a boring, tedious burden. Begin by allocating about a half hour to writing your field notes for each hour you spend in the field site.

The notes must be neat and organized because you will return to them over and over again. Once written, the notes are private and valuable. You must treat them with care and protect confidentiality. Members have the right to remain anonymous, and researchers often use *pseudonyms* (false names) in notes. Field notes may be of interest to hostile parties, blackmailers, or legal officials, so some researchers write field notes in code.

Your state of mind, level of attention, and conditions in the field affect note taking. Begin with relatively short one- to three-hour periods in the field before writing notes. Johnson (1975:187) remarked:

The quantity and quality of the observational records vary with the field worker's feelings of restedness or exhaustion, reactions to particular events, relations with others, consumption of alcoholic beverages, the number of discrete observations, and so forth.

Types of Field Notes. Field researchers take notes in many ways (see Figure 13.3).[38] The recommendations here (also see Box 13.5) are suggestions. Full field notes have several types or levels. Five levels will be described. It is usually best to keep all the notes for an observation period together and to distinguish types of notes by separate pages. Some researchers include inferences with direct observations if they are set off by a visible device such as brackets or colored ink. The quantity of notes varies across types. For example, six hours in the field might result in 1 page of jotted notes, 40 pages of direct observation, 5 pages of researcher inference, and 2 pages total for methodological, theoretical, and personal notes.

Jotted Notes. It is nearly impossible to take good notes in the field. Even a known observer in a public setting looks strange when furiously writing. More important, when looking down and writing, the researcher cannot see and hear what is happening. The attention given to note writing is taken from field observation where it belongs. The specific setting determines whether any notes in the field can

---

BOX **13.5** **Recommendations for Taking Field Notes**

1. Record notes as soon as possible after each period in the field, and do not talk with others until observations are recorded.
2. Begin the record of each field visit with a new page, with the date and time noted.
3. Use jotted notes only as a temporary memory aid, with keywords or terms, or the first and last things said.
4. Use wide margins to make it easy to add to notes at any time. Go back and add to the notes if you remember something later.
5. Plan to type notes and keep each level of notes separate so it will be easy to go back to them later.
6. Record events in the order in which they occurred, and note how long they lasted (e.g., a 15-minute wait, a one-hour ride).
7. Make notes as concrete, complete, and comprehensible as possible.
8. Use frequent paragraphs and quotation marks. Exact recall of phrases is best, with double quotes; use single quotes for paraphrasing.
9. Record small talk or routines that do not appear to be significant at the time; they may become important later.

10. "Let your feelings flow" and write quickly without worrying about spelling or "wild ideas." Assume that no one else will see the notes, but use pseudonyms.
11. Never substitute tape recordings completely for field notes.
12. Include diagrams or maps of the setting, and outline your own movements and those of others during the period of observation.
13. Include the researcher's own words and behavior in the notes. Also record emotional feelings and private thoughts in a separate section.
14. Avoid evaluative summarizing words. Instead of "The sink looked disgusting," say, "The sink was rust-stained and looked as though it had not been cleaned in a long time. Pieces of food and dirty dishes looked as though they had been piled in it for several days."
15. Reread notes periodically and record ideas generated by the rereading.
16. Always make one or more backup copies, keep them in a locked location, and store the copies in different places in case of fire, flood, or theft.

---

be taken. The researcher may be able to write, and members may expect it, or he or she may have to be secretive (e.g., go to the restroom).

Jotted notes are written in the field. They are short, temporary memory triggers such as words, phrases, or drawings taken inconspicuously, often scribbled on any convenient item (e.g., napkin, matchbook). They are incorporated into direct observation notes but are never substituted for them.

Direct Observation Notes. The basic source of field data are notes a researcher writes immediately after leaving the field, which he or she can add to later. The notes should be ordered chronologically with the date, time, and place on each entry. They serve as a detailed description of what the researcher heard and saw in concrete, specific terms. To the ex-

tent possible, they are an exact recording of the particular words, phrases, or actions.

Your memory improves with practice, and you can soon remember exact phrases from the field. Verbatim statements should be written with double quote marks to distinguish them from paraphrases. Dialogue accessories (nonverbal communication, props, tone, speed, volume, gestures) should be recorded as well. Record what was actually said and do not clean it up; include ungrammatical speech, slang, and misstatements (e.g., write, "Uh, I'm goin' home, Sal," not "I am going home, Sally").

Put concrete details in notes, not summaries. For example, instead of "We talked about sports," write "Anthony argued with Sam and Jason. He said that the Cubs would win next week because they traded for a new shortstop, Chiappetta. He also said that the team was better than the Mets, who he thought had inferior infielders. He cited last week's game where the Cubs won against Boston by 8 to 3." You should note who was present, what happened,

---

Jotted notes   Field notes inconspicuously written while in the field site on whatever is convenient in order to "jog the memory" later.

where it occurred, when, and under what circumstances. New researchers may not take notes because "nothing important happened." An experienced researcher knows that events when "nothing happened" can reveal a lot. For example, members may express feelings and organize experience into folk categories even in trivial conversations.

Researcher Inference Notes. You should listen to members in order to "climb into their skin" or "walk in their shoes."[39] This involves a three-step process: listen without applying analytical categories; compare what is heard to what was heard at other times and to what others say; then apply your own interpretation to infer or figure out what it means. In ordinary interaction, we do all three steps simultaneously and jump quickly to our own inferences. A field researcher learns to look and listen without inferring or imposing an interpretation. His or her observations without inferences go into **direct observation notes**.

You can record inferences in a separate section that is keyed to direct observations. We never see social relationships, emotions, or meaning. We see specific physical actions and hear words, then use background cultural knowledge, clues from the context, and what is done or said to assign social meaning. For example, we do not see *love* or *anger;* we see and hear specific actions (red face, loud voice, wild gestures, obscenities) and draw inferences from them (the person is angry).

We constantly infer social meaning on the basis of what we see and hear, but not always correctly. For example, my niece visited me and accompanied me to a store to buy a kite. The clerk at the cash register smiled and asked her whether she and her "Daddy" (looking at me) were going to fly the kite that day. The clerk observed our interaction, then inferred a father/daughter, not an uncle/niece relationship. She saw and heard a male adult and a female child, but she inferred the social meaning incorrectly.

You want to keep inferred meaning separate from direct observation because the meaning of actions is not always self-evident. Sometimes, people try to deceive others. For example, an unrelated couple register at a motel as Mr. and Mrs. Smith. More frequently, social behavior is ambiguous or multiple meanings are possible. For example, I see a White male and female, both in their late twenties, get out of a car and enter a restaurant together. They sit at a table, order a meal, and talk with serious expressions in hushed tones, sometimes leaning forward to hear each other. As they get up to leave, the woman, who has a sad facial expression and appears ready to cry, is briefly hugged by the male. They then leave together. Did I witness a couple breaking up, two friends discussing a third, two people trying to decide what to do because they have discovered that their spouses are having an affair with each other, or a brother and sister whose father just died? The **separation of inference** allows multiple meanings to arise on rereading direct observation notes. If you record inferred meaning without separation, you lose other possible meanings.

Analytic Memos. Researchers make many decisions about how to proceed while in the field. Some acts are planned (e.g., to conduct an interview, to observe a particular activity, etc.) and others seem to occur almost out of thin air. Field researchers keep methodological ideas in analytic notes to record their plans, tactics, ethical and procedural decisions, and self-critiques of tactics.

Theory emerges in field research during data collection and when reviewing field notes. Analytic notes have a running account of a researcher's attempts to give meaning to field events. He or she thinks out loud in the notes by suggesting links between ideas, creating hypotheses, proposing conjectures, and developing new concepts.

Analytic memos are part of the theoretical notes. They are systematic digressions into theory, where a researcher elaborates on ideas in depth, expands on ideas while still in the field, and modifies

---

Direct observation notes   Field research notes that attempt to include all details and specifics of what the researcher heard or saw in a field site, and are written to permit multiple interpretations later.

Separation of inference   A field researcher writes direct observation notes in a way that keeps what was observed separate from what was inferred or believed to have occurred.

Analytic memos   Notes a qualitative researcher takes while developing more abstract ideas, themes, or hypotheses from an examination of details in the data.

or develops more complex theory by rereading and thinking about the memos.

Personal Notes. As discussed earlier, personal feelings and emotional reactions become part of the data and color what a researcher sees or hears in the field. A researcher keeps a section of notes that is like a personal diary. He or she records personal life events and feelings in it ("I'm tense today, I wonder if it's because of the fight I had yesterday with . . ."; "I've got a headache on this gloomy, overcast day").

Personal notes provide a way to cope with stress; they are a source of data about personal reactions; they help to evaluate direct observation or inference notes when the notes are later reread. For example, if you were in a good mood during observations, it might color what you observed.

Maps and Diagrams. Field researchers often make maps and draw diagrams or pictures of the features of a field site.[40] This serves two purposes: It helps organize events in the field and it helps convey a field site to others. For example, a researcher observing a bar with 15 stools may draw and number 15 circles to simplify recording (e.g., "Yosuke came in and sat on stool 12; Phoebe was already on stool 10"). Field researchers find three types of maps helpful: spatial, social, and temporal. The first helps orient the data; the latter two are preliminary forms of data analysis. A *spatial map* locates people, equipment, and the like in terms of geographical physical space to show where activities occur (Figure 13.4a). A *social map* shows the number or variety of people and the arrangements among them of power, influence, friendship, division of labor, and so on (Figure 13.4b). A *temporal map* shows the ebb and flow of people, goods, services, and communications, or schedules (Figure 13.4c).

Machine Recordings to Supplement Memory. Tape recorders and videotapes can be helpful supplements in field research. They never substitute

for field notes or a researcher's presence in the field. They cannot be introduced into all field sites and can be used only after a researcher develops rapport. Recorders and videotapes provide a close approximation to what occurred and a permanent record that others can review. They help a researcher recall events and observe what does not happen, or nonresponses, which are easy to miss. Nevertheless, these items create disruption and an increased awareness of surveillance. Researchers who rely on them must address associated problems (e.g., ensure that batteries are fresh and there are enough blank tapes). Also, relistening to or viewing tapes can be time consuming. For example, it may take over 100 hours to listen to 50 hours recorded in the field. Transcriptions of tape are expensive and not always accurate; they do not always convey subtle contextual meanings or mumbled words.[41]

Interview Notes. If a researcher conducts field interviews (to be discussed), he or she keeps the interview notes separate.[42] In addition to recording questions and answers, he or she creates a **face sheet.** This is a page at the beginning of the notes with information such as the date, place of interview, characteristics of interviewee, content of the interview, and so on. It helps the interviewer when rereading and making sense of the notes.

Data Quality

The Meaning of Quality. What does the term *high-quality data* mean in field research, and what does a researcher do to get such data?[43] For a quantitative researcher, high-quality data are reliable and valid; they give precise, consistent measures of the same "objective" truth for all researchers. An interpretive approach suggests a different kind of data quality. Instead of assuming one single, objective truth, field researchers hold that members subjectively interpret experiences within a social context. What a member takes to be true results from social interaction and interpretation. Thus, high-quality field data capture such processes and provide an understanding of the member's viewpoint.

A field researcher does not eliminate subjective views to get quality data; rather, quality data include

---

Face sheet   A page at the beginning of interview or field notes with information on the date, place of observations, interviews, the context, and so on.

a. Spatial Map

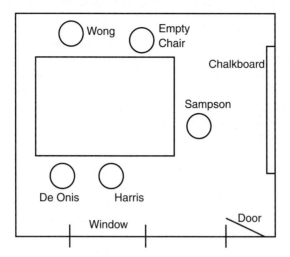

b. Social Map

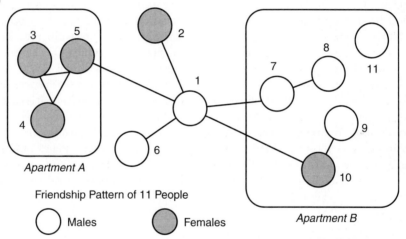

Friendship Pattern of 11 People

○ Males   ● Females

Apartment A

Apartment B

c. Temporal Map

Day of Week, Buzz's Bar

	Mon	Tue	Wed	Thr	Fri	Sat
Open 10:00	Old Drunks	Old Drunks	Old Drunks	Old Drunks	Skip Work or Leave Early	Going to Fish
5:00	Football Watchers	Neighbors and Bridge Players	Softball Team (All-Male Night)	Young Crowd	Loud Music, Mixed Crowd	Loners and No Dates
Close 1:00						

FIGURE 13.4   Types of Maps Used in Field Research

his or her subjective responses and experiences. Quality field data are detailed descriptions from the researcher's immersion and authentic experiences in the social world of members.[44]

Reliability in Field Research. The reliability of field data addresses the question: Are researcher observations about a member or field event internally and externally consistent? **Internal consistency** refers to whether the data are plausible given all that is known about a person or event, eliminating common forms of human deception. In other words, do the pieces fit together into a coherent picture? For example, are a member's actions consistent over time and in different social contexts?

External consistency is achieved by verifying or cross-checking observations with other, divergent sources of data. In other words, does it all fit into the overall context? For example, can others verify what a researcher observed about a person? Does other evidence confirm the researcher's observations?

Reliability in field research also includes what is not said or done, but is expected or anticipated. Such omissions or null data can be significant but are difficult to detect. For example, when observing a cashier end her shift, you notice that the money in a drawer is not counted. You may notice the omission only if other cashiers always count money at the end of the shift (see the discussion of negative case method in Chapter 15).

Reliability in field research depends on your insight, awareness, suspicions, and questions. You look at members and events from different angles (legal, economic, political, personal) and mentally ask questions: Where does the money come from for that? What do those people do all day?

Internal consistency A way to achieve data reliability in field research in which a researcher examines the plausibility of data to see whether they form a coherent whole, fit all else that is known about a person or event, and avoid common forms of deception.

External consistency A way to achieve reliability of data in field research in which the researcher cross-checks and verifies qualitative data using multiple sources of information.

You depend on what members tell you. This makes the credibility of members and their statements part of reliability. To check member credibility, you must ask: Does the person have a reason to lie? Is she in a position to know that? What are the person's values and how might that shape what she says? Is he just saying that to please me? Is there anything that might limit his spontaneity?

Take subjectivity and context into account as you evaluate credibility. A person's statements or actions are affected by subjective perceptions. Statements are made from a particular point of view and colored by an individual's experiences. Instead of evaluating each statement to see whether it is true, you may find statements useful in themselves. Even inaccurate statements and actions can be revealing.

As mentioned before, actions and statements are shaped by the context in which they appear. What is said in one setting may differ in other contexts. For example, when asked, "Do you dance?" a member may say no in a public setting full of excellent dancers, but yes in a semiprivate setting with few dancers and different music. It is not that the member is lying but that the answer is shaped by the context.

Other obstacles to reliability include behaviors that can mislead a researcher: misinformation, evasions, lies, and fronts.[45] *Misinformation* is an unintended falsehood caused by the uncertainty and complexity of life. For example, nurses in a hospital state something as "official hospital policy" when, in fact, there is no such written policy.

Evasions are intentional acts of not revealing information. Common evasions include not answering questions, answering a different question than was asked, switching topics, or answering in a purposefully vague and ambiguous manner. For example, a salesman appears uncomfortable when the topic of using call girls to get customers comes up at a dinner party. He says, "Yes, a lot of people use them." But later, alone, after careful questioning, the salesman is drawn out and reveals that he himself uses the practice.

Lies are untruths intended to mislead or to give a false view. For example, a gang member gives the researcher a false name and address, or a church minister gives an inflated membership figure in order to look more successful. Douglas (1976:73) noted, "In all other research settings I've known about in any detail, lying was common, both among members and to researchers, especially about the things that were really important to the members."

Fronts are shared and learned lies and deceptions. They can include the use of physical props and collaborators. For example, a bar is really a place to make illegal bets. The bar appears legitimate and sells drinks, but its true business is revealed only by careful investigation. Fronts are not always malicious. A common example is that of Santa Claus—a "front" put on for small children.

Validity in Field Research. Validity in field research comes from a researcher's analysis and data as accurate representations of the social world in the field. Replicability is not a criterion because field research is virtually impossible to replicate. Essential aspects of the field change: The social events and context change, the members are different, the individual researcher differs, and so on. There are four kinds of validity or tests of research accuracy: ecological validity, natural history, member validation, and competent insider performance.

Ecological validity is the degree to which the social world described by a researcher matches the world of members. It asks: Is the natural setting described relatively undisturbed by the researcher's presence or procedures? A study has ecological validity if events would have occurred without a researcher's presence.

Natural history is a detailed description of how the project was conducted. It is a full and candid disclosure of a researcher's actions, assumptions, and procedures for others to evaluate. A study is valid in terms of natural history if outsiders see and accept the field site and the researcher's actions.

Member validation occurs when a researcher takes field results back to members, who judge their adequacy. A study is member valid if members recognize and understand the researcher's description as reflecting their intimate social world. Member validation has limitations because conflicting perspectives in a setting produce disagreement with researcher's observations, and members may object when results do not portray their group in a favor-

able light. In addition, members may not recognize the description because it is not from their perspective or does not fit with their purposes.[46]

Competent insider performance is the ability of a nonmember to interact effectively as a member or pass as one. This includes the ability to tell and understand insider jokes. A valid study gives enough of a flavor of the social life in the field and sufficient detail so that an outsider can act as a member. Its limitation is that it is not possible to know the social rules for every situation. Also, an outsider might be able to pass simply because members are being polite and do not want to point out social mistakes.[47]

Focusing and Sampling

Focusing. The field researcher first gets a general picture, then focuses on a few specific problems or issues (see Figure 13.5).[48] A researcher decides on specific research questions and develops hypotheses only after being in the field and experiencing it firsthand. At first, everything may be relevant; later, however, he or she selectively focuses attention on specific questions and themes.

Fronts   When one or more people in a field site engage in actions and say things that give an impression or appearance that differs from what is actually occurring.

Ecological validity   Demonstrating the authenticity and trustworthiness of a study by showing that the researcher's descriptions of the field site match those of the members and that the field researcher's presence was not a disturbance.

Natural history   A method field researchers use to demonstrate the authenticity and trustworthiness of a study by fully disclosing actions and procedures in depth as they occurred over time.

Member validation   A method field researchers use to demonstrate the authenticity and trustworthiness of a study by having the people who were studied read and confirm as being true that which the researchers have reported.

Competent insider performance   A method field researchers use to demonstrate the authenticity and trustworthiness of a study by the researcher "passing" as a member of the group under study.

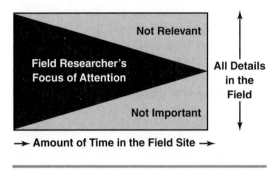

FIGURE 13.5   **Focusing in Field Research**

Sampling. Field research sampling differs from survey research sampling, although sometimes both use snowball sampling (see Chapter 8).[49] A field researcher uses *theoretical sampling* guided by developing theory. Field researchers sample times, situations, types of events, locations, types of people, or contexts of interest.

For example, a researcher samples time by observing a setting at different times. He or she observes at all times of the day, on every day of the week, and in all seasons to get a full sense of how the field site stays the same or changes. It is often best to overlap when sampling (e.g., to have sampling times from 7:00 A.M. to 9:00 A.M., from 8:00 A.M. to 10:00 A.M., from 9:00 A.M. to 11:00 A.M., etc.).

A researcher samples locations because one location may give depth, but a narrow perspective. Sitting or standing in different locations helps the researcher get a sense of the whole site. For example, the peer-to-peer behavior of schoolteachers usually occurs in a faculty lounge, but it also occurs at a local bar or cafe when teachers gather or in a classroom temporarily used for a teacher meeting. In addition, researchers trace the paths of members to various field locations.

Field researchers sample people by focusing their attention or interaction on different kinds of people (old-timers and newcomers, old and young, males and females, leaders and followers). As a researcher identifies types of people, or people with opposing outlooks, he or she tries to interact with and learn about all types.

For example, you might sample three kinds of field events: routine, special, and unanticipated.

Routine events (e.g., opening up a store for business) happen every day and should not be considered unimportant simply because they are routine. Special events (e.g., annual office party) are announced and planned in advance. They focus member attention and reveal aspects of social life not otherwise visible. Unanticipated events are those that just happen to occur while a researcher is present (e.g., unsupervised workers when the manager gets sick and cannot oversee workers at a store for a day). In this case, you see something unusual, unplanned, or rare by chance.

THE FIELD RESEARCH INTERVIEW

So far, you have learned how field researchers observe and take notes. They also interview members, but field interviews differ from survey research interviews. This section introduces the field interview.

The Field Interview

Field researchers use unstructured, nondirective, indepth interviews, which differ from formal survey research interviews in many ways (see Table 13.1).[50] The field interview involves asking questions, listening, expressing interest, and recording what was said.

The field interview is a joint production of a researcher and a member. Members are active participants whose insights, feelings, and cooperation are essential parts of a discussion process that reveals subjective meanings. "The interviewer's presence and form of involvement—how she or he listens, attends, encourages, interrupts, digresses, initiates topics, and terminates responses—is integral to the respondent's account" (Mishler, 1986:82).

Field research interviews go by many names: unstructured, depth, ethnographic, open ended, informal, and long. Generally, they involve one or more people being present, occur in the field, and are informal and nondirective (i.e., the respondent may take the interview in various directions).[51]

A field interview involves a mutual sharing of experiences. You might share your background to build trust and encourage the informant to open up, but do not force answers or use leading questions.

TABLE 13.1   Survey Interviews versus Field Research Interviews

TYPICAL SURVEY INTERVIEW	TYPICAL FIELD INTERVIEW
1 It has a clear beginning and end.	1. The beginning and end are not clear. The interview can be picked up later.
2. The same standard questions are asked of all respondents in the same sequence.	2. The questions and the order in which they are asked are tailored to specific people and situations.
3. The interviewer appears neutral at all times.	3. The interviewer shows interest in responses, encourages elaboration.
4. The interviewer asks questions, and the respondent answers.	4. It is like a friendly conversational exchange, but with more interviewer questions.
5. It is almost always with one respondent alone.	5. It can occur in group setting or with others in area, but varies.
6. It has a professional tone and businesslike focus; diversions are ignored.	6. It is interspersed with jokes, asides, stories, diversions, and anecdotes, which are recorded.
7 Closed-ended questions are common, with infrequent probes.	7. Open-ended questions are common, and probes are frequent.
8. The interviewer alone controls the pace and direction of the interview.	8. The interviewer and member jointly control the pace and direction of the interview.
9. The social context in which the interview occurs is ignored and assumed to make little difference.	9. The social context of the interview is noted and seen as important for interpreting the meaning of responses.
10. The interviewer attempts to mold the communication pattern into a standard framework.	10. The interviewer adjusts to the member's norms and language usage.

Sources: Adapted from Briggs (1986), Denzin (1989), Douglas (1985), Mishler (1986), Spradley (1979a).

You want to encourage and guide a process of mutual discovery.

In field interviews, members express themselves in the forms in which they normally speak, think, and organize reality. You want to retain members' jokes and narrative stories in their natural form and do not repackage them into a standardized format. Focus on the member's perspective and experiences. In order to stay close to the member's experience, ask questions in terms of concrete examples or situations—for example, "Could you tell me things that led up to your quitting in June?" instead of "Why did you quit your job?"

Field interviews occur in a series over time. Begin by building rapport and steering conversation away from evaluative or highly sensitive topics. Avoid probing inner feelings until intimacy is es-

tablished, and even then, expect apprehension. After several meetings, you may be able to probe more deeply into sensitive issues and seek clarification of less sensitive issues. In later interviews, you may return to topics and check past answers by restating them in a nonjudgmental tone and asking for verification—for example, "The last time we talked, you said that you started taking things from the store after they reduced your pay. Is that right?"

The field interview is a "speech event," closer to a friendly conversation than the stimulus/response model found in a survey research interview (see Chapter 10). You are familiar with a friendly conversation, which has its own informal rules and the following elements: (1) a greeting ("Hi, it's good to see you again"); (2) the absence of an explicit goal or purpose (we don't say, "Let's now discuss what we did last weekend"); (3) avoidance of explicit repetition (we don't say, "Could you clarify what you said about . . ."); (4) question asking ("Did you see the race yesterday?"); (5) expressions of interest ("Really? I wish I could have been there!"); (6) expressions of ignorance ("No, I missed it. What happened?"); (7) turn taking, so the encounter is balanced (one person does not always ask questions and the other only answer); (8) abbreviations ("I missed the Derby, but I'm going to the Indy," not "I missed the Kentucky Derby horse race but I will go to the Indianapolis 500 automotive race"); (9) a pause or brief silence when neither person talks is acceptable; (10) a closing (we don't say, "Let's end this conversation"; instead, we give a verbal indicator before physically leaving—"I've got to get back to work now. See ya tomorrow.").

The field interview differs from a friendly conversation. It has an explicit purpose—to learn about the informant and setting. A researcher includes explanations or requests that diverge from friendly conversations. For example, he or she may say, "I'd like to ask you about . . . ," or "Could you look at this and see if I've written it down right?" The field interview is less balanced. A higher proportion of questions come from the researcher, who expresses more ignorance and interest. Also, it includes repetition, and a researcher asks the member to elaborate on unclear abbreviations.[52]

Field research interviewers watch for markers. A **marker** in a field interview is "a passing reference made by a respondent to an important event or feeling state" (Weiss, 1994:77). For example, during an interview with a 45-year-old physician, the interviewee mentions casually, while describing having difficulty in a high school class, "It was about that time that my sister was seriously injured in a car accident." Maybe the person never said anything about the sister or the accident before. By

dropping it in, the respondent is indicating it was an important event at the time. A researcher should pick up on a marker and later may ask, "Earlier, you mentioned that your sister was seriously injured in a car accident. Could you tell me more about that?" Most importantly, the interviewer listens. He or she does not interrupt frequently, repeatedly finish the respondent's sentences, offer associations (e.g., "Oh, that is just like X"), insist on finishing asking a question that the respondent has begun to answer, fight for control over the interview process, or stay fixed with a line of thought and ignore new leads.[53]

Life History

Life history, life story, or a biographical interview is a special type of field interviewing. It overlaps with oral history (see Chapter 14).[54] There are multiple purposes for stories of the past and these may shape the forms of interview. In a **life history interview,** researchers interview and gather documentary material about a particular individual's life, usually someone who is old. "The concept of *life story* is used to designate the retrospective information itself without the corroborative evidence often implied by the term *life history*" (Tagg, 1985:163). Researchers ask open-ended questions to capture how the person understands his or her own past. Exact accuracy in the story is less critical than the story itself. Researchers recognize that the person may reconstruct or add present interpretations to the past; the person may "rewrite" his or her story. The main purpose is to get at how the respondent sees/remembers the past, not just some kind of objective truth (see Box 13.6).

Researchers sometimes use a life story grid in which they ask the person what happened at various dates and in several areas of life. A grid may consist of categories such as migration, occupation, education, or family events for each of ten different ages in the person's life. Researchers often supplement the interview information with artifacts (e.g., old photos) and may present them during the interview to stimulate discussion or recollection. "Life writing as an empirical exercise feeds on data: letters, documents, interviews" (Smith, 1994:290). McCracken (1988:20) gave an example of how

Marker   A passing reference by a person in a field site that actually indicates a very important event or feeling.

Life history interview   Open-ended interview with one person who describes his or her entire life. It can be considered a subtype of oral history.

BOX **13.6** The Life History or Life Story Interview

Life history or life story interviews usually involve two to ten open-ended interviews, usually recorded, of 60 to 90 minutes. These interviews serve several purposes. First, they can assist the informant being interviewed in reconstructing his or her life memories. Retelling and remembering one's life events as a narrative story can have therapeutic benefits and pass on personal wisdom to a new generation. Second, these interviews can create new qualitative data on the life cycle, the development of self, and how people experience events that can be archived and added to similar data (e.g., The Center for Life Stories at University of Southern Maine is such an archive). Third, life story interviews can provide the interviewer with an in-depth look at another's life. This is often an enriching experience that creates a close personal relationship and encourages self-reflection in ways that enhance personal integrity. Steps in the process are as follows:

1. The researcher prepares with background reading, refines his or her interview skills, contacts the informant, gets permission for the interview, and promises anonymity.
2. The researcher conducts a series of interviews, audio- or video-recording them. The interviewer suspends

any prior history with an informant and gives his or her total respect, always showing sincere interest in what another says. He or she asks open-ended questions, but is flexible and never forces a question. The interviewer acts as a guide, knowing when to ask a question that will open up stories; gives intense attentiveness, and is completely nonjudgmental and supportive. Often, the interviewer offers photographs or objects to help spark memories and past feelings.

3. The researcher transcribes the recorded interviews in four stages: (a) prepares a summary of each tape; (b) makes a verbatim transcription, with minor editing (e.g., adds sentences, paragraphs, etc.) and stage directions (e.g., laughter, coughing, etc.); (c) reviews the whole transcript for clarity of meaning and does further editing and minor rearranging; and (d) has the informant review the transcript for any corrections and modifications.
4. The researcher sends a note of appreciation to the informant and prepares a commentary on major themes and/or sends it to an archive.

Source: Adapted from Atkinson, 1998.

objects aided the interview by helping him understand how the person being interviewed saw things. When interviewing a 75-year-old woman in her living room, McCracken initially thought the room just contained a lot of cluttered physical objects. After having the woman explain the meaning of each item, it was clear that she saw each as a memorial or a memento. The room was a museum to key events in her life. Only after the author looked at the objects in this new way did he begin to see the furniture and objects not as inanimate things but as objects that radiated meaning.

Sometimes, researchers find an existing archive with a person; other times, they search out the documents and create an archive. Locating such documentary data can be a tremendous task, followed by reviewing, cataloging, and organizing the information. The interview and documentary data together form the basis of the life story.

Types of Questions in Field Interviews

Field researchers ask three types of questions in a field interview: descriptive, structural, and contrast questions. All are asked concurrently, but each type is more frequent at a different stage in the research process (see Figure 13.6). During the early stage, ask descriptive questions and gradually add structural questions until, in the middle stage after analysis has begun, they make up a majority of the questions. Ask contrast questions in the middle of a study and increase them until, by the end, you ask them more than any other type.[55]

A researcher asks a *descriptive question* to explore the setting and learn about members. Descriptive questions can be about time and space—for example, "Where is the bathroom?" "When does the delivery truck arrive?" "What happened Monday night?" They can also be about

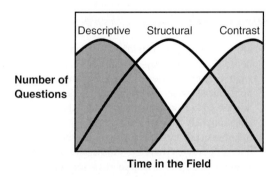

Number of Questions / Time in the Field

FIGURE 13.6 Types of Questions in Field Research Interviews

people and activities: "Who is sitting by the window?" "What is your uncle like?" "What happens during the initiation ceremony?" They can be about objects: "When do you use a saber saw?" "Which tools do you carry with you on an emergency water leak job?" Questions asking for examples or experiences are descriptive questions—for example, "Could you give me an example of a great date?" "What were your experiences as a postal clerk?" Descriptive questions may ask about hypothetical situations: "If a student opened her book during the exam, how would you deal with it?" Another type of descriptive question asks members about the argot of the setting: "What do you call a deputy sheriff?" (The answer is a "county Mountie.")

A researcher uses a *structural question* after spending time in the field and starting to analyze data, especially with a domain analysis (to be discussed in Chapter 15). It begins after a researcher organizes specific field events, situations, and conversations into categories. For example, a researcher's observations of a highway truck-stop restaurant revealed that the employees informally classify customers who patronize the truck stop. In a preliminary analysis, he or she creates a conceptual category of kinds of customers and has members verify the categories with structural questions.

One way to pose a structural question is to ask the members whether a category includes elements

in addition to those already identified by a researcher—for example, "Are there any types of customers other than regulars, greasers, pit stoppers, and long haulers?" In addition, a researcher asks for confirmation: "Is a greaser a type of customer that you serve?" "Would you call a customer who . . . a greaser?" "Would a pit stopper ever eat a three-course dinner?"

The *contrast question* builds on the analysis that has been verified by structural questions. Questions focus on similarities or differences between elements in categories or between categories as the researcher asks members to verify similarities and differences: "You seem to have a number of different kinds of customers come in here. I've heard you call some customers 'regulars' and others 'pit stoppers.' How are a regular and a pit stopper alike?" or "Is the difference between a long hauler and a greaser that the greaser doesn't tip?" or "Two types of customers just stop to use the restroom—entire families and a lone male. Do you call both pit stoppers?"

Informants

An informant or key actor in field research is a member with whom a field researcher develops a relationship and who tells about, or informs on, the field.[56] Who makes a good informant? The ideal informant has four characteristics (see Box 13.7).

You may interview several types of informants. Contrasting types of informants who provide useful perspectives include rookies and old-timers, people in the center of events and those on the fringes of activity, people who recently changed status (e.g., through promotion) and those who are static, frustrated or needy people and happy or secure people, the leader in charge and the subordinate who follows. Expect mixed and inconsistent messages when you interview a range of informants.

Interview Context

Field researchers recognize that a conversation in a private office may not occur in a crowded lunch-

1. The informant who is totally familiar with the culture and is in position to witness significant events makes a good informant. He or she lives and breathes the culture and engages in routines in the setting without thinking about them. The individual has years of intimate experience in the culture; he or she is not a novice.
2. The individual is currently involved in the field. Ex-members who have reflected on the field may provide useful insights, but the longer they have been away from direct involvement, the more likely it is that they have reconstructed their recollections.
3. The person can spend time with the researcher. Interviewing may take many hours, and some members are simply not available for extensive interviewing.
4. Nonanalytic individuals make better informants. A nonanalytic informant is familiar with and uses native folk theory or pragmatic common sense. This is in contrast to the analytic member, who preanalyzes the setting, using categories from the media or education. Even members educated in the social sciences can learn to respond in a nonanalytic manner, but only if they set aside their education and use the member perspective.

room.[57] Often, interviews take place in the member's home environment so that he or she is comfortable. This is not always best. If a member is preoccupied or there is no privacy, a researcher will move to another setting (e.g., restaurant or university office).

The interview's meaning is shaped by its Gestalt or whole interaction of a researcher and a member in a specific context. Also, a researcher notes nonverbal forms of communication (e.g., shrugs, gestures, etc.) that add meaning.

LEAVING THE FIELD

Work in the field can last for a few weeks to a dozen years.[58] In either case, at some point work in the field ends. Some researchers suggest that the end comes naturally when theory building ceases or reaches a closure; others feel that fieldwork could go on without end and that a firm decision to cut off relations is needed.

Experienced field researchers anticipate a process of disengaging and exiting the field. Depending on the intensity of involvement and the length of time in the field, the process can be disruptive or emotionally painful for both the researcher and the members. A researcher may experience the emotional pain of breaking intimate friendships when leaving the field. He or she may feel guilty and depressed immediately before and after leaving. He or she may find it difficult to let go because of personal and emotional entanglements. If the involvement in the field was intense and long, and the field site differed from his or her native culture, the researcher may need months of adjustment before feeling at home with his or her original cultural surroundings.

Once you decide to leave—because the project reaches a natural end and little new is being learned, or because external factors force it to end (e.g., end of a job, gatekeepers order the researcher out, etc.)—choose a method of exiting. You can leave by a quick exit (simply not return one day) or slowly withdraw, reducing involvement over weeks. You also need to decide how to tell members and how much advance warning to give.

The exit process depends on the specific field setting and the relationships developed. In general, let members know a short period ahead of time. You should fulfill any bargains or commitments that were built up and leave with a clean slate. Sometimes, a ritual or ceremony, such as a going-away party or shaking hands with everyone, helps signal the break for members. Maintaining friendships with members after exiting is also advocated and is preferred by feminist researchers.

Leaving affects members. Some may feel hurt or rejected because a close social relationship is ending. They may react by trying to pull you back into the field and make you more of a member, or they may become angry and resentful. They may grow cool and distant because of an awareness that the you really are an outsider. In any case, fieldwork is not finished until the process of disengagement and exiting is complete.

Focus Groups

The focus group is a special qualitative research technique in which people are informally "interviewed" in a group-discussion setting.[59] Focus group research has rapidly grown in the past 20 years. The procedure is that a researcher gathers together 6 to 12 people in a room with a moderator to discuss a few issues. Most focus groups last about 90 minutes. The moderator is trained to be nondirective and to facilitate free, open discussion by all group members (i.e., not let one person dominate the discussion). Group members should be homogenous, but not include close friends or relatives. In a typical study, a researcher uses four to six separate groups. Focus group topics might include public attitudes (e.g., race relations, workplace equality), personal behaviors (e.g., dealing with AIDS), a new product (e.g., breakfast cereal), or a political candidate. Researchers often combine focus groups with quantitative research, and the procedure has its own specific strengths and weaknesses (see Box 13.8).

Several years ago, I conducted an applied study on why parents and students chose to attend a private high school. In addition to collecting quantitative survey data, I formed six focus groups, each with 8 to 10 students from the high school. A trained college-student moderator asked questions, elicited comments from group members, and prevented one person from dominating discussions. The six groups were co-ed and contained members of either one grade level or two adjacent grades (e.g., freshmen and sophomores). Students discussed their reasons for attending the high school and whether specific factors were important. I tape-recorded the discussions, which lasted about 45 minutes, then analyzed the tapes to understand what the students saw as important to their decisions. In addition, the data helped when interpreting the survey data.

BOX **13.8** **Advantages and Limitations of Focus Groups**

ADVANTAGES

- The natural setting allows people to express opinions/ideas freely.
- Open expression among members of marginalized social groups is encouraged.
- People tend to feel empowered, especially in action-oriented research projects.
- Survey researchers are provided a window into how people talk about survey topics.
- The interpretation of quantitative survey results is facilitated.
- Participants may query one another and explain their answers to each others.

LIMITATIONS

- A "polarization effect" exists (attitudes become more extreme after group discussion).
- Only one or a few topics can be discussed in a focus group session.
- A moderator may unknowingly limit open, free expression of group members.
- Focus group participants produce fewer ideas than in individual interviews.
- Focus group studies rarely report all the details of study design/procedure.
- Researchers cannot reconcile the differences that arise between individual-only and focus group–context responses.

ETHICAL DILEMMAS OF FIELD RESEARCH

The direct personal involvement of a field researcher in the social lives of other people raises many ethical dilemmas. The dilemmas arise when a researcher is alone in the field and has little time to make a moral decision. Although he or she may be aware of general ethical issues before entering the field, they arise unexpectedly in the course of observing and interacting in the field. We will look at five ethical issues in field research: deception, confidentiality, involvement with deviants, the powerful, and publishing reports.[60]

Deception

The most hotly debated of the ethical issues arising from deception is that of covert versus overt field research.[61] Deception arises in several ways in field research: The research may be covert; or may assume a false role, name, or identity; or may mislead members in some way. Some support it and see it as necessary for entering into and gaining a full knowledge of many areas of social life. Others oppose it and argue that it undermines a trust between researchers and society.[62] Although its moral status is questionable, there are some field sites or activities that can only be studied covertly (see Chapter 15).

Covert research is never preferable and never easier than overt research because of the difficulties of maintaining a front and the constant fear of getting caught. As Lofland and Lofland (1995:35) noted, "As in all other ethical dilemmas of naturalistic research, we believe that the ethically sensitive, thoughtful and knowledgeable investigator is the best judge of whether covert research is justified."

Confidentiality

A researcher learns intimate knowledge that is given in confidence. He or she has a moral obligation to uphold the confidentiality of data. This includes keeping information confidential from others in the field and disguising members' names in field notes. Sometimes a field researcher cannot directly quote a person in a research report. One strategy is instead of reporting the source as an informant, the researcher can find documentary evidence that says the same thing and use the document (e.g., an old memo, a newspaper article, etc.) as the source of the information.

Involvement with Deviants

Researchers who conduct field research on people who engage in illegal, immoral, or unethical behavior face additional dilemmas. They know of and are sometimes involved in illegal activity. Fetter-

man (1989) called this **guilty knowledge.** Such knowledge is of interest not only to law enforcement officials but also to other field site members. The researcher faces a dilemma of building trust and rapport with the members, yet not becoming so involved as to violate his or her basic personal moral standards. Usually, the researcher makes an explicit arrangement with the deviant members.

The Powerful

Many field researchers study those without power in society (e.g., street people, the poor, children, and lower-level workers in bureaucracies). Powerful elites can easily block access and have effective gatekeepers. Researchers are criticized for ignoring the powerful. At the same time, they are criticized by the powerful for being biased in favor of the less powerful. Becker (1970c) explained this by the **hierarchy of credibility,** which says that those who study the powerless criminals or low-level subordinates in an organization are viewed as biased, whereas those with authority are assumed to be credible. Most people assume that those at or near the top of organizations have the right to define the way things are going to be, that they have a broader view and are in a position to do something. Thus, "the sociologist who favors officialdom will be spared the accusation of bias" (Becker, 1970c:20). When field researchers become immersed in the world of the less powerful and understand that point of view, they are expressing a rarely heard perspective. They may be accused of bias because they give a voice to parts of society that are not otherwise heard.

Guilty knowledge   When a researcher learns of illegal, unethical, or immoral actions by the people in the field site that are not widely known.

Hierarchy of credibility   Situations in which a researcher who learns much about weaker members of society whose views are rarely heard is accused of "bias" while the views of powerful people are accepted as "unbiased" based on their high social status.

Publishing Field Reports

The intimate knowledge you obtain and report creates a dilemma between the right of privacy and the right to know. You cannot publicize member secrets, violate privacy, or harm reputations. Yet, if you cannot publish anything that might offend or harm someone, what you learned will remain hidden, and it may be difficult for others to believe the report if critical details are omitted.

Some researchers suggest asking members to look at a report to verify its accuracy and to approve of their portrayal in print. For marginal groups (e.g., addicts, prostitutes, crack users), this may not be possible, but researchers must always respect member privacy. On the other hand, censorship or self-censorship can be a danger. A compromise position is that truthful but unflattering material may be published only if it is essential to the researchers' larger arguments.[63]

CONCLUSION

In this chapter, you learned about field research and the field research process (choosing a site and gaining access, relations in the field, observing and collecting data, and the field interview). Field researchers begin data analysis and theorizing during the data collection phase.

You can now appreciate implications of saying that in field research, the researcher is directly involved with those being studied and is immersed in a natural setting. Doing field research usually has a greater impact on the researcher's emotions, personal life, and sense of self than doing other types of research. Field research is difficult to conduct, but it is a way to study parts of the social world that otherwise could not be studied.

Good field research requires a combination of skills. In addition to a strong sense of self, the best field researchers possess an incredible ability to listen and absorb details, tremendous patience, sensitivity and empathy for others, superb social skills, a talent to think very quickly "on one's feet," the ability to see subtle interconnections among people/events, and a superior ability to express oneself in writing.

Field research is strongest when a researcher studies a small group of people interacting in the present. It is valuable for micro-level or small-group face-to-face interaction. It is less effective when the concern is macro-level processes and social structures. It is nearly useless for events that occurred in the distant past or processes that stretch across decades. Historical-comparative research, discussed in the next chapter, is better suited to investigating these types of concerns.

KEY TERMS

acceptable incompetent
access ladder
analytic memos
appearance of interest
argot
attitude of strangeness
breaching experiment
competent insider performance
defocusing
direct observation notes
ecological validity
ethnography

ethnomethodology
external consistency
face sheet
field site
focus group
freeze outs
fronts
gatekeeper
go native
guilty knowledge
hierarchy of credibility
internal consistency

jotted notes
life history interview
marker
member validation
natural history
naturalism
normalize social research
separation of inference
social breakdown
thick description

REVIEW QUESTIONS

1. What were the two major phases in the development of the Chicago school, and what are the journalistic and anthropological models?

2. List 5 of the 10 things the "methodological pragmatist" field researcher does.

3. Why is it important for a field researcher to read the literature before beginning fieldwork? How does this relate to defocusing?

4. Identify the characteristics of a field site that make it a good one for a beginning field researcher.

5. How does the "presentation of self" affect a field researcher's work?

6. What is the attitude of strangeness, and why is it important?

7. What are relevant considerations when choosing roles in the field, and how can the degree of researcher involvement vary?

8. Identify three ways to ensure quality field research data.

9. Compare differences between a field research and a survey research interview, and between a field interview and a friendly conversation.

10. What are the different types or levels of field notes, and what purpose does each serve?

NOTES

1. See Lofland and Lofland (1995:6,18–19).

2. For studies of these sites or topics, see Neuman (2000:345–346). On studies of children or schools, see Corsaro (1994), Corsaro and Molinari (2000), Eder (1995), Eder and Kinney (1995), Kelle (2000), and Merten (1999). On studies of homeless people, see Lankenau (1999), and on studies of female strippers, see Wood (2000).

3. For a background in the history of field research, see Adler and Adler (1987:8–35), Burgess (1982a), Douglas (1976:39–54), Holy (1984), and Wax (1971:21–41). On the Chicago school, see Blumer (1984) and Faris (1967).

4. Ethnography is described in Agar (1986), Franke (1983), Hammersley and Atkinson (1983), Sanday (1983), and Spradley (1979a:3–12; 1979b:3–16).

5. See Geertz (1973, 1979) on "thick description." Also see Denzin (1989:159–160) for additional discussion.

6. For more on ethnomethodology, see Cicourel (1964), Denzin (1970), Leiter (1980), Mehan and Wood (1975), and Turner (1974). Also see Emerson (1981:357–359) and Lester and Hadden (1980) on the relationship between field research and ethnomethodology. Garfinkel (1974a) discussed the origins of the term *ethnomethodology*.

7. The misunderstandings of people resulting from the disjuncture of different cultures is a common theme.

8. For a general discussion of field research and naturalism, see Adler and Adler (1994), Georges and Jones (1980), Holy (1984), and Pearsall (1970). For discussions of contrasting types of field research, see Clammer (1984), Gonor (1977), Holstein and Gubrium (1994), Morse (1994), Schwandt (1994), and Strauss and Corbin (1994).

9. See Georges and Jones (1980:21–42) and Lofland and Lofland (1995:11–15).

10. Johnson (1975:65–66) has discussed defocusing.

11. See Lofland (1976:13–23) and Shaffir and colleagues (1980:18–20) on feeling marginal.

12. See Adler and Adler (1987:67–78).

13. See Hammersley and Atkinson (1983:42–45) and Lofland and Lofland (1995:16–30).

14. Jewish researchers have studied Christians (Kleinman, 1980), Whites have studied African Americans (Liebow, 1967), and adult researchers have become intimate with youngsters (Fine, 1987; Fine and Glassner, 1979; Thorne and Luria, 1986). Also see Eichler (1988), Hunt (1989), and Wax (1979) on the role of race, sex, and age in field research.

15. See Douglas and Rasmussen (1977) and Yancey and Rainwater (1970).

16. Roy (1970) argued for the "Ernie Pyle" role based on his study of union organizing in the southern United

States. In this role, named after a World War II battle journalist, the researcher "goes with the troops" as a type of participant as observer. Trice (1970) discussed the advantages of an outsider role. Schwartz and Schwartz (1969) discussed various roles.

17. For more on gatekeepers and access, see Beck (1970:11–29), Bogdan and Taylor (1975:30–32), and Wax (1971:367).

18. Adapted from Gray (1980:311). See also Hicks (1984) and Schatzman and Strauss (1973:58–63).

19. Negotiation in the field is discussed in Gans (1982), Johnson (1975:58–59, 76–77), and Schatzman and Strauss (1973:22–23).

20. On entering and gaining access to field sites with deviant groups, see Becker (1970a:31–38), Hammersley and Atkinson (1983:54–76), Lofland and Lofland (1995:31–41), and West (1980). Elite access is discussed by Hoffman (1980).

21. See Lofland and Lofland (1995:12).

22. For more on roles in field settings, see Barnes (1970:241–244), Emerson (1981:364), Hammersley and Atkinson (1983:88–104), Warren and Rasmussen (1977), and Wax (1979). On dress, see Bogdan and Taylor (1975:45) and Douglas (1976).

23. See Strauss (1987:10–11).

24. See Georges and Jones (1980:105–133) and Johnson (1975:159). Clarke (1975) noted that it is not necessarily "subjectivism" to recognize this in field research.

25. See Gurevitch (1988), Hammersley and Atkinson (1983), and Schatzman and Strauss (1973:53) on "strangeness" in field research.

26. See Douglas (1976), Emerson (1981:367–368), and Johnson (1975:124–129) on being patient, polite, and considerate.

27. See Wax (1971:13).

28. For discussions of ascribed status (and, in particular, gender) in field research, see Adler and Adler (1987), Ardener (1984), Ayella (1993), Denzin (1989:116–118), Douglas (1976), Easterday and associates (1982), Edwards (1993), Lofland and Lofland (1995:23), and Van Maanen (1982).

29. See Gans (1982), Goward (1984b), and Van Maanen (1983b:282–286).

30. See Douglas (1976:216) and Corsino (1987).

31. For discussion of "normalizing," see Gans (1982: 57–59), Georges and Jones (1980:43–164), Hammersley and Atkinson (1983:70–76), Harkens and Warren (1993), Johnson (1975), and Wax (1971). Mann (1970) discussed how to teach members about a researcher's role.

32. The acceptable incompetent or learner role is discussed in Bogdan and Taylor (1975:46), Douglas (1976), Hammersley and Atkinson (1983:92–94), Lofland and Lofland (1995:56), and Schatman and Strauss (1973:25).

33. See Warren and Rasmussen (1977) for a discussion of cross-sex tension.

34. Also see Adler and Adler (1987:40–42), Bogdan and Taylor (1975:35–37), Douglas (1976), and Gray (1980:321).

35. See Bogdan and Taylor (1975:50–51), Lofland and Lofland (1995:57–58), Shupe and Bromley (1980), and Wax (1971).

36. See Johnson (1975:105–108).

37. See Becker and Geer (1970), Spradley (1979a, 1979b), and Schatzman and Strauss (1973) on argot.

38. For more on recording and organizing data, see Bogdan and Taylor (1975:60–73), Hammersley and Atkinson (1983:144–173), and Kirk and Miller (1986:49–59).

39. See Schatzman and Strauss (1973:69) on inference.

40. See Denzin (1989:87), Lofland and Lofland (1995: 197–201), Schatzman and Strauss (1973:34–36), and Stimson (1986) on maps in field research.

41. See Albrecht (1985), Bogdan and Taylor (1975:109), Denzin (1989:210–233), and Jackson (1987) for more on taping in field research.

42. See Burgess (1982b), Lofland and Lofland (1995: 89–98), and Spradley (1979a, 1979b) on notes for field interviews.

43. For additional discussion of data quality, see Becker (1970b), Dean and Whyte (1969), Douglas (1976:7), Kirk and Miller (1986), and McCall (1969).

44. Douglas (1976:115) argued that it is easier to "lie" with "hard numbers" than with detailed observations of natural settings.

45. Adapted from Douglas (1976:56–104).

46. See Bloor (1983) and Douglas (1976:126).

47. For more on validity in field research, see Briggs (1986:24), Bogdan and Taylor (1975), Douglas (1976), Emerson (1981:361–363), and Sanjek (1990).

48. See Lofland (1976) and Lofland and Lofland (1995:99–116) on focusing. Spradley (1979b:100–111) also provides helpful discussion.

49. See Denzin (1989:71–73, 86–92), Glaser and Strauss (1967), Hammersley and Atkinson (1983: 45–53), Honigmann (1982), and Weiss (1994:25–29) on sampling in field research.

50. Discussion of field interviewing can be found in Banaka (1971), Bogdan and Taylor (1975:95–124), Briggs (1986), Burgess (1982c), Denzin (1989:103–120), Dou-

glas (1985), Lofland and Lofland (1995:78–88), Spradley (1979a), and Whyte (1982).

51. See Fontana and Frey (1994).

52. For more on comparisons with conversations, see Briggs (1986:11), Spradley (1979a:56–68), and Weiss (1994:8).

53. See Weiss (1994:78).

54. See Atkinson (1998), Denzin (1989:182–209), Nash and McCurdy (1989), Smith (1994), and Tagg (1985) on life history interviews.

55. The types of questions are adapted from Spradley (1979a, 1979b).

56. Field research informants are discussed in Dean and associates (1969), Kemp and Ellen (1984), Schatzman and Strauss (1973), Spradley (1979a:46–54), and Whyte (1982).

57. Interview contexts are discussed in Hammersley and Atkinson (1983:112–126) and in Schatzman and Strauss (1973:83–87). Briggs (1986) argued that nontraditional

populations and females communicate better in unstructured interviews.

58. Altheide (1980), Bogdan and Taylor (1975:75–76), Lofland and Lofland (1995:61), Maines and colleagues (1980), and Roadburg (1980) discuss leaving the field.

59. For a discussion of focus groups, see Bischoping and Dykema (1999), Churchill (1983:179–184), Krueger (1988), Labaw (1980:54–58), and Morgan (1996).

60. See Lofland and Lofland (1995:26, 63, 75, 168–177), Miles and Huberman (1994:288–297), and Punch (1986).

61. Covert, sensitive study is discussed in Ayella (1993), Edwards (1993), and Mitchell (1993).

62. See Douglas (1976), Erikson (1970), and Johnson (1975).

63. See Barnes (1970), Becker (1969), Fichter and Kolb (1970), Goward (1984a), Lofland and Lofland (1995: 204–230), Miles and Huberman (1994:298–307), and Wolcott (1994) on publishing field research results.

Historical-Comparative Research

> *Sociological explanation is necessarily historical. Historical sociology is thus not some special kind of sociology; rather, it is the essence of the discipline.*
> —Philip Abrams, *Historical Sociology*, p. 2

> *Thinking without comparisons is unthinkable. And, in the absence of comparisons, so is all scientific thought and all scientific research. No one should be surprised that comparisons, implicit and explicit, pervade the work of social scientists and have done from the beginning.*
> —Guy Swanson, "Frameworks for Comparative Research," p. 145

Social scientific explanations of major societal processes—terrorism, a nation going to war, growing poverty, sources of inequality, rising immigration rates, urban decay—rely on studies that use historical and comparative research. In addition, historical-comparative (H-C) research (also called comparative-historical) brings clarity to many methodological concerns found in other forms of research, and researchers use it to address many ex-

citing questions in social research. Nonetheless, students sometimes find historical-comparative studies difficult to understand, even when such studies do not use complex statistics and have only words or maps. The reason may be that topics and issues explored with H-C research often are outside the everyday experiences of most students, especially if they are monolingual and monocultural; that is, familiar with only their own language and culture, or lacking a solid background in history. In addition, basic researchers, moreso than applied researchers, use historical-comparative research. This is because it can reveal processes over long time periods and across societies, and it addresses many central issues in general theory (Mahoney, 2004b). This makes H-C research vital to the expansion of fundamental knowledge, but students who are just beginning to acquire social science knowledge may not yet recognize its contributions.

The classic social thinkers in the nineteenth century, such as Émile Durkheim, Karl Marx, and Max Weber, who founded the social sciences, used a historical and comparative method. This method is used extensively in several areas of sociology (e.g., social change, political sociology, social movements, and social stratification) and has been applied in many others, as well (e.g., religion, criminology, gender issues, race relations, and family). Although much social research focuses on current social life in one country, historical and/or comparative studies have become more common in recent years.

A SHORT HISTORY OF HISTORICAL-COMPARATIVE RESEARCH

The nineteenth-century founders of sociology conducted historical-comparative (H-C) research, blending together sociology, history, political science, and economics. Beginning around World War I, historical-comparative research declined as the social sciences separated. Comparative research was increasingly conducted by anthropologists and historical research by historians. Sociologists conducted little historical-comparative research between World War I and the 1950s. There were a few exceptions, however. Marc Bloch, George Homans, Robert Merton, and Karl Polanyi all produced H-C works that had great influence.[1]

Scholarly interest in comparative research increased after World War II with improved international communication, the breakup of colonial empires, and a world leadership role for the United States. A few H-C studies of major significance appeared during the 1950s.[2]

Several factors stimulated a return to H-C research. First, some historians (e.g., Lee Benson, Robert W. Fogel, Richard Jensen, and Stephen Thernstrom) imported quantitative techniques from the social sciences, increasing the interchange between history and the social sciences. Statistical studies of mobility, railroad expansion, and voting showed historians the power of quantitative data and gave quantitative researchers new questions to address with their techniques. Second, survey techniques were exported from the United States and used to study different nations. New methodological issues and questions arose from attempts to use quantitative techniques for cross-national generalizations.

Third, the historical-comparative works of Max Weber and Karl Marx were translated and made available in English for the first time. "The translation of Weber probably did more to influence the writing of history in the 1960s than any other single influence from the social sciences" (Stone, 1987:13). Fourth, several H-C studies appeared that made important theoretical advances.[3] In the 1970s, several new models of how to do H-C research appeared.[4]

H-C grew into a vital force during the 1980s. In 1983, a section on it was formed in the American Sociological Association (ASA). In his presidential address to the ASA, Melvin Kohn (1987) said that cross-national research was experiencing a revival after being nearly abandoned in the 1930s. Hunt (1989:1) remarked, "Historical sociology has become one of the most important subfields of sociology, and perhaps the fastest growing." Articles using some form of historical-comparative research appeared in leading scholarly journals. For example, about 40 percent of the articles published in the most prestigious U.S. sociology journals after 1990 were historical or comparative in some sense.[5]

RESEARCH QUESTIONS APPROPRIATE FOR HISTORICAL-COMPARATIVE RESEARCH

Historical-comparative research is a powerful method for addressing big questions: How did major societal change take place? What fundamental features are common to most societies? Why did current social arrangements take a certain form in some societies but not in others? For example, historical-comparative researchers have addressed the questions of what caused societal revolutions in China, France, and Russia (Skocpol, 1979); how major social institutions, such as medicine, have developed and changed over two centuries (Starr, 1982); how basic social relationships, such as feelings about the value of children, change (Zelizer, 1985); why public policy toward treatment of the elderly developed in one way instead of another in the United States (Quadagno, 1988); and what caused the failure of a mass political movement in the United States that advocated greater equality and democracy (McNall, 1988).[6]

Historical-comparative research is suited for examining the combinations of social factors that produce a specific outcome (e.g., civil war). It is also appropriate for comparing entire social systems to see what is common across societies and what is unique, and to study long-term societal change. An H-C researcher may apply a theory to specific cases to illustrate its usefulness. For example, if France has highly centralized power and high political dissatisfaction, whereas the United States is low on both centralized power and political dissatisfaction, a researcher can begin to build a causal account relating centralized power and dissatisfaction. Changes within a country over time in centralization of power and dissatisfaction can verify causal links.[7]

Historical-comparative research can strengthen conceptualization and theory building. By looking at historical events or diverse cultural contexts, a researcher can generate new concepts and broaden his or her perspectives. Concepts are less likely to be restricted to a single historical time or to a single culture. General concepts can be grounded in the experiences of people living in specific cultural and historical contexts.[8]

A difficulty in reading H-C studies is that one needs a knowledge of the past or other cultures to fully understand them. Readers limited to knowing about their own cultures or contemporary times alone may find it difficult to understand the H-C studies or classical theorists. For example, it is difficult to understand Karl Marx's "The Communist Manifesto"

without a knowledge of the conditions of feudal Europe and the world in which Marx was writing. In that time and place, serfs lived under severe oppression. Feudal society included caste-based dress codes in cities and a system of peonage that forced serfs to give a large percent of their product to landlords. The one and only Church had extensive landholdings, and tight familial ties existed among the aristocracy, landlords, and Church. Modern readers might ask, Why did the serfs not flee if conditions were so bad? The answer requires an understanding that serfs had little chance to survive in European forests living on roots, berries, and hunting. Also, no one would aid a fleeing serf refugee because the traditional societies did not embrace strangers, but feared them. To understand H-C studies by classical theorists, "one must appreciate what they took for granted as characteristic of their time and their interpretations of the past" (Tuchman, 1994:310).

THE LOGIC OF HISTORICAL-COMPARATIVE RESEARCH

Confusion over terms reigns in H-C research. Researchers call what they do historical, comparative, or historical-comparative, but mean different things. The key question is: Is there a distinct historical-comparative method and logic, or is there just social research that happens to examine social life in the past or in several societies?

The Logic of Historical-Comparative Research and Quantitative Research

Quantitative versus Historical-Comparative Research. A source of the confusion is that some H-C researchers use a positivist, quantitative approach to study historical or comparative issues. Others rely on the qualitative, interpretative, or critical approaches. According to Ragin and Zaret (1983), a Durkheimian (or positivist) approach and a Weberian (or interpretative) approach to H-C research use different logics.[9]

This confusion is summarized by Øyen (1990:7):

The vocabulary for distinguishing between different kinds of comparative research is redundant and not

TABLE 14.1   Logically Possible Kinds of Historical-Comparative Research

TIME DIMENSION AND KIND OF DATA	COMPARATIVE DIMENSION		
	Single Nation*	Few Nations	Many Nations
One Time in Past			
Quantatitive	1	2	3
Qualitative	4	5	6
Across Time			
Quantitative	7	8	9
Qualitative	10	11	12
Present			
Quantitative	13	14	15
Qualitative	16	17	18

*Nation different than researcher's and audience of results for present time.

very precise. Concepts such as cross-country, cross-national, cross-societal, cross-systemic, cross-institutional, as well as trans-national, trans-societal, trans-cultural, and comparisons on the macro-level, are used both as synonymous with comparative research in general and as denoting specific kinds of comparisons.

Historical-comparative research can be organized along three dimensions. First, does the researcher focus on what occurs in one nation or a small set of nations, or does the researcher attempt to study many nations? Second, how does the researcher involve time or history? Does he or she focus on a single time period in the past, examine events across many years, or study the present or a recent time period? Finally, does the researcher rely primarily on quantitative or qualitative data? If we cross-classify the three dimensions, we get a typology of 18 logically possible kinds of H-C research (see Table 14.1). No wonder there is so much confusion over what constitutes H-C research.

Most social research is in cells 1, 4, 5, 7, 8, 10, 11, 13, 14, 15, and 16. This includes all of the single-nation column.

Many H-C studies try to identify universal or near-universal processes, that is, social processes or relationships operating across all human societies,

or at least within a major type of society (i.e., highly industrial, agricultural) for a long time period (Ember and Ember, 2001). Studies that consider data for only one society or a brief time period have limited generalizability, and we cannot say with confidence whether an explanation based on such data applies only to that one society or is found across most human societies, or whether it is specific to one time point or holds across a stretch of history.

For example, a study might find that economic inequality is associated with higher property crime in major Australian cities in 2005. We do not know whether this is something unique to Australia in the beginning of the twenty-first century. If we find that economic inequality and crime rates are highly associated in the cities of Australia, the United States, Great Britain, and Canada, our findings are far stronger. If we find this correlation held in the 1950s and 1980s as well, it is also more generalizable. The comparison set is still limited to English-speaking industrialized nations with an Anglo culture in the recent historical era. If we can add Brazil, Egypt, France, Turkey, and South Korea and go back to 1900 and find the same relationship, the generalization gets much stronger.

Some researchers try to get data for many of the world's 170 nations, such as Beckfield's (2003) research on inequality that considered 90 nations, Schofer's (2004) data on over 120 nations for a study of the world expansion of science, Sung's (2003) study of women's political participation that included 99 countries, and Tsutsui and Wotipka's (2004) study of international human rights organizations with 77 nations. However, data on many societies are unavailable or not comparable, so most comparative studies are limited to between 10 and 20 nations. For example, Brady (2003) studied politics and welfare in 16 rich nations, Chang (2004) examined sex segregation in 16 developing countries, Mahoney (2003) (discussed in Chapter 2) looked at 15 South American nations, Moller and colleagues (2003) examined poverty in 14 advanced countries, Sutton (2004) studied imprisonment in 15 nations, and van Tubergen and associates (2004) looked at immigrant policy in 18 countries. Other researchers focus on comparing two or three cases.

BOX **14.1** Women of the Klan

In *Women of the Klan,* Kathleen Blee (1991) noted that, prior to her research, no one had studied the estimated 500,000 women in the largest racist, right-wing movement in the United States. She suggested that this may have been due to an assumption that women were apolitical and passive. Her six years of research into the unknown members of a secret society over 60 years previous shows the ingenuity needed in historical-sociological research.

Blee focused on the state of Indiana, where as many as 32 percent of White Protestant women were members of the Ku Klux Klan at its peak in the 1920s. In addition to reviewing published studies on the Klan, her documentary investigation included newspapers, pamphlets, and unpublished reports. She conducted library research on primary and secondary materials at over half a dozen college, government, and historical libraries. The historical photographs, sketches, and maps in the book give readers a feel for the topic.

Finding information was difficult. Blee did not have access to membership lists. She identified Klan women by piecing together a few surviving rosters, locating newspaper obituaries that identified women as Klan members, scrutinizing public notices or anti-Klan documents for the names of Klan women, and interviewing surviving women of the Klan.

To locate survivors 60 years after the Klan was active, Blee had to be persistent and ingenious. She mailed a notice about her research to every local newspaper, church bulletin, advertising supplement, historical society, and public library in Indiana. She obtained 3 written recollections, 3 unrecorded interviews, and 15 recorded interviews. Most of her informants were over age 80. They recalled the Klan as an important part of their lives. Blee verified parts of their memories through newspaper and other documentary evidence.

Membership in the Klan remains controversial. In the interviews, Blee did not reveal her opinions about the Klan. Although she was tested, Blee remained neutral and did not denounce the Klan. She stated, "My own background in Indiana (where I lived from primary school through college) and white skin led informants to assume—lacking spoken evidence to the contrary—that I shared their worldview" (p. 5). She did not find Klan women brutal, ignorant, and full of hatred. Blee got an unexpected response to a question on why the women had joined the Klan. Most were puzzled by the question. To them it needed no explanation—it was just "a way of growing up" and "to get together and enjoy."

For example, Fretzer (2000) looked at public attitudes toward immigration in France, Germany, and the United States; Gangl (2004) compared welfare state policies and unemployment in Germany and the United States; Marx (1998) (discussed in Chapter 2) studied race relations in Brazil, South Africa, and the United States; whereas Tobin and associates (1989) looked at preschools in Japan, the United States, and China. Last, studies focus on one location but are implicitly comparative (see Box 14.5 later in this chapter).

Many studies focus on the present, but others look at one society at one point in the past, such as Einwohner's (2003) study of Warsaw, Poland, in 1943 (discussed in Chapter 3), Emigh's (2003) study on fifteenth-century Tuscany (discussed in Chapter 15), or Blee's study of women in 1920s Indiana (see Box 14.1). Often, researchers focus on a 20–30 year time period. For example, Ruef

(2004) studied agricultural forms in the U.S. South 1860–1880. Olzak and Shanahan (2003) looked at racial conflict in the United States 1869–1924 (see Box 14.2), and Sutton (2004) studied imprisonment in 15 nations 1960–1990. A few look at long time periods, such as Lachman's (2003) study of elites in four European states, 1500s to 1700s, Mahoney's (2003) study of South America across two centuries (described in Chapter 2), or Behrens and colleagues' (2003) study of voting disenfranchisement in the United States 1850–2002 (discussed in Chapter 3).

The Logic of Historical-Comparative Research and Interpretive Research

A distinct, qualitative historical-comparative type of social research differs from the positivist approach. It also differs from an extreme interpretive approach,

BOX **14.2** Seeing Past Events in a New Light, Racial Boundaries in the United States

H-C researchers reorganize data and use theory to see events in new ways. Olzak and Shanahan (2003) did this in a study of past racial conflicts in the United States. They noted that before 1870, the U.S. racial divide was between Whites, understood as people from a few northwestern European countries, and all others, and Whites alone had full citizenship. After an 1870 law granted citizenship rights to African Americans and large-scale immigration from southern or eastern Europe and Asia, the line between being White and others began to blur. In the 1890s, southern and eastern Europeans (e.g., Italians) were called colored and lynched as blacks, and Asians who tried to become naturalized citizen were turned down by the courts using a 1790 law that limited U.S. citizenship to "white persons."

Competition theory states that when racial barriers weaken between two groups in the same social-economic position, competition and conflict between the groups will grow. The authors argued that legal action affecting the dominant racial group's exclusive position can increase intergroup conflict. They examined historical records of racial-ethnic relations and immigration, information on new laws and court rulings, and newspaper reports of racial conflict in 76 local settings between 1869 and 1924. They documented patterns of White attacks on Asian and African Americans and found that laws clarifying racial divisions and reinforcing a new "White" identity to include all people of European ancestry were associated with greater attacks on African Americans and Asians. U.S. courts rulings sharpened a new racial division, placing all European-origin immigrants on one side, and African Americans and Asians on the other. Mob attacks and the court rulings or new laws were dual strategies to exclude non-Whites, with the legal action legitimating attacks on non-Whites. The authors concluded, as a result of the legal policy, "race became a master identity for newcomers and racial boundaries become salient to many types of interaction" (p. 506).

which some field researchers, cultural anthropologists, and traditional historians advocate.

Historical-comparative researchers who use case studies and qualitative data may depart from positivist principles. Case studies, even on one nation, can be very important. Without case studies, scholars "would continue to advance theoretical arguments that are inappropriate, outdated, or totally irrelevant for a specific region" (Bradshaw and Wallace, 1995:155). Case studies can elaborate historical processes and specify concrete historical details.

Scholars who adopt the positivist approach to social science criticize the historical-comparative approach for using a small number of cases. Such scholars believe that historical-comparative research cannot produce the types of probabilistic causal generalizations that they take as being indicators of a "true" (i.e., positivist) science.[10]

Like interpretive field research, H-C research focuses on culture, tries to see through the eyes of those being studied, reconstructs the lives of the people studied, and examines particular individuals or groups. An extreme interpretive position goes beyond a desire to see the world through the eyes of others. It says that an empathic understanding of the people being studied is the primary goal of social research. It avoids causal statements, systematic concepts, or theoretical models. An extreme interpretive approach assumes that each social setting is unique and that comparisons are impossible. It re-creates specific subjective experiences and describes particulars. As Stone (1987:31) noted, traditional history "deals with a particular problem and a particular set of actors at a particular time and a particular place."

A distinct H-C approach borrows from ethnography and cultural anthropology, and some varieties of H-C attempt to re-create the reality of another time or place. Yet, borrowing from the strengths of ethnography does not require adopting the extreme interpretive approach.[11]

A Distinct Historical-Comparative Approach

The distinct historical-comparative research method combines a sensitivity to specific historical or cultural contexts with theoretical generalization.

TABLE 14.2   Summary of a Comparison of Approaches to Research: The Qualitative versus Quantitative Distinction

TOPIC	BOTH FIELD AND H-C	QUANTITATIVE
Researcher's perspective	Include as an integral part of the research process	Remove from research process
Approach to data	Immersed in many details to acquire understanding	Precisely operation-alize variables
Theory and data	Grounded theory, dialogue between data and concepts	Deductive theory tested with empirical data
Present findings	Translate a meaning system	Test hypotheses
Action/structure	People act and construct meaning but within structures	Social forces shape behavior
Laws/generalization	Limited generalizations that depend on context	Discover universal, context-free laws

FEATURES OF DISTINCT H-C RESEARCH APPROACH

TOPIC	HISTORICAL-COMPARATIVE RESEARCHER'S APPROACH
Evidence	Reconstructs from fragments and incomplete evidence
Distortion	Guards against using own awareness of factors outside the social or historical context
Human role	Includes the consciousness of people in a context and uses their motives as causal factors
Causes	Sees cause as contingent on conditions, beneath the surface, and due to a combination of elements
Micro/macro	Compares whole cases and links the micro to macro levels or layers of social reality
Cross-contexts	Moves between concrete specifics in a context and across contexts for more abstract comparisons

Historical-comparative researchers may use quantitative data to supplement qualitative data and analysis. The logic and goals of H-C research are closer to those of field research than to those of traditional positivist approaches (see Table 14.2).

Similarities to Field Research. First, both H-C research and field research recognize that the researcher's point of view is an unavoidable part of research. Both involve interpretation, which introduces the interpreter's location in time, place, and worldview. Historical-comparative research does not try to produce a single, unequivocal set of objective facts. Rather, it is a confrontation of old with new or of different worldviews. It recognizes that a researcher's reading of historical or comparative evidence is influenced by an awareness of the past and by living in the present.

Second, both field and H-C research examine a great diversity of data. In both, the researcher becomes immersed in data to gain an empathic understanding of events and people. Both capture subjective feelings and note how everyday, ordinary activities signify important social meaning.

The researcher inquires, selects, and focuses on specific aspects of social life from the vast array of events, actions, symbols, and words. An H-C researcher organizes data and focuses attention on the basis of evolving concepts. He or she examines rituals and symbols that dramatize culture (e.g., parades, clothing, placement of objects, etc.) and investigates the motives, reasons, and justifications for behaviors. For example, Burrage and Corry (1981) measured changes in occupation status in London between the fourteenth and seventeenth centuries using records of the official order of appearance of guilds at major public events (parades, pageants, feasts, royal visits, etc.).[12]

Third, both field and H-C researchers often use *grounded theory*. Theory usually emerges during the process of data collection. Both examine the data without beginning with fixed hypotheses. Instead, they develop and modify concepts and theory through a dialogue with the data, then apply theory to reorganize the evidence. Thus, data collection and theory building interact. Thompson (1978:39) called this "a dialogue between concept and evidence, a dialogue conducted by successive hypotheses, on the one hand, and empirical research on the other."[13]

Next, both field and H-C research involve a type of translation. The researcher's meaning system usually differs from that of the people he or she studies, but he or she tries to penetrate and understand their point of view. Once the life, language, and perspective of the people being studied have been mastered, the researcher "translates" it for others who read his or her report.

Fifth, both field and H-C researchers focus on action, process, and sequence and see time and process as essential. Both are sensitive to an ever-present tension between agency, the fluid-social action and changing social reality, and structure, the fixed regularities and patterns that shape social actions and perceptions. Both see social reality simultaneously as something created and changed by people and as imposing a restriction on human choice.[14]

Sixth, generalization and theory are limited in field and H-C research. Historical and cross-cultural knowledge is incomplete and provisional, based on selective facts and limited questions. Neither deduces propositions or tests hypotheses in order to uncover fixed laws. Likewise, replication is unrealistic because each researcher has a unique perspective and assembles a unique body of evidence. Instead, researchers offer plausible accounts and limited generalizations.

Unique Features of Historical-Comparative Research. Despite its many similarities to field research, some important differences distinguish H-C research. As the title to David Lowenthal's *The Past Is a Foreign Country* (1985) suggests, research on the past and on an alien culture share much in common.

First, the evidence for H-C research is usually limited and indirect. Direct observation or involvement by a researcher is often impossible. An H-C researcher reconstructs what occurred from the evidence. Historical evidence depends on the survival of data from the past, usually in the form of documents (e.g., letters and newspapers). The researcher is limited to what has not been destroyed and what leaves a trace, record, or other evidence behind.

Historical-comparative researchers interpret the evidence. The researcher becomes immersed in and absorbs details about a context. For example, a researcher examining the family in the past or a distant country needs to be aware of the full social context (e.g., the nature of work, forms of communication, transportation technology, etc.). He or she looks at maps and gets a feel for the laws in effect, the condition of medical care, and common social practices. For example, the meaning of "a visit by a family member" is affected by conditions such as roads of dirt and mud, the inability to call ahead of time, and the lives of people who work on a farm with animals that need constant watching.

Another feature is that a researcher's reconstruction of the past or another culture is easily distorted. Compared to the people being studied, a researcher is usually more aware of events occurring prior to the time studied, events occurring in places other than the location studied, and events that occurred after the period studied. This awareness gives the researcher a greater sense of coherence than was experienced by those living in the past or in an isolated social setting. "In short, historical explanation surpasses any understanding while events are still occurring. The past we reconstruct is more coherent than the past when it happened" (Lowenthal, 1985:234). A researcher's broader awareness can create the illusion that things happened because they had to, or that they fit together neatly.

A researcher cannot easily see through the eyes of those being studied. Knowledge of the present and changes over time can distort how events, people, laws, or even physical objects are perceived. For example, the old buildings that survive into the present are more permanent and solid than those that did not survive. Moreover, a surviving building looks different in 2005 than it did in 1805 because of the context in which it appears. When the 1805 building was newly built and standing among similar buildings, the people living at the time saw it differently than people do in the the twenty-first century. They experienced building styles differently, and the building did not appear as something preserved in an old style in the context of newer buildings from the subsequent two hundred years.

Historical-comparative researchers recognize the capacity of people to learn, make decisions, and act on what they learn to modify the course of events. When conscious people are involved, lawlike generalizations that hold across societies are limited.[15] For example, if a group of people are aware of or gain consciousness of their own past history and avoid the mistakes of the past, they may act consciously to alter the course of events. Of course, people will not necessarily learn or act on what they have learned, and if they do act they will not necessarily be successful. Nevertheless, people's capacity to learn introduces indeterminacy into historical-comparative explanations.

An H-C researcher wants to find out whether the people involved saw various courses of action as plausible. Thus, the worldview and knowledge of those people is a conditioning factor, shaping what the people being studied saw as possible or impossible. The researcher asks whether people were conscious of certain things. For example, if an army knew an enemy attack was coming and so decided to cross a river in the middle of the night, the action

"crossing the river" would have a different meaning than in the situation in which the army did not know the enemy was approaching.

Historical-comparative research takes a contingent view of causality. An H-C researcher often uses combinational explanations. They are analogous to a chemical reaction in which several ingredients (chemicals, oxygen) are added together under specified conditions (temperature, pressure) to produce an outcome (explosion). This differs from a linear causal explanation. The logic is more "A, B, and C appeared together in time and place, then D resulted" than "A caused B, and B caused C, and C caused D." Ragin (1987:13) summarized:

> Most comparativists, especially those who are qualitatively oriented, are interested in specific historical sequences or outcomes and their causes across a set of similar cases. Historical outcomes often require complex, combinational explanations, and such explanations are very difficult to prove in a manner consistent with the norms of mainstream quantitative social science.

For example, Max Weber's explanations gave cultural factors equal weight to economic, demographic, or social structural factors. Weber employed a combination of causal factors through the ideal type, which was neither a deductive formal theory to test, nor an inductive, problem-specific theory.[16]

Historical-comparative research focuses on whole cases versus separate variables across cases. A researcher approaches the whole as if it has multiple layers. He or she grasps surface appearances as well as reveals the general, hidden structures, unseen mechanisms, or causal processes.

A historical-comparative researcher integrates the micro (small-scale, face-to-face interaction) and macro (large-scale social structures) levels. Instead of describing micro-level or macro-level processes alone, the researcher describes both levels or layers of reality and links them to each other.[17] For example, an H-C researcher examines the details of individual biographies by reading diaries or letters to get a feel for the individuals: the food they ate, their recreational pursuits, their clothing, their sicknesses, their relations with friends, and so on. He or she links this micro-level view to macro-level processes: increased immigration, mechanization of production, proletarianization, tightened labor markets, and the like.

H-C research shifts between a specific context and a general comparison. A researcher examines specific contexts, notes similarities and differences, then generalizes. He or she then looks again at the specific contexts using the generalizations.

Comparative researchers compare across cultural-geographic units (e.g., urban areas, nations, societies, etc.).[18] Historical researchers investigate past contexts, usually in one culture (e.g., periods, epochs, ages, eras, etc.), for sequence and comparison.[19] Of course, a researcher can combine both to investigate multiple cultural contexts in one or more historical contexts. Yet, each period or society has its unique causal processes, meaning systems, and social relations. This produces a creative tension between the concrete specifics in a context and the abstract ideas a researcher uses to make links across contexts.

The use of transcultural concepts in comparative analysis is analogous to the use of transhistorical ones in historical research.[20] In comparative research, a researcher translates the specifics of a context into a common, theoretical language. "The comparative investigator can thus be regarded as fighting a continuous struggle between the 'culture-boundness' of system-specific categories and the 'contentlessness' of system-inclusive categories" (Smelser, 1976:178).

The Annales School. H-C research draws from the **Annales school,**[21] a research method associated with a group of French historians (e.g., Marc Bloch, Fernand Braudel, Lucien Febvre, and Emmanuel Le Roy Ladurie), and named after the scholarly journal *Annales: Économies, Sociétés, Civilisations,* founded in 1929. The school's orientation can be summarized by four interrelated characteristics.

One characteristic is the school's synthetic, totalizing, holistic, or interdisciplinary approach. Annales researchers combine geography, ecology, economics, and demography with cultural factors to give a total picture of the past. They blend together the diverse conditions of material life and

collective beliefs or culture into a comprehensive reconstruction of the past civilization.

A second characteristic is illustrated by a French term of the school, the **mentalities** of an era. This term is not directly translatable into English. It means a distinctive worldview, perspective, or set of assumptions about life—the way that thinking was organized, or the overall pattern of conscious and unconscious cognition, belief, and values that prevailed in an era. Thus, researchers try to discover the overall arrangement of thought in a historical period that shaped subjective experience about fundamental aspects of reality: the nature of time, the relationship of humans to the physical environment, how truth is created, and the like.

The Annales approach mixes concrete historical specificity and abstract theory. Theory takes the form of models or deep underlying structures, which are causal or organizing principles that account for everyday events. Annales historians look for both the deep-running currents that shape the surface events and individual actions.

A last characteristic is an interest in long-term structures or patterns. In contrast to traditional historians who focus on particular individuals or events over short time spans, from several years to a few decades, Annales historians examine long-term changes, over periods of a century or more, in the fundamental way that social life is organized. They use the term **longue durée**. It means a long duration or a historical era in geographic space (e.g., feudalism in western Europe, or the fifteenth to eighteenth centuries in the Mediterranean region).

Annales school A group of French historians that developed a research approach is that holistic, blends attention to the concrete specificity of daily life with abstract theory building, and considers long-term society-wide structural change.

Mentalities An Annales school idea meaning a pattern of everyday consciousness and assumptions about ordinary life that pervades during a particular historical period.

Longue durée An Annales school idea meaning a long period of time, often a century or longer, across which fundamental patterns or structures in social life remain stable and shape daily life.

To do this, a researcher must adopt a unique orientation toward history.

The Annales school has influenced H-C research in several ways. It puts events in a broader context, builds theory about underlying structures, and emphasizes a sensitivity to the different subjective consciousness of the past. Finally, it encourages a holistic integration of diverse types of data.

STEPS IN A HISTORICAL-COMPARATIVE RESEARCH PROJECT

In this section, we turn to the process of doing H-C research. Conducting historical-comparative research does not involve a rigid set of steps and, with only a few exceptions, it does not use complex or specialized techniques.

Conceptualizing the Object of Inquiry

An H-C researcher begins by becoming familiar with the setting and conceptualizes what is being studied. He or she may start with a loose model or set of preliminary concepts and apply them to a specific setting. The provisional concepts contain implicit assumptions or organizing categories that he or she uses to see the world, "package" observations, and search through evidence.

If a researcher is not already familiar with the historical era or comparative settings, he or she conducts an orientation reading (reading several general works). This will help the researcher grasp the specific setting, assemble organizing concepts, subdivide the main issue, and develop lists of questions to ask.[22] Concepts and evidence interact to stimulate research. For example, Skocpol (1979) began her study of revolution with puzzles in macrosociological theory and the histories of specific revolutions. The lack of fit between histories of revolutions and existing theories stimulated her research.

Whether or not a researcher is conscious and explicit about it, he or she organizes specific details

into analytic categories. Researchers find it best to recognize this process explicitly and avoid the **Baconian fallacy.** Named for Francis Bacon (1561–1626), it is assuming that a researcher operates without preconceived questions, hypotheses, ideas, assumptions, theories, paradigms, postulates, prejudices, or presumptions of any kind.

Locating Evidence

Next, a researcher locates and gathers evidence through extensive bibliographic work. A researcher uses many indexes, catalogs, and reference works that list what libraries contain. For comparative research, this means focusing on specific nations or units and on particular kinds of evidence within each. The researcher frequently spends many weeks searching for sources in libraries, travels to several different specialized research libraries, and spends months or years reading books and articles. Comparative research often involves learning one or more foreign languages.

As the researcher masters the literature and takes detailed notes, he or she completes many specific tasks: creating a bibliography list (on cards or computer) with complete citations, taking notes that are neither too skimpy nor too extensive (i.e., more than one sentence but less than dozens of pages of quotes), and developing a file on themes or working hypotheses.

A researcher adjusts initial concepts, questions, or focus on the basis of what he or she discovers in the evidence. New issues and questions arise as he or she reads and considers a range of research reports at different levels of analysis (e.g., general context and detailed narratives on specific topics) and multiple studies on a topic, crossing topic boundaries. For example, Quadagno's (1988) study of old-age and welfare programs started with an interest in the history of U.S. programs for the aged. She began with government records on programs for the elderly. Soon, she discovered the importance of southern political pressure, so she spent months learning about southern U.S. history. As the issue unfolded, she examined the literature on social programs. Then, as her inquiry expanded, she read theoretical and empirical discussions showing con-

---

Baconian fallacy The fallacy of assuming that a researcher can operate without any preconceived questions, ideas, assumptions, theories, or presumptions.

nections to other social welfare programs. They suggested a comparison with extensive western European programs. In western Europe, organized labor is represented by the social democratic parties, which shaped most social programs in those countries. Therefore, Quadagno's research turned to U.S. labor history. The records of labor officials and labor history led her to examine the actions of employers and the power of the private sector. She stated, "I moved back and forth between theory and archival materials, with each new set of empirical observations guiding my generalizations about factors shaping welfare policy" (1988:x).

Evaluating Quality of Evidence

As an H-C researcher gathers evidence, he or she asks two questions: How relevant is the evidence to emerging research questions and evolving concepts? How accurate and strong is the evidence?

The question of relevance is a difficult one. As the focus of research shifts, evidence that was not relevant can become relevant. Likewise, some evidence may stimulate new avenues of inquiry and a search for additional confirming evidence.

An H-C researcher reads evidence for three things: the implicit conceptual framework, particular details, and empirical generalizations (factual statements on which there is agreement). He or she evaluates alternative interpretations of evidence and looks for "silences," or cases where the evidence fails to address an event, topic, or issue. For example, when examining a group of leading male merchants, a researcher may find documents that ignore their wives and many servants.

Researchers try to avoid fallacies in the evidence. Fischer (1970) provided an extensive list of such fallacies. For example, the fallacy of *pseudoproof* is a failure to place something into its full context. The evidence might state that there was a 50 percent increase in income taxes, but its impact is not meaningful outside of a context. The researcher must ask: Did other taxes decline? Did income increase? Did the tax increase apply to all income? Was everyone affected equally? Another fallacy to avoid with historical evidence is **anachronism**, when an event appears to have occurred before or

after the time it actually did. A researcher should be precise about the sequence of events and note discrepancies in dating events in evidence.

Organizing Evidence

As a researcher gathers evidence and locates new sources, he or she begins to organize the data. Obviously, it is unwise to take notes madly and let them pile up haphazardly. A researcher begins a preliminary analysis by noting low-level generalizations or themes. For example, in a study of revolution, a researcher develops a theme: The rich peasants supported the old regime. He or she can record this theme in his or her notes and later assign it significance.

Next, a researcher organizes evidence, using theoretical insights to stimulate new ways to organize data and for new questions to ask of evidence (see Box 14.2).

The interaction of data and theory means that a researcher goes beyond a surface examination of the evidence to develop new concepts by critically evaluating the evidence based on theory. For example, a researcher reads a mass of evidence about a protest movement. The preliminary analysis organizes the evidence into a theme: People who are active in protest interact with each other and develop shared cultural meanings. He or she examines theories of culture and movements, then formulates a new concept: "oppositional movement subculture."

Synthesizing

The next step is the process of synthesizing evidence. The researcher refines concepts and moves toward a general explanatory model after most of the evidence is in. Old themes or concepts are revised, and new ones are created. Concrete events give meaning to concepts. The researcher looks for patterns across time or units, and draws out similarities and differences with analogies. He or she

Anachronism An error whereby a historical-comparative researcher locates an event before or after when it actually occurred.

organizes divergent events into sequences and groups them together to create a larger picture. Plausible explanations are then developed that subsume both concepts and evidence into a coherent whole. The researcher then reads and rereads notes and sorts and resorts them on the basis of organizing schemes. He or she looks for links or connections he or she sees while looking at the evidence in different ways.

Synthesis links specific evidence with an abstract model of underlying relations or causal mechanisms. Researchers may use metaphors. For example, mass frustration leading to a revolution is "like an emotional roller coaster drop" in which things seem to be getting better, and then there is a sudden letdown after expectations have risen very fast. The models are sensitizing devices.

A researcher often looks for new evidence to verify specific links that appear only after an explanatory model is developed. He or she evaluates how well the model approximates the evidence and adjusts it accordingly. He or she goes back and forth from the abstract to the concrete (see Chapter 15).

The major task for the historical-comparative researcher is organizing and giving new meaning to evidence. Skocpol (1979:xiv) argued:

> The comparative historian's task—and potential distinctive scholarly contribution—lies not in revealing new data about particular aspects of the large time periods and distinctive places surveyed, but rather in establishing the interest and prima facie validity of an overall argument about causal regularities across various historical cases.

Historical-comparative researchers also identify critical indicators and supporting evidence for themes or explanations. A **critical indicator** is unambiguous evidence, which is usually sufficient for inferring a specific theoretical relationship. Researchers seek these indicators for key parts of an explanatory model. Indicators critically confirm a

---

Critical indicator A clear, unambiguous measure or indicator of a concept in a specific cultural or historical setting.

Historiography Approaches, with assumptions, emphases, and a theoretical point of view, that historians use when writing historical studies.

---

theoretical inference and occur when many details suggest a clear interpretation. For example, a critical indicator of hostility between two nations is a formal declaration of war. A critical indicator of the rising political power of a social group is the formation of formal organizations with a large membership identified with the group and advocating its position. In contrast to a critical indicator is supporting evidence, evidence for less central parts of a model. It builds the overall background or context. The evidence is less abundant or weaker, and lacks a clear and unambiguous theoretical interpretation.

Writing a Report

The last step is to combine evidence, concepts, and synthesis into a research report. The way in which the report is written is key in H-C research. Assembling evidence, arguments, and conclusions into a report is always a crucial step; but more than in quantitative approaches. The careful crafting of evidence and explanation makes or breaks H-C research. A researcher distills mountains of evidence into exposition and prepares extensive footnotes. She or he weaves together evidence and arguments to communicate a coherent, convincing picture to readers (see Chapter 16).

DATA AND EVIDENCE IN HISTORICAL CONTEXT

Types of Historical Evidence

History means the events of the past (e.g., it is *history* that the French withdrew troops from Vietnam), a record of the past (e.g., a *history* of French involvement in Vietnam), and a discipline that studies the past (e.g., a department of *history*).[23] **Historiography** is the method of doing historical research or of gathering and analyzing historical evidence. Historical sociology is a part of historical-comparative research. It

> is an approach to historical data, a style of historiography, that seeks to explain and understand the past in terms of sociological models and theories. . . . Alternatively, historical data may be used to illustrate and test the validity of sociological con-

BOX **14.3** Using Archival Data

The archive is the main source for primary historical materials. Archives are accumulations of documentary materials (papers, photos, letters, etc.) in private collections, museums, libraries, or formal archives.

LOCATION AND ACCESS

Finding whether a collection exists on a topic, organization, or individual can be a long, frustrating task of many letters, phone calls, and referrals. If the material on a person or topic does exist, it may be scattered in multiple locations. Gaining access may depend on an appeal to a family member's kindness for private collections or traveling to distant libraries and verifying one's reason for examining many dusty boxes of old letters. Also, the researcher may discover limited hours (e.g., an archive is open only four days a week from 10 A.M. to 5 P.M., but the researcher needs to inspect the material for 40 hours).

SORTING AND ORGANIZATION

Archive material may be unsorted or organized in a variety of ways. The organization may reflect criteria that are unrelated to the researcher's interests. For example, letters and papers may be in chronological order, but the researcher is interested only in letters to four professional colleagues over three decades, not daily bills, family correspondence, and so on.

TECHNOLOGY AND CONTROL

Archival materials may be in their original form, on microforms, or, more rarely, in an electronic form. Researchers may be allowed only to take notes, not make copies, or they may be allowed only to see select parts of the whole collection. Researchers become frustrated with the limitations of having to read dusty papers in one specific room and being allowed only to take notes by pencil for the few hours a day the archive is open to the public.

TRACKING AND TRACING

One of the most difficult tasks in archival research is tracing common events or persons through the materials. Even if all material are in one location, the same event or relationship may appear in several places in many forms. Researchers sort through mounds of paper to find bits of evidence here and there.

DRUDGERY, LUCK, AND SERENDIPITY

Archival research is often painstaking slow. Spending many hours pouring over partially legible documents can be very tedious. Also, researchers will often discover holes in collections, gaps in a series of papers, or destroyed documents. Yet, careful reading and inspection of previously untouched material can yield startling new connections or ideas. The researcher may discover unexpected evidence that opens new lines of inquiry (see Elder et al., 1993, and Hill, 1993).

---

cepts, principles and theories. (Mariampolski and Hughes, 1978:104–105)

Researchers draw on four types of historical evidence: primary sources, secondary sources, running records, and recollections.[24] Traditional historians rely heavily on primary sources. H-C researchers often use secondary sources or the different data types in combination. For example, Quadagno (1984) examined the U.S. Social Security Act to evaluate theories of political power. Of the 47 sources she cited for evidence, 23 were primary sources (letters, memos, official reports, newspaper or magazine articles of the period), 3 were recollections (memoirs or oral histories), and 21 were secondary sources (books by historians and other researchers).

Primary Sources. The letters, diaries, newspapers, movies, novels, articles of clothing, photographs, and so forth of those who lived in the past and have survived to the present are **primary sources.** They are found in archives (a place where documents are stored), in private collections, in family closets, or in museums (see Box 14.3). Today's documents and objects (our letters, television programs, commercials, clothing, automobiles) will be primary sources for future historians. An example of a classic primary source is a bundle of yellowed

Primary sources Qualitative or quantitative data about past events or social life that were created and used in the past time period.

letters written by a husband away at war to his wife and found in an attic by a researcher. For example, in a book on poverty in one Kentucky community, Billings and Blee's (2000) data included manuscripts from a federal census (1850 to 1910) for both individuals and agriculture as well as tax rolls, deeds, wills, and court records; newspapers; state accounting board records; letters and reports by visiting preachers; and official data at the county and state level. They were able to link individuals, relationships, and households to create longitudinal files on individuals and families for a 60-year period.

Published and unpublished written documents are the most important types of primary source. Researchers find them in their original form or preserved in microfiche or on film. They are often the only surviving record of the words, thoughts, and feelings of people in the past. Written documents are helpful for studying societies and historical periods with writing and literate people. A frequent criticism of written sources is that they were largely written by elites or those in official organizations; thus, the views of the illiterate, the poor, or those outside official social institutions may be overlooked. For example, it was illegal for slaves in the United States to read or write, and thus written sources on the experience of slavery have been indirect or difficult to find.

The written word on paper was the main medium of communication prior to the widespread use of telecommunications, computers, and video

technology to record events and ideas. In fact, the spread of forms of communication that do not leave a permanent physical record (e.g., telephone conversations, computer records, and television or radio broadcasts), and that have largely replaced letters, written ledgers, and newspapers, may make the work of future historians more difficult.

Secondary Sources. Primary sources have realism and authenticity, but the practical limitation of time can restrict research on many primary sources to a narrow time frame or location. To get a broader picture, many H-C researchers use **secondary sources,** the writings of specialist historians who have spent years studying primary sources.

In his article on elites in early modern Europe, of Lachmann's (2003) 82 references, 72 were secondary historical sources and 10 were theoretical works. Emigh (2003) used 129 references for her 32-page journal article on fifteenth-century Tuscany. Of these references, 43 were works on theory or general history in early Europe. The remaining 86 references were secondary historical sources, 23 of which were written in Italian.

Running Records. **Running records** consist of files or existing statistical documents maintained by organizations. An example of a running record is a file in a country church that contains a record of every marriage and every death from 1910 to the present. Roy (1983) used running records when he studied the boards of directors of major U.S. corporations between 1886 and 1905. His evidence came from 150 primary documents, official reports and statistics, and annual business reference books, some of which are still being published.

Recollections. The statements or writings of individuals about their past lives or experiences based on memory are **recollections.** These can be in the form of memoirs, autobiographies, or interviews. Because memory is imperfect, recollections are often distorted in ways that primary sources are not. For example, Blee (1991) interviewed a woman in her late eighties about being in the Ku Klux Klan (see Box 14.1).

In gathering **oral history,** a type of recollection, a researcher conducts unstructured interviews

Secondary sources Qualitative data and quantitative data used in historical research. Information about events or settings are documented or written later by historians or others who did not directly participate in the events or setting.

Running records Existing statistics research based on files, records, or documents that are maintained in a relatively consistent manner over a long period of time.

Recollections Statements or writings about past experiences collected after time has passed and based on a memory or stimulated by a review of old objects, photos, or notes.

Oral history A recollection in which a person is interviewed about the events, beliefs, or feelings in the past that he or she experienced.

BOX **14.4** Seven Deadly Sins of Memory

Schacter (2001) observed that memory loss or mistaken memory takes several forms:

1. *Transience.* Experiencing the slow, continuous decay of memory over time, such that the more distance in the past an event occurred, the less detail is recalled about it
2. *Absent-mindedness.* Focusing on one idea or thing so much that it misdirects one's attention so that other, often simple things, are forgotten (e.g., focusing on a major project but forgetting to pick up the car keys)
3. *Blocking.* Searching unsuccessfully for information that the person possesses but cannot recall despite trying to do so at the moment (often phrased as "it is on the tip of my tongue")
4. *Misattribution.* Mistaking fantasy for reality, or what one heard from a friend or what one saw in a movie for one's own experience
5. *Suggestibility.* Being asked questions in such a way that a person begins to distort his or her memory and believe things happened that did not happen
6. *Bias.* Recalling things in a distorted way, often interjecting ideas, feelings, or beliefs that occurred later in time, or after the remembered event, into it
7. *Persistence.* Being unable to forget something despite trying

with people about their lives or events in the past. This approach is especially valuable for nonelite groups or the illiterate. The oral history technique began in the 1930s and now has a professional association and scholarly journal devoted to it.[25]

Studies on memory suggest caution when a researcher uses oral history or recollections (see Box 14.4). As Schacter (2001:9) remarked,

> We tend to think of memories as snapshots from family albums that, if stored properly, could be retrieved in precisely the same condition in which they were put away. But we now know that we do not record our experience in the way a camera records them. . . . We extract key elements of our experience and store them. We then recreate or reconstruct our experiences rather than retrieve copies of them. Sometimes, in the process of reconstructing we add

on feelings, beliefs, or even knowledge we have obtained after the experience.

Some people "rewrite" the past to make it more consistent with current beliefs or remember the past in a self-enhancing way (i.e., inaccurately recall themselves in a more positive way). Older adults (usually beginning sometime in their 50s) tend to lose the memory of specific details about past events more than do younger people. More highly educated, mentally active older adults show less memory loss, but some degree of individual or collective memory distortion is relatively frequent.[26]

Research with Secondary Sources

Uses and Limitations. Social researchers often use secondary sources, the books and articles written by specialist historians, as evidence of past conditions.[27] As Skocpol (1984:382) remarked, the use of such materials is not systematized, and "comparative historical sociologists have not so far worked out clear, consensual rules and procedures for the valid use of secondary sources as evidence." Secondary sources have limitations and need to be used with caution.

The limitations of secondary historical evidence include problems of inaccurate historical accounts and a lack of studies in areas of interest. Such sources cannot be used to test hypotheses. Post facto (after-the-fact) explanations cannot meet positivist criteria of falsifiability, because few statistical controls can be used and replication is impossible.[28] Yet, historical research by others plays an important role in developing general explanations, among its other uses. For example, such research substantiates the emergence and evolution of tendencies over time.[29]

Potential Problems. The many volumes of secondary sources present a maze of details and interpretations for an H-C researcher. He or she must transform the mass of descriptive studies into an intelligible picture. This picture needs to be consistent with and reflective of the richness of the evidence. It also must bridge the many specific time periods or locales. The researcher faces potential problems with secondary sources.

One problem is in reading the works of historians.[30] Historians do not present theory-free, objective "facts." They implicitly frame raw data, categorize information, and shape evidence using concepts. The historian's concepts are often a mixture drawn from journalism, the language of historical actors, ideologies, philosophy, everyday language in the present, and social science. They may be vague, applied inconsistently, and not mutually exclusive nor exhaustive. For example, a historian describes a group of people in a nineteenth-century town as upper class. But he or she never defines the term and fails to link it to a theory of social classes. The methodological problem is that the historian's implicit theories constrain the evidence. A social researcher tries to find evidence for explanations that may be contrary to ones implicitly used by historians in secondary sources by reading through a disorderly set of concepts to reach the evidence.

A second problem is that the historian's selection procedure is not transparent. Historians select some information from all possible evidence. As Carr (1961:138) noted, "History therefore is a process of selection in terms of historical significance . . . from the infinite oceans of facts the historian selects those which are significant for his purpose." Yet, the H-C researcher does not know how this was done. Without knowing the selection process, a historical-comparative researcher must rely on the historian's judgments, which can contain biases.[31] For example, a historian reads 10,000 pages of newspapers, letters, and diaries, then boils down this information into summaries and selected quotes in a 100-page book. An H-C researcher does not know whether information that the historian left out is relevant for his or her purposes.

The typical historian's research practice also introduces an individualist bias. A heavy reliance on primary sources and surviving artifacts combines with an atheoretical orientation to produce a focus on the actions of specific people. This particularistic, micro-level view directs attention away from integrating themes or patterns. An emphasis on the activities of specific individuals is a type of theoretical orientation.[32]

A third issue is in the organization of the evidence. Historians organize evidence as they write *narrative history* (see Box 14.5). This compounds problems of undefined concepts and the selection of evidence.

In the historical narrative, the writer organizes material chronologically around a single coherent "story." Each part of the story is connected to each other part by its place in the time order of events. Together, all the parts form a unity or whole. Conjuncture and contingency are key elements of the narrative form—that is, if X (or X plus Z) occurred, then Y would occur, and if X (or X plus Z) had not occurred, something else would have followed. The contingency creates a logical interdependency between earlier and later events.

With its temporal logic, the narrative organization differs from quantitative explanation in which the researcher identifies statistical patterns to infer causes.

A difficulty of the narrative is that the organizing tool—time order or position in a sequence of events—does not alone denote theoretical or historical causality. In other words, the narrative meets only one of the three criteria for establishing causality (see Chapter 3)—that of temporal order. Narrative method can obscure underlying causal models or processes when a historian includes events in the narrative that have no causal significance. He or she adds them to enrich the background or context, to add color. Likewise, he or she presents events that have no immediate causal impact, events with a delayed causal impact, or events that are temporarily "on hold."

Also, few narrative historians explicitly state how combination or interaction effects operate. For example, the historian discusses three conditions for an event. Yet, rarely do readers know whether all three conditions must operate together to have a causal impact, but no two conditions alone, or no single condition alone, creates the same impact.[33]

The narrative organization can create conflicting findings. The H-C researcher must read though weak concepts, unknown selection criteria, and unclear casual logic. Beneath the narrative may reside the historian's social theory, but it remains implicit and hidden.

A last problem is that a historian is influenced by historiographic schools, personal beliefs, social

BOX **14.5** The Narrative in History

Many historians write in the traditional narrative form, which can be a secondary source for the H-C researcher.

CHARACTERISTICS OF THE NARRATIVE FORM

1. It tells a story or tale, with a plot and subplots, watersheds, and climaxes.
2. It follows a chronological order and sequence of events.
3. It focuses on specific individuals, not on structures or abstract ideas.
4. It is primarily particular and descriptive, not analytic and general.
5. It presents events as unique, unpredictable, and contingent.

STRENGTHS OF THE NARRATIVE FORM

1. It is colorful, interesting, and entertaining to read.
2. It gives an overall feel for life in a different era, so that readers get the sense that they were there.

3. It communicates the way people in the past subjectively experienced reality and helps readers identify emotionally with people in the past.
4. It surrounds individuals and specific events with a mix of many aspects of social reality.

WEAKNESSES OF THE NARRATIVE FORM

1. It hides causal theories and concepts or leaves them implicit.
2. It uses rhetoric, ordinary language, and commonsense logic to persuade, and therefore is subject to logical fallacies of semantic distortion and various rhetorical devices.
3. It tends to ignore the normal or ordinary for the unique, dramatic, extraordinary, or unusual.
4. It rarely builds on previous knowledge and does little to create general knowledge.
5. It tends to be overly individualistic, overstating the role of particular people and their ability to shape events voluntarily.

theories, and current events at the time the research is conducted.

Historians writing today examine primary materials differently from how those writing in the 1920s did. In addition, there are various schools of historiography (e.g., diplomatic, demographic, ecological, psychological, Marxist, intellectual, etc.) that have their own rules for seeking evidence and asking questions. Carr (1961:54) warned, "Before you study history, study the historian. . . . Before you study the historian, study his historical and social environment."

Research with Primary Sources

The historian is a major issue when a researcher uses secondary sources. When using primary sources, a major issue is that only a fraction of everything written or used in the past has survived into the present. Moreover, what survived is a nonrandom sample of what once existed. Lowenthal (1985:191–192) observed, "The surviving residues of past thoughts and things represent a

tiny fraction of previous generations' contemporary fabric."

Historical-comparative researchers attempt to read primary sources with the eyes and assumptions of a contemporary who lived in the past. They "bracket" or hold back knowledge of subsequent events and modern values. Cantor and Schneider (1967:46) wrote, "If you do not read the primary sources with an open mind and an intention to get inside the minds of the writings and look at things the way *they* saw them, you are wasting your time."

For example, when reading a source produced by a slaveholder, moralizing against slavery or faulting the author for not seeing its evil is not worthwhile. The H-C researcher holds back moral judgments and becomes a moral relativist while reading primary sources. He or she must "think and believe like his subjects, discover how they performed in their own eyes" (Shafer, 1980:165).

Another problem is that locating primary documents is a time-consuming task. A researcher must search through specialized indexes and travel to archives or specialized libraries. Primary sources

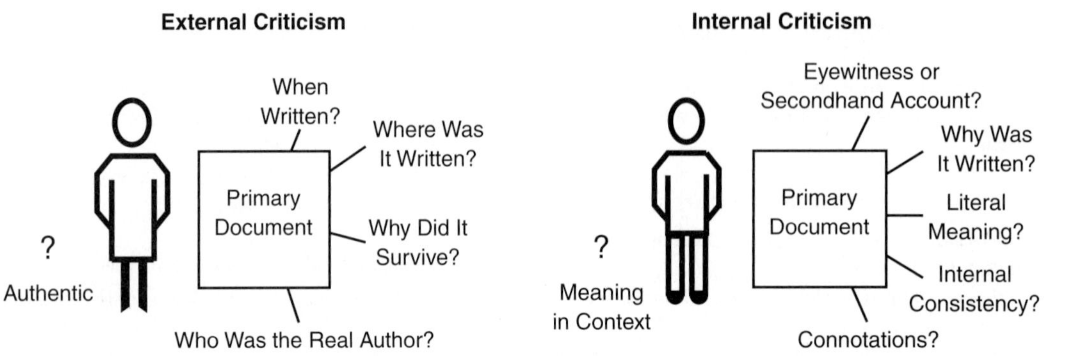

External Criticism

When Written?
Where Was It Written?
Primary Document
Why Did It Survive?
? Authentic
Who Was the Real Author?

Internal Criticism

Eyewitness or Secondhand Account?
Why Was It Written?
Primary Document
Literal Meaning?
Internal Consistency?
? Meaning in Context
Connotations?

FIGURE 14.1   Internal and External Criticism

are often located in a dusty, out-of-the-way room full of stacked cardboard boxes containing masses of fading documents. These may be incomplete, unorganized, and in various stages of decay. Once the documents or other primary sources are located, the researcher evaluates them by subjecting them to external and internal criticism (see Figure 14.1).

External criticism means you evaluate the authenticity of a document itself to be certain that it is not a fake or a forgery. Criticism involves asking: Was the document created when it is claimed to have been, in the place where it was supposed to be, and by the person who claims to be its author? Why was the document produced to begin with, and how did it survive?

Once the document passes as being authentic, you use **internal criticism,** an examination of the document's contents to establish credibility. You

External criticism Checking the authenticity of primary historical sources by accurately locating the place and time of its creation (e.g., it is not a forgery).

Internal criticism A way to establish the authenticity and credibility of primary historical sources and determine its accuracy as an account of what occurred in the past.

Bowdlerization A deliberate distortion of the past designed to protect the appearance a particular (usually favorable) image.

Nonsource-based knowledge General knowledge available to a researcher based on reasoning or an in-depth awareness of historical circumstances.

evaluate whether what is recorded was based on what the author directly witnessed or is secondhand information. This requires examining both the literal meaning of what is recorded and the subtle connotations or intentions. You note other events, sources, or people mentioned in the document and ask whether they can be verified. You examine implicit assumptions or value positions, and the relevant conditions under which the document was produced is noted (e.g., during wartime or under a totalitarian regime). Also consider language usage at the time and the context of statements within the document to distill a meaning.

Many types of distortions can appear in primary documents. One is **bowdlerization**—a deliberate distortion designed to protect moral standards or furnish a particular image. For example, a photograph is taken of the front of a building. Trash and beer cans are scattered all around this building, and the paint is faded. The photograph, however, is taken of the one part of the building that has little trash and is framed so that the trash does not show; darkroom techniques make the faded paint look new. Another example is the practice of including famous people who did not actually attend a party in newspaper society column reports of the parties of well-to-do people.[34]

In addition to primary and secondary sources, historical researchers use what Topolski (1976) called **nonsource-based knowledge.** This is knowledge available to a researcher about the past that does not originate in a specific primary document or secondary source. It can be based on logical reasoning. For example, persons A and B are a married couple in a monogamous society that values sexual fidelity. When B has an affair. A is likely to become jealous. It is also knowledge of previous significant events that shape the context of what is studied. For instance, a researcher studying France in the late 1920s is aware that a large proportion of French males in the 18- to 40-year-old age group were killed a few years earlier in World War I. Current knowledge, too, can help in understanding past events. For example, a researcher knows that the Black Plague was a disease spread by fleas carried by rats and due to poor sanitary conditions, but people in the past were unaware of the cause of this disease.

COMPARATIVE RESEARCH

Types of Comparative Research

A Comparative Method. Problems in other types of research are magnified in a comparative study.[35] Holt and Turner (1970:6) said, "In principle, there is no difference between comparative cross-cultural research and research conducted in a single society. The differences lie, rather, in the magnitude of certain types of problems." Comparative research is more of a perspective or orientation than a separate research technique. In this section, we consider its strengths.

A comparative perspective exposes weaknesses in research design and helps you improve the quality of research. The focus of comparative research is on similarities and differences between units.

Comparative research reveals aspects of social life that are general across units (e.g., cultures), as opposed to being limited to one unit alone. All researchers want to generalize to some degree. Positivist researchers are interested in discovering general laws or patterns of social behavior that hold across societies. But most positivist research is not comparative. Ragin (1994a:107) observed:

> Comparative researchers examine patterns of similarities and differences across cases and try to come to terms with their diversity. . . . Quantitative researchers also examine differences among cases, but with a different emphasis, the goal is to explain the covariation of one variable with another, usually across many cases. . . . The quantitative researcher typically has only broad familiarity with the cases.

The comparative orientation improves measurement and conceptualization. Concepts developed by researchers who conduct research across several social units or settings are less likely to apply only to a specific culture or setting. It is difficult for a researcher to detect hidden biases, assumptions, and values until he or she applies a concept in different cultures or settings. Different social settings provide a wider range of events or behavior. The range in one culture is narrower than for human behavior in general, so research in a single culture focuses on a restricted range of possible social activity. For example, two researchers, Hsi-Ping and Abdul, examine the relationship between the age at which a child is weaned and the onset of emotional problems. Hsi-Ping looks only at U.S. data, which show a range from 5 to 15 months at weaning and indicate that emotional problems increase steadily as age of weaning increases. She concludes that late weaning causes emotional problems. Abdul looks at data from 10 cultures and discovers a range from 5 to 36 months at weaning. He finds that the rate of emotional problems rises with age of weaning until 18 months; it then peaks and falls to a lower level. Abdul arrives at more accurate conclusions: Emotional problems are likely for weaning between the ages of 6 and 24 months, but weaning either earlier or later reduces the chances of emotional problems. Hsi-Ping reached false conclusions about the relationship because of the narrow range of weaning age in the United States.

Comparative research can eliminate or offer alternative explanations for causal relationships. For example, Weil (1985) looked at the relationship between years of schooling and intolerance. Past research found such a relationship in the United States, and most researchers thought that education generally broadened perspectives and increased tolerance. Weil, who looked for the relationship in other nations (1985:470), concluded that the relationship "is weaker, nonexistent, or sometimes even reverse in nonliberal democracies or countries that did not have liberal-democratic regime forms in earlier decades, compared to countries which have been liberal democratic for some time." In other words, a certain type of government is a necessary condition for the relationship. Education does not have a universal effect of increasing tolerance; rather, education socializes people to their country's official values. Where the official values are for tolerance, education increases tolerance; elsewhere, it does not have that effect.

Comparative research is more difficult, more costly, and more time consuming than research that is not comparative. The types of data that can be collected and problems with equivalence (to be discussed) are also frequent problems.

Comparative researchers can rarely use random sampling. Sufficient information is not available for all of the approximately 160 nations in the world. It is unavailable for a nonrandom subset (poor countries, nondemocratic countries, etc.). In addition, can a researcher treat all nations as equal units when some have over a billion people and others only 100,000? The small number of cases creates a tendency for researchers to particularize and see each case as unique, limiting generalization. For example, a researcher examines five cases (e.g., countries), but the units differ from each other in 20 ways. It is difficult to test theory or determine relationships when there are more different characteristics than units.

Comparative researchers can apply, not test, theory, and can make only limited generalizations. Despite the ability to use combinational theory and to consider cases as wholes in H-C research, rigorous theory testing or experimental research is rarely possible. For example, a researcher interested in the effects of economic recessions cannot cause one group of countries to have a recession while others do not. Instead, the researcher waits until a recession occurs and then looks at other characteristics of the country or unit.

Four Types. Kohn (1987) has discussed four types of comparative research. The first two fit into a distinct H-C approach, the third uses a positivist approach, and the last is a unique approach.[36]

When conducting **case-study comparative research,** you compare particular societies or cultural units and do not make broad generalizations. Examples of questions addressed by this type are as follows: How do Canada and the United States differ? How did people experience old age in Japan, Taiwan, and Korea? In what ways are the educational systems of the United States and Russia alike and different? A researcher intensively examines a limited number of cases, where the "case" is a culturally defined group. By examining in depth a small number of cases, or just one, there is relatively little need to be concerned about the equivalence of units (see Box 14.6). This method is helpful for identifying factors that are constant or that vary among a few cases.[37]

When doing **cultural-context research** you study cases that are surrogates for types of societies or units. The study by Anthony Marx (1998) on race relations in the United States, South Africa, and Brazil mentioned in Chapter 2 is a good example of cultural-context research. He examined some common ideas, race relations, official policies, and laws related to race in three different cultural settings. He did not arbitrarily or randomly choose the three nations for study. He chose them because they represented three different types of racial regimes or systems for organizing relations among racial groups. Each provided a different kind of cultural context in which Marx could examine common themes, patterns, and processes.

In the third type of comparative research, the nation is the unit of analysis. In **cross-national research,** you measure variables across many nations.

Case-study comparative research Comparative research in which a researcher compares one or two particular cultures (or cultural units such as regions) in depth.

Cultural-context research Comparative research focused on a small number of societies or cultures that represents theoretical types that are compared to permit generalizations to other societies of those same types.

Cross-national research Comparative research with data (usually quantitative) for several variables is examined across many nations and statistically analyzed.

Classic anthropological studies often involve field research in another culture. One such study describes a neighborhood of day laborers in Tokyo (Fowler, 1996). In a city known for its clean, safe streets, high cost of living, and busy lifestyle, this is a neighborhood often overlooked by tourists as well as by most Japanese. Its population is overwhelming male, consisting of men who primarily work in low-wage, unstable construction jobs. The author was an American male who spoke fluent Japanese and was married to a Japanese woman. He came across the neighborhood accidentally and studied it for 16 months, using classic field research techniques. Except for one night, he lived outside the area, returning home at night by train. His book-length report includes numerous situations, conversations, quotes, maps, and photographs. It is implicitly comparative, not only because the author was a foreigner writing in a different language for a foreign audience but also in how he explains the social relations, customs, and categories of the neighborhood using colorful details that place it in (and yet somewhat separate from) the rest of the larger culture in which it existed. The author conveys an empathetic understanding of the neighborhood men and their subculture by giving many concrete descriptions, but he situates the descriptions in the larger Japanese culture and the Tokyo urban culture. He presents historical and other contextual information and makes references to somewhat parallel places in other countries such as in the United States.

Nations are not mentioned by name, but you look at variation across nations, converting unique features of nations into variables. For statistical analysis, the cross-national researcher needs information on 40 to 50 nations. Although there are nearly 150 independent nation-states, data are rarely available for more than 50 nations.

Transnational research is a type of comparative research in which you use a multination unit (e.g., a region of the globe such as the Third World) and focus on the relations among blocs of nations as units. You do not see nations as isolated entities but as parts of an international system. Wallerstein's (1974) research on the long-term development of a "world system" since the 1400s illustrates this type of research. His writings spawned a new school of thought, world system theory, which has stimulated additional H-C research.

The Units Being Compared

Culture versus Nation. For convenience, comparative researchers often use the nation-state as a unit of analysis. The nation-state is the major unit used in thinking about the divisions of people across the globe today. Although it is a dominant unit in current times, it is neither an inevitable nor a permanent one; in fact, it has been around for only about 300 years.

The nation-state is a socially and politically defined unit. In it, one government has sovereignty (i.e., military control and political authority) over populated territory. Economic relations (e.g., currency, trade, etc.), transportation routes, and communication systems are integrated within territorial boundaries. The people of the territory usually share a common language and customs, and there is usually a common educational system, legal system, and set of political symbols (e.g., flag, national anthem, etc.). The government claims to represent the interests of all people in the territory under its control.

The nation-state is frequently a surrogate for culture, which is more difficult to define as a concrete, observable unit. *Culture* refers to a common identity among people based on shared social relations, beliefs, and technology. Cultural differences in language, custom, traditions, and norms often follow national lines. In fact, sharing a common culture is a major factor causing the formation of distinct nation-states.

Transnational research Comparative research that examines and compares multination units.

The boundaries of a nation-state may not match those of a culture. In some situations, a single culture is divided into several nations; in other cases, a nation-state contains more than one culture. Over the past centuries, boundaries between cultures and distinct vibrant cultures have been destroyed, rearranged, or diffused as territory around the world was carved into colonies or nation-states by wars and conquest. For example, European empires imposed arbitrary boundaries over several cultural groups in nations that were once colonies.[38] Likewise, new immigrants or ethnic minorities are not always assimilated into the dominant culture in a nation. For example, one region of a nation may have people with a distinct ethnic background, language, customs, religion, social institutions, and identity (e.g., the province of Quebec in Canada). Such intranational cultures can create regional conflict, because ethnic and cultural identities are the basis for nationalism.[39]

The nation-state is not always the best unit for comparative research. You should ask: What is the relevant comparative unit for my research question—the nation, the culture, a small region, or a subculture? For example, a research question is: Are income level and divorce related (i.e., are higher income people less likely to divorce?)? A group of people with a distinct culture, language, and religion live in one region of a nation. Among them, income and divorce are not related; elsewhere in the nation, however, where a different culture prevails, income and divorce are related. If you use the nation-state as the unit, the findings could be ambiguous and the explanation weak. Instead of assuming that each nation-state has a common culture, you may find that a unit smaller than the nation-state is more appropriate.

Nevertheless, boundaries between cultures or subcultures are difficult to operationalize. Cultures are hard to define, are constantly evolving, and have boundaries that blend into each other. Except for

cases of border disputes, boundaries between nations are less ambiguous, but they, too, change over time. There is no easy answer. The issue of the appropriate unit to use remains a serious one.

Galton's Problem. The issue of the units of comparison is related to a problem named after Sir Francis Galton (1822–1911), who raised an issue at the Royal Anthropological Institute in 1889 regarding a paper by E. B. Taylor. When researchers compare units or their characteristics, they want the units to be distinct and separate from each other. If the units are not different but are actually the subparts of a single larger unit, then researchers will find spurious relationships. For example, the units are the states and provinces in Canada, France, and the United States; a researcher discovers a strong association between speaking English and having the dollar as currency, or speaking French and using the franc as currency. Obviously, the association exists because the units of analysis (i.e., states or provinces) are subparts of larger units (i.e., nations). The features of the units are due to their being parts of larger units and not to any relationship among the features. Social geographers also encounter this because many social and cultural features diffuse across geographic space.

Galton's problem is an important issue in comparative research because cultures rarely have fixed boundaries.[40] It is hard to say where one culture ends and another begins, whether one culture is distinct from another, or whether the features of one culture have diffused to another over time. Galton's problem occurs when the relationship between two variables in two different units is actually due to a common origin, and they are not truly distinct units (see Figure 14.2).

Galton's problem originated with regard to comparisons across cultures, but it applies to historical comparisons also. It arises when a researcher asks whether units are really the same or different in different historical periods. For example, is the Cuba of 1885 the same country as the Cuba of 1985? Do 100 years since the end of Spanish colonialism, the rise of U.S. influence, independence, dictatorship, and a communist revolution fundamentally change the unit?

Galton's problem The potential problem of finding correlations or associations among characteristics in multiple cases or units, when the characteristics diffused from a single source and the units (e.g., countries, cultures) are not really independent cases.

Data in Cross-Cultural Research

Comparative Field Research. Many comparative researchers use field research and participant observation in cultures other than their own. Anthropologists are specially trained and prepared for this type of research. The exchange of methods between anthropological and field research suggests that there are small differences between field research in one's own society and in another culture. Field research in a different culture is usually more difficult and places more requirements on the researcher.

Existing Sources of Qualitative Data. Comparative researchers can use secondary sources. For example, a researcher who conducts a comparative study of the Brazilian, Canadian, and Japanese educational systems can read studies by researchers from many countries, including Brazil, Canada, and Japan, which describe the education systems in the three nations.

There may have been 5,000 different human cultures throughout human history; about 1,000 of them have been studied by social researchers. A valuable source of ethnographic data on different cultures is the **Human Relations Area Files (HRAF)** and the related *Ethnographic Atlas.*[41] The HRAF is a collection of field research reports that anthropologist George Murdock began to gather and organize in 1938. It brings together information from ethnographic studies on various cultures, most of which are primitive or small tribal groupings. Extensive information on nearly 300 cultures has been organized by social characteristics or practices (e.g., infant feeding, suicide, childbirth, etc.). A study on a particular culture is divided up, and its information on a characteristic is grouped with that from other studies. This makes it easy to compare many cultures on the same characteristic. For example, a researcher interested in inheritance can learn that of 159 different cultures in which it has been studied, 119 have a patrilineal form (father to son), 27 matrilineal (mother to daughter), and 13 mixed inheritance.

Researchers can use the HRAF to study relationships among several characteristics of different cultures. For example, to find out whether sexual assault against women, or rape, is associated with

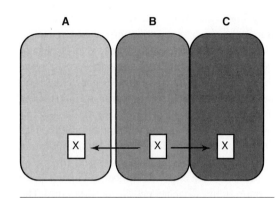

FIGURE 14.2   Galton's Problem. *Galton's problem* occurs when a researcher observes the same social relationship (represented by X) in different settings or societies (represented as A, B, and C) and falsely concludes that the social relationship arose independently in these different places. The researcher may believe he or she has discovered a relationship in three separate cases. But the actual reason for the occurrence of the social relation may be a shared or common origin that has diffused from one setting to others. This is a problem because the researcher who finds a relationship (e.g., a marriage pattern) in distinct settings or units of analysis (e.g., societies) may believe it arose independently in different units. This belief suggests that the relationship is a human universal. The researcher may be unaware that in fact it exists because people have shared the relationship across units.

patriarchy (i.e., the holding of power and authority by males), a researcher can examine the presence of sexual assault and the strength of patriarchy in many cultures.

Using the HRAF does have limitations, however. First, the quality of the original research reports depends on the initial researcher's length of time in the field, familiarity with the language, and prior experience, as well as on the explicitness of the research report. In addition, the range of behavior observed by the initial researcher and the depth of inquiry can

Human Relations Area Files (HRAF) An extensive catalog and comprehensive collection of ethnographies on many cultures (mostly preliterate) that permits a researcher to compare across cultural units.

vary. For example, a researcher may say that in culture X the children are not punished, when in fact children are punished, but in private, and it is the public punishment of children that is taboo. In addition, the categorization of characteristics in the HRAF can be crude. For example, the importance of sorcery in a culture could be coded on a scale from highly important to not very important. Another limitation involves the cultures that have been studied. Western researchers have made contact with and conducted field research on a limited number of cultures prior to these cultures' contact with the outside world. The cultures studied are not a representative sample of all the human cultures that existed. In addition, Galton's problem (discussed earlier) can be an issue.

Cross-National Survey Research. Survey research was discussed in Chapter 10. This section examines issues that arise when a researcher uses the survey technique in other cultures.[42] The limitations of a cross-cultural survey are not different in principle from those of a survey within one culture. Nevertheless, they are usually so much greater in magnitude and severity that a researcher must carefully consider whether the survey is the best method in a setting.

Survey research in a different culture requires that the researcher possess an in-depth knowledge of its norms, practices, and customs. Without such an in-depth knowledge, it is easy to make serious errors in procedure and interpretation. Knowing another language is not enough. A researcher needs to be multicultural and thoroughly know the culture in addition to being familiar with the survey method. Substantial advance knowledge about the other culture is needed prior to entering it or planning the survey. Close cooperation with the native people of the other culture is also essential.

A researcher's choice of the cultures or nations to include in a cross-cultural survey should be made on both substantive (e.g., theoretical, research question) and practical grounds. Each step of survey research (question wording, data collection, sampling, interviewing, etc.) must be tailored to the culture in which it is conducted. One critical issue is how the people from the other culture experience the survey. In some cultures, the survey and interviewing itself may be a strange, frightening experience, analogous to a police interrogation.

Sampling for a survey is also affected by the cultural context. Comparative survey researchers must consider whether accurate sampling frames are available, the quality of mail or telephone service, and transportation to remote rural areas. They need to be aware of such factors as how often people move, the types of dwellings in which people live, the number of people in a dwelling, the telephone coverage, or typical rates of refusal. Researchers must tailor the sampling unit to the culture and consider how basic units, such as the family, are defined in that culture. Special samples or methods for locating people for a sample may be required. For example, in his survey in India, Elder (1973) reported that he undersampled people living in servant quarters located behind middle- and upper-income homes.

Although researchers have conducted surveys across cultures and languages for decades, and such surveys have been more frequent in the recent years, they are still learning about the complex methodological issues involved in cross-cultural survey design and question writing.[43] Problems or concerns encountered when conducting a survey in one's own culture are greatly magnified when two or more cultures are included. Direct language translation is rarely adequate, and many issues of equivalence are involved (equivalence is discussed later in this chapter).

First, the comparative survey researcher must be very culturally aware. One issue is topic sensitivity. Topics that are noncontroversial in one culture may be highly sensitive or even taboo in another. As Smith (2004) noted, topic sensitivity varies widely by culture. Alcohol use is more sensitive in Islamic than in Judeo-Christian cultures, political questions about the Communist Party are forbidden in China, and cohabitation is common in Sweden but still socially sensitive elsewhere. Cultural settings imply other differences. One can ask about the emperor in Japan or the queen in Great Britain but not in the United States or Germany. In some African and Islamic societies, asking about a man's wife should be phrased in the plural. The researcher needs to know regional variations, such as in Scottish law a person can be found guilty, not proven, or innocent but in English law somone is guilty or not guilty. As Braun (2003) emphasized, respondents will interpret questions in their own known context, and fill in meaning using local knowledge, assumptions, and interpretations, even when the question originated in a different cultural-language setting. For example, asking, "If the mother works, does the child suffer?" can vary by culture. Respondents may envision the child as an infant or a 5-year-old. Their reaction can vary widely if their society has many part-time jobs with flexible hours near home widely available to mothers and there is an extensive system of free, high-quality child-care versus living where mothers must work full-time some distance away with few or very expensive child-care facilities. What may appear to be the same, even in the same language, may not have the same meaning. The English term *Social Security* is used in Australia, Britain, Canada, Ireland, and the United States but has a different meaning in each country and refers to different government programs.

Second, patterns and styles of communication vary by culture. The pace of talk and use of silence vary both culturally and linguistically. Social desirability (see Chapter 10), the response set or yes saying, and public willingness to answer survey questions vary significantly by culture.[44] In addition to the questions themselves, response scales (e.g., strongly agree, disagree, etc.) vary widely across languages and cultural settings. King and colleagues (2004) described a method of using short vignettes to anchor responses within a specific cultural setting. For example, asking about someone being elderly or middle aged may vary by societal context. In one society, middle aged may mean 30 years old and elderly may mean 45 because of high death rates, whereas in another people think of 50 years old as middle aged and 70 as elderly. Likewise, rather than ask a respondent whether the amount of political say he or she has is "None at all, A little, or A lot," King and associates (2004) suggested that a researcher first provide a set of concrete stories, or vignettes, and ask a respondent to match his or her response to a vignette. For example, in the standard Likert-form question–response, Mexicans may say they have less political influence than do Chinese.

This may be even though Mexico has a far more open political system with voting that has thrown out the ruling party, while China is a one-party totalitarian state. When given five vignettes about their likely response to poor-quality local drinking water—from supporting opposition candidates, to initiating a petition, to feeling it is worthless to vote, to asking local leaders for help, to suffering in silence—the respondents in Mexico and China may answer in ways that better reflect their actual political influence. Researchers can statistically calibrate general responses with a few vignettes.

Interviewing requires special attention in cross-cultural situations. Selection and training of interviewers depends on the education, norms, and etiquette of the other culture. The interview situation raises issues such as norms of privacy, ways to gain trust, beliefs about confidentiality, and differences in dialect. For example, in some cultures, an interviewer must spend a day in informal discussion before achieving the rapport needed for a short formal interview.

Comparative researchers need to be aware of a version of social desirability bias—the **courtesy bias.** It occurs when strong cultural norms cause respondents to hide anything unpleasant or give answers that the respondent thinks that the interviewer wants. Respondents may seriously understate or overstate some characteristics (e.g., income, accomplishments, education) because of cultural norms. In addition, the manner in which answers are given (e.g., tone of voice, situation, etc.) may change their meaning (see Box 14.7).

Access can be a serious issue in cultures in which cultural norms limit openness or protect privacy. In addition, the researcher's origin from another country or culture may be a significant barrier in itself. Specific problems involve knowing what agencies and individuals to contact, the appropriate procedures for making contacts (e.g., a formal letter of introduction), how to maintain goodwill (e.g., gift giving), and the effects of such arrangements

---

Courtesy bias When very strong cultural norms exist to "maintain face" or hide unpleasant information from others, including social researchers.

BOX **14.7** **Cross-Cultural Answers to Survey Questions**

The meaning of a statement or answer to a question often depends on the customs of a culture, the social situation, and the manner in which the answer is spoken. The manner of answering can reverse the different meanings of the same answer based on the manner in which the answer was spoken.

MANNER IN WHICH ANSWER SPOKEN	ANSWER TO QUESTION	
	Yes	No
Polite	No	Yes
Emphatic	Yes	No

Source: Adapted from Hymes (1970:329).

CHART 14.1   **Cross-Cultural Survey Question Design**

QUESTION SOURCE	ADVANTAGE	DISADVANTAGE
Adapt or adopt existing question	Easy, inexpensive, and fast	Often language and cultural suitability problems
New question methods	High cultural suitability, few language problems	High development cost, more time required

Source: Adapted from Harkness, van de Vijver, and Johnson, (2003:25).

on the quality and comparability of research. In some cultures, bribery, family connections, or the approval of local political authorities are required for access to sampling frames, certain sections of a town, or specific respondents. In addition, a researcher may have to take special precautions to protect the confidentiality and integrity of data once they have been collected.

Survey Questionnaires and Multiple Languages. Most survey researchers use an "ask-the-same-question" approach, in which they use an existing question or develop a question in one language and then translate or adopt it into another language. An alternative is to design new questions for multiple languages from the beginning. There is a trade-off between adopting existing questions and creating new ones (see Chart 14.1) that suggests developing new questions is preferred for better quality survey research.

Adapting questions appears straightforward without changes in meaning, such as making minor adjustments as in changing the word *stomach* to *tummy* when a question is adapted to children. However, there are many possible pitfalls. Ideally, translators are familiar with survey questionnaire design and the concepts a researcher is attempting to measure. Beyond words, a researcher must be

aware of what is left unstated or implied. For example, the question, "Can you open the door?" can mean an ability, or it can be a request, depending on the language and context in which it appears. Grammatical gender is an issue in many languages. German has three, whereas French, Italian, and Spanish have two. In some languages gendered grammar marks the speaker's gender; in others it indicates the target about whom one is speaking. For example, you might not be able to ask about a "friend" without specifying gender. The English question, "Who is your best friend?" requires asking two questions, "Who is your best male friend?" "Who is your best female friend?" Certain occupations, such as secretary, may be so strongly gendered that asking about whether a male or female has the job is very awkward. Other statuses are embedded in terms. In some languages, such as Japanese, you cannot ask about someone's brother or sister without specifying whether it is an older or younger brother or sister.

Even what appears to be the same word (e.g., friend, *Freund*, *amigo*) carries different connotations and cultural meanings. For example, *liberty* in English and *liberté* in French translate as being the same, but they have different meanings because of historical context and political-ideational context. Language and cultural differences may exist within the same country. The English word *education* in the United States primarily refers to academic subjects, whereas the similar word *educación* used among Spanish-speaking immigrants includes learning social skills not normally included in the content of the English use of the term *education*.

Comparative researchers often use a technique called **back translation** to achieve lexicon equivalence.[45] In back translation, a phrase or question is translated from one language to another and then back again. For example, a phrase in English is translated into Korean and then independently translated from Korean back into English. A researcher then compares the first and second English versions. For example, in a study to compare knowledge of international issues by U.S. and Japanese college students, the researchers developed a questionnaire in English. They next had a team of Japanese college faculty translate the questionnaire into Japanese. Some changes were made in the questionnaire. When they used back translation, they discovered "30 translating errors, including some major ones" (Cogan et al., 1988:285).

Back translation does not help when words for a concept do not exist in a different language (e.g., there is no word for *trust* in Hindi, for *loyalty* in Turkish, or for *good quarrel* in Thai). Thus, translation may require complex explanations, or a researcher may not be able to use certain concepts.

Increasingly, researchers advise against simple translation including back translation because it cannot catch all problems. Harkness (2003:42) noted that the German phrase, *Das Leben in vollen Zügen geißen,* was translated into English as "Enjoy life in full trains." This was accurate and not caught by back translation techniques. The actual meaning in English is, "Live life to the full" (British English) or "Live life to the fullest" (American English). This is because the word *Zügen* has two meanings, one of which is trains. She argues (Harkness 2003:35), "Whenever possible, translation should be integrated into the study design. In practice, however, translation rarely is seen as part of questionnaire design and usually is treated as an addendum." Modern cross-cultural communication and translation theory suggests using an intergrated approach, with a team of translators checking survey wording with techniques, such as cognitive interviews and focus groups, to discuss the actual meanings of survey questions. Researchers should avoid **safari research**—the tendency of a research team from one culture to develop a project and measures in its own cultural-language context, then impose them onto another culture. The alternative is joint research with a multicultural research team.

Back translation is one of several sequential methods that starts with a questionnaire that was written in one language and created from a single cultural perspective.[46] It is then translated into a new language for use in different cultural setting (see Box 14.8 and Figure 14.3). Newer methods involve parallel or simultaneous survey development. From the beginning, a team of researchers and translators writes questions in multiple languages and designs questionnaires for use in multiple cultural settings. Such new methods are likely to avoid many past questionnaire translation problems.

Western Cultural Bias

Most social research is conducted by people who live, work, or have been educated in any one of a handful of societies in which advanced Western culture is dominant. This creates a danger of a **Western cultural bias** and ethnocentrism. As Myrdal (1973:89) concluded, "A Western approach must be regarded as a biased approach."

Each culture has its own assumptions, modes of thought, orientation toward time, and fundamental

---

Back translation Written material is translated into a second language, translated back to the original language by a different translator, then the original writing and the translated versions are compared.

Safari research When researchers from one culture impose their perspectives, ideas, and issues onto another culture and treat the studied culture as only an exotic object to be studied.

Western cultural bias A bias in comparative research that is organized around the outlook and perspective of advanced Western societies that is largely insensitive to local, non-Western cultural issues, values, or perspectives.

BOX **14.8** Approaches to Cross-Cultural Survey Translation

1. *Translation-on-the-fly.* Researchers develop and pilot test a questionnaire in one language. Bilingual interviewers are employed and translate each question and response during interviews.
2. *Single translation.* Researchers develop and pilot test a questionnaire in one language. A skilled translator converts it from the original language to a target language.
3. *Back translation.* Researchers develop and pilot test a questionnaire in one language. A translator takes it from the original language to a target language. The translated questionnaire is next translated back to the original language by a second translator. The results are compared with the original questionnaire and adjustments made.
4. *Parallel translation.* A multicultural group develops a questionnaire with two or more translators independently translating a questionnaire. Each translator incorporates input from multiple target cultural-language sources. Later, the questionnaires

are coordinated and adjusted based on a review and adjudication by a multicultural/lingual team. The questionnaires are then pilot tested in multiple cultural-language contexts.
5. *Simultaneous development.* A team of translators and researchers from different languages/cultures work together, discussing the meanings of concepts and terms in the several languages with alternative translations. The questionnaire items are created for multiple languages/cultural contexts through a decentering process sensitive to *emic/etic* distinctions, with culturally specific and multiple-culture ideas/terms. An independent multicultural/lingual team reviews and adjudicates questionnaires in multiple languages. The questionnaires are pilot tested with bilingual-cultural and monolingual-cultural respondents.

Sources: See Smith (2004), Harkness, van de Vijver, and Johnson (2003), Harkness, Pennell, and Schoua-Glusberg (2004).

---

values about human life. All these influence thinking and social relations. If social researchers were totally free of culture or had a unique professional culture apart from any specific culture, then cultural bias would not be an issue. But this is unrealistic. It is too easy for researchers to believe that their assumptions, concepts, findings, and values—which are colored by Western culture—apply universally to all people in the world.

A comparative approach encourages researchers to ask questions that challenge their own cultural tradition.[47] In addition, a comparative perspective stimulates researchers to look beyond surface appearances. They may just be symptoms of deeper beliefs, values, and relationships. By becoming multicultural, a researcher gains a better awareness of problems in doing social research and of Western bias, and can produce improved social research as a result.

An Inverted Focus. Researchers outside the United States, and some within it, criticize U.S. social science for being "inverted" or too self-

centered. American theories and ways to conduct social research became dominant during the years following World War II, and many Americans arrogantly assumed this was natural because their methods and theories were the best. This problem is compounded by the U.S. global economic, military, and political dominance and by the international strength of popular and commercial U.S. culture.

Unfortunately, many researchers only see concerns from the viewpoint of their own cultural values and beliefs, citing only research that was conducted in the United States. Too often, they ignore concerns relevant to the rest of the world and overlook studies conducted by scholars outside the United States (Connell, 1990).

The "inverted" focus causes two problems. First, the vast research establishment in the United States produces a large majority of the world's empirical social science research. An inverted focus distorts understanding about social relations around the planet. It shows conditions or events only through the lens of U.S. culture, which can create

Translation on-the-Fly

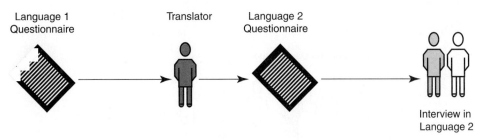

Single Translation

Back Translation

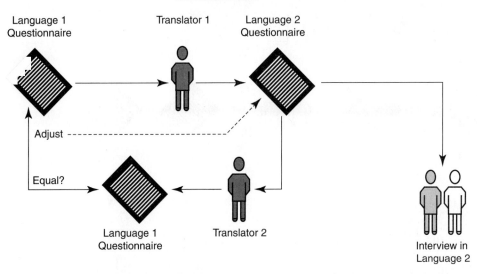

FIGURE 14.3   Cross-Cultural Survey Translation

(continued)

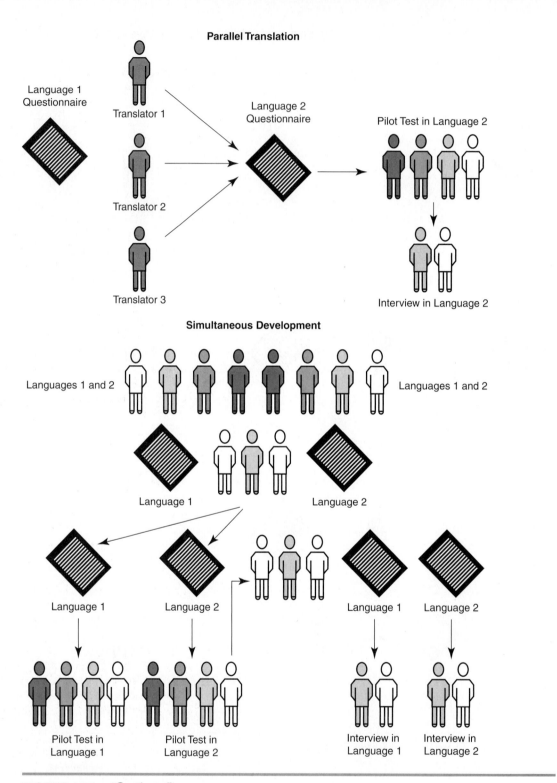

FIGURE 14.3 (Continued)

misinterpretations or misunderstanding of larger global issues as well as the concerns of people in different cultural settings. Second, many researchers, especially those who adopt a positivist approach, believe they are discovering universal laws of human behavior. If they formulate research questions based on the views of only one culture, study only one culture, and cite studies conducted in only one culture, their results are not universal. They are building a national rather than a global social science. U.S. researchers cannot generalize beyond the national context except when justified by comparative research, and they need to guard against ethnocentricism.[48]

Certain issues, methods, or theories may be limited and apply to one nation or a very few nations, whereas other issues, methods, and theories may be truly universal to all humanity. Thus, it may be beneficial to think in terms of having both national and universal social sciences.[49] The claim that sociology and other fields are universal sciences that discover principles for all people is often overstated. This claim is true only to the extent that researchers regularly use cross-national methods and ideas and make cross-cultural comparisons an integral part of their research designs.

Anthropologists distinguish emic from etic concepts and approaches.[50] Although it is an overly simple dichotomy, it helps to clarify comparative research issues. An **emic** approach analyzes cultural elements in terms of a native's explicit or implicit categories and meaning system. It is the "insider's" or "native's" interpretation of customs or beliefs. Emic concepts are ones developed and used within a specific cultural setting, and they may not exist elsewhere. They are perceptions and understandings appropriate by the insider's culture. An **etic** approach analyzes cultural elements in terms of cultural-neutral, comparative categories and principles. It applies the external researcher's interpretation of events, customs, or beliefs and focuses on meaning from a decontextualized perspective. Etic concepts are universal in the international scientific community or are widely shared across many cultures. Comparative social researchers recognize and apply both the emic and etic approaches. They try not only to understand and see the world from the insider's view

of a specific cultural setting but also to be able to transcend that setting to establish linkages among and communicate across diverse cultural settings.

EQUIVALENCE IN HISTORICAL-COMPARATIVE RESEARCH

The Importance of Equivalence

Equivalence is a critical issue in all research.[51] It is the issue of making comparisons across divergent contexts, or whether a researcher, living in a specific time period and culture, correctly reads, understands, or conceptualizes data about people from a different historical era or culture. Without equivalence, a researcher cannot use the same concepts or measures in different cultures or historical periods, and this makes comparison difficult, if not impossible. It is similar to the problems that arise with measurement validity in quantitative research.

The equivalence issue varies on a continuum. At one extreme, a researcher discovers something that is totally foreign to his or her experience (e.g., head-hunting and cannibalism) or that is unique to a particular time or culture. At the opposite extreme, there are subtle differences, which are easily overlooked but could affect comparisons. For example, Elder (1973:127) noted this problem when translating the term *friend* across three European languages:

> *Take* friend *in English*, Freund *in German, and* amigo *in Spanish. Technically, they translate identically. Yet the German* Freund *refers to a few deep, personal associates; the English* friend *refers to a somewhat less intense and wider range of acquaintances; and the Spanish* amigo *refers to a very wide range of persons, some of whom might have been met only that day. Thus, the question, "How many friends do you have?" is asking something different in all three languages.*

Emic Concepts or approaches are ones developed and used within a specific cultural setting, and they may not exist elsewhere.

Etic Concepts or approaches that are universal in the international scientific community or widely shared across multiple cultural settings.

Types of Equivalence

The equivalence issue has implications for H-C research. A researcher might misunderstand or misinterpret events in a different era or culture. Assuming that the (emic) interpretation is correct, a researcher may find it difficult to conceptualize and organize the events to make comparisons across times or places (etic). If he or she fully grasps another time or culture (emic), a researcher may still find it difficult to communicate with others from his or her own time and culture (emic). The equivalence issue can be divided into four subtypes: lexicon equivalence, contextual equivalence, conceptual equivalence, and measurement equivalence.

Lexicon Equivalence. **Lexicon equivalence** is

the correct translation of words and phrases, or finding a word that means the same thing as another word. This is clearest between two languages. For example, in many languages and cultures there are different forms of address and pronouns for intimates (e.g., close friends and family members) and subordinates (e.g., younger persons and lower-status people) from those used in unknown or public settings or for persons of higher social status. There are no directly equal linguistic forms of speech in English, although the idea of close personal versus public relations exists in English-speaking cultures. In such languages, switching pronouns when saying "How are you today?" might indicate a change in status or in the social relationship. One would have to indicate it in another, perhaps nonverbal, way if speaking in English.

Lexicon equivalence can be significant in historical research because the meaning of words changes over time, even in the same language. The greater the distance in time, the greater the chance that an expression will have a different meaning or

connotation. For example, today the word *weed* refers to unwanted plants or to marijuana, but in Shakespeare's era, the word meant clothing.

A sensitivity to subtle changes in language use can be crucial when a researcher tries to understand the perspective of other people. For example, Sewell (1980) found that differences in how people living about a century and a half ago used certain terms helped him to understand changes in their consciousness and social experiences. However, Jones (1983:24) noted, "Harnessing elementary insights derived from theories of language to problems of substantive historical interpretation is in . . . an extremely primitive state."

Contextual Equivalence. **Contextual equiva-**

lence is the correct application of terms or concepts in different social or historical contexts. It is an attempt to achieve equivalence within specific contexts. For example, in cultures with different dominant religions, a religious leader (e.g., priest, minister, or rabbi) can have different roles, training, and authority. In some contexts, priests are full-time male professionals who are wealthy, highly esteemed, well-educated community leaders and also wield political power. In other contexts, a priest is anyone who rises above others in a congregation on a temporary basis but is without power or standing in the community. Priests in such a context may be less well educated, have low incomes, and be viewed as sincere spiritual people. A researcher who asks about "priests" without noticing the context could make serious errors in interpretations.

Context also applies across historical eras. For example, *attending college* has a different meaning today than in a historical context in which only the richest one percent of the population attended college, most colleges had fewer than 500 students, all were private all-male institutions that did not require a high school diploma for entry, and a college curriculum consisted of classical languages and moral training. Attending college 100 years ago was not the same as it is today; the historical context has altered the meaning of attending college.

Conceptual Equivalence. The ability to use the

same concept across divergent cultures or historical

Lexicon equivalence Finding equivalent words or phrases to express the identical meaning in different languages or in the translation from one language to another.

Contextual equivalence The issue of whether social roles, norms, or situations across different cultures or historical periods are equivalent or can be compared.

eras is **conceptual equivalence.** Researchers live within specific cultures and historical eras. Their concepts are based on their experiences and knowledge from their own culture and era. Researchers may try to stretch their concepts by learning about other cultures or eras, but their views of other cultures or eras are colored by their current life situations. This creates a persistent tension and raises the question: Can a researcher create concepts that are simultaneously true reflections of life experiences in different cultures or eras and that also make sense to him or her?

The issue of a researcher's concept is a special case of larger emic and etic issues, because concepts can be incompatible across different time periods or cultures. Is it possible to create concepts that are true, accurate, and valid representations of social life in two or more cultural or historical settings that are very different? For example, Thompson (1967) argued that the subjective experience of time and its measurement were radically different in the preindustrial period. The concept of punctuality or of the workday had a very different meaning or did not exist at all. The researcher interested in comparing work in the late twentieth and the early sixteenth centuries is comparing apples and oranges. For example, the word *class* exists in many societies, but the system of classes (i.e., the role of income, wealth, job, education, status, relation to means of production), the number of classes, the connotations of being in a particular class, and class categories or boundaries differ across societies. This makes the study of social class across societies difficult.[52]

At times, the same or a similar concept exists across cultures but in different forms or degrees of strength. For example, in many Asian societies, there is a marked difference between the outward, public presentation and definition of self and the private, personal presentation and the definition of self. What one reveals and shows externally is often culturally detached from true, internal feelings. Some languages mark this linguistically, as well. The idea of a distinct self for public, nonfamily, or nonprivate situations exists in Western cultures, as well, but it is much weaker and less socially significant. In addition, many Western cultures assume that the inner self is "real" and should be revealed, an assumption that is not always shared cross-culturally.

At other times, there is no direct cultural equivalent. For example, there is no direct Western conceptual equivalent for the Japanese *ie*. It is translated as family system, but as Hendry (2003:26) explained, "The whole notion of 'family system' was a concept created in the face of outside influence to explain Japanese behavior in a comparative context." The *ie* includes a continuing line of familial descent going back generations and continuing into the future. Its meaning is closer to a European lineage "house" among the feudal nobility than the modern household or even an extended family. It includes ancestors, going back many generations, and future descendants, with branches created by noninheriting male offspring (or adopted sons). It can also include a religious identity and property-holding dimensions (as land or a business passed down for generations). It can include feelings of obligation to one's ancestors and feelings to uphold any commitments they may have made. The *ie* is also embedded in a web of hierarchical relationships with other *ie* and suggests social position or status in a community. For various reasons, the U.S. occupation forces in Japan after World War II legally abolished the *ie* and tried to impose a very different, alien cultural concept, that of the nuclear family.

Conceptual equivalence also applies to the study of different historical eras. For example, income is very different in a historical era with a largely noncash society in which most people grow their own food, make their own furniture and clothing, or barter goods. Where money is rarely used, it makes no sense to think of income as the number of dollars earned. Counting hogs, acres of land, pairs of shoes, servants, horse carriages, and the like may be more appropriate. Likewise, poor people today may have finished eight years of school; may own a black-and-white television; may live in a small, run-down house; and may own a rusted, battered, 15-year-old automobile. Being poor in a past era may have meant sleeping in barns with animals, begging on the streets, being near starvation, never attending

Conceptual equivalence The issue of whether the same ideas or concepts occur across divergent cultural or historical settings.

school, and owning only the clothing on one's back. Yet, despite the material differences, in terms of the specific societies and the concept of poverty, the poor of today and yesterday may be equivalent.

Measurement Equivalence. **Measurement equivalence** means equal measures of the same concept in different settings. If a researcher develops a concept appropriate to different contexts, the question remains: Are different measures necessary in different contexts for the same concept? Armer (1973:52) defined this idea as follows: "equivalence with respect to measurement refers to whether the instruments used in separate societies in fact measure the same concept, regardless of whether the manifest content and procedures are identical or not." He argued that it may be necessary to use different indicators in different contexts. A researcher might measure the same concept using an attitude survey in one culture but field research in another. The issue then becomes: Can a researcher compare results based on different indicators?

The measurement equivalence issue suggests that an H-C researcher must examine many sources of partial evidence in order to measure or identify a theoretical construct. When evidence exists in fragmentary forms, he or she must examine extensive quantities of indirect evidence in order to identify constructs. Noting this type of process in his study of early nineteenth-century French works, Sewell (1980:9) remarked:

> *The ideas we were pursuing were stated partially and in fragments, written down in the heat of the action, often by an unknown person or by groups of persons, and are available only in the most heterogeneous forms—in manifestations, records of debates at meetings, posts, satirical prints, statutes of associations, pamphlets, and so on. In such situations the coherence of the thought lies not in particular texts . . . but in the entire ideological discourse constituted by a large number of individually fragmentary and incomplete statements, gestures, images and actions.*

Measurement equivalence Creating or locating measures that will accurately represent the same construct or variable in divergent cultural or historical settings.

ETHICS

Historical-comparative research shares many of the ethical concerns found in nonreactive research techniques.

The use of primary historical sources occasionally raises special ethical issues. First, it is difficult to replicate research based on primary material. The researcher's selection criteria for use of evidence and external criticism of documents places a burden on the integrity of the individual researcher. Novick (1988:220) suggested:

> *The historian has seen, at first hand, a great mass of evidence, often unpublished. The historian develops an interpretation of this evidence based on years of immersion in the material—together, of course, with the perception apparatus and assumptions he or she brings to it. Historians employ devices, the footnote being the most obvious example, to attain for their work something approaching "replicability," but the resemblance is not all that close.*

Errors in documentation or the failure to document primary sources sufficiently may create an accusation of fraud against historians, especially from opposing historiographic schools.[53]

Second, the right to protect privacy may interfere with the right to gather evidence. A person's descendants may want to destroy or hide private papers or evidence of scandalous behavior. Major political figures (e.g., presidents and top administrators) may want to hide embarrassing official documents.[54]

Comparative researchers must be sensitive to cultural and political issues of cross-cultural interaction. They need to learn what is considered offensive within a culture. Sensitivity means showing respect for the traditions, customs, and meaning of privacy in a host country. For example, it may be taboo for a man to interview a married woman without her husband present.

In general, a researcher who visits another culture wants to establish good relations with the host country's government. It is unwise to take data out of the country without giving something (e.g., results) in return. At times, the military or political interests of the researcher's home nation or the researcher's personal values may conflict with official policy in the host nation. A researcher may be suspected of being a spy or may be under pressure from his or her home country to gather covert information.

Sometimes, the researcher's presence or findings may cause diplomatic problems. For example, a researcher who examines abortion practices in a country, then declares that official government policy is to force many women to have abortions, can expect serious controversy. Likewise, a researcher who is sympathetic to the cause of groups who oppose the government may be imprisoned or asked to leave the country. Social researchers who conduct research in another country should be aware of such issues and the potential consequences of their actions.

Many comparative researchers from "rich," highly industrialized nations who conduct applied economic development research in "poor" industrializing nations emphasize using participatory action research (see Chapter 2). This is as much for practical as ethical reasons. Development researchers learned that unless they work closely with local people, incorporate their popular beliefs, and gain their cooperation and support, the applied research projects are unlikely to be successful or sustained.[55] In addition to usual issues with applied research and learning to respect local customs and culture, this often means the researcher, as part of doing the research project, must include teaching local people elements of research design. The researcher needs to demonstrate in very basic, visual terms the logic of research and the impact of a project (e.g., use new food-storage methods, eliminate parasites, improve drinking water, etc.) on local living conditions.

CONCLUSION

In this chapter, you have learned methodological principles for an inquiry into historical and comparative materials. The H-C approach is appropriate when asking big questions about macro-level change, or for understanding social processes that operate across time or across several societies. Historical-comparative research can be carried out in several ways, but a distinct qualitative H-C approach is similar to that of field research in important respects.

Historical-comparative research involves a different orientation toward research more than it means applying specialized techniques. Some specialized techniques are used, such as the external criticism of primary documents or back translation. Nevertheless, the most vital feature is how a researcher approaches a question, probes data, and moves toward explanations.

Historical-comparative research is more difficult to conduct than research that is neither historical nor comparative, but the difficulties are present to a lesser degree in other types of social research. For example, issues of equivalence exist to some degree in all social research. In H-C research, however, the problems cannot be treated as secondary concerns. They are at the forefront of how research is conducted and determine whether a research question can be answered.

KEY TERMS

anachronism	cultural-context research	mentalities
Annales school	emic	nonsource-based knowledge
back translation	etic	oral history
Baconian fallacy	external criticism	primary sources
bowdlerization	Galton's problem	recollections
case-study comparative research	historiography	running records
conceptual equivalence	Human Relations Area Files (HRAF)	safari research
contextual equivalence	internal criticism	secondary sources
courtesy bias	lexicon equivalence	transnational research
critical indicator	longue durée	Western cultural bias
cross-national research	measurement equivalence	

REVIEW QUESTIONS

1. What are some of the unique features of historical-comparative research?
2. What are the similarities between field research and H-C research?
3. What is the Annales school, and what are three characteristics or terms in its orientation toward studying the past?
4. What is the difference between a critical indicator and supporting evidence?
5. What questions are asked by a researcher using external criticism?
6. What are the limitations of using secondary sources?
7. What was Galton's problem and why is it important in comparative research?
8. What strengths or advantages are there to using a comparative method in social research?
9. In what ways is cross-national survey research different from survey research within one's own culture?
10. What is the importance of equivalence in H-C research, and what are the four types of equivalence?

NOTES

1. The early works include the following: Marc Bloch, *Feudal society,* transl. L. A. Manyon (Chicago: University of Chicago Press, 1961; original 1939–1940); George Homans, *English villagers of the thirteenth century* (Cambridge, MA: Harvard University Press, 1941); Robert K. Merton, *Science, technology and society in seventeenth century England* (New York: Harper & Row, 1970; originally published in 1938); and Karl Polanyi, *The great transformation,* revised ed. (Boston: Beacon, 1957; originally published in 1957).

2. They included Robert Bellah's *Tokugawa Religion* (1957), Reinhard Bendix's *Work and Authority in Industry* (1956), and Neil Smelser's *Social Change in the Industrial Revolution* (1959).

3. Three such works include Charles Tilly's *The Vendee* (1964), Barrington Moore Jr.'s *The Social Origins of Dictatorship and Democracy* (1966), and E. P. Thompson's *The Making of the English Working Class* (1963). Tilly's study of France in the 1790s combined quantitative logic and new historical data. Moore's study of England, India, Japan, Germany, the United States, and the former Soviet Union traced how combinations of events and coalitions of social groups caused some nations to develop democractic and others nondemocratic governments. Thompson's study on England prior to 1840 examined the lives, words, and actions of ordinary people. "The inspiration for a good deal of the new social history came from E. P. Thompson's (1963) *The Making of the English Working*

Class. Surely, no work in European history ever so profoundly and so rapidly influenced American historians" (Novick, 1988:440).

4. Some influential works of this period include Anderson (1974a, 1974b), Hector (1975), Paige (1975), Skocpol (1979), Tilly and colleagues (1975), and Wallerstein (1974).

5. This is a large increase over the previous period (1985–1989) when it was about 28 percent. By contrast, the percentage of historical or comparative articles in the journals between 1976 and 1978 was about 18 percent. Additional information on the history of historical-comparative research can be found in Calhoun (1996), Johnson (1982), Kohn (1987, especially footnote 1), Lipset (1968), Novick (1988), Roy (1984), Skocpol (1984), Dennis Smith (1991), Warwick and Osherson (1973), and Zaret (1978).

6. See Mahoney (1999) for major works of historical-comparative research.

7. For a discussion of differences between generalizations and analysis across temporal units and cultural units, see Firebaugh (1980) and Smelser (1976).

8. See Calhoun (1996), McDaniel (1978), Przeworski and Teune (1970), and Stinchcombe (1978) for additional discussion.

9. Brown (1978), Johnson (1982), Lloyd (1986), McLennan (1981:66–71), and Nowak (1989) provided discussions of the relationship between positivist and

nonpositivist approaches to historical-comparative research, and the turn toward a realist philosophy of science. See Murphey (1973) with regard to historical research. For comparative research, see Hymes (1970) and Mehan (1973).

10. See Goldthrope (1991, 1997), Lieberson (1991), and Treiman (1977). Counterarguments are made by Burawoy (1977), Goldstone (1997), Mahoney (1999), and Rueschemeyer and Stephens (1997).

11. For more on borrowing from anthropology, see Biersack (1989), Desan (1989), Johnson (1982), Sewell (1980), Stone (1987), and Walters (1980).

12. See also Desan (1989), Griswold (1983), and Ryan (1989) for discussions of ritual and cultural symbolism.

13. Also see Carr (1961:35, 69), McDaniel (1978), Novick (1988:604), and Ragin (1987:164–166) on the dialogue metaphor.

14. For additional discussion, see Sewell (1987).

15. See Roth and Schluchter (1979:205).

16. See Kalberg (1994).

17. For an additional discussion of the penetration of surface events, see Bloch (1953:13), Lloyd (1986), McLennan (1981:42–44), and Sewell (1987).

18. See Naroll (1968) for a discussion of difficulties in creating distinctions. Also see Whiting (1968).

19. See the discussion on periodization in Chapter 15.

20. Transhistorical concepts are discussed by others, such as Bendix (1963), Przeworski and Teune (1970), and Smelser (1976).

21. For more on the Annales school, see Braudel (1980), Darnton (1978), Hunt (1989), Lloyd (1986), and McLennan (1981).

22. Orientation reading is discussed in Shafer (1980: 46–48).

23. Shafer (1980:2) discussed this in greater depth.

24. See Lowenthal (1985:187).

25. For additional information on oral history, see Dunaway and Baum (1984), Sitton and colleagues (1983), and P. Thompson (1978). Also see Prucha (1987:78–80) for a guide to major collections of oral histories in the United States.

26. See Schacter (1995) and Schacter (2001:20–21).

27. Bendix (1978:16) distinguished between the *judgments* of historians and the *selections* of sociologists.

28. Merton (1957:93–94) discussed the limitation of post facto interpretations.

29. For a discussion of law versus tendency in historical social theory, see Applebaum (1978b) and McLennan (1981:75). Murphey (1973:86) provided a useful discussion of the issues.

30. The word *read,* as used here, means to bring a theoretical framework and analytic purpose to the text. Specific details and the historian's interpretations are read "through" (i.e., passed, but not without notice) in order to discover patterns of relations in underlying structures. See Sumner (1979) for discussion. This relates to the objectivity question in historiography in Novick (1988) and Winkler (1989).

31. Bonnell (1980:161), Finley (1977:132), and Goldthorpe (1977:189–190) discussed how historians use concepts. Selection in this context is discussed by Abrams (1982:194) and Ben-Yehuda (1983).

32. See Barzun and Graff (1970), Braudel (1980), Cantor and Schneider (1967), Novick (1988), or Shafer (1980). Most focus on the assembly of historical details that are documented in artifacts, including those of collective biography. This focuses attention on specific historical actors, their actions and motives, so it takes on an individualistic-voluntaristic slant, and studies become ideographic accounts of micro behavior. See also Block (1977), Laslett (1980), and MacIver (1968).

33. The narrative is discussed in Abbott (1992), Gallie (1963), Gotham and Staples (1996), Griffin (1993), McLennan (1981:76–87), Runciman (1980), and Stone (1987:74–96).

34. For more on the use and evaluation of primary sources, see Barzun and Graff (1970:63–128). Cantor and Schneider (1967:22–91), Dibble (1963), Mariampolski and Hughes (1978), Milligan (1979), Platt (1981), Shafer (1980:127–170), and Topolski (1976). Bloch's (1953:79–137) discussion of historical criticism is still valuable today.

35. For more on the strengths and limitations of comparative research, see Anderson (1973), Holt and Turner (1970), Kohn (1987), Ragin (1987), Smelser (1976), Vallier (1971a, 1971b), Walton (1973), and Whiting (1968).

36. Similar classifications are provided in Bollen and associates (1993), Chase-Dunn (1989:309–333), and Ragin (1994a). Also see Ragin (1989) for a critique of Kohn's typology.

37. See Ragin (1987:49–50).

38. For example, Eric Wolf's (1982) study of the cultures or civilizations around the world between 1400 and 1900 illustrates the existence of many separate cultures and civilizations prior to European colonization and the rise of nation-states.

39. For examples, see Hector (1975) and See (1986).

40. See Elder (1973) and Whiting (1968) on Galton's problem.

41. For more on the *Human Relations Area Files* and the *Ethnographic Atlas,* see Murdock (1967, 1971) and Whiting (1968).

42. For more on comparative survey research, see Burton and White (1987), Elder (1973), Frey (1970), Verba

(1971), Warwick and Lininger (1975), and Williamson and colleagues (1982:315–319). For an additional discussion of access issues, see Armer (1973:59) and Form (1973).

43. See Harkness, van de Vijver, and Johnson (2003) and Smith (2003, 2004).

44. Couper and de Leeuw (2003) discuss nonresponse, and Johnson and van de Vijver (2003) describe social desirability issues.

45. For more on back translation, see Anderson (1973), Grimshaw (1973), and Hymes (1970).

46. See Harkness, van de Vijver, and Johnson (2003).

47. See Frey (1970), Grimshaw (1973), and McDaniel (1978).

48. See also Bradshaw and Wallace (1996).

49. See Hiller (1979).

50. See Ember (1977), Harris (1976), and Headland and associates (1990).

51. For additional discussions of equivalence, see Anderson (1973), Armer (1973), Frey (1970), Holt and Turner (1970), Przeworski and Teune (1970, 1973), and Warwick and Osherson (1973).

52. See Hazelrigg (1973).

53. See Novick (1988:612–622) for an extensive discussion of the David Abraham case.

54. For a discussion of archived data, see Odette and Mautner (2004) and Richardson and Godfrey (2003).

55. See Mikkelsen (1995).

Analysis of Qualitative Data

Much of the best work in sociology has been carried out using qualitative methods without statistical tests. This has been true of research areas ranging from organization and community studies to microstudies of face to face interaction and macrostudies of the world system. Nor should such work be regarded as weak or initial "exploratory" approaches to those topics.
—Randall Collins, "Statistics versus Words," p. 340

Qualitative data are in the form of text, written words, phrases, or symbols describing or representing people, actions, and events in social life. Qualitative researchers rarely use statistical analysis. Their data analysis can be systematic and logically rigorous, although in a different way from quantitative or statistical analysis.

In the past, few qualitative researchers explained how they analyzed data. In fact, a common criticism of qualitative research was that data analysis was not made explicit or open to inspection. Qualitative data analysis has moved to a more ex-

plicit and systematic step-by-step approach.[1] Nevertheless, no single qualitative data analysis approach is widely accepted.

This chapter is divided into four parts. We first examine similarities and differences between qualitative and quantitative data analysis. Next, we look at how researchers use coding and concept/theory building in the process of analyzing qualitative data. Third, we review some of the major analytic strategies researchers deploy and ways they think about linking qualitative data with theory. We also look at what researchers do not see, or how they use the absence of direct, observable evidence in an explanation. Last, we briefly review other techniques researchers use to manage and examine patterns in the qualitative data they have collected.

COMPARING METHODS OF DATA ANALYSIS

Qualitative and quantitative forms of data analysis have similarities and differences.

Similarities

First, for data in both styles, researchers infer from the empirical details of social life. To *infer* means to pass a judgment, to use reasoning, and to reach a conclusion based on evidence. In both forms of data analysis, the researcher carefully examines empirical information to reach a conclusion based on reasoning and simplifying the complexity in the data. There is some abstraction or distance from the data, but this varies by the style of research. Both forms of data analysis anchor statements about the social world in a inquiry that has adequacy (i.e., it is faithful to the data). "In qualitative research, *adequacy* refers to the amount of data collected, rather than to the number of subjects as in quantitative research. Adequacy is attained when sufficient data has been collected that saturation occurs" (Morse, 1994:230, emphasis in original).

A second similarity is that both forms of analysis involve a public method or process. Researchers systematically record or gather data, making their actions accessible to others. Both types of researchers collect large amounts of data. They describe the data and document how they collected and examined it. The degree to which the method is standardized and visible may vary, but all researchers reveal their study design in some way. "Research designs in qualitative research are not always made explicit, but they are at least implicit in every piece of research" (King et al., 1994:118).

Next, comparison is a central process to all data analysis, qualitative or quantitative. All social researchers compare the evidence they have gathered internally or with related evidence. Researchers identify multiple process, causes, properties, or mechanisms within the evidence. They then look for patterns—similarities and differences, aspects that are alike and unlike:

> *[Qualitative] researchers examine patterns of similarities and differences across cases and try to come to terms with their diversity. . . . Quantitative researchers also examine differences among cases, but with a different emphasis, the goal is to explain the covariation of one variable with another, usually across many cases. . . . The quantitative researcher typically has only broad familiarity with the cases. (Ragin, 1994a:107)*

Fourth, in both qualitative and quantitative forms of data analysis, researchers strive to avoid errors, false conclusions, and misleading inferences. Researchers are also alert for possible fallacies or illusions. They sort through various explanations, discussions, and descriptions, and evaluate merits of rivals, seeking the more authentic, valid, true, or worthy among them.

Differences

First, quantitative researchers choose from a specialized, standardized set of data analysis techniques. Hypothesis testing and statistical methods are similar across different social research projects or across the natural and social sciences. Quantitative analysis is highly developed and builds on applied mathematics. By contrast, qualitative data analysis is less standardized. The wide variety in qualitative research is matched by the many approaches to data analysis. Qualitative research is often inductive. Researchers rarely know the specifics of data analysis when they begin a project. Schatzman and Strauss (1973:108) remarked, "Qualitative analysts do not often enjoy the operational advantages of their quantitative cousins in being able to predict their own analytic processes; consequently, they cannot refine and order their raw data by operations built initially into the design of research."

A second difference is that quantitative researchers do not begin data analysis until they have collected all of the data and condensed them into numbers. They then manipulate the numbers in order to see patterns or relationships. Qualitative researchers look for patterns or relationships, early in a research project, while they are still collecting data. The results of early data analysis guide subsequent data collection. Thus, analysis is less a distinct final stage of research than a dimension of research that stretches across all stages.

Another difference is the relation to social theory. Quantitative researchers manipulate numbers that represent empirical facts in order to test an abstract hypothesis with variable constructs. By contrast, qualitative researchers create new concepts and theory by blending together empirical evidence and abstract concepts. Instead of testing a hypothesis, a qualitative analyst may illustrate or color in evidence showing that a theory, generalization, or interpretation is plausible.

The fourth difference is the degree of abstraction or distance from the details of social life. In all data analysis, a researcher places raw data into categories that he or she manipulates in order to identify patterns. In quantitative analysis, this process is clothed in statistics, hypotheses, and variables. Quantitative researchers assume that social life can be measured by using numbers, then manipulate the numbers with statistics to reveal features of social life.

Qualitative analysis does not draw on a large, well-established body of formal knowledge from mathematics and statistics. The data are relatively imprecise, diffuse, and context-based, and can have more than one meaning. This is not seen as a disadvantage.

> *Words are not only more fundamental intellectually; one may also say that they are necessarily superior to mathematics in the social structure of the discipline. For words are a mode of expression with greater open-endedness, more capacity for connecting various realms of argument and experience, and more capacity for reaching intellectual audiences. (Collins, 1984:353)*

Explanations and Qualitative Data

A qualitative researcher does not have to choose between a rigid idiographic/nomothetic dichotomy—that is, between describing specifics and verifying universal laws. Instead, a researcher develops explanations or generalizations that are close to concrete data and contexts. He or she usually uses a lower level, less abstract theory, which is grounded in concrete details. He or she may build new theory to create a realistic picture of social life and stimulate understanding more than to test a causal hypotheses. Explanations tend to be rich in detail, sensitive to context, and capable of showing the complex processes or sequences of social life. The explanations may be causal, but this is not always the case. The researcher's goal is to organize specific details into a coherent picture, model, or set of interlocked concepts.

Qualitative explanations can be either highly unlikely or plausible. The researcher supplies supportive evidence to eliminate some theoretical explanations from consideration, and to increase the plausibility of others.

Qualitative analysis can eliminate an explanation by showing that a wide array of evidence contradicts it. The data might support more than one explanation, but *all* explanations will not be consistent with it. In addition to eliminating less plausible explanations, qualitative data analysis helps to verify a sequence of events or the steps of a process. This temporal ordering is the basis of finding associations among variables, and it supports causal arguments.

Some qualitative researchers are almost entirely descriptive and avoid theoretical analysis. In general, it is best to make theories and concepts explicit. Without an analytic interpretation or theory provided by the researcher, the readers of qualitative research may use their own everyday, taken-for-granted ideas. Their commonsense framework is likely to contain implicit assumptions, biases, ethnocentrism, and ill-defined concepts from dominant cultural values.[2]

CODING AND CONCEPT FORMATION

Qualitative researchers often use general ideas, themes, or concepts as tools for making generalizations. Qualitative analysis often has nonvariable concepts or simple nominal-level variables.

Conceptualization

Quantitative researchers conceptualize variables and refine concepts as part of the process of measuring variables. By contrast, qualitative researchers form new concepts or refine concepts that are grounded in the data. Concept formation is an integral part of data analysis and begins during data collection. Thus, conceptualization is one way that a qualitative researcher organizes and makes sense of data.

A qualitative researcher analyzes data by organizing it into categories on the basis of themes, concepts, or similar features. He or she develops new concepts, formulates conceptual definitions, and examines the relationships among concepts. Eventually, he or she links concepts to each other in terms of a sequence, as oppositional sets (X is the opposite of Y), or as sets of similar categories that he or she interweaves into theoretical statements. Researchers form concepts as they read through and ask critical questions of data (e.g., field notes, historical documents, secondary sources, etc.). The questions can come from the abstract vocabulary of a discipline such as sociology—for example: Is this a case of class conflict? Was role conflict present in that situation? Is this a social movement? Questions can also be logical—for example: What was the sequence of events? How does the way it happened here compare to over there? Are these the same or different, general or specific cases?[3]

In qualitative research, ideas and evidence are mutually interdependent. This applies particularly to case-study analysis. Cases are not given preestablished empirical units or theoretical categories apart from data; they are defined by data and theory. By analyzing a situation, the researcher organizes data and applies ideas to create or specify a case. Making or creating a case, called *casing,* brings the data and theory together (casing was discussed in Chapter 7). Determining what to treat as a case resolves a tension or strain between what the researcher observes and his or her ideas about it. "Casing viewed as a methodological step, can occur at any phase of the research process, but occurs especially at the beginning of the project and at the end" (Ragin, 1992b:218).

Coding Qualitative Data

When quantitative researcher codes data, he or she arranges measures of variables into a machine-readable form for statistical analysis. Coding data has a different meaning and role in qualitative research. A researcher organizes the raw data into conceptual categories and creates themes or concepts. Instead of a clerical data management task, qualitative coding is an integral part of data analysis. It is guided by the research question and leads to new questions. It frees a researcher from entanglement in the details of the raw data and encourages higher-level thinking about them. It also moves him or her toward theory and generalizations:

> *Codes are tags or labels for assigning units of meaning to the descriptive or inferential information compiled during a study. Codes usually are attached to "chunks" of varying size—words, phases, sentences or whole paragraphs, connected or unconnected to a specific setting. (Miles and Huberman, 1994:56)*

Coding is two simultaneous activities: mechanical data reduction and analytic categorization of data. The researcher imposes order on the data (see Box 15.1). "Contrasted with the weeks and weeks in which she will be engaged in mechanical processing, the truly analytic moments will occur during bursts of insight or pattern recognition" (Wolcott, 1994:24). Coding data is the hard work of reducing large mountains of raw data into small, manageable piles. In addition to making the data manageable, coding allows a researcher to quickly retrieve relevant parts of it. Between the moments of thrill and inspiration, a great deal of coding qualitative data, or filework, can be wearisome and tedious.

Strauss (1987) defined three kinds of qualitative data coding. The researcher reviews the data on three occasions, using a different coding each time. Strauss (1987:55) warned, "Coding is the most difficult operation for inexperienced researchers to understand and to master."[4]

BOX **15.1**   Themes and Coding Qualitative Data

"A good thematic code is one that captures the qualitative richness of the phenomenon. It is usable in the analysis, the interpretation, and the presentation of research" (Boyatzis, 1998:31). To code data into themes, a researcher first needs to learn how "to see" or recognize themes in the data. Seeing themes rests on four abilities: (1) recognizing patterns in the data, (2) thinking in terms of systems and concepts, (3) having tacit knowledge or in-depth background knowledge (e.g., it helps to know Greek myths to understand Shakespeare's plays), and (4) possessing relevant information (e.g., one needs to know a lot about rock musicians and music to code themes about a rock music concert) (see Boyatzis, 1998:7–8).

Three errors to avoid when coding (see Schwandt, 1997:17) are staying at a descriptive level only (not being analytic), treating coding as a purely mechanical process, and keeping codes fixed and inflexible. Codes have five parts: a one- to three-word label or name, a definition with a main characteristic, a "flag" description of how to recognize the code in the data, any exclusions or qualification, and an example.

Illustration

Label.   Gender-role disputes are an example.

Definition.   Interpersonal verbal disagreements are an example, as are conflicts or disputes over what is proper or acceptable behavior for males and females in their interactions together or separately because he or she is male or female.

Flag.   An example would be sarcastic remarks, jokes, or disagreements (very mild to angry arguments) over what a male or female should do because he or she is male or female.

Qualifications.   Only disputes among same gendered persons are considered. Any type of behavior (verbal or nonverbal) can be the target of a dispute. Interactions among overtly homosexual and transgendered persons are not included.

Example.   Outside a classroom, Sara and Jessica, 16 years old, discuss their dates last night. Sara says, "We went out for pizza—of course he paid." Jessica remarks, "Of course? You mean you expect the guy to pay?" Sara answers, "Oh, forget it."

Open Coding. **Open coding** is performed during a first pass through recently collected data. The researcher locates themes and assigns initial codes in a first attempt to condense the mass of data into categories. He or she slowly reads field notes, historical sources, or other data, looking for critical terms, central people, key events, or themes, which are then noted. Next, he or she writes a preliminary concept or label at the edge of a note card or computer record and highlights it with a different color or in some similar way. The researcher is open to creating new themes and to changing these initial codes in subsequent analysis. A theoretical framework helps if it is used in a flexible manner.

Open coding brings themes to the surface from deep inside the data. The themes are at a low level of abstraction and come from the researcher's initial research question, concepts in the literature, terms used by members in the social setting, or new thoughts stimulated by immersion in the data. As Schatzman and Strauss (1973:121) warned, it is important for researchers to see abstract concepts in concrete data and to move back and forth between abstract concepts and specific details:

> *Novices occasionally, if not characteristically, bog down in their attempts to utilize substantive levers [i.e., concepts of a discipline] because they view them as real forms. Experienced researchers and scholars more often see through these abstract devices to the ordinary, empirical realities they represent; they are thereby capable of considerable conceptual mobility. Thus, we urge the novice in analysis to convert relatively inert abstractions into stories—even with plots.*

Open coding   A first coding of qualitative data in which a researcher examines the data to condense them into preliminary analytic categories or codes.

An example of this is found in LeMasters's (1975) field research study of a working-class tavern when he found that marriage came up in many conversations. If he open coded field notes, he might have coded a block of field notes with the theme *marriage*. Following is an example of hypothetical field notes that can be open coded with the theme *marriage:*

> I wore a tie to the bar on Thursday because I had been at a late meeting. Sam noticed it immediately and said. "Damn it, Doc. I wore one of them things once—when I got married—and look what happened to me! By God, the undertaker will have to put the next one on." I ordered a beer, then asked him, "Why did you get married?" He replied, "What the hell you goin' to do? You just can't go on shacking up with girls all your life—I did plenty of that when I was single" with a smile and wink. He paused to order another beer and light a cigarette, then continued, "A man, sooner or later, likes to have a home of his own, and some kids, and to have that you have to get married. There's no way out of it—they got you hooked." I said, "Helen [his wife] seems like a nice person." He returned, "Oh, hell, she's not a bad kid, but she's a goddamn woman and they get under my skin. They piss me off. If you go to a party, just when you start having fun, the wife says 'let's go home.'" (Adapted from LeMasters, 1975:36–37)

Historical-comparative researchers also use open coding. For example, a researcher studying the Knights of Labor, an American nineteenth-century movement for economic and political reform, reads a secondary source about the activities of a local branch of the movement in a specific town. When reading and taking notes, the researcher notices that the Prohibition party was important in local elections and that temperance was debated by members of the local branch. The researcher's primary interest is in the internal structure, ideology, and growth of the Knights movement. Temperance is a new and unexpected category. The researcher codes the notes with the label "temperance" and includes it as a possible theme.

Although some researchers suggest that you begin coding with a list of concepts, researchers generate most coding themes while reading data notes. Regardless of whether you begin with a list of themes, you make a list of themes *after* open coding. Such a list serves three purposes:

1. It helps you see the emerging themes at a glance.
2. It stimulates you to find themes in future open coding.
3. You can use the list to build a universe of all themes in the study, which you reorganize, sort, combine, discard, or extend in further analysis.

Qualitative researchers vary in how completely and in how much detail they code. Some code every line or every few words; others code paragraphs or pages. Some of the data are not coded and are dross or left over. The degree of detail in coding depends on the research question, the "richness" of the data, and the researcher's purposes (see Box 15.2).

Open-ended coding extends to analytic notes or memos that a researcher writes to himself or herself while collecting data. Researchers should write memos on their codes (see the later discussion of analytic memo writing).

Axial Coding. This is a "second pass" through the data. During open coding, you focus on the actual data and assign code labels for themes. There is no concern about making connections among themes or elaborating the concepts that the themes represent. By contrast, in **axial coding,** you begin with an organized set of initial codes or preliminary concepts. In this second pass, you focus on the initial coded themes more than on the data. Additional codes or new ideas may emerge during this pass, and you should note them; but your primary task is to review and examine initial codes. You move toward organizing ideas or themes and identify the axis of key concepts in analysis.

Miles and Huberman (1994:62) have warned:

> Whether codes are created and revised early or late is basically less important than whether they have some conceptual and structural order. Codes should relate to one another in coherent, study-important ways; they should be part of a governing structure.

Axial coding   A second stage of coding of qualitative data in which a researcher organizes the codes, links them, and discovers key analytic categories.

BOX **15.2** The Process of Coding Qualitative Data

Coding qualitative data, whether it is in the form of observational field notes, video or audio recordings, open-ended interviews, or detailed historical documents, is a challenge despite attempts by Strauss (1987) and others to systematize and simplify the process, making it appear as a fixed three-step sequence with open, axial, and selective coding. Some researchers rely on text-coding software programs (see discussion later in this chapter) that force them to create codes, but the software is just one tool in a larger coding process.

Weston and associates (2001) described their coding process in detail. Weston worked as part of a six-person research team and noted that team collaboration helped to make coding processes more explicit. The ideal associated with grounded theory that a researcher begins with a completely open mind and without prior expectations is just that, an ideal. In reality, a person's academic training, awareness of concepts and theoretical assumptions, and expectations from the audience who will read the research report shape data coding. In Weston's study, the process began with one researcher on the team creating a coding system that had four codes based on a first reading of open-ended interview transcript data. The system had a definition for each coded idea and rules with examples for converting raw data into codes. Others on the research team then used the system to code selections of raw data. Based on experiences with this preliminary system, they revised the coding system and added subtypes of the original codes. The process was repeated several times with the team members individually coding raw data, meeting together to discuss coding, and revising the coding system. After months of coding and meetings, the initial four codes became three master concepts with two of the three containing two types and each type having four to seven more refined codes. This yielded 34 coding distinctions. Over the next two years, the research team applied the system to hundreds of pages of raw data. Team members continued the process of reflecting on codes, meeting to discuss coding, and refining the system. Eventually their coding system had four tiers—three master concepts, seven types under the master concepts, two subtypes within three of the seven types, and several refined codes within each of the subtypes. In total, they created 58 codes.

Over the next two years, as they continued to examine the data and present findings to the scientific community, the team kept on refining and adjusting the coding system. They were following a strategy of *successive approximation* (see later in this chapter). A few new codes emerged and system's structure shifted a little, but four years into the project, after hundreds of hours of meetings and repeated passes through the raw data, the coding system stabilized. As you see, a coding system can be more than a way to code raw data. It offers a system of analysis that provides a structured interpretation. By the way, Weston's research topic was improving university teaching, and the team's data were from detailed open-ended interviews with six professors gathered during one semester.

During axial coding, ask about causes and consequences, conditions and interactions, strategies and processes, and look for categories or concepts that cluster together. You should ask questions such as: Can I divide existing concepts into subdimensions or subcategories? Can I combine several closely related concepts into one more general one? Can I organize categories into a sequence (i.e., A, then B, then C), or by their physical location (i.e., where they occur), or their relationship to a major topic of interest? For example, a field researcher studying working-class life divides the general issue of marriage into subparts (e.g., engagement, weddings). He or she marks all notes involving parts of marriage and then relates marriage to themes of sexuality, division of labor in household tasks, views on children, and so on. When the theme reappears in different places, the researcher makes comparisons so he or she can see new themes (e.g., men and women have different attitudes toward marriage).

In the example of historical research on the Knights of Labor, a researcher looks for themes related to temperance. He or she looks for discussions of saloons, drinking or drunkenness, and relations between the movement and political parties that support or oppose temperance. Themes that cluster around temperance could also include drinking as a form of recreation, drinking as part of ethnic culture, the views of different religions on drinking, and gender differences regarding drinking.

Axial coding not only stimulates thinking about linkages between concepts or themes but it also raises new questions. It can suggest dropping some themes or examining others in more depth. In addition, it reinforces the connections between evidence and concepts. As you consolidate codes, you may find evidence in many places for core themes and build a dense web of support in the qualitative data for them. This is analogous to the idea of multiple indicators described with regard to reliability and measuring variables. The connection between a theme and data is strengthened by multiple instances of empirical evidence.[5]

Selective Coding. By the time you are ready for this last pass through the data, you have identified the major themes of the research project. **Selective coding** involves scanning all the data and previous codes. Look selectively for cases that illustrate themes and make comparisons and contrasts after most or all data collection is complete. Begin after you have well-developed concepts and have started to organize the overall analysis around several core generalizations or ideas. For example, a researcher studying working-class life in a tavern decides to make gender relations a major theme. In selective coding, the researcher goes through his or her field notes, looking for differences in how men and women talk about dating, engagements, weddings, divorce, extramarital affairs, or husband/wife relations. He or she then compares male and female attitudes on each part of the theme of marriage.

Likewise, the researcher studying the Knights of Labor decides to make the movement's failure to form alliances with other political groups a major theme. The researcher goes through his or her notes looking for compromise and conflict between the

Knights and other political parties, including temperance groups and the Prohibition party. The array of concepts and themes that are related to temperance in axial coding helps him or her discover how the temperance issue facilitated or inhibited alliances.

During selective coding, major themes or concepts ultimately guide the search. You reorganize specific themes identified in earlier coding and elaborate more than one major theme. For example, in the working-class tavern study, the researcher examines opinions on marriage to understand both the theme of gender relations and the theme of different stages of the life cycle. He or she does this because marriage can be looked at both ways. Likewise, in the Knights of Labor study, the researcher can use temperance to understand the major theme of failed alliances and also to understand another theme, sources of division within the movement that were based on ethnic or religious differences among members.

Analytic Memo Writing

Qualitative researchers are always writing notes. Their data are recorded in notes, they write comments on their method or research strategy in notes, and so on. They are compulsive note-takers, keep their notes organized in files, and create many files with different kinds of notes: a file on methodological issues (e.g., locations of sources or ethical issues), a file of maps or diagrams, a file on possible overall outlines of a final report or chapter, a file on specific people or events, and so on.

The *analytic memo* is a special type of note (discussed in Chapter 13).[6] It is a memo or discussion of thoughts and ideas about the coding process that you write to yourself. Each coded theme or concept forms the basis of a separate memo, and the memo contains a discussion of the concept or theme. Rough theoretical ideas form the beginning of analytic memos.

The analytic memo forges a link between the concrete data or raw evidence and more abstract, theoretical thinking (see Figure 15.1). It contains your reflections on and thinking about the data and coding. Add to the memo and use it as you pass

Selective coding A last stage in coding qualitative data in which a researcher examines previous codes to identify and select data that will support the conceptual coding categories that were developed.

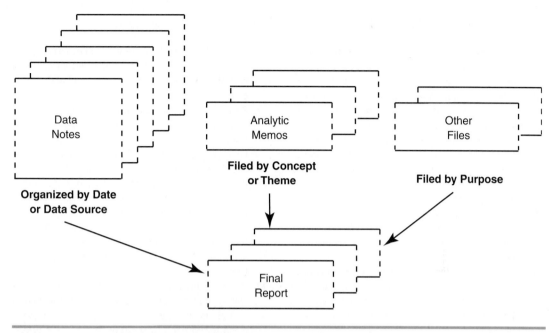

FIGURE 15.1   Analytic Memos and Other Files

through the data with each type of coding. The memos form the basis for analyzing data in the research report. In fact, rewritten sections from good-quality analytic memos can become sections of the final report.

The technology involved in writing analytic memos is simple: pen and paper, a few notebooks, a stack of file folders, and photocopies of notes. Some researchers use computers, but it is not necessary. There are many ways to write analytic memos; each researcher develops his or her own style or method. Some concrete suggestions based on the experience of other researchers are provided in Box 15.3. Some researchers make multiple copies of notes, then cut them and place parts of a copy into an analytic memo file. This works well if the physical files are large and analytic memos are kept distinct within the file (e.g., on different-colored paper or placed at the beginning). Other researchers list within the analytic memo file locations in the data notes where a theme appears. Then it is easy to move between the analytic memo and the data. Because data notes contain highlighted or

marked themes, it is easy to find specific sections in the data. An intermediate strategy is to keep a running list of locations where a major theme appears in the data, but also include copies of a few key sections of the notes for easy reference.[7]

As you review and modify analytic memos, discuss ideas with colleagues and return to the literature with a focus on new issues. Analytic memos may help to generate potential hypotheses, which you can add and drop as needed. The also help you develop new themes or modify coding systems.

Outcroppings

Many qualitative researchers operate on the assumption that the empirical evidence they gather is related to both their theoretical ideas and structures beneath observable reality. The relationship, modeled in Figure 15.2, suggests that a reseacher's data are only samples of everything that happens on the visible, surface level. The researcher uses the data to generate and evaluate theories and generalizations. At the same time, he or she assumes that

BOX **15.3** Suggestions for Analytic Memo Writing

1. Start to write memos shortly after you begin data collection, and continue memo writing until just before the final research report is completed.
2. Put the date on memo entries so that you can see progress and the development of thinking. This will be helpful when rereading long, complicated memos, because you will periodically modify memos as research progresses and add to them.
3. Interrupt coding or data recording to write a memo. Do not wait and let a creative spark or new insight fade away—write it down.
4. Periodically read memos and compare memos on similar codes to see whether they can be combined, or whether differences between codes can be made clearer.
5. Keep a separate file for memos on each concept or theme. All memo writing on that theme or concept is kept together in one file, folder, or notebook. Label it with the name of the concept or theme so it can be located easily. It is important to be able to sort or reorganize memos physically as analysis progresses, so you should be able to sort the memos in some way.
6. Keep analytic memos and data notes separate because they have different purposes. The data are evidence. The analytic memos have a conceptual,

theory-building intent. They do not report data, but comment on how data are tied together or how a cluster of data is an instance of a general theme or concept.
7. Refer to other concepts within an analytic memo. When writing a memo, think of similarities to, differences between, or causal relationships to other concepts. Note these in the analytic memo to facilitate later integration, synthesis, and analysis.
8. If two ideas arise at once, put each in a separate memo. Try to keep each distinct theme or concept in a separate memo and file.
9. If nothing new can be added to a memo and you have reached a point of saturation in getting any further data on a theme or concept, indicate that in the memo.
10. Develop a list of codes or labels for the memos. This will let you look down the list and see all the themes of memos. When you periodically sort and regroup memos, reorganize this list of memo labels to correspond to the sorting.

Sources: Adapted from Miles and Huberman (1994:72–76), Lofland and Lofland (1995:193–194), and Strauss (1987: 127–129). Also see Lester and Hadden (1980).

---

beneath the outer surface of reality lie deeper social structures or relationships.

The surface reality that we see only partially reflects what goes on unseen, beneath the surface. Events on the surface are **outcroppings,** to use a term from geology (see Fetterman, 1989:68). In geology, an outcropping is the part of bedrock that is exposed on the surface for people to see. It is the outward manifestation of central, solid features of the land. Geologists study outcroppings to get clues about what lies beneath the surface.

There are many things we cannot directly observe in the social world. We cannot observe a deep loving relationship between two people. We can see

its outward manifestation in a kiss, specific deeds of affection, and acts of kindness. Likewise, we cannot directly observe a social structure such as social class. We can see its outward signs in differences in how people act, their career assumptions, their material possessions, and so forth. Sometimes, we are misled by outward observation. Researchers use qualitative data analysis to examine and organize the observable data so that social theories reflect not only the surface level of reality but also, more importantly, the deeper structures and forces that may lie unseen beneath the surface.

Outcropping   An aspect of qualitative data analysis in which a researcher recognizes some event or feature as representing deeper structural relations.

ANALYTIC STRATEGIES FOR QUALITATIVE DATA

Techniques of coding, memo writing, and looking for outcroppings are generic approaches to the

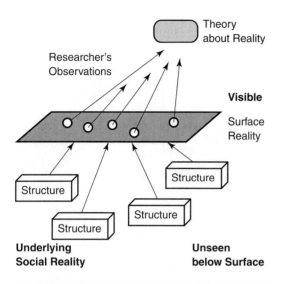

Theory about Reality

Researcher's Observations

Visible

Surface Reality

Structure

Structure

Structure

Structure

Underlying Social Reality

Unseen below Surface

FIGURE 15.2   Theory, Surface Reality, and Underlying Structures

analysis of qualitative data. Most qualitative researchers use them to some degree, often combined with a more specific strategy for the analysis of qualitative data. In this section you will learn about strategies researchers use to analyze qualitative data: the ideal type, successive approximation, the illustrative method, domain analysis, analytic comparison, narrative analysis, and negative case method.

Compared to the analysis of quantitative data, strategies for qualitative data are more diverse, less standardized, and less explicitly outlined by researchers. As Mahoney (1999:1192–1193) noted, "The absence of methodological explicitness has made it difficult for many readers to fully understand and appreciate the arguments of [qualitative data] researchers." Some researchers only use one strategy, whereas others combine several together. Mahoney (1999:1191) remarked, "Each methodological strategy and combination carries its owns strengths and limitations, no one approach is inherently better than the rest."

In general, *data analysis* means a search for patterns in data—recurrent behaviors, objects, phases, or ideas. Once a pattern is identified, it is in-

terpreted in terms of a social theory or the setting in which it occurred. This allows the qualitative researcher to move from the description of a historical event or social setting to a more general interpretation.

A source of confusion is that data take multiple forms in various stages of qualitative research. For example, field research data include raw sense data that a researcher experiences, recorded data in field notes, and selected or processed data that appear in a final report (see Figure 15.3). Data analysis involves examining, sorting, categorizing, evaluating, comparing, synthesizing, and contemplating the coded data as well as reviewing the raw and recorded data.

Ideal Types

Max Weber's *ideal type* is used by many qualitative researchers. Ideal types are models or mental abstractions of social relations or processes. They are pure standards against which the data or "reality" can be compared. An ideal type is an artificial device used for comparison, because no reality ever fits an ideal type. For example, a researcher develops a mental model of the ideal democracy or an ideal college beer party. These abstractions, with lists of characteristics, do not describe any specific democracy or beer party; nevertheless, they are useful when applied to many specific cases to see how well each case measures up to the ideal.

Weber's method of ideal types also complements Mills's method of agreement (see analytic comparison). With the method of agreement, a researcher's attention is focused on what is common across cases, and he or she looks for common causes in cases with a common outcome. By itself, the method of agreement implies a comparison against actual cases. This comparison of cases could also be made against an idealized model. A researcher could develop an ideal type of a social process or relationship, then compare specific cases to it.

Qualitative researchers have used ideal types in two ways: to contrast the impact of contexts and as analogy.

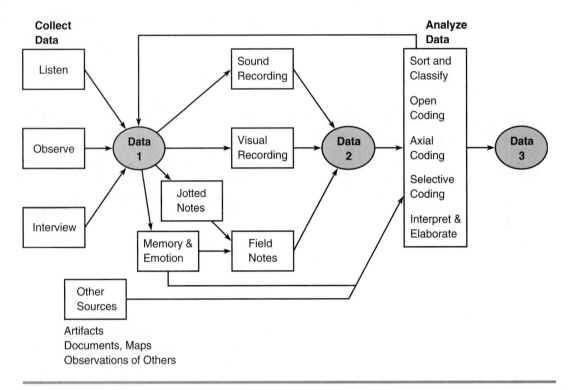

FIGURE 15.3   Data in Field Research. (Data 1 = Raw sense data, experiences of researcher; Data 2 = Recorded data, physical record of experiences; Data 3 = Selected, processed data in a final report)

Source: Adapted from Ellen (1984a:214).

Contrast Contexts. Researchers who adopt a strongly interpretive approach may use ideal types to interpret data in a way that is sensitive to the context and cultural meanings of members. They do not test hypotheses or create a generalizable theory, but use the ideal type to bring out the specifics of each case and to emphasize the impact of the unique context.[8]

Researchers making contrasts between contexts often choose cases with dramatic contrasts or distinctive features. For example, in *Work and Authority in Industry,* Reinhard Bendix (1956) compared management relations in very different contexts, Czarist Russia and industrializing England.

When comparing contexts, some researchers do not use the ideal type to illustrate a theory in different cases or to discover regularities. Instead, they accentuate the specific and the unique. By contrast, other researchers use ideal types to show how unique features shape the operation of general processes. As Skocpol and Somers (1980:178) explained:

Above all, contrasts are drawn between or among individual cases. Usually such contrasts are developed with the aid of references to broad themes or orienting questions or ideal type concepts. Themes and questions may serve as frameworks for pointing out differences among cases. Ideal types may be used as sensitized devices—benchmarks against which to establish the particular features of each case.

Thus, one use of the ideal type is to show how specific circumstances, cultural meanings, and the perspectives of specific individuals are central for understanding a social setting or process. The ideal type becomes a foil against which unique contextual features can be more easily seen.

Analogies. Ideal types are also used as analogies to organize qualitative data. An *analogy* is a statement that two objects, processes, or events are similar to each other. Researchers use them to communicate ideas and to facilitate logical comparisons. Analogies transmit information about patterns in data by referring to something that is already known or an experience familiar to the reader. Analogies can describe relationships buried deep within many details and are a shorthand method for seeing patterns in a maze of specific events. They make it easier to compare social processes across different cases or settings.[9] For example, a researcher says that a room went silent after person X spoke and "a chill like a cold gust of air" spread through it. This does not mean that the room temperature dropped or that a breeze was felt, but it succinctly expresses a rapid change in emotional tone. Likewise, a researcher reports that gender relations in society Y were such that women were "viewed like property and treated like slaves." This does not mean that the legal and social relations between genders were identical to those of slave owner and slave. It implies that an ideal type of a slave-and-master relationship would show major similarities to the evidence on relations between men and women if applied to society Y.

Ideal type analogies used to analyze qualitative data operate as a heuristic device (i.e., a device that helps one learn or see). Analogies are especially valuable when researchers attempt to make sense of or explain data by referring to a deep structure or an underlying mechanism.[10] Ideal types do not provide a definitive test of an explanation. Rather, they guide the conceptual reconstruction of the mass of details into a systematic format.

Successive Approximation

This method involves repeated iterations or cycling through steps, moving toward a final analysis. Over time, or after several iterations, a researcher moves from vague ideas and concrete details in the data toward a comprehensive analysis with generalizations. This is similar to coding discussed earlier.

A researcher begins with research questions and a framework of assumptions and concepts. He or she then probes into the data, asking questions of the evidence to see how well the concepts fit the evidence and reveal features of the data. He or she also creates new concepts by abstracting from the evidence and adjusts concepts to fit the evidence bet-

ter. The researcher then collects additional evidence to address unresolved issues that appeared in the first stage, and repeats the process. At each stage, the evidence and the theory shape each other. This is called **successive approximation** because the modified concepts and the model approximate the full evidence and are modified over and over to become successively more accurate.

Each pass through the evidence is provisional or incomplete. The concepts are abstract, but they are rooted in the concrete evidence and reflect the context. As the analysis moves toward generalizations that are subject to conditions and contingencies, the researcher refines generalizations and linkages to reflect the evidence better.[11]

The Illustrative Method

Another method of analysis uses empirical evidence to illustrate or anchor a theory. With the **illustrative method,** a researcher applies theory to a concrete historical situation or social setting, or organizes data on the basis of prior theory. Preexisting theory provides the **empty boxes.** The researcher sees whether evidence can be gathered to fill them.[12] The evidence in the boxes confirms or rejects the theory, which he or she treats as a useful device for interpreting the social world. The theory can be in the form of a general model, an analogy, or a sequence of steps.[13]

There are three variations of the illustrative method. One is *case clarification*. The theoretical model illuminates or clarifies a specific case or single situation. The case becomes understandable by applying the theory to it. A second is *parallel demonstration*. A researcher juxtaposes multiple

Successive approximation A method of qualitative data analysis in which the researcher repeatedly moves back and forth between the empirical data and the abstract concepts, theories, or models, adjusting theory and refining data collection each time.

Illustrative method A method of qualitative data analysis in which a researcher takes the theoretical concepts and treats them as empty boxes to be filled with specific empirical examples and descriptions.

Empty boxes The conceptual categories in an explanation used as part of the illustrative method.

cases (i.e., units or time periods) to show that the theory operates in multiple cases. The researcher can illustrate theory with specific material from multiple cases. An example of parallel demonstration is found in Paige's (1975) study of rural class conflict. Paige first developed an elaborate model of conditions that cause class conflict, and then provided evidence to illustrate it from Peru, Angola, and Vietnam. This demonstrated the applicability of the model in several cases.

A third use of successive approximation is *pattern matching* (Mahoney 2000b). A researcher matches the observations from one case with the pattern or concepts derived from theory or other studies. It allows for partial theory falsification; it narrows the range of possible explanations by eliminating some ideas, variables, or patterns from consideration.

A single case study with the illustrative method does not permit a strong test or verification of an explanation. This is because data from one case can illustrate the empty boxes from several competing explanations. In addition, finding evidence to illustrate an empty box using one case does not build a generalized explanation. A general explanation requires evidence from numerous cases.

Domain Analysis

Ethnographer James Spradley (1979a, 1979b) developed **domain analysis,** an innovative and comprehensive approach for analyzing qualitative data. A key part of his system, which is an organized structure for qualitative data analysis, is described here.

Domain analysis   A method of qualitative data analysis in which a researcher describes and reveals the structure of a cultural domain.

Cultural domain   A cultural setting or site in which people regularly interact and develop a set shared understandings or "miniculture" that can be analyzed.

Folk domain   A cultural domain based on the argot and categories used by the people being studied in a field site.

Mixed domain   A cultural domain that combines the argot and categories of members under study with categories developed by a researcher for analysis.

Spradley defined the basic unit in a cultural setting as a **cultural domain,** an organizing idea or concept. His system is built on analyzing domains. Domains are later combined into taxonomies and broader themes to provide an overall interpretation of a cultural scene or social setting. Cultural domains have three parts: a cover term, included terms, and a semantic relationship. The *cover term* is simply the domain's name. *Included terms* are the subtypes or parts of the domain. A *semantic relationship* tells how the included terms fit logically within the domain. For example, in the domain of a witness in a judicial setting, the cover term is "witness." Two subtypes or included terms are "defense witness" and "expert witness." The semantic relationship is "is a kind of." Thus, an expert witness and a defense witness are kinds of witnesses. Other semantic relationships are listed in Chart 15.1.

Spradley's system was developed by analyzing the argot of members in ethnographic field research, but it can be extended to other qualitative research. For example, Zelizer (1985) studied the changing social value of children by examining documents on attitudes and behaviors toward a child's death in the late nineteenth century. She could have used a domain analysis in which "attitude toward child's death" was a domain, and the statements of various attitudes she discovered in documents were included terms. The attitudes could be organized by the semantic relationship "is a kind of."

Spradley identified three types of domains: folk domains, mixed domains, and analytic domains. **Folk domains** contain terms from the argot of the members in a social setting. To use them, a researcher pays close attention to language and usage. The domain uses the relationship among terms from a subculture's argot or in the language of historical actors to identify cultural meaning:

Mixed domains contain folk terms, but the researcher adds his or her own concepts. For example, kinds of runners are named by the terminology of runners (e.g.. long-distance runner, track people, etc.), but a researcher observes other types of people for whom no term exists in the argot. He or she gives them labels (e.g., infrequent visitors, newcomers, amateurs, etc.).

CHART 15.1 Forms of Relationships in Cultural Domains

SEMANTIC RELATIONSHIP	EXAMPLE OF USE
is a kind of	A bus *is a kind of* motor vehicle [kinds of vehicles].
is a part of/is a place in	A tire *is a part of* a car [parts of cars].
is a way to	Cheating *is a way to* get high grades in school [ways students get high grades].
is used for	A train *is used for* transporting goods [ways to transport goods].
is a reason for	High unemployment *is a reason for* public unrest [reasons for public unrest].
is a stage of	The charge *is a stage of* a battle [stages of battle].
is a result of/is a cause of	A coal power plant *is a cause of* acid rain [causes of acid rain].
is a place for	A town square *is a place for* a mob to gather [places where mobs gather].
is a characteristic of	Wearing spiked, colored hair *is a characteristic of* punks [characteristics of punks].

Analytic domains contain terms from the researcher and social theory. They are most helpful when the meanings in a setting are tacit, implicit, or unrecognized by participants. The researcher infers meaningful categories and identifies patterns from observations and artifacts, then assigns terms to them.

Domains are constructed from data notes. You read your notes, looking for common semantic relationships (e.g., is a kind of place, is a kind of person, is a kind of feeling, etc.) in order to find them. You proceed by identifying a list of cover terms. In the examples, a witness in a judicial setting or an attitude toward a child's death are cover terms. Once you have a list of cover terms, you next organize the information from the notes as included terms. Prepare a worksheet for each domain relationship. The worksheet contains the cover term,

the list of included terms, and the semantic relationship. An example worksheet is shown in Box 15.4.

Next, you locate your examples of the domain relationship from your notes. The analysis proceeds until all relevant domains have been identified. You then organize the domains by comparing their differences and similarities. Finally, reorganize domains into typologies or taxonomies and reexamine the domains to create new, broader domains that include other domains as included terms.

Spradley's domain analysis formalizes six steps common to other forms of qualitative data analysis. A researcher (1) rereads data notes full of details, (2) mentally repackages details into organizing ideas, (3) constructs new ideas from notes on the subjective meanings or from the researcher's organizing ideas, (4) looks for relationships among ideas and puts them into sets on the basis of logical similarity, (5) organizes them into larger groups by comparing and contrasting the sets of ideas, and (6) reorganizes and links the groups together with broader integrating themes. The process builds up from specifics in the notes to an overall set of logical relationships.[14]

Analytic Comparison

The British philosopher and theorist John Stuart Mill (1806–1873) developed a logic of comparison that is still in wide use today. His method of agreement and method of difference form the basis for **analytic comparison**.[15] Researchers can use the ideal type, successive approximation, the illustrative method, and domain analysis to examine qualitative data from a single case or from multiple cases; however, for analytic comparison multiple cases are required. Analytic comparison uses a quasi-experimental approach that combines deductive with inductive theorizing. Basically, a researcher identifies many factors for a

Analytic domain A cultural domain developed by a researcher using categories or terms he or she developed to understand a social setting.

Analytic comparison Qualitative data analysis in which a researcher uses the method of agreement and the method of difference to discover casual factors that affect an outcome among a set of cases.

BOX **15.4** Example of Domain Analysis Worksheet

1. Semantic relationship: <u>Strict inclusion</u>
2. Form: <u>X (is a kind of) Y</u>
3. Example: <u>An oak (is a kind of) tree</u>

INCLUDED TERMS	SEMANTIC RELATIONSHIP	COVER TERM
<u>laundromat</u> <u>hotel lobby</u> <u>motor box</u> <u>orchard</u>	is a kind of ⟶	<u>flop</u>
<u>flophouse</u> <u>under bridge</u> <u>box car</u> <u>alley</u> <u>public toilet</u> <u>steam grate</u>		

Structural questions: <u>Would you call an alley a flop?</u>

INCLUDED TERMS	SEMANTIC RELATIONSHIP	COVER TERM
<u>trusty</u> <u>ranger</u> <u>bull cook</u> <u>mopper</u>	is a kind of ⟶	<u>jail inmate</u>
<u>head trusty</u> <u>lockup</u> <u>bullet man</u> <u>sweeper</u> <u>lawn man</u> <u>inmate's barber</u>		

Structural questions: <u>Would you call a trusty a type of jail inmate?</u>

set of cases, sorts through logical combinations of factors, and compares them across cases. In certain ways, analytic comparison shares features with statistical reasoning more than with quantitative data analysis. It is even used with rational decision-making models, such that particular combinations of factors may make certain choices appear to be rational for people, whereas other combinations do not.

Analytic comparison sometimes is called nominal comparison because the factors in the qualitative data are often at a nominal level of measurement, but might be ordinal. The researcher organizes data for a set of cases (often three to ten cases) into many mutually exclusive and exhaustive factors. When analytic comparison is formalized using a computer program (QCA for Qualitative Comparative Analysis, to be discussed later in this chapter), a researcher first constructs what logicians and mathematicians call a truth table. A truth table contains all the logically possible combinations of factors and outcomes among cases. This information is frequently organized as a chart (see Box 15.5) that looks similar to a Guttman scale (discussed in Chapter 7). The real strength of analytic comparison is that it helps researchers identify the combination of factors, often measured at the nominal level, that are associated with an outcomes among a small number of cases.

Ragin (1994b) contrasted case-oriented, analytic comparison with traditional variable-oriented statistical analysis. He noted that case-oriented comparison "sees cases as meaningful but complex configurations of events and structures, and treats cases a singular, whole entities purposefully selected" (p. 300). Analytic comparison almost always involves qualitative data from a small number of cases and adopts an intensive (i.e., a great many in-depth details about a few cases) rather than an extensive (i.e., a few details about a great many cases) data analysis strategy. Moreover, explanation in analytic comparison tends to be interpretative or structural rather than nomothetic. Analytic comparison emphasizes the effect of particular configurations of conditions in cases or context. It allows different causal factors to pro-

BOX **15.5** **Example of Method of Agreement and Difference:**
Theda Skocpol's Theory of Revolution

	CAUSAL FACTOR		OUTCOME
CASE	*State Breakdown*	*Peasant Revolt*	*Revolution?*
France	Yes	Yes	Yes
Russia 1917	Yes	Yes	Yes
China	Yes	Yes	Yes
England	Yes	No	No
Russia 1905	No	Yes	No
Germany	No	No	No
Prussia	No	No	No
Japan	No	No	No

Source: Adapted from Mahoney 1999, Table 1.

duce an outcome and considers highly complex outcomes that have qualitative differences.[17]

Method of Agreement. The **method of agreement** focuses attention on what is common across cases. You establish that cases have a common outcome, then try to locate a common cause, although other features of the cases may differ. The method proceeds by a process of elimination. You eliminate features as possible causes if they are not shared across cases that have a common outcome. For example, you look at four cases. All four share two common features, but they also differ in many respects. You look for one or more common causes to explain the common outcome in all cases. At the same time, you eliminate alternative possibilities and identify a few primary causal factors so that you can argue that, despite the differences, the critical similarities exist.

Method of Difference. You can use the **method of difference** alone or in conjunction with the method of agreement. The method of difference is usually stronger and is a "double application" of the method of agreement. First, locate cases that are similar in many respects but differ in a few crucial ways. Next pinpoint features whereby a set of cases is similar with regard to an outcome and causal features, and another set whereby the cases differ on outcomes and causal features. The method of difference reinforces information from positive cases

(e.g., cases that have common causal features and outcomes) with negative cases (e.g., cases lacking the outcome and causal features). Thus, you look for cases that have many of the causal features of positive cases but lack a few key features and have a different outcome.

An Example. Theda Skocpol (1979) used analytic comparison, combined with other techniques (e.g., the narrative), in her famous study of social revolutions (1979).[18] She used the method of agreement to identify a set of common causes that were present in three cases of revolution (France, Russia, and China). She used the method of difference to show how nonrevolutionary cases (England, Russia in 1905, Japan, Germany, and Prussia) lacked a cause and did not experience a revolution. She identified two primary causes of revolution: a breakdown of the state, especially the military and government administration when subjected to foreign pressures, and widespread peasant revolts against landlords.

Method of agreement A method of qualitative data analysis in which a researcher compares characteristics that are similar across cases that share a significant outcome.

Method of difference A method of qualitative data analysis in which a researcher compares characteristics among cases in which some cases share a significant outcome but others do not, and the researcher focuses on the differences among cases.

BOX **15.6** Analytic Comparison to Study the Success and Failure of Homeless Organizations

Cress and Snow (1996) used analytic comparison to analyze field-research data (1,500 pages of field notes) that they had gathered on 15 social movement organizations to help homeless people in eight U.S. cities. They identified four general types of resources—moral, material, information, and human—that the movements could have. They measured a movement organization's resources by whether it had 14 specific resources, at least two for each of the four types. For example, a specific moral resource was a public statement of support by an external organization, material support included supplies such as paper or telephone service, information support included people who were experienced at

running meetings, and human support included individuals who volunteered time on a regular basis and followed orders.

The researchers classified whether the movement organizations were *viable* (seven were and eight were not), meaning that the organization had survived for one year or more during which meetings were held at least twice a month. They found that nine specific resources were necessary or the organization would fail, as well as combinations of the five other resources. The development of the 15 organizations followed one of three "paths" based on the combination of the nine necessary and the five "other" resources.

Another example of analytic comparison is provided in Box 15.6.

Narrative Analysis

Narrative, and the related idea of analyzing a sequence of events, has multiple meanings and is used in anthropology, archaeology, history, linguistics, literary criticism, political science, psychology, and sociology.[19] We encountered narrative in Chapter 14 on historical-comparative research where it referred to a form of historical writing. In addition, a narrative refers to a type of qualitative data, a form of inquiry and data gathering, a way to discuss and present data, a set of qualitative data analysis techniques, and a kind of theoretical explanation. As Griffin (1992a:419) observed, "Narrative is both a rhetorical form and a generic, logical form of explanation that merges theorized description of an event with its explanation."

Despite the diversity of its uses, a *narrative* shares six core elements:[20] (1) telling a story or tale (i.e., presenting unfolding events from a point of

view), (2) a sense of movement or process (i.e., a before and after condition), (3) interrelations or connections within a complex, detailed context, (4) an involved individual or collectivity that engages in action and makes choices, (5) coherence or the whole holds together, and (6) the temporal sequencing of a chain of events. Next we briefly consider several kinds of narrative, then turn to examine, **narrative analysis,** a type of qualitative data analysis.

As raw data, a narrative refers to the condition of social life. Narratives are how people organize their everyday practices and subjective understandings, and they appear in oral or written texts to express the understandings. It is a quality of lived experience and a form by which people construct their identities and locate themselves in what is happening around them, at the micro and macro levels.[21] *Narrative text* is a story-like format people apply to organize and express meaning and understandings in social life. "Schooling, clinics, counseling centers, correctional facilities, hospitals, support groups, and self-help organizations, among many other sites for storing experience, provide narrative frameworks for conveying personal experience through time"(Gubrium and Holstein, 1998:164). Narratives appear in stories in novels, poems, myths, epic tales, dramatic performances, film, newspaper or media reports, sermons, oral histories, interviews, and in

Narrative analysis Both a type of historical writing that tells a story and a type of qualitative data analysis that presents a chronologically linked chain of events in which individual or collective social actors have an important role.

the telling of events of a person's life. More than a form of expression, narrative is also a practice. *Narrative practice* is the story-like form through which people subjectively experience and give meaning to their daily lives and their actions in the world. A narrative organizes information, events, and experiences that flow across time, providing a story line or plot from a particular point of view. The point of view is that of a motivated actor who expresses intentions. The narrative plot is embedded in a complex constellation of particular details, making universal generalizations difficult.

For example, in a study of Caracas, Venezuela, Smilde (2003) emphasized the narrative in the beliefs of local Pentecostal churches. A local group of men used the stories in the Pentecostal narrative to reinterpret their life experiences and it shaped their daily lives. The men adapted and used the narrative to reorganize their understandings of ongoing life events and it gave a new coherence to events. Thus, the narrative blended a religious conversion with a new self-understanding and helped the men to reinterpret their past actions and guide their current activities. Thus, more than the telling of a story, the narrative helped them construct identity and find meaning in life.

Narrative inquiry is method of investigation and data collection that tries to retain a narrative-like quality that exists in social life. The researcher using narrative inquiry tries to capture people's ordinary lived experience without disrupting, destroying, or reducing its narrative character. The researcher's inquiry is self-reflective; that is, the researcher places him or herself in a flow of events and self-consciously becomes a part of the "plot." The research sees inquiry itself—engaging participant-observers in a field setting or examining historical-comparative documents—in narrative terms; that is, as a tale with a sense of movement and a coherent sequence of events about an engaged social actor in a specific context.

A *narrative style* of presenting and describing data grows out of the interpretative social science approach. It is sometimes called "storytelling" (Berger and Quinney, 2004). This mode of presentation blends description, empathetic understanding, and interpretation. It seeks to dissolve any gap between the researcher and those being researched, making the researcher an integral aspect of the description, discussion, and interpretation in a study. Researcher and researched coparticipate in creating/gathering data and in reflecting on it, so the researcher's life and those of the people being studied are interwoven. The researcher, as an individual social actor, is inseparable from the research process and from data presentation. His or her personal biography and life situation are a part of the story format in which data are presented, discussed, and interpreted. Besides "giving voice" to the people who are studied, the researcher's voice, presence, and subjectivity are also included. The researcher is a storyteller, not a disembodied voice or detached observer; rather, a storyteller whose emotions, personal experiences, and life events are a part of the story that is being told.

Last, narrative is a method for analyzing data and providing an explanation. This take several forms and goes by several names—such as analytic narrative, narrative explanation, narrative structural analysis, or sequence analysis.[22] Besides recognizing the core elements of a narrative (listed earlier), researchers who use *narrative analysis* techniques try to systematically "map out" the narrative and give it a formalized grammar/structure. They not only recognize the narrative character of social life but also analyze data in ways that retain and unveil that character. They portray the narrative as an outline or model that also serves as an explanation.

Some authors apply a few analytic concepts to qualitative data, whereas others employ complex logical systems to detect or outline the structure of a narrative, often with the aid of computer software. As a researcher examines and analyzes qualitative data for its narrative form and elements—whether it is an individual's life history, a particular historical event, the evolution of an organization over the years, or a macro-level historical process—he or she focuses on events (rather than variables, individuals, or cases), connections among events, and temporal features, such as the order, pace, duration, and frequency. The researcher treats the sequence of events itself as an object of inquiry.

Franzosi (1998) argued that once researchers recognize narrative within data, they try to extract and preserve it without destroying its meaning-making ability or structure. They also look for what Abell (2004:293) called "action linkages"—that is, how a social actor engages in actions to transform one condition or situation into another or, simply put, makes things happen. As they map the structure of a narrative's sequence, the mapping operates as both a mode of data analysis and a type of explanation, that is, an answer to the question, Why do events occur as they do? Some feel narrative explanations are not causal, but others believe narrative analysis is causal explanation, although perhaps involving a different type of causality, one that is common in a traditional positivist science approach.[23]

Tools of Narrative Analysis.   We next examine three analytic tools qualitative researchers use in narrative analysis, path dependency, periodization, and historical contingency.

   Path dependency refers to how a unique beginning can trigger a sequence of events and create a deterministic path that is followed in the chain of subsequent events. The path constrains or limits the direction of the ongoing events that follow. In explanations that use path dependency, the outcome is highly sensitive to events that occurred very early in the process. Path dependency explanations emphasize how the choices of one period limit future options, shape later choices, and even accelerate events toward future crises in which options may be restricted.[24]

   When building a path-dependent explanation, a researcher starts with an outcome. He or she then shows how the outcome follows from a sequence of prior events. As he or she traces back and demonstrates each event's effect on another, the researcher goes backward in the process to initial events or conditions. The initial conditions a researcher identifies are a "historical fork in the road" (Haydu, 1998:352).

> **Path dependency**   An analytic idea used in narrative analysis that explains a process or chain of events as having a beginning that triggers a structured sequence, such that the chain of events follows an identifiable trajectory over time.

Explanations that use path dependency assume that the processes that generated initial events, a social relationship, or institution may differ from the processes that keep it going. There may be one explanation for the "starting event," and another for the path of subsequent events. Researchers often explain the starting event as the result of a contingent process (i.e., a specific and unique combination of factors in a particular time and place that may never repeat). In addition, causal processes in one historical period may not operate in another. "There is no good reason to assume that findings from one period support causal claims for another period" (Haydu, 1998:345).

   There are two types of path dependency: self-reinforcing and reactive sequence.[25] A researcher using a *self-reinforcing* path dependency explanation looks at how, once set into motion, events continue to operate on their own, or propel later events in a direction that resists external factors. Thus, the initial "trigger event" constrains, or places limits on, the direction of a process. Once a process begins, "inertia" comes into play to continue the process along the same path or track.

   A classic example of inertia is the QWERTY pattern of letters on a keyboard. The pattern is inefficient. It takes longer for the fingers to hit keys than alternative patterns, and it is difficult to learn. QWERTY was created over a century ago to work with the first crude, slow mechanical typewriters. Inventors designed a keyboard pattern that would slow human typists to prevent the early machine from jamming. Later, mechanical typewriters improved, and they were replaced by electric typewriters and electronic keyboards. The old keyboard pattern became unnecessary and obsolete, but it continues to this day. The inertia to use an obsolete, inefficient, and slow system is strong. It overwhelms the efforts needed to change existing machinery and people to a rational, faster keyboard system. Social institutions are similar. Once social relations and institutions are created in specific form (e.g., decentralized with many local offices), it is difficult to change them, even if they are no longer efficient in current conditions.

   The *reactive sequence* path dependency emphasizes a different process. Researchers focus on how each event responds to an immediately preceding one. Thus, instead of tracing a process back to its origins, the researcher examines each step in the process to see how one step influences the next one. The interest is in whether the moving sequence of events transforms or reverses the flow of direction from the initial event. The path does not have to be unidirectional or linear; it can "bend" or even reverse course to negate its previous direction.

One way to see reactive sequence path dependency is that a sequence of events can be like a pendulum that swings back and forth. A single event may set into motion a reaction that changes or reverses the direction of the events that preceded it. For example, as part of the long process of the U.S. civil rights movement, the assassination of Martin Luther King Jr. triggered more vigorous civil rights law enforcement and an expansion of welfare programs. Events had been moving in the direction of greater social equality, reduced discrimination, and expanded legal rights. Yet, vigorous civil rights enforcement and welfare expansion disrupted existing status and power relations. This created tensions that triggered a backlash by resentful Whites. The White backlash tried to restrict or reverse civil rights law enforcement and cut back social welfare programs. A reaction to events in the sequence reversed the direction of its path.

A historical-comparative researcher believes that historical reality has discontinuous stages or steps. He or she may divide 100 years of history into periods by breaking continuous time into discrete units or periods and define the periods theoretically. This is known as **periodization.** Theory helps him or her identify what is significant and what is common within periods or between different periods. As Carr (1961:76) remarked, "The division of history into periods is not a fact, but a necessary hypothesis." The breaks between periods are artificial; they are not natural in history, but they are not arbitrary.

The researcher cannot determine the number and size of periods and the breaks between them until after the evidence has been examined. He or she may begin with a general idea of how many periods to create and what distinguishes them, but will adjust the number and size of the periods and the location of the breaks after reviewing the evidence. He or she then reexamines the evidence with added

data, readjusts the periodization, and so forth. After several cycles, he or she approximates a set of periods in 100 years on the basis of successively theorizing and looking at evidence.

Historical contingency refers to a unique combination of particular factors or specific circumstances that may not be repeated. The combination is idiosyncratic and unexpected from the flow of prior conditions. As Mahoney (2000a:513) explained, "Contingency refers to the inability of theory to predict or explain, either deterministically or probabilistically, the occurrence of a specific outcome. A contingent event is therefore an occurrence that was not expected to take place." A contingent situation may be unexpected, but once it occurs, it can profoundly influence subsequent events. Because many possible idiosyncratic combinations of events occur, a researcher uses theory to identify important contingent events for an explanation.

A *critical juncture* is often a part of historical contingency. Researchers explain how several viable options may exist at a specific point in time. Once one option is selected by the coming together of many ideosyncratic events, it has a powerful continuing influence. Researchers combine historical contingency and path dependency. See Box 15.7.

One example is Roy's (1997) explanation of the modern corporation. He argued that the preexisting power relations among investors and government officials in the mid-nineteenth century did not inevitably cause the large private corporation to rise to prominence. A unique set of factors at a particular time and place favored its appearance. Once the institution of the large modern corporation appeared, it encouraged the ascendance of certain groups and fostered new power arrangements that operated to maintain the corporation form. An elite of financiers, wealthy investors, and executives rose

---

Periodization Dividing the flow of time in social reality into segments or periods. A field researcher might discover parts or periods in an ongoing process (e.g., typical day, yearly cycle).

Historical contingency An analytic idea in narrative analysis that explains a process, event, or situation by referring to the specific combination of factors that came together in a particular time and place.

BOX **15.7** **Path Dependency, Critical Junctures, and Historical Contingency**

Researchers combine the concepts of path dependency and conjunction in narrative analysis to discover how a specific short-term combination of circumstances can set subsequent events off along a new trajectory, and they try to identify these "critical junctures" or historical turning points. Kiser and Linton (2002) used this idea in their study of France from 1515 to 1789, and noted, "Particular historical turning points change the relationships between variables" (p. 905). They focused on rebellions again taxation in France. Tax revolts occurred in about 20 percent of the years 1515 to 1789. The taxes were primarily gathered to pay for ongoing wars (wars took place in 65 percent of the time period). The Fronde was a set of large-scale revolts (1648 to 1653) that the king's army successfully suppressed. Prior to the Fronde, tax increases and offensive wars regularly generated local revolts, but after it they very rarely did. The theoretical implication is that researchers may find that one set of causal relations are stable and operate for a time period but find little evidence for them in another period. Moreover, researchers might identify a specific event or short-term period that operates as a critical juncture or tipping point after which important relations dramatically shift and then begin to operate differently. It is a pattern of continuity along a path that is interrupted at a juncture and then is redirected to a new trajectory.

in power and benefited from the private corporation form of business organization. They actively supported it through new laws, government rules, financial relations, and other conditions. The corporation form sustained their growing power and privilege. Thus, a "chance" coming together of events at one time selected a particular form of business organization among alternatives; it was not inevitable. Once established, this form set into motion dynamics that perpetuated it into the future and altered surrounding conditions, making alternatives

less viable. It reinforced new sociopolitical arrangements and realigned economic power in ways that undermined the alternatives to it. Thus, the corporate form of organization created a path on which the events that followed in time depended.

The path dependency may be self-reinforcing to continue with inertia along one direction, or particular events might set off a reaction that alters its direction. Along the flowing sequence of events across time, periodic critical junctures may occur. The process or conditions that were initially set into motion may resist change, or the contingent conditions may be powerful enough to trigger a major change in direction and initiate a new path of events.

Negative Case Method

Most researchers focus on what is evident in the data and what has happened. Yet, at times they study what is *not* explicit in the data or what did *not* happen. At first studying what is not there may appear counterintuitive, but an alert observer who is aware of all the clues notices what is missing as well as what is there. In the story "Silver Blaze," Sherlock Holmes solved a mystery when he noticed that a guard dog did not bark during the theft of an expensive racehorse, suggesting that the watchdog knew the thief. When what was expected did not occur, it was important information.

Negative evidence takes many forms (see Box 15.8). It includes silences, absences, and omissions. For example, a field researcher notices that no one of a certain age, race, or gender is present in a social setting. This absence can be very revealing about the nature of the setting. Likewise, a researcher notices money lying on the floor, yet no one picks it up. The failure to pick it up can be an important clue. A historical-comparative researcher notices that there are not reports of a kind of crime (e.g., hate crime, child abuse) in certain locations or times. He or she may find that the absence of reports or incidences of the crime can be equally important as their presence.

The **negative case method** is a way to systematically examine the absence of what is expected.[26] It combines the method of difference from analytic comparison with deviant case analysis. In deviant case analysis, a researcher focuses attention on a

Negative case method A method of qualitative data analysis in which a research focuses on a case that does not conform to theoretical expectations and uses details from that case to refine theory.

BOX **15.8** Types of Negative Evidence

1. *Events that do not occur.* Some events are expected to occur on the basis of past experience, but do not. For example, research on the Progressive Era of U.S. history found that large corporations did not veto moderate labor reform legislation. Such a veto was expected after they had showed hostility toward labor for years. Instead, they actually encouraged the reform because it would quiet growing labor unrest.

   Likewise, nondecisions may occur when powerful groups do not participate directly in events because their powerful positions shape which issues arise. For example, a city has terrible air pollution, but there is no public action on the problem, because "everyone" implicitly recognizes the power of polluting industry over jobs, tax revenue, and the community's economy. The polluting industry does not have to oppose local regulations over pollution, because no such regulations are ever proposed.

2. *Events of which the population is unaware.* Some activities or events are not noticed by people in a setting or by researchers. For example, at one time the fact that employers considered a highly educated woman only for clerical jobs was not noticed as an issue. Until societal awareness of sexism and gender equality grew, few saw this practice as limiting the opportunities of women. Another example is that country-western song writers deny writing with a formula. Despite their lack of awareness, a formula is apparent through a content analysis of lyrics. The fact that members or participants in a setting are unaware of an issue does not mean that a researcher should ignore it or fail to look for its influence.

3. *Events the population wants to hide.* People may misrepresent events to protect themselves or others. For example, elites often refuse to discuss unethical behavior and may have documents destroyed or held from public access for a long period. Likewise, for many years, cases of incest went unreported in part because they violated such a serious taboo that incest was simply hushed up.

4. *Overlooked commonplace events.* Everyday, routine events set expectations and create a taken-for-granted attitude. For example, television programs appear so often in conversations that they are rarely noticed. Because most people have a television set and watch TV regularly, only someone who rarely watches television or who is a careful analyst may notice the topic. Or a researcher observes a historical period in which cigarette smoking is common. He or she may become aware only if he or she is a nonsmoker or lives in a period when smoking has become a public health issue.

5. *Effects of a researcher's preconceived notions.* Researchers must take care not to let their prior theoretical framework or preconceived notions blind them to contrary events in a social setting. Strong prior notions of where to look and what data are relevant may inhibit a researcher from noticing other relevant or disconfirming evidence. For example, a researcher expects violent conflict between drug addicts and their children and notices it immediately, but fails to see that they also attempt to form a loving relationship.

6. *Unconscious nonreporting.* Some events appear to be insignificant and not worthy of being reported in the mind of a researcher. Yet, if detailed observations are recorded, a critical rereading of notes looking for negative cases may reveal overlooked events. For example, at first a researcher does not consider company picnics to be important. However, after rereading data notes and careful consideration, he or she realizes that they play an important symbolic role in building a sense of community.

7. *Conscious nonreporting.* Researchers may omit aspects of the setting or events to protect individuals or relations in the setting. For example, a researcher discovers an extramarital affair involving a prominent person but wishes to protect the person's good name and image. A more serious problem is a breach of ethics. This occurs when a researcher fails to present evidence that does not support his or her argument or interpretation of data. Researchers should present evidence that both supports and fails to confirm an interpretation. Readers can then weigh both types of evidence and judge the support for the researcher's interpretation.

Source: Lewis and Lewis (1980).

few cases among a great many (including quantitative data sets) that do not conform to the general pattern. These unusual cases can be used to understand processes or generate new ideas.

In negative case methodology, a researcher uses detailed knowledge of one particular case that does not conform to what would be expected based on a theory that has supporting evidence from many other cases. The single negative case is then used to reexamine the theory, noticing lapses or problems in it. Insights from the negative case are then used to revise the theory.

For example, Emigh (2003) observed that fifteenth-century Tuscany, at the peak of the highly developed northern Italian Renaissance culture, had all the preconditions predicted by major theories for producing a rapid "take off" to industrial capitalism—efficient agriculture, well-developed commercial manufacturing, no feudal nobility, a large urban economy, and a stable political organization. Yet, it did not happen. Emigh asked why it was a negative case and gained an in-depth knowledge of the one negative case. She was then able to uncover previously unknown factors (about local rural investment) that the major theories did not take into account.

The types of analytic strategies used in qualitative analysis are summarized graphically in Figure 15.4.

OTHER TECHNIQUES

Qualitative researchers use many analysis techniques. Here, we briefly look at other techniques to illustrate the variety.

Network Analysis

The idea of social networks was discussed in Chapter 3 with network theory and in Chapter 8 with snowball sampling. Qualitative researchers often "map" the connections among a set of people, organizations, events, or places. Using sociograms and similar mapping techniques, they can discover, analyze, and display sets of relations. For example, in a company, Harry gives Sue orders, Sue and Sam consult and help one another. Sam gets materials from Sandra. Sandra socializes with Mary. Researchers find that networks help them see and understand the structure of complex social relations.[27]

Time Allocation Analysis

Time is an important resource. Researchers examine the way people or organizations spend or invest time to reveal implicit rules of conduct or priorities. Researchers document the duration or amount of time devoted to various activities. Similar to the time budget survey discussed in Chapter 10, qualitative researchers examine the duration or amount of time devoted to activities. An analysis of how people, groups, or organizations allocate the valuable resources they control (such as time, space, money, prestige) can reveal a lot about their real, as contrasted with officially professed, priorities. Often, people are unaware of or do not explicitly acknowledge the importance of an activity on which they spent time. For example, a researcher notices that certain people are required to wait before seeing a person, while others do not wait. The researcher may analyze the amount of time, who waits, what they do while waiting, and whether they feel waiting is just. Or the researcher documents that people say that a certain celebration in a corporation is not important. Yet, everyone attends and spends two hours at the event. The collective allocation of two hours during a busy week for the celebration signals its latent or implicit importance in the culture of the corporation.[28]

Flowchart and Time Sequence

In addition to the amount of time devoted to various activities, researchers analyze the order of events or decisions. Historical researchers have traditionally focused on documenting the sequence of events, but comparative and field researchers also look at flow or sequence. In addition to when events occur, researchers use the idea of a decision tree or flowchart to outline the order of decisions, to understand how one event or decision is related to others. For

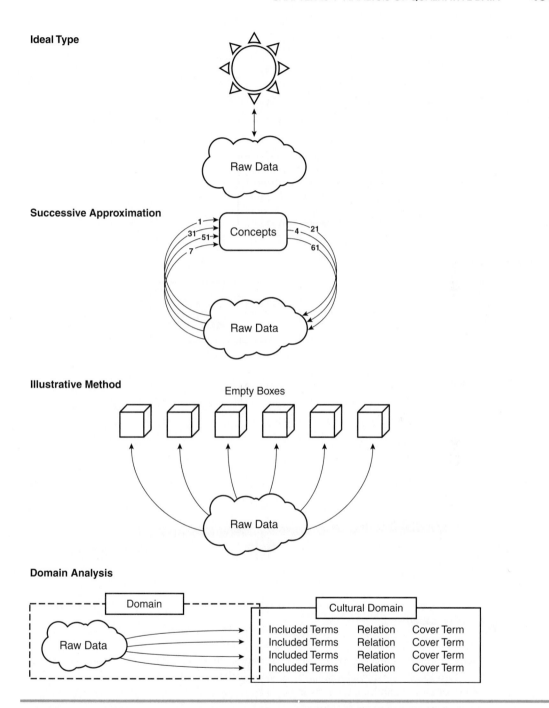

FIGURE 15.4   Summary of Analytic Strategies Used in Qualitative Data Analysis

(continued)

Analytic Comparison

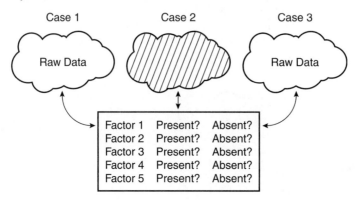

Narrative Analysis

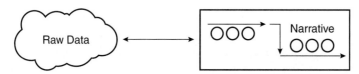

Negative Case Method

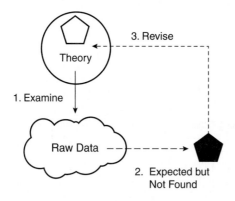

FIGURE 15.4   (Continued)

example, an activity as simple as making a cake can be outlined (see Figure 15.5). The idea of mapping out steps, decisions, or events and looking at their interrelationship has been applied to many settings. For example, Brown and Canter (1985) developed a detailed flowchart for house-buying behavior. They divided it into 50 steps, with a time line and many actors (e.g., involved buyer, financial official,

surveyor, buyer's attorney, advertising firm/realtor, seller, seller's attorney).[29]

Multiple Sorting Procedure

Multiple sorting is a technique similar to domain analysis that a researcher can use in field research or oral history. Its purpose is to discover how people

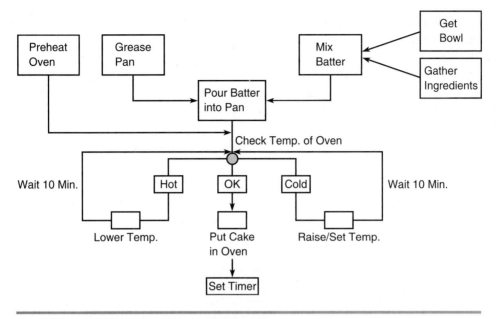

FIGURE 15.5   Partial Flowchart of Cake Making

categorize their experiences or classify items into systems of similar or different. Multiple sorting procedure has been adopted by cognitive anthropologists and psychologists. It can be used to collect, verify, or analyze data. Here is how it works. You give those being studied a list of terms, photos, places, names of people, and so on, and ask them to organize the lists into categories or piles. The subjects or members use categories of their own devising. Once sorted, you ask about the criteria used. The subjects are then given the items again and asked to sort them in other ways they may think of them. There is a similarity to Thurstone scaling (Chapter 7) in that people sort items, but here, the number of piles and type of items differ. More significantly, the purpose of the sorting is not to create a uniform scale but to discover the variety of ways people understand the world. For example (Canter et al., 1985:90), a gambler sorts a list of eight gambling establishments five times. Each sort had three to four categories. One of the sorts organized them based on "class of casino" (high to low). Other sorts were based on "frills," "size of stake," "make me money," and "personal preference." By examining the sorts, you see how others organize their worlds.[30]

Diagrams

Qualitative researchers have moved toward presenting their data analysis in the form of diagrams and charts. Diagrams and charts help them organize ideas and systematically investigate relations in the data, as well as communicate results to readers. Researchers use spatial or temporal maps (see Chapter 13), typologies (see Chapter 3), or sociograms. For example, in his study of Little League baseball, Fine (1987) used sociograms to present the social relations among players.

Quantitative researchers use many different graphs, tables, charts, and pictorial devices to present information. In addition to taxonomies, maps, and lists, they suggested the use of flowcharts, organizational charts, causal diagrams, and various lists and grids to illustrate analysis (see Figure 15.6).

Maps

Quantitative and qualitative researchers place their data on maps to help them see spatial relations and to supplement or reinforce results from other data

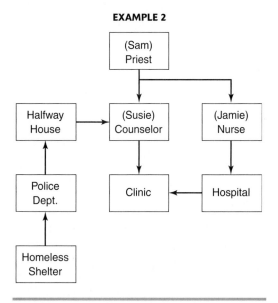

EXAMPLE 1

Person	Worked before College	Part-Time Job in College	Pregnant Now	Had Own Car
John	Yes	Yes	N/A	No
Mary	Yes	DK	No	Yes
Martin	No	Yes	N/A	Yes
Yoshi	Yes	No	Yes	Yes

DK = don't know, N/A = not applicable

EXAMPLE 2

FIGURE 15.6 Examples of the Use of Diagrams in Qualitative Analysis

analysis. For example, Ballen and Richardson (2002) used maps of France and United States to examine data on geographic patterns in suicide rates and support theories of social integration and imitation from Émile Durkheim. Kiser and Linton (2002) presented a map of France with sites of rebellions marked in their study (see Box 15.7). Villarreal (2002, 2004) used a map of Mexico in his study of violence and social-political change. McVeigh and colleagues (2003) showed a map of counties across the United States in their study of differences in local hate crime law enforcement. Myers and Caniglia (2004) used a map of regions in the United States in their study of whether protest events were reported in major newspapers. Griswold and Wright (2004) labeled areas of a U.S. map as part of their study of the endurance of distinct regional cultures. Although maps can be helpful in analyzing and presenting data to bolster an explanation, as a visual representation of information they can also be misleading and should be used with care (see Monmonier, 1996).

Software for Qualitative Data

Quantitative researchers have used computers for four decades to generate tables, graphs, and charts to analyze and present numerical data. By contrast, qualitative researchers moved to computers and diagrams only in the past 10 years.[31] A researcher who enters notes in a word-processing program may quickly search for words and phrases that can be adapted to coding data and linking codes to analytic memos. Word processing can also help a researcher revise and move codes and parts of field notes.

Here, we will consider software specifically created for qualitative data analysis. Many are new and are quickly changing. New computer programs are continuously being developed or modified, and most come with highly detailed and program-specific user manuals, so the review here does not go into detail about specific software. It covers only the major approaches to qualitative data analysis at this time.

Text Retrieval. Some programs perform searches of text documents, similar to the search function in word-processing software. The specialized text retrieval programs are faster and have the capability of finding close matches, slight misspellings, similar sounding words, or synonyms. For example, when a researcher looks for the keyword *boat,* the program might also tell whether any of the following appeared: *ship, battleship, frigate, rowboat, schooner, vessel, yacht, steamer, ocean liner, tug, canoe, skiff, cutter, aircraft carrier, dinghy, scow, galley, ark, cruiser, destroyer, flagship,* and *submarine.* In addition, some programs permit the combination of words or phrases using logical terms *(and, or, not)* in what are called *Boolean searches.* For example, a researcher may search long documents for when the keywords *college student* and *drinking* and *smoking* occur within four sentences of one another, but only when the word *fraternity* is not present in the block of text. This Boolean search uses *and* to seek the intersection of *college student* with either of two behaviors that are connected by the logical term *or*, whereas the logical search word *not* excludes situations in which the term *fraternity* appears.

Most programs show the keyword or phrase and the surrounding text. The programs may also permit a researcher to write separate memos or add short notes to the text. Some programs count the keywords found and give their location. Most programs create a very specific index for the text, based only on the terms of interest to the researcher.

Textbase Managers. Textbase managers are similar to text retrieval programs. The key difference is their ability to organize or sort information about search results. Many programs create subsets of text data that help a researcher compare and sort notes by a key idea or to add factual information. For example, where the data are detailed notes on interviews, a researcher can add information on the date and length of the interview, gender of interviewee, location of interview, and so on. The researcher can then sort and organize each interview or part of the interview notes using a combination of keywords and added information.

In addition, some programs have *Hypertext* capability. Hypertext is a way of linking terms to other information. It works such that clicking the mouse on one term causes a new screen (one that has related information) to appear. The researcher can identify keywords or topics and link them together in the text. For example, a field researcher wants to examine the person Susan and the topic of hair (including haircuts, hairstyles, hair coloring, and hats or hair coverings). The researcher can use Hypertext to connect all places Susan's name appears to discussions of hair. By the mouse clicking on Susan's name, one block of text quickly jumps to another in the notes to see all places where Susan and the hair topic appear together.

Some textbase manager software creates cross-tabulation or scatterplot cross-classifications from information in text documents. For example, students keep journals on a course. They write their feelings about each day using one of four categories (boring, stimulating, challenging, or creative). The students also describe the major activities of each day (e.g., group work, discussion, watch videotape,

---

BOX **15.9** **Using a Computer Program in the Analysis of Tape-Recorded Qualitative Data**

Smith and Short (2001) observed that qualitative data analysis software has immensely increased the efficiency in coding raw qualitative data. The software helps researchers assign a code to data, organize codes, and retrieve linked codes and data. Most of the programs use data in the form of written text. Researchers with audio or video files first had to convert their data into a written transcript before using the software. Smith and Short described a system for coding tape-recorded data in which they used the counter on a recorder/player to index data and then tied counter location information to a location counter (via a spreadsheet) in the software. This location information was linked to the software's code generating and recording system. Their approach works with analog or digitally recorded audio or video data. By leaving the data in raw form and having a stable counter for recordings, they could analyze data without having to create a written transcript.

---

lecture, or demonstration). A researcher can cross-classify student feelings by activity. By adding other information (e.g., male or female), the researcher can see how students with different characteristics felt about various activities and examine whether the feelings changed with the topic being presented or the time during the academic year.

Code-and-Retrieve Programs. Researchers often assign codes or abstract terms to qualitative data (text field notes, interview records, and video or audiotape transcripts). Code-and-retrieve programs allow a researcher to attach codes to lines, sentences, paragraphs, or blocks of text. The programs may permit multiple codes for the same data. In addition to attaching codes, most programs also allow the researcher to organize the codes. For example, a program can help a researcher make outlines or "trees" of connections (e.g., trunks, branches, and twigs) among the codes, and among the data to which the codes refer. The qualitative data are rearranged in the program based on the researcher's codes and the relations among codes that a researcher specifies (see Box 15.9).

Code-Based Theory Builders. Qualitative researchers are often interested in the evaluation and generation of theory. Code-based theory builders require that a researcher first assign codes to the data. The programs provide ways for manipulating or drawing contrasts and comparisons among the codes. The relationships among the codes then become the basis for a researcher to test or generate theory.

The types of relations created among the codes may vary by program. A program may permit *if-then* type of logical relations or used in event-structure analysis. For example, Corsaro and Heise (1990) described how they coded field research data on young children into separate events. They then examined the logical sequence and relations among the events to search for principles or a "grammar" of implicit rules. They looked for rules that guided the sequencing, combination, or disconnection among events. The computer software ETHNO asks for logical connections among the events (e.g., time order, necessary precondition, co-occurrence, etc.), then shows the pattern among events.

In contrast to other qualitative programs, code-based theory builders have a powerful ability to manipulate codes to reveal patterns or show relations in data that are not immediately evident. It becomes easier for researchers to compare and classify categories of data. The program QCA (Qualitative Comparative Analysis) uses Boolean logic or algebra to help a researcher analyze the characteristics of several cases and apply the method of difference and method of agreement. It performs algebraic computations to identify common and unique characteristics among a set of cases. The algebra is not difficult but it can be time consuming and subject to human error without the program.

Conceptual Network Builders. This category of programs helps a researcher build and test theory by presenting graphic displays or networks. The displays do more than diagram data; they help organize a researcher's concepts or thinking about the data. The programs use nodes, or key concepts, that the researcher identifies in data. They then show links or relationships among the nodes. Most programs give graphic presentations with boxes or circles and connected by lines with arrows. The output looks similar to a flowchart diagram, with a web or network of connections among concepts. For example, the data might be a family tree in which the relationships among several generations of family members are presented. Relations among family members (X is a sibling of Y, Z is married to Y, G is an offspring of X) can be used to discuss and analyze features of the network.

Event-Structure Analysis

Many qualitative researchers organize data chronologically in a narrative analysis. **Event-structure analysis (ESA)** is a method to help researchers organize the sequence of events in ways that facilitate seeing causal relations. The method and a computer program used with it (called ETHNO) were first used for field research data, but it can be used for historical data, as well. In ESA, the researcher first organizes the data into events, then places the events in a temporal sequence.[32]

ESA is narrative analysis in which the researcher outlines a set of links between events that happened. He or she separates what had to happen before other events from what could have happened. The computer program forces the researcher to answer questions about the logical relationships among events. For example, a situation has events A, B, C, X, and Y. The researcher is asked: Must event A occur prior to X causing Y (i.e., Is A a necessary precondition for the X:Y causal relationship?) or would X affect Y without A? If it is required, A must recur before X will again affect Y again. This process forces a researcher to explain whether the causal relation between two events is a unique and one-time relation or a recurring relationship that can be repeated either indefinitely or a limited number of cycles.

> **Event-structure analysis (ESA)** Qualitative data analysis, often conducted with computer software, that forces a researcher to specify the links among a sequence of many events. It clarifies causal relationships by asking whether one event logically had to follow another, or it just happened to follow.

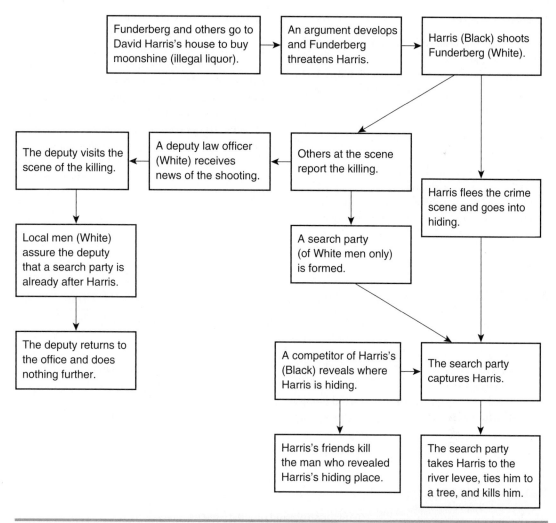

FIGURE 15.7   Example of Event-Structure Analysis of the Lynching of David Harris
Source: Adapted from Griffin (1993).

Event-structure analysis has limitations. It does not provide the theory or causal logic; the researcher must supply that. It only creates maps or diagrams (with the computer program) that make it easier to see relationships. When the researcher makes a decision about logically possible relations, ESA clarifies a chain of events and highlights those that might have been different. ESA does not have a place for enduring social structures that frame the action of event sequences: The researcher adds more traditional analysis.

Griffin's (1993) analysis of a lynching illustrates ESA. Based on many oral histories, a book, and newspaper reports, he reconstructed the sequence of events surrounding the lynching of David Harris in Bolivar County, Mississippi, in April 1930. After answering many yes/no questions about possible linkages among a long series of events and analyzing the linkages, Griffin was able to conclude that the critical factor was the inaction of the local deputy who could have stopped the process. An abbreviated summary of the ESA diagram is presented in Figure 15.7.

CONCLUSION

In this chapter, you have learned how researchers analyze qualitative data. In many respects, qualitative data are more difficult to deal with than data in the form of numbers. Numbers have mathematical properties that let a researcher use statistical procedures. Qualitative analysis requires more effort by an individual researcher to read and reread data notes, reflect on what is read, and make comparisons based on logic and judgment.

Most forms of qualitative data analysis involve coding and writing analytic memos. Both are labor-intensive efforts by the researcher to read over data carefully and think about them seriously. In addition, you learned about methods that researchers have used for the analysis of qualitative data. They are a sample of the many methods of qualitative data analysis. You also learned about the importance of thinking about negative evidence and events that are not present in the data.

This chapter ends the section of the book on research design, data collection, and data analysis. Social research also involves preparing reports on a research project, which is addressed in the next chapter.

KEY TERMS

analytic comparison	folk domain	negative case method
analytic domain	historical contingency	open coding
axial coding	illustrative method	outcropping
cultural domain	method of agreement	path dependency
domain analysis	method of difference	periodization
empty boxes	mixed domain	selective coding
event-structure analysis	narrative analysis	successive approximation

REVIEW QUESTIONS

1. Identify four differences between quantitative and qualitative data analysis.
2. How does the process of conceptualization differ in qualitative and quantitative research?
3. How does data coding differ in quantitative and qualitative research, and what are the three kinds of coding used by a qualitative researcher?
4. What is the purpose of analytic memo writing in qualitative data analysis?
5. Describe *successive approximation.*
6. What are the *empty boxes* in the illustrative method and how are they used?
7. What is the difference between the method of agreement and the method of difference? Can a researcher use both together? Explain why or why not.
8. What are the parts of a domain and how are they used in domain analysis?
9. What are the major features of a narrative?
10. Why is it important to look for negative evidence, or things that do not appear in the data, for a full analysis?

NOTES

1. See Miles and Huberman (1994) and Ragin (1987). These should not be confused with statistical techniques for "qualitative" data (see Haberman, 1978). These are sophisticated statistical techniques (e.g., logit and log linear) for quantitative variables where the data are at the nominal or ordinal level. They are better labeled as techniques for categorical data.

2. Sprague and Zimmerman (1989) discuss the importance of an explicit theory.

3. See Hammersley and Atkinson (1983:174–206) for a discussion of questions.

4. See Boyatzis (1998), Lofland and Lofland (1995: 192–193), Miles and Huberman (1994:57–71), Sanjek (1990:388–392), and Wolcott (1994) for additional discussions of coding.

5. See also Horan (1987) and Strauss (1987:25) for multiple indicator measurement models with qualitative data.

6. For more on memoing, see Lester and Hadden (1980), Lofland and Lofland (1995:193–197), Miles and Huberman (1994:72–77), and Strauss (1987:107–129).

7. Also see Barzun and Graff (1970:255–274), Bogdan and Taylor (1975), Lofland and Lofland (1984:131–140), Shafer (1980:171–200), Spradley (1979a, 1979b), and Schatzman and Strauss (1973:104–120) on notes and codes.

8. See Skocpol (1984) and Skocpol and Somers (1980).

9. For a discussion of analogies and models, see Barry (1975), Glucksmann (1974), Harré (1972), Hesse (1970), and Kaplan (1964).

10. For a discussion of the importance of analogies in social theory, see Lloyd (1986:127–132) and Stinchcombe (1978).

11. For more on successive approximation and a debate over it, see Applebaum (1978a), McQuaire (1978, 1979), Paul Thompson (1978), Wardell (1979), and Young (1980).

12. For a discussion of empty boxes, see Bonnell (1980) and Smelser (1976).

13. For a discussion of the illustrative method, see Bonnell (1980) and Skocpol (1984). Bogdan and Taylor (1975:79) describe a similar method.

14. See Coffrey et al. (2002) for an example of domain analysis.

15. For a discussion of methods of difference and agreement, see Ragin (1987:36–42), Skocpol (1984), Skocpol and Somers (1980), and Stinchcombe (1978:25–29).

16. See Mahoney (1999) on a nominal comparison.

17. See Griffin (1993) and Mahoney (1999).

18. See Mahoney (1999) for a discussion of Skocpol.

19. On various uses see Abbott (1995) and Franzosi (1998)

20. The six core elements are derived from discussion of narrative in the following: Abell (2001, 2004), Abbott (1995, 2001), Büthe (2002), Franzosi (1998), Griffin (1992, 1993), Gubrium and Holstein (1998), Haydu (1998), Mahoney (2000), Pedriana (2005), Sewell (1992, 1996), and Stryker (1996).

21. On narrative as a condition of social life, see Abbott (2001) and Somers (1994).

22. Abell (2004:288) remarked, "Although the term narrative and cognate concepts . . . are widely used . . . no settled definition is yet established." Some of the terms used include the following: analytic narrative (Pedriana, 2005), causal narrative (Sewell, 1996), comparative narrative (Abell, 2001), event structural analysis (Griffin, 1993), historical narrative (Mahoney, 2000b), narrative explanation (Abell, 2004), sequence analysis (Abbott, 1995), and structural analysis of narrative (Franzosi, 1998).

23. On debates about causality in narrative analysis and narrative as explanation, see Abbott (2001:290), Abell (2004), Büthe (2002), Griffin (1993), and Mahoney (2000b). For debate about the narrative, see Haydu (1998), Mahoney (1999), Sewell (1996), and Stryker (1996). Researchers such as Goldthrope (1991, 1997) and Lieberson (1991) question the approach, whereas Goldstone (1997) and Rueschemeyer and Stephens (1997) defend its utility.

24. See Haydu (1998:353).

25. Mahoney (2000a) gives a detailed description of the path dependency method and provides many examples of its use. Altman (2000) provides a discussion from the economics literature. Also see Blute (1997) and Pedriana (2005).

26. See Becker and Geer (1982) and Emigh (1997) on the negative case method. Blee and Billings (1986) discuss analyzing "silences" and unnoticed features in ethnographic or historical text.

27. See Sanjek (1978) and Werner and Schoepfle (1987a).

28. See Gross (1984) and Miles and Huberman (1994:85, 119–126).

29. See Lofland and Lofland (1995:199–200) and Werner and Schoepfle (1987a:130–146).

30. See Canter and associates (1985) and Werner and Schoepfle (1987a:180–181).

31. See Dohan and Sanchez-Jankowski (1998) and Weitzman and Miles (1995) for a comprehensive review of software programs for qualitative data analysis. Also see Fielding and Lee (1991) and Richards and Richards (1994).

32. For a more in-depth discussion of event-structure analysis, see Abbott (1992), Griffin (1993), Griffin and Ragin (1994), Heise (1991), and Issac and colleagues (1994).

CHAPTER 16

Writing the Research Report and the Politics of Social Research

> But that's our business: to arrange ideas in so rational an order that another person can make sense of them. We have to deal with that problem on two levels. We have to arrange the ideas in a theory or narrative, to describe causes and conditions that lead to the effects that we want to explain, and do it in an order that is logically and empirically correct. . . . Finally, we want our prose to make the order we have constructed clear. We don't want imperfection in our prose to interfere with our readers' understanding. These two jobs converge and cannot be separated.
>
> —Howard Becker, *Writing for Social Scientists*, p. 133

In the previous chapters, we have looked at how to design studies, gather data, and analyze the data. Yet, a research project is not complete until the researcher shares the results with others. Communicating results and how a study was conducted is a critical last step in the research process. It is usually in the form of a written report. In Chapter 1, we saw how the norm of communalism emphasizes that researchers make public how they conducted their research and their findings. In Chapter 5, we saw how to locate previous studies in the scholarly literature. In this chapter, you will learn about writing a research report.

Conducting a study and reporting its results can create controversy. As noted in Chapter 5, doing research can raise contentious ethical issues. Ethical issues largely involve protecting research subjects, maintaining integrity while doing research, and dealing with pressure from research sponsors. Social research also involves political issues that can

be even more contentious. The politics of social research can affect how one conducts a study and disseminates findings from it, and how others try to use or misuse research findings.

This chapter combines two topics: writing a research report and the politics of social research. Writing a research report requires mastering relatively straightforward, noncontroversial rules and skills. The central issues in the politics of social research are not straightforward. They include issues such as the freedom of a researcher to conduct a study and to prepare the report without interference from powerful social groups. There are rules for writing reports and codes of ethics, but there is no code or rules for research politics.

Social research may be imperfect, but its ultimate goals are to discover knowledge, expand understanding, and seek truth. Social researchers want to clearly and openly share the method and findings of their research with the scientific community and beyond. Political controversies develop when powerful groups or institutions try to block inquiry, prevent the free flow of new knowledge, place limits on the search for truth, or misuse and selectively ignore research findings. They usually do this to advance their own nonscientific goals and purposes.

In the first part of this chapter, we examine how to write both quantitative and qualitative reports. Researchers need to take the writing process very seriously. They must explain both how they conducted a study and the findings in a research report. In the second part of the chapter, we look at the politics of social research. We consider attempts by powerful groups or governments to limit what researchers study, how they conduct a research study, and where they disseminate results. We end by looking at the concepts of objectivity and value freedom.

THE RESEARCH REPORT

Why Write a Report?

After a researcher completes a project or a significant phase of a large project, it is time to communicate the findings to others through a research report. One can learn a lot about writing a research report by reading many reports and taking a course in scientific and technical writing.

A research report is a written document (or oral presentation based on a written document) that communicates the methods and findings of a research project to others. It is more than a summary of findings; it is a record of the research process. A researcher cannot wait until the research is done to think about the report; he or she must think ahead to the report and keep careful records while conducting research. In addition to findings, the report includes the reasons for initiating the project, a description of the project's steps, a presentation of data, and a discussion of how the data relate to the research question or topic.

The report tells others what you, the researcher, did, and what you discovered. It is a way of disseminating knowledge. As you saw in Chapter 1, the research report plays a significant role in binding together the scientific community. Other reasons for writing a report are to fulfill a class or job assignment, to meet an obligation to an organization that paid for the research, to persuade a professional group about specific aspects of a problem, or to tell the general public about findings. Communicating with the general public is rarely the primary method for communication of scientific results; it is usually a second stage of dissemination.

The Writing Process

Your Audience. Professional writers say: Always know for whom you are writing. This is because communication is more effective when it is tailored to a specific audience. You should write a research report differently depending on whether the primary audience is an instructor, students, professional social scientists, practitioners, or the general public. It goes without saying that the writing should be clear, accurate, and well organized.

Instructors assign a report for different reasons and may place requirements on how it is written. In general, instructors want to see writing and an organization that reflect clear, logical thinking. Student reports should demonstrate a solid grasp of substantive and methodological concepts. A good way to do this is to use technical terms explicitly *when appropriate;* they should not be used excessively or incorrectly.

When writing for students, it is best to define technical terms and label each part of the report. The discussion should proceed in a logical, step-by-step manner with many specific examples. Use straightforward language to explain how and why you conducted the various steps of the research project. One strategy is to begin with the research question, then structure the report as an answer.

Scholars do not need definitions of technical terms or explanations of why standard procedures (e.g., random sampling) were used. They are most interested in how the research is linked to abstract theory or previous findings in the literature. They want a condensed, detailed description of research design. They pay close attention to how variables are measured and the methods of data collection. Scholars like a compact, tightly written, but extensive section on data analysis, with a meticulous discussion of results.

Practitioners prefer a short summary of how the study was conducted and results presented in a few simple charts and graphs. They like to see an outline of alternative paths of action implied by results with the practical outcomes of pursuing each path. Practitioners must be cautioned not to overgeneralize from the results of one study. It is best to place the details of research design and results in an appendix.

When writing for the general public, use simple language, provide concrete examples, and focus on the practical implications of findings for social problems. Do not include details of research design or of results, and be careful not to make unsupported claims when writing for the public. Informing the public is an important service, which can help nonspecialists make better judgments about public issues.

Style and Tone. Research reports are written in a narrow range of styles and have a distinct tone. Their purpose is to communicate clearly the research method and findings.

Style refers to the types of words chosen by the writer and the length and form of sentences or paragraphs used. *Tone* is the writer's attitude or relation toward the subject matter. For example, an informal, conversational style (e.g., colloquial words, idioms, clichés, and incomplete sentences) with a personal tone (e.g., these are my feelings) is appropriate for writing a letter to a close friend, but not for research reports. Research reports have a formal and succinct (saying a lot in few words) style. The tone expresses distance from the subject matter; it is professional and serious. Field researchers sometimes use an informal style and a personal tone, but this is the exception. Avoid moralizing and flowery language. The goal is to inform, not to advocate a position or to entertain.

A research report should be objective, accurate, and clear. Check and recheck details (e.g., page references in citations) and fully disclose how you conducted the research project. If readers detect carelessness in writing, they may question the research itself. The details of a research project can be complex, and such complexity means that confusion is always a danger. It makes clear writing essential. Clear writing can be achieved by thinking and rethinking the research problem and design, explicitly defining terms, writing with short declarative sentences, and limiting conclusions to what is supported by the evidence.

Organizing Thoughts. Writing does not happen magically or simply flow out of a person when he or she puts pen to paper (or fingers to keyboard) although many people have such an illusion. Rather, it is hard work, involving a sequence of steps and activities that result in a final product. Writing a research report is not radically different from other types of writing. Although some steps differ and the level of complexity may be greater, most of what a good writer does when writing a long letter, a poem, a set of instructions, or a short story applies to writing a research report.

First, a writer needs something about which to write. The "something" in the research report includes the topic, research question, design and measures, data collection techniques, results, and implications. With so many parts to write about, organization is essential. The most basic tool for organizing writing is the outline. Outlines help a writer ensure that all ideas are included and that the relationship between them is clear. Outlines are made up of topics (words or phrases) or sentences. Most of us are familiar with the basic form of an outline (see Figure 16.1).

Outlines can help the writer, but they can also become a barrier if they are used improperly. An outline is simply a tool to help the writer organize ideas. It helps (1) put ideas in a sequence (e.g., what will be said first, second, and third); (2) group related ideas together (e.g., these are similar to each other, but differ from those); and (3) separate the more general, or higher-level, ideas from more specific ideas, and the specific ideas from very specific details.

Some students feel that they need a complete outline before writing, and that once an outline is prepared, deviations from it are impossible. Few writers begin with a complete outline. The initial outline is sketchy because until you write everything down, it is impossible to put all ideas in a sequence, group them together, or separate the general from the specific. For most writers, new ideas develop or become clearer in the process of writing itself.

FIGURE 16.1   Form of Outline

I. First major topic	One of the most important
A. Subtopic of topic I	Second level of importance
1. Subtopic of A	Third level of importance
a. Subtopic of 1	Fourth level of importance
b. Subtopic of 1	"
(1) Subtopic of b	Fifth level of importance
(2) Subtopic of b	"
(a) Subtopic of (2)	Sixth level of importance
(b) Subtopic of (2)	"
i. Subtopic of (b)	Seventh level of importance
ii. Subtopic of (b)	"
2. Subtopic of A	Third level of importance
B. Subtopic of topic I	Second level of importance
II. Second major topic	One of the most important

A beginning outline may differ from the final outline by more than degree of completeness. The process of writing may not only reveal or clarify ideas for the writer but also stimulate new ideas, new connections between ideas, a different sequence, or new relations between the general and the specific. In addition, the process of writing may stimulate reanalysis or a reexamination of the literature or findings. This does not mean beginning all over again. Rather, it means keeping an open mind to new insights and being candid about the research project.

Back to the Library. Few researchers finish their literature review before completing a research project. The researcher should be familiar with the literature before beginning a project, but will need to return to the literature after completing data collection and analysis, for several reasons. First, time has passed between the beginning and the end of a research project, and new studies may have been published. Second, after completing a research project, a researcher will know better what is or is not central to the study and may have new questions in mind when rereading studies in the literature. Finally, when writing the report, researchers may find that notes are not complete enough or a detail is missing in the citation of a reference source. The visit to the library after data collection is less extensive and more selective or focused than that conducted at the beginning of research.

When writing a research report, researchers frequently discard some of the notes and sources that were gathered prior to completing the research project. This does not mean that the initial library work and literature review were a waste of time and effort. Researchers expect that some of the notes (e.g., 25 percent) taken before completing the project will become irrelevant as the project gains focus. They do not include notes or references in a report that are no longer relevant, for they distract from the flow of ideas and reduce clarity.

Returning to the library to verify and expand references focuses ideas. It also helps avoid plagiarism. **Plagiarism** is a serious form of cheating, and many universities expel students caught engaging in it. If a professional ever plagiarizes in a scholarly journal, it is treated as a very serious offense.[1] Take careful notes and identify the exact source of phrases or ideas to avoid unintentional plagiarism. Cite the sources of both directly quoted words and paraphrased ideas. For direct quotes, include the location of the quote with page numbers in the citation.

Using another's written words and failing to give credit is wrong, but paraphrasing is less clear.

Plagiarism   "Stealing" another's ideas by using the words and the ideas of another without properly documenting the original source.

Paraphrasing is not using another's exact words; it is restating another's ideas in your own words, condensing at the same time. Researchers regularly paraphrase, and good paraphrasing requires a solid understanding of what is being paraphrased. It means more than replacing another's words with synonyms; paraphrasing is borrowing an idea, boiling it down to its essence, and giving credit to the source.[2]

The Writing Process

Writing is a process. The way to learn to write is by writing.[3] It takes time and effort, and it improves with practice. There is no single correct way to write, but some methods are associated with good writing. The process has three steps:

1. *Prewriting.* Prepare to write by arranging notes on the literature, making lists of ideas, outlining, completing bibliographic citations, and organizing comments on data analysis.
2. *Composing.* Get your ideas onto paper as a first draft by freewriting, drawing up the bibliography and footnotes, preparing data for presentation, and forming an introduction and conclusion.
3. *Rewriting.* Evaluate and polish the report by improving coherence, proofreading for mechanical errors, checking citations, and reviewing voice and usage.

Many people find that getting started is difficult. Beginning writers often jump to the second step and end there, which results in poor-quality writing. **Prewriting** means that a writer begins with

Paraphrasing Restating an author's ideas in one's own words and giving proper credit to the original source.

Prewriting An early step in the writing process during which a writer organizes notes, makes lists of ideas, outlines thoughts, and makes certain that bibliographic citations are complete.

Freewriting An initial step in the writing process in which the writer tries to get his or her ideas down on paper as quickly as possible, not worrying about grammar or spelling.

a file folder full of notes, outlines, and lists. You must think about the form of the report and audience. Thinking time is important. It often occurs in spurts over a period of time before the bulk of composing begins.

Some people become afflicted with a strange ailment when they sit down to compose writing. It is known as *writer's block*—a temporary inability to write. It comes when the mind goes blank, the fingers freeze, and panic sets in. Writers from beginners through experts occasionally experience it. If you experience it, calm down and work on overcoming it (see Box 16.1).

Numerous writers begin to compose by **freewriting,** a process of sitting down and writing down everything you can as quickly as it enters into your mind. Freewriting establishes a link between a rapid flow of ideas in the mind and writing. When you freewrite, you do not stop to reread what you wrote, you do not ponder the best word, you do not worry about correct grammar, spelling, or punctuation. You just put ideas on paper as quickly as possible to get and keep the creative juices or ideas flowing. You can later clean up what you wrote.

Writing and thinking are so intertwined that it is impossible to know where one ends and the other begins. This means that if you plan to sit and stare at the wall, the computer output, the sky, or whatever until all thoughts become totally clear before beginning, you will rarely get anything written. The thinking process can be ignited during the writing itself.

Rewriting. Perhaps one in a million writers is a creative genius who can produce a first draft that communicates with astounding accuracy and clarity. For the rest of us mortals, writing means that rewriting—and rewriting again—is necessary. For example, Ernest Hemingway is reported to have rewritten the end of *Farewell to Arms* 39 times.[4] It is not unusual for a professional researcher to rewrite a report a dozen times. Do not become discouraged. If anything, rewriting reduces the pressure; it means you can start writing soon and get out a rough draft that you can polish later. Plan to rewrite a draft at least three or four times. A draft is a complete report, from beginning to end, not a few rough notes or an outline.

BOX **16.1** Suggestions for Ending Writer's Block

1. *Begin early.* Do not procrastinate or wait until the last minute. This not only gives you time to come back to the task but also reduces the tension because you have time to write a poor-quality first draft that can be improved upon. Shafer (1980:205) chided, "Writing is hard work, and the excuses authors find for postponing it are legendary." Set yourself a deadline for a first draft that is at least a week before the final deadline, and keep it!
2. *Take a break, then return.* Some writers find that if they take a walk, get a snack, read a newspaper, and come back to the task a half hour later, the block is gone. Small diversions, if they remain small and short term, can help on occasion.
3. *Begin in the middle.* You do not have to begin at the beginning. Begin in the middle and just start writing, even if does not seem to be directly relevant. It may be easier to get to your topic once the writing/thinking process is moving.
4. *Engage in personal magic rituals.* Some people have unusual habits or rituals that they engage in before writing (e.g., washing dishes, clearing a desk, sharpening pencils). These can serve as mental triggers to help you get started. Do what gets you started writing.
5. *Break it into small parts.* Do not feel that you have to sit down and complete the writing task as a whole. Begin with pieces that come easily to you and stitch together the pieces later.
6. *Do not expect perfection.* Write a draft, which means that you can throw away, revise, and change what you wrote. It is always easier to revise a rough draft than to create perfect writing the first time.

Rewriting helps a writer express himself or herself with a greater clarity, smoothness, precision, and economy of words. When rewriting, the focus is on clear communication, not pompous or complicated language. As Leggett and colleagues (1965:330) stated, "Never be ashamed to express a simple idea in simple language. Remember that the use of complicated language is not in itself a sign of intelligence."

Rewriting means slowly reading what you have written and, if necessary, out loud to see whether it sounds right. It is a good idea to share your writing with others. Professional writers have others read and criticize their writing. New writers soon learn that friendly, constructive criticism is very valuable. Sharing your writing with others may be difficult at first. It means exposing your written thoughts and encouraging criticism. Yet, the purpose of the criticism is to clarify writing, and the critic is doing you a favor.

Rewriting involves two processes: revising and editing. **Revising** is inserting new ideas, adding supporting evidence, deleting or changing ideas, moving sentences around to clarify meaning, or strengthening transitions and links between ideas. **Editing** means cleaning up and tightening the more mechanical aspects of writing, such as spelling, grammar, usage, verb tense, sentence length, and paragraph organization. When you rewrite, go over a draft and revise it brutally to improve it. This is easier if some time passes between a draft and rewriting. Phrases that seemed satisfactory in a draft may look fuzzy or poorly connected after a week or two (see Box 16.2).

Even if you have not acquired typing skills, it is a good idea to type, or print out if you use a word processor, at least one draft before the final draft. This is because it is easier to see errors and organization problems in a clean, typed draft. Feel free to cut and paste, cross out words, or move phrases on the printed copy.

Revising A step in the writing process, part of rewriting, in which a writer adds ideas or evidence, and deletes, rearranges, or changes ideas to improve clarity and better communicate meaning.

Editing A step in the writing process, part of rewriting, in which a writing cleans up and tightens the language, checks grammar (e.g., verb agreement, usage), adjusts sentence length, and reorganizes paragraphs to improve communication and strengthen style.

BOX **16.2** Suggestions for Rewriting

1. *Mechanics.* Check grammar, spelling, punctuation, verb agreement, verb tense, and verb/subject separation with each rewrite. Remember that each time new text is added, new errors can creep in. Mistakes are not only distracting but they also weaken the confidence readers place in the ideas you express.

2. *Usage.* Reexamine terms, especially key terms, when rewriting to see whether you are using the exact word that expresses your intended meaning. Do not use technical terms or long words unnecessarily. Use the plain word that best expresses meaning. Get a thesaurus and use it. A *thesaurus* is an essential reference tool, like a dictionary, that contains words of similar meaning and can help you locate the exact word for a meaning you want to express. Precise thinking and expression requires precise language. Do not say *average* if you use the *mean.* Do not say *mankind* or *policeman* when you intend *people* or *police officer.* Do not use *principal* for *principle.*

3. *Voice.* Writers of research reports often make the mistake of using the passive instead of the active voice. It may appear more authoritative, but passive voice obscures the actor or subject of action. For example, the passive, *The relationship between grade in school and more definite career plans was confirmed by the data* is better stated as the active, *The data confirm the relationship between grade in school and more definite career plans.* The passive, *Respondent attitude toward abortion was recorded by an interviewer* reads easier in the active voice: *An interviewer recorded respondent attitude toward abortion.* Also avoid unnecessary qualifying language, such as *seems to* or *appears to.*

4. *Coherence.* Sequence, steps, and transitions should be logically tight. Try reading the entire report one paragraph at a time. Does the paragraph contain a unified idea? A topic sentence? Is there a transition between paragraphs within the report?

5. *Repetition.* Remove repeated ideas, wordiness, and unnecessary phrases. Ideas are best stated once, forcefully, instead of repeatedly in an unclear way. When revising, eliminate deadwood (words that add nothing) and circumlocution (the use of several words when one more precise word will do). Directness is preferable to wordiness. The wordy phrase, *To summarize the above, it is our conclusion in light of the data that X has a positive effect of considerable magnitude on the occurrence of Y, notwithstanding the fact that Y occurs only on rare occasions,* is better stated, *In sum, we conclude that X has a large positive effect on Y, but Y occurs infrequently.* As Selvin and Wilson (1984) warned, verbose and excessive words or qualifiers make it difficult to understand what is written.

6. *Structure.* Research reports should have a transparent organization. Move sections around as necessary to fit the organization better, and use headings and subheadings. A reader should be able to follow the logical structure of a report.

7. *Abstraction.* A good research report mixes abstract ideas and concrete examples. A long string of abstractions without the specifics is difficult to read. Likewise, a mass of specific concrete details without periodic generalization also loses readers.

8. *Metaphors.* Many writers use metaphors to express ideas. Phrases such as *the cutting edge, the bottom line,* and *penetrating to the heart* are used to express ideas by borrowing images from other contexts. Metaphors can be an effective method of communication, but they need to be used sparingly and with care. A few well-chosen, consistently used, fresh metaphors can communicate ideas quickly and effectively; however, the excessive use of metaphors, especially overused metaphors (e.g., *the bottom line*), is a sloppy, unimaginative method of expression.

Good typing skills and an ability to use a word processor are extremely valuable when writing reports and other documents. Serious professionals find that the time they invest into building typing skills and learning to use a word processor pays huge dividends later. Word processors not only make editing much easier but also check spelling and offer synonyms. In addition, there are programs that check grammar. You cannot rely on the computer program to do all the work, but it makes writing easier. The speed and ease that a word processor offers is so dramatic that few people who become skilled at using one ever go back to writing by hand or typing.

One last suggestion: Rewrite the introduction and title after completing a draft so that they accurately reflect what is said.[5] Titles should be short and descriptive. They should communicate the topic and the major variables to readers. They can describe the type of research (e.g., "An experiment on . . .") but should not have unnecessary words or phrases (e.g., "An investigation into the . . .").

The Quantitative Research Report

The principles of good writing apply to all reports, but the parts of a report differ depending on whether the research is quantitative or qualitative. Before writing any report, read reports on the same kind of research for models.

We begin with the quantitative research report. The sections of the report roughly follow the sequence of steps of a research project.[6]

Abstract or Executive Summary. Quantitative research reports begin with a short summary or abstract. The size of an abstract varies; it can be as few as 50 words (this paragraph has 75 words) or as long as a full page. Most scholarly journal articles have abstracts on the first page of the article. The abstract has information on the topic, the research problem, the basic findings, and any unusual research design or data collection features.

Reports of applied research that are written for practitioners have a longer summary called the **executive summary.** It contains more detail than an article abstract and includes the implications of research and major recommendations made in the report. Although it is longer than an abstract, an executive summary rarely exceeds four or five pages.

Abstracts and executive summaries serve several functions: For the less interested reader, they tell what is in a report; for readers looking for specific information, they help the reader determine whether the full report contains important information. Readers use the abstract or summary to screen information and decide whether the entire report should be read. It gives serious readers who intend to read the full report a quick mental picture of the report which makes reading the report easier and faster.

Presenting the Problem. The first section of the report defines the research problem. It can be placed in one or more sections with titles such as "Introduction," "Problem Definition," "Literature Review," "Hypotheses," or "Background Assumptions." Although the subheadings vary, the contents include a statement of the research problem and a rationale for what is being examined. Here, you explain the significance of and provide a background to the research question. Explain the significance of the research by showing how different solutions to the problem lead to different applications or theoretical conclusions. Introductory sections frequently include a context literature review and link the problem to theory. Introductory sections also define key concepts and present conceptual hypotheses.

Describing the Methods. The next section of the report describes how you designed the study and collected the data. It goes by several names (e.g., "Methods," "Research Design," or "Data") and may be subdivided into other parts (e.g., "Measures," "Sampling," or "Manipulations"). It is the most important section for evaluating the methodology of the project. The section answers several questions for the reader:

1. What type of study (e.g., experiment, survey) was conducted?
2. Exactly how were data collected (e.g., study design, type of survey, time and location of data collection, experimental design used)?
3. How were variables measured? Are the measures reliable and valid?
4. What is the sample? How many subjects or respondents are involved in the study? How were they selected?
5. How were ethical issues and specific concerns of the design dealt with?

Executive summary A summary of a research project's findings placed at the beginning of report for an applied, nonspecialist audience, usually a little longer than an abstract.

Results and Tables. After describing how data were collected, methods of sampling, and measurement, you then present the data. This section presents—it does not discuss, analyze, or interpret the data. Some researchers combine the "Results" section with the next section, called "Discussion" or "Findings."

You must make choices in how to present the data.[7] When analyzing the data, you look at dozens of univariate, bivariate, and multivariate tables and statistics to get a feel for the data. This does not mean that you include every statistic or table in a final report. Rather, select the minimum number of charts or tables that fully inform the reader. Use data analysis techniques to summarize the data and test hypotheses (e.g., frequency distributions, tables with means and standard deviations, correlations, and other statistics).

You want to give a complete picture of the data without overwhelming the reader—not provide data in excessive detail nor present irrelevant data. Readers can make their own interpretations. Detailed summary statistics belong in appendixes.

Discussion. In the discussion section, give the reader a concise, unambiguous interpretation of its meaning. The discussion is not a selective emphasis or partisan interpretation; rather, it is a candid discussion of what is in the results section. The discussion section is separated from the results so that a reader can examine the data and arrive at different interpretations. Grosof and Sardy (1985:386) warned, "The arrangement of your presentation should reflect a strict separation between data (the record of your observations) and their summary and analysis on one hand, and your interpretations, conclusion, and comment on the other."

Beginning researchers often find it difficult to organize a discussion section. One approach is to organize the discussion according to hypotheses, discussing how the data relate to each hypothesis. In addition, researchers should discuss unanticipated

findings, possible alternative explanations of results, and weaknesses or limitations.

Drawing Conclusions. You should restate the research question and summarize findings in the conclusion. Its purpose is to summarize the report, and it is sometimes titled "Summary."

The only sections after the conclusion are the references and appendixes. The references section contains only sources that were referred to in the text or notes of the report. Appendixes, if used, usually contain additional information on methods of data collection (e.g., questionnaire wording) or results (e.g., descriptive statistics). The footnotes or endnotes in quantitative research reports expand or elaborate on information in the text. Use them sparingly to provide secondary information that clarifies the text. They should not distract from the flow of the reading.

The Qualitative Research Report

Compared to quantitative research, it is more difficult to write a report on qualitative social research. It has fewer rules and less structure. Nevertheless, the purpose is the same: to clearly communicate the research process and the data collected through the process.

Quantitative reports present hypotheses and evidence in a logically tight and condensed style. By contrast, qualitative reports tend to be longer, and book-length reports are common (see Box 16.3).

Field Research. Field research reports rarely follow a fixed format with standard sections, and theoretical generalizations and data are not separated into distinct sections.[8] Generalizations are intertwined with the evidence, which takes the form of detailed description with frequent quotes.

Researchers balance the presentation of data and analysis to avoid an excessive separation of data from analysis, called the **error of segregation.** This occurs when researchers separate data from analysis so much that readers cannot see the connection.[9]

The tone of field research reports is less objective and formal, and more personal. Field research reports may be written in the first person (i.e., using

Error of segregation   A mistake when writing qualitative research in which a writer creates too large of a separation between empirical details and abstract theorizing.

BOX **16.3** **Why Qualitative Research Reports Are Longer**

1. The data in a qualitative report are more difficult to condense. Data are in the form of words, pictures, or sentences and include many quotes and examples.
2. Qualitative researchers try to create a subjective sense of empathy and understanding among readers in addition to presenting factual evidence and analytic interpretations. Detailed descriptions of specific settings and situations help readers better understand or get a feel for settings. Researchers attempt to transport the reader into the subjective worldview and meaning system of a social setting.
3. Qualitative researchers use less standardized techniques of gathering data, creating analytic categories, and organizing evidence. The techniques applied may be particular to individual researchers or unique settings. Thus, researchers explain what they did and why, because it has not been done before.
4. Exploring new settings or constructing new theory is a common goal in qualitative research. The development of new concepts and examination of relationships among them adds to the length of reports. Theory flows out of evidence, and detailed descriptions demonstrate how the researcher created interpretations.
5. Qualitative researchers may use more varied writing styles, which increases length. They have greater freedom to employ literary devices to tell a story or recount a tale.

Field researchers face a data reduction dilemma when presenting evidence. Most data are in the form of an enormous volume of field notes, but a researcher cannot directly share all the observations or recorded conversations with the readers. For example, in their study of medical students, *Boys in White*, Becker and Geer had about 5,000 pages of single-spaced field notes. Field researchers include only about 5 percent of their field notes in a report as quotes. The remaining 95 percent is not wasted; there is just no room for it. Thus, writers select quotes and indirectly convey the rest of the data to readers.

There is no fixed organization for a field research report, although a literature review often appears near the beginning. There are many acceptable organizational forms. Lofland (1976) suggests the following:

1. Introduction
   a. Most general aspects of situation
   b. Main contours of the general situation
   c. How materials were collected
   d. Details about the setting
   e. How the report is organized
2. The situation
   a. Analytic categories
   b. Contrast between situation and other situations
   c. Development of situation over time
3. Strategies
4. Summary and implications

Devices for organizing evidence and analysis also vary a great deal.[11] For example, writers can organize the report in terms of a *natural history* (see Chapter 13), an unfolding of events as you discovered them, or as a chronology, following the developmental cycle or career of an aspect of the setting or people in it. Another possibility is to organize the report as a **zoom lens,** beginning broadly and then focusing increasingly narrowly on a specific topic. Statements can move from universal statements about all cultures, to general statements about a

the pronoun *I*) because the researcher was directly involved in the setting, interacted with the people studied, and was the measurement "instrument." The decisions or indecisions, feelings, reactions, and personal experiences of the researcher are parts of the field research process.

Field research reports often face more skepticism than quantitative reports do. This makes it essential to assess an audience's demands for evidence and to establish credibility. The key is to provide readers with enough evidence so that they believe the recounted events and accept the interpretations as plausible. A degree of selective observation is accepted in field research, so the critical issue is whether other observers could reach the same conclusion if they examined the same data.[10]

Zoom lens   A method of organizing a field research report in which the author begins broadly with a topic, then increasingly focuses it more narrowly and specifically.

specific cultures, to statements about a specific cultural scene, to specific statements about an aspect of culture, to specific statements about specific incidents.[12]

Field researchers also organize reports by themes. A writer chooses between using abstract analytic themes and using themes from the categories used by the people who were studied. The latter gives readers a vivid description of the setting and displays knowledge of the language, concepts, categories, and beliefs of those being written about.[13]

Field researchers discuss the methods used in the report, but its location and form vary. One technique is to interweave a description of the setting, the means of gaining access, the role of the researcher, and the subject/researcher relationship into the discussion of evidence and analysis. This is intensified if the writer adopts what Van Maanen (1988:73) called a "confessional" style of writing. A chronological, zoom lens, or theme-based organization allows placing the data collection method near the beginning or the end. In book-length reports, methodological issues are usually discussed in a separate appendix.

Field research reports can contain transcriptions of tape recordings, maps, photographs, or charts illustrating analytic categories. They supplement the discussion and are placed near the discussion they complement. Qualitative field research can use creative formats that differ from the usual written text with examples from field notes. Photographs give a visual inventory of the settings described in the text and present the meanings of settings in the terms of those being studied. For example, field research articles have appeared in the form of all photographs, a script for a play, or a documentary film.[14]

Direct, personal involvement in the intimate details of a social setting heightens ethical concerns. Researchers write in a manner that protects the privacy of those being studied and helps prevent the publication of a report from harming those who were studied.[15] They usually change the names of members and exact locations in field reports. Personal involvement in field research leads researchers to include a short autobiography. For example, in the appendix to *Street Corner Society* the author, William Foote Whyte, gave a detailed account of the occupations of his father and grandfather, his hobbies and interests, the jobs he held, how he ended up going to graduate school, and how his research was affected by his getting married.

Historical-Comparative Research. There is no single way to write a report on historical-comparative research. Most frequently, researchers "tell a story" or describe details in general analytic categories. The writing usually goes beyond description and includes limited generalizations and abstract concepts.

Historical-comparative (H-C) researchers rarely describe their methods in great detail. Explicit sections of the report or an appendix that describes the methods used are unusual. Occasionally, a book-length report contains a bibliographic essay that discusses major sources used. More often, numerous detailed footnotes or endnotes describe the sources and evidence. For example, a 20-page report on quantitative or field research typically has 5 to 10 notes, whereas an H-C research report of equal length may have 40 to 60 notes.

Historical-comparative reports can contain photographs, maps, diagrams, charts, or tables of statistics throughout the report and in the section that discusses evidence that relates to them. The charts, tables, and so forth supplement a discussion or give the reader a better feel for the places and people being described. They are used in conjunction with frequent quotes as one among several types of evidence. Historical-comparative reports rarely summarize data to test specific hypotheses as quantitative research does. Instead, the writer builds a web of meaning or descriptive detail and organizes the evidence itself to convey interpretations and generalizations.

There are two basic modes of organizing historical-comparative research reports: by topic and chronologically. Most writers mix the two types. For example, information is organized chronologically within topics or organized by topic within chronological periods. Occasionally other forms of organization are used—by place, by individual person, or by major events. If the report is truly comparative, the writer has additional options, such as making comparisons within topics. Box 16.4 provides a sample of some techniques used by

BOX **16.4** Features to Consider in the Historical-Comparative Research Report

1. *Sequence.* Historical-comparative researchers are sensitive to the temporal order of events and place a series of events in order to describe a process. For example, a researcher studying the passage of a law or the evolution of a social norm may break the process into a set of sequential steps.
2. *Comparison.* Comparing similarities and differences lies at the heart of comparative-historical research. Make comparisons explicit and identify both similarities and differences. For example, a researcher comparing the family in two historical periods or countries begins by listing shared and nonshared traits of the family in each setting.
3. *Contingency.* Researchers often discover that one event, action, or situation depends on or is conditioned by others. Outlining the linkages of how one event was contingent on others is critical. For example, a researcher examining the rise of local newspapers notes that it depended on the spread of literacy.
4. *Origins and consequences.* Historical-comparative researchers trace the origins of an event, action, organization, or social relationship back in time, or follow its consequences into subsequent time periods. For example, a researcher explaining the end of slavery traces its origins to many movements, speeches, laws, and actions in the preceding fifty years.
5. *Sensitivity to incompatible meaning.* Meanings change over time and vary across cultures. Historical-comparative researchers ask themselves whether a word or social category had the same meaning in the past as in the present or whether a word in one culture has a direct translation in another culture. For example, a college degree had a different meaning in a historical era when it was extremely expensive and less than 1 percent of the 18- to 22-year-old population received a degree compared to the late twentieth century, when college became relatively accessible.
6. *Limited generalization.* Overgeneralization is always a potential problem in historical-comparative research. Few researchers seek rigid, fixed laws in historical, comparative explanation. They qualify statements or avoid strict determination. For example, instead of a blanket statement that the de-

struction of the native cultures in areas settled by European Whites was the inevitable consequence of advanced technological culture, a researcher may list the specific factors that combined to explain the destruction in particular social-historical settings.
7. *Association.* The concept of association is used in all forms of social research. As in other areas, historical-comparative researchers identify factors that appear together in time and place. For example, a researcher examining a city's nineteenth-century crime rate asks whether years of greater migration into the city are associated with higher crime rates and whether those arrested tended to be recent immigrants.
8. *Part and whole.* It is important to place events in their context. Writers of historical-comparative research sketch linkages between parts of a process, organization, or event and the larger context in which it is found. For example, a researcher studying a particular political ritual in an eighteenth-century setting describes how the ritual fit within the eighteenth-century political system.
9. *Analogy.* Analogies can be useful. The overuse of analogy or the use of an inappropriate analogy is dangerous. For example, a researcher examines feelings about divorce in country X and describes them as "like feelings about death" in country Y. This analogy requires a description of "feelings about death" in country Y.
10. *Synthesis.* Historical-comparative researchers often synthesize many specific events and details into a comprehensive whole. Synthesis results from weaving together many smaller generalizations and interpretations into coherent main themes. For example, a researcher studying the French Revolution synthesizes specific generalizations about changes in social structure, international pressures, agricultural dislocation, shifting popular beliefs and problems with government finances into a compact, coherent explanation. Researchers using the narrative form summarize the argument in an introduction or conclusion. It is a motif or theme embedded within the description. Thus, theoretical generalizations are intertwined with the evidence and appear to flow inductively out of the detailed evidence.

historical-comparative researchers to organize evidence and analysis.[16]

Some H-C researchers mimic the quantitative research report and use quantitative research techniques. They extend quantitative research rather than adopt a distinct historical-comparative research method. Their reports follow the model of a quantitative research report.

You learned about narrative analysis in Chapter 15. Researchers who use this strategy often adopt a narrative style of report writing. Researchers who use the narrative style organize data chronologically and try to "tell a story" around specific individuals and events.

The Research Proposal

What Is the Proposal? A research proposal is a document that presents a plan for a project to reviewers for evaluation. It can be a supervised project submitted to instructors as part of an educational degree (e.g., a master's thesis or a Ph.D. dissertation), or it can be a research project proposed to a funding agency. Its purpose is to convince reviewers that you, the researcher, are capable of successfully conducting the proposed research project. Reviewers have more confidence that a planned project will be successfully completed if the proposal is well written and organized, and if you demonstrate careful planning.

The proposal is similar to a research report, but it is written before the research project begins. A proposal describes the research problem and its importance, and gives a detailed account of the methods that will be used and why they are appropriate.

The proposal for quantitative research has most of the parts of a research report: a title, an abstract, a problem statement, a literature review, a methods or design section, and a bibliography. It lacks results, discussion, and conclusion sections. The proposal has a plan for data collection and analysis (e.g., types of statistics). It frequently includes a

> **Grantsmanship**   Strategies and skills of locating appropriate funding sources and preparing quality proposals to fund research.

schedule of the steps to be undertaken and an estimate of the time required for each step.

Proposals for qualitative research are more difficult to write because the research process itself is less structured and preplanned. The researcher prepares a problem statement, literature review, and bibliography. He or she demonstrates an ability to complete a proposed qualitative project in two ways. First, the proposal is well written, with an extensive discussion of the literature, significance of the problem, and sources. This shows reviewers familiarity with qualitative research and the appropriateness of the method for studying the problem. Second, the proposal describes a qualitative pilot study. This demonstrates motivation, familiarity with research techniques, and ability to complete a report about unstructured research.

Proposals to Fund Research. The purpose of a research grant is to provide the resources needed to help complete a worthy project. Researchers whose primary goal is to use funding for personal benefit or prestige, to escape from other activities, or to build an "empire" are less successful. The strategies of proposal writing and getting grants has become an industry called **grantsmanship.**

There are many sources of funding for research proposals. Colleges, private foundations, and government agencies have programs to award grants to researchers. Funds may be used to purchase equipment, to pay your salary or that of others, for research supplies, for travel to collect data, or for help with the publication of results. The degree of competition for a grant varies a great deal, depending on the source. Some sources fund more than 3 out of 4 proposals they receive, others fund fewer than 1 in 20.

There are many sources of funding for social research, but there may be no source willing to fund a specific project. You need to investigate funding sources and ask questions: What types of projects are funded—applied versus basic research, specific topics, or specific research techniques? What are the deadlines? What kind (e.g., length, degree of detail, etc.) of proposal is necessary? How large are most grants? What aspects (e.g., equipment, personnel, travel, etc.) of a project are or are not funded? There are many sources of information on funding sources. Librarians or officials who are responsible for research grants at a college are good resource people. For example, private foundations are listed in an annual publication, *The Foundation Directory. The Guide to Federal Funding for Social Scientists* lists sources in the U.S. government. In the United States, there are many newsletters on funding sources and national computerized databases that subscribers can search for funding sources. Some agencies periodically issue **requests for proposals (RFPs)** that ask for proposals to conduct research on a specific issue. Researchers need to learn about funding sources, because it is essential to send the proposal to an appropriate source in order to be successful.[17]

Researchers need to show a track record of past success in the proposal, especially if they are going to be in charge of the project. The researcher in charge of a research project is the **principal investigator (PI)** or project director. Proposals usually include a curriculum vitae or academic resumé, letters of support from other researchers, and a record of past research. Reviewers feel safer investing funds in a project headed by someone who already has research experience than in a novice. One can build a track record with small research projects or by assisting an experienced researcher before seeking funding as a principal investigator.

The reviewers who evaluate a proposal judge whether the proposal project is appropriate to the funding source's goals. Most funding sources have guidelines stating the kinds of projects they fund. For example, programs that fund basic research have the advancement of knowledge as a goal. Programs to fund applied research often have improvements in the delivery of services as a goal. Instructions specify page length, number of copies, deadlines, and the like. Follow all instructions exactly. Why would reviewers give thousands of dollars to a researcher to carry out a complicated research project if he or she cannot even follow instructions on the page length of a proposal?

Proposals should be neat and professional looking. The instructions usually ask for a detailed plan for the use of time, services, and personnel. These should be clearly stated and realistic for the project. Excessively high or low estimates, unnec-

---

BOX 16.5 Factors Associated with a Successful Research Proposal

1. It addresses an important research question. It builds on prior knowledge and represents a substantial advance of knowledge for basic research. It documents a major social problem and holds promise for solutions for applied research.
2. It follows all instructions, is well written, and is easy to follow, with clearly stated objectives.
3. It completely describes research procedures that include high standards of research methodology, and it applies research techniques that are appropriate to the research question.
4. It includes specific plans for disseminating the results and evaluating whether the project has met its objectives.
5. The project is well designed and shows serious planning. It has realistic budgets and schedules.
6. The researcher has the necessary experience or background to complete the project successfully.

---

essary add-ons, or omitted essentials will lower how reviewers evaluate a proposal. Creating a budget for a proposed project is complicated and usually requires technical assistance. For example, pay rates, fringe benefit rates, and so on that must be charged may not be easy to obtain. It is best to consult a grants officer at a college or an experienced proposal writer. In addition, endorsements or clearances of regulations are often necessary (e.g., IRB approval; see Chapter 5). Proposals should also include specific plans for disseminating results (e.g., publications, presentations before professional groups, etc.) and a plan for evaluating whether the project met its objectives (see Box 16.5).

The proposal is a kind of contract between researcher and the funding source. Funding agencies often require a final report, including details on how funds were spent, the findings, and an evaluation of

---

Request for proposals (RFP) An announcement by a funding organization that it is willing to fund research and it is soliciting written plans of research projects.

Principal investigator (PI) The person who is primarily in charge of research on a project that is sponsored or funded by an organization.

whether the project met its objectives. Failure to spend funds properly, complete the project described in the proposal, or file a final report may result in a researcher being barred from receiving future funding or facing legal action. A serious misuse of funds may result in the banning of others at the same institution from receiving future funding.

The process of reviewing proposals after they are submitted to a funding source takes anywhere from a few weeks to almost a year, depending on the funding source. In most cases, reviewers rank a large group of proposals, and only highly ranked proposals receive funding. A proposal often undergoes a peer review in which the reviewers know the proposer from the vitae in the proposal, but the proposer does not know the reviewers. Sometimes a proposal is reviewed by nonspecialists or nonresearchers. Instructions on preparing a proposal indicate whether to write for specialists in a field or for an educated general audience. A proposal may be evaluated by more than one group of reviewers. In general, proposals that ask for larger amounts of money receive closer review.

If a proposal is funded, celebrate, but only for a short time. If the proposal is rejected, which is more likely, do not despair. Most proposals are rejected the first or second time they are submitted. Many funding sources provide written reviewer evaluations of the proposal. Always request them if they are provided. Sometimes, a courteous talk on the telephone with a person at the funding source will reveal the reasons for rejection. Strengthen and resubmit a proposal on the basis of the reviewer's comments. Most funding sources accept repeated resubmissions of revised proposals, and proposals that have been revised may be stronger in subsequent competitions.

THE POLITICS OF SOCIAL RESEARCH

The naïve, innocent view of social research suggests that conducting and writing about research is a pure process that operates in a sociopolitical vacuum, totally insulated from the pressures or concerns of the larger society. A more realistic view is that re-searchers must be prepared to deal with an array of ethical and political concerns. The ethical researcher protects subjects, conducts research honestly in accordance with codes of ethics, avoids interference from sponsors, and disseminates results in an open, clear manner. The politics of social research overlaps with many issues in sponsored research (discussed in Chapter 5). In addition, researchers face economically or politically powerful groups in society or the government who attempt to limit what they can study, how they conduct research, or how they disseminate the findings of research.

Limits on What Researchers Study

Direct Limits on Research. Governments or powerful groups in society may try to restrict free scientific inquiry. In nondemocratic societies, control over or the censorship of social research is the rule, not the exception. This is particularly the case with politically sensitive topics, including public opinion surveys. Thus, in past years in China, eastern Europe, South Africa, Taiwan, and other places, social researchers have been suspect, limited to "safe" topics, or forced to support official government policy.[18] In a number of countries, the study of sociology itself was banned as subversive after a military coup. In an extreme case, 40 percent of German scientists were dismissed from their jobs for political reasons when the Nazis "purified" universities and research centers in 1937.[19] Hundreds of professors and researchers in the United States who did not publicly swear to anticommunism and collaborate with the McCarthy investigations of the 1950s were purged. At that time, people who objected to mandatory loyalty oaths, supported racial integration, or advocated the teaching of sex education were suspected of subversion and threatened with dismissal. For instance, at the University of California alone, 25 professors were fired for refusing to sign a loyalty oath.[20]

Two possible limitations on social research are (1) gatekeepers who control access to data or subjects and (2) controls over how official statistics are collected. Gatekeepers can limit what is studied and may want to protect themselves or their organizations from criticism or embarrassment. They often limit access to subjects or areas with which they have concerns. For example, in 1997, the U.S. Army dropped several questions from a 153-item questionnaire on sexual harassment that was being sent to 9,000 soldiers. The reason for eliminating 6 questions was that "senior Army officials feared that the responses could be highly embarrassing to the Army" (Schmitt, 1997). Two researchers who were consultants on the project, a social anthropologist and a law professor, were upset. One said that preliminary results from an early version of the questionnaire suggested that sexual harassment at military bases was correlated with responses to the questions that asked about certain soldier behaviors (e.g., going to strip clubs, watching X-rated movies, etc.). Gatekeeper army officials did not want the potentially embarrassing information collected.

Another limitation involves official or existing statistics that government or other large organizations collect. Whether agencies collect information and how they collect it can affect research findings. Often, political factors affect how phenomena (e.g., unemployment, income, educational success, poverty level, etc.) are defined in official statistics and whether such data are collected.[21]

Hundreds of social scientists regularly rely on the data collected by the U.S. Census Bureau for conducting demographic, economic, and other studies. The original purpose of a census was to allocate elected representatives among states and districts. Later, the Census Bureau gathered information for making policy decisions, for providing social programs, and for distributing government funds based on the population size of an area. Over the years, it has become a major source of social science information and a clearinghouse for official statistics on many topics. Serious distortions (e.g., systematic overcounts or undercounts of some people or areas) weakens research findings based on Census Bureau statistics, prevents full democratic representation, and undermines a fair distribution of social programs or funds (see discussion in Chapter 11).

Some social researchers, especially those who rely on existing statistics, depend on the government to supply information or documents. In the United States, the Paperwork Reduction Act of 1980 created an Office of Information and Regulatory Af-

fairs to determine whether it was necessary to collect information and maintain records. The act resulted in fewer publications from government-sponsored research. In addition, the law had been "used on occasion to restrict information not supportive of executive branch policy goals" (Shattuck and Spence, 1988:47). For example, in the health field, research projects with an environmental focus that indirectly criticized business or government policy were more likely to be rejected for publication under "paperwork reduction" justification than those with a traditional disease focus that indirectly blamed the victim.

In the name of cost cutting, government agencies stopped collecting information, removed information from public circulation, and shifted information collection to private businesses. The number of outlets of the U.S. government publishing offices were cut and prices were raised. Bureaucratic decisions not to collect information can have policy implications.

Limits Due to the Influence of Politicians. Unfortunately, some people outside the scientific community attack social research when it disagrees with their social or political values. A politician or journalist may hear about a research project in a controversial area or may misinterpret the project, then use the occasion to attract publicity. For example, Professor Harris Rubin at the University of Southern Illinois intended to investigate the effects of THC (the active agent in marijuana) on sexual arousal. Almost no scientific evidence existed, only contradictory myths. He very carefully followed all procedures and clearances, and the research project was funded by the National Institute of Mental Health in 1975. A conservative congressperson learned of the research topic from nearby newspapers and introduced an amendment in Congress to prohibit further funding. In addition, all funds for the project were to be repaid to the federal government. Despite arguments that politicians should not interfere with legitimate research, funding was cut. Politicians are afraid to support social research if an opposing candidate could make a case to voters that the government appeared to be paying for students to "get stoned and watch porno films."[22] In 1989,

BOX **16.6** **U.S. Congressmen Question Research Funding**

In 1998, Representative Marshall Sanford of South Carolina said he wanted to cut National Science Foundation (NSF) funding for studies of questionable "scientific value." Apparently believing he was a better judge of scientific value than the scientific community, he cited studies about automatic teller machines and billiards. NSF officials observed that the research to which the congressman referred, the abbreviation *ATM* stood for *asynchronous transfer modes,* a high-speech data technique, not *automatic teller machines,* and *billiards* is a term physicists use in atomic theory for a subatomic particle, not the game as the congressman had assumed. Representative Sanford, along with a representative from California, indicated a desire to punish the NSF for supporting what they deemed unnecessary, wasteful studies. These included why people risk their resources to join social groups, differences between the social behavior of men and women, and why potential political candidates decide to run for office. Other congress members defended the NSF and noted that such criticisms were the result of faulty, sloppy research by the politicians, not the type of research the NSF supports through its peer-review process (Lederman, 1998).

noted that the project was not canceled because of questions about its scientific quality or importance; rather, it was an ideologically based decision that "we don't need to know this."[24]

Public attacks on social research, even non-controversial but misunderstood research, hurts all researchers. Politicians may "kill" research that the scientific community recognizes as legitimate, or they promote pet projects that have little scientific value. Researchers who apply for government funds sometimes restate their project in terms that do not attract attention. The public ridicule of researchers or the denial of research funds also encourages self-censorship and fosters a negative public opinion about social research.

National Security and Limits on Social Research. Military secrecy and national security became major issues in the United States during World War I and World War II. Most of the concern was with technology to create weapons, but social researchers have been limited in their study of foreign nations, issues of military interest, and research into government itself. U.S. security agencies such as the National Security Administration and the Central Intelligence Agency (CIA) have influenced social and natural science research into the Cold War period of the 1950s.

There was significant political influence over U.S. social science research about non-Western societies during the Cold War era, especially from the late 1940s to the mid-1960s. Intelligence and security agencies worked closely and clandestinely with most research centers and scholarly associations. During that period, security and military government agencies and a few politicized foundations provided most funds for social research about other societies, and officials monitored the writings and statements of researchers for conformity with government policy. Researchers who secretly worked for or cooperated with the government agencies tended to receive research funding and see their careers advance. Independent researchers or those who asked questions about official policy rarely saw research funds and faced career limitations. Conducting research that contradicted official policy was almost impossible.[25]

funding for a major national survey on sexual behavior to combat the AIDS epidemic was blocked in Congress by members who did not believe that it was proper for researchers to inquire into human sexual behavior (see Box 16.6).[27]

A research project on teenage sex conducted by the National Institutes of Health (NIH) was canceled in 1991 after action by the U.S. Senate. The study was to survey 24,000 teens about their social activities, family life, and sexual behavior, in order to provide background for understanding AIDS and other sexually transmitted diseases. Many researchers said they did not want to speak out on the issue for fear that they would become the target of attack by political groups. Some who spoke out said that the ability of a small minority with an extreme political ideology to kill important research was "a scandalous act" and "frightening." One researcher

One government research project in the 1960s created a great controversy. The U.S. Army funded **Project Camelot,** which involved respected social researchers who went to Chile to study political insurgency and mobilization. Several aspects of the project created controversy. First, the project's goal was to find out how to prevent peasants and disadvantaged groups in Third World countries from taking independent political action to oppose a dictator. Such counterinsurgency research is usually conducted by the Central Intelligence Agency. The researchers were accused of using their skills and knowledge to advance military interests against disadvantaged Third World people. Second, some researchers were unaware of the source of funds. Third, the people and the government of Chile were not informed about the project. Once they discovered it, they asked that it end and that all researchers leave.[26]

By the late 1960s and 1970s, freedom to conduct research expanded, restrictions on researchers were relaxed, and the government classified fewer documents. The U.S. Congress passed the *Freedom of Information Act (FOIA)* in 1966 and strengthened it in 1974. The law opened many government documents to scholars and members of the public if they filed requests with government agencies. The trend toward greater openness of information and freedom of research was reversed in the 1980s. The U.S. government limited the publication of information, expanded the range of classified documents, and made less information publicly available. This has restrained academic inquiry, scientific progress, and democratic decision making.[27]

In the 1980s, the definition of national security was broadened, the system for classifying government documents was expanded, and new limits were imposed on research into "sensitive areas," even if no government agency or funds are involved. It became easier to classify information and classify documents that were already in the public domain. In addition, military and security officials could restrict researchers from outside the United States from attending scholarly meetings or visiting U.S. classrooms, libraries, and research centers.[28]

In the past, CIA undercover agents have posed as social researchers to get information in foreign nations. Until 1986, the CIA had a blanket rule barring researchers from disclosing CIA sponsorship of their research. At that time, the rule was loosened to cover only cases where the CIA believed such disclosure "would prove damaging to the United States." For example, a Harvard professor had a contract with the CIA not to reveal that the agency paid for the research for a scholarly book on U.S. foreign policy.[29]

Cross-national research involves unique issues. The research community condemns the use of undercover agents in the guise of researchers and the practice of hiding the source of funding for research. Researchers have developed ethical guidelines for conduct in other nations, which specify cooperation with host officials, the protection of subjects, and leaving information in the host nation. Nevertheless, a researcher may find interference from his or her own government, or the researcher's respect for the basic human rights of the people being studied in a nondemocratic society may lead him or her to hide information from the host government involved.[30]

During the 30 years from 1970 to 2001, social researchers had significant independence and academic freedom to study various societies. However, in the United States political changes appearing since the September 11, 2001, terrorist attacks may point to a return to greater government monitoring and influence over social research on other nations.

Indirect Limits through Control over Research Funding.
The most common way that politics shapes social research is through control over funds for doing research. This is similar to the issues involved in sponsored research. Large-scale research projects can be expensive, costing as much as a million dollars. The funds often come from private sources or governments.

Most officials recognize that an open and autonomous social scientific community is the best path to unbiased, valid knowledge. The peer-review

Project Camelot A controversial social research project in Chile funded by the U.S. Army in the 1960s that violated ethical principles and raised major political concerns.

process promotes autonomous research because proposals for funds to conduct research submitted to a government agency are reviewed by researcher peers who evaluate the proposal on its scientific merit. Although the government funds most basic research, research itself is conducted at many colleges, universities, and research centers across the nation.

The sums for social research are tiny compared with the amounts spent by large corporations on research or to government funding for natural science or military research. In the United States, most social research funding comes from the federal government, with university and private foundation funding limited in amount, scope, and number. Thus, for large projects, researchers are forced to go to the government for funding.

Prior to World War II in the United States, a few private foundations set up by wealthy families (Carnegie, Ford, Rockefeller, and Sage) funded most sociological research. The foundations sought information about the serious social problems that appeared with early industrialism. They also wanted to discourage links between radicals and social researchers and protect established social institutions. After a number of years, "the production of social science research thus becomes regularized or routinized, and its connection with sponsoring organizations becomes obscured from the public's view" (Seybold, 1987:197). Private foundation funds redirected social research efforts away from its early focus that was applied, action oriented, critical, neighborhood centered, and involved participation by subjects and toward a focus that was detached, professional, positivist, and academic. After World War II, government research funding expanded. Private foundations maintained a role setting research priorities through the 1960s, when federal government funds surpassed private funds.[31] Government research funds grew, but funding for the social sciences and sociology remained tiny. In the United States, research funding for sociology has been less than 1 percent of federal funding for basic research.

In the United States, social research funding is available from several federal agencies, including National Science Foundation, Department of Defense, Agriculture Department, Commerce Depart-ment, Department of Housing and Urban Development, Department of Education, National Endowment for the Humanities, Small Business Administration, Department of Justice, Department of Labor, and the many institutes under the Department of Health and Human Services. The federal government itself employs researchers. Most social research is conducted at colleges and universities or independent research institutes.

The primary funding source for social research in the United States (the National Science Foundation; NSF) supported only basic positivist research early in its history for political reasons. Nonpositivist social research and applied studies were excluded to win backing from natural scientists, to counter popular perceptions that social science was "fluff," and to repel charges by ideological conservatives that social science was "left-wing." In addition, the NSF avoided supporting research on controversial topics (e.g., sex, political power, etc.). This was due to a fear, in the political climate of the 1950s and 1960s, that the study of such topics could create political problems that would jeopardize obtaining government funds for social science research.

The decision to allocate funds to various agencies for social research and the applied/basic split varies from year to year and is determined by political processes. Although the scientific review committees within the NSF and NIH evaluate the scientific merit of submitted proposals, political officials decide the total amount of funds available, and whether funds must be used for applied or basic research. Politicians set priorities, so conflicts between the political parties or ideological interests affect the amount of research funding available and how it can be spent (see Box 16.7).

Funding for social science research in the National Science Foundation declined 24 percent between 1976 and 1980 in constant dollars. Despite an outcry, funding dropped another 17 percent between 1980 and 1983. This was because political leaders thought that too many research results supported the policies of their opponents. Applied research was also reduced. In response, the professional associations of several social science disciplines joined together to form a lobbying

BOX **16.7** Political Influence on Crime Research in the United States

Savelsberg and colleagues (2002) asked whether political pressures in the United States altered the direction of social research on crime issues between 1951 and 1993. They looked at scholarly journal articles and asked whether shifts in politics affected research through funds for research and whether changing the organization of academic fields in colleges and universities influenced the theories used (i.e., individual problems versus social forces or inequalities), topics examined (e.g., street crime and illegal drugs versus white-collar crimes), and crime perspectives applied (i.e., micro-level enforcement versus macro level or understanding criminal behavior) of articles. They found that funding by agencies that tried to advance a political agenda and new academic departments created to be better aligned and more responsive to political interests rather than acting as an independent research community both had an effect on what types of studies were conducted. Nonetheless, while funding and new organizational units affected which topics researchers studied and which theories they tested, these factors did not affect whether data supported the theories. Thus, political forces did influence the theories, topics, and perspectives to which researchers devoted attention and efforts, but political factors did not influence how researchers designed or conducted the research studies.

organization: the *Consortium of Social Science Associations (COSSA).* COSSA was able to reduce the size of some cuts.[32]

The funding for social research may be unchanged for 80 years. Funds from the private Social Science Research Council in the late 1920s, once adjusted for inflation and the size of academic profession, were probably greater than funding for social science research from the National Science Foundation now.[33]

Political values are relevant when money is allocated for research on certain questions and priorities. For example, politicians decide that money is allocated for applied research to demonstrate how "burdensome" the costs of regulation are for large corporations, but none is available to investigate the benefits of regulation for consumers. They increase funds to study crime committed by drug addicts, but eliminate funds to study crime by corporate executives. They make available new funds for research on how to promote entrepreneurship, while cutting back funds to study the human consequences of social program cutbacks.[34]

Funds for basic research can promote specific theoretical or value perspectives. For example, funds may be allocated to study how individual attributes correlate with undesirable social behaviors, while no funding exists for investigating structural and community factors. By focusing on some research questions and limiting alternatives, political groups try to shape the research that is conducted.

Many issues that social researchers address bear directly on social beliefs, values, and policies. Political groups set priorities for these issues that are distinct from those of the scientific community. This has both positive and negative effects. It ensures that the concerns of politicians or vocal public groups are addressed and that social problems that politically influential groups define as important get researched. If scientific research does not support a popular public myth (e.g., that capital punishment has a deterrent effect or that women who have abortions suffer psychological harm), funds are repeatedly allocated to try to discover evidence that will confirm popular beliefs, while scientifically central issues go unfunded.

The scientific community has substantial freedom to define what should be researched, but problems affecting less politically vocal groups or issues for which there is no lobby receive limited research funding. This imbalance of funding creates an imbalance in knowledge across issues. Eventually, there is substantial knowledge on the issues of interest to powerful political groups, while their opponents are weakened by a lack of knowledge.

In the United States, a research proposal that has undergone rigorous peer review for its scientific merit might still be rejected by politicians, who may not even have read the proposal, because they dislike a research topic for political-ideological reasons. Members of the U.S. Congress have reduced money for the major research agency, the National Science Foundation, because they disliked particular social research projects that the agency had funded based on purely scientific grounds.[35]

Earmarked or "Pork Barrel" Funding for Research.

Beginning in the 1990s, U.S. politicians increasingly circumvented the scientific peer-review process to allocate government financial support for research. The politicians earmarked or targeted money for specific projects at particular universities and research institutes. The politicians allocated funds based on political favoritism, instead of relying on competition among proposals based on research quality or merit as evaluated by informed members of the scientific community. It appears that "pork barrel" politics—the process by which politicians distribute money to major government projects not based on importance or being a high priority, but because they bring money to the businesses and supporters in a politician's home district—had spread to the funding of research.

Increasingly, researchers in some states or electoral districts receive substantial funding, while others get almost nothing, based on political connections rather than on scientific merit. For example, the State University of New York at Buffalo received $12 million to conduct research on traffic injuries in a noncompetitive, political decision. Between 1989 and 1993, the amount of research funds politically earmarked doubled; it then remained stable of a few years. Since 1996, it has grown rapidly and increased fivefold. The *Chronicle of Higher Education* reports that 2001 was a record year for such pork barrel spending; it was the largest one-year increase since records were kept. By 2001, it had topped $2 billion.

The politicized allocation of government research funds puts pressure on universities and research institutes to court favor with influential politicians. For example, in 1995, New Hampshire received no earmarked research funds. Then in 1999, after New Hampshire Republican Senator Judd Gregg became the chairman of an appropriations subcommittee, researchers in New Hampshire benefited as their state leaped to the seventh highest in receiving government funds. When Senator John McCain tried to end pork barrel spending for research in 2001, the U.S. Senate defeated his mea-

sure 87 to 12. Many politicians are "proud of pork" and brag about the money they "bring home" based on political favoritism not scientific merit. To obtain research funds, universities and research institutes increasingly find that they must devote efforts to courting political favor and lobbying, instead encouraging researchers to prepare a research proposal that will be scientifically competitive in the peer-review process.[36]

Many research institutes and universities have turned to private donors (wealthy individuals, corporations, or foundations) for research funds. Funding from private donors often comes with strings attached. For example, a private donor withdrew $450,000 because a researcher at the university that received the money had publicly criticized a policy that the donor favored.[37] Some donors want to support independent research with no strings, but many use the donated funds to create subtle pressure to advance a pet policy position, ideological stand, or political agenda. Universities and research institutes try to avoid limitations on research funding from private donators, but they must balance needed "hard cash" from a donor against abstract ideals, such as a researcher's freedom to conduct and publish any research that advances knowledge. They resolve the difficulty of returning or rejecting a donor's funds by agreeing to limits on open, free inquiry.

Limits on the Dissemination of Knowledge.

A major norm of the scientific community says to publicly distribute knowledge. Powerful groups or institutions can impinge on social research by limiting the flow of information, restricting publication, or silencing researchers.

A 1997 news report illustrates the suppression of research findings. A pharmaceutical company that had a widely used drug for thyroid problems prohibited a university research team from publishing its research results that showed the drug to be ineffective. In exchange for research funds, the researchers had signed a contract giving the company a right to veto publications. Other studies show that when drug companies fund research, 98 percent of the time the published findings show that the drugs are effective. This number is far higher than when the drug companies are not the funding

"These projected figures are a figment of our imagination. We hope you like them."

source. Some believe that negative findings about new products get suppressed when millions of dollars for a company are involved. Researchers may be given stock or financial incentives to show positive findings or to delay the release of findings. More than half of university researchers who received money from drug or biotechnology companies stated that private donors exerted influence on how they did their work.

Research on medicine or biotechnology is not the only area where profits and disseminating research findings come into conflict. In 1997, a Cornell University professor testified for 10 minutes at a town meeting about the labor practices of the largest nursing home corporation in the United States—Beverly Enterprises, which operates 700 nursing homes. The professor's testimony was backed up by years of research and documented by congressional reports, newspaper reports, court records, interviews, and other scholars. In 1998, the company sued the professor for $225,000 for defaming it and demanded years of research documents and notes. This is called a **SLAPP (Strategic Lawsuits Against Public Participation) suit** and its purpose is to stop public testimony. The practice began in the 1970s, when companies issued "strategic lawsuits" to silence opposition on controversial issues.

In other cases, a study of corporate crime was delayed and the results changed after the threat of a lawsuit by managers who had been interviewed in the study; the publication of a study of a boarding school was stopped due to a possible lawsuit after school officials wanted to change what they had said in interviews and make other changes in the book because they disagreed with the researcher's finding; and an article was changed after a researcher threatened a lawsuit over the exposure conflicts that occurred among researchers during a study conducted by a team of researchers.[38]

Between 2002 and 2004 serious charges were made that the federal government of the United States restricted the release of scientific information that contradicted or failed to support the administration's policy positions. These included censoring data on the efficacy of condoms, blocking evidence that showed abstinence is not as effective as sex education, and directing the National Cancer Institute to post a claim on its website stating that abortion promotes breast cancer, although a major study showed no connection. In addition, it had reports on global warming removed from distribution based on the objections from political advisers, not scientists. The Environmental Protection Agency said it would not analyze pollution studies that contradicted official administration policy. A U.S. Department of Agriculture researcher who looked at how to decrease the odor of swine farms through diet developed applications that detected air contaminants. Unintentionally, the study also showed that large-scale hog confinements regularly violated federal pollution limits and produced antibiotic-resistant bacteria. A member of the hog industry learned of the research and contacted the researcher's supervisor, who in turn forbade him from delivering findings at a research conference or submit his study to scientific journals.[39] However, this is not as drastic as the jailing of survey researchers by Iran's government because they found results showing a large majority of the Iranian

SLAPP suit Wealthy, powerful organizations use this to intimidate researchers and stop them from publicly expressing ideas or revealing information.

BOX **16.8** A Summary of Political Issues

DIRECT LIMITS ON RESEARCH

1. The government (or vigilante groups) bans, fires, jails, or threatens professors and researchers who study unpopular topics, openly discuss "forbidden" ideas, or make statements that they oppose.
2. Officials in government agencies or large organizations block access to official documents or statistical information, or try to restrict how official data are gathered or made publicly available.
3. Politicians and those in high office criticize, attack, or put public pressure to block legitimate social research that they disagree with on personal, religious, or ideological grounds.
4. Officials try to block or censor research because they believe it might hinder national security or they clandestinely try to control social research for their own military or secret intelligence gathering purposes.

INDIRECT LIMITS ON RESEARCH THROUGH FUNDING

1. Limits or cuts in funding for research prevent the production of new knowledge that might challenge ideological beliefs or political views.
2. Controls over the topics or issues receiving research funding redirect new knowledge so that it will provide support for certain policy positions.

3. Pork barrel spending by politicians circumvents the peer-review processes and allocates research funds based on political favoritism or on rewarding friends in one's home district, instead of being based on competition by scientific merit.
4. Limits are placed on the techniques, tools, or services that researchers can use to fulfill political objectives and are unrelated to the scientific research process, yet add costs, time, or complications to conducting research.

LIMITS ON OR BIAS IN THE DISSEMINATION OF RESEARCH RESULTS

1. Researchers are threatened with legal action or penalties if they speak freely in a public forum or openly publish the findings of their research.
2. Prior review or screening is required by nonscientists (i.e., corporate or political officials) before a researcher is allowed to share research findings with the scientific community or public.
3. Officials and other influential people promote research findings that the scientific community considers to be seriously defective, weak, or inadequate but that advance their political agenda.

---

people wanted to improve relations with the United States, which was again the Iranian government's policy (see Box 16.8).

The Dissemination of Findings

What do you do with your research findings? Positivist researchers recognize two areas in which values legitimately come into play. First, researchers can select a topic area or research question. Although there are "frontier" areas of inquiry in topic areas, researchers can choose a research question on the basis of personal preference.[40]

> **Models of relevance** A set of ideal types of ways social researchers understand the purposes of conducting research and the use of research results.

Second, once research is completed, researchers' values shape where they disseminate their findings. They are expected to report findings to the scientific community, and funding agencies require a report, but beyond these requirements, it is up to the researcher.

Models of Relevance. What happens when the research completed involves an ethical-political concern that Rule (1978a, 1978b) has called **models of relevance?** Rule reviewed the positions that social researchers took toward their research and its use and argued that the positions can be collapsed into five basic types (see Box 16.9).

The models of relevance are ideal types of the positions social scientists take. Is the researcher a technician, who produces valid, reliable information about how society works, to be used by others?

BOX **16.9 Models of Relevance**

1. *No net effects.* Social science findings produce no greater social good. Several famous social scientists who argue this are William Graham Sumner, Vilfredo Pareto, Herbert Spencer, Edward Banfield, and James Q. Wilson. These conservative social scientists see the products of research as capable of being used for anyone's self-interest and believe that, in the long run, as much harm as good has come from the greater knowledge social science yields.

2. *Direct and positive effects.* Social science knowledge results in an improvement for all. Liberal social scientists, such as Robert Merton, who adopt this stance see knowledge about social relations leading to a more rational world. Research results on social problems help us understand the social world much better, enabling us to know how we can modify it toward some greater good. For example, Lindblom and Cohen (1979) urged a redirection of social science toward what they see as social problem solving.

3. *Special constituency, the proletariat.* Social science should be used to advance the interests and position of the working class. This is the Marxist model of the appropriate use of social research. According to it, all social science falls into three categories: the trivial, that which helps the bourgeoisie, and that which aids the proletariat. Consistent with a critical science approach, research findings should be used to advocate and defend the interests of the working class and assist workers by exposing and combatting exploitation, oppression, injustice, and repression.

4. *Special constituency, the uncoopted.* Social science should be used to aid any disadvantaged or under- privileged group in society. This model, associated with Karl Mannheim and C. Wright Mills, is more general than the Marxian position. It sees many social groups as lacking power in society (women, consumers, racial minorities, gays, the poor, etc.) and argues that these groups are oppressed by the powerful in society who have access to education, wealth, and knowledge. The social researcher should defend those who lack a voice in society and who are manipulated by those in power. The powerful can use or purchase social science research for their own ends. Because they have a unique role in society and are in a position to learn about all areas of society, social researchers have an obligation to help the weak and share knowledge with them.

5. *Special constituency, the government.* Social science's proper role is to aid the decision makers of society, especially public officials. This model has been expressed by Senator Daniel Patrick Moynihan and in official NSF policy reports, and is common in nondemocratic societies. It is similar to the second model (direct and positive effects), but adds the assumption that government is in the best position to make use of social research findings and is fully committed to eradicating social problems. It is also similar to the first (no net effects) model but implies "selling" or providing findings to the highest bidder within the limits of national loyalty. It assumes that the government operates in the best interests of everyone, and that researchers have a patriotic duty to give what they learn to those with political power.

Or does the researcher belong to an independent community of professionals who have a say in what research questions are asked and how results are used? On a continuum, one extreme is the amoral researcher who lacks any concern or control over research or its use. He or she supplies the knowledge that others request and nothing more. This was the stance many scientists in Nazi Germany used to justify collaboration with Nazi practices later classified as "crimes against humanity." He or she "just follows orders" and "just does the job" but asks "no questions." At the other extreme are researchers who have total control over research and its use.

The approaches to social science discussed in Chapter 4 are associated with different models of relevance, as are different political views.[41] Positivists tend to follow the "direct and positive effects" or "special constituency, the government" model. The interpretive researcher follows the "no net effects" or the "uncoopted" model. Critical social scientists follow the "special constituency, the proletariat" or "special constituency, the uncoopted" models.

The models are ideal types. Specific researchers or research projects cross between models. For example, Whyte (1986) described research on employee ownership as crossing between three constituencies (the proletariat, the uncoopted, and the government) and as having direct and positive effects.

Since Rule developed models of relevance, a new model has appeared with the growth of non-government, private **think tanks** in the United States. This sixth model is *special constituency, wealthy individuals, and corporations.* It states social research can reflect a researcher's personal political values and advance the political goals of wealthy groups who seek to maintain or expand their power. The think tanks are research and publicity organizations funded by wealthy individuals, corporations, and political groups. For example, the Manhattan Institute, Cato Institute, Heritage Foundation, and American Enterprise Institute grew dramatically from the early 1980s to the 1990s. They advance a political viewpoint and use social research or pseudoscience among other means. Think tanks pay researchers, sponsor research reports, and draw public attention to results that support their political viewpoint (see Box 16.10).

Think tank studies vary in quality, lack peer review, and are short on solid evidence but long on suggestions. The audience for this research is not the scientific community, and the primary goal is not to advance knowledge. Rather, think tank researchers conduct policy-oriented studies with an ideological viewpoint in an attempt to shape public thinking and influence political debate. Many receive significant media publicity, fame, and fortune, although their research may be inferior and lacks scientific peer review. At the same time, traditional social scientists who operate with meager funds, but who lack connections to the mass media, find that their more rigorous, careful studies of the same public issues get overlooked. The public and policy officials are often overwhelmed by the publicity of think tank research results.

After Findings Are Published. The communalism norm of the scientific community says make

---

Think tank   An organization (usually nonprofit, nongovernment) in which one or more researchers, writers, journalists, and others develop, refine, elaborate, and publicize ideas about policy issues.

BOX **16.10** **Ethics, Politics, and the Misuse of Survey Research**

In a highly unusual move, the leading professional public opinion organization, the American Association for Public Opinion Research (AAPOR), sharply criticized two organizations that engaged in blatant unethical behavior with survey research to advance narrow political goals. In 1997, the Association found that Frank Luntz of Luntz Research Corporation "repeatedly refused to make public essential factors about his research." His surveys showed strong public support for a Republican Party proposal called "Contract with America" in November 1994 that other researchers did not find. Luntz widely publicized his findings, but refused to disclose basic methodological information, as required in ethical surveys.

Three years later, the AAPOR criticized Campaign Tel, Ltd. for a gross violation of confidentiality. Campaign Tel used a list with names and telephone numbers of registered Wisconsin voters and claimed to be conducting a survey. In fact, the company turned over detailed information on survey responses and phone number to the Wisconsin Republican Party. The AAPOR states that it "strongly condemns any practice that poses as a survey and elicits information from a respondent for any purpose other than legitimate survey research." In this case, the company posed as a legitimate survey organization, but was really a partisan get-out-the-vote effort of a political campaign. The company misrepresented its true nature. By the time the AAPOR had detected and documented the unethical behavior, Campaign Tel ceased to exist.

Source: See AAPOR website www.aapor.org/main1.html.

---

findings public. Once findings are part of the public domain, the researcher loses control over them. This means that others can use the findings for their own purposes. Although the researcher may have chosen a topic based on his or her values, once the findings are published, others can use them to advance opposing values.

For example, a researcher wants to increase the political rights of a Native American tribe. He or she studies the tribe's social practices, including social barriers to their achieving greater power in the community. Once the findings are published, members of the tribe can use the results to break down barriers. Yet, opponents can use the same findings to restrict the power of the tribe and to reinforce the barriers.

Findings That Influence Future Behavior.
Did you ever do something differently than before because of research findings you read? If so, you are not alone. Sometimes the dissemination of findings affect social behavior. One example is the effect of political poll results. Public opinion polls affect the political preferences of voters; that is, parts of the population change their views to correspond to what opinion polls say they have found.[42]

Other social research findings can affect behavior. In fact, the dissemination of research findings may affect behavior in a way that negates or alters the original findings. For example, a study finds that professionals are likely to put a great deal of stress on the academic achievement of their children. This creates highly anxious, unhappy children. If professionals read the findings, they may alter their child-rearing behavior. Then another study, years later, might find that professionals are not likely to rear their children to achieve in academic areas any more than other groups do.

Researchers have several responses to research findings that affect social behavior:

1. They ruin predictability and regularity of human social behavior, undermining replication.
2. Only trivial behaviors are changed, so this is an issue only to researchers working in very narrow applied areas.
3. Human behavior can change because there are few unalterable laws of human behavior, and people will use knowledge in the public domain to change their lives.

In any case, social research has not uncovered the full complexity of human relations and behavior. Even if it did, and such knowledge were fully and accurately disseminated to the entire population, social researchers would still have to study which human behaviors change and how (see Box 16.11).

After years of research, the scientific community occasionally arrives at an international consensus on an issue. Major science organizations proclaim that an overwhelming majority of research evidence favors a specific position on an applied issue (e.g., the level of arsenic in drinking water that is safe). This does not mean that the scientists have proof. Recall that scientists use the term differently than most other people. They have exceedingly high standards for *proof* and do not use the term for empirical questions, because it implies absolute certainty and closure.

Scientific consensus means that after carefully reviewing numerous studies conducted over many years and weighing all the evidence, in the judgment of nearly all informed scientists, there little doubt about an issue (e.g., a far lower level of arsenic is needed for public health and safety). The scientific community seeks to contribute to larger society, to advance the "common good" or "public interest," by making their consensus known on an issue that will benefit the general public's health and safety.

When a major politician announces no change in government policy until the science is clear or there is proof, it misleads the public about science. In reality, pressures from special interests and political ideology are probably driving the politician's decision. A public announcement that misrepresents how science operates and its role in public policy may serve to conceal political reasons behind a policy decision (*Economist,* 2001).

Academic Freedom.
Most students have heard about academic freedom, but few understand it. **Academic freedom** is the existence of an open and largely unrestricted atmosphere for the free exchange of ideas and information. In open democratic societies, many people value intellectual freedom and believe in providing scholars with freedom from interference. This idea is based on the belief

Academic freedom   A guarantee that researchers and/or teachers are free to examine all topics and discuss all ideas without any restrictions, threats, or interference from people or authorities outside the community of teachers, scholars, and scientists.

that fundamental democratic institutions, the advance of unbiased knowledge, and freedom of expression require a free flow of ideas and information.

Academic freedom is related to the autonomy of research. New ideas for research topics, the interpretation of findings, the development of theories or hypotheses, and the open discussion of ideas require academic freedom.

Academic freedom in colleges, universities, and research institutes provides a context for the free discussion and open exchange of ideas that scientific research requires. For knowledge to advance, researchers, professors, and students need a setting in which they feel free to advance or debate diverse, and sometimes unpopular, opinions or positions—a setting in which people are not afraid to explore a full range of ideas in open discussion, in classrooms, in public talks, or in publications.

The importance of academic freedom is demonstrated by the paucity of social research in places where it is nonexistent. The major threat to academic freedom comes from social or political groups that want to restrict discussion or impose a point of view. Restrictions on academic freedom limit the growth of knowledge about society and undermine the integrity of the research process.

Academic freedom was a significant issue in the late nineteenth and early twentieth centuries, when the social sciences were institutionalized in universities. In the early years, professors lost their jobs because political officials or economic elites disliked the views expressed in their classrooms or publications. Famous scholars in the early period of American social science, like Thorsten Veblen, were forced out of several colleges because of what they said in the classroom or ideas they wrote about. The development of tenure, the idea that faculty could not be fired after a long probationary period without a very good reason, advanced academic freedom but did not guarantee complete academic freedom. Professors and researchers have been fired for advocating unpopular ideas.[43]

Political attacks on social science are not new. They illustrate the conflict between the independent pursuit of knowledge and the views of political groups who want to impose their beliefs. These attacks raise the question: How autonomous should so-cial science be from the values in the larger culture? The findings of social research frequently conflict with social beliefs based on nonscientific knowledge systems such as religion or political ideology. Galileo faced this issue about 400 years ago, before natural science was accepted. His astronomical findings, based on free-thinking science, contradicted official Church doctrine. Galileo was forced to recant his findings publicly, under the threat of torture. Silencing him slowed the advance of knowledge for a generation. The challenges of evolutionary theory also illustrate how scientific knowledge and popular beliefs conflict with one another.

Academic freedom is integral to good research. Scientific research involves more than knowing technical information (e.g., how to draw a random sample); it requires a spirit of free and open discussion, criticism on the basis of scientific merit irrespective of values, and inquiry into all areas of social life. These values are threatened when academic freedom is restricted.

OBJECTIVITY AND VALUE FREEDOM

Some argue that social science must be as objective and unbiased as the natural sciences; others maintain that value-free, objective social science is impossible. Part of the confusion is because each term has at least two alternative definitions. Sometimes, two different terms share the same definition (see Box 16.12).

The positivist approach holds that science is value free, unbiased, and objective. It collapses the definitions together. Value neutrality is guaranteed by logical-deductive, formal theory and a complete separation of facts from value-based concepts. The scientific community is free of prejudice and governed by free and open discussion. With complete value freedom and objectivity, science reveals the one and only, unified, unambiguous truth.

Max Weber, Alvin Gouldner, and Karl Mannheim are three major nonpositivist social thinkers who discussed the role of the social scientist in society. Weber (1949) argued that the fact/value separation is not clear in the social sciences. He suggested that value-laden theories de-

BOX **16.12** Objective, Value Free, and Unbiased

1. *Objective:*
   a. Opposite of *subjective;* external, observable, factual, precise, quantitative
   b. Logical; created by an explicit rational procedure; absence of personal or arbitrary decisions; follows specific preestablished rules
2. *Value Free:*
   a. Absence of any metaphysical values or assumptions; devoid of a priori philosophical elements; amoral
   b. Lack of influence from personal prejudice or cultural values; devoid of personal opinion; no room for unsupported views; neutral
3. *Unbiased:*
   a. Nonrandom error eliminated; absence of systematic error; technically correct
   b. Lack of influence from personal prejudice or cultural values; devoid of personal opinion; no room for unsupported views; neutral

fine social facts or socially meaningful action. Thus, social theories necessarily contain value-based concepts, because all concepts about the social world are created by members of specific cultures. The cultural content of social concepts cannot be purged, and socially meaningful action makes sense only in a cultural context. For example, when social researchers study racial groups, they are not interested in the biological differences between races. Race is a social concept; it is studied because the members of a culture attach social meaning to racial appearance. Race would be meaningless if people did not attach such a social meaning to observable racial differences.

Other social researchers have built on Weber's ideas. For example, Moore (1973) asked whether majority-group (e.g., Anglo, White) researchers, as "outsiders," can accurately study racial minorities, because their questions, assumptions, and interests come from a dominant, nonminority perspective. Are the culture, values, and belief system of the dominant White culture appropriate for asking important questions and really understanding the subculture of racial minorities? Similar concerns have been raised

regarding gender.[44] Being from a different culture may not preclude researching a group, but it calls for extra care and sensitivity from a researcher.

Weber (1949) also argued that social scientists cannot avoid taking stands on social issues they study. Researchers *must* be unbiased (i.e., neutral and devoid of personal opinion and unsupported views) when applying accepted research techniques and focus on the means or mechanisms of how the social world works, not on ends, values, or normative goals. A researcher's values must be separate from the findings, and he or she should advocate positions on specific issues only when speaking as a private citizen.

Gouldner (1976) attacked the notion of value-free, objective social science. He argued that value freedom was used in the past to disguise specific value positions. In fact, value freedom is itself a value—a value in favor of "value free." Gouldner said that complete value freedom was impossible and that scientists and other professionals use the term to hide their own values. He recommended making values explicit. A researcher can be motivated to do research by a desire to do more than dispassionately study the world. The researcher who is motivated by a strong moral desire to effect change need not invalidate good research practice.

Mannheim (1936) also questioned the ideas of *value neutrality* and *objectivity.* He saw the intellectuals of a society, especially those involved in social research, as occupying a unique social role. A person's social location in society shapes his or her ideas and viewpoints. Yet, social researchers are separate from others and are less shaped by their social position because they try to learn the viewpoints of other people and empathize with all parts of society. Social researchers are not beholden to powerful elites, and they are also less subject to shifts in popular opinion, fads, and crazes. They can and should adopt a **relational position**—a position apart from any other specific social group, yet in touch with all groups. They should be detached or

Relational position Karl Mannheim's idea that professional academic researchers and intellectuals occupy a unique social position and are detached from the major groups in society, which puts them in the best position to develop unbiased knowledge.

marginal in society, yet have connections with all parts of society, even parts that are often overlooked or hidden.

CONCLUSION

Clearly communicating results is part of the larger scientific enterprise, as are the ethics and politics of social research. The "solutions" to the political issues that social researchers face are threefold. First, researchers need to be aware of such issues, be aware of potential dangers, and adopt a realistic view of sociopolitical environment instead of a naive view of social research. Second, researchers need to form self-defense organizations that can

work with others to advocate for the independence of research from outside pressures. Third, researchers need to educate the general public and leaders of major institutions about the value and importance of independent social research.

I want to end this chapter by urging you, as a consumer of social research or a new social researcher, to be self-aware. Be aware of the place of the researcher in society and of the societal context of social research itself. Social researchers, and sociologists in particular, bring a unique perspective to the larger society. Social researchers have a responsibility and need an awareness of how the social sciences acquired their current place in society.

KEY TERMS

academic freedom	models of relevance	relational position
editing	paraphrasing	request for proposals (RFP)
error of segregation	plagiarism	revising
executive summary	prewriting	SLAPP suit
freewriting	principal investigator (PI)	think tank
grantsmanship	Project Camelot	zoom lens

REVIEW QUESTIONS

1. Discuss the relationship among prewriting, freewriting, rewriting, editing, and composing in the process of writing a research report.

2. What are the primary differences in the organization of a quantitative versus a qualitative research report?

3. How is a proposal to conduct research similar to and different from a final research report?

4. What types of limitations on social research come from the actions of politicians?

5. In what ways can control over funding influence the types of issues being researched?

6. How might the criteria used by government or private donors that provide funds for research differ from criteria used by peers in the scientific community?

7. What trends are there in U.S. government funding for research over the past 20 years, and how might they be influencing the research that is being conducted?

8. What is the source of Rule's models of relevance and what is their usefulness?

9. How does academic freedom support or contradict a relational position?

10. What are the meanings of doing objective and value-free research?

NOTES

1. See "Plagiarism Case Documented," in American Sociological Association *Footnotes,* 17(2) (February 1989), p. 2, or "Noted Harvard Psychiatrist Resigns Post after Faculty Group Finds He Plagiarized," in *Chronicle of Higher Education,* 35(15) (December 7, 1989), p. 1.

2. From Sociology Writing Group (1991).

3. For suggestions on writing, see Donald and colleagues (1983) and Leggett and colleagues (1965).

4. From Sociology Writing Group (1991:40).

5. See Fine (1988) for this and other suggestions on writing.

6. See Mullins (1977:11–30) for a discussion of outlines and the organization of quantitative research reports. Also see Williams and Wolfe (1979:85–116) for good hints on how to organize ideas in a paper.

7. Grosof and Sardy (1985:386–389) have provided suggestions on how to explain quantitative findings.

8. Lofland (1974) inductively discovered what he identifies as five major writing styles for reporting field research (generic, novel, elaborated, eventful, and interpenetrated) and discusses how they are evaluated.

9. The error of segregation is discussed in Lofland and Lofland (1984:146).

10. See Becker and Geer (1982:244) and Schatzman and Strauss (1973:130) for a discussion of this and related issues.

11. See Hammersley and Atkinson (1983) and Van Maanen (1988).

12. Discussed in Spradley (1970:162–167).

13. See Van Maanen (1988:13).

14. See Dabbs (1982) and Jackson (1978).

15. For a discussion of ethical concerns in writing field research reports, see Becker (1969), Punch (1986), and Wax (1971).

16. See Barzun and Graff (1970) and Shafer (1980) for excellent suggestions on writing about historical research.

17. For more on writing proposals to fund research projects, see Bauer (1988), Locke and associates (1987), and Quarles (1986). A somewhat dated but useful short introduction to proposal writing is Krathwohl (1965).

18. For Russian social science research, see Keller (1988, 1989) and Swafford (1987). Also see "Soviet Sociologist Calls Attention for Her Science," American Sociological Association *Footnotes* (April 1987), p. 2.

19. See Greenberg (1967:71).

20. For more on the decade of the 1950s and its effect on social researchers, see Caute (1978:403–430), Goldstein (1978:360–369), and Schrecker (1986).

21. See Block and Burns (1986) and Starr (1987).

22. See Bermant (1982:138). Nelkin (1982a) provided a general discussion of "forbidden" topics in social science research.

23. "Sex Survey Is Dealt a Setback," *New York Times* (July 26, 1989), p. 7.

24. See Stephen Burd, "Scientists Fear Rise of Intrusion in Work Supported by NIH," in *Chronicle of Higher Education* (October 2, 1991), p. Alff.

25. See Cumings (1997), Sanders (1979), and Simpson (1993) on U.S. government influence on area studies and internationally related academic research during the Cold War era.

26. Project Camelot is described in Horowitz (1965).

27. See Dickson (1984), Nelkin (1982b), and Shattuck and Spence (1988:2).

28. See Shattuck and Spence (1988) and Josephson (1988). Also see "Librarians Charge Plan Would Cut Flow of Data," *New York Times* (February 21, 1989).

29. For more on the CIA and social researchers, see Shattuck and Spence (1988:39–40) and Stephenson (1978).

30. For sensitive situations involving cross-national research, see Fuller (1988) and Van den Berge (1967).

31. For discussion, see Bannister (1987), Blumer (1991b), D'Antonio (1992), Hyman (1991), Ross (1991), and Seybold (1987).

32. See Dynes (1984) on COSSA.

33. The SSRC spent $20 million for the social sciences from 1924 to 1928 (Gieger, 1986:152) compared to $136 million allocated in 1989 by the NSF for the social sciences (D'Antonio, 1992). In the late 1920s, the number of academic social scientists was about one-tenth and a dollar purchased over six times more. The number of social science doctorates—including psychology, teaching, or conducting basic research—in 1986 was about 129,000 (Science and Engineering Personnel: A National Overview, Document NSF 90-310). The size of the higher educational faculty in all academic fields in 1930 was under 83,000 (Historical Statistics of the United States, 1970, Table H696). The $20 million over four years in the 1920s, or $5 million per year, would be equivalent to roughly $300 million in 1990. The median family income before taxes in 1929 was $2,335 (Historical Statistics, Table G308).

34. For more on the effects of politics and funding cuts on social research in the 1980s, see Cummings (1984), Himmelstein and Zald (1984), and Zuiches (1984). For more general discussion of the effect of funding on research, see Galliher and McCartney (1973) and Dickson (1984).

35. See "NIH FY 1991 Budget Rescinded by $3.1 Million, Congress Objects to 31 Research Projects Funded by NSF," *The Blue Sheet* (F-D-C Reports, Inc.) (May 27, 1992), p. 3.

36. Brainard and Borrego (2003), Brainard and Southwick (2001), Cordes (1998), Payne (2003a, 2003b), and Savage (2001) on rapidly increasing pork barrel academic spending.

37. See Golder (1996).

38. On the issue of influence over researchers, see Punch (1986:18–19; 49–69). Also see Lawrence Altman, "Experts See Bias in Drug Data," *New York Times* (April 29, 1997), and Sheryl Gay Stolberg, "Gifts to Science Researchers Have Strings, Study Finds," *New York Times* (April 1, 1998). On the nursing home "slap suit," see Steven Greenhouse, "Cornell Professor Fights a Slander Suit," *New York Times* (April 1, 1998), and news report of Morning Edition, National Public Radio (April 27, 1998).

39. See Block (2003), Clymer (2002), Krider (2004), Lee (2003), and Union of Concerned Scientists (2004).

40. For more discussion on how researchers select research questions or problems, see Gieryn (1978) and Zuckerman (1978).

41. See Brym (1980) on role of intellectuals in society.

42. Marsh (1984), Noelle-Neumann (1974, 1984) and Price (1989) discussed the effects of research results on subsequent public behavior and opinion.

43. Bartiz (1960), Schrecker (1986), Schwendinger and Schwendinger (1974), and Silva and Slaughter (1980) discuss the history of social researchers in society.

44. Committees on the Status of Women in Sociology (1986).

American Sociological Association Code of Ethics

INTRODUCTION

The American Sociological Association's (ASA's) Code of Ethics sets forth the principles and ethical standards that underlie sociologists' professional responsibilities and conduct. These principles and standards should be used as guidelines when examining everyday professional activities. They constitute normative statements for sociologists and provide guidance on issues that sociologists may encounter in their professional work.

ASA's Code of Ethics consists of an Introduction, a Preamble, five General Principles, and specific Ethical Standards. This Code is also accompanied by the Rules and Procedures of the ASA Committee on Professional Ethics which describe the procedures for filing, investigating, and resolving complaints of unethical conduct.

The Preamble and General Principles of the Code are aspirational goals to guide sociologists toward the highest ideals of sociology. Although the Preamble and General Principles are not enforceable rules, they should be considered by sociologists in arriving at an ethical course of action and may be considered by ethics bodies in interpreting the Ethical Standards.

The Ethical Standards set forth enforceable rules for conduct by sociologists. Most of the Ethical Standards are written broadly in order to apply to sociologists in varied roles, and the application of an Ethical Standard may vary depending on the context. The Ethical Standards are not exhaustive. Any conduct that is not specifically addressed by this Code of Ethics is not necessarily ethical or unethical.

Note: This code of ethics is from the American Sociological Association, approved by the ASA membership in June 1997.

Membership in the ASA commits members to adhere to the ASA Code of Ethics and to the Policies and Procedures of the ASA Committee on Professional Ethics. Members are advised of this obligation upon joining the Association and that violations of the Code may lead to the imposition of sanctions, including termination of membership. ASA members subject to the Code of Ethics may be reviewed under these Ethical Standards only if the activity is part of or affects their work-related functions, or if the activity is sociological in nature. Personal activities having no connection to or effect on sociologists' performance of their professional roles are not subject to the Code of Ethics.

PREAMBLE

This Code of Ethics articulates a common set of values upon which sociologists build their professional and scientific work. The Code is intended to provide both the general principles and the rules to cover professional situations encountered by sociologists. It has as its primary goal the welfare and protection of the individuals and groups with whom sociologists work. It is the individual responsibility of each sociologist to aspire to the highest possible standards of conduct in research, teaching, practice, and service.

The development of a dynamic set of ethical standards for a sociologist's work-related conduct requires a personal commitment to a lifelong effort to act ethically; to encourage ethical behavior by students, supervisors, supervisees, employers, employees, and colleagues; and to consult with others as needed concerning ethical problems. Each sociologist supplements, but does not violate, the values and rules specified in the Code of Ethics based on guidance drawn from personal values, culture, and experience.

GENERAL PRINCIPLES

The following General Principles are aspirational and serve as a guide for sociologists in determining ethical courses of action in various contexts. They exemplify the highest ideals of professional conduct.

Principle A: Professional Competence

Sociologists strive to maintain the highest levels of competence in their work; they recognize the limitations of their expertise; and they undertake only those tasks for which they are qualified by education, training, or experience. They recognize the need for ongoing education in order to remain professionally competent; and they utilize the appropriate scientific, professional, technical, and administrative resources needed to ensure competence in their professional activities. They consult with other professionals when necessary for the benefit of their students, research participants, and clients.

Principle B: Integrity

Sociologists are honest, fair, and respectful of others in their professional activities—in research, teaching, practice, and service. Sociologists do not knowingly act in ways that jeopardize either their own or others' professional welfare. Sociologists conduct their affairs in ways that inspire trust and confidence; they do not knowingly make statements that are false, misleading, or deceptive.

Principle C: Professional and Scientific Responsibility

Sociologists adhere to the highest scientific and professional standards and accept responsibility for their work. Sociologists understand that they form a community and show respect for other sociologists even when they disagree on theoretical, methodological, or personal approaches to professional activities. Sociologists value the public trust in sociology and are concerned about their ethical behavior and that of other sociologists that might compromise that trust. While endeavoring always to be collegial, sociologists must never let the desire to be collegial outweigh their shared responsibility for ethical behavior. When appropriate, they consult with colleagues in order to prevent or avoid unethical conduct.

Principle D: Respect for People's Rights, Dignity, and Diversity

Sociologists respect the rights, dignity, and worth of all people. They strive to eliminate bias in their professional activities, and they do not tolerate any forms of discrimination based on age; gender; race; ethnicity; national origin; religion; sexual orientation; disability; health conditions; or marital, domestic, or parental status. They are sensitive to cultural, individual, and role differences in serving, teaching, and studying groups of people with distinctive characteristics. In all of their work-related activities, sociologists acknowledge the rights of others to hold values, attitudes, and opinions that differ from their own.

Principle E: Social Responsibility

Sociologists are aware of their professional and scientific responsibility to the communities and societies in which they live and work. They apply and make public their knowledge in order to contribute to the public good. When undertaking research, they strive to advance the science of sociology and to serve the public good.

ETHICAL STANDARDS

1. Professional and Scientific Standards

Sociologists adhere to the highest possible technical standards that are reasonable and responsible in their research, teaching, practice, and service activities. They rely on scientifically and professionally derived knowledge; act with honesty and integrity; and avoid untrue, deceptive, or undocumented statements in undertaking work-related functions or activities.

2. Competence

(a) Sociologists conduct research, teach, practice, and provide service only within the boundaries of their competence, based on their education, training, supervised experience, or appropriate professional experience.

(b) Sociologists conduct research, teach, practice, and provide service in new areas or involving new techniques only after they have taken reasonable steps to ensure the competence of their work in these areas.

(c) Sociologists who engage in research, teaching, practice, or service maintain awareness of current scientific and professional information in their fields of activity, and undertake continuing efforts to maintain competence in the skills they use.

(d) Sociologists refrain from undertaking an activity when their personal circumstances may interfere with their professional work or lead to harm for a student, supervisee, human subject, client, colleague, or other person to whom they have a scientific, teaching, consulting, or other professional obligation.

3. Representation and Misuse of Expertise

(a) In research, teaching, practice, service, or other situations where sociologists render professional judgments or present their expertise, they accurately and fairly represent their areas and degrees of expertise.

(b) Sociologists do not accept grants, contracts, consultation, or work assignments from individual or organizational clients or sponsors that appear likely to require violation of the standards in this Code of Ethics. Sociologists dissociate themselves from such activities when they discover a violation and are unable to achieve its correction.

(c) Because sociologists' scientific and professional judgments and actions may affect the lives of others, they are alert to and guard against personal, financial, social, organizational, or political factors that might lead to misuse of their knowledge, expertise, or influence.

(d) If sociologists learn of misuse or misrepresentation of their work, they take reasonable steps to correct or minimize the misuse or misrepresentation.

4. Delegation and Supervision

(a) Sociologists provide proper training and supervision to their students, supervisees, or employees and take reasonable steps to see that such persons perform services responsibly, competently, and ethically.

(b) Sociologists delegate to their students, supervisees, or employees only those responsibilities that such persons, based on their education, training, or experience, can reasonably be expected to perform either independently or with the level of supervision provided.

5. Nondiscrimination

Sociologists do not engage in discrimination in their work based on age; gender; race; ethnicity; national origin; religion; sexual orientation; disability; health conditions; marital, domestic, or parental status; or any other applicable basis proscribed by law.

6. Non-exploitation

(a) Whether for personal, economic, or professional advantage, sociologists do not exploit persons over whom they have direct or indirect supervisory, evaluative, or other authority such as students, supervisees, employees, or research participants.

(b) Sociologists do not directly supervise or exercise evaluative authority over any person with whom they have a sexual relationship, including students, supervisees, employees, or research participants.

7. Harassment

Sociologists do not engage in harassment of any person, including students, supervisees, employees, or research participants. Harassment consists of a single intense and severe act or of multiple persistent or pervasive acts which are demeaning, abusive, offensive, or create a hostile professional or workplace environment. Sexual harassment may include sexual solicitation, physical advance, or verbal or non-verbal conduct that is sexual in nature. Racial harassment may include unnecessary, exaggerated, or unwarranted attention or attack, whether verbal or non-verbal, because of a person's race or ethnicity.

8. Employment Decisions

Sociologists have an obligation to adhere to the highest ethical standards when participating in employment related decisions, when seeking employment, or when planning to resign from a position.

8.01 Fair Employment Practices

(a) When participating in employment-related decisions, sociologists make every effort to ensure equal opportunity and fair treatment to all full- and part-time employees. They do not discriminate in hiring, promotion, salary, treatment, or any other conditions of employment or career development on the basis of age; gender; race; ethnicity; national origin; religion; sexual orientation; disability; health conditions; marital, domestic, or parental status; or any other applicable basis proscribed by law.

(b) When participating in employment-related decisions, sociologists specify the requirements for hiring, promotion, tenure, and termination and communicate these requirements thoroughly to full- and part-time employees and prospective employees.

(c) When participating in employment-related decisions, sociologists have the responsibility to be informed of fair employment codes, to communicate this information to employees, and to help create an atmosphere upholding fair employment practices for full- and part-time employees.

(d) When participating in employment-related decisions, sociologists inform prospective full- and part-time employees of any constraints on research and publication and negotiate clear understandings about any conditions that may limit research and scholarly activity.

8.02 Responsibilities of Employees

(a) When seeking employment, sociologists provide prospective employers with accurate and complete information on their professional qualifications and experiences.

(b) When leaving a position, permanently or temporarily, sociologists provide their employers with adequate notice and take reasonable steps to reduce negative effects of leaving.

9. Conflicts of Interest

Sociologists maintain the highest degree of integrity in their professional work and avoid conflicts of interest and the appearance of conflict. Conflicts of interest arise when sociologists' personal or financial interests prevent them from performing their professional work in an unbiased manner. In research, teaching, practice, and service, sociologists are alert to situations that might cause a conflict of interest and take appropriate action to prevent conflict or disclose it to appropriate parties.

9.01 Adherence to Professional Standards

Irrespective of their personal or financial interests or those of their employers or clients, sociologists adhere to professional and scientific standards in (1) the collection, analysis, or interpretation of data; (2) the reporting of research; (3) the teaching, professional presentation, or public dissemination of sociological knowledge; and (4) the identification or implementation of appropriate contractual, consulting, or service activities.

9.02 Disclosure

Sociologists disclose relevant sources of financial support and relevant personal or professional relationships that may have the appearance of or potential for a conflict of interest to an employer or client, to the sponsors of their professional work, or in public speeches and writing.

9.03 Avoidance of Personal Gain

(a) Under all circumstances, sociologists do not use or otherwise seek to gain from information or material received in a confidential context (e.g., knowledge obtained from reviewing a manuscript or serving on a proposal review panel), unless they have authorization to do so or until that information is otherwise made publicly available.

(b) Under all circumstances, sociologists do not seek to gain from information or material in an employment or client relationship without permission of the employer or client.

9.04 Decisionmaking in the Workplace

In their workplace, sociologists take appropriate steps to avoid conflicts of interest or the appearance of conflicts, and carefully scrutinize *potentially biasing* affiliations or relationships. In research, teaching, practice, or service, such potentially biasing affiliations or relationships include, but are not limited to, situations involving family, business, or close personal friendships or those with whom sociologists have had strong conflict or disagreement.

9.05 Decisionmaking Outside of the Workplace

In professional activities outside of their workplace, sociologists in *all* circumstances abstain from engaging in deliberations and decisions that allocate or withhold benefits or rewards from individuals or institutions if they have *biasing* affiliations or relationships. These biasing affiliations or relationships are: 1) current employment or being considered for employment at an organization or institution that could be construed as benefiting from the decision; 2) current officer or board member of an organization or institution that could be construed as benefiting from the decision; 3) current employment or being considered for employment at the same organization or institution where an individual could benefit from the decision; 4) a spouse, domestic partner, or known relative who as an individual could benefit from the decision; or 5) a current business or professional partner, research collaborator, employee, supervisee, or student who as an individual could benefit from the decision.

10. Public Communication

Sociologists adhere to the highest professional standards in public communications about their professional services, credentials and expertise, work products, or publications, whether these communications are from themselves or from others.

10.01 Public Communications

(a) Sociologists take steps to ensure the accuracy of all public communications. Such public communications include, but are not limited to, directory listings; personal resumes or curriculum vitae; advertising; brochures or printed matter; interviews or comments to the media; statements in legal proceedings; lectures and public oral presentations; or other published materials.

(b) Sociologists do not make public statements that are false, deceptive, misleading, or fraudulent, either because of what they state, convey, or suggest or because of what they omit, concerning their research, practice, or other work activities or those of persons or organizations with which they are affiliated. Such activities include, but are not limited to, false or deceptive statements concerning sociologists' (1) training, experience, or competence; (2) academic degrees; (3) credentials; (4) institutional or association affiliations; (5) services; (6) fees; or (7) publications or research findings. Sociologists do not make false or deceptive statements concerning the scientific basis for, results of, or degree of success from their professional services.

(c) When sociologists provide professional advice or comment by means of public lectures, demonstrations, radio or television programs, prerecorded tapes, printed articles, mailed material, or other media, they take reasonable precautions to ensure that (1) the statements are based on appropriate research, literature, and practice; and (2) the statements are otherwise consistent with this Code of Ethics.

10.02 Statements by Others

(a) Sociologists who engage or employ others to create or place public statements that promote their work products, professional services, or other activities retain responsibility for such statements.

(b) Sociologists make reasonable efforts to prevent others whom they do not directly engage, employ, or supervise (such as employers, publishers, sponsors, organizational clients, members of the media) from making deceptive statements concerning their professional research, teaching, or practice activities.

(c) In working with the press, radio, television, or other communications media or in advertising in the media, sociologists are cognizant of potential conflicts of interest or appearances of such conflicts (e.g., they do not provide compensation to employees of the media), and they adhere to the highest standards of professional honesty (e.g., they acknowledge paid advertising).

11. Confidentiality

Sociologists have an obligation to ensure that confidential information is protected. They do so to ensure the integrity of research and the open communication with research participants and to protect sensitive information obtained in research, teaching, practice, and service. When gathering confidential information, sociologists should take into account the long-term uses of the information, including its potential placement in public archives or the examination of the information by other researchers or practitioners.

11.01 Maintaining Confidentiality

(a) Sociologists take reasonable precautions to protect the confidentiality rights of research participants, students, employees, clients, or others.

(b) Confidential information provided by research participants, students, employees, clients, or others is treated as such by sociologists even if there is no legal protection or privilege to do so. Sociologists have an obligation to protect confidential information, and not allow information gained in confidence from being used in ways that would unfairly compromise research participants, students, employees, clients, or others.

(c) Information provided under an understanding of confidentiality is treated as such even after the death of those providing that information.

(d) Sociologists maintain the integrity of confidential deliberations, activities, or roles, including, where applicable, that of professional committees, review panels, or advisory groups (e.g., the ASA Committee on Professional Ethics).

(e) Sociologists, to the extent possible, protect the confidentiality of student records, performance data, and personal information, whether verbal or written, given in the context of academic consultation, supervision, or advising.

(f) The obligation to maintain confidentiality extends to members of research or training teams and collaborating organizations who have access to the information. To ensure that access to confidential information is restricted, it is the responsibility of researchers, administrators, and principal investigators to instruct staff to take the steps necessary to protect confidentiality.

(g) When using private information about individuals collected by other persons or institutions, sociologists protect the confidentiality of individually identifiable information. Information is private when an individual can reasonably expect that the information will not be made public with personal identifiers (e.g., medical or employment records).

11.02 Limits of Confidentiality

(a) Sociologists inform themselves fully about all laws and rules which may limit or alter guarantees of confidentiality. They determine their ability to guarantee absolute confidentiality and, as appropriate, inform research participants, students, employees, clients, or others of any limitations to this guarantee at the outset consistent with ethical standards set forth in 11.02(b).

(b) Sociologists may confront unanticipated circumstances where they become aware of information that is clearly health- or life-threatening to research participants, students, employees, clients, or others. In these cases, sociologists balance the importance of guarantees of confidentiality with other principles in this Code of Ethics, standards of conduct, and applicable law.

(c) Confidentiality is not required with respect to observations in public places, activities conducted in public, or other settings where no rules of privacy are provided by law or custom. Similarly, confidentiality is not required in the case of information available from public records.

11.03 Discussing Confidentiality and Its Limits

(a) When sociologists establish a scientific or professional relationship with persons, they discuss (1) the relevant limitations on confidentiality, and (2) the foreseeable uses of the information generated through their professional work.

(b) Unless it is not feasible or is counter-productive, the discussion of confidentiality occurs at the outset of the relationship and thereafter as new circumstances may warrant.

11.04 Anticipation of Possible Uses of Information

(a) When research requires maintaining personal identifiers in data bases or systems of records, sociologists delete such identifiers before the information is made publicly available.

(b) When confidential information concerning research participants, clients, or other recipients of service is entered into databases or systems of records available to persons without the prior consent of the relevant parties, sociologists protect anonymity by not including personal identifiers or by employing other techniques that mask or control disclosure of individual identities.

(c) When deletion of personal identifiers is not feasible, sociologists take reasonable steps to determine that appropriate consent of personally-identifiable individuals has been obtained before they transfer such data to others or review such data collected by others.

11.05 Electronic Transmission of Confidential Information

Sociologists use extreme care in delivering or transferring any confidential data, information, or communication over public computer networks. Sociologists are attentive to the problems of maintaining confidentiality and control over sensitive material and data when use of technological innovations, such as public computer networks, may open their professional and scientific communication to unauthorized persons.

11.06 Anonymity of Sources

(a) Sociologists do not disclose in their writings, lectures, or other public media confidential, personally identifiable information concerning their research participants, students, individual or organizational clients, or other recipients of their service which is obtained during the course of their work, unless consent from individuals or their legal representatives has been obtained.

(b) When confidential information is used in scientific and professional presentations, sociologists disguise the identity of research participants, students, individual or organizational clients, or other recipients of their service.

11.07 Minimizing Intrusions on Privacy

(a) To minimize intrusions on privacy, sociologists include in written and oral reports, consultations, and public communications only information germane to the purpose for which the communication is made.

(b) Sociologists discuss confidential information or evaluative data concerning research participants, students, supervisees, employees, and individual or organizational clients only for appropriate scientific or professional purposes and only with persons clearly concerned with such matters.

11.08 Preservation of Confidential Information

(a) Sociologists take reasonable steps to ensure that records, data, or information are preserved in a confidential manner consistent with the requirements of this Code of Ethics, recognizing that ownership of records, data, or information may also be governed by law or institutional principles.

(b) Sociologists plan so that confidentiality of records, data, or information is protected in the event of the sociologist's death, incapacity, or withdrawal from the position or practice.

(c) When sociologists transfer confidential records, data, or information to other persons or organizations, they obtain assurances that the recipients of the records, data, or information will employ measures to protect confidentiality at least equal to those originally pledged.

12. Informed Consent

Informed consent is a basic ethical tenet of scientific research on human populations. Sociologists do not involve a human being as a subject in research without the informed consent of the subject or the subject's legally authorized representative, except as otherwise specified in this Code. Sociologists recognize the possibility of undue influence or subtle pressures on subjects that may derive from researchers' expertise or authority, and they take this into account in designing informed consent procedures.

12.01 Scope of Informed Consent

(a) Sociologists conducting research obtain consent from research participants or their legally authorized representatives (1) when data are collected from research participants through any form of communication, interaction, or intervention; or (2) when behavior of research participants occurs in a private context where an individual can reasonably expect that no observation or reporting is taking place.

(b) Despite the paramount importance of consent, sociologists may seek waivers of this standard when (1) the research involves no more than minimal risk for research participants, and (2) the research could not practicably be carried out were informed consent to be required. Sociologists recognize that waivers of consent require approval from institutional review boards or, in the absence of such boards, from another authoritative body with expertise on the ethics of research. Under such circumstances, the confidentiality of any personally identifiable information must be maintained unless otherwise set forth in 11.02(b).

(c) Sociologists may conduct research in public places or use publicly available information about individuals (e.g., naturalistic observations in public places, analysis of public records, or archival research) without obtaining consent. If, under such circumstances, sociologists have any doubt whatsoever about the need for informed consent, they consult with institutional review boards or, in the absence of such boards, with another authoritative body with expertise on the ethics of research before proceeding with such research.

(d) In undertaking research with vulnerable populations (e.g., youth, recent immigrant populations, the mentally ill), sociologists take special care to ensure that the voluntary nature of the research is understood and that consent is not coerced. In all other respects, sociologists adhere to the principles set forth in 12.01(a)–(c).

(e) Sociologists are familiar with and conform to applicable state and federal regulations and, where applicable, institutional review board requirements for obtaining informed consent for research.

12.02 Informed Consent Process

(a) When informed consent is required, sociologists enter into an agreement with research participants or their legal representatives that clarifies the nature of the research and the responsibilities of the investigator prior to conducting the research.

(b) When informed consent is required, sociologists use language that is understandable to and respectful of research participants or their legal representatives.

(c) When informed consent is required, sociologists provide research participants or their legal representatives with the opportunity to ask questions about any aspect of the research, at any time during or after their participation in the research.

(d) When informed consent is required, sociologists inform research participants or their legal representatives of the nature of the research; they indicate to participants that their participation or continued participation is voluntary; they inform participants of significant factors that may be expected to influence their willingness to participate (e.g., possible risks and benefits of their participation); and they explain other aspects of the research and respond to questions from prospective participants. Also, if relevant, sociologists explain that refusal to participate or withdrawal from participation in the research involves no penalty, and they explain any foreseeable consequences of declining or withdrawing. Sociologists explicitly discuss confidentiality and, if applicable, the extent to which confidentiality may be limited as set forth in 11.02(b).

(e) When informed consent is required, sociologists keep records regarding said consent. They recognize that consent is a process that involves oral and/or written consent.

(f) Sociologists honor all commitments they have made to research participants as part of the informed consent process except where unanticipated circumstances demand otherwise as set forth in 11.02(b).

12.03 Informed Consent of Students and Subordinates

When undertaking research at their own institutions or organizations with research participants who are students or subordinates, sociologists take special care to protect the prospective subjects from adverse consequences of declining or withdrawing from participation.

12.04 Informed Consent with Children

(a) In undertaking research with children, sociologists obtain the consent of children to participate, to the extent that they are capable of providing such consent, except under circumstances where consent may not be required as set forth in 12.01(b).

(b) In undertaking research with children, sociologists obtain the consent of a parent or a legally authorized guardian. Sociologists may seek waivers of parental or guardian consent when (1) the research involves no more than minimal risk for the research participants, and (2) the research could not practicably be carried out were consent to be required, or (3) the consent of a parent or guardian is not a reasonable requirement to protect the child (e.g., neglected or abused children).

(c) Sociologists recognize that waivers of consent from a child and a parent or guardian require approval from institutional review boards or, in the absence of such boards, from another authoritative body with expertise on the ethics of research. Under such circumstances, the confidentiality of any personally identifiable information must be maintained unless otherwise set forth in 11.02(b).

12.05 Use of Deception in Research

(a) Sociologists do not use deceptive techniques (1) unless they have determined that their use will not be harmful to research participants; is justified by the study's prospective scientific, educational, or applied value; and that equally effective alternative procedures that do not use deception are not feasible, and (2) unless they have obtained the approval of institutional review boards or, in the absence of such boards, with another authoritative body with expertise on the ethics of research.

(b) Sociologists never deceive research participants about significant aspects of the research that would affect their willingness to participate, such as physical risks, discomfort, or unpleasant emotional experiences.

(c) When deception is an integral feature of the design and conduct of research, sociologists attempt to correct any misconception that research participants may have no later than at the conclusion of the research.

(d) On rare occasions, sociologists may need to conceal their identity in order to undertake research that could not practicably be carried out were they to be known as researchers. Under such circumstances, sociologists undertake the research if it involves no more than minimal risk for the research participants and if they have obtained approval to proceed in this manner from an institutional review board or, in the absence of such boards, from another authoritative body with expertise on the ethics of research. Under such circumstances, confidentiality must be maintained unless otherwise set forth in 11.02(b).

12.06 Use of Recording Technology

Sociologists obtain informed consent from research participants, students, employees, clients, or others prior to videotaping, filming, or recording them in any form, unless these activities involve simply naturalistic observations in public places and it is not anticipated that the recording will be used in a manner that could cause personal identification or harm.

13. Research Planning, Implementation, and Dissemination

Sociologists have an obligation to promote the integrity of research and to ensure that they comply with the ethical tenets of science in the planning, implementation, and dissemination of research. They do so in order to advance knowledge, to minimize the possibility that results will be misleading, and to protect the rights of research participants.

13.01 Planning and Implementation

(a) In planning and implementing research, sociologists minimize the possibility that results will be misleading.

(b) Sociologists take steps to implement protections for the rights and welfare of research participants and other persons affected by the research.

(c) In their research, sociologists do not encourage activities or themselves behave in ways that are health- or life-threatening to research participants or others.

(d) In planning and implementing research, sociologists consult those with expertise concerning any special population under investigation or likely to be affected.

(e) In planning and implementing research, sociologists consider its ethical acceptability as set forth in the Code of Ethics. If the best ethical practice is unclear, sociologists consult with institutional review boards or, in the absence of such review processes, with another authoritative body with expertise on the ethics of research.

(f) Sociologists are responsible for the ethical conduct of research conducted by them or by others under their supervision or authority.

13.02 Unanticipated Research Opportunities

If during the course of teaching, practice, service, or non-professional activities, sociologists determine that they wish to undertake research that was not previously anticipated, they make known their intentions and take steps to ensure that the research can be undertaken consonant with ethical principles, especially those relating to confidentiality and informed consent. Under such circumstances, sociologists seek the approval of institutional review boards or, in the absence of such review processes, another authoritative body with expertise on the ethics of research.

13.03 Offering Inducements for Research Participants

Sociologists do not offer excessive or inappropriate financial or other inducements to obtain the participation of research participants, particularly when it might coerce participation. Sociologists may provide incentives to the extent that resources are available and appropriate.

13.04 Reporting on Research

(a) Sociologists disseminate their research findings except where unanticipated circumstances

(e.g., the health of the researcher) or proprietary agreements with employers, contractors, or clients preclude such dissemination.

(b) Sociologists do not fabricate data or falsify results in their publications or presentations.

(c) In presenting their work, sociologists report their findings fully and do not omit relevant data. They report results whether they support or contradict the expected outcomes.

(d) Sociologists take particular care to state all relevant qualifications on the findings and interpretation of their research. Sociologists also disclose underlying assumptions, theories, methods, measures, and research designs that might bear upon findings and interpretations of their work.

(e) Consistent with the spirit of full disclosure of methods and analyses, once findings are publicly disseminated, sociologists permit their open assessment and verification by other responsible researchers with appropriate safeguards, where applicable, to protect the anonymity of research participants.

(f) If sociologists discover significant errors in their publication or presentation of data, they take reasonable steps to correct such errors in a correction, a retraction, published errata, or other public fora as appropriate.

(g) Sociologists report sources of financial support in their written papers and note any special relations to any sponsor. In special circumstances, sociologists may withhold the names of specific sponsors if they provide an adequate and full description of the nature and interest of the sponsor.

(h) Sociologists take special care to report accurately the results of others' scholarship by using correct information and citations when presenting the work of others in publications, teaching, practice, and service settings.

13.05 Data Sharing

(a) Sociologists share data and pertinent documentation as a regular practice. Sociologists make their data available after completion of the project or its major publications, except where proprietary agreements with employers, contractors, or clients preclude such accessibility or when it is impossible to share data and protect the confidentiality of the data or the anonymity of research participants (e.g., raw field notes or detailed information from ethnographic interviews).

(b) Sociologists anticipate data sharing as an integral part of a research plan whenever data sharing is feasible.

(c) Sociologists share data in a form that is consonant with research participants' interests and protect the confidentiality of the information they have been given. They maintain the confidentiality of data, whether legally required or not; remove personal identifiers before data are shared; and if necessary use other disclosure avoidance techniques.

(d) Sociologists who do not otherwise place data in public archives keep data available and retain documentation relating to the research for a reasonable period of time after publication or dissemination of results.

(e) Sociologists may ask persons who request their data for further analysis to bear the associated incremental costs, if necessary.

(f) Sociologists who use data from others for further analyses explicitly acknowledge the contribution of the initial researchers.

14. Plagiarism

(a) In publications, presentations, teaching, practice, and service, sociologists explicitly identify, credit, and reference the author when they take data or material verbatim from another person's written work, whether it is published, unpublished, or electronically available.

(b) In their publications, presentations, teaching, practice, and service, sociologists provide acknowledgment of and reference to the use of others' work, even if the work is not quoted verbatim or paraphrased, and they do not present others' work as their own whether it is published, unpublished, or electronically available.

15. Authorship Credit

(a) Sociologists take responsibility and credit, including authorship credit, only for work they have actually performed or to which they have contributed.

(b) Sociologists ensure that principal authorship and other publication credits are based on the relative scientific or professional contributions of the individuals involved, regardless of their status. In claiming or determining the ordering of authorship, sociologists seek to reflect accurately the contributions of main participants in the research and writing process.

(c) A student is usually listed as principal author on any multiple authored publication that substantially derives from the student's dissertation or thesis.

16. Publication Process

Sociologists adhere to the highest ethical standards when participating in publication and review processes when they are authors or editors.

16.01 Submission of Manuscripts for Publication

(a) In cases of multiple authorship, sociologists confer with all other authors prior to submitting work for publication and establish mutually acceptable agreements regarding submission.

(b) In submitting a manuscript to a professional journal, book series, or edited book, sociologists grant that publication first claim to publication except where explicit policies allow multiple submissions. Sociologists do not submit a manuscript to a second publication until after an official decision has been received from the first publication or until the manuscript is withdrawn. Sociologists submitting a manuscript for publication in a journal, book series, or edited book can withdraw a manuscript from consideration up until an official acceptance is made.

(c) Sociologists may submit a book manuscript to multiple publishers. However, once sociologists have signed a contract, they cannot withdraw a manuscript from publication unless there is reasonable cause to do so.

16.02 Duplicate Publication of Data

When sociologists publish data or findings that they have previously published elsewhere, they accompany these publications by proper acknowledgment.

16.03 Responsibilities of Editors

(a) When serving as editors of journals or book series, sociologists are fair in the application of standards and operate without personal or ideological favoritism or malice. As editors, sociologists are cognizant of any potential conflicts of interest.

(b) When serving as editors of journals or book series, sociologists ensure the confidential nature of the review process and supervise editorial office staff, including students, in accordance with practices that maintain confidentiality.

(c) When serving as editors of journals or book series, sociologists are bound to publish all manuscripts accepted for publication unless major errors or ethical violations are discovered after acceptance (e.g., plagiarism or scientific misconduct).

(d) When serving as editors of journals or book series, sociologists ensure the anonymity of reviewers unless they otherwise receive permission from reviewers to reveal their identity. Editors ensure that their staff conform to this practice.

(e) When serving as journal editors, sociologists ensure the anonymity of authors unless and until a manuscript is accepted for publication or unless the established practices of the journal are known to be otherwise.

(f) When serving as journal editors, sociologists take steps to provide for the timely review of all manuscripts and respond promptly to inquiries about the status of the review.

17. Responsibilities of Reviewers

(a) In reviewing material submitted for publication, grant support, or other evaluation purposes, sociologists respect the confidentiality of the process and the proprietary rights in such information of those who submitted it.

(b) Sociologists disclose conflicts of interest or decline requests for reviews of the work of others where conflicts of interest are involved.

(c) Sociologists decline requests for reviews of the work of others when they believe that the review process may be biased or when they have questions about the integrity of the process.

(d) If asked to review a manuscript, book, or proposal they have previously reviewed, sociologists make it known to the person making the request (e.g., editor, program officer) unless it is clear that they are being asked to provide a reappraisal.

18. Education, Teaching, and Training

As teachers, supervisors, and trainers, sociologists follow the highest ethical standards in order to ensure the quality of sociological education and the integrity of the teacher-student relationship.

18.01 Administration of Education Programs

(a) Sociologists who are responsible for education and training programs seek to ensure that the programs are competently designed, provide the proper experiences, and meet all goals for which claims are made by the program.

(b) Sociologists responsible for education and training programs seek to ensure that there is an accurate description of the program content, training goals and objectives, and requirements that must be met for satisfactory completion of the program.

(c) Sociologists responsible for education and training programs take steps to ensure that graduate assistants and temporary instructors have the substantive knowledge required to teach courses and the teaching skills needed to facilitate student learning.

(d) Sociologists responsible for education and training programs have an obligation to ensure that ethics are taught to their graduate students as part of their professional preparation.

18.02 Teaching and Training

(a) Sociologists conscientiously perform their teaching responsibilities. They have appropriate skills and knowledge or are receiving appropriate training.

(b) Sociologists provide accurate information at the outset about their courses, particularly regarding the subject matter to be covered, bases for evaluation, and the nature of course experiences.

(c) Sociologists make decisions concerning textbooks, course content, course requirements, and grading solely on the basis of educational criteria without regard for financial or other incentives.

(d) Sociologists provide proper training and supervision to their teaching assistants and other teaching trainees and take reasonable steps to ensure that such persons perform these teaching responsibilities responsibly, competently, and ethically.

(e) Sociologists do not permit personal animosities or intellectual differences with colleagues to foreclose students' or supervisees' access to these colleagues or to interfere with student or supervisee learning, academic progress, or professional development.

19. Contractual and Consulting Services

(a) Sociologists undertake grants, contracts, or consultation only when they are knowledgeable about the substance, methods, and techniques they plan to use or have a plan for incorporating appropriate expertise.

(b) In undertaking grants, contracts, or consultation, sociologists base the results of their professional work on appropriate information and techniques.

(c) When financial support for a project has been accepted under a grant, contract, or consultation, sociologists make reasonable efforts to complete the proposed work on schedule.

(d) In undertaking grants, contracts, or consultation, sociologists accurately document and appropriately retain their professional and scientific work.

(e) In establishing a contractual arrangement for research, consultation, or other services, sociologists clarify, to the extent feasible at the outset, the nature of the relationship with the individual, organizational, or institutional client. This clarification includes, as appropriate, the nature of the services to be performed, the probable uses of the services provided, possibilities for the sociologist's future use of the work for scholarly or publication purposes, the timetable for delivery of those services, and compensation and billing arrangements.

20. Adherence to the Code of Ethics

Sociologists have an obligation to confront, address, and attempt to resolve ethical issues according to this Code of Ethics.

20.01 Familiarity with the Code of Ethics

Sociologists have an obligation to be familiar with this Code of Ethics, other applicable ethics codes, and their application to sociologists' work. Lack of awareness or misunderstanding of an ethical standard is not, in itself, a defense to a charge of unethical conduct.

20.02 Confronting Ethical Issues

(a) When sociologists are uncertain whether a particular situation or course of action would violate the Code of Ethics, they consult with other sociologists knowledgeable about ethical issues, with ASA's Committee on Professional Ethics, or with other organizational entities such as institutional review boards.

(b) When sociologists take actions or are confronted with choices where there is a conflict between ethical standards enunciated in the Code of Ethics and laws or legal requirements, they make known their commitment to the Code and take steps to resolve the conflict in a responsible manner by consulting with colleagues, professional organizations, or the ASA's Committee on Professional Ethics.

20.03 Fair Treatment of Parties in Ethical Disputes

(a) Sociologists do not discriminate against a person on the basis of his or her having made an ethical complaint.

(b) Sociologists do not discriminate against a person based on his or her having been the subject of an ethical complaint. This does not preclude taking action based upon the outcome of an ethical complaint.

20.04 Reporting Ethical Violations of Others

When sociologists have substantial reason to believe that there may have been an ethical violation by another sociologist, they attempt to resolve the issue by bringing it to the attention of that individual if an informal resolution appears appropriate or possible, or they seek advice about whether or how to proceed based on this belief, assuming that such

Note: This revised edition of the ASA Code of Ethics builds on the 1989 edition of the Code and the 1992 version of the American Psychological Association's Ethical Principles of Psychologists and Code of Conduct.

activity does not violate any confidentiality rights. Such action might include referral to ASA's Committee on Professional Ethics.

20.05 Cooperating with Ethics Committees

Sociologists cooperate in ethics investigations, proceedings, and resulting requirements of the American Sociological Association. In doing so, they make reasonable efforts to resolve any issues of confidentiality. Failure to cooperate may be an ethics violation.

20.06 Improper Complaints

Sociologists do not file or encourage the filing of ethics complaints that are frivolous and are intended to harm the alleged violator rather than to protect the integrity of the discipline and the public.

Table of Randomly Selected Five-Digit Numbers

10819	85717	64540	95692	44985	88504	50298	20830	67124	20557
28459	13687	50699	62110	49307	84465	66518	08290	96957	45050
19105	52686	51336	53101	81842	20323	71091	78598	60969	74898
35376	72734	13951	27528	36140	42195	25942	70835	45825	49277
93818	84972	66048	83361	56465	65449	87748	95405	98712	97183
35859	82675	87301	71211	78007	99316	25591	63995	40577	78894
66241	89679	04843	96407	01970	06913	19259	72929	82868	50457
44222	37633	85262	65308	03252	36770	51640	18333	33971	49352
54966	75662	80544	48943	87983	62759	55698	41068	35558	60870
43351	15285	38157	45261	50114	35934	05950	11735	51769	07389
11208	80818	78325	14807	19325	41500	01263	09211	56005	44250
71379	53517	15553	04774	63452	50294	06332	69926	20592	06305
63162	41154	78345	23645	74235	72054	84152	27889	76881	58652
17457	68490	19878	04981	83667	00053	12003	84614	14842	29462
28042	42748	55801	94527	21926	07901	89855	21070	80320	91153
32240	24201	24202	45025	07664	11503	97375	83178	26731	45568
87288	22996	67529	38344	29757	74161	16834	40238	48789	99995
39052	23696	42858	85695	50783	51790	80882	97015	81331	76819
71528	74553	32294	86652	15224	07119	45327	69072	64572	07658
76921	04502	78240	89519	02621	40829	88841	66178	01266	10906
45889	22839	77794	94068	85709	96902	19646	40614	03169	45434
10486	79308	75231	33615	42194	49397	91324	79553	66976	83861
42051	14719	80056	74811	58453	04526	90724	36151	09168	04291
47919	11314	80282	09297	02824	59530	31237	26311	62168	46591
19634	40589	28985	40577	33213	52852	17556	85342	66881	18944
10265	45549	38771	38740	48104	63990	73234	19398	33740	97345
74975	33526	36190	25201	19239	06254	02198	99109	01005	20983
37677	76778	15736	57675	81153	59651	69262	89250	75156	59164
18774	15979	26466	80236	65400	24272	02088	09307	33426	11230
93728	14965	85141	27821	53791	38728	66369	29415	55330	99228
34212	15590	41336	23614	26153	19466	44176	80885	00015	40077
81984	54478	45226	97338	14064	45768	13538	49093	05691	69720
72755	15743	00552	89374	85400	37392	26598	71917	64275	16125
13162	57044	75982	15819	23385	40860	51585	44542	39656	91139
64686	62224	34124	79171	73909	26196	54057	63264	72089	06658
00157	64594	03178	75774	32315	34443	37224	85593	55251	42666
84194	83591	82152	24311	22414	43244	81542	31491	42075	17275
05776	60399	65218	89299	20273	30071	53077	18853	56652	63896
33365	18314	81074	49433	10884	75467	56085	14731	98085	60895
67928	38976	38480	59980	23156	72335	33489	59420	67819	51874

64394	45154	81851	54228	73095	97217	16908	90242	92869	17311
73000	20948	57065	70195	87563	41590	85047	71743	94916	50534
63555	03388	96638	16591	13641	73342	59131	63144	63587	62084
84005	02035	08182	16395	44928	08897	44750	71378	67522	20180
42593	35102	14577	38102	60403	04540	53992	27069	69574	76682
49519	49517	88147	83375	87045	57466	91259	06680	45586	36257
42149	01579	83056	19423	28165	25620	68035	17919	09120	59078
66192	98427	10152	96970	89990	34604	49632	46533	63362	43151
16124	88620	87074	37851	77131	73855	03740	10306	63858	04349
35492	47334	57189	26465	70078	14477	00881	00929	86907	73764
54503	40155	94734	20689	32475	62851	13216	21419	95502	36783
88063	53451	15642	67345	06935	70644	68570	79176	31975	83082
83689	14426	40357	34906	56282	96104	83796	57663	88627	17521
40393	72810	00681	15351	28858	72086	99090	39741	17914	27385
76648	61322	06817	64674	50317	52373	78223	84222	14021	43432
42091	27088	37686	88033	68007	71009	24018	49568	64351	94130
78925	41509	14319	92389	85492	40880	01487	85509	48316	62618
61915	98081	87996	53798	51485	38912	85858	43392	64678	44458
29504	66960	42645	54547	20615	77035	79942	33972	46112	78290
90170	97643	46284	34591	42692	72933	66166	98389	37460	14545
96439	06806	76714	80084	57685	37447	44901	64699	89142	64657
98365	28725	84376	50634	79289	31106	71351	10533	57545	27399
74794	91013	89791	54236	02369	35317	31103	82481	52256	94510
37499	85907	16293	17673	13373	06599	50138	19860	46716	36928
77530	25960	33671	54383	25144	82627	99266	75134	96539	47242
67990	35106	05214	82928	39824	11128	31390	76293	52809	54881
07355	29187	09357	94498	69697	92515	89812	90794	44738	46806
40716	05787	68975	38937	44033	50064	25582	09428	10220	42455
97748	64395	13937	60406	99182	92720	80805	26242	81943	40341
83682	18775	60095	78600	03994	30313	21418	58563	47258	75582
73506	30672	18213	37887	26698	87700	75784	86878	74004	88636
36274	02333	43132	93725	87912	90341	74601	77001	30717	60002
73508	00852	94044	98474	12621	91655	55258	85551	76122	68052
06488	12362	60020	66902	90734	73689	22382	40896	09028	72925
20201	31560	98885	32275	46818	76114	07959	65639	33267	98595
49947	13114	06773	06454	95070	26564	08974	11640	76202	86105
79928	50600	06586	72129	37233	02564	83265	32579	21234	83535
76360	86412	36240	20210	17692	80482	67007	15474	23198	74250
54601	84643	66759	57661	16434	61708	93185	75957	61056	90678
23441	63863	95238	59665	55789	26180	12566	58645	15125	76707
47093	90509	48767	09874	23363	84954	09789	30178	28804	93294
93603	11580	94163	85561	71328	88735	69859	84563	25579	52858
68812	15299	99296	45906	37303	49507	70680	74412	96425	38134
69023	84343	36736	52659	90751	20115	89920	44995	17109	96613
76913	03158	83461	27842	03903	34683	89761	80564	45806	88009
99426	99643	00749	79376	44910	27490	59668	93907	73112	46365
59429	08121	06954	28120	17606	22482	91924	00401	16459	15570
38121	05358	01205	00662	73934	97834	56917	64058	05148	87599
97781	32170	99914	75565	79802	38905	17167	08196	46043	72094
79068	21760	78832	93795	67798	54968	87328	46494	74338	89805
46601	04015	00484	39366	56233	22622	90706	02327	60807	39009

Sample of Data Archives and Resources for Secondary Analysis

Dozens of social science data archives around the world provide researchers free or inexpensive access to quantitative data. The Inter-University Consortium for Political and Social Research (University of Michigan) and the Social Sciences Data Collection (University of California at San Diego) are good starting places. Social science data archives and other sources in the following list are generally available in English and have Internet sites. The list is not comprehensive, because new archives and sources are being created or changing location.

Social Science Data Archives and Sources

Archivio Dati e Programmi per le Scienze Sociali, ADPSS (Italy)

Australian Consortium for Social and Political Research Incorporated

Behavioral Risk Factor Surveillance System (U.S.A.)

Belgian Archives for the Social Sciences, BASS

Centers for Disease Control and Prevention and Health Promotion (U.S.A.)

Central Archive for Empirical Social Research (Cologne, Germany)

Central Intelligence Agency (U.S.A.)

Centre d'Informatisation des Données Socio-Politiques/Banque de Données Socio-Politiques, CIDSP/BDSP (France)

Centre for Applied Social Surveys (University of Southhampton, U.K.)

Centre for Ethnic Studies (University of Montreal, Canada)

Centre for International Statistics at the Canadian Council on Social Development

Children of the National Longitudinal Survey of Youth (U.S.A.)

Council of European Social Sciences Data Archives, CESSDA

Danish Data Archives, DDA

Data and Program Library Service, DPLS (University of Wisconsin at Madison)

Data Archive (University of Essex, U.K.)

Estonian Social Science Data Archive

European Centre for Analysis in the Social Sciences (University of Essex, U.K.)

European Research Centre on Migration and Ethnic Relations (ERCOMER)

General Social Survey (National Opinion Research Center, University of Chicago)

Health Retirement Study & Survey of Asset & Health Dynamics among the Oldest Old (U.S.A.)

Indian Social Science Research Center Data Archive, SSDA-IND (India)

Institute for Social Development & Policy Research (Seoul National University, South Korea)

Institute for Social Research in Social Science and Louis Harris Data Center (University of North Carolina)

Institute for Social Science Research, Social Science Data Archive (University of California at Los Angeles)

Inter-University Consortium for Political and Social Research, ICPSR (University of Michigan)

Israel Social Sciences Data Archive

Jerusalem Social Sciences Data Archive, SSDA-IL (Israel)

Lijphart Elections Archive (University of California, San Diego)

Luxembourg Income Study

Mexican Migration Project (U.S.A.)

National Election Studies (University of Michigan)

National Institute of Child Health and Human Development (U.S.A.)

National Institute on Aging (U.S.A.)

National Longitudinal Study of Adolescent Health (U.S.A.)

National Survey of Families and Households (U.S.A.)

Netherlands Historical Data Archive, NHDA

New Zealand Social Science Research Data and Information Services Centre

Norwegian Social Sciences Data Archive, NSD

Panel Study of Income Dynamics (U.S.A.)

Population Studies Center (University of Michigan)

Roper Center for Public Opinion Research (University of Connecticut)

Scandinavian Research Council for Criminology (University of Iceland)

Social Indicators of Development (University of North Carolina, Charlotte)

Social Science Data Archives (Australian National University)

Social Science Data Archives (Norway)

Social Science Data Services (Brown University)

Social Science Japan Data Archive (Institute of Social Science, University of Tokyo)

Social Science Research Centre (University of Hong Kong)

Social Sciences Data Collection (University of California at San Diego)

Social Stratification and Social Mobility survey (Japan)

Sociology of Development Research Centre (University of Bielefeld, Germany)

South African Data Archive

State of the Nation's Cities (Center for Urban Policy Research, Rutgers University)

Statistical Data Locators (Nanyang Technological University, Singapore)

Statistics Canada

Supreme Court Decisions Server (U.S.A.)

Swedish Social Science Data Service (Goteborg University, Sweden)

Swiss Information and Data Archive Service for the Social Sciences, SIDOS

United Nations Crime and Justice Information Network

United Nations Statistics

United States Department of Justice, Bureau of Justice Statistics

United States Department of Labor, Bureau of Labor Statistics, National Longitudinal Surveys

Wiener Institut für Sozialwissenschaftliche Dokumentation und Metodik, WISDOM (Austria)

Wisconsin Longitudinal Study (University of Wisconsin at Madison)

World Bank Statistics

World-Systems Archive (University of Colorado at Boulder)

Zentralarchiv für Empirische Sozialforschung an der Universität zu Köln (Germany)

Measurement Theory and Specialized Techniques for Index and Scale Construction

This appendix covers two more technical topics in quantitative measurement, although at an elementary level. The first is a general approach to measurement based on logical or mathematical-type theory. The second is a set of advanced statistical techniques that require the use of computer programs. Although the topics themselves are advanced for the beginning student of social research, the presentation here lays a foundation for further study and it provides a basis for understanding if the techniques appear in scholarly journal articles.

INTRODUCTION TO MEASUREMENT THEORY

Measurement theory is the name for a body of mathematical and methodological theory on reliability, validity, and related topics.[1] Measurement theory gets quite technical, but a general introductory summary of its core assumption can help you understand the principles of good measurement. Measurement theory is based on the idea that an empirical measure of a concept reflects three components: (1) the true construct or an absolutely perfect measure of it, (2) systematic error, and (3) random error. People can see only the empirical measure; the three components are unobserved, hypothetical ideas about what measurement involves. The parts of measurement can be symbolically expressed as follows:

X *Observation:* The empirical indicator or observation
T *True measure:* Ideal, pure construct
S *Systematic error:* Bias; any error that is not random

R *Random error:* Nonsystematic, unavoidable, chance errors

Thus, measurement theory assumes that a specific observation is made up of the construct and of two components that are called errors because they represent deviations from the true construct. If this is put in the form of an equation, it becomes:

$$X = T + S + R$$

This equation is the core of measurement theory. In plain English, it states that an empirical observation by a researcher actually comprises three unseen sources: the construct plus two kinds of potential errors or possible sources of deviation from the true construct.

In the preceding section, you saw that perfect measurement validity is a perfect match between an empirical indicator and the construct it indicates (or its theoretical definition). The measurement theory equation states that an empirical observation and the construct are equal when there are no measurement errors—that is, when the two components that represent potential errors equal zero. Thus, using the equation and measurement theory, we can restate the definition of perfect measurement validity as $X = T$. Researchers use the equation to think about and improve validity by focusing their attention on the two possible types of errors, S and R, and how to get them to equal zero.

Let us focus on the R, or random error, part of the equation first. Probability theory from mathematics says that in the long run, over enough cases, the R becomes zero and drops out of the equation. In the language of statistical theory, the random error has an *expected value* of zero. Without getting into complex probability theory, this happens because errors that are truly random cancel each other out in the long run. Various mathematical proofs and empirical tests show that over a very large number of separate events (e.g., several million), truly random processes stabilize around a true value and errors become zero. For example, I flip a perfectly balanced coin in a truly random way for 10 million times. The "errors"—or in this situation, getting more heads than tails or vice versa—will disappear. I can be extremely certain that my flipping will result in 50 percent heads and 50 percent tails. Another example is that of driving a car at a constant speed. Assume that I have a valid and reliable speedometer and I try to drive exactly 50 kilometers per hour, no more and no less. I will be slightly above this speed at some times and slightly below it at other times. If my errors are truly random, the speeds over and under 50 kilometers per hour will cancel each other, or the expected value of the deviations above and below the speed will be zero and my speed will be 50 kilometers per hour. Researchers do not worry a lot about random error. They assume that there is always some random error, but that, over enough replications or cases, it can be safely ignored.

Once we ignore random error, an observation *(X)* equals the true construct *(T)* and systematic or nonrandom error *(S)*. Systematic error is a potentially avoidable error that distorts results in a systematic manner. An example of a systematic error can be a poorly worded question that causes most respondents to answer in a particular way, or an interviewer's attempts to get respondents to answer in a particular way. Systematic error is at the heart of validity and reliability. It prevents indicators from measuring what they claim to measure (i.e., the true construct). Thus, another way to think about improving measurement is to eliminate systematic error or *bias*.[2]

Systematic error shows how causal inferences from empirical data can be in error. What was said earlier about measurement validity can be restated as validity when the observed measure *(X)* equals the true measure *(T)*. $X = T$ when the systematic error *(S)* is zero.

There are many possible sources of systematic errors. For example, a lack of stability reliability is a type of systematic error. My bathroom scale lacks stability reliability because the spring in it is getting weaker, so I appear to be getting lighter with each successive measurement of my weight. This error in measuring my weight is a type of systematic error that undermines validity. In the example of driving 50 kilometers per hour, my random errors may cancel each other out, but if my speedometer was systematically showing a lower speed, my observation would not be a valid measure. The measurement theory equation is a way to show that any measurement bias or deviation (i.e., nonzero value for systematic error) reduces measurement validity.

Specialized Techniques

Researchers can choose from numerous advanced statistical techniques to help them in constructing quantitative indexes and scales. Some techniques help researchers test for unidimensionality among indicators, some provide researchers with weight for indicators that are being combined into an index, and some help researchers sort and divide a very large number of indicators. The three briefly summarized in this appendix are examples of the powerful techniques available. You will need to acquire a background in statistics and learn to use computer programs before you will be able to use these techniques.

The purpose of introducing you to the techniques is twofold. First, you may encounter them in the methods, analysis, or results sections of scholarly journal articles. This introduction will help you understand why they are being used. Second, the logic of the techniques reinforces the basic principles of measurement and index or scale construction that you have already learned. The logic illustrates how the principles are extended to complex, sophisticated applications. Although the three techniques use advanced statistics, their logic is consistent with basic measurement principles.

Factor Analysis

Factor analysis is a group of sophisticated statistical techniques that require a computer to conduct.[3] Statistical training is necessary to use factor analysis properly. Improperly used, it creates nonsense. Factor analysis helps researchers construct indexes, test the unidimensionality of scales, assign weights to items in an index, and statistically reduce a large number of indicators to a smaller set. The statistical theory and algebra on which factor analysis is based is beyond the level of this book, but its conceptual principles are not difficult to grasp. The fundamental logic of factor analysis is based on the idea that it is possible to manipulate statistically the empirical relationships among several indicators to reveal a common unobserved factor or hypothetical construct.

When conducting factor analysis, a researcher begins with a number of items he or she believes to measure a single construct. At least five indicators are recommended. The indicators should be measured at the ordinal, interval, or ratio level. The interval or ratio level is preferred, and extra caution is necessary for ordinal-level measurement. The researcher gives the factor analysis computer program characteristics of the variables and technical information. The factor analysis results tell a researcher how well the items or indicators relate to an underlying factor or hypothetical construct. For example, factor analysis results tell the researcher whether the items all load, or are associated with, one or more than one factor.

Factor analysis also produces factor scores, which can be used as weights in creating an index. These scores represent how strongly each indicator is associated with the unobserved factor. For example, I conduct an Australian survey in which there were 16 Likert scale items that measure attitudes toward Japan. I use factor analysis to tell me whether the 16 items are explained by two factors. For example, 5 attitude items load on a factor that indicates a fear of military conflict construct. The other 11 items load on a factor that indicates antagonism toward a different racial group. The meaning of a factor comes from looking at the items that load on it. I can combine each set of items into two separate indexes of attitudes toward Japan.

Q-Sort Analysis

Q-sort analysis is a close relative of factor analysis.[4] Like factor analysis, the technique requires statistical background beyond the scope of this book. It illustrates an interesting scaling logic as well.

Q-sort methodology uses *ipsative scoring,* as opposed to *normative scoring,* which is used in most scaling or index techniques. With normative scoring, a person rates each item in an index or scale independently. With ipsative scoring, a person is forced to decide between the items, so a decision on one item affects other items.

For example, I rank movie stars. When I choose an actor as number one, it means that no other actor can be number one. The decision about one item (i.e., the number-one actor) affects or limits my decision about other items. This is ipsative scoring. By contrast, with normative scoring, I rate a list of actors from "highly like" to "highly dislike," as with a Likert scale. I could rate several actors "highly like." My decision to rate one actor does not limit my decisions about rating others.

Q-sort analysis begins with people ranking statements about a concept or object. In a manner somewhat like Thurstone scaling, people are given a large number of statements (e.g., 30 to 50) and asked to sort them. The statements are taken from popular writings on a topic, everyday conversations, television programs, and the like, and should represent diverse ways people think about a topic.

Instead of piles along one continuum, the Q-sort technique has people place statements into boxes in a grid that varies along two continua. There are as many boxes in the grid as there are statements. Each statement goes into one box. One continuum (e.g., right to left) indicates how positive or negative a person feels about the statement. The other continuum (e.g., up and down) indicates the strength of commitment to the positive or negative feelings about statements. The decision to place a statement in a box excludes placing any other statements in the same location. The raw data for Q-sort are the statements as they are organized in the grid.

In factor analysis, the researcher enters the data from many indicators, and the computer program produces a small number of factors. In Q-sort analysis, the researcher enters the grid location of statements, and the computer program identifies clusters or sets of people. Thus, Q-sort analysis shows which people organize statements in similar ways.

Q-sort analysis identifies how people organize their thinking on a topic on the basis of how they organized statements in the grid. It gives a researcher a map of major positions on an issue held by people. For example, 20 people place 45 statements about Arab-Israeli relations into a grid. The results of Q-sort analysis show a researcher that the 20 people think about Arab-Israeli relations in one of three main ways: (1) a concern for Israeli security and fear of Arabs, (2) frustration with U.S. support for Israel and resentment toward Israel, or (3) a feeling that the world balance of power depends on what happens with Israel and its neighbors.

Cluster Analysis

As with factor and Q-sort analysis, cluster analysis is a sophisticated statistical technique that will be described only briefly and in general terms.[5]

Cluster analysis is a technique for organizing information or items measuring a variable. It statistically organizes relationships among a large number of items and places them into groups. The grouping or classification procedure uses statistical techniques like those in factor analysis and Q-sort analysis. The technique groups items by similarity and difference.

Factor analysis results tell a researcher how each item relates to one or more unobserved factors. Results look like a list of items with a number next to each; the number is the association between an item and a factor. Results from Q-sort analysis tell a researcher how people organize statements and show that people organize statements in a small number of ways. Results consist of the list of people with a number next to each person representing the degree to which a person followed one of a few patterns for organizing statements.

Cluster analysis results, by contrast, are in the form of a graph or picture, which resembles a tree diagram because it looks like the branches of a tree. Lines extend from a trunk, to large branches, to smaller branches, and so forth to tiny twigs. There are several levels of branching. The branching diagram shows a researcher which items are similar to each other and which are different. Each item in the cluster analysis represents a tiny twig, and the pattern of connections illustrates similarity and differences. Two items that share connections to a common nearby branch are more similar than two items that share no common branch until they reach the trunk.

For example, a researcher asks mental patients 556 true/false statements in a personality test. Cluster analysis organizes the 566 items into "twigs" of a tree diagram. There are four major levels of branching: twigs to small branches, small branches to medium branches, medium branches to large branches, and large branches to the trunk. At each level, the branching shows groups of items that represent psychological disorders, or shows how sets of psychological disorders form common psychotic types. A research examines the pattern of branching to see how the answers to items form groups and how the groups can, in turn, be grouped.

NOTES

1. See Blalock (1982) and Zeller and Carmines (1980) for more in-depth discussions of measurement theory in the social sciences.
2. See Carmines and Zeller (1979:13–15) and Nunnally (1978).
3. Factor analysis is discussed in Kim and Mueller (1978). For more technical discussions, see Bohrnstedt and Borgatta (1981) and Jackson and Borgatta (1981). Duncan (1984:209–216) offers a critique of factor analysis.
4. Q-sort analysis is discussed in Brown (1980, 1986), McKeown (1988), and Nunnally (1978:544–558).
5. Cluster analysis is introduced in Aldenderfer and Blashfield (1984). Also see Bailey (1983) and Lorr (1983) for social science applications.

Evaluation Research

Evaluation research is the most widely used type of applied research. Researchers use it to learn whether a program or activity accomplished its intended objectives (see Chapter 2). The program or activity could be a drug-treatment program, a program to assist battered women, a neighborhood crime-watch program, or a class in school. There are specialized courses, journals, or books on evaluation research (or program evaluation) and a professional association, the American Evaluation Association, but evaluation research is not a different kind of research. Evaluation research can be quantitative or qualitative; it can involve existing statistics, experimental design, surveys, historical documents, or field observation.

The audience for evaluation research can differ from other social research. It is rarely academics, but rather "stakeholders," or parties with a stake in a program such as policymakers, beneficiaries, citizens, sponsors, people who work with a program or deliver services, and competing organizations.

Evaluation research rapidly grew in the United States in the late 1960s to provide "hard data" on many newly created government social programs. The primary reason for the growth of evaluation research was political (see Chapter 16). Critics of the programs demanded empirical evidence that programs were working, or accomplishing their objectives, and not a "waste of money." A second reason for the growth of evaluation research was that program administrators wanted to compare and measure the effectiveness of alternative programs or methods of delivering services. Evaluation research also expanded because more people were experienced with social research and had the capacity to conduct an independent systematic study of programs.

The large number of new programs by government (at the federal, state, and local levels) and nonprofit organizations spawned companies that specialized in conducting evaluation research. The companies hired sociologists, psychologists, political scientists, social workers, and education researchers. After very rapid growth in the 1970s, evaluation research sharply declined in the 1980s. One estimate suggests a 37 percent decline between 1980 and 1984 in U.S. federal government funds for evaluation research (Miller 1991), due to a mix of hostility toward all social programs and a desire to cut spending. Paradoxically, many of the people who had demanded evaluation research because they were skeptical about social programs in the 1970s sought to cut evaluation research in the 1980s when it showed that the programs they disliked were achieving objectives. As you can see, evaluation research can be contentious, but most evaluation researchers focus on doing quality research to produce results people can believe.

FORMULATING THE PROBLEM

The first step in evaluation research, as in any research project, is to formulate the problem. For evaluation, problem formulation may originate with an organization or with people external to those who design and operate the program under evaluation. In other words, outsiders may impose evaluation and use it to judge a program and/or the people involved with it. Such outside evaluation can make the people who design and run a program nervous.

Of course, many programs also conduct ongoing self-evaluation for self-improvement.

A basic issue in evaluation research is: What should we evaluate? One can evaluate the process and procedures used in a program, the program personnel (including their background, competence, training, etc.), and/or a program's short-term and long-term outcomes. Frequently, disagreement arises because different people (e.g., funding agencies, clients, coworkers, administrators, other organizations) believe a program should be achieving different objectives, or they assign very different priorities to similar objectives. For example, parties involved in evaluating a college course might suggest divergent objectives for evaluating it, such as the following:

Student: Was the course fun, exciting, and interesting? Was it not too very difficult, and neither too slow or too fast paced?

Teacher: Did students learn the all the material in the course? Was the mix of instructional methods and materials and motivational techniques highly effective?

Teacher's colleagues: Was the teacher effective at imparting the most current knowledge, attitudes, and skills to students, and thus effective in preparing them for other courses?

Administrator: Did the teacher follow all procedures (e.g., turn in grades on time) and teach an efficient number of students, and are the students satisfied (no complaints/ problems)?

Employer: Did the students learn the skills/ attitudes that are needed in the workplace?

A critical first task for an evaluation researcher is to identify a range of objectives (outcomes and processes) wanted by a diversity of parties involved in a program. For example, a researcher evaluating a homeless shelter might find that the homeless people served, nearby business owners, other charitable social services, city officials, and workers at the shelter each has a different set of objectives for the program. The official goals or objectives in program documents may be of limited use because they are often phased in vague, idealistic terms, can be con-

tradictory, or may be designed as "window dressing" to appease an external audience and not represent the real ongoing situation.

Early in the evaluation process, a researcher needs to identify all relevant parties and contact each separate from one another to learn potential evaluation criteria or program objectives from that party's point of view. This means a researcher must study a program or organization to identify relevant parties, then use various techniques, such the focus group (see Chapter 13), to discover how each sees the program and what each believe its objectives and priorities should be.

A researcher needs to be aware that some parties may be suspicious of the evaluation process. If one is conducting a legitimate, honest, fair, and independent evaluation, the researcher needs to assure all involved of his or her integrity and that the evaluation is not a "smoke screen" for a decision that has already been made. For example, people receiving benefits from a program may justify fear that the evaluation will result in the cutting of their benefits and hesitate to cooperate with a researcher. Past misuse of evaluation can lead to cynicism or freeze outs (see Chapter 13).

After the researcher has contacted a range of parties involved, obtained objectives from each, and assembled a list of various objectives, he or she next consolidates and organizes the list. A researcher might find that different parties state the same objective in different ways, or want the same objective but have different time frames. Parties might favor contradictory objectives. For example, a student might want a course to be easy to pass, whereas a teacher wants it to "weed out" weak students.

Usually, it is best to retain contradictory evaluation objectives when they reflect the opposing interests of the diverse parties involved. To do otherwise would be to silence or censor certain parties or points of view. For example, one party says the objective of a homeless shelter is to keep homeless people off the street or make them invisible. If a researcher ignores objectives by other parties (e.g., empower the homeless, improve their quality of life, provide the homeless with a safe haven), the researcher could produce a misleading evaluation of the shelter's "success." Sometimes one party may try to stop a researcher from evaluating objectives other than his or hers, which raises ethical concerns (see Chapters 5 and 16). Likewise, researchers must be sensitive to situations in which parties try to hide or distort information because they believe its inclusion in an evaluation might bring them harm.

MEASURABLE OBJECTIVES

After identifying a complete list of objectives, the researcher's next step is to develop measures for each. A researcher needs to conceptualize and define each objective clearly and then create an empirical measure for it (see Chapter 7).

The researcher can often measure some objectives with existing statistical sources or "social indictors" that are built into the ongoing monitoring of activities (see Chapter 11). For example, evaluation data might include the number of students and their grades in a course, the number of clients who visit an agency, the number and type of staff who work in an office, the number of cases reported to police, and so on. The data may be in official public records, private routine bureaucratic records, or case files or files on specific people (e.g., employee hiring and job performance record) (see "running records" in Chapter 14). For example, in evaluating a library program, the records routinely kept of books checked out can become a source of evaluation data. The researcher needs to negotiate access to various types of records and ensure confidentiality.

Evaluation researchers sometimes create a survey questionnaire to access the views or opinions of affected people (see Chapter 10). Researchers use surveys to learn the level of satisfaction with service, the beliefs of people, or whether opinions have changed. A researcher should be aware that measuring *beliefs* about program objectives can differ from measuring objectives directly. For example, a teacher surveys students and asks, "Do you think you learned a lot?" This is different from an independent measure of student learning (e.g., scores on a test, ability to demonstrate certain skills). Sometimes the two kinds of measures produce the same results, but not always.

Many evaluation researchers hold that the experimental or quasi-experimental design (see Chapter 9) is the ideal approach for evaluation research. One reason is that experimental research makes it easy to specify causes, or connect the program to achieving an objective. Often in evaluation research, it is difficult to specify whether the program was the only or true cause of attaining an objective. Measuring objectives before and after an intervention or program makes attribution of cause easier. It is often very difficult to pinpoint the cause for an objective. Supporters of an evaluated program will claim that the program is the real cause, whereas opponents are likely to say it is due to a nonprogram factor. For example, students taking a course learn a great deal about a country, one of the course objectives. The evaluator asks, was it due to the course alone or to events beyond the course, as in the History Effect (see Chapter 9). If, during the course, the country students were learning about was attacked and the mass media widely reported on the country, it may be a mistake to attribute achieving the objective to the course alone.

Another reason evaluators like experimental research is that it controls for external conditions. Researchers want to know whether success or failure to reach objectives is caused by the program or due to circumstances outside of the program. This is ideally achieved with an experiment that controls for threats to internal validity. Nevertheless, in field experiments, control is often difficult to achieve. For example, a homeless shelter program may have reducing the number of homeless people on the street as an objective. Yet, a severe economic recession may impoverish many more people, making them homeless. Under such conditions, the program cannot be "blamed" for not achieving its objective.

Under ideal conditions, evaluation researchers begin to measure objectives before a program begins and to control all external factors as potential explanations. In addition, they evaluate both during a program's operation, formative evaluation, as well as at the end of a program, summative evaluation (see Chapter 2). In reality, they often evaluate after a program began and cannot get "pretest" data, are unable to control many potential others causes, and can only do summative evaluation.

In addition to measuring objectives, many evaluation researchers add an exploratory dimension.

The researcher may be curious and interested in outcomes or parts of the program and its processes that no one identifies, but which he or she notices during the process of evaluation. Sometimes the researcher may anticipate a latent or "hidden objective" based on reviewing the research literature of similar programs. The researcher also needs to be sensitive to unexpected outcomes that a program causes. For example, a researcher evaluates a program that is designed to stop pregnant mothers from using illegal drugs. She or he may find during an in-depth interview that the mothers stay away from rehabilitation services and prenatal health programs as a result of the program because they fear arrest. In this situation, the program's unanticipated outcome (staying away from health services to assist the mothers) may be more powerful or significant than its official objective—to stop pregnant women from using illegal drugs.

QUALITATIVE VERSUS QUANTITATIVE EVALUATION RESEARCH

Evaluation researchers can include qualitative data (i.e., photos, field observation, document study, and/or in-depth open-ended interviewing) as well as quantitative data as part of program evaluation. Qualitative data may allow a researcher to document difficult-to-quantify objectives. For example, a researcher evaluating a college course conducts in-depth open interviews. The researcher discovers that a few students say the class "changed entire my life" or "changed how I think about the world," although such information may not register on standard quantitative evaluation indicators. A researcher in the field observing a group of people in a program may see high levels of social interaction and mutual emotional support among the clients served by a program. This might be an important objective for the clients, although it may not be an official objective or one expressed by the clients.

A researcher can evaluate a program with regard to long- and short-term objectives. Long-term program objectives are much more difficult to evaluate and often impossible to document within the time period of the evaluation study. In addition, the short- and long-term objectives do not always complement one another. The short-term objective of "satisfaction" with services delivered may contradict a long-term goal of permanent ad significant personal change in clients.

Evaluation researchers often encounter program supporters who say no one can evaluate this program because it has imprecise objectives (e.g., give someone greater independence) and a long time frame to achieve them (e.g., 10 years after the program). The best an evaluation researcher can do in such situations is to operationalize the objectives with multiple qualitative and quantitative indictors, identify many intermediate steps or processes that suggest movement toward the long-term objective, and document the "momentum" of process toward reaching the objectives. For example, a professor states, "My classes prepare students not for their first job, but their third job out; I give students a set of critical reasoning skills, organizational attitudes, and in-depth communication abilities that slowly appear years later." To evaluate whether this is occurring, a researcher does not have to wait 10 years to see how many of the students become successful. The researcher can begin by identifying early operational indicators of each skill area and see whether the professor's students are learning them. The researcher could also do alumni and employer surveys to find out whether the skills are used in subsequent years.

Few evaluation researchers worry greatly about theory. Most evaluation research is not theoretically oriented but has more of a technocratic orientation (see Chapter 6). Brickmayer (2000) argued for theory-based evaluation that moves beyond the "did it work?" questions to why did it work or did not work. Theory-based evaluation uses evaluation to build a base of theoretically based knowledge for program improvement. Beyond determining the degree to which a program achieves each objective, in theory-based evaluation a researcher tries to specify why. For example, a researcher wants to evaluate a statewide antismoking mass media campaign that targets young teens. The researcher finds that the media campaign has only limited, short-term effects. The hypothesized relationship between media message, belief change, and change in smoking behavior may be too simplistic. The researcher may find that smoking beliefs change, but behavior stays the same because of other factors (e.g., peer pressure, countervailing images of glamour in the media). The evaluation researcher can use the findings about the interconnection among media messages, belief, and behavior to build a more general theory about how media messages affect social behaviors.

AFTER THE EVALUATION

After gathering data about each objective, a researcher needs to judge how well a program has reached the objectives and communicate his or her results. Often, reaching objectives, especially for nonquantitative or long-term objectives, is partial or requires the researcher to provide a detailed explanation. Short-term, quantitative objectives are usually easier to evaluate and report on. For example, it is easier to state whether an accident prevention program reduced accidents by 15 percent over two months than whether an education program prepared people with valuable life skills they will use over the next two decades. The researcher needs to carefully organize and document statements made in the report with data (see Chapter 16).

Others may use, ignore, or misuse the results of evaluation research. A researcher cannot always prevent the evaluation results from being ignored or misused, but can do several things to reduce their likelihood. First, a researcher is less likely to have an evaluation ignored or misused if he or she includes clear policy-related implications in the research report. Concrete recommendations with specific time lines are difficult to ignore. Second, a researcher is less likely to have problems if the report includes multiple types of data and methods of gathering data. It is easier to ignore or select one isolated item from a survey than it is to ignore or selectively choose one item from a rich, multifaceted report. Last, the researcher should widely distribute the report to various stakeholders or parties involved. Delivering the evaluation report to a single person or office makes its easy to bury the report or select items from it. Wide distribution gives many people with diverse views an opportunity to read and respond to it. Wider distribution also includes delivering the results in multiple formats: a short and long version, a written report, and several oral presentations.

Bibliography

Abell, Peter. (2001). Causality and low-frequency complex events. *Sociological Methods and Research,* 30: 57–80.

Abell, Peter. (2004). Narrative explanation. *Annual Review of Sociology,* 30:287–310.

Abbott, Andrew. (1988). *The system of professions: An essay on the division of expert labor.* Chicago: University of Chicago Press.

Abbott, Andrew. (1992). From causes to events: Notes on narrative positivism. *Sociological Methods and Research,* 20:428–455.

Abbott, Andrew. (1995). Sequence analysis. *Annual Review of Sociology,* 21:93–113.

Abbott, Andrew. (2001). *Time matters: On theory and method.* Chicago: University of Chicago Press.

Abelson, Robert P., Elizabeth F. Loftus, and Anthony G. Greenwald. (1992). Attempts to improve the accuracy of self-reports of voting. In *Questions about questions: Inquiries into the cognitive bases of surveys,* edited by J. Turner, pp. 138–153. New York: Russell Sage Foundation.

Abrams, Philip. (1982). *Historical sociology.* Ithaca, NY: Cornell University Press.

Abt, Charles. (1979). Government constraints on evaluation quality. In *Improving evaluation,* edited by L. Datta and R. Perloff. Beverly Hills, CA: Sage.

Achen, Christopher H. (1982). *Interpreting and using regression.* Beverly Hills, CA: Sage.

Adams, Gerald R., and Jay D. Schvaneveldt. (1985). *Understanding research methods.* New York: Longman.

Adler, Patricia A. (1985). *Wheeling and dealing.* New York: Columbia University Press.

Adler, Patricia A., and Peter Adler. (1983). Shifts and oscillations in deviant careers: The case of upper-level drug dealers and smugglers. *Social Problems,* 31:195–207.

Adler, Patricia A., and Peter Adler. (1987). *Membership roles in field research.* Beverly Hills, CA: Sage.

Adler, Patricia A., and Peter Adler. (1993). Ethical issues in self-censorship: Ethnographic research on sensitive topics. In *Research on sensitive topics,* edited by C. Renzetti and R. Lee, pp. 249–266. Thousand Oaks, CA: Sage.

Adler, Patricia A., and Peter Adler. (1994). Observational techniques. In *Handbook of qualitative research,* edited by N. Denzin and Y. Lincoln, pp. 377–392. Thousand Oaks, CA: Sage.

Adorno, Theodor W. (1976a). Sociology and empirical research. In *The positivist dispute in German sociology,* edited by T. Adorno et al., trans. Glyn Adey and David Frisby, pp. 68–86. New York: Harper & Row.

Adorno, Theodor W. (1976b). The logic of the social sciences. In *The positivist dispute in German sociology,* edited by T. Adorno et al., trans. Glyn Adey and David Frisby, pp. 87–104. New York: Harper & Row.

Agar, Michael. (1980). Getting better quality stuff: Methodological competition in an interdisciplinary niche. *Urban Life,* 9:34–50.

Agar, Michael. (1986). *Speaking of ethnography.* Beverly Hills, CA: Sage.

Agger, Ben. (1991). Critical theory, poststructuralism, postmodernism: Their sociological relevance. *Annual Review of Sociology,* 17:105–131.

Agnew, Neil McK., and Sandra W. Pyke. (1991). *The science game: An introduction to research in the social sciences,* 5th ed. Englewood Cliffs, NJ: Prentice-Hall.

Albrecht, Gary L. (1985). Videotape safaris: Entering the field with a camera. *Qualitative Sociology,* 8:325–344.

Aldenderfer, Mark S., and Roger K. Blashfield. (1984). *Cluster analysis.* Beverly Hills, CA: Sage.

Alderson, Arthur, and Jason Beckfield. (2004). Power and position in the world city system. *American Journal of Sociology,* 109:811–851.

Alford, Robert R. (1998). *The craft of inquiry: Theories, method, evidence.* New York: Oxford University Press.

Allison, Paul D. (2001). *Missing data.* Thousand Oaks CA: Sage.

Almgren, Gunnar, Avery Guest, George Imerwahr, and Michael Spittel. (1998). Joblessness, family disruption, and violent death in Chicago, 1970–1990. *Social Forces,* 76: 1465–1494.

Almond, Gabriel A., and Sidney Verba. (1963). *The civic culture.* Princeton, NJ: Princeton University Press.

Altheide, David L. (1980). Leaving the newsroom. In *Fieldwork experience,* edited by W. B. Shaffir, R. Stebbins, and A. Turowetz, pp. 301–310. New York: St. Martin's Press.

Altman, Morris. (2000). A behavioral model of path dependency: The economics of profitable inefficiency and market failure. *Journal of Socio-Economics,* 29:127–145.

Alvarez, R. Michael, and Tara Butterfield. (2000). The resurgence of nativism in California? The case of Proposition 187 and illegal immigration. *Social Science Quarterly,* 81:167–179.

Alwin, Duane F. (1977). Making errors in surveys. *Sociological Methods and Research,* 6:131–150.

Alwin, Duane F. (1988). The general social survey: A national data resource for the social sciences. *PS: Political Science and Politics,* 21:90–94.

Alwin, Duane F., and David J. Jackson. (1980). Measurement models for response errors in surveys: Issues and applications. In *Sociological methodology, 1980,* edited by S. Leinhardt. San Francisco: Jossey-Bass.

Alwin, Duane F., and Jon A. Krosnick. (1985). The measurement of values in surveys: A comparison of ratings and rankings. *Public Opinion Quarterly,* 49:535–552.

American Sociological Association. (1997). *American Sociological Association style guide,* 2nd ed. Washington, DC: American Sociological Association.

Aminzade, Ronald. (1984). Capitalist industrialization and patterns of industrial protest: A comparative urban study of nineteenth century France. *American Sociological Review,* 49:437–453.

Anderson, Andy B., Alexander Basilevsky, and Derek P. J. Hum. (1983). Measurement: Theory and techniques. In *Handbook of survey research,* edited by P. Rossi, J. D. Wright, and A. Anderson, pp. 231–287. New York: Academic Press.

Anderson, Barbara A., Brian D. Silver, and Paul R. Abramson. (1988). The effects of the race of interviewer on race-related attitudes of black respondents in SRC/CPS national election studies. *Public* Opinion *Quarterly,* 52:289–324.

Anderson, Elijah. (1989). Jelly's place. In *In the field,* edited by C. Smith and W. Kornblum, pp. 9–20. New York: Praeger.

Anderson, N. (1923). *The hobo.* Chicago: University of Chicago Press.

Anderson, Perry. (1974a). *Linkages of the absolutist state.* London: New Left Books.

Anderson, Perry. (1974b). *Passages from antiquity to feudalism.* London: New Left Books.

Anderson, R. Bruce W. (1973). On the comparability of meaningful stimuli in cross-cultural research. In *Comparative research methods,* edited by D. Warwick and S. Osherson, pp. 149–186. Englewood Cliffs, NJ: Prentice-Hall.

Andorka, Rudolf. (1987). Time budgets and their uses. *Annual Review of Sociology,* 13:149–164.

Andren, Gunnar. (1981). Reliability and content analysis. In *Advances in content analysis,* edited by K. Rosengren, pp. 43–67. Beverly Hills, CA: Sage.

Andrews, Frank M., Laura Klem, Terrence Davidson, Patrick O'Malley, and Willard Rodgers. (1981). *A guide for selecting statistical techniques for analyzing social science data.* Ann Arbor: Institute for Social Research, University of Michigan.

Andrews, Tracy, Vickie D. Ybarra, and Teresa Miramontes. (2002). Negotiating survival: Undocumented Mexican immigrant women in the Pacific Northwest. *Social Science Journal,* 39:431–449.

Applebaum, Richard. (1978a). Marxist method: Structural constraints and social praxis. *American Sociologist,* 13:73–81.

Applebaum, Richard. (1978b). Marx's theory of the falling rate of profit. *American Sociological Review,* 43:67–80.

Aquilino, William S. (1993). Effects of spouse presence during the interview on survey response concerning marriage. *Public Opinion Quarterly,* 57:358–376.

Aquilino, William S., and Leonard Losciuto. (1990). Effects of interview mode on self-reported drug use. *Public Opinion Quarterly,* 54:362–395.

Archer, Margaret, R. Bhaskar, A. Collier, T. Lawson, and A. Norrie, eds. (1998). *Critical realism: Essential readings.* New York: Routledge.

Archibald, Randall C. (May 25, 1998). Knowledge scare on cost of college study finds. *New York Times.*

Ardener, Shirley. (1984). Gender orientations in fieldwork. In *Ethnographic research: A guide to general conduct,* edited by R. F. Ellen, pp. 118–129. Orlando: Academic Press.

Ariès, E. (1977). Male–female interpersonal styles in all male, all female, and mixed groups. In *Beyond sex roles,* edited by A. Sargent, pp. 292–299. Boulder, CO: West.

Armer, Michael. (1973). Methodological problems and possibilities in comparative research. In *Comparative social research,* edited by M. Armer and A. D. Grimshaw, pp. 49–79. New York: Wiley.

Aronson, Elliot, and J. Merrill Carlsmith. (1968). Experimentation in social psychology. In *The handbook of social psychology, Vol. 2: Research methods,* edited by G. Lindzey and E. Aronson, pp. 1–78. Reading, MA: Addison-Wesley.

Atkinson, Robert. (1998). *The life story interview.* Thousand Oaks, CA: Sage.

Auriat, Nadia. (1993). My wife knows best: A comparison of event dating accuracy between the wife, the husband, the couple, and the Belgium population register. *Public Opinion Quarterly,* 57:165–190.

Auster, Carol J. (1985). Manual for socialization: Examples from Girl Scout handbooks, 1913–1984. *Qualitative Sociology,* 8:359–367.

Ayella, Marybeth. (1993). "They must be crazy:" Some of the difficulties in researching cults. In *Research on sensitive topics,* edited by C. Renzetti and R. Lee, pp. 108–124. Thousand Oaks, CA: Sage.

Babbie, Earl. (1989). *The practice of social research,* 5th ed. Belmont, CA: Wadsworth.

Babbie, Earl. (1990). *Survey research methods,* 2nd ed. Belmont, CA: Wadsworth.

Babbie, Earl. (1998). *The practice of social research,* 8th ed. Belmont, CA: Wadsworth.

Backstrom, Charles H., and Gerald Hursh-Cesar. (1981). *Survey research,* 2nd ed. New York: Wiley.

Bailey, Kenneth D. (1983). Sociological classification and cluster analysis. *Quality and Quantity,* 17:251–268.

Bailey, Kenneth D. (1984). A three-level measurement model. *Quality and Quantity,* 18:225–245.

Bailey, Kenneth D. (1986). Philosophical foundations of sociological measurement: Notes on the three-level model. *Quality and Quantity,* 20:327–337.

Bailey, Kenneth D. (1987). *Methods of social research,* 3rd ed. New York: Free Press.

Bailey, Kenneth D. (1988). Ethical dilemmas in social problems research: A theoretical framework. *American Sociologist,* 19:121–137.

Bailey, Kenneth D. (1992). Typologies. In *Encyclopedia of Sociology,* Vol. 4, edited by E. and M. Borgatta, pp. 2188–2194. New York: Macmillan.

Bakanic, Von, Clark McPhail, and Rita Simon. (1987). The manuscript review and decision-making process. *American Sociological Review,* 52:631–642.

Bakanic, Von, Clark McPhail, and Rita Simon. (1989). Mixed messages:

Referees' comments on the manuscripts they review. *Sociological Quarterly,* 30:639–654.

Ball, Michael, and Gregory W. H. Smith. (1992). *Analyzing visual data.* Thousand Oaks, CA: Sage.

Ball, Richard A., and G. David Curry. (1995). The logic of definition in criminology: Purposes and methods for defining "gangs." *Criminology,* 33:225–245.

Ballen, Robert D., and Kelly K. Richardson. (2002). Social integration, imitation and the geographic patterning of suicide. *American Sociological Review,* 873–888.

Banaka, William H. (1971). *Training in depth interviewing.* New York: Harper & Row.

Bannister, Robert C. (1987). *Sociology and scientism: The American quest for objectivity, 1880–1940.* Chapel Hill: University of North Carolina Press.

Barber, Jennifer S., and William G. Axinn. (1998). Gender attitudes and marriage among young women. *Sociological Quarterly,* 39:11–31.

Bardack, Nadia R., and Francis T. McAndrew. (1985). The influence of physical attractiveness and manner of dress on success in a simulated personnel decision. *Journal of Social Psychology,* 125:777–778.

Barlow, Melissa Hickman, David E. Barlow, and Theodore G. Chiricos. (1995). Economic conditions and ideologies of crime in the media: A content analysis of crime news. *Crime and Deliquency,* 41:3–19.

Barnes, Barry. (1974). *Scientific knowledge and sociological theory.* Boston: Routledge and Kegan Paul.

Barnes, J. A. (1970). Some ethical problems in modern fieldwork. In *Qualitative methodology,* edited by W. J. Filstead, pp. 235–251. Chicago: Markham.

Barnes, J. A. (1979). *Who should know what? Social science, privacy and ethics.* New York: Cambridge University Press.

Barry, Brian. (1975). On analogy. *Political Studies,* 23:208–224.

Bart, Pauline. (1987). Seizing the means of reproduction: An illegal feminist abortion collective—How and why it worked. *Qualitative Sociology,* 10:339–357.

Bart, Pauline, and Linda Frankel. (1986). *The student sociologist's handbook,* 4th ed. New York: Random House.

Bartiz, Loren. (1960). *Servants of power: A history of the use of social science in American industry.* Middletown, CT: Wesleyan University Press.

Barton, Allen H. (1995). Asking why about social problems: Ideology and causal models in the public mind. *International Journal of Public Opinion Research,* 7:299–327.

Barzun, Jacques, and Henry F. Graff. (1970). *The modern researcher,* rev. ed. New York: Harcourt, Brace and World.

Bateson, Nicholas. (1984). *Data construction in social surveys.* Boston: George Allen and Unwin.

Bauer, David G. (1988). *The "how to" grants manual,* 2nd ed. New York: Macmillan.

Bauer, Raymond, ed. (1966). *Social indicators.* Cambridge, MA: MIT Press.

Bausell, R. Barker. (1994). *Conducting meaningful experiments: Forty steps to becoming a scientist.* Thousand Oaks, CA: Sage.

Bayless, David L. (1981). Twenty-two years of survey research at the Research Triangle: 1959–1980. In *Current topics in survey sampling,* edited by D. Krewski, R. Platek, and J. N. K. Rao, pp. 87–103. New York: Academic Press.

Beasley, David. (1988). *How to use a research library.* New York: Oxford University Press.

Beatty, Paul. (1995). Understanding the standardization. *Journal of Official Statistics,* 11:147–160.

Beck, Bernard. (1970). Cooking welfare stew. In *Pathways to data,* edited by R. W. Habenstein, pp. 7–29. Chicago: Aldine.

Becker, Howard. (1967). Whose side are we on? *Social Problems,* 14: 239–247.

Becker, Howard S. (1969). Problems in the publication of field studies. In *Issues in participant observation,* edited by G. McCall and J. L. Simmons, pp. 260–275. Reading, MA: Addison-Wesley.

Becker, Howard S. (1970a). Practitioners of vice and crime. In *Pathways to data,* edited by R. W. Habenstein, pp. 30–49. Chicago: Aldine.

Becker, Howard S. (1970b). Problems of inference and proof in participant observation. In *Qualitative methodology: Firsthand involvement with the social world,* edited by W. J. Filstead, pp. 189–201. Chicago: Markham.

Becker, Howard S. (1970c). Whose side are we on? In *Qualitative methodology,* edited by W. J. Filstead, pp. 15–26. Chicago: Markham.

Becker, Howard S. (1986). *Writing for social scientists: How to start and finish your thesis, book or article.* Chicago: University of Chicago Press.

Becker, Howard S. (1993). How I learned what a crock was. *Journal of Contemporary Ethnography,* 22:28–35.

Becker, Howard S. (1998). *Tricks of the trade: How to think about your research while you're doing it.* Chicago: University of Chicago Press.

Becker, Howard S., and Blanche Geer. (1970). Participant observation and interviewing: A comparison. In *Qualitative methodology,* edited by W. J. Filstead, pp. 133–142. Chicago: Markham.

Becker, Howard S., and Blanche Geer. (1982). Participant observation: The analysis of qualitative field data. In *Field research: A sourcebook and field manual,* edited by R. G. Burgess, pp. 239–250. Boston: George Allen and Unwin.

Becker, Howard S., Blanche Geer, Everett C. Hughes, and Anselm Strauss. (1961). *Boys in white: Student culture in medical school.* Chicago: University of Chicago Press.

Becker, Howard S., Michal M. McCall, and Lori V. Morris. (1989). Theatres and communities: Three scenes. *Social Problems,* 36:93–116.

Beckfield, Jason. (2003). Inequality in the world polity. *American Sociological Review,* 68:401–424.

Beecher, H. K. (1970). *Research and the individual: Human studies.* Boston: Little, Brown.

Behrens, Angela, Christopher Uggen, and Jeff Manza. (2003). Ballot manipulation and the "menace of negro domination." *American Sociological Review,* 109:559–605.

Belenky, Mary Field, Blythe McVicker Clinchy, Nancy Rule Goldberger, and Jill Mattuck Tarule. (1986). *Women's ways of knowing: The development of self, voice and mind.* New York: Basic Books.

Bellah, Robert N. (1957). *Tokugawa religion.* Glencoe, IL: Free Press.

Belli, Robert F., et al. (1999). Reducing vote overreporting in surveys: Social desirability, memory failure and source monitoring. *Public Opinion Quarterly,* 63:90–108.

Ben-David, Joseph. (1971). *The scientist's role in society.* Englewood Cliffs, NJ: Prentice-Hall.

Ben-Yehuda, Nachman. (1983). History, selection and randomness—Towards an analysis of social historical explanations. *Quality and Quantity,* 17: 347–367.

Bendix, Reinhard. (1956). *Work and authority in industry.* New York: Wiley.

Bendix, Reinhard. (1963). Concepts and generalizations in comparative sociological studies. *American Sociological Review,* 28:91–116.

Bendix, Reinhard. (1978). *Kings or people: Power and the mandate to rule.* Berkeley: University of California Press.

Benton, Ted. (1977). *Philosophical foundations of the three sociologies.* Boston: Routledge and Kegan Paul.

Berelson, B. (1952). *Content analysis in communication research.* Glencoe, IL: Free Press.

Berg, Bruce L. (1989). *Qualitative research methods.* Boston: Allyn and Bacon.

Berger, Peter. (1963). *An invitation to sociology: A humanistic perspective.* Garden City, NY: Anchor.

Berger, Peter, and Thomas Luckman. (1967). *The social construction of reality: A treatise in the sociology of knowledge.* Garden City, NY: Anchor.

Berger, Ronald, and Richard Quinney. (2004). *Storytelling sociology: Narrative as social inquiry.* Boulder CO: Lynne Reinner.

Berinsky, Adam J. (1999). The two faces of public opinion. *American Journal of Political Science,* 43:1209–1230.

Berk, Richard A. (1983). An introduction to sample selection bias in sociological data. *American Sociological Review,* 48:386–397.

Berk, Richard A. (1995). Publishing evaluation research. *Contemporary Sociology,* 24:9–12.

Berland, Gretchen K., et al. (2001). Health information on the Internet. *JAMA: Journal of the American Medical Association,* 285:2612–2622.

Bermant, Gordon. (1982). Justifying social science research in terms of social benefit. In *Ethical issues in social science research,* edited by T. Beauchamp, R. Faden, R. J. Wallace, and L. Walters, pp. 125–142. Balti-

more: Johns Hopkins University Press.

Bernard, H. Russell. (1988). *Research methods in cultural anthropology.* Newbury Park, CA: Sage.

Bernard, H. Russell, Peter Killworth, David Kronenfeld, and Lee Sailer. (1984). The problem of information accuracy: The validity of retrospective data. *Annual Review of Anthropology,* 13:495–517.

Bernstein, Robert, A. Chadha, and R. Montjoy. (2001). Overreporting voting: Why it happens and why it matters. *Public Opinion Quarterly,* 65:22–44.

Best, Joel. (2001). *Damned lies and statistics.* Berkeley: University of California Press.

Bhaskar, Roy. (1975). *A realist theory of science.* Atlantic Highlands, NJ: Humanities.

Bhaskar, Roy. (2003). *From science to emancipation: Alienation and enlightenment.* Thousand Oaks CA: Sage.

Biersack, Aletta. (1989). Local knowledge, local history: Geertz and beyond. In *The new cultural history,* edited by L. Hunt, pp. 72–96. Berkeley: University of California Press.

Billings, Dwight B., and Kathleen Blee. (2000). *The road to poverty.* Cambridge University Press.

Binson, Diane, and Joseph Catania. (1998). Respondents' understanding of the words in sexual behavior questions. *Public Opinion Quarterly,* 62:190–208.

Bischoping, Katherine, and Jennifer Dykema. (1999). Toward a social psychological programme for improving focus group methods of developing questionnaires. *Journal of Official Statistics,* 15:495–516.

Bishop, George F. (1987). Experiments with the middle response alternative in survey questions. *Public Opinion Quarterly,* 51:220–232.

Bishop, George. (1992). Qualitative analysis of question-order and context effects. In *Context effects in social and psychological research,* edited by N. Schwarz and S. Sudman, pp. 149–162. New York: Springer-Verlag.

Bishop, George F., R. W. Oldendick, and A. J. Tuchfarber. (1983). Effects of filter questions in public opinion surveys. *Public Opinion Quarterly,* 47:528–546.

Bishop, George F., R. W. Oldendick, and A. J. Tuchfarber. (1984). What must my interest in politics be if I just told you "I don't know"? *Public Opinion Quarterly,* 48:510–519.

Bishop, George F., R. W. Oldendick, and A. J. Tuchfarber. (1985). The importance of replicating a failure to replicate: Order effects on abortion items. *Public Opinion Quarterly,* 49:105–114.

Bishop, George F., A. J. Tuchfarber, and R. W. Oldendick. (1986). Opinions on fictitious issues: The pressure to answer survey questions. *Public Opinion Quarterly,* 50:240–251.

Bittman, Michael, and Judy Wajcman. (2000). The rush hour: The character of leisure time and gender equity. *Social Forces,* 79:165–190.

Blaikie, Norman. (1993). *Approaches to social enquiry.* Cambridge, MA: Polity.

Blalock, Hubert M., Jr. (1968). The measurement problem: A gap between the language of theory and research. In *Methodology in social research,* edited by H. Blalock and A. Blalock, pp. 5–27. New York: McGraw-Hill.

Blalock, Hubert M., Jr. (1969). *Theory construction: From verbal to mathematical formulations.* Englewood Cliffs, NJ: Prentice-Hall.

Blalock, Hubert M., Jr. (1979a). Measurement and conceptualization problems: The major obstacle to integrating theory and research. *American Sociological Review,* 44:881–894.

Blalock, Hubert M., Jr. (1979b). *Social statistics,* 2nd ed. New York: McGraw-Hill.

Blalock, Hubert M., Jr. (1982). *Conceptualization and measurement in the social sciences.* Beverly Hills, CA: Sage.

Blalock, Hubert M., Jr., and Ann B. Blalock, eds. (1968). *Methodology in social research.* New York: McGraw-Hill.

Blankenship, Albert B. (1977). *Professional telephone surveys.* New York: McGraw-Hill.

Blau, Judith R. (1978). Sociometric structure of a scientific discipline. *Research in Sociology of Knowledge, Sciences and Art,* 1:191–206.

Blee, Kathleen M. (1991). *Women of the Klan: Racism and gender in the 1920s.* Berkeley: University of California Press.

Blee, Kathleen M., and Dwight B. Billings. (1986). Reconstructing daily life in the past: An hermeneutical approach to ethnographic data. *Sociological Quarterly,* 27:443–462.

Bleicher, Josef. (1980). *Contemporary hermeneutics.* Boston: Routledge and Kegan Paul.

Bloch, Marc. (1953). *The historian's craft,* trans. Peter Putnam. New York: Vintage.

Block, Fred. (1977). Beyond corporate liberalism. *Social Problems,* 24: 353–361.

Block, Fred, and Gene A. Burns. (1986). Productivity as a social problem: The uses and misuses of social indicators. *American Sociological Review,* 51:767–780.

Block, Jennifer. (2003). Science gets sacked. *Nation,* 277(6):5–7.

Bloor, Michael J. (1983). Notes on member validation. In *Contemporary field research,* edited by R. M. Emerson, pp. 156–171. Boston: Little, Brown.

Blum, Debra E. (1989). A dean is charged with plagiarizing a dissertation for his book on Muzak. *Chronicle of Higher Education,* 35:A17.

Blume, Stuart S. (1974). *Toward a political sociology of science.* New York: Free Press.

Blumer, M. (1984). *The Chicago school of sociology.* Chicago: University of Chicago.

Blumer, Martin. (1991a). W. E. B. DuBois as a social investigator: The Philadelphia Negro 1889. In *The social survey in historical perspective, 1880–1940,* edited by M. Blumer, K. Bales, and K. Sklar, pp. 170–188. New York: Cambridge University Press.

Blumer, Martin. (1991b). The decline of the social survey movement and the rise of American empirical sociology. In *The social survey in historical perspective, 1880–1940,* edited by M. Blumer, K. Bales, and K. Sklar, pp. 271–315. New York: Cambridge University Press.

Blumer, Martin. (1992). The growth of applied sociology after 1945: The prewar establishment of the postwar infrastructure. In *Sociology and its publics: The forms and fates of disciplinary organization,* edited by T. C. Halliday and M. Janowitz, pp. 317–346. Chicago: University of Chicago.

Blumer, Martin, K. Bales, and K. Sklar. (1991). The social survey in histori-cal perspective. In *The social survey in historical perspective, 1880–1940,* edited by M. Blumer, K. Bales, and K. Sklar, pp. 1–48. New York: Cambridge University Press.

Blumstein, Alfred. (1974). Seriousness weights in an index of crime. *American Sociological Review,* 39:854–864.

Blute, Marion. (1997). History versus science: The evolutionary solution. *Canadian Journal of Sociology,* 22: 345–364.

Bogardus, Emory S. (1959). *Social distance.* Yellow Springs, OH: Antioch Press.

Bogdan, Robert, and Steven J. Taylor. (1975). *Introduction to qualitative research methods: A phenomenological approach to the social sciences.* New York: Wiley.

Bohrnstedt, George. (1992a). Reliability. In *Encyclopedia of Sociology,* Vol. 3, edited by E. and M. Borgatta, pp. 1626–1632. New York: Macmillan.

Bohrnstedt, George. (1992b). Validity. In *Encyclopedia of Sociology,* Vol. 4, edited by E. and M. Borgatta, pp. 2217–2222. New York: Macmillan.

Bohrnstedt, George W., and Edgar F. Borgatta, eds. (1981). *Social measurement: Current issues.* Beverly Hills, CA: Sage.

Bohrnstedt, George, and David Knoke. (1994). *Statistics for social data analysis,* 3rd ed. Itasca, IL: Peacock.

Bollen, Kenneth A., Barbara Entwisle, and Arthur S. Alderson. (1993). Macrocomparative research methods. *Annual Review of Sociology,* 19:321–351.

Bolton, Ruth N., and Tina Bronkhorst. (1996). Questionnaire pretesting: Computer-assisting coding of concurrent protocols. In *Answering questions,* edited by N. Schwarz and S. Sudman, pp. 37–64. San Francisco: Jossey-Bass.

Bond, Charles F., Jr., and Evan L. Anderson. (1987). The reluctance to transmit bad news: Private discomfort or public display? *Journal of Experimental Social Psychology,* 23:176–187.

Bonnell, Victoria E. (1980). The uses of theory, concepts and comparison in historical sociology. *Comparative Studies in Society and History,* 22:156–173.

Borgatta, Edgar F., and George W. Bohrnstedt. (1980). Level of measurement: Once over again. *Socio-logical Methods and Research,* 9:147–160.

Boruch, Robert F. (1982). Methods for revolving privacy problems in social research. In *Ethical issues in social science research,* edited by T. Beauchamp, R. Faden, R. J. Wallace, and L. Walters, pp. 292–313. Baltimore: Johns Hopkins University Press.

Boswell, Terry, and Cliff Brown. (1999). The scope of general theory. *Sociological Methods and Research,* 28:154–185.

Bottomore, Thomas. (1984). *The Frankfurt School.* New York: Travistock.

Bouchard, Thomas J., Jr. (1976). Unobtrusive measures: An inventory of uses. *Sociological Methods and Research,* 4:267–300.

Bourgeois, Philippe. (1996). *In search of respect: Selling crack in El Barrio.* New York: Cambridge University Press.

Boyatzis, Richard E. (1998). *Transforming qualitative information: Thematic analysis and code development.* Thousand Oaks, CA: Sage.

Bradburn, Norman M. (1983). Response effects. In *Handbook of survey research,* edited by P. Rossi, J. Wright, and A. Anderson, pp. 289–328. Orlando, FL: Academic.

Bradburn, Norman M., and Carrie Miles. (1979). Vague qualifiers. *Public Opinion Quarterly,* 43:92–101.

Bradburn, Norman M., and Seymour Sudman. (1980). *Improving interview method and questionnaire design.* San Francisco: Jossey-Bass.

Bradburn, Norman M., and Seymour Sudman. (1988). *Polls and surveys: Understanding what they tell us.* San Francisco: Jossey-Bass.

Bradshaw, York W., and Michael Wallace. (1996). *Global inequalities.* Thousand Oaks, CA: Pine Forge Press.

Bradsher, Keith. (2002). *High and mighty.* New York: Public Affairs.

Brady, David. (2003). The politics of poverty. *Social Forces,* 82:557–588.

Brainard, Jeffrey, and Ron Southwick. (August 10, 2001). A record year at the federal trough: Colleges feast on $1.67 billion in earmarks. *Chronicle of Higher Education.*

Brainard, Jeffrey, and Anne Borrego. (September 26, 2003). Academic pork barrel tops $2 billion for first time. *Chronicle of Higher Education.*

Brannigan, Augustine. (1992). Postmodernism. *Encyclopedia of Sociology,*

Vol. 3, edited by E. and M. Borgatta, pp. 1522–1525. New York: Macmillan.

Braudel, Fernand. (1980). *On history,* trans. Sarah Matthews. Chicago: University of Chicago Press.

Braun, Michael. (2003). Communication and cognition. In *Cross-cultural survey methods,* edited by Janet Harkness, Fons Van de Vijver, and Peter Mohler, pp. 57–67. Hoboken NJ: Wiley.

Bredo, Eric, and Walter Feinberg, eds. (1982). *Knowledge and values in social and educational research.* Philadelphia: Temple University Press.

Brehm, John. (1993). *The phantom respondents: Opinion surveys and political representation.* Ann Arbor: University of Michigan Press.

Brehm, John. (1994). Stubbing our toes for a foot in the door? Prior contact, incentives and survey response. *International Journal of Public Opinion Research,* 6:45–63.

Brenner, Michael. (1985). Survey interviewing. In *The research interview: Uses and approaches,* edited by M. Brenner, J. Brown, and D. Canter, pp. 9–36. New York: Academic Press.

Brenner, Michael, Jennifer Brown, and David Canter, eds. (1985). *The research interview: Uses and approaches.* Orlando, FL: Academic Press.

Brickmayer, Johanna D. (2000). Theory-based evaluation in practice. *Evaluation Review,* 24:407–423.

Briggs, Charles L. (1986). *Learning now to ask: A sociolinguistic appraisal of the role of the interview in social science research.* New York: Cambridge University Press.

Brinberg, David, and Joseph E. McGrath. (1982). A network of validity concepts. In *Forms of validity in research,* edited by D. Brinberg and L. Kidder, pp. 5–21. San Francisco: Jossey-Bass.

Brint, Steven. (1994). *In an Age of Experts: The changing role of professionals in politics and public life.* Princeton, NJ: Princeton University Press.

Britton, Dana M. (1990). Homophobia and homosociality: An analysis of boundary maintenance. *Sociological Quarterly,* 31:423–440.

Broad, W. J., and N. Wade. (1982). *Betrayers of the truth.* New York: Simon and Schuster.

Brodsky, Stanley L., and H. O'Neal Smitherman. (1983). *Handbook of scales for research in crime and delinquency.* New York: Plenum.

Brody, Charles J. (1986). Things are rarely black or white: Admitting gray into the converse model of attitude stability. *American Journal of Sociology,* 92:657–677.

Brown, Jennifer, and David Canter. (1985). The uses of explanation in the research interview. In *The research interview: Uses and approaches,* edited by M. Brenner, J. Brown, and D. Canter, pp. 217–245. New York: Academic Press.

Brown, Richard Harvey. (1978). Symbolic realism and sociological thought. In *Structure, consciousness and history,* edited by R. H. Brown and S. M. Lyman, pp. 14–37. New York: Cambridge University Press.

Brown, Richard Harvey. (1989). *Social science as civic discourse: Essays on the invention, legitimation and uses of social theory.* Chicago: University of Chicago Press.

Brown, Steven R. (1980). *Political subjectivity: Applications of Q methodology in political science.* New Haven, CT: Yale University Press.

Brown, Steven R. (1986). Q technique and method: Principles and procedures. In *New tools for social scientists: Advances and applications in research methods,* edited by W. D. Berry and M. Lewis-Beck, pp. 57–76. Beverly Hills, CA: Sage.

Brym, Robert J. (1980). *Intellectuals and politics.* Boston: George Allen and Unwin.

Burawoy, Michael. (1977). Social structure, homogenization, and the process of status attainment in the United States and Great Britain. *American Journal of Sociology,* 82:1031–1042.

Burawoy, Michael. (1985). Karl Marx and the satanic mills: Factory politics under early capitalism in England, the United States, and Russia. *American Journal of Sociology,* 90: 247–282.

Burawoy, Michael. (1989). Two methods in search of science: Skocpol versus Troksky. *Theory and Society,* 18:759–806.

Burawoy, Michael, et al. (2004). Public sociologies. *Social Problems,* 51: 103–131.

Burawoy, Michael. (1990). Marxism as science: Historical challenges and

theoretical growth. *American Sociological Review,* 55:775–793.

Burawoy, Michael. (1991). The extended case method. In *Ethnography unbound: Power and resistance in the modern metropolis,* edited by M. Burawoy et al., pp. 271–287. Berkeley: University of California Press.

Burawoy, Michael. (1998). The extended case method. *Sociological Theory,* 16:4–33.

Burgess, Robert G. (1982a). Approaches to field research. In *Field research,* edited by R. G. Burgess, pp. 1–11. Boston: George Allen and Unwin.

Burgess, Robert G. (1982b). Keeping field notes. In *Field research,* edited by R. G. Burgess, pp. 191–194. Boston: George Allen and Unwin.

Burgess, Robert G. (1982c). The unstructured interview as a conversation. In *Field research,* edited by R. G. Burgess, pp. 107–110. Boston: George Allen and Unwin.

Burke, Peter. (1980). *Sociology and history.* Boston: George Allen and Unwin.

Burke, Peter. (1992). *History and social theory.* Ithaca, NY: Cornell University Press.

Burnstein, Leigh, Howard E. Freeman, and Peter H. Rossi, eds. (1985). *Collecting evaluation data: Problems and solutions.* Beverly Hills, CA: Sage.

Burrage, Michael C., and David Corry. (1981). At sixes and sevens: Occupational status in the city of London from the 14th to the 17th century. *American Sociological Review,* 46:375–392.

Burton, Michael L., and Douglas R. White. (1987). Cross-cultural surveys today. *Annual Review of Anthropology,* 16:143–160.

Büthe, Tim. (2002). Taking temporality seriously: Modeling history and the use of narratives as evidence. *American Political Science Review,* 96: 481–493.

Byrne, Noel. (1978). Sociotemporal considerations of everyday life suggested by an empirical study of the bar milieu. *Urban Life,* 6:417–438.

Calhoun, Craig. (1996). The rise and domestication of historical sociology. In *The historical turn in the human sciences,* edited by T. J. McDonald, pp. 305–337. Ann Arbor: University of Michigan Press.

Camic, Charles. (1980). The institutionalization of the role of scientist:

England in the seventeenth century and ancient Greece. *Comparative Social Research,* 3:271–285.

Camic, Charles, and Yu Xie. (1994). The statistical turn in American social science: Columbia University, 1890–1915. *American Sociological Review,* 59:773–805.

Campbell, Donald T., and D. W. Fiske. (1959). Convergent and discriminant validation by the multitrait-multimethod matrix. *Psychological Bulletin,* 56:81–105.

Campbell, Donald T., and Julian C. Stanley. (1963). *Experimental and quasi-experimental designs for research.* Chicago: Rand McNally.

Campbell, John P., Richard L. Daft, and Charles L. Hulin. (1982). *What to study: Generating and developing research questions.* Beverly Hills, CA: Sage.

Cancian, Francesca M., and Cathleen Armstead. (1992). Participatory research. In *Encyclopedia of Sociology,* Vol. 3, edited by E. and M. Borgatta, pp. 1427–1432. New York: Macmillan.

Cannell, Charles F., and Robert L. Kahn. (1968). Interviewing. In *Handbook of social psychology,* 2nd ed., Vol. 2, edited by G. Lindzey and E. Aronson, pp. 526–595. Reading, MA: Addison-Wesley.

Cannell, Charles F., Peter V. Miller, and Lois Oksenberg. (1981). Research on interviewing techniques. In *Sociological methodology, 1981,* edited by S. Leinhardt, pp. 389–436. San Francisco: Jossey-Bass.

Canter, David, Jennifer Brown, and Linda Goat. (1985). Multiple sorting procedure for studying conceptual systems. In *The research interview: Uses and approaches,* edited by M. Brenner, J. Brown, and D. Canter, pp. 79–114. New York: Academic Press.

Cantor, Norman F., and Richard I. Schneider. (1967). *How to study history.* New York: Thomas Y. Crowell.

Caplan, Arthur L. (1982). On privacy and confidentiality in social science research. In *Ethical issues in social science research,* edited by T. Beauchamp, R. Faden, R. J. Wallace, and L. Walters, pp. 315–327. Baltimore: Johns Hopkins University Press.

Cappell, Charles L., and Thomas M. Guterbock. (1992). Visible colleges: The social and conceptual structure of sociology specialties. *American Sociological Review,* 57:266–273.

Capron, Alexander Morgan. (1982). Is consent always necessary in social science research? In *Ethical issues in social science research,* edited by T. Beauchamp, R. Faden, R. J. Wallace, and L. Walters, pp. 215–231. Baltimore: Johns Hopkins University Press.

Carl, Jim. (1994). Parental choice as national policy in England and the United States. *Comparative Education Review,* 38:294–322.

Carley, Michael. (1981). *Social measurement and social indicators: Issues of policy and theory.* London: George Allen and Unwin.

Carmines, E., and R. Zeller. (1979). *Reliability and validity assessment.* Beverly Hills, CA: Sage.

Carney, Thomas F. (1972). *Content analysis: A technique for systematic inference from communications.* Winnipeg: University of Manitoba Press.

Carr, Edward Hallett. (1961). *What is history?* New York: Vintage.

Carr-Hill, Roy A. (1984a). The political choice of social indicators. *Quality and Quantity,* 18:173–191.

Carr-Hill, Roy A. (1984b). Radicalising survey methodology. *Quantity and Quality,* 18:275–292.

Catania, Joseph, D. Dinson, J. Canahola, L. Pollack, W. Hauck, and T. Coates. (1996). Effects of interviewer gender, interviewer choice and item wording on responses to questions concerning sexual behavior. *Public Opinion Quarterly,* 60:345–375.

Caute, David. (1978). *The great fear.* New York: Touchstone.

Cerulo, Karen A. (1989). Sociopolitical control and the structure of national symbols: An empirical analysis of anthems. *Social Forces,* 68:76–99.

Chadwick, Bruce A., Howard M. Bahr, and Stan L. Albrecht. (1984). *Social science research methods.* Englewood Cliffs, NJ: Prentice-Hall.

Chafetz, Janet Saltzman. (1978). *A primer on the construction and testing of theories in sociology.* Itasca, IL: Peacock.

Chambers, Marcia. (October 22, 1986). Jesuit priest standing by the survey that Vatican attempted to suppress. *New York Times.*

Chang, Mariko Lin. (2004). Cross-national variation in sex segregation in sixteen developing countries. *American Sociological Review,* 69:114–137.

Channels, Noreen L. (1993). Anticipating media coverage: Methodological decisions regarding criminal justice research. In *Research on sensitive topics,* edited by C. Renzetti and R. Lee, pp. 267–280. Thousand Oaks, CA: Sage.

Charmaz, Kathy. (2003). Grounded theory: Objectivist and constructionist methods. In *Strategies of qualitative inquiry,* 2nd ed., edited by N. Denzin and Y. Lincoln, pp. 249–291. Thousand Oaks CA: Sage.

Chase-Dunn, Christopher. (1989). *Global formation: Structures of the world economy.* Cambridge, MA: Blackwell.

Chavez, Leo R. (2001). *Covering immigration: Popular images and politics of the nation.* Berkeley: University of California Press.

Chebat, Jean-Charles, and Jacques Picard. (1988). Receivers' self-acceptance and the effectiveness of two-sided messages. *Journal of Social Psychology,* 128:353–362.

Chicago manual of style for authors, editors and copywriters, 13th ed., revised and expanded. (1982). Chicago: University of Chicago Press.

Christian, Leah Melani, and Don A. Dillman. (2004). The influence of graphic and symbolic language manipulations on response to self-administered questions. *Public Opinion Quarterly,* 68:57–80.

Christian, Sue Ellen, and Maria Knight Lapinski. (2003). Support for the contact hypothesis: High school students' attitudes toward Muslims post 9–11. *Journal of Intercultural Communication Research,* 32:247–263.

Christians, Clifford G. (2003). Ethics and politics in qualitative research. In *The Landscape of qualitative research,* 2nd ed., edited by N. Denzin and Y. Lincoln, pp. 208–244. Thousand Oaks CA: Sage.

Church, Allan H. (1993). Estimating the effect of incentives on mail survey response rates: A meta analysis. *Public Opinion Quarterly,* 57:62–80.

Churchill, Gilbert A., Jr. (1983). *Marketing research: Methodological foundations,* 3rd ed. New York: Dryden.

Cicourel, Aaron. (1964). *Method and measurement in sociology.* Glencoe, IL: Free Press.

Cicourel, Aaron. (1973). *Cognitive sociology.* London: Macmillan.

Cicourel, Aaron. (1982). Interviews, surveys, and the problem of ecological validity. *American Sociologist,* 17:11–20.

Clammer, John. (1984). Approaches to ethnographic research. In *Ethnographic research: A guide to general conduct,* edited by R. F. Ellen, pp. 63–85. Orlando: Academic Press.

Clark, Herbert H., and Michael F. Schober. (1992). Asking questions and influencing answers. In *Questions about questions: Inquiries into the cognitive bases of surveys,* edited by J. Turner, pp. 15–48. New York: Russell Sage Foundation.

Clarke, Michael. (1975). Survival in the field: Implications of personal experience in field work. *Theory and Society,* 2:95–123.

Clemens, Elizabeth, and Walter Powell. (1995). Careers in print: Books, journals, and scholarly reputations. *American Journal of Sociology,* 101:433–497.

Clogg, Clifford C., and D. O. Sawyer. (1981). A comparison of alternative models for analyzing the scalability of response patterns. In *Sociological methodology 1981,* edited by S. Leinhardt, pp. 240–280. San Francisco: Jossey-Bass.

Clubb, Jerome M., E. Austin, C. Geda, and M. Traugott. (1985). Sharing research data in the social sciences. In *Sharing research data,* edited by S. Fineberg, M. Martin, and M. Straf, pp. 39–88. Washington, DC: National Academy Press.

Cogan, Johan, Judith Torney-Purta, and Douglas Anderson. (1988). Knowledge and attitudes toward global issues: Students in Japan and the United States. *Comparative Education Review,* 32:283–297.

Cohen, Patricia Cline. (1982). *A calculating people: The spread of numeracy in early America.* Chicago: University of Chicago Press.

Cohen, Stephen R. (1991). The Pittsburg survey and the social survey movement: A sociological road not taken. In *The social survey in historical perspective, 1880–1940,* edited by M. Blumer, K. Bales, and K. Sklar, pp. 245–268. New York: Cambridge University Press.

Cole, Jonathan R., and Stephen Cole. (1973). *Social stratification in science.* Chicago: University of Chicago Press.

Cole, Stephen. (1978). Scientific reward systems: A comparative analysis. *Research in the Sociology of Knowledge, Science and Art,* 1:167–190.

Cole, Stephen. (1983). The hierarchy of the sciences? *American Journal of Sociology,* 89:111–139.

Cole, Stephen. (1994). Why sociology doesn't make progress like the natural sciences. *Sociological Forum,* 9:133–154.

Cole, Stephen, Jonathan Cole, and Gary A. Simon. (1981). Chance and consensus in peer review. *Science,* 214:881–885.

Coleman, James, and Thomas Hoffer. (1987). *Public and private schools: The impact of community.* New York: Basic Books.

Collins, H. M. (1983). The sociology of scientific knowledge: Studies of contemporary science. *American Review of Sociology,* 9:265–285.

Collins, Randall. (1984). Statistics versus words. *Sociological Theory,* 2:329–362.

Collins, Randall. (1986). Is 1980s sociology in the doldrums? *American Journal of Sociology,* 91: 1336–1355.

Collins, Randall. (1988). *Theoretical sociology.* New York: Harcourt Brace Jovanovich.

Collins, Randall. (1989). Sociology: Proscience or anti-science? *American Sociological Review,* 54:124–139.

Collins, Randall. (1994). Why the social sciences won't become high-consensus, rapid-discovery science. *Sociological Forum,* 9:155–177.

Collins, Randall, and Sal Restivo. (1983). Development, diversity and conflict in the sociology of science. *Sociological Quarterly,* 24:185–200.

Comaroff, John, and Jean Comaroff. (1992). *Ethnography and the historical imagination.* Boulder, CO: Westview.

Committees on the Status of Women in Sociology. (1986). *The treatment of gender in research.* Washington, DC: American Sociological Association.

Connell, R. W. (1990). Notes on American sociology and American power. In *Sociology in America,* edited by H. Gans, pp. 265–271. Thousand Oaks, CA: Sage.

Conrad, Frederick, and Michael Schober. (2000). Clarifying question meaning in a household telephone survey. *Public Opinion Quarterly,* 64:1–28.

Contrad, Peter, and Shulamit Reinharz. (1984). Computers and qualitative data: Editors' introductory essay. *Qualitative Sociology,* 7:3–15.

Converse, Jean M. (1984). Strong arguments and weak evidence: The open/closed questioning controversy of the 1940s. *Public Opinion Quarterly,* 48:267–282.

Converse, Jean M. (1987). *Survey research in the United States: Roots and emergence, 1890–1960.* Berkeley: University of California Press.

Converse, Jean M., and Stanley Presser. (1986). *Survey questions: Handcrafting the standardized questionnaire.* Beverly Hills, CA: Sage.

Cook, Judith A., and Mary Margaret Fonow. (1990). Knowledge and women's interests: Issues of epistemology and methodology in feminist sociological research. In *Feminist research methods,* edited by J. McCarl Nielsen, pp. 69–93. Boulder, CO: Westview.

Cook, Thomas D., and Donald T. Campbell. (1979). *Quasi-experimentation: Design and analysis issues for field settings.* Chicago: Rand McNally.

Cooper, Harris M. (1984). *The integrative research review: A systematic approach.* Beverly Hills, CA: Sage.

Corsaro, William A. (1988). Routines in the peer culture of American and Italian nursery school children. *Sociology of Education,* 61:1–14.

Corsaro, William A. (1992). Cross-cultural analysis. In *Encyclopedia of Sociology,* Vol. 1, edited by E. and M. Borgatta, pp. 390–395. New York: Macmillan.

Corsaro, William. (1994). Discussion, debate, and friendship processes: Peer discourse in U.S. and Italian nursery schools. *Sociology of Education,* 67:1–26.

Corsaro, William A., and David Heise. (1990). Event structure models from ethnographic data. *Sociological Methodology,* 20:1–57.

Corsaro, William, and Luisa Molinari. (2000). Priming events and Italian children's transition from preschool to elementary school: Representations and action. *Social Psychology Quarterly,* 63:16–33.

Corsino, Louis. (1987). Fieldworkers blues: Emotional stress and research underinvolvement in fieldwork settings. *Social Science Journal,* 24: 275–285.

Coser, Lewis. (1981). The uses of classical sociological theory. In *The future of the sociological classics,* edited by Buford Rhea, pp. 170–182. Boston: George Allen and Unwin.

Costner, Herbert L. (1969). Theory, deduction and rules of correspondence. *American Journal of Sociology,* 75:245–263.

Costner, Herbert L. (1985). Theory, deduction and rules of correspondence. In *Causal models in the social sciences,* 2nd ed., edited by H. M. Blalock, Jr., pp. 229–250. New York: Aldine.

Cotter, Patrick R., Jeffrey Cohen, and Philip B. Coulter. (1982). Race of interview effects in telephone interviews. *Public Opinion Quarterly,* 46:278–286.

Couch, Carl J. (1987). Objectivity: A crutch and club for bureaucrats/subjectivity: A haven for lost souls. *Sociological Quarterly,* 28:105–118.

Couper, Mick. (1997). Survey introductions and data quality. *Public Opinion Quarterly,* 61:317–338.

Couper, Mick. (2000). Review: Web surveys. *Public Opinion Quarterly,* 64:464–495.

Couper, Mick, and Edith de Leeuw. (2003). Nonresponse in cross-cultural and cross-national surveys. In *Cross-cultural survey methods,* edited by J. Harkness, F. Van de Vijver, and P. Mohler, pp. 157–179. Hoboken NJ: Wiley.

Couper, Mick, and Robert Groves. (2004). Introductory interactions in telephone surveys and nonresponse. In *Standardization and tacit knowledge,* edited by Douglas W. Maynard, et al., pp. 161–177. New York: Wiley.

Couper, Mick, and Benjamin Rowe. (1996). Evaluation of a computer assisted self-interview component in a computer-assisted personal interview survey. *Public Opinion Quarterly,* 60:89–105.

Couper, Mick P., Eleanor Singer, et al. (1998). Participation in the 1990 decennial census. *American Politics Quarterly,* 26:59–81.

Couper, Mick, Eleanor Singer, and Roger Tourangeau. (2003). Understanding the effects of audio-CASI on self-reports of sensitive behavior. *Public Opinion Quarterly,* 67:385–395.

Couper, Mick, Roger Tourangeau, and Kristin Kenyon. (2004). Picture this! Exploring visual effects on web surveys. *Public Opinion Quarterly,* 68:255–266.

Couper, Mick P., Michael Traugott, and Mark Lamias. (2001). Web survey design and administration. *Public Opinion Quarterly,* 65:230–253.

Cox, Stephen, and William Davidson. (1995). A meta-analysis of alternative education programs. *Crime and Delinquency,* 41:219–230.

Cozby, Paul C. (1984). *Using computers in the behavioral sciences.* Palo Alto, CA: Mayfield.

Craib, Ian. (1984). *Modern social theory: From Parsons to Habermas.* New York: St. Martin's Press.

Crane, Diana. (1967). The gatekeepers of science: Some factors affecting the selection of articles for scientific journals. *American Sociologist,* 2:195–201.

Crane, Diana. (1972). *Invisible colleges.* Chicago: University of Chicago Press.

Crespi, Irving. (1987). Surveys as legal evidence. *Public Opinion Quarterly,* 51:84–91.

Cress, Daniel M., and David A. Snow. (1996). Mobilization at the margins: Resources, benefactors, and the viability of homeless social movement organizations. *American Sociological Review,* 61:1089–1109.

Creswell, John W. (1994). *Research design: Qualitative and quantitative approaches.* Thousand Oaks, CA: Sage.

Croyle, Robert T., and Elizabeth Loftus. (1992). Improving episodic memory performance of survey respondents. In *Questions about questions: Inquiries into the cognitive bases of surveys,* edited by J. Turner, pp. 95–101. New York: Russell Sage Foundation.

Crozat, Matthew. (1998). Are the times a-changin'? Assessing the acceptance of protest in Western democracies. In *The movement society,* edited by D. Meyer and S. Tarrow, pp. 59–81. Totowa, NJ: Rowman and Littlefield.

Cullen, Francis T., Bruce Link, and Craig Polanzi. (1982). The seriousness of crime revisited: Have attitudes toward white collar crime changed? *Criminology,* 20:83–102.

Cumings, Bruce. (1997). Boundary displacement: Area studies and international studies during and after the Cold War." *Bulletin of Concerns of Asian Scholars,* 29:6–26.

Cummings, Scott. (1984). The political economy of funding for social science research. *Sociological Inquiry,* 54:154–170.

Curran, Daniel J., and Sandra Cook. (1993). Doing research in post-Tiananmen China. In *Research on sensitive topics,* edited by C. Renzetti and R. Lee, pp. 71–81. Thousand Oaks, CA: Sage.

Czaja, Ronald, Johnny Blair, and Jutta P. Sebestik. (1982). Respondent selection in a telephone survey: A comparison of three techniques. *Journal of Marketing Research,* 19:381–385.

Dabbs, James M., Jr. (1982). Making things visible. In *Varieties of qualitative research,* edited by J. Van Maanen, J. Dabbs, Jr., and R. R. Faulkner, pp. 31–64. Beverly Hills, CA: Sage.

Dale, Angela, S. Arber, and Michael Procter. (1988). *Doing secondary analysis.* Boston: Unwin Hyman.

Danermark, Berth, M. Ekström, L. Jakobsen, and J. Karlsson. (2002). *Explaining society.* New York: Routledge.

D'Antonio, William V. (August 1989). Executive office report: Sociology on the move. *ASA Footnotes,* 17, p. 2.

D'Antonio, William V. (1992). Recruiting sociologists in a time of changing opportunities. In *Sociology and its publics: The forms and fates of disciplinary organization,* edited by T. Halliday and M. Janowitz, pp. 99–136. Chicago: University of Chicago Press.

Danziger, Kurt. (1988). The question of identity: Who participated in psychological experiments? In *The rise of experimentation in American psychology,* edited by J. Morawski, pp. 35–52. New Haven, CT: Yale University Press.

Danziger, Sandra K. (1979). On doctor watching: Fieldwork in medical settings. *Urban Life,* 7:513–532.

Darnton, Robert. (1978). The history of *mentalities.* In *Structure, consciousness and history,* edited by R. H. Brown and S. M. Lyman, pp. 106–136. New York: Cambridge University Press.

Davis, Darren W. (1997). The direction of race of interviewer effects among African-Americans: Donning the black mask. *American Journal of Political Science,* 41:309–322.

Davis, Fred. (1959). The cabdriver and his fare: Facets of a fleeting relationship. *American Journal of Sociology,* 65:158–165.

Davis, Fred. (1973). The Martian and the convert: Ontological polarities in social research. *Urban Life,* 2:333–343.

Davis, James A. (1985). *The logic of causal order.* Beverly Hills, CA: Sage.

Davis, James A. (1992). Changeable weather in a cooling climate atop the liberal plateau: Conversion and replacement in forty-two general social survey items, 1972–1989." *Public Opinion Quarterly,* 56:261–306.

Davis, James A., and Tom W. Smith. (1986). *General social surveys 1972–1986 cumulative codebook.* Chicago: National Opinion Research Center, University of Chicago.

Davis, James A., and Tom W. Smith. (1992). *The NORC General Social Survey: A user's guide.* Newbury Park, CA: Sage.

Dawes, R. M., and T. W. Smith. (1985). Attitude and opinion measurement. In *Handbook of social psychology,* 3rd ed., Vol. 1, edited by G. Lindzey and E. Aronson, pp. 509–566. New York: Random House.

Dean, John P., Robert L. Eichhorn, and Lois R. Dean. (1969). Fruitful informants for intensive interviewing. In *Issues in participant observation,* edited by G. McCall and J. L. Simmons, pp. 142–144. Reading, MA: Addison-Wesley.

Dean, John P., and William Foote Whyte. (1969). How do you know if the informant is telling the truth? In *Issues in participant observation,* edited by G. McCall and J. L. Simmons, pp. 105–115. Reading, MA: Addison-Wesley.

Deegan, Mary Jo. (1988). *Jane Addams and the men of the Chicago School, 1892–1918.* New Brunswick: Transaction.

De Heer, Wim. (1999). International response trends: Results from an international survey. *Journal of Official Statistics,* 15:129–142.

DeLamater, John, and Pat MacCorquodale. (1975). The effects of interview schedule variations on reported sexual behavior. *Sociological Methods and Research,* 4:215–236.

Dellinger, Kirsten, and Christine Williams. (2002). The locker room and the dorm room. *Social Problems* 49:242–57.

DeMaio, Theresa J. (1980). Refusals: Who, where and why? *Public Opinion Quarterly,* 44:223–233.

DeMaio, Theresa J. (1984). Social desirability and survey measurement: A review. In *Surveying subjective phenomena,* Vol. 2, edited by C. Turner and E. Martin, pp. 257–282. New York: Russell Sage Foundation.

Denzin, Norman K. (1970). Symbolic interactionism and ethnomethodology. In *Understanding everyday life,* edited by J. Douglas, pp. 261–286. Chicago: Aldine.

Denzin, Norman K. (1989). *The research act: A theoretical introduction to sociological methods,* 3rd ed. Englewood Cliffs, NJ: Prentice-Hall.

Denzin, Norman K., and Kai Erikson. (1982). On the ethics of disguised observation: An exchange. In *Social research ethics,* edited by M. Blume. New York: Macmillan.

Denzin, Norman K., and Yvonna S. Lincoln, eds. (1994). Introduction: Entering the field of qualitative research. In *Handbook of qualitative research,* pp. 1–18. Thousand Oaks, CA: Sage.

Denzin, Norman K., and Yvonna S. Lincoln. (2003a). Introduction. In *Strategies of Qualitative Inquiry,* 2nd ed., edited by N. Denzin and Y. Lincoln, pp. 1–45. Thousand Oaks CA: Sage.

Denzin, Norman K., and Yvonna S. Lincoln. (2003b). Introduction. In *The landscape of qualitative research,* 2nd ed., edited by N. Denzin and Y. Lincoln, pp. 1–45. Thousand Oaks CA: Sage.

Derksen, Linda, and John Gartell. (1992). Scientific explanation. In *Encyclopedia of sociology,* Vol. 4, edited by E. and M. Borgatta, pp. 1711–1720. New York: Macmillan.

Desan, Susanne. (1989). Crowds, community and ritual in the work of E. P. Thompson and Natalie Davis. In *The new cultural history,* edited by L. Hunt, pp. 24–46. Berkeley: University of California Press.

Devault, Marjorie L. (1990). Talking and listening from women's standpoint: Feminist strategies for interviewing and analysis. *Social Problems,* 37:96–116.

deVaus, D. A. (1986). *Surveys in social research.* Boston: George Allen and Unwin.

Dexter, Lewis A. (1970). *Elite and specialized interviewing.* Evanston, IL: Northwestern University Press.

Diamond, Sigmund. (1988). Informed consent and survey research: The FBI and the University of Michigan Survey Research Center. In *Surveying social life: Papers in honor of Herbert H. Hyman,* edited by H. O'Gorman, pp. 72–99. Middletown, CT: Wesleyan University Press.

Dibble, Vernon K. (1963). Four types of inference from documents to events. *History and Theory,* 3:203–221.

Dickson, David. (1984). *The new politics of science.* Chicago: University of Chicago Press.

Diener, Edward, and Rick Crandall. (1978). *Ethics in social and behavioral research.* Chicago: University of Chicago Press.

Dijkstra, Wil, and Johannes van der Zouwen, eds. (1982). *Response behavior in the survey interview.* New York: Academic Press.

Dillman, Don A. (1978). *Mail and telephone surveys: The total design method.* New York: Wiley.

Dillman, Don A. (1983). Mail and other self-administered questionnaires. In *Handbook of survey research,* edited by P. Rossi, J. Wright, and A. Anderson, pp. 359–377. Orlando, FL: Academic Press.

Dillman, Don A. (1991). The design and administration of mail surveys. *Annual Review of Sociology,* 17: 225–249.

Dillman, Don A. (2000). *Mail and Internet surveys: The tailored design method,* 2nd ed. New York: Wiley.

Dillman, Don, and Cleo Redline. (2004). Testing paper self-administered questionnaires. In *Methods for testing and evaluating survey questionnaires,* edited by Stanley Presser et al., pp. 299–318. New York: Wiley.

Dillman, Don A., Eleanor Singer, Jon Clark, and James Treat. (1996). Effects of benefits, appeals, mandatory appeals and variations in statements of confidentiality on completion rates for census questionnaires. *Public Opinion Quarterly,* 60:376–389.

Dohan, Daniel, and Martin Sanchez-Jankowski. (1998). Using computers to analysis ethnographic field data. *Annual Review of Sociology,* 24:477–498.

Donald, Robert B. et al. (1983). *Writing clear paragraphs,* 2nd ed. Englewood Cliffs, NJ: Prentice-Hall.

Dooley, David. (1984). *Social research methods.* Englewood Cliffs, NJ: Prentice-Hall.

Douglas, Jack D. (1976). *Investigative social research.* Beverly Hills, CA: Sage.

Douglas, Jack D. (1985). *Creative interviewing.* Beverly Hills, CA: Sage.

Douglas, Jack D., and Paul K. Rasmussen. (1977). *The nude beach.* Beverly Hills, CA: Sage.

Drass, Kriss. (1980). The analysis of qualitative data: A computer program. *Urban Life,* 9:332–353.

Dressler, William H. (1991). *Stress and adaptation in the context of culture: Depression in a southern black community.* Albany: State University of New York Press.

DuBois, W. E. Burghardt. (1899). *The Philadelphia Negro.* New York: Benjamin Bloom.

Dukes, Richard, Tara Bisel, Karoline Borega, Eligio Lobato, and Matthew Owens. (2003). Expressions of love, sex, and hurt in popular songs: A content analysis of all-time greatest hits." *The Social Science Journal,* 40:643–650.

Dunaway, David K., and Willa K. Baum, eds. (1984). *Oral history.* Nashville, TN: Association for State and Local History.

Duncan, Otis Dudley. (1975). *Introduction to structural equation models.* New York: Academic Press.

Duncan, Otis Dudley. (1984). *Notes on social measurement: Historical and critical.* New York: Russell Sage Foundation.

Duncan, Otis Dudley, and Magnus Stenbeck. (1988). No opinion or not sure? *Public Opinion Quarterly,* 52:513–525.

Duneier, Mitchell. (1999). *Sidewalk.* New York: Farrar, Straus and Giroux.

Durkheim, Émile. (1938). *Rules of the sociological method,* trans. Sarah Solovay and John Mueller, edited by G. Catlin. Chicago: University of Chicago Press.

Dykema, Jennifer, and Nora Cate Schaeffer. (2000). Events, instruments, and reporting errors. *American Sociological Review,* 65:619–629.

Dynes, Russell R. (1984). The institutionalization of COSSA. *Sociological Inquiry,* 54:211–229.

Earl, Jennifer, Andres Martin, John McCarthy, and Sarah Soule. (2004). The use of newspaper data in the study of collective behavior. *Annual Review of Sociology,* 30:65–80.

Easterday, Lois, Diana Papademas, Laura Schorr, and Catherine Valentine. (1982). The making of a female researcher: Role problems in fieldwork. In *Field research,* edited by

R. G. Burgess, pp. 62–67. Boston: George Allen and Unwin.

Eastrope, Gary. (1974). *History of social research methods.* London: Longman.

Eckberg, Douglas Lee, and Lester Hill, Jr. (1979). The paradigm concept and sociology. *American Sociological Review,* 44:937–947.

Economist. (2001) What's your poison? *The Economist,* March 31, 2001.

Eder, Donna. (1981). Ability grouping as a self-fulfilling prophecy: A microanalysis of teacher–student interaction. *Sociology of Education,* 54: 151–162.

Eder, Donna. (1985). The cycle of popularity: Interpersonal relations among female adolescents. *Sociology of Education,* 58:154–165.

Eder, Donna. (1995). *School talk: Gender and adolescent culture.* New Brunswick, NJ: Rutgers University Press.

Eder, Donna, and David Kinney. (1995). The effect of middle school extracurricular activities on adolescents' popularity and peer status. *Youth and Society,* 26:298–325.

Edward, G. Franklin. (1974). E. Franklin Frazier. In *Black sociologists: Historical and contemporary perspectives,* edited by J. Blackwell and M. Janowitz, pp. 85–117. Chicago: University of Chicago Press.

Edwards, Allen L. (1957). *Techniques of attitude scale construction.* New York: Appleton-Century-Crofts.

Edwards, Rosalind. (1993). An education in interviewing: Placing the researcher and research. In *Research on sensitive topics,* edited by C. Renzetti and R. Lee, pp. 181–196. Thousand Oaks, CA: Sage.

Egerton, Muriel. (2002). Higher education and civic engagement. *British Journal of Sociology,* 53:603–621.

Eichler, Margrit. (1988). *Nonsexist research methods: A practical guide.* Boston: George Allen and Unwin.

Einwohner, Rachel. (2003). Opportunity, honor, and action in the Warsaw Ghetto uprising of 1943. *American Journal of Sociology,* 109:650–675.

Elder, Glen H., Jr., Eliza Pavalko, and Elizabeth Clipp. (1993). *Working with archival data: Studying lives.* Thousand Oaks, CA: Sage.

Elder, Joseph W. (1973). Problems of cross-cultural methodology: Instrumentation and interviewing in India. In *Comparative social research,*

edited by M. Armer and A. D. Grimshaw, pp. 119–144. New York: Wiley.

Eliasoph, Nina. (1998). *Avoiding politics: How Americans produce apathy in everyday life.* New York: Cambridge University Press.

Ellen, R. F., ed. (1984a). *Ethnographic research: A guide to general conduct.* Orlando: Academic Press.

Ellen, R. F. (1984b). Some other interactionist methods. In *Ethnographic research: A guide to general conduct,* edited by R. F. Ellen, pp. 273–293. Orlando: Academic Press.

Ember, Carol R. (1977). Cross-cultural cognitive studies. *Annual Review of Anthropology,* 6:33–56.

Ember, Carol R., and Melvin Ember. (2001). *Cross cultural research methods.* Lanham MD: Altamira Press.

Emerson, Robert M. (1981). Observational field work. *Annual Review of Sociology,* 7:351–378.

Emerson, Robert M. (1983). Introduction. In *Contemporary field research,* edited by R. M. Emerson, pp. 1–16. Boston: Little, Brown.

Emerson, Robert M., Rachel Fretz, and Linda Shaw. (1995). *Writing ethnographic field notes.* Chicago: University of Chicago Press.

Emigh, Rebecca Jean. (1997). The power of negative thinking: The use of negative case methodology in the development of sociological theory. *Theory and Society,* 26:649–684.

Emigh, Rebecca Jean. (2003). Economic interests and structural relations: The underdevelopment of capitalism in fifteenth-century Tuscany. *American Journal of Sociology,* 108:1075–1113.

Ennis, James G. (1992). The social organization of sociological knowledge: Modeling the intersection of specialties. *American Sociological Review,* 57:259–265.

ERIC. (October 1, 1976). The faculty work week at the University of Connecticut. ERIC Database# ED142157.

Erikson, Kai T. (1970). A comment on disguised observation in sociology. In *Qualitative methodology,* edited by W. J. Filstead, pp. 252–260. Chicago: Markham.

Erikson, Kai T. (1978). *Everything in its path.* New York: Touchstone.

Eschholz, Sarah, and Jana Bufkin. (2001). Crime in the movies: Investigating the efficacy of measures of both sex and gender for predicting victimization and offending in film. *Sociological Forum,* 16: 655–676.

Eschholz, Sarah, Jana Bufkin, and Jenny Long. (2001). Symbolic reality bites: Women and racial/ethnic minorities in modern film. *Sociological Spectrum,* 22:299–334.

Evans, Peter, and John D. Stephens. (1989). Studying development since the sixties: The emergence of a new comparative political economy. *Theory and Society,* 17:713–746.

Fantasia, Rick. (1988). *Cultures of solidarity: Consciousness, action and contemporary American workers.* Berkeley: University of California Press.

Faris, R. E. L. (1967). *Chicago sociology, 1920–1932.* San Francisco: Chandler.

Fay, Brian. (1975). *Social theory and political practice.* London: George Allen and Unwin.

Fay, Brian. (1987). *Critical social science: Liberation and its limits.* Ithaca, NY: Cornell University Press.

Featherman, David L., and Richard C. Rockwell. (1992). Social science research council. In *Encyclopedia of sociology,* Vol. 4, edited by E. and M. Borgatta, pp. 1942–1945. New York: Macmillan.

Ferriss, Abbott L. (1988). The uses of social indicators. *Social Forces,* 66:601–617.

Fetterman, David M. (1989). *Ethnography: Step by step.* Newbury Park, CA: Sage.

Fetzer, Joel S. (2000). *Public attitudes toward immigration in the United States, France and Germany.* New York: Cambridge University Press.

Fichter, Joseph H., and William L. Kolb. (1970). Ethical limitations on sociological reporting. In *Qualitative methodology,* edited by W. J. Filstead, pp. 261–270. Chicago: Markham.

Fielding, Nigel G., and Raymond M. Lee, eds. (1991). *Using computers in qualitative research.* Newbury Park, CA: Sage.

Fine, Gary Alan. (1979). Small groups and culture creation: The idioculture of Little League baseball teams. *American Sociological Review,* 44: 733–745.

Fine, Gary Alan. (1980). Cracking diamonds: Observer role in Little League baseball settings and the acquisition of social competence. In *Fieldwork experience,* edited by

W. B. Shaffir, R. A. Stebbins, and A. Turowetz, pp. 117–132. New York: St. Martin's Press.

Fine, Gary Alan. (1987). *With the boys: Little League baseball and preadolescent culture.* Chicago: University of Chicago Press.

Fine, Gary Alan. (1988). The ten commandments of writing. *The American Sociologist,* 19:152–157.

Fine, Gary Alan. (1990). Organizational time: The temporal experience of restaurant kitchens. *Social Forces,* 69:95–114.

Fine, Gary Alan. (1992). The culture of production: Aesthetic choices and constraints in culinary work. *American Journal of Sociology,* 97: 1268–1294.

Fine, Gary Alan. (1996). *Kitchens: The culture of restaurant work.* Berkeley: University of California Press.

Fine, Gary Alan. (1999). Field labor and ethnographic reality. *Journal of Contemporary Ethnography,* 28:532–540.

Fine, Gary Alan, and Barry Glassner. (1979). Participant observation with children: Promise and problems. *Urban Life,* 8:153–174.

Finkel, Steven E., Thomas M. Guterbock, and Marian J. Borg. (1991). Race-of-interviewer effects in a preelection poll: *Virgina* 1989. *Public Opinion Quarterly,* 55:313–330.

Finley, M. I. (Summer 1977). Progress in historiography. *Daedalus,* pp. 125–142.

Finsterbusch, Kurt, and Annabelle Bender Motz. (1980). *Social research for policy decisions.* Belmont, CA: Wadsworth.

Finsterbusch, Kurt, and C. P. Wolf. (1981). *Methodology of social impact assessment.* Stroudsburg, PA: Hutchinson Ross.

Firebaugh, Glenn. (1980). Cross-national versus historical regression models. *Comparative Social Research,* 3:333–344.

Firebaugh, Glenn, and Kevin Chen. (1995). Vote turnout of nineteenth amendment women: The enduring effect of disenfranchisement. *American Journal of Sociology,* 100:972–996.

Fischer, Claude S. (1992). *America calling: A social history of the telephone to 1940.* Berkeley: University of California Press.

Fischer, Claude S. et al. (1996). *Inequality by design: Cracking the bell curve myth.* Princeton, NJ: Princeton University Press.

Fischer, David H. (1970). *Historians' fallacies: Towards a logic of historical thought.* New York: Harper & Row.

Fischer, Frank. (1985). Critical evaluation of public policy: A methodological case study. In *Critical theory and public life,* edited by J. Forester, pp. 231–257. Cambridge, MA: MIT Press.

Fiske, Donald W. (1982). Convergent-discriminant validation in measurements and research strategies. In *Forms of validation in research,* edited by D. Brinberg and L. H. Kidder, pp. 72–92. San Francisco: Jossey-Bass.

Fiske, Edward B. (July 12, 1989). The misleading concept of "average" on reading tests changes, and more students fall below it. *New York Times.*

Fletcher, Colin. (1974). *Beneath the surface: An account of three styles of sociological research.* Boston: Routledge and Kegan Paul.

Flick, Uwe. (1998). *An introduction to qualitative research.* Thousand Oaks, CA: Sage.

Flora, Cornelia Butler. (1979). Changes in women's status in women's magazine fiction: Differences by social class. *Social Problems,* 26:558–569.

Foddy, William. (1993). *Constructing questions for interviews and questionnaires: Theory and practice in social research.* New York: Cambridge University Press.

Foddy, William. (1995). Probing: A dangerous practice in social surveys? *Quality and Quantity,* 29:73–86.

Fontana, Andrea, and James H. Frey. (1994). Interviewing: The art of science. In *Handbook of qualitative research,* edited by N. Denzin and Y. Lincoln, pp. 361–376. Thousand Oaks, CA: Sage.

Form, Willam H. (1973). Field problems in comparative research. In *Comparative social research,* edited by M. Armer and A. D. Grimshaw, pp. 83–117. New York: Wiley.

Foster, Gary S., Richard L. Hummel, and Donald J. Adamchak. (1998). Patterns of conception, natality and mortality from midwestern cemeteries: A sociological analysis of historical data. *Sociological Quarterly,* 39:473–490.

Fowler, Edward. (1996). *San'ya blues: Laboring life in contemporary Tokyo.* Ithaca, NY: Cornell University Press.

Fowler, Floyd J., Jr. (1984). *Survey research methods.* Beverly Hills, CA: Sage.

Fowler, Floyd J., Jr. (1992). How unclear terms can affect survey data. *Public Opinion Quarterly,* 56:218–231.

Fowler, Floyd J. (2004). The case for more split-sample experiments in developing survey instruments. In *Methods for testing and evaluating survey questionnaires,* edited by Stanley Presser et al., pp. 173–188. New York: Wiley.

Fowler, Floyd Jackson, and Charles Cannell. (1996). Using behavioral coding to identify cognitive problems with survey questions. In *Answering Questions,* edited by N. Schwarz and S. Sudman, pp. 15–36. San Francisco: Jossey-Bass.

Fox, James Alan, and Paul E. Tracy. (1986). *Randomized response: A method for sensitive surveys.* Beverly Hills, CA: Sage.

Fox, John. (1992). Statistical graphics. In *Encyclopedia of Sociology,* Vol. 4, edited by E. and M. Borgatta, pp. 2054–2073. New York: Macmillan.

Fox, Richard, Melvin R. Crask, and Jonghoon Kim. (1988). Mail survey response rate: A meta-analysis of selected techniques for inducing response. *Public Opinion Quarterly,* 52:467–491.

Franke, Charles O. (1983). Ethnography. In *Contemporary field research,* edited by R. M. Emerson, pp. 60–67. Boston: Little, Brown.

Franke, Richard H., and James D. Kaul. (1978). The Hawthorne experiments: First statistical interpretation. *American Sociological Review,* 43: 623–643.

Frankel, Martin. (1983). Sampling theory. In *Handbook of survey research,* edited by P. Rossi, J. Wright, and A. Anderson, pp. 21–67. Orlando, FL: Academic Press.

Franzosi, Roberto. (1998). Narrative analysis—or why (and how) sociologists should be interested in narrative. *Annual Review of Sociology,* 24: 517–554.

Frazier, E. Franklin. (1957). *The black bourgeoisie.* Glencoe, IL: Free Press.

Frechette-Schrader, Kristin. (1994). *Ethics of scientific research.* Lanham, MD: Rowland and Littlefield.

Freeman, Howard. (1983). *Applied sociology.* San Francisco: Jossey-Bass.

Freeman, Howard. (1992). Evaluation research. In *Encyclopedia of Sociology,* Vol. 2, edited by E. and M. Borgatta, pp. 594–598. New York: Macmillan.

Freeman, Howard, and Merrill J. Shanks, eds. (1983). The emergence of computer assisted survey research. *Sociological Methods and Research,* 23:115–230.

Freidson, Eliot. (1986). *Professional powers: A study of the institutionalization of formal knowledge.* Chicago: University of Chicago Press.

Freidson, Eliot. (1994). *Professionalism reborn: Theory, prophecy and policy.* Chicago: University of Chicago Press.

Freire, Paulo. (1970). *Pedagogy of the oppressed,* trans. Myra Bergman Ramos. New York: Seabury.

Frey, Frederick W. (1970). Cross-cultural survey research in political science. In *The methodology of comparative research,* edited by R. Holt and J. Turner, pp. 173–294. New York: Free Press.

Frey, James H. (1983). *Survey research by telephone.* Beverly Hills, CA: Sage.

Friedrichs, Robert W. (1970). *A sociology of sociology.* New York: Free Press.

Frost, Peter, and Ralph Stablein, eds. (1992). *Doing exemplary research.* Newbury Park, CA: Sage.

Fuchs, Stephan, and Jonathan H. Turner. (1986). What makes a science "mature"? Patterns of organizational control in scientific production. *Sociological Theory,* 4:143–150.

Fuller, Linda. (1988). Fieldwork in forbidden terrain: The U.S. state and the case of Cuba. *American Sociologist,* 19:99–120.

Fumento, Michael. (August, 1998). Road rage versus reality. *Atlantic Monthly,* 282:12–17.

Futrell, Robert, and Pete Simi. (2004). Free spaces, collective identity, and the persistence of U.S. White Power activism. *Social Problems* 51:16–42.

Galaskiewicz, Joseph. (1985). Professional networks and the institutionalization of a single mind set. *American Sociological Review,* 50:639–658.

Galaskiewicz, Joseph. (1987). The study of a business elite and corporate philanthropy in a United States metropolitan area. In *Research methods for elite studies,* edited by G. Moyser and M. Wagstaffe, pp. 147–165. Boston: George Allen and Unwin.

Galaskiewicz, Joseph, and Stanley Wasserman. (1993). Social network analysis: Concepts, methodology and directions for the 1990s. *Sociological Methods and Research,* 22:3–22.

Gallie, W. B. (1963). The historical understanding. *History and Theory,* 3:149–202.

Galliher, John F., and James L. McCartney. (1973). The influence of funding agencies on juvenile delinquency research. *Social Problems,* 21:77–90.

Gamson, William A. (1992). *Talking politics.* Cambridge: Cambridge University Press.

Ganahl, Dennis, Thomas Prinsen, and Sara Baker Netzley. (2003). Content analysis of prime time commercials: A contextual framework of gender representation. *Sex Roles: A Journal of Research,* 49:545–551.

Gangl, Markus. (2004). Welfare states and the scar effects of unemployment. *American Journal of Sociology,* 109:1319–1364.

Gans, Herbert J. (1982). The participant observer as a human being: Observations on the personal aspects of fieldwork. In *Field research,* edited by R. G. Burgess, pp. 53–61. Boston: George Allen and Unwin.

Garfinkel, Harold. (1967). *Studies in ethnomethodology.* Englewood Cliffs, NJ: Prentice-Hall.

Garfinkel, Harold. (1974a). The origins of the term "ethnomethodology." In *Ethnomethodology,* edited by R. Turner, pp. 15–18. Middlesex: Penguin.

Garfinkel, Harold. (1974b). The rational properties of scientific and common sense activities. In *Positivism and sociology,* edited by A. Giddens, pp. 53–74. London: Heinemann.

Gartell, C. David, and John W. Gartell. (1996). Positivism in sociological practice, 1967–1990. *Canadian Review of Sociology and Anthropology,* 33:143–159.

Gartell, C. David, and John W. Gartell. (2002). Positivism in sociological research: USA and UK (1966–1990). *British Journal of Sociology,* 53: 639–657.

Gaskell, George, Daniel Wright, and Colm O'Muircheartaigh. (2000). Telescoping landmark events. *Public Opinion Quarterly,* 64:77–89.

Gaston, Jerry. (1978). *The reward system in British and American science.* New York: Wiley.

Geer, John G. (1988). What do open-ended questions measure? *Public Opinion Quarterly,* 52:365–371.

Geertz, Clifford. (1973). *The interpretation of cultures.* New York: Basic Books.

Geertz, Clifford. (1979). From the native's point of view: On the nature of anthropological understanding. In *Interpretive social science: A reader,* edited by P. Rabinow and W. Sullivan, pp. 225–242. Berkeley: University of California Press.

Geiger, Roger L. (1986). *To advance knowledge: The growth of American research universities, 1900–1940.* New York: Oxford University Press.

Georges, Robert A., and Michael O. Jones. (1980). *People studying people.* Berkeley: University of California Press.

Gephart, Robert P., Jr. (1988). *Ethnostatistics: Qualitative foundations for quantitative research.* Newbury Park, CA: Sage.

Gibbs, Jack. (1989). Conceptualization of terrorism. *American Sociological Review,* 54:329–340.

Giddens, Anthony. (1976). *New rules of sociological method: Positivist critique of interpretative sociologies.* New York: Basic Books.

Giddens, Anthony. (1978). Positivism and its critics. In *A history of sociological analysis,* edited by T. Bottomore and R. Nisbet. New York: Basic Books.

Giddens, Anthony. (1994). Elites and power. In *Social stratification: Class, race & gender in sociological perspective,* edited by D. Grusky, pp. 170–174. Boulder, CO: Westview.

Gieryn, Thomas F. (1978). Problem retention and problem change in science. In *The sociology of science,* edited by J. Gaston. San Francisco: Jossey-Bass.

Gilbert, Margaret. (1992). *On social facts.* Princeton, NJ: Princeton University Press.

Gillespie, Richard. (1988). The Hawthorne experiments and the politics of experimentation. In *The rise of experimentation in American psychology,* edited by J. Morawski, pp. 114–137. New Haven, CT: Yale University Press.

Gillespie, Richard. (1991). *Manufacturing knowledge: A history of the Hawthorne experiments.* New York: Cambridge University Press.

Gilljam, Mikael, and David Granberg. (1993). Should we take Don't Know for an answer? *Public Opinion Quarterly,* 57:348–357.

Glaser, Barney, and Anselm Strauss. (1967). *The discovery of grounded theory.* Chicago: Aldine.

Glaser, Barney, and Anselm Strauss. (1968). *A time for dying.* Chicago: Aldine.

Glasser, Gerald J., and Gale O. Metzger. (1972). Random digit dialing as a method of telephone sampling. *Journal of Marketing Research,* 9:59–64.

Glucksmann, Miriam. (1974). *Structuralist analysis in contemporary social thought: A comparison of the theories of Claude Levi-Strauss and Louis Althusser.* Boston: Routledge and Kegan Paul.

Gold, Raymond L. (1969). Roles in sociological field observation. In *Issues in participant observation,* edited by G. J. McCall and J. L. Simmons, pp. 30–38. Reading, MA: Addison-Wesley.

Golden, Tim. (December 9, 1996). Universities find donors sometimes impose a price. *New York Times.*

Goldstein, Kenneth M., and M. Kent Jennings. (2002). The effect of advance letters on cooperation in a list sample telephone survey. *Public Opinion Quarterly,* 66:608–617.

Goldstein, Robert Justin. (1978). *Political repression in modern America.* New York: Schenckman.

Goldstone, Jack A. (1997). Methodological issues in comparative macrosociology. *Comparative Social Research,* 16: 107–120.

Goldthorpe, John. (1977). The relevance of history to sociology. In *Sociological research methods,* edited by M. Bulmer, pp. 178–191. London: Macmillan.

Goldthorpe, John. (1991). The uses of history in sociology: Reflections on some recent tendencies. *British Journal of Sociology,* 42:211–230.

Goldthorpe, John H. (1997). Current issues in comparative macrosociology: A debate on methodological issues. *Comparative Social Research,* 16:1–26.

Gonor, George. (1977). "Situation" versus "frame": The "interactionist" and the "structuralist" analysis of everyday life. *American Sociological Review,* 42:854–867.

Goode, Erica. (February 5, 2002) A rare day: The movies get mental illness right. *New York Times.*

Gorden, Raymond. (1980). *Interviewing: Strategy, techniques and tactics,* 3rd ed. Homewood, IL: Dorsey Press.

Gorden, Raymond. (1992). *Basic interviewing skills.* Itasca, IL: Peacock.

Gordon, David F. (1987). Getting close by staying distant: Fieldwork with

proselytizing groups. *Qualitative Sociology,* 10:267–287.

Gordon, Randall A., T. A. Bindrim, M. L. McNicholas, and T. L. Walden. (1988). Perceptions of blue-collar and white-collar crime: The effect of defendant race on simulated juror decisions. *Journal of Social Psychology,* 128:191–197.

Gorelick, Sherry. (1991). Contradictions of feminist methodology. *Gender and Society,* 5:459–477.

Gotham, Kevin Fox, and William G. Staples. (1996). Narrative analysis and the new historical sociology. *Sociological Quarterly,* 37:481–502.

Gould, Roger V. (1991). Multiple networks and mobilization in the Paris Commune, 1871. *American Sociological Review,* 56:716–729.

Gouldner, Alvin. (1970). *The coming crisis of Western sociology.* New York: Basic Books.

Gouldner, Alvin W. (1976). The dark side of the dialectic: Toward a new objectivity. *Sociological Inquiry,* 46:3–16.

Goward, Nicola. (1984a). Publications on fieldwork experiences. In *Ethnographic research: A guide to general conduct,* edited by R. F. Ellen, pp. 88–100. Orlando: Academic Press.

Goward, Nicola. (1984b). Personal interaction and adjustment. In *Ethnographic research: A guide to general conduct,* edited by R. F. Ellen, pp. 100–118. Orlando: Academic Press.

Gowda, Rajeev, and Jeffrey C. Fox, eds. (2002). *Judgments, decisions, and public policy.* New York: Cambridge University Press.

Goyder, John C. (1982). Factors affecting response rates to mailed questionnaires. *American Sociological Review,* 47:550–554.

Graham, Sandra. (1992). Most of the subjects were white and middle class: Trends in published research on African Americans in selected APA journals, 1970–1989. *American Psychologist,* 47:629–639.

Granovetter, Mark. (1976). Network sampling: Some first steps. *American Journal of Sociology,* 81:1287–1303.

Grant, Linda, Kathryn B. Ward, and Xue Lan Rong. (1987). Is there an association between gender and methods of sociological research? *American Sociological Review,* 52:856–862.

Gray, Bradford H. (1982). The regulatory context of social and behavioral research. In *Ethical issues in social science research,* edited by T. Beauchamp, R. Faden, R. J. Wallace, and L. Walters, pp. 329–354. Baltimore: Johns Hopkins University Press.

Gray, Paul S. (1980). Exchange and access in field work. *Urban Life,* 9:309–331.

Greenberg, Daniel S. (1967). *The politics of pure science.* New York: New American Library.

Greenwald, Howard P. (1992). Ethics in social research. In *Encyclopedia of sociology,* Vol. 2., edited by E. and M. Borgatta, pp. 584–588. New York: Macmillan.

Greenwood, Davydd, and Marten Levin. (2003). Reconstructing the relationships between universities and society through action research. In *The landscape of qualitative research,* 2nd ed., edited by N. Denzin and Y. Lincoln, pp. 131–166. Thousand Oaks CA: Sage.

Griffin, Larry J. (1992a). Temporality, events and explanation in historical sociology. *Sociological Methods and Research,* 20:403–427.

Griffin, Larry J. (1992b). Comparative-historical analysis. In *Encyclopedia of sociology,* Vol. 1, edited by E. and M. Borgatta, pp. 263–271. New York: Macmillan.

Griffin, Larry J. (1993). Narrative, event structure analysis and causal interpretation in historical sociology. *American Journal of Sociology,* 98:1094–1133.

Griffin, Larry J., and Charles Ragin. (1994). Some observations on formal methods of qualitative analysis. *Sociological Methods and Research,* 23:4–22.

Griffin, Larry J., Michael E. Wallace, and Beth A. Rubin. (1986). Capitalist resistance to the organization of labor before the New Deal: Why? How? Success? *American Sociological Review,* 51:147–167.

Grimshaw, Allen D. (1973). Comparative sociology. In *Comparative social research,* edited by M. Armer and A. Grimshaw, pp. 3–48. New York: Wiley.

Grinnell, Frederick. (1987). *The scientific attitude.* Boulder, CO: Westview.

Griswold, Wendy. (1983). The devil's techniques: Cultural legitimation and social change. *American Sociological Review,* 48:668–680.

Griswold, Wendy. (1987). A methodological framework for the sociology of culture. In *Sociological methodology, 1987,* edited by C. Clogg, pp. 1–35. San Francisco: Jossey-Bass.

Griswold, Wendy. (1994). *Cultures and societies in a changing world.* Thousand Oaks, CA: Pine Forge Press.

Griswold, Wendy, and Nathan Wright. (2004). Cowbirds, locals, and the dynamic endurance of regionalism. *American Journal of Sociology,* 109:1411–1451.

Groff, Ruth. (2004). *Critical realism, post-positivism, and the possibility of knowledge.* New York: Routledge.

Grosof, Miriam, and Hyman Sandy. (1985). *A research primer for the social and behavioral sciences.* Orlando: FL: Academic Press.

Gross, Daniel R. (1984). Time allocation: A tool for the study of cultural behavior. *Annual Review of Anthropology,* 13:519–558.

Groves, Robert M. (1996). How do we know what we think they think is really what they think? In *Answering Questions,* edited by N. Schwarz and S. Sudman, pp. 389–402. San Francisco: Jossey-Bass.

Groves, Robert M., and Mick Couper. (1996). Contact level uniqueness and cooperation in face-to-face surveys. *Journal of Official Statistics,* 12: 63–83.

Groves, Robert M., and Mick Couper. (1998). *Nonresponse in household interview surveys.* New York: Wiley.

Groves, Robert M., Nancy H. Fultz, and Elizabeth Martin. (1992). Direct questioning about comprehension in a survey setting. In *Questions about questions: Inquiries into the cognitive bases of surveys,* edited by J. Turner, pp. 49–61. New York: Russell Sage Foundation.

Groves, Robert M., and Robert L. Kahn. (1979). *Surveys by telephone: A national comparison with personal interviews.* New York: Academic Press.

Groves, Robert M., and Nancy Mathiowetz. (1984). Computer assisted telephone interviewing: Effects on interviewers and respondents. *Public Opinion Quarterly,* 48:356–369.

Groves, Robert M., Stanley Presser, and Sarah Dipko. (2004). The role of topic interest in survey participation decisions. *Public Opinion Quarterly,* 68:2–31.

Groves, Robert M., Eleanor Singer, and Amy Corning. (2000). Leverage-saliency theory of survey participation. *Public Opinion Quarterly,* 64:299–308.

Guba, Egon G., and Yvonna S. Lincoln. (1994). Competing paradigms in qualitative research. In *Handbook of qualitative research,* edited by N. Denzin and Y. Lincoln, pp. 105–117. Thousand Oaks, CA: Sage.

Gubrium, Jaber F., and James A. Holstein. (1992). Qualitative methods. *Encyclopedia of sociology,* Vol. 3, edited by E. and M. Borgatta, pp. 1577–1582. New York: Macmillan.

Gubrium, Jaber F., and James A. Holstein. (1998). Narrative practice and the coherence of personal stories. *Sociological Quarterly,* 39:163–187.

Gurevitch, Z. D. (1988). The other side of the dialogue: On making the other strange and the experience of otherness. *American Journal of Sociology,* 93:1179–1199.

Gurney, Joan Neff. (1985). Not one of the guys: The female researcher in a male-dominated setting. *Qualitative Sociology,* 8:42–62.

Gusfield, Joseph. (1976). The literary rhetoric of science: Comedy and pathos in drinking driver research. *American Sociological Review,* 41:16–34.

Gustavsen, Bjørn. (1986). Social research as participatory dialogue. In *The use and abuse of social science,* edited by F. Heller, pp. 143–156. Beverly Hills, CA: Sage.

Gustin, Bernard H. (1973). Charisma, recognition and the motivation of scientists. *American Journal of Sociology,* 86:1119–1134.

Gutterbock, Thomas M. (1997). Review: Why *Money* magazine's "Best Places" keep changing. *Public Opinion Quarterly,* 61:339–355.

Guttman, Louis. (1950). The basis for scalogram analysis. In *Measurement and prediction,* edited by S. A. Stouffer, L. Buttman, E. A. Suchman, P. F. Lazarfeld, S. A. Star, and J. A. Clausen, pp. 60–90. Princeton, NJ: Princeton University Press.

Guttman, Louis. (1970). A basis for scaling qualitative data. In *Attitude measurement,* edited by G. Summers, pp. 174–186. Chicago: Rand McNally.

Guy, Rebecca F., Charles E. Edgley, Ibtihaj Arafat, and Donald E. Allan.

(1987). *Social research methods: Puzzles and solutions.* Boston: Allyn and Bacon.

Haberman, Shelby J. (1978). *Analysis of qualitative data.* New York: Academic Press.

Habermas, Jurgen. (1971). *Knowledge and human interests.* Boston: Beacon.

Habermas, Jurgen. (1973). *Theory and practice.* Boston: Beacon.

Habermas, Jurgen. (1976). *Legitimation crisis.* Boston: Beacon.

Habermas, Jurgen. (1979). *Communication and the evolution of society.* Boston: Beacon.

Habermas, Jurgen. (1988). *On the logic of the social sciences.* Oxford: Polity.

Hagan, John. (1990). The gender stratification of income inequality among lawyers. *Social Forces,* 63:835–855.

Hage, Jerald. (1972). *Techniques and problems of theory construction in sociology.* New York: Wiley.

Hagstrom, Warren. (1965). *The scientific community.* New York: Basic Books.

Hakim, Catherine. (1987). *Research design: Strategies and choices in the design of social research.* Boston: Allen and Unwin.

Halfpenny, Peter. (1979). The analysis of qualitative data. *Sociological Review,* 27:799–823.

Halfpenny, Peter. (1982). *Positivism and sociology: Explaining social life.* London: George Allen and Unwin.

Hallin, Daniel C. (1985). The American news media: A critical theory perspective. In *Critical theory and public life,* edited by J. Forester, pp. 121–146. Cambridge, MA: MIT Press.

Hallowell, Lyle. (1985). *Ethical and legal problems of research: Professional workshop.* Presentation at the American Sociological Association annual meeting, Washington, DC, August 26.

Hammersley, Martyn. (1992). *What's wrong with ethnography? Methodological explorations.* New York: Routledge.

Hammersley, Martyn. (1995). Theory and evidence in qualitative research. *Quality and Quantity,* 29:55–66.

Hammersley, Martyn. (2000). Varieties of social research: A typology. *International Journal of Social Research Methodology,* 3:221–229.

Hammersley, Martyn, and Paul Atkinson. (1983). *Ethnography: Principles in practice.* London: Tavistock.

Hannan, Michael T. (1985). Problems of aggregation. In *Causal models in the social sciences,* 2nd ed., edited by H. Blalock, Jr., pp. 403–439. Chicago: Aldine.

Harari, Herbert, Oren Harari, and Robert V. White. (1985). The reaction to rape by American bystanders. *Journal of Social Psychology,* 125:653–658.

Harding, Sandra. (1986). *The science question in feminism.* Ithaca, NY: Cornell University Press.

Hargens, Lowell L. (1991). Impressions and misimpressions about sociology journals. *Contemporary Sociology,* 20:343–349.

Hargens, Lowell L. (1988). Scholarly consensus and journal rejection rates. *American Sociological Review,* 53:139–151.

Harkens, Shirley, and Carol Warren. (1993). The social relations of intensive interviewing: Constellations of strangeness and science. *Sociological Methods and Research,* 21:317–339.

Harkness, Janet. (2003). Questionnaire in translation. In *Cross-cultural survey methods,* edited by J. Harkness, F. Van de Vijver, and P. Mohler, pp. 35–56. Hoboken NJ: Wiley.

Harkness, Janet, Beth-Ellen Pennell, and Alisu Schoua-Glusberg. (2003). Survey questionnaire translation and assessment. In *Methods for testing and evaluating survey questionnaires,* edited by S. Presser et al., pp. 453–473. New York: Wiley.

Harkness, Janet, Fons van de Vijver, and Timothy Johnson. (2003). Questionnaire design in comparative research. In *Cross-cultural survey methods,* edited by J. Harkness, F. Van de Vijver, and P. Mohler, pp. 19–34. Hoboken, NJ: Wiley.

Harper, Douglas. (1982). *Good company.* Chicago: University of Chicago Press.

Harper, Douglas. (1987). *Working knowledge.* Chicago: University of Chicago Press.

Harper, Douglas. (1994). On the authority of the image: Visual methods at the crossroads. In *Handbook of qualitative research,* edited by N. Denzin and Y. Lincoln, pp. 403–412. Thousand Oaks, CA: Sage.

Harré, Rom. (1972). *The philosophies of science.* London: Oxford University Press.

Harré, R., and P. F. Secord. (1979). *The explanation of social behavior.* Totowa, NJ: Littlefield, Adams.

Harrington, Brooke. (2003). The social psychology of access in ethnographic research. *Journal of Contemporary Ethnography,* 32:592–625.

Harris, Benjamin. (1988). Key words: A history of debriefing in social psychology. In *The rise of experimentation in American psychology,* edited by J. Morawski, pp. 188–212. New Haven, CT: Yale University Press.

Harris, Marvin. (1976). History and significance of the emic/etic distinction. *Annual Review of Anthropology,* 5:329–350.

Harvey, Lee. (1990). *Critical social research.* London: Urwin Hyman.

Hastings, Philip K., and Dean R. Hodge. (1986). Religious and moral attitude trends among college students, 1948–84. *Social Forces,* 65:370–377.

Hauck, Matthew, and Michael Cox. (1974). Locating a sample by random digit dialing: Some hypotheses and a random sample. *Public Opinion Quarterly,* 38:253–260.

Hayano, David M. (1982). *Poker faces: The life and work of professional card players.* Berkeley: University of California Press.

Haydu, Jeffrey. (1998). Making use of the past: Time periods as cases to compare and as sequences of problem solving. *American Journal of Sociology,* 104:339–371.

Hazelrigg, Lawrence E. (1973). Aspects of the measurement of class consciousness. In *Comparative social research,* edited by M. Armer and A. D. Grimshaw, pp. 219–246. New York: Wiley.

Headland, Thomas, Kenneth Pike, and Marvin Harris, eds. (1990). *Emics and etics: The insider/outsider debate.* Beverly Hills CA: Sage.

Hearnshaw, L. S. (1979). *Cyril Burt: Psychologist.* London: Holder and Stoughten.

Heberlein, Thomas A., and Robert Baumgartner. (1978). Factors affecting response rates to mailed questionnaires: A quantitative analysis of the published literature. *American Sociological Review,* 43:447–462.

Heberlein, Thomas A., and Robert Baumgartner. (1981). Is a questionnaire necessary in a second mailing? *Public Opinion Quarterly,* 45:102–107.

Heckathorn, Douglas D. (1997). Respondent-driven sampling: A new approach to the study of hidden populations. *Social Problems,* 44: 174–199.

Heckathorn, Douglas D. (2002). Respondent-driven sampling II: Deriving valid population estimates from chain-referral samples of hidden populations. *Social Problems,* 49:11–35.

Hector, Michael. (1975). *Internal colonialism.* Berkeley: University of California Press.

Hegtvedt, Karen A. (1992). Replication. In *Encyclopedia of sociology,* Vol. 3, edited by E. and M. Borgatta, pp. 1661–1663. New York: Macmillan.

Heise, David. (1965). Semantic differential profiles for 1,000 most frequent English words. *Psychological Monographs,* 70, No. 8.

Heise, David. (1970). The semantic differential and attitude research. In *Attitude measurement,* edited by G. Summers, pp. 235–253. Chicago: Rand McNally.

Heise, David. (1974). Some issues in sociological measurement. In *Sociological methodology, 1973–74,* edited by H. L. Costner, pp. 1–16. San Francisco: Jossey-Bass.

Heise, David, ed. (1981). *Microcomputers in social research.* Beverly Hills, CA: Sage.

Heise, David. (1991). Event structure analysis. In *Using computers in qualitative research,* edited by N. Fielding and R. Lee, pp. 136–163. Newbury Park, CA: Sage.

Held, David. (1980). *Introduction to critical theory: Horkheimer to Habermas.* Berkeley: University of California Press.

Heller, Nelson B., and J. Thomas McEwen. (1973). Applications of crime seriousness information in police departments. *Journal of Criminal Justice,* 1:241–253.

Hendry, Joy. (1987). *Understanding Japanese society.* New York: Croom Helm.

Hendry, Joy (2003) *Understanding Japanese Society,* 3rd ed. New York: Routledge.

Henry, Gary T. (1990). *Practical sampling.* Newbury Park, CA: Sage.

Henry, Gary T. (1995). *Graphing data: Techniques for display and analysis.* Thousand Oaks, CA: Sage.

Herbert, Bob. (December 19, 2003) Change the channel. *New York Times.*

Herrera, C. D. (1999). Two arguments for "covert methods" in social research.

British Journal of Sociology, 50:331–343.

Herrnstein, Richard, and Charles Murray. (1994). *The bell curve: Intelligence and class structure in American life.* New York: Free Press.

Herting, Jerald R. (1985). Multiple indicator models using LISREL. In *Causal models in the social sciences,* 2nd ed., edited by H. Blalock, Jr., pp. 263–320. New York: Aldine.

Herting, Jerald R., and Herbert L. Costner. (1985). Re-specification in multiple indicator models. In *Causal models in the social sciences,* 2nd ed., edited by H. Blalock, Jr., pp. 321–394. Chicago: Aldine.

Herzberger, Sharon D. (1993). The cyclical pattern of child abuse: A study of research methodology. In *Research on sensitive topics,* edited by C. Renzetti and R. Lee, pp. 33–51. Thousand Oaks, CA: Sage.

Herzog, A. Regula, and Jerald G. Bachman. (1981). Effects of questionnaire length on response quality. *Public Opinion Quarterly,* 45:549–559.

Hesse, Mary B. (1970). *Models and analogies in science.* Notre Dame, IN: Notre Dame Press.

Hicks, David. (1984). Getting into the field and establishing routines. In *Ethnographic research: A guide to general conduct,* edited by R. F. Ellen, pp. 192–199. Orlando: Academic Press.

Higher Education Research Institute. (2004). *Recent findings.* www.gseis .ucla.edu/heri/findings.html

Hill, Michael R. (1993). *Archival strategies and techniques.* Thousand Oaks, CA: Sage.

Hiller, Harry H. (1979). Universality of science and the question of national sociologies. *American Sociologist,* 14:124–135.

Himmelstein, Jerome L., and Mayer Zald. (1984). American conservatism and government funding of the social sciences and arts. *Sociological Inquiry,* 54:171–187.

Hindess, Barry. (1973). *The use of official statistics in sociology: A critique of positivism and ethnomethodology.* New York: Macmillan.

Hippler, Hans J., and Norbert Schwarz. (1986). Not forbidding isn't allowing: The cognitive basis of the forbid–allow asymmetry. *Public Opinion Quarterly,* 50:87–96.

Hirschman, Albert O. (1970). *Exit, voice, and loyalty: Response to de-*

cline in firms, organizations and states. Cambridge, MA: Harvard University Press.

Hochschild, Arlie. (1978). *The unexpected community: Portrait of an old age subculture.* Berkeley: University of California Press.

Hochschild, Arlie. (1983). *The managed heart.* Berkeley: University of California Press.

Hochschild, Jennifer L. (1981). *What's fair? American beliefs about distributive justice.* Cambridge, MA: Harvard University Press.

Hodson, Randy. (1998). Organizational ethnographies: An underutilized resource in the sociology of work. *Social Forces,* 76:1173–208.

Hoffmann, Joan Eakin. (1980). Problems of access in the study of social elites and boards of directors. In *Fieldwork experience,* edited by W. B. Shaffir, R. A. Stebbins, and A. Turowetz, pp. 45–56. New York: St. Martin's Press.

Holbrook, Allyson, Melanie Green, and Jon Krosnick. (2003). Telephone versus face-to-face interviewing of national probability samples with long questionnaires. *Public Opinion Quarterly,* 67:79–125.

Hollander, Myles, and Frank Proschan. (1984). *The statistical exorcist: Dispelling statistics anxiety.* New York: Marcel Decker.

Hollis, Martin. (1977). *Models of man: Philosophical thoughts on social action.* New York: Cambridge University Press.

Holstein, James A., and Jaber F. Gubrium. (1994). Phenomenology, ethnomethodology and interpretative practice. In *Handbook of qualitative research,* edited by N. Denzin and Y. Lincoln, pp. 262–272. Thousand Oaks, CA: Sage.

Holsti, Ole R. (1968a). Content analysis. In *Handbook of social psychology,* 2nd ed., Vol. 2, edited by G. Lindzey and E. Aronson, pp. 596–692. Reading, MA: Addison-Wesley.

Holsti, Ole R. (1968b). *Content analysis for the social sciences and humanities.* Reading, MA: Addison-Wesley.

Holt, Robert T., and John E. Turner. (1970). The methodology of comparative research. In *The methodology of comparative research,* edited by R. Holt and J. Turner, pp. 1–20. New York: Free Press.

Holub, Robert C. (1991). *Jürgen Habermas: Critic in the public sphere.* New York: Routledge.

Holy, Ladislav. (1984). Theory, methodology and the research process. In *Ethnographic research: A guide to general conduct,* edited by R. F. Ellen, pp. 13–34. Orlando: Academic Press.

Homan, Roger. (1980). The ethics of covert methods. *British Journal of Sociology,* 31:46–57.

Honan, William H. (Jan. 22, 1997). Scholars attack public school TV program. *New York Times.*

Honigmann, John J. (1982). Sampling in ethnographic fieldwork. In *Field research,* edited by R. G. Burgess, pp. 79–90. Boston: Allen and Unwin.

Horan, Patrick. (1987). Theoretical models in social history research. *Social Science History,* 11:379–400.

Horn, Robert V. (1993). *Statistical indicators for the economic and social sciences.* Cambridge: Cambridge University Press.

Hornsby-Smith, M. P. (1974). The working life of the university lecturer. *Universities Quarterly,* 28:149–164.

Hornstein, Gail A. (1988). Quantifying psychological phenomena: Debates, dilemmas and implications. In *The rise of experimentation in American psychology,* edited by J. Morawski, pp. 1–34. New Haven, CT: Yale University Press.

Horowitz, Irving Louis. (1965). The life and death of Project Camelot. *Transaction,* 3:3–7, 44–47.

House, Ernest R. (1980). *Evaluating with validity.* Beverly Hills, CA: Sage.

Hoy, David Couzens. (1994). *Critical theory.* Cambridge, MA: Blackwell.

Hoynes, William. (May/June 1997). News for a captive audience extra. <http://www.fair.org/extra/9705/ch1-hoynes.html> November 2, 1998.

Hubbard, Raymond, and Eldon Little. (1988). Promised contributions to charity and mail survey responses: Replication with extension. *Public Opinion Quarterly,* 52:223–230.

Huck, Schuyler W., and Howard M. Sandler. (1979). *Rival hypotheses: Alternative interpretations of data based conclusions.* New York: Harper & Row.

Humphreys, Laud. (1975). *Tearoom trade: Impersonal sex in public places,* enlarged ed. Chicago: Aldine.

Hunt, Lynn. (1989). Introduction. In *The new cultural history,* edited by L.

Hunt, pp. 1–22. Berkeley: University of California Press.

Hunt, Morton. (1997). *How science takes stock: The story of meta-analysis.* New York: Russell Sage Foundation.

Hunter, John E., Frank L. Schmidt, and Gregg B. Jackson. (1982). *Meta-analysis: Cumulating research findings across studies.* Beverly Hills, CA: Sage.

Hyman, Herbert H. (1975). *Interviewing in social research.* Chicago: University of Chicago Press.

Hyman, Herbert H. (1991). *Taking society's measure: A personal history of survey research.* New York: Russell Sage.

Hymes, Dell. (1970). Linguistic aspects of comparative political research. In *The methodology of comparative research,* edited by R. Holt and J. Turner, pp. 295–341. New York: Free Press.

Hymes, Dell. (1983). *Essays in the history of linguistic anthropology.* Philadelphia: John Benjamins Publishers.

Inverarity, James M. (1976). Populism and lynching in Louisiana, 1889–1896: A test of Erikson's theory of the relationship between boundary crisis and repressive justice. *American Sociological Review,* 41:262–280.

Isaac, Larry W., and Larry J. Griffin. (1989). A historicism in time series analysis of historical process: Critique, redirection, and illustrations from U.S. labor history. *American Sociological Review,* 54:873–890.

Isaac, Larry W., Debra A. Street, and Stan J. Knapp. (1994). Analyzing historical contingency with formal methods: The case of the "relief explosion" and 1968. *Sociological Methods and Research,* 23:114–141.

Jackson, Bruce. (1978). Killing time: Life in the Arkansas penitentiary. *Qualitative Sociology,* 1:21–32.

Jackson, Bruce. (1987). *Fieldwork.* Urbana: University of Illinois Press.

Jackson, David J., and Edgar F. Borgatta, eds. (1981). *Factor analysis and measurement in sociological research.* Beverly Hills, CA: Sage.

Jacob, Herbert. (1984). *Using published data: Errors and remedies.* Beverly Hills, CA: Sage.

Jaeger, Richard M. (1983). *Statistics as a spectator sport.* Beverly Hills, CA: Sage.

Jennings, M. Kent, and Vicki Zeitner. (2003). Internet use and civic engagement: A longitudinal analysis. *Public Opinion Quarterly,* 67: 311–334.

Johnson, Bruce. (1982). Missionaries, tourists and traders. *Studies in Symbolic Interaction,* 4:115–150.

Johnson, David Richard, and James C. Creech. (1983). Ordinal measures in multiple indicator models: A simulation study of categorization error. *American Sociological Review,* 48:398–407.

Johnson, David W., and Roger T. Johnson. (1985). Relationships between black and white students in intergroup cooperation and competition. *Journal of Social Psychology,* 125: 421–428.

Johnson, John M. (1975). *Doing field research.* New York: Free Press.

Johnson, P. Timonty, James G. Hougland, Jr., and Richard R. Clayton. (1989). Obtaining reports of sensitive behavior: A comparison of substance-use reports from telephone and face-to-face interviews. *Social Science Quarterly,* 70:173–183.

Johnson, Stephen D. (1985). Religion as a defense in a mock-jury trial. *Journal of Social Psychology,* 125: 213–220.

Johnson, Timothy, and Fons van de Vijver. (2003). Social desireability in cross-cultural research. In *Cross-cultural survey methods,* edited by J. Harkness, F. Van de Vijver, and P. Mohler, pp. 195–206. Hoboken NJ: Wiley.

Jones, Gareth Stedman. (1976). From historical sociology to theoretical history. *British Journal of Sociology,* 27:295–305.

Jones, Gareth Stedman. (1983). *Languages of class.* New York: Cambridge University Press.

Jones, J. H. (1981). *Bad blood: The Tuskegee syphilis experiment.* New York: Free Press.

Jones, Wesley H. (1979). Generalizing mail survey inducement methods: Populations' interactions with anonymity and sponsorship. *Public Opinion Quarterly,* 43:102–111.

Jordan, Lawrence A., Alfred C. Marcus, and Leo G. Reeder. (1980). Response styles in telephone and household interviewing: A field experiment. *Public Opinion Quarterly,* 44:210–222.

Jordan, Stephen M., and Daniel Layzell. (1992). A case study of faculty workload issues in Arizona: Implications for state higher education policy. Policy Paper. Denver, CO: Education Commission of the States.

Josephson, Paul R. (Nov. 1, 1988). The FBI menaces academic freedom. *New York Times.*

Junker, Buford H. (1960). *Field work.* Chicago: University of Chicago Press.

Juster, F. Thomas, and Kenneth C. Land, eds. (1981). *Social accounting systems: Essays on the state of the art.* New York: Academic Press.

Kalberg, Stephen. (1994). *Max Weber's comparative-historical sociology.* Chicago: University of Chicago Press.

Kalmijn, Matthijus. (1991). Shifting boundaries: Trends in religious and educational homogamy. *American Sociological Review,* 56:786–801.

Kalton, Graham. (1983). *Introduction to survey sampling.* Beverly Hills, CA: Sage.

Kandel, Denise B. (1980). Drug and drinking behavior among youth. *Annual Review of Sociology,* 6: 235–265.

Kandel, William, and Douglas S. Massey. (2002). The culture of mexican migration: A theoretical and empirical analysis. *Social Forces,* 80:981–1004.

Kane, Emily W., and Laura J. MacAulay. (1993). Interview gender and gender attitudes. *Public Opinion Quarterly,* 57:1–28.

Kaplan, Abraham. (1964). *The conduct of inquiry: Methodology for behavioral science.* New York: Harper & Row.

Kaplowitz, Michael, Timothy Hadlock, and Ralph Levine. (2004). A comparison of web and web survey response rates. *Public Opinion Quarterly,* 68:94–101.

Karp, David A. (1973). Hiding in pornographic bookstores: A reconsideration of the nature of urban anonymity. *Urban Life,* 1:427–452.

Karp, David A. (1980). Observing behavior in public places: Problems and strategies. In *Fieldwork experience,* edited by W. B. Shaffir, R. A. Stebbins, and A. Turowetz, pp. 82–97. New York: St. Martin's Press.

Karweit, Nancy, and Edmund D. Meyers, Jr. (1983). Computers in survey research. In *Handbook of survey research,* edited by P. Rossi, J. Wright,

and A. Anderson, pp. 379–414. Orlando, FL: Academic Press.

Katovich, Michael A., and Ron L. Diamond. (1986). Selling time: Situated transactions in a noninstitutional setting. *Sociological Quarterly,* 27:253–271.

Katz, Jay. (1972). *Experimentation with human beings.* New York: Russell Sage Foundation.

Keat, Russell. (1981). *The politics of social theory: Habermas, Freud and the critique of positivism.* Chicago: University of Chicago Press.

Keat, Russell, and John Urry. (1975). *Social theory as science.* London: Routledge and Kegan Paul.

Keeter, Scott. (1995). Estimating telephone noncoverage bias with a telephone survey. *Public Opinion Quarterly,* 59:196–217.

Keeter, Scott, et al. (2000). Consequences of reducing non-response in a national telephone survey. *Public Opinion Quarterly,* 64:125–148.

Kelle, Helga. (2000). Gender and territoriality in games played by nine- to twelve-year-old schoolchildren. *Journal of Contemporary Ethnography,* 29:164–197.

Keller, Bill. (May 27, 1988). Ups and downs of conducting the poll. *New York Times.*

Keller, Bill. (January 19, 1989). Prying where it counts: Into census. *New York Times.*

Keller, Evelyn Fox. (1983). *A feeling for the organism: The life and work of Barbara McClintock.* New York: W. H. Freeman.

Keller, Evelyn Fox. (1985). *Reflections on gender and science.* New Haven, CT: Yale University Press.

Keller, Evelyn Fox. (1990). Gender and science. In *Feminist research methods,* edited by J. McCarl Nielsen, pp. 41–57. Boulder, CO: Westview.

Kelly, Erin L. (2003). The strange history of employer-sponsored child care. *American Journal of Sociology,* 109:606–649.

Kelman, Herbert. (1982). Ethical issues in different social science methods. In *Ethical issues in social science research,* edited by T. Beauchamp, R. Faden, R. J. Wallace, and L. Walters, pp. 40–99. Baltimore: Johns Hopkins University Press.

Kemmis, Stephen, and Robin McTaggart. (2003). Participatory action research. In *Strategies of qualitative*

inquiry, 2nd ed., edited by N. Denzin and Y. Lincoln, pp. 336–396. Thousand Oaks CA: Sage.

Kemp, Jeremy, and R. F. Ellen. (1984). Informants. In *Ethnographic research: A guide to general conduct,* edited by R. F. Ellen, pp. 224–236. Orlando: Academic Press.

Kent, Stephen A. (1992). Historical sociology. In *Encyclopedia of sociology,* Vol. 2, edited by E. and M. Borgatta, pp. 837–843. New York: Macmillan.

Kercher, Kyle. (1992). Quasi-experimental research designs. In *Encyclopedia of sociology,* Vol. 3, edited by E. and M. Borgatta, pp. 1595–1613. New York: Macmillan.

Kerlinger, Fred N. (1979). *Behavioral research: A conceptual approach.* New York: Holt, Rinehart and Winston.

Kidder, Louise H. (1982). Face validity from multiple perspectives. In *Forms of validity in research,* edited by D. Brinberg and L. Kidder, pp. 41–57. San Francisco: Jossey-Bass.

Kidder, Louise H., and Charles M. Judd. (1986). *Research methods in social relations,* 5th ed. New York: Holt, Rinehart and Winston.

Kiecolt, K. Jill, and Laura E. Nathan. (1985). *Secondary analysis of survey data.* Beverly Hills, CA: Sage.

Kim, Jae-On, and Charles W. Mueller. (1978). *Introduction to factor analysis: What it is and how to do it.* Beverly Hills, CA: Sage.

Kimmel, Allan J. (1988). *Ethics and values in applied social research.* Newbury Park, CA: Sage.

Kincheloe, Joe L., and Peter L. McLaren. (1994). Rethinking critical theory and qualitative research. In *Handbook of qualitative research,* edited by N. Denzin and Y. Lincoln, pp. 138–157. Thousand Oaks, CA: Sage.

King, Desmond. (1998). The politics of social research: Institutionalizing public funding regimes in the United States and Britain. *British Journal of Political Science,* 28:415–444.

King, Gary, Robert O. Keohane, and Sidney Verba. (1994). *Designing social inquiry: Scientific inference in qualitative research.* Princeton, NJ: Princeton University Press.

King, Gary, C. Murray, J. Salomon, and A. Tandon. (2004). Enhancing the validity and cross-cultural comparability of measurement in survey research. *American Political Science Review,* 98:191–207.

Kirk, Jerome, and Marc L. Miller. (1986). *Reliability and validity in qualitative research.* Beverly Hills, CA: Sage.

Kiser, Edgar, and April Linton. (2002). The hinges of history: State making and revolt in early modern France. *American Sociological Review,* 62:889–910.

Kish, L. (1965). *Survey sampling.* New York: Wiley.

Kleinman, Sherry. (1980). Learning the ropes as fieldwork analysis. In *Fieldwork experience,* edited by W. B. Shaffir, R. A. Stebbins, and A. Turowetz, pp. 171–183. New York: St. Martin's Press.

Kleinman, Sherry, and Martha A. Copp. (1993). *Emotions and field work.* Thousand Oaks, CA: Sage.

Knapp, Peter. (1990). The revival of macrosociology: Methodological issues of discontiuity in comparative-historical theory. *Sociological Forum,* 5:545–567.

Knäuper, Bärbel. (1999). The impact of age and education on response order effects in attitude measurement. *Public Opinion Quarterly,* 63:347–370.

Koch, Nadine S., and Jolly A. Emrey. (2001). The Internet and opinion measurement: Surveying marginalized populations. *Social Science Quarterly,* 82:131–138.

Kohn, Melvin L. (1987). Cross-national research as an analytic strategy. *American Sociological Review,* 52:713–731.

Kohn, Melvin L., ed. (1989). *Cross-national research in sociology.* Newbury Park, CA: Sage.

Koretz, Daniel. (Summer 1988). Arriving in Lake Wobegon: Are standardized tests exaggerating achievement and distorting instruction? *American Educator,* 12:8–15.

Kraemer, Helena Chmura, and Sue Thiemann. (1987). *How many subjects? Statistical power analysis in research.* Newbury Park, CA: Sage.

Krathwohl, D. R. (1965). *How to prepare a research proposal.* Syracuse, NY: Syracuse University Bookstore.

Krider, Dylan Otto. (2004). Politicized science. *Dissent,* 51:45–48.

Krippendorff, Klaus. (1980). *Content analysis: An introduction to its methodology.* Beverly Hills, CA: Sage.

Krosnick, Jon. (1992). The impact of cognitive sophistication and attitude importance on response-order and question-order effects. In *Context effects,* edited by N. Schwarz and Sudman, pp. 203–218. New York: Springer-Verlag.

Krosnick, Jon, and Robert P. Abelson. (1992). The case for measuring attitude strength in surveys. In *Questions about questions: Inquiries into the cognitive bases of surveys,* edited by J. Turner, pp. 177–203. New York: Russell Sage Foundation.

Krosnick, Jon, and Duane F. Alwin. (1988). A test of the form-resistant correlation hypothesis: Ratings, rankings and the measurement of values. *Public Opinion Quarterly,* 52:526–538.

Krosnick, Jon A., et al. (2002). The impact of "no opinion" response options on data quality. *Public Opinion Quarterly,* 66:371–403.

Krueger, Richard A. (1988). *Focus groups: A practical guide for applied research.* Beverly Hills, CA: Sage.

Krysan, Maria. (2002). Community undesirability in black and white. *Social Problems,* 49:521–543.

Kuhn, Thomas S. (1970). *The structure of scientific revolutions,* 2nd ed. Chicago: University of Chicago Press.

Kuhn, Thomas S. (1979). The relations between history and the history of science. In *Interpretive social science: A reader,* edited by P. Rabinow and W. Sullivan. Berkeley: University of California Press.

Kusserow, Richard P. (March 1989). *Misconduct in scientific research.* Report of the Inspector General of the U.S. Department of Health and Human Services. Washington, DC: Department of Health and Human Services.

Kviz, Frederick J. (1984). Bias in a directory sample for mail survey of rural households. *Public Opinion Quarterly,* 48:801–806.

Labaw, Patricia J. (1980). *Advanced questionnaire design.* Cambridge, MA: Abt Books.

Lachmann, Richard. (1988). Graffiti as career and ideology. *American Journal of Sociology,* 94:251–272.

Lachmann, Richard. (1989). Elite conflict and state formation in 16th and 17th century England and France. *American Sociological Review,* 54:141–162.

Lachmann, Richard. (2003). Elite Self-interest and economic decline in early modern Europe. *American Sociological Review,* 68:346–372.

Lacy, Dean. (2001). A theory of nonseparable preferences in survey responses. *American Journal of Political Science,* 45:239–258.

Lagemann, Ellen Condliffe. (1989). *The politics of knowledge: The Carnegie Corporation, philanthropy and public policy.* Chicago: University of Chicago.

Land, Kenneth. (1992). Social indicators. In *Encyclopedia of sociology,* Vol. 4, edited by E. and M. Borgatta, pp. 1844–1850. New York: Macmillan.

Lane, Michael. (1970). *Structuralism.* London: Jonathan Cape.

Lang, Eric. (1992). Hawthorne effect. In *Encyclopedia of sociology,* Vol. 2, edited by E. and M. Borgatta, pp. 793–794. New York: Macmillan.

Lankenau, Stephen E. (1999). Stronger than dirt. *Journal of Contemporary Ethnography,* 28:288–318.

Laslett, Barbara. (1980). Beyond methodology. *American Sociological Review,* 45:214–228.

Laslett, Barbara. (1992). Gender in/and social history. *Social Science History,* 16:177–196.

Lavoie, Francine, Line Robitaille, and Hebert Martine. (2000). Teen dating relationships and aggression: An exploratory study. *Violence Against Women,* 6:6–36.

Layder, Derek. (1993). *New strategies in social research.* Cambridge, MA: Polity.

Lazarsfeld, Paul F., and Jeffrey G. Reitz. (1975). *An introduction to applied sociology.* Amsterdam: Elsevier.

Lazere, Donald, ed. (1987). *American media and mass culture: Left perspectives.* Berkeley: University of California Press.

Leal, David L., and Frederick Hess. (1999). Survey bias on the front porch: Are all subjects interviewed equally? *American Politics Quarterly,* 27: 468–487.

Lee, Alfred McClung. (1978). *Sociology for whom?* New York: Oxford University Press.

Lee, Barrett, Chad Farrell, and Bruce Link. (2004). Revisiting the contact hypothesis. *American Sociological Review* 69: 40–63.

Lee, Harper. (1960). *To kill a mockingbird.* New York: Warner Books.

Lee-Treweek, Geraldine, and Stephanie Linkogle, eds. (2000). *Danger in the field.* New York: Routledge.

Leggett, Glenn, C. David Mean, and William Charvat. (1965). *Prentice-Hall handbook for writers,* 4th ed. Englewood Cliffs, NJ: Prentice-Hall.

Leiter, Kenneth. (1980). *A primer on ethnomethodology.* New York: Oxford University Press.

LeMasters, E. E. (1975). *Blue collar aristocrats.* Madison: University of Wisconsin Press.

Lemert, Charles. (1979). Science, religion and secularization. *Sociological Quarterly,* 20:445–461.

Lemert, Charles, ed. (1981). *French sociology: Rupture and renewal since 1968.* New York: Columbia University Press.

Lenzer, Gertrud, ed. (1975). *Auguste Comte and positivism: Essential writings.* New York: Harper & Row.

Lester, Marilyn, and Stuart C. Hadden. (1980). Ethnomethodology and grounded theory methodology: An integration of perspective and method. *Urban Life,* 9:3–33.

Levine, Joel H. (1993). *Exceptions are the rule: An inquiry into methods in the social sciences.* Boulder, CO: Westview.

Lewis, George H., and Jonathan F. Lewis. (1980). The dog in the night-time: Negative evidence in social research. *British Journal of Sociology,* 31:544–558.

Lieberson, Stanley. (1985). *Making it count: The improvement of social research and theory.* Berkeley: University of California Press.

Lieberson, Stanley. (1991). Small N's and big conclusions: An examination of the reasoning of comparative studies based on a small number of cases. *Social Forces,* 70:307–320.

Lieberson, Stanley, Susan Dumais, and Shyon Baumann. (2000). The instability of androgynous names: The symbolic maintenance of gender boundaries. *American Journal of Sociology,* 105:1249–1287.

Liebetrau, Albert M. (1983). *Measures of association.* Beverly Hills, CA: Sage.

Liebman, Robert, John R. Sutton, and Robert Wuthnow. (1988). Exploring social sources of denominationalism: Schisms in American Protestant denominations, 1890–1980. *American Sociological Review,* 53:343–352.

Liebow, Elliot. (1967). *Talley's corner.* Boston: Little, Brown.

Lifton, Robert J. (1986). *Nazi doctors.* New York: Basic Books.

Light, Richard J., and David B. Pillemer. (1984). *Summing up: The science of reviewing research.* Cambridge, MA: Harvard University Press.

Likert, Rensis. (1970). A technique for the measurement of attitudes. In *Attitude measurement,* edited by G. Summers, pp. 149–158. Chicago: Rand McNally.

Lindblom, Charles E., and David K. Cohen. (1979). *Usable knowledge: Social science and social problem solving.* New Haven, CT: Yale University Press.

Lindzey, Gardner, and Donn Byrne. (1968). Measurement of social choice and interpersonal attractiveness. In *The handbook of social psychology,* Vol. 2: Research methods, edited by G. Lindzey and E. Aronson, pp. 452–525. Reading, MA: Addison-Wesley.

Link, Michael W., and Robert Oldendick. (1999). Call screening: Is it really a problem for survey research. *Public Opinion Quarterly,* 63:577–589.

Lipset, Seymour Martin. (1968). History and sociology: Some methodological considerations. In *Sociology and history: Methods,* edited by S. M. Lipset and R. Hofstadter, pp. 20–58. New York: Basic Books.

Little, Daniel. (1991). *Varieties of social explanation: An introduction to the philosophy of science.* Boulder, CO: Westview.

Lloyd, Christopher. (1986). *Explanation in social history.* New York: Basil Blackwell.

Locke, Lawrence F., Warren Wyrick Spirduso, and Stephen J. Silverman. (1987). *Proposals that work: A guide for planning dissertations and grant proposals,* 2nd ed. Beverly Hills, CA: Sage.

Lofland, John. (1974). Styles of reporting qualitative field research. *American Sociologist,* 9:101–111.

Lofland, John. (1976). *Doing social life: The qualitative study of human interaction in natural settings.* New York: Wiley.

Lofland, John, and Lyn H. Lofland. (1984). *Analyzing social settings,* 2nd ed. Belmont, CA: Wadsworth.

Lofland, John, and Lyn H. Lofland. (1995). *Analyzing social settings,* 3rd ed. Belmont, CA: Wadsworth.

Lofland, Lyn H. (1972). Self management in public settings: Parts I and II. *Urban Life,* 1:93–108, 217–231.

Loftus, Elizabeth, Mark Klinger, Kyle Smith, and Judith Fiedler. (1990). A tale of two questions: Benefit of asking more than one question. *Public Opinion Quarterly,* 54:330–345.

Loftus, Elizabeth, Kyle D. Smith, Mark R. Klinger, and Judith Fiedler. (1992). Memory and mismemory of health events. In *Questions about questions: Inquiries into the cognitive bases of surveys,* edited by J. Turner, pp. 102–137. New York: Russell Sage Foundation.

Long, J. Scott. (1976). Estimation and hypothesis testing in linear models containing measurement error: A review of Joreskog's model for the analysis of covariance structures. *Sociological Methods and Research,* 5:157–206.

Long, J. Scott. (1978). Productivity and academic positions in a scientific career. *American Sociological Review,* 43:889–908.

Longino, Helen E. (1990). *Science as social knowledge: Values and objectivity in scientific inquiry.* Princeton, NJ: Princeton University Press.

Lorr, Maurice. (1983). *Cluster analysis for social scientists: Techniques for analyzing and simplifying complex blocks of data.* San Francisco: Jossey-Bass.

Lovin-Smith, Lynn, and Charles Brody. (1989). Interruptions in group discussions: The effects of gender and group composition. *American Sociological Review,* 54:424–435.

Lowenthal, David. (1985). *The past is a foreign country.* New York: Cambridge University Press.

Lu, Shun, and Gary Alan Fine. (1995). The presentation of ethnic authenticity: Chinese food as a social accomplishment. *Sociological Quarterly,* 36:535–553.

Luebke, Barbara F. (1989). Out of focus: Images of men and women in newspaper photographs. *Sex Roles,* 20: 121–133.

Lyberg, Lars, et al. (1997). *Survey measurement and process quality.* New York: Wiley.

Lynd, Robert S. (1964). *Knowledge for what? The place of social science in American culture.* New York: Grove. (Originally published in 1939 by Princeton University Press.)

MacFarlane, Alan. (1977). *Reconstructing historical communities.* New York: Cambridge University Press.

MacIver, A. M. (1968). Levels of explanation in history. In *Readings in the philosophy of the social sciences,* edited by M. Brodbeck, pp. 304–316. New York: Macmillan.

MacKeun, Michael B. (1984). Reality, the press and citizens' political agendas. In *Surveying subjective phenomena,* Vol. 2, edited by C. Turner and E. Martin, pp. 443–473. New York: Russell Sage Foundation.

Magaña, Lisa, and Robert Short. (2002). The social construction of Mexican and Cuban immigrants by politicians. *The Review of Policy Research,* 19:78–94.

Mahoney, James. (1999). Nominal, ordinal, and narrative appraisal in macrocausal analysis. *American Journal of Sociology,* 104:1154–1196.

Mahoney, James. (2000a). Path dependence in historical sociology. *Theory and Society,* 9:507–548.

Mahoney, James. (2000b). Strategies of causal inference in small-N analysis. *Sociological Methods and Research,* 28:387–424.

Mahoney, James. (2003). Long-run development and the legacy of colonialism in Spanish America. *American Journal of Sociology,* 109: 50–106.

Mahoney, James. (2004a). Comparative-historical methodology. *Annual Review of Sociology,* 30:81–101.

Mahoney, James. (2004b). Revisiting general theory in historical sociology. *Social Forces,* 83:459–489.

Maier, Mark H. (1991). *The data game: Controversies in social science statistics.* Armonk, NY: M. E. Sharpe.

Maines, David R., William Shaffir, and Allan Turowetz. (1980). Leaving the field in ethnographic research. In *The fieldwork experience: Qualitative approaches to social research,* edited by W. B. Shaffir, R. Stebbins, and A. Turowetz, pp. 261–280. New York: St. Martin's Press.

Maloney, Dennis M. (1984). *Protection of human research subjects: A practical guide to federal laws and regulations.* New York: Plenum.

Mann, Floyd C. (1970). Human relations skills in social research. In *Qualitative methodology,* edited by W. J. Filstead. Chicago: Markham.

Mannheim, Karl. (1936). *Ideology and utopia.* New York: Harcourt, Brace and World.

Mariampolski, Hyman, and Dana C. Hughes. (1978). The use of personal documents in historical sociology. *The American Sociologist,* 13:104–113.

Marradi, Alberto. (1981). Factor analysis as an aid in the formation and refinement of empirically useful concepts. In *Factor analysis and measurement in social research: A multi-dimensional perspective,* edited by D. Jackson and E. Borgatta, pp. 11–50. Beverly Hills, CA: Sage.

Marsh, Catherine. (1982). *The survey method: The contribution of surveys to sociological explanation.* Boston: George Allen and Unwin.

Marsh, Catherine. (1984). Do polls affect what people think? In *Surveying subjective phenomena,* Vol. 2, edited by C. Turner and E. Martin, pp. 565–592. New York: Russell Sage Foundation.

Marshall, Catherine. (1985). Appropriate criteria of trustworthiness and goodness for qualitative research on educational organizations. *Quality and Quantity,* 19:353–373.

Marshall, Catherine, and Gretchen B. Rossman. (1989). *Designing qualitative research.* Beverly Hills, CA: Sage.

Marshall, Susan E. (1986). In defense of separate spheres: Class and politics in the antisuffrage movement. *Social Forces,* 65:327–351.

Martin, Elizabeth. (1985). Surveys as social indicators: Problems of monitoring trends. In *Handbook of survey research,* edited by P. Rossi, J. Wright, and A. Anderson, pp. 677–743. Orlando, FL: Academic.

Martin, Elizabeth. (1999). Who knows who lives here? *Public Opinion Quarterly,* 63:200–236.

Martin, Elizabeth. (2004). Vignettes and respondent debriefing for questionnaire design. In *Methods for testing and evaluating survey questionnaires,* edited by Stanley Presser et al., pp. 149–172. New York: Wiley.

Martin, Jay. (1973). *The dialectical imagination.* Boston: Little, Brown.

Martin, John L., and Laura Dean. (1993). Developing a community sample of gay men for an epidemiological study of AIDS. In *Research on sensitive topics,* edited by C. Renzetti and R. Lee, pp. 82–100. Thousand Oaks, CA: Sage.

Marvasti, Amir B. (2004). *Qualitative research in sociology.* Thousand Oaks CA: Sage.

Marx, Anthony W. (1998). *Making race and nation: A comparison of the United States, South Africa and Brazil.* New York: Cambridge University Press.

Marx, Karl, and Friedrich Engels. (1947). *The German ideology, Parts I & III,* edited with introduction by R. Pascal. New York: International Publishers.

Masterman, Margaret. (1970). The nature of a paradigm. In *Criticism and the growth of knowledge,* edited by I. Lakatos and A. Musgrove, pp. 59–90. Cambridge: Cambridge University Press.

May, Reuben A. Buford. (2001). *Talking at Trena's.* New York: New York University Press.

Mayer, Charles S., and Cindy Piper. (1982). A note on the importance of layout in self-administered questionnaires. *Journal of Marketing Research,* 19:390–391.

Mayer, Susan. (2002). How economic segregation affects children's educational attainment. *Social Forces,* 81:153–176.

Mayhew, Bruce H. (1980). Structuralism versus individualism, Part I: Shadowboxing in the dark. *Social Forces,* 59:335–375.

Mayhew, Bruce H. (1981). Structuralism versus individualism, Part II: Ideological and other obfuscations. *Social Forces,* 59:627–648.

Maynard, Douglas W., and Nora Cate Schaeffer. (2004). Refusal conversion and tailoring. In *Standardization and tacit knowledge,* edited by Douglas W. Maynard, et al., pp. 219–239. New York: Wiley.

McCabe, Donald L. (1992). The influence of situational ethics on cheating among college students. *Sociological Inquiry,* 62:365–374.

McCall, George. (1969). Quality control in participant observation. In *Issues in participant observation,* edited by G. McCall and J. L. Simmons, pp. 128–141. Reading, MA: Addison-Wesley.

McCall, George. (1984). Systematic field observation. *Annual Review of Sociology,* 10:263–282.

McCall, Michal. (1980). Who and where are the artists? In *The fieldwork experience: Qualitative approaches to social research,* edited by William B. Shaffir, R. Stebbins, and A. Turowetz, pp. 145–158. New York: St. Martin's Press.

McCarthy, Thomas. (1978). *The critical theory of Jurgen Habermas.* Cambridge, MA: MIT Press.

McCartney, James L. (1984). Setting priorities for research: New politics for the social sciences. *Sociological Quarterly,* 25:437–455.

McCarty, John A., and L. J. Shrum. (2000). The measurement of personal values in survey research: A test of alternative rating procedures. *Public Opinion Quarterly,* 64:271–298.

McConaghy, Maureen. (1975). Maximum possible error in Guttman scales. *Public Opinion Quarterly,* 39:343–357.

McCracken, Grant. (1988). *The long interview.* Thousand Oaks, CA: Sage.

McDaniel, Timothy. (1978). Meaning and comparative concepts. *Theory and Society,* 6:93–118.

McDiarmid, Garnet. (1971). *Teaching prejudice: A content analysis of social studies textbooks authorized for use in Ontario.* Ontario: Ontario Institute for Studies in Education.

McFarland, Daniel A. (2004). Resistance as a social drama. *American Journal of Sociology,* 109:1249–1318.

McFarland, Sam G. (1981). Effects of question order on survey responses. *Public Opinion Quarterly,* 45: 208–215.

McGrath, Joseph, Joanne Martin, and Richard A. Kulka. (1982). *Judgment calls in research.* Beverly Hills, CA: Sage.

McIver, John P., and Edward G. Carmines. (1981). *Unidimensional scaling.* Beverly Hills, CA: Sage.

McKee, J. McClendon, and David J. O'Brien. (1988). Question order effects on the determinants of subjective well being. *Public Opinion Quarterly,* 52:351–364.

McKelvie, Stuart J., and Linda A. Schamer. (1988). Effects of night, passengers and sex on driver behavior at stop signs. *Journal of Social Psychology,* 128:658–690.

McKeown, Bruce. (1988). *Q methodology.* Thousand Oaks, CA: Sage.

McLaren, Lauren M. (2003). Anti-immigrant prejudice in Europe: Contact, threat perception, and preferences for the exclusion of migrants. *Social Forces,* 81:909–936.

McLennan, Gregor. (1981). *Marxism and the methodologies of history.* London: Verso.

McMurtry, John. (1978). *The structure of Marx's world view.* Princeton, NJ: Princeton University Press.

McNall, Scott G. (1988). *The road to rebellion.* Chicago: University of Chicago Press.

McQuaire, Donald. (1978). Marx and the method of successive approximations. *Sociological Quarterly,* 20:431–435.

McQuaire, Donald. (1979). Reply to Wardell. *Sociological Quarterly,* 20: 431–435.

McVeigh, Rory. (2004). Structural ignorance and organized racism in the United States. *Social Forces,* 82:895–936.

McVeigh, Rory, Michael Welch, and Thoroddur Bjarnason. (2003). Hate crime reporting as a successful social movement outcome. *American Sociological Review,* 68:843–867.

Meadows, A. J. (1974). *Communication in science.* Toronto: Butterworths.

Mehan, Hugh. (1973). Assessing children's language using abilities (with discussion). In *Comparative social research,* edited by M. Armer and A. Grimshaw, pp. 309–345. New York: Wiley.

Mehan, Hugh, and Houston Wood. (1975). *The reality of ethnomethodology.* New York: Wiley.

Melbin, Murray. (1978). Night as frontier. *American Sociological Review,* 43:3–22.

Mendelberg, Tali. (1997). Executing Hortons: Racial crime and the 1988 presidential campaign. *Public Opinion Quarterly,* 61:134–157.

Mendenhall, William, Lyman Ott, and Richard L. Scheaffer. (1971). *Elementary survey sampling.* Belmont, CA: Duxbury Press.

Merten, Don E. (1999). Enculturation into secrecy among junior high school girls. *Journal of Contemporary Ethnography,* 28:107–138.

Merton, Robert K. (1957). *Social theory and social structure.* New York: Free Press.

Merton, Robert K. (1967). *On theoretical sociology: Five essays, old and new.* New York: Free Press.

Merton, Robert K. (1970). *Science, technology and society in seventeenth century England.* New York: Harper & Row.

Merton, Robert K. (1973). *The sociology of science.* Chicago: University of Chicago Press.

Meyer, Katrina A. (1998). Faculty workload studies: Perspectives, needs, and future directions. ASHE-ERIC Higher Education Report, Vol. 26, No. 1. Washington, DC: Office of Educational Research and Improvement.

Mikkelsen, Britha. (1995). *Methods for development work and research: A guide for practitioners.* Thousand Oaks, CA: Sage.

Milem, Jeffrey F., Joseph Berger, and Eric Dey. (2000). Faculty time allocation: A study of change over twenty years. *Journal of Higher Education,* 71:454–475.

Miles, Matthew B., and A. Michael Huberman. (1994). *Qualitative data analysis,* 2nd ed. Thousand Oaks, CA: Sage.

Milgram, Stanley. (1963). Behavioral study of obedience. *Journal of Abnormal and Social Psychology,* 6:371–378.

Milgram, Stanley. (1965). Some conditions of obedience and disobedience to authority. *Human Relations,* 18:57–76.

Milgram, Stanley. (1974). *Obedience to authority.* New York: Harper & Row.

Miller, Delbert C. (1991). *Handbook of research design and social measurement,* 5th ed. Newbury Park, CA: Sage.

Miller, Gale. (1992). Case studies. In *Encyclopedia of sociology,* Vol. 1, edited by Edgar and Marie Borgatta, pp. 167–172. New York: Macmillan.

Miller, J. Mitchell, and Richard Tewksbury, eds. (2000). *Extreme methods: Innovative approaches to social science research.* New York: Addison Wesley, Longman.

Miller, Richard. (1987). *Fact and method: Explanation, confirmation and reality in the natural and social sciences.* Princeton, NJ: Princeton University Press.

Miller, William L. (1983). *The survey method in the social and political sciences: Achievements, failures and prospects.* London: Frances Pinter.

Milligan, John D. (1979). The treatment of historical source. *History and Theory,* 18:177–196.

Mills, C. Wright. (1959). *The sociological imagination.* New York: Oxford University Press.

Miringoff, Marc, and Marque-Luisa Miringoff. (1999). *The social health of the nation: How America is really doing.* New York: Oxford University Press.

Mishler, Elliot G. (1986). *Research interviewing: Context and narrative.* Cambridge, MA: Harvard University Press.

Mitchell, Alison. (May 17, 1997). Survivors of Tuskegee study get apology from Clinton. *New York Times.*

Mitchell, J. Clyde. (1984). Case studies. In *Ethnographic research: A guide to general conduct,* edited by R. F. Ellen, pp. 237–241. Orlando, FL: Academic Press.

Mitchell, Mark, and Janina Jolley. (1988). *Research design explained.* New York: Holt, Rinehart and Winston.

Mitchell, Richard G., Jr. (1993). *Secrecy and fieldwork.* Thousand Oaks, CA: Sage.

Mitroff, Ian. (1974). Norms and counter-norms in a select group of the Apollo moon scientists: A case study of ambivalence of scientists. *American Sociology Review,* 39:579–595.

Moller, Stephanie, D. Bradley, E. Huber, F. Nielsen, and J. Stephens. (2003). Determinants of relative poverty in advanced capitalist democracies. *American Sociological Review,* 68:22–51.

Molotch, Harvey, William Freudenburg, and Krista Paulsen. (2000). History repeats itself, but how? City character, urban tradition, and the accomplishment of place. *American Sociological Review,* 65:791–823.

Monaghan, Peter. (April 7, 1993a). Facing jail, a sociologist raises question about a scholar's right to protect sources. *Chronicle of Higher Education,* p. A10.

Monaghan, Peter. (May 26, 1993b). Sociologist is jailed for refusing to testify about research subject. *Chronicle of Higher Education,* p. A10.

Monaghan, Peter. (September 1, 1993c). Sociologist jailed because he "wouldn't snitch" ponders the way research ought to be done. *Chronicle of Higher Education,* pp. A8–A9.

Monmonier, Mark. (1996). *How to lie with maps,* 2nd ed. Chicago: University of Chicago Press.

Mooney, Linda, and Robert B. Gramling. (1991). Asking threatening questions and situational framing: The effects of decomposing survey items. *Sociological Quarterly,* 32:277–288.

Moore, Barrington, Jr. (1966). *The social origins of dictatorship and democracy.* Boston: Beacon Press.

Moore, Joan. (1973). Social constraints on sociological knowledge: Academic and research concerning minorities. *Social Problems,* 21:65–77.

Moore, R. J. (2004). Managing troubles in answering survey questions: Respondents' uses of projective reporting. *Social Psychology Quarterly,* 67:50–69.

Morgan, David L. (1996). Focus groups. *Annual Review of Sociology,* 22: 129–152.

Morgan, Laurie A. (1998). Glass-ceiling effect or cohort effect? A longitudinal study of the gender earnings gap for engineers, 1982–1989. *American Sociological Review,* 63:479–483.

Morrow, Raymond Allan. (1994). *Critical theory and methodology.* Thousand Oaks, CA: Sage.

Morse, Janice M. (1994). Designing funded qualitative research. In *Handbook of qualitative research,* edited by N. Denzin and Y. Lincoln, pp. 220–235. Thousand Oaks, CA: Sage.

Moser, C. A., and G. Kalton. (1972). *Survey methods in social investigation.* New York: Basic Books.

Mostyn, Barbara. (1985). The content analysis of qualitative research data: A dynamic approach. In *The research interview: Uses and approaches,* edited by M. Brenner, J. Brown, and D. Canter, pp. 115–145. New York: Academic Press.

Mulkay, Michael. (1979). *Science and the sociology of knowledge.* London: George Allen and Unwin.

Mullins, Carolyn J. (1977). *A guide to writing and publishing in the social and behavioral sciences.* New York: Wiley.

Mullins, Nicholas C. (1971). *The art of theory: Construction and use.* New York: Harper & Row.

Mullins, Nicholas C. (1973). *Theory and theory groups in American sociology.* New York: Harper & Row.

Murdock, George P. (1967). Ethnographic atlas. *Ethnology,* 6:109–236.

Murdock, George P. (1971). *Outline of cultural materials,* 4th ed. New Haven, CT: Human Relations Area Files.

Murphey, Murray G. (1973). *Our knowledge of the historical past.* Indianapolis: Bobbs-Merrill.

Musick, Marc A., John Wilson, and William Bynum. (2000). Race and formal volunteering: The differential effects of class and religion. *Social Forces,* 78:1539–1571.

Myerhoff, Barbara. (1989). So what do you want from us here? In *In the field,* edited by C. Smith and W. Kornblum, pp. 83–90. New York: Praeger.

Myers, Daniel J., and Beth S. Caniglia. (2004). All the rioting that's fit to print. *American Sociological Review,* 69:519–543.

Myers, Gloria, and A. V. Margavio. (1983). The black bourgeoisie and reference group change: A content analysis of *Ebony. Qualitative Sociology,* 6:291–307.

Myrdal, Gunnar. (1973). The beam in our eyes. In *Comparative research methods,* edited by D. Warwick and S. Osherson, pp. 89–99. Englewood Cliffs, NJ: Prentice-Hall.

Nadeau, Richard, Richard Miemi, and Jeffrey Levine. (1993). Innumeracy about minority population. *Public Opinion Quarterly,* 57:332–347.

Namenwirth, J. Z. (1970). Prestige newspapers and assessment of elite opinions. *Journalism Quarterly,* 47:318–323.

Narayan, Sowmya, and John A. Krosnick. (1996). Education moderates some response effects in attitude measurement. *Public Opinion Quarterly,* 60:58–88.

Naroll, Raoul. (1968). Some thoughts on comparative method in cultural anthropology. In *Methodology in social research,* edited by H. Blalock and A. Blalock, pp. 236–277. New York: McGraw-Hill.

Nash, Jeffrey E., and David W. McCurdy. (1989). Cultural knowledge and systems of knowing. *Sociological Inquiry,* 59:117–126.

Nederhof, Anton J. (1986). Effects of research experiences of respondents. *Quality and Quantity,* 20:277–284.

Nelkin, Dorothy. (1982a). Forbidden research: Limits on inquiry in the social sciences. In *Ethical issues in social science research,* edited by Tom L. Beauchamp, R. Faden, R. J. Wallace, and L. Walters, pp. 163–174. Baltimore: Johns Hopkins University Press.

Neuberg, Leland Gerson. (1988). Distorted transmission: A case study in the diffusion of "social scientific" research. *Theory and Society,* 17:487–526.

Neuman, W. Lawrence. (1992). Gender, race and age differences in student definitions of sexual harassment. *Wisconsin Sociologist,* 29:63–75.

Neuman, W. Lawrence. (2000). *Social research methods: Qualitative and quantitative approaches,* 4th ed. Boston: Allyn and Bacon.

Neuman, W. Russell, Marion R. Just, and Ann N. Crigler. (1992). *Common knowledge: News and the construction of political meaning.* Chicago: University of Chicago Press.

Noelle-Neumann, Elisabeth. (1974). Spiral of silence: A theory of public opinion. *Journal of Communication,* 24:43–51.

Noelle-Neumann, Elisabeth. (1984). *The spiral of silence: Public opinion our social skin.* Chicago: University of Chicago Press.

Norris, M. (1981). Problems in the analysis of soft data and some suggested solutions. *Sociology,* 15:337–351.

Norusis, Marija J. (1986). *The SPSS-X guide to data analysis.* Chicago: SPSS, Inc.

Novick, Peter. (1988). *That noble dream: The "objectivity question" and the American historical profession.* New York: Cambridge University Press.

Nowak, Stefan. (1989). Comparative studies and social theory. In *Cross-national research in sociology,* edited by M. Kohn, pp. 34–56. Newbury Park, CA: Sage.

Nowotny, Helga, and Hilary Rose, eds. (1979). *Counter-movements in the sciences.* Boston: D. Reidel.

Nunnally, Jum C. (1978). *Psychometric theory.* New York: McGraw-Hill.

Oakley, Ann. (1981). Interviewing women: A contradiction in terms. In *Doing feminist research,* edited by H. Roberts, pp. 30–61. London: Routledge.

O'Brien, Robert M. (1992). Levels of analysis. In *Encyclopedia of sociology,* Vol. 3, edited by E. and M. Borgatta, pp. 1107–1112. New York: Macmillan.

Odette, Parry, and Natasha Mautner. (2004). Whose data are they anyway? *Sociology,* 38:139–152.

O'Donnell, John M. (1985). *The origins of behaviorism: American psychology, 1870–1920.* New York: New York University Press.

Oesterle, Sabrina, Monica Kirkpatrick Johnson, and Jeylan T. Mortimer. (2004). Volunteerism during the transition to adulthood: A life course perspective. *Social Forces,* 82: 1123–1149.

Offe, Claus. (1981). The social sciences: Contract research or social movements? *Current Perspectives on Social Theory,* 2:31–37.

Oksenberg, Lois, Lerita Coleman, and Charles F. Cannell. (1986). Interviewers' voices and refusal rates in telephone surveys. *Public Opinion Quarterly,* 50:97–111.

Oliker, Stacey J. (1994). Does workfare work? Evaluation research and workfare policy. *Social Problems,* 41:195–211.

Olsen, Marvin E., and Michael Micklin, eds. (1981). *Handbook of applied sociology.* New York: Praeger.

Olsen, Virginia. (1994). Feminism and models of qualitative research. In *Handbook of qualitative research,* edited by N. Denzin and Y. Lincoln, pp. 158–174. Thousand Oaks, CA: Sage.

Olzak, Susan, and Suzanne Shanahan. (2003). Racial policy and racial conflict in the United States, 1869–1924. *Social Forces,* 82:481–518.

Ong, Andy S. J., and Colleen A. Ward. (1999). The effects of sex and power schemas, attitudes toward women, and victim resistance on rape attributions. *Journal of Applied Social Psychology,* 29:362–376.

Orbuch, Terri, and Sandra L. Eyster. (1997). Divison of labor among black couples and white couples. *Social Forces,* 76:301–332.

Orloff, Ann Shola. (1993). *The politics of pensions: A comparative analysis of Britain, Canada and the United States, 1880–1940.* Madison: University of Wisconsin Press.

Osgood, C. E., G. Suci, and H. Tannenbaum. (1957). *The measurement of meaning.* Urbana: University of Illinois Press.

Ostrom, Thomas M., and Katherine M. Gannon. (1996). Exemplar generation: Assessing how respondents give meaning to rating scales. In *Answering Questions,* edited by N. Schwarz and S. Sudman, pp. 293–318. San Francisco: Jossey-Bass.

O'Sullivan, Katherine. (1986). *First world nationalisms.* Chicago: University of Chicago Press.

Øyen, Else. (1990). The imperfection of comparisons. In *Comparative methodology: Theory and practice in international social research,* edited by E. Øyen, pp. 1–18. Newbury Park, CA: Sage.

Paige, Jeffrey M. (1975). *Agrarian revolution.* New York: Free Press.

Parcel, Toby L. (1992). Secondary data analysis and data archives. In *Encyclopedia of sociology,* Vol. 4, edited by E. and M. Borgatta, pp. 1720–1728. New York: Macmillan.

Patrick, Steven, Robert Marsh, Wade Bundy, Susan Mimura, and Tina Perkins. (2004). Control group study of juvenile diversion programs. *Social Science Journal* 41:129–35.

Paulos, John Allen. (2001). *Innumeracy: Mathematical illiteracy and its consequences.* New York: Hill and Wang.

Payne, A. Abigail. (2003a). The effects of congressional appropriation committee membership on the distribution of federal research funding to universities. *Economic Inquiry,* 41: 325–345.

Payne, A. Abigail. (2003b). The role of politically motivated subsidies on university research activities. *Educational Policy,* 17:12–37.

Pearsall, Marion. (1970). Participant observation as role and method in behavioral research. In *Qualitative methodology,* edited by W. J. Filstead, pp. 340–352. Chicago: Markham.

Pearson, Michael Ross, and Robyn M. Dawes. (1992). Personal recall and the limits of retrospective questions in surveys. In *Questions about questions: Inquiries into the cognitive bases of surveys,* edited by J. Turner, pp. 65–94. New York: Russell Sage Foundation.

Pedriana, Nicholas. (2005). Rational choice, structural context, and increased return. *Sociological Methods and Research,* 33:349–382.

Peterson, Robert A. (1984). Asking the age question: A research note. *Public Opinion Quarterly,* 48:379–383.

Pettit, Becky, and Bruce Western. (2004). Mass imprisonment and the life course. *American Sociological Review,* 69:151–169.

Pfohl, Stephen. (1990). Welcome to the parasite cafe: Postmodernity as a social problem. *Social Problems,* 37:421–442.

Phillips, Bernard. (1985). *Sociological research methods: An introduction.* Homewood, IL: Dorsey.

Phillips, D. C. (1987). *Philosophy, science and social inquiry: Contemporary methodological controversies in social science and related applied fields of research.* New York: Pergamon.

Phillips, Derek. (1971). *Knowledge from what?* Chicago: Rand McNally.

Pierson, Paul. (2000). Increased return, path dependence, and the study of politics. *American Political Science Review,* 94:251–267.

Piliavin, Irving M., J. Rodin, and Jane A. Piliavin. (1969). Good samaritanism: An underground phenomenon? *Journal of Personality and Social Psychology,* 13:289–299.

Platt, Jennifer. (1981). Evidence and proof in documentary research. *Sociological Review,* 29:31–66.

Poe, Gail S., et al. (1988). "Don't know" boxes in factual questions in a mail questionnaire: Effects on level and quality of response. *Public Opinion Quarterly,* 52:212–222.

Pollner, Melvin, and Richard Adams. (1997). The effect of spouse presence on appraisals of emotional support and household strain. *Public Opinion Quarterly,* 61:615–626.

Popper, Karl. (1959/1934). *The logic of scientific discovery.* New York: Basic Books.

Popovich, P. M., B. J. Licata, D. Nokovich, T. Martelli, and S. Zoloty. (1986) "Assessing the incidence and perceptions of sexual harassment behaviors among American undergraduates." *Journal of Psychology* 120:387–396.

Porter, Stephen, and Michael Whitcomb. (2003). The impact of contact type on web survey response rates. *Public Opinion Quarterly,* 67:579–588.

Porter, Theodore M. (1995). *Trust in numbers: The pursuit of objectivity in science and the public life.* Princeton, NJ: Princeton University Press.

Pottick, Kathleen, and Paul Lerman. (1991). Maximizing survey response rates for hard-to-reach inner-city populations. *Social Science Quarterly,* 72:172–180.

Presser, Stanley. (1984). Is inaccuracy on factual survey items item-specific or respondent-specific? *Public Opinion Quarterly,* 48:344–355.

Presser, Stanley. (1990). Measurement issues in the study of social change. *Social Forces,* 68:856–868.

Presser, Stanley, Johnny Blair, and Timothy Triplett. (1992). Survey sponsorship, response rates and response effects. *Social Science Quarterly,* 73: 699–702.

Prewitt, Kenneth. (1983). Management of survey organizations. In *Handbook of social research,* edited by P. Rossi, J. Wright, and A. Anderson, pp. 123–143. Orlando, FL: Academic Press.

Price, Vincent. (1989). Social identification and public opinion: Effects of communicating group conflict. *Public Opinion Quarterly,* 53: 197–224.

Prior, Lindsay. (2003). *Using documents in social research.* Thousand Oaks CA: Sage.

Prucha, Francis Paul. (1987). *Handbook for research in American history: A guide to bibliographies and other reference works.* Lincoln: University of Nebraska Press.

Przeworski, Adam, and Henry Teune. (1970). *The logic of comparative inquiry.* New York: Wiley.

Przeworski, Adam, and Henry Teune. (1973). Equivalence in cross-national research. In *Comparative research methods,* edited by D. Warwick and S. Osherson, pp. 119–137. Englewood Cliffs, NJ: Prentice-Hall.

Punch, Maurice. (1986). *The politics and ethics of fieldwork.* Beverly Hills, CA: Sage.

Pusey, Michael. (1987). *Jügen Habermas.* New York: Tavistock.

Pyke, Sandra W., and Neil McK. Agnew. (1991). *The science game,* 5th ed. Englewood Cliffs, NJ: Prentice-Hall.

Quadagno, Jill S. (1984). Welfare capitalism and the Social Security Act of 1935. *American Sociological Review,* 49:632–648.

Quadagno, Jill S. (1988). *The transformation of old age security.* Chicago: University of Chicago Press.

Quarles, Susan D., ed. (1986). *Guide to federal funding for social scientists.* New York: Russell Sage Foundation.

Rabinow, Paul, and William M. Sullivan. (1979). The interpretative turn: Emergence of an approach. In *Interpretative social science: A reader,* edited by P. Rabinow and W. Sullivan, pp. 1–24. Berkeley: University of California Press.

Ragin, Charles C. (1987). *The comparative method.* Berkeley: University of California Press.

Ragin, Charles. (1989). New directions in comparative research. In *Cross-national research in sociology,* edited by M. Kohn, pp. 57–76. Newbury Park, CA: Sage.

Ragin, Charles C. (1992a). Introduction: Cases of "what is a case?" In *What is a case: Exploring the foundations of social inquiry,* edited by C. Ragin and H. Becker, pp. 1–18. New York: Cambridge University Press.

Ragin, Charles C. (1992b). Casing and the process of social inquiry. In *What is a case: Exploring the foundations of social inquiry,* edited by C. Ragin and H. Becker, pp. 217–226. New York: Cambridge University Press.

Ragin, Charles C. (1994a). *Constructing social research.* Thousand Oaks, CA: Pine Forge Press.

Ragin, Charles C. (1994b). Introduction to qualitative comparative analysis. In *The comparative political economy of the welfare state,* edited by Thomas Janoski and Alexander Hicks, pp. 299–319. New York: Cambridge University Press.

Ragin, Charles C., and David Zaret. (1983). Theory and method in comparative research. *Social Forces,* 61:731–754.

Rampton, Sheldon, and John Stauber. (2001). *Trust us, we're experts.* New York: Putnam.

Rathje, W. L., and W. W. Hughes. (1976). The garbage project as nonreactive approach: Garbage in-garbage out. In *Perspective on attitude assessment: Surveys and their alternatives,* edited by H. W. Sinaiko and L. A. Broeding. Champaign, IL: Pendleton Publications.

Rathje, William, and Cullen Murphy. (1992). *Rubbish: The archaeology of garbage.* New York: Vintage.

Ravo, Nick. (October 14, 1996). Index of Social Well-Being is at the lowest in 25 years. *New York Times.*

Reason, Peter. (1994). Three approaches to participative inquiry. In *Handbook of qualitative research,* edited by N. Denzin and Y. Lincoln, pp. 324–339. Thousand Oaks, CA: Sage.

Reese, Stephen, W. Danielson, P. Shoemaker, T. Chang, and H. Hsu. (1986). Ethnicity of interview effects among Mexican Americans and Anglos. *Public Opinion Quarterly,* 50:563–572.

Reingold, Beth, and Richard Wike. (1998). Confederate symbols, southern identity, and racial attitudes: The case of the Georgia state flag. *Social Science Quarterly,* 79:568–580.

Reinharz, Shulamit. (1979). *On becoming a social scientist.* San Francisco: Jossey-Bass.

Reinharz, Shulamit. (1992). *Feminist methods in social research.* New York: Oxford University Press.

Reskin, Barbara. (1977). Scientific productivity and the reward structure of science. *American Sociological Review,* 42:491–504.

Reynolds, Paul Davidson. (1971). *A primer in theory construction.* Indianapolis: Bobbs-Merrill.

Reynolds, Paul Davidson. (1979). *Ethical dilemmas and social science research.* San Francisco: Jossey-Bass.

Reynolds, Paul Davidson. (1982). *Ethics and social science research.* Englewood Cliffs, NJ: Prentice-Hall.

Richards, Thomas J., and Lyn Richards. (1994). Using computers in qualitative research. In *Handbook of qualitative research,* edited by N. Denzin and Y. Lincoln, pp. 445–462. Thousand Oaks, CA: Sage.

Richardson, Jane, and Barry Godfrey. (2003). Towards ethical practice in the use of archived transcripted interviews. *International Journal of Social Research Methodology,* 6:347–355.

Ricoeur, Paul. (1970). The model of the text: Meaningful action considered as a text. In *Interpretive social science: A reader,* edited by P. Rabinow and W. Sullivan, pp. 73–102. Berkeley: University of California Press.

Ridgeway, Cecilia, and Kristan Glasgow Erickson. (2000). Creating and spreading status beliefs. *American Journal of Sociology,* 106:579–615.

Rind, Bruce, and David Strohmetz. (1999). Effect on restaurant tipping of a helpful message written on the back of customers' checks. *Journal of Applied Social Psychology,* 29:139–144.

Risman, Barbara J. (2001). Calling the bluff of value-free science. *American Sociological Review,* 66:605–618.

Ritzer, George. (1975). *Sociology: A multi-paradigm science.* Boston: Allyn and Bacon.

Roadburg, Alan. (1980). Breaking relationships with field subjects: Some problems and suggestions. In *Fieldwork experience,* edited by W. B. Shaffir, R. Stebbins, and A. Turowetz, pp. 281–291. New York: St. Martin's Press.

Roberts, Carl W. (1989). Other than counting words: A linguistic approach to content analysis. *Social Forces,* 68:147–177.

Robertson, John A. (1982). The social scientist's right to research and the IRB system. In *Ethical issues in social science research,* edited by T. L. Beauchamp, R. Faden, R. J. Wallace, and L. Walters, pp. 356–372. Baltimore: Johns Hopkins University Press.

Robinson, John P., Jerrold G. Rusk, and Kendra B. Head. (1972). *Measures of political attitudes.* Ann Arbor: Center for Political Studies, Institute for Social Research, University of Michigan.

Robinson, John P., and Philip R. Shaver. (1969). *Measures of social psychological attitudes.* Ann Arbor: Survey Research Center, Institute for Social Research, University of Michigan.

Roderick, Rick. (1986). *Habermas and the foundations of critical theory.* New York: St. Martin's Press.

Roethlisberger, F. J., and W. J. Dickenson. (1939). *Management and the worker.* Cambridge, MA: Harvard University Press.

Rose, Gerry. (1982). *Deciphering social research.* Beverly Hills, CA: Sage.

Rosen, Lawrence. (1995). The creation of the Uniform Crime Report: The role of social science. *Social Science History,* 19:215–238.

Rosenau, Pauline Marie. (1992). *Postmodernism and the social sciences.* Princeton, NJ: Princeton University Press.

Rosenberg, Morris. (1968). *The logic of survey analysis.* New York: Basic Books.

Rosenthal, Robert. (1984). *Meta-analytic procedures for social research.* Beverly Hills, CA: Sage.

Rosnow, Ralph L. (1981). *Paradigms in transition: The methodology of social inquiry.* New York: Oxford University Press.

Ross, Dorothy. (1991). *The origins of American social science.* New York: Cambridge University Press.

Ross, James, S. Laston, P. Pelto, and L. Muna. (2002). Exploring explanatory models of women's reproductive health in rural Bangladesh. *Culture, Health and Sexuality,* 4:173–190.

Rossi, Peter H., ed. (1982). *Standards for evaluation practice.* San Francisco: Jossey-Bass.

Rossi, Peter H., and Howard E. Freeman. (1985). *Evaluation: A systematic approach,* 3rd ed. Beverly Hills, CA: Sage.

Rossi, Peter H., James D. Wright, and Eleanor Weber-Burdin. (1982). *Natural hazards and public choice.* New York: Academic Press.

Rossi, Robert J., and Kevin J. Gilmartin. (1980). *The handbook of social indicators: Sources, characteristics and analysis.* New York: Garland STPM Press.

Roth, Guenther, and Wolfgang Schluchter. (1979). *Max Weber's vision of history: Ethics and methods.* Berkeley: University of California Press.

Roy, Donald. (1970). The study of southern labor union organizing campaigns. In *Pathways to data,* edited by R. W. Habenstein, pp. 216–244. Chicago: Aldine.

Roy, William G. (1983). The unfolding of the interlocking directorate structure of the United States. *American Sociological Review,* 48:248–257.

Roy, William G. (1984). Class conflict and social change in historical perspective. *Annual Review of Sociology,* 10:483–506.

Roy, William G. (1997). *Socializing capital: The rise of the large industrial corporation in America.* Princeton, NJ: Princeton University Press.

Roy, William. (2001). *Making societies.* Thousand Oaks CA: Pine Forge Press.

Rubin, Herbert J. (1983). *Applied social research.* Columbus, OH: Charles E. Merrill.

Ruef, Martin. (2004). The demise of an organizational form: Emancipation and plantation agriculture in the American South, 1860–1880. *American Journal of Sociology,* 109:1365–1410.

Rueschemeyer, Dietrich, Evelyne Huber Stephens, and John D. Stephens. (1992). *Capitalist development and democracy.* Chicago: University of Chicago Press.

Rueschemeyer, Dietrich, and John Stephens. (1997). Comparing historical sequences: A powerful tool for causal analysis. *Comparative Social Research,* 16:55–72.

Rule, James. (1978a). *Insight and social betterment: A preface to applied social science.* New York: Oxford University Press.

Rule, James. (1978b). Models of relevance: The social effects of sociology. *American Journal of Sociology,* 84:78–98.

Runciman, W. G. (1980). Comparative sociology or narrative history. *European Journal of Sociology,* 21: 162–178.

Runyon, Richard P., and Audry Haber. (1980). *Fundamentals of behavioral statistics.* Reading, MA: Addison-Wesley.

Ryan, Mary. (1989). The American parade. In *The new cultural history,* edited by L. Hunt, pp. 131–153. Berkeley: University of California Press.

Ryder, Norman B. (1992). Cohort analysis. In *Encyclopedia of sociology,* Vol. 1, edited by E. and M. Borgatta, pp. 227–231. New York: Macmillan.

Sabia, Daniel R., Jr., and Jerald T. Wallulis. (1983). *Changing social science: Changing theory and other critical perspectives.* Albany: State University of New York at Albany.

Sagarin, Edward. (1973). The research setting and the right not to be researched. *Social Problems,* 21: 52–64.

Sanchez, Maria Elena. (1992). Effects of questionnaire design on the quality of survey data. *Public Opinion Quarterly,* 56:206–217.

Sanday, Peggy Reeves. (1983). The ethnographic paradigm(s). In *Qualitative methodology,* edited by J. Van Maanen, pp. 19–36. Beverly Hills, CA: Sage.

Sanders, Jane. (1979). *Cold war on the campus: Academic freedom at the University of Washington, 1946–64.* Seattle: University of Washington Press.

Sanders, Jimy, Victor Nee, and Scott Sernau. (2002). Asian immigrants' reliance on social ties in a multiethnic labor market. *Social Forces,* 81: 281–314.

Sanjek, Roger. (1978). A network method and its uses in urban anthropology. *Human Organization,* 37:257–268.

Sanjek, Roger. (1990). On ethnographic validity. In *Field notes: The makings of anthropology,* edited by R. Sanjek, pp. 385–418. Ithaca, NY: Cornell University Press.

Savage, James. (2001). *Funding science in America: Congress, universities, and the politics of the academic pork barrel.* New York: Cambridge University Press.

Savelsberg, Joachim, Ryan King, and Lara Cleveland. (2002). Politicized scholarship? Science on crime and the state. *Social Problems,* 49: 327–48.

Saxe, Leonard, and Michelle Fine. (1981). *Social experiments: Methods for design and evaluation.* Beverly Hills, CA: Sage.

Sayer, Andrew. (1992). *Method in social science: A realist approach,* 2nd ed. New York: Routledge.

Schacter, Daniel L, ed. (1995). *Memory distortion: How minds, brains, and societies reconstruct the past.* Cambridge, MA: Harvard University Press.

Schacter, Daniel L. (2001). *The seven deadly sins of memory: How the mind forgets and remembers.* Boston: Houghton Mifflin.

Schaefer, David, and Don A. Dillman. (1998). Development of a standard e-mail methodology. *Public Opinion Quarterly,* 62:378–397.

Schaffer, Nora Cate. (1980). Evaluating race-of-interviewer effects in a na-

tional survey. *Sociological Methods and Research,* 8:400–419.

Schaeffer, Nora Cate. (2004). Conversation with a purpose—or conversation? In *Standardization and tacit knowledge,* edited by Douglas W. Maynard et al., pp. 95–123. New York: Wiley.

Schaeffer, Nora Cate, and Stanley Presser. (2003). The science of asking questions. *Annual Review of Sociology,* 29:65–88.

Schatzman, Leonard, and Anselm L. Strauss. (1973). *Field research: Strategies for a natural sociology.* Englewood Cliffs, NJ: Prentice-Hall.

Scheibe, Karl E. (1988). Metamorphosis in the psychologist's advantage. In *The rise of experimentation in American psychology,* edited by J. Morawski, pp. 53–71. New Haven, CT: Yale University Press.

Scheuch, Erwin K. (1990). The development of comparative research: Towards causal explanations. In *Comparative methodology,* edited by E. Øyen, pp. 19–37. Newbury Park, CA: Sage.

Schmeling, Sharon L., and Mike Miller. (August 11, 1988). Whistleblower wins suit against UW. *Capital Times* (Madison, Wisconsin).

Schmitt, Eric. (June 27, 1997). Army criticized on survey on harrassment. *New York Times.*

Schneider, Mark A. (1987). Culture-as-text in the work of Clifford Geertz. *Theory and Society,* 16:809–883.

Schober, Michael, and Frederick G. Conrad. (1997). Does conversational interviewing reduce survey measurement error? *Public Opinion Quarterly,* 61:576–602.

Schober, Michael, and Frederick Conrad. (2004). A collaborative view of standardized survey interview. In *Standardization and tacit knowledge,* edited by Douglas W. Maynard et al., pp. 67–94. New York: Wiley

Schofer, Evan. (2004). "Cross-national differences in the expansion of science, 1970–1990." *Social Forces* 83:215–48.

Schrager, Laura, and James Short. (1980). How serious a crime? Perceptions of organizational and common crimes. In *White collar crime,* edited by G. Geis and E. Stotland, pp. 14–31. Beverly Hills, CA: Sage.

Schrecker, Ellen. (1986). *No ivory tower: McCarthyism and the university.* New York: Oxford University Press.

Schuessler, Karl. (1982). *Measuring social life feelings.* San Francisco: Jossey-Bass.

Schuman, Howard. (1992). Context effects: State of the past/state of the art. In *Context effects in social and psychological research,* edited by N. Schwarz and S. Sudman, pp. 5–20. New York: Springer-Verlag.

Schuman, Howard, and Lawrence Bobo. (1988). Survey-based experiments on white racial attitudes towards racial integration. *American Journal of Sociology,* 94:273–299.

Schuman, Howard, and Jean M. Converse. (1971). Effects of black and white interviewers on black response in 1968. *Public Opinion Quarterly,* 65:44–68.

Schuman, Howard, and Otis Dudley Duncan. (1974). Questions about attitude survey questions. In *Sociological methodology, 1973–1974,* edited by H. Costner, pp. 232–251. San Francisco: Jossey-Bass.

Schuman, Howard, and Jacob Ludwig. (1983). The norm of even-handedness in surveys as in life. *American Sociological Review,* 48:112–120.

Schuman, Howard, and Stanley Presser. (1977). Question wording as an independent variable in survey analysis. *Sociological Methods and Research,* 6:151–170.

Schuman, Howard, and Stanley Presser. (1979). The open and closed question. *American Sociological Review,* 44:692–712.

Schuman, Howard, and Stanley Presser. (1981). *Questions and answers in attitude surveys: Experiments on question form, wording and content.* New York: Academic Press.

Schwandt, Thomas A. (1994). Constructivist, interpretivist approaches to human inquiry. In *Handbook of qualitative research,* edited by N. Denzin and Y. Lincoln, pp. 118–137. Thousand Oaks, CA: Sage.

Schwandt, Thomas A. (1997). *Qualitative inquiry: A dictionary of terms.* Thousand Oaks, CA: Sage.

Schwartz, David. (1997). *Culture and power: The sociology of Pierre Bourdieu.* Chicago: University of Chicago Press.

Schwartz, Howard, and Jerry Jacobs. (1979). *Qualitative sociology: A method to the madness.* New York: Free Press.

Schwartz, Morris, and Charlotte Green Schwartz. (1969). Problems in field observation. In *Issues in participant observation,* edited by G. J. McCall and J. L. Simmons, pp. 89–105. Reading, MA: Addison-Wesley.

Schwarz, Norbert, and Hans-J. Hippler. (1995). Subsequent questions may influence answers to preceding questions in mail surveys. *Public Opinion Quarterly,* 59:93–97.

Schwarz, Norbert, Bäurbel Knäuper, Hans-J. Hippler, Elizabeth Noelle-Neumann, and Leslie Clark. (1991). Rating scales: Numeric values may change the meaning of scale labels. *Public Opinion Quarterly,* 55:570–582.

Schwarz, Norbert, and Seymour Sudman. (1992). *Context effects in social and psychological research.* New York: Springer-Verlag.

Schwarz, Norbert, and Seymour Sudman. (1994). *Autobiographical memory and the validity of retrospective reports.* New York: Springer-Verlag.

Schwendinger, H., and J. Schwendinger. (1974). *Sociologists of the chair.* New York: Basic Books.

Scott, William A. (1968). Attitude measurement. In *The handbook of social psychology, Vol. 2: Research methods,* edited by G. Lindzey and E. Aronson, pp. 204–273. Reading, MA: Addison-Wesley.

Sears, David O. (1986). College sophomores in the laboratory: Influences of a narrow data base on social psychology's view of human nature. *Journal of Personality and Social Psychology,* 51: 515–530.

Sellin, Thorsten, and Marvin E. Wolfgang. (1964). *The measurement of delinquency.* New York: Wiley.

Selvin, Hanan C., and Everett K. Wilson. (1984). On sharpening sociologists' prose. *Sociological Quarterly,* 25: 205–223.

Sepstrup, P. (1981). Methodological developments in content analysis. In *Advances in content analysis,* edited by K. Rosengren, pp. 133–158. Beverly Hills, CA: Sage.

Sewell, William H., Jr. (1980). *Work and revolution in France.* New York: Cambridge University Press.

Sewell, William H., Jr. (1987). Theory of action, dialectic, and history: Comment on Coleman. *American Journal of Sociology,* 93:166–171.

Sewell, William H., Jr. (1992). Introduction: Narratives and social identities. *Social Science History,* 16:479–488.

Sewell, William H., Jr. (1996). Three temporalities: toward an eventful sociology. In *The historical turn in the human sciences,* edited by T. McDonald, pp. 245–280. Ann Arbor: University of Michigan Press.

Seybold, Peter. (1987). The Ford Foundation and the transformation of political science. In *The structure of power in America,* edited by M. Schwartz, pp. 185–198. New York: Holmes and Meier.

Shafer, Robert Jones. (1980). *A guide to historical method,* 3rd ed. Homewood, IL: Dorsey.

Shaffir, William B., Robert A. Stebbins, and Allan Turowetz. (1980). Introduction. In *Fieldwork experience,* edited by W. B. Shaffir, R. Stebbins, and A. Turowetz, pp. 3–22. New York: St. Martin's Press.

Shattuck, John, and Muriel Morisey Spence. (1988). *Government information controls: Implications for scholarship, science and technology.* Washington, DC: Association of American Universities.

Shaw, C. (1930). *The jack roller.* Chicago: University of Chicago Press.

Sheatsley, Paul B. (1983). Questionnaire construction and item writing. In *Handbook of social research,* edited by P. Rossi, J. Wright, and A. Anderson, pp. 195–230. Orlando, FL: Academic Press.

Shihadeh, Edward S., and Graham Ousey. (1998). Industrial restructuring and violence: The link between entry-level jobs, economic deprivation, and black and white homicide. *Social Forces,* 77:185–206.

Shupe, Anston D., Jr., and David G. Bromley. (1980). Walking a tightrope: Dilemmas of participation observation of groups in conflict. *Qualitative Sociology,* 2:3–21.

Sieber, Joan, ed. (1982). *The ethics of social research: Fieldwork, regulation, and publication.* New York: Springer-Verlag.

Sieber, Joan E. (1992). *Planning ethically responsible research: A guide for students and internal review boards.* Thousand Oaks, CA: Sage.

Sieber, Joan E. (1993). The ethics and politics of sensitive research. In *Research on sensitive topics,* edited by C. Renzetti and R. Lee, pp. 14–26. Thousand Oaks, CA: Sage.

Sieber, Sam D. (1973). The integration of fieldwork and survey methods.

American Journal of Sociology, 78:1335–1359.

Sigelman, Lee. (1982). The uncooperative interviewee. *Quality and Quantity,* 16:345–353.

Sigelman, Lee, and Richard Niemi. (2001). Innumeracy about minority populations: African Americans and Whites compared. *Public Opinion Quarterly,* 65:86–94.

Silva, Edward T., and Sheila Slaughter. (1980). Prometheus bound: Limits of social science professionalization. *Theory and Society,* 9:781–819.

Silverman, David. (1972). Some neglected questions about social reality. In *New directions in sociological theory,* edited by P. Filmer et al. Cambridge, MA: MIT Press.

Silverman, David. (1993). *Interpreting qualitative data.* Thousand Oaks, CA: Sage.

Simpson, Christopher. (1993). U.S. mass communication research and counterinsurgency after 1945: An investigation of the construction of scientific "reality." In *Ruthless criticism: New perspectives in U.S. communication history,* edited by William Solomon and Robert McChesney. Minneapolis: University of Minnesota Press.

Singer, Benjamin D. (1989). The criterial crisis of the academic world. *Sociological Inquiry,* 59:127–143.

Singer, Eleanor. (1978). Informed consent: Consequences for response rate and response quality in social survey. *American Sociological Review,* 43:144–162.

Singer, Eleanor. (1988). Surveys in the mass media. In *Surveying social life: Papers in honor of Herbert H. Hyman,* edited by H. O'Gorman, pp. 413–436. Middletown, CT: Wesleyan University Press.

Singer, Eleanor. (1999). The effect of incentives. *Journal of Official Statistics,* 15:217–230.

Singer, Eleanor, and Martin R. Frankel. (1982). Informed consent procedures in telephone interviews. *American Sociological Review,* 47:416–426.

Singer, Eleanor, Robert Groves, and Amy Corning. (1999). Differential incentives: Beliefs about practices, perceptions of equity and effects on survey participation. *Public Opinion Quarterly,* 63:251–260.

Singer, Eleanor, and Luane Kohnke-Aguirre. (1979). Interviewer expectation effects: A replication and extension. *Public Opinion Quarterly,* 43:245–260.

Singer, Eleanor, John Van Hoewyk, and Mary Maher. (1998). Does the payment of incentives create expectation effects? *Public Opinion Quarterly,* 62:152–164.

Singer, Eleanor, John Van Hoewyk, and Mary Maher. (2000). Experiments with incentives in telephone surveys. *Public Opinion Quarterly,* 64: 171–188.

Singer, Eleanor, Dawn R. Von Thurn, and Ester R. Miller. (1995). Confidentiality assurances and response: A quantitative review of the experimental literature. *Public Opinion Quarterly,* 59:66–77.

Singleton, Royce, Jr., B. Straits, Margaret Straits, and Ronald McAllister. (1988). *Approaches to social research.* New York: Oxford University Press.

Sitton, Thad, G. Mehaffy, and O. L. Davis, Jr. (1983). *Oral history.* Austin: University of Texas Press.

Skidmore, William. (1979). *Theoretical thinking in sociology,* 2nd ed. New York: Cambridge University Press.

Sklar, Kathryn Kish. (1991). Hull House maps and papers: Social science as women's work in the 1890s. In *The social survey in historical perspective, 1880–1940,* edited by M. Blumer, K. Bales, and K. Sklar, pp. 111–147. New York: Cambridge University Press.

Skocpol, Theda. (1979). *States and social revolutions.* New York: Cambridge University Press.

Skocpol, Theda. (1984). Emerging agendas and recurrent strategies in historical sociology. In *Vision and method in historical sociology,* edited by T. Skocpol, pp. 356–392. Cambridge: Cambridge University Press.

Skocpol, Theda. (1988). The "uppity generation" and the revitalization of macroscopic sociology: Reflections at mid-career of a woman from the sixties. *Theory and Society,* 17:627–644.

Skocpol, Theda, and Margaret Somers. (1980). The uses of comparative history in macrosocial inquiry. *Comparative Studies in Society and History,* 22:174–197.

Skog, Ole-Jorgen. (2003). Alcohol consumption and fatal accidents in Canada, 1950–1998. *Addition,* 98:883–893.

Slater, Phil. (1977). *Origin and significance of the Frankfurt School.* Boston: Routledge and Kegan Paul.

Smart, Barry. (1976). *Sociology, phenomenology, and Marxian analysis: A critical discussion of the theory and practice of a science of society.* Boston: Routledge and Kegan Paul.

Smelser, Neil J. (1959). *Social change in the industrial revolution.* Chicago: University of Chicago Press.

Smelser, Neil J. (1976). *Comparative methods in the social sciences.* Englewood Cliffs, NJ: Prentice-Hall.

Smelser, Neil J. (1991). Internationalization of social science knowledge. *American Behavioral Scientist,* 35:65–91.

Smilde, David. (2003). Skirting the instrumental paradox: Intentional belief through narrative in Latin American Pentecostalism. *Qualitative Sociology,* 26:313–329.

Smith, Calvin, and Patricia Short. (2001). Integrating technology to improve the efficiency of qualitative data analysis. *Qualitative Sociology,* 24:401–408.

Smith, Christopher. (1995). Asian New York: The geography and politics of diversity. *International Migration Review,* 29:59–84.

Smith, Dennis. (1991). *The rise of historical sociology.* Philadelphia: Temple University Press.

Smith, George W., and Dorothy E. Smith. (1998). The ideology of "fag": The high school experience of gay students. *Sociological Quarterly,* 39: 289–308.

Smith, James Allen. (1991). *The idea brokers: Think tanks and the new policy elite.* New York: Free Press.

Smith, Louis M. (1994). Biographical method. In *Handbook of qualitative research,* edited by N. Denzin and Y. Lincoln, pp. 286–305. Thousand Oaks, CA: Sage.

Smith, Mary Lee, and Gene V. Glass. (1987). *Research and evaluation in education and the social sciences.* Englewood Cliffs, NJ: Prentice-Hall.

Smith, Robert B. (1987). Linking quality and quantity. Part I: Understanding and explanation. *Quantity and Quality,* 21:291–311.

Smith, Robert B. (1988). Linking quality and quantity, Part II: Surveys as formalizations. *Quantity and Quality,* 22:3–30.

Smith, Rogers M. (1996). Science, nonscience and politics. In *The historic turn in the human sciences,* edited by T. McDonald, pp. 119–159. Ann Arbor: University of Michigan Press.

Smith, Tom W. (1984). The subjectivity of ethnicity. In *Surveying subjective phenoemona,* Vol. 2, edited by C. Turner and E. Martin, pp. 117–128. New York: Russell Sage Foundation.

Smith, Tom W. (1987). That which we call welfare by any other name would smell sweeter: An analysis of the impact of question wording on response patterns. *Public Opinion Quarterly,* 51:75–83.

Smith, Tom W. (1989). Random probes of GSS questions. *International Journal of Public Opinion Research,* 1:305–325.

Smith, Tom W. (1992). Thoughts on the nature of context effects. In *Context effects in social and psychological research,* edited by N. Schwarz and S. Sudman, pp. 163–184. New York: Springer-Verlag.

Smith, Tom W. (1995). Trends in nonresponse rates. *International Journal of Public Opinion Research,* 7: 156–171.

Smith, Tom W. (2002). The Muslim population of the United States. *Public Opinion Quarterly,* 66:404–417.

Smith, Tom W. (2003). Developing comparable questions in cross-national surveys. In *Cross-cultural survey methods,* edited by J. Harkness, F. Van de Vijver, and P. Mohler, pp. 69–91. Hoboken NJ: Wiley.

Smith, Tom W. (2004). Developing and evaluating cross-national survey instruments. In *Methods for testing and evaluating survey questionnaires,* edited by S. Presser et al., pp. 431–452. New York: Wiley.

Sniderman, Paul M., and Michael Gray Hagen. (1985). *Race and inequality: A study in American values.* Chatham, NJ: Chatham House.

Sniderman, Paul M., and Douglas Grob. (1996). Innovation in experimental design in attitude surveys. *Annual Review of Sociology,* 22:377–399.

Snow, David A., Susan G. Baker, Leon Anderson, and Michael Martin. (1986b). The myth of pervasive mental illness among the homeless. *Social Problems,* 33:407–423.

Snow, David A., E. Burke Bochford, Jr., Steven K. Worden, and Robert D. Benford. (1986a). Frame alignment process, micromobilization and movement participation. *American Sociological Review,* 51: 464–481.

Sobal, Jeffery. (1984). The content of survey introductions and the provision of informed consent. *Public Opinion Quarterly,* 48:788–793.

Sociology Writing Group, UCLA. (1991). *A guide to writing sociology papers,* 2nd ed. New York: St. Martin's Press.

Sohn-Rethel, Alfred. (1978). *Intellectual and manual labor: A critique of epistemology.* New York: Macmillan.

Somers, Margaret R. (1994). Reclaiming the epistemological "other": Narrative and the social construction of identity. In *Social theory and the politics of identity,* edited by Craig Calhoun, pp. 37–99. Cambridge MA: Blackwell.

Sonquist, J. A., and C. Dunkelberg. (1977). *Survey and opinion research: Procedures for processing and analysis.* Englewood Cliffs, NJ: Prentice-Hall.

Spector, Paul E. (1981). *Research designs.* Beverly Hills, CA: Sage.

Spector, Paul E. (1992). *Summated rating scale construction.* Newbury Park, CA: Sage.

Spradley, James P. (1970). *You owe yourself a drunk.* Boston: Little, Brown.

Spradley, James P. (1979a). *The ethnographic interview.* New York: Holt, Rinehart and Winston.

Spradley, James P. (1979b). *Participant observation.* New York: Holt, Rinehart and Winston.

Spradley, James P., and B. J. Mann. (1975). *The cocktail waitress.* New York: Wiley.

Sprague, Joey, and Mary K. Zimmerman. (1989). Quality and quantity: Reconstructing feminist methodology. *American Sociologist,* 20:71–86.

Stack, Carol. (1989). Doing research in the flats. In *In the field,* edited by C. Smith and W. Kornblum, pp. 21–26. New York: Praeger.

Stack, Steven. (1987). Celebrities and suicide: A taxonomy and analysis, 1948–1983. *American Sociological Review,* 52:401–412.

Staggenborg, Susan. (1988). "Hired hand research" revised. *American Sociologist,* 19:260–269.

Stake, Robert E. (1994). Case studies. In *Handbook of qualitative research,* edited by N. Denzin and Y. Lincoln, pp. 236–247. Thousand Oaks, CA: Sage.

Starr, Paul. (1982). *The social transformation of American medicine.* New York: Basic Books.

Starr, Paul. (1987). The sociology of official statistics. In *The politics of numbers,* edited by W. Alonso and P. Starr, pp. 7–58. New York: Russell Sage Foundation.

Stech, Charlotte G. (1981). Trends in nonresponse rates, 1952–1979. *Public Opinion Quarterly,* 45:40–57.

Steensland, Brian, J. Park, M. Regnerus, L. Robinson, W. Wilcox, and R. Woodberry. (2000). The measure of American religion: Toward improving the state-of-the-art. *Social Forces,* 79:291–318.

Stempel, G., III. (1971). Visibility of blacks in news and news-picture magazines. *Journalism Quarterly,* 48:337–339.

Stephens, John. (1989). Democratic transition and breakdown in western Europe, 1870–1939: A test of the Moore thesis. *American Journal of Sociology,* 94:1019–1077.

Stephens, Mary Ann Parris, N. S. Cooper, and J. M. Kinney. (1985). The effects of effort on helping the physically disabled. *Journal of Social Psychology,* 125:495–503.

Stephenson, Richard M. (1978). The CIA and the professor: A personal account. *American Sociologist,* 13:128–133.

Stern, Paul C. (1979). *Evaluating social science research.* New York: Oxford University Press.

Stevens, Carla, and Micah Dial, eds. (1994). Preventing the misuse of evaluation. *New Directions for Program Evaluation, 64.* San Francisco: Jossey-Bass.

Stevenson, Richard W. (October 16, 1996). U.S. to revise its estimate of layoffs. *New York Times.*

Stewart, David W. (1984). *Secondary research: Information sources and methods.* Beverly Hills, CA: Sage.

Stewart, Donald E. (1983). *The television family.* Melborne: Institute of Family Studies.

Stimson, Gerry B. (1986). Place and space in sociological fieldwork. *The Sociological Review,* 34:641–656.

Stinchcombe, Arthur L. (1968). *Constructing social theories.* New York: Harcourt, Brace and World.

Stinchcombe, Arthur L. (1973). Theoretical domains and measurement, Part 1. *Acta Sociologica,* 16:3–12.

Stinchcombe, Arthur L. (1978). *Theoretical methods in social history.* New York: Academic Press.

Stoecker, Randy. (1993). The federated frontstage structure and localized social movements: A case study of the Ceder-Riverside neighborhood move-ment. *Social Science Quarterly,* 74:169–184.

Stoecker, Randy. (1999). Are academics irrelevant? Roles for scholars in participatory research. *American Behavioral Scientist,* 42:840–854.

Stoianovich, Traian. (1976). *French historical method.* Ithaca, NY: Cornell University Press.

Stone, Lawrence. (1987). *The past and present revisited.* Boston: Routledge and Kegan Paul.

Stone, Philip, et al. (1966). *The general inquirer: A computer approach to content analysis in the behavioral sciences.* Cambridge, MA: MIT Press.

Stone, Philip J., and Robert P. Weber. (1992). Content analysis. In *Encyclopedia of sociology,* Vol. 1, edited by E. and M. Borgatta, pp. 290–295. New York: Macmillan.

Stoner, Norman W. (1966). *The social system of science.* New York: Holt, Rinehart and Winston.

Strack, Fritz. (1992). "Order effects" in survey research. In *Context effects in social and psychological research,* edited by N. Schwarz and S. Sudman, pp. 23–24. New York: Springer-Verlag.

Strauss, Anselm. (1987). *Qualitative analysis for social scientists.* New York: Cambridge University Press.

Strauss, Anselm, and Juliet Corbin. (1990). *Basics of qualitative research: Grounded theory procedures and techniques.* Newbury Park, CA: Sage.

Strauss, Anselm, and Juliet Corbin. (1994). Grounding theory methodology: An overview. In *Handbook of qualitative research,* edited by N. Denzin and Y. Lincoln, pp. 273–285. Thousand Oaks, CA: Sage.

Stryker, Robin. (1996). Beyond history versus theory: Strategic narrative and sociological explanation. *Sociological Methods and Research,* 24: 304–352.

Suchman, Luch, and Brigitte Jordan. (1992). Validity and the collaborative construction of meaning in face-to-face surveys. In *Questions about questions: Inquiries into the cognitive bases of surveys,* edited by J. Turner, pp. 241–267. New York: Russell Sage Foundation.

Sudman, Seymour. (1976a). *Applied sampling.* New York: Academic Press.

Sudman, Seymour. (1976b). Sample surveys. *Annual Review of Sociology,* 2:107–120.

Sudman, Seymour. (1983). Applied sampling. In *Handbook of survey research,* edited by P. Rossi, J. Wright, and A. Anderson, pp. 145–194. Orlando, FL: Academic Press.

Sudman, Seymour, and Norman M. Bradburn. (1983). *Asking questions: A practical guide to questionnaire design.* San Francisco: Jossey-Bass.

Sudman, Seymour, and Norman M. Bradburn. (1987). The organizational growth of public opinion research in the United States. *Public Opinion Quarterly,* 51:S67-S78.

Sudman, Seymour, Norman M. Bradburn, and Norbert Schwarz. (1996). *Thinking about answers: The ap-plication of cognitive processes to survey research.* San Francisco: Jossey-Bass.

Sullivan, John L., and Stanley Feldman. (1979). *Multiple indicators: An introduction.* Beverly Hills, CA: Sage.

Suls, Jerry M., and Ralph L. Rosnow. (1988). Concerns about artifacts in psychological experiments. In *The rise of experimentation in American psychology,* edited by J. Morawski, pp. 153–187. New Haven, CT: Yale University Press.

Sumner, Colin. (1979). *Reading ideologies.* New York: Academic Press.

Sung, Hung-En1 (2003). "Fairer sex of fairer system? Gender and corruption revisited." *Social Forces* 82:703–723.

Suppe, Frederick, ed. (1977). *The structure of scientific theories,* 2nd ed. Urbana: University of Illinois Press.

Survey Research Center, Institute for Social Research. (1976). *Interviewer's manual,* rev. ed. Ann Arbor: University of Michigan.

Sutton, John R. (1991). The political economy of madness: The expansion of the asylum in progressive America. *American Sociological Review,* 56:665–678.

Sutton, John R. (2000). Imprisonment and social classification in five common-law democracies, 1955–1985. *American Journal of Sociology,* 106:350–386.

Sutton, John R. (2004). The political economy of imprisonment in affluent Western democracies, 1960–1990. *American Sociological Review,* 69:170–189.

Swanborn, Peter G. (1996). A common base for quality control criteria in quantitative and qualitative research. *Quality and Quantity,* 30:19–35.

Swanson, Guy E. (1971). Frameworks for comparative research. In *Comparative methods in sociology,* edited by I. Vallier, pp. 141–203. Berkeley: University of California Press.

Swartz, David. (1997). *Culture and power: The sociology of Pierre Bourdieu.* Chicago: University of Chicago Press.

Swidler, Ann. (1986). Culture in action: Symbols and strategies. *American Sociological Review,* 51: 273–286.

Tagg, Stephen K. (1985). Life story interviews and their interpretation. In *The research interview: Uses and approaches,* edited by M. Brenner, J. Brown, and D. Canter, pp. 163–199. New York: Academic Press.

Tanur, Judith H., ed. (1992). *Questions about questions: Inquiries into the cognitive bases of surveys.* New York: Russell Sage Foundation.

Tanur, Judith M. (1983). Methods for large scale surveys and experiments. In *Sociological Methodology, 1983–1984,* edited by S. Leinhardt, pp. 1–71. San Francisco: Jossey-Bass.

Tarnai, John, and D. Dillman. (1992). Questionnaire context as a source of response differences in mail and telephone surveys. In *Context effects,* edited by N. Schwarz and S. Sudman, pp. 115–129. New York: Springer-Verlag.

Tarnai, John, and Danna L. Moore. (2004). Methods for testing and evaluating computer-assisted questionnaires. In *Methods for testing and evaluating survey questionnaires,* edited by S. Presser et al., pp. 319–335. New York: Wiley.

Tashakkori, Abbas, and Charles Teddlie. (1998). *Mixed methodology: Combining qualitative and quantitative approaches.* Thousand Oaks, CA: Sage.

Taylor, Charles. (1979). Interpretation and the sciences of man. In *Interpretative social science: A reader,* edited by P. Rabinow and W. Sullivan, pp. 25–72. Berkeley: University of California Press.

Taylor, Charles Lewis, ed. (1980). *Indicator systems for political, economic and social analysis.* Cambridge, MA: Oelgeschlager, Gunn and Hain.

Taylor, Marcia Freed. (1994). Ethical considerations in European cross-national research. *International Social Science Journal,* 46:523–532.

Taylor, Steven. (1987). Observing abuse: Professional ethics and personal morality in field research. *Qualitative Sociology,* 10:288–302.

Thompson, E. P. (1963). *The making of the English working class.* New York: Vintage.

Thompson, E. P. (1967). Time, work-discipline, and industrial capitalism. *Past and Present,* 38:56–97.

Thompson, E. P. (1978). *The poverty of theory and other essays.* New York: Monthly Review Press.

Thompson, Paul. (1978). *The voice of the past: Oral history.* New York: Oxford University Press.

Thorne, Barrie, and Zella Luria. (1986). Sexuality and gender in children's daily world. *Social Problems,* 33:176–190.

Thrasher, F. M. (1927). *The gang.* Chicago: University of Chicago Press.

Thurstone, L. L. (1970). Attitudes can be measured. In *Attitude measurement,* edited by G. Summers, pp. 127–141. Chicago: Rand McNally.

Tilly, Charles. (1964). *The vendee.* Cambridge, MA: Harvard University Press.

Tilly, Charles. (1981). *As sociology meets history.* New York: Academic Press.

Tilly, Charles, Louise Tilly, and Richard Tilly. (1975). *The rebellious century, 1830–1930.* Cambridge, MA: Harvard University Press.

Tobin, Joseph, David Wu, and Dana Davidson. (1989). *Preschool in three cultures.* New Haven CT: Yale University Press.

Todorov, Alexander. (2000a). Context effects in national health surveys. *Public Opinion Quarterly,* 64:65–76.

Todorov, Alexander. (2000b). The accessibility and applicability of knowledge: Predicting context effects in national surveys. *Public Opinion Quarterly,* 64:429–451.

Topolski, Jerzy. (1976). *Methodology of history,* trans. Olgierd Wojtasiewicz. Boston: D. Reidel.

Toulmin, Stephen. (1953). *The philosophy of science: An introduction.* New York: Harper & Row.

Tourangeau, Roger. (1992). Context effects on responses to attitude questions. In *Context effects in social and psychological research,* edited by N. Schwarz and S. Sudman, pp. 35–47. New York: Springer-Verlag.

Tourangeau, Roger. (2004a). Survey research and societal change. *Annual Review of Psychology,* 55:775–801.

Tourangeau, Roger. (2004b). Experimental design considerations for testing and evaluating questionnaires. In *Methods for testing and evaluating survey questionnaires,* edited by Stanley Presser et al., pp. 209–224. New York: Wiley.

Tourangeau, Roger, Mick Couper, and Frederick Conrad. (2004). Spacing, position, and order. *Public Opinion Quarterly,* 68:368–393.

Tourangeau, Roger, and Tom Smith. (1996). Asking sensitive questions: The impact of data collection mode, question format and question context. *Public Opinion Quarterly,* 60:275–304.

Tourangeau, Roger, et al. (1997). Who lives here? *Journal of Official Statistics,* 13:1–18.

Tourangeau, Roger, Darby Steiger and David Wilson. (2002). Self-Administered Questions by Telephone. *Public Opinion Quarterly,* 66:265–278.

Traugott, Michael W. (1987). The importance of persistence in respondent selection for preelection surveys. *Public Opinion Quarterly,* 51:48–57.

Treiman, Michael. (1977). Towards methods for a quantitative comparative sociology: A reply to Burawoy. *American Journal of Sociology,* 82:1042–1056.

Trice, H. M. (1970). The "outsider's" role in field study. In *Qualitative methodology,* edited by W. J. Filstead, pp. 77–82. Chicago: Markham.

Tropp, Richard A. (1982). A regulatory perspective on social science research. In *Ethical issues in social science research,* edited by T. Beauchamp, R. Faden, R. J. Wallace, and L. Walters, pp. 391–415. Baltimore: Johns Hopkins University Press.

Trovato, Frank. (1998). The Stanley cup of hockey and suicide in Quebec, 1951–1992. *Social Forces,* 77: 105–126.

Trussell, Norm, and Paul Lavrakas. (2004). The influence of incremental increases in token cash. *Public Opinion Quarterly,* 68:368–393.

Tsutsui, Kiyoteru, and Christine Min Wotipka. (2004). Global civil society and international human rights movement. *Social Forces,* 83:587–620.

Tuchman, Gaye. (1994). Historical social science: Methodologies, methods and meanings. In *Handbook of qualitative research,* edited by N. Denzin and Y. Lincoln, pp. 306–323. Thousand Oaks, CA: Sage.

Tucker, Clyde. (1983). Interviewer effects in telephone interviewing. *Public Opinion Quarterly,* 47:84–95.

Tufte, Edward. (1983). *The visual display of quantitative information.* Cheshire, CT: Graphics Press.

Tufte, Edward. (1991). *Envisioning information,* rev. ed. Cheshire, CT: Graphics Press.

Tuma, Nancy B., and Andrew Grimes. (1981). A comparison of models of role orientations of professionals in a research oriented university. *Administrative Science Quarterly,* 21:187–206.

Turner, Charles. (1984). Why do surveys disagree? Some preliminary hypotheses and some disagreeable examples. In *Surveying subjective phenomena,* Vol. 2, edited by C. Turner and E. Martin, pp. 157–214. New York: Russell Sage Foundation.

Turner, Charles, and Elizabeth Martin, eds. (1984). *Surveying subjective phenomena,* Vol. 1. New York: Russell Sage Foundation.

Turner, Jonathan H. (1985). In defense of positivism. *Sociological Theory,* 3:24–30.

Turner, Jonathan H. (1992). Positivism. In *Encyclopedia of sociology,* Vol. 3, edited by E. and M. Borgatta, pp. 1509–1512. New York: Macmillan.

Turner, Roy. (1974). *Ethnomethodology.* Middlesex: Penguin.

Turner, Stephen P. (1980). *Sociological explanation as translation.* New York: Cambridge University Press.

Turner, Stephen P. (1991). The world of academic quantifiers: The Columbia University family and its connections. In *The social survey in historical perspective, 1880–1940,* edited by M. Blumer, K. Bales, and K. Sklar, pp. 269–290. New York: Cambridge University Press.

Turner, Stephen Park, and Jonathan H. Turner. (1991). *The impossible science: An institutional analysis of American sociology.* Newbury Park, CA: Sage.

Union of Concerned Scientists. (2004). *Scientific integrity in policy making.* Cambridge MA: Union of Concerned Scientists.

Useem, Michael. (1976a). Government influence on the social science paradigm. *Sociological Quarterly,* 17: 146–161.

Useem, Michael. (1976b). State production of social knowledge: Patterns of government financing of academic social research. *American Sociological Review,* 41:613–629.

Valentine-French, Suzanne, and H. Lorraine Radtke. (1989). Attributions of responsibility for an incident of sexual harassment in a university setting. *Sex Roles,* 21:545–555.

Valentino, Nicholas A. (1999). Crime news and the priming of racial attitudes during evaluations of the president. *Public Opinion Quarterly,* 63:293–320.

Vallier, Ivan, ed. (1971a). *Comparative methods in sociology: Essays on trends and applications.* Berkeley: University of California Press.

Vallier, Ivan. (1971b). Empirical comparisons of social structure. In *Comparative methods in sociology,* edited by I. Vallier, pp. 203–263. Berkeley: University of California Press.

Van den Berg, Harry, and Cees Van der Veer. (1985). Measuring ideological frames of references. *Quality and Quantity,* 19:105–118.

Van den Berge, Pierre L. (1967). Research in South Africa: The story of my experiences with tyranny. In *Ethics, politics and social research,* edited by G. Sjøberg. New York: Schenckman.

Van der Zouwen, Johannes, and Johannes Smit. (2004). Evaluating survey questions by analyzing patterns of behavior codes and question-answer sequences. In *Methods for testing and evaluating survey questionnaires,* edited by Stanley Presser et al., pp. 109–130. New York: Wiley.

Van Maanen, John. (1973). Observations on the making of policemen. *Human Organization,* 32:407–418.

Van Maanen, John. (1982). Fieldwork on the beat. In *Varieties of qualitative research,* edited by J. Van Maanen, J. Dabbs, Jr., and R. Faulkner, pp. 103–151. Beverly Hills, CA: Sage.

Van Maanen, John. (1983a). Epilogue: Qualitative methods reclaimed. In *Qualitative methodology,* edited by J. Van Maanen, pp. 247–268. Beverly Hills, CA: Sage.

Van Maanen, John. (1983b). The moral fix: On the ethics of fieldwork. In *Contemporary field research,* edited by R. M. Emerson, pp. 269–287. Boston: Little, Brown.

Van Maanen, John. (1988). *Tales of the field: On writing ethnography.*

Chicago: University of Chicago Press.

Van Poppel, Frans, and L. Day. (1996). A test of Durkheim's theory of suicide—Without committing the "ecological fallacy." *American Sociological Review,* 61:500–507.

Van Tubergen, Frank, Ineke Maas, and Henk Flap. (2004). The economic incorporation of immigrants in 18 western societies. *American Sociological Review,* 69:704–727.

Vaughan, Diane. (1992). Theory elaboration: The heuristics of case analysis. In *What is a case? Exploring the foundations of social inquiry,* edited by C. Ragin and H. Becker, pp. 173–202. Cambridge: Cambridge University Press.

Vaughan, Ted R. (1967). Government intervention in social research: Political and ethical dimensions of the Wichita jury recordings. In *Ethics, politics and social research,* edited by G. Sjøberg. New York: Schenckman.

Veltmeyer, Henry. (1978). Marx's two methods of sociological analysis. *Sociological Inquiry,* 48:101–112.

Verba, Sidney. (1971). Cross-national survey research. In *Comparative methods in sociology,* edited by I. Vallier, pp. 309–356. Berkeley: University of California Press.

Verba, Sidney, and Gary R. Orren. (1985). *Equality in America: The view from the top.* Cambridge, MA: Harvard University Press.

Vidich, Arthur Joseph, and Joseph Bensman. (1968). *Small town in mass society,* rev. ed. Princeton, NJ: Princeton University Press.

Villarreal, Andrés. (2002). Political competition and violence in Mexico. *American Sociological Review,* 67: 477–498.

Villarreal, Andrés. (2004). The social ecology of rural violence. *American Journal of Sociology,* 110:349–399.

Villenas, Sofia. (1996). The colonizer/colonized Chicana ethnographer: Identity, marginalization, and co-optation in the field. *Harvard Educational Review,* 66:711–731.

Villenas, Sofia. (2001). Latina mothers and small-town racisms: Creating narratives of dignity and moral education in North Carolina. *Anthropology and Education Quarterly,* 32: 3–28.

Wade, Nicholas. (1976). IQ and heredity: Suspicion of fraud beclouds classic experiment. *Science,* 194: 916–919.

Waksberg, J. (1978). Sampling methods for random digit dialing. *Journal of the American Statistical Association,* 73:40–46.

Wald, Matthew. (July 1, 2004). Any Saturday on highways ranks close to deadly holidays. *New York Times.*

Walder, Andrew G. (2003). Elite opportunity in transitional economies. *American Sociological Review,* 68:899–916.

Wallace, Walter. (1971). *The logic of science in sociology.* Chicago: Aldine.

Wallerstein, Immanuel. (1974). *The modern world system.* New York: Academic Press.

Walsh, David. (1972). Varieties of positivism. In *New directions in sociological theory,* edited by P. Filmer et al. Cambridge, MA: MIT Press.

Walster, Elaine. (1965). The effect of self-esteem on romantic liking. *Journal of Experimental Social Psychology,* 1:194–197.

Walters, Ronald G. (1980). Signs of the times. *Social Research,* 47:537–556.

Walton, John. (1973). Standardized case comparison. In *Comparative social research,* edited by M. Armer and A. Grimshaw, pp. 173–191. New York: Wiley.

Walton, John. (1992a). *Western times and water wars: State, culture and rebellion in California.* Berkeley: University of California Press.

Walton, John. (1992b). Making the theoretical case. In *What is a case? Exploring the foundations of social inquiry,* edited by C. Ragin and H. Becker, pp. 121–138. Cambridge: Cambridge University Press.

Ward, Benjamin. (1972). *What's wrong with economics.* New York: Basic Books.

Ward, Kathryn B., and Linda Grant. (1985). The feminist critique and a decade of published research in sociology journals. *Sociological Quarterly,* 26:139–158.

Wardell, Mark L. (1979). Marx and his method: A commentary. *Sociological Quarterly,* 20:425–436.

Warner, R. Stephen. (1971). The methodology of Marx's comparative analysis of modes of production. In *Comparative methods in sociology,* edited by I. Vallier, pp. 49–74. Berkeley: University of California Press.

Warren, Carol A. B., and Paul K. Rasmussen. (1977). Sex and gender in field research. *Urban Life,* 6: 349–369.

Warwick, Donald P. (1982). Types of harm in social science research. In *Ethical issues in social science research,* edited by T. Beauchamp, R. Faden, R. J. Wallace, and L. Walters, pp. 101–123. Baltimore: Johns Hopkins University Press.

Warwick, Donald P., and Charles A. Lininger. (1975). *The sample survey: Theory and practice.* New York: McGraw-Hill.

Warwick, Donald P., and Samuel Osherson. (1973). Comparative analysis in the social sciences. In *Comparative research methods,* edited by D. Warwick and S. Osherson, pp. 3–11. Englewood Cliffs, NJ: Prentice-Hall.

Watters, John K., and Patrick Biernacki. (1989). Targeted sampling: Options for the study of hidden populations. *Social Problems,* 36:416–430.

Wax, Rosalie H. (1971). *Doing fieldwork: Warnings and advice.* Chicago: University of Chicago Press.

Wax, Rosalie H. (1979). Gender and age in fieldwork and fieldwork education: No good thing is done by any man alone. *Social Problems,* 26: 509–522.

Webb, Eugene J., Donald T. Campbell, Richard D. Schwartz, Lee Sechrest, and Janet Belew Grove. (1981). *Nonreactive measures in the social sciences,* 2nd ed. Boston: Houghton Mifflin.

Weber, Max. (1949). *The methodology of the social sciences,* trans. and edited by E. Shils and H. Finch. New York: Free Press.

Weber, Max. (1974). Subjectivity and determinism. In *Positivism and sociology,* edited by A. Giddens, pp. 23–32. London: Heinemann.

Weber, Max. (1978). *Economy and society,* Vol. 1, edited by G. Roth and C. Wittich. Berkeley: University of California Press.

Weber, Max. (1981). Some categories of interpretative sociology. *Sociological Quarterly,* 22:151–180.

Weber, Robert P. (1983). Measurement models for content analysis. *Quality and Quantity,* 17:127–149.

Weber, Robert P. (1984). Computer assisted content analysis: A short primer. *Qualitative Sociology,* 7:" 126–149.

Weber, Robert P. (1985). *Basic content analysis.* Beverly Hills, CA: Sage.

Weeks, M. F., and R. P. Moore. (1981). Ethnicity of interviewer effects on ethnic respondents. *Public Opinion Quarterly,* 45:245–249.

Weil, Frederick D. (1985). The variable effects of education on liberal attitudes. *American Sociological Review,* 50:458–474.

Weinberg, Steven. (May 31, 2001). Can science explain everything? Anything? *New York Review of Books,* 48, 47–50.

Weinstein, Deena. (1979). Fraud in science. *Social Science Quarterly,* 59:639–652.

Weiss, Carol H. (1972). *Evaluation research: Methods of assessing program effectiveness.* Englewood Cliffs, NJ: Prentice-Hall.

Weiss, Janet A., and Judith E. Gruber. (1987). The managed irrelevance of educational statistics. In *The politics of numbers,* edited by W. Alonso and P. Starr, pp. 363–391. New York: Russell Sage Foundation.

Weiss, Robert S. (1994). *Learning from strangers: The arts and method of qualitative interview studies.* New York: Free Press.

Weitzman, Eben, and Matthew Miles. (1995). *Computer programs for qualitative data analysis.* Thousand Oaks, CA: Sage.

Wells, Gary L., and Elizabeth A. Olson. (2003). Eyewitness testimony. *Annual Review of Psychology,* 54: 277–295.

Wells, Gary L., Elizabeth Olson, and Steve Charman. (2003). Distorted retrospective eyewitness reports as functions of feedback and delay. *Journal of Experimental Psychology, Applied,* 9:42–52.

Wenger, G. Clare, ed. (1987). *The research relationship: Practice and politics in social policy research.* Boston: Allen and Unwin.

Wentworth, Ellen J. (1993). *Survey responses: An evaluation of their validity.* New York: Academic Press.

Werner, Oswald, and G. Mark Schoepfle. (1987a). *Systematic fieldwork, Vol. 1: Foundations of ethnography and interviewing.* Beverly Hills: Sage.

Werner, Oswald, and G. Mark Schoepfle. (1987b). *Systematic fieldwork, Vol. 2: Ethnographic analysis and data management.* Beverly Hills: Sage.

West, W. Gordon. (1980). Access to adolescent deviants and deviance. In *Fieldwork experience,* edited by W. B. Shaffir, R. A. Stebbins, and A. Turowetz, pp. 31–44. New York: St. Martin's Press.

Westmarland, Louise. (2000). Taking the flak: Operational policing, fear, and violence. In *Danger in the field,* edited by G. Lee-Treweek and S. Linkogle, pp. 26–42. New York: Routledge.

Weston, Cynthia, T. Gandell, J. Beauchamp, L. McAlpine, C. Wiseman, and C. Beauchamp. (2001). Analyzing interview data: The development and evolution of a coding system. *Qualitative Sociology,* 24:381–400.

Whalley, Peter. (1984). Deskilling engineers? The labor process, labor markets, and labor segmentation. *Social Problems,* 32:117–132.

Whiting, John W. M. (1968). Methods and problems in cross-cultural research. In *The handbook of social psychology,* 2nd ed., edited by G. Lindzey and E. Aronson, pp. 693–728. Reading, MA: Addison-Wesley.

Whyte, William Foote. (1955). *Street corner society: The social structure of an Italian slum,* 2nd ed. Chicago: University of Chicago Press.

Whyte, William Foote. (1982). Interviewing in field research. In *Field research,* edited by R. G. Burgess, pp. 111–122. Boston: George Allen and Unwin.

Whyte, William Foote. (1984). *Learning from the field: A guide from experience.* Beverly Hills: Sage.

Whyte, William Foote. (1986). On the uses of social science research. *American Sociological Review,* 51:555–563.

Whyte, William F. (1989). Advancing scientific knowledge through participatory action research. *Sociological Forum,* 4:367–385.

Wieder, D. Lawrence. (1977). Ethnomethodology and ethnosociology. *Mid-American Review of Sociology,* 2:1–18.

Wiedmer, Terry L. (1993). Perspectives on scholarship in education: Undergraduate and graduate students' views on faculty scholarship. Paper at the American Educational Research Association meeting, Atlanta, GA.

Wigginton, Eliot, ed. (1972). *Foxfire book.* New York: Doubleday.

Wilcox, Clyde, Lee Sigelman, and Elizabeth Cook. (1989). Some like it hot: Individual differences in responses to group feeling thermometers. *Public Opinion Quarterly,* 53:246–257.

Wilhelm, Brenda. (1998). Changes in cohabitation across cohorts: The influ-

ence of political activism. *Social Forces,* 77:289–310.

Williams, Bill. (1978). *A sampler on sampling.* New York: Wiley.

Williams, Carol I., and Gary K. Wolfe. (1979). *Elements of research: A guide for writers.* Palo Alto, CA: Mayfield.

Williams, L. Susan, Sandra Alvarez, and Kevin Andrade Hauck. (2002). My name is not Maria: Young Latinas seeking home in the heartland. *Social Problems,* 49:563–584.

Williams, Terry, and E. Dunlap. (1992). Personal safety in dangerous places. *Journal of Contemporary Ethnography,* 21:343–375.

Williamson, John B., David Karp, John Dalphin, and Paul Gray. (1982). *The research craft.* Boston: Little and Brown.

Willimack, Diane K., Howard Schuman, Beth-Ellen Pennell, and James M. Lepkowski. (1995). Effects of prepaid non-monetary incentives on response rates and response quality in face-to-face survey. *Public Opinion Quarterly,* 59:78–92.

Willis, Gordon B. (2004). Cognitive interviewing revisited. In *Methods for testing and evaluating survey questionnaires,* edited by Stanley Presser et al., pp. 23–44. New York: Wiley.

Willis, Paul. (1977). *Learning to labor: How working class kids get working class jobs.* New York: Columbia University Press.

Wilson, John. (1982). Realist philosophy as a foundation for Marx's social theory. *Current Perspectives in Social Theory,* 3:243–263.

Wilson, Thomas P. (1970). Normative and interpretive paradigms in sociology. In *Understanding everyday life: Toward the reconstruction of sociological knowledge,* edited by J. Douglas, pp. 57–79. New York: Aldine.

Wilson, Timothy D., and Elizabeth W. Dunn. (2004). Self-knowledge: Its limits, value, and potential for improvement. *Annual Review of Psychology,* 55:493–518.

Wilson, Timothy, Suzzane J. LaFleur, and D. Eric Anderson. (1996). The validity and consequence of verbal reports about attitudes. In *Answering questions,* edited by N. Schwarz and S. Sudman, pp. 91–114. San Francisco: Jossey-Bass.

Wimberly, Dale W. (1990). Investment dependence and alternative explanations of third world mortality: A cross-national study. *American Sociological Review,* 55:75–91.

Winkler, Karen J. (January 11, 1989). Dispute over validity of historical approaches pits traditionalists against advocates of new methods. *Chronicle of Higher Education,* pp. A4ff.

Winston, Chester. (1974). *Theory and measurement in sociology.* New York: Wiley.

Wolcott, Harry F. (1994). *Transforming qualitative data: Description, analysis and interpretation.* Thousand Oaks, CA: Sage.

Wolf, Eric R. (1982). *Europe and the people without history.* Berkeley: University of California Press.

Wood, Elizabeth Anne. (2000). Work-ing in the fantasy factory. *Journal of Contemporary Ethnography,* 29:5–32.

Woodrum, Eric. (1984). "Mainstreaming" content analysis in social science: Methodological advantages, obstacles, and solutions. *Social Science Research,* 13:1–19.

Wright, Debra L., William S. Aquilino, and Andrew J. Supple. (1998). A comparison of computer-assisted and paper-and-pencil administered questionnaires in a survey on smoking, alcohol and drug use. *Public Opinion Quarterly,* 62:311–353.

Wright, Erik O. (1978). *Class, crisis and state.* London: New Left Books.

Wright, James D., and Peter H. Rossi, eds. (1981). *Social science and natural hazards.* Cambridge, MA: Abt Books.

Wuthnow, Robert. (1979). The emergence of modern science and world system theory. *Theory and Society,* 8:215–243.

Wuthnow, Robert. (1987). *Meaning and moral order: Explorations in cultural analysis.* Berkeley: University of California Press.

Wysong, Earl, Richard Aniskiewicz, and David Wright. (1994). Truth and DARE: Tracking drug education

from graduation and symbolic politics. *Social Problems,* 41:448–468.

Yammarino, Francis, Steven Skiner, and Terry Childers. (1991). Understanding mail survey response behavior: A meta-analysis. *Public Opinion Quarterly,* 55:613–640.

Yancey, William L., and Lee Rainwater. (1970). Problems in the ethnography of the urban underclasses. In *Pathways to data,* edited by R. W. Habenstein, pp. 245–269. Chicago: Aldine.

Yeo, Eileen James. (1991). The social survey in social perspective, 1830–1930. In *The social survey in historical perspective, 1880–1940,* edited by M. Blumer, K. Bales, and K. Sklar, pp. 49–65. New York: Cambridge University Press.

Yin, Robert K. (1988). *Case study research,* rev. ed. Newbury Park, CA: Sage.

Young, T. R. (1980). Comment on the McQuaire–Wardell debate. *Sociological Quarterly,* 21:459–462.

Yow, Valerie Raleigh. (1994). *Recording oral history: A practical guide for social scientists.* Thousand Oaks, CA: Sage.

Yu, J., and H. Cooper. (1983). A quantitative review of research design effects on response rates to questionnaires. *Journal of Marketing Research,* 20:36–44.

Zaller, John, and Stanley Feldman. (1992). A simple theory of survey responses: Answering questions versus revealing preferences. *American Journal of Political Science,* 36: 579–616.

Zane, Anne, and Euthemia Matsoukas. (1979). Different settings, different results? A comparison of school and home responses. *Public Opinion Quarterly,* 43:550–557.

Zaret, David. (1978). Sociological theory and historical scholarship. *The American Sociologist,* 13:114–121.

Zeisel, Hans. (1985). *Say it with figures,* 6th ed. New York: Harper & Row.

Zelizer, Viviana A. (1985). *Pricing the priceless child.* New York: Basic Books.

Zeller, Richard, and Edward G. Carmines. (1980). *Measurement in the social sciences: The link between theory and data.* New York: Cambridge University Press.

Ziman, John. (1968). *Public knowledge: An essay concerning the social dimension of science.* New York: Cambridge University Press.

Ziman, John. (1976). *The force of knowledge: The scientific dimension of society.* New York: Cambridge University Press.

Zimbardo, Philip G. (1972). Pathology of imprisonment. *Society,* 9:4–6.

Zimbardo, Philip G. (1973). On the ethics of intervention in human psychological research. *Cognition,* 2: 243–256.

Zimbardo, Philip G., et al. (April 8, 1973). The mind is a formidable jailer: A pirandellian prison. *New York Times Magazine,* 122:38–60.

Zimbardo, Philip G., et al. (1974). The psychology of imprisonment: Privation, power and pathology. In *Doing unto others,* edited by Z. Rubin. Englewood Cliffs, NJ: Prentice-Hall.

Zipp, John F., and Joann Toth. (2002). She said, he said: The impact of spousal presence in survey research. *Public Opinion Quarterly,* 66:209–234.

Zuckerman, Harriet. (1972). Interviewing an ultra-elite. *Public Opinion Quarterly,* 36:159–175.

Zuckerman, Harriet. (1978). Theory choice and problem choice in science. In *Sociology of science,* edited by J. Gaston, pp. 65–95. San Francisco: Jossey-Bass.

Zuiches, James J. (1984). The organization and funding of social science in the NSF. *Sociological Inquiry,* 54:188–210.

Name Index

Subject Index

Scholarly Journals in the Social Sciences in English

GENERAL SOCIAL SCIENCE

American Behavioral Scientist
Annals of the American Academy of Political and Social Science
Evaluation Practice (American Evaluation Association)
Evaluation Review
Human Relations
Public Opinion Quarterly (American Association for Public Opinion)
Rationality and Society
Social Science Journal (Western Social Science Association)
Social Science Quarterly (Southwestern Social Science Association)
Theory and Society

ANTHROPOLOGY

American Anthropologist (American Anthropological Association)
American Ethnologist (American Ethnological Society)
Critique of Anthropology
Ethnology
Human Organization (Society for Applied Anthropology)
Mankind Quarterly (Institute for the Study of Man)

CRIMINOLOGY/SOCIOLOGY OF LAW

Contemporary Crisis
Crime and Delinquency (National Council on Crime and Delinquency)
Crime, Law and Social Change
Criminal Justice and Behavior (American Association of Correctional Psychologists)
Criminology (American Society of Criminology)
Journal of Criminal Law and Criminology
Journal of Research in Crime and Delinquency (National Council on Crime and Delinquency)
Journal of Quantitative Criminology
Law and Social Inquiry (American Bar Association)
Law and Society Review (Law and Society Association)
Social Justice: A Journal of Crime, Conflict and World Order

RACE/ETHNIC RELATIONS

Ethnic Forum
Ethnic Groups
Ethnic and Racial Studies
Hispanic Journal of Behavioral Sciences
Journal of American Ethnic History
Journal of Black Studies
Negro Educational Review
Phylon: The Atlanta University Review of Race and Culture
Race and Class (Institute of Race Relations)
Review of Black Political Economy (National Economic Association)

COMPARATIVE-HISTORICAL RESEARCH

Comparative Political Studies
Comparative Studies in Society and History
Cross-Cultural Research
Development and Change
Economic Development and Cultural Change
International Journal of Comparative Sociology
International Journal of Contemporary Sociology
International Migration Review
Journal of Cross-Cultural Psychology
Review (Fernand Braudel Center)
Social Science History

POLITICAL SCIENCE/POLITICAL SOCIOLOGY

American Journal of Political Science (Midwest Political Science Association)
American Political Science Review (American Political Science Review)
American Politics Quarterly
British Journal of Political Science
Canadian Journal of Political Science (Canadian Political Science Association; also in French)
Journal of Conflict Resolution
Journal of Political and Military Sociology
Journal of Politics (Southern Political Science Association)
Political Methodology
Political Science Quarterly (Academy of Political Science)
Politics and Society
Review of Radical Political Economics (Union for Radical Political Economics)
Western Political Quarterly (Western Political Science Association)